MW00640341

Annals of Communism

Each volume in the series Annals of Communism will publish selected and previously inaccessible documents from former Soviet state and party archives in a narrative that develops a particular topic in the history of Soviet and international communism. Separate English and Russian editions will be prepared. Russian and Western scholars work together to prepare the documents for each volume. Documents are chosen not for their support of any single interpretation but for their particular historical importance or their general value in deepening understanding and facilitating discussion. The volumes are designed to be useful to students, scholars, and interested general readers.

STALIN'S MASTER NARRATIVE

A Critical Edition of the

HISTORY
OF THE
COMMUNIST PARTY
OF THE
SOVIET UNION
(BOLSHEVIKS):
SHORT COURSE

EDITED BY
David Brandenberger and Mikhail Zelenov

Yale UNIVERSITY PRESS
NEW HAVEN AND LONDON

Special thanks to the Russian State Archive of Socio-Political History (RGASPI) for its assistance and photographs.

The English translation is adapted from the *History of the Communist Party of the Soviet Union (Bolsheviks)* published in Moscow by the State Foreign Languages Publishing House in 1939.

Yale University Press books may be purchased in quantity for educational, business, or promotional use. For information, please e-mail sales.press@yale.edu (U.S. office) or sales@yaleup.co.uk (U.K. office).

Set in Minion Pro type by Newgen.
Printed in the United States of America.

Library of Congress Control Number: 2018953985
ISBN 978-0-300-15536-5 (hardcover : alk. paper)

A catalogue record for this book is available from the British Library.

This paper meets the requirements of ANSI/NISO Z39.48-1992 (Permanence of Paper).

10 9 8 7 6 5 4 3 2 1

Yale University Press gratefully acknowledges the financial support given for this publication by the John M. Olin Foundation, the Lynde and Harry Bradley Foundation, the Historical Research Foundation, Roger Milliken, the Rosentiel Foundation, Lloyd H. Smith, Keith Young, the William H. Donner Foundation, Joseph W. Donner, Jeremiah Milbank, the David Woods Kemper Memorial Foundation, and the Smith Richardson Foundation.

Contents

Acknowledgments

This critical edition has benefited from a number of long- and short-term grants provided by the International Research and Exchanges Board, with funds supplied by the National Endowment for the Humanities and the United States Department of State under the auspices of the Russian, Eurasian, and East European Research Program (Title VIII); the National Endowment for the Humanities; the US Department of State's Fulbright Program; and the School of Arts and Sciences at the University of Richmond.

Aspects borrow from chapters two, seven, and nine of David Brandenberger's 2011 Propaganda State in Crisis: Ideology, Indoctrination, and Terror under Stalin, 1927–1941. We would like to thank Yale University Press for permission to reprint portions of this book. We would also like to acknowledge our gratitude to a number of colleagues who have read and commented upon aspects of this manuscript, particularly Lars Lih, Erik van Ree, and Peter Blitstein. Discussions with Sandra Dahlke, O. A. Kuchkina, George Enteen, David Priestland, Ronald Grigor Suny, K. A. Boldovskii, and V. V. Kondrashin came at important junctures, as did support from Jonathan Brent, Vadim Staklo, William Frucht, and Mary Pasti at Yale University Press, Jay Harward and Anita Hueftle at Newgen North America, and A. K. Sorokin at the former Central Party Archive in Moscow.

A Note on Conventions

The transliteration of titles, terms, surnames, and geographic locations in this volume's introduction, notes, and index follows a modified version of the US Library of Congress system in which hard and soft signs are dropped, "ye" is used for "e," "y" for "ii," and so on, to accommodate a broad readership. Exceptions occur in quotations taken from other sources and in the bibliographic citations, which follow Library of Congress conventions strictly. In order to improve readability, frequent terms like "the Party" are not capitalized in the text.

Within the text of the SHORT COURSE itself, the transliteration of titles, terms, surnames, and geographic locations follows an arcane and somewhat idiosyncratic house style practiced by the U.S.S.R.'s Foreign Languages Publishing House in the late 1930s. Peculiarities in grammar, punctuation, and capitalization (including the titles of chapters and subchapters) also stem from the need to conform to this original house style.

Throughout the text of this critical edition, struck-through characters, words, sentences, and entire paragraphs capture J. V. Stalin's personal excision of material written originally by Ye. M. Yaroslavsky and P. N. Pospelov. The use of italics denotes Stalin's editorial interpolations into the text. Any exceptions to these rules are identified and explained in individual footnotes. Because of the need to reserve italics to represent Stalin's editing, this critical edition renders all book titles, foreign words and phrases, and dramatic emphases in a combination of large and small capital letters. Square brackets contain notations added by the editors of this critical edition.

Selected Terms, Acronyms, and Abbreviations

For a complete list and glosses of terms, historical events, and personalities referred to in this volume, see the index.

Agitprop	Central Committee Directorate of Agitation and Propaganda
artel	cooperative
ataman	chief of a Cossack regiment
bek	noble title among Central Asian peoples
bey	noble title among Central Asian peoples
Cheka	secret police (1918–1922)
CPSU(B)	Communist Party of the Soviet Union (Bolsheviks)
dekulakization	elimination of "prosperous" elements of the peasantry (1929–1932)
IMEL	Marx-Engels-Lenin Institute
komsomol	young communist league
kulak	"prosperous" peasant
kvostism	expression meaning "to follow in the tail"
muzhik	male peasant
nepman	entrepreneur during New Economic Policy (1921–1928)
NKVD	secret police (1934–1946)
Orgburo	Central Committee Organizational Bureau
Politburo	Central Committee Political Bureau
RSDLP	Russian Social-Democratic Labor Party
Sovnarkom	Council of People's Commissars
SRs	Socialist-Revolutionary Party
subbotnik	voluntary Saturday work
uyezd	district
volost	district
White Guards	anti-Bolshevik forces during Russian Civil War (1918–1921)

Weights and Measures

centner	approx. 112 pounds (50.8 kilograms)
dessiatin	approx. 2.7 acres (10,925 square meters)
pood	approx. 36 pounds (16.3 kilograms)
verst	approx. 3,500 feet (1 kilometer)

Archival Repository Acronyms and Abbreviations

Acronyms

APRF	Arkhiv Prezidenta Rossiiskoi Federatsii (the former Politburo Archive of the Central Committee, presently the Presidential Archive of the Russian Federation)
RGANI	Rossiiskii gosudarstvennyi arkhiv noveishei istorii (the former "Current" Archive of the Central Committee, presently the Russian State Archive of Recent History)
RGASPI	Rossiiskii gosudarstvennyi arkhiv sotsial'no-politicheskoi istorii (the former Central Party Archive, presently the Russian State Archive of Socio-Political History)
RGVA	Rossiiskii gosudarstvennyi voennyi arkhiv (Russian State Military Archive)
TsAOPIM	Tsentral'nyi arkhiv obshchestvenno-politicheskoi istorii Moskvy (Central Archive of the Socio-Political History of Moscow)

Abbreviations

f.	FOND (collection)
op.	OPIS' (inventory)
d.	DELO (file)
dd.	DELA (files)
l.	LIST (folio)
ll.	LISTY (folios)
ob	OBROROT (verso)

STALIN'S MASTER NARRATIVE

Editors' Introduction

THE HISTORICAL CONTEXT

History of the Communist Party of the Soviet Union (Bolsheviks): Short Course was the central text of the Stalin-era ideological canon. Compulsory reading for Soviet citizens of all walks of life, it was ubiquitous in the U.S.S.R. between 1938 and 1956. Over forty million copies of the book circulated in over a dozen languages, with hundreds of thousands more appearing in places as far-flung as Warsaw, Prague, Budapest, Beijing, London, Paris, and New York.[1] What's more, the Short Course governed all references to the Soviet historical experience, not only in public school textbooks and more academic scholarship, but on the theatrical stage and silver screen as well. Even the display cases of the country's museums were arranged in conformity with the new storyline. The Short Course was, in other words, the U.S.S.R.'s master narrative—a hegemonic statement on history, philosophy, and ideology that scripted Soviet society for the better part of a generation. Abroad, the book enjoyed a similar role among Moscow-aligned communist parties and fellow travelers; after 1945, it served as a blueprint for socialist development in the U.S.S.R.'s new Eastern European satellites, the People's Republic of China, and the Democratic People's Republic of Korea. Ultimately, the Short Course ought to be considered one of the most influential books of the twentieth century.

J. V. Stalin has traditionally been credited with authorship of the Short Course, despite the fact that it was officially attributed to an anonymous Central Committee editing commission. Some commentators have gone so far as to suggest that it should be read as Stalin's autobiography, if not his personal Mein Kampf.[2] This critical edition of the Short Course demonstrates that such accounts fundamentally mischaracterize Stalin's relationship to the book, insofar as he neither wrote it from scratch nor interpolated his own personal experiences into its narrative. That said, Stalin did repeatedly meddle in the compilation of its broader storyline as it took shape during the early to mid-1930s. And during his editing of the *Short Course* itself, Stalin rewrote vast stretches of the history of the Bolshevik revolutionary movement, recasting early interparty rivalries, the party's seizure of power in 1917, and the formation and development of Soviet statehood. He reframed the saga of collectivization, industrialization, and the Great Terror. He crafted what was probably the most significant ideological statement of his career for the book's fourth chapter. In aggregate, his editing of the text effectively reinterpreted the official party line on subjects such as Soviet internationalism, the Comintern, the national question, and the nature of grassroots participation in the revolution and socialist construction, among many others.

Ultimately, the *Short Course* ought to be recognized as one of the most important texts for the study of Stalinism, the party canon, and modern communism as a whole. It offers a unique perspective on Stalin's plans for the transformation of Soviet identity and the society's historical imagination. Perhaps most provocatively, the *Short Course* and its editing offer unprecedented insight into the nature of Stalin's *mentalité* and his understanding of history, agency, and Marxism-Leninism itself.

1. Stalin's Letter to *Proletarskaya revolyutsiya* and the Mobilization of Party Historians. The New Priority of Party History after the Kirov Murder. The Reorganization of Agitprop and Its Textbook Brigades

Despite its centrality to the era, the *Short Course* has only recently begun to receive sustained analysis in modern scholarly literature.[3] Specialists tend to date its origins to 1931, when Stalin denounced party historians as "archive rats" in a letter to the journal *Proletarskaya revolyutsiya* and called for a new approach to party education that would emphasize accessibility and popular indoctrination.[4] What was needed was apparently something that Henry Steele Commager has referred to as a "usable past"—the recasting of party history in an instrumental, mobilizational light. In retrospect, it is clear that this was to be accomplished by replacing the anonymous, materialist schemata of the 1920s with an animated, heroic, and patriotic historical narrative. That said, the general secretary and his comrades-in-arms were surprisingly vague about what precisely they expected from leading historians such as Ye. M. Yaroslavsky, V. G. Knorin, and N. N. Popov, and the latter struggled to bring the existing canon into conformity with the party's demands. In the end, they produced little during the early 1930s that withstood the test of time.[5]

As is well known, the murder of S. M. Kirov in December 1934 provided Stalin with a casus belli to wage war against the remnants of the left Zinovievite opposition. Less well known is the fact that the murder also served as the premise for renewed intervention within the party educational system. Official calls in January 1935 demanded that all indoctrinational efforts henceforth be structured around the Bolsheviks' historic struggle with the internal party opposition.[6] PRAVDA followed up on this directive two months later by chastising state publishing houses for their attempts to get by with new editions of obsolete instructional texts. Not only did these texts fail to supply information now judged to be critical for promoting vigilance within party ranks, but they were still encumbered by excessive schematicism and attention to anonymous social forces.[7]

In the midst of this discussion in the press, A. I. Stetsky summoned leading members of the ideological establishment to his Central Committee department of culture and propaganda for a wide-ranging discussion of the crisis.[8] The next day, Yaroslavsky wrote a letter to Stalin in which he conceded that much of the miserable state of party education was attributable to the inaccessibility of its textual materials. He proposed to rectify the situation by reorganizing party education into a centralized, three-tiered system. On the most basic level, neophytes would study a curriculum structured around a short, animated, still-to-be-written textbook that would flank vital information about party history with illustrated material on the party's "heroism and people." Students would then move on to material organized around a textbook like Knorin's 1934 SHORT HISTORY OF THE CPSU(B), "although here it would be necessary to avoid schematicism" and "liven up" the narrative. Finally, the most politically mature party members would study their history according to a detailed, two-volume text that would devote two-thirds of its narrative to the post-1917 period. Yaroslavsky offered his recently republished HISTORY OF THE CPSU(B) as an example of such an advanced reader. Key to the success of this proposal, Yaroslavsky averred, would be input from the party hierarchy on the priorities around which this new generation of texts was to be constructed.[9]

Internal party reports, combined with Yaroslavsky's lobbying and criticism in the press, pushed Stalin and his entourage to correct the situation not only on the textbook front but throughout the party educational establishment as a whole. In late March 1935, the general secretary gave an extended speech to the Orgburo in which he assailed the quality of party education and adopted Yaroslavsky's call for a three-tiered indoctrinational system. At that same meeting, the party leadership passed a Central Committee resolution calling for new infrastructure, greater discipline, and more accountability—an initiative quickly seconded by the Leningrad party organization, which was still reeling from the Kirov murder.[10] Evidently unsatisfied with these measures, the hierarchs took further action between April and June. First, directives were issued instructing all local party organizations to update and verify their membership rolls in order to purge slackers, criminals, deviationists, and "dead souls" from their ranks.[11] Second, Stetsky's massive Central Committee apparatus was broken up into five smaller departments dedicated to more focused work on agitation and propaganda, state publishing and the press, cultural enlightenment, school policy, and science.[12] Third, Stalin and the other Central Committee secretaries met to draw up a new, more detailed agenda for party history textbooks. Fourth, the hierarchs passed yet another Central Committee resolution that reiterated the need for improvements in history instruction among party members. Courses, classes, and reading circles had to be rethought; curricular materials had to be redesigned.[13] The repeated issuance of such decrees during the mid-1930s testifies both to the continuing priority of such efforts and to a growing impatience over their fulfillment.

Most important among these measures was probably Stalin's meeting about party education efforts with other Central Committee secretaries during the spring of 1935—a little-understood event that is described only obliquely in correspondence between Stetsky, Yaroslavsky, and the general secretary himself. It was apparently at this meeting that a whole array of textbook projects was either commissioned or re-endorsed. B. M. Volin and S. B. Ingulov were instructed to combine forces on a coauthored political grammar. Knorin, Yaroslavsky, and P. N. Pospelov were to produce a new, collectively written popular history for mass audiences. A larger brigade of authors who had been working on a four-volume academic history of the party at the Marx-Engels-Lenin Institute (IMEL) since 1932 was to continue to soldier forward, flanked by a second brigade that was to produce a shorter, two-volume history for grassroots propagandists and party activists.[14]

In some senses, these measures signaled a fresh start on the ideological front. In others, however, they spoke of continued weakness. Four years after Stalin's letter to *Proletarskaya revolyutsiya*, the party leadership had placed responsibility for its new initiatives in the hands of three people who had repeatedly failed to deliver breakthroughs in the past. True, all were quintessential insiders: Knorin was an important Comintern official who had just been appointed to be Stetsky's deputy at Agitprop; Yaroslavsky sat on several prominent editorial boards and the Party Control Commission; Pospelov edited the party's ideological journal *Bolshevik* with the other two. But none of them had any new ideas on how to combine the party hierarchy's demands for an accessible, animated historical narrative with a sophisticated explication of Marxist-Leninist theory. Predictably, although this troika succeeded in cobbling together a massive new two-volume text by the end of 1935—*The History of the CPSU(B): A Popular Textbook*—it failed to win Stalin's approval.[15] Archival material detailing Stalin's reaction to this text has not survived, but it is likely that at least two things aroused his displeasure. First, although the *Popular Textbook* was considerably more dynamic and evocative than its predecessors, it was very long and—despite its title—not really suitable for mass audiences. Second, it was dominated by a verbose play-by-play narrative that offered little in the way of larger observations, generalizations, or lessons associated with the party's historical experience. In other words, the book did not satisfy the party's need for a didactic work that would rally opinion at the grass roots. Stalin's dismissal of the POPULAR TEXTBOOK left its authors little choice but to return to the drawing board in search of a genuinely popular approach to party history.[16]

2. The Ideological Establishment during the Great Terror. Stalin's Reorganization of the Party's Educational System. Chaos within the Textbook Brigades. Stalin's Rewriting of Party History

These problems with party education were compounded in mid-1936 by the advent of the Great Terror. This purge precipitated demands for an explanation for the persistence of opposition within the party, first on the left and then on the right. At the same time, widespread arrests within the upper ranks of the party, state bureaucracy, and military stripped the historical narrative of its protagonists and heroes. Authors who were involved in the development of new textbooks during these years must have looked on helplessly as wave after wave of the Terror swept away the leading lights of the party, realizing that it would be virtually impossible to compile a grand narrative on party history under such conditions. At first, authors like Yaroslavsky appear to have confronted the challenge that the Terror posed to their developing narratives merely by removing mention of party members as they fell.[17] In time, however, the randomness of the purge revealed this to be an exercise in futility—there was simply no way to anticipate who would be the next to be arrested, and this transformed the historians' work into a game of Russian roulette. Aware of the penalty for allowing enemies of the people into print and unwilling to gamble on their ability to predict who within the party would survive the purge, historians simply began to delete all mention of those who were not fixtures of Stalin's inner circle (e.g., V. M. Molotov, L. M. Kaganovich, K. Ye. Voroshilov, N. I. Yezhov), long-dead martyrs (Kirov, M. V. Frunze, F. E. Dzerzhinsky), members of the Soviet Olympus (A. G. Stakhanov, V. K. Blyukher, I. D. Papanin, V. P. Chkalov), or already-condemned enemies of the people (L. D. Trotsky, G. E. Zinoviev, L. B. Kamenev).[18] In the end, this methodology offered the best chance of constructing a narrative that the censor would pass, albeit at the cost of abandoning all pretense of a dynamic storyline animated by a diverse variety of inspirational heroes.

Unsurprisingly, as the Terror mounted, so too did calls from all levels of the party for a canonical textbook that could serve as an almanac or reference book in troubled times.[19] Stalin stoked this sense of ideological panic in his infamous speech at the party's 1937 February–March Central Committee plenum, where he blamed the rank and file's lack of vigilance on their poor understanding of the official line. "Master Bolshevism," he commanded. Prioritize "the political training of our cadres." These demands contributed not only to the tension in the air, but to a formal resolution calling for further educational reform. Stalin capitalized on this mandate shortly after the plenum's conclusion, forwarding a proposal to the Politburo for a two-tier system of "Party" and "Leninist" courses for discussion in early April.[20]

Amid the orgy of arrests that followed the plenum, Yaroslavsky hurriedly submitted to Stalin a draft of a new textbook that he had spent the past year developing. Stalin asked Stetsky to look at it and the latter promptly tore the manuscript apart.[21] Stalin took a close look at Stetsky's report and then rescheduled the Politburo's discussion of party educational reform in order to first sketch out his own broad critique of recent work on the subject. The end result was a terse memorandum that showed no awareness of the effect that the purges were having on the field:

> I think that our textbooks on party history are unsatisfactory for three main reasons. They are unsatisfactory because they present party history without connection to the country's history; because simple discussion of events and facts in the struggle with tendencies [in the party] is given without the necessary Marxist explanations; and because [the texts] suffer from an incorrect formulation and an incorrect periodization of events.

Continuing, Stalin noted that particularly the struggle with factionalism required more attention: already a major characteristic of the Bolshevik experience, the subject was now to become its defining feature. The purpose of this focus was obviously twofold, providing a historically informed explanation for the ongoing search for hidden enemies within the party while at the same time justifying Stalin's demands for heightened political vigilance. Much more attention was also to be given to prerevolutionary Russian political and economic history, which would inform the context and imperative of otherwise obscure interparty debates. Accounts of the postrevolutionary period were to be similarly bolstered. According to Stalin, every chapter and major division of the texts was to be prefaced with pertinent information on Russo-Soviet state history in order to ensure that the books would not read like some "light and unintelligible story about bygone affairs." He concluded his memorandum with a table that laid out in unambiguous terms what he considered to be the correct periodization of the party's historical experience.[22]

Stalin circulated this memorandum among his colleagues in the Politburo and then assembled the group for a meeting in mid-April with specialists like Knorin, Popov, B. M. Tal, L. Z. Mekhlis, and A. I. Ugarov. Two resolutions emerged from this meeting—the first established a commission to organize Stalin's two-tiered training courses and the second outlined the curricular materials that the courses would require. Surviving archival evidence suggests that the lower-tier "Party" courses were to emphasize an accessible, populist line focusing on the U.S.S.R.'s usable past, Soviet patriotism, and the personality cult, and were to rely upon revised editions of Yaroslavsky's and Knorin's well-known textbooks on party history. The upper-tier "Leninist" courses, by contrast, were to stress a more rigorously orthodox approach to party ideology and utilize a new flagship text to be coauthored by Knorin, Yaroslavsky, and Pospelov.[23] Officially freed of all other commitments, this troika was given four months to produce the new catechism.[24]

Few traces of Knorin, Yaroslavsky, and Pospelov's collaboration survive from early that summer—something that is rather curious for a group that had just been tasked with such an important assignment.[25] Yaroslavsky, however, had been upset by Stetsky's review of his SHORT HISTORY and focused closely on the Politburo-commissioned revisions to his well-known SKETCHES ON THE HISTORY OF THE CPSU(B).[26] Knorin wrote an explanatory article about Stalin's views on party history for several leading party journals and then also probably began revising his 1934 textbook.[27] Pospelov spent his time on another piece that was perhaps intended for the IMEL's single remaining textbook brigade.[28] Such behavior is odd enough to provoke questions about what was preventing the troika from focusing exclusively on its central mandate. Were the historians intimidated by the nature of the assignment? Did personal rivalries complicate their collaborative work? Did they somehow believe that they could satisfy the party hierarchy with a revised version of their 1935 POPULAR TEXTBOOK?

Perhaps the best explanation for the troika's peculiar behavior stems from the Terror's savage assault on the Soviet elite, which during the spring and early summer of 1937 was consuming not only historic individuals, but historians themselves. Colleagues like G. S. Zaidel, G. S. Fridlyand, N. N. Vanag, Z. B. Lozinsky, O. A. Lidak, V. M. Dalin, S. A. Piontkovsky, S. M. Dubrovsky, T. M. Dubynya, I. V. Frolov, N. M. Voitinsky, and A. I. Urazov all "disappeared" as arrests swept through the profession.[29] Popov's exposure as an "enemy of the people" on June 17 abruptly closed the books on the IMEL textbook project that he was supervising.[30] And the arrest of Knorin himself a week later likely drove Yaroslavsky and Pospelov to despair as it threatened their project with total collapse.[31] This probably indicates why so little archival material survives from the troika's work during these months, inasmuch as Knorin's arrest either forced Yaroslavsky and Pospelov to turn over hundreds of pages of notes and drafts to the NKVD or destroy this paper trail themselves. Internal IMEL reports indicate that this wave of repression within the ideological establishment left the institute almost totally paralyzed.[32]

Days after Knorin's arrest, Yaroslavsky submitted to Stalin a new version of his SKETCHES ON THE HISTORY OF THE CPSU(B) that he had revised for the lower-tier "Party" courses that were scheduled to launch that fall. In an accompanying letter, Yaroslavsky claimed that he had been focusing all of his energies on this work recently (probably a poorly concealed attempt to distance himself from the fallen Knorin) and announced his readiness to begin work on the more advanced narrative for the upper-tier courses with Pospelov.[33] Stalin took a look at his 800-page typescript, had it laid out in publishers' galleys, and then lightly edited it before passing it on to Stetsky.[34] The general secretary must have given it a relatively positive appraisal, because while Stetsky's eventual review was critical, it focused on narrow questions of fact and interpretation rather than more fundamental flaws. Stalin accepted the constructive tone of the report and forwarded it to the rest of the Politburo members for their sanction.[35]

In the end, Yaroslavsky's manuscript was judged to be too long and too choked with factual detail for use with mass audiences.[36] That said, the party hierarchy had few other choices. The IMEL's four-volume academic history had collapsed in 1936 and its shorter project had just been crippled by Popov's "unmasking." Knorin's arrest had doomed both his lower-tier textbook and the flagship text that he was to write with Yaroslavsky and Pospelov. This forced the party hierarchy to delay the launch of Stalin's new educational system and to press Yaroslavsky for revisions to his lower-tier manuscript—decisions that suspended his plans to develop a more advanced text.[37] To help with this time-consuming work, Stetsky commandeered a brigade of remaining specialists at the IMEL—Pospelov, V. G. Sorin, M. S. Volin, and others—to help Yaroslavsky with the redrafting. As Yaroslavsky would later remember, "a whole group took responsibility for these issues. Comrade [A. A.] Zhdanov even said along the way that 'a whole collective farm' had taken shape around the project."[38] For his part, Yaroslavsky appears to have returned to the project willingly, understandably reluctant to lose favor with the party hierarchy. The weight of the task bore down on him, however; as he later recalled: "after that project was presented [to Stalin] and after it was looked over by members of the Politburo, we were told: 'Make it twice as short, so that it will run no more than 240 pages in length.' This was a very difficult task—you can't just scrunch this sort of thing down—and it took an awful lot of work."[39]

Indeed, it was only in November 1937 that Yaroslavsky succeeded in returning his lower-tier manuscript—now in its second incarnation and retitled HISTORY OF THE CPSU(B): A SHORT TEXTBOOK—to the party hierarchy.[40] Thoroughly reworked and half its former size, the book prioritized accessibility through references to Soviet patriotism, the personality cult, and the usable past (to the extent to which this was still possible). Although the SHORT TEXTBOOK contained a fairly narrow, selective cast of protagonists and malefactors, it was otherwise a surprisingly rich and detailed account. Lenin and Stalin loomed particularly large, of course, both because they animated an otherwise impersonal narrative and because Yaroslavsky had long harbored dreams of writing a biography of the general secretary.[41]

When Stalin found time to look at the manuscript in late 1937 or early 1938, he judged it to be worth reviewing and ordered it circulated among members of his inner circle. That said, if Stalin did not object to the overall approach to party history embodied in the text, he did reject Yaroslavsky's plodding historical introduction and hasty conclusion. After editing the first few pages of the introduction himself, he asked Pospelov to write a more theoretical one.[42] Stalin heavily revised this draft and then met with Zhdanov and Pospelov twice in early March, even as the Third Moscow Trial was deciding the fates of N. I. Bukharin, A. I. Rykov, and their "co-conspirators."[43] Ultimately, it was decided to equip the textbook with only a minimalistic introduction and shift the theory to its conclusion.[44] Stalin's notes from this session suggest that he was utterly obsessed by the notion of an omnipresent conspiracy that state prosecutor A. Ya. Vyshinsky was presenting at the Bukharin trial:

1. All non-com[munist] parties in the working class—the S[ocialist] R[evolutionarie]s, Mensheviks, Anarcho-Syndicalists, *and so on*—became counter-rev[olutionary] BOURGEOIS parties even before the Oct[ober] Revolution and *thereafter turned into* agents of intern[ational] espionage agencies.
2. All *oppositionist* currents within our party ~~turned~~—the Trotskyites, ~~leftists,~~ rightists (Bukharin-Rykov), "leftists" (Lominadze, Shatskin), "work[ers'] oppos[ition]" (Shlyapn[ikov], Medvedev and o[thers]), "democr[atic] centralists" (Sapronov), and nationalists of every stripe and republic of the U.S.S.R.—became enemies of the people and agents (spies) of intern[ational] espionage agencies in the course of the struggle.
3. How did this come about?
   a. These oppositionist currents were in [illegible].
   b. Then, having been defeated in an ideological sense and having lost their footing within the working class, they turned for aid to the imperialists and became spies in the pay of their espionage agencies.[45]

As is visible from these directives, Stalin was unsatisfied by the textbook's treatment of the party's struggle with the external opposition. The treachery of the Mensheviks, SRs, and other socialists needed to be given a greater sense of historicity: if at first, before October 1917, they had secretly served the domestic Russian bourgeoisie, after the revolution they switched their allegiance to foreign paymasters abroad. This explained the persistence of their double-dealing as well as their resistance to the Bolshevik cause even after their own defeat. Equally disconcerting was the textbook's failure to make sense of the oppositionist currents within the Bolshevik party itself. Referring obliquely to the paranoiac revelations of the Third Moscow Trial, Stalin instructed Pospelov and Yaroslavsky to focus on how all dissenting Bolshevik factions on the left and the right had joined together after their defeat to continue their struggle with the party's leadership. Lacking popular support at home, this unholy alliance was described as entering into a conspiracy with the enemies of the U.S.S.R. abroad, revealing the full extent of its ideological and moral bankruptcy.

Taken together, these themes were to define Yaroslavsky and Pospelov's revisions to the textbook's conclusion. Stalin also clearly expected the historians to work back through the rest of the manuscript, interpolating details into earlier chapters that would foreshadow the unmasking of the entire conspiracy in early 1938. Although demanding, these instructions were much more specific than what Yaroslavsky and Pospelov had received in the past and they responded energetically to the task at hand. Pospelov played such an important role in these revisions that Yaroslavsky added his name to the book's title page when it was laid out in publisher's galleys in late March.[46]

Ye. M. Yaroslavsky and P. N. Pospelov at work, late 1930s. RGASPI, f. 629, op. 1, d. 141, l. 22.

On April 3, Stalin met with Zhdanov and Pospelov to discuss this third draft, now known as THE HISTORY OF THE CPSU(B): A SHORT COURSE.[47] Zhdanov's notes from the meeting suggest that the general secretary remained unsatisfied with the book's conclusion—particularly its treatment of how the party's enemies shifted from mere opposition to treason and conspiracy.

> ALMOST READY
>
> Pick apart the other parties
>
> Provide a reading list
>
> In the conclusion:
>
> Which parties and which groups encircled the working class and how did the party overcome them?
>
> THE HISTORY OF THE PARTY is the history of the struggle with and destruction of other parties.
>
> In the conclusion, LIST OFF how ALL OF THEM were defeated.
>
> So that people will understand Lenin and grasp what the parties were in 1917.
>
> These parties [illegible] in the history of the civil war.
>
> ABOUT STALIN'S SINGLE PARTY.
>
> This is why history exists. All the other parties were on the other side. Lenin said that this is a law.
>
> Go over how the hostile parties became bourgeois parties even before October and about the tendencies (how the De[mocratic]C[entralist]s became c[ounter]-r[evolutionary] groups).
>
> The basic line is what Lenin said at the Tenth Party Congress: that once they were ideologically defeated and after they had lost their foothold within the working class, they looked to the imperialists for help.
>
> And [they became] mercenary spies of their intelligence services.
>
> Criticism is necessary. Factionalism is not necessary.[48]

In the wake of this meeting, Zhdanov asked Pospelov to prepare at least two more drafts of the conclusion.[49] Unsatisfied with this work, Zhdanov apparently then asked Pospelov to refashion what he had written into a long passage for interpolation into the existing conclusion.[50] This addition, along with a handful of other revisions, were incorporated into Yaroslavsky and Pospelov's fourth version of the manuscript, which was sent to Stalin on April 24.[51]

Many associated with the work on the textbook were quite confident that the book was now ready for publication. Not only had Stalin read the first three versions of the text and commented upon the latter two, but he was also known to have skimmed the fourth version right after receiving it—a quick read-through that produced only a few critical comments.[52] Yaroslavsky was con-

Stalin at his writing desk, late 1930s. RGASPI, f. 558, op. 11, d. 1650, l. 20.

fident enough to describe the book as forthcoming in a speech at the Higher Party School in May; Zhdanov did the same in Leningrad in June.[53] Stalin acted as if the ordeal was nearly over as well. First, he appointed an editorial commission to proofread the SHORT COURSE manuscript. Second, in the same Politburo resolution, he called for an array of other "short courses" to be written on geography, world history, and the history of the U.S.S.R.[54] Third, Stalin even began to lightly edit the textbook's last chapters and conclusion.[55]

Perhaps because Stalin expected this editing to be quite straightforward, he began proofreading the galleys systematically only in late May. According to Yaroslavsky, he quickly became very frustrated. Cursing that "no 'collective farm' will ever be able to get this right," the general secretary decided to rewrite much of the book himself.[56] As he explained to his inner circle in a letter later that August:

> Of the HISTORY OF THE CPSU(B)'s 12 chapters, it turned out to be necessary to fundamentally revise 11 of them. Only the 5th chapter ended up not needing fundamental revisions. I did this in order to underscore and emphasize theoretical moments in the party's history in view of our cadres' weakness in the area of theory and in view of the pressing need to begin liquidating this weakness. It was this reasoning that led to the need to fundamentally revise the book. Were it not for this reasoning, the book, of course, would not have demanded such revisions.[57]

As mild and almost apologetic as Stalin's letter was, the new draft that he now sent to his colleagues and to Yaroslavsky and Pospelov made it clear that he had objected to a lot more than just the previous draft's treatment of Marxist-Leninist theory. What was the underlying logic to Stalin's intervention? Key to understanding his insertions and excisions is the chaos of the Terror, which delayed both the launch of the two-tiered party educational system and the broader party history catechism as well. Indeed, it had taken nearly a year for Yaroslavsky and Pospelov to complete just their plodding lower-tier text! Unsatisfied with what Yaroslavsky and Pospelov had delivered but unable to wait any longer for the planned flagship narrative, Stalin apparently decided to rewrite what they had written into something usable at all levels of the party organization.[58]

Archival evidence indicates that one of the things Stalin objected to in Yaroslavsky and Pospelov's narrative was its tendency to over-encumber the reader with historical minutiae—something that led the general secretary to ruthlessly strike out wordiness and digressions that did not contribute directly to the overall story. He also cut dozens of paragraphs and scores of parenthetical references relating to himself and his career—changes that did not eliminate the personality cult from the text, but did prevent it from eclipsing other major thematic priorities.

In place of all this excessive detail, Stalin did two things. First, he altered the narrative's interpretive position on a number of key themes, from the Bolsheviks' prerevolutionary standoff with other opposition parties to the nature of the October 1917 revolution and the postrevolutionary struggle to build Soviet power. (Many of these revisions are discussed at length below in the Critical Edition section of this Introduction.) Second, Stalin attempted to interpolate into the text the theoretical red thread that he claimed was absent in Yaroslavsky and Pospelov's account. Although he did this throughout the manuscript, this new priority is most visible in Chapter Four and the conclusion, where he added an entirely new philosophical section on dialectical materialism, and a set of broader theoretical reflections on the party's historical experience.

Aside from the general secretary's elevation of theory and depreciation of the personality cult, perhaps the most eye-catching part of his thematic interventions concerned the book's explanation for the Great Terror. During March and April 1938, Stalin had instructed Yaroslavsky and Pospelov to interpolate evidence into the text of the omnipresent left-right conspiracy that had just been uncovered by the Third Moscow Trial in order to explain problems associated with collectivization, industrialization, and the party's hold on power. In each case, examples of poor agricultural policy, kulak resistance, industrial wrecking, consumer shortages, and factional activity were to be tied to the Trotskyite-Bukharinite opposition and their capitalist masters abroad. Ultimately, this recourse to conspiracy as a way of explaining domestic shortcomings created a claustrophobic narrative of tension, vulnerability, and fear in the face of a resourceful, relentless enemy.[59]

When Stalin began to work through this material a few months later, however, he appears to have found the omnipresent conspiracy paradigm inexpedient, if not totally unpersuasive. Reversing himself from earlier that spring, Stalin now cut vast stretches of text from the manuscript with an eye toward reducing the intensity and immediacy of the threat presented in Yaroslavsky and Pospelov's manuscript. Not only did the general secretary strike out much of the detail and discussion devoted to the crises in industry, agriculture, and party life, but he also quashed the attribution of these crises to a dynamic, centralized opposition at home or abroad. Stalin also removed discussion of the Comintern and class struggle outside of the U.S.S.R. in places like Germany and Spain, stifling the contention that there was a worldwide capitalist conspiracy under way against socialism.[60] What Yaroslavsky and Pospelov had depicted as a tight and interconnected narrative of organized wrecking and criminal activity was transformed by Stalin into a much more disorganized set of crises associated with the building of socialism.

This is not to say, of course, that Stalin completely rewrote the Short Course's broad conclusion that the struggle against the domestic opposition was to be treated on par with the struggle against hostile enemies abroad. Indeed, all these forces—internal and external—were described in the book's final chapter as having come together in a broad conspiratorial cabal with the intent of toppling the Soviet regime and reincorporating the lands of the U.S.S.R. back into the capitalist system. But Stalin's editing reduced the actuality of this plot by decoupling it from the specific crises that the regime had faced during the early to mid-1930s, transforming it from a concrete threat into a more abstract menace. He also rolled back the immediacy of the conspiracy by suggesting that any malevolent plans already in motion had been arrested by the Third Moscow Trial. Stalin then completed his narrative on the Terror by quickly seguing into an uplifting discussion of Soviet representative democracy, denying his readers any opportunity for hand-wringing or doubt.

If Stalin's downgrading of the Terror altered the whole emplotment of party history, another dimension of his revisions affected how it was to be framed for public consumption. As noted above, during the summer of 1938 the general secretary stripped the Short Course of much of its play-by-play narrative in favor of a more dehistoricized focus on the grand dynamics, themes, and patterns of party history—"theory," as Stalin put it. In his subsequent August letter to his colleagues, he justified this return to Marxist-Leninist schematicism by citing the party rank and file's weakness in theory—something that he claimed to necessitate the purge of huge amounts of factual material and commentary on dozens of beloved Soviet heroes from Old Bolshevik revolutionaries and Red Army commanders to champion workers, peasants, record-setting aviators, and Arctic explorers. By the time he finished editing the text, Stalin had removed mention of over half of Yaroslavsky and Pospelov's entire cast of characters. Theory, according to the general secretary, was more important to Soviet society than the exploits of mere mortals, no matter how heroic or inspiring.

This assertion of the importance of theory was not without precedent, of course—during the 1930s, Stalin had repeatedly demanded that his cadres complement technical training with a better understanding of Marxism-Leninism. At the 1937 February-March plenum, Stalin returned to the need to master theory—something he associated with ideological vigilance—and this issue clearly remained on his mind in the summer of 1938.[61] Two areas were apparently of particular concern. First, cadres were to master what Stalin referred to in early drafts of his revisions as "the law on the party's development." Put another way, what was it that distinguished Lenin's movement from its rivals and how did it persevere in its commitment to revolution and socialism both before and after 1917? Second, cadres were to finally appreciate the centrality of "socialism in one country" to the Soviet experiment. Unsurprisingly, this theory had loomed large in Yaroslavsky and Pospelov's narrative; now, however, it absolutely dominated the party's historical experience. Socialism in one country was apparently what Lenin had focused on after the collapse of the Second International during the First World War. Socialism in one country explained the course of the revolution, the civil war, and the New Economic Policy (NEP). Socialism in one country defined the scale and timing of industrialization and collectivization. And socialism in one country would determine the nature of state policy in the future, whether concerning the economy, the society, or the defense of the U.S.S.R.

Of course, such priorities account for only part of Stalin's motives for rewriting the text, insofar as they ignore the fact that the general secretary had spent the first half of the 1930s demanding that the ideological establishment develop precisely what he now proposed to abandon: an animated, accessible, and heroic approach to party propaganda and ideology.[62] They also ignore the circumstances under which this style of mobilization ground to a halt after mid-1936, when many of the leading lights of the Soviet Olympus were consumed by the unfolding purge of the party, state, and Red Army. In other words, Stalin's return to theory in 1938 ought not to be viewed in an ideological vacuum. Rather, it is necessary to view this decision as having been predicated at least in part by Stalin's realization that the Terror had compromised the party's ability to use heroes to personify the official line.

Stalin's declaration of the need to prioritize theory over the heroic may also stem from his ongoing frustration with the excesses of the personality cult, which he periodically suspected of eclipsing more sophisticated forms of party propaganda. Stalin was, of course, well aware of the role that charismatic leadership played in the U.S.S.R., uniting an otherwise disorganized and restive society under the aegis of a larger-than-life leader. That said, he is also known to have lashed out at the cult during the 1930s when it focused too tightly on him as a person instead of as the symbolic personification of party and state leadership.[63] This explains why he deleted so much of Yaroslavsky and Pospelov's hagiographic commentary devoted to his person from the narrative; it also explains his removal of similarly passionate paeans to the likes of Voroshilov, Molotov, and other leading Bolshevik personages.

Yaroslavsky and Pospelov's rhetorical excess may likewise explain Stalin's most puzzling editorial decision, which cut almost all discussion of Soviet patriotism from the text. Like his turn against Soviet heroes and the personality cult, Stalin's opposition to the manuscript's celebration of patriotic loyalty to the U.S.S.R. appears to contradict his encouragement of this sort of sloganeering earlier in the decade.[64] What's more, although mention of Soviet patriotism in official mass culture had been inhibited between 1936 and 1938 by the Terror's repression of specific patriots, the emotion itself remained very much an active referent in regime propaganda. Stalin's cutting of the SHORT COURSE's numerous invocations of patriotism, therefore, probably stemmed from the verbose, flowery form in which these statements were made rather than from any misgivings over their actual content. As noted above, Yaroslavsky and Pospelov had never written about patriotism in their earlier party histories (perhaps out of a sense of ideological discomfort with this rather questionably Marxist concept) and their invocations of the emotion here were expressed in shrill, clichéd terms that detracted from the textbook's persuasive appeal. As with other rhetorical clutter in the text, Stalin was quick to cut such formulaic commentary. That said, if Stalin stripped this rhetoric out of the text on account of its forced nature, he failed to replace it with a more sincere discussion of the positive role of patriotism in Soviet society. In the long run, this had the effect of decoupling the SHORT COURSE from the broader dynamics of interwar Soviet propaganda and mass culture and limited its overall accessibility, especially among mass audiences.

When Stalin wrote to his colleagues about his revisions to the SHORT COURSE in August 1938, he also sent them copies of the text for proofreading. For the most part, the party hierarchs reported only favorable impressions; any critical observations were almost always confined to minor questions of style and mechanics.[65] True, Molotov, A. I. Mikoian, M. I. Kalinin, and G. I. Petrovsky proposed a handful of more substantial corrections (and Molotov twice asked not to be credited with other people's accomplishments), but such quibbles were largely ignored.[66] Yaroslavsky and Pospelov also enthusiastically participated in this round of editing, even though Stalin had replaced their names on the book's title page with an anonymous formula attributing the text to "A Commission of the CPSU(B) Central Committee."[67] Yaroslavsky wrote excitedly to Stalin that the textbook would play "an enormous role in the masses' Bolshevik education." That said, he expressed concern over the amount of biographical material that had ended up on the proverbial cutting-room floor:

> . . . I do have one observation of substance, however. Literally every mention of your name and information about your public service has been excised from the textbook's first two chapters. This is of course an illustration of your great modesty, which is a wonderful trait for any Bolshevik to have. But you belong to history and your participation in the party's construction must be fully depicted. I attempted to do just this in the version of the textbook that we turned in to the Central Committee.[68]

Pospelov, too, hailed the new manuscript, particularly the way that it treated the elusive subject of theory:

> When you read and reread the first two chapters, you see how incomplete the galleys were that we submitted to the Central Committee, both in terms of form and content. You especially sense the weakness of the old material when it came to illuminating the theoretical moments of the party's history, which now, after your fundamental revisions, are advanced as a top priority.

Pospelov likewise voiced concern about the removal of the text's commentary on the prerevolutionary Bolshevik organizations of the Caucasus and Stalin's role therein.[69] Days later, both historians followed up these initial letters with a series of corrections and clarifications that Stalin found quite useful while resolving remaining problems with the text.[70] That said, he proved unwilling to reconsider his decision to downgrade the role of the personality cult in the text.

Determined to release the textbook without further delay, Stalin then summoned Molotov, Zhdanov, Pospelov, Yaroslavsky, and L. Ya. Rovinsky, an editor at Pravda, to his Kremlin office for a series of nightly editorial meetings between September 8 and 18.[71] Each evening, they would fine-tune a single chapter of the text in preparation for its serialization in the newspaper the next morning. Yaroslavsky described the meetings later in vivid terms:

> I must say that I've seen an awful lot of editorial sessions in my 40 years of party work, but never in my life have I seen such editing, nor in general such attention to scholarship or the printed word. [. . .] Every day, at about 5 or 6 o'clock in the evening [*sic*, actually much closer to midnight], the editorial commission would assemble in Stalin's office. [. . .] Every line was subjected to discussion. Comrade Stalin took every kind of correction very seriously, even down to the last comma, and discussed it all.[72]

According to Pospelov, the nightly sessions also afforded Stalin an opportunity to reminisce about how he and his comrades-in-arms had studied party history in the olden days.[73] Final endorsement at the end of each exhausting session cleared the way for PRAVDA to publish the SHORT COURSE ON THE HISTORY OF THE CPSU(B) in eleven full-page centerfold installments in mid-September 1938. Few events during the years of the Great Terror captivated Stalin and his comrades-in-arms to the degree to which the completion of the SHORT COURSE did.

3. Launch of the SHORT COURSE. Early Confusion and Controversy. A Newly Bifurcated Party Educational System. Reorganization of Propaganda and Agitation during the War

Unsurprisingly, the SHORT COURSE's appearance was greeted by major excitement and a massive publicity campaign.[74] PRAVDA declared that "the duty of every Bolshevik, no matter whether a party member or not, is to commit to the serious, attentive, dogged study" of the new volume, described parenthetically as "an irreplaceable guide for mastering Bolshevism." Hints in the press of Stalin's personal involvement in the project—"the enormous theoretical work accomplished by the Central Committee and personally by the party chief and genius of humanity, Comrade Stalin"—guaranteed it unquestionable authority. PRAVDA called upon the entire party to immerse itself in the text, redoubling its efforts to master party history.[75] Massive initial printings of the SHORT COURSE in book form confirmed the scale of the investment that the party hierarchy was making.[76]

This combination of popular anticipation and official fanfare assured the SHORT COURSE canonical status even before the passage of a corresponding Politburo resolution later that year.[77] This authority was reinforced by the routine invocation of the text in the press and newsreel during the remainder of the interwar period.[78] Citation of the textbook became a key part of authoritative commentary on subjects from history and philosophy to art, literature, and the sciences.[79] Within the broader reaches of Soviet mass culture, the SHORT

Course had a similar effect on literary criticism and repertoire for the theatrical stage and silver screen. Ultimately, its narrative came to govern everything from party and Komsomol entrance exams to the arrangement of exhibits in the Central Lenin Museum.[80]

As triumphal as the textbook's launch was, however, it took place against the backdrop of profound confusion and paralysis within the party educational system. As noted above, the Politburo had ratified plans for a two-tier set of "Party" and "Leninist" courses in 1937 that were designed to differentiate between mass indoctrinational activities and higher party education—plans that were wrecked after Knorin's arrest and Yaroslavsky's failure to immediately deliver a usable lower-tier text. When Stalin moved to personally complete the lower-level text that Yaroslavsky eventually supplied with Pospelov, he appears to have rewritten it in a bid to produce a single master narrative that would be appropriate for all audiences. Abandoning his plans for a multi-tier party educational system, Stalin allowed the party press to advertise the Short Course as a canonical text fit for all.

Stalin's eleventh-hour redesign of the Short Course limited its accessibility, however, not only because of its new emphasis on theory and depreciation of conventional propaganda tropes, but because his editing left the text uneven, incompletely hybridized, and sometimes impenetrably schematic. Within a few weeks of the text's release, Stalin appears to have realized that the Short Course was more difficult than he had intended, perhaps while presiding over a conference of propagandists that was hurriedly convened at the end of September 1938. Backtracking on the issue of the text's intended readership, Stalin suddenly criticized Pravda, Izvestiya, and Komsomolskaya pravda for overselling the book on the mass level. As important as the book was, he now claimed that it was chiefly intended for party executives and upwardly mobile activists. This evasive position is visible in the transcript from the first day of the conference, when the general secretary interrupted one of his comrades-in-arms as the latter attempted to define who was to study the book:

Zhdanov: This task is connected with the means by which not only our cadres in party propaganda will master Bolshevism, but our state cadres, administrative cadres, [those in] cooperatives, and students within [the country's] youth . . .

Stalin: [interrupting] . . . and employees . . .

Zhdanov: . . . [and] people who have a direct relationship to government, as one cannot run a government like ours without keeping abreast of such things, without being well-grounded in theoretical knowledge.[81]

Aware of the ambiguousness of this directive, Stalin attempted to clarify his position in another speech at the close of the conference:

> To whom is this book addressed? It is addressed to our cadres and not to ordinary workers on the shop floor, nor to ordinary employees in institutions, but to the cadres whom Lenin described as professional revolutionaries. This book is addressed to our administrative cadres. They, most of all, need to go and work on their theory; after that, everyone else can. One cannot forget, you know, that in our plants and factories we have youth who are studying [in addition to working], and that these people are the future leaders of our state.[82]

Still ambiguous and internally inconsistent, this position was reiterated by Stalin again at an October Politburo meeting where the SHORT COURSE was placed in the center of indoctrinational efforts for party personnel. Apparently almost everyone of any importance in the U.S.S.R. was to master the text sooner or later—from bureaucrats and bookkeepers to brigadiers on the shop floor. "Even Comrade Khrushchev should," quipped Stalin, teasing the Ukrainian party boss for his folksy lack of sophistication. Khrushchev, in actual fact, probably epitomized Stalin's "cadres" better than the general secretary even realized. After all, like Khrushchev, many members of the party and state administration had had only a few years of formal schooling and were, for all intents and purposes, only functionally literate.[83] A survey of party administrators at the provincial, regional, city, and local level had revealed in 1937 that three-quarters of them had the equivalent of only an elementary school education.[84] This meant that many of Stalin's leading party cadres would struggle to understand the SHORT COURSE, much less master it.[85]

This assessment of the abilities of the party's rank and file corresponds closely to concerns expressed by specialists at the above-mentioned September 1938 propagandists' conference. Although the SHORT COURSE was conceptually striking, it downgraded or abandoned three themes that had defined party propaganda since the early to mid-1930s: heroism, the personality cult, and Soviet patriotism. Many involved in party indoctrination had come to regard these emphases as vital to the official line's accessibility and were unsure about how else to popularize the text. Typical were the views of a propagandist named Shlensky, who noted at the conference that although the SHORT COURSE was "an encyclopedia of everything known about issues concerning Marxism-Leninism," it paid insufficient attention to important individuals in party history. Auxiliary material or a specialized curriculum was needed, according to Shlensky, to structure audiences' work on the text and guarantee its accessibility.[86]

Stalin responded impatiently to such suggestions when he took the floor at the end of the conference, reiterating that the SHORT COURSE was intended to focus on large, theoretical questions rather than minutiae. More dramatically, he criticized the party's long-standing reliance on a heroic approach to party history:

> Until now, party history has been written from a different perspective. I don't want to insult or hound the authors of these history textbooks—these are people who've worked conscientiously and done much for the good of our party—but all the same, the path they've taken, the path which our textbooks have taken, just won't do. They've attempted to train and educate people by example, by celebrating exemplary individuals. Not everyone did this, but most did. And even now, Comrade Shlensky notes that the book gives insufficient treatment to the role of specific individuals. But since when is that what is at stake? We were presented with this sort of a draft text and we fundamentally revised it. [Originally,] this draft textbook was for the most part based on exemplary individuals—those who were the most heroic, those who escaped from exile and how many times they escaped, those who suffered in the name of the cause, etc., etc.
>
> But should a textbook really be designed like that? Can we really use such a thing to train and educate our cadres? We ought to base our cadres' training on ideas, on theory. What is theory? Theory is knowledge of the laws of historical development. If we possess such knowledge, then we'll have real cadres, but if the people don't possess this knowledge, they won't be cadres—they'll be just empty spaces.
>
> What do exemplary individuals really give us? I don't want to pit ideas and individuals against one another—sometimes it's necessary to refer to individuals, but we should refer to them only as much as is really necessary. It's ideas that really matter, not individuals—ideas, in a theoretical context.[87]

Unwilling to compromise on this issue during the conference, Stalin reiterated his position again at the Politburo in early October.[88] Shlensky had probably hoped that the SHORT COURSE would shore up official propaganda efforts, which had suffered during the Terror, and supply a new pantheon of heroes that could be used to personify the party line. Stalin rebuffed this notion, demonstrating a strong belief in the mobilizational power of theory and profound doubt over the potential of Soviet heroism to serve as party propaganda in the wake of the purges.

If Stalin's dismissal of Shlensky's concerns was unexpected, another of his directives at the conference was probably no less shocking. The general secretary had long been frustrated by the party educational system, which despite its massive scale was famously disorganized, inefficient, and riddled with incompetence. Listening to the propagandists detail its many shortcomings at the conference, Stalin apparently came to the conclusion that the Short Course made much of this educational system redundant. Couldn't individual study of the Short Course, complemented by an occasional tutorial or lecture, accomplish official goals with greater reliability? Wouldn't self-study not only foster a direct relationship between audience and text, but also eliminate the need for poorly educated middlemen? Such reasoning led Stalin to propose at the end of the conference a radical redesign of the party's indoctrinational system that would close the majority of its reading circles and political literacy courses and replace them with a curriculum that would enable Soviet citizens to study party ideology on their own.[89] Unsurprisingly, the conference participants proved unwilling to contradict this proposal.

Two weeks later, when the Politburo assembled to discuss Stalin's proposed reform of the party educational system, the general secretary reiterated his objections to the way party indoctrinational efforts had been structured around specific heroic personalities rather than more universal theoretical laws. An educational strategy that had apparently left party cadres poorly trained and insufficiently vigilant, it had been exacerbated by weak grassroots-level instruction and supporting materials. Referring to the Short Course as a panacea for this crisis, Stalin offered the textbook as a template for a whole new generation of handbooks, brochures, and reference materials and called for party education to be organized tightly around it. Lectures, tutorials, and individual study were henceforth to replace most of the reading circles and courses that had defined earlier indoctrinational efforts; leading party cadres and the intelligentsia were to master the Short Course on their own. A Central Committee resolution was promulgated in mid-November that passed these reforms into law.[90]

Stalin's reorientation of the party educational system seriously complicated the launch of the Short Course. The abandonment of traditional propaganda tropes and indoctrinational infrastructure, compounded by the Short Course's own awkwardness and schematicism, made mastery of the text extremely difficult. Many attempted to learn the text by rote; others appear to have given up. Unable to resolve these issues, the ideological establishment was quickly forced to resort to measures that contradicted the spirit, if not the letter, of the new educational law. By late 1939, a new array of ad hoc study circles and informal courses had come to rival the scale of the previous network. These forums were complemented by dozens of improvised auxiliary texts and readers that were likewise designed to aid in the mastery of the Short Course.[91] Even more intriguing was the return of propaganda tropes based on heroes, patriotism, and the personality cult, which had never fully disappeared from Soviet mass culture and which now supplied content to the grassroots groups in order to make party history more accessible.[92]

In time, these auxiliary courses and texts led to a de facto bifurcation of party indoctrinational efforts that was reminiscent of Stalin's stillborn two-tier system from 1937. Propagandists at the grassroots level again stressed the tried and true mobilizational themes of the mid-1930s, aided by a new retrenchment of the personality cult (particularly after the publication of two new Stalin biographies in late 1939).[93] These grassroots efforts were also now augmented by a major new drive that framed party history within the context of the Russian national past and the thousand-year history of Russian statehood.[94] More elite mobilizational efforts, by contrast, focused on ideologically orthodox themes revolving around Marxism-Leninism, a materialist reading of party history, and Stalin's own schematic theory of the party. This bifurcation of party educational efforts after 1938 was never explicitly acknowledged, but it does explain the persistence of such varied mobilization tropes and devices throughout Soviet society during the late interwar period.

The SHORT COURSE, it should be said, straddled this bifurcation rather awkwardly, being too abstract and complex for mass audiences and too rigid and dogmatic for better-educated ones. Readers at the grass roots must have found the text particularly disconcerting, not only because it was difficult to master, but because it made little or no mention of Soviet heroism, patriotism, or russocentrism, three of the most ubiquitous themes in official prewar mass culture. Frustrated by this disconnect and by broader problems of accessibility, grassroots agitators and instructors wrote to party authorities for advice. What was to be prioritized as one studied this book? What were the red threads that had to be traced throughout the narrative? Were some parts of the book more important than others or were readers expected to master this "encyclopedia of Bolshevism" in its entirety?

No less than Yaroslavsky himself tried to play down the confusion associated with the SHORT COURSE in early January 1939 while addressing a Komsomol Central Committee conference. "It seems to me," he began, "that many here have gotten mixed up and are exaggerating the difficulties to be found in the study of the history of the party, Bolshevism, Marxism, and Leninism." Dismissing issues of accessibility and abstraction, Yaroslavsky urged agitators and lecturers merely to paraphrase the textbook's contents to their audiences in more colloquial terms. If done correctly, this approach would allow them to present the text in "popularized and simple" terms without actually simplifying the overarching message of the book at all.[95]

Persistent questions led Yaroslavsky to return to the subject later that year with more detailed, thoughtful advice. Speaking anecdotally, he noted that when he taught party history, he found it useful to communicate to his students a sweeping vision of the era: "You need to provide a living, representative picture of the period surrounding the subjects under examination, to recreate the epoch's aroma, as it were, so that the listener can get a sense of the epoch." This approach to popularization apparently required two things. First, Yaroslavsky complemented the SHORT COURSE with an array of supplemental materials and visual aids. Second, he personally supplied details and perspectives not covered in the official narrative. These pedagogical methods, Yaroslavsky averred, opened up the historico-philosophical world of the SHORT COURSE to even the least prepared of audiences.[96]

As reasonable as such pedagogical strategies may seem, they were considerably less effective than Yaroslavsky believed. According to G. V. Shumeiko, an Agitprop staffer and one-time assistant to Pospelov, the Central Committee received numerous complaints between 1938 and 1940 about Yaroslavsky from his students, who found his macro approach to party history disconcerting and who couldn't understand why his lectures strayed so far from the official curriculum. Unaware of Yaroslavsky's central role in the writing of the party canon, they speculated that he might be speaking from old, outdated lecture notes. Perhaps he hadn't fully appreciated the sea change in the party educational system that the SHORT COURSE had precipitated? Some requested that he be instructed to base his lectures more explicitly on the new orthodoxy. Others, guided by an exaggerated sense of political vigilance, even denounced the historian for deviating from the party line. As Shumeiko explains,

> Yaroslavsky's position as lecturer was complicated by the fact that he often got sidetracked with stories about the various stages of party history and filled these stories with mention of great names, which intentionally or unintentionally equated Stalin with other participants of the revolutionary past. I myself witnessed quite a dramatic scene [while investigating these reports] at a lecture of Yaroslavsky's in the Lenin auditorium of the Miusskaya Square party school. Comments could be heard echoing from the audience during the lecture such as: "Illuminate the facts according to the SHORT COURSE—what you are saying is not depicted there!"
>
> The old man, trying to remain calm, answered that he had personally witnessed the events that he was describing.
>
> "So what?" echoed from the hall. "There is an official interpretation."[97]

As is visible from this dramatic standoff, Yaroslavsky's grand vision of party history and his invocation of famous names and reputations from the past unnerved his students in the wake of the purges. Although frustrated by the SHORT COURSE's narration of party history, they knew enough to fear unofficial interpretations—even those of leading party historians. Forced to choose between an interpretation that they could understand but not fully trust and another that they could trust but not fully understand, most chose the latter.

If a majority of Soviet citizens ultimately tried to learn at least part of the SHORT COURSE by rote, some attempted to alert party authorities to the text's deficiencies. A collective farmer from Rostov, for instance, wrote to Agiprop that the book would be more engaging if it provided more biographical detail on Stalin—a comment that unintentionally reveals the degree to which he and his contemporaries had come to conflate party history with the personality cult. Another Soviet citizen agreed that the text could be more animated and recommended that sections be added in the next printing that would detail the heroism and patriotic valor of Soviet troops on the Manchurian border and in Poland, Finland, and the Baltic states between 1938 and 1940. A schoolteacher complained that the SHORT COURSE's fourth chapter was so convoluted and choked with obscure philosophical references that it simply had to be rewritten; failure to do so would result in misunderstandings and perhaps even unintentional heresy during class discussions. Others likewise complained about the complexity of the text and recommended that state publishing houses produce more auxiliary materials to aid readers with terminology and vital primary sources. Similarly flustered, yet another voice from the grass roots confessed that the text was so difficult that he doubted his generation would be able to master it without special classes.[98] But although all of these suggestions were diligently filed away for safekeeping in the Central Committee archives, there is no evidence that any of them ever received serious consideration. Indeed, aside from the quiet removal of mention of two fallen party members from the text—N. I. Yezhov and F. I. Goloshchekin—the SHORT COURSE was not updated or revised before the start of the war.

In spite of the problems associated with the SHORT COURSE's launch, the textbook reigned supreme over party indoctrination efforts during the last years of the interwar period. The party hierarchy stood behind the new catechism and everywhere one looked, the text loomed large, whether in libraries and public lectures, reading circles and study groups, or newspaper editorials and book reviews. When the All-Union Agricultural Exhibition opened in 1939 to showcase Soviet economic and cultural achievements, the pavilion devoted to the state publishing industry dedicated an entire room to the SHORT COURSE in a building flanked by a larger-than-life statue of a worker on a pillar holding aloft a copy of the book. To mark the second anniversary of the text's appearance, the Central Newsreel Studio in Moscow released a documentary film entitled A MIGHTY WEAPON OF BOLSHEVISM, which included shots of Stalin at his writing desk, copies of the SHORT COURSE rolling off the printing press, and readers enthusiastically working through the book. Juxtaposition of these scenes against images of crowds celebrating the October Revolution on Red Square and tour groups visiting the reorganized Lenin Museum tied the book to famous public rituals and sites.[99]

Indeed, it was only the crisis following the Nazi invasion in June 1941 that forced the ideological establishment to alter its approach to popular indoctrination. New directives dispensed with the system's de facto bifurcation and allowed patriotic, russocentric sloganeering to eclipse wartime references to party history, Marxism-Leninism, and even the personality cult.[100] As a result, the Short Course faded from public view. But as dramatic as this turnabout was, it would be a mistake to regard it as a wholesale ideological retreat from Soviet socialism to Russian nationalism. In 1944, when the situation at the front finally turned to the Soviets' advantage, Agitprop officials began to

Скульптура рабочего на обелиске у павильона «Печать».

Statue of a worker raising a copy of the Short Course up to the sky at the State Publishing Pavilion of the prewar All-Union Agricultural Exhibition, 1939. From Pavilon Pechat': Putevoditel' (Moscow: Sel'khozgiz, 1940), 5.

revive the ideologically orthodox dimensions of the party's indoctrinational program. Agitprop chief G. F. Aleksandrov proposed as early as that March to reorient new educational efforts around the SHORT COURSE. The first priority, according to the Agitprop boss, was to begin republishing the textbook and other Marxist-Leninist classics that had been neglected since the early days of the war. Second, the press was to again afford a prominent place to articles on party history. Third, new research was needed to provide an official narrative on party history between 1938 and 1944, as the SHORT COURSE had nothing to say about the recent past. B. M. Volin reiterated these proposals in a letter to G. M. Malenkov later that year.[101]

4. The Postwar Ideological Revival. Discussions of a Second Edition of the SHORT COURSE. Reorganization of the Party Educational System. Mass Culture. Stalin's Death

In the months that followed victory in 1945, the party leadership returned to championing the cause of ideological orthodoxy.[102] Administrative norms and standards of personal conduct that had been relaxed amid the exigencies of war were now restored and a politicized sense of vigilance again became the order of the day. Massive printings of the SHORT COURSE accompanied this change, releasing millions of new copies of the prewar text into circulation—a somewhat peculiar decision that was offset by large print runs of Stalin's wartime speeches.[103]

This new stress on ideological orthodoxy coincided with a similarly renewed emphasis on the Stalin cult. As the veneration of the general secretary rose to new heights in early 1946, Malenkov proposed to the Politburo that the IMEL take up the long-delayed publication of Stalin's collected works. Most striking about Malenkov's otherwise rather predictable missive was the fact that it proposed to include the whole SHORT COURSE within the new series rather than just Stalin's famous subsection on dialectical and historical materialism. In other words, authorship of the SHORT COURSE was to be reassigned to the general secretary alone.[104] Stalin accepted Malenkov's proposal and drafted a Politburo decision that was approved immediately; PRAVDA announced the new publication plans on January 20.[105]

For some within the ideological establishment, the inclusion of the SHORT COURSE in Stalin's collected works merely confirmed rumors about the book's authorship that had circulated in Soviet society since 1938. That said, it did raise an array of technical questions for IMEL staffers. Would the forthcoming volume merely reprint the 1938 edition in new bindings? Would it feature a new title page in order to clarify the book's authorship? Would it correct other errors that had been identified in the narrative since 1938? Would the narrative be rewritten in the first person or updated to cover the late prewar and wartime periods?

Although incomplete, the IMEL's postwar archives indicate that in the wake of this Politburo decision, the institute conducted a review of all the SHORT COURSE's reported shortcomings in order to identify corrections needed for a new edition. By the fall of 1946, 21 pages of factual errors, inaccurate translations, and lapses in grammar and stylistics had been compiled. That October, this list was forwarded to Stalin along with publisher's galleys for the textbook that been reformatted to match the layout of the general secretary's WORKS.[106] Three months later, in January 1947, Aleksandrov and P. N. Fedoseyev sent Stalin an additional 150-page typescript designed to update the SHORT COURSE's narrative through 1945. Much of this material focused on international security concerns and included new paragraphs on the betrayal of Czechoslovakia in 1938, the failure of collective security in 1939, and the connection of these developments to the signing of the Molotov-Ribbentrop treaty. Other new sections detailed prewar Japanese aggression against the U.S.S.R., the "Winter War" with Finland, and the U.S.S.R.'s annexation of territory along its western borders in 1939–1940. Aleksandrov and Fedoseyev also supplied a new chapter on the Second World War that cast the conflict as the U.S.S.R.'s nearly single-handed struggle with Nazi Germany. It also stressed new themes with relevance to the emerging Cold War, particularly the dynamic nature of Soviet patriotism at home and the duplicity of the U.S.S.R.'s wartime allies abroad.[107] After Aleksandrov and Fedoseyev were dismissed from Agitprop in 1947, D. T. Shepilov rewrote their new chapters as his own, changing very little in the process.[108]

Stalin did not hurry to respond to the IMEL and Agitprop proposals and this caused work on the SHORT COURSE to grind to a halt. The general secretary was, of course, very busy during the late 1940s, preoccupied not only with the everyday affairs of state, but with the production of other canonical books including the first volumes of his collected works and the second edition of his official SHORT BIOGRAPHY.[109] He also devoted an enormous amount of time to a collectively written textbook on Marxist-Leninist political economy.[110] That said, Stalin's relative silence in regard to the SHORT COURSE is puzzling in light of the book's continuing priority.

The general secretary did not, of course, completely neglect the issue during those years. He read the proposals forwarded to him from the IMEL and Agitprop in 1946 and 1947.[111] He also lightly edited two copies of the original 1938 text, experimenting with a new title page and outlining preliminary revisions to Chapter Twelve concerning the origins of the Second World War.[112] But even as he thought about a second edition, he rebuffed S. I. Vavilov's 1949 proposal to insert the entire text of the SHORT COURSE into the seventh volume of the postwar GREAT SOVIET ENCYCLOPEDIA. According to Vavilov, Stalin objected to the idea on a number of levels. "What? Print the entire book?" he apparently asked. "Why? For whom? No more than a twentieth of the book would be worth printing, as the rest of it is intended for party executives and appeals only to a very narrow set of interests. And much of it has become obsolete; moreover, it doesn't include the last ten years." When Vavilov persisted, asking Stalin to recommend someone who could perform the needed updating, the general secretary declared the whole initiative to be premature.[113]

Similar confusion is visible in the archival record in the years that followed. Between 1950 and 1951, the IMEL again prepared the SHORT COURSE for inclusion in Stalin's WORKS. Most striking about this new set of galleys is the fact that it disregarded almost all of the editorial refinements done since 1946.[114] At first glance, this would seem to suggest that Stalin had finally decided against updating the original 1938 text. That said, the general secretary still refused to authorize the release of this volume within his collected works—a delay that suggests some sort of lingering doubt, either concerning the issue of authorship or the need for an updated second edition. It is possible, of course, that Stalin had a clear sense of what he wanted and intended to return to the book when he found the time. More likely, however, is that he found the prospect of revising the text overwhelming, inasmuch as the events of the past decade—particularly those during the war and early postwar years—were difficult to reconcile with the trajectory of the SHORT COURSE's prewar narrative.[115] Unfortunately, the party archives do not explain why Stalin failed to take charge of the postwar party canon as he had in 1938. In the end, the only clear decision that Stalin made in regard to the SHORT COURSE was to repeatedly authorize new printings of the original freestanding 1938 edition.[116]

While puzzling, such misfires did not affect the dominance that the original edition enjoyed over Soviet society during the late 1940s and early 1950s. Millions of copies of this dated volume were published in the U.S.S.R. during these years, matched by millions more throughout Eastern Europe and Asia.[117] The ubiquity of the SHORT COURSE was further reinforced by its central role in a vast new network of officially sanctioned study circles, discussion clubs, and night schools, as well as the appearance of dozens of auxiliary texts and continuous coverage in the press.[118] It even found its way into newsreels, poster art, and popular fiction.[119]

At the same time that these elements of party education and mass culture were reinforcing the SHORT COURSE's authority, they were playing another, more subtle role as well. As noted above, one of the peculiarities of the 1938 SHORT COURSE was its silence in regard to a number of the period's most important ideological priorities—particularly Soviet patriotism, official

"Study the Great Path of the Lenin-Stalin Party!" (B. Berezovsky, 1951). One of Stalin's "cadres" studies party history through the SHORT COURSE alongside a plaster bas relief of Lenin, Stalin, Dzerzhinsky, and Sverdlov rallying a revolutionary crowd. Unopened volumes from Lenin's and Stalin's collected works lie on his library desk.

russocentrism, and the wartime experience.[120] For some, this lack of populist sloganeering must have been quite disorienting. Perhaps for this very reason, many of the auxiliary texts written during the early postwar period went to considerable lengths to frame the SHORT COURSE's prewar sensibilities within

Study circle on the SHORT COURSE, "Universal" Artel, Kurgan, 1949. Photograph from private collection of V. V. Shevtsov.

the realities of postwar propaganda.[121] In the end, this new amalgam of party history and patriotism was probably more successful in advancing the SHORT COURSE and its agenda than its awkwardly bifurcated prewar predecessor. The accessibility of the text was probably also eased by the emergence of better-educated party and state cadres, who were more prepared to handle the SHORT Course's abstraction and schematicism.

So central was the SHORT COURSE to the early postwar canon that even the death of Stalin in March 1953 did not undermine its authority.[122] Ironically, Stalin's death actually provided the IMEL—or the IMELS, as the Marx-Engels-Lenin-Stalin Institute was now to be known—with an opportunity to revive its work on the SHORT COURSE as part of a larger effort to publish the last volumes of the late leader's WORKS. After all, the party leadership remained committed to the project and Stalin was no longer in a position to delay the process. The IMELS archives reveal that the institute spent the spring of 1953 preparing an edition of the SHORT COURSE that would preserve the book's prewar scope but correct its factual errors, mistranslations, and problems with stylistics and grammar.[123] In May, galleys were sent to the party leadership for its approval and tentative plans were made to publish the volume in 1954.[124]

Although little is known about the Central Committee Presidium's decision-making process during the second half of 1953, the IMELS learned late that December that the party leadership was debating a major policy change.

Apparently, the Presidium was considering the idea of dropping the SHORT COURSE from Stalin's collected works and publishing it separately in a new edition.[125] Such a decision would distance Stalin from the text's authorship and effectively restore credit for the book to its original Central Committee editing commission; the late leader's official participation in the volume would again be limited to authorship of the section on dialectical and historical materialism. The Presidium ratified this policy change shortly thereafter and instructed the IMELS to reorganize its plans for the last volumes of Stalin's WORKS. Volume 15, devoted to the SHORT COURSE, was to be eliminated; volume 16, covering 1941–1953, was to be renumbered; and volume 14, covering the 1934–1941 period, was to be expanded by some 44 pages in order to accommodate Stalin's now-orphaned philosophical tract.[126]

Why did the Presidium prioritize this about-face in 1953–1954? At first glance, this posthumous demotion of Stalin from his position as historian-in-chief would seem to anticipate the process of de-Stalinization that later defined Khrushchev's so-called "Thaw." But such a conclusion seems unlikely, inasmuch as the party leaders remained committed to the Stalin-era canon (something clear from their plans to publish the final volumes of Stalin's WORKS and the long-overdue textbook on political economy). Instead, the explanation seems to have been much more pragmatic: authorship of the SHORT COURSE had to be reassigned if a second edition of the textbook was still to be contemplated. After all, how could the text be revised or updated if its sole author were dead? Successful rerelease of the SHORT COURSE required a return to the original story that the text had been written collectively by an anonymous Central Committee editing commission.[127]

Once the issue of the SHORT COURSE's authorship had been resolved, the party leadership returned to more technical questions regarding a second edition. In March 1955, the Presidium assigned the task of drawing up plans for the revisions to Pospelov, who was now a Central Committee secretary.[128] Fragmentary evidence suggests that the editing was to proceed on three different levels. All basic errors would be corrected. Alterations to the original narrative would also be permitted when warranted. Finally, Chapter Twelve would be reworked in order to link the book's prewar content to four new chapters on the war and postwar recovery.[129]

Although the IMELS probably expected to devote the second half of 1955 to the SHORT COURSE, Pospelov and the Presidium were slow to supply the institute with instructions on the needed revisions. As a result, the IMELS failed to even assemble a new editorial brigade until November.[130] Even so, the institute's director vowed to ready a working draft of the new edition to present to the Twentieth Party Congress in February 1956.[131] Needless to say, such promises proved impossible to fulfill. As it turned out, this was probably just as well.

5. The Central Committee Commission on Stalin-Era Repression. The Twentieth Party Congress and Khrushchev's "Secret Speech." De-Stalinization within the Party History Establishment. Glasnost' and the Call for a More Critical View of Party History

As is well known, it was at the Twentieth Party Congress that the authority of the SHORT COURSE was first officially challenged in connection with Stalin's cult of personality. Ironically, this was probably precipitated by none other than Pospelov, who had been tapped by Khrushchev in late December 1955 to chair a Central Committee commission on the rehabilitation of prominent party members repressed during the Terror. Pospelov's hurried report, presented to the Central Committee Presidium less than a week before the congress was to open in early February 1956, focused tightly on the abuses and excesses of the 1934–1940 period. Perhaps because of his personal involvement in the SHORT COURSE, Pospelov proved unwilling to criticize the reigning historical narrative, acknowledging only that many of the "anti-Soviet organizations, blocs and various centers" had been fabrications of the secret police. Aside from this, Pospelov declined to question the broader contours of party history, particularly its handling of the Trotskyite left, the Bukharinite right, and various domestic enemies such as the kulaks, capitalist holdovers, and bourgeois nationalists. He also declined to cross-examine other costly dimensions of the interwar period, such as shock industrialization and collectivization.[132]

Even with these ideological blinders, Pospelov's report still shocked the party leaders, who appear to have been stunned by the sheer scale and systematic nature of the Terror. Molotov, Kaganovich, and Voroshilov conceded that the report ought to be shared with the congress, but only if counterbalanced by an affirmation of Stalin's service to party and state. Such a nuancing of Pospelov's findings was necessary, claimed Kaganovich, "so as not to blacken thirty years of history" and compromise the present party leadership. After a spirited debate, it was decided that Khrushchev ought to present Pospelov's original report to a closed forum at the end of the congress.[133]

Days later, on the opening day of the congress, Khrushchev hinted in his keynote address about what was to come by criticizing several aspects of recent party history including the personality cult and other episodes of "arbitrariness and illegality." Party ideology, Khrushchev added, was also an area in need of major reform, particularly in regard to educational and indoctrinational efforts.[134] It fell to Mikoian, however, to begin the assault in earnest in his official report on party ideology. Particularly interesting was his criticism of the SHORT COURSE, which he attacked first for its failings as a propaganda vehicle:

> The Central Committee's report is clear on the unsatisfactory state of our propaganda work. One of the main reasons for this is that as a rule we study Marxism-Leninism only according to the SHORT COURSE. This is, of course, not right. The wealth of Marxist-Leninist thought cannot be captured within the limited scope of our party's history, much less within a single short course on the subject. To do this, there should be several theoretical textbooks created especially for our comrades with different levels of preparation. That's the first thing. Second, the present SHORT COURSE cannot be considered satisfactory because, at the very least, it doesn't cover the past twenty-odd years of party life. How can our lack of an official historical narrative covering the past two decades be justified?

Mikoian thus began his attack by targeting the SHORT COURSE's traditional vulnerabilities—its inaccessibility to the rank and file and its dated content. Refusing to limit himself to these well-known weaknesses, however, Mikoian then denounced its uncritical triumphalism:

> If our historians were to start studying the facts and episodes from party history during the Soviet period—those covered in the SHORT COURSE—in a profound and serious way, and if they did some good digging in the archives and in historical documents rather than just in the official press, they'd be able to do a better job of illuminating many of the facts and events mentioned in the SHORT COURSE from a truly Leninist point of view.

Complaining specifically about the lack of decent scholarship on the revolution, civil war, and Soviet state building, Mikoian called for new studies that would "show all the sides of our Soviet Fatherland rather than just its heavily lacquered façade." In the absence of such scholarship, he said, it was impossible to escape the conclusion that this was "the most backward area of our ideological work."[135] Although greeted with applause during the congress, Mikoian's speech was apparently so jarring that his own brother approached him afterward to question his judgment. "It's a shame that you gave such a speech," he apparently exclaimed. "You are basically right, but many delegates are unhappy and are complaining about you. Why did you need to attack Stalin like that? Why are you taking the initiative here when no one else is talking about it?"[136]

Khrushchev, of course, fully supported Mikoian's line of attack and planned to develop it further in his "Secret Speech" at end of the congress. Authorized by the Presidium to present Pospelov's findings, Khrushchev found the latter's indictment too reserved and expanded the scope of the exposé over the course of several days.[137] When done, Khrushchev's report began as Pospelov's had, presenting a Marxist critique of the personality cult and then using Lenin's invocation of Stalin's personal shortcomings in his long-suppressed "Testament" as a segue toward a broader condemnation of the general secretary's "violations of socialist legality." Accepting Pospelov's dating of the outset of this lawlessness to 1934, Khrushchev expanded his focus past 1940 and into the early 1950s. He also expanded the scope of the indictment itself, attacking party history for its whitewash of an array of injustices. Interparty democracy had been undermined. Collective leadership had been quashed. Lenin's testament had been suppressed. The party had been debased from the vanguard of the working class into an instrument of tyranny. History itself had been co-opted. For Khrushchev, this dysfunction was epitomized by the SHORT COURSE:

> Does this book correctly depict the party's efforts in the socialist transformation of our country, in the construction of a socialist society, in the industrialization and collectivization of our country? Does it correctly depict the other steps taken by the party, which unerringly followed the path outlined by Lenin? No—the book speaks principally about Stalin, about his speeches and about his reports. Everything is tied to his name without the smallest exception.
>
> And when Stalin himself claimed that he himself wrote the SHORT COURSE ON THE HISTORY OF THE CPSU(B), this arouses nothing less than indignation. Can a Marxist-Leninist really write about himself in such a way, praising himself to the skies?[138]

Perhaps the most famous indictment of the SHORT COURSE, this accusation about Stalin's ostensibly craven need for self-aggrandizement ignored enormous amounts of evidence to the contrary and mischaracterized the general secretary's editing of the text in ways that persist to the present day.[139]

Khrushchev went on to talk about many other things in his Secret Speech, but returned to the SHORT COURSE in his concluding recommendations. Reminding his audience of the textbook's supposedly single-minded celebration of Stalin and its concomitant neglect of party and society, he called for a new approach to party history:

> In all our ideological work, it is necessary to restore and seriously develop Marxism-Leninism's most important teachings about the role of the people as the agent of history and the creator of all of humanity's material and spiritual wealth, and about the Marxist party's decisive role in the revolutionary struggle for the transformation of society and the victory of communism.

> In connection with this, we have a lot of critical work to do from a Marxist-Leninist perspective in order to review and correct erroneous opinions connected to the personality cult that have become very common in history, philosophy, economics, and other scholarly fields, as well as in literature and the arts. In particular, it is necessary to do everything possible to create a textbook on the history of the party that will be put together from an objectively Marxist point of view: textbooks on the history of Soviet society and books on the history of the civil war and the Great Patriotic War must also be developed.[140]

Khrushchev's case against Stalin was, then, considerably more ambitious than the indictment offered by the Pospelov commission. What's more, Khrushchev, together with Mikoian, had effectively stripped the Short Course of its sacrosanct status and authority. That said, Khrushchev was not quite as dismissive of the Stalinist historical narrative as Mikoian had been. Although Khrushchev called for new work on the revolution, civil war, socialist construction, and Second World War, he focused on Stalin's role in these histories rather than on their broader, triumphalist nature. He also did not challenge traditional characterizations of the Trotskyites and Bukharinites as double-dealing traitors (although he did suggest that the threat that these groups had posed had been exaggerated). Neither did he rehabilitate the Mensheviks or other groups such as the kulaks and bourgeois nationalists. And like Pospelov, he shielded Soviet economic adventurism during the first Five-Year Plan from criticism by dating the outset of Stalin's crimes to December 1934. Khrushchev's rejection of the text's political violence and personality cult, in other words, did not prevent him from leaving much of the rest of it intact.

Unsurprisingly, even Khrushchev's limited criticism of Stalin and the Short Course paralyzed Soviet indoctrinational efforts after word of his speech was disseminated among the party rank and file. This confusion was heightened when party authorities proved unable to clarify for grassroots-level instructors and propagandists what changes they could expect in the official line.[141] Indeed, it would take many months of professional infighting for party historians and educators to finally establish what de-Stalinization really meant for the U.S.S.R.'s usable past.[142] When a new generation of textbooks finally began to emerge at the end of this process in 1958, the new historical narrative followed Khrushchev's interpretation very closely. The new textbooks erased Stalin from the annals of party history and reassigned credit for all "his" accomplishments to the party as a whole; they also reduced the attention cast toward other prominent historical personalities on both sides of the revolutionary divide.[143] But aside from this rather mechanistic reassignment of historical agency, the new official line preserved much of Stalin's master narrative.

Thus even after it was formally dropped from the canon, the SHORT COURSE continued to influence the writing of party and state history in the U.S.S.R. Aspects of the textbook's approach to Marxism-Leninism would also shape the official histories of communist regimes in Eastern Europe for years to come, albeit in a similarly unacknowledged form.[144] In Moscow, some historians attempted to challenge this legacy during the early 1960s, only to be rebuffed during the conservative backlash following Khrushchev's ouster. Shortly thereafter, a Central Committee department head even went so far as to propose returning the SHORT COURSE to print.[145] In the end, a compromise was reached that curtailed all public discussion about Stalin—whether positive or negative—in official scholarship and mass culture. This effectively stifled all debate over the personality cult for a generation; it also stymied any further reform of party history, effectively prolonging the SHORT COURSE's influence over the discipline by two more decades.

This taboo was broken only in 1988, when M. S. Gorbachev called for a more critical appraisal of Stalinism within the context of his glasnost-driven struggle with the party's old guard. Ironically, this turnabout returned the SHORT COURSE to the limelight exactly fifty years after it had first occupied center stage. Now, however, instead of being hailed as an "encyclopedia of Bolshevism," it was condemned in equally hyperbolic terms as an "encyclopedia of dogma."[146] Reviving criticism voiced at the Twentieth Party Congress, Gorbachev's partisans pressed on, declaring the textbook to have distorted more than just the 1934–1938 period. As N. N. Maslov put it, the problem was pathological:

> The worst result of the publication and canonization of the SHORT COURSE was the establishment in party history of untruthful, falsified ideas and positions, skewed evaluations of historical episodes and phenomena, distorted descriptions of historical facts, and dogmatic and vulgarized theory. Party historians inevitably fell into hypocrisy and self-deception as they helped establish Stalin's cult of personality and created for him an aura of greatness and infallibility. Serious work with historical sources was not necessary in order to write such history—indeed, sources only got in the way. Nor was historiography needed as the past and multicolored present perished at the hands of these party historians—all that was necessary was a single, dead schema. Methodology, which is designed to aid in the search for historical truth, was also forgotten, inasmuch as it too was superfluous in this realm of untruthful thought.[147]

Official endorsement of this sort of criticism invited new investigations into subjects that had been previously off limits, such as industrialization and

"A people who forget its history is doomed to repeat it" (L. Kovaleva, 1988). The SHORT COURSE looms over a traditional Russian village, threatening to crush it with the weight of party history. Key dates are identified with red bookmarks—1929, 1934, 1937, etc. The politicized atmosphere of the period is visible in the fact that two of the bookmarks—1948 and 1952—refer to years not even covered in the book.

collectivization. It also opened the door to a broader reconceptualization of the Soviet usable past—something that led D. A. Volkogonov to conclude the following year that the SHORT COURSE had left deep scars on the society's historical consciousness. The textbook, he argued, had taught Soviet society to assume a passive, submissive relationship toward political authority. It had trained Soviet citizens to believe that the party was always correct and that any shortcomings or problems interfering with the realization of the official line were the result of sabotage and wrecking on the part of the U.S.S.R.'s foes. Equally pernicious, the SHORT COURSE had apparently indoctrinated the society into seeing change as legitimate only when implemented on a sudden, revolutionary scale; reform and restructuring, by contrast, had come to be regarded with suspicion as something proffered only by double-dealers and outright enemies.[148]

While Maslov and Volkogonov were probably right about the legacy of the official historical line as a whole, their singular focus on the SHORT COURSE appears today to be rather simplistic and reductionist. That said, their views in 1988 were really no more hyperbolic than those offered by Khrushchev in 1956 or Stalin in 1938. All three, after all, saw the text as a political symbol and mobilization device as well as a historical narrative. For Stalin, the text was the key to a theory of party history that combined universal elements of Marxism-Leninism with the specificity of the party's revolutionary experience. For Khrushchev, the textbook offered a useful explanation of the past that needed only to be purged of its political violence and cult-like fascination with Stalin. Gorbachev's adherents went much further in their symbolic pillorying of the SHORT COURSE, blaming it for all the complexities of the 1917–1991 period in order to displace the heavy burden of this tragic history. Each of these attempts to create an official historical line on the past ultimately failed, however, leaving Soviet and then post-Soviet society to search for a usable past to the present day.

Ubiquitous during the Stalin period and enormously influential even after its fall, the SHORT COURSE occupies a unique place in the history of Marxism, ideology, propaganda, and political indoctrination. One of the most frequently published ideological tracts in world history, it also looms large as one of the Stalin period's great pyrrhic victories, on par with the completion of the first Five-Year Plan, the excavation of the Baltic–White Sea Canal, and even the construction of Soviet socialism itself. Notorious to the present day because of its politicization and dogmatism, the SHORT COURSE has long escaped proper understanding as both a historic text and a historical narrative. This edition, therefore, fills a gaping void in the literature and provides answers to many long-standing questions about the nature of Stalinism and the Stalin era.

THE CRITICAL EDITION

This critical edition of the SHORT COURSE surveys Stalin's revisions to Yaroslavsky and Pospelov's final April 1938 prototype party history. It comprises at least three undated rounds of Stalin's editing conducted in mid-1938, totaling several thousand pages of handwritten marginalia, typescript, and publisher's galleys.[149] This edition also details all other known interventions into the text—mostly technical and stylistic recommendations made to Stalin by Yaroslavsky, Pospelov, and his Politburo comrades-in-arms in August 1938 on the eve of the SHORT COURSE's publication.[150]

A daunting task, the aggregation of this archival documentation was complicated by the fact that a considerable portion of Stalin's draft materials, including intermediate copies of a number of chapters, appears to have been discarded along the way. Indeed, the incompleteness of this archival record has confounded researchers since its declassification in the 1990s. Such circumstances led the editors of the present volume to conclude that the only way to produce a comprehensive accounting of Stalin's editorial interventions would be to base this critical edition on a textual comparison of Yaroslavsky and Pospelov's final April 1938 prototype and the version of the SHORT COURSE that was published in September 1938. This textual analysis was then cross-checked against surviving archival documentation to ensure accuracy.

An unusual solution to the problem, this methodology allows the present edition to capture both the nature and scope of Stalin's interventions within a single volume. The editors have opted against distinguishing between the general secretary's individual rounds of editing, both because of the incompleteness of the archival record and because such archeographic complexity would render this critical edition unreadable to all but a handful of specialists. Scholars requiring such detail should consult the original archival materials preserved at the former Central Party Archive in Moscow.[151]

1. Stalin as Editor-in-Chief

The archival record indicates that Stalin worked on Yaroslavsky and Pospelov's final prototype party history alone between April and August 1938, with the assistance of only a small pool of typists.[152] Inasmuch as Stalin's office calendar reveals that he received an unusually small number of visitors in mid-May, mid-June, and early July, it seems reasonable to conclude that it was during those times that he retired to his dacha to focus on the SHORT COURSE.[153]

Surviving material reveals Stalin to have been a demanding editor who disliked historical writing that focused on minutiae at the expense of the big picture. He also had little patience for wordiness; florid, metaphorical language; hyperbole; digressions; and literary devices like foreshadowing. I. I. Mints described the experience of working with Stalin in 1935 on the editing of another book, THE HISTORY OF THE CIVIL WAR IN THE U.S.S.R., in terms that inform the general secretary's revisions to the SHORT COURSE three years later:

Stalin was pedantically interested in formal exactitude. He replaced "Piter" in one place with "Petrograd," "February in the Countryside" as a chapter title (he thought that suggested a landscape) with "The February Bourgeois-Democratic Revolution," [and] "Land" as a chapter title (a "modernism," he called it) with "The Mounting Agrarian Movement." Grandiloquence was mandatory too. "October Revolution" had to be replaced by "The Great Proletarian Revolution."[154]

Other aspects of Stalin's work on the SHORT COURSE display similar hallmarks of an experienced but amateur editor. As is well known from his personal library and archive, Stalin fancied himself to be a wordsmith of sorts and read with red pencil in hand, compulsively altering word choice and the phrasing of passages that he felt could be expressed more effectively. Elsewhere, the general secretary rewrote clauses, sentences, paragraphs, and even entire sections of the text, but he did this in a way that amounted to little more than intensive line editing. That is, if Stalin frequently streamlined and sharpened argumentation, it was much more infrequently that he would reorganize the material at hand in a more thoroughgoing fashion. Equally rare was Stalin's addition of anything new to the SHORT COURSE, aside from a few sections like his famous exegesis on dialectical and historical materialism in Chapter Four. And although it is true that he altered a number of the book's central themes—emphasizing, for instance, the red thread of socialism in one country at the expense of the threat of omnipresent conspiracy—even this was done in a rather crude and inconsistent way. The end result was a book that was incompletely recast and unevenly rewritten, without the subtlety, consistency, or accessibility that one would expect from such a crucial text. If anything, Stalin's editing exacerbated the SHORT COURSE's formulaic nature and schematicism and thus produced a party catechism that many found difficult to read and even more difficult to understand.

2. Stalin's Revision of Yaroslavsky and Pospelov's Prototype Party History

The following chapter summaries outline both the history that Yaroslavsky and Pospelov presented to Stalin in April 1938 and the alterations that the general secretary subsequently made to the narrative. Inasmuch as Stalin introduced literally thousands of editorial changes into the text, these short sketches address only the most important of his interventions.

Introduction

As originally conceived, the SHORT COURSE was to begin with a sweeping philosophical treatise that Stalin rejected when he examined the second version of Yaroslavsky and Pospelov's history in late 1937 or early 1938. He first asked Pospelov to redraft the introduction and then attempted to rewrite this statement himself before becoming frustrated with its length and inaccessibility.[155] Yaroslavsky and Pospelov subsequently opened their third and fourth versions of the textbook with just a few pages of early party history at the beginning of the book's first chapter. This writing traced the party's origins to the 1880s before casting the organization in diametrical opposition to other Marxist, socialist, and bourgeois groups that it denounced as "enemies of the people." The Bolsheviks matured in the context of their struggle with these enemies—the party's left and right opposition, the broader non-Bolshevik socialist opposition, and other nonsocialist opponents including monarchists, capitalists, kulaks, and non-Russian national liberation movements. The party's mettle was also tested by the revolutions of 1905 and 1917 and the demands of building and defending socialism. Familiarity with Bolshevik history was held to contribute to the resolution of this ongoing struggle, inasmuch as the party's historical experience was governed by universal laws of societal development.

When Stalin turned to edit Yaroslavsky and Pospelov's text, he detached this opening statement from their first chapter and fashioned it into a short, freestanding introduction to the whole book. Aside from routine attention to terminology, Stalin also made more substantive alterations to the piece. Perhaps most importantly, he struck out epithets categorizing the party's various opponents as enemies of the people and replaced them with less hyperbolic Marxist-Leninist terms such as "petty bourgeoisie," "opportunists," and "nationalists." He concluded by reappraising the heuristic value of party history, noting that the lessons to be learned from the book were based on practical experience rather than just abstract theory.

Chapter One (1883–1901)

As noted above, Yaroslavsky and Pospelov's first chapter originally began with a short introduction to party history before providing a more detailed sketch of Russian socioeconomic underdevelopment during the nineteenth century. Serfdom oppressed a large part of the population, even after its formal abolition in 1861. The non-Russian peoples of the empire were even more hard-pressed, as they faced intensive russification in addition to other sorts of oppression. Yaroslavsky and Pospelov quoted Stalin as saying that such oppression was "inhuman and barbarous."

Capitalist development after 1861 accelerated rapidly, leading to the polarization of agrarian society into protocapitalist peasants (the so-called kulaks) and the poor peasantry. Economic exploitation in the cities impoverished the working class, leading to demonstrations and strikes, which stimulated the growth of a major labor movement. Such unrest was less visible in the countryside, in part because of the peasants' monarchistic deference to the tsar.

Marxism was introduced into Russia by G. V. Plekhanov as a challenge to other earlier forms of socialism. Plekhanov and his Emancipation of Labor group struggled in particular against the populist Narodniks, questioning whether this group's peasant constituency was truly socialist and whether the populists' advocacy of terrorism could actually precipitate revolutionary change.

V. I. Lenin hailed Plekhanov for his rout of the Narodniks and introduction of Marxist Social Democracy in Russia. That said, Yaroslavsky and Pospelov made it clear that Lenin still criticized Plekhanov for his proposal to ally his small movement with the bourgeoisie instead of with the peasantry. In 1895, Lenin formed the League of Struggle for the Emancipation of the Working Class in St. Petersburg in order to combine the economic fight for better wages and working conditions with political calls for revolution. Exiled to Siberia from 1895 to 1900, Lenin fought with former allies who wished to focus exclusively on economic issues—a Marxist heresy called Economism. He also campaigned against a new group of Legal Marxists as well as Narodnik holdovers. Upon his return from exile, Lenin departed for Europe to found the newspaper ISKRA in order to give the revolutionary movement a clearer general line.

According to Yaroslavsky and Pospelov, one of the few places where ideological confusion did not reign supreme during these years was in Transcaucasia. There Stalin and other local Marxists founded several thriving Social-Democratic organizations. Inspired by Lenin's League of Struggle, these groups were notable for their loyalty to his revolutionary line and their close connection with the grassroots labor movement.

As noted above, when Stalin began editing Chapter One, he detached its opening paragraphs to create a freestanding introduction to the entire book. He then expanded aspects of Chapter One, adding detail about the peasants' difficult existence in the countryside and cutting commentary on the non-Russian peoples, including even his own statement about how the Russian empire had been uniquely oppressive toward its minorities.[156] Through this editing, Stalin heightened the contrast between the peasantry and the emergent industrial proletariat, which possessed more of a sense of internal solidarity and militancy. He also underscored the vanguardist line that held that despite the proletariat's progressive nature, it would not be able to realize its revolutionary destiny without a party to supply organization and leadership. Interestingly, he cut mention of the peasants' traditional monarchism, perhaps in order to emphasize their readiness to follow the working class and its party.

Next, Stalin reduced the amount of attention devoted to Plekhanov. In particular, he revised a poorly written section of text in order to clarify the role of the individual in the Marxist historical process. He also adjusted commentary on the Narodniks to stress their failure to understand the materialist factors that would govern the coming revolution.[157]

When Stalin turned to Lenin's activities in the League for Struggle, he reduced his mentor's practical role in labor organizing and styled him instead as a theoretician. According to Stalin, Lenin distinguished himself by refuting Plekhanov, the Economists, the Narodniks, and the Legal Marxists. Particularly important was Lenin's contention that the peasants were a natural ally of the working class, despite their political naïveté.

Perhaps most dramatic within this editorial process was Stalin's elimination of all commentary on his own prerevolutionary career in the Transcaucasian underground and virtually all its detail on local Social-Democratic organizations, both in Transcaucasia and elsewhere. Such cuts, which even deleted the names of prominent Old Bolsheviks, continued through Chapter Five and had the effect of concentrating historical agency around Lenin and the Bolshevik movement's central institutions.

Stalin also scaled back the discussion of unlikely alliances in the text. The Narodniks, according to Yaroslavsky and Pospelov, had aligned with kulaks in the countryside after their defeat, while the Economists had actively courted the bourgeoisie. Stalin reduced the prominence of such claims, evidently unimpressed with the text's recourse to mass conspiracy as an explanatory paradigm.

Chapter Two (1901–1904)

Yaroslavsky and Pospelov began their second chapter with an overview of a period that was marked by international economic crisis, unemployment, and a rise in labor militancy. Students, the liberal urban and rural bourgeoisie, and the non-Russian nationalities were also restive. Yaroslavsky and Pospelov explained the more limited militancy among the peasantry by noting that many remained monarchists and believed that the tsar was a good person surrounded by bad advisers.

This wave of urban unrest, according to Yaroslavsky and Pospelov, signaled that Russia now stood at the epicenter of the worldwide revolutionary movement. Industrialization was proceeding more rapidly in Russia than elsewhere, conditions were more oppressive, and the working class was more aware of how little it had to lose. That said, the Social-Democratic movement found it difficult to act in a concerted fashion, as it had to operate underground and contend with challenges ranging from secret police infiltration to the popularity of reformist socialism (Economism).

Iskra criticized the Economists and called for order, discipline, and a rational approach to consciousness-building. This position was repeated in Lenin's book What Is To Be Done? At the same time that Iskra challenged the Economists, it also attacked the Socialist Revolutionaries for their adoption of a Narodnik-like program of peasant insurrection. Peasant socialism, according to Yaroslavsky and Pospelov, was a recipe for kulak domination of the countryside, while peasant terrorism would undermine the rest of the revolutionary movement. ISKRA's success in this struggle was apparently visible in agitational work carried out on the ground by Stalin and his comrades in Tiflis, Baku, and Batumi.

ISKRA set the stage for a 1903 congress where the Russian Social-Democratic Labor Party (RSDLP) officially took shape. There, participants debated the ISKRA program, questioning whether the working class was really conscious enough to lead the revolution, whether the peasantry could be rallied to the cause, and whether national self-determination should be championed. Lenin attempted to limit the party's membership and enforce a greater sense of discipline to defend against opportunism from within and police penetration from without. L. D. Trotsky and Yu. O. Martov opposed Lenin, believing that the party needed to accept all those wishing to join. They also resisted Lenin's insistence upon an alliance with the peasantry, asserting that it would be more natural to work with the liberal bourgeoisie. Outflanked on these issues, Lenin won two minor debates when the Jewish Bund suddenly quit the congress. Finding his faction briefly in the majority, Lenin and his comrades adopted the sobriquet of the Bolsheviks and labeled Martov's faction the Mensheviks.

After the congress, the Bolshevik-Menshevik split worsened. The Mensheviks seized ISKRA and made inroads within the Second International abroad. Lenin countered with a new broadside, ONE STEP FORWARD, TWO STEPS BACK, in which he accused the Mensheviks of acting in the interests of the liberal bourgeoisie and intelligentsia and then reasserted the need for a party vanguard and rigorous discipline. He also called for more agitation, a new newspaper (VPERYOD), and another party congress.

When Stalin turned to edit Chapter Two, he reduced the degree to which striking workers were able to express political grievances on their own. This, according to Stalin, was something that they could articulate only with the help of the party. He also revised commentary on the restiveness of the non-Russian regions and the countryside, removing all discussion of the former and deemphasizing the latter.

At the same time, Stalin deleted much of the broader international context for the Russian revolutionary situation, rendering it effectively sui generis. He also cut mention of the revolutionary movement's infiltration by police spies and nonrevolutionary moderates, emphasizing instead the threat that the Economists and Legal Marxists posed by refusing Lenin's call for tighter party organization and discipline.

When Stalin turned to ISKRA, which had enjoyed considerable historical agency in Yaroslavsky and Pospelov's narrative, he subordinated the newspaper to Lenin and transformed the party leader into the chapter's central actor. According to Stalin, it was Lenin who founded the newspaper, wrote its key articles, and used it to define party priorities. Stalin reinforced Lenin's primacy in the chapter by deleting a major subsection on the SRs. He cut commentary on the work of professional revolutionaries in local party organizations as well, deleting mention not only of himself, but of over a dozen other Old Bolsheviks. He also rewrote much of the text's treatment of the 1903 party congress in order to reduce Yaroslavsky and Pospelov's detailed commentary on the positions of Lenin's rivals. Stalin concluded the chapter by arguing that the emergent rift within Russian Social Democracy was more serious than just a question of rival tendencies—the party had ruptured into two separate political groups.

Chapter Three (1904–1907)

In the race to partition China at the end of the nineteenth century, Russian and Japanese interests collided over the Korean peninsula and Manchuria. According to Yaroslavsky and Pospelov, the tsarist government welcomed this conflict, assuming that a quick war abroad would help it suppress revolutionary discontent at home. The Mensheviks also supported the war (making common cause with not only the liberal bourgeoisie but also the industrialists and landlords). The Bolsheviks, by contrast, believed that a major military defeat would weaken the state and strengthen the revolutionary movement.

In December 1904, Stalin organized a major strike in Baku that set the stage for the coming revolution. In January 1905, a priest named Father Georgy Gapon convinced striking workers in St. Petersburg to march on the Winter Palace—something that Yaroslavsky and Pospelov claimed was a provocation designed to allow the police to suppress the activists. Despite Bolshevik warnings, the march culminated with a massacre on Palace Square. "Bloody Sunday," as the event was subsequently known, triggered strikes and protest throughout the empire.

The Bolsheviks set up urban and rural committees (Soviets) to coordinate a mass uprising. Menshevik, Social-Revolutionary (SR), and Anarchist activists also campaigned within society, confusing the situation. According to Yaroslavsky and Pospelov, such divisions encouraged the tsar to use both carrot and stick to restore order: a consultative "Bulygin" Duma was proposed at the same time that orders were given for the launch of punitive military expeditions. In this, Nicholas II relied on the panicky liberal bourgeoisie and its Cadet party, which went over to the tsar in exchange for a share of political power.

The Mensheviks supported the Bulygin Duma, while the Bolsheviks called for a boycott and continued protest. Concerned about this lack of coordination, Lenin convened a new party congress. Both there and in his subsequent Two Tactics of Social-Democracy in the Democratic Revolution,

Lenin argued that there were only two possible outcomes for the revolution. If the uprising were successful, it would depose the tsar, form a dictatorship of the proletariat and peasantry, and transition Russia into a democratic republic. Such a bourgeois revolution, Lenin believed, would organically "grow over" into socialism as the proletariat became more conscious and organized. If the uprising failed, the end result would be an alliance between the tsar and the liberal bourgeoisie, a rout of revolutionary forces, and a worsening of labor conditions. Victory, Lenin averred, required workers to play a vanguard role in an alliance with the peasantry.

According to Yaroslavsky and Pospelov, the Mensheviks objected to these tactics and demanded that the unrest follow the course established by all nineteenth-century bourgeois revolutions. Apparently only a spontaneous working-class revolution could be considered truly Marxist. Trotsky added that the revolution would have to be "permanent"—that is, supported by similar risings throughout the industrial world. Such unrealistic demands would effectively surrender the revolution to its enemies.

Bolshevik pragmatism, by contrast, yielded results. Indeed, party-coordinated uprisings that summer drove the tsar to take increasingly desperate measures that fall. First, he issued the Manifesto of October 17, which promised a legislative Duma and civil rights. Second, he mobilized all the forces at his disposal to suppress worker unrest, even deploying Black-Hundred vigilantes and soldiers returning home after the conclusion of a hasty peace with Japan.

Striking St. Petersburg workers ignored the tsar's manifesto and convened a Soviet of People's Deputies to coordinate the uprising—an objective that Yaroslavsky and Pospelov claimed was compromised when Trotsky took command of the body. Bolshevik leadership in the Moscow Soviet, by contrast, precipitated a full-scale armed uprising. Lenin returned to Russia from exile in November in order to join Stalin and other local activists engaged in arming the working class. Unfortunately, the revolutionaries in Moscow did not receive support from the city garrison or the St. Petersburg Soviet and were quickly routed.

In the wake of this debacle, the divided RSDLP assembled at its Fourth Party Congress in April 1906. As in the past, Lenin proposed limiting the party's membership and strengthening its work among the peasantry. The Mensheviks prevailed in this debate, however, and won control of the party's Central Committee and Iskra. This led Lenin to form a Bolshevik party center in order to operate independently of the main RSDLP institutions.

The Bolsheviks boycotted the First State Duma, resisting calls for accommodation and conciliation. The Mensheviks and SRs, by contrast, campaigned actively for the liberal bourgeois Cadet Party. The tsar was dissatisfied with the resulting legislature and called new elections. This time, the Bolsheviks took part in order to use the Duma podium to disseminate revolutionary propaganda. The Mensheviks again urged their constituents to support the Cadets. The Second Duma proved to be even more radical and the tsar dismissed it as well. The Third Duma, elected under a newly restrictive franchise, dutifully supported Prime Minister P. A. Stolypin as he suppressed the remains of the revolutionary movement. According to this telling of events, history had proven Lenin right about the perils of accommodation and conciliation.

Yaroslavsky and Pospelov argued that although the 1905 revolution rivaled the 1871 Paris Commune in revolutionary importance, it was undermined by several factors. First, despite the Bolsheviks' best efforts, the peasants lacked proper leadership. Their reluctance to join the rebellious workers also affected Bolshevik efforts within the peasant-dominated army. Second, neither the workers' rebellion nor the RSDLP had been adequately organized. Third, the Bolsheviks found their revolutionary line undermined at every turn by both the conciliatory, opportunistic Mensheviks and the duplicitous Cadets. Quoting Lenin's evaluation of the revolution as a "dress rehearsal," Yaroslavsky and Pospelov reasoned that without 1905, the revolution of 1917 would have failed, as would have revolutions in the Ottoman Empire, Persia, and China.

As with other chapters, when Stalin turned to Chapter Three, he added material designed to make the narrative more accessible—additional explanation, restatement, and repetition of major themes. Thematically, he also altered the narrative, removing material about the human cost of the Russo-Japanese war, lest it reflect unfavorably upon the Bolsheviks' defeatist position vis-à-vis Japan. He also edited the narrative on the Bloody Sunday massacre in order to reduce the Bolsheviks' direct involvement in the fiasco.

During the revolutionary events of 1905, Stalin stripped the names of leading Old Bolsheviks from the narrative (including his own) in order to place Lenin at the center of the story, flanked by a maturing party organization. As the Old Bolsheviks were cut from the text, so too were regional party organizations and activists, especially in non-Russian locales. This editing had the effect of seriously undercutting Yaroslavsky and Pospelov's discussion of working-class initiative, agency, and heroism during 1905.

In his revisions to the revolutionary narrative itself, Stalin stressed the need for a worker-led bourgeois democratic revolution, a worker-peasant alliance, and the "growing over" of the bourgeois democratic revolution into a socialist one. He also underscored the Bolshevik-Menshevik schism, although he shifted the text's focus away from the Mensheviks' theoretical program—especially Trotsky's permanent revolution thesis—in order to emphasize the group's real-world refusal to take up arms and challenge its counterrevolutionary bourgeois allies. Finally, Stalin added analysis that justified the Bolsheviks' decision to boycott the elections to the First State Duma but then to participate in those that followed.

More generally, Stalin redirected the text away from descriptions of the unsuccessful revolution in order to focus on a broader evaluation of the events. Dividing the revolution into two periods, he argued that at first, as the tide of revolution rose against the weak tsar, the revolutionary movement proved strong enough to sweep away the Bulygin Duma and threaten the regime. During the second period, however, after the conclusion of the war with Japan, the tsar managed co-opt the frightened bourgeoisie, divide the workers, neutralize the peasantry, and crush the uprising.

Stalin also drew larger conclusions about the experience of 1905, deleting Yaroslavsky and Pospelov's rhapsodic world-historical comparisons to the Paris Commune and 1917 in order to focus on more practical, domestic lessons. The liberal bourgeoisie had demonstrated itself to be incapable of playing its historic Marxist role of overthrowing the feudal regime. The Mensheviks were little better, having abandoned revolution in favor of a conciliatory, reformist position. Only the working class, led by the Bolsheviks and assisted by the peasantry, was truly capable of carrying out a bourgeois democratic revolution and then transitioning to socialism.

Chapter Four (1908–1912)

Chapter Four began with an overview of the postrevolutionary "years of reaction" that opened with the election of the conservative Third State Duma. According to Yaroslavsky and Pospelov, economic stability obscured the fact that Russian "monopoly capitalism" remained underdeveloped and dependent on foreign markets. Political stability masked disarray within the opposition's ranks. The Cadets, who had earlier opposed the tsar, were now so afraid of revolution that they behaved like monarchists. Many Social-Democratic deputies were arrested; those who remained at large were silenced by Stolypin's persecution of left-leaning parties and peasant activists. Quoting Stalin, Yaroslavsky and Pospelov wrote that "the victory of the lash and darkness was complete." Just a handful of Bolsheviks held seats in the Duma; the only other radicals—the agrarian Trudoviks—epitomized their rural constituency by vacillating between the Bolsheviks and Cadets.

Political repression affected society as well, especially in the countryside. Yaroslavsky and Pospelov argued that this was part of a larger tsarist bid to encourage the kulaks to break away from the traditional peasant commune. According to Lenin, the regime sought to develop rural bourgeois support to match similar constituencies in urban areas. Together, these alliances signaled the decomposition of the once-mighty autocracy into a weaker, transitionary "bourgeois monarchy."

Repression after 1905 forced Lenin back into exile and drove many fellow travelers to either join forces with the tsarist system, align with more moderate opposition groups, or leave politics altogether. Stalin's organization in Baku persevered, although it too had to contend with treachery within the RSDLP, particularly from Menshevik "Liquidators" who proposed to abolish the party's illegal organizations. Stalin endured numerous arrests and terms of internal exile during these years, managing to escape back to underground work each time.

According to Yaroslavsky and Pospelov, Stalin's struggle against Menshevik Liquidatorism represented only part of the Bolsheviks' agenda after 1905. He also confronted insecure Bolsheviks known as the Otzovists, who had lost faith in everyday revolutionary politics and sought refuge in escapist philosophy and religious thought. Yaroslavsky and Pospelov explained the behavior of the Liquidators and Otzovists by highlighting their bourgeois social origins.

This struggle was further complicated by the August Bloc, Trotsky's 1912 bid to reconcile the Bolsheviks and Mensheviks. According to Yaroslavsky and Pospelov, this was an example of Trotsky's double-dealing, as his actual goal was to undermine the revolutionary movement. They credited Stalin with first exposing Trotsky's deception and then calling for a new party congress, a new newspaper, and a separate organizational center.

The August Bloc ultimately forced Lenin to convene a party conference in Prague in 1912 to formally break away from the Menshevik-dominated RSDLP. Independence would allow the Bolsheviks to operate without the distraction of the double-dealers, conciliators, and opportunists who had long divided Russian Social Democracy. Stalin was elected to the Central Committee and appointed head of the Russian bureau in absentia (he had been arrested in Russia while helping organize the conference). Shortly thereafter, Stalin again escaped from detention and returned to organizing party activities, the new newspaper Pravda, and the Bolshevik faction in the Duma.

Yaroslavsky and Pospelov concluded the chapter by noting the importance of the Prague conference, as it freed the Bolsheviks to purge their ranks and assume their rightful place at the forefront of the revolutionary labor movement.[158] Revolution in 1917 would not have been possible if the movement had still been debilitated by the Mensheviks and their divisiveness, opportunism, and liquidatorism.

Stalin began editing Chapter Four by cutting down discussion of Stolypin's reprisals, deleting even his own assessment of their brutality. He also deleted the contention that Stolypin's agricultural reforms had been designed to foster a rural bourgeoisie to match those urban groups allied with the tsar. Rewriting material on secret police infiltration during these years, he deleted the tenuous allegation that some of these provocateurs would continue to undermine the party until 1937–1938. As before, Stalin excised material on his underground party organizations in Transcaucasia—five full paragraphs of detail. Similar material on other Old Bolsheviks was also cut. These excisions, as well as others later in the chapter, reduced Stalin's profile in the narrative and shifted historical agency to the party organization as a whole.

More important for Chapter Four was Stalin's revision of Yaroslavsky and Pospelov's treatment of the fellow travelers who had drifted from the revolutionary cause after 1905. Highlighting Lenin's critique of these intellectuals' indulgence in philosophical and religious idealism in MATERIALISM AND EMPIRIO-CRITICISM, Stalin then embarked on a major explanation of the theoretical essence of Marxism-Leninism. Such a discussion had been missing from the textbook since Stalin had cut it from the SHORT COURSE's second version in early 1938.[159]

The end result of Stalin's intervention was an entirely new, freestanding, twenty-five-page exegesis on dialectical and historical materialism that laid out what he viewed as the core tenets of Marxist-Leninist thought.[160] It began by distinguishing the dialectical method from metaphysics, and then noted that because everything in existence builds upon previous developments, any dialectical investigation of the world had to be historical in nature. Such investigations also had to be materialist, as they focused on the objective truth reflected in concrete phenomena, stages of development, and relationships governed by scientific law. The fact that all such natural and social phenomena were connected meant that socialism—a materially grounded theory of societal development—was an inherently scientific form of analysis.

For Stalin, social thought and culture arose from material conditions, which were in turn defined by both their period's economic mode of production and society's relationship to that production. This was a subtle process rather than a vulgar, mechanistic one and allowed for the simultaneous existence of obsolete, moribund ideas and progressive, advanced theory stemming from the process of material change. Stalin justified this conclusion about the nature of historical materialism with an extended discussion of Marx's stages of economic development. In the end, Stalin argued that because Marxist-Leninist theory was grounded in the laws of the natural and social orders, it was uniquely suited to serve as a practical guide for making sense of the world.

When Stalin returned to editing Yaroslavsky and Pospelov's text, he emphasized Lenin's choice of tactics, which combined illegal activity with legal activism. Stressing the struggle against the Liquidators and Otzovists, Stalin struck out the text's explanation for the emergence of these groups and their philosophical tenets, effectively stifling their voices within the narrative. When the text turned to the August Bloc, Stalin simplified the text's critique of this coalition. Emphasizing Trotsky's duplicitousness, he expanded upon Lenin's theoretical engagement with the bloc while removing discussion of the practical challenges that it created for the party.

In his revisions to the Prague conference, Stalin rewrote entire passages to emphasize the Bolsheviks' moral obligation to break with the Mensheviks, Liquidators, and Otzovists. Once independent of these rivals, the Bolsheviks would be free to become a new type of party that could pursue a revolutionary Leninist agenda without compromise. Stressing the centrality of this decision to the future of the Bolshevik movement, he transformed this section from a summary of the opposition's transgressions into a celebration of Lenin's corrective.

In the aftermath of the conference, Stalin cut all discussion of his own service at the head of the party's Russian bureau. He also excised a whole section on Lenin's struggle for a left-wing coalition within the Second International. Finally, he altered Yaroslavsky and Pospelov's official explanation for the Bolsheviks' perseverance between 1905 and 1912, arguing that it was the party members' faith in Marxism rather than their connection to the people that had kept the movement on the revolutionary path.

Chapter Five (1912–1914)

Yaroslavsky and Pospelov opened Chapter Five by noting that although the working class was humbled in 1905, its commitment to revolutionary change rose again after 1911. This restiveness reemerged elsewhere in society as well. Peasants rebelled against their landlords. Soldiers and sailors mutinied against their officers. Such activism confirmed the correctness of the Bolshevik line.

The Bolsheviks' commitment to legal forms of agitation during these years was visible in their investment in PRAVDA, which disseminated the party line. Stalin noted in his articles that conditions in the country were reminiscent of 1905 and that it was time for the proletariat to lead the way forward, in league with the poor peasantry. Legal Bolshevik work also led the party to participate in the elections to the Fourth Duma, where Lenin gained six seats with which to denounce the autocracy, condemn police brutality, expose industrialists' exploitation of the working class, and demand land reform. Such agitation expanded the party's influence in workers' clubs and other grassroots organizations. According to Yaroslavsky and Pospelov, by 1913, the Bolsheviks controlled many of the trade unions in Moscow and St. Petersburg and were making major inroads among women, youth, and other constituencies.

The party also continued its struggle against the Trotskyites, Liquidators, Otzovists, SRs, and others within the August Bloc. Aside from this group's questionable commitment to the revolution, its stance on the national question also aroused Bolshevik ire. Historically, the tsars had pursued a policy of russification, limiting the linguistic and cultural expression of Ukrainians and other non-Russians. This led to the emergence of bourgeois activists, whose nationalist rallying calls divided the restive working class against itself. Within the Social-Democratic movement, this nationalism was particularly palpable among the Mensheviks and the Jewish Bund. Rosa Luxemburg and Polish Social Democracy, by contrast, denied the relevance of the national question to the revolution. The Bolsheviks condemned both of these positions, defending every nation's right to self-determination while claiming that modern states could counter separatist tendencies by ensuring national equality. Lenin and Stalin saw the downtrodden nationalities as allies in the coming revolution—something Stalin theorized in his famous 1913 article "Marxism and the National Question."

Between 1912 and 1914, tensions between the imperialist powers precipitated feverish preparations for war. At the same time, revolutionary tensions in Russia found reflection in mass strikes in Britain and France and new labor militancy in Germany. According to Yaroslavsky and Pospelov, only the wave of patriotic jingoism that accompanied the outbreak of World War I prevented a repeat of the 1905 uprising throughout Europe.

Stalin engaged with Chapter Five on a number of levels, initially focusing on readability and the removal of superfluous detail and hyperbole. In the section on PRAVDA, Stalin rewrote two sentences in order to share responsibility for the founding of the paper with other Bolsheviks and to reduce his overall role in the newspaper's production. Adding material on PRAVDA's coverage of the plight of the peasantry and the worker-peasant alliance, he attributed the paper's success to its commitment to Lenin's line rather than to its working-class advocacy.

In regard to the Fourth Duma, Stalin removed material on his role in the electoral campaign. He proved equally uninterested in other sorts of local organizing, whether concerning women's mobilization or labor insurance campaigns. As before, he dramatically reduced the text's attention to issues such as the national question and rival party platforms. Such deletions redirected readers' attention to the central party organization, as Stalin likely intended.

Toward the conclusion of the chapter, Stalin stressed that Bolshevik success amid the rising tide of labor activism between 1913 and 1914 stemmed from its leaders' correct understanding of Marxist-Leninist theory and the larger historical context. Agreeing with Yaroslavsky and Pospelov that this movement was swept away by the wave of patriotic fervor that accompanied the start of World War I, he argued that this did not depreciate the importance of the party's victories over Trotsky, the Liquidators, and the Otzovists. Stalin even allowed himself a rare moment of foreshadowing in order to note that this experience would play an important role in the party's struggle for power in 1917.

Chapter Six (1914–March 1917)

According to Yaroslavsky and Pospelov, although the First World War was an imperialist conflict, it was styled as a defensive one by the bourgeoisie and opportunistic socialist elements. Social Democracy and the Second International thus betrayed the cause, insofar as they ought to have either condemned the conflict or used it to precipitate revolutionary class war.

Russia's entrance into the conflict was linked to imperial dreams of territorial annexation and a dependency upon British and French finance capital. According to Yaroslavsky and Pospelov, the domestic Russian bourgeoisie and landlord class supported the war in exchange for profitable contracts and an excuse to crush organized labor. They rallied around the tsar, as did the Cadets, the Mensheviks, and SRs, calling upon the workers and peasants to renounce their struggle in the name of "class peace." But the revolutionary working class, under the leadership of the Bolshevik Party, continued its struggle against the autocracy, assisted by the most conscious representatives of the peasantry and non-Russian nationalities.

In exile, Lenin tried to organize a new International with radicals such as Rosa Luxemburg that would transform the imperialist world war into global revolution. At home, the Bolsheviks also agitated against the war, whether in the press, on the street, or within the Duma. They denounced the defense of "national interests," fomented labor unrest, and called for the workers and peasants to turn their weapons against the capitalist system.

Lenin hoped that these tactics would be adopted by Social Democrats elsewhere in the world. He laid out many of his views on the war in his 1916 book, Imperialism, The Highest Stage of Capitalism, where he argued that imperialism, through its ruthless pursuit of finance capital and new markets, had created zones of uneven development and extreme exploitation. This fueled not only labor unrest at home, but anti-colonial movements on the periphery. According to Lenin, the time was ripe for an alliance between the industrial proletariat and anti-colonial insurgents that would break the capitalist system where it was the weakest.

Lenin was challenged by an array of opponents—Mensheviks, Trotskyites, and even leading Bolsheviks—who combined forces to resist him. N. I. Bukharin questioned the necessity of undermining the state; he and G. L. Pyatakov also dismissed the right of ethnic self-determination in a statement that Lenin believed would weaken the appeal of the revolution in the colonial world. L. B. Kamenev and G. Ye. Zinoviev undermined Lenin's antiwar position by sympathizing with pro-war socialist opportunists.

Stalin supported Lenin from internal exile in Turukhansk, exposing local Mensheviks, Trotskyites, and Anarchists. He also convened a meeting of the party's Russian bureau in order to discipline Kamenev. Many other underground party organizations continued to function during the war as well, agitating against the imperialist conflict.

In 1915 and 1916, military and economic setbacks precipitated unrest in urban and rural areas. The non-Russian nationalities joined the workers and peasants in their discontent, resulting in a major uprising in Kazakhstan in 1916. The bourgeoisie, in league with Britain and France, realized that popular unrest might topple the government and also began to look for alternatives to the tsar.

In early 1917, work stoppages in Petrograd turned into a general, city-wide strike as the Bolsheviks' militancy overshadowed Menshevik calls for moderation. According to Yaroslavsky and Pospelov, on February 26, 1917, the Bolshevik party organization issued a manifesto calling for armed struggle against the tsar and the formation of a provisional revolutionary government. The workers rallied to this manifesto, as did the Petrograd garrison and other military units, and the resulting February bourgeois-democratic revolution quickly toppled the tsar.

As in 1905, Soviets emerged as the administrative arm of the revolution. Workers and soldiers sent their deputies to the Soviets, trusting that these councils would end the war and then address other revolutionary issues. But while the Bolsheviks were leading the street protests, the Mensheviks and SRs infiltrated the Soviets in order to stem the radical tide and support their bourgeois allies. The Mensheviks and SRs in the Executive Committee of the Petrograd Soviet secretly conspired with the Duma to form a Provisional Government headed by former tsarist servitors, Octobrists, Cadets, and a lone SR, A. F. Kerensky.

This government represented the newly ascendant bourgeoisie and ruled in tandem with the Menshevik- and SR-dominated Petrograd Soviet in an awkward arrangement known as "dual power." Yaroslavsky and Pospelov noted that because of the political inexperience of the workers and peasants, the bourgeoisie and its "socialist" allies were able to trick the population into supporting the war in the name of defending the new republic. As a result, the first task of the Bolshevik party became the exposure of the imperialist nature of this "defensism." The party did this by reopening its newspapers, mobilizing the masses, and devoting special attention to women, youth, and the worker-peasant alliance. Exposure of this defensism would allow the Bolsheviks to challenge the Mensheviks' and SRs' hold over the Soviets.

Yaroslavsky and Pospelov concluded the chapter by noting that the war had exposed the corrupt nature of the Second International and Social Democracy as a whole. Only the Bolshevik party had proved ready and willing to rally the working class against capitalism, war, and the Mensheviks, SRs, and Anarchists. The treachery of these latter groups left the Bolsheviks with no other choice than to advance toward the second stage of the revolution in order to overthrow the capitalist bourgeoisie and its "socialist" allies.

When Stalin turned to Chapter Six, he began by reducing the attention that Yaroslavsky and Pospelov had cast on grassroots worker unrest on the eve of the war and to local party activism once the conflict started. Reassigning historical agency to the party organization as a whole, he again deleted commentary on his own work as well as that of an array of other Old Bolsheviks. The only major exception to this rule was Bolshevik agitation within the army, as party support within the ranks would help differentiate victory in 1917 from the defeats of 1905.[161] Discussion of the War Industry Committees was also preserved, as these public-private organizations epitomized the growing influence of the bourgeoisie and their exploitation of Menshevik support in the trade unions.

Internationally, Stalin rewrote the European socialists' response to the war in order to demonstrate that Lenin had foreseen the collapse of the Second International. Deleting mention of Luxemburg, Stalin stressed the uniqueness of the Bolsheviks' stance against the war and the uniformity of their opponents' slide into opportunism and then "social chauvinism." He also expounded upon Lenin's IMPERIALISM, THE HIGHEST STAGE OF CAPITALISM, particularly its theoretical groundwork for Marxist revolution in a single country. Stalin deleted most of the detail on the positions espoused by Trotsky, Zinoviev, Kamenev, and Bukharin on war, revolution, and the national question—editing that left the oppositionists seeming both petty and inarticulate.

Stalin rewrote much of Yaroslavsky and Pospelov's treatment of the February revolution in order to stress three things. First, he underscored the decisive impact of the war not only on nation-states and national economies, but on international Social Democracy. Only the Bolshevik movement had withstood this test and resisted the temptation of opportunism and social chauvinism. Second, he emphasized the destructive effect of the war on Russia—on its population, economy, and daily life itself. Such a bitter experience had aroused the population and stimulated the revolutionary movement. Third, Stalin rewrote Yaroslavsky and Pospelov's discussion of the bourgeoisie's loss of faith in the tsar in order to scale back Britain and France's role in the planning of its palace coup.

In Stalin's editing of the February Revolution itself, he stressed precision and stylistics. He also stressed the importance of the worker-peasant alliance and the duplicity of the Mensheviks and SRs as they co-opted the Soviets. In the aftermath of the revolution, Stalin simplified the agenda that Yaroslavsky and Pospelov had outlined for the Bolsheviks. The party was to focus on exposing the bourgeois, imperialist nature of the Provisional Government before contesting the Mensheviks' and SRs' dominance in the Soviets. Stalin assigned this task to the Bolsheviks' newly reopened newspapers and deleted mention of mobilization work among soldiers, women, and youth.

In the chapter's conclusion, Stalin strengthened its condemnation of the Second International for supporting the war and betraying the working class. Only the Bolsheviks had remained loyal to the cause and therefore were able to rally their constituents against the war-weakened autocracy. But while the Bolsheviks toppled the old regime in February 1917, the revolution remained incomplete. This was because they were not yet strong enough to stop the Mensheviks and SRs from deceiving the masses in league with the bourgeois Provisional Government.

Chapter Seven (April 1917–1918)

Yaroslavsky and Pospelov opened their treatment of the lead-up to the October 1917 Revolution by focusing on the Provisional Government's refusal to address popular demands for bread, land, and peace out of loyalty to domestic and foreign capital. It also refused to alter oppressive tsarist-era policies in regard to the non-Russian peoples, especially in Transcaucasia, Ukraine, and Finland. Even so, many people continued to back the Provisional Government, due to the Mensheviks' and SRs' duplicity and their own political inexperience.

During this period, the Bolshevik party emerged from the revolutionary underground with only 45,000 members. Lenin was abroad and other leaders including Stalin were just returning from internal exile. According to Yaroslavsky and Pospelov, as the party reconstituted itself, it focused on exposing Menshevik and SR treachery and radicalizing Soviets throughout the country. Stalin denounced Bolsheviks such as Kamenev, who supported the Provisional Government, and called instead for the arming of the workers, the creation of a Red Guard, and continuation of the revolution. Lenin returned to Russia in early April and elaborated upon these positions in his famous April Theses. In order to distinguish the party from its rivals, Lenin called for the Bolsheviks to fully break with the RSDLP and form a Third International. These proposals provoked a storm of criticism from the bourgeoisie, Mensheviks, and SRs, as well as from a few Bolsheviks.

Weeks later, the Provisional Government sparked public protest by reassuring its foreign allies that it remained committed to the war. Although the party supported these demonstrations, its Petrograd committee went further to demand the government's overthrow—something Lenin felt was premature. According to Yaroslavsky and Pospelov, these protests ultimately forced the Provisional Government into a tighter embrace with the bourgeoisie, Mensheviks, and SRs.

Two months after the February Revolution, the Bolshevik ranks had doubled in size to some 80,000. At the Seventh Party Conference, Lenin reiterated his calls to focus on the Soviets, the peasantry, and the treachery of the Mensheviks and SRs. Stalin presented a report to the conference on nationality policy that defended Lenin's position on self-determination, noting as he had in 1916 that the non-Russian peoples were natural Bolshevik allies. Kamenev and A. I. Rykov opposed Lenin's call for radicalizing the Soviets; Zinoviev opposed Lenin's calls for a new international; and Pyatakov spoke out against Lenin on the national question as he and Bukharin had before.

In June, the First All-Russian Congress of Soviets convened. This forum was dominated by Menshevik and SR delegates, who defended their support for the Provisional Government by claiming that there was no revolutionary party ready to assume power. This led Lenin to issue his famous repartee: "There is such a party!"

Shortly thereafter, the Provisional Government launched a new military offensive in order to placate its foreign allies and strengthen its position vis-à-vis the Bolsheviks. According to Yaroslavsky and Pospelov, defeat at the front and renewed public protest at home led the Provisional Government and its Menshevik and SR allies to look for ways to eliminate the Bolshevik party. When angry crowds filled the streets in early July, the government decided to blame the party for the unrest. The Bolshevik leadership attempted to restrain what it felt were premature protests; even so, the Provisional Government called for the arrest of the party's leaders, the seizure of its printing presses, and the closure of its organization. Accusations of treason forced Lenin into hiding in Finland—a decision that Yaroslavsky and Pospelov credited with saving him from being assassinated, as Luxemburg and Karl Liebknecht would be a year later. This bid to crush the Bolshevik Party marked the end of dual power and the emergence of a united counterrevolutionary bourgeois government.

The Sixth Party Congress convened in secret in late July, now representing 240,000 members. Stalin, speaking in Lenin's place, announced that the rightward shift of the Provisional Government now prevented a peaceful socialist revolution, despite the party's growth and its successes in the Soviets. An armed revolt was the only remaining option. Several oppositionists objected to this assessment. The Trotskyite Ye. A. Preobrazhensky suggested that any revolution would have to wait for a similar situation to mature in the West. Bukharin questioned whether the peasants could be counted upon to support the working class. Rykov and Kamenev challenged the timing of the revolt. Others urged Lenin to surrender to the authorities, publicly encouraging him to embarrass the Provisional Government from the prisoner's dock while privately hoping that the trial would end with his execution. Stalin prevailed at the congress and established an agenda for the uprising and subsequent worker control of factories, cooption of trade unions, and peasant land seizures. It was also there that Trotsky's

Mezhraiontsy group was admitted to the party, including a number of double-dealers like Trotsky who only pretended to commit to the party's platform.

Having consolidated power during the July Days protests, the bourgeoisie was now determined to eliminate the Bolsheviks. General L. G. Kornilov called for the closure of the Soviets and staged a coup d'état that Kerensky initially supported. According to Yaroslavsky and Pospelov, the Bolsheviks' defeat of this counterrevolutionary bid for power, which demonstrated the party's continuing viability as well as the true sympathies of the Provisional Government and its Menshevik and SR allies.

Kornilov's defeat, combined with worsening economic conditions, won the Bolsheviks still more popular support. According to Yaroslavsky and Pospelov, as the Mensheviks, SRs, and Anarchists lost influence, they became embittered and transformed from opportunistic bourgeois sympathizers into full-scale counterrevolutionary organizations. Only a small faction of Left SRs continued to support the revolution. Thus the Bolsheviks now had to struggle with the Mensheviks, SRs, and Anarchists in the same way that they were contending with the Provisional Government.

That fall, Lenin emerged from hiding in order to present plans for a seizure of power to the party's Central Committee. Kamenev and Zinoviev objected and claimed that the Bolsheviks were still too weak, unintentionally revealing their preference for the bourgeois status quo. Trotsky recommended that the revolution be delayed until the Second Congress of Soviets, giving the Provisional Government time to react. Shortly after Lenin's proposal was accepted, Kamenev and Zinoviev denounced the uprising in the Menshevik press; Trotsky later leaked its date and time.

When the Provisional Government mobilized to counter the Bolshevik threat on October 24, the party staged its coup d'état. Leading Bolsheviks fanned out across the country while in Petrograd, Stalin assembled a Bolshevik Revolutionary Military Center to direct the Petrograd Soviet's Revolutionary Military Committee in overthrowing the Provisional Government.[162] The next day, Lenin turned power over to the Second Congress of Soviets.

The Mensheviks, Right SRs, and Bundists walked out of the congress to protest the coup. The Bolsheviks and their Left SR allies then ratified the advent of Soviet power and adopted Lenin's decrees on peace and land. They also appointed the first Soviet government, the Council of People's Commissars, with Lenin as chair. Yaroslavsky and Pospelov conceded that the revolution did face some resistance, despite its popularity among the people. Most notoriously, Kamenev, Zinoviev, and several supporters quit the Council of People's Commissars after demanding that Mensheviks and SRs be allowed to join the government. They were briefly replaced by several Left SRs.

Between late 1917 and early 1918, Soviet power was established throughout the old empire—Ukraine, southern Russia, the Urals region, Siberia, Finland, and the Baltics. According to Yaroslavsky and Pospelov, this victory stemmed from three factors. First, the Provisional Government had lost all its credibility among the workers and peasants. This stemmed from Kerensky's commitment to continuing the war and his refusal to pursue land reform or support workers' control of industry. Second, such policies gave rise to a close worker-peasant alliance. Third, this worker-peasant alliance broke with its previous support for the Mensheviks, SRs, and other conciliators and rallied around the Bolshevik party.

The Bolshevik victory in 1917 inspired similar worker revolts in Finland, Germany, and Austro-Hungary in 1918 and the establishment of Soviet governments in Hungary and Bavaria in 1919. Unfortunately, Yaroslavsky and Pospelov averred, all of these revolutions failed due to the weakness of local communist parties and the treachery of their Social-Democratic rivals.

The Bolsheviks continued to face opposition at home as well. In the face of resistance from the bourgeoisie and its allies within the old state bureaucracy and among the Mensheviks and SRs, the party decided to nationalize industry, annul the tsarist debt, abolish social estates and gender inequality, and create two new institutions—the All-Russian Extraordinary Commission for the Struggle with the Counterrevolution (the Cheka) and the Red Army. These measures dealt a blow to the domestic and foreign bourgeoisie and won the party support among toilers across the world.

At the same time that the Bolsheviks were eliminating social inequalities, they also proclaimed a new nationality policy that liberated non-Russians from the oppression they had faced under the tsar and Provisional Government. Lenin and Stalin's "Declaration of the Rights of the Peoples of Russia" announced this new policy, as did Stalin's "To All Working Muslims of Russia and the East." A Commissariat of Nationalities was established to advance a new nationality policy under Stalin's direct leadership.

According to Yaroslavsky and Pospelov, when elections to the Constituent Assembly were held, the Bolsheviks prevailed within key constituencies. That said, the overall majority went to other parties, in part because the SRs had organized the voting before the October Revolution. The Bolsheviks allowed the Constituent Assembly to convene in order to demonstrate to the society how little the Mensheviks and SRs had to offer. This hostile body was then shuttered when it refused to ratify the Soviet government's early decrees.

Next, the Soviet government ended the war by signing the Treaty of Brest-Litovsk, despite the resistance of Trotsky and the "Left Communists" (Bukharin, Pyatakov, and K. B. Radek). According to Yaroslavsky and Pospelov, Lenin conceded that the treaty was onerous, but argued that it would provide the Bolsheviks with the "breathing space" needed to consolidate power, strengthen the country's defenses, and reinforce its relationship with the peasantry. Later, the Trotskyites and Left Communists confessed at the 1938 trial of the Anti-Soviet "Bloc of Rights and Trotskyites" to having aimed to wreck the peace treaty, assassinate Lenin and Stalin, and overthrow the government. To this end, they even entered into negotiations with the Polish nationalist J. Pilsudski.

Having expropriated the capitalists, Lenin now called for the foundation of a socialist economy. In the cities, labor discipline was needed, as was good management, technical expertise, leveled wages, and measures to combat profiteering. In the countryside, the party focused on destroying the counterrevolutionary kulaks, who were refusing to sell grain at fixed prices. According to Yaroslavsky and Pospelov, these initiatives were resisted by the Left Communists and Left SRs, who denounced the new management practices, defended the kulaks, and called into question the building of socialism in one country. When they were rebuffed by the Fifth Congress of Soviets in June 1918, the Left SRs rose in rebellion and attempted to assassinate the German ambassador to provoke a new war. Later, at the trial of the Anti-Soviet "Bloc of Rights and Trotskyites," it was revealed that Bukharin and Trotsky had supported this treachery as well.

Yaroslavsky and Pospelov concluded the chapter by noting that under Lenin and Stalin, the party had built a mass following of workers and peasants by remaining true to the revolutionary cause and by exposing the bourgeois nature of the Mensheviks, SRs, and Anarchists. The party had also prevailed over opposition within its own ranks that questioned whether socialism could be built in one country. Ultimately, the October Revolution had delivered a major victory, stripping the bourgeoisie of its control over the means of production and transforming the factories, railroads, and banks into public property. It freed the country from its semi-colonial status and involvement in the imperialist war. And it allowed the party to form a proletarian dictatorship under the Soviets to usher in a new era of global socialist revolution.

When Stalin turned to Chapter Seven, he began by emphasizing the Provisional Government's lack of interest in popular demands for bread, land, and peace. Nor would these issues receive attention in the Petrograd Soviet, which had been co-opted by the Mensheviks and SRs. At the same time, he cut detail on popular resentment over these actions, reducing the historical agency that Yaroslavsky and Pospelov had granted to the grass roots. Discussion of non-Russian discontent after the February Revolution was likewise excised, suggesting that Stalin had decided to downgrade the degree to which the national question contributed to the October Revolution.[163]

In Stalin's revisions to the party's experience after February 1917, he noted that Kamenev and others had initially supported the Provisional Government and its continuation of the war. Stalin was careful to distinguish this position from the one he adopted with Molotov and "the majority of the Party," which anticipated Lenin's rejection of dual power. For much of the rest of the chapter, Stalin stressed the importance of central party leadership in general and Lenin's directions in particular. He spent considerably less time on lower-level party organizations, cutting detail on work at the grass roots, among women and youth, and within the Red Guard.[164]

In his treatment of the July Days crisis, Stalin deleted Yaroslavsky and Pospelov's suggestion that the protests had been deliberately used to entrap the Bolsheviks. This reversal offers another early indication of Stalin's waning interest in the conspiratorial thinking that framed the second half of Yaroslavsky and Pospelov's narrative. Stalin also challenged another key aspect of the original account concerning the summer of 1917. As noted above, Yaroslavsky and Pospelov had argued that Kornilov's attempted coup signaled that counterrevolutionary forces had seized the initiative within the army and the Provisional Government. Stalin disagreed, contending that this revanche was only illusory and revealed weakness rather than strength.

Stalin made only minor changes to Yaroslavsky and Pospelov's account of the October Revolution itself. He simplified the name of the Bolsheviks' Revolutionary Military Fighting Center to the Party Center. He reduced his own role in the narrative and added mention of several more Old Bolsheviks including Molotov, Dzerzhinsky, and Yaroslavsky. He replaced Yaroslavsky and Pospelov's term "coup d'état" with "uprising." And he reduced the degree to which the Bolsheviks relied upon the Left SRs to consolidate power.

Yaroslavsky and Pospelov had explained the Bolsheviks' victory with reference to an exclusively domestic set of factors. Stalin challenged this interpretation when he received their final galleys on April 24, writing in the margins that their explanation should be based on his 1924 article "The October Revolution and the Tactics of the Russian Communists." The authors attempted to satisfy the general secretary's request by quoting his article verbatim. Accordingly, the Bolsheviks' victory stemmed from three external factors and six internal ones. First among the external factors was the fact that the world's major imperialist powers were preoccupied with the world war. Second, the ongoing war led many in foreign lands to sympathize with the Russian revolution's call for peace. Third, a revolutionary crisis was maturing abroad among the working class that brought the Bolsheviks tangible support in both the West and the East. Among the internal factors, first was the fact that the revolution was supported by a majority of the Russian working class. Second, it also enjoyed the support of the poor peasants and soldiers. Third, it was led by an experienced and disciplined party. Fourth, the Bolsheviks faced relatively weak internal opponents, whether the increasingly powerless bourgeoisie, the frightened landlords, or the bankrupt Mensheviks and SRs. Fifth, the breadth of Russia allowed the Bolsheviks room to maneuver. And sixth, the Bolsheviks were able to acquire the resources to arm and supply their movement.

During the summer of 1938, Stalin rewrote these conclusions into a more straightforward set of five points that downplayed the influence of the international context and eliminated the role played by the working-class movement abroad. He also deleted mention of Luxemburg and Liebknecht's 1919 German revolution, as well as similar unrest in Hungary and Bavaria in 1919—changes that transformed the October revolution into an almost purely Russian affair.

This heavy focus on central Russian events was complemented by Stalin's continuing depreciation of the role that the national question played in the seizure and consolidation of power. Striking a lengthy paragraph on how the revolution had overthrown the previous colonial regime, guaranteed equality for ethnic and Muslim minorities, and facilitated the independence of Ukraine and Finland, he rewrote the surrounding text in such a way as to mention the non-Russian peoples only parenthetically in a list of various constituencies whom the Bolsheviks had successfully rallied to the cause. The "Declaration of the Rights of the Peoples of Russia" was similarly lumped together into an inventory of social reforms enacted by the Bolsheviks once in power. This editing transformed the revolution into an event that was emancipatory mainly in class terms; it also transformed the subsequent loss of Ukraine, Finland, Poland, and the Baltic provinces from a national issue into a purely territorial one.

When Stalin turned to the Treaty of Brest-Litovsk, he argued that the treaty negotiations had been betrayed by Trotsky and the Left Communists. Stressing the treacherous nature of this alliance, he underscored Yaroslavsky and Pospelov's contention that the conspirators had intended to restart the war with Germany, assassinate Lenin and himself, and form a new government along with the Left SRs.

As he concluded work on the narrative on 1917, Stalin again deleted commentary focusing on his personal contribution to the revolution. As before, he either reassigned his historical agency to Lenin or emphasized the party's vanguardist role. Stalin also rewrote passages to stress the bourgeois opportunism of the Mensheviks, SRs, and Anarchists before the revolutions of 1917. According to Stalin, it was only after October that they despaired over their loss of popular support and became wholly counterrevolutionary. He then further reduced the conspiratorial nature of the opposition by cutting mention of foreign participation in the anti-party plot. This, combined with reduced commentary on support for the revolution abroad and in the non-Russian regions, gave the narrative an unmistakably centralized, domestic focus.[165]

Chapter Eight (1918–1920)

Yaroslavsky and Pospelov dated the outset of the Civil War to mid-1918, when the international bourgeoisie attempted to quash the revolution and Lenin's establishment of a socialist economy. This bid was assisted by the Mensheviks, SRs, Anarchists, and "bourgeois nationalists" from the Jewish Bund, Ukrainian Petlyurites, Georgian Mensheviks, Azeri Mussavatists, and Armenian Dashnaks. Imperial Germany initiated this struggle in 1917–1918 with its colonization of Ukraine and Finland and recruitment of allies within the nascent White movement. After Germany's defeat, Britain, France, and other members of the Entente supplanted this aid with support for counterrevolution in the north, on the lower Volga, and in Siberia. They also assisted nationalists in Georgia and Azerbaidzhan. This foreign participation in the Civil War was vital, as domestic anti-Bolshevik forces were not strong enough to challenge Soviet power on their own.

To counter the threat, the party deployed the Red Army against its White opponents, the Cheka against foreign-fomented terrorism, and grain supply detachments against kulak-led economic sabotage. Stalin distinguished himself in the Red Army while Dzerzhinsky served valiantly at the head of the Cheka.

According to Yaroslavsky and Pospelov, the threat that the revolution posed to the capitalist world became clear after the collapse of Imperial Germany and Austro-Hungary in November 1918. Quickly, Soviet power was established in Estonia, Latvia, Lithuania, Belorussia, Ukraine, and the Caucasus. In Germany, communists under Liebknecht and Luxemburg staged a rebellion in Berlin before being betrayed by local Social Democrats. In 1919, communists briefly took power in Hungary and Bavaria, while other movements emerged in Switzerland, France, Poland, and elsewhere. Lenin had been proven right about the international revolutionary situation and convened the first congress of the Third International—the Comintern—to coordinate communist parties worldwide.

At the Eighth Party Congress, Lenin called for international worker movements to expel all opportunistic and nationalistic Social Democrats from their ranks. He also sought support for war communism, central planning, the worker-peasant alliance, the use of "bourgeois" specialists in the economy and Red Army, and a nationality policy founded upon self-determination. Bukharin and Pyatakov opposed Lenin's position on self-determination, questioning whether it would really secure non-Russian support for the party. Lenin also clashed with the Military Opposition, a group of radical Bolsheviks who had been alienated by Trotsky's deference to tsarist-era specialists within the ranks. With Stalin's help, Lenin prevailed in these debates.

Yaroslavsky and Pospelov then outlined the Civil War according to a schema organized around the campaigns of A. V. Kolchak and N. N. Yudenich,

A. I. Denikin and Yudenich, and Pilsudski and P. N. Wrangel. During the first campaign, in early 1919, Kolchak and his foreign allies assembled a force that threatened the Soviet republic's access to grain, oil, and coal. His forces were thrown back by the Red Army under M. V. Frunze despite Trotsky's attempt to sabotage the offensive. Stalin blunted Yudenich's advance on Petrograd, accelerating the final defeat of Kolchak.

During the summer of 1919, the Entente launched a second campaign against the Soviet republic, headed by Denikin in the south and Yudenich and Polish forces in the west. According to Yaroslavsky and Pospelov, Trotsky proposed to attack Denikin across the Don Steppe from Tsaritsyn in a treacherous maneuver designed to wreck the Red Army. Stalin made a counterproposal to attack Denikin's forces in the Donetsk Basin from Kharkov that won the Bolsheviks a key victory.

Denikin's defeat gave the Bolsheviks a respite that allowed attention to be cast toward war communism and the organization of economic planning, food supply, labor discipline, and the worker-peasant alliance. According to Yaroslavsky and Pospelov, grain requisitioning during the Civil War was understood to be a long-term loan that would be paid back to the peasantry after the construction of socialism.

Denikin's defeat also allowed Lenin to convene the Ninth Party Congress in 1920, where he proposed to reinforce labor discipline and economic centralization by extending party control over the trade unions. He was opposed by a loose alliance of Left Communists and new party members drawn from the ranks of the Mensheviks, SRs, and non-Russian bourgeois nationalists. These oppositionists asserted their right to oppose Lenin's initiatives under the principle of "Democratic Centralism," a party tradition that encouraged internal discussion and debate. This led Yaroslavsky and Pospelov to label them bourgeois fellow travelers rather than genuine Bolsheviks—an issue of particular concern for the Ukrainian communist party. Lenin defeated the Democratic Centralists at the congress and instructed the Ukrainian party to purge its ranks.

In 1920, Poland launched the third campaign of the Civil War with an Entente-backed invasion of Ukraine that coincided with Wrangel's advance northward from Crimea. Thrown back by a Red Army counterattack, the Poles retreated to the gates of Warsaw, where Yaroslavsky and Pospelov noted that Trotsky cheated the Bolsheviks of a decisive victory. The Red Army had greater success elsewhere, defeating Wrangel at Perekop and establishing Soviet power in Transcaucasia, eastern Siberia, Karelia, and Turkestan.

These victories increased interest in communism within the European working class, even among Social Democrats and Anarcho-Syndicalists. That said, the rightist and leftist views that these activists brought with them as they joined foreign communist parties threatened the coherence of the Comintern line. At the Second Comintern Congress, Lenin demanded a new approach to membership that would contain the spread of such petty bourgeois views.

In their final analysis of the Bolsheviks' Civil War record, Yaroslavsky and Pospelov credited Lenin and Stalin with creating an effective party organization capable of leading the worker-peasant alliance to victory, whether at the center, the grass roots, or behind enemy lines. Resolve at the front was matched by discipline and vigilance at home. Economic transformation and national liberation in the non-Russian regions also played key roles, as did the identification of a new cadre of leading Bolsheviks—K. Ye. Voroshilov, M. V. Frunze, S. M. Kirov, G. K. Ordzhonikidze, V. I. Chapaev, and N. A. Shchors. Such developments inspired working-class movements abroad and stood in stark contrast to the treacherous record of the Mensheviks, SRs, Anarchists, and other bourgeois parties. Although these groups had enjoyed some measure of popularity before 1917, their loss of social support during the revolution had led them to surrender their principles and sell out to the international bourgeoisie.

When Stalin turned to editing the Civil War, he stressed the idea that rather than being all-powerful, the counterrevolution was a wartime contingency of international and domestic forces too weak to oppose the revolution on their own. Focusing on Britain and France instead of Germany, he contended that these countries were threatened by the specter of Bolshevik-inspired rebellion at home. For that reason, they recruited allies within the Soviet republic from among the defeated classes who wished to depose the Bolsheviks and rejoin the capitalist system and its imperialist war. For Stalin, this dialectical approach to understanding the counterrevolution was important enough to justify displacement of a lot of factual material about the war (including virtually everything about his personal role in the events).

If Stalin retained quite a bit of the text's narrative structure, he made a number of eye-catching cuts. Detail on domestic anti-Soviet rebellions was reduced, as were allegations about these movements' foreign sponsors. Stalin even deleted Yaroslavsky and Pospelov's revelation that Trotsky's errors against Kolchak and Denikin had been intentional sabotage. Predictably, Stalin cut discussion of his own participation in the defeat of Yudenich; Frunze likewise disappeared from the narrative about Kolchak. Only Voroshilov and S. M. Budyonny gained a bit of attention in the text's discussion of Denikin's rout.

Stalin's editing was even more severe elsewhere in the chapter. He cut down the focus on nationality policy at the Eighth Party Congress and deleted most of the text's discussion of war communism, grain requisitioning, labor discipline, and the worker-peasant alliance. He likewise stripped the text of several pages on trade unions, Democratic Centralism, and the role that these oppositionists would later play in counterrevolutionary plots. Such deletions again suggest that Stalin had lost interest in the oppositionists and their platforms by the summer of 1938.

Stalin broadened the text's account of the Polish war, especially concerning questionable decisions made by Trotsky and M. N. Tukhachevsky. When attention turned to Wrangel, Stalin added a line about his alliance with the Anarchist N. I. Makhno and then deleted discussion of his loss to Frunze at Perekop. In the text on the final stages of the war, Stalin cut mention of the struggle in Turkestan against the Basmachi but added a line on the defeat of bourgeois Azeri, Armenian, and Georgian nationalists. Chiefly interested in the domestic military dimensions of the Civil War, he reduced or cut commentary at the end of the chapter on the international situation and the Comintern. He also deleted the attention that Yaroslavsky and Pospelov had cast on grassroots party organizations in order to focus on the relationship between the central party organization and the front.

Recasting the text's conclusions about the Bolshevik victory, Stalin briefly waxed rhapsodic about the odds that the party had faced at the start of the Civil War. According to his accounting of the lessons to be learned from the conflict, the Bolsheviks had won because of the party's ability to mobilize the workers and peasants and establish a reliable army. Within the Red Army itself, confidence in the Bolshevik cause and the party's leadership led to superior discipline and unity, as well as a broad sense of self-sacrifice. Working-class commanders and heroes within the ranks dealt punishing blows to the Whites that were matched by partisan warfare behind enemy lines. In the end, this unity of purpose within the revolutionary republic not only provided for a domestic victory against the counterrevolution, but rallied foreign workers to the Soviet cause as well.

Chapter Nine (1921–1925)

At the end of the Civil War, the Soviet economy was in ruins. The Civil War had also aggravated class tensions—peasants resented ongoing grain requisitioning and workers complained about postwar shortages and unemployment. According to Yaroslavsky and Pospelov, these tensions were exploited by holdovers from among the White Guards, Mensheviks, SRs, Anarchists, and bourgeois nationalists, who continued to enjoy foreign support. Kulak uprisings in Siberia, Ukraine, and Tambov presaged the Kronstadt mutiny in March 1921. This last uprising was crushed by Voroshilov and the Red Army, but illustrated the dire conditions in which the Soviet republic found itself.

According to Lenin, the economic crisis, combined with the vestiges of capitalism in the countryside, posed a greater threat to the country than the Civil War. The solution was large-scale industrialization and electrification, which were necessary for a modern socialist economy. To accomplish this, the peasants would have to turn away from petty bourgeois profiteering. Trade unions would have to support central state objectives. Party members too would have to commit to the leadership's priorities, particularly those who only recently had belonged to other socialist and nationalist parties.

Trotsky challenged Lenin from the left over the issue of the peasantry and trade unions, calling for a harder line. From the right, Lenin was attacked by the Workers' Opposition and Democratic Centralists, who questioned the party's leading role in the proletarian dictatorship. According to Yaroslavsky and Pospelov, such oppositional activity was driven by these groups' alliance with the petty bourgeoisie, kulaks, and other holdovers who wished to restore capitalism. Trotsky began working for German espionage at this time, as did his lieutenants. The full extent of this vast left-right conspiracy would be exposed only in March 1938 at the trial of the "Bloc of Rights and Trotskyites."

At the Tenth Party Congress, Lenin passed a resolution outlawing such factionalism. He also launched NEP in order to resolve the economic crisis. Grain requisitioning would be abolished in order to allow the peasantry to return to the market. Private manufacturing in the urban economy would likewise be tolerated until the public sector grew stronger. This congress also saw Stalin present a major report on nationality policy in which he argued that it was not enough to have liberated the non-Russian nationalities. Now the party needed to adopt compensatory programs to promote their economic and political development and eliminate the heritage of tsarist-era oppression. The party also needed to condemn both Russian dominant-nation nationalism and local nationalistic sentiment within the former colonies. According to Yaroslavsky and Pospelov, if Russian Great Power chauvinism was bad because of its imperialist connotations, the latter was worse, as it promoted separatism that ultimately posed a direct threat to the unity of the U.S.S.R.

NEP drew criticism from some within the party for restoring capitalism even as others complained that it did not make enough concessions to the market. Lenin demonstrated the effectiveness of the policy at the Eleventh Party Congress, however, pointing to improvements in the economy and the worker-peasant alliance. This congress also saw Stalin elevated to general secretary of the party.

According to Yaroslavsky and Pospelov, the Trotskyites and Bukharinites continued to express doubts about the party's ability to build socialism on its own and contended that large sectors of the economy should be ceded to foreign capitalists in exchange for needed capital. The Trotskyites went further and called for intensified exploitation of the peasantry in order to generate more funds. The Twelfth Party Congress rejected these proposals, which were subsequently revealed to have been treacherous bids to undermine the stability of the republic.

Despite the formation of an all-union structure for the U.S.S.R. in 1922, the party faced a resurgence of bourgeois nationalism in non-Russian regions. Georgian communists in particular were running roughshod over smaller ethnic groups in Transcaucasia with the support of the Trotskyites, Bukharinites, and Ukrainian communists. Shortly after the exposure of the Georgian affair, bourgeois nationalists in Tatarstan were revealed to be plotting to secede from the U.S.S.R. with the help of foreign espionage agencies. Again, Yaroslavsky and Pospelov warned that local nationalism would continue to threaten the U.S.S.R. in the future.

Continuing economic weakness at home and the failure of revolution abroad allowed the Trotskyites another opportunity to undermine the party. Taking advantage of Lenin's declining health, they argued along with the Democratic Centralists, Left Communists, and Workers' Opposition that the ban on factionalism should be rescinded. Stalin defended party discipline and unity at the Thirteenth Party Congress. Later, when Trotsky expanded this attack by publishing his article "The Lessons of October," Stalin counterattacked with a lecture entitled "The Foundations of Leninism." In this presentation, Stalin denounced Trotsky's political program for its Menshevik-like doubts about the worker-peasant alliance and the building of socialism in the U.S.S.R.

Amid this struggle, Lenin died on January 21, 1924. As his heir, Stalin took charge of the leader's commemoration, vowing to maintain Lenin's commitment to the party, the proletarian dictatorship, the worker-peasant alliance, the former colonial peoples, the Red Army, and the Comintern. According to Yaroslavsky and Pospelov, so many rank-and-file workers and peasants joined the party in the wake of the leader's death (the so-called Lenin Levy) that it permanently transformed the organization's makeup.

Restoration of the economy in 1925–1926 demonstrated that on a domestic level, the country had been able to develop a socialist economy. On the international level, this accomplishment would remain tenuous until the international proletariat rose up to free the U.S.S.R. of its capitalist encirclement. Trotsky, working in league with capitalists abroad, stubbornly denied that socialism could be built in one country. Bukharin and his allies likewise attempted to undermine the party line, supporting further concessions to kulak entrepreneurs. Zinoviev and Kamenev, who publicly supported the party line, also attempted to undermine it from behind the scenes.

At the Fifteenth Party Congress, Stalin reported that while economic conditions were improving, it was necessary to redouble industrialization efforts. Stalin was opposed by the Zinovievites, who now embraced a Trotskyite position questioning the worker-peasantry alliance and socialism in one country. He was also opposed by Bukharinite demands for a softer line on the kulaks. According to Yaroslavsky and Pospelov, this resistance stemmed from the emergence of a grand conspiracy linking the Trotskyites, Zinovievites, Bukharinites, and nationalists together with the remnants of the bourgeoisie, kulaks, Mensheviks, SRs, Economists, and Liquidators. These oppositionists focused their wrath on Stalin because of his unwavering commitment to the Leninist cause. Stalin dealt the conspirators a major defeat at the congress and renewed the party's commitment to industrialization and the worker-peasant alliance.

When Stalin turned to edit Chapter Nine, he observed that although the party faced an array of social, economic, and political problems, none of them were serious enough to pose an immediate threat to the Soviet republic. Stalin then rewrote the party's response to these challenges, shifting the discussion from an open-ended debate over a variety of policy options to a much more narrow account of NEP's specific implementation. According to his version of the events, Lenin and the party enjoyed greater command over the situation, while the opposition became less organized and articulate. Stalin likewise cut talk of a left-right conspiracy, foreign espionage, weaknesses in local party organizations, and other issues that foreshadowed the 1936–1938 trials.

During the discussion of the Tenth Party Congress, Stalin clarified Yaroslavsky and Pospelov's characterization of party policy. Conceding that war communism had been implemented prematurely, he cast NEP as a temporary tactical retreat designed to allow the party to begin building socialism. In regard to the opposition that NEP faced within the party, Stalin stressed the differences that divided the dissenters rather than the commonalities that united them. Indeed, in Stalin's mind, the only thing that the dissenters shared was a poor grasp of Marxism and a stubborn refusal to recognize the correctness of the Bolsheviks' position.

Stalin also reframed the text's treatment of nationality policy. First, he cut mention of the concrete measures needed to offset the legacy of tsarist oppression. Second, he altered the text's treatment of dominant-nation and local nationalism. Yaroslavsky and Pospelov had criticized dominant-nation nationalism with reference to Russian Great Power chauvinism before 1917; Stalin blunted this criticism by highlighting the fact that other nations beside the Russians had also run roughshod over their neighbors—something he illustrated with the 1922 Georgian scandal. He then downgraded the whole issue of the bourgeois nationalist threat by stripping the Tatar plot of its concrete details and foreign paymasters and deleting Yaroslavsky and Pospelov's prophecy regarding the danger that such conspiracies would pose in the future. Stalin's deletions in subsequent chapters would continue to depreciate this dimension of the national question.

When Stalin turned back to the economy, he focused on the Trotskyites' role in fomenting dissent. Deleting virtually all of the commentary on their actual policy proposals, he instead emphasized the group's inherent hostility toward the party itself. So intent was Stalin on silencing the opposition that he even cut most of the text's discussion of his own famous response to Trotsky's "Lessons of October."

In his commentary on Lenin's death, Stalin reduced mention of the Lenin Levy and his own status as heir apparent. Instead, he emphasized more central issues such as how the Thirteenth Party Congress renewed the party's commitment to NEP. In the subsequent discussion of socialism in one country, he retained Yaroslavsky and Pospelov's approach to the issue, but stripped the text of objections offered by what his party historians had described as an emergent left-right conspiracy of Trotsky, Bukharin, Zinoviev, and Kamenev. This editing diminished the threat posted by the opposition as the party pressed forward with industrialization and the worker-peasant alliance.

Chapter Ten (1926–1929)

After NEP's stabilization, industrialization became the party's chief priority. Heavy industry was especially needed, as it was critical to the defense of the U.S.S.R. Yaroslavsky and Pospelov illustrated this point by quoting Stalin's famous 1931 warning: "We are fifty to one hundred years behind the advanced countries. We must make good this distance in ten years. Either we manage it, or they will crush us."

Initial successes in industrialization unnerved the capitalists abroad. In May 1927, the British broke off diplomatic and trade relations and dispatched agents to undermine the new socialist economy. Shortly thereafter, the Soviet ambassador to Poland was assassinated. Soviet representatives were attacked in Berlin, Beijing, Shanghai, and Tientsin. At home, Trotsky—now an agent of British intelligence—stoked this tension.

The party responded to the 1927 War Scare by initiating trade agreements, non-aggression pacts, and proposals for world disarmament. It expanded the state sector of the economy in urban areas in order to crowd out the capitalist "nepmen" while rolling back kulak influence in the countryside. According to Yaroslavsky and Pospelov, the urban bourgeoisie resisted, seeking to undermine plans for socialism in one country with the Trotskyites and their foreign allies. The kulaks offered similar resistance with help from their Bukharinite allies.

Yaroslavsky and Pospelov went into considerable detail in regard to the Trotskyite opposition, outlining its membership, policy proposals, and political tactics. This necessitated a long discussion of the group's standoff with Stalin at the Fifteenth Party Congress and Seventh Comintern Plenum in 1926; its attempts to exacerbate the 1927 War Scare and undermine the Comintern line on China; and its bid to stage public protests during the tenth anniversary celebrations of the October Revolution. Like the August Bloc, the Trotskyites and their

Zinovievite allies espoused doubts about the party line—in this case concerning socialism in one country. But according to Yaroslavsky and Pospelov, the Trotskyites' ideological opposition to party policy also masked a deeper form of treachery: a conspiracy with fascists and imperialists abroad to undermine Soviet power and return the U.S.S.R. to the capitalist system. This deception illustrated the full extent of the Trotskyites' degeneration from an oppositional movement into a gang of double-dealing enemy agents.

Of course, the emergence of such a massive conspiracy under the direction of foreign paymasters presented Yaroslavsky and Pospelov with a major problem. How were they to explain the failure of Stalin and the party leadership to appreciate the scale of this threat until 1936–1938? Apparently, this group had been very successful at using leftist rhetoric to mask its true intentions. What's more, much of the party's rank and file had failed to treat the opposition with sufficient caution. This lack of vigilance slowed the investigations that ultimately exposed the full extent of this group's treachery.

In the second half of the chapter, Yaroslavsky and Pospelov outlined the party's efforts to modernize agriculture and ensure a stable supply of grain at fixed prices. Predictably, these efforts met with fierce kulak resistance, insofar as Stalin had warned that class antagonism would rise as socialism neared. But now, Bukharin and the rightists emerged as a second opposition group to challenge the state's efforts in the countryside. They questioned the party's accelerated plans for industrialization and collectivization and warned that a hardline policy against the kulaks would undermine the worker-peasant alliance. Such expressions of doubt later turned out to mask more nefarious goals as the Bukharinites aligned with the Trotskyites and Zinovievites in order to defeat Soviet power and bring about the restoration of capitalism. When this conspiracy was exposed in 1929, the Bukharinites publicly repented while privately continuing with their double-dealing. Ultimately, they plotted against the party not only with the Trotskyites, but with bourgeois nationalists in the republics and fascists abroad.

Interpreting these struggles with the opposition as a sign of weakness, the capitalist powers applied new pressure on the Soviet republic, especially in the Far East. The U.S.S.R. responded by turning the tables on its enemies, waging a diplomatic campaign for world peace while deploying the Red Army to the Chinese border under V. K. Blyukher. This produced a wave of support within the western working class that the Comintern exploited in order to extract trade concessions from countries like Great Britain.

The chapter concluded with the launch of the First Five Year Plan, the advent of machine-tractor stations, and the emergence of new forms of labor heroism oriented around a campaign of competitive "socialist emulation." Rank-and-file party members and workers played a dynamic role in this process, participating not only in production and plan fulfillment, but in the safeguarding of the economy against sabotage by class enemies.

When Stalin turned to editing Chapter Ten, he reframed the context for the whole economic transformation in order to emphasize the degree to which it was a natural outgrowth of the party's Leninist program. This involved more attention to planning and less to the opposition. Trotsky, Stalin now clarified, was not actually an agent of British intelligence, even if his views did coincide with those of the foreign bourgeoisie. What's more, the Trotskyites were less menacing than originally depicted, insofar as their ties were limited to the Zinovievites and the defeated domestic bourgeoisie and did not yet extend to the Bukharinite right. Even more importantly, Stalin deleted much of the text's discussion of the Trotskyites' platform and their subversive activities—editing that reduced their overall profile in the story by recasting them as deceptive spoilers rather than genuine rivals. When the narrative shifted to collectivization, Stalin also reframed the Bukharinite opposition, casting doubt on the rightists' ability, circa 1929, to mobilize kulak insurgents or forge an alliance with the Trotskyites, bourgeois nationalists, or foreign espionage agencies.

Regarding the launch of the First Five Year Plan, Stalin reframed the narrative in order to cut mention of grassroots initiatives promoting everything from machine-tractor stations to labor heroism. Such detail gave way to a new focus on the central party organization. Even more fundamental, however, was Stalin's decision to mute the role of the foreign threat in the party's pursuit of industrialization and agricultural development. If Yaroslavsky and Pospelov had linked the economic transformation to the exigencies of national defense, Stalin now tied it to longer-range goals associated with the building of socialism. Soviet power was to be recast as proactive rather than reactive as it pursued priorities determined by the dictates of Leninism.

Chapter Eleven (1930–1934)

In 1929, as the U.S.S.R. built socialism, the capitalist world descended into economic crisis. According to Yaroslavsky and Pospelov, Stalin predicted that the capitalists would turn to fascism at home and imperialism abroad in order to hold on to power. Indeed, Japan seized Manchuria and threatened the Soviet republic. In Germany, fascists took power in 1933, suppressed communist and working-class activists, and began preparations for war as well. According to Yaroslavsky and Pospelov, the fascist cause was aided within the U.S.S.R. by a left-right conspiracy of Trotskyites, Zinovievites, and Bukharinites, who engaged in espionage and terrorism along with Menshevik holdovers. Bourgeois specialists in industry and nationalists in the republics likewise did the fascists' bidding. Kulaks, too, engaged in economic wrecking and counterrevolution.

Despite this sabotage, the collective farm movement of the late 1920s experienced considerable success, thanks to support from the state and its machine-tractor stations. According to Yaroslavsky and Pospelov, this convinced the middle peasantry to rally to Soviet power, which in turn allowed official policy to shift from merely restricting kulak influence to actually eliminating the kulaks as a class. Stalin outlined his plans for collectivization and dekulakization shortly thereafter, dismissing the Bukharinites' objections as anti-Marxist opportunism. Stalin's plans, based on Lenin's theoretical work, were ratified by the Central Committee in early 1930.

The party carefully established appropriate collectivization targets for each region and warned local officials not to exceed these norms. According to Yaroslavsky and Pospelov, many nevertheless became "dizzy with success" and either made mistakes or behaved so coercively that they risked antagonizing the peasantry and undermining collectivization itself. Other officials—concealed Bukharinites and Trotskyites—deliberately alienated the peasantry by implementing a distorted version of the plan. Stalin and the party took concrete steps to rein in these abuses and defend the peasantry. While most of the excesses stemmed from the "right deviation," Stalin reminded the party that the "left deviation" was implicated as well. Yaroslavsky and Pospelov quoted Stalin as noting that this was one of the most dangerous periods in party history.

At the Sixteenth Party Congress in mid-1930, Stalin expressed satisfaction with the progress of industrialization, but called for more ambitious targets. The congress approved his proposal to complete the current Five Year Plan in four years. According to Yaroslavsky and Pospelov, only the oppositionist Rightist-"Leftist" Bloc objected to this decision and called for a slower pace recommended by Bukharin. Such "reasonable" objections were eventually revealed to be double-dealing, inasmuch as this group actually intended to weaken the U.S.S.R. on behalf of German and Japanese fascism. Indeed, the bloc was just one of several left-right conspiracies working to undermine the U.S.S.R. in order to return the country to the world capitalist system.

Like industrialization, collectivization required attention. Much of the countryside was quickly collectivized, but only in a formal sense. Kulak resistance also remained a major problem, whether in terms of overt terrorism or covert wrecking. The latter issue was especially important, as kulak agents had wormed their way into administrative positions in order to sabotage infrastructure, investment, and planning. They in turn were supported by Bukharinites in the Commissariat of Agriculture and the scientific establishment. This forced the party to redouble its efforts to increase vigilance, expose kulaks, and defend socialist property. It also led the party to reiterate its commitment to rural prosperity, inasmuch as Stalin considered that to be key to the transformation of the agricultural economy.

Dogged work ultimately allowed the First Five-Year Plan to be completed in four years. Waxing rhapsodic about this victory, Yaroslavsky and Pospelov contrasted the U.S.S.R.'s economic transformation with the crisis that still gripped the capitalist world. Financing industrialization had proven possible, the economy was booming, unemployment had been eliminated, and standards of living were improving. According to Yaroslavsky and Pospelov, backward Russia was now becoming one of the world's most technically and economically advanced countries. They quoted Stalin as proclaiming this victory to be important both at home and abroad, inasmuch as it refuted doubts about the possibility of building socialism in one country.

As Stalin announced the launch of the Second Five Year Plan, he warned that although the opposition had suffered severe defeats, it was by no means vanquished. Indeed, it was axiomatic that as the Soviet state neared socialism, the opposition would resist with increasing desperation. Continued vigilance and careful leadership would be necessary in order to guard against both sabotage and administrative excesses that the enemy might exploit.

In 1934, the Seventeenth Party Congress hailed the construction of a socialist foundation for the economy. Stalin congratulated the party on its accomplishments and outlined the agenda for the Second Five Year Plan in a speech that Kirov termed "the most brilliant document of the epoch." Bukharin, Rykov, Zinoviev, Kamenev, and M. P. Tomsky made repentant speeches at the congress, but this public behavior merely masked continued double-dealing in private. According to Yaroslavsky and Pospelov, these oppositionists were upset by the party's show of unity and support for Stalin and conspired with foreign fascists to assassinate Kirov and the rest of the party leadership in order to make the U.S.S.R. vulnerable to attack. Their betrayal was so thorough that when Zinoviev and Kamenev were arrested for Kirov's murder in late 1934, the rest continued to deceive and dissemble, concealing their treacherous connection to Trotsky and fascist intelligence services abroad. The full scale of this conspiracy would be exposed only in 1936–1938.

Yaroslavsky and Pospelov concluded the chapter by summarizing the accomplishments of the period. Industry had laid the foundation for a fully socialist economy. Agriculture had been collectivized in a successful campaign marked by the elimination of the kulaks as a class. And it was these victories that spurred the surrounding capitalist countries to conspire with the Trotskyites, Zinovievites, and Bukharinites to assassinate the party leadership, undermine the U.S.S.R.'s defenses, and prepare the country for a return to capitalism.

When Stalin turned to Chapter Eleven, he expanded the discussion of the capitalist economic crisis abroad. He noted how the crisis had induced Japan and Germany to prepare for war but clarified that their opponents would be Great Britain, France, and the US rather than the U.S.S.R. Along the way, he removed detail about Germany's rout of its domestic communist movement, emphasizing instead how the German Social Democrats were to blame for allowing Hitler to come to power. He also deleted the connection between the rise of fascism and increasing domestic oppositional activity in the U.S.S.R.

Stalin generally agreed with Yaroslavsky and Pospelov about the success of the collective farm movement at the end of the 1920s, disputing only the exaggerated role that the machine-tractor stations had played in winning over the peasantry. Instead, he stressed that it was broad grassroots support for dekulakization that accounted for the movement's popularity. Outlining this transformation of agriculture, Stalin cut much of the left and right opposition out of the story—particularly the Bukharinites' objections. As in previous chapters, this sort of editing muzzled the oppositionists, transforming their policy protests into inarticulate treachery.

At the same time that Stalin was reducing the detail afforded to the opposition, he also reduced mention of excesses attributed to local officials. Claims that hidden Bukharinites and Trotskyites were deliberately antagonizing the peasantry were cut as well. Ultimately, this editing led Stalin to remove even his own statements about the near and present danger that accompanied the collectivization campaign itself, normalizing the movement into little more than a particularly difficult phase in the U.S.S.R.'s complex economic transformation.

Stalin agreed with Yaroslavsky and Pospelov's assessment that the country's economic agenda required a redoubling of effort around 1930. Surveying the obstacles encountered during collectivization, he rejected the way Yaroslavsky and Pospelov blamed these problems on the Rightist-"Leftist" Bloc and other oppositional conspiracies. Conceding that some kulak sabotage had occurred, he asserted that most of the difficulties actually stemmed from an underappreciation of the importance of technology. Modern problems required modern solutions, and backwardness could undermine the whole process of socialist construction.

Toward the end of the chapter, Stalin cut much of the triumphalism about the completion of the First Five Year Plan. He replaced this celebration with a terse summary of what had been accomplished: the country had shifted from peasant agriculture to an industrial economy; capitalist elements had been driven from both industry and agriculture; the industrial sector had eliminated unemployment; and the collective farm system had put an end to rural poverty. And all of this had been done while freeing the population from exploitation and oppression. Stalin also struck out Yaroslavsky and Pospelov's warnings about an anticipated rise in sabotage and wrecking, replacing paragraphs of exacting detail with the passing caution that hostile capitalist and bourgeois nationalist elements remained at large in the U.S.S.R.

Having depreciated the Trotskyite and Bukharinite opposition for much of the period, Stalin reversed course toward the conclusion of Chapter Eleven in order to explain the assassination of Kirov in December 1934. Indulging in surprisingly bitter invective that was more emotional than it was rigorous or persuasive, Stalin asserted that the success of the country's economic transformation had driven the Trotskyites and Bukharinites mad with envy. Unable to reconcile themselves to their loss of popular support, they turned to wrecking and sabotage under the cover of double-dealing.

According to Stalin, the party had seen through the Trotskyites' and Bukharinites' repentant speeches at the Seventeenth Party Congress. That said, the party had not realized that these groups were prepared to go so far as to try to kill Kirov and the rest of the party leadership. Again, Stalin lapsed into verbal abuse, referring to Trotsky as Judas and acknowledging for the first time the connection between domestic left-right conspirators and German and Japanese fascism. Stalin did not afford much meaning to this plotting, but he did grant it an auxiliary role in the overall narrative.

The importance of Stalin's editing of this chapter is hard to exaggerate. Rejecting Yaroslavsky and Pospelov's account of a highly organized, omnipresent conspiracy acting on foreign orders, Stalin disentangled the Trotskyites and Bukharinites from the narrative of grassroots resistance and wrecking. Kulaks and other bourgeois elements, according to Stalin, had instinctively rebelled against collectivization and industrialization and then waged a losing battle against this economic transformation. Their instinctive struggle was almost entirely separate from the nefarious activity occurring at the same time within the ranks of the political opposition. There, Trotskyites, Bukharinites, SRs, Mensheviks, and bourgeois nationalists found themselves increasingly isolated and irrelevant, able only to express moral support for the kulaks and capitalist holdovers. According to Stalin, it was bitterness and spite rather than foreign paymasters that caused these groups to decompose from political oppositionists into saboteurs and terrorists. Fascinatingly, if Yaroslavsky and Pospelov had placed this left-right conspiracy at the center of all anti-Soviet activity since 1917, Stalin condescendingly characterized its various factions as increasingly impotent and disconnected from Soviet reality. Their collaboration with fascist espionage agencies and willingness to engage in ever more desperate acts of subterfuge was less a sign of their strength than of their weakness.

As Stalin was rewriting the centrality of the political opposition to the party's historical experience, he was also downgrading the importance of this resistance to the overall story of Soviet economic transformation. In Stalin's telling, industrialization and collectivization were now better grounded in theory and practice from the very start. Their implementation was more orderly and better planned and their success less dependent on outside factors. What Yaroslavsky and Pospelov had described as a defensive battle, complicated by pervasive wrecking, elaborate conspiracies, and foreign-sponsored terrorism, was normalized in Chapter Eleven into just one more stage in the difficult struggle to build Soviet socialism.

Chapter Twelve (1935–1937)

Continuing economic crisis in the mid-1930s drove the capitalist world to desperate measures. According to Yaroslavsky and Pospelov, more and more leaders embraced fascism at home in order to control the working class. Abroad, they relied on imperialism to maintain their hold on power. A quarter of the world's population was thus engulfed in war by 1937.

According to Yaroslavsky and Pospelov, the U.S.S.R. rebuffed these international tensions with a peaceful foreign policy backed up by a strong defense. It exposed the fascists' warmongering and poor treatment of their own populations. It supported the Chinese, who were suffering under Japanese occupation, and stood up for the Spanish people after the start of their country's civil war. In response, the fascists plotted an attack on the U.S.S.R. and collaborated with the Trotskyites, Bukharinites, and bourgeois nationalists in order to undermine the Soviet economy, cripple the Red Army, and hasten the restoration of capitalism.

In the meantime, the U.S.S.R.'s economic transformation neared completion. According to Yaroslavsky and Pospelov, a world-class industrial base had been built, backed up by a modern agricultural sector. Stalin now called for the previous period's emphasis on technology to be complemented by a new focus on personnel. The Stakhanovite movement soon emerged to champion labor heroism and productivity—something that quickly inspired other sorts of valor in areas ranging from aviation to Arctic exploration. Yaroslavsky and Pospelov identified many of these "new people" by name, saluting them as role models for the entire society.

According to Yaroslavsky and Pospelov, this economic transformation literally revolutionized agrarian society, bringing culture and prosperity to the post-kulak village. These accomplishments were hailed at a series of official receptions held for leading agricultural workers in 1935 and 1936. Conditions in urban areas were similarly transformed, leading to improvements in living standards, housing, health, cultural life, and education. Yaroslavsky and Pospelov then returned to the subject of Stakhanovism to provide extended commentary on specific heroes of the movement who promoted efficiency and technical know-how. This discussion of economic success was complemented by attention to Soviet society's newfound unity and the "Friendship of the Peoples" that now bound the country's various ethnic groups together. This stress on domestic unity was mirrored by another subsection focusing on the Comintern's promotion of the Popular Front abroad.

Societal transformation on this level, averred Yaroslavsky and Pospelov, necessitated a new constitution. Predictably, the new social contract, which was ratified in December 1936, recognized both the leading role of the party and the progressive character of the working class, "the most revolutionary, conscious, and organized" class in the U.S.S.R.

Yaroslavsky and Pospelov then outlined the climax of the party's struggle with the opposition. Reminding their readers that the Bolsheviks' opponents had sold out to the fascists abroad after losing popular support at home, Yaroslavsky and Pospelov warned that recruitment of such renegades would continue as long as the U.S.S.R. remained within a capitalist encirclement. They then surveyed recent victories over the opposition, beginning with the Trotskyites, whose leaders were convicted in August 1936 and January 1937 of conspiring to bring down Soviet power and partition the country into German, Japanese, and Polish colonies. The Trotskyites were then tied to an even larger left-right conspiracy with the Bukharinites and bourgeois nationalists during the February–March 1937 Central Committee plenum—a plot that also apparently included Menshevik and SR holdovers. The following summer, another major conspiracy was uncovered within the Red Army high command. Exposure of these cabals resulted in the trial of the "Bloc of Trotskyites and Rights" in March 1938, which demonstrated the full nature of the left-right threat to the U.S.S.R. It also confirmed the prophetic nature of Stalin's many demands for vigilance and a more cautious approach to party membership.

At the same time that the party was rooting out the left and right opposition, it was revising its own internal norms and practices. Particularly targeted for reform were domestic elections. During the First Five Year Plan, officials had developed an excessive fixation with technology and had become bureaucratized, ideologically lax, and insufficiently vigilant. Now, they would be held to a higher standard. This renewed commitment to ideological orthodoxy increased popular confidence in party rule and its building of socialism in one country. It also rallied the population around the party's concrete achievements in industrialization and collectivization—achievements without precedent either under the tsar or among the U.S.S.R.'s rivals abroad. Confirmation of this new spirit of unity in Soviet society was captured in the successful elections to the Supreme Soviet in December 1937.

Yaroslavsky and Pospelov concluded the chapter with an extensive section crediting Stalin with the U.S.S.R.'s economic transformation. Turning Marxist theory into reality, he had utilized Lenin's work on the proletarian dictatorship to produce breakthroughs in everything from industrialization and collectivization to nationality policy. This was complemented by Stalin's own teaching on the escalating threat of class conflict as the society embraced socialism—an axiom that enabled the population to vigilantly defend the accomplishments of Soviet power.

When Stalin turned to Chapter Twelve, he reframed Yaroslavsky and Pospelov's treatment of international tensions caused by the Great Depression. Ignoring the fascist states' suppression of their own populations, he focused on their attack on British, French, and US interests, arguing that such aggression heralded the beginning of a second world war. Intent on casting this emergent war as a conflict between capitalist countries, Stalin cut all mention of any imminent threat to the U.S.S.R. To this end, he deleted discussion of domestic Trotskyite and Bukharinite terrorism committed on behalf of foreign paymasters. He also reduced the potential for future conflict between the U.S.S.R. and its neighbors in the narrative by cutting detail on Soviet diplomatic efforts against fascism and in support of the Chinese and Spanish people.

Stalin then expanded Yaroslavsky and Pospelov's summary of the U.S.S.R.'s industrial and agricultural transformation. He proved only marginally interested in the social dimension of this transformation, however, and rewrote the section on the Stakhanovite movement in order to shift its attention from an emphasis on prosperity to one on productivity. Elsewhere in the chapter, he reduced attention to improved living and working conditions, as well as the effect that these gains had on morale and everyday heroism in society. Many of Yaroslavsky and Pospelov's role models disappeared from the text at the same time. The subsection on the Friendship of the Peoples was likewise deleted, as was one concerning the Comintern's Popular Front.[166]

Stalin agreed with Yaroslavsky and Pospelov that the building of socialism required a new constitution, but deleted their discussion of the leading role that this document assigned to the party and the working class. This editing is hard to explain at first glance, as Stalin had consistently expanded the leading role of the party in the narrative even as he reduced the historical agency assigned to the grass roots. Perhaps he felt that at this point in the story, the role of the party was obvious and the role of the working class better left unsaid.

Stalin's most dramatic editing concerned the struggle with the opposition. Here, he struck out Yaroslavsky and Pospelov's description of the renegades' various attempts to sabotage the ongoing socialist construction. He dropped discussion of plots within the Red Army, cut huge amounts of detail about the other conspiracies, and then lumped together the few traitors who remained as if to say that there was no longer any real distinction between the Trotskyites, Bukharinites, and bourgeois nationalists. Lapsing again into invective as he had in Chapter Eleven, Stalin heaped abuse on the "Bloc of Trotskyites and Rights" for their unprincipled left-right cabal and audacity to plot against the U.S.S.R.

Such isolated stretches of undisguised contempt and anger provide an eye-catching counterpoint to Stalin's otherwise sober and dispassionate editing.

At least as important as Stalin's new account of the defeat of the "Bloc of Trotskyites and Rights" was the degree to which his overall treatment of the struggle with the opposition differed from what was originally supplied by Yaroslavsky and Pospelov. If the latter two had spent the last five chapters developing a broad narrative of omnipresent conspiracy, according to which a highly organized group of insurgents with foreign backing had engaged in widespread wrecking and terror, Stalin recast the opposition as inarticulate traitors who were more desperate and craven than they were actually threatening. He did this by calling into question the effectiveness of the left-right conspiracy, whether as a group of political saboteurs or as the leaders of a broader insurgency involving the now-defeated kulaks and capitalist holdovers. Yaroslavsky and Pospelov had narrated a tale of claustrophobic tension, double-dealing, and omnipresent peril; now, Stalin offered in its place a much more conventional story of predictable but ultimately futile resistance to socialist construction. Stalin clearly wanted the readers of the SHORT COURSE to view the opposition with disgust and indignation, but he did not wish to undermine their confidence in the party and its leadership in the process.[167]

Yaroslavsky and Pospelov had concluded the chapter by using the reform of party elections to reiterate the importance of vigilance and ideological orthodoxy. Stalin rewrote this section to contend that these reforms had ushered in a new era in Soviet democracy. He used this new emplotment to shift focus away from the Great Terror and toward the December 1937 Supreme Soviet elections, which he represented as no less than a watershed moment in Soviet history. For Stalin, the elections proved that unity had been achieved in Soviet society through the construction of socialism and the purge of oppositional elements. This was such a key point that he decided to end the chapter right there, deleting Yaroslavsky and Pospelov's triumphalist summary of the party's economic transformation, its defeat of the opposition, and its celebration of his own leadership throughout the period.[168]

Conclusion

Yaroslavsky and Pospelov began the conclusion to the SHORT COURSE with a summary of the lessons to be learned from the narrative. First, the Bolsheviks had been victorious because of their discipline and promotion of the people's interests. Second, the Bolsheviks were unique in this regard and had had to overcome consistent opposition from the Mensheviks, SRs, and Anarcho-Syndicalists, who gravitated toward the bourgeoisie even before becoming embittered over their loss of popular support. Third, the Bolsheviks had also prevailed against bourgeois factions within the party itself—the Trotskyites, the Bukharinites, the Workers' Opposition, and the Democratic Centralists—all of whom had eventually combined forces against Soviet power. Fourth, Bolshevik success in this struggle stemmed from party members' ability to combine orthodox Marxist-Leninist theory with the flexible, real-world implementation of this knowledge. Fifth, the Bolsheviks' success was also attributable to their willingness to engage in self-criticism—something related to their mastery of theory and practice. Sixth, the Bolsheviks benefited from their strong relationship with society itself, not only leading the people, but following them as well.

Attempting to offer more personal advice on individual communist conduct, Yaroslavsky and Pospelov essentially reformulated their initial postulates. According to the history of the party, every Bolshevik was to look to the past, the people, and Marxist-Leninist theory for advice regarding the present and future. Bolsheviks were also to keep watch for hidden enemies in order to defend societal unity and socialist construction. Such lessons would allow the party to maintain its vanguardist role both within Soviet society and the worldwide revolutionary movement.

Predictably, Stalin rewrote much of the conclusion to emphasize his own sense of the party's priorities. First, he argued that party history validated the Bolsheviks' revolutionary militancy and refusal to compromise with other questionably Marxist movements. Second, he contended that such a rigorous position was only possible due to the party's mastery of Marxism-Leninism and its creative use of this theory in practice. Third, party history required the Bolsheviks to aggressively pursue the elimination of their opponents, whether Mensheviks, SRs, Anarchists, or bourgeois nationalists. Fourth, party history likewise required the Bolsheviks to struggle ceaselessly against compromising, opportunistic elements within their own ranks. Finally, party history demanded that the Bolsheviks routinely engage in self-criticism and maintain close ties with the people as a whole in order to remain true to the revolutionary cause.

Evident here is Stalin's promotion of Marxist-Leninist theory and depreciation of the struggle with the opposition. This change of priorities is clear from his reordering of the lessons to be learned from the SHORT COURSE; it is even more visible in the sheer amount of text on the opposition that Stalin deleted from the conclusion in order to make his case for the centrality of theory in the party's historical experience. This turnabout epitomized Stalin's overall reimagination of the party's historical experience quite effectively: if Yaroslavsky and Pospelov had depicted the struggle with the opposition as the red thread running throughout party history, Stalin now argued that the principal lesson to be learned related to the symbiotic relationship between Leninism in theory and Leninism in practice. The Bolsheviks' mastery of this lesson was epitomized by their successful rallying of the society together to defeat its enemies and build socialism in one country.

THE TRANSLATION

This critical edition is based on the official English translation of the SHORT COURSE, published in the U.S.S.R. in 1939.[169] One of a dozen translations produced under the auspices of the Comintern and the State Foreign Languages Publishing House, it was commissioned by the Politburo in mid-September 1938 as part of a larger effort to make the SHORT COURSE available to non-Russian speakers worldwide.[170] A historical document in its own right, this translation was chosen as the basis for this edition due to the enormous international influence it has wielded since its first printing.

Archival documents reveal that the responsibility for this translation was assigned in 1938 to an editorial team under the supervision of M. M. Borodin, an Old Bolshevik best known for his tenure as the editor-in-chief of the English-language newspaper MOSCOW NEWS. Leading consultants to the project included I. E. Chernov, a high-ranking editor at the TASS Wire Service, and the radical Scottish communist J. R. Campbell, who was in Moscow at the time serving as a liaison between the Comintern and the Communist Party of Great Britain. Two prominent translators—the head of the publishing house's English department, A. I. Fainberg, and the British communist John Evans—performed the work itself, assisted by D. L. Fromberg, I. B. Lasker-Grinberg, and L. I. Davidovich.[171] The imperfect, idiosyncratic nature of their rendering of the SHORT COURSE into English probably stems from the fact that nearly all of these specialists were Russian-born "re-émigrés" who had learned English while living abroad in either Great Britain or the United States before returning to the U.S.S.R. during the 1920s. An American employee of the publishing house in the 1930s recalled later in her memoirs that these staffers typically worked on important ideological texts such as the SHORT COURSE under very tense conditions.[172]

On the pages that follow, the text of the SHORT COURSE is rendered in conventional typeface wherever its final version can be traced back to Yaroslavsky and Pospelov's final April 1938 prototype history. Book titles and emphases in the text are rendered in capital letters, as per the official 1939 translation, as are parenthetical editorial statements ("—ED.") from the first edition. Stalin's editing and textual interpolations are indicated through the use of italics. His editorial excisions are represented in type that has literally been struck through—an unconventional style of presentation that graphically captures some of the violence with which the general secretary disemboweled party history. All of the editorial changes outlined in the volume are Stalin's; all

Table 1. Representation of Stalin's editing

original sentence fragment	Later, when the Civil War broke out, the Bolshevik party . . .
simple deletion	Later, when the Civil War broke out, the ~~Bolshevik~~ party . . .
deletion plus decapitalization	Later, when ~~the Civil~~ *war* broke out, the party . . .
deletion plus capitalization	~~Later,~~ *W*hen war broke out, the party . . .
simple interpolation	When war broke out, the *Bolshevik* party . . .
interpolation plus decapitalization	*But w*hen war broke out, the Bolshevik party . . .
simple word or phrase replaced	But when war broke out, the Bolshevik ~~party~~ *movement* . . .
sentence division plus capitalization	~~But when~~ *W*ar broke out. *T*he Bolshevik movement . . .
edit suggested by someone else	War broke out. The Bolshevik ~~movement~~ *party*[1] . . .
parenthetical note	*(. . . —Ed.)*

corrections and deletions that were suggested by other members of the general secretary's inner circle are identified by footnotes and explained in the volume's scholarly apparatus.

As this is a complex text to represent in print, several caveats are necessary to keep in mind before proceeding. First, as noted above, this critical edition is a synthetic text that aggregates at least three discrete rounds of Stalin's editing during the summer of 1938. It therefore tracks Stalin's overall revisions to the Short Course without attempting to distinguish between his editing from draft to draft. Second, this edition has gone to great lengths to restore to the text all the material that Stalin cut from Yaroslavsky and Pospelov's final April 1938 prototype, inasmuch as the general secretary's excisions are often as important as his interpolations. In cases where Stalin deleted text in order to replace it with his own additions, the deletions are always rendered first, followed by his new text. Third, although this edition is based on the official 1939 English version of the Short Course, everything that Stalin excised from the April 1938 prototype has had to be translated from scratch before being restored to the text. Considerable effort has been made to translate this new material according to the conventions of the original 1939 edition, including its slightly stilted, literal renderings, its idiosyncratic use of colloquialisms, and its inconsistent capitalization and spelling rules. Original typesetting errors have been retained, as have nonstandard usages such as the adjective "Whiteguard" and noun "technique," which Moscow-based translators regularly conflated with "technology" during the 1930s.[173] Finally, the organization at the center of this story is referred to here as the Communist Party of the Soviet Union (Bolsheviks)—CPSU(B)—a turn of phrase that was used in foreign propaganda from the 1920s until its official Russian renaming in 1952.[174]

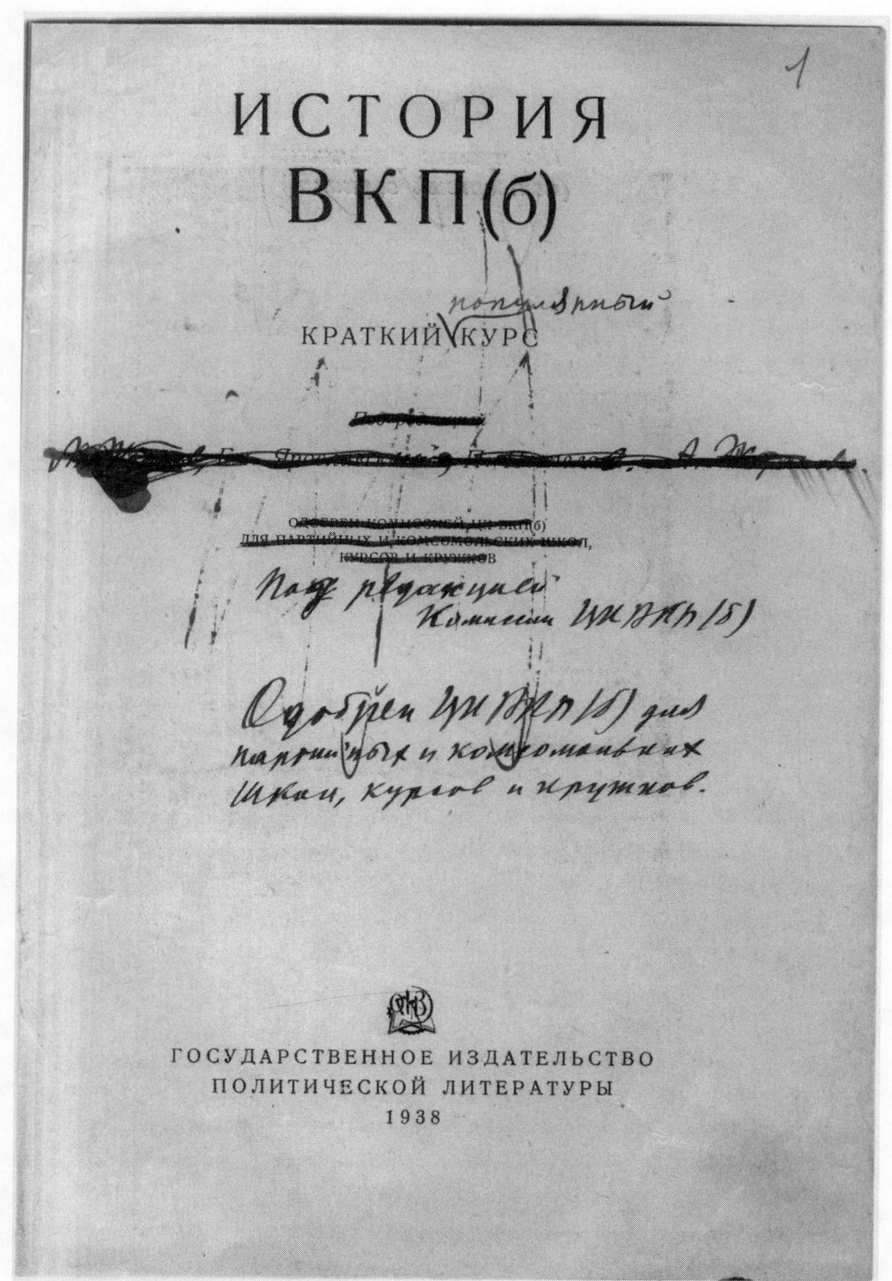

1

ИСТОРИЯ
ВКП(б)

популярный

КРАТКИЙ КУРС

~~Одобрен Комиссией ЦК ВКП(б)~~
~~для партийных и комсомольских школ,~~
~~курсов и кружков~~

Под редакцией
Комиссии ЦК ВКП(б)

Одобрен ЦК ВКП(б) для
партийных и комсомольских
школ, курсов и кружков.

ГОСУДАРСТВЕННОЕ ИЗДАТЕЛЬСТВО
ПОЛИТИЧЕСКОЙ ЛИТЕРАТУРЫ
1938

Title page with Stalin's editing from the late summer of 1938. RGASPI, f. 558, op. 11, d. 1217, l. 1.

HISTORY
OF THE
COMMUNIST PARTY
OF THE
SOVIET UNION
/BOLSHEVIKS/

SHORT ~~*POPULAR*~~ COURSE

EDITED BY

~~*A. Zhdanov*, Em. Yaroslavsky and P. Pospelov, *A. Zhdanov*~~[1]

A COMMISSION OF THE C.C. OF THE C.P.S.U.(B.)

AUTHORIZED BY

~~A COMMISSION OF~~ THE C.C. OF THE C.P.S.U.(B.), *1938*

~~FOR PARTY AND YOUNG COMMUNIST LEAGUE SCHOOLS, COURSES AND STUDY CIRCLES~~

Contents

CHAPTER TWO

Formation of the Russian Social-Democratic Labour Party. ~~and the~~ Appearance of the Bolshevik and the Menshevik Groups within the Party (1901–1904)

1. Upsurge of the Revolutionary Movement in Russia ~~at the Beginning of the Twentieth Century~~ *in 1901–04*

2. ~~Lenin's Iskra in the Struggle for the Formation of a Proletarian Party.~~ *Lenin's Plan for the Building of a Marxist Party. Opportunism of the "Economists." Iskra's Fight for Lenin's Plan. Lenin's Book What Is To Be Done? Ideological Foundations of the Marxist Party*

~~3.~~ ~~Stalin—Founder of the Leninist-Iskra Organization in Transcaucasia~~

3.~~4.~~ Second Congress of the ~~R.S.D.L.P.~~ *Russian Social-Democratic Labour Party. Adoption of Program and Rules and Formation of a Single Party. Differences at the Congress and Appearance of Two Trends within the Party: the Bolshevik and the Menshevik*

~~5.~~ ~~Appearance within the Party of Bolshevik and Menshevik Factions.~~

4.~~6.~~ ~~The Bolshevik Struggle for the Party with the Mensheviks and Conciliators in 1903–04~~ *Splitting Activities of the Menshevik Leaders and Sharpening of the Struggle within the Party after the Second Congress. Opportunism of the Mensheviks. Lenin's Book, One Step Forward, Two Steps Back. Organizational Principles of the Marxist Party.*

Brief Summary

CHAPTER THREE

The Mensheviks and the Bolsheviks in the Period of the Russo-Japanese War and the First Russian Revolution (1904–1907)

1. Russo-Japanese War. *Further Rise of the Revolutionary Movement in Russia. Strikes in St. Petersburg. Workers' Demonstration before the Winter Palace on January 9, 1905. Demonstration Fired Upon. Outbreak of the Revolution*

~~2.~~ ~~January 9, 1905—Beginning of the Revolution~~

2.~~3.~~ ~~From January 9 to the General Strike.~~ *Workers' Political Strikes and Demonstrations. Growth of the Revolutionary Movement among the Peasants. Revolt on the Battleship "Potemkin"*

3.~~4.~~ ~~Two Tactics in the Bourgeois-Democratic Revolution—Those of the Bolsheviks and Mensheviks.~~ *Tactical Differences between Bolsheviks*

CHAPTER FOUR

The Mensheviks and the Bolsheviks in the Period of the Stolypin Reaction. ~~and~~ *T*he Bolsheviks Constitute Themselves as an Independent ~~Social-Democratic~~ *Marxist* Party (1908–1912)

CHAPTER FIVE

The Bolshevik Party during the New Rise of the Working-Class Movement before the First Imperialist War (1912–1914)

CHAPTER SIX

The Bolshevik Party in the Period of the Imperialist War. ~~And~~ The Second ~~Russian~~ Revolution *in Russia* (1914–~~February~~–March 1917)

3. *Theory and* Tactics of the Bolsheviks *Party* ~~during the Years of the Imperialist War~~ *on the Question of War, Peace and Revolution*

~~4. Bolshevik Work in Russia during the War Years~~

4.~~5.~~ ~~Growth of the Revolutionary Movement and Crisis in the Country on the Eve of the February Revolution.~~ *Defeat of the Tsarist Army. Economic Disruption. Crisis of Tsardom*

5.~~6.~~ The February ~~Bourgeois-Democratic~~ Revolution ~~of 1917~~. *Fall of Tsardom. Formation of Soviets of Workers' and Soldiers' Deputies. Formation of the Provisional Government. Dual Power*

~~7. Creation of the Soviets of Workers' and Soldiers' Deputies~~

Brief Summary

CHAPTER SEVEN

The Bolshevik Party in the Period of Preparation and Realization of the October Socialist Revolution (April 1917–1918)

1. Situation in the Country after the ~~Victory of the Second Russian~~ February Revolution. *Party Emerges from Underground and Passes to Open Political Work. Lenin Arrives in Petrograd. Lenin's April Theses. Party's Policy of Transition to Socialist Revolution*

~~2. The Bolshevik Party after the Bourgeois-Democratic February Revolution~~

2.~~3.~~ ~~First Crisis of Power.~~ *Beginning of the Crisis of the Provisional Government.* April Conference *of the Bolshevik Party*

3.~~4.~~ ~~Struggle of the Bolsheviks for the Masses~~ *Successes of the Bolshevik Party in the Capital. Abortive Offensive of the Armies of the Provisional Government. Suppression of the July Demonstration of Workers and Soldiers*

~~5. The Demonstration of July 3–5 and Its Suppression by the Provisional Government~~

4.~~6.~~ The Bolshevik Party Adopts the Course of Preparing for Armed Uprising. Sixth Party Congress

5.~~7.~~ *General* Kornilov's Plot ~~and Its~~ *against the Revolution*. Suppression *of the Plot. Petrograd and Moscow Soviets Go Over to the Bolsheviks*

~~8. Organization of the Storm (September–October 1917)~~

6.~~9.~~ ~~Preparation and Carrying-Out of the Armed Uprising.~~ *October Uprising in Petrograd and Arrest of the Provisional Government. Second Congress of Soviets and Formation of the Soviet Government. Decrees of the Second Congress of Soviets on Peace and Land.* Victory of the ~~October~~ Socialist Revolution. *Reasons for the Victory of the Socialist Revolution*

~~10. Second All-Russian Congress of Soviets (November 7–8, 1917). Formation of the Council of People's Commissars under Lenin's Command~~

7.~~11.~~ Struggle of the Bolshevik Party to Consolidate the Soviet Power. *Peace of Brest-Litovsk. Seventh Party Congress*

~~12. Struggle of the Bolshevik Party for an End to the Imperialist War~~

8.~~13.~~ Lenin's Plan for *the Initial Steps in* Socialist Construction ~~(Spring of 1918)~~. *Committees of the Poor Peasants and the Curbing of the Kulaks. Revolt of the "Left" Socialist-Revolutionaries and Its Suppression. Fifth Congress of Soviets and Adoption of the Constitution of the R.S.F.S.R.*

~~14. Creation of Committees of the Poor, Struggle with the Kulaks and Development of the Socialist Revolution in the Countryside~~

Brief Summary

CHAPTER EIGHT
The Bolshevik Party in the Period of *Foreign Military Intervention and* Civil War (1918–1920)

1. ~~International Imperialism and the Soviet Republic. The Year 1918.~~ *Beginning of Foreign Military Intervention. First Period of the Civil War*

2. *Defeat of Germany in the War.* Revolution in Germany ~~and Austro-Hungary. Establishment~~ *Founding* of the ~~Communist~~ *Third* International. Eighth Party Congress

~~3. Eighth Party Congress~~

3.~~4.~~ *Extension of Intervention. Blockade of the Soviet Country.* ~~Defeat of the First and Second Kolchak Campaigns~~ *Kolchak's Campaign and Defeat. Denikin's Campaign and Defeat. A Three-Months' Respite. Ninth Party Congress*

~~5. War Communism~~

~~6. A Brief Respite toward the Beginning of the 1920s. The Party's Struggle with the "Democratic-Centralism" Anti-Party Group~~

4.~~7.~~ ~~Third Campaign of the Entente, White Poles and Wrangel (1920)~~ *Polish Gentry Attack Soviet Russia. General Wrangel's Campaign. Failure of the Polish Plan. Rout of Wrangel. End of the Intervention*

~~8. Party Work during the Civil War Years~~

~~9. The Bolshevik Party—the Chief and Organizer of the Victory of the Proletarian Dictatorship during the Civil War~~

5. How and Why the Soviet Republic Defeated the Combined Forces of British-French-Japanese-Polish Intervention and of the Bourgeois-Landlord-Whiteguard Counter-Revolution in Russia

Brief Summary

CHAPTER NINE
The Bolshevik Party in the Period of Transition to the Peaceful Work of Economic Restoration (1921–1925)

1. Soviet Republic after the *Defeat of the Intervention and* End of the Civil War. *Difficulties of the Restoration Period*

2. *Party* Discussion on the Trade Unions ~~and the Party's Crisis~~. *Tenth Party Congress. Defeat of the Opposition. Adoption of the New Economic Policy (NEP)*

~~3. Tenth Party Congress of the Bolsheviks~~

3.~~4.~~ ~~The Bolshevik Party during~~ The *First* ~~Years~~ *Results* of NEP. *Eleventh Party Congress. Formation of the Union of Soviet Socialist Republics. Lenin's Illness. Lenin's Co-operative Plan. Twelfth Party Congress*

4.~~5.~~ Struggle ~~of the Party against the Trotskyite Opposition in 1923–24~~ *against the Difficulties of Economic Restoration. Trotskyites Take Advantage of Lenin's Illness to Increase Their Activity. New Party Discussion. Defeat of the Trotskyites. Death of Lenin. The Lenin Enrolment. Thirteenth Party Congress*

~~6. Lenin's Death. Stalin's Oath~~

5.~~7.~~ The Soviet Union towards the End of the Restoration Period. *The Question of Socialist Construction and the Victory of Socialism in Our Country. Zinoviev-Kamenev "New Opposition." Fourteenth Party Congress. Policy of Socialist Industrialization of the Country*

~~8. Fourteenth Party Congress—the Congress of Industrialization~~

Brief Summary

2. *Further Progress of Industry and Agriculture in the U.S.S.R. Second Five-Year Plan Fulfilled Ahead of Time. Reconstruction of Agriculture and Completion of Collectivization. Importance of Cadres. Stakhanov Movement. Rising Standard of Welfare. Rising Cultural Standard. Strength of the Soviet Revolution*

~~2.~~ ~~Strengthening Socialist Productive Relations~~

~~3.~~ ~~Rise of the Working People's Well-Being~~

~~4.~~ ~~The Stakhanovite Movement and the Struggle for Socialist Labour Productivity~~

~~5.~~ ~~The U.S.S.R.'s Great Friendship of the Peoples~~

~~6.~~ ~~Seventh Comintern Congress (June–August 1935)~~

3.~~7.~~ *Eighth Congress of Soviets. Adoption of the* New ~~Stalinist~~ Constitution *of the U.S.S.R.*

4.~~8.~~ ~~Defeat~~ *Liquidation* of the ~~Counter-Revolutionary~~ *Remnants of the* Bukharin-Trotsky ~~Germano-Japanese~~ Gang of Spies, ~~Saboteurs,~~ Wreckers and ~~Terrorists~~ *Traitors to the Country. Preparations for the Election of the Supreme Soviet of the U.S.S.R. Broad Inner-Party Democracy as the Party's Course. Election of the Supreme Soviet of the U.S.S.R.*

~~9.~~ ~~The Bolshevik Party's Further Struggle for the Strengthening of Its Ranks. C.P.S.U.(B.) Central Committee Plenum (February–March 1937)~~

~~10.~~ ~~Elections to the Supreme Soviet (December 12, 1937)~~

Conclusion

Explanation of Terms[2]

~~A Guide to the Literature on the SHORT COURSE ON THE HISTORY OF THE C.P.S.U.(B.)~~[3]

~~CHAPTER ONE~~

~~The Struggle for the Creation of a Marxist Social-Democratic Party in Russia~~

~~(FROM THE FORMATION OF PLEKHANOV "EMANCIPATION OF LABOUR" GROUP—1883—TO THE APPEARANCE OF THE FIRST ISSUES OF ISKRA—1900–1901)~~

Introduction

The Communist Party of the Soviet Union (Bolsheviks) has traversed a long and glorious road, leading from the first tiny Marxist circles and groups that appeared in Russia in the eighties of the past century to the great Party of the Bolsheviks, which *now* directs the first Socialist State of Workers and Peasants in the world.

The C.P.S.U.(B.) grew up on the basis of the working-class movement in pre-revolutionary Russia; it sprang from the Marxist circles and groups which had established connection with the working-class movement and imparted to it a Socialist consciousness. The C.P.S.U.(B.) has always been guided by the revolutionary teachings of Marxism-Leninism. In the new conditions of the era of imperialism, imperialist wars and proletarian ~~Socialist~~ revolution*s*, its leaders *further* developed the teachings of Marx and Engels and raised them to a new level.

The C.P.S.U.(B.) grew; *and* gained strength~~, and became tempered~~ in a ~~stubborn~~ fight over fundamental principles waged against the ~~enemies of Marxism-Leninism~~ *petty-bourgeois parties* within the working-class movement—the Socialist-Revolutionaries (and earlier still, against their predecessors, the Narodniks), the Mensheviks, Anarchists and bourgeois nationalists *of all shades*—and, within the Party itself, against *the Menshevik, opportunist trends*—the Trotskyites, Bukharinites, *nationalist deviators* and other anti-Leninist groups.

The C.P.S.U.(B.) gained strength and became tempered in the ~~sharpest class~~ *revolutionary* struggle against all enemies of the working class and of all working people—against landlords, capitalists, kulaks, wreckers, spies, against all the mercenaries of the surrounding capitalist states.

1

И С Т О Р И Я В К П (б).

КРАТКИЙ КУРС.

В в е д е н и е.

Всесоюзная Коммунистическая партия(большевиков) прошла долгий и славный путь от первых маленьких марксистских кружков и групп, появившихся в России в 80-х годах прошлого столетия, до великой партии большевиков, руководящей ныне первым в мире социалистическим государством рабочих и крестьян.

ВКП(б) выросла на основе рабочего движения в дореволюционной России из марксистских кружков и групп, которые связались с рабочим движением и внесли в него социалистическое сознание. ВКП(б) руководствовалась и руководствуется революционным учением марксизма-ленинизма. Ее вожди в новых условиях эпохи империализма, империалистических войн и пролетарских революций развили дальше учение Маркса и Энгельса, подняли его на новую ступень.

ВКП(б) росла крепла и закалялась в упорной принципиальной борьбе с врагами марксизма-ленинизма внутри рабочего движения – эсерами (а еще раньше с их предшественниками – народниками), меньшевиками, анархистами, буржуазными националистами, а внутри партии – с троцкистами, бухаринцами и прочими антиленинскими группами.

First page of the Introduction with Stalin's editing from the summer of 1938. RGASPI, f. 558, op. 11, d. 1209, l. 1.

The history of the C.P.S.U.(B.) is the history of three revolutions: the *bourgeois-democratic* revolution of 1905, the *bourgeois-democratic* revolution of February 1917, and the Socialist revolution of October 1917.

The history of the C.P.S.U.(B.) is the history of the overthrow of tsardom, of the overthrow of the power of the landlords and capitalists; *it is the history of the rout of the armed foreign intervention during the Civil War;* it is the history of the building of the Soviet state and of Socialist society in our country.

The study of the history of the C.P.S.U.(B.) enriches us with the ~~knowledge~~ *experience* of the fight for Socialism waged by the workers and peasants of our country.

The study of the history of the C.P.S.U.(B.), the history of the struggle of our Party against all enemies of Marxism-Leninism, against all enemies of the working people, helps us to MASTER BOLSHEVISM and sharpens our political vigilance.

The study of the heroic history of the Bolshevik Party arms us with a knowledge of the laws of social development and of the political struggle, with a knowledge of the motive forces of revolution.

The study of the history of the C.P.S.U.(B.) ~~adds to~~ *strengthens* our certainty of the ultimate ~~triumph~~ *victory* of the great cause of the Party of Lenin-Stalin, the victory of Communism ~~in our country and~~ throughout the world.

This book ~~narrates~~ *sets forth* briefly the history of the Communist Party of the Soviet Union (Bolsheviks).

CHAPTER ONE

The Struggle for the Creation of a Social-Democratic Labour Party in Russia (1883–1901)

1. *Abolition of Serfdom and* the Development of *Industrial* Capitalism in Russia ~~at the End of the Nineteenth Century~~. *Rise of the Modern Industrial Proletariat. First Steps of the Working-Class Movement*

Tsarist Russia entered the path of capitalist development later than other countries. Prior to the sixties of the past century there were very few mills and factories in Russia. Manorial estates based on serfdom constituted the prevailing form of economy. ~~In 1861, the tsarist government, frightened by the peasant rebellions against the landlords, was compelled to abolish serfdom.~~ There could be no real development of industry under serfdom. The involuntary labour of the serfs in agriculture was of low productivity. The whole course of economic development made the abolition of serfdom imperative. *In 1861, the tsarist government, weakened by defeat in the Crimean War, and frightened by the peasant revolts against the landlords, was compelled to abolish serfdom.*

But even after serfdom had been abolished the landlords continued to oppress the peasants. In the process of "emancipation" they robbed the peasants by inclosing, cutting off, considerable portions ~~(from 1/5 to 1/3)~~ of the land previously used by the peasants. These cut-off portions of land were called by the peasants OTREZKI (cuts). The peasants were compelled to pay about 2,000,000,000 rubles to the landlords as the redemption price for their "emancipation."

After serfdom had been abolished the peasants were obliged to rent land from the landlords on most onerous terms. In addition to paying money rent, the peasants were often compelled by the landlord to cultivate without remuneration a definite portion of his land with their own implements and horses.[1] *This was called* OTRABOTKI *or* BARSHCHINA *(labour rent, corvée). In most cases the peasants were obliged to pay the landlords rent in kind in the amount of one-half of their harvests. This was known as* ISPOLU *(half and half system).*

3

- 3 -

Изучение истории ВКП(б) укрепляет уверенность в окончательной победе великого дела партии Ленина - Сталина, победе коммунизма во всем мире.

Книга эта кратко ~~рассказывает~~ излагает историю Всесоюзной Коммунистической партии (большевиков).

ГЛАВА I

БОРЬБА ЗА СОЗДАНИЕ СОЦИАЛ-ДЕМОКРАТИЧЕСКОЙ РАБОЧЕЙ ПАРТИИ В РОССИИ.

(1883 - 1901 гг.)

~~(От образования плехановской группы "Освобождение труда" - 1883 год - до появления первых номеров "Искры" - 1900-1901 годы)~~

1. Отмена крепостного права и развитие промышленного капитализма в России. Появление современного промышленного пролетариата. Первые шаги рабочего движения.

~~В 1861 году~~ Царское правительство, (ослабленное военным поражением во время Крымской кампании и запуганное) ~~боясь~~ крестьянскими "бунтами" против помещиков, вынуждено ~~было~~ оказалось в 1861 году отменить крепостное право. Весь ход экономического развития России толкал к уничтожению крепостного права. Подневольный, крепостной труд давал низкую производительность в сельском хозяйстве. При крепостном праве не могла по-настоящему развиваться промышленность.

Но и после отмены крепостного права помещики продолжали угнетать крестьян. Помещики ограбили крестьян, отняв, отрезав у них при "освобождении" зна-

First page of Chapter One with Stalin's editing from the summer of 1938. RGASPI, f. 558, op. 11, d. 1209, l. 3.

Thus the situation remained almost the same as it had been under serfdom, the only difference being that the peasant was now personally free, [and] could not be bought and sold like a chattel.

The landlords bled the backward peasant farms white by various methods of extortion (rent, fines~~, usury and so on~~). Owing to the oppression of the landlords the bulk of ~~this~~ *the* peasantry were unable to improve their farms. Hence the extreme backwardness of agriculture in pre-revolutionary Russia, which led to frequent crop failures and famines.

The survivals of serfdom, crushing taxation ~~(taxes)~~ and the redemption payments to the landlords, which not infrequently exceeded the income of the peasant household, ruined the peasants, reduced them to pauperism and forced them to quit their villages in search of a livelihood. They went to work in the mills and factories. This was a source of cheap labour power for the manufacturers.

Over the workers and peasants stood a veritable army of sheriffs, deputy sheriffs, gendarmes, constables, rural police, who protected the tsar, the capitalists and the landlords ~~and bullied~~ *from* the toiling *and exploited* people. Corporal punishment existed right up to 1903. Although serfdom had been abolished the peasants were flogged for the slightest offence and for the non-payment of taxes. Workers were ~~brutally~~ manhandled by the police and the Cossacks, especially during strikes, when the workers downed tools because their lives had been made intolerable by the manufacturers. Under the tsars the workers and peasants had no political rights whatever. The tsarist autocracy was the worst enemy of the people.

Tsarist Russia was a prison of nations.[2] The numerous non-Russian nationalities ~~(about 100,000,000 total)~~ were entirely devoid of rights and were subjected to constant insult and humiliation of every kind. The tsarist government taught the Russian population to look down upon the native peoples of the national regions as an inferior ~~thing~~ *race*, officially referred to them as INORODTSI (aliens), and fostered contempt and hatred of them. The tsarist government deliberately fanned national discord, instigated one nation against another, engineered Jewish pogroms and, in Transcaucasia, incited Tatars and Armenians to massacre each other.

Nearly all, *if not all,* government posts in the national regions were held by Russian officials. All business in government institutions and in the courts was conducted ~~only~~ in the Russian language. It was forbidden to publish newspapers and books in the languages of the non-Russian nationalities or to ~~even talk~~ *teach* in the schools in the native tongue. The tsarist government strove to extinguish every spark of national culture and pursued a policy of forcible "Russification." Tsardom was a hangman and torturer of the non-Russian peoples.

~~". . . tsarist Russia," said Comrade Stalin, "was the home of every kind of oppression—capitalist, colonial and militarist—in its most inhuman and barbarous form." (Stalin, Questions of Leninism, 10th Russ. ed., p. 4.)~~

After the ~~peasant reforms of 1861~~ *abolition of serfdom*, the development of *industrial* capitalism in Russia proceeded at a ~~very~~ *fairly* rapid pace in spite of the fact that it was still hampered by survivals of serfdom. During the twenty-five years, 1865–90, the number of workers employed in large mills and factories and on the railways increased from 706,000 to 1,433,000, or more than doubled.

Large-scale capitalist industry in Russia began to develop even more rapidly in the nineties. ~~In 1900–1903,~~ *By the end of that decade* the number of workers employed in the large mills and factories, in the mining industry and on the railways amounted in the fifty European provinces of Russia alone to 2,207,000, and in the whole of Russia to 2,792,000 persons. ~~(Lenin, Collected Works, Russ. ed., Vol. III, p. 388.) The production of bituminous coal, oil and metallurgy was distinguished by particularly stormy growth during the nineties. In ten years (1890–1900), iron smelting increased more than three times.~~

This was a modern industrial proletariat, radically different from the workers employed in the factories of the period of serfdom and from the workers in small, handicraft and other kinds of industry, both because of the spirit of solidarity prevailing among the workers in big capitalist enterprises and because of their militant revolutionary qualities.

The industrial boom of the nineties was chiefly due to intensive railroad construction. During the course of the decade (1890–1900) over 21,000 versts of new railway line were laid. The railways created a big demand for metal (for rails, locomotives and cars), and also for increasing quantities of fuel—coal and oil. *This led to the development of the metal and fuel industries.*

In pre-revolutionary Russia, as in all capitalist countries, periods of industrial boom alternated with industrial crises, stagnation, which severely affected the working class and condemned hundreds of thousands of workers to unemployment and poverty.

Although the development of capitalism *in Russia* proceeded fairly rapidly ~~in Russia~~ after the abolition of serfdom, nevertheless, in economic development ~~she~~ *Russia* lagged considerably behind other capitalist countries. The vast majority of the population was still engaged in agriculture. In his celebrated work, The Development of Capitalism in Russia, Lenin cited significant figures from the general census of the population of 1897 which showed that about five-sixths of the total population were engaged in agriculture, ~~or about 97,000,000 people (including their families)~~ and only one-sixth in large and small industry, trade, on the railways and waterways, in building work, lumbering, and so on~~, or about 21,700,000 people (including their families)~~.

~~These figures graphically demonstrate~~ *This shows* that *although capitalism was developing in* Russia ~~had already become a capitalist country. But at the same time~~, she was still[3] an agrarian, economically backward country, a petty-bourgeois country, that is, a country in which low-productive *individual* peasant farming based on small ownership still predominated.

~~From the point of view of capitalism, there were new, modern classes as well as old, pre-capitalist classes in pre-revolutionary Russia. The fundamentally new classes were the proletariat and industrial bourgeoisie, which began to grow rapidly after the fall of serfdom. In pre-emancipation Russia, these classes were insignificant and did not enjoy great significance. The old, pre-capitalist classes were the feudal landlord class, the peasant class and a large strata of petty handicraftsmen and artisans.~~

~~At the end of the nineties, no fewer than 4,000,000 people worked in petty artisanal industry. Of them, about 2,000,000—according to Lenin's calculations—had already turned into hired labour, engaged in putting out work at home for the capitalists. The remaining 2,000,000 artisans still worked independently as petty proprietors. They could also be referred to as a pre-capitalist class.~~

Capitalism was developing not only in the towns but also in the countryside. The peasantry, ~~this~~ *the* most numerous class in pre-revolutionary Russia, was undergoing a process of disintegration, of cleavage~~:~~. *F*rom among the more well-to-do peasants there was emerging an upper layer of kulaks, the rural bourgeoisie, while on the other hand many peasants were being ruined, and the number of poor peasants, rural proletarians and semi-proletarians, was on the increase. As to the middle peasants, their number decreased from year to year.

In 1903 there were about ten million peasant households in Russia. In his pamphlet entitled To the Village Poor, Lenin calculated that of this total~~—10,000,000 households—there were~~ not less than ~~three to~~ three and a half million households *consisted* of peasants possessing no horses. These were the poorest peasants who usually sowed ~~a tenth, or in many cases, only two tenths~~ *only a small part* of their land, leased the rest to the kulaks, and themselves left to seek other sources of livelihood. The position of these peasants came nearest to that of the proletariat. Lenin called them rural proletarians or semi-proletarians.

On the other hand, one and a half million rich, kulak households (out of a total of ten million peasant households) concentrated in their hands half the total sown area of the peasants. This peasant bourgeoisie was growing rich by grinding down the poor and middle peasantry and profiting from the toil of agricultural labourers, *and was developing into rural capitalists.*

The working class of Russia began to awaken already in the seventies, and *especially in* the eighties, and started a struggle against the capitalists. Exceedingly hard was the lot of the workers in tsarist Russia. In the ~~seventies and~~ eighties the working day in the mills and factories was not less than 12 1/2 hours, and in the textile industry reached 14 to 15 hours. The exploitation of female and child labour was widely resorted to. Children worked the same hours as adults, but, like the women, received a much smaller wage. Wages were ~~very~~ *inordinately* low. The majority of the workers were paid seven or eight rubles per month. The most highly paid workers in the metal works and foundries received no more than 35 rubles per month. There were no regulations for the protection of labour, with the result that workers were maimed and killed in large numbers. Workers were not insured, and all medical services had to be paid for. Housing conditions were appalling. In the factory-owned barracks, workers were crowded as many as 10 or 12 to a small ~~room (cell)~~ *"cell."* In paying wages, the manufacturers often cheated the workers, compelled them to make their purchases in the factory-owned shops at exorbitant prices, and mulcted them in fines.

The workers began to take a common stand and present joint demands to the factory owner[4] for the improvement of their intolerable conditions. They would down tools and ~~not return before the owner had satisfied their demands, that is~~[5] go on strike. The earlier strikes in the seventies and eighties were usually provoked by excessive fines, cheating and swindling of the workers over wages, and reductions in the rates of pay~~, etc~~.

In the earlier strikes, the workers, driven to despair, would sometimes smash machinery, break factory windows and wreck factory-owned shops and factory offices.

The more advanced workers began to realize that if they were to be successful in their struggle against the capitalists, they needed organization. Workers' unions began to arise.

In 1875 the South Russian Workers' Union was formed in Odessa. This first workers' organization lasted eight or nine months and was then smashed by the tsarist government.

~~But no amount of persecution from the tsarist government was able to stop the labour movement.~~ In 1878 the Northern Union of Russian Workers was formed in St. Petersburg, headed by Khalturin, a carpenter, and Obnorsky, a fitter. The program of the Union ~~explicitly~~ stated that its aims and objects were similar to those of the Social-Democratic labour parties of the West. The ultimate aim of the Union was to bring about a Socialist revolution—"the overthrow of the existing political and economic system, as an extremely unjust system." Obnorsky, one of the founders of the Union, had lived abroad for some time and had there acquainted himself with the activities of the Marxist

Social-Democratic parties and of the First International, which was directed by Marx. This circumstance left its impress on the program of the Northern Union of Russian Workers. The immediate aim of the ~~Northern~~ Union ~~of Russian Workers~~ was to win political liberty and political rights for the people (freedom of speech, press, assembly, etc.). The immediate demands also included a reduction of the working day.

The membership of the Union reached 200, and it had about as many sympathizers. It began to take part in workers' strikes, to lead them ~~in the strike at the New Cotton Mill and elsewhere~~. The tsarist government smashed this workers' union too.

But the working-class movement continued to grow, spreading from district to district. The eighties were marked by a large number of strikes. In the space of five years (1881–86) there were as many as 48 strikes involving 80,000 workers.

An exceptional part in the history of the revolutionary movement was played by the big strike that broke out at the Morozov mill in Orekhovo-Zuyevo in 1885.

About 8,000 workers were employed at this mill. Working conditions grew worse from day to day: there were five wage cuts between 1882 and 1884, and in the latter year rates were reduced by 25 per cent at one blow. In addition, Morozov, the manufacturer, tormented the workers with fines. It was revealed at the trial which followed the strike that of every ruble earned by the workers, from 30 to 50 kopeks went into the pocket of the manufacturer in the form of fines. ~~Finally,~~ *T*he workers could not stand this robbery any longer and in January 1885 went out on strike. The strike had been organized beforehand. It was led by a politically advanced worker, Pyotr Moiseyenko, who had been a member of the Northern Union of Russian Workers and already had some revolutionary experience. On the eve of the strike Moiseyenko and others of the more class-conscious weavers drew up a number of demands for presentation to the mill owners; they were endorsed at a secret meeting of the workers. The chief demand was the abolition of the rapacious fines.

This strike was suppressed by armed force. Over 600 workers were arrested and scores of them committed for trial.

Similar strikes broke out in ~~four~~ *the* mills of Ivanovo-Voznesensk in 1885.

In the following year the tsarist government was compelled by its fear of the growth of the working-class movement ~~and strikes (especially the Morozov strike)~~ to promulgate a law on fines which provided that the proceeds from fines were not to go into the pockets of the manufacturers but were to be used for the needs of the workers themselves. ~~After that, the mill owners were not able to rob and cheat the workers so insolently.~~

The Morozov and other strikes taught the workers that a great deal could be gained by organized struggle. The working-class movement began to produce capable leaders and organizers who staunchly championed the interests of the working class.

At the same time, on the basis of the growth of the working-class movement and under the influence of the working-class movement of Western Europe, the first Marxist organizations began to arise in Russia.

2. ~~Spread of Marxism~~ *Narodism (Populism) and Marxism* in Russia. *Plekhanov and* ~~The~~ *His* "Emancipation of Labour" Group. Its *Plekhanov's* Fight against ~~the Narodniks~~ *Narodism. Spread of Marxism in Russia*

Prior to the appearance of the Marxist groups revolutionary work in Russia was carried on by the Narodniks (Populists), who were opponents of Marxism.

The first *Russian*[6] Marxist group ~~formed~~ *arose* ~~in Russia~~[7] in 1883. This was the "Emancipation of Labour" group formed by G. V. Plekhanov abroad, in Geneva ~~(Switzerland)~~, where he had been obliged to take refuge from the persecution of the tsarist government for his revolutionary activities.

Previously Plekhanov had himself been a Narodnik. But having studied Marxism while abroad, he broke with Narodism and became an outstanding propagandist of Marxism.

The "Emancipation of Labour" group did a great deal to disseminate Marxism in Russia. They translated works of Marx and Engels into Russian—The Communist Manifesto, Wage-Labour and Capital, Socialism: Utopian and Scientific, etc.—had them printed abroad and circulated them secretly in Russia. Plekhanov, *Zasulich, Axelrod* and other members of this group also wrote a number of ~~books and brochures~~ *works* explaining the teachings of Marx and Engels, the ideas of scientific Socialism.

~~Before Marx and Engels, there were outstanding thinkers who dreamed of the restructuring of human society, of the elimination of inequality and exploitation and man's exploitation of his fellow man. But these people, who called themselves Socialists, dreamed of attaining Socialism without class struggle. They thought that it would be possible to "persuade" the exploitative classes, the bourgeoisie and the landlords, to voluntarily surrender their wealth and power.~~[8]

Marx and Engels, the great teachers of the proletariat, were the first to explain ~~in their scholarly works~~ that, *contrary to the opinion of the utopian Socialists,* Socialism was not the invention of dreamers *(utopians)*, but the inevitable outcome of the development of modern *capitalist* society. They showed that the capitalist system *would fall, just as serfdom had fallen, and that capitalism* was creating its own gravedigger in the person of the proletariat. They showed that only the class struggle of the proletariat, only the victory of the proletariat over the bourgeoisie, would rid humanity of ~~the calamities that were oppressing it~~ *capitalism and exploitation.*

Marx and Engels taught the proletariat to be conscious of its own strength, ~~and~~ to be conscious of its class interests *and to unite for a determined struggle against the bourgeoisie.* ~~"Marxism is the scientific expression of the fundamental interests of the working class" (Stalin). In his book Capital,~~ Marx *and Engels* discovered the ~~economic~~ laws of ~~advancing~~ *development* of capitalist society and proved scientifically that the development of ~~the contradictions of~~ capitalist society, and the class struggle going on within it, must inevitably lead ~~this society~~ to ~~collapse~~ *the fall of capitalism*, to the ~~revolution~~ *victory* of the proletariat, to the DICTATORSHIP OF THE PROLETARIAT.

Marx and Engels taught that ~~to overthrow~~ *it was impossible to get rid of* the power of capital and to convert capitalist property into public property ~~was possible for~~ *by peaceful means, and that* the working class *could achieve this* only by revolutionary violence *against the bourgeoisie, by a* PROLETARIAN REVOLUTION, by establishing its own political rule—the dictatorship of the proletariat~~. The task of this period was to~~—*which must* crush *the resistance of* the exploiters and create a new, classless, Communist society.

~~Marx and Engels personally led the revolutionary struggle of the working class and helped it to organize. During the Revolution of 1848, Marx and Engels stood at the head of the revolutionary German workers. Even before the Revolution of 1848, they formed the Communist League and wrote the famous Communist Manifesto. In this manifesto, they said that the proletariat had nothing to lose in the revolution except for its chains and had the whole world to win. Their militant call, "Workers of the World, Unite!" became the banner for workers of the entire world. Marx, with Engels's help, led the First International, or the "International Workingman's Association," which was organized in 1864.~~

~~After the fall of the Paris Commune (1871), the First International soon ceased to exist. But the labour movement and the spread of Marxist ideas developed even more broadly in a variety of countries.~~

Marx and Engels taught that the industrial proletariat is the most revolutionary and therefore the most advanced class in capitalist society, and that only a class like the proletariat could rally around itself all the forces discontented with capitalism and lead them in the storming of capitalism. But in order to vanquish the old world and create a new, classless society, the proletariat must have its own working-class party, which Marx and Engels called the Communist Party.

It was to the dissemination of the views of Marx and Engels that the first Russian Marxist group, Plekhanov's "Emancipation of Labour" group, devoted itself.

The "Emancipation of Labour" group raised the banner of Marxism in the Russian press abroad at a time when no Social-Democratic movement in Russia yet existed. It was first necessary to prepare the theoretical, ideological ground for such a movement. The chief ideological obstacle to the spread of Marxism and of the Social-Democratic movement was the Narodnik views which at that time ~~still~~ prevailed among *the advanced workers and* the revolutionary-minded intelligentsia.

As capitalism developed in Russia the working class became a powerful *and advanced* force that was capable of waging an organized *revolutionary* struggle. But the leading role of the working class was not understood by the Narodniks. The Russian ~~Populist Revolutionaries of the seventies~~ *Narodniks* erroneously held that the principal revolutionary force was *not the working class, but* the peasantry, and that the rule of the tsar and the landlords could be overthrown by means of peasant revolts alone. The Narodniks *did not know the working class and* did not realize that the peasants alone were incapable of ~~ever~~ vanquishing tsardom and the landlords without an alliance with the working class and without its guidance. *The Narodniks did not understand that the working class was the most revolutionary and the most advanced class of society.*

The Narodniks ~~of the seventies~~ first endeavoured to rouse the peasants for a struggle against the tsarist government. With this purpose in view, young revolutionary intellectuals donned peasant ~~or worker~~ garb~~, sometimes quickly learned some artisanal trade~~ and flocked to the countryside—"to the people," as it used to be called. Hence the term "Narodnik," from the word NAROD, the people. But they found no backing among the peasantry, *for they did not have a proper knowledge or understanding of the peasants either*. The majority of them were arrested by the police. Thereupon the Narodniks decided to continue the struggle against the tsarist autocracy single-handed, without the people, *and this led to even more serious mistakes.*

A secret Narodnik society known as "Narodnaya Volya" ("People's Will") began to plot the assassination of the tsar. On March 1, 1881, members of the "Narodnaya Volya" succeeded in killing Tsar Alexander II with a bomb. But the people did not benefit from this in any way. The assassination of individuals could not bring about the overthrow of the tsarist autocracy or the abolition of the landlord class. The assassinated tsar was replaced by another, Alexander III, under whom the conditions of the workers and peasants became still worse.

The method of combating tsardom ~~selected~~ *chosen* by the Narodniks, namely, by the assassination of individuals, by individual terrorism, was wrong and ~~very~~ detrimental to the revolution. The policy of individual terrorism was based on the erroneous Narodnik theory of active "heroes" and a passive "mob," which awaited exploits from the "heroes." This false theory maintained that it is only outstanding individuals who make history, while the masses, *the people, the class,* ~~or~~ the "mob," as the Narodnik writers contemptuously called them, are incapable of conscious, organized activity and can only blindly follow the "heroes." For this reason the Narodniks abandoned mass revolutionary work among the peasantry and the working class and changed to *individual* terrorism. They induced one of the most prominent revolutionaries of the time, Stepan Khalturin, to give up his work of organizing a revolutionary workers' union and to devote himself entirely to terrorism.

By these assassinations of individual representatives of the class of exploiters, assassinations that were of no benefit to the revolution, the Narodniks diverted the attention of the working people from the struggle against that ~~entire~~ class as a whole ~~and~~. *They* hampered the ~~formation of an alliance of workers and peasants~~ *development of the revolutionary initiative and activity of the working class and the peasantry.*

~~The Narodniks' actions were detrimental because~~ *T*he Narodniks prevented the working class from understanding its leading role in the revolution and retarded the creation of ~~a Marxist labour~~ *an independent* party *of the working class.*

Although the Narodniks' secret organization had been smashed by the tsarist government, Narodnik views continued to persist for a long time among the revolutionary-minded intelligentsia. The surviving Narodniks stubbornly resisted the spread of Marxism in Russia and hampered the organization of the working class. ~~Narodism was the most evil enemy of Marxism.~~

Marxism in Russia ~~grew and became stronger~~ *could therefore grow and gain strength only* by combating Narodism~~, exposing the whole erroneous and harmful nature of the Narodniks' teaching and their terroristic tactics, which precluded the organization of a mass party~~.

The "Emancipation of Labour" group launched ~~criticism of~~ *a fight against* the erroneous views of the Narodniks and showed how greatly their views and methods of struggle were prejudicing the working-class movement.

In his writings directed against the Narodniks, Plekhanov showed that their views had nothing in common with scientific Socialism, even though they called themselves Socialists.

Plekhanov was the first to give a ~~profound~~ Marxist criticism of ~~all~~ the erroneous views of the Narodniks. Delivering ~~daring~~ *well-aimed* blows at the Narodnik ~~foolishness~~ *views,* Plekhanov at the same time developed a brilliant defence of the Marxist views.

What were the major errors of the Narodniks which Plekhanov hammered at with such destructive effect?

First,[9] the Narodniks asserted that capitalism was ~~an "accident"~~ *something "accidental"* in Russia, that it would not develop, and that therefore the proletariat would not *grow and* develop either.

Secondly,[10] the Narodniks did not regard the working class as the foremost class ~~(the hegemon)~~ in the revolution. They dreamed of attaining Socialism without the proletariat. They considered that the principal revolutionary force was the peasantry—*led by the intelligentsia—and the peasant commune, which they regarded as the embryo and foundation of Socialism.*

Thirdly,[11] the Narodniks' view of the whole course of human history was erroneous and harmful. *They neither knew nor understood the laws of the economic and political development of society. In this respect they were quite backward.* According to them, history was made *not by classes, and not by the struggle of classes, but* by outstanding individuals—"heroes"—who were blindly followed by the masses, ~~or~~ the "mob," *the people, the classes.*

In ~~the struggle against~~ *combating and exposing* the Narodniks Plekhanov wrote a number of ~~remarkable~~ Marxist works which were instrumental in rearing and educating the Marxists in Russia. Such works of his as SOCIALISM AND THE POLITICAL STRUGGLE, OUR DIFFERENCES, ON THE DEVELOPMENT OF THE MONISTIC VIEW OF HISTORY, ~~TOWARD THE QUESTION OF THE ROLE OF THE INDIVIDUAL IN HISTORY, and an array of others~~ cleared the way for the victory of ~~a Marxist movement~~ *Marxism* in Russia~~, for the development of scientific Socialism~~.

In his works Plekhanov expounded ~~brilliantly upon~~ the basic principles of Marxism. Of particular importance was his ON THE DEVELOPMENT OF THE MONISTIC VIEW OF HISTORY, *published in 1895.* Lenin said that this book served to "rear a whole generation of Russian Marxists." (Lenin, COLLECTED WORKS, Russ. ed., Vol. XIV, p. 347.)

In his writings aimed against the Narodniks, Plekhanov showed that it was absurd to put the question the way the Narodniks did: should capitalism develop in Russia or not? As a matter of fact Russia HAD ALREADY ENTERED the path of capitalist development, Plekhanov said, producing facts to prove it, and there was no force that could divert her from this path.

The task of the revolutionaries was not to ARREST the development of capitalism in Russia—that they could not do anyhow. Their task was to secure the support of the powerful revolutionary force brought into being by the development of capitalism, namely, the working class~~; their task was~~, to develop its class-consciousness, *to organize it, and to help it to create its own working-class party.*

~~"We must take advantage of the ongoing socio-economic turnover in Russia in the interests of the revolution and the working population," Plekhanov wrote in his work OUR DIFFERENCES, referring to the rapid development of capitalism.~~

Plekhanov also shattered the second major error of the Narodniks, namely, their denial of the role of the proletariat as the ~~leader (the hegemon)~~ *vanguard* in the revolutionary struggle. The Narodniks looked upon the rise of the proletariat in Russia as something in the nature of a "historical misfortune," and spoke of the "ulcer of proletarianism." Plekhanov, championing the teachings of Marxism, showed that they were fully applicable to Russia and that *in spite of the numerical preponderance of the peasantry and the relative numerical weakness of the proletariat,* it was on the proletariat and on its growth that the revolutionaries should base their chief hopes.

Why on the proletariat ~~and not on the peasantry~~?

Because the proletariat, ~~according to Plekhanov, was a GROWING, developing class,~~ *although it was still numerically small, was a labouring class which was connected with the MOST ADVANCED form of economy, large-scale production, and* which *for this reason* had a great future before it.

Because the proletariat, as a class, was GROWING from year to year, was DEVELOPING politically, [*it*] *easily lent itself to organization*[12] *owing to the conditions of labour prevailing in large-scale production, and was the most revolutionary class owing to its proletarian status, for it had nothing to lose in the revolution*[13] *but its chains.*

The case was different with the peasantry.

The peasantry (meaning here the individual peasants, each of whom worked for himself—ED.[14]*), despite its*[15] *numerical strength, was a labouring class that was connected with the MOST BACKWARD form of economy, small-scale production, owing to which it had not and could not have any great future before it.*

~~But the peasantry was a class that was not only not growing, but which was gradually SPLITTING UP into kulaks (the bourgeoisie) and poor and landless peasants (semi-proletarians and rural proletarians).~~ *Far from growing as a class, the peasantry was splitting up more and more into bourgeois (kulaks) and poor peasants (proletarians and semi-proletarians). Moreover, being scattered, it lent itself less easily than the proletariat to organization, and, consisting of small owners, it joined the revolutionary movement less readily than the proletariat.*[16]

~~The Narodniks announced that Socialism in Russia would come not through the dictatorship of the proletariat, but through the peasant commune, which they regarded as the embryo of Socialism.~~

~~What was the commune, which survived from the time of serfdom?~~

~~Peasant land was considered not to be the property of individual peasants, but of the village or land community in question. Generally speaking, this land was redivided every twelve years or so according to the number of souls, or mouths to feed, in each peasant household at the time of the redivision. These allotments of communal land were not allowed to be bought or sold. It was because of such customs that the Narodniks concluded that the peasants must be innate Socialists.~~

~~The Narodniks forgot, however, that the agriculture that was conducted on these allotments of communal land was conducted individually, rather than collectively. They closed their eyes to the fact that the poor peasants who possessed no horses had nothing with which to work their land, and that the poor peasants and the peasants of little means had to surrender a large part of their allotment to the kulaks for virtually nothing. The kulak felt himself to be superior within the commune and could exploit the poor and middle peasants at will. The commune was also convenient for the tsarist government. The tsarist government introduced "collective responsibility" for the collection of the state's taxes, according to which the entire village or commune was responsible for the total sum due.~~

The Narodniks maintained[17] *that Socialism in Russia would come not through the dictatorship of the proletariat, but through the peasant commune, which they regarded as the embryo and basis of Socialism. But the commune was neither the basis nor the embryo of Socialism, nor could it be, because the commune was dominated by the kulaks—the bloodsuckers who exploited the poor peasants, the agricultural labourers and the economically weaker middle peasants. The formal existence of communal land ownership and the periodical redivision of the land according to the number of mouths in each peasant household did not alter the situation in any way. Those members of the commune used the land who owned draught cattle, implements and seed, that is, the well-to-do middle peasants and kulaks. The peasants who possessed no horses, the poor peasants, the small peasants generally, had to surrender their land to the kulaks and to hire themselves out as agricultural labourers. As a matter of fact, the peasant commune was a convenient means of masking the dominance of the kulaks and an inexpensive instrument in the hands of the tsarist government for the collection of taxes from the peasants on the basis of collective responsibility. That was why tsardom left the peasant commune intact. It was absurd to regard a commune of this character as the embryo or basis of Socialism.*

~~The Narodniks did not understand that the peasant himself did not aim for Socialism and that the initiative for the Socialist restructuring of society could come only from the working class, which would lead the peasantry along with it. The Narodniks aimed to preserve and immortalize petty-bourgeois peasant agriculture, out of which capitalism would inevitably emerge. This is why Lenin wrote that there was "NOT A GRAN (one of the smallest possible units of measurement—ED.) of Socialism" in Narodism. (Lenin, COLLECTED WORKS, Russ. ed., Vol. XV, p. 466.)~~

~~Plekhanov and especially Lenin demonstrated that the rapid development of capitalism was also occurring in the countryside and demonstrated the total futility of the Narodniks' dreams for the land commune as the path to~~

~~Socialism. Plekhanov and then Lenin demonstrated that only the working class could be an advanced revolutionary class.~~

~~Plekhanov developed a critique of the Narodniks' theory of active "heroes" and the passive, blind "mob." In the struggle with the Narodniks, Plekhanov laid out the Marxist explanation on the role of the individual in history.~~

~~The Narodniks claimed that history is made by only individual, outstanding personalities—"heroes"—and that the masses are a blind force that is incapable of any sort of creativity—something like an enormous number of zeros. Therefore, the Narodniks never aimed to raise the revolutionary consciousness of the masses and organize them for the struggle against tsardom, but instead went over to individual terrorism.~~

~~In his works, Plekhanov defended the fundamental tenets of Marxism, saying that the development of human society ultimately occurs through the development of material productive forces and changes in the mode of material production. Societal relations change on this basis as well. The revolutionary's task is to understand in which direction society is developing and what is growing and maturing in social life and what is dying out and decomposing.~~

~~Marxism, or dialectical materialism, aims for the elimination of classes and the destruction of the capitalist system and capitalist society. The teachings of Marxism itself appeared only when the elimination of classes and capitalism became a historical imperative. Marxism, wrote Plekhanov, appeals not to individual "heroic" loners, but to the working class, which is to become the genuine hero of the next historical period. The complete destruction of wage slavery and the capitalist system is in the interests of the working class. Thus Marxism expresses the fundamental interests of the working class.~~

~~But Marxism does not deny the role of outstanding individuals in history. Marx wrote that it is precisely people who make their own history. But they do not make it in any old way that might occur to them. Every new generation must confront the specific conditions of material production and social relations which were already present as that generation came into being.~~

Plekhanov shattered the third major error of the Narodniks as well, namely, that "heroes," outstanding individuals, and their ideas played a prime role in social development, and that the role of the masses, the "mob," the people, classes, was insignificant. Plekhanov accused the Narodniks of IDEALISM, and showed that the truth lay not with idealism, but with the MATERIALISM of Marx and Engels.

Plekhanov expounded and substantiated the view of Marxist materialism. In conformity with Marxist materialism, he showed that in the long run the development of society is determined not by the wishes and ideas of outstanding individuals, but by the development of the material conditions of existence of society, by the changes in the mode of production of the material wealth required for the existence of society, by the changes in the mutual relations of classes in the pro-

duction of material wealth, by the struggle of classes for place and position in the production and distribution of material wealth. It was not ideas that determined the social and economic status of men, but the social and economic status of men that determined their ideas. Outstanding individuals[18] *may become nonentities if their ideas and wishes run counter to the economic development of society, to the needs of the foremost class; and vice versa, outstanding people may really become outstanding individuals if their ideas and wishes correctly express the needs of the economic development of society, the needs of the foremost class.*

In answer to the Narodniks' assertion that the masses are nothing but a mob, and that it is heroes who make history and convert the mob into a people, the Marxists affirmed that it is not heroes that make history, but history that makes heroes, and that, consequently, it is not heroes who create a people, but the people who create heroes and move history onward. Heroes,[19] outstanding individuals, ~~and great people are only worth something~~ *may play an important part in the life of society only* in so far as they ~~can~~ *are capable of* correctly understand*ing* ~~these social conditions~~ *the conditions of development of society* and the ways of changing them for the better. *Heroes, outstanding individuals,*[20] *may become ridiculous and useless failures if they do not correctly understand the conditions of development of society and go counter to the historical needs of society in the conceited belief that they are "makers" of history.*

To this category of ill-starred heroes belonged the Narodniks.

> ~~"The more or less slow change of 'economic conditions' occasionally places before society the imperative of a more or less rapid transformation of its institutions. This transformation never takes place "on its own." It always demands the intervention of MEN, who are thus confronted with great social tasks. And it is those men who contribute more than others to the resolution of these tasks who are called great men. . . .~~
>
> ~~A great man is great not because his special qualities allow him to leave a personal mark on great historical events, but because he possesses special qualities that make him uniquely capable of serving the great social needs of his time, needs which have arisen as a result of general and particular causes. Carlyle, in his well-known work on heroes, refers to great men as BEGINNERS. This is a very apt choice of words. The great man is a beginner because he sees FURTHER than others and desires things MORE STRONGLY.~~
>
> ~~He resolves scientific tasks which have been posed by the preceding progress of the intellectual development of society. He identifies new social needs created by the preceding development of social relations. He takes upon himself the initiative to satisfy these needs," wrote Plekhanov in his famous article, TOWARD THE QUESTION OF THE ROLE OF~~

~~THE INDIVIDUAL IN HISTORY (Plekhanov, WORKS, Russ. ed., vol. VIII, p. 306, 304–305).~~

Plekhanov's ~~work~~ *writings*~~, the dissemination of the works of Marx and Engels by the "Emancipation of Labour" group~~ *and the fight he waged against the Narodniks* thoroughly undermined their influence among the revolutionary intelligentsia. But the ideological destruction of Narodism was still far from complete. It was left to Lenin to deal the final blow to Narodism, as an enemy of Marxism~~, in the nineties~~.

Soon after the suppression of the "Narodnaya Volya" Party the majority of the Narodniks renounced the revolutionary struggle against the tsarist government ~~and the landlords~~ and began to preach a policy of reconciliation and agreement with ~~them~~ *it*. In the eighties and nineties the Narodniks began to ~~openly~~ voice the interests of the kulaks[21] ~~and the prosperous peasantry~~.

The "Emancipation of Labour" group prepared two drafts of a program for a Russian Social-Democratic party (the first in 1884 and the second in 1887). This was a very important preparatory step in the formation of a Marxist Social-Democratic party in Russia.

~~The contributions of the "Emancipation of Labour" group to the cause of propagandizing Marxism and founding Social-Democracy in Russia were great. Lenin underscored more than once that Plekhanov was the FOUNDER of the Marxist Social-Democratic Party in Russia. During the time when Plekhanov remained a consistent Marxist, he enjoyed totally exceptional authority and popularity within the proletarian party. But when Plekhanov began to stumble in a political sense and deviate from the proletarian line, the workers broke with Plekhanov and forgot about him.~~

~~After Plekhanov slid into opportunism once and for all, Lenin wrote: "His personal contributions in the past were enormous. Over the course of twenty years, from 1883–1903, he supplied a mass of superior works." (Lenin, COLLECTED WORKS, Russ. ed., Vol. XVII, p. 416.) In 1921, Lenin pointed out that it would be impossible to become a fully conscious communist without studying Plekhanov's philosophical work, "as it is the best of the international literature on Marxism."~~

~~Marxist groups and reading circles began to quickly develop in various cities during the second half of the 1880s. The most important of them were the Blagoyev group in St. Petersburg, Fedoseyev's reading circle in Kazan and Brusnev's group in St. Petersburg. All of these reading circles and groups prioritized the study of Marx's works and prepared to conduct propaganda. The Brusnev group succeeded in organizing the first celebration of May Day in Russia in 1891. 70–80 advanced workers from St. Petersburg took part in that first~~

~~May Day celebration. Several worker-propagandists gave speeches which were then secretly printed and disseminated. The Marxist reading circles and groups in Russia worked on literature that they received from abroad from the "Emancipation of Labour" group.~~

But at the same time the "Emancipation of Labour" group ~~had~~ *was guilty of* some very serious ~~shortcomings~~ *mistakes.* Its first draft program still contained vestiges of the Narodnik views; it countenanced the tactics of individual terrorism. *Furthermore,* Plekhanov failed to take into account that *in the course of the revolution* the proletariat could and should lead the peasantry ~~in the revolutionary struggle~~, and that only in an alliance with the peasantry could the proletariat gain the victory over tsardom. Plekhanov *further* considered that the *liberal* bourgeoisie was a force that could give support, albeit unstable support, to the revolution~~.~~; *b*ut as to the peasantry, in some of his writings ~~Plekhanov~~ *he* discounted it entirely, declaring ~~this~~, for instance, *that*:

> "Apart from the bourgeoisie and the proletariat we perceive no social forces in our country in which oppositional or revolutionary combinations might find support." (Plekhanov, Works, Russ. ed., Vol. III, p. ~~120~~ *119*.)

These erroneous views were the germ of Plekhanov's future Menshevik views.

Neither the "Emancipation of Labour" group nor the Marxist circles of that period ~~in Russia~~ had yet any practical connections with the working-class movement.[22] It was a period in which the theory of Marxism, the ideas of Marxism, and the *principles of the* Social-Democratic program were just appearing and gaining a foothold in Russia. In the decade of 1884–94 the Social-Democratic movement still existed in the form of small separate groups and circles which had no connections, *or very scant connections,* with the *mass* working-class movement. Like an infant still unborn but already developing in its mother's womb, the Social-Democratic movement, as Lenin wrote, was in the "PROCESS OF FŒTAL DEVELOPMENT."

The "Emancipation of Labour" group, Lenin said, "only laid the theoretical foundations for the Social-Democratic movement and made the first step towards the working-class movement."

The task of uniting Marxism ~~and Socialism~~ and the working-class movement in Russia, *and of correcting the mistakes of the "Emancipation of Labour" group* ~~was solved by~~ *fell to* Lenin. ~~Lenin organized a group and then the Bolshevik Party and led the working class and peasantry in the struggle with the tsarist government, landlords and bourgeoisie.~~

~~The first RUDIMENT of the revolutionary proletarian party was the "League of Struggle for the Emancipation of the Working Class," organized by Lenin in St. Petersburg.~~

3. Beginning of Lenin's Revolutionary Activities. St. Petersburg League of Struggle for the Emancipation of the Working Class

Vladimir Ilyich Ulyanov (Lenin), the ~~great chief of the working class and~~ founder of Bolshevism, was born in the city of Simbirsk (now Ulyanovsk) in 1870 ~~and began his revolutionary activity as a seventeen year-old boy~~. In 1887 Lenin entered the Kazan University, but was soon arrested and expelled from the university for taking part in the revolutionary student movement. In Kazan Lenin joined a Marxist circle formed by one Fedoseyev. Lenin later removed to Samara and soon afterwards the first Marxist circle in that city was formed with Lenin as the central figure. Already in those days Lenin amazed everyone by his thorough knowledge of Marxism.

At the end of 1893 Lenin removed to St. Petersburg. His very first utterances in the Marxist circles of that city made ~~the~~ *a* deep~~est~~ impression on their members. His extraordinarily profound knowledge of Marx, his ability to apply Marxism to the economic and political situation of Russia at that time, his ardent and unshakable belief in the victory of the workers' cause, and his *outstanding* talent as an organizer made Lenin the acknowledged leader of the St. Petersburg Marxists.

Lenin enjoyed the warm affection of the politically advanced workers whom he taught in the circles.

"Our lectures," says the worker Babushkin recalling Lenin's teaching activities in the workers' circles, "were of a very lively and interesting character; we were all very pleased with these lectures and constantly admired the wisdom of our lecturer."

~~Lenin taught the workers to connect the struggle for their everyday interests to greater political tasks.~~

In 1895 Lenin united all the *Marxist* workers' circles in St. Petersburg (there were already about twenty of them) into a single League of Struggle for the Emancipation of the Working Class. He thus prepared the way for the founding of a ~~genuinely~~ revolutionary Marxist workers' party. ~~Under the influence of the St. Petersburg League of Struggle for the Emancipation of the Working Class, similar leagues were organized in other cities.~~

Lenin put before the League of Struggle the task of forming closer connections with the mass working-class movement and of giving it political leadership. Lenin proposed to pass from the PROPAGANDA of Marxism among the few politically advanced workers who gathered in the propaganda circles to political AGITATION among the broad masses of the working class on issues of the day. *This turn towards mass agitation was of profound importance for the subsequent development of the working-class movement in Russia.* ~~Lenin even got involved in all the minor details of the workers' lives. He wrote leaflets and brochures for the workers (for instance, on fines and strikes) and mobilized them for the stubborn struggle with the capitalists and tsarist government.~~

The nineties were a period of industrial boom. The number of workers was ~~also~~ increasing. The working-class movement was ~~also~~ gaining strength. In the period of 1895–99, according to incomplete data, not less than 221,000 workers ~~already~~ took part in strikes. *The working-class movement was becoming an important force in the political life of the country.* ~~In this way,~~ The course of events was ~~all the more~~ corroborating the view which the Marxists had championed against the Narodniks, *namely, that the working class was to play the leading role in the revolutionary movement.*

Under Lenin's guidance, the League of Struggle for the Emancipation of the Working Class linked up the struggle of the workers for economic demands—improvement of working conditions, shorter hours and higher wages—with the political struggle *against tsardom*. The League of Struggle ~~assisted the workers in staging successful strikes and directed strikes itself~~ *educated the workers politically.*

Under Lenin's guidance, the St. Petersburg League of Struggle for the Emancipation of the Working Class was the first body in Russia that began to UNITE SOCIALISM WITH THE WORKING-CLASS MOVEMENT. When a strike broke out in some factory, the League of Struggle, which through the members of its circles was kept well posted on the state of affairs in the factories, immediately responded by issuing leaflets and Socialist proclamations. These leaflets exposed the oppression of the workers by the manufacturers, explained how the workers should fight for their interests, and set forth the workers' demands. The leaflets told the plain truth about *the ulcers of capitalism*, the poverty of the workers, their intolerably hard working day of 12 to 14 hours, and their utter lack of rights. They also put forward *appropriate* political demands ~~to be addressed by the tsarist government~~. With the collaboration of the worker Babushkin, Lenin at the end of 1894 wrote the first agitational leaflet of this kind and an appeal to the workers of the Semyannikov Works in St. Petersburg who were on strike. In the autumn of 1895 Lenin wrote a leaflet for the men and women strikers of the Thornton Mills. These mills belonged to English owners who were making millions in profits out of them. The working day in these mills exceeded 14 hours, while the wages of a weaver were about 7 rubles per month. The workers won the strike. In a short space of time the League of Struggle printed dozens of such leaflets and appeals to the workers of various factories. Every leaflet greatly helped to stiffen the spirit of the workers. They saw that the Socialists were helping and defending them. ~~On the other hand, the tsarist government and mill owners were frightened by the appearance of these Socialist leaflets, which had never played a role in earlier strikes.~~

In the summer of 1896 a strike of 30,000 textile workers, led by the League of Struggle, took place in St. Petersburg. The chief demand was for shorter hours. This strike forced the tsarist government to pass, on June 2, 1897, a law limiting the working day to 11 1/2 hours. Prior to this the working day was not limited ~~by anything~~ *in any way.*

In December 1895 Lenin was arrested by the tsarist government and placed in prison. ~~At the same time, G. M. Krzhizhanovsky and an array of other leading workers within the League of Struggle were arrested—the so-called "old fellows" who had laid the foundation of the organization.~~ But even in prison he did not discontinue his revolutionary work. He assisted the League of Struggle with advice and direction and wrote pamphlets and leaflets for it~~, which were secretly smuggled out of prison~~. There he wrote a pamphlet entitled ON STRIKES and a leaflet entitled TO THE TSARIST GOVERNMENT, exposing its savage despotism. There too Lenin drafted a program for the party (he used milk as an invisible ink and wrote between the lines of a book on medicine).

~~At the end of 1896, the "young" revolutionaries who had temporarily become the leaders of the League of Struggle after the arrest of the "old fellows," adopted an erroneous line. They announced that it was necessary to rally the workers to only an economic struggle against individual capitalists and to renounce the political struggle against the entire tsarist system. These people came to be called "Economists." Lenin waged the most decisive struggle against the Economists.~~

~~Lenin's~~ *The* St. Petersburg League of Struggle gave a powerful impetus to the amalgamation of ~~individual~~ *the* workers' circles in other cities and regions *of Russia* into similar leagues. ~~Thus at the end~~ *In the middle* of the nineties Marxist organizations arose in Transcaucasia. In 1894 a Workers' Union was formed in Moscow. Towards the end of the nineties a Social-Democratic Union was formed in Siberia. In the nineties Marxist groups arose in Ivanovo-Voznesensk, Yaroslavl and Kostroma and subsequently merged to form the Northern Union of the Social-Democratic Party. In the second half of the nineties Social-Democratic groups and unions were formed in Rostov-on-Don, Ekaterinoslav, Kiev, Nikolayev, Tula, Samara, Kazan, Orekhovo-Zuyevo and other cities.

The importance of the St. Petersburg League of Struggle for the Emancipation of the Working Class consisted in the fact that, as Lenin said, it was the first *real* RUDIMENT OF A REVOLUTIONARY PARTY WHICH WAS BACKED BY THE WORKING-CLASS MOVEMENT.

Lenin drew on the revolutionary experience of the St. Petersburg League of Struggle in his subsequent work of creating a Marxist Social-Democratic party in Russia.

After the arrest of Lenin and his close associates, the leadership of the St. Petersburg League of Struggle changed considerably. New people appeared who called themselves the "young" and Lenin and his associates the "old fellows." These people pursued an erroneous political line. They declared that the workers should be called upon to wage only an economic struggle against their employers; as for the political struggle, that was the affair of the liberal bourgeoisie, to whom the leadership of the political struggle should be left.

These people came to be called "Economists."

They were the first group of compromisers and opportunists within the ranks of the Marxist organizations in Russia.

4. Lenin's Struggle against Narodism and "Legal Marxism." *Lenin's Idea of an Alliance of the Working Class and the Peasantry. First Congress of the Russian Social-Democratic Labour Party*

Although Plekhanov had already in the eighties dealt the chief blow to the Narodnik system of views, at the beginning of the nineties Narodnik views still found sympathy among certain sections of the revolutionary youth. Some of them continued to hold that Russia could avoid the capitalist path of development and that the principal role in the revolution would be played by the peasantry, and not by the working class. The Narodniks that still remained did their utmost to prevent the spread of Marxism in Russia, fought the ~~Social-Democrats~~ *Marxists* ~~in a war of words and print~~ and endeavoured to discredit them in every way. Narodism had to be completely SMASHED ideologically if the further spread of Marxism and the creation of a Social-Democratic party were to be assured.

This task was performed by Lenin.

In his ~~well-known~~ book, WHAT THE "FRIENDS OF THE PEOPLE" ARE AND HOW THEY FIGHT AGAINST THE SOCIAL-DEMOCRATS (1894), Lenin thoroughly exposed the true character of the *Narodniks, showing that they were* false "friends of the people" ~~and the harmful and erroneous nature of their views~~ *actually working against the people.*

Essentially, the Narodniks of the nineties had long ago renounced all revolutionary struggle against the tsarist government. The liberal Narodniks preached reconciliation with the tsarist government. "They think," Lenin wrote in reference to the Narodniks of that period, "that if they simply plead with this government nicely enough and humbly enough, it will put everything right." (Lenin, SELECTED WORKS, Eng. ed., Vol. I, p. 413.)

The Narodniks of the nineties shut their eyes to the condition of the poor peasants, to the class struggle in the countryside, *and to the exploitation of the poor peasants by the kulaks,* and sang praises to the development of kulak farming. *As a matter of fact* they voiced the interests of the kulaks.

At the same time, the Narodniks in their periodicals baited the ~~Russian~~ Marxists. They deliberately distorted and falsified the views of the Russian Marxists and claimed that the latter desired the ruin of the countryside and wanted "every muzhik to be stewed in the factory kettle." Lenin exposed the falsity of the Narodnik criticism and pointed out that it was not a matter of the "wishes" of the Marxists, but of the fact that capitalism was actually developing in Russia and that this development was inevitably accompanied by a growth of the proletariat. And the proletariat would be the gravedigger of the capitalist system.

Lenin showed that it was the Marxists and not the Narodniks who were the real friends of the people, that it was the Marxists who wanted to throw off the capitalist and landlord yoke, to destroy tsardom.

In his book, What the "Friends of the People" Are, Lenin *for the first time* advanced the ~~task~~ *idea* of a revolutionary alliance of the workers and peasants *as the principal means of overthrowing tsardom, the landlords and the bourgeoisie.*

In a number of his writings *during this period* Lenin criticized the methods ~~and approaches (ways and means)~~ of political struggle ~~that had been~~ employed by *the principal Narodnik group,* the "Narodnaya Volya," and later by *the successors of the Narodniks,* the Socialist-Revolutionaries—especially the tactics of individual terrorism. Lenin considered these tactics harmful to the revolutionary movement, for they substituted the struggle of individual heroes for the struggle of the masses. They signified a lack of confidence in the ~~uprising~~ *revolutionary movement* of the people.

> ~~"Terror," Lenin wrote, "was a conspiracy of the intellectual groups. Terror was utterly unconnected with any sort of popular sentiment. Terror did not prepare any kind of militant leader for the masses. Terror was the result and also the symptom and complement of disbelief in the uprising. . . ." (Lenin, Collected Works, Russ. ed., Vol. IX, p. 26.)~~

In the book, What the "Friends of the People" Are and How Do They Fight Against the Social-Democrats, Lenin ~~lays out~~ *outlined* the *main* tasks of the *Russian* ~~revolutionary~~ Marxists. *In his opinion,* the~~ir~~ first duty *of the Russian Marxists* was to weld the disunited Marxist circles into a *united* Socialist workers' party. He *further* pointed out that it would be the working class of Russia ~~that would lead all the working people and all those oppressed by the tsarist regime~~, *in alliance with the peasantry,* that would overthrow the tsarist autocracy~~. After that, wrote Lenin~~, *after which* the Russian proletariat, *in alliance with the labouring and exploited masses,* would, along with the proletariat of other countries, take the straight road of open political struggle to the victorious Communist revolution.[23]

Thus, over forty years ago, Lenin correctly ~~and precisely~~ pointed out to the working class its path of struggle, ~~pointed to~~ *defined* its role as ~~the leader (the hegemon) of all the democratic elements~~ *the foremost revolutionary force in society, and that of the peasantry as the ally of the working class.*

The struggle waged by Lenin and his followers against Narodism led to the latter's complete ideological defeat already in the nineties.

Of immense significance, too, was Lenin's struggle against "legal Marxism." It usually happens with big social movements in history that transient "fellow-travelers" fasten on them. The "LEGAL MARXISTS," as they were called, were such fellow-travelers. Marxism began to spread widely throughout Russia; and so we find bourgeois intellectuals decking themselves out in a Marxist garb. They published their articles in newspapers and periodicals that were legal, that is, allowed by the tsarist government. That is why they came to be called "legal Marxists."

After their own fashion, they too fought Narodism. But they tried to make use of this fight and of the banner of Marxism in order to subordinate and adapt the working-class movement to the interests of bourgeois society, to the interests of the bourgeoisie. They cut out the very core of Marxism, namely, the doctrine of the proletarian revolution and the dictatorship of the proletariat. One prominent legal Marxist, Peter Struve, extolled the bourgeoisie, and instead of calling for a revolutionary struggle *against capitalism*, urged that "we acknowledge our lack of culture and go to capitalism for schooling."

In the fight against the Narodniks Lenin considered it permissible to come to a temporary agreement with the "legal Marxists" *in order to use them against the Narodniks, as*, for example, for the joint publication of a collection of articles directed against the Narodniks. At the same time, however, Lenin was unsparing in his criticism of the "legal Marxists" and exposed their liberal bourgeois nature.

~~Lenin called the "legal Marxists" the "CONDUCTORS OF BOURGEOIS INFLUENCE OVER THE PROLETARIAT."~~

Many of these fellow-travelers later became Constitutional-Democrats (the principal party *of the Russian bourgeoisie*), and during the Civil War out-and-out Whiteguards. ~~Struve was, for instance, a minister under Wrangel in 1920.~~

~~5. Beginning of Comrade Stalin's Revolutionary Activity~~

~~At the end of the nineties, the working-class revolutionary movement grew to encompass the Russian periphery including the Caucasus, where Comrade Stalin led the revolutionary struggle of the working class and the formation of Marxist Social-Democratic organizations.~~

~~The Caucasus was a site of Russian tsardom's predatory national-colonial policy, which was attempting to uproot all the dreams of freedom among the~~

peoples of Transcaucasia through its representatives—the generals, governor-generals and the Transcaucasian ruling elite—the Georgian princes, Turkish beks, etc. In Transcaucasia, survivals of serfdom, oppressive land relations and so on persisted like nowhere else until the Revolution of 1905. This is why in Transcaucasia, the revolutionary movement encompassed the broad masses.

There was a firm base in Transcaucasia for the formation of revolutionary Marxist Bolshevik organizations. The industrial proletariat grew swiftly in Baku, where the production of oil was developing quickly, and in Batum, where the oil was refined. There were also a good number of industrial workers in Tiflis (in the railroad machine shops).

But here there was also a more semi-artisanal proletariat, working in small workshops, trade enterprises, and so on. This stratum provided a nurturing base for the Mensheviks and the petty-bourgeois nationalist parties. Therefore, the struggle for Lenin's line, which the Transcaucasian Bolsheviks were waging under the leadership of Comrade Stalin, was stubborn and difficult.

The spread of Marxism in Transcaucasia began in the first half of the nineties. In 1893, the "Mesame-Dasi" (Social-Democratic) group was organized. It was heterogeneous in composition. Aside from opportunistic elements, it included a group of revolutionary Marxists. In 1895 the revolutionary Marxist Alexander TSULUKIDZE joined this group, as did Lado (Vladimir) KETSKHOVELI, a well-known organizer and Marxist devotee of the working class. In 1898, Comrade STALIN joined this group. It was this revolutionary Marxist group personified by Stalin, Ketskhoveli and Tsulukidze that gave a start to revolutionary Social-Democracy in Transcaucasia.

Already in 1897, as a seventeen year-old youth, Stalin headed a revolutionary Marxist reading circle among the students of the Tiflis seminary and was expelled from this seminary for revolutionary activities. At this time, he was also connected to an illegal, secret Social-Democratic organization and took part in the secret meetings of workers at the Tiflis railroad machine shops. In 1898–1900, Tiflis's central Social-Democratic group conducted an enormous amount of revolutionary propaganda and organizational work among the workers. Like Lenin during the formation of St. Petersburg's League of Struggle, Comrade Stalin personally conducted an enormous amount of propaganda work in the workers' study circles, enjoying the workers' greatest respect and love. During this period, Stalin led more than eight Social-Democratic worker study circles in Tiflis.

One of the participants in these study circles, the senior worker Comrade Khurtsilayev, recalled in his memoirs how skilfully Comrade Stalin had trained the workers in a political sense and how he taught them about the revolutionary struggle. Stalin played a practical role in leading their strikes:

~~"The study circle lessons were very lively and interesting. In a simple, understandable way, Comrade Stalin told us about the workers' tasks in the struggle with the autocracy and taught us basic political literacy. The participants of our reading circle, inspired by their leader, waited impatiently for an opportunity to put into practice everything that the party and our teacher had prepared us for.~~

~~The opportunity soon appeared. A strike began in the railroad machine shops. We, of course, took part in it. And how we rejoiced when Comrade Stalin assigned to us the struggle with strikebreakers. He assigned us posts on all the streets that led to the factory. Here, we were to take all necessary measures in order to prevent strikebreakers from reaching the machine shops.~~

~~We spent nearly a year in Comrade Stalin's study circle. Over the course of that time, we learned a lot and became battle-hardened for our whole lives. Comrade Stalin left a deep mark on every one of us as a role model." ("The Great Chief and Teacher," in the collection Old Workers' Stories of the Great Chief, Russ. ed., pp. 26–27.)~~

~~In the period between 1898–1900, the leading central Social-Democratic group of the Tiflis organization arose and took shape under Comrade Stalin. This political and organizational work concluded with the founding in 1901 of the first elected Tiflis committee of the Social-Democratic organization. This Leninist-oriented committee was created at the initiative of Comrade Stalin.~~

~~In the history of the Bolshevik Party, Comrade Stalin's activity in forming revolutionary Marxist Social-Democratic organizations in Transcaucasia had great significance.~~

6. First Congress of the R.S.D.L.P.

~~National Social-Democratic organizations were founded in the nineties.~~ *Along with the Leagues of Struggle in St. Petersburg, Moscow, Kiev and other places, Social-Democratic organizations arose also in the western national border regions of Russia.* ~~In 1898, a semi-Narodnik organization arose in Poland—the Polish Socialist Party (P.P.S.)—which behaved like a petty-bourgeois, nationalist party. It quickly gave rise to~~ *In the nineties the Marxist elements in the Polish nationalist party broke away to form* the Social-Democratic Party of Poland and Lithuania ~~under Rosa Luxembourg~~. At the end of the nineties Latvian Social-Democratic organizations were formed, and in October 1897 the Jewish General *Social-Democratic* Union—known as the Bund—was founded in the western provinces of Russia. ~~The Bund was never a consistent Marxist~~

~~organization. It worked chiefly among handicraftsmen and salesmen. The Bund eventually allied with the Mensheviks and played a conciliatory, opportunistic role.~~

In 1898 several of the Leagues of Struggle—those of St. Petersburg, Moscow, Kiev and Ekaterinoslav—together with the Bund made the first attempt to unite and form a *Social-Democratic* party. For this purpose they summoned the First Congress of the Russian Social-Democratic Labour Party (R.S.D.L.P.), which was held in Minsk in March 1898. ~~It did not, however, turn out to be possible to create a party at this congress.~~

The First Congress of the R.S.D.L.P. was attended by only nine persons. *Lenin was not present because at that time he was living in exile in Siberia.* The Central Committee of the Party elected at the congress was very soon arrested. The Manifesto published in the name of the congress was in many respects unsatisfactory. It evaded the question of the conquest of political power by the proletariat, ~~it did not bring up the struggle for a democratic republic,~~ it made no mention of the hegemony ~~(leadership)~~ of the proletariat, and *said nothing about* the allies of the proletariat in its ~~political~~ struggle *against tsardom and the bourgeoisie.*

In its decisions and in its Manifesto the congress announced the formation of the Russian Social-Democratic Labour Party.

It is this *formal act, which played a great revolutionary propagandist role,* that ~~constitutes~~ *constituted* the significance of the First Congress of the R.S.D.L.P.[24]

But *although the First Congress had been held,* in reality no Marxist Social-Democratic Party was as yet formed in Russia. The ~~First~~ *c*ongress did not succeed in uniting the separate Marxist circles and organizations and welding them together organizationally. There was still no common line of action in the*ir* work ~~of the local organizations~~, nor was there a *party* program, party rules or a single leading centre.

For *this and for* a number of other reasons, the ideological confusion in the *local* ~~Marxist~~ organizations ~~even increased.~~ *began to increase, and this created favourable ground for the growth w*ithin the working-class movement *of* the opportunist trend known as "Economism" ~~grew stronger for a time~~.

It required several years of intense effort on the part of Lenin and of Iskra (Spark), the newspaper he founded, before this confusion could be overcome, the opportunist vacillations put an end to, and the way prepared for the formation of the Russian Social-Democratic Labour Party ~~(R.S.D.L.P.)~~.

~~The Leninist newspaper Iskra (The Spark) prepared for the formation of the Bolshevik Party, which at first existed in the form of a group or a faction of the R.S.D.L.P.~~

5.~~7.~~ Lenin's Fight against ~~the Economists~~ *"Economism."* ~~First Issue of~~ *Appearance of Lenin's Newspaper* ISKRA

Lenin was not present at the First Congress of the R.S.D.L.P. He was at that time in exile in Siberia, in the village of Shushenskoye, where he had been banished by the tsarist government after a long period of imprisonment in St. Petersburg in connection with the prosecution of the League of Struggle.

But Lenin continued his revolutionary activities even while in exile. There he finished a highly important scientific work, THE DEVELOPMENT OF CAPITALISM IN RUSSIA, which completed the ideological destruction of Narodism. *There, too, h*e wrote his *well-known* pamphlet, THE TASKS OF THE RUSSIAN SOCIAL-DEMOCRATS.

~~While still in exile, Lenin gave the Economists a decisive rebuff.~~ *Although Lenin was cut off from direct, practical revolutionary work, he nevertheless managed to maintain some connections with those engaged in this work; he carried on a correspondence with them from exile, obtained information from them and gave them advice. At this time Lenin was very much preoccupied with the "Economists." He realized better than anybody else that "Economism" was the main nucleus of compromise and opportunism, and that if "Economism" were to gain the upper hand in the working-class movement, it would undermine the revolutionary movement of the proletariat and lead to the defeat of Marxism.*

Lenin therefore started a vigorous attack on the "Economists" as soon as they appeared on the scene.

The "Economists" ~~said~~ *maintained* that the workers should ~~limit themselves to only the ECONOMIC struggle,~~ *engage only in the economic struggle;* ~~"the struggle for another five kopeks," as it was said at the time.~~ *as to t*he *p*olitical struggle, ~~the struggle for political rights,~~ *that* should be left to the liberal bourgeoisie~~—the liberal professors, lawyers and other such people, the Economists said~~, *whom the workers should support*. ~~But the Economists did not want to understand that the liberal bourgeoisie—that is, that part of the bourgeoisie that was somewhat dissatisfied with the tsarist government—would not struggle at all for the workers' rights nor for the overthrow of tsardom, but only in order to obtain concessions and rights for themselves. More than that, the liberal bourgeoisie was weak and cowardly and did not frighten tsardom. Renouncing the independent proletarian political organization and the independent political demands of the workers, the Economists played into the hands of the bourgeoisie and tsarist government. Therefore Lenin referred to the Economists as the CONDUCTORS OF BOURGEOIS INFLUENCE OVER THE PROLETARIAT.~~ *In Lenin's eyes this tenet was a desertion of Marxism, a denial of the necessity for an independent political party of the working class, an attempt to convert the working class into a political appendage of the bourgeoisie.*

In 1899 a group of "Economists" (Prokopovich, Kuskova and others, who later became Constitutional-Democrats) issued a manifesto in which they opposed ~~the~~ revolutionary ~~teachings of~~ Marxism, and insisted that the idea of an independent political party of the proletariat and of independent political demands by the working class be renounced. The "Economists" ~~said~~ *held* that the ~~Russian Marxists only had to aid in the working class's economic struggle and support the liberal bourgeoisie~~ *political struggle was a matter for the liberal bourgeoisie, and that as far as the workers were concerned, the economic struggle against the employers was enough for them.*

When Lenin acquainted himself with this opportunist document he called a conference of Marxist political exiles living in the vicinity. Seventeen of them met and, *headed by Lenin,* issued a *trenchant* protest denouncing the views of the "Economists."

This protest, which was written by Lenin, was circulated among the Marxist organizations *all over the country* and played ~~a large political~~ *an outstanding* part *in the development of Marxist ideas and of the Marxist party in Russia.*

The Russian "Economists" advocated the same views as the opponents of Marxism in the Social-Democratic parties abroad *who were known as the Bernsteinites, that is, followers of the opportunist Bernstein.*

Lenin's struggle against the "Economists" was therefore at the same time a struggle against opportunism on an international scale.

The fight against "Economism," the fight for the creation of ~~a revolutionary~~ *an independent* political party of the proletariat, was chiefly waged by ISKRA, the *illegal* newspaper founded by Lenin.

~~This struggle was serious because the Economists at the end of the nineties and the beginning of the new century enjoyed well-known influence over the more backward part of the workers, especially over the workers connected with the countryside (many of these half-peasant half-workers thought only about how to earn enough for a horse or a cow before returning to the countryside).~~

~~The Economists' line enjoyed similar support among the better-paid worker elite, the so-called "labour aristocracy."~~

~~This brief wide influence of the Economists likewise facilitated the success of an array of Economist strikes at the end of the nineties, when it was easier to win concessions from individual mill owners due to the conditions of industrial growth.~~

At the beginning of 1900, Lenin and other members of the League of Struggle returned from their Siberian exile to Russia. Lenin conceived the idea of founding a big ~~continuously circulating~~ illegal Marxist newspaper on an all-Russian scale. The numerous small Marxist circles and organizations which already existed in Russia were not yet linked up. At a moment when, in the words of Comrade Stalin, "amateurishness and the parochial outlook of the circles were corroding the Party from top to bottom, when ideological confusion was the characteristic feature of the internal life of the Party," the creation of an illegal newspaper on an all-Russian scale was the chief task of the Russian revolutionary Marxists. Only such a newspaper could link up the disunited Marxist organizations and prepare the way for the creation of a real party.

But such a newspaper could not be published in tsarist Russia owing to police persecution. Within a month or two at most the tsar's sleuths would get on its track and smash it. Lenin therefore decided to publish the newspaper abroad. There it was printed on very thin but durable paper and secretly smuggled into Russia. Some of the issues of Iskra were reprinted in Russia by secret printing plants in Baku, Kishinev and Siberia.

In the autumn of 1900 Lenin went abroad to make arrangements with the comrades in the "Emancipation of Labour" group for the publication of a political newspaper on an all-Russian scale. The idea had been worked out by Lenin in all its details while he was in exile. On his way back from exile he had held a number of conferences on the subject in Ufa, Pskov, Moscow and St. Petersburg. Everywhere he made arrangements with the comrades about codes for secret correspondence, addresses to which literature could be sent, and so on, and discussed with them plans for the future struggle.

The tsarist government scented a most dangerous enemy in Lenin. Zubatov, an officer of gendarmes in the tsarist Okhrana, expressed the opinion in a confidential report that "there is nobody bigger than Ulyanov [Lenin] in the revolution today," ~~and recommended having~~ *in view of which he considered it expedient to have* Lenin assassinated.

Abroad, Lenin came to an arrangement with the "Emancipation of Labour" group, namely, with Plekhanov, Axelrod and V. Zasulich, for the publication of Iskra under joint auspices. The whole plan of publication from beginning to end had been worked out by Lenin. ~~Almost all of the leading articles on the issues of party organization in the first and successive issues of Iskra belonged to Lenin.~~

The first issue of Iskra appeared abroad in December 1900. The title page bore the epigraph: "The Spark Will Kindle a Flame." These words were taken from the reply of the Decembrists to the poet Pushkin who had sent greetings to them in their place of exile in Siberia.

And indeed, from the spark (Iskra) started by Lenin there *subsequently* flamed up the great revolutionary conflagration in which the tsarist monarchy of the landed nobility, and the power of the bourgeoisie were reduced to ashes.

Brief Summary

The Marxist Social-Democratic Labour Party in Russia was formed in a struggle waged in the first place against Narodism and its views, which were erroneous and harmful to the cause of revolution.

Only by ideologically shattering the views of the Narodniks was it possible to clear the way for a Marxist workers' party in Russia. A decisive blow to Narodism was dealt by Plekhanov and his "Emancipation of Labour" group in the eighties.

Lenin completed the ideological defeat of Narodism and dealt it the final blow in the nineties.

The "Emancipation of Labour" group, founded in 1883, did a great deal for the dissemination of Marxism in Russia; it laid the theoretical foundations for Social-Democracy and took the first step to establish connection with the working-class movement.

With the development of capitalism in Russia the ~~number of~~ industrial proletariat rapidly grew *in numbers*. In the middle of the eighties the ~~growing~~ working class adopted the path of organized struggle, of mass ~~organized~~ action ~~(the Morozov strike of 1885)~~ *in the form of organized strikes*. ~~In this way, the Russian Marxists' contention that the working class was the head of the revolutionary forces was confirmed.~~ But the Marxist circles and groups *only carried on propaganda and did not realize the necessity for passing to mass agitation among the working class; they therefore* still had no practical connection with the working-class movement and did not lead it.

The St. Petersburg League of Struggle for the Emancipation of the Working Class, which Lenin formed in 1895 and which started mass agitation among the workers and led mass strikes, marked a new stage—*the transition to mass agitation among the workers and* the union of Marxism with the working-class movement. The St. Petersburg League of Struggle for the Emancipation of the Working Class was the rudiment of a revolutionary proletarian party in Russia. *The formation of the St. Petersburg League of Struggle was followed by the formation of* ~~revolutionary~~ Marxist organizations ~~formed~~ in all the principal industrial centres ~~and~~ *as well as* in the border regions. ~~An organization of revolutionary Marxists arose under the leadership of Comrade Stalin in Transcaucasia.~~

In 1898 at the First Congress of the R.S.D.L.P. the first, ~~still~~ *although* unsuccessful, attempt was made to unite the Marxist Social-Democratic organizations into a party. But this congress did not yet create a party: there was neither a party program nor party rules; there was no single leading centre, and there was scarcely any connection between the separate Marxist circles and groups.

In order to unite and link together the separate Marxist organizations *into a single party*, Lenin put forward and carried out a plan for the founding of Iskra, the first newspaper of the revolutionary Marxists on an all-Russian scale.

The principal opponents to the creation of a single political working-class party at that period were the "Economists." They denied the necessity for such a party. They fostered the disunity and amateurish methods of the separate groups. It was against them that Lenin and the newspaper Iskra *organized by him directed their blows.*

The appearance of the first issues of Iskra (1900–01) marked a transition to a new period—a period in which a *single* Russian Social-Democratic Labour Party was really formed from the disconnected *groups and* circles ~~and groups~~.

CHAPTER TWO

Formation of the Russian Social-Democratic Labour Party. ~~and the~~ Appearance of the Bolshevik and the Menshevik Groups within the Party (1901–1904)

1. Upsurge of the Revolutionary Movement in Russia ~~at the Beginning of the Twentieth Century~~ *in 1901–04*

The end of the nineteenth century in Europe was marked by an industrial crisis. It soon spread to Russia. During the period of the crisis (1900–03) about 3,000 large and small enterprises were closed down and over 100,000 workers thrown on the streets. The wages of the workers that remained employed were sharply reduced. The insignificant concessions previously wrung *from the capitalists* as the result of stubborn economic strikes were now withdrawn.

Industrial crisis and unemployment did not halt or weaken the working-class movement. On the contrary, the workers' struggle ~~took on~~ *assumed* an increasingly revolutionary character. From economic strikes, the workers ~~went on~~ *passed* to political strikes, and ~~the workers organized~~ *finally to* demonstrations, ~~going into the streets with political demands, with the slogan of toppling the autocracy~~ *put forward political demands for democratic liberties, and raised the slogan, "Down with the tsarist autocracy!"* ~~All the workers in a large number of cities organized May Day demonstrations and strikes.~~

A May Day strike at the Obukhov munitions plant in St. Petersburg in 1901 resulted in a bloody encounter between the workers~~, police~~ and troops. ~~But~~ *T*he only weapons the workers could oppose to the armed forces of the tsar were stones and lumps of iron. The stubborn resistance of the workers was broken. This was followed by savage reprisals: about 800 workers were arrested, and many were cast into prison or condemned to penal servitude and exile. But the heroic "Obukhov defence" made a profound impression on the workers of Russia and called forth a wave of sympathy among ~~Western European workers~~ *them.*

In March 1902 *big strikes and* a demonstration of workers took place in Batum, organized by the Batum Social-~~Democrats~~ *Democratic Committee* ~~under the leadership of Comrade Stalin~~. The Batum demonstration stirred up the workers and peasants of Transcaucasia.

-51-　　51

ГЛАВА II

ОБРАЗОВАНИЕ РОССИЙСКОЙ СОЦИАЛ-ДЕМОКРАТИЧЕСКОЙ РАБОЧЕЙ ПАРТИИ. ПОЯВЛЕНИЕ ВНУТРИ ПАРТИИ ФРАКЦИЙ БОЛЬШЕВИКОВ И МЕНЬШЕВИКОВ.

(1901-1904 годы)

1. Под"ем революционного движения в России в 1901-1904 годах.

В конце XIX столетия в Европе разразился промышленный кризис. Кризис этот вскоре захватил и Россию. За годы кризиса - 1900-1903 - закрылось до 3 тысяч крупных и мелких предприятий. На улицу было выброшено свыше 100 тысяч рабочих. Заработная плата оставшимся на предприятиях рабочим резко сокращалась. Незначительные уступки, вырванные ранее рабочими (у капиталистов) в упорных экономических стачках, были теперь обратно взяты капиталистами.

Промышленный кризис, безработица не остановили и не ослабили рабочего движения. Наоборот, борьба рабочих стала принимать все более революционный характер. От экономических стачек рабочие стали переходить к политическим стачкам. Наконец, рабочие переходят к демонстрациям, выставляют политические требования о демократических свободах, выставляют лозунг: "долой царское самодержавие".

В 1901 году первомайская стачка на военном Обуховском заводе в Петербурге превратилась в кровавое столкновение между рабочими и войсками. Вооруженным

First page of Chapter Two with Stalin's editing from the summer of 1938. RGASPI, f. 558, op. 11, d. 1209, l. 5.

In 1902 a big strike broke out in Rostov-on-Don as well. The first to come out were the railwaymen, who were soon joined by the workers of many factories. The strike agitated all the ~~Rostov~~ workers. As many as 30,000 would gather at meetings held outside the city limits on several successive days. At these meetings Social-Democratic proclamations were read aloud and speakers addressed the workers. The police and the Cossacks were powerless to disperse these meetings, attended as they were by many thousands. When several workers were killed *by the police*, a huge procession of working people attended their funeral on the following day. Only by summoning troops from surrounding cities ~~could~~ *was* the tsarist government *able to* suppress the strike ~~and the revolutionary actions of the Rostov workers by military force~~. The struggle of the Rostov workers was led by the Don Committee of the R.S.D.L.P.

The strikes that broke out in 1903 were of even larger dimensions. ~~General~~ *Mass political* strikes took place that year in the south, sweeping Transcaucasia (Baku, Tiflis, Batum) and the large cities of the Ukraine (Odessa, Kiev, Ekaterinoslav). ~~Over two-hundred thousand workers took part in these strikes. The labour movement at the start of the twentieth century involved large masses of the workers. It~~ *The strikes* became increasingly stubborn~~, conscious~~ and better organized. Unlike earlier actions of the working class, the political struggle of the workers was nearly everywhere directed by the Social-Democratic committees ~~that followed ISKRA~~.

The working class of Russia was rising to wage a ~~political~~ *revolutionary* struggle against the tsarist regime~~—the power of the landlords and capitalists~~.

The working-class movement influenced the peasantry. In the spring and summer of 1902 a peasant movement broke out in the Ukraine (Poltava and Kharkov provinces) and in the Volga region. The peasants set fire to landlords' mansions, seized their land, and killed the detested ZEMSKY NACHALNIKS (rural prefects) and landlords. Troops were sent to quell the rebellious peasants. Peasants were shot down, hundreds were arrested, and their leaders and organizers were flung into prison, *but the revolutionary peasant movement continued to grow.* ~~The peasant movement was defeated. The majority of the peasants still believed in the tsar. There were cases in which officers threatened to use force as they ordered crowds to disperse and the peasants cried back at them: "You're lying! You'd not dare shoot! The Tsar has not allowed it!" The peasants still did not understand that it was necessary to eliminate the tsarist power and unite with the workers for victory.~~

The ~~mass~~ revolutionary actions of the workers and peasants ~~at the start of the twentieth century and the growth of the emancipation movement of the nationalities oppressed by the tsar—all of this~~ indicated that revolution was maturing and drawing near in Russia.

~~The winds of the revolutionary storms were felt everywhere. The revolution in Russia was to begin earlier than in any other country. Therefore, the centre of the revolutionary movement shifted from the Western European countries to Russia at the beginning of the twentieth century. It was not a coincidence that it was in Russia at this time that the most revolutionary party in the world was born and began to develop—the Bolshevik Party. It was not a coincidence that Russia was the motherland of Bolshevism.~~

~~Lenin and the Iskra-ites devoted a lot of attention to the peasants and their struggle. In 1903, Lenin wrote a brochure entitled To the Village Poor. In this brochure and in an array of other articles, Lenin called upon the peasants to ally with the workers in the struggle against tsardom. Lenin explained to the poor in the countryside how they ought to struggle against the landlords and capitalists. Lenin wrote in his brochure that:~~

> ~~". . . all the Russian workers and all the village poor ought TO WAGE A STRUGGLE FROM BOTH SIDES WITH BOTH HANDS: with one hand, STRUGGLE AGAINST ALL THE BOURGEOISIE in an alliance with all the workers, and with the other hand, STRUGGLE AGAINST ALL THE STATE OFFICIALS AND THE LANDLORD-SERFHOLDERS in an alliance with all the peasants. The first step in the countryside ought to be the full emancipation of the peasants, the assurance of all civil rights and the creation of peasant committees for the return of all confiscated land. Our final step both in the city and in the countryside ought to be THE SEIZURE OF ALL THE LAND AND MILLS FROM THE LANDLORDS AND BOURGEOISIE AND THE CONSTRUCTION OF A SOCIALIST SOCIETY." (Lenin, Collected Works, Russ. ed., Vol. V, pp. 299–300, 307.)~~

~~At the same time that the worker and peasant movement was growing, so too was the emancipatory revolutionary movement of the nationalities oppressed by the tsar, especially in Transcaucasia, Poland and the Baltic provinces.~~

Under the influence of the *revolutionary* struggle of the workers the *opposition* movement of the students against the government assumed ~~a much~~ greater intensity. In retaliation for the student demonstrations and strikes, the government ~~began to~~ shut down the universities, ~~began to fling~~ *flung* hundreds of students into prison ~~and exile~~, and finally conceived the idea of sending recalcitrant students into the army as common soldiers. In response, the students of all the universities organized a general strike in the winter of 1901–02. About thirty thousand students were involved in this strike.

The ~~strengthening of the~~ revolutionary movement of the workers and peasants, *and especially the reprisals against the students,* also induced the liberal bourgeois~~ie~~ and the liberal landlords who sat on what was known as the Zemstvos to ~~speak out and express their dissatisfaction with the tsarist government~~ *bestir themselves and to raise their voices in "protest" against the "excesses" of the tsarist government in repressing their student sons.*

The Zemstvo liberals had their stronghold in the Zemstvo boards. ~~What was a Zemstvo?~~ These were local government bodies which had charge of purely local affairs affecting the rural population (~~for instance,~~ the ~~construction~~ *building* of roads, ~~and part of the construction of~~ hospitals and schools). ~~The landlords gave the orders in the Zemstvo boards; the Zemstvo boards were elected at landlord assemblies in each province or district and made policy in the interests of the landlords. Thus, for instance, taxes for local Zemstvo needs were assessed only from peasant households as the landlords' territory was exempted from this taxation. Part of the Zemstvo boards were composed of liberal landlords, that is, those who were somewhat dissatisfied with the tsarist government and its appointed officials. These liberal landlords wanted to limit the power of the tsar with some sort of body elected by the landlords and capitalists.~~ The liberal landlords *played a fairly prominent part on the Zemstvo boards. They* were closely associated with the *liberal* bourgeois~~ie~~, *in fact* [*they*] *were almost merged with them,* ~~as~~ *for* they themselves were beginning to abandon methods based on survivals of serfdom for capitalist methods of farming on their estates, *as being more profitable.* ~~The liberal bourgeoisie and liberal landlords, who soon formed the liberal Cadet party, were dissatisfied with the tsarist government and its officials.~~ *Of course, both these groups of liberals supported the tsarist government; but they were opposed to the "excesses" of tsardom, fearing that these "excesses" would only intensify the revolutionary movement.* ~~But~~ *While they feared the "excesses" of tsardom,* they feared revolution even more. *In protesting against these "excesses," the liberals pursued two aims: first, to "bring the tsar to his senses," and secondly, by donning a mask of "profound dissatisfaction" with tsardom, to gain the confidence of the people, and to get them, or part of them, to break away from the revolution, and thus undermine its strength.*

Of course, the Zemstvo liberal movement offered no menace whatever to the existence of tsardom; nevertheless, it served to show that all was not well with the "eternal" pillars of tsardom.

In 1902 the ~~liberal bourgeoisie organized~~ *Zemstvo liberal movement led to* the *formation of the bourgeois* "Liberation" group, the nucleus of the future principal party of the bourgeoisie *in Russia*—the Constitutional-~~Democrats~~ *Democratic Party.* ~~P. Struve was the organizer of the "Liberation" group, having much earlier been active as a legal Marxist who had even written the manifesto for the First Conference of the R.S.D.L.P.~~

Perceiving that the movement of the workers and peasants was sweeping the country in a formidable torrent, the tsarist government did everything it could ~~in order~~ to stem the ~~dangerous~~ revolutionary tide. Armed force was used with increasing frequency to suppress the workers' strikes and demonstrations; the bullet and the knout became the government's usual reply to the actions of the workers and peasants; prisons and places of exile were filled to overflowing.

While tightening up the measures of repression, the tsarist government tried *at the same time to resort to other, non-repressive and more "flexible," measures* to divert the workers from the revolutionary movement. Attempts were made to create bogus workers' organizations under the aegis of the gendarmes and police. ~~The activities of these organizations~~ *They* were dubbed *organizations of* "police socialism" or ~~ZUBATOVISM~~ *Zubatov organizations* (after the name of a colonel of gendarmerie, Zubatov, who was the founder of these police-controlled workers' organizations). Through its agents the OKHRANA tried to get the workers to believe that the tsarist government was itself prepared to assist them in securing the satisfaction of ~~a few of~~ their economic demands. "Why engage in politics, why make a revolution, when the tsar himself is ~~siding with~~ *on the side of* the workers?"—Zubatov agents would insinuate *to the workers.* Zubatov organizations were formed in several cities. On the model of these organizations and with the same purposes in view, an organization known as the Assembly of Russian Factory Workers of St. Petersburg was formed in 1904 by a priest by the name of Gapon.

But the attempt of the tsarist OKHRANA to gain control over the working-class movement failed. The tsarist government proved unable *by such measures* to cope with the *growing* working-class movement. The rising *revolutionary* ~~labour~~ movement *of the working class* swept these police-controlled organizations from its path.

~~The formation of a Marxist labour party in Russia took place in conditions that differed from those within which labour parties formed in the West.~~

~~There, in the Western capitalist countries, proletarian parties formed in the wake of the bourgeois revolutions and were able to exist openly (legally). In Russia, formation of the proletarian party took place under a fierce tsarist regime on the eve of the bourgeois-democratic revolution.~~

~~Bourgeois elements (legal Marxists, Economists) joined the Marxist party organizations who had never even thought about the struggle for Socialism and who simply wanted to use the working class to complete the Bourgeois Revolution in the interests of the bourgeoisie. These people wanted the workers' assistance in order to replace the tsarist government or, at the very least, to obtain from the tsarist government political freedoms and concessions for the liberal bourgeoisie.~~

~~On the other hand, the best revolutionaries from the Marxist reading circles and groups were on the run from the tsarist gendarmes. This occurred at the same time that the growing, spontaneous labour movement was demanding~~

~~leadership from allied organizations of steadfast revolutionaries. They could instill a sense of Socialist consciousness within the mass labour movement and rebuff the bourgeois elements who were joining the Marxist organizations.~~

~~Lenin laid out an ingenious plan for the formation of a proletarian party in Russia that would be able to prepare the working class and all the labouring people to storm the tsarist autocracy, and after the fall of tsardom, to mount the Socialist revolution and the dictatorship of the proletariat. This plan was accepted by the majority of the revolutionary Marxists who were engaged in practical revolutionary work in Russia.~~

~~Lenin's all-Russian newspaper Iskra connected the various Marxist reading circles and groups together. Iskra rebuffed the alien, bourgeois elements that had penetrated into the labour movement. Iskra put an end to the disorder and amateurism within the labour movement, that is, to the conditions in which every Marxist reading circle operated on its own, as a petty handicraftsman would, and to the conditions in which the technique and scale of Party work were very weak.~~

~~With the help of Iskra, the basis was laid for a firm, secret (conspiratorial), centralized organization of revolutionaries that would not be destroyed by the tsarist government.~~

2. ~~Lenin's Iskra in the Struggle for the Formation of a Proletarian Party.~~ *Lenin's Plan for the Building of a Marxist Party. Opportunism of the "Economists." Iskra's Fight for Lenin's Plan. Lenin's Book What Is To Be Done? Ideological Foundations of the Marxist Party*

Notwithstanding the fact that the First Congress of the Russian Social-Democratic Party had been held in 1898, and that it had announced the formation of the Party, no real party was as yet created. There was no party program or party rules. The Central Committee of the Party elected at the First Congress was arrested and never replaced, for there was nobody to replace it. Worse still, the ideological confusion and lack of organizational cohesion of the Party became even more marked after the First Congress.

While the years 1884–94 were a period of victory over Narodism and of ideological preparation for the formation of a Social-Democratic Party, and the years 1894–98 a period in which an attempt, although unsuccessful, was made to weld the separate Marxist organizations into a Social-Democratic Party, the period immediately following 1898 was one of increased ideological and organizational confusion within the Party. The victory gained by the Marxists over Narodism and the revolutionary actions of the working class, which proved that the Marxists were right, stimulated the sympathy of the revolutionary youth for Marxism. Marxism became the fashion. This resulted in an influx into the

Marxist organizations of throngs of young revolutionary intellectuals, who were weak in theory and inexperienced in political organization, and who had only a vague, and for the most part incorrect, idea of Marxism, derived from the opportunist writings of the "legal Marxists" with which the press was filled. This resulted in the lowering of the theoretical and political standard of the Marxist organizations, in their infection with the "legal Marxist" opportunist tendencies, and in the aggravation of ideological confusion, political vacillation and organizational chaos.

The rising tide of the working-class movement and the obvious proximity of revolution demanded a united and centralized party of the working class which would be capable of leading the revolutionary movement. But the local Party organizations, the local committees, groups and circles were in such a deplorable state, and their organizational disunity and ideological discord so profound, that the task of creating such a party was one of immense difficulty.

The difficulty ~~of forming a proletarian party in Russia was enormous~~ *lay not only in the fact that t*he Party had to be built under the fire of ~~the most~~ savage persecution by the tsarist government~~. The best Party workers were being pursued by the police~~, *which every now and then robbed the organizations of their finest workers whom it* condemned to exile, imprisonment and penal servitude~~. The tsarist government cast its net of spies everywhere and sowed provocateurs into the Marxist organizations in order to turn the revolutionaries over into the gendarmes' hands~~, *but also in the fact that a large number of the local committees and their members would have nothing to do with anything but their local, petty practical activities, did not realize the harm caused by the absence of organizational and ideological unity in the Party, were accustomed to the disunity and ideological confusion that prevailed within it, and believed that they could get along quite well without a united centralized party.*

If a centralized party was to be created, this backwardness, inertia, and narrow outlook of the local bodies had to be overcome.

But this was not all. There was a fairly large group of people within the Party who had their own press—the RABOCHAYA MYSL *(Workers' Thought) in Russia and* RABOCHEYE DELO *(*WORKERS' CAUSE*) abroad—and who were trying to justify on theoretical grounds the lack of organizational cohesion and the ideological confusion within the Party, frequently even lauding such a state of affairs, and holding that the plan for creating a united and centralized political party of the working class was unnecessary and artificial.*

These were the "Economists" and their followers.

Before a united political party of the proletariat could be created, the "Economists" had to be defeated.

It was to this task and to the building of a working-class party that Lenin addressed himself.

How to begin the building of a united party of the working class was a question on which opinions differed. Some thought that the building of the Party should be begun by summoning the Second Congress of the Party, which would unite the local organizations and create the Party. Lenin was opposed to this. He held that before convening a congress it was necessary to make the aims and objects of the Party clear, to ascertain what sort of a party was wanted, to effect an ideological demarcation from the "Economists," to tell the Party honestly and frankly that there existed two different opinions regarding the aims and objects of the Party—the opinion of the "Economists" and the opinion of the revolutionary Social-Democrats—to start a wide campaign in the press in favour of the views of revolutionary Social-Democracy—just as the "Economists" were conducting a campaign in their own press in favour of their own views—and to give the local organizations the opportunity to make a deliberate choice between these two trends. Only after this indispensable preliminary work had been done could a Party Congress be summoned.

Lenin put it plainly:

> *"Before we can unite, and in order that we may unite, we must first of all draw firm and definite lines of demarcation." (Lenin, SELECTED WORKS, Eng. ed., Vol. II, p. 45.)*

~~What was needed was to create a firm, secret (conspiratorial) organization of revolutionaries that could withstand police attacks and at the same time be closely connected to the masses. Such an organization was built by Lenin's ISKRA.~~

Lenin accordingly held that the building of a political party of the working class should be begun by the founding of a militant political newspaper on an all-Russian scale, which would carry on propaganda and agitation in favour of the views of revolutionary Social-Democracy—that the establishment of such a newspaper should be the first step in the building of the Party.

In his well-known article, "Where to Begin?" Lenin outlined a concrete plan for the building of the Party, a plan which was later expanded in his famous work WHAT IS TO BE DONE?

> *"In our opinion," wrote Lenin in this article, "the starting point of our activities, the first practical step towards creating the organization desired (that is, the formation of a party—ED.), finally, the main thread following which we would be able to develop, deepen and expand that organization unswervingly, should be the establishment of a political newspaper on an all-Russian scale. . . . Without it we cannot systematically carry on that all-embracing propaganda and agitation, consistent in principle, which*

> *form the chief and constant task of Social-Democrats in general, and the particularly urgent task of the present moment when interest in politics, in questions of Socialism, has been aroused among the widest sections of the population." (Ibid., p. 19.)*

Lenin considered that such a newspaper would serve not only to weld the Party ideologically, but also to unite the local bodies within the Party organizationally. The network of agents and correspondents of the newspaper, representing the local organizations, would provide a skeleton around which the Party could be built up organizationally. For, Lenin said, "a newspaper is not only a collective propagandist and collective agitator, but also a collective organizer."

> *"This network of agents," writes Lenin in the same article, "will form the skeleton of precisely the organization we need, namely, one that is sufficiently large to embrace the whole country, sufficiently wide and many-sided to effect a strict and detailed division of labour; sufficiently tried and tempered to be able unswervingly to carry on* ITS OWN *work under all circumstances, at all 'turns' and in all contingencies; sufficiently flexible to be able to avoid open battle against an enemy of overwhelming strength, when he has concentrated all his forces at one spot, and yet able to take advantage of the awkwardness of this enemy and to attack him whenever and wherever least expected." (Ibid., pp. 21–2.)*

ISKRA *was to be such a newspaper.*

And ISKRA *did indeed become such a political newspaper on an all-Russian scale which prepared the way for the ideological and organizational consolidation of the Party.*

As to the structure and composition of the Party itself, Lenin considered that it should consist of two parts: a) a close circle of regular cadres of leading Party workers, chiefly professional revolutionaries, that is, Party workers free from all occupation except Party work and possessing the necessary minimum of theoretical knowledge, political experience, organizational practice and the art of combating the tsarist police and of eluding them; and b) a broad network of local Party organizations and a large number of Party members enjoying the sympathy and support of hundreds of thousands of working people.

> *"I assert," Lenin wrote,[1] "1) that no revolutionary movement can endure without a stable organization of leaders that maintains continuity; 2) that the wider the masses spontaneously drawn into the struggle . . . the more urgent the need of such an organization, and the more solid this[2] organization must be . . . 3) that such an organization must consist chiefly of*

people professionally engaged in revolutionary activity; 4) that in an autocratic state the more we CONFINE *the membership of such organization to people who are professionally engaged in revolutionary activity and who have been professionally trained in the art of combating the political police, the more difficult will it be to wipe out such an organization, and 5) the* GREATER *will be the number of people of the working class and of the other classes of society who will be able to join the movement and perform active work in it." (Ibid., pp. 138–39.)*

~~*And further:*~~

~~"A worker agitator who is at all gifted and "promising" MUST NOT be left to work eleven hours a day in a factory. We must arrange that he be maintained by the Party; that he may go underground in good time; that he change the place of his activity, if he is to enlarge his experience, widen his outlook, and be able to hold out for at least a few years in the struggle against the gendarmes. As the spontaneous rise of their movement becomes broader and deeper, the working-class masses promote from their ranks not only an increasing number of talented agitators, but also talented organisers, propagandists, and "practical workers" in the best sense of the term (of whom there are so few among our intellectuals who, for the most part, in the Russian manner, are somewhat careless and sluggish in their habits). When we have forces of specially trained worker-revolutionaries who have gone through extensive preparation (and, of course, revolutionaries "of all arms of the service"), no political police in the world will then be able to contend with them, for these forces, boundlessly devoted to the revolution, will enjoy the boundless confidence of the widest masses of the workers." *(Ibid., p. 142.)*~~[3]

As to the character of the Party that was being built up and its role in relation to the working class, as well as its aims and objects, Lenin held that the Party should form the[4] *vanguard of the working class, that it should be the guiding force of the working-class movement, co-ordinating and directing the class struggle of the proletariat.*[5] *The ultimate goal of the Party was the overthrow of capitalism and the establishment of Socialism. Its immediate aim was the overthrow of tsardom and the establishment of a democratic order. And inasmuch as the overthrow of capitalism was impossible without the preliminary overthrow of tsardom, the principal task of the Party at the given moment was to rouse the working class and the whole people for a struggle against tsardom, to develop a revolutionary movement of the people against it, and to overthrow it as the first and serious obstacle in the path of Socialism.*[6]

"History," Lenin wrote,[7] *"has now confronted us with an immediate task which is the* MOST REVOLUTIONARY *of all the* IMMEDIATE *tasks that confront the proletariat of any country. The fulfilment of this task, the destruction of the most powerful bulwark not only of European but also (it may now be said) of Asiatic reaction would make the Russian proletariat the vanguard of the international revolutionary proletariat." (Ibid., p. 50.)*

And further:

"We must bear in mind that the struggle with the government for partial demands, the winning of partial concessions, are only petty skirmishes with the enemy, petty encounters on the outposts, whereas the decisive engagement is still to come. Before us, in all its strength, stands the enemy's fortress, which is raining shot and shell upon us and mowing down our best fighters. We must capture this fortress; and we shall capture it if we unite all the forces of the awakening proletariat with all the forces of the Russian revolutionaries into one party, which will attract all that is alive and honest in Russia. And only then will the great prophecy of Pyotr Alexeyev, the Russian worker revolutionary, be fulfilled: 'the muscular arm of the working millions will be lifted, and the yoke of despotism, guarded by the soldiers' bayonets, will be smashed to atoms!'" (Lenin, COLLECTED WORKS, *Russ. ed., Vol. IV, p. 59.)*

Such was Lenin's plan for the creation of a party of the working class in autocratic tsarist Russia.

~~Lenin's ISKRA also had enemies within the labour movement. Bolshevism matured in the struggle of Lenin's ISKRA against "Economism." This is what the opportunistic movement was called that claimed that the workers should wage only a purely economic struggle, that is, that they should aim for wage increases, a shorter working day, etc. The Economists denied the working class's political struggle and its leadership role. They announced that the political struggle against the tsarist autocracy must be led by the liberal bourgeoisie and that the working class must follow the bourgeoisie and not carry out its own policies.~~

The "Economists" showed no delay in launching an attack on Lenin's plan.

They asserted that the general political struggle against tsardom was a matter for all classes, but primarily for the bourgeoisie, and that therefore it[8] *was of no serious interest to the working class, for the chief interest of the workers lay in the economic struggle against the employers for higher wages, better working conditions,*[9] *etc. The primary and immediate aim of the Social-Democrats*[10] *should therefore be not a political struggle against tsardom, and not the overthrow of tsardom, but the organization of the "economic struggle of the workers against the employers and the government." By the economic struggle against the government they meant a struggle for better factory legislation. The "Economists" claimed that in this way it would be possible "to lend the economic struggle itself a political character."*

~~The Economists believed that the Social-Democrats' task was to support only those demands which were spontaneous, that is, only those that the workers themselves put forward during the strikes that took place. The Economists were against the characterization of the spontaneous labour movement as Socialist, conscious or revolutionary. They were against the idea that the Party would lead the working class.~~

~~The Economists wanted the Social-Democratic Party organizations to plod behind the backward part of the workers like a tail; they wanted to restrict the workers' struggle to only economic demands placed before individual mill owners. The Economists did not want to understand that without a political struggle and revolution, it would be impossible to seriously improve the economic condition of the working class in any way.~~[11]

The "Economists" no longer dared openly to contest the need for a political party of the working class. But they considered that it should not be the guiding force of the working-class movement, that it should not interfere in the spontaneous movement of the working class, let alone direct it, but that it should follow in the wake of this movement, study it and draw lessons from it.

The "Economists" furthermore asserted that the role of the conscious element in the working-class movement, the organizing and directing role of Socialist consciousness and Socialist theory,[12] *was insignificant, or almost insignificant; that the Social-Democrats should not elevate the minds of the workers to the level of Socialist consciousness, but, on the contrary, should adjust themselves and descend to the level of the average, or even of the more backward sections of the working class, and that the Social-Democrats should not try to impart a Socialist consciousness to the working class, but should wait until the spontaneous movement of the working class arrived of itself at a Socialist consciousness.*

~~Exposing the whole madness of the Economists' "khvostism" (to follow in the tail), Iskra tried to raise ever broader strata of the working class to the level of the advanced ones. It explained the political tasks of the working class as the vanguard in the struggle for democracy against the tsarist autocracy. Iskra wrote about the imperative of the struggle for political freedoms, the eight-hour working day, the overthrow of tsardom, and then the overthrow of the entire capitalist system.~~

As regards Lenin's plan for the organization of the Party, the "Economists" regarded it almost as an act of violence against the spontaneous movement.

In the struggle with the Economists and later with the Mensheviks, Lenin and Stalin defended the idea that the task of Social-Democracy was to introduce political consciousness into the spontaneous labour movement. In his 1905 brochure BRIEFLY ABOUT THE PARTY'S DIFFERENCES, Comrade Stalin explained the imperative of introducing Socialist consciousness into the spontaneous labour movement in this way.

> "What is scientific Socialism without the labour movement?—asked Comrade Stalin. "It is a compass—he replied—that when left unused can only rust and then must be thrown overboard.
>
> What is the labour movement without Socialism?
>
> A ship without a compass . . . .
>
> But combine the two, and you will have a ship that can speed to distant shores according to a trusted route and, in spite of the storms, reach its pier."

Just like the Economists wanted the workers to limit themselves to only an economic struggle against individual capitalists, they also resisted the creation of a militant, all-Russian, centralized party organization. But only this, commanded by one of the centres of the all-Russian Party organization, would be able to lead a successful struggle against the tsarist government. The Economists had already defended the preservation of their "amateurism," that is, the complete disassociation of local Marxist organizations from one-another when every reading circle worked on its own, as a petty handicraftsman would. At the start of the 1900s, the Economists enjoyed a majority in the local party organizations. Their views were dangerous for the revolutionary cause; had they not been defeated, it would have been impossible to even think about the creation of a genuinely proletarian party or its leading role in the revolution.

The significance of Lenin's work WHAT IS TO BE DONE? was especially great in the struggle with the "Economists." This programmatic book of Lenin's, which appeared in March 1902, made up an entire era in the history of the struggle for the formation of the Bolshevik Party.

In his book WHAT IS TO BE DONE? Lenin defeated the Economists, who had wanted to lure the young proletarian party that was still taking shape into the bog of opportunism. The substance of this opportunism consisted in renouncing revolutionary struggle while being in league with the bourgeoisie. Opportunism was sacrificing the fundamental interests of the masses for the temporary interests of an insignificant minority of workers; in other words, it was an alliance of a part of the workers with the bourgeoisie against the proletarian masses. This line was also supported by the Economists.

~~In the struggle with the Economists, Lenin laid out his plan for the formation of a militant proletarian party that would serve as the VANGUARD of the working class. Lenin outlined his grandiose plan for the formation of a proletarian party that would genuinely be capable of "overturning" Russia and leading the proletariat to seize power.~~

In the columns of ISKRA, and especially in his celebrated work WHAT IS TO BE DONE?, Lenin launched a vehement attack against this opportunist philosophy of the "Economists" and demolished it.

1) Lenin showed[13] *that to divert the working class from the general political struggle against tsardom and to confine its task to that of the economic struggle against the employers and the government, while leaving both employers and government intact, meant to condemn the workers to eternal slavery. The*[14] *economic struggle of the workers against the employers and the government was a trade union struggle for better terms in the sale of their labour power to the capitalists. The workers, however, wanted to fight not only for better terms in the sale of their labour power to the capitalists, but also for the abolition of the capitalist system itself which condemned them to sell their labour power to the capitalists and to suffer exploitation.*[15] *But the workers could not develop their struggle against capitalism, their struggle for Socialism to the full, as long as the path of the working-class movement was barred by tsardom, that watchdog of capitalism. It was therefore the immediate task of the Party and of the working class to remove tsardom from the path and thus clear the way to Socialism.*[16]

2) Lenin showed that to extol the spontaneous process in the working-class movement, to deny that the Party had a leading role to play, to reduce its role to that of a recorder of events, meant to preach khvostism (following in the tail), to preach the conversion of the Party into a tail-piece of the spontaneous process, into a passive force of the movement, capable only of contemplating the spontaneous process and allowing events to take their own course. To advocate this meant working for the destruction of the Party, that is, leaving the working class without a party—that is, leaving the working class unarmed. But to leave the working class unarmed when it was faced by such enemies as tsardom, which was armed to the teeth, and the bourgeoisie, which was[17] *organized on modern lines and had its own party to direct its struggle against the working class, meant to betray the working class.*

3) Lenin showed that to bow in worship of the spontaneous working-class movement and to belittle the importance of consciousness, of Socialist consciousness and Socialist theory, meant, in the first place, to insult the workers, who were drawn to consciousness as to light; in the second place, to lower the value of theory in the eyes of the Party, that is, to depreciate the instrument which helped the Party to understand the present and foresee the future; and, in the third place, it meant to sink completely and irrevocably into the bog of opportunism.

> *"Without a revolutionary theory," Lenin said, "there can be no revolutionary movement. . . . The role of vanguard can be fulfilled only by a party that is guided by the most advanced theory." (Lenin,* SELECTED WORKS, *Eng. ed., Vol. II, pp. 47, 48.)*

4) Lenin showed that the "Economists" were deceiving the working class when they asserted that a Socialist ideology could arise from the spontaneous movement of the working class, for in reality the Socialist ideology arises not from the spontaneous movement, but from science. By denying the necessity of[18] *imparting a Socialist consciousness to the working class, the "Economists" were clearing the way for bourgeois ideology, facilitating its introduction and dissemination among the working class, and, consequently, they were burying the idea of union between the*[19] *working-class movement and Socialism, thus helping the bourgeoisie.*[20]

> *"All worship of the spontaneity of the labour movement," Lenin said, "all belittling of the role of 'the conscious element,' of the role of the party of Social-Democracy,* MEANS, ALTOGETHER IRRESPECTIVE OF WHETHER THE BELITTLER LIKES IT OR NOT, STRENGTHENING THE INFLUENCE OF THE BOURGEOIS IDEOLOGY AMONG THE WORKERS." *(Ibid., p. 61.)*
>
> *And further:*
>
> *"The only choice is: either the bourgeois or the Socialist ideology. There is no middle course. . . . Hence to belittle the Socialist ideology* IN ANY WAY, TO TURN AWAY FROM IT IN THE SLIGHTEST DEGREE *means to strengthen the bourgeois ideology." (Ibid., p. 62.)*

5) Summing up all these mistakes of the "Economists," Lenin came to the conclusion that they did not want a[21] *party of social revolution for the emancipation of the working class from capitalism, but a*[22] *party of "social reform," which presupposed the preservation of capitalist rule, and that, consequently, the "Economists" were reformists*[23] *who were betraying the fundamental interests of the proletariat.*

6) Lastly, Lenin showed that "Economism" was not an accidental phenomenon in Russia, but that the "Economists" *were an instrument of bourgeois influence upon the working class, that they* had allies in the West-European Social-Democratic parties *in the person of the revisionists, the followers of the opportunist Bernstein.* ~~At this time,~~ The opportunist trend in Social-Democratic parties was gaining strength in Western Europe; on the plea of "freedom to criticize" Marx, it demanded a "revision" of the Marxist doctrine (hence the term ~~for this trend~~ "revisionism"); *it demanded renunciation of the revolution, of Socialism and of the dictatorship of the proletariat.* ~~The revisionists announced~~

~~that the Social-Democrats must transform from a party of social revolution into a democratic party of modest social reforms. They unconditionally rejected the idea of a proletarian dictatorship. The revisionists tried to convince the working class that its task was only to struggle for more advantageous conditions for the sale of their labour to the capitalists and wage increases and not for the destruction of the entire system of capitalist wage slavery. The chieftain of the revisionists, Bernstein, advanced the slogan: "the movement is everything and the ultimate goal is nothing." In other words, according to the revisionists, modest reforms (like, for instance, legislation limiting the length of the working day), the economic struggle for better pay, etc., were all that Social-Democracy was to aim for. And the ultimate goal, Socialism, was "nothing."~~ *Lenin showed that t*he Russian "Economists" were ~~also~~ pursuing a similar ~~political~~ policy of renunciation of the revolutionary struggle, *of Socialism and of the dictatorship of the proletariat.*

~~Lenin demonstrated the decisive meaning of this principled struggle against a retreat from Marxism and for a revolutionary theory. In order to be the genuine vanguard of the working class, the Party had to be armed with a revolutionary theory that pointed to the route toward liberating the working class from the capitalist yoke.~~

> ~~"Without a revolutionary theory, there can be no revolutionary movement. . . . THE ROLE OF THE VANGUARD CAN ONLY BE FULFILLED BY A PARTY THAT IS LED BY ADVANCED THEORY," wrote Lenin in his book WHAT IS TO BE DONE? (Lenin, COLLECTED WORKS, Russ. ed., Vol. IV, p. 380.)~~

~~Lenin pointed out that the Party was the conscious, advance guard of the working class, its vanguard. The strength of this vanguard was ten or a hundred times greater that its numbers. This vanguard was to introduce Socialist consciousness into the working-class masses and elevate the masses to the level of the proletariat's class interests. The Party had to explain to the working class about its fundamental interests, which included the overthrow of the capitalist system and how to reach these goals.~~

~~Lenin advanced a plan to rally local Marxist Social-Democratic reading circles and groups together into a militant, all-Russian Party organization, led by a single centre. Only such a centralized and disciplined organization would be able to successfully struggle with the tsarist government and prepare the working-class forces for revolution. This working-class Party had to be constructed on the basis of the revolutionary consciousness and activism of each one of its members. Its nucleus had to be an organization of professional revolutionaries, that is, people who devoted all their strength to the revolutionary cause.~~

~~Lenin pointed out that what was most necessary for the creation of such a Party was an all-Russian newspaper. ISKRA became such a newspaper. The newspaper would be a collective propagandist and agitator. It would facilitate the ideological defeat of the enemies within the labour movement. The newspaper would defend the purity of the revolutionary theory and refine the Party program. The newspaper would forge ideological unity through its genuine, active preparations for the upcoming revolution. The newspaper was not only a collective propagandist and agitator, but a collective organizer. Local Party workers would unite around it as they would around an all-Party cause, writing to the newspaper, supplying dispatches and facilitating its dissemination. The isolation of individual organizations, when each was concerned only about its own local affairs, would be exchanged for efforts to connect all of these organizations together and rally them around a single, common Party task. This, according to Lenin, was how to forge organized unity.~~

~~During the period in which the Party was organized, when the multitude of local Marxist reading circles and groups in existence were not yet connected with one another and when the Economists wanted to reduce the workers' struggle to the struggle for a "fiver," the most important cause was the formation of a militant, all-Russian illegal (secret) newspaper. ISKRA's activity and its struggle with "khvostism" and the Economists' "amateurish approach" laid the foundation for the formation of a genuinely proletarian party in Russia. In his book WHAT IS TO BE DONE?, Lenin generalized about the entire experience of the political struggle with the Economists. The book WHAT IS TO BE DONE had the most significant influence on the advanced workers of Russia. It is impossible to become a conscious Marxist-Leninist without familiarizing oneself with that book.~~

~~The struggle with the Economists was very important because it was in this struggle that the question concerning which path the proletarian party in Russia was to take would be resolved. The path of revolutionary struggle or the path of opportunism, denial of the working class's political struggle and the adaptation of its line to the interests of the bourgeoisie? The Economists pushed for the latter path.~~

Such were the main theoretical principles expounded by Lenin in WHAT IS TO BE DONE?

As a result of the wide circulation of this book, by the time of the Second Congress of the Russian Social-Democratic Party, that is, within a year after its publication (it appeared in March 1902), nothing but a distasteful memory remained of the ideological stand of "Economism," and to be called an "Economist" was regarded by the majority of the members of the Party as an insult.

It was a complete ideological defeat for "Economism," for the ideology of opportunism, KHVOSTISM and spontaneity.

But this does not exhaust the significance of Lenin's WHAT IS TO BE DONE?

The historic significance of this celebrated book lies in the fact that in it Lenin:

1) For the first time in the history of Marxist thought, laid bare the ideological roots of opportunism, showing that they principally consisted in[24] *worshipping the spontaneous*[25] *working-class movement and belittling the role of Socialist consciousness in the working-class movement;*

2) Brought out the great importance of theory, of consciousness, and of the Party as a revolutionizing and guiding force of the spontaneous working-class movement;

3) Brilliantly substantiated the fundamental Marxist thesis that a Marxist party is a union of the working-class movement with Socialism;

4) Gave a brilliant exposition[26] *of the ideological foundations of a Marxist party.*

The theoretical theses expounded in WHAT IS TO BE DONE? *later became the foundation of the ideology of the Bolshevik Party.*

Possessing such a wealth of theory, ISKRA *was able to, and actually did, develop an extensive campaign for Lenin's plan for the building of the Party, for mustering its forces, for calling the Second Party Congress, for revolutionary Social-Democracy, and against the "Economists," revisionists, and opportunists of all kinds.*

~~Lenin's ISKRA ideologically defeated the Economists. Aside from the Economists, ISKRA also waged a struggle with the Socialist-Revolutionaries.~~

~~At the start of the 1900s, the populist Socialist-Revolutionary party took shape in connection with the strengthening of the peasant movement. This petty-bourgeois party spoke out against the teachings of revolutionary Marxism.~~

~~Lenin declared the most decisive and merciless war against the Socialist-Revolutionaries. Lenin saw the Socialist-Revolutionaries' fundamental harm in the fact that they presented themselves as Socialists, although they had never actually been Socialists. The Socialist-Revolutionaries advanced an agrarian program for the "Socialization" of the land. The essence of this program consisted of the following: the land was to be divided among the peasants without affecting private ownership of the instruments and means of production, while capitalism was to be preserved in the city. And the Socialist-Revolutionaries considered this to be a Socialist program!~~

~~Lenin exposed the Socialist-Revolutionaries. He pointed out that the Socialist-Revolutionaries were deceiving the peasants with their program for "Socializing" the land by claiming that this program provided for Socialism. On the contrary, the Socialist-Revolutionaries' program resulted in the strengthening of private property in the countryside rather than its destruction, as well as the strengthening of the kulaks and the development and strengthening of capitalism in Russia.~~

~~Lenin criticized with particular intensity the Socialist-Revolutionaries' preaching about individual terrorism as the "highest form" of struggle. Terrorists actually interfered with the mass struggle against tsardom. They distracted the workers' attention and strength away from the only correct path—the path of organized struggle. The path was cleared towards the formation of a revolutionary labour party in the struggle with the Socialist-Revolutionary terrorists.~~

~~Iskra gave a clear and precise answer to all the questions about the country's political life. Iskra's dispatches and articles showed the horrific oppression of the tsarist government, the brutal torture of the working people, the savage police beatings, the whipping of the peasants during tax collection, the mass drafting of students into the army, etc., on the basis of concrete examples. Iskra wrote in detail about the revolutionary demonstrations. Iskra showed the growing displeasure with the tsarist government within the various strata and classes of society and instilled in them a hatred for tsardom. Iskra introduced the working class to the conscious realization that they must be the vanguard for democracy and the popular masses' chieftain in the struggle against tsardom. Iskra worked out the working class's point of view on all these political issues.~~

One of the most important things that Iskra did was to draft a program for the Party. The program of a workers' party, *as we know,* is a brief, *scientifically formulated* statement of the aims and objects of the struggle of the working class. The program defines both the ultimate goal of the revolutionary movement of the proletariat, and the demands for which the party fights while on the way to the achievement of the ultimate goal. *The drafting of a program was therefore a matter of prime importance.*

During the drafting ~~and discussion~~ of the program ~~there were~~ *serious* ~~very major~~ differences *arose* on the editorial board of Iskra ~~with~~ *between* Lenin, on the one hand, and Plekhanov and other members of the board, on the other. These differences and disputes almost led to a complete rupture between Lenin and Plekhanov. But matters did not come to a head at that time. Lenin secured the inclusion in the *draft* program of a most important clause on the dictatorship of the proletariat and of a clear statement on the leading role of the working class in ~~relation to the working masses~~ *the revolution*.

It was Lenin, too, who drew up the whole agrarian section of the program. Already at that time Lenin was in favour of the nationalization of the land, but he considered it necessary in the first stage of the struggle to put forward the demand for the return to the peasants of the otrezki, that is, those portions of the land which had been cut off the peasants' land by the landlords at the time of "emancipation" of the peasants. Plekhanov *was* opposed *to* the demand for the nationalization of the land.

~~Lenin focused on rallying the peasantry to the revolution; Plekhanov underestimated the peasantry's revolutionary potential.~~

The disputes between Lenin and Plekhanov over the Party program to some extent ~~decided beforehand~~ *determined* the future differences between the Bolsheviks and the Mensheviks. ~~It was only thanks to the fact that Lenin's important corrections were ratified that the program became the militant program of the revolutionary party.~~

~~In the struggle against the Economists, Socialist-Revolutionaries and other enemies within the labour movement, Iskra depended on the help and support of its supporters in Russia. Lenin stubbornly and tirelessly built the Iskra organization. Lenin devoted all of his attention and energy to Iskra and its organization. In Iskra, he wrote all the fundamental, programmatic articles, personally worked through all the dispatches and notices that Russian workers had submitted and edited the entire newspaper. Lenin maintained a broad correspondence in Iskra's name with local Party organizations and individual Social-Democrats. This correspondence was conducted in secret (using codes) and required enormous effort. N. K. Krupskaya, who was the secretary of the Iskra editorial board, helped Lenin with all of this work. On Lenin's orders, Iskra's agents and plenipotentiaries—Litvinov, Stopani, Gusev, N. Bauman, Zemlyachka and others—traveled around to local organizations, evading the persecution of tsarist detectives and exposing local Economists. They won over local Social-Democratic committees and strengthened the new Party organizations. The severe conditions of the underground and the struggle with numerous enemies forged professional revolutionaries who were ready to sacrifice themselves in the name of revolutionary work.~~

~~In the history of the Bolshevik Party, professional revolutionaries played an enormous role. Lenin and Stalin, most of all, served as models for the professional revolutionary. Lenin and Stalin personified the best qualities of the proletarian revolutionaries—ideological integrity and a refusal to compromise in the struggle with those who would retreat from Marxism and the revolutionary line; selfless devotion to the cause of communism; iron Party discipline; a connection with the broad masses; and the wisdom to not only teach the masses, but to learn from them as well.~~

~~One of these noteworthy professional revolutionaries was Yakov Mikhailovich Sverdlov, who was consumed while working on the construction of the Party and Soviet state. Other such professional revolutionaries also died at their glorious battle stations: Felix Edmundovich Dzerzhinsky, the iron knight of the revolution; Sergei Mironovich Kirov, villainously murdered by the Trotskyite-Bukharinite gang; and Valerian Vladimirovich Kuibyshev, who was similarly ruined by these monsters. Sergo Ordjonikidze and Mikhail Vasilyevich Frunze were professional revolutionaries. Such a professional revolution-~~

ary was Ivan Vasilyevich Babushkin, who worked with Lenin already in the League of Struggle for the Emancipation of the Working Class and who was shot by tsarist butchers in Siberia during the revolution of 1905. The majority of the leaders of the Party and Soviet government belong to this group of professional revolutionaries who were trained in the strict school of Bolshevik struggle.

A mighty organization of professional revolutionaries took shape in Russia around the newspaper ISKRA. Lenin showed the advanced workers of Russia that their struggle for the victory of the ISKRA plan had international significance. He showed that great historical tasks stood before the working class. In his work WHAT IS TO BE DONE?, Lenin wrote prophetically:

> "History has now placed before us an immediate task, which is THE MOST REVOLUTIONARY of all the IMMEDIATE tasks lying before the proletariat in whatever country you might choose. Realization of this task—the destruction of the most powerful base of not only European, but also (as we can say today) Asian reaction—will make the Russian proletariat the vanguard of the international revolutionary proletariat." (Lenin, COLLECTED WORKS, Russ. ed., Vol. IV, p. 382.)

3. Stalin—Founder of the Leninist-ISKRA Organization in Transcaucasia

A mighty ISKRA organization took shape in Transcaucasia. Its founder was Comrade Stalin.

Stalin occupied a place within the leading ranks, alongside Lenin, in the struggle for a working class revolutionary party in our country. Even then, at the dawn of the construction of the Bolshevik Party, Stalin clearly saw who his chieftain and teacher was. Here is how Comrade Stalin reminisced on this topic in a speech to the Kremlin cadets' banquet in honor of Lenin's memory:

> "My acquaintance with Lenin's revolutionary activity at the end of the 1890s and especially after 1901, after the publication of ISKRA, led me to the conviction that we had in Lenin a truly unusual person. He was not at that time simply a Party leader in my mind—he was practically its founder, because he alone understood the inner essence and pressing needs of our Party. When I compared him to the other leaders of our Party, it always seemed to me that Lenin's comrades in arms—Plekhanov, Martov, Axelrod and others—stood a full head shorter than Lenin, and that Lenin in comparison to them was not simply a leader, but a leader of a higher type, a mountain eagle, who knew no fear in the strug-

~~gle and in bravely leading the Party forward along the untraveled paths of the Russian revolutionary movement."~~

~~It was at about this time that Lenin and Stalin first became acquainted with one another, albeit from afar. The life and activity of Lenin and Stalin converged tightly in the struggle for the revolutionary cause.~~

~~Comrade Stalin, with his militant comrades-in-arms Lado Ketskhoveli and A. Tsulukidze and the Russian Social-Democrats who were in Tiflis—V. Kurnatovsky and others—built a Leninist, ISKRA-ist Social-Democratic organization in Transcaucasia. On Comrade Stalin's initiative, the First Congress of the Tiflis Social-Democratic organization was called in November 1901. The conference elected the first Tiflis committee of the R.S.D.L.P., which included Comrade Stalin.~~

~~Comrade Stalin did not limit his work to just Tiflis. Following a decision of the Tiflis organization, Lado Ketskhoveli went to Baku to strengthen the local Social-Democratic organization and found an illegal print shop. It was in this print shop in September 1901 that the first issue was published of BRDZOLA (THE STRUGGLE)—the militant organ of the Transcaucasian Social-Democrats, a group within which Comrade Stalin played the most active role. Comrade Stalin went to Batum at the end of November 1901 for work. In Batum, Comrade Stalin entered into contact with the advanced workers and organized reading circles in all the major enterprises. He himself led 11 reading circles, founded a print shop, wrote leaflets and facilitated their publication and distribution not only in Batum, but in other regions of Georgia. A month later, Stalin had already prepared the groundwork for the formation of an ISKRA organization in Batum. On the evening of January 1, 1902, the Batum Social-Democratic Organization was created by representatives of the reading circles under the leadership of Comrade Stalin.~~

~~Under Comrade Stalin's leadership, the Batum committee organized workers' strikes. On March 9, 1902, a demonstration of Batum workers took place under Comrade Stalin's leadership. About six thousand people took part in it. The demonstration was fired upon by soldiers, and about 500 participants were arrested and expelled from Batum. On March 9, the day of the victims' funerals, Comrade Stalin organized a second political demonstration. These events in Batum had enormous significance for the rallying of the revolutionary movement throughout Transcaucasia. Soon, on April 5 (18, New Style), 1902, Comrade Stalin was arrested and imprisoned. As with Lenin, prison did not prevent Stalin from helping those who remained at large to conduct revolutionary work. Sensing in Comrade Stalin a terrible revolutionary strength, the tsarist government banished him to far Siberia, to the village of Novaya Uda in the Balagansk district of Irkutsk province. Despite Comrade Stalin's arrest and~~

~~subsequent banishment, his work of training revolutionary Social-Democrats never ceased. In 1903, the Baku, Batum and Tiflis committees united to form the Transcaucasian Social-Democratic Workers' League. Under the leadership of Comrades Tskhakaya and Stalin, a militant proletarian party organization was built in Transcaucasia. Revolutionary workers of various nationalities united within it—Russians, Georgians, Armenians and Turks. Later, Lenin referred to the Transcaucasian organization as a model of proletarian internationalism.~~

3.4. Second Congress of the ~~R.S.D.L.P.~~ *Russian Social-Democratic Labour Party. Adoption of Program and Rules and Formation of a Single Party. Differences at the Congress and Appearance of Two Trends within the Party: the Bolshevik and the Menshevik*

Thus the triumph of Lenin's principles and the successful struggle waged by Iskra *for Lenin's plan of organization brought about all the principal conditions necessary for the creation of a party, or, as it was said at the time, of a real party. The* Iskra *trend gained the upper hand among the Social-Democratic organizations in Russia. The Second Party Congress could now be summoned.*

The Second Congress of the R.S.D.L.P. opened on July 17 (30, New Style), 1903. It was held abroad, in secret. It first met in Brussels, but the Belgian police requested the delegates to leave the country. Thereupon the congress transferred its sittings to London.

Forty-three delegates in all, representing 26 organizations, assembled at the congress. Each committee was entitled to send two delegates, but some of them sent only one. The 43 delegates commanded 51 votes between them.

The chief purpose of the congress was "to create a real party on that basis of principles and organization which had been advanced and elaborated by Iskra." (Lenin, Selected Works, Eng. ed., Vol. II, p. 412.) ~~It was in this way that Lenin defined the main task of the Second Congress in his historic, eternal work One Step Forward, Two Steps Back. It was impossible to realize without struggle.~~

The composition of the congress was heterogeneous. *The avowed "Economists" were not represented, because of the defeat they had suffered. But they had since disguised their views so artfully that they managed to smuggle several of their delegates into the congress. Moreover, the Bund delegates differed only ostensibly from the "Economists"; in reality they supported the "Economists."*

Thus ~~It~~ *the congress* was attended not only by supporters of Iskra, but also by its adversaries. Thirty-three of the delegates, that is, the majority, were supporters of Iskra. But not all those who considered themselves Iskra-ists were real Leninist Iskra-ists. The delegates fell into several groups. The supporters of Lenin, or the firm Iskra-ists, commanded 24 votes; nine of the Iskra-ists followed Martov; these were ~~"soft"~~ *unstable* Iskra-ists. Some of the delegates vacillated between Iskra and its opponents; they commanded 10 votes *and constituted the Centre.* The ~~extreme~~ *avowed* opponents of Iskra commanded 8 votes (3 "Economists" and 5 Bundists). A split in the ranks of the Iskra-ists would be enough to give the enemies of Iskra~~, who had gathered 27 votes against 24,~~ the upper hand.

It will therefore be seen how complex the situation was at the congress. Lenin expended a great deal of energy to ensure the victory of Iskra.

The most important item on the agenda was the adoption of the *Party* program. ~~The workers' party program was a brief explanation of the goals and tasks of the working class's struggle. It determined both the ultimate goal of the revolutionary movement and the demands that the Party was struggling for on the path to this ultimate goal. The fundamental idea of the Iskra draft program was the idea of the proletarian dictatorship. This program did not suit the opportunists.~~ *The chief point which, during the discussion of the program, aroused the objections of the opportunist section of the congress was the question of the dictatorship of the proletariat.* ~~The Economist Akimov spoke out against the program in especially heated terms. Trotsky also spoke out against the dictatorship of the proletariat. Trotsky announced that the dictatorship of the proletariat would be possible only after the Party merged with the working class. In other words, Trotsky was demanding the elimination of the Party, without which it would be impossible to realize the dictatorship of the proletariat or reinforce it. Trotsky likewise announced that the dictatorship of the proletariat would be possible only when the working class represented the majority in the country. This meant that Trotsky was actually against the proletarian dictatorship. We know that even now, 20 years after the October Socialist revolution, the working class still does not make up the majority of the country, and yet the proletarian dictatorship has already existed for 20 years in the USSR. The pseudo-Cadet and Economist Akimov completely agreed with Trotsky. Lurking within his position at the Second Conference were the roots of the brutal struggle that was led by Trotsky—a fascist agent and the most evil enemy of the people.~~ *There were a number of other items in the program on which the opportunists did not agree with the revolutionary section of the congress. But they decided to put up the main fight on the question of the dictatorship of the proletariat, on the plea that the programs of a number of foreign Social-Democratic parties contained no clause on the dictatorship of the proletariat, and that therefore the program of the Russian Social-Democratic Party could dispense with it too.*

The opportunists also ~~spoke out at the congress against other points in the program. They~~ objected to the inclusion in the Party program of demands on the peasant question. These people did not want revolution; they, therefore, fought shy of the ally of the working class—the peasantry—and adopted ~~a hostile~~ *an unfriendly* attitude towards it.

The Bundists and the Polish Social-Democrats objected to the right of nations to self-determination. Lenin ~~and Stalin~~ had always taught that the working class must combat national oppression. To object to the inclusion of this demand in the program ~~meant~~ *was tantamount to a proposal* to renounce proletarian internationalism and to become accomplices in ~~tsardom~~ *national oppression*.

Lenin made short work of all these ~~opportunists~~ *objections*.

The congress adopted the program proposed by ISKRA.

This program ~~was divided into~~ *consisted of* two parts: a maximum program and a minimum program. The maximum program dealt with the principal aim of the working-class party, namely, ~~to complete~~ the Socialist revolution, ~~to~~ *the* overthrow *of* the power of the capitalists, *and* ~~to~~ *the* establish*ment of* the dictatorship of the proletariat ~~and to build a Socialist society~~. The minimum program dealt with the *immediate* aims of the Party, *aims to be achieved* before the overthrow of the capitalist system and the establishment of the dictatorship of the proletariat~~. The Party considered the bourgeois-democratic revolution to be its most immediate task~~, namely, the overthrow of the tsarist autocracy, the establishment of a democratic republic, the introduction of an 8-hour working day, the abolition of all survivals of serfdom in the countryside, and the restoration to the peasants of the cut-off lands (OTREZKI) of which they had been deprived by the landlords ~~during the destruction of serfdom~~.

Subsequently, the Bolsheviks ~~laid out~~ *replaced* the demand *for the return of the OTREZKI by the demand* for the confiscation of all the landed estates.

~~In order to complete the Socialist revolution and establish the proletarian dictatorship, it was necessary first of all to be victorious in the bourgeois-democratic revolution—to overthrow the power of the tsar and landlords.~~

The program adopted by the Second Congress was the revolutionary program of the working class's party.

It remained in force until the Eighth *Party* Congress, held after the victory of the proletarian revolution, when our Party adopted a new Program. ~~At Lenin's suggestion, all the parts of the old program where the contradictions of capitalist society were discussed were carried over into the new Program, as was the imperative of establishing the proletarian dictatorship.~~

~~For the realization of all of these great tasks and the leadership of the growing revolutionary movement of workers and peasants, it was necessary to correctly organize the Party. The congress allocated a lot of time to the issues of party building. Lenin gave the report on the Party Rules. It was on account of these Rules that the struggle at the congress got as sharp as it did. The organizational question was fundamental to the Second Congress.~~

~~5. Appearance within the Party of Bolshevik and Menshevik Factions.~~

~~Organizational differences were one of the major reasons for the Party's split at the conference into two factions (groups): THE BOLSHEVIKS AND MENSHEVIKS. What was the essence of this disagreement?~~

~~Lenin suggested that the first paragraph of the Party Rules ought to be expressed as follows: "Anyone can be a Party member who recognizes its program and who supports the Party both in material terms and in terms of personal participation in one of the Party's organizations." The Party, Lenin said, was the vanguard detachment of the working class, as well as its leader and chieftain. Only those who were selflessly devoted to the revolution and who would steadfastly struggle for the workers' cause could be in the Party.~~

~~People could be considered Party members if they deferred to the Party, acknowledged Party discipline to be obligatory, and devoted themselves entirely to the cause of the Party and Socialism. Every member of the Party had to belong to some kind of organization. In such an organization, the Party member received militant training and became tempered and tested in his work. This understanding of membership equipped the Party with better quality people—numerically fewer, but of higher quality and more steadfast. This relationship to the Party meant that those joining were completely on the Party's side, entirely for the Party in every sense and ready to subordinate all their actions to the demands of the Party.~~

~~Lenin's formulation of the first paragraph of the Rules made it harder for non-proletarian elements to gain entrance to the Party. "Our task—said Lenin at the conference—is to protect the firm, restrained and pure nature of our Party. We must attempt to raise the rank and significance of Party membership higher and higher and higher. (Lenin, COLLECTED WORKS, Russ. ed., Vol. VI, p. 33.)~~

~~Against Lenin spoke out the "soft" ISKRAites—the future Mensheviks Martov, Trotsky and several others. All of the opportunists joined them. The Martovites suggested accepting into the Party all takers. They suggested that everyone who promised to contribute something should be invited to join the Party, even those who did not belong to a Party organization or submit to Party discipline.~~

Having adopted the program, the Second Party Congress proceeded to discuss the draft of the Party Rules. Now that the congress had adopted a program and had laid the foundation for the ideological unity of the Party, it had also to adopt Party Rules so as to put an end to amateurishness and the parochial outlook of the circles, to organizational disunity and the absence of strict discipline in the Party.

The adoption of the program had gone through comparatively smoothly, but fierce disputes arose at the congress over the Party Rules. The sharpest differences arose over the formulation of the first paragraph of the rules, dealing with Party membership. Who could be a member of the Party, what was to be the composition of the Party, what was to be the organizational nature of the Party, an organized whole or something amorphous?—such were the questions that arose in connection with the first paragraph of the rules. Two different formulations contested the ground: Lenin's formulation, which was supported by Plekhanov and the firm ISKRA*-ists; and Martov's formulation, which was supported by Axelrod, Zasulich, the unstable* ISKRA-ISTS*, Trotsky, and all the avowed opportunists at the congress.*

According to Lenin's formulation, one could be a member of the Party who accepted its program, supported it financially, and belonged to one of its organizations. Martov's formulation, while admitting that acceptance of the program and financial support of the Party were indispensable conditions of Party membership, did not, however, make it a condition that a Party member should belong to one of the Party organizations, maintaining that a Party member need not necessarily belong to a Party organization.

Lenin regarded the Party as an ORGANIZED *detachment, whose members cannot just enrol themselves in the Party, but must be admitted into the Party by one of its organizations, and hence must submit to Party discipline. Martov, on the other hand, regarded the Party as something organizationally* AMORPHOUS*, whose members enrol themselves in the Party and are therefore not obliged to submit to Party discipline, inasmuch as they do not belong to a Party organization.*

Thus, unlike Lenin's formulation, ~~the Menshevik~~ *Martov's* formulation ~~of the first paragraph of the Rules~~ would throw the door of the Party wide open to *unstable* non-proletarian elements. On the eve of the bourgeois-democratic revolution there were people among the bourgeois intelligentsia ~~(liberal professors, etc.)~~ who for a while sympathized with the revolution. From time to time they might even render some small service~~, for instance, allowing revolutionaries to spend the night in their apartments~~ *to the Party*. But such people would not join an organization, submit to Party discipline, carry out ~~all~~ Party tasks and run the accompanying risks. Yet Martov and the other Mensheviks proposed to regard such people as Party members, and to accord them the right and opportunity to influence Party affairs. They even proposed *to grant*[27] *any striker the right* to "enrol" ~~every striker~~ *himself* in the Party, although non-Socialists, *Anarchists and Socialist-Revolutionaries* also took part in strikes.

~~The Menshevik proposal weakened the working class party and made it possible for alien people, random "fellow travelers" and those hostile to Socialism from the ranks of the liberal bourgeoisie to penetrate into the Party. The Leninists stood for a militant, proletarian party, while the Martovites stood for a petty-bourgeois, opportunistic party.~~

And so it was that instead of a monolithic and militant party with a clearly defined organization, for which Lenin and the Leninists fought at the congress, the

Martovites wanted a heterogeneous and loose, amorphous party, which could not be a militant party with firm discipline because of its heterogeneous character, if for no other reason.

~~The alliance of all the opportunists~~ *The breaking away of the unstable* Iskra-*ists from the firm* Iskra-ists, *their alliance with the Centrists, joined as they were by the avowed opportunists,* turned the balance *in favour of Martov* on this point. By 28 votes to 22, with one abstention, the congress adopted Martov's formulation of the first paragraph of the Rules. ~~Only at the Third R.S.D.L.P. Congress would this decision be rescinded and would Lenin's first paragraph of the Rules be ratified.~~

~~Lenin's struggle for the first paragraph of the Rules, as the future experience of the Party would show, had enormous historical significance. The Bolshevik Party, built on a foundation of Leninism, was transformed into a mighty revolutionary force. The Menshevik party, a group of bourgeois lackeys, sank to the bottom of the counter-revolutionary pit.~~

~~The Second Congress made decisions on the issue of the relationship to the liberal bourgeoisie. The Leninists attacked the opportunists on this issue of the relationship to the liberals. The opportunists, led by Martov and Trotsky, proposed that the workers conclude an alliance for the struggle with tsardom not with the working peasantry, but with the liberal bourgeoisie. Lenin and his supporters exposed the harm proposed by Martov and Trotsky. The Leninists demonstrated that it was impossible to depend on the bourgeoisie, who might switch sides and betray the people. Lenin and the Bolsheviks said that the working class had to side with the peasantry and lead it into battle against tsardom.~~

~~During the period of the Second Congress, the Party completed its famous ABOUT-FACE away from temporary agreements with liberals like Struve and toward a struggle-to-the-death with the liberal bourgeoisie. During the years of preparation for the struggle with tsardom, a few liberals dressed up in Marxist costume. Now, as the revolution approached ever closer, the liberal bourgeoisie stripped off its Legal Marxist finery and began to build its own bourgeois political organization. Struve became the chieftain of the liberal bourgeois group "Liberation." In a resolution that the Bolsheviks supported at the Second Congress, the anti-revolutionary, anti-social character of Struve's group was underscored.~~

~~Why did the Bolsheviks relate to the liberal bourgeoisie with such distrust? The liberal bourgeoisie was incapable of waging a struggle for the total defeat of tsardom and the landlords. Now that open struggle for the defeat of tsardom had begun, it was necessary to wage a decisive struggle with the liberal bourgeoisie as well. The Mensheviks (including Plekhanov) proved to be incapable~~

~~of waging this struggle against the liberal bourgeoisie. On the contrary, they aimed to subordinate the working class to the liberal bourgeoisie's influence.~~

~~Differing views on the question of organization and the liberal bourgeoisie formed the basis for a PRINCIPLED struggle between the Bolsheviks and Mensheviks. The Bolshevik Party was forged and tempered in this struggle for the Leninist revolutionary line.~~

After the split in the ranks of the Iskra-ists over the first paragraph of the Rules the struggle at the congress became still more acute. The congress was coming to the last item on the agenda—the elections of the leading institutions of the Party: the editorial board of the central organ of the Party (Iskra), and the Central Committee. However, before the elections were reached, certain incidents occurred which changed the alignment of forces.

In connection with the Party Rules, the congress had to deal with the question of the Bund. The Bund laid claim to a special ~~place~~ *position* within the Party. It demanded to be recognized as the sole representative of the Jewish workers *in Russia*. To comply with this demand would have meant to divide the workers *in the Party organizations* according to nationality, and to renounce common *territorial class* organizations of the workers. The congress rejected the *system of organization on* national lines proposed by the Bund.[28] Thereupon the Bundists quit the congress. Two "Economists" also left the congress when the latter refused to recognize their Foreign League as the representative of the Party abroad.

The departure of these seven opportunists altered the balance of forces at the congress in favour of the Leninists.

From the very outset Lenin focussed his attention on the composition of the central institutions of the Party. He deemed it necessary that the Central Committee should be ~~elected from~~ *composed of* staunch and consistent revolutionaries. The Martovites strove to secure the predominance of unstable, opportunist elements on the Central Committee. The majority of the congress supported Lenin on this question. The Central Committee that was elected consisted of Lenin's followers.

On Lenin's proposal, Lenin, Plekhanov and Martov were elected to the editorial board of Iskra. ~~But~~ Martov had demanded the election of all the six former members of *the* Iskra *editorial board* at the congress, *the majority of whom were Martov's followers*. This demand was rejected by the majority of the congress. The three proposed by Lenin were elected. Martov thereupon announced that he would not join the editorial board of the central organ.

~~Lenin, as one can see, led the majority of the Iskra-ites at the congress. Lenin's supporters were elected to the Central Committee and Iskra editorial board.~~

Thus, by its vote on the ~~centres~~ *central institutions of the Party,* the congress sealed *the defeat of Martov's followers and* the victory of Lenin's ~~principles~~ *followers.*

From that time on, Lenin's followers, who received the majority of votes in the elections at the congress, have been called Bolsheviks (from BOLSHINSTVO, majority), and Lenin's opponents, who received the minority of votes, have been called Mensheviks (from MENSHINSTVO, minority).

~~It appears at first glance that the congress split over the question of elections to the central institutions of the Party. But if one looks at the total sum of the differences, then the split at the Second Congress took place over the issue of how to build the Party. Lenin and the Bolsheviks believed that it was necessary to create a militant, centralized Party, capable of taking charge of the working class and leading it to victory over tsardom and the bourgeoisie. And the party that Martov and Trotsky proposed to found was only able to trudge at the tail of the spontaneous labour movement and would have become an appendage of the bourgeois parties.~~

~~The Second Congress had enormous significance for Party history.~~

Summing up the work of the Second Congress, the following conclusions may be drawn:

1) The congress sealed the victory of Marxism over "Economism," over open opportunism.

2) The congress adopted a Program and Rules ~~of the Party~~, *created the Social-Democratic Party, and thus built the framework of a single party.*

~~The congress created the Party's central institutions: the Central Committee and the Central Organ. At the Second Congress, the revolutionary party of the working class thus took shape: the Russian Social-Democratic Labour Party. This Party was born in the conditions of a bitter struggle for Lenin's revolutionary line, under enemy fire.~~

~~After the Second Congress, the division of the Social-Democratic Party into the Bolsheviks and Mensheviks began. In the struggle for the Party, Lenin created the Bolshevik group. Led by Lenin, the Bolsheviks defended and solidified the victory of ISKRA's ideological and organizational foundations at the congress. The Bolsheviks demonstrated that they were able to wage their struggle against the opportunists to the end—to a split and a break with them.~~

3) The congress revealed the existence of grave differences over questions of organization which divided the Party into two sections, the Bolsheviks and the Mensheviks, of whom the former championed the organizational principles of revolutionary Social-Democracy, while the latter sank into the bog of organizational looseness and of opportunism.

4) The congress showed that the place of the old opportunists, the "Economists," who had already been defeated by the Party, was being taken by new opportunists, the Mensheviks.

5) The congress did not prove equal to its task in matters of organization, showed vacillation, and at times even gave the preponderance to the Mensheviks; and although it corrected its position towards the end, it was nevertheless unable to expose the opportunism of the Mensheviks on matters of organization and to isolate them in the Party, or even to put such a task before the Party.

This latter circumstance proved one of the main reasons why the struggle between the Bolsheviks and the Mensheviks, far from subsiding after the congress, became even more acute.

~~4.6. The Bolshevik Struggle for the Party with the Mensheviks and Conciliators in 1903–04~~ *Splitting Activities of the Menshevik Leaders and Sharpening of the Struggle within the Party after the Second Congress. Opportunism of the Mensheviks. Lenin's Book, ONE STEP FORWARD, TWO STEPS BACK. Organizational Principles of the Marxist Party.*

After the Second Congress the struggle within the Party became even more acute. The ~~opportunists~~ *Mensheviks* did their utmost to frustrate the ~~fundamental result~~ *decisions* of the *Second* Congress ~~to create a revolutionary party~~ *and to seize the central institutions of the Party. They demanded that their representatives be included in the editorial board of ISKRA and in the Central Committee in such numbers as would give them a majority on the editorial board and parity with the Bolsheviks on the Central Committee. As this ran directly counter to the decisions of the Second Congress, the Bolsheviks rejected the Mensheviks' demand. Thereupon t*he Mensheviks, secretly from the Party, created their own anti-Party factional organization, headed by Martov, Trotsky and Axelrod~~.~~ ~~They set for themselves the task of seizing the Party centre and destroying the Party. The majority of the local Social-Democratic organizations in Russia approved of Lenin's line at the Second Congress and supported the Bolsheviks. The Mensheviks waged a rabid struggle against Lenin's revolutionary line.~~*, and, a*s Martov wrote, ~~they~~ "broke into revolt against Leninism." ~~The Mensheviks were able to lure to their side the majority of the foreign part of the Party, where intellectuals prevailed among the émigrés.~~ *The methods they adopted for combating the Party were, as Lenin expressed it, "to disorganize the whole Party work, damage the cause, and hamper all and everything."* ~~The Mensheviks won a decisive majority at the congress~~ *They entrenched themselves* in the Foreign League of Russian Social-Democrats, *nine-tenths of whom were émigré intellectuals isolated from the work in Russia, and from this position they opened fire on the Party, on Lenin and the Leninists.*

The Mensheviks received considerable help from Plekhanov. At the Second Congress Plekhanov sided with Lenin. But after the Second Congress he ~~became afraid of a struggle with~~ *allowed* the Mensheviks *to intimidate him with threats of a split*. He ~~wanted~~ *decided* to “make peace” with the Mensheviks at all costs. It was the deadweight of his earlier opportunist mistakes that dragged Plekhanov down to the Mensheviks. From an advocate of reconciliation with the opportunist Mensheviks he soon became a ~~rabid opportunist~~ *Menshevik himself*. Plekhanov demanded that all ~~four of~~ the former Menshevik editors of the Iskra who had been rejected by the congress be included in the editorial board. Lenin, of course, could not agree to this and resigned from the Iskra editorial board in order to entrench himself in the Central Committee of the Party and to strike at the opportunists from this position. Acting by himself, and in defiance of the will of the congress, Plekhanov co-opted the ~~four~~ former Menshevik editors to the editorial board of Iskra. From that moment on, beginning with the 52nd issue of Iskra, the Mensheviks converted it into their own organ and began to propagate their opportunist views in its columns ~~and its line~~.

~~The Mensheviks found support in the Second International. After the death of Engels, the parties of the Second International did not want to wage a struggle with opportunism. These parties put up with the most insolent opportunists within their ranks, who openly spoke out against the revolutionary teachings of Marx and Engels. These parties tolerated people within their ranks who said that the Social-Democratic party must renounce Socialist revolution and the struggle for the proletarian dictatorship and limit itself to an everyday, petty struggle for “reforms” and small compromises from the bourgeoisie on behalf of the workers while preserving the capitalist system.~~

~~It was for this reason that the parties of the Second International and their leaders did not wish to wage a struggle with the opportunists and enemies of Marxism. These parties had passed over in an ideological sense and betrayed the fundamental interests of the working class to become reformist and non-revolutionary parties.~~

~~Inasmuch as the leaders of the Second International themselves (Kautsky, Bebel and others) did not want to struggle with the open opportunists, they extended all of their sympathy to the Mensheviks. They did not understand the uncompromising, principled struggle with opportunism that the Bolsheviks were waging and were frightened of it. Even the representatives of the left wing of the Second International (Rosa Luxembourg, for instance) did not understand the Bolsheviks and frequently supported the Mensheviks.~~

~~But Lenin knew that the Bolsheviks’ policies were the only correct Marxist ones and he firmly continued his revolutionary line with the support of the local organizations in Russia.~~

Ever since then Lenin’s Bolshevik Iskra has been known in the Party as the old Iskra, and the Menshevik, opportunist Iskra as the new Iskra.

When it passed into the hands of the Mensheviks, Iskra became a weapon in the fight against Lenin and the Bolsheviks, and an organ for the propaganda of

Menshevik opportunism, primarily on questions of organization. Joining forces with the "Economists" and the Bundists, the Mensheviks started a campaign in the columns of Iskra, *as they said, against Leninism. Plekhanov could not stick to his position as an advocate of conciliation, and soon he too joined the campaign. This was bound to happen by the very logic of things: whoever insists on a conciliatory attitude towards opportunists is bound to sink to opportunism himself. There began to flow from the columns of the new* Iskra, *as from a cornucopia, articles and statements claiming that the Party ought not to be an organized whole; that free groups and individuals should be allowed within its ranks without any obligation to submit to the decisions of its organs; that every intellectual who sympathized with the Party, as well as "every striker" and "every participant in a demonstration," should be allowed to declare himself a Party member; that the demand for obedience to all the decisions of the Party was "formal and bureaucratic"; that the demand that the minority must submit to the majority meant the "mechanical suppression" of the will of Party members; that the demand that all Party members—both leaders and rank-and-filers—should equally observe Party discipline meant establishing "serfdom" within the Party; that what "we" needed in the Party was not centralism but anarchist "autonomism" which would permit individuals and Party organizations not to obey the decisions of the Party.*

This was unbridled propaganda of organizational license, which would undermine the Party principle and Party discipline; it was glorification of the individualism of the intelligentsia, and a justification of the anarchist contempt of discipline.

The Mensheviks were obviously trying to drag the Party back from the Second Congress to the old organizational disunity, to the old parochial outlook of the circles and the old amateurish methods.

A vigorous rebuff had to be given the Mensheviks.

~~In May 1904, Lenin spoke out with his programmatic work One Step Forward, Two Steps Back, which addressed the Party's Menshevik crisis.~~

~~In this work, Lenin, struggling with the Mensheviks, further developed his Marxist-Leninist teaching on the proletarian party, the most important parts of which he had already laid out in the book What Is To Be Done?~~

~~Lenin demonstrated that the differences concerning the first paragraph of the Rules had grown over in the hands of the Mensheviks into a system of opportunistic views on organizational issues. And this question was a question of life and death for the Party at that time. The Mensheviks wanted to erase all the boundaries between Party-mindedness and non-party mindedness. The Mensheviks wanted to replace the proletarian, militant Party, with its clearly marked boundaries, its clear program, its clear line on political behavior, its firm discipline and its subordination of local organizations to the Party centre, with some sort of diffuse, formless, lifeless organization. The Mensheviks~~

~~depreciated the idea of Party-mindedness; they essentially wanted to leave the proletariat without an independent party and in this way submit it to the liberal bourgeoisie on the eve of the approaching 1905 revolution.~~

~~Lenin brilliantly saw through the Mensheviks' "plan" and attacked it with all of his might, warning the Party of the danger and harm posed by the Menshevik plan.~~

~~The Mensheviks basically tried to destroy the Party that was created by the Second Congress, objecting to Party discipline and the idea that the Party was to be an ORGANIZED detachment within which the minority submitted to the majority and within which all the Party organizations submitted to the Party centre. After the Second Congress, which represented a step forward toward the formation of a genuine Party, the Mensheviks, as Lenin put it, took two steps back. The Mensheviks wanted to return to the period of "amateurish approaches" when every Marxist reading circle in Russia acted on its own, without submitting to anyone else.~~

~~Ostensibly in the workers' interests, the Mensheviks announced that they were against Party discipline and the definition of boundaries in the Party.~~

~~Lenin exposed the total deceit of the Mensheviks' contention and demonstrated that the Mensheviks were in fact acting in the interests of the BOURGEOIS INTELLIGENTSIA, which was averse to and fearful of proletarian discipline and organization.~~

~~Lenin condemned the Mensheviks' "aristocratic anarchism." He explained that the workers were not afraid of discipline because the high technical development of modern large-scale industry had accustomed workers to discipline in order to work together. The intelligentsia, as a special stratum of modern capitalist society, was another matter. This stratum was characterized by INDIVIDUALISM and an inability to work according to organizational discipline, as well as its general weakness and unsteadiness. The nature of the intelligentsia was inseparably connected to the everyday conditions of its existence and the terms of its income, which in many senses resembled that of a PETTY-BOURGEOIS LIFESTYLE (independent work or work done in a very small collective, etc.).~~

~~Lenin underscored that it was impossible to combine the Party as a vanguard detachment of the working class with the whole class itself. The most conscious and active sons of the working class could become Party members. This vanguard detachment was to preserve its close connection to the masses at all times and not break away from them. Only then would the Party be able to lead the whole class, steadily ELEVATING ever broader strata to the level of consciousness possessed by the vanguard detachment.~~

This rebuff was administered by Lenin in his celebrated book, ONE STEP FORWARD, TWO STEPS BACK, published in May 1904.

The following are the main organizational principles which Lenin expounded in his book, and which afterwards came to form the organizational foundations of the Bolshevik Party.

1) The Marxist Party is a part, a detachment, of the working class. But the working class has many detachments, and hence not every detachment of the working class can be called a party of the working class. The Party differs from other detachments of the working class primarily by the fact that it is not an ordinary detachment, but the VANGUARD *detachment, a* CLASS-CONSCIOUS DETACHMENT, *a* MARXIST *detachment of the working class, armed with a knowledge of the life of society, of the laws of its development and of the laws of the class struggle, and for this reason able to lead the working class and to direct its struggle. The Party must therefore not be confused with the working class, as the part must not be confused with the whole. One cannot demand that every striker be allowed to call himself a member of the Party, for whoever confuses Party and class lowers the level of consciousness of the Party to that of "every striker," destroys the Party as the class-conscious vanguard of the working class. It is not the task of the Party to* LOWER *its level to that of "every striker," but to elevate the masses of the workers, to* ELEVATE *"every striker" to the level of the Party.*[29]

> "We are the party of a class," ~~Lenin wrote in this work ONE STEP FORWARD, TWO STEPS BACK~~ *Lenin wrote,*[30] "and therefore ALMOST THE ENTIRE CLASS (and in times of war, in the period of civil war, the entire class) should act under the leadership of our Party, should adhere to our Party as closely as possible. But it would be Manilovism (smug complacency) and 'KHVOSTISM' (following in the tail) to think that at any time under capitalism the entire class, or almost the entire class, would be able to rise to the level of consciousness and activity of its vanguard, of its Social-Democratic Party. *No sensible Social-Democrat has ever yet doubted that under capitalism even the trade union organizations (which are more primitive and more comprehensible to the undeveloped strata) are unable to embrace the entire, or almost the entire working class. To forget the distinction between the vanguard and the whole of the masses which gravitate towards it, to forget the constant duty of the vanguard to raise ever wider strata to this most advanced level, means merely to deceive oneself, to shut one's eyes to the immensity of our tasks, and to narrow down these tasks.*" (Lenin, COLLECTED WORKS, Russ. ed., Vol. VI, pp. 205–06.)

2) The Party is not only the vanguard, the class-conscious detachment of the working class, but also an ORGANIZED *detachment of the working class, with its own discipline, which is binding on its members. Hence Party members must necessarily be members of some organization of the Party. If the Party were not an* ORGANIZED *detachment of the class, not a* SYSTEM OF ORGANIZATION, *but a mere agglomeration of persons*[31] *who declare themselves to be Party members but do not belong to any Party organization and therefore are* NOT ORGANIZED, *hence not obliged to obey Party decisions, the Party would never have a united will, it could never achieve the united action of its members, and, consequently, it would be unable to direct the struggle of the working class. The Party can*[32] *lead the practical struggle of the working class and direct it towards one aim only if all its members are* ORGANIZED *in one common detachment, welded together by unity of will, unity of action and unity of discipline.*

The objection raised by the Mensheviks that in that case many intellectuals—for example, professors, university and high school students, etc.—would remain outside the ranks of the Party, since they would not want to join any of the organizations of the Party, either because they shrink from Party discipline, or, as Plekhanov said at the Second Congress, because they consider it "beneath their dignity to join some local organization"—this Menshevik objection recoiled on the heads of the Mensheviks themselves; for the Party does not need members who shrink from Party discipline and fear to join the Party organization. Workers did not fear discipline and organization, and they willingly join the organization if they have made up their minds to be Party members. It is the individualistic intellectuals who fear discipline and organization, and they would indeed remain outside the ranks of the Party. But that was all to the good, for the Party would be spared that influx of unstable elements, which had become particularly marked at that time, when the bourgeois democratic revolution was on the upgrade.

> *"When I say," Lenin wrote, "that the Party should be a* SUM *(and not a mere arithmetical sum, but a complex) of* ORGANIZATIONS. . . . *I thereby express clearly and precisely my wish, my demand, that the Party, as the vanguard of the class, should be as* ORGANIZED *as possible, that the Party should admit to its ranks only such elements as* LEND THEMSELVES TO AT LEAST A MINIMUM OF ORGANIZATION. . . ." *(Ibid., p. 203.)*

And further:

> *"Martov's formulation* OSTENSIBLY *defends the interests of the broad strata of the proletariat, but* IN FACT, *it serves the interests of the* BOURGEOIS INTELLECTUALS, *who fight shy of proletarian discipline and organization. No one will undertake to deny that it is* PRECISELY ITS INDIVIDUALISM *and incapacity for discipline and organization that in general distinguish* THE INTELLIGENTSIA AS A SEPARATE STRATUM *of modern capitalist society." (Ibid., p. 212.)*

And again:

> *"The proletariat is not afraid of organization and discipline. . . . The proletariat will do nothing to have the worthy professors and high school students, who do not want to join an organization, recognized as Party members merely because they work under the control of an organization. . . . It is not the proletariat, but* CERTAIN INTELLECTUALS *in our Party who lack* SELF-TRAINING *in the spirit of organization and discipline." (Ibid., p. 307.)*

3) The Party is not merely an organized detachment, but "the HIGHEST OF ALL FORMS OF ORGANIZATION*" of the working class, and it is its mission* TO GUIDE *all the other organizations of the working class. As the highest form of organization, consisting of the finest members of the class, armed with an advanced theory, with knowledge of the laws of the class struggle and with the experience of the revolutionary movement, the Party has every opportunity*[33] *of guiding—and is obliged to guide—*[34] *all the other organizations of the working class.* ~~Summing up the struggle with the Mensheviks over the question of organization, Lenin pointed out that by destroying party organization and discipline, the Mensheviks aspired TO BLUNT the proletariat's weapon of class struggle.~~ *The attempt of the Mensheviks to belittle and depreciate the leading role of the Party tends to weaken all the other organizations of the proletariat which are guided by the Party, and, consequently, to weaken and disarm the proletariat, for* "in its struggle for power the proletariat has no other weapon but organization"~~—this was the way in which Lenin concluded his famous work ONE STEP FORWARD, TWO STEPS BACK~~. (Lenin, SELECTED WORKS, Eng. ed., Vol. II, p. 466.)

4) The Party is an EMBODIMENT OF THE CONNECTION *of the vanguard of the working class* WITH THE WORKING CLASS MILLIONS. *However fine a vanguard the Party may be, and however well it may be organized, it cannot exist and develop without connections with the non-Party masses, and without multiplying and strengthening these connections.*[35] *A party which shuts itself up in its own shell, isolates itself from the masses, and loses, or even relaxes, its connections with its class is bound to lose the confidence and support of the masses, and, consequently, is surely bound to perish. In order to live to the full and to develop, the Party must multiply its connections with the masses*[36] *and win the confidence*[37] *of the millions of its class.*[38]

> *"In order to be a Social-Democratic* PARTY*," Lenin said, "we must win the* SUPPORT *precisely of the* CLASS*." (Lenin,* COLLECTED WORKS*, Russ. ed., Vol. VI, p. 208.)*

5) In order to function properly and to guide the masses systematically, the Party must be organized on the principle of CENTRALISM, *having one set of rules and uniform Party discipline, one leading organ—the Party Congress, and in the intervals between congresses—the Central Committee of the Party; the minority must submit to the majority, the various organizations must submit to the centre, and lower organizations to higher organizations. Failing these conditions, the party of the working class cannot be a real party and cannot carry out its tasks in guiding the class.*

Of course, as under the tsarist autocracy the Party existed illegally, the Party organizations could not in those days be built up on the principle of election from below, and as a consequence, the Party had to be strictly conspiratorial. But Lenin considered that this TEMPORARY *feature in the life of our Party would at once lapse with the elimination of tsardom, when the Party would become open and legal, and the Party organizations would be built up on the principles of democratic elections, of* DEMOCRATIC CENTRALISM.

> *"FORMERLY," Lenin wrote, "our Party was not a formally organized whole, but only the sum of separate groups, and, therefore, no other relations except those of ideological influence were possible between these groups.* NOW *we have become an organized Party, and this implies the establishment of authority, the transformation of the power of ideas into the power of authority, the subordination of lower Party bodies to higher Party bodies." (Ibid., p. 291.)*

Accusing the Mensheviks of organizational nihilism and of aristocratic anarchism which would not submit to the authority of the Party and its discipline, Lenin wrote:

> *"This aristocratic anarchism is particularly characteristic of the Russian nihilist. He thinks of the Party organization as a monstrous 'factory'; he regards the subordination of the part to the whole and of the minority to the majority as 'serfdom' . . . division of labour under the direction of a centre evokes from him a tragi-comical outcry against people being transformed into 'wheels and cogs' (to turn editors into contributors being considered a particularly atrocious species of such transformation); mention of the organizational rules of the Party calls forth a contemptuous grimace and the disdainful remark (intended for the 'formalists') that one could very well dispense[39] with rules altogether." (Lenin,* SELECTED WORKS, *Eng. ed., Vol. II, pp. 442–43.)*

6) In its practical work, if it wants to preserve the UNITY *of its ranks, the Party must impose a* COMMON *proletarian discipline,* EQUALLY *binding on all Party members, both leaders and rank-and-file. Therefore there should be no division within the Party into the "chosen few," on whom discipline is not binding, and the "many," on whom discipline is binding. If this condition is not observed, the integrity of the Party and the unity of its ranks cannot be maintained.*

> *"The complete[40] absence of* SENSIBLE *arguments on the part of Martov and Co. against the editorial board appointed by the congress," Lenin wrote, "is best of all shown by their own catchword: 'We are not serfs!' . . . The mentality of the bourgeois intellectual, who regards himself as one of the 'chosen few' standing above mass organization and mass discipline, is expressed here with remarkable clarity. . . . It seems to the individualism of the intelligentsia . . . that* ALL *proletarian organization and discipline is* SERFDOM.*" (Lenin,* COLLECTED WORKS, *Russ. ed., Vol. VI, p. 282.)*
>
> *And further:*
>
> *"As we proceed with the building of a* REAL *party, the class-conscious worker must learn to distinguish the mentality of the soldier of the proletarian army from the mentality of the bourgeois intellectual who makes a display of anarchist phraseology, he must learn to* DEMAND *that the duties of a Party member be fulfilled not only by the rank-and-filers, but by the 'people at the top' as well." (Lenin,* SELECTED *Works, Eng. ed., Vol. II, pp. 445–46.)*

Summing up his analysis of the differences, and defining the position of the Mensheviks as "opportunism in matters of organization," Lenin considered that one of the gravest sins of Menshevism lay in its underestimation of the importance of party ORGANIZATION *as a weapon of the proletariat in the struggle for its emancipation. The Mensheviks held that the party* ORGANIZATION *of the proletariat was of no great importance for the victory of the revolution. Contrary to the Mensheviks, Lenin held that the* IDEOLOGICAL *unity of the proletariat alone was* NOT ENOUGH *for victory; if victory was to be won, ideological unity would have to be "*CONSOLIDATED*" by the "material unity of* ORGANIZATION*" of the proletariat. Only on this condition, Lenin considered, could the proletariat become an invincible force.*

> *"In its struggle for power," Lenin wrote, "the proletariat has no other weapon but organization. Disunited by the rule of anarchic competition in the bourgeois world, ground down by forced labour for capital, constantly thrust back to the 'lower depths' of utter destitution, savagery and degeneration, the proletariat can become, and inevitably will become, an invincible force only when its ideological unification by the principles of Marxism*

> *is consolidated by the material unity of an organization which will weld millions of toilers into an army of the working class. Neither the decrepit rule of Russian tsardom, nor the senile rule of international capital will be able to withstand this army." (Ibid., p. 466.)*

With these prophetic words Lenin concludes his book.

Such were the fundamental organizational principles set forth by Lenin in his famous book, ONE STEP FORWARD, TWO STEPS BACK.

The importance of this book lies primarily in the fact that it successfully upheld the Party principle against the circle principle, and the Party against the disorganizers; that it smashed the opportunism of the Mensheviks on questions of organization, and laid the organizational foundations of the Bolshevik Party.

But this does not exhaust its significance. Its historic significance lies in the fact that in it Lenin, for the first time in the history of Marxism, elaborated the DOCTRINE OF THE PARTY *as the leading* ORGANIZATION *of the proletariat, as the principal* WEAPON *of the proletariat, without which the struggle for the dictatorship of the proletariat cannot be won.*

The circulation of Lenin's book, ONE STEP FORWARD, TWO STEPS BACK, *among the Party workers led the majority of the local organizations to rally to the side of Lenin.*

But the more closely the organizations rallied around the Bolsheviks, the more malicious became the behaviour of the Menshevik leaders.

In the summer of 1904, ~~as a result of the conciliatory attitude toward them by several members of the Party's Central Committee (Noskov, Krassin)~~ *thanks to Plekhanov's assistance and the treachery of Krassin and Noskov, two demoralized Bolsheviks,* the Mensheviks captured *the majority on* the Central Committee. ~~On the pages of ISKRA, the Mensheviks hounded Lenin and the Bolsheviks. But Lenin was supported by a group of battle-tempered Bolshevik revolutionaries, who were working locally in Russia. Stalin was imprisoned and then banished to Siberia during the Second Congress period. At the beginning of 1904, Comrade Stalin escaped from exile and rallied the Transcaucasian Party organizations around Lenin. Led by Comrade Stalin, the Caucasus Committee demanded the convening of the Third Party Congress. Comrade Stalin exposed the Mensheviks and conciliators and formed Bolshevik committees.~~ *It was obvious that the Mensheviks were working for a split. The loss of* ISKRA *and of the Central Committee put the Bolsheviks in a difficult position. It became necessary for them to organize their own Bolshevik newspaper. It became necessary to make arrangements for a new Party congress, the Third Congress, so as to set up a new Central Committee and to settle accounts with the Mensheviks.*

And this is what the Bolsheviks, headed by Lenin, set to work to do.

The Bolsheviks started a campaign for the summoning of the Third Party Congress. In August 1904, under Lenin's guidance, a conference of twenty-two Bolsheviks was held in Switzerland. The conference adopted an appeal ~~written by Lenin~~ addressed "To the Party." This appeal served the Bolsheviks as a program in their struggle for the summoning of the Third Congress. At three regional conferences of ~~the~~ *Bolshevik* Committees ~~of the Majority~~ (Southern, Caucasian and Northern), a Bureau of Committees of the Majority was elected, which undertook the practical preparations for the ~~new~~ Third Party Congress.

On January 4, 1905, the first issue of the Bolshevik newspaper Vperyod (Forward) appeared~~, which continued the old Iskra line and prepared the working class for revolutionary struggle~~.

Thus two separate groups arose within the Party, the Bolsheviks and the Mensheviks, each with its own central body and its own press.

~~The Bolshevik organizations took shape and became tempered in the struggle for the Leninist line after the Second Congress and in the struggle for the Third Congress. The Bolsheviks emerged victorious and succeeded in convening the Third Congress.~~

Brief Summary

In the period 1901–04, with the growth of the revolutionary working-class movement, the Marxist Social-Democratic organizations in Russia grew and gained strength. In the stubborn struggle over principles, waged against the "Economists," the revolutionary line of Lenin's Iskra gained the victory~~, as did Lenin's plan for organizing the proletarian party~~, and the ideological confusion and "amateurish methods of work" were overcome.

Iskra linked up the scattered Social-Democratic circles and groups and prepared the way for the convocation of the Second Party Congress. At the Second Congress, held in 1903, the Russian Social-Democratic Labour Party was formed, a Party Program and Rules were adopted, and the central leading organs of the Party were set up.

In the struggle waged at the Second Congress for the complete victory of the Iskra trend in the R.S.D.L.P. there emerged ~~factions~~ *two* ~~(~~groups~~)~~—the Bolshevik~~s~~ *group* and the Menshevik~~s~~ *group*.

The chief differences *between the Bolsheviks and the Mensheviks after the Second Congress* centred round ~~the~~ question~~s~~ of organization.

~~The Mensheviks struggled against the formation of the sort of proletarian party that would be able to make the proletariat into the hegemon (leader) of the bourgeois-democratic revolution, and, subsequently, lead it to the Socialist revolution.~~

~~Attempting to interfere with the formation of a militant proletarian party, the Mensheviks did things in such a way as to subordinate the labour movement to the liberal bourgeoisie.~~

~~The Bolsheviks defended Lenin's plan for organizing the proletarian party as a vanguard and organized detachment of the working class, as explained by Lenin in his works What Is To Be Done? and One Step Forward, Two Steps Back.~~

The Mensheviks drew closer to the "Economists" and took their place within the Party. For the time being the opportunism of the Mensheviks revealed itself in questions of organization. The Mensheviks were opposed to a militant revolutionary party of the type advocated by Lenin. They wanted a loose, unorganized, KHVOSTIST party. They worked to split the ranks of the Party. With Plekhanov's help, they seized Iskra and the Central Committee, and used these central organs for their own purposes—to split the Party.

Seeing that the Mensheviks were threatening a split, the Bolsheviks adopted measures to curb the splitters; they mustered the local organizations to back the convocation of a Third Congress, and they started their own newspaper, Vperyod.

Thus,[41] on the eve of the first Russian revolution, *when the Russo-Japanese war had already begun,*[42] the Bolsheviks and the Mensheviks acted as two ~~different political currents in the Russian Social-Democratic Labour Party~~ *separate political groups.*[43]

CHAPTER THREE[1]

The Mensheviks and the Bolsheviks in the Period of the Russo-Japanese War and the First Russian Revolution (1904–1907)

1. Russo-Japanese War. *Further Rise of the Revolutionary Movement in Russia. Strikes in St. Petersburg. Workers' Demonstration before the Winter Palace on January 9, 1905. Demonstration Fired Upon. Outbreak of the Revolution*

At the end of the nineteenth century the imperialist states began an ~~especially~~ intense struggle for mastery of the Pacific and for the partition of China. Tsarist Russia, too, took part in this struggle. In 1900, tsarist troops together with Japanese, German, British~~,~~ *and* French ~~and other~~ troops suppressed with unparalleled cruelty an uprising of the Chinese people *directed against the foreign imperialists. Even before this t*he tsarist government had compelled China to surrender to Russia the Liaotung Peninsula with the fortress of Port Arthur. Russia secured the right to build railways on Chinese territory. A railway was built in Northern Manchuria—the Chinese-Eastern Railway—and Russian troops were stationed there to protect it. Northern Manchuria fell under the military occupation of tsarist Russia. Tsardom was advancing towards Korea. The Russian bourgeoisie was making plans for founding a "Yellow Russia" in Manchuria.

Its annexations in the Far East brought tsardom into conflict with another marauder, Japan, which had rapidly become an imperialist country and was also bent on annexing territories on the Asiatic continent, in the first place at the expense of China. Like tsarist Russia, Japan was striving to lay her hands on Korea and Manchuria. Already at that time Japan dreamed of seizing Sakhalin and the Russian Far East. Great Britain, who feared the growing strength of tsarist Russia in the Far East, secretly sided with Japan. War between Russia and Japan was brewing. The tsarist government was pushed to this war by ~~a part of~~ the *big* bourgeoisie, which was seeking new markets, and by the more reactionary ~~part~~ *sections* of the landlord class.

Without waiting for the tsarist government to declare war, Japan started hostilities herself. She had a good espionage service in Russia and anticipated

ГЛАВА III

МЕНЬШЕВИКИ И БОЛЬШЕВИКИ В ПЕРИОД РУССКО-ЯПОНСКОЙ ВОЙНЫ И ПЕРВОЙ РУССКОЙ РЕВОЛЮЦИИ

(1904—1907 годы)

Русско-японская война.

С конца XIX столетия империалистические государства начали особенно усиленную борьбу за господство на Тихом океане, за раздел Китая. В этой борьбе участвовала и царская Россия. В 1900 году царские войска совместно с японскими, германскими, английскими, французскими и другими с невиданной жестокостью подавили народное восстание в Китае. Царское правительство вынудило Китай передать России Ляодунский полуостров с крепостью Порт-Артур. Россия добилась права строить железные дороги на китайской территории. Была построена железная дорога в Северной Манчжурии—Китайская восточная железная дорога (КВЖД) и введены русские войска для защиты ее. Северная Манчжурия подверглась военной оккупации со стороны царской России. Царизм подбирался к Корее. Русская буржуазия строила планы создания «Желтороссии» в Манчжурии.

В своих захватах на Дальнем Востоке царизм столкнулся с другим хищником—Японией, которая быстро превратилась в империалистическую страну и тоже стремилась к захватам на Азиатском материке, в первую очередь за счет Китая. Япония, так же как и царская Россия, стремилась забрать себе Корею и Манчжурию. Япония уже и тогда мечтала о захвате Сахалина и Дальнего Востока. Англия, которая побаивалась усиления царской России на Дальнем Востоке, втайне была на стороне Японии. Назревала русско-японская война. К этой войне толкала царское правительство часть буржуазии, искавшей новых рынков, и наиболее реакционная часть помещиков.

Не дожидаясь, пока царское правительство объявит войну, Япония первая начала ее. Располагая хорошей разведкой в России, Япония рассчитала, что в этой борьбе будет иметь неподготовленного противника. Не объявляя войны, Япония в январе 1904 года напала на русскую крепость Порт-Артур. Находившемуся в Порт-Артуре русскому флоту причинены были серьезные потери. Так началась русско-японская война. Царское правительство рассчитывало, что война поможет ему укрепить свое политическое положение и остановить революцию, но Война еще более расшатала царизм.

Плохо вооруженная и обученная, руководимая бездарными и продажными генералами, русская армия стала терпеть одно пора-

50

First page of Chapter Three with Stalin's editing from the summer of 1938. RGASPI, f. 558, op. 11, d. 1209, l. 101.

that her foe would be unprepared for the struggle. In January 1904, without declaring war, Japan *suddenly* attacked the Russian fortress of Port Arthur and *inflicted* heavy losses ~~were inflicted~~ on the Russian fleet lying in the harbour.

That is how the Russo-Japanese War began.

The tsarist government reckoned that the war would help to strengthen its political position and to check the revolution. But ~~the opposite happened~~ *it miscalculated*. The tsarist regime was shaken more than ever by the war.

Poorly armed and trained, and commanded by incompetent and corrupt generals, the Russian army suffered defeat after defeat. ~~The soldier masses heroically fought and died during the fighting.~~

Capitalists, government officials and generals grew rich on the war. Peculation was rampant. The troops were ~~very~~ poorly supplied. When the army was short of ammunition, it would receive, as if in derision, carloads of icons. The soldiers said bitterly: "The Japanese are giving it to us with shells; we're to give it to them with icons." Special trains, instead of being used to evacuate the wounded, were loaded with property looted by the tsarist generals.

The Japanese besieged and subsequently captured Port Arthur. After inflicting a number of defeats on the tsarist army, they finally routed it near Mukden. In this battle the tsarist army of 300,000 men lost about 120,000 men, killed, wounded or taken prisoner. This was followed by the utter defeat and destruction in the Straits of Tsushima of the tsarist fleet dispatched from the Baltic to relieve Port Arthur. *The defeat at* Tsushima was disastrous: of the twenty warships dispatched by ~~Tsarist Russia~~ *the tsar*, thirteen were sunk or destroyed and four captured ~~by the Japanese~~. Tsarist Russia had definitely lost the war.

The tsarist government was compelled to conclude an ignominious peace with Japan. Japan seized Korea and deprived Russia of Port Arthur and of half the Island of Sakhalin.

The people had not wanted the war and realized how harmful it would be for the country. They paid heavily for the backwardness of tsarist Russia. ~~This predatory war cost the people 110,000 dead and crippled and 150,000 wounded.~~

The Bolsheviks and the Mensheviks adopted different attitudes towards the war.

The Mensheviks, ~~like~~ *including* Trotsky, were sinking to a position of defending the "fatherland" *of the tsar*, the landlords and the capitalists.

The Bolsheviks, headed by Lenin, ~~already then~~ *on the other hand*, held that the defeat of the tsarist government in this predatory war would *be useful, as it would* weaken tsardom and strengthen the revolution~~ary movement~~.

The defeats of the tsarist armies opened the eyes of the masses to the rottenness of tsardom. Their hatred for the tsarist regime grew daily more intense. The fall of Port Arthur meant the beginning of the fall of the autocracy, Lenin wrote.

The tsar wanted to use the war to stifle the revolution. He achieved the very opposite. The Russo-Japanese War hastened the outbreak of the revolution.

~~2. January 9, 1905—Beginning of the Revolution~~

~~As we have seen, there were grounds to spare for revolution.~~ In tsarist Russia the capitalist yoke was aggravated by the yoke of tsardom. The workers not only suffered from capitalist exploitation, from inhuman toil, but, in common with the whole people, suffered from a lack of all rights. The politically advanced workers therefore strove to lead the revolutionary movement of all the democratic elements in town and country against tsardom. The peasants were in dire need owing to lack of land and the numerous survivals of serfdom, and lived in a state of bondage to the landlords and kulaks. The nations inhabiting tsarist Russia groaned beneath a double yoke—that of their own landlords and capitalists and that of the Russian landlords and capitalists. The *economic* crisis of 1900–03 had aggravated the hardships of the toiling masses; the war intensified them still further. The war defeats added fuel to the hatred of the masses for tsardom. The patience of the people was coming to an end.

As we see, there were grounds enough and to spare for revolution.

In December 1904 a huge and well-organized strike of workers took place in Baku, led by ~~Comrade Stalin~~ *the Baku Committee of the Bolsheviks.* The strike ended in a victory for the workers and a collective agreement was concluded ~~with~~ *between* the *oilfield workers and* owners, the first of its kind in the history of the working-class movement in Russia.

The Baku strike marked the beginning of a revolutionary rise in Transcaucasia *and in various parts of Russia.*

> "The Baku strike was the signal for the glorious actions in January and February all over Russia." (STALIN.)

This strike was like a clap of thunder heralding a great revolutionary storm.

The revolutionary storm broke with the events of January 9 (22, New Style), 1905, *in St. Petersburg.*

On January 3, 1905, a strike began at the biggest of the St. Petersburg plants, the Putilov (now the Kirov) Works. The strike was caused by the dismissal of four workers. It grew rapidly and was joined by other St. Petersburg mills and factories. The strike became general. The movement grew formidable. The tsarist government decided to crush it while it was still in its earliest phase.

In 1904, prior to the Putilov strike, the police had used the services of an agent-provocateur, a priest by the name of Gapon, to form an organization of the workers known as the Assembly of Russian Factory Workers. This organization had its branches in all the districts of St. Petersburg. When the strike broke out the priest Gapon at the meetings of his society put forward a treacherous plan: all the workers were to gather on January 9 and, carrying church banners and portraits of the tsar, to march in peaceful procession to the Winter Palace and present a petition to the tsar stating their needs. The tsar would appear before the people, listen to them and satisfy their demands. Gapon undertook to assist the tsarist Okhrana by providing a pretext for firing on the workers and drowning the working-class movement in blood. But this police plot recoiled on the head of the tsarist government.

The petition was discussed at workers' meetings where amendments were made. Bolsheviks spoke at these meetings *without openly announcing themselves as such*. Under their influence, the petition was supplemented by demands for freedom of the press, freedom of speech, freedom of association for the workers, the convocation of a Constituent Assembly for the purpose of changing the political system of Russia, equality of all before the law, separation of church from the state, termination of the war, an 8-hour working day, *and* the handing over of the land to the peasants ~~and an array of other demands~~. ~~These demands corresponded to those found in the R.S.D.L.P. program.~~

At these meetings the Bolsheviks explained to the workers that liberty could not be obtained by petitions to the tsar, but ~~liberty~~ would have to be won by force of arms. The Bolsheviks warned the workers that they would be ~~shot down~~ *fired upon*. But they were unable to prevent the procession to the Winter Palace. A large part of the workers still believed that the tsar would help them. The movement had taken a strong hold on the masses.

The petition of the St. Petersburg workers ~~was written to say~~ *stated*:

> "We, the workingmen of St. Petersburg, our wives, our children and our helpless old parents, have come to Thee, our Sovereign, to seek truth and protection. We are poverty-stricken, we are oppressed, we are burdened with unendurable toil; we suffer humiliation and are not treated like human beings. . . . We have suffered in patience, but we are being driven deeper and deeper into the slough of poverty, lack of rights and ignorance; we are being strangled by despotism and tyranny. . . . Our patience is exhausted. The dreaded moment has arrived when we would rather die than bear these intolerable sufferings any longer. . . ."

Early in the morning of January 9, 1905, the workers marched to the Winter Palace where the tsar *was* then ~~lived~~ *residing*. They came with their whole families—wives, children and old folk—carrying portraits of the tsar and church banners. They chanted hymns as they marched. They were unarmed. Over 140,000 persons gathered in the streets.

They met with a hostile reception from Nicholas ~~the Bloody~~ *II. He* gave orders to fire upon the unarmed workers. That day over a thousand workers were killed and more than two thousand wounded by the tsar's troops. The streets of St. Petersburg ran with workers' blood.

The Bolsheviks had marched with the workers. Many of them were ~~shot down~~ *killed* or arrested. There, in the streets running with workers' blood, the Bolsheviks explained to the workers who it was that bore the guilt for this heinous crime *and how he was to be fought.*

January 9 came to be known as "Bloody Sunday." On that day the workers received a bloody lesson. It was their faith in the tsar that was riddled by bullets on that day. They came to realize that they could win their rights only by struggle. That evening barricades ~~began to go up~~ *were already being erected* in the working-class districts. ~~The Bolsheviks took charge of the workers.~~ *The workers said: "The tsar gave it to us; we'll now give it to him!"*

The fearful news of the tsar's bloody crime spread far and wide. The whole working class, the whole country was stirred by indignation and abhorrence. There was not a town where the workers did not strike in protest against the tsar's villainous act and did not put forward political demands. The workers now ~~went out onto~~ *emerged into* the streets with the slogan, "Down with autocracy!" In January the number of strikers reached the immense figure of 440,000. More workers came out on strike in one month than during the whole preceding decade. The working-class movement rose to an unprecedented height.

~~Thus~~ Revolution in Russia had begun.

~~2.3. From January 9 to the General Strike.~~ *Workers' Political Strikes and Demonstrations. Growth of the Revolutionary Movement among the Peasants. Revolt on the Battleship "Potemkin"*

After January 9 ~~1905~~ the revolutionary struggle of the workers ~~did not die down~~ *grew more acute and assumed a political character. The workers began to pass from economic strikes and sympathy strikes to political strikes, to demonstrations, and in places to armed resistance to the tsarist troops.* Particularly stubborn and well organized were the strikes in the big cities such as St. Petersburg, Moscow, Warsaw, Riga and Baku, where large numbers of workers were concentrated. The metal workers marched in the front ranks of the fighting proletariat. By their strikes, the vanguard of the workers stirred up the less class-conscious sections and roused the whole working class to the struggle. The influence of the ~~R.S.D.L.P.~~ *Social-Democrats* grew rapidly.

The May Day demonstrations in a number of towns were marked by clashes with police and troops. In Warsaw, the demonstration was fired upon and several hundred persons were killed or wounded. At the call of the Polish Social-

Democrats the workers replied to the shooting in Warsaw by a general protest strike. Strikes and demonstrations did not cease throughout the month of May. In that month over 200,000 workers went on strike *throughout Russia.* General strikes broke out in Baku, Lodz and Ivanovo-Voznesensk. More and more frequently the strikers and demonstrators clashed with the tsarist troops. Such clashes took place in a number of cities—Odessa, Warsaw, Riga, Lodz and others.

Particularly acute was the struggle in Lodz, a large Polish industrial centre. The workers erected scores of barricades in the streets of Lodz and for three days (June 22–24, 1905) battled in the streets against the tsarist troops. Here armed ~~uprising~~ *action* merged with a general strike. Lenin regarded these battles as the first armed action of the workers in Russia.

The outstanding strike that summer was that of the workers of Ivanovo-Voznesensk. It lasted for about two and a half months, from the end of May to the beginning of August 1905. About 70,000 workers, among them many women, took part in the strike. It was led by the Bolshevik Northern Committee. Thousands of workers gathered almost daily outside the city on the banks of the River Talka. At these meetings they discussed their needs. The workers' meetings were addressed by Bolsheviks. ~~The workers listened to the revolutionary speeches of the orators—Frunze and others—with enormous interest.~~ In order to crush the strike, the tsarist authorities ordered the troops to disperse the workers and to fire upon them. Several scores of workers were killed and several hundred wounded. A state of emergency was proclaimed in the city. But the workers remained firm and would not return to work. They and their families starved, but would not surrender. It was only extreme exhaustion that in the end compelled them to return to work. The strike steeled the workers. It was an example of the courage, staunchness, endurance and solidarity of the working class. It was a real political education for the workers of Ivanovo-Voznesensk.

During the strike the workers of Ivanovo-Voznesensk ~~put forward~~ *set up* a Council of Representative*s* ~~Deputies~~, which was actually one of the first Soviets of Workers' Deputies in Russia.

The workers' *political* strikes stirred up the whole country.

Following the town, the countryside began to rise. In the spring, peasant unrest broke out. The peasants marched in great crowds against the landlords, raided their estates, sugar refineries and distilleries, and set fire to their palaces and manors. In a number of places the peasants seized the land, resorted to wholesale cutting down of forests, and demanded that the landed estates be turned over to the people. They seized the landlords' stores of grain and other products and divided them among the starving. The landlords fled in panic to the towns. The tsarist government ~~sent out~~ *dispatched* soldiers and Cossacks to crush the peasants' revolts. The troops fired on the peasants, arrested the "ringleaders" and flogged and tortured them. But the peasants would not cease their struggle.

The peasant movement spread ever wider in the central parts of Russia, ~~and~~ the Volga region*, and in Transcaucasia, especially in Georgia*. ~~But the peasant rebellions developed even further in the national regions. In Georgia, especially in Guri, almost all of the peasantry rose up. The peasants began to seize the landed estates. They ceased to fulfill their obligations to their landlords and obey the tsarist authorities. In the villages, peasant committees appeared that took charge of everything. In Latvia and Esthonia, the landless peasants rebelled. In the Ukraine and Byelorussia, the peasant struggle for the land also grew.~~

The ~~Social-Democratic Bolsheviks~~ *Social-Democrats* penetrated *deeper* into the countryside. The Central Committee *of the Party* issued an appeal to the peasants entitled: "To You, Peasants, We Address Our Word!" ~~as well as other leaflets.~~ The Social-Democratic committees in the Tver, Saratov, Poltava, Chernigov, Ekaterinoslav, *Tiflis* and many other provinces issued appeals to the peasants. In the villages, the Social-Democrats would arrange meetings, organize circles among the peasants, and set up peasant committees. In the summer of 1905 strikes of agricultural labourers ~~and poor peasants~~, organized by Social-Democrats, occurred in many places.

But this was only the beginning of the peasant struggle. The peasant movement affected only 85 uyezds (districts), or roughly one-seventh of the total number of uyezds in the European part of tsarist Russia.

~~The emancipation movement developed among the oppressed nationalities as well—the Poles, the peoples of Transcaucasia, the Ukrainians, the Tatars and others.~~

The movement of the workers and peasants and the *series of* reverses *suffered by the Russian troops* in the Russo-Japanese War had its influence on the armed forces. This bulwark of tsardom began to totter.

In June 1905 a revolt broke out on the POTEMKIN, a battleship of the Black Sea Fleet. The battleship was at that time stationed near Odessa, where a general strike of the workers was in progress. The insurgent sailors wreaked vengeance on their more detested ~~command staff~~ *officers* and brought the vessel to Odessa. The battleship POTEMKIN had gone over to the side of the revolution.

Lenin attributed immense importance to this revolt. He considered it necessary for the Bolsheviks to assume the leadership of this movement and to link it up with the movement of the workers, peasants and the local garrisons~~, especially along the Black Sea coast~~.

The tsar dispatched several warships against the POTEMKIN, but the sailors of these vessels refused to fire on their insurgent comrades. For several days the red ensign of revolution waved from the mast of the battleship POTEMKIN. But at that time, in 1905, the Bolshevik Party was not the only party leading the movement, as was the case later, in 1917. There were quite a number of Mensheviks, Socialist-Revolutionaries and Anarchists on board the POTEMKIN. Consequently, although individual Social-Democrats took part in the revolt, it lacked proper and sufficiently experienced leadership. At decisive moments part of the sailors wavered. The other vessels of the Black Sea Fleet did not join the revolt of the POTEMKIN. Having run short of coal and provisions, the revolutionary battleship was compelled to make for the Rumanian shore and there surrender to the authorities.

The ~~heroic~~ revolt of the sailors on the battleship POTEMKIN ended in defeat. The sailors who subsequently fell into the hands of the tsarist government were committed for trial. Some were executed and others condemned to exile and penal servitude. But the revolt in itself was an event of the utmost importance. The POTEMKIN revolt was the first instance of mass revolutionary action in the army and navy, the first occasion on which a large unit of the armed forces of the tsar sided with the revolution. This revolt made the idea of the army and navy joining forces with the working class, *the people,* more comprehensible to and nearer to the heart of the workers and peasants, and especially of the soldiers and sailors themselves ~~during the days of the rebellion~~.

~~Attempts by the masses to deliver an armed rebuff to the tsar's troops became more and more frequent. In an array of places actual street fighting began between the people and the troops—battles at the barricades. The fighting turned into an uprising. The workers demonstrated ideal forms of heroism and revolutionary enthusiasm.~~

The workers' recourse to mass political strikes and demonstrations, the growth of the peasant movement, the armed clashes between the people and the police and troops, and, finally, the revolt in the Black Sea Fleet, all went to show that conditions were ripening for an armed uprising of the people. ~~The position of the bourgeoisie was different. The liberals started to appeal more and more frequently to the tsar with letters and draft proposals outlining necessary reforms. They were forced to embrace this cause by the revolution and their fears in the face of it.~~ *This stirred the liberal bourgeoisie into action. Fearing the revolution, and at the same time frightening the tsar with the spectre of revolution, it sought to come to terms with the tsar against the revolution; it demanded slight reforms "for the people" so as to "pacify" the people, to split the forces of the revolution and thus avert the "horrors of revolution."* ~~In their letters to the tsar, the bourgeoisie defended their own bourgeois class interests rather than the interests of the people. Thus while they were deciding at a February 1905 congress of Zemstvo officials in Moscow to give up some of their land for compensation,~~

~~some liberal landlords said out-loud:~~ "Better part with some of our land than part with our heads," *said the liberal landlords. The liberal bourgeoisie was preparing to share power with the tsar.* ~~The liberal bourgeois party—the Constitutional Democratic Party—issued its demands: "compensation for the land at a just rate." Of course, this was the "justice" of the owners, the landlords. The Constitutional Democrats' program proposed a deal between the liberals and tsardom: there would be no republic or returning the land to the peasants, but there would be an upper house of parliament, where the honorable landlords, capitalists, bishops and major tsarist officials would preside.~~ "The proletariat is fighting; the bourgeoisie is stealing towards power,"~~—thus~~ Lenin wrote *in those days* in reference to the tactics of the working class and the tactics of the liberal bourgeoisie.

The tsarist government ~~attempted to take care of~~ *continued to suppress* the ~~developing revolutionary movement~~ *workers and peasants* with ferocious brutality. *But it could not help seeing that it would never cope with the revolution by repressive measures alone. Therefore, without abandoning measures of repression, it resorted to a policy of manoeuvring.* ~~At that time, tsardom attempted to distract the masses from revolution by enflaming national animosities. Jewish pogroms were organized by the police in an array of cities and Armenian-Tatar massacres were provoked in Baku.~~ *On the one hand, with the help of its agents-provocateurs, it incited the peoples of Russia against each other, engineering Jewish pogroms and mutual massacres of Armenians and Tatars.* ~~Attempting to deceive the masses, the tsar promised to convene a Duma. This Duma (known as the Bulygin Duma after the person who designed it, the tsarist minister Bulygin) was not granted any legislative powers and was supposed to be just a consultative assembly for the landlords and bourgeoisie under the tsar.~~ *On the other hand, it promised to convene a "representative institution" in the shape of a ZEMSKY SOBOR or a State Duma, and instructed the Minister Bulygin to draw up a project for such a Duma, stipulating, however, that it was to have no legislative powers. All these measures were adopted in order to split the forces of revolution and to sever from it the moderate sections of the people.*

~~The Bolsheviks spoke out against the tsar's efforts to deceive the masses. They advanced the slogans: "Down with the consultative Duma!" "Boycott the Duma!" and "Down with the tsarist government!" Millions of people followed the Bolsheviks' call to boycott the Duma. And the Bulygin Duma was never convened. The revolutionary vortex swept it away.~~

The Bolsheviks declared a boycott of the Bulygin Duma with the aim of frustrating this travesty of popular representation.[2]

The Mensheviks, on the other hand, decided not to sabotage the Duma and considered it necessary to take part in it.

~~3.4. Two Tactics in the Bourgeois-Democratic Revolution—Those of the Bolsheviks and Mensheviks~~ *Tactical Differences between Bolsheviks and Mensheviks. Third Party Congress. Lenin's* TWO TACTICS OF SOCIAL-DEMOCRACY IN THE DEMOCRATIC REVOLUTION. *Tactical Foundations of the Marxist Party*

~~When the revolution began in Russia, Lenin was in emigration in Switzerland. At the first news of the January 9 events, the Bolsheviks personified by Lenin judged these events to mark the beginning of the revolution.~~

~~In his letters and articles, Lenin pointed out that the nascent revolution conferred great responsibility upon the Social-Democratic Party. It was necessary to organize their forces and agree on the forms and means of struggle. And if before the revolution Lenin demanded the convention of the Third Party Congress, then all the more insistently did he advance this demand now. The demand for the quickest possible convention of the congress was supported by the overwhelming majority of the party organizations in Russia.~~

The revolution had set in motion all classes of society. The turn in the political life of the country caused by the revolution dislodged them from their old wonted positions and compelled them to regroup themselves in conformity with the new situation. Each class and each party endeavoured to work out its tactics, its line of conduct, its attitude towards other classes, and its attitude towards the government. Even the tsarist government found itself compelled to devise new and unaccustomed tactics, as instanced by the promise to convene a "representative institution"—the Bulygin Duma.

The Social-Democratic Party, too, had to work out its tactics. This was dictated by the growing tide of the revolution. It was dictated by the practical questions that faced the proletariat and brooked no delay: organization of armed uprising, overthrow of the tsarist government, creation of a provisional revolutionary government, participation of the Social-Democrats in this government, attitude towards the peasantry and towards the liberal bourgeoisie, etc. The Social-Democrats had to work out for themselves carefully considered and uniform Marxist tactics.

But owing to the opportunism of the Mensheviks and their splitting activities, the Russian Social-Democratic Party was at that time divided into two groups. The split could not yet be considered complete, and FORMALLY *the two groups were not yet two separate parties; but* IN REALITY *they very much resembled two separate parties, each with its own leading centre and its own press.*

What helped to widen the split was the fact that to their old differences with the majority of the Party over ORGANIZATIONAL *questions the Mensheviks added new differences, differences over* TACTICAL *questions.*

The absence of a united party resulted in the absence of uniform party tactics.

A way out of the situation may have been found by immediately summoning another congress, the Third Congress of the Party, establishing common tactics and binding the minority to carry out in good faith the decisions of the congress, the decisions of the majority. This was what the Bolsheviks proposed to the Mensheviks. But the Mensheviks would not hear of summoning the Third Congress. Considering it a crime to leave the Party any longer without tactics endorsed by the Party and binding upon all Party members, the Bolsheviks decided to take the initiative of convening the Third Congress into their own hands.

All the Party organizations, both Bolshevik and Menshevik, were invited to the congress. But the Mensheviks refused to take part in the Third Congress and decided to hold one of their own. As the number of delegates at their congress proved to be small, they called it a conference, but actually it was a congress, a Menshevik party congress, whose decisions were considered binding on all Mensheviks.

The Third Congress of the ~~R.S.D.L.P.~~ *Russian Social-Democratic Party* met in London in April 1905. It was attended by 24 delegates representing 20 Bolshevik ~~Party~~ Committees. All the larges~~t committees in Russia~~ *organizations of the Party* were represented~~: St. Petersburg, the Urals, Odessa, Saratov, Tula, Tver, Nizhni Novgorod, Nikolayevsk, the north-west region and the Caucasus Union. This was the first purely Bolshevik congress. The Mensheviks refused to attend the Third Congress~~.

The congress condemned the Mensheviks as "a section that had split away from the Party" and passed on to the business on hand, the working out of the tactics of the Party.

At the same time that this congress was held ~~in London~~, the Mensheviks ~~convened~~ *held* their ~~Menshevik~~ conference in Geneva.

"Two congresses—two parties," was the way Lenin summed up the situation. ~~But the split with the Mensheviks was still not allowed to result in a complete and total dissolution of the formal alliance with them at the Third Party Congress. This happened later, at the Prague Conference (1912). The Third Congress still considered it to be possible to maintain a formal alliance with the Mensheviks, in order to expose the conciliators' policy within the framework of the unified party and strip away the portion of the workers who still remained on the Mensheviks' side.~~

Both the congress and the conference virtually discussed the same tactical questions, but the decisions they arrived at were diametrically opposite. The two sets of resolutions adopted by the congress and the conference respectively revealed the whole depth of the tactical difference between the Third Party Congress and the Menshevik conference, between the Bolsheviks and the Mensheviks.

Here are the main points of these differences.

TACTICAL LINE OF THE THIRD PARTY CONGRESS. The congress held that despite the bourgeois-democratic character of the revolution in progress, despite the fact that it could not at the given moment go beyond the limits of what was possible within the framework of capitalism, it was primarily the proletariat that was interested in its complete victory, for the victory of this revolution would enable the proletariat to organize itself, to grow politically, to acquire experience and competence in political leadership of the toiling masses, and to proceed from the bourgeois revolution to the Socialist revolution.

Tactics of the proletariat designed to achieve the complete victory of the bourgeois-democratic revolution could find support only in the peasantry, for the latter could not settle scores with the landlords and obtain possession of their lands without the complete victory of the revolution. The peasantry was therefore the natural ally of the proletariat.

The liberal bourgeoisie was not interested in the complete victory of this revolution, for it needed the tsarist regime as a whip against the workers and peasants, whom it feared more than anything else, and it would strive to preserve the tsarist regime, only somewhat restricting its powers. The liberal bourgeoisie would therefore attempt to end matters by coming to terms with the tsar on the basis of a constitutional monarchy.

The revolution would win only if headed by the proletariat; if the proletariat, as the leader of the revolution, secured an alliance with the peasantry; if the liberal bourgeoisie were isolated; if the Social-Democratic Party took an active part in the organization of the uprising of the people against tsardom; if, as the result of a successful uprising, a provisional revolutionary government were set up that would be capable of destroying the counter-revolution root and branch and convening a Constituent Assembly representing the whole people; and if the Social-Democratic Party did not refuse, the circumstances being favourable, to take part in the provisional revolutionary government in order to carry the revolution to its conclusion.

Tactical line of the Menshevik conference. Inasmuch as the revolution was a bourgeois revolution, only the liberal bourgeoisie could be its leader. The proletariat should not establish close relations with the peasantry, but with the liberal bourgeoisie. The chief thing was not to frighten off the liberal bourgeoisie by a display of revolutionary spirit and not to give it a pretext to recoil from the revolution, for if it were to recoil from the revolution, the revolution would be weakened.

It was possible that the uprising would prove victorious; but after the triumph of the uprising the Social-Democratic Party should step aside so as not to frighten away the liberal bourgeoisie. It was possible that as a result of the uprising a provisional revolutionary government would be set up; but the Social-Democratic Party should under no circumstances take part in it, because this government would not be Socialist in character, and because—and this was the chief thing—by its participation in this government and by its revolutionary spirit, the Social-

Democratic Party might frighten off the liberal bourgeoisie and thus undermine the revolution.

It would be better for the prospects of the revolution if some sort of representative institution were convened, of the nature of a Zemsky Sobor *or a State Duma, which could be subjected to the pressure of the working class from without so as to transform it into a Constituent Assembly or impel it to convene a Constituent Assembly.*

The proletariat had its own specific, purely wage-worker interests, and it should attend to these interests only and not try to become the leader of the bourgeois revolution, which, being a general political revolution, concerned all classes and not the proletariat alone.

Such, in brief, were the two tactics of the two groups of the Russian Social-Democratic Labour Party.

~~We have seen how different the views of the Mensheviks and Bolsheviks were regarding the organization of the Party. The Mensheviks attempted to interfere with the creation of a militant proletarian party. The Mensheviks wanted to strip the working class of its weapon—the party organization—on the eve of the approaching Revolution of 1905. The Bolsheviks defended the Leninist plan of organizing a militant, centralized party as the vanguard detachment of the working class.~~

~~When the Revolution of 1905 began, the disagreements and principled struggle between the Mensheviks and Bolsheviks heated up with new strength. These were disagreements regarding Social-Democracy's tactics in the bourgeois-democratic revolution.~~

~~Tactics were what the Party called its political behavior—its character, direction and means of political activity. Tactical decisions and resolutions were made by the Party congresses and conferences in order to precisely determine the Party's political conduct in light of new tasks or political circumstances. Such a new set of political circumstances was created by the start of the Russian Revolution of 1905.~~

~~In his remarkable work Two Tactics of Social-Democracy in the Democratic Revolution, Lenin showed all the fundamental differences between how the Mensheviks and Bolsheviks viewed the Revolution of 1905 and the role of the proletariat, bourgeoisie and peasantry therein.~~

In his historic book, Two Tactics of Social-Democracy in the Democratic Revolution, *Lenin gave a classical criticism of the tactics of the Mensheviks and a brilliant substantiation of the Bolshevik tactics.*

This book appeared in July 1905, that is, two months after the Third Party Congress. One might assume from its title that Lenin dealt in it only with tactical questions relating to the period of the bourgeois-democratic revolution and had only the Russian Mensheviks in mind. But as a matter of fact when he criticized the tactics of the Mensheviks he at the same time exposed the tactics of international opportunism; and when he substantiated the Marxist tactics in the period of the bourgeois revolution and drew the distinction between the bourgeois revolution and the Socialist revolution, he at the same time formulated the fundamental principles of the Marxist tactics in the period of transition from the bourgeois revolution to the Socialist revolution.

The fundamental tactical principles expounded by Lenin in his pamphlet, Two Tactics of Social-Democracy in the Democratic Revolution, *were as follows:*

1) The main tactical principle, one that runs through Lenin's whole book, is that the proletariat can and must be the leader *of the bourgeois democratic revolution, the* guiding force *of the bourgeois-democratic revolution in Russia.*

Lenin admitted the bourgeois character of this revolution, for, as he said, "it is incapable of directly *overstepping the bounds of a mere democratic revolution." However, he held that it was not a revolution of the upper strata, but a people's revolution, one that would set in motion the whole people, the whole working class, the whole peasantry. Hence the attempts of the Mensheviks to belittle the significance of the bourgeois revolution for the proletariat, to depreciate the role of the proletariat in it, and to keep the proletariat away from it were in Lenin's opinion a betrayal of the interests of the proletariat.*

> *"Marxism," Lenin said, "teaches the proletarian not to keep aloof from the bourgeois revolution, not to be indifferent to it, not to allow the leadership of the revolution to be assumed by the bourgeoisie, but, on the contrary, to take a most energetic part in it, to fight most resolutely for consistent proletarian democracy, for carrying the revolution to its conclusion." (Lenin,* Selected Works, *Vol. III, p. 77.)*
>
> *"We must not forget," Lenin says further, "that there is not, nor can there be, at the present time, any other means of bringing Socialism nearer, than complete political liberty, than a democratic republic." (Ibid., p. 122.)*

Lenin foresaw ~~the possibility of a two-way~~ *two possible outcomes of the* revolution:

a) ~~First Outcome~~: *Either it would end in a* decisive victory over tsardom, *in* the overthrow of tsardom ~~by means of a successful armed uprising and the establishment of a provisional revolutionary government. This government would be a revolutionary democratic dictatorship of the proletariat and peasantry. Its tasks would be the establishment of a democratic republic, the confiscation of the landed estates for the peasantry, the implementation of the 8-hour working day for the workers and the merciless struggle with the counter-revolution~~ *and the establishment of a democratic republic*;

b) ~~Second Outcome:~~ *Or, i*f the forces ~~and organization of the workers and peasants~~ were inadequate ~~for an armed overthrow of tsardom and revolution~~, *it might end in* a ~~pathetic~~ deal between *the tsar and* the ~~liberal~~ bourgeoisie ~~and tsardom~~ *at the expense of the people,* ~~and the introduction of a~~ *in some sort of* curtailed constitution, ~~which would not grant political rights to the people~~ *or, most likely, in some caricature of a constitution.*

~~The Bolsheviks said that for a decisive victory of the revolution over tsardom, it was necessary that the proletariat take command of the popular revolution.~~

The proletariat was ~~vitally~~ interested in the ~~completion of the democratic revolution, the establishment of a democratic republic, the winning of political rights and liberties and the 8-hour working day~~ *better outcome of the two, that is, in a decisive victory over tsardom.* ~~This would have eased the proletariat's subsequent struggle for Socialism.~~ *But such an outcome was possible only if the proletariat succeeded in becoming the leader and guide of the revolution.*

~~The proletariat was able to count on the support of the peasantry, which was also vitally interested in the completion of the democratic revolution, the confiscation of the landed estates, and the establishment of a democratic republic.~~

~~The Bolsheviks, both during the Revolution of 1905 and after its defeat, treated the peasant struggle for land with the greatest significance and looked upon the peasantry as a major revolutionary force.~~

> ~~"10,000,000 peasant households have 73,000,000 dessiatins of land. 28,000 noble and dirty-faced landlords have 63,000,000 dessiatins. This is the basic backdrop against which the peasantry's struggle for land is developing," wrote Lenin in the book The Agrarian Program of Social-Democracy in the First Russian Revolution (Lenin, Collected Works, Russ. ed., Vol. XI, p. 337).~~

~~Therefore, the Bolsheviks advanced as their first priority the creation of an alliance of workers and peasants for the overthrow of tsardom. The Bolsheviks aimed to instill revolutionary consciousness into the spontaneous, disjointed peasant movement. The Bolsheviks did not avert their eyes from the fact that "naive monarchism" was still strong among the peasantry—that is, the belief in the "tsar-little father." Such a belief had even been held by a part of the St. Petersburg workers before January 9, 1905. The Bolsheviks introduced to the peasant masses the slogan calling for the overthrow of the tsar, the establishment of a democratic republic and the creation of a revolutionary worker-peasant government. In the decisions of the Third Party Congress, the Bolsheviks said that the peasants must immediately create revolutionary committees on the local level and seize the landed estates without compensation.~~

~~The Bolsheviks explained the traitorous conduct of the liberal bourgeoisie (the Constitutional Democrats) to the workers and peasants. The Constitutional Democrats attempted to disrupt the development of the revolution. The Constitutional Democrats assumed for themselves the false name "The Party of Popular Liberty," but in fact struggled against the people's winning of political rights. The Constitutional Democrats were for the preservation of the tsarist monarchy and against a democratic republic. They aimed to conclude a sweetheart deal with tsardom and secure a curtailed constitution, according to which tsardom would concede a part of its powers to the bourgeoisie and liberal landlords.~~

~~The Constitutional Democrats represented the class interests of the bourgeoisie and liberal landlords. And the Russian bourgeoisie had no interest in the overthrow of tsardom and the establishment of a democratic republic. On the contrary, it was interested in the preservation of the tsarist autocracy which assisted it in its exploitation of the workers by putting down the workers' strikes with armed force. The Russian bourgeoisie was dependent on the tsarist government in a materialist sense, due to its receipt of lucrative state orders. The Russian bourgeoisie feared the rising revolutionary power of the proletariat and aimed for only a minor restriction of the tsarist autocracy. The liberal landlords feared that in the case of a decisive victory of the revolution, the peasantry would take its land away without compensation.~~

~~This is why the liberal bourgeoisie was not able to move the revolution forward and be the chief (the hegemon) of the democratic revolution. Only the proletariat could be the chief of a truly popular revolution against tsardom and the survivals of serfdom. This is how the Bolsheviks posed the question that produced all their tactics during the Revolution of 1905 and all the decisions of the Third Party Congress.~~

~~The Mensheviks claimed that the chief (the hegemon) of the nascent revolution ought to be the liberal bourgeoisie. The Mensheviks said that the main task of the proletariat in the revolution was to not scare the bourgeoisie with its demands, so that the bourgeoisie would not be startled by the revolution. In order to "not frighten" the bourgeoisie, the Mensheviks refused, for instance, to advance the revolutionary slogan calling for a democratic republic. This refusal to advance the slogan for a democratic republic at this decisive moment at the beginning of the revolution revealed that the Mensheviks were lined up behind the Constitutional Democrats, who were against a democratic republic and for a "constitutional" monarchy. The Mensheviks did not want the working class to play any sort of independent role in the revolution and only to support the liberal bourgeoisie, following them about like a tail. The Mensheviks were against completing the democratic revolution.~~

~~The Revolution of 1905 was actually a bourgeois, or more precisely a bourgeois-democratic revolution. This means that its first task could not be the overthrow of the capitalist system. The establishment of a democratic republic, the confiscation of the landed estates and the introduction of the 8-hour working day did not mean the elimination of the private ownership of the means of production, the mills and the factories, and so therefore did not leave the bounds of the capitalist system. But completion of the democratic revolution would have eased the conditions of all the working people, freeing them from the unbearable oppression of tsardom, and it would have eased the working class's transfer over to the Socialist revolution. This is why the proletariat was not able to remain on the sidelines during the bourgeois-democratic revolution and had to take charge of it.~~

~~The Mensheviks declared like a parrot that since the revolution was a bourgeois one, it should be led by the bourgeoisie. The Mensheviks cited the previous bourgeois revolutions (the Revolution of 1789–1793 in France, the Revolution of 1848 in Germany) as examples where the bourgeoisie did genuinely play a leadership role. But the Mensheviks did not want to recognize that the situation in Russia in 1905 was fundamentally different than the conditions of the eighteenth and nineteenth century European bourgeois revolutions. Lenin fully exposed the meaninglessness of the Mensheviks' historical comparison, demonstrating that the Mensheviks were deviating from Marxism in not wanting to see the different circumstances between the previous bourgeois revolutions and the Revolution of 1905.~~

~~Lenin frequently invoked the well-known Marxist maxim that "THE TRUTH IS CONCRETE," or, in other words, that any theoretical idea needs to be verified in practice. Lenin taught that Marxism demands precise examination (analysis) of the new circumstances and conditions in which the proletariat is struggling, as well as the special character of each historical period.~~

~~During the previous bourgeois revolutions in the West, the proletariat was still a small class in numerical terms and large-scale industry was not yet developed. The proletariat was weak, divided and disorganized; it was not yet consciousness in a class-sense of its special tasks in the revolution. Therefore, the proletariat went along with the bourgeoisie, which used the proletariat as a weapon for the attainment of its bourgeois goals. The bourgeoisie during the West-European revolutions of the eighteenth and nineteenth centuries was capable of revolutionary struggle against tsardom and the class of feudal landlords. It could have brought along with it the small proletariat and peasantry.~~

~~The situation in Russia at the start of the twentieth century was completely different. The Russian proletariat had become already quite a large class. It had shown its revolutionary strength in an array of strikes and demonstrations. Its~~

~~class consciousness was on the rise; it had its own party, which it had lacked in the previous bourgeois revolutions. The Russian bourgeoisie feared the proletariat more than it did tsardom. The Russian bourgeoisie needed tsardom as an ally against the proletariat.~~

~~This is why the Russian bourgeoisie was incapable of waging a decisive struggle against tsardom or being the chief (the hegemon) of the bourgeois-democratic revolution. The Bolsheviks proved that it was capable only of making a deal with tsardom.~~

~~Comrade Stalin defended and developed these Leninist maxims in his public speeches during the Revolution of 1905.~~

~~The profound, principled foundation for all the disagreements between the Bolsheviks and Mensheviks concerned the question of tactics during the Revolution of 1905. Was the leading role (the hegemony) in the bourgeois-democratic revolution to belong to the proletariat or the bourgeoisie? Was the democratic revolution to be completed or limited by a deal between the Constitutional Democrats and tsardom?~~

~~The Bolsheviks and Mensheviks answered these fundamental questions about the revolution in different ways. This disagreement grew to encompass all tactical questions.~~

> *"The outcome of the revolution," Lenin said, "depends on whether the working class will play the part of a subsidiary to the bourgeoisie, a subsidiary that is powerful in the force of its onslaught against the autocracy but impotent politically, or whether it will play the part of leader of the people's revolution." (Ibid., p. 41.)*

Lenin maintained that the proletariat had every POSSIBILITY *of escaping the fate of a subsidiary to the bourgeoisie, and of becoming the leader of the bourgeois-democratic revolution. This possibility, according to Lenin, arises from the following.*

First, "the proletariat, being, by virtue of its very position, the most advanced and the only consistently revolutionary class, is for that very reason called upon to play the leading part in the general democratic revolutionary movement in Russia." (Lenin, COLLECTED WORKS*, Russ. ed., Vol. VIII, p. 75.)*

Secondly, the proletariat has its own political party, which is independent of the bourgeoisie and which enables the proletariat to weld itself "into a united and independent political force." (Ibid., p. 75.)

*Thirdly, the proletariat is more interested than the bourgeoisie in a decisive victory of the revolution, in view of which "*IN A CERTAIN SENSE *the bourgeois revolution is* MORE ADVANTAGEOUS *to the proletariat than to the bourgeoisie." (Ibid., p. 57.)*

> *"It is to the advantage of the bourgeoisie," Lenin wrote, "to rely on certain remnants of the past as against the proletariat, for instance, on the monarchy, the standing army, etc. It is to the advantage of the bourgeoisie if the bourgeois revolution does not too resolutely sweep away all the remnants of the past, but leaves some of them, i.e., if this revolution is not fully consistent, if it is not complete and if it is not determined and relentless. . . . It is of greater advantage to the bourgeoisie if the necessary changes in the direction of bourgeois democracy take place more slowly, more gradually, more cautiously, less resolutely, by means of reforms and not by means of revolution . . . if these changes develop as little as possible the independent revolutionary activity, initiative and energy of the common people, i.e., the peasantry and especially the workers, for otherwise it will be easier for the workers, as the French say, 'to hitch the rifle from one shoulder to the other,' i.e., to turn against the bourgeoisie the guns which the bourgeois revolution will place in their hands, the liberty which the revolution will bring, the democratic institutions which will spring up on the ground that is cleared of serfdom. On the other hand, it is more advantageous for the working class if the necessary changes in the direction of bourgeois democracy take place by way of revolution and not by way of reform; for the way of reform is the way of delay, of procrastination, of the painfully slow decomposition of the putrid parts of the national organism. It is the proletariat and the peasantry that suffer first of all and most of all from their putrefaction. The revolutionary way is the way of quick amputation, which is the least painful to the proletariat, the way of the direct removal of the decomposing parts, the way of fewest concessions to and least consideration for the monarchy and the disgusting, vile, rotten and contaminating institutions which go with it." (Lenin, SELECTED WORKS, Vol. III, pp. 75–6.)*
>
> *"That," Lenin continues, "is why the proletariat fights in the front ranks for a republic and contemptuously rejects silly and unworthy advice to take care not to frighten away the bourgeoisie." (Ibid., p. 108.)*

In order to convert the POSSIBILITY of the proletarian leadership of the revolution into a REALITY, in order that the proletariat might ACTUALLY become the leader, the guiding force of the bourgeois revolution, at least two conditions were needed, according to Lenin.

First, it was necessary for the proletariat to have an ally who was interested in a decisive victory over tsardom and who might be disposed to accept the leadership of the proletariat. This was dictated by the very idea of leadership, for a leader ceases to be a leader if there is nobody to lead, a guide ceases to be a guide if there is nobody to guide. Lenin considered that the peasantry was such an ally.

Secondly, it was necessary that the class which was fighting the proletariat for the leadership of the revolution and striving to become its sole leader, should be forced out of the arena of leadership and isolated. This too was dictated by the very idea of leadership, which precluded the possibility of there being two leaders of the revolution. Lenin considered that the liberal bourgeoisie was such a class.

> *"Only the proletariat can be a consistent fighter for democracy," Lenin said. "It may become a victorious fighter for democracy only if the peasant masses join its revolutionary struggle." (Ibid., p. 86.)*
>
> *And further:*
>
> *"The peasantry includes a great number of semi-proletarian as well as petty-bourgeois elements. This causes it also to be unstable and compels the proletariat to unite in a strictly class party. But the instability of the peasantry differs radically from the instability of the bourgeoisie, for at the present time the peasantry is interested not so much in the absolute preservation of private property as in the confiscation of the landed estates, one of the principal forms of private property. While this does not cause the peasantry to become Socialist or cease to be petty-bourgeois, the peasantry is capable of becoming a whole-hearted and most radical adherent of the democratic revolution. The peasantry will inevitably become such if only the progress of revolutionary events, which is enlightening it, is not interrupted too soon by the treachery of the bourgeoisie and the defeat of the proletariat. Subject to this condition, the peasantry will inevitably become a bulwark of the revolution and the republic, for only a completely victorious revolution can give the peasantry* EVERYTHING *in the sphere of agrarian reforms—everything that the peasants desire, of which they dream, and of which they truly stand in need." (Ibid., pp. 108–09.)*

Analysing the objections of the Mensheviks, who asserted that these Bolshevik tactics "will compel the bourgeois classes to recoil from the cause of the revolution and thus curtail its scope," and characterizing these objections as "tactics of betrayal of the revolution," as "tactics which would convert the proletariat into a wretched appendage of the bourgeois classes," Lenin wrote:

> *"Those who really understand the role of the peasantry in the victorious Russian revolution would not dream of saying that the sweep of the revolution would be diminished if the bourgeoisie recoiled from it. For, as a matter of fact, the Russian revolution will begin to assume its real sweep, will really assume the widest revolutionary sweep possible in the epoch of*

> *bourgeois-democratic revolution, only when the bourgeoisie recoils from it and when the masses of the peasantry come out as active revolutionaries side by side with the proletariat. In order that it may be consistently carried to its conclusion, our democratic revolution must rely on such forces as are capable of paralysing the inevitable inconsistency of the bourgeoisie, i.e., capable precisely of 'causing it to recoil from the revolution.'" (Ibid., p. 110.)*

Such is the main tactical principle regarding the proletariat as the leader of the bourgeois revolution, the fundamental tactical principle regarding the hegemony (leading role) of the proletariat in the bourgeois revolution, expounded by Lenin in his book, TWO TACTICS OF SOCIAL-DEMOCRACY IN THE DEMOCRATIC REVOLUTION.

This was a new line of the Marxist party on questions of tactics in the bourgeois-democratic revolution, a line fundamentally different from the tactical lines hitherto existing in the arsenal of Marxism. The situation before had been that in the bourgeois revolution—in Western Europe, for instance—it was the bourgeoisie that played the leading part, the proletariat willy-nilly playing the part of its subsidiary, while the peasantry was a reserve of the bourgeoisie. The Marxists considered such a combination more or less inevitable, at the same time stipulating that the proletariat must as far as possible fight for its own immediate class demands and have its own political party. Now, under the new historical conditions, according to Lenin, the situation was changing in such a way that the proletariat was becoming the guiding force of the bourgeois revolution, the bourgeoisie was being edged out of the leadership of the revolution, while the peasantry was becoming a reserve of the proletariat.

The claim that Plekhanov "also stood" for the hegemony of the proletariat is based upon a misunderstanding. Plekhanov flirted with the idea of the hegemony of the proletariat and was not averse to recognizing it in words—that is true. But in reality he was opposed to this idea in its essence. The hegemony of the proletariat implies the leading role of the proletariat in the bourgeois revolution, accompanied by a policy of ALLIANCE *between the proletariat and the peasantry and a policy of* ISOLATION *of the liberal bourgeoisie; whereas Plekhanov, as we know, was* OPPOSED *to the policy of isolating the liberal bourgeoisie,* FAVOURED *a policy of* AGREEMENT *with the liberal bourgeoisie, and was* OPPOSED *to a policy of alliance between the proletariat and the peasantry. As a matter of fact, Plekhanov's tactical line was the Menshevik line which rejected the hegemony of the proletariat.*

~~Take the question of the ARMED UPRISING. The tsarist government was the first to begin the civil war by shooting down the unarmed, peaceful workers' demonstration on January 9. It continued by firing on unarmed strikers and demonstrators in an array of cities. In retaliation, a variety of separate, spontaneous armed uprisings against tsardom began in a variety of cities.~~

~~The most important task of the proletarian party was to organize the uprising against tsardom and arm the working class.~~

~~The Bolsheviks' Third Party Congress of the R.S.D.L.P. announced that the revolutionary movement had already brought about the necessary armed uprising and that the proletariat had to take part in that uprising in the most energetic of ways, as that would decide the fate of the Russian revolution. The congress pointed out that the Party must take the most energetic measures in order to arm the proletariat and personally direct the uprising. The Bolsheviks issued a militant slogan on practical preparations for the uprising and proposed to this end to form special groups of party workers.~~

~~On the basis of the decisions of the Third Party Congress, the Bolsheviks organized armed squads of workers and supplied them with military training and weapons. This work was led by Lenin and Stalin. Comrade Litvinov spent a lot of energy on the technical preparations for the uprising and the delivery of weapons. The Bolsheviks' militant activities were developed and prepared by such revolutionary organizers as Klim Voroshilov, Sergo Ordjonikidze, Valerian Kuibyshev, Sergey Kirov and Mikhail Frunze. Legendary heroes of the revolution such as "Kamo" (Petrosyan) were known for this work.~~

~~The Party created military organizations which conducted revolutionary propaganda and agitation among the tsarist troops. The Party secretly published special newspapers for the army and navy.~~

~~The issue of the general strike had a large significance. The leaders of the Second International and the Russian Mensheviks had a negative view of the general strike. The Third Party Congress underscored the significance of the general strike as the most important means of struggle and pointed to the imperative of transforming it into an uprising. This Bolshevik tactic completely justified itself in the revolution. The October general strike grew into an uprising in December 1905.~~

~~The Mensheviks denied the imperative of ORGANIZING an armed uprising. They assured the workers that it was not possible to organize an uprising and that it would take place on its own, spontaneously. The Mensheviks opposed technical-military preparations for the uprising and effectively refused to arm the workers.~~

~~The Mensheviks attempted to distract the workers from preparing for the uprising and from revolutionary methods of struggle. Thus, in the fall of 1905, for instance, when the mass strikes were leading to the maturation of a general, political strike, and when the transformation of the general, political strike into an armed uprising was at hand, the Mensheviks called upon the workers to participate in the elections to the so-called "Bulygin," or "Consultative" Duma. Proposing to take part in the elections to such a Duma at the moment when the revolutionary movement was in the middle of an uprising, the Mensheviks~~

~~encouraged the workers to believe that the working class would be able to win political rights from the tsarist government by peaceful means. The Bolsheviks proposed to the workers that they boycott the Bulygin Duma and prepare for the general strike and the armed uprising. The October 1905 general strike swept away the caricatured Bulygin Duma, within which the Mensheviks wanted to take part.~~

~~The Bolsheviks said that the realization of a democratic republic in Russia was possible only as the result of a victorious popular uprising. The organ of this uprising was the PROVISIONAL REVOLUTIONARY GOVERNMENT, which, according to the Bolsheviks, was to be a revolutionary-democratic dictatorship of the proletariat and peasantry. The Bolsheviks considered it possible for representatives of the party of the proletariat to take part in such a worker-peasant government, in order to realize the proletariat's leadership of the democratic revolution and defend the revolutionary demands of the working class.~~

~~The Mensheviks believed that all the power in the new government ought to belong to the liberal bourgeoisie. Such a government, according to the Mensheviks, could be created without an uprising by some sort of a representative institution like the Bulygin Duma or the so-called ZEMSKY SOBOR, which the tsar had earlier wanted to form. The Mensheviks announced that Social-Democracy should not participate in the organization of a provisional revolutionary government and should not send its representatives in order to advance the revolutionary demands of the working class. This is because it would "STARTLE THE BOURGEOIS CLASSES AND FORCE THEM TO BACK AWAY FROM THE CAUSE OF THE REVOLUTION AND THUS WEAKEN ITS IMPACT." This is literally what the Transcaucasus Menshevik conference wrote in its April 1905 resolution, having received full approval from the Menshevik newspaper ISKRA.~~

> ~~"This resolution," wrote Lenin, "is shameful, since it expresses (aside from the will and consciousness of those writing it, who have taken up a position on the slippery slope of opportunism) treachery in regard to the interests of the working class that lie in the hands of the bourgeoisie. This resolution illuminates the transformation of the proletariat into a tail of the bourgeoisie during the epoch of the democratic revolution." (Lenin, COLLECTED WORKS, Russ. ed., Vol. VIII, p. 193.)~~

2) Lenin considered that the most effective means of overthrowing tsardom and achieving a democratic republic was a victorious armed uprising of the people. Contrary to the Mensheviks, Lenin held that "the general democratic revolutionary movement has ALREADY BROUGHT ABOUT THE NECESSITY *for an armed uprising," that "the organization of the proletariat for uprising" had already "been placed on the order of the day as one of the essential, principal and* INDISPENS-

ABLE tasks of the Party," and that it was necessary "to adopt the MOST ENERGETIC measures to arm the proletariat and to ensure the possibility of directly leading the uprising." (Lenin, COLLECTED WORKS, Russ. ed., Vol. VIII, p. 75.)

To guide the masses to an uprising and to turn it into an uprising of the whole people, Lenin deemed it necessary to issue such slogans, such appeals to the masses as would set free their revolutionary initiative, organize them for insurrection and disorganize the machinery of power of tsardom. He considered that these slogans were furnished by the tactical decisions of the Third Party Congress, to the defence of which his book TWO TACTICS OF SOCIAL-DEMOCRACY IN THE DEMOCRATIC REVOLUTION was devoted.

The following, he considered, were these slogans:

a) "Mass political strikes, which may be of great importance at the beginning and in the very process of the insurrection" (ibid., p. 75);

b) "Immediate realization, in a revolutionary way, of the 8-hour working day and of the other immediate demands of the working class" (ibid., p. 47);

c) "Immediate organization of revolutionary peasant committees in order to carry out" in a revolutionary way "all the democratic changes," including the confiscation of the landed estates (ibid., p. 88);

d) Arming of the workers.

Here two points are of particular interest:

First, the tactics of realizing IN A REVOLUTIONARY WAY the 8-hour day in the towns, and the democratic changes in the countryside, that is, a way which disregards the authorities, disregards the law, which ignores both the authorities and the law, breaks the existing laws and establishes a new order by unauthorized action, as an accomplished fact. This was a new tactical method, the use of which paralysed the machinery of power of tsardom and set free the activity and creative initiative of the masses. These tactics gave rise to the revolutionary strike committees in the towns and the revolutionary peasant committees in the countryside, the former of which later developed into the Soviets of Workers' Deputies and the latter into the Soviets of Peasants' Deputies.

Secondly, the use of MASS POLITICAL STRIKES, the use of general political strikes, which later, in the course of the revolution, were of prime importance in the revolutionary mobilization of the masses. This was a new and very important weapon in the hands of the proletariat, a weapon hitherto unknown in the practice of the Marxist parties and one that subsequently gained recognition.

Lenin held that following the victorious uprising of the people the tsarist government should be replaced by a provisional revolutionary government. It would be the task of the provisional revolutionary government to consolidate the conquests of the revolution, to crush the resistance of the counter-revolution and to give effect to the minimum program of the Russian Social-Democratic Labour Party. Lenin maintained that unless these tasks were accomplished, a decisive victory over tsardom would be impossible. And in order to accomplish these tasks and achieve a decisive victory over tsardom, the provisional revolutionary government would have to be not an ordinary kind of government, but a government of the dictatorship of the victorious classes, of the workers and peasants; it would have to be a revolutionary dictatorship of the proletariat and peasantry. Citing Marx's well-known thesis that "after a revolution every provisional organization of the state requires a dictatorship, and an energetic dictatorship at that," Lenin came to the conclusion that if the provisional revolutionary government was to ensure a decisive victory over tsardom, it could be nothing else but a dictatorship of the proletariat and peasantry.

> *"A decisive victory of the revolution over tsardom is* THE REVOLUTIONARY-DEMOCRATIC DICTATORSHIP OF THE PROLETARIAT AND THE PEASANTRY," *Lenin said. ". . . And such a victory will be precisely a dictatorship, i.e., it must inevitably rely on military force, on the arming of the masses, on an uprising and not on institutions of one kind or another, established in a 'lawful' or 'peaceful' way. It can be only a dictatorship, for the realization of the changes which are urgently and absolutely indispensable for the proletariat and the peasantry will call forth the desperate resistance of the landlords, of the big bourgeoisie, and of tsardom. Without a dictatorship it is impossible to break down that resistance and to repel the counter-revolutionary attempts. But of course it will be a democratic, not a Socialist dictatorship. It will not be able (without a series of intermediary stages of revolutionary development) to affect the foundations of capitalism. At best it may bring about a radical redistribution of landed property in favour of the peasantry, establish consistent and full democracy, including the formation of a republic, eradicate all the oppressive features of Asiatic bondage, not only in village but also in factory life, lay the foundation for a thorough improvement in the position of the workers and for a rise in their standard of living, and—last but not least—carry the revolutionary conflagration into Europe. Such a victory will by no means as yet transform our bourgeois revolution into a Socialist revolution; the democratic revolution will not directly overstep the bounds of bourgeois social and economic relationships; nevertheless, the significance of such a victory for the future development of Russia and of the whole world will be immense. Nothing will raise the revolutionary energy of the world proletariat so much, nothing will shorten the path leading to its complete victory to such an extent, as this decisive victory of the revolution that has now started in Russia." (Lenin,* SELECTED WORKS, *Vol. III, pp. 82–3.)*

As to the attitude of the Social-Democrats towards the provisional revolutionary government and as to whether it would be permissible for them to take part in it, Lenin fully upheld the resolution of the Third Party Congress on the subject, which reads:

> *"Subject to the relation of forces, and other factors which cannot be exactly determined beforehand, representatives of our Party may participate in the provisional revolutionary government for the purpose of relentless struggle against all counter-revolutionary attempts and of the defence of the independent interests of the working class; an indispensable condition for such participation is that the Party should exercise strict control over its representatives and that the independence of the Social-Democratic Party, which is striving for a complete Socialist revolution and, consequently, is irreconcilably hostile to all the bourgeois parties, should be strictly maintained; whether the participation of Social-Democrats in the provisional revolutionary government prove possible or not, we must propagate among the broadest masses of the proletariat the necessity for permanent pressure to be brought to bear upon the provisional government by the armed proletariat, led by the Social-Democratic Party, for the purpose of defending, consolidating and extending the gains of the revolution." (Ibid., pp. 46–7.)*

As to the Mensheviks' objection that the provisional government would still be a bourgeois government, that the Social-Democrats could not be permitted to take part in such a government unless one wanted to commit the same mistake as the French Socialist Millerand when he joined the French bourgeois government, Lenin parried this objection by pointing out that the Mensheviks were here mixing up two DIFFERENT *things and were betraying their inability to treat the question as Marxists should. In France it was a question of Socialists taking part in a* REACTIONARY *bourgeois government at a time when* THERE WAS NO *revolutionary situation in the country, which made it incumbent upon the Socialists not to join such a government; in Russia, on the other hand, it was a question of Socialists taking part in a* REVOLUTIONARY *bourgeois government fighting for the* VICTORY OF THE REVOLUTION *at a time when the revolution was* IN FULL SWING, *a circumstance which would make it* PERMISSIBLE *for, and, under favourable circumstances,* INCUMBENT *upon the Social-Democrats to take part in such a government in order to strike at the counter-revolution not only "from below," from without, but also "from above," from within the government.*

~~The Bolsheviks' and Mensheviks' relationship to THE PEASANT MOVEMENT also differed on a fundamental level. The Bolsheviks saw in the revolutionary peasantry the only ally for the proletariat that was even somewhat reliable and powerful. The Mensheviks by contrast placed all their hopes on the liberal bourgeoisie. They did not want to rally the peasantry to revolution. They denied the peasantry's revolutionary role. The Mensheviks spoke out against the~~

~~organization of peasant committees and their seizure of the landed estates. They advised the peasants to peacefully await the future Constituent Assembly's decision on the land question. This is also how they acted in 1917. Their slogan at that time also was: "Don't Touch the Landlords and Capitalists." The Mensheviks were against the creation of a revolutionary worker-peasant government.~~

~~Such were the two different tactics of the Bolsheviks and Mensheviks, which had been outlined already at the start of the Revolution of 1905 and which guided each faction over the course of the revolution.~~

~~The Bolsheviks revealed themselves to be firm, steadfast revolutionaries, who passionately aimed to complete the democratic revolution under the leadership (hegemony) of the proletariat in alliance with the peasantry.~~

~~The Mensheviks were conciliators with the bourgeoisie and did not want to complete the democratic revolution. They plodded in line behind the Constitutional Democrats like a tail. The Mensheviks objected to the working class and its party conducting an independent political line during the revolution and wanted to subordinate the proletariat to the influence of the liberal bourgeoisie.~~

~~The Bolsheviks and Mensheviks formally belonged to the same Social-Democratic Party. The Mensheviks formally recognized the same program that the Bolsheviks did, which had been approved at the Second Party Congress. However, the Mensheviks' whole political conduct indicated that they recognized the program IN WORDS ONLY. And political parties and political leaders are judged not by their words, but BY THEIR DEEDS. The Mensheviks' deeds were such that in order to suit the Constitutional Democrats, they refused to support the militant revolutionary slogan on the struggle for a democratic republic, so as not to "scare" the bourgeoisie. And this slogan, incidentally, was in the Party program.~~

~~Lenin pointed out in his famous work TWO TACTICS OF SOCIAL-DEMOCRACY IN THE DEMOCRATIC REVOLUTION that the Mensheviks were nearing the "Liberators" (the Constitutional Democrats) in a PRACTICAL, POLITICAL sense. Lenin said bluntly that the Mensheviks were actually moving the revolution not forward, but BACKWARD.~~

> ~~"What is the point of their recognizing the program which demands a republican alternative to the autocracy when there is no slogan calling for a struggle for the republic in the tactical resolution, which determines the tasks of the Party in the revolutionary moment for the present and near future," wrote Lenin in regard to the Mensheviks. (Lenin, COLLECTED WORKS, Russ. ed., Vol. VIII, p. 53.)~~

~~In contrast to the Mensheviks, the Bolsheviks provided the sort of slogans that moved the revolution FORWARD. The Bolsheviks provided militant revo-~~

lutionary slogans which illuminated the path of revolutionary struggle for the workers and peasants and ignited their will toward victory.

Lenin pointed out in TWO TACTICS that a revolutionary party can and must play an enormous, genuine, leading and coordinating role in history if it recognizes the material conditions for a revolutionary coup d'état and takes charge of the vanguard class. This is what the Marxists teach—the materialist understanding of history. The Bolsheviks took into account the material conditions for a coup, the interests of the various classes and the imperative of an armed uprising and its organization. The Bolsheviks took command of the vanguard class—the proletariat—and moved the revolution forward with their revolutionary slogans and tactics.

The Mensheviks dismissed the Marxist, materialistic understanding of history, not wanting to understand the genuine, leading, and organizational role of the proletarian party in the revolution. The Mensheviks, by contrast, PUT A BRAKE on the revolution with all of their tactics, acting in the interest of the bourgeoisie.

Already in the course of the Revolution of 1905, the important uniqueness of Bolshevism-Leninism had begun to appear—FAITH IN THE MASSES and faith that the masses were capable of acting as the active creator of the new social order.[3]

Concluding his immortal work TWO TACTICS OF SOCIAL-DEMOCRACY IN THE DEMOCRATIC REVOLUTION, Lenin wrote the following inspirational words:

> "'Revolutions are the locomotives of history,' said Marx. Revolution is a holiday for the oppressed and exploited. Never have the popular masses been able to take such an active role in the creation of the new social order as during a revolution. At such times the people are capable of wonders, from the perspective of the narrow, bourgeois standard on gradual progress. But it is necessary that the leaders of the revolutionary parties define their tasks more broadly and daringly at such a time, so that their slogans are always at the head of the masses' revolutionary activity, serving as a lighthouse for them and showing them our democratic and Socialist ideal in its full height and glory, showing them the shortest, straightest path to full, unconditional, decisive victory." (Lenin, COLLECTED WORKS, Russ. ed., Vol. VIII, p. 104.)

5. Leninist Position on the Question of the Bourgeois-Democratic Revolution Passing into a Socialist One

Lenin taught that the establishment of the revolutionary-democratic dictatorship of the proletariat and peasantry would be merely a temporary, transitional task.

*3) While advocating the victory of the bourgeois revolution and the achievement of a democratic republic, Lenin had not the least intention of coming to a halt in the democratic stage and confining the scope of the revolutionary movement to the accomplishment of bourgeois-democratic tasks. On the contrary, Lenin maintained that f*ollowing upon the ~~resolution of this task~~ *accomplishment of the democratic tasks*, the proletariat *and the other exploited masses* would have to ~~develop~~ *begin* a struggle, this time for the SOCIALIST revolution. *Lenin knew this and regarded it as the duty of Social-Democrats to do everything to make t*he *bourgeois-*democratic revolution ~~had to~~ PASS INTO the Socialist revolution. *Lenin held that the dictatorship of the proletariat and the peasantry was necessary not in order to* END *the revolution at the point of consummation of its victory over tsardom, but in order to* PROLONG *the state of revolution as much as possible, to destroy the last remnants of counter-revolution, to make the flame of revolution spread to Europe, and, having in the meantime given the proletariat the opportunity of educating itself politically and organizing itself into a great army, to begin the direct transition to the Socialist revolution.*

~~Lenin pointed out that the complete victory of the democratic revolution, the overthrow of tsardom and the elimination of landed estates and feudal property rights would mark the beginning of a decisive struggle for a Socialist coup d'état and the eradication of capitalist exploitation.~~

~~In the place of the slogan about the revolutionary democratic dictatorship of the proletariat and peasantry, the Party would have to disseminate a slogan about the SOCIALIST dictatorship of the proletariat, that is, about a total Socialist coup d'état.~~

~~During the democratic coup d'état, the proletariat would rely on the entire peasantry, because the entire peasantry was interested in the elimination of feudal landlord property rights to the land. During the execution of the Socialist coup d'état the proletariat would be able draw in semi-proletarian elements of the population and rely on the poor peasantry.~~

~~During the execution of the final stages of the Socialist coup d'état, the proletariat would have to overcome unsteady elements within peasantry and smallholders. The proletariat, depending on the poor peasantry, would have to develop the struggle against the rural bourgeoisie (the kulaks) and strengthen its alliance with the middle peasantry.~~

~~In his work TWO TACTICS OF SOCIAL-DEMOCRACY IN THE DEMOCRATIC REVOLUTION, Lenin developed an ingenious plan for the bourgeois-democratic revolution to pass into a Socialist one.~~

Dealing with the scope of the bourgeois revolution, and with the character the Marxist party should lend it, Lenin wrote:

"The proletariat must carry to completion the democratic revolution, by allying to itself the mass of the peasantry in order to crush by force the resistance of the autocracy and to paralyse the instability of the bourgeoisie. The proletariat must accomplish the Socialist revolution by allying to itself the mass of the semi-proletarian elements of the population in order to crush by force the resistance of the bourgeoisie and to paralyse the instability of the peasantry and the petty bourgeoisie.[4] *Such are the tasks of the proletariat, which the new* ISKRA-ISTS *(that is, Mensheviks—*ED.*) always present so narrowly in their arguments and resolutions about the scope of the revolution.*" (~~Lenin, SELECTED WORKS, Vol. III,~~ *Ibid.*, pp. 110–11.)

And further:

"At the head of the whole of the people, and particularly of the peasantry—for complete freedom, for a consistent democratic revolution, for a republic! At the head of all the toilers and the exploited—for Socialism! Such must in practice be the policy of the revolutionary proletariat, such is the class slogan which must permeate and determine the solution of every tactical problem, of every practical step of the workers' party during the revolution." (Ibid., p. 124.)

In order to leave nothing unclear, two months after the appearance of the TWO TACTICS *Lenin wrote an article entitled "Attitude of Social-Democrats to the Peasant Movement," in which he explained:*

"From the democratic revolution we shall at once, and just in accordance with the measure of our strength, the strength of the class-conscious and organized proletariat, begin to pass to the Socialist revolution. *We stand for uninterrupted revolution. We shall not stop half way.*" (~~Lenin, SELECTED WORKS, Vol. III,~~ *Ibid.*, p. 145.)

This was a new line in the question of the relation between the bourgeois revolution and the Socialist revolution, a new theory of a regrouping of forces around the proletariat, towards the end of the bourgeois revolution, for a direct transition to the Socialist revolution—the theory of the bourgeois-democratic revolution PASSING INTO *the Socialist revolution.*

In working out this new line, Lenin based himself, first, on the well-known thesis of uninterrupted revolution advanced by Marx at the end of the forties of the last century in the Address to the Communist League, and, secondly, on the well-known idea of the necessity of combining the peasant revolutionary movement with the proletarian revolution which Marx expressed in a letter to Engels in 1856, saying that: "the whole thing in Germany will depend on the possibility of backing the proletarian revolution by some second edition of the Peasants' War." However, these brilliant ideas of Marx were not developed subsequently in the works of Marx and Engels, while the theoreticians of the Second International did their utmost to bury them and consign them to oblivion. To Lenin fell the task of bringing these[5] *forgotten ideas of Marx to light and restoring them to their full rights. But in restoring these Marxian ideas, Lenin did not—and could not—confine himself to merely repeating them, but developed them further and moulded them into a harmonious theory of Socialist revolution by introducing a new factor, an* INDISPENSABLE *factor of the Socialist revolution, namely, an* ALLIANCE *of the proletariat with the semi-proletarian elements of town and country as a* CONDITION *for the victory of the proletarian revolution.*

This line confuted the tactical position of the West-European Social-Democratic parties who took it for granted that after the bourgeois revolution the peasant masses, including the poor peasants, would necessarily desert the revolution, as a result of which the bourgeois revolution would be followed by a prolonged INTERVAL, *a long "lull" lasting fifty or a hundred years, if not longer, during which the proletariat would be "peacefully" exploited and the bourgeoisie would "lawfully" enrich itself until the time came round for a new revolution, a Socialist revolution.*

This was a new theory which held that the SOCIALIST *revolution would be accomplished not by the proletariat in isolation as against the* WHOLE *bourgeoisie, but by the proletariat as the leading class which would have as* ALLIES *the semi-proletarian elements of the population, the "toiling and exploited millions."*

According to this theory the hegemony of the proletariat in the bourgeois revolution, the proletariat BEING IN ALLIANCE *with the peasantry, would grow into the hegemony of the proletariat in the Socialist revolution, the proletariat now* BEING IN ALLIANCE *with the other labouring and exploited masses, while the democratic dictatorship of the proletariat and the peasantry would prepare the ground for the Socialist dictatorship of the proletariat.*

It refuted the theory current among the West-European Social-Democrats who denied the revolutionary potentialities of the semi-proletarian masses of town and country and took for granted that "apart from the bourgeoisie and the proletariat we perceive no social forces in our country in which oppositional or revolutionary combinations might find support" (these were Plekhanov's words, typical of the West-European Social-Democrats).

The West-European Social-Democrats held that in the Socialist revolution the proletariat would stand ALONE, *against the* WHOLE *bourgeoisie,* WITHOUT *allies, against ALL the non-proletarian classes and strata. They would not take account of the fact that capital exploits not only the proletarians but also the semi-proletarian millions of town and country, who are crushed by capitalism and who may become allies of the proletariat in the struggle for the emancipation of society from the capitalist yoke. The West-European Social-Democrats therefore held that conditions were not yet ripe for a Socialist revolution in Europe, that the conditions could be considered ripe only when the proletariat became the majority of the nation, the majority of society, as a result of the further economic development of society.*

This spurious anti-proletarian standpoint of the West-European Social-Democrats was completely upset by Lenin's theory of the Socialist revolution.

Lenin's theory did not yet contain any direct conclusion regarding the possibility of a victory of Socialism in one country, taken singly. But it did contain all, or nearly all, the fundamental elements necessary for the drawing of such a conclusion sooner or later.

As we know, Lenin arrived at this conclusion ten years later, in 1915.

Such are the fundamental tactical principles expounded by Lenin in his historic book, TWO TACTICS OF SOCIAL-DEMOCRACY IN THE DEMOCRATIC REVOLUTION.

The historic significance of this book consists above all in the fact that in it Lenin ideologically shattered the petty-bourgeois tactical line of the Mensheviks, armed the working class of Russia for the further development of the bourgeois-democratic revolution, for a new onslaught on tsardom, and put before the Russian Social-Democrats a clear perspective of the necessity of the bourgeois revolution passing into the Socialist revolution.

But this does not exhaust the significance of Lenin's book. Its invaluable significance consists in that it enriched Marxism with a new theory of revolution and laid the foundation for the revolutionary tactics of the Bolshevik Party with the help of which in 1917 the proletariat of our country achieved the victory over capitalism.

~~The Trotskyites subsequently slandered Lenin with the claim that he and the Bolsheviks had supposedly only spoken out about the bourgeois revolution passing into a Socialist one in 1917—that they had "rearmed" themselves. In fact, as we know, it was already in 1894 that Lenin wrote in his book WHAT IS A 'FRIEND OF THE PEOPLE?' that having overthrown the tsar, the proletariat would have to follow a direct path of political struggle toward the Socialist revolution. The victory of the bourgeois-democratic revolution for the Bolsheviks would mean the immediate transition over to the struggle for the Socialist revolution. The Bolsheviks struggled for this transition in 1905 and 1917.~~

~~The Mensheviks were afraid and did not want either a Socialist revolution or a full victory of the democratic revolution over tsardom. Moreover, they were against the transition from a bourgeois revolution to a Socialist one.~~

~~One of the most malicious Mensheviks at the time was Trotsky. Trotskyism was one of the most harmful varieties of Menshevism. Trotsky tried in every way to mask his Menshevik views with pseudo-revolutionary phrases. He called his point of view the "theory of permanent (that is, uninterrupted) revolution." This false "theory" gave rise to the slogan of revolution WITHOUT THE PEASANTRY, which led to the rupture and defeat of the revolution because the working class could not stage a successful revolution without the peasant alliance. As with all Mensheviks, Trotsky did not want to rally the peasantry to revolution and was against the worker-peasant alliance. He denied the dictatorship of the proletariat, which was impossible without the worker-peasant alliance. Trotsky announced that the victory of the working class in the revolution would be only temporary, and that the working class would inevitably end up in a hostile clash with the broad peasant masses.~~

~~Trotsky instilled in the workers a lack of faith in their own power, announcing that revolutionary Russia could not survive in the face of conservative Europe. He was against the revolutionary-democratic dictatorship of the proletariat and peasantry during the Revolution of 1905. Trotsky wanted the formation of a liberal-Menshevik government after the revolution—something like MacDonald's so-called British "Labour" government, which, as is well-known, conducted bourgeois policy.~~

~~Trotsky was worse and more harmful than the other Mensheviks because he concealed his bourgeois, counter-revolutionary essence with pseudo-revolutionary phrases.~~

~~In this way, during the Revolution of 1905, the Bolsheviks and Mensheviks spoke out with different views and tactics regarding the revolution. The Bolsheviks represented the interests of the working class, the leader of the revolution. The Mensheviks attempted to subordinate the working class to the bourgeoisie. Within the working class, there was no unity. The most conscious and revolutionary part of the workers took the Bolsheviks' side. The other part of the workers, who didn't fully understand their own interests, continued to follow the Mensheviks on a leash. The Mensheviks deceived this part of the working class with Socialist phrases.~~

4.~~6.~~ Further Rise of the Revolution. ~~The October General~~ *All-Russian* Political Strike *of October 1905. Retreat of Tsardom. The Tsar's Manifesto. Rise of the Soviets of Workers' Deputies*

By the autumn of 1905 the revolutionary movement had swept the whole country and gained tremendous momentum.

On September 19 a ~~general~~ printers' strike broke out in Moscow. It spread to St. Petersburg and a number of other cities. In Moscow itself the printers' strike was supported by the workers in other industries and developed into a ~~universal~~ *general political* strike.

In the beginning of October a strike started on the Moscow-Kazan Railway. Within two days it was joined by all the railwaymen of the Moscow railway junction and soon all the railways of the country were in the grip of the strike. The postal and telegraph services came to a standstill. In various cities of Russia the workers gathered at huge meetings and decided to down tools. The strike spread to factory after factory, mill after mill, city after city, and region after region. The workers were joined by the minor employees, students and intellectuals—lawyers, engineers and doctors.

The October *political* strike became an ~~universal~~ *all-Russian* strike which embraced *nearly* the whole country, including the most remote districts, and *nearly* all the workers, including the most backward strata. ~~More than half a~~ *About one* million ~~mill~~ *industrial* workers alone took part in the general *political* strike, not counting the large number of railwaymen, postal and telegraph employees and others. The whole life of the country came to a standstill. The government was paralysed.

The working class headed the struggle of the masses against the autocracy.

The Bolshevik slogan of a mass political strike had borne fruit.

The October general strike revealed the power and might of the proletarian movement and compelled the mortally frightened tsar~~ist government~~ to issue ~~its~~ *his* Manifesto of October 17, 1905. This Manifesto promised the people "the unshakable foundations of civil liberty: real inviolability of person, and freedom of conscience, speech, assembly and association." It promised to convene a legislative Duma and to extend the franchise to all classes of the population.

Thus, Bulygin's deliberative Duma was swept away by the tide of revolution. The Bolshevik tactics of boycotting the Bulygin Duma proved to have been right.

~~The large industrial bourgeoisie hurried to support the tsar and conclude an agreement with him. They formed the Octobrist Party (The Union of October Seventeenth).~~

*Nevertheless, t*he Manifesto of October 17 was a fraud on the people, *a trick of the tsar to gain some sort of respite in which to lull the credulous and to win time to rally his forces and then to strike at the revolution*. In words the tsarist government promised liberty, but actually it granted nothing substantial. *So far, p*romises were all that the workers and peasants had received from the government. Instead of the broad political amnesty which was expected, on October 21 amnesty was granted to only a *small* section of political prisoners. At the same time, *with the object of dividing the forces of the people,* the government engineered a number of sanguinary Jewish pogroms, in which ~~several~~ *many* thousand*s of* people perished; ~~more than ten thousand were maimed or wounded.~~ *and i*n order to crush the revolution ~~the tsarist government~~ *it* created police-controlled gangster organizations known as the League of the Russian People and the League of Michael the Archangel. These organizations, in which a prominent part was played by reactionary landlords, merchants, priests, *and* semi-criminal elements of the vagabond type ~~and various intoxicated rabble~~, were ~~called~~ *christened* by the people "Black-Hundreds." The Black-Hundreds, with the support of the police, openly manhandled and murdered *politically advanced workers,* ~~revolutionaries and even several liberally minded people,~~ *revolutionary intellectuals and students,* burned ~~buildings filled with people there for meetings, like in Tomsk, where on the order of the "Black Hundreds" and the priests, several hundred people were burned to death in a building where a meeting was underway~~ *down meeting places and fired upon assemblies of citizens. These so far were the only results of the tsar's Manifesto.*

There was a *popular* song at the time ~~about this Manifesto~~ which ran:

> "The tsar caught fright, issued a Manifesto:
> Liberty for the dead, for the living—arrest."

~~Nikolay Ernestovich Bauman, one of the most important Bolshevik organizers, was killed by the Black Hundreds in Moscow on October 18. Bauman's funeral on October 20, 1905, turned into a demonstration of grandiose proportions previously unheard of in Russia. Enormous throngs of people stretched across Moscow, from the Technical School to the Vagankovsk cemetery, and more and more new organizations joined the procession en route. Speeches were given at the grave site. The police and troops watched for those returning from the funeral and fell upon them. Many were killed and wounded.~~

The Bolsheviks explained to the masses that the Manifesto of October 17 was a trap. They branded the conduct of the government after the promulgation of the Manifesto as provocative. The Bolsheviks called the workers to arms, to prepare for armed uprising.

The workers set about forming fighting squads with greater energy than ever. It ~~was~~ *became* clear to them that the first victory of October 17, wrested by the general political strike, demanded of them further efforts, the continuation of the struggle for the ~~final~~ overthrow of tsardom.

Lenin regarded the Manifesto of October 17 as an expression of a certain *temporary* equilibrium of forces: the proletariat and the peasantry, having wrung the Manifesto from the tsar, WERE STILL NOT STRONG ENOUGH to overthrow tsardom, WHEREAS TSARDOM WAS NO LONGER ABLE to rule by the old methods alone and had been compelled to give a paper promise of ~~liberty~~ *"civil liberties" and a "legislative" Duma.*

~~7. Soviets of Workers' Deputies~~

In those stormy ~~October~~ days *of the October political strike,* in the fire of the struggle *against tsardom*, the revolutionary creative initiative of the working-class masses forged a new and powerful weapon—the Soviets *of Workers' Deputies*.

The Soviets of Workers' Deputies—which were assemblies of delegates from all mills and factories—represented a type of mass political organization of the working class which the world had never seen before. The Soviets that first arose in 1905 were the PROTOTYPE of the Soviet power which the proletariat, led by the Bolshevik Party, set up in 1917. The Soviets were a new revolutionary form of the creative initiative of the people~~;~~. *T*hey were set up exclusively by the revolutionary sections of the population, in defiance of all laws and prescripts of ~~the monarchy~~ *tsardom*~~;~~. *T*hey were a manifestation of the independent action of the people who were rising to fight tsardom.

The Bolsheviks regarded the Soviets as the embryo of revolutionary power ~~and contended~~. *They maintained* that the~~ir~~ strength and significance *of the Soviets* would depend solely on the strength and success of the uprising.

The Mensheviks regarded the Soviets neither as embryonic organs of revolutionary power nor as organs of uprising. They looked upon the Soviets as organs of local self-government, in the nature of ~~the Zemstvos~~ *democratized municipal government bodies*.

~~The disputes between the Bolsheviks and Mensheviks about the role and significance of the Soviets during the first revolution showed to a significant extent that the Mensheviks opposed the revolutionary Soviets. The Mensheviks demonstrated this conclusively in 1917, when they became enemies of the Soviet power.~~

In St. Petersburg, elections to the Soviet~~s~~ of Workers' Deputies took place in all the mills and factories on October 13 (26, New Style) 1905. The first meeting of the Soviet was held that night. Moscow followed St. Petersburg in forming a Soviet of Workers' Deputies.

The St. Petersburg Soviet of Workers' Deputies, being the Soviet of the most important industrial and revolutionary centre of Russia, the capital of the tsarist empire, ought to have played a decisive role in the Revolution of 1905. However, it did not perform its task, ~~because the Mensheviks under Trotsky took over its leadership~~ *owing to its bad, Menshevik leadership*. ~~In the Soviet, Trotsky supplied slogans which harmed the revolution, calling for instance for the evacuation of troops from St. Petersburg. The Mensheviks in the Soviet did not pay attention to the need for revolutionary work among the tsarist troops and did not prepare for an uprising.~~ *As we know, Lenin had not yet arrived in St. Petersburg; he was still abroad. The Mensheviks took advantage of Lenin's absence to make their way into the St. Petersburg Soviet and to seize hold of its leadership. It was not surprising under such circumstances that the Mensheviks Khrustalev, Trotsky, Parvus and others managed to turn the St. Petersburg Soviet against the policy of an uprising. Instead of bringing the soldiers into close contact with the Soviet and linking them up with the common struggle, they demanded that the soldiers be withdrawn from St. Petersburg. The Soviet, instead of arming the workers and preparing them for an uprising, just marked time and was against preparations for an uprising.*

Altogether different was the role ~~in the revolution~~ played *in the revolution* by the Moscow Soviet of Workers' Deputies. *From the very first the Moscow Soviet pursued a thoroughly revolutionary policy.* The leadership of the Moscow Soviet was in the hands of the Bolsheviks. ~~With its help~~ *Thanks to them, side by side with the Soviet of Workers' Deputies*, there arose in Moscow a Soviet of Soldiers' Deputies. The Moscow Soviet became an organ of armed uprising.

In the period October to December 1905, Soviets of Workers' Deputies were set up in a number of large towns and in ~~the major~~ *nearly all the* working-class centres. Attempts were made to organize Soviets of Soldiers' and Sailors' Deputies and to unite them with the Soviets of Workers' Deputies. In some localities Soviets of Workers' and Peasants' Deputies were formed ~~(Alapaikha, Tagil)~~.

The influence of the Soviets was tremendous. In spite of the fact that they ~~were just embryonic organs,~~ often arose spontaneously, lacked definite structure and were loosely organized, they acted as a governmental power. Without legal authority, they introduced freedom of the press and an 8-hour working day. They called upon the people not to ~~give money~~ *pay taxes* to the tsarist government. In some cases they confiscated government funds and used them for the needs of the revolution.

~~The Bolsheviks allocated a lot of attention and energy to the Soviets. Lenin said that in establishing the Soviets, the working class took a step of enormous world-historical importance for the first time since the 1871 Paris Commune. Comrade Stalin said in his speech to the First All-Union Meeting of Stakhanovites that "the movement for the Soviets of Workers' Deputies, which was begun in 1905 by the workers of Moscow and Leningrad, led in the end to the defeat of capitalism and the victory of Socialism in one sixth of the world."~~

5.~~8.~~ December Armed Uprising. *Defeat of the Uprising. Retreat of the Revolution. First State Duma. Fourth (Unity) Party Congress*

During October and November 1905 the revolutionary struggle of the masses went on developing with intense vigour. ~~In November, 325,000 workers went on strike.~~ Workers' strikes continued.

The struggle of the peasants against the landlords assumed wide dimensions in the autumn of 1905. The peasant movement embraced over one-third of the uyezds of the country. The provinces of Saratov, Tambov, Chernigov, *Tiflis, Kutais* and several others were the scenes of veritable peasant revolts. Yet the onslaught of the peasant masses was still inadequate. ~~The peasants, as Lenin pointed out, burned down only 2,000 of 30,000 landed estates, that is only one fifteenth of what they should have destroyed.~~ The peasant movement lacked organization and leadership.

Unrest increased also among the soldiers in a number of cities—Tiflis, Vladivostok, Tashkent, Samarkand, Kursk, Sukhum, Warsaw, Kiev, and Riga. Revolts broke out in Kronstadt and among the sailors of the Black Sea Fleet in Sevastopol (November 1905). But the revolts were isolated, and the tsarist government was able to suppress them.

Revolts in units of the army and navy were frequently provoked by the brutal conduct of the officers, by bad food ("bean riots"), and similar causes. The bulk of the sailors and soldiers in revolt did not yet clearly realize the necessity for the overthrow of the tsarist government, for the ~~most~~ energetic prosecution of the armed struggle. They were still too peaceful and complacent; they frequently made the mistake of releasing officers who had been arrested at the outbreak of the revolt, and would allow themselves to be placated by the promises and coaxing of their superiors. ~~The tsarist government played for time, gathered reinforcements and broke up the rebel forces. After that followed the harshest suppression and execution of the rebels.~~

The revolutionary movement had approached the verge of armed insurrection. ~~Tirelessly,~~ *T*he Bolsheviks called upon the masses ~~from the January days of 1905~~ to rise in arms against the tsar and the landlords, and explained to them that this was ~~imperative and~~ inevitable. The Bolsheviks worked indefatigably in preparing for ~~and organizing the~~ armed uprising. Revolutionary work was carried on among the soldiers and sailors, and military organizations of the Party were set up in the armed forces. Workers' fighting squads were formed in a number of cities, and their members taught the use of arms. The purchase of arms from abroad and the smuggling of them into Russia was organized, prominent members of the Party taking part in arranging for their transportation. ~~A. M. Gorky helped the Bolsheviks in this affair.~~[6]

In November 1905 Lenin returned to Russia. He took a direct part in the preparations for armed uprising, while keeping out of the way of the tsar's gendarmes and spies. His articles in the Bolshevik newspaper, NOVAYA ZHIZN (NEW LIFE), served to guide the Party in its day-to-day work.

At this period Comrade Stalin was carrying on tremendous revolutionary work in Transcaucasia. He exposed and lashed the Mensheviks ~~and other~~ *as* foes *of the revolution and* of the armed uprising. He resolutely prepared the workers for the decisive battle against the autocracy. *Speaking* at a meeting of workers in Tiflis *on the day the tsar's Manifesto was announced,* Comrade Stalin said:

> "What do we need in order to really win? We need three things: first—~~what we need is~~ arms, second—arms, third—arms and arms again!"

In December 1905 a Bolshevik Conference was held in Tammerfors, Finland. *Although the Bolsheviks and Mensheviks formally belonged to one Social-Democratic Party, they actually constituted two different parties, each with its own leading centre.* At this conference Lenin and Stalin met for the first time. Until then they had maintained contact by correspondence and through comrades.

~~Reminiscing later about his first meeting with Lenin at the Tammerfors Conference, Comrade Stalin wrote:~~

> ~~"The two speeches that Lenin gave at the conference on current events and the agrarian question were remarkable. Unfortunately, they have not survived. They were inspiring speeches which roused the whole conference into a state of stormy excitement. Lenin's speeches were distinguished from those of more common "parliamentary" orators by his unusually strong sense of conviction, the simplicity and clarity of his argumentation, his terse and easily understood phrases and his lack of affect, dizzying gestures and theatrical phrases designed for show.~~
>
> ~~But it wasn't this aspect of Lenin's speeches that captivated me at the time. What captivated me was the overwhelming logical power of Lenin's speeches, which were somewhat terse, but which took hold of his audience on a fundamental level, slowly electrifying it, and then, as they say, completely overpowering it." (Stalin, ON LENIN, Russ. ed., pp. 50–1.)~~

Of the decisions of the Tammerfors Conference, the following two should be noted: one on the restoration of the unity of the Party, which had virtually been split into two parties, and the other on the boycott of the First Duma, known as the Witte Duma.

As *by that time* the armed uprising had already begun in Moscow, the conference, on Lenin's advice, hastily completed its work and dispersed to enable the ~~Bolsheviks~~ *delegates* to ~~actively~~ participate *personally in the uprising.*

~~We have already seen that the revolutionary struggle grew over into an armed uprising.~~ *But* the tsarist government ~~also prepared for a decisive battle~~ *was not dozing either. It too was preparing for a decisive struggle.* Having concluded ~~a deal with a part of the bourgeoisie (The Union of October Seventeenth)~~ *peace with Japan, and thus lessened the difficulties of its position*, the *tsarist* government assumed the ~~decisive~~ offensive against the workers and peasants. It declared martial law in a number of provinces where peasant revolts were rife, issued the brutal commands "take no prisoners" and "spare no bullets," and gave orders for the arrest of the leaders of the revolutionary movement and the dispersal of the Soviets *of Workers' Deputies* ~~and the strike committees~~.

In reply to this, the Moscow Bolsheviks and the Moscow Soviet of Workers' ~~and Soldiers'~~ Deputies which they led, and which was connected with the broad masses of the workers, ~~conducted~~ *decided to make* ~~active~~ *immediate* preparations for armed uprising. On December 5 (18) the Moscow Bolshevik Committee resolved to call upon the Soviet to declare a general *political* strike with the object of turning it into an uprising *in the course of the struggle*. This decision was supported at mass meetings of the workers. The Moscow Soviet responded to the will of the working class and unanimously resolved to start a general political strike ~~in order to transform it into an armed uprising~~.

When the Moscow proletariat began the revolt, it had a fighting organization of about one thousand combatants, more than half of whom were Bolsheviks. *In addition t*here were fighting squads in several of the Moscow ~~enterprises~~ *factories. In all, the insurrectionaries had a force of about two thousand combatants. The workers expected to neutralize the garrison and to win over a part of it to their side.*

The political strike started *in Moscow* on December 7 (20). However, ~~it was not yet a general one~~ *efforts to spread it to the whole country failed*; it met with inadequate support in St. Petersburg, and this reduced the chances of success of the uprising from the very outset. The Nikolayevskaya (now the October) Railway remained in the hands of the tsarist government. Traffic on this line was not suspended, which enabled the government to transfer regiments of the Guard from St. Petersburg to Moscow for the suppression of the uprising.

In Moscow itself the garrison vacillated ~~on the eve and during the beginning of the uprising~~. *The workers had begun t*he uprising ~~had begun~~ partly in expectation of receiving support from the~~se regiments~~ *garrison*. But the revolutionaries had delayed too long, and the government managed to cope with the unrest ~~among the troops~~ *in the garrison*.

The first barricades appeared in Moscow on December 9 (22). Soon ~~many~~ *the* streets of the city were covered with barricades. The tsarist government ~~did not hesitate to use artillery fire in the capital~~ *brought artillery into action*. It concentrated a force many times exceeding the strength of the insurrectionaries. For nine days on end several thousand armed workers waged a heroic fight. It was only by bringing regiments from St. Petersburg, Tver and the Western Territory that the tsarist government was able to crush the uprising. On the very eve of the fighting the leadership of the uprising was partly arrested and partly isolated. The members of the Moscow Bolshevik Committee were arrested. The armed action took the form of disconnected uprisings of separate districts. ~~Lacking~~ *Deprived of* a directing centre, and lacking a ~~strictly developed~~ *common* plan of operations *for the whole city*, the districts mainly confined themselves to defensive action. This was the chief source of weakness of the Moscow uprising and one of the causes of its defeat, as Lenin later pointed out.

The ~~struggle~~ *uprising* assumed a particularly stubborn and bitter character in the Krasnaya Presnya district *of Moscow*. This was the main stronghold and centre of the uprising. Here the best of the fighting squads, led by Bolsheviks, were concentrated. *But* Krasnaya Presnya was suppressed by fire and sword; it was drenched in blood and ablaze with the fires caused by artillery. The Moscow uprising was crushed~~, despite all the heroism that was shown by the revolting workers~~.

The ~~Moscow~~ uprising was not ~~alone~~ *confined to Moscow*. Revolutionary uprisings broke out in a number of other cities and districts. There were armed uprisings in Krasnoyarsk, Molotovilikha (Perm), Novorossisk, Sormovo, Sevastopol and Kronstadt.

The oppressed nationalities of Russia also rose in armed struggle. Nearly the whole of Georgia was up in arms. ~~Under the leadership of Comrade Stalin, the workers and peasants of the Caucasus bravely fought with the tsarist troops.~~ A big uprising took place in the Ukraine, in the cities of Gorlovka, Alexandrovsk and Lugansk (now Voroshilovgrad) in the Donetz Basin. ~~The Lugansk workers were led by the young metal worker Klim Voroshilov.~~ A stubborn struggle was waged in Latvia. In Finland the workers formed their Red Guard and rose in revolt.

But all these uprisings, like the uprising in Moscow, were crushed with inhuman ferocity by the autocracy.

~~Why did the armed December uprising conclude with a defeat for the workers?~~

~~Lenin and Stalin explained the reasons for this defeat.~~

~~The peasantry did not support the uprising at the right time. Many peasants still believed in the tsar. Therefore, part of the army shot down the rebels. There were not enough supportive and coordinated actions among the workers themselves. The uprising was not properly set up and organized. It was not uniform and began in different regions of Russia at different times. In Georgia, the uprising heated up when in Moscow it had already been suppressed. In Siberia, the workers took up arms significantly later than in Moscow. The Siberian organization turned out to be insufficiently strong to make use of the enormous dissatisfaction among the soldiers returning from Manchuria.~~

~~The Mensheviks under Trotsky who sat in the St. Petersburg Soviet were against the uprising and did not prepare for it. The Mensheviks did not support the revolting Moscow workers and undermined the uprising in St. Petersburg. The revolting Moscow workers did not have enough weapons. There were also not enough well-trained Red military forces who might have led the uprising. The rebels took the path of defence instead of offence. A genuine struggle to bring troops over onto the side of the rebels was not developed.~~

~~What sort of evaluation did the Mensheviks and Bolsheviks give to the December uprising?~~

The appraisals of the December armed uprising given by the Mensheviks and the Bolsheviks differed.

"They should not have taken to arms," was the rebuke the Menshevik Plekhanov flung at the Party after the uprising. The Mensheviks argued that ~~there actually hadn't been~~ a*n* ~~popular~~ uprising *was unnecessary and pernicious, that it could be dispensed with in the revolution, that success could be achieved not by armed uprising, but by peaceful methods of struggle.* ~~They tried in every way to depreciate and ridicule it, attempting to show that the path toward revolt was an unreliable, deceptive path of struggle.~~

~~The Bolsheviks did not relate to the uprising in this way. For them,~~ *The Bolsheviks branded this stand as treachery. They maintained that* the experience of the Moscow armed uprising had but confirmed that the working class could wage a successful armed struggle. In reply to Plekhanov's rebuke—"they should not have taken to arms"—Lenin said:

> "On the contrary, we should have taken to arms more resolutely, energetically and aggressively; we should have explained to the masses that it was impossible to confine ourselves to a peaceful strike and that a fearless and relentless armed fight was indispensable." (Lenin, SELECTED WORKS, Vol. III, p. 348.)

~~The Bolsheviks considered the armed struggle of the Russian workers that December to have been the greatest proletarian movement since the 1871 Paris Commune.~~

~~9. Bolsheviks and Mensheviks after the December Uprising~~

The uprising of December 1905 was the climax of the ~~first~~ revolution. The tsarist autocracy ~~dealt the revolution a major blow~~ *defeated the uprising. Thereafter the revolution took a turn and began to recede. The tide of revolution gradually subsided.*

The *tsarist* government hastened to take advantage of this defeat to deal the final blow to the revolution. The tsar's hangmen and jailers began their bloody work. Punitive expeditions raged in Poland, Latvia, Esthonia, Transcaucasia and Siberia. ~~In their orders, the Minister-Hangmen wrote: "The arrests have not accomplished their objectives and it is impossible to try hundreds of thousands of people. . . . We suggest that the mutineers be destroyed by force of arms and that their homes be set on fire in the case of resistance;" "Arrest fewer and shoot more;" "Use firepower, not persuasion."~~

But the revolution was ~~far from~~ *not yet* crushed. The workers and revolutionary peasants retreated slowly, putting up a fight. New sections of the workers were drawn into the struggle. Over a million workers took part in strikes in 1906; 740,000 in 1907. The peasant movement embraced about one-half of the uyezds of tsarist Russia in the first half of 1906, and one-fifth in the second half of the year. Unrest continued in the army and navy.

~~So what was the condition in which the Party found itself?~~

~~At the beginning of the Revolution of 1905, the R.S.D.L.P. was but a small, secret organization, an alliance of underground reading circles. During the revolutionary year, thousands of workers joined the Party. It became a mass party. During this time, the workers won from the tsarist autocracy the freedom of assembly and speech. Just in St. Petersburg, there were three Social-Democratic dailies which appeared in print runs of 50,000 to 100,000 copies apiece. Between October and December 1905, many hundreds of thousands of workers followed the Bolsheviks. The Bolshevik organizations grew and became stronger due to the workers. Those who followed the Mensheviks in large numbers were from the petty bourgeoisie, the intelligentsia and the artisanal strata of the proletariat.~~

~~Over the course of 1905, the struggle between the Bolsheviks and the Mensheviks continued without interruption. It continued after the December uprising as well. The Mensheviks considered the December defeat to be the end of the revolution. The Bolsheviks looked upon it differently. They considered the time to have come for a temporary break and that it was necessary for the renewed preparation of forces, for a new armed uprising. The Bolsheviks, therefore, struggled for the expansion of the revolution and its new upsurge.~~

The tsarist government, in combating the revolution, did not confine itself to repressive measures. Having achieved its first successes by repressive measures, it decided to deal a fresh blow at the revolution by convening a new Duma, a "legislative" Duma. It hoped in this way to sever the peasants from the revolution and thus put an end to it. ~~Especially sharp was the emergence of disagreement between the Bolsheviks and Mensheviks over the question of the First State Duma.~~ In December 1905~~, after the armed uprising had already begun,~~ the tsarist government promulgated a law providing for the convocation of a *new*, a *"legislative"* Duma *as distinct from the old, "deliberative" Bulygin Duma, which had been swept away as the result of the Bolshevik boycott*. The tsarist election law was ~~an insult to the popular masses~~ *of course anti-democratic*. Elections were not universal. Over half the population—for example, women and over two million workers—were deprived of the right of vote altogether. Elections were not equal. The electorate was divided into four curias, as they were called: the agrarian (landlords), the urban (~~for the most part, the~~ bourgeoisie), the peasant and the worker curias. Election was not direct, but by several stages. ~~The population voted for electors, and then they selected representatives from their own milieu.~~ There was actually no secret ballot. The election law ensured the *overwhelming* preponderance in the Duma of a ~~small~~ handful of landlords and capitalists over the millions of workers and peasants.

The tsar intended to make use of the Duma to divert the masses from the revolution. In those days a large proportion of the peasants believed that they could obtain land through the Duma. The Constitutional-Democrats, Mensheviks and Socialist-Revolutionaries ~~supported the deception of the~~ *deceived* workers and peasants by stating that the system the people needed could be obtained without uprising, without revolution. It was to fight this fraud on the people that the Bolsheviks announced and pursued the tactics of ~~an active~~ boycotting the First State Duma. *This was in accordance with the decision passed by the Tammerfors Conference.* ~~The Mensheviks, however, called upon the workers to side with the Constitutional Democrats in the Duma elections.~~

In their fight *against tsardom*, the workers demanded *the* unity *of the forces of the Party*, the unification of the party of the proletariat. *Armed with the decision of the Tammerfors Conference on unity, t*he Bolsheviks supported this demand of the workers and proposed to the Mensheviks ~~an alliance—the convocation of~~ *that* a unity congress *of the Party be called*. Under the pressure of the workers, the Mensheviks had to consent to unification.

Lenin was in favour of unification, but only of such unification as would not cover up the ~~fundamental~~ differences that existed over the problems of the revolution ~~between the Bolsheviks and Mensheviks~~. Considerable damage was done to the Party by the conciliators (Bogdanov, Krassin and others), who tried to prove that ~~there were~~ no serious differences *existed* between the Bolsheviks and the Mensheviks. Lenin fought the conciliators, insisting that ~~at the congress~~ the Bolsheviks should come *to the congress* with their own platform, so that the workers might clearly see what the position of the Bolsheviks was and on what basis unification was being effected. The Bolsheviks ~~even~~ drew up such a platform ~~on all the revolutionary questions~~ *and submitted it to the Party members for discussion.*

The Fourth Congress of the R.S.D.L.P., known as the Unity Congress, met in Stockholm (Sweden) in April 1906. It was attended by 111 delegates with right of vote, representing 57 local organizations of the Party. In addition, there were representatives from the national Social-Democratic parties: 3 from the Bund, 3 from the Polish ~~and Lithuanian~~ Social-Democratic Party, and 3 from the Lettish Social-Democratic organization.

Owing to the smash-up of the Bolshevik organizations during and after the December uprising, not all of them were able to send delegates. Moreover, during the "days of liberty" of 1905, the Mensheviks had admitted into their ranks a large number of petty-bourgeois intellectuals who had nothing whatever in common with revolutionary Marxism. It will suffice to say that the Tiflis Mensheviks (and there were very few industrial workers in Tiflis) sent as many delegates to the congress as the largest of the proletarian organizations, the St. Petersburg organization. ~~This is why~~ *The result was that* at the Stockholm Congress the Mensheviks ~~made up~~ *had* a majority, *although, it is true, an insignificant one.*

This composition of the congress determined the Menshevik character of the decisions on a number of questions. ~~The Mensheviks knew that the Lettish and Polish Social-Democrats were close to the Bolsheviks in their views. Therefore, the Mensheviks took advantage of their majority in order to delay the question of admitting the national Social-Democratic organizations into the R.S.D.L.P. until the end of the conference.~~

Only FORMAL unity was effected at this congress. In reality, the Bolsheviks and the Mensheviks retained their own views and their own independent organizations.

The chief questions discussed at the Fourth ~~(Unity)~~ Congress were the agrarian question, the current situation and the class tasks of the proletariat, policy towards the State Duma, and organizational questions.

Although the Mensheviks constituted the majority at this congress they were obliged to agree to Lenin's formulation of the first paragraph of the Party Rules *dealing with Party membership*, in order not to antagonize the workers.

On the agrarian question, Lenin advocated the NATIONALIZATION of the land. He held that the nationalization of the land would be possible only with the victory of the revolution, after tsardom had been overthrown. Under such circumstances the nationalization of the land would make it easier for the proletariat, in alliance with the poor peasants, to pass to the Socialist revolution. Nationalization of the land meant the confiscation of all the landed estates ~~by the revolutionary peasant committees~~ without compensation *and turning them over to the peasantry*. The Bolshevik agrarian program called upon the peasants to rise in revolution against the tsar and the landlords.

The Mensheviks took up a different position. They advocated a program of MUNICIPALIZATION. According to this program, the landed estates were not to be placed at the disposal of the village communities, not even given to the village communities for use, but were to be placed at the disposal of the municipalities (that is, the local organs of self-government, or Zemstvos), and each peasant was to RENT as much of this land as he could afford.

The Menshevik program of municipalization was ~~not only incorrect, but~~ *one of compromise, and therefore* prejudicial to the revolution. It ~~didn't~~ *could not* mobilize the peasants for a revolutionary struggle and was not designed to achieve the complete abolition of landlord property rights in land. The Menshevik program was designed to stop the revolution halfway~~, and not go all the way~~. The Mensheviks did not want to rouse the peasants for revolution. ~~Two LINES—PROLETARIAN AND PETTY BOURGEOIS—THUS APPEARED IN THE QUESTION ON THE AGRARIAN PROGRAM.~~

The Menshevik program received the majority of the votes at the congress.

The Mensheviks particularly betrayed their anti-proletarian, opportunist nature during the discussion of the resolution on the current situation and on the State Duma. The Menshevik Martynov frankly spoke in opposition to the hegemony ~~(leadership)~~ of the proletariat in the revolution. Comrade Stalin, replying to the Mensheviks, put the matter very bluntly:

> "Either the hegemony of the proletariat, or the hegemony of the democratic bourgeoisie—that is how the question stands in the Party, that is where we differ." ~~(VERBATIM REPORT OF THE FOURTH (UNITY) CONGRESS OF THE R.S.D.L.P., Russ. ed., 1934, p. 235.)~~

~~Comrade Stalin proved that the Bolsheviks' tactics, designed to organize a new uprising, were the only correct and militant tactics. They would rouse the workers and rally them to the revolution. The Mensheviks' tactics lulled the workers to sleep.~~

As to the State Duma, the Mensheviks extolled it in their resolution as the best means of solving the problems of the revolution and of liberating the people from tsardom. The Bolsheviks, on the contrary, regarded the Duma as an impotent appendage of tsardom, as a screen for the evils of tsardom, which the latter would discard as soon as it proved inconvenient.

The Central Committee elected at the Fourth Congress consisted of three Bolsheviks and six Mensheviks. The editorial board of the central press organ was formed entirely of Mensheviks.

It was clear that the internal Party struggle would continue. ~~For the Bolsheviks it became clear that it was imperative for them to have their own centre. At a meeting of the Bolshevik delegates, such a centre was formed. Lenin, gathering together the Bolshevik deputies, gave them specific orders on how to keep control of themselves and how to conduct work in order to win over to their side the majority of the organizations and the organized workers.~~

~~The Mensheviks emerged victorious at the Fourth Party Congress. But Lenin did not give up hope. He was convinced that the Bolsheviks' victory over the opportunists was near and passed on this conviction to all the Bolsheviks.~~

After the Fourth Congress the conflict between the Bolsheviks and the Mensheviks broke out ~~even more~~ *with new vigour*. In the local organizations, which were formally united, reports on the congress were often made by two speakers: one from the Bolsheviks and another from the Mensheviks. The result of the discussion of the~~se~~ two lines was that *in most cases* the majority of the ~~Party~~ members *of the organizations* sided with the Bolsheviks.

Events proved that the Bolsheviks were right. The Menshevik Central Committee elected at the Fourth Congress increasingly ~~showed~~ *revealed* its opportunism and its utter inability to lead the revolutionary struggle of the masses. In the summer and autumn of 1906 the *revolutionary* struggle of the masses took on new vigour. Sailors' revolts broke out in Kronstadt and Sveaborg; the peasants' struggle against the landlords flared up. Yet the Menshevik Central Committee issued opportunist slogans, which the masses did not follow.

6. Dispersion of the First State Duma. Convocation of the Second State Duma. Fifth Party Congress. Dispersion of the Second State Duma. Causes of the Defeat of the First Russian Revolution

~~During the summer of 1906, the tsar dismissed the First State Duma and scheduled elections for a second one. Because the circumstances had changed and the revolutionary wave had begun to subside, the Bolsheviks ceased to use the slogan calling for a Duma boycott.~~

As the First State Duma did not prove docile enough, the tsarist government dispersed it in the summer of 1906. The government resorted to even more drastic repressions against the people, extended the ravaging activities of the punitive expeditions throughout the country, and announced its decision of shortly calling a Second State Duma. The tsarist government was obviously growing more insolent. It no longer feared the revolution, for it saw that the revolution was on the decline.

The Bolsheviks had to decide whether to participate in the Second Duma or to boycott it. By boycott, the Bolsheviks usually meant an active boycott, and not the mere passive abstention from voting in the elections. The Bolsheviks regarded active boycott as a revolutionary means of warning the people against the attempts of the tsar to divert them from the path of revolution to the path of tsarist "constitution," as a means of frustrating these attempts and organizing a new onslaught of the people on tsardom.

The experience of the boycott of the Bulygin Duma had shown that a boycott was "the only correct tactics, as fully proved by events." (Lenin, SELECTED WORKS,

Vol. III, p. 393.) This boycott was successful because it not only warned the people against the danger of the path of tsarist constitutionalism but frustrated the very birth of the Duma. The boycott was successful because it was carried out DURING THE RISING TIDE *of the revolution and was supported by this tide, and not when the revolution was receding. The summoning of the Duma could be frustrated only during the* HIGH TIDE *of the revolution.*

The boycott of the Witte Duma, i.e., the First Duma, took place after the December uprising had been defeated, when the tsar proved to be the victor, that is, at a time when there was reason to believe that the revolution had begun to recede.

> *"But," wrote Lenin, "it goes without saying that at that time there were as yet no grounds to regard this victory (of the tsar—*ED.*) as a decisive victory. The uprising of December 1905 had its sequel in a series of disconnected and partial military uprisings and strikes in the summer of 1906. The call to boycott the Witte Duma was a call to concentrate these uprisings and make them general." (Lenin,* COLLECTED WORKS*, Russ. ed., Vol. XII, p. 20.)*

The boycott of the Witte Duma was unable to frustrate its convocation although it considerably undermined its prestige and weakened the faith of a part of the population in it. The boycott was unable to frustrate the convocation of the Duma because, as subsequently became clear, it took place at a time when the revolution was receding, when it was on the decline. For this reason the boycott of the First Duma in 1906 was unsuccessful. In this connection Lenin wrote in his famous pamphlet, "LEFT-WING" COMMUNISM, AN INFANTILE DISORDER:

> *"The Bolshevik boycott of 'parliament' in 1905 enriched the revolutionary proletariat with highly valuable political experience and showed that in combining legal with illegal, parliamentary with extraparliamentary forms of struggle, it is sometimes useful and even essential to reject parliamentary forms. . . . The boycott of the 'Duma' by the Bolsheviks in 1906 was however a mistake, although a small and easily remediable one. . . . What applies to individuals applies—with necessary modifications—to politics and parties. Not he is wise who makes no mistakes. There are no such men nor can there be. He is wise who makes not very serious mistakes and who knows how to correct them easily and quickly. (Lenin,* COLLECTED WORKS*, Russ. ed., Vol. XXV, pp. 182–83.)*

As to the Second State Duma, Lenin held that in view of the changed situation and the decline of the revolution, the Bolsheviks "must reconsider the question of boycotting the State Duma." (Lenin, SELECTED WORKS*, Vol. III, p. 392.)*

> *"History has shown," Lenin wrote, "that when the Duma assembles opportunities arise for carrying on useful agitation both from within the Duma and, in connection with it, outside—that the tactics of joining forces with the revolutionary peasantry against the Constitutional-Democrats can be applied in the Duma." (Ibid., p. 396.)*

All this showed that one had to know not only how to advance resolutely, to advance in the front ranks, when the revolution was in the ascendant, but also how to retreat properly, to be the last to retreat, when the revolution was no longer in the ascendant, changing one's tactics as the situation changed; to retreat not in disorder, but in an organized way, calmly and without panic, utilizing every minute opportunity to withdraw the cadres from under enemy fire, to reform one's ranks, to muster one's forces and to prepare for a new offensive against the enemy.

The Bolsheviks decided to take part in the elections to the Second Duma.

But the Bolsheviks ~~went~~ *did not go* to the Duma *for the purpose of carrying on organic "legislative" work inside it in a bloc with the Constitutional-Democrats, as the Mensheviks did, but* for the purpose of utilizing it as a platform in the interests of the revolution.

The Menshevik Central Committee, *on the contrary,* urged that election agreements be formed with the Constitutional-Democrats, and that support be given to the Constitutional-Democrats in the Duma, *for in their eyes the Duma was a legislative body that was capable of bridling the tsarist government.*

The majority of the Party organizations expressed themselves against *the policy of* the Menshevik Central Committee.

The Bolsheviks demanded that a new ~~extraordinary~~ Party congress be called.

In May 1907 the Fifth Party Congress met in London. At the time of this congress the R.S.D.L.P. (together with the national Social-Democratic organizations) had a membership of nearly 150,000. In all, 336 delegates attended the congress, of whom 105 were Bolsheviks and 97 Mensheviks. The remaining delegates represented the national Social-Democratic organizations—the Polish and Lettish Social-Democrats and the Bund—which had been admitted into the R.S.D.L.P. at the previous congress.

~~The Menshevik~~ Trotsky tried to knock together a group of his own at the congress, *a centrist, that is, semi-Menshevik, group,* but could get no following.

As the Bolsheviks had the support of the Poles and the Letts, they had a *stable* majority at the congress.

One of the main questions at issue at the congress was that of policy towards the bourgeois parties. There had already been a struggle between the Bolsheviks and Mensheviks on this question at the Second Congress. The Fifth Congress gave a Bolshevik estimate of all the non-proletarian parties—*Black-Hundreds,*

~~the Rightists,~~ Octobrists (Union of October 17), Constitutional-Democrats and Socialist-Revolutionaries—and formulated the Bolshevik tactics to be pursued in regard to ~~them~~ *these parties.*

~~What was the Bolshevik line in regard to the other parties?~~ The ~~Fifth~~ congress ~~issued the directive~~ *approved the policy of the Bolsheviks and decided* to wage a relentless struggle both against the Black-Hundred parties—the League of the Russian People, the monarchists, the Council of the United Nobility—and against the Octobrists, the Commercial and Industrial Party and the Party of Peaceful Renovation. All these parties were outspokenly counter-revolutionary.

As regards the liberal bourgeoisie, the Constitutional-Democratic Party, the congress ~~also~~ recommended a ~~merciless struggle with them~~ *policy of uncompromising exposure*; the false and hypocritical "democracy" of the Constitutional-Democratic Party was to be exposed and the attempts of the liberal bourgeoisie to gain control of the peasant movement combated.

As to the so-called Narodnik or Trudovik parties (the Popular Socialists, the Trudovik Group and the Socialist-Revolutionaries), the congress recommended that their attempts to mask themselves as Socialists be exposed. At the same time the congress considered it permissible now and then to conclude agreements with these parties for a joint and simultaneous attack on tsardom and the ~~treacherous, liberal~~ *Constitutional-Democratic* bourgeoisie, inasmuch as these parties were at that time democratic parties and expressed the interests of the petty bourgeoisie of town and country.

~~The Bolsheviks were victorious at the Fifth Party Congress on all the fundamental issues. But the struggle at the congress was very bitter. The Mensheviks tried to undermine the congress in every way: on every issue, they demanded roll-call votes and proposed dozens of amendments.~~

Even before this congress, the Mensheviks had proposed that a so-called "labour congress" be convened. The Mensheviks' idea was to call a congress at which Social-Democrats, Socialist-Revolutionaries and Anarchists~~, as well as all trade unions, workers' co-operatives and clubs and so on,~~ should all be represented. This *"labour"* congress was to form something in the nature of a "non-partisan party," or a "broad" *petty-bourgeois* labour party *without a program*. Lenin ~~and Stalin~~ exposed this as a pernicious attempt on the part of the Mensheviks to liquidate the *Social-Democratic* Labour Party and to dissolve the vanguard of the working class in the petty-bourgeois mass. The congress vigorously condemned the Menshevik call for a "labour congress."

Special attention was devoted at the congress to the subject of the trade unions. The Mensheviks advocated "neutrality" of the trade unions; in other words, they were opposed to *the* Party ~~leadership~~ *playing a leading role* in them. The congress rejected the Mensheviks' motion and adopted the resolution submitted by the Bolsheviks. This resolution stated that the Party must gain the ideological *and political* leadership in the trade unions.

The Fifth Congress was a big victory for the Bolsheviks in the working-class movement. But the Bolsheviks did not allow this to turn their heads; nor did they rest on their laurels. That was not what Lenin taught them. The Bolsheviks knew that ~~decisive~~ *more* fighting with the Mensheviks was still to come.

In an article entitled "Notes of a Delegate" *which appeared in 1907*, Comrade Stalin ~~summarized~~ *assessed* the results of the congress *as follows*:

> "The actual unification of the advanced workers of all Russia into a single all-Russian party under the banner of REVOLUTIONARY Social-Democracy—that is the significance of the London Congress, that is its general character."

In *t*his article ~~on the Fifth (London) Party Congress of the R.S.D.L.P.,~~ Comrade Stalin cited ~~very important~~ data showing the COMPOSITION of the congress. They show that the Bolshevik delegates were sent to the congress chiefly by the big industrial centres (St. Petersburg, Moscow, the Urals, Ivanovo-Voznesensk, etc.), whereas the Mensheviks got their mandates from districts where small production prevailed, where artisans, semi-proletarians predominated, as well as from ~~several~~ *a number of* purely rural areas.

> "Obviously," says Comrade Stalin, summing up the results of the congress, "the tactics of the Bolsheviks are the tactics of the proletarians in big industry, the tactics of those areas where the class contradictions are especially clear and the class struggle especially acute. Bolshevism is the tactics of the real proletarians. On the other hand, it is no less obvious that the tactics of the Mensheviks are primarily the tactics of the handicraft workers and the peasant semi-proletarians, the tactics of those areas where the class contradictions are not quite clear and the class struggle is masked. Menshevism is the tactics of the semi-bourgeois elements among the proletariat. So say the figures." (VERBATIM REPORT OF THE FIFTH CONGRESS OF THE R.S.D.L.P., Russ. ed., 1935, pp. xi and xii.)

When the tsar dispersed the First Duma he expected that the Second Duma would be more docile. But the Second Duma, too, belied his expectations. The tsar thereupon decided to disperse it, too, and to convoke a Third Duma on a more restricted franchise, in the hope that this Duma would prove more amenable.

Shortly after the Fifth Congress, the tsarist government effected what is known as the COUP D'ETAT of June 3. On June 3, 1907, the tsar dispersed the Second State Duma. The sixty-five deputies of the Social-Democratic group in the Duma were arrested and exiled to Siberia. A new election law was promulgated. The rights of the workers and peasants were still further curtailed. ~~The autocracy went on a decisive offensive against the revolution.~~ *The tsarist government continued its offensive.*

The tsar's Minister Stolypin ~~organized~~ *intensified* the campaign of bloody reprisals against the workers and peasants. ~~Tens of~~ *T*housands of revolutionary workers and peasants were shot by punitive expeditions, or hanged~~, without trial~~. In the tsarist dungeons revolutionaries were tortured mentally and physically. Particularly savage was the persecution of the working-class organizations, especially the Bolsheviks. The tsar's sleuths were searching for Lenin, who was living in hiding in Finland. They wanted to wreak their vengeance on the leader of the revolution. In December 1907 Lenin managed at great risk to make his way abroad and again became an exile.

The dark period of the Stolypin reaction set in.

~~**10. Reasons for the Revolution's Defeat**~~

The first Russian revolution thus ended in ~~temporary~~ defeat.

~~An array of~~ *The* causes that contributed to this defeat ~~was~~ *were* as follows:

1) ~~First of all—~~*I*n the revolution, there was still no ~~strong and~~ stable alliance of the workers and peasants *against tsardom*. The peasants rose in struggle against the landlords and ~~they were influenced by the revolutionary labour movement~~ *were willing to join in an alliance with the workers against them.* But they did not yet realize that the landlords ~~and~~ *could not be overthrown unless the tsar were overthrown, they did not realize that* the tsar ~~were~~ *was* acting hand-in-hand *with the landlords,* and large numbers of the peasants still had faith in the tsar *and placed their hopes in the tsarist State Duma*. That is why a considerable section of the peasants were disinclined to join in alliance with the workers for the overthrow of tsardom. The peasants had more faith in the compromising Socialist-Revolutionary Party than in the real revolutionaries—the Bolsheviks. As a result, the struggle of the peasants against the landlords was not sufficiently organized. Lenin said:

> "The peasants' actions were too scattered, too unorganized and not sufficiently aggressive, and that was one of the fundamental causes of the defeat of the revolution." (Lenin, COLLECTED WORKS, Russ. ed., Vol. XIX, p. 354.)

2) The disinclination of a large section of the peasants to join the workers for the overthrow of tsardom also influenced the conduct of the army, which largely consisted of peasants' sons clad in soldiers' uniforms. Unrest and revolt broke out in certain units of the tsar's army, but the majority of the soldiers still assisted the tsar in suppressing the strikes and uprisings of the workers.

3) Neither was the action of the workers sufficiently concerted. The advanced sections of the working class started a heroic revolutionary struggle in 1905. The more backward sections—the workers in the less industrialized provinces, those who lived in the villages—came into action more slowly. Their participation in the revolutionary struggle became particularly active in 1906, but by then the vanguard *of the working class* had already been considerably weakened.

4) The working class was the foremost and principal force of the revolution; but the necessary unity and solidarity in the ranks of the party of the working class were lacking. The R.S.D.L.P.—the party of the working class—was split into two groups ~~(factions)~~: the Bolsheviks and the Mensheviks. The Bolsheviks pursued a consistent revolutionary line and called upon the workers to overthrow tsardom. The Mensheviks, by their compromising tactics, hampered the revolution, *confused the minds of large numbers of workers and split the working class*. Therefore, the workers did not always act concertedly in the revolution, and the working class ~~in 1905~~, still ~~lacked the ability to~~ *lacking unity within its own ranks, could not* become the real ~~head (hegemon)~~ *leader* of the revolution ~~and enjoy the recognition of the peasant masses.~~ ~~The Party still lacked the strength to combine together the three fundamental currents of the revolutionary movement: the workers, peasants and soldiers.~~

~~After the defeat of the Revolution of 1905, the Bolsheviks continued to wage a struggle for the formation and strengthening of the worker-peasant alliance in the bourgeois-democratic revolution in the name of the hegemony of the proletariat, which was achieved during the second Russian revolution of February 1917. It was not only the counter-revolutionary landlords, capitalists and clergy that assisted the tsar in suppressing the revolution, but the liberal bourgeoisie, who betrayed the promises that they had given in their own announcements and programs.~~

5) The tsarist autocracy received help in crushing the Revolution of 1905 from the West-European imperialists. The foreign capitalists feared for their investments in Russia and for their huge profits. Moreover, they feared that if the Russian revolution were to succeed the workers of other countries would rise in revolution, too. ~~This is why~~ *T*he West-European imperialists *therefore* came to the assistance of the hangman-tsar. The French bankers ~~gave a lot of gold~~ *granted a big loan* to the tsar for the suppression of the revolution. The German ~~emperor~~ *kaiser* kept a large army in readiness to intervene in aid of the Russian tsar.

6) The conclusion of peace with Japan in September 1905 was ~~also~~ of *considerable* help to the tsar. Defeat in the war and the menacing growth of the revolution had induced the tsar to hasten the signing of peace. The loss of the war weakened tsardom. The conclusion of peace strengthened the position of the tsar.

In 1905–07, tsardom turned out to be stronger than the revolution. The autocracy was able to hold off the attack of the popular masses. Tsardom gathered its forces together and temporarily suppressed the revolution.

11. Historical Significance of the First Russian Revolution

The significance of the Revolution of 1905 was enormous. It was a great school of political struggle for the workers and peasants. All the classes and parties showed their true colors in this revolution. The workers and peasants saw who was their friend and who was their enemy. In one year, the workers traveled quite a path from the peaceful march to the tsar in January 1905 to the armed uprising in December. They accumulated enormous experience in the staging of general strikes and armed uprisings.

Lenin pointed out that the UNIQUENESS of the first Russian revolution consisted in the fact that "it was BOURGEOIS-DEMOCRATIC, according to its social content, but PROLETARIAN according to its means." (Lenin, *Collected Works*, Russ. ed., Vol. XIX, p. 345.) The most immediate goal of the first Russian Revolution of 1905 was the overthrow of tsardom, the victory of a democratic republic, the 8-hour working day and the confiscation of the landed estates. Realization of these objectives would have meant the victory of the bourgeois-democratic revolution, but not a socialist one, because the capitalist system would still not have been destroyed.

In this bourgeois-democratic revolution, the working class served at the VANGUARD force. The main means of struggle with tsardom was the proletariat's means of struggle—the strike that transforms into an uprising.

In the flame of revolution workers and peasants from all the peoples of Russia grew closer and laid the steady foundations of a militant worker-peasant alliance. Through their personal experience, the workers and peasants were persuaded of the Bolsheviks' correctitude. They were convinced that the Bolsheviks were speaking the truth when they demonstrated the imperative of a worker-peasant alliance, an armed overthrow of the autocracy and the formation of organs of revolutionary power. As a result of the revolution, the Bolsheviks' influence over the masses grew significantly. The Revolution of 1905 played the greatest role in the preparation for the great October victory of 1917. Lenin frequently said that without "the dress rehearsal" of 1905, the victory of the October 1917 Revolution would have been impossible. The Revolution of 1905 advanced a new form of organization for the masses and the embryonic organs of power—the Soviets.

~~The Revolution of 1905 had enormous international significance. Practically all the fundamental questions of the world revolution—the armed uprising and the dictatorship of the proletariat—factored into this struggle. The revolutionary creativity of the Russian workers led to the formation of the Soviets. Millions of workers and peasants throughout the world today study the experience of the First Russian Revolution. As Lenin wrote, "The forms of struggle must serve as a lighthouse for the cause of training new generations of fighters."~~

~~The Revolution of 1905 also had a direct and powerful effect on the revolutionary movement around the world. Under its influence, hundreds of millions of oppressed working people in the East were rallied to the revolutionary struggle. Revolutions occurred in Turkey, Persia and China. Under its influence, the strike wave in Western Europe shot upward. Powerful street protests and an unheard-of upsurge in the strike movement—this was the way in which the West-European workers responded to our revolution. The demarcation between revolutionary and opportunist elements of the Second International likewise became stronger.~~

~~The Revolution of 1905 therefore left a deep impression on the whole of human history.~~

Brief Summary

~~In the course of the Revolution of 1905, the Bolsheviks had to defend the revolutionary line in a stubborn, principled struggle with the Mensheviks.~~

~~The Mensheviks' tactics were based on the idea that leadership (hegemony) in the bourgeois-democratic revolution of 1905 should belong to the liberal bourgeoisie, as it had in previous bourgeois revolutions in the West. The Mensheviks retreated from Marxism, not wanting to see a difference between the historical circumstances of the Revolution of 1905 and previous bourgeois revolutions.~~

~~The Mensheviks were actually against the uprising and the proletariat's leading role therein; they refused to engage in practical preparations for the uprising or the arming of the workers.~~

~~The Mensheviks were on a leash held by the Constitutional Democrats, who wanted to conclude an agreement with the autocracy instead of overthrowing tsardom. Already in the Revolution of 1905, the Mensheviks acted as conciliators in regard to the bourgeoisie, betraying the fundamental interests of the working class and aiming to subordinate the working class to the influence of the bourgeoisie. The Mensheviks were against a worker-peasant alliance and did not want to rally the peasantry to revolution.~~

~~The Mensheviks did not want to bring about the realization of the democratic-bourgeois revolution.~~

~~The Bolsheviks waged an uncompromising, principled struggle with the conciliators—the Mensheviks. In their tactics, the Bolsheviks based their struggle on the idea that the leading role (the hegemonic role) in the 1905 bourgeois-democratic revolution must belong to the proletariat.~~

~~The Bolsheviks advanced the slogan for a revolutionary-democratic dictatorship of the proletariat and peasantry, a revolutionary worker-peasant government that was to take shape as the result of a victorious popular uprising against tsardom. Before this revolutionary government, the Bolsheviks advanced the tasks of bringing about the realization of the democratic revolution, a democratic republic, the confiscation of the landed estates, the 8-hour working day and the other working-class demands, as well as the suppression of all attempts at counter-revolution. The Bolsheviks struggled for the realization of the worker-peasant alliance.~~

~~The Bolsheviks led the practical preparations for the uprising, armed the workers and fought on the barricades.~~

~~The Bolsheviks believed that realizing the democratic revolution would ease the proletariat's struggle for a socialist coup d'état. The leadership (hegemony) of the proletariat in the democratic revolution was the embryonic, transitional step toward the dictatorship of the proletariat. Lenin held that the bourgeois-democratic revolution would pass into a socialist revolution in accord with the strength and consciousness of the organized proletariat.~~

~~The conciliatory tactics of the Mensheviks, who still enjoyed the following of a part of the workers, instilled doubt within the working class and prevented the workers from acting concertedly against tsardom. This was one of the reasons for the defeat of the Revolution of 1905.~~

~~Despite the defeat of the Revolution of 1905, the Bolsheviks did not lose faith in the masses. The Bolsheviks exhaustively used the experience of the Revolution of 1905, the grim lessons of defeat, for further struggle against tsardom and capitalism. The experience of the Revolution of 1905 was of decisive significance for the victory of the February Bourgeois-Democratic Revolution of 1917 and for the victory of the October Socialist Revolution of 1917.~~

The first Russian revolution constituted a whole historical stage in the development of our country. This historical stage consisted of two periods: the first period, when the tide of revolution rose from the general political strike in October to the armed uprising in December and took advantage of the weakness of the tsar, who had suffered defeat on the battlefields of Manchuria, to sweep away the Bulygin Duma and wrest concession after concession from the tsar; and the second period, when tsardom, having recovered after the conclusion of peace with Japan, took advantage of the liberal bourgeoisie's fear of the revolution, took advantage of the vacillation of the peasants, cast them a sop in the form of the Witte Duma, and passed to the offensive against the working class, against the revolution.

In the short period of only three years of revolution (1905–07) the working class and the peasantry received a rich political education, such as they could not have received in thirty[7] *years of ordinary peaceful development. A few years of revolution made clear what could not be made clear in the course of decades of peaceful development.*

The revolution disclosed that tsardom was the sworn enemy of the people, that tsardom was like the proverbial hunchback whom only the grave could cure.

The revolution showed that the liberal bourgeoisie was seeking an alliance with the tsar, and not with the people, that it was a counter-revolutionary force, an agreement with which would be tantamount to a betrayal of the people.

The revolution showed that only the working class could be the leader of the bourgeois-democratic revolution, that it alone could force aside the liberal Constitutional-Democratic bourgeoisie, destroy its influence over the peasantry, rout the landlords, carry the revolution to its conclusion and clear the way for Socialism.

Lastly, the revolution showed that the labouring peasantry, despite its vacillations, was the only important force capable of forming an alliance with the working class.

Two lines were contending within the R.S.D.L.P. during the revolution, the line of the Bolsheviks and the line of the Mensheviks. The Bolsheviks took as their course the extension of the revolution, the overthrow of tsardom by armed uprising, the hegemony of the working class, the isolation of the Constitutional-Democratic bourgeoisie, an alliance with the peasantry, the formation of a provisional revolutionary government consisting of representatives of the workers and peasants, the victorious completion of the revolution. The Mensheviks, on the contrary, took as their course the liquidation of the revolution. Instead of overthrowing tsardom by uprising, they proposed to reform and "improve" it; instead of the hegemony of the proletariat, they proposed the hegemony of the liberal bourgeoisie; instead of an alliance with the peasantry, they proposed an alliance with the Constitutional-Democratic bourgeoisie; instead of a provisional government, they proposed a State Duma as the centre of the "revolutionary forces" of the country.

Thus the Mensheviks sank into the morass of compromise and became vehicles of the bourgeois influence on the working class, virtual agents of the bourgeoisie within the working class.

The Bolsheviks proved to be the only revolutionary Marxist force in the Party and the country.

It was natural that, in view of such profound differences, the R.S.D.L.P. proved in fact to be split into two parties, the party of the Bolsheviks and the party of the Mensheviks. The Fourth Party Congress changed nothing in the actual state of affairs within the Party. It only preserved and somewhat strengthened FORMAL *unity in the Party. The Fifth Party Congress took a step towards* ACTUAL *unity in the Party, a unity achieved under the banner of Bolshevism.*

Reviewing the revolutionary movement, the Fifth Party Congress condemned the line of the Mensheviks as one of compromise, and approved the Bolshevik line as a revolutionary Marxist line. In doing so it once more confirmed what had already been confirmed by the whole course of the first Russian revolution.

The revolution showed that the Bolsheviks knew how to advance when the situation demanded it, that they had learned to advance in the front ranks and to lead the whole people in attack. But the revolution also showed that the Bolsheviks knew how to retreat in an orderly way when the situation took an unfavourable turn, when the revolution was on the decline, and that the Bolsheviks had learned to retreat properly, without panic or commotion, so as to preserve their cadres, rally their forces, and, having reformed their ranks in conformity with the new situation, once again to resume the attack on the enemy.

It is impossible to defeat the enemy without knowing how to attack properly.

It is impossible to avoid utter rout in the event of defeat without knowing how to retreat properly, to retreat without panic and without confusion.

CHAPTER FOUR

The Mensheviks and the Bolsheviks in the Period of the Stolypin Reaction. and *T*he Bolsheviks Constitute Themselves as an Independent Social-Democratic Labour *Marxist* Party (1908–1912)

1. Stolypin Reaction. *Disintegration among the Oppositional Intelligentsia. Decadence. Desertion of a Section of the Party Intelligentsia to the Enemies of Marxism and Attempts to Revise the Theory of Marxism. Lenin's Rebuttal of the Revisionists in His MATERIALISM AND EMPIRO-CRITICISM AND HIS DEFENCE of the Theoretical Foundations of the Marxist Party*

The Second State Duma was dissolved by the tsarist government on June 3, 1907. This is customarily referred to in Russian history as the COUP D'ETAT of June 3. The tsarist government issued a new law on the elections to the Third State Duma, and thus violated its own Manifesto of October 17, 1905, which stipulated that new laws could be issued only with the consent of the Duma. The members of the Social-Democratic group in the *Second* Duma were committed for trial; the representatives of the working class were condemned to penal servitude and exile.

The new election law that was published by the government was so drafted as to increase considerably the number *of representatives* of the landowners, landlords and the commercial and industrial bourgeoisie in the Duma. At the same time the representation of the peasants and workers, small as it was, was reduced to a fraction of its former size.

Black-Hundreds and Constitutional-Democrats preponderated in the Third Duma. Of a total of 442 deputies, 171 were Rights (Black-Hundreds), 113 were Octobrists or members of kindred groups, 101 were Constitutional-Democrats or members of kindred groups, 13 were Trudoviki, and 18 were Social-Democrats (see Lenin's article "The Third Duma," COLLECTED WORKS, Russ. ed., Vol. XII, p. 94).

The Rights (so called because they occupied the benches on the right-hand side of the Duma) represented the very worst enemies of the workers and peasants—the Black-Hundred feudal landlords, who had subjected the peasants to mass floggings and shootings during the suppression of the peasant uprisings

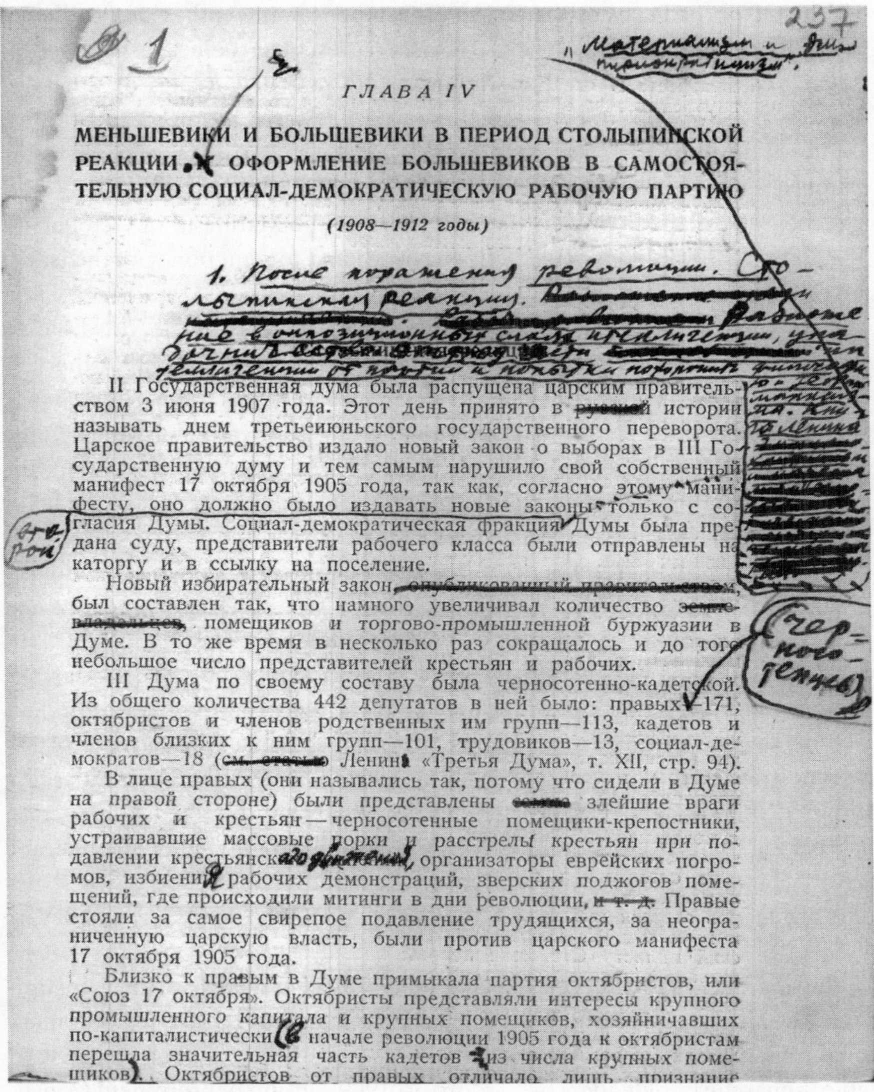

ГЛАВА IV

МЕНЬШЕВИКИ И БОЛЬШЕВИКИ В ПЕРИОД СТОЛЫПИНСКОЙ РЕАКЦИИ. ОФОРМЛЕНИЕ БОЛЬШЕВИКОВ В САМОСТОЯТЕЛЬНУЮ СОЦИАЛ-ДЕМОКРАТИЧЕСКУЮ РАБОЧУЮ ПАРТИЮ

(1908—1912 годы)

II Государственная дума была распущена царским правительством 3 июня 1907 года. Этот день принято в русской истории называть днем третьеиюньского государственного переворота. Царское правительство издало новый закон о выборах в III Государственную думу и тем самым нарушило свой собственный манифест 17 октября 1905 года, так как, согласно этому манифесту, оно должно было издавать новые законы только с согласия Думы. Социал-демократическая фракция Думы была предана суду, представители рабочего класса были отправлены на каторгу и в ссылку на поселение.

Новый избирательный закон, опубликованный правительством, был составлен так, что намного увеличивал количество землевладельцев, помещиков и торгово-промышленной буржуазии в Думе. В то же время в несколько раз сокращалось и до того небольшое число представителей крестьян и рабочих.

III Дума по своему составу была черносотенно-кадетской. Из общего количества 442 депутатов в ней было: правых—171, октябристов и членов родственных им групп—113, кадетов и членов близких к ним групп—101, трудовиков—13, социал-демократов—18 (см. статью Ленина «Третья Дума», т. XII, стр. 94).

В лице правых (они назывались так, потому что сидели в Думе на правой стороне) были представлены самые злейшие враги рабочих и крестьян — черносотенные помещики-крепостники, устраивавшие массовые порки и расстрелы крестьян при подавлении крестьянского движения, организаторы еврейских погромов, избиения рабочих демонстраций, зверских поджогов помещений, где происходили митинги в дни революции, и т. д. Правые стояли за самое свирепое подавление трудящихся, за неограниченную царскую власть, были против царского манифеста 17 октября 1905 года.

Близко к правым в Думе примыкала партия октябристов, или «Союз 17 октября». Октябристы представляли интересы крупного промышленного капитала и крупных помещиков, хозяйничавших по-капиталистически (в начале революции 1905 года к октябристам перешла значительная часть кадетов из числа крупных помещиков). Октябристов от правых отличало лишь признание

Fragment of first page of Chapter Four with Stalin's editing from the summer of 1938. RGASPI, f. 558, op. 11, d. 1210, l. 237.

movement, and organizers of Jewish pogroms, of the manhandling of demonstrating workers and of the brutal burning of premises where meetings were being held during the revolution~~, etc~~. The Rights stood for the most ruthless suppression of the working people, and for the unlimited power of the tsar; they were opposed to the tsar's Manifesto of October 17, 1905.

The Octobrist Party, or the Union of October Seventeenth, closely adhered to the Rights in the Duma. The Octobrists represented the interests of big industrial capital, and of the big landlords who ran their estates on capitalist lines (at the beginning of the Revolution of 1905 a large number of the big landlords belonging to the Constitutional-Democratic Party went over to the Octobrists). The only thing that distinguished the Octobrists from the Rights was their acceptance—*only in words at that*—of the Manifesto of October 17. The Octobrists fully supported *both*[1] the home and foreign policy of the tsarist government.

The Constitutional-Democratic Party had fewer seats in the Third Duma than in the First and Second Dumas. This was due to ~~the fact that the voting rights possessed by the urban masses (employees, part of the merchants, etc.), who had voted for the Constitutional-Democrats in the previous Duma elections after having been deceived by their false "democratic" promises, were now significantly limited. Moreover, there was~~ the transfer of part of the landlord vote from the Constitutional-Democrats to the Octobrists.

There was a small group of petty-bourgeois democrats, known as Trudoviki, in the Third Duma. They vacillated between the Constitutional-Democrats and the labour democrats (Bolsheviks). Lenin pointed out that although the Trudoviki in the Duma were extremely weak, they ~~still~~ represented the MASSES, the peasant masses. The vacillation of the Trudoviki between the Constitutional-Democrats and the labour democrats was an inevitable consequence of the class position of the small owners. Lenin set before the Bolshevik deputies, the labour democrats, the task of "helping the weak petty-bourgeois democrats, of wresting them from the influence of the liberals, of rallying the democratic camp against the counter-revolutionary Constitutional-Democrats, and not only against the Rights. . . ." (Lenin, COLLECTED WORKS, Russ. ed., Vol. XV, p. 486.)

During the Revolution of 1905, and especially after its defeat, the Constitutional-Democrats increasingly revealed themselves as a counter-revolutionary force. Discarding their "democratic" mask more and more, they acted like veritable monarchists, defenders of tsardom. In 1909 a group of prominent Constitutional-Democrat writers ~~(among whom was Struve, the formal "Legal Marxist," with whom we are already familiar)~~ published a volume of articles entitled VEKHI (LANDMARKS) in which, on behalf of the bourgeoisie, they thanked the tsar for crushing the revolution. Cringing and fawning upon the tsarist government, the government of the knout and the gallows, the Constitutional-Democrats bluntly stated in this book that "we should bless this government, which alone, with its bayonets and jails, protects us (the liberal bourgeoisie) from the ire of the people."

Having dispersed the Second State Duma and disposed of the Social-Democratic group of the Duma, the tsarist government zealously set about destroying the political and economic organizations of the proletariat. Convict prisons, fortresses and places of exile were filled to overflowing with revolutionaries. They were brutally beaten up in the prisons, ~~and frightfully~~ tormented and tortured. The Black-Hundred terror raged unchecked. The tsar's Minister Stolypin set up gallows ~~everywhere,~~ all over the country. Several thousand revolutionaries were executed. In those days the gallows was known as the "Stolypin necktie."

~~To completely crush the revolution, the tsarist government continued to dispatch punitive expeditions, which executed thousands of people without trial and flogged the peasants in the countryside en masse. "The victory of the lash and darkness was complete"—this was how Comrade Stalin characterized political life in Russia after the crushing of the Revolution of 1905.~~

In its efforts to crush the revolutionary movement of the workers *and* peasants~~, soldiers and sailors,~~ the tsarist government could not confine itself to acts of repression, punitive expeditions, shootings, jailings and sentences of penal servitude. It perceived with alarm that the naive faith of the peasants in "the little father, the tsar" was steadily vanishing. ~~The tsarist government~~ *It* therefore resorted to a broad manoeuvre.[2] It conceived the idea of creating a solid support for itself in the countryside, in the large class of rural bourgeoisie—the kulaks.

On November 9, 1906, Stolypin issued a new agrarian law enabling the peasants to leave the communes and to set up separate farms. Stolypin's agrarian law ~~destroyed~~ *broke down*[3] the system of communal land ~~ownership~~ *tenure*. The peasants were invited to take possession of their allotments as private property and to withdraw from the communes. They could now sell their allotments, which they were not allowed to do before. When a peasant left his commune the latter was obliged to allot land to him in a single tract (KHUTOR, ~~or~~[4] OTRUB).

The rich peasants, the kulaks, now had the opportunity to buy up the land of the poor ~~peasantry~~ *peasants* at low prices. Within a few years after the promulgation of the law, over a million ~~members of the~~ poor ~~peasantry~~ *peasants* had lost their land altogether and had been completely ruined. As the poor ~~peasantry~~ *peasants* lost their land the number of kulak farmholds grew ~~to about a million~~. These were sometimes regular estates employing hired labour—farm hands—on a large scale. The government compelled the peasants to allot the best land of the communes to the kulak farmers.

During the "emancipation" of the peasants the landlords[5] had robbed the peasants of their land; now the kulaks[6] ~~robbed~~ *began to rob* the communes of their land, securing the best plots and buying up the allotments of poor peasants at low prices.

The tsarist government advanced large loans to the kulaks for the purchase of land and the outfitting of their farms. Stolypin wanted to turn the kulaks into small landlords, into loyal defenders of the tsarist autocracy.

In the nine years 1906–15 alone, over two million households withdrew from the communes.

~~The tsarist government of the feudal landlords entered into an agreement with the bourgeoisie in October 1905. Now, the tsarist government wanted to base itself on the rural bourgeoisie and the kulaks without ceasing to represent the landlords as its first priority. The tsarist monarchy, in Lenin's words, was "decomposing and making another step toward turning into a bourgeois monarchy." As is well known, the first step to this end was the reform of 1861, which eliminated serfdom.~~

As a result of the Stolypin policy the condition of the peasants with small land allotments, and of the poor peasants, grew worse than ever. The process of differentiation among the peasantry became more marked. The peasants began to come into collision with the kulak farmers.

At the same time, the peasants ~~were surprised~~ *began to realize* that they would never gain possession of the landed estates as long as the tsarist government and the State Duma of the landlords and Constitutional-Democrats existed.

~~In the nine years 1906–15 alone, over two million households withdrew from the communes.~~

During the period when kulak farmholds were being formed in large numbers (1907–09), the peasant movement began to decline, but soon after, in 1910, 1911, and later, owing to the clashes between the members of the village communes and the kulak farmers, the peasant movement against the landlords and the kulak farmers grew in intensity.

There were big changes *also* in ~~the country's economy~~ *industry* after the revolution. *The concentration of industry in the hands of increasingly powerful capitalist groups proceeded much more rapidly.* Even before the Revolution of 1905, the capitalists ~~in Russia~~ had begun to form associations with the object of raising prices ~~and strengthening the pressure on the workers~~ *within the country and of using the super-profits thus obtained for the encouragement of export trade so as to enable them to dump goods abroad at low prices and to capture foreign markets*. These capitalist associations (monopolies) were called trusts[7] and syndicates.[8] After the revolution ~~the trusts and syndicates~~ *their number* became still greater ~~and greater~~. There was also an increase in the number of big banks, *whose role in industry became more important*. The flow of foreign capital into Russia increased.

~~In other words,~~ *Thus* capitalism in Russia was turning into monopoly capitalism, imperialist[9] capitalism, on a growing scale. ~~The big bourgeoisie represented by the Octobrist Party (and the Constitutional-Democrats) pushed the tsarist government to seize foreign markets and to take Persia, Constantinople and Galicia. In the Third Duma, it was the Octobrist Party that inspired the imperialistic policy of the tsarist government.~~

After several years of stagnation ~~in Russian industry,~~ ~~after 1910 it~~ *industry* began to revive: the output of coal, metal, oil, textiles and sugar increased. Grain exports assumed large dimensions.

Although Russia at that time made *some* ~~economic~~ *industrial* progress, ~~but~~ *she* was still backward compared with Western Europe, and still dependent on foreign capitalists. Russia did not produce machinery and machine tools—they were imported ~~by capitalists~~ from abroad. She had no *automobile industry or* chemical industry; ~~Russia had no knowledge of~~ *she did not produce* artificial fertilizers. Russia also lagged behind other capitalist countries in the manufacture of armaments.

Pointing to the low level of consumption of metals in Russia as an indication of the country's backwardness, Lenin wrote ~~in 1913~~:

> "In the half-century following the emancipation of the peasants the consumption of iron in Russia has increased five-fold; yet Russia remains an incredibly and unprecedentedly backward country, poverty-stricken and semi-barbaric, equipped with modern implements of production to one-fourth the extent of England, one-fifth the extent of Germany, and one-tenth the extent of America." (Lenin, Collected Works, Russ. ed., Vol. XVI, p. 543.)

One direct result of ~~pre-revolutionary~~ Russia's economic and political backwardness was the dependence both of Russian ~~tsardom as well as Russian~~ capitalism *and of tsardom itself* on West-European capitalism.

This found expression in the fact that such highly important branches of industry as coal, oil, *electrical equipment,* ~~fuel~~ and metallurgy were in the hands of foreign capital, *and* that tsarist Russia had to import nearly all her machinery and equipment from abroad.

It also found expression in the fettering foreign loans. To pay interest on these loans tsardom squeezed hundreds of millions of rubles out of the people annually.

It moreover found expression in the secret treaties *with Russia's "allies,"* by which the tsarist government undertook in the event of war to ~~supply~~ *send* millions of Russian soldiers *to support the "allies" on the imperialist fronts and* to protect the tremendous profits of the British and French capitalists.

~~During the years of reaction, the tsarist gendarmerie continuously conducted brigand-like raids on workers' organizations, overran and closed hundreds of trade unions every year and arrested and exiled trade union workers.~~

The period of the Stolypin reaction was marked by particularly savage assaults on the working class by the gendarmerie and police, the tsarist agents-provocateurs and Black-Hundred ruffians. But it was not only the underlings of the tsar who harassed and persecuted the workers. ~~At this time, the Union of Mill and Factory Owners advanced an~~ *No less zealous in this respect were the factory and mill owners, whose* offensive ~~across the whole front~~ against the working class ~~THAT~~ became particularly aggressive in the years of industrial stagnation and increasing unemployment. The factory owners declared mass lockouts and drew up black lists of class-conscious workers who took an active part in strikes. Once a person was blacklisted he could never hope to find employment in any of the plants belonging to the manufacturers' association in that particular branch of industry. Already in 1908 wage rates were cut by 10 to 15 per cent. The working day was everywhere increased to ~~11~~ *10* or 12 hours. The system of rapacious fines again flourished.

The defeat of the Revolution of 1905 started a process of disintegration and degeneration in the ranks of the fellow-travelers of the ~~first~~ revolution. ~~Especially profound were the disintegration and~~ Degenerate *and decadent* tendencies *grew particularly marked* among the intelligentsia. The fellow-travelers who came from the bourgeois ~~and petty-bourgeois~~ camp to join the ~~revolutionary party of the proletariat~~ *movement* during the upsurge of the revolution deserted the Party in the days of reaction. Some of them joined the camp of the open enemies of the revolution, others entrenched themselves in such legally functioning working-class societies as still survived, and endeavoured to divert the proletariat from the path of revolution and to ~~destroy and eliminate~~ *discredit* the revolutionary party of the proletariat. Deserting the revolution the fellow-travelers tried to win the good graces of the reactionaries and to live in peace with tsardom.

The tsarist government took advantage of the defeat of the revolution to enlist the more cowardly and self-seeking fellow-travelers of the revolution as agents-provocateurs. These vile Judases were sent by the tsarist OKHRANA into the working class and Party organizations, where they spied from within and betrayed revolutionaries~~, condemning them to death, hard labour and banishment.~~ ~~Part of these provocateurs concealed themselves so well that they were not exposed in 1917, after the fall of tsardom. A few of them were only unmasked by the N.K.V.D. in 1937–38.~~

~~During the years of reaction,~~ The *offensive of the* counter-revolution was waged on the ideological front as well. There appeared a whole horde of ~~BOURGEOIS~~ *fashionable* writers who *"criticized" Marxism, and "demolished" it,* mocked and scoffed at the revolution, extolled treachery, and lauded sexual depravity under the guise of the "cult of individuality."

In the realm of philosophy *increasing attempts were made to "criticize" and revise Marxism; there also appeared* all sorts of religious trends ~~and clericalism grew stronger~~, camouflaged by ~~scientific obscurantism~~ *pseudo-scientific theories.*

"Criticizing" Marxism became fashionable.

~~In this way, the bourgeoisie~~ *All these gentlemen, despite their multifarious colouring,* pursued one *common* aim: to divert the masses from the revolution.

~~Only one revolutionary party bravely struggled against all this "abomination of desolation" and did not roll up the banner of revolution in the face of the counter-revolution's attack. This was the Bolsheviks, led by Lenin, who formed during this period into an independent Social-Democratic Labour Party (the Bolsheviks).~~

~~2. Bolshevik Activity during the Years of Reaction~~

~~The tsarist government fell upon the Bolshevik Party with particular force. Bolshevik Party organizations were destroyed and newspapers closed. Only in Baku was Comrade Stalin able to publish a few issues of the newspaper GUDOK (WHISTLE), despite all the police persecution. The Baku proletariat, in the path of the reactionary offensive, conducted defencist mass worker strikes, in which tens of thousands of workers took part. These strikes had a large political significance, holding off the counter-revolutionary attack. Lenin said in regard to the Baku proletariat's 1908 strikes: "these mass strikes were the Last of the Mohicans." (Lenin, COLLECTED WORKS, Russ. ed., Vol. XV, p. 33.)~~

~~After the London R.S.D.L.P. Congress, Lenin was no longer able to stay in either Russia or Finland. The police and gendarmes were now spending more effort hunting him down in order to arrest him. Lenin was forced once again to travel abroad into emigration. Now it would again be necessary to direct the Bolsheviks' revolutionary work from far away, from abroad.~~

~~But these years of Lenin's emigration, between the first and second Russian revolutions, were years of the sharpest struggle for the Party and for its ideological purity. These were years of struggle against decadence and DISBELIEF IN THE REVOLUTIONARY CAUSE, against the attempt of the Mensheviks to eliminate and destroy the revolutionary proletarian party. These were years of struggle for the preservation of the old Bolshevik cadres and the training of the new ones who entered the ranks of the Party during these grim years of reaction.~~

~~Comrade Stalin's activity during this period had a very great significance for the Party. The tsarist government did not give Comrade Stalin a chance to work freely within the Party organization for a very long period of time. He en-~~

dured numerous arrests and banishments during these years between the first and second revolutions. But with his iron will, Comrade Stalin was inseparable from the revolution and the Party and several times broke out of the confinement of his distant exile in order to return to revolutionary work.

On March 25, 1908, Comrade Stalin was arrested in Baku (under the name Nizharadze) and was sent to Bailovsk prison and then banished to the town of Solvychegodsk in the Vologda region. He stayed there until June 24, 1909, when he was able to escape from exile. On March 23, 1910, Stalin was again arrested in Baku; after an extended period in prison, he was banned from living in the Caucasus territory for five years and banished once again (for the third time) to the Vologda region. In July 1911, Comrade Stalin again escaped from exile. This time, he was able to work in freedom for just a few months; on September 9, 1911, Comrade Stalin was arrested in St. Petersburg and again banished to the town of Solvychegodsk in the Vologda region. Here he remained until 1912. In February 1912, Comrade Stalin escaped from exile and conducted revolutionary work in St. Petersburg, but was arrested already on April 22 and banished to the Narymsk territory for four years. This was at the beginning of summer in 1912; later that summer, Comrade Stalin escaped from Narymsk and returned to revolutionary work in St. Petersburg.

In March 1913, Comrade Stalin was again arrested in St. Petersburg and on June 1913 he was banished to the Turukhansk territory under surveillance for four years. This was his sixth and final banishment. He would be freed from this exile by the second Russian February Revolution.

Entirely devoted to the cause of the working class, Comrade Stalin conducted major work in directing the Bolshevik organizations and constructing the Party during the time when he was not in captivity.

Major work was also done during the period by Y. M. Sverdlov. Arrested in 1906, he was held in a fortress until 1909. In the fall of 1909, he was released from the fortress and returned to revolutionary work in Moscow. Already in December 1909, however, he was back under arrest and banished to Narymsk. From this place of exile, he escaped several months later and returned to revolutionary work in St. Petersburg. Arrested in November 1910, he was sent back to the Narymsk territory. He attempted to escape several more times from Narymsk, but each time the tsarist government stopped him en route and it was only on his fifth attempt that he was able to get away and return to St. Petersburg, where he served as a member of the Party's Central Committee until March 1913. In June 1913, he was banished to the Turukhansk territory, whence he was freed only by the February 1917 Revolution.

Even driven into far-off exile, the Bolsheviks did not cease their revolutionary work. Thus the tsarist police reported about Comrade Molotov, who in 1909–10 was in exile in the Vologda region: "being an active Party worker

~~among the exiles, he maintained a correspondence with Party officials in other cities and aimed to create a Social-Democratic faction in the city of Vologda from forces in the city—railroad workers from the junction and repair shops."~~

~~Comrades Voroshilov, Kuibyshev and many others advanced this kind of revolutionary work in exile as well.~~

~~Indestructible faith in the Party, the revolution and the power of the working class gave the Bolsheviks the will to struggle in the most grim of times. The revolutionary Bolsheviks were forced to hide for years at a time in the underground and live under assumed names, without means or contact with their families, nor a place of their own to live, and with tsarist spies forever at their heels. They spent time in prison and exile, escaped and again picked up their selfless work.~~

~~Prison and exile were not able to break the Bolsheviks. In prison, the Bolsheviks frequently endured beatings. Thus, in 1908, a company of soldiers of the Salyansk regiment beat up political prisoners in the Bailovsk prison in Baku, where Comrade Stalin was being held, on the orders of the prison command. When the prisoners were forced to "run the gauntlet," Stalin walked through the rain of clubs with a book in his hands with his head held high. Comrade Stalin's courage and resilience bolstered the morale of the rest of the prisoners.~~

~~Despite the defeat of the first revolution, the defeat of the worker and peasant movements, the defeat of the proletarian and peasant organizations and the retreat of a significant portion of the intelligentsia from the revolution, the Bolshevik organization preserved its faith in the proletarian banner. The tough Bolshevik cadres, trained by Lenin and Stalin, were able to restore the proletarian party's organization after its defeat by the counter-revolution and to prepare the working class for a new revolutionary rising.~~

~~Lenin lived during these years abroad: first in Switzerland, and then after 1910 in Paris, and then Cracow. On the eve of the imperialist war, he was living in Poronin, on the Austrian border; during the imperialist war, he broke out of the Poronin prison and lived in Switzerland.~~

~~Lenin edited the illegal newspaper Proletary (Proletarian), which was the leading organ for all Bolshevik Party organizations.~~

~~Lenin maintained correspondence and personal contact with the leaders of the Bolshevik Party organizations in Russia; he continuously aided them with instructions, literature, and so on. Abroad, Lenin organized a whole array of meetings with leading party workers in Russia and his work during the years of emigration had a decisive importance for the preservation of the Bolshevik Party. In the village of Longjumeau near Paris, Lenin organized a party school, where Party workers from Russia studied. Lenin himself gave lectures at this school. Among the two dozen Party workers who graduated from the Longjumeau school was Sergo Ordjonikidze.~~

Decadence and scepticism also affected a section of the Party intelligentsia, those who considered themselves Marxists but had never held firmly to the Marxist position. Among them were writers like Bogdanov, Bazarov, Lunacharsky (who had sided with the Bolsheviks in 1905), Yushkevich and Valentinov (Mensheviks). They launched their "criticism" simultaneously against the philosophical foundations of Marxist theory, i.e., against dialectical materialism, and against the fundamental Marxist principles of historical science, i.e., against historical materialism. This criticism differed from the usual criticism in that it was not conducted openly and squarely, but in a veiled and hypocritical form under the guise of "defending" the fundamental positions of Marxism. These people claimed that in the main they were Marxists, but that they wanted to "improve" Marxism—by ridding it of certain of its fundamental[10] principles. In reality, they were hostile to Marxism, for they tried to undermine its theoretical foundations, although they hypocritically denied their hostility to Marxism and two-facedly continued to style themselves Marxists. The danger of this hypocritical criticism lay in the fact that it was calculated to deceive rank-and-file members of the Party and might lead them astray. The more hypocritical grew this criticism, which aimed at undermining the theoretical foundations of Marxism, the more dangerous it was to the Party, for the more it merged with the general campaign of the reactionaries against the Party, against the revolution. Some of the intellectuals who had deserted Marxism went so far as to advocate the founding of a new religion (these were known as "god-seekers" and "god-builders").[11]

It became urgent for the Marxists to give a fitting retort to these renegades from Marxist theory, to tear the mask from their faces and thoroughly expose them, and thus safeguard the theoretical foundations of the Marxist Party.

One might have thought that this task would have been undertaken by Plekhanov and his Menshevik friends who regarded themselves as "eminent Marxist theoreticians." But they preferred to fire off one or two insignificant critical notes of the newspaper type and quit the field.

It was Lenin who accomplished this task in his famous book MATERIALISM AND EMPIRIO-CRITICISM, *published in 1909.*

> *"In the course of less than half a year," Lenin wrote, "four books devoted mainly and almost entirely to attacks on dialectical materialism have made their appearance. These include first and foremost* STUDIES IN *(?—it would have been more proper to say 'against')* THE PHILOSOPHY OF MARXISM *(St. Petersburg, 1908), a symposium by Bazarov, Bogdanov, Lunacharsky, Berman, Helfond, Yushkevich and Suvorov; Yushkevich's* MATERIALISM AND CRITICAL REALISM; *Berman's* DIALECTICS IN THE LIGHT OF THE MODERN THEORY OF KNOWLEDGE *and Valentinov's* THE PHILOSOPHIC CONSTRUCTIONS OF MARXISM. *... All these people, who, despite the sharp*

> *divergence of their political views, are united in their hostility toward dialectical materialism, at the same time claim to be Marxists in philosophy! Engels' dialectics is 'mysticism,' says Berman. Engels' views have become 'antiquated,' remarks Bazarov casually, as though it were a self-evident fact. Materialism thus appears to be refuted by our bold warriors, who proudly allude to the 'modern theory of knowledge,' 'recent philosophy' (or 'recent positivism'), the 'philosophy of modern natural science,' or even the 'philosophy of natural science of the twentieth century.'" (Lenin, SELECTED WORKS, Vol. XI, p. 89.)*

Replying to Lunacharsky, who, in justification of his friends—the revisionists in philosophy—said, "perhaps we have gone astray, but we are seeking," Lenin wrote:

> *"As for myself, I too am a 'seeker' in philosophy. Namely, the task I have set myself in these comments (i.e., MATERIALISM AND EMPIRIO-CRITICISM—ED.) is to find out what was the stumbling block to these people who under the guise of Marxism are offering something incredibly muddled, confused and reactionary." (Ibid., p. 90.)*

But as a matter of fact, Lenin's book went far beyond this modest task. Actually, the book is something more than a criticism of Bogdanov, Yushkevich, Bazarov and Valentinov and their teachers in philosophy, Avenarius and Mach, who endeavoured in their writings to offer a refined and polished idealism as opposed to Marxist materialism; it is at the same time a defence of the theoretical foundations of Marxism—dialectical and historical materialism—and a materialist generalization of everything important and essential acquired by science, and especially the natural sciences, in the course of a whole historical period, the period from Engels' death to the appearance of Lenin's MATERIALISM AND EMPIRIO-CRITICISM.

Having effectively criticized in this book the Russian empirio-criticists and their foreign teachers, Lenin comes to the following conclusions regarding philosophical and theoretical revisionism:

1) *"An ever subtler falsification of Marxism, an ever subtler presentation of anti-materialist doctrines under the guise of Marxism—this is the characteristic feature of modern revisionism in political economy, in questions of tactics and in philosophy generally." (Ibid., p. 381.)*
2) *"The whole school of Mach and Avenarius is moving towards idealism." (Ibid., p. 405.)*
3) *"Our Machians have all got stuck in idealism." (Ibid., p. 395.)*

4) *"Behind the gnosiological scholasticism of empirio-criticism it is impossible not to see the struggle of parties in philosophy, a struggle which in the last analysis expresses the tendencies and ideology of the antagonistic classes in modern society." (Ibid., p. 406.)*
5) *"The objective, class role of empirio-criticism reduces itself to nothing but that of servitor of the fideists (the reactionaries who hold faith above science—Ed.[12]) in their struggle against materialism in general and historical materialism in particular." (Ibid., p. 406.)*
6) *"Philosophical idealism is . . . a road to clerical obscurantism." (Ibid., p. 84.)*

In order to appreciate the tremendous part played by Lenin's book in the history of our Party and to realize what theoretical treasure Lenin safeguarded from the motley crowd of revisionists and renegades of the period of the Stolypin reaction, we must acquaint ourselves, if only briefly, with the fundamentals of dialectical and historical materialism.

This is all the more necessary because dialectical and historical materialism constitute the theoretical basis of Communism, the theoretical foundations of the Marxist party, and it is the duty of every active member of our Party to know these principles and hence to study them.

What, then, is

1) Dialectical materialism?

2) Historical materialism?

2. Dialectical and Historical Materialism

Dialectical materialism is the world outlook of the Marxist-Leninist party.[13] It is called dialectical materialism because its approach to the phenomena of nature, its method of studying and apprehending them, is DIALECTICAL, *while its interpretation of the phenomena of nature, its conception of these phenomena, its theory, is* MATERIALISTIC.

Historical materialism is the extension of the principles of dialectical materialism to the study of social life, an application of the principles of dialectical materialism to the phenomena of the life of society, to the study of society and its history.

When describing their dialectical method, Marx and Engels usually refer to Hegel as the philosopher who formulated the main features of dialectics. This, however, does not mean that the dialectics of Marx and Engels is identical with the dialectics of Hegel. As a matter of fact, Marx and Engels took from the Hegelian dialectics only its "rational kernel," casting aside its idealistic shell, and developed it further so as to lend it a modern scientific form.

> *"My dialectic method," says Marx, "is fundamentally not only different from the Hegelian, but is its direct opposite. To Hegel, the process of thinking, which, under the name of 'the Idea,' he even transforms into an independent subject, is the demiurge (creator) of the real world, and the real world is only the external, phenomenal form of 'the Idea.' With me, on the contrary, the ideal is nothing else than the material world reflected by the human mind, and translated into forms of thought." (Karl Marx, CAPITAL, Vol, I, p. xxx, George Allen & Unwin Ltd., 1938.)*

When describing their materialism, Marx and Engels usually refer to Feuerbach as the philosopher who restored materialism to its rights. This, however, does not mean that the materialism of Marx and Engels is identical with Feuerbach's materialism. As a matter of fact, Marx and Engels took from Feuerbach's materialism its "inner kernel," developed it into a scientific-philosophical theory of materialism and cast aside its idealistic and religious-ethical encumbrances. We know that Feuerbach, although he was fundamentally a materialist, objected to the name materialism. Engels more than once declared that "in spite of the materialist foundation, Feuerbach remained bound by the traditional idealist fetters," and that "the real idealism of Feuerbach becomes evident as soon as we come to his philosophy of religion and ethics." (Karl Marx, SELECTED WORKS, Vol. I, pp. 439, 442.)

Dialectics comes from the Greek DIALEGO, to discourse, to debate. In ancient times dialectics was the art of arriving at the truth by disclosing the contradictions in the argument of an opponent and overcoming these contradictions. There were philosophers in ancient times who believed that the disclosure of contradictions in thought and the clash of opposite opinions was the best method of arriving at the truth. This dialectical method of thought, later extended to the phenomena of nature, developed into the dialectical method of apprehending nature, which regards[14] the phenomena of nature as being in constant movement and undergoing constant change, and the development of nature as the result of the development of the contradictions in nature, as the result of the interaction[15] of opposed forces in nature.

In its essence, dialectics is the direct opposite of metaphysics.[16]

1) The principal features of the Marxist DIALECTICAL METHOD are as follows:

a) Contrary to metaphysics, dialectics does not regard nature as an accidental agglomeration of things, of phenomena, unconnected with, isolated from, and independent of, each other, but as a connected and integral whole, in which things, phenomena, are organically connected with, dependent on, and determined by, each other.

The dialectical method therefore holds that no phenomenon in nature can be understood if taken by itself, isolated from surrounding phenomena, inasmuch as any phenomenon in any realm of nature may become meaningless to us if it is not considered in connection with the surrounding conditions, but divorced from them; and that, vice versa, any phenomenon can be understood and explained if considered in its inseparable connection with surrounding phenomena, as one conditioned by surrounding phenomena.

b) Contrary to metaphysics, dialectics holds that nature is not a state of rest and immobility, stagnation and immutability, but a state of continuous movement and change, of continuous renewal and development, where something is always arising and developing, and something always disintegrating and dying away.

The dialectical method therefore requires that phenomena should be considered not only from the standpoint of their interconnection and interdependence, but also from the standpoint of their movement, their change, their development, their coming into being and going out of being.

The dialectical method regards as important primarily not that which at the given moment seems to be durable and yet is already beginning to die away, but that which is arising and developing, even though at the given moment it may appear to be not durable, for the dialectical method considers invincible[17] *only that which is arising and developing.*

> *"All nature," says Engels, "from the smallest thing to the biggest, from a grain of sand to the sun, from the protista (the primary living cell—Ed.) to man, is in a constant state of coming into being and going out of being, in a constant flux, in a ceaseless state of movement and change." (F. Engels, Dialectics of Nature.)*

Therefore, dialectics, Engels says, "takes things and their perceptual images essentially in their inter-connection, in their concatenation, in their movement, in their rise and disappearance." (Ibid.)

c) Contrary to metaphysics, dialectics does not regard the process of development as a simple process of growth, where quantitative changes do not lead to qualitative changes, but as a development which passes from insignificant and imperceptible quantitative changes to open, fundamental changes, to qualitative changes; a development in which the qualitative changes occur not gradually, but rapidly and abruptly, taking the form of a leap from one state to another; they occur not accidentally but as the natural result of an accumulation of imperceptible and gradual quantitative changes.

The dialectical method therefore holds that the process of development should be understood not as movement in a circle, not as a simple repetition of what has already occurred, but as an onward and upward movement, as a transition from an old qualitative state to a new qualitative state, as a development from the simple to the complex, from the lower to the higher:

> *"Nature," says Engels, "is the test of dialectics, and it must be said for modern natural science that it has furnished extremely rich and daily increasing materials for this test, and has thus proved that in the last analysis nature's process is dialectical and not metaphysical, that it does not move in an eternally uniform and constantly repeated circle, but passes through a real history. Here prime mention should be made of Darwin, who dealt a severe blow to the metaphysical conception of nature by proving that the organic world of today, plants and animals, and consequently man too, is all a product of a process of development that has been in progress for millions of years." (F. Engels, ANTI-DÜHRING.)*

Describing dialectical development as a transition from quantitative changes to qualitative changes, Engels says:

> *"In physics . . . every change is a passing of quantity into quality, as a result of quantitative change of some form of movement either inherent in a body or imparted to it. For example, the temperature of water has at first no effect on its liquid state; but as the temperature of liquid water rises or falls, a moment arrives when this state of cohesion changes and the water is converted in one case into steam and in the other into ice. . . . A definite minimum current is required to make a platinum wire glow; every metal has its melting temperature; every liquid has a definite freezing point and boiling point at a given pressure, as far as we are able with the means at our disposal to attain the required temperatures; finally, every gas has its critical point at which, by proper pressure and cooling, it can be converted into a liquid state. . . . What are known as the constants of physics (the point at which one state passes into another—ED.) are in most cases nothing but designations for the nodal points at which a quantitative (change) increase or decrease of movement causes a qualitative change in the state of the given body, and at which, consequently, quantity is transformed into quality." (DIALECTICS OF NATURE.)*

> *Passing to chemistry, Engels continues:*

> *"Chemistry may be called the science of the qualitative changes which take place in bodies as the effect of changes of quantitative composition. This was already known to Hegel. . . . Take oxygen: if the molecule contains*

> *three atoms instead of the customary two, we get ozone, a body definitely distinct in odour and reaction from ordinary oxygen. And what shall we say of the different proportions in which oxygen combines with nitrogen or sulphur, and each of which produces a body qualitatively different from all other bodies!" (Ibid.)*

Finally, criticizing Dühring, who scolded Hegel for all he was worth, but surreptitiously borrowed from him the well-known thesis that the transition from the insentient world to the sentient world, from the kingdom of inorganic matter to the kingdom of organic life, is a leap to a new state, Engels says:

> *"This is precisely the Hegelian nodal line of measure relations, in which, at certain definite nodal points, the purely quantitative increase or decrease gives rise to a* QUALITATIVE LEAP *for example, in the case of water which is heated or cooled, where boiling-point and freezing point are the nodes at which—under normal pressure—the leap to a new aggregate state takes place, and where consequently quantity is transformed into quality." (F. Engels,* ANTI-DÜHRING.*)*

d) Contrary to metaphysics, dialectics holds that internal contradictions are inherent in all things and phenomena of nature, for they all have their negative and positive sides, a past and a future, something dying away and something developing; and that the struggle between these opposites, the struggle between the old and the new, between that which is dying away and that which is being born, between that which is disappearing and that which is developing, constitutes the internal content of the process of development, the internal content of the transformation of quantitative changes into qualitative changes.

The dialectical method therefore holds that the process of development from the lower to the higher takes place not as a harmonious unfolding of phenomena, but as a disclosure of the contradictions inherent in things and phenomena, as a "struggle" of opposite tendencies which operate on the basis of these contradictions.

> *"In its proper meaning," Lenin says, "dialectics is the study of the contradiction* WITHIN THE VERY ESSENCE OF THINGS.*" (Lenin,* PHILOSOPHICAL NOTEBOOKS*, Russ. ed., p. 263.)*

And further:

> *"Development is the 'struggle' of opposites." (Lenin,* SELECTED WORKS*, Vol. XI, pp. 81–2.)*

Such, in brief, are the principal features of the Marxist dialectical method.

It is easy to understand how immensely important is the extension of the principles of the dialectical method to the study of social life and the history of society, and how immensely important is the application of these principles to the history of society and to the practical activities of the party of the proletariat.

If there are no isolated phenomena in the world, if all phenomena are interconnected and interdependent, then it is clear that every social system and every social movement in history must be evaluated not from the standpoint of "eternal justice" or some other preconceived idea, as is not infrequently done by historians, but from the standpoint of the conditions which gave rise to that system or that social movement and with which they are connected.

The slave system would be senseless, stupid and unnatural under modern conditions. But under the conditions of a disintegrating primitive communal system, the slave system is a quite understandable and natural phenomenon, since it represents an advance on the primitive communal system.

The demand for a bourgeois-democratic republic when tsardom and bourgeois society existed, as, let us say, in Russia in 1905, was a quite understandable, proper and revolutionary demand, for at that time a bourgeois republic would have meant a step forward. But now, under the conditions of the U.S.S.R., the demand for a bourgeois-democratic republic would be a meaningless and counter-revolutionary demand, for a bourgeois republic would be a retrograde step compared with the Soviet republic.

Everything depends on the conditions, time and place.

It is clear that without such a HISTORICAL *approach to social phenomena, the existence and development of the science of history is impossible, for only such an approach saves the science of history from becoming a jumble of accidents and an agglomeration of most absurd mistakes.*

Further, if the world is in a state of constant movement and development, if the dying away of the old and the upgrowth of the new is a law of development, then it is clear that there can be no "immutable" social systems, no "eternal principles" of private property and exploitation, no "eternal ideas" of the subjugation of the peasant to the landlord, of the worker to the capitalist.

Hence the capitalist system can be replaced by the Socialist system, just as at one time the feudal system was replaced by the capitalist system.

Hence we must not base our orientation on the strata of society which are no longer developing, even though they at present constitute the predominant force, but on those strata which are developing and have a future before them, even though they at present do not constitute the predominant force.

In the eighties of the past century, in the period of the struggle between the Marxists and the Narodniks, the proletariat in Russia constituted an insignificant minority of the population, whereas the individual peasants constituted the vast majority of the population. But the proletariat was developing as a class, whereas the peasantry as a class was disintegrating. And just because the proletariat was developing as a class the Marxists based their orientation on the proletariat. And they were not mistaken, for, as we know, the proletariat subsequently grew from an insignificant force into a first-rate historical and political force.

Hence, in order not to err in policy, one must look forward, not backward.

Further, if the passing of slow quantitative changes into rapid and abrupt qualitative changes is a law of development, then it is clear that revolutions made by oppressed classes are a quite natural and inevitable phenomenon.

Hence the transition from capitalism to Socialism and the liberation of the working class from the yoke of capitalism cannot be effected by slow changes, by reforms, but only by a qualitative change of the capitalist system, by revolution.

Hence, in order not to err in policy, one must be a revolutionary, not a reformist.

Further, if development proceeds by way of the disclosure of internal contradictions, by way of collisions between opposite forces on the basis of these contradictions and so as to overcome these contradictions, then it is clear that the class struggle of the proletariat is a quite natural and inevitable phenomenon.

Hence we must not cover up the contradictions of the capitalist system, but disclose and unravel them; we must not try to check the class struggle but carry it to its conclusion.

Hence, in order not to err in policy, one must pursue an uncompromising proletarian class policy, not a reformist policy of harmony of the interests of the proletariat and the bourgeoisie, not a compromisers' policy of "the growing of capitalism into Socialism."

Such is the Marxist dialectical method when applied to social life, to the history of society.

As to Marxist philosophical materialism, it is fundamentally the direct opposite of philosophical idealism.

2) The principal features of Marxist philosophical MATERIALISM *are as follows:*

a) Contrary to idealism, which regards the world as the embodiment of an "absolute idea," a "universal spirit," "consciousness," Marx's philosophical materialism holds that the world is by its very nature MATERIAL, *that the multifold phenomena of the world constitute different forms of matter in motion, that interconnection and interdependence of phenomena, as established by the dialectical method, are a law of the development of moving matter, and that the world develops in accordance with the laws of movement of matter and stands in no need of a "universal spirit."*

> *"The materialist world outlook," says Engels, "is simply the conception of nature as it is, without any reservations." (MS of* LUDWIG FEUERBACH.*)*

Speaking of the materialist views of the ancient philosopher Heraclitus, who held that "the world, the all in one, was not created by any god or any man, but was, is and ever will be a living flame, systematically flaring up and systematically dying down," Lenin comments: "A very good exposition of the rudiments of dialectical materialism." (Lenin, PHILOSOPHICAL NOTEBOOKS, Russ. ed., p. 318.)

b) Contrary to idealism, which asserts that only our mind really exists, and that the material world, being, nature, exists only in our mind, in our sensations, ideas and perceptions, the Marxist materialist philosophy holds that matter, nature, being, is an objective reality existing outside and independent of our mind; that matter is primary, since it is the source of sensations, ideas, mind, and that mind is secondary, derivative, since it is a reflection of matter, a reflection of being; that thought is a product of matter which in its development has reached a high degree of perfection, namely, of the brain, and the brain is the organ of thought; and that therefore one cannot separate thought from matter without committing a grave error. Engels says:

> *"The question of the relation of thinking to being, the relation of spirit to nature is the paramount question of the whole of philosophy. . . . The answers which the philosophers gave to this question split them into two great camps. Those who asserted the primacy of spirit to nature . . . comprised the camp of IDEALISM. The others, who regarded nature as primary, belong to the various schools of MATERIALISM." (Karl Marx, SELECTED WORKS, Vol. I, pp. 430–31.)*

And further:

> *"The material, sensuously perceptible world to which we ourselves belong is the only reality. . . . Our consciousness and thinking, however suprasensuous they may seem, are the product of a material, bodily organ, the brain. Matter is not a product of mind, but mind itself is merely the highest product of matter." (Ibid., p. 435.)*

Concerning the question of matter and thought, Marx says:

> *"IT IS IMPOSSIBLE TO SEPARATE THOUGHT FROM MATTER THAT THINKS. Matter is the subject of all changes." (Ibid., p. 397.)*

Describing the Marxist philosophy of materialism, Lenin says:

> *"Materialism in general[18] recognizes objectively real being (matter) as independent of consciousness, sensation, experience. . . . Consciousness is*

only the reflection of being, at best, an approximately true (adequate, ideally exact) reflection of it." (Lenin, SELECTED WORKS, Vol. XI, p. 378.)

And further:

(a) "Matter is that which, acting upon our sense-organs, produces sensation; matter is the objective reality given to us in sensation. . . . Matter, nature, being, the physical—is primary, and spirit, consciousness, sensation, the psychical—is secondary." (Ibid., pp. 208, 209.)
(b) "The world picture is a picture of how matter moves and of how 'MATTER THINKS.[19]'" (Ibid., p. 403.)
(c) "The brain is the organ of thought." (Ibid., p. 125.)

c) Contrary to idealism, which denies the possibility of knowing the world and its laws, which does not believe in the authenticity of our knowledge, does not recognize objective truth, and holds that the world is full of "things-in-themselves" that can never be known to science, Marxist philosophical materialism holds that the world and its laws are fully knowable, that our knowledge of the laws of nature, tested by experiment and practice, is authentic knowledge having the validity of objective truth, and that there are no things in the world which are unknowable, but only things which are still not known, but which will be disclosed and made known by the efforts of science and practice.

Criticizing the thesis of Kant and other idealists that the world is unknowable and that there are "things-in-themselves" which are unknowable, and defending the well-known materialist thesis that our knowledge is authentic knowledge, Engels writes:

"The most telling refutation of this as of all other philosophical fancies is practice, viz., experiment and industry. If we are able to prove the correctness of our conception of a natural process by making it ourselves, bringing it into being out of its conditions and using it for our own purposes into the bargain, then there is an end of the Kantian 'thing-in-itself.' The chemical substances produced in the bodies of plants and animals remained such 'things-in-themselves' until organic chemistry began to produce them one after another, whereupon the 'thing-in-itself' became a thing for us, as for instance, alizarin, the colouring matter of the madder, which we no longer trouble to grow in the madder roots in the field, but produce much more cheaply and simply from coal tar. For three hundred years the Copernican solar system was a hypothesis, with a hundred, a thousand or ten thousand chances to one in its favour, but still always a hypothesis. But when Leverrier, by means of the data provided by this system, not only deduced

> *the necessity of the existence of an unknown planet, but also calculated the position in the heavens which this planet must necessarily occupy, and when Galle really found this planet, the Copernican system was proved." (Karl Marx, SELECTED WORKS, Vol. I, pp. 432–33.)*

Accusing Bogdanov, Bazarov, Yushkevich and the other followers of Mach of fideism, and defending the well-known materialist thesis that our scientific knowledge of the laws of nature is authentic knowledge, and that the laws of science represent objective truth, Lenin says:

> *"Contemporary fideism does not at all reject science; all it rejects is the 'exaggerated claims' of science, to wit, its claim to objective truth. If objective truth exists (as the materialists think), if natural science, reflecting the outer world in human 'experience,' is alone capable of giving us objective truth, then all fideism is absolutely refuted." (Lenin, SELECTED WORKS, Vol. XI, p. 189.)*

Such, in brief, are the characteristic features of the Marxist philosophical materialism.

It is easy to understand how immensely important is the extension of the principles of philosophical materialism to the study of social life, of the history of society, and how immensely important is the application of these principles to the history of society and to the practical activities of the party of the proletariat.

If the connection between the phenomena of nature and their interdependence are laws of the development of nature, it follows, too, that the connection and interdependence of the phenomena of social life are laws of the development of society, and not something accidental.

Hence social life, the history of society, ceases to be an agglomeration of "accidents," and becomes the history of the development of society according to regular laws, and the study of the history of society becomes a science.

Hence the practical activity of the party of the proletariat must not be based on the good wishes of "outstanding individuals," not on the dictates of "reason," "universal morals," etc., but on the laws of development of society and on the study of these laws.

Further, if the world is knowable and our knowledge of the laws of development of nature is authentic knowledge, having the validity of objective truth, it follows that social life, the development of society, is also knowable, and that the data of science regarding the laws of development of society are authentic data having the validity of objective truths.

Hence the science of the history of society, despite all the complexity of the phenomena of social life, can become as precise a science as, let us say, biology, and capable of making use of the laws of development of society for practical purposes.

Hence the party of the proletariat should not guide itself in its practical activity by casual motives, but by the laws of development of society, and by practical deductions from these laws.

Hence Socialism is converted from a dream of a better future for humanity into a science.

Hence the bond between science and practical activity, between theory and practice, their unity, should be the guiding star of the party of the proletariat.

Further, if nature, being, the material world, is primary, and mind, thought, is secondary, derivative; if the material world represents objective reality existing independently of the mind of men, while the mind is a reflection of this objective reality, it follows that the material life of society, its being, is also primary, and its spiritual life secondary, derivative, and that the material life of society is an objective reality existing independently of the will of men, while the spiritual life of society is a reflection of this objective reality, a reflection of being.

Hence the source of formation of the spiritual life of society, the origin of social ideas, social theories, political views and political institutions, should not be sought for in the ideas, theories, views and political institutions themselves, but in the conditions of the material life of society, in social being, of which these ideas, theories, views, etc., are the reflection.

Hence, if in different periods of the history of society different social ideas, theories, views and political institutions are to be observed; if under the slave system we encounter certain social ideas, theories, views and political institutions, under feudalism others, and under capitalism others still, this is not to be explained by the "nature," the "properties" of the ideas, theories, views and political institutions themselves but by the different conditions of the material life of society at different periods of social development.

Whatever is the being of a society, whatever are the conditions of material life of a society, such are the ideas, theories, political views and political institutions of that society.

In this connection, Marx says:

> *"It is not the consciousness of men that determines their being, but, on the contrary, their social being that determines their consciousness." (Karl Marx, SELECTED WORKS, Vol. I, p. 356.)*

Hence, in order not to err in policy, in order not to find itself in the position of idle dreamers, the party of the proletariat must not base its activities on abstract "principles of human reason," but on the concrete conditions of the material life of society, as the determining force of social development; not on the good wishes of "great men," but on the real needs of development of the material life of society.

The fall of the utopians, including the Narodniks, Anarchists and Socialist-Revolutionaries, was due, among other things, to the fact that they did not recognize the primary role which the conditions of the material life of society play in the development of society, and, sinking to idealism, did not base their practical activities on the needs of the development of the material life of society, but, independently of and in spite of these needs, on "ideal plans" and "all-embracing projects" divorced from the real life of society.

The strength and vitality of Marxism-Leninism lie in the fact that it does base its practical activity on the needs of the development of the material life of society and never divorces itself from the real life of society.

It does not follow from Marx's words,[20] however, that social ideas, theories, political views and political institutions are of no significance in the life of society, that they do not reciprocally affect social being, the development of the material conditions of the life of society. We have been speaking so far of the ORIGIN *of social ideas, theories, views and political institutions, of* THE WAY THEY ARISE, *of the fact that the spiritual life of society is a reflection of the conditions of its material life. As regards the* SIGNIFICANCE *of social ideas, theories, views and political institutions, as regards their* ROLE *in history, historical materialism, far from denying them, stresses the role and importance of these factors in the life of society, in its history.*

There are different kinds of social ideas and theories. There are old ideas and theories which have outlived their day and which serve the interests of the moribund forces of society. Their significance lies in the fact that they hamper the development, the progress of society. Then there are new and advanced ideas and theories which serve the interests of the advanced forces of society. Their significance lies in the fact that they facilitate the development, the progress of society; and their significance is the greater the more accurately they reflect the needs of development of the material life of society.[21]

New social ideas and theories arise only after the development of the material life of society has set new tasks before society. But once they have arisen they become a most potent force which facilitates the carrying out of the new tasks set by the development of the material life of society, a force which facilitates the progress of society. It is precisely here that the tremendous organizing, mobilizing and transforming value of new ideas, new theories, new political views and new political institutions manifests itself. New social ideas and theories arise precisely because they are necessary to society, because it is IMPOSSIBLE *to carry out the urgent tasks of development of the material life of society without their organizing, mobilizing and transforming action. Arising out of the new tasks set by the development of the material life of society, the new social ideas and theories force their way through, become the possession of the masses, mobilize and organize them against the moribund forces of society, and thus facilitate the overthrow of these forces which hamper the development of the material life of society.*

Thus social ideas, theories and political institutions, having arisen on the basis of the urgent tasks of the development of the material life of society, the development of social being, themselves then react upon social being, upon the material life of society, creating the conditions necessary for completely carrying out the urgent tasks of the material life of society, and for rendering its further development possible.

In this connection, Marx says:

> *"Theory becomes a material force as soon as it has gripped[22] the masses." (Zur Kritik der Hegelschen Rechtsphilosophie.)*

Hence, in order to be able to influence the conditions of material life of society and to accelerate their development and their improvement, the party of the proletariat must rely upon such a social theory, such a social idea as correctly reflects the needs of development of the material life of society, and which is therefore capable of setting into motion broad masses of the people and of mobilizing them and organizing them into a great army of the proletarian party, prepared to smash the reactionary forces and to clear the way for the advanced forces of society.

The fall of the "Economists" and Mensheviks was due among other things to the fact that they did not recognize the mobilizing, organizing and transforming role of advanced theory, of advanced ideas and, sinking to vulgar materialism, reduced the role of these factors almost to nothing, thus condemning the Party to passivity and inanition.

The strength and vitality of Marxism-Leninism are derived from the fact that it relies upon an advanced theory which correctly reflects the needs of development of the material life of society, that it elevates theory to a proper level, and that it deems it its duty to utilize every ounce of the mobilizing, organizing and transforming power of this theory.

That is the answer historical materialism gives to the question of the relation between social being and social consciousness, between the conditions of development of material life and the development of the spiritual life of society.[23]

It now remains to elucidate the following question: what, from the viewpoint of historical materialism, is meant by the "conditions of material life of society" which in the final analysis determine the physiognomy of society, its ideas, views, political institutions, etc.?

What, after all, are these "conditions of material life of society," what are their distinguishing features?

There can be no doubt that the concept "conditions of material life of society" includes, first of all, nature which surrounds society, geographical environment, which is one of the indispensable and constant conditions of material life of society and which, of course, influences the development of society. What role does geographical environment play in the development of society? Is geographical environment the chief force determining the physiognomy of society, the character of the social system of men, the transition from one system to another?

Historical materialism answers this question in the negative.

Geographical environment is unquestionably one of the constant and indispensable conditions of development of society and, of course, influences the development of society, accelerates or retards its development. But its influence is not the DETERMINING *influence, inasmuch as the changes and development of society proceed at an incomparably faster rate than the changes and development of geographical environment. In the space of three thousand years three different social systems have been successively superseded in Europe: the primitive communal system, the slave system and the feudal system. In the Eastern part of Europe, in the U.S.S.R., even four social systems have been superseded. Yet during this period geographical conditions in Europe have either not changed at all, or have changed so slightly that geography takes no note of them. And that is quite natural. Changes in geographical environment of any importance require millions of years, whereas a few hundred or a couple of thousand years are enough for even very important changes in the system of human society.*

It follows from this that geographical environment cannot be the chief cause, the DETERMINING *cause of social development, for that which remains almost unchanged in the course of tens of thousands of years cannot be the chief cause of development of that which undergoes fundamental changes in the course of a few hundred years.*

Further, there can be no doubt that the concept "conditions of material life of society" also includes growth of population, density of population of one degree or another, for people are an essential element of the conditions of material life of society, and without a definite minimum number of people there can be no material life of society. Is not growth of population the chief force that determines the character of the social system of man?

Historical materialism answers this question too in the negative.

Of course, growth of population does influence the development of society, does facilitate or retard the development of society, but it cannot be the chief force of development of society, and its influence on the development of society cannot be the DETERMINING *influence because, by itself, growth of population does not furnish the clue to the question why a given social system is replaced precisely by such and such a new system and not by another, why the primitive communal system is succeeded precisely by the slave system, the slave system by the feudal system, and the feudal system by the bourgeois system, and not by some other.*

If growth of population were the determining force of social development, then a higher density of population would be bound to give rise to a correspondingly higher type of social system. But we do not find this to be the case. The density of population in China is four times as great as in the U.S.A., yet the U.S.A. stands higher than China in the scale of social development, for in China a semi-feudal system still prevails, whereas the U.S.A. has long ago reached the highest stage of development of capitalism. The density of population in Belgium is nineteen times as great as in the U.S.A., and twenty-six times as great as in the U.S.S.R. Yet the U.S.A. stands higher than Belgium in the scale of social development; and as for the U.S.S.R., Belgium lags a whole historical epoch behind this country, for in Belgium the capitalist system prevails, whereas the U.S.S.R. has already done away with capitalism and has set up a Socialist system.

It follows from this that growth of population is not, and cannot be, the chief force of development of society, the force which DETERMINES *the character of the social system, the physiognomy of society.*

What, then,[24] *is the chief force in the complex of conditions of material life of society which determines the physiognomy of society, the character of the social system, the development of society from one system to another?*

This force, historical materialism holds, is the METHOD OF PROCURING THE MEANS OF LIFE *necessary for human existence, the* MODE OF PRODUCTION OF MATERIAL VALUES*—food, clothing, footwear, houses, fuel, instruments of production,*[25] *etc.—which are indispensable for the life of development of society.*

In order to live, people must have food, clothing, footwear, shelter, fuel, etc.; in order to have these material values, people must produce them; and in order to produce them, people must have the instruments of production with which food, clothing, footwear, shelter, fuel,[26] *etc., are produced; they must be able to produce these instruments and to use them.*

The INSTRUMENTS OF PRODUCTION[27] *wherewith material values are produced, the people*[28] *who operate the instruments of production and carry on the production of material values thanks to a certain* PRODUCTION EXPERIENCE *and* LABOUR SKILL*—all these elements jointly constitute the* PRODUCTIVE FORCES *of society.*

But the productive forces are only one aspect of production, only one aspect of the mode of production, an aspect that expresses the relation of men to the objects and forces of nature which they make use of for the production of material values. Another aspect of production, another aspect of the mode of production, is the relation of men to each other in the process of production, men's RELATIONS OF PRODUCTION. *Men carry on a struggle against nature and utilize*[29] *nature for the production of material values not in isolation from each other, not as separate individuals, but in common, in groups, in societies. Production, therefore, is at all times and under all conditions social production. In the production of material values men enter into mutual relations of one kind or another within production, into relations of production of one kind or another. These may be relations of co-operation and mutual help between people who are free from exploitation; they may be relations of domination and subordination*[30]*; and, lastly, they may be transitional from one form of relations of production to another. But whatever the character of the relations of production may be, always and in every system, they constitute just as essential an element of production as the productive forces of society.*

> *"In production," Marx says, "men not only act on nature but also on one another. They produce only by co-operating in a certain way and mutually exchanging their activities. In order to produce, they enter into definite connections and relations with one another and only within these social connections and relations does their action on nature, does production, take place." (Karl Marx, SELECTED WORKS, Vol. I, p. 264.)*

Consequently, production, the mode of production, embraces both the productive forces of society and men's relations of production, and is thus the embodiment of their unity in the process of production of material values.

ONE OF THE FEATURES[31] *of production is that it never stays at one point for a long time and is always in a state of change and development, and that, furthermore, changes in the mode of production inevitably call forth changes in the whole social system, social ideas, political views and political institutions—they call forth a reconstruction of the whole social and political order. At different stages of development people make use of different modes of production, or, to put it more crudely, lead different manners of life. In the primitive commune there is one mode of production, under slavery there is another mode of production, under feudalism a third mode of production, and so on. And, correspondingly, men's social system, the spiritual life of men, their views and political institutions also vary.*

Whatever is the mode of production of a society, such in the main is the society itself, its ideas and theories, its political views and institutions.

Or, to put it more crudely, whatever is man's manner of life, such is his manner of thought.[32]

This means that the history of development of society is above all the history of the development of production, the history of the modes of production which succeed each other in the course of centuries, the history of the development of productive forces and people's relations of production.

Hence the history of social development is at the same time the history of the producers of material values themselves, the history of the labouring masses who are the chief force in the process of production and who carry on the production of material values necessary for the existence of society.

Hence, if historical science is to be a real science, it can no longer reduce the history of social development to the actions of kings and generals, to the actions of "conquerors" and "subjugators" of states, but must above all devote itself to the history of the producers of material values, the history of the labouring masses, the history of peoples.

Hence the clue to the study of the laws of history of society must not be sought in men's minds, in the views and ideas of society, but in the mode of production practised by society in any given historical period; it must be sought in the economic life of society.

Hence the prime task of historical science is to study and disclose the laws of production, the laws of development of the productive forces and of the relations of production, the laws of economic development of society.

Hence, if the party of the proletariat is to be a real party, it must above all acquire a knowledge of the laws of development of production, of the laws of economic development of society.

Hence, if it is not to err in policy, the party of the proletariat must both in drafting its program and in its practical activities proceed primarily from the laws of development of production, from the laws of economic development of society.

A SECOND FEATURE[33] *of production is that its changes and development always begin with changes and development of the productive forces, and, in the first place, with changes and development of the instruments of production. Productive forces are therefore the most mobile and revolutionary element of production. First the productive forces of society change and develop, and then,* DEPENDING *on these changes and* IN CONFORMITY WITH THEM, *men's relations of production, their economic relations, change. This, however, does not mean that the relations of production do not influence the development of the productive forces and that the latter are not dependent on the former. While their development is dependent on the development of the productive forces, the relations of production in their turn react upon the development of the productive forces, accelerating or retarding it. In this connection it should be noted that the relations of production cannot for too long a time lag behind and be in a state of contradiction to the growth of the productive forces, inasmuch as the productive forces can develop in full measure only when the relations of production correspond to the character, the state of the productive forces and allow full scope for their development. Therefore, however much the relations of production may lag behind the development of the productive forces, they must, sooner or later, come into correspondence with—and actually do come into correspondence with—the level of development of the productive forces, the character of the productive forces. Otherwise we would have a fundamental violation of the unity of the productive forces and the relations of production within the system of production, a disruption of production as a whole, a crisis of production, a destruction of productive forces.*

An instance in which the relations of production do not correspond to the character of the productive forces, conflict with them, is the economic crises in capitalist countries, where private capitalist ownership of the means of production is in glaring incongruity with the social character of the process of production, with the character of the productive forces. This results in economic crises, which lead to the destruction of productive forces. Furthermore, this incongruity itself constitutes the economic basis of social revolution, the purpose of which is to destroy the existing relations of production and to create new relations of production corresponding to the character of the productive forces.

In contrast, an instance in which the relations of production completely correspond to the character of the productive forces is the Socialist national economy of the U.S.S.R., where the social ownership of the means of production fully corresponds to the social character of the process of production, and where, because of this, economic crises and the destruction of productive forces are unknown.

Consequently, the productive forces are not only the most mobile and revolutionary element in production, but are also the determining element in the development of production.

Whatever are the productive forces such must be the relations of production.

While the state of the productive forces furnishes an answer to the question—with what instruments of production do men produce the material values they need?—the state of the relations of production furnishes the answer to another question—who owns the MEANS OF PRODUCTION *(the land, forests, waters, mineral resources, raw materials, instruments of production, production premises, means of transportation and communication, etc.), who commands the means of production, whether the whole of society, or individual persons, groups, or classes which utilize them for the exploitation of other persons, groups or classes?*

Here is a rough picture of the development of productive forces from ancient times to our day. The transition from crude stone tools to the bow and arrow, and the accompanying transition from the life of hunters to the domestication of animals and primitive pasturage; the transition from stone tools to metal tools (the iron axe, the wooden plough fitted with an iron colter, etc.), with a corresponding[34] *transition to tillage and agriculture; a further improvement in metal tools for the working up of materials, the introduction of the blacksmith's bellows, the introduction of pottery, with a corresponding development of handicrafts, the separation of handicrafts from agriculture, the development of an independent handicraft industry and, subsequently, of manufacture; the transition from handicraft tools to machines and the transformation of handicraft and manufacture into machine industry; the transition to the machine system and the rise of modern large-scale machine industry—such is a general and far from complete picture of the development of the productive forces of society in the course of man's history. It will be clear that the development and improvement of the instruments of production were effected by men who were related to production, and not independently of men; and, consequently, the change and development of the instruments of production were accompanied by a change and development of men, as the most important element of the productive forces, by a change and development of their production experience, their labour skill, their ability to handle the instruments of production.*

In conformity with the change and development of the productive forces of society in the course of history, men's relations of production, their economic relations also changed and developed.

Five MAIN *types of relations of production are known to history: primitive communal, slave, feudal, capitalist and Socialist.*

The basis of the relations of production under the primitive communal system is that the means of production are socially owned. This in the main corresponds to the character of the productive forces of that period. Stone tools, and, later, the bow and arrow, precluded the possibility of men individually combating the forces of nature and beasts of prey. In order to gather the fruits of the forest, to catch fish, to build some sort of habitation, men were obliged to work in common if they did not want to die of starvation, or fall victim to beasts of prey or to neighbouring societies. Labour in common led to the common ownership of the means of production, as well as of the fruits of production. Here the conception of private ownership of the means of production did not yet exist, except for the personal ownership of certain implements of production which were at the same time means of defence against beasts of prey. Here there was no exploitation, no classes.

The basis of the relations of production under the slave system is that the slave owner owns the means of production; he also owns the worker in production—the slave,[35] *whom he can sell, purchase, or kill as though he were an animal. Such relations of production in the main correspond to the state of the productive forces of that period. Instead of stone tools, men now have metal tools at their command; instead of the wretched and primitive husbandry of the hunter,*[36] *who knew neither pasturage, nor tillage, there now appear pasturage, tillage, handicrafts, and a division of labour between these branches of production. There appears the possibility of the exchange of products between individuals and between societies, of the accumulation of wealth in the hands of a few, the actual accumulation of the means of production in the hands of a minority, and the possibility of subjugation*[37] *of the majority*[38] *by a minority and their conversion into slaves. Here we no longer find the common and free*[39] *labour of all members of society in the production process—here there prevails the forced labour of slaves, who are exploited by the non-labouring slave owners. Here, therefore, there is no common ownership of the means of production or of the fruits of production. It is replaced by private ownership. Here the slave owner appears as the prime and principal property owner in the full sense of the term.*

Rich and poor, exploiters and exploited, people with full rights and people with no rights, and a fierce class struggle between them—such is the picture of the slave system.

The basis of the relations of production under the feudal system is that the feudal lord owns the means of production and does not fully own the worker in production—the serf, whom the feudal lord can no longer kill, but whom he can buy and sell. Alongside of feudal ownership there exists individual ownership by the peasant and the handicraftsman of his implements of production and his private enterprise based on his personal labour. Such relations of production in the main correspond to the state of the productive forces of that period. Further improvements in the smelting and working of iron; the spread of the iron plough and the loom; the further development of agriculture, horticulture, viniculture and dairying; the appearance of manufactories alongside of the handicraft workshops—such are the characteristic features of the state of the productive forces.

The new productive forces demand that the labourer shall display some kind of initiative in production and an inclination for work, an interest in work. The feudal lord therefore discards the slave, as a labourer who has no interest in work and is entirely without initiative, and prefers to deal with the serf, who has his own husbandry, implements of production, and a certain interest in work essential for the cultivation of the land and for the payment in kind of a part of his harvest to the feudal lord.

Here private ownership is further developed. Exploitation is nearly as severe as it was under slavery—it is only slightly mitigated. A class struggle between exploiters and exploited is[40] *the principal feature of the feudal system.*

The basis of the relations of production under the capitalist system is that the capitalist owns the means of production, but not the workers in production—the wage labourers, whom the capitalist can neither kill nor sell because they are personally free, but who are deprived of means of production and, in order not to die of hunger, are obliged to sell their labour power to the capitalist and to bear the yoke of exploitation. Alongside of capitalist property in the means of production, we find, at first on a wide scale, private property of the peasants and handicraftsmen[41] *in the means of production, these peasants and handicraftsmen no longer being serfs, and their private property being based on personal labour. In place of the handicraft workshops and manufactories there appear huge mills and factories equipped with machinery. In place of the manorial estates tilled by the primitive*[42] *implements of production*[43] *of the peasant, there now appear large capitalist farms run on scientific lines*[44] *and supplied with agricultural machinery.*

The new productive forces require that the workers in production shall be better educated and more intelligent than the downtrodden and ignorant serfs, that they be able to understand machinery and operate it properly. Therefore, the capitalists prefer to deal with wage workers who are free from the bonds of serfdom and who are educated enough to be able properly to operate machinery.

But having developed productive forces to a tremendous extent, capitalism has become enmeshed in contradictions which it is unable to solve. By producing larger and larger quantities of commodities, and reducing their prices, capitalism intensifies competition, ruins the mass of small and medium private owners, converts them into proletarians and reduces their purchasing power, with the result that it becomes impossible to dispose of the commodities produced. On the other hand, by expanding production and concentrating millions of workers in huge mills and factories, capitalism lends the process of production a social character and thus undermines its own foundation,[45] *inasmuch as the social character of the process of production demands the social ownership of the means of production; yet the means of production remain private capitalist property, which is incompatible with the social character of the process of production.*

These irreconcilable contradictions between the character of the productive forces and the relations of production make themselves felt in periodical crises of overproduction, when the capitalists, finding no effective demand for their goods owing to the ruin of the mass of the population which they themselves have brought about, are compelled to burn products, destroy manufactured goods, suspend[46] *production, and destroy productive forces at a time when millions of people are forced to suffer unemployment and starvation, not because there are not enough goods, but because there is an overproduction of goods.*

This means that the capitalist relations of production have ceased to correspond to the state of productive forces of society and have come into irreconcilable contradiction with them.

This means that capitalism is pregnant with revolution, whose mission it is to replace the existing capitalist[47] *ownership of the means of production by Socialist ownership.*[48]

This means that the main feature of the capitalist system is a most acute class struggle between the exploiters and the exploited.

The basis of the relations of production under the Socialist system, which so far has been established only in the U.S.S.R., is the social ownership of the means of production. Here there are no longer exploiters and exploited. The goods produced are distributed according to labour performed, on the principle: "He who does not work, neither shall he eat." Here the mutual relations of people in the process of production are marked by comradely co-operation and the Socialist mutual assistance of workers who are free from exploitation. Here the relations of produc-

tion fully correspond to the state of productive forces, for the social[49] *character of the process of production is reinforced by the social*[50] *ownership of the means of production.*

For this reason Socialist production in the U.S.S.R. knows no periodical crises of overproduction and their accompanying absurdities.

For this reason, the productive forces here develop at an accelerated pace, for the relations of production that correspond to them offer full scope for such development.

Such is the picture of the development of men's relations of production in the course of human history.

Such is the dependence of the development of the relations of production on the development of the production forces of society, and primarily, on the development of the instruments of production, the dependence by virtue of which the changes and development of the productive forces sooner or later lead to corresponding changes and development of the relations of production.

> *"The use and fabrication of instruments of labour (by instruments of labour Marx has in mind primarily*[51] *instruments of production.—Ed.)," says Marx, "although existing in the germ among certain species of animals, is specifically characteristic of the human labour-process, and Franklin therefore defines man as a tool-making animal. Relics of bygone instruments of labour possess the same importance for the investigation of extinct economic forms of society, as do fossil bones for the determination of extinct species of animals. It is not the articles made, but how they are made, and by what instruments that enables us to distinguish different economic epochs. . . . Instruments of labour not only supply a standard of the degree of development to which human labour has attained but they are also indicators of the social conditions under which that labour is carried on." (Karl Marx, Capital, Vol. I, p. 159.)*
>
> *And further:*
>
> *a) "Social relations are closely bound up with productive forces. In acquiring new productive forces men change their mode of production; and in changing their mode of production, in changing the way of earning their living, they change all their social conditions. The hand-mill gives you society with the feudal lord; the steam-mill, society with the industrial capitalist." (Karl Marx, The Poverty of Philosophy, p. 92.)*
>
> *b) "There is a continual movement of growth in productive forces, of destruction in social relations, of formation in ideas; the only immutable thing is the abstraction of movement." (Ibid., p. 93.)*

Speaking of historical materialism as formulated in the COMMUNIST MANIFESTO, *Engels says:*

> *"Economic production and the structure of society of every historical epoch necessarily arising therefrom constitute the foundation for the political and intellectual history of that epoch; . . . consequently ever since the dissolution of the primeval communal ownership of land all history has been a history of class struggles, of struggles between exploited and exploiting, between dominated and dominating classes at various stages of social evolution; . . . this struggle, however, has now reached a stage where the exploited and oppressed class (the proletariat) can no longer emancipate itself from the class which exploits and oppresses it (the bourgeoisie), without at the same time forever freeing the whole of society from exploitation, oppression and class struggles." (Preface to the German edition of The Communist Manifesto—Karl Marx,* SELECTED WORKS, *Vol. I, pp. 192–93.)*

A THIRD FEATURE[52] *of production is that the rise of new productive forces and of the relations of production corresponding to them does not take place separately from the old system, after the disappearance of the old system, but within the old system; it takes place not as a result of the deliberate and conscious activity of man, but spontaneously, unconsciously, independently of the will of man. It takes place spontaneously and independently of the will of man for two reasons.*

First, because men are not free to choose one mode of production or another, because as every new generation enters life it finds productive forces and relations of production already existing as the result of the work of former generations, owing to which it is obliged at first to accept and adapt itself to everything it finds ready made in the sphere of production in order to be able to produce material values.

Secondly, because, when improving one instrument of production or another, one element of the productive forces or another, men do not realize, do not understand or stop to reflect what social results these improvements will lead to, but only think of their everyday interests, of lightening their labour and of securing some direct and tangible advantage for themselves.

When, gradually and gropingly, certain members of primitive communal society passed from the use of stone tools to the use of iron tools, they, of course, did not know and did not stop to reflect what social results this innovation would lead to; they did not understand or realize that the change to metal tools meant a revolution in production, that it would in the long run lead to the slave system. They simply wanted to lighten their labour and secure an immediate and tangible advantage; their conscious activity was confined within the narrow bounds of this everyday personal interest.

When, in the period of the feudal system, the young bourgeoisie of Europe began to erect, alongside of the small guild workshops, large manufactories, and thus advanced the productive forces of society, it, of course, did not know and did not stop to reflect what social consequences this innovation would lead to; it did not realize or understand that this "small" innovation would lead to a regrouping of social forces which was to end in a revolution both against the power of kings, whose favours it so highly valued, and against the nobility, to whose ranks its foremost representatives not infrequently[53] *aspired. It simply wanted to lower the cost of producing goods, to throw large quantities of goods on the markets of Asia and of recently discovered America, and to make bigger profits. Its conscious activity was confined within the narrow bounds of this commonplace practical aim.*

When the Russian capitalists, in conjunction with foreign capitalists, energetically implanted modern large-scale machine industry in Russia, while leaving tsardom intact and turning the peasants over to the tender mercies of the landlords, they, of course, did not know and did not stop to reflect what social consequences this extensive growth of productive forces would lead to, they did not realize or understand that this big leap in the realm of the productive forces of society would lead to a regrouping of social forces that would enable the proletariat to effect a union with the peasantry and to bring about a victorious Socialist revolution. They simply wanted to expand industrial production to the limit, to gain control of the huge home market, to become monopolists, and to squeeze as much profit as possible out of the national economy. Their conscious activity did not extend beyond their commonplace, strictly practical interests. Accordingly, Marx says:

> *"In the social production which men carry on (that is, in the production of the material values necessary to the life of men—Ed.) they enter into definite relations that are indispensable and independent (EMPHASIS ADDED—Ed.)*[54] *of their will; these relations of production correspond to a definite stage of development of their material forces of production." (Karl Marx, SELECTED WORKS, Vol. I, p. 356.)*

This, however, does not mean that changes in the relations of production, and the transition from old relations of production to new relations of production proceed smoothly, without conflicts, without upheavals. On the contrary,[55] *such a transition usually*[56] *takes place by means of the revolutionary overthrow of the old relations of production and the establishment of new relations of production. Up to a certain period the development of the productive forces and the changes in the realm of the relations of production proceed spontaneously, independently of the will of men. But that is so only up to a certain moment, until the new and developing productive forces have reached a proper state of maturity. After the new productive forces have matured, the existing relations of production and their upholders—the ruling classes—become that "insuperable" obstacle which can only be removed by the conscious action of the new classes,*[57] *by the forcible acts of these classes, by revolution. Here there stands out in bold relief the* TREMENDOUS *role of new social ideas, of new political institutions, of a new political power, whose mission it is to abolish by force the old relations of production. Out of the conflict between the new productive forces and the old relations of production, out of the new economic demands of society there arise new social ideas; the new ideas organize and mobilize the masses; the masses become welded into a new political army, create a new revolutionary power, and make use of it to abolish by force the old system of relations of production, and firmly to establish the new system. The spontaneous process of development yields place to the conscious actions of men, peaceful development to violent upheaval, evolution to revolution.*

> *"The proletariat," says Marx, "during its contest with the bourgeoisie is compelled, by the force of circumstances, to organize itself as a class . . . by means of a revolution, it makes itself the ruling class, and, as such, sweeps away by force the old conditions of production." (*THE COMMUNIST MANIFESTO*—Karl Marx,* SELECTED WORKS*, Vol. I, p. 228.)*
>
> *And further:*
>
> *a) "The proletariat will use its political supremacy to wrest, by degrees, all capital from the bourgeoisie, to centralize all instruments of production in the hands of the state, i.e., of the proletariat organized as the ruling class; and to increase the total of productive forces as rapidly as possible." (Ibid., p. 227.)*
> *b) "Force is the midwife of every old society pregnant with a new one." (Karl Marx,* CAPITAL*, Vol. I, p. 776.)*

Here is the brilliant formulation of the essence of historical materialism given by Marx in 1859 in his historic Preface to his famous book, CRITIQUE OF POLITICAL ECONOMY*:*

> *"In the social production which men carry on they enter into definite relations that are indispensable and independent of their will; these relations of production correspond to a definite stage of development of their mate-*

rial forces of production. The sum total of these relations of production constitutes the economic structure of society—the real foundation, on which rises a legal and political superstructure and to which correspond definite forms of social consciousness. The mode of production in material life determines the social, political and intellectual life process in general. It is not the consciousness of men that determines their being, but, on the contrary, their social being that determines their consciousness. At a certain stage of their development, the material forces of production in society come in conflict with the existing relations of production, or—what is but a legal expression for the same thing—with the property relations within which they have been at work before. From forms of development of the forces of production these relations turn into their fetters. Then begins an epoch of social revolution. With the change of the economic foundation the entire immense superstructure is more or less rapidly transformed. In considering such transformations a distinction should always be made between the material transformation of the economic conditions of production which can be determined with the precision of natural science, and the legal, political, religious, aesthetic or philosophic—in short, ideological forms in which men become conscious of this conflict and fight it out. Just as our opinion of an individual is not based on what he thinks of himself, so can we not judge of such a period of transformation by its own consciousness; on the contrary, this consciousness must be explained rather from the contradictions of material life, from the existing conflict between the social forces of production and the relations of production. No social order ever disappears before all the productive forces for which there is room in it have been developed; and new higher relations of production never appear before the material conditions of their existence have matured in the womb of the old society itself. Therefore, mankind always sets itself only such tasks as it can solve; since, looking at the matter more closely, we will always find that the task itself arises only when the material conditions necessary for its solution already exists or are at least in the process of formation." (Karl Marx, SELECTED WORKS, Vol. I, pp. 356–57.)

Such is Marxist materialism as applied to social life, to the history of society.

Such are the principal features of dialectical and historical materialism.

It will be seen from this what a theoretical treasure was safeguarded by Lenin for the Party and protected from the attacks of the revisionists and renegades, and how important was the appearance of Lenin's book, MATERIALISM AND EMPIRIO-CRITICISM, for the development of our Party.

3. ~~Bolshevik and Menshevik Evaluation of the Prospects for Revolution.~~ *Bolsheviks and Mensheviks in the Period of the Stolypin Reaction.* Struggle of the Bolsheviks against the Liquidators and Otzovists

During the years of reaction, the work in the Party organizations was ~~much~~ *far* more difficult than during the preceding period of development of the ~~1905~~ revolution. The Party membership had sharply declined. Many of the petty-bourgeois ~~"~~fellow-travelers~~"~~ of the Party, especially the intellectuals, deserted its ranks from fear of persecution by the tsarist government ~~and loss of belief in the revolution~~.

Lenin pointed out that at such moments revolutionary parties should perfect their knowledge. During the period of rise of the revolution they learned how to advance; during the period of reaction they should learn how to retreat properly, *how to go underground, how to preserve and strengthen the illegal party, how to make use of legal opportunities, of all legally existing, especially mass, organizations in order to strengthen their connections with the masses.*

The Mensheviks retreated in panic, not believing that a new rise in the tide of revolution was possible; they disgracefully renounced ~~all~~ the revolutionary demands of the program and the revolutionary slogans of the Party; they wanted to liquidate,[58] to abolish, the revolutionary illegal ~~organization of the~~ party *of the proletariat*. For this reason, Mensheviks *of this type* came to be known as LIQUIDATORS.

Unlike the Mensheviks, the Bolsheviks were certain that within the next few years there would be a rise in the tide of revolution, and held that it was the duty of the Party to prepare the masses for this new rise. The fundamental problems of the revolution had not been solved. The peasants had not obtained the landlords' land, the workers had not obtained the 8-hour day, the tsarist autocracy, so detested by the people, had not been overthrown, and it had again suppressed the meagre political liberties which the people had wrung from it in 1905. Thus the causes which had given rise to the Revolution of 1905 still remained in force. That is why the Bolsheviks were certain that there would be a new rise of the revolutionary movement, prepared for it and mustered the forces of the working class ~~after the defeat of the first Russian revolution~~.

The Bolsheviks derived their certainty ~~in~~ *that*[59] a new rise in the tide of the revolution *was inevitable also*[60] from the fact that the Revolution of 1905 had taught the working class to fight for its rights in mass revolutionary struggle.[61] During the period of reaction ~~and~~, *when the capitalists took* the offensive ~~of capital~~, the workers could not forget these lessons of 1905. Lenin quoted letters from workers in which they told how factory owners were again oppressing and humiliating them, and in which they said: "WAIT, ANOTHER 1905 WILL COME!"

The fundamental ~~revolutionary~~ *political* aim of the Bolsheviks remained ~~the same that~~ *what* it had been *in 1905*, namely, to overthrow tsardom, to carry the bourgeois-democratic revolution to its conclusion and ~~then~~ to proceed to the Socialist revolution. Never for a moment did the Bolsheviks forget this ~~basic~~ aim, and they continued to put before the masses the principal revolutionary slogans—a democratic republic, the confiscation of the landed estates, and an 8-hour day.

But the TACTICS of the Party could not remain what they had been during the rising tide of the revolution in 1905. For example, it would have been wrong in the immediate future to call the masses to a general political strike or to an armed uprising, for the revolutionary movement was on the decline, the working class was in a state of extreme fatigue, *and the position of the reactionary classes had been strengthened considerably*. The Party had to reckon with ~~THIS FACT AND~~ the new situation. ~~It would have been incorrect to continue with the tactic of boycotting the Duma; it was necessary to take part in the Duma and use the legal opportunities to agitate during elections and from the Duma tribune. Offensive tactics had to be exchanged for a tactical retreat, but a retreat that was done correctly in order to preserve the revolutionary army and its morale and military readiness as much as possible.~~ *Offensive tactics had to be replaced by defensive tactics, the tactics of mustering forces, the tactics of withdrawing the cadres underground and of carrying on the work of the Party from underground, the tactics of combining illegal work with work in the legal working-class organizations.*

And the Bolsheviks proved able to accomplish this.

> "We knew how to work during the long years preceding the revolution. Not for nothing do they say that we are as firm as a rock. The Social-Democrats have formed a proletarian party which will not lose heart at the failure of the first armed onslaught, will not lose its head, and will not be carried away by adventures," wrote Lenin. (Lenin, COLLECTED WORKS, Russ. ed., Vol. XII, p. 126.)

The Bolsheviks ~~under Lenin and Stalin~~ strove to preserve and strengthen the illegal Party organizations. But at the same time they deemed it essential to utilize every legal opportunity, every legal opening to maintain and preserve connections with the masses *and thus strengthen the Party*.

> "This was a period when our Party turned from the open revolutionary struggle against tsardom to roundabout methods of struggle, to the utilization of each and every legal opportunity—from mutual aid societies to the Duma platform. This was a period of retreat after we had been

defeated in the Revolution of 1905. This turn made it incumbent upon us to master new methods of struggle, in order to muster our forces and resume the open revolutionary struggle against tsardom." (~~Concluding Words of Comrade~~ J. Stalin ~~at the Fifteenth Party Congress~~, VERBATIM REPORT OF THE FIFTEENTH PARTY CONGRESS, Russ. ed., pp. 366–67, 1935.)

The surviving legal organizations served as a sort of screen for the underground organizations of the Party and as a means of maintaining connections with the masses. In order to preserve their connections with the masses, the Bolsheviks made use of the trade unions and other legally existing public organizations, such as sick benefit societies, workers' co-operative societies, clubs, educational societies and People's Houses. The Bolsheviks made use of the platform of the State Duma to expose the policy of the tsarist government, to expose the Constitutional-Democrats, and to win the support of the peasants for the proletariat. The preservation of the illegal Party organization, and the direction of all other forms of political ~~struggle~~ *work* through this organization, enabled the Party to pursue a correct line and to muster forces in preparation for a new rise in the tide of revolution.

The Bolsheviks carried out their revolutionary line in a fight on TWO FRONTS, a fight against the two varieties of opportunism *within the Party*[62]—against the LIQUIDATORS, *who were open adversaries of the Party*, and against what were known as the OTZOVISTS, *who were concealed foes of the Party.*

The Bolsheviks, headed by Lenin, waged a relentless struggle against liquidationism from the very inception of this opportunist trend. Lenin pointed out that the Liquidators were ~~a sign of bourgeois influence on the proletariat~~ *agents of the liberal bourgeoisie within the Party.*

In December 1908, the Fifth (*All*-Russian) Conference of the R.S.D.L.P. was held in Paris. On Lenin's motion, this conference ~~decisively~~ condemned liquidationism, that is, the attempts of a certain section of the Party intellectuals (Mensheviks) "to liquidate the existing organization of the R.S.D.L.P. and to replace it at all costs, even at the price of down-right renunciation of the program, tactics and traditions of the Party, by an amorphous association functioning legally." (RESOLUTIONS OF THE C.P.S.U.[B.], Russ. ed., Part I, p. 128.)

The conference called upon all Party organizations to wage a resolute struggle against the attempts of the Liquidators.

But the Mensheviks did not abide by this decision of the ~~Fifth Party~~ conference and increasingly committed themselves to liquidationism, betrayal of the revolution, and collaboration with the Constitutional-Democrats. The Mensheviks were more and more openly renouncing the revolutionary program of the proletarian Party, ~~for instance on~~ the demands for a democratic republic,

~~on the demand~~ for an 8-hour day *and for the confiscation of the landed estates*~~, etc~~. They wanted, at the price of ~~totally~~ renouncing the program and tactics of the Party, to obtain the consent of the tsarist government to the existence of an open, legal, supposedly "labour" party ~~(in reality the party was something akin to the Zubatov organization)~~. They were prepared to make peace with and to adapt themselves to the Stolypin regime. That is why the Liquidators were also called the "Stolypin Labour Party."

~~In his "Letter from the Caucasus," written in 1909, Comrade Stalin said that the Mensheviks were demanding "that our program be adapted to that of the Constitutional-Democrats," exposing the Tiflis Mensheviks, who were the most open in their decision to renounce the revolutionary program and eliminate the proletarian party. The Mensheviks announced that the proletariat could not count on the support of the peasantry, that the proletariat could not lead the revolution itself, and therefore that its task amounted just to supporting the moderate Constitutional-Democratic bourgeoisie.~~

> ~~"In a word, in the place of the leading party of the proletariat, which was also leading the peasantry, there is the leadership role of the Constitutional-Democratic bourgeoisie, leading the proletariat by the nose.~~
>
> ~~Such are the 'new' tactics of the Tiflis Mensheviks," wrote Comrade Stalin. (LENIN AND STALIN, Russ. ed., Vol. 1, p. 529.)~~

~~Using the Tiflis Mensheviks as an example, Comrade Stalin exposed the existence of all-Russian Menshevik liquidationism. Lenin was in full agreement with the lethal critique that Comrade Stalin addressed to the Mensheviks. Lenin wrote soon thereafter that the Caucasian Menshevik Zhordanya "confirmed in this article some of the more serious accusations made by the author of the 'Letter from the Caucasus,' Comrade K. S." (Comrade Stalin, in other words).~~

Besides fighting the overt adversaries of the revolution, the Liquidators, *who were headed by Dan, Axelrod, and Potressov, and assisted by Martov, Trotsky and other Mensheviks,* the Bolsheviks also waged a relentless struggle against *the covert Liquidators,* the Otzovists, who camouflaged their opportunism by "Left" phraseology. Otzovists was the name given to certain former Bolsheviks who demanded the recall (OTZYV means recall) of the workers' deputies from the State Duma and the discontinuation of work in legally existing organizations altogether.

~~The Otzovist trend arose within the camp of those who supported the incorrect tactic of boycotting the Third State Duma and refused to participate in the Duma elections.~~

~~Lenin spoke out decisively against the boycott of the Duma elections and explained the mistakes of the boycotters, who did not understand that a change~~

~~in circumstances demands a change in tactics for the Bolsheviks. If in the heat of the 1905 revolution, in the heat of the armed uprising, it had been necessary to refuse to participate in the elections to the Bulygin Duma in order not to distract the masses from the armed uprising, now it was necessary to take part in the elections. It was necessary to use the elections for revolutionary agitation among the masses and to steadily assemble the revolutionary forces.~~

In 1908 a number of Bolsheviks~~—those who supported the boycott—~~demanded the recall of the Social-Democratic deputies from the State Duma. Hence, they were called Otzovists. The Otzovists formed their own group (Bogdanov, Lunacharsky, Alexinsky, Pokrovsky, *Bubnov* and others) which started a struggle against Lenin and Lenin's line. The Otzovists *stubbornly* refused to work in the trade unions and other legally existing societies. In doing so they did great injury to the workers' cause. The Otzovists were driving a wedge between the Party and the working class, tending to deprive the Party of its connections with the non-party masses; they wanted to seclude themselves within the underground organization, yet at the same time they placed it in jeopardy by denying it the opportunity of utilizing legal cover. The Otzovists did not understand that in the State Duma, and through the State Duma, the Bolsheviks could influence the peasantry, could expose the policy of the tsarist government and the policy of the Constitutional-Democrats, who were trying to gain the following of the peasantry by fraud. The Otzovists hampered the mustering of forces for a new advance of the revolution. The Otzovists were therefore "Liquidators inside-out": they ~~destroyed~~ *endeavoured to destroy* the possibility of utilizing the legally existing organizations and, in fact, renounced proletarian leadership of the ~~whole revolutionary movement~~ *broad non-party masses*, renounced revolutionary ~~STRUGGLE~~ *work*.

A conference of the enlarged editorial board of the Bolshevik newspaper PROLETARY, *summoned* in 1909 *to discuss the conduct of the Otzovists,* condemned them. The Bolsheviks announced that they had nothing in common with the Otzovists and ~~drove~~ *expelled* them ~~out of~~ *from* the Bolshevik ~~faction~~ *organization.*

~~What can explain the appearance of the Liquidators and the Otzovists in the period of reaction? We know that the working class in Russia was not homogeneous and that it had a thin petty-bourgeois stratum. The petty-bourgeois elements showed a lack of resilience when the labour movement experienced difficulties or when it was necessary to make a change. After the defeat of the revolution, it was necessary to stage an organized retreat, rebuild the ranks, change tactics and adapt to the new conditions of work while defending the revolutionary program. This is what the Bolsheviks did. But the Liquidators and Otzovists expressed the doubts of the Bolsheviks' petty-bourgeois stratum.~~

~~They were the conductors of bourgeois influence over the proletariat as the Economists and legal Marxists had been before them.~~

~~After the Revolution of 1905, the bourgeoisie entered into an agreement with tsardom, once and for all, becoming true counter-revolutionary forces. It would be profitable for the bourgeoisie if the workers would renounce the revolutionary struggle with tsardom. And the Menshevik-Liquidators were conducting precisely this policy of renouncing the revolutionary struggle with tsardom and the capitalist class. The Menshevik-Liquidators served as direct agents of the bourgeoisie in the labour movement. "The Liquidators are petty-bourgeois intelligentsia who have been sent by the bourgeoisie to carry their liberal debauchery into the workers' milieu," said Lenin.~~

~~The Otzovists essentially ended up on this path of renouncing the revolutionary struggle as well, as they aimed to separate the revolutionary party from the masses and in this way weaken it.~~ Both the Liquidators and the Otzovists were nothing but ~~bourgeois and~~ petty-bourgeois fellow-travelers[63] of the proletariat and its Party. When times were hard for the ~~proletarian party~~ *proletariat* the true character of the Liquidators and Otzovists became revealed with particular clarity.

~~The Otzovists began to preach teachings in the realm of philosophy which were hostile to Marx and Engels. Lenin dealt them a decisive rebuff, having demonstrated in a specially written book (Lenin, COLLECTED WORKS, Russian ed., Vol. XIII) the bourgeois, clerical essence of the Otzovists' philosophy.~~

~~The Otzovists actually slid toward an odd defence of religion and began to preach of the proletariat's need for a new religion, the construction of its own God and the search for its own religion. For this, they were known as the "god-builders" and "god-seekers." Lenin and all the Bolsheviks waged a determined struggle against the god-builders and god-seekers.~~

~~At the end of 1909, the Otzovists, god-builders and god-seekers aligned together into an independent organization, the group "VPERYOD." This group had its own tactical program and organized its own party school, first on the island of Capri and then in Bologna (Italy).~~

~~Lenin waged an uncompromising struggle against this group. A portion of the VPERYODists (Lunacharsky, Pokrovsky) eventually returned to the Bolshevik Party. And some of them left our party for good (Stanislav Volsky, Bazarov, Bogdanov, Alexinsky and others).~~

~~In this period, Kamenev, Zinoviev, Tomsky and Rykov assumed a conciliatory position toward the "Left" opportunists. They supported the Otzovists. Behind Lenin's back, Kamenev wrote to Bogdanov, who had been expelled from the party, about how he had supported Bogdanov's idealistic philosophy since 1905. This was not the first time that this double-dealer had conspired with the enemies of Bolshevism behind Lenin's back.~~

4. Struggle of the Bolsheviks against Trotskyism ~~and Conciliationism~~. *Anti-Party August Bloc*

At a time when ~~Lenin and Stalin~~ *the Bolsheviks* were waging a relentless struggle on two fronts—against the ~~Menshevik-~~Liquidators and against the ~~"Liquidators of the Left" (~~Otzovists~~)~~—defending the consistent line of the proletarian party, Trotsky ~~wholly sided with~~ *supported* the Menshevik Liquidators ~~and advanced a treacherous policy~~. It was at this period that Lenin branded him "Judas Trotsky." Trotsky formed a group of writers in Vienna (Austria) and began to publish an allegedly non-factional, but in reality Menshevik newspaper. "Trotsky behaves like a most despicable careerist and factionalist. . . . He pays lip service to the Party, but behaves worse than any other factionalist," wrote Lenin ~~in August 1909~~ *at the time*.

Later, in 1912, Trotsky organized the August Bloc,[64] a bloc of all the ~~non-Bolshevik~~ *anti-Bolshevik* groups and trends directed against *Lenin and* the Bolshevik Party. The Liquidators and the Otzovists united in this anti-Bolshevik bloc, thus demonstrating their kinship. Trotsky and the Trotskyites took up a liquidationist stand on all fundamental issues. *But* ~~At the time, Trotsky appeared as a centrist—that is, he tried to conceal his opportunism—as Kautsky had in the Second International,~~ *Trotsky masked* his liquidationism ~~through revolutionary rhetoric~~ *under the guise of Centrism, that is, conciliationism; he claimed that he belonged to neither the Bolsheviks nor the Mensheviks and that he was trying to reconcile them*. In this connection, Lenin said that Trotsky was more vile and pernicious than the open Liquidators, because he was trying to deceive the workers into believing that he was "above factions," whereas in fact he entirely supported the Menshevik Liquidators. The Trotskyites were the principal group that fostered Centrism ~~in Russia~~.

> "Centrism," ~~pointed out~~ *writes* Comrade Stalin, "is a political concept. Its ideology is one of adaptation, of subordination of the interests of the proletariat to the interests of the petty-bourgeoisie WITHIN ONE COMMON PARTY. This ideology is alien and abhorrent to Leninism." (Stalin, LENINISM, Vol. II, "The Industrialization of the Country and the Right Deviation in the C.P.S.U.," p. 97.)

~~And~~[65] *At* this period Kamenev, Zinoviev and Rykov were actually *covert* agents of Trotsky, for they ~~looked upon him in a conciliatory way and~~ often helped him against Lenin. With the aid of Zinoviev, Kamenev, Rykov and other ~~conciliators with Trotskyism~~ *covert allies of Trotsky*, a Plenum of the Central Committee was convened in January 1910 AGAINST LENIN'S WISHES. By that time the composition of the Central Committee had changed owing to the arrest of a number of Bolsheviks, and the ~~conciliators~~ *vacillating elements* were able to force through anti-Leninist decisions. Thus, it was decided at this plenum to close down the Bolshevik newspaper PROLETARY and to give financial support to Trotsky's newspaper PRAVDA, published in Vienna. Kamenev joined the editorial board of Trotsky's newspaper and together with Zinoviev strove to make it the organ of the Central Committee.

It was only on Lenin's insistence ~~along with the firm Bolsheviks~~ that the January ~~1910~~ Plenum of the Central Committee adopted a resolution condemning liquidationism and otzovism, but here too Zinoviev and Kamenev insisted on Trotsky's proposal that the Liquidators should not be referred to as such.

It turned out as Lenin had foreseen and forewarned: only the Bolsheviks obeyed the decision of the plenum of the Central Committee and closed down their organ, PROLETARY, whereas the Mensheviks continued to publish their *factional* liquidationist newspaper GOLOS SOTSIAL-DEMOKRATA (VOICE OF THE SOCIAL-DEMOCRAT).

~~The Bolshevik centre's hands were tied. It was condemned to forced inaction at a time when what was necessary was intensive work on the restoration of the Party. These grim circumstances came about as a result of conciliators with the Bolshevik ranks, who in this way served as the direct ACCOMPLICES OF OPPORTUNISM.~~

~~Kamenev and Zinoviev interfered with the Leninist struggle on two fronts and negotiated with representatives of Polish Social-Democracy (Varsky and Tyshkoy) behind Lenin's back about "putting pressure" on Lenin and forcing him to renounce the two-front struggle with the opportunists.~~

Lenin's position was fully supported by *Comrade* Stalin who published a ~~second~~ *special* article ~~"Letter from the Caucasus"~~ in SOTSIAL-DEMOKRAT, No. 11, ~~February 13 (26), 1910,~~ in which he condemned the conduct of the ~~Conciliators with~~ *accomplices of* Trotskyism, and spoke of the necessity of putting an end to the abnormal situation created within the Bolshevik group by the treacherous conduct of ~~the conciliators with Trotskyism and liquidationism~~ *Kamenev, Zinoviev and Rykov*. The article ~~also~~ advanced as *immediate* tasks what was later carried into effect at the Prague *Party* Conference, namely, convocation of a general Party conference, publication of a Party newspaper appearing legally, and creation of a*n illegal* practical Party centre in Russia. Comrade Stalin's article was based on decisions of the Baku Committee, which fully supported Lenin.

~~It is possible to see through the example of the conduct of the conciliators toward Trotskyism and liquidationism that conciliation always had been a dangerous opportunistic deviation from the general Party line. The conciliators were agents of Menshevism, Trotskyism and the Rights within the Party's ranks.~~

~~Trotsky, Kamenev, Zinoviev, Rykov and other opportunists formed an unprincipled bloc of various opportunistic groups on the basis of their renunciation of the revolutionary tasks. Lenin took a firm position on gathering together all revolutionary Social-Democratic elements and all those able to take part in the struggle against liquidationism. On this basis, a militant agreement was reached between the Bolsheviks and the "Menshevik Party Members"—this is what those Mensheviks were called who along with Plekhanov defended the point of view that it was imperative to maintain the party's illegal revolutionary organizations.~~

~~Did this militant agreement mean that the Bolsheviks made any compromises with the Menshevik Party Members, who were struggling at that time against liquidationism? No, of course not. This unity of action was created on the basis of revolutionary Marxism. In December 1911, Lenin explained this bloc (union) as a form of the united front of all party members against all Liquidators.~~

To counteract Trotsky's anti-Party August Bloc, which consisted exclusively of anti-Party elements, from the Liquidators and Trotskyites to the Otzovists and "god-builders," a Party bloc was formed consisting of people who wanted to preserve and strengthen the illegal proletarian Party. This bloc consisted of the Bolsheviks, headed by Lenin, and a small number of pro-Party Mensheviks, headed by Plekhanov. Plekhanov and his group of pro-Party Mensheviks, while maintaining the Menshevik position on a number of questions, emphatically dissociated themselves from the August Bloc and the Liquidators and sought to reach agreement with the Bolsheviks. Lenin accepted Plekhanov's proposal and consented to a temporary bloc with him against the anti-Party elements on the ground that such a bloc would be advantageous to the Party and fatal to the Liquidators.

Comrade Stalin fully ~~approved of~~ *supported* this bloc. He was in exile ~~in the Vologda region~~ at the time and *from there* wrote a letter to Lenin ~~from Solvychegodsk~~, saying:

> "In my opinion the line of the bloc (Lenin-Plekhanov) is the only ~~normal~~ *correct* one: 1) this line, and it alone, answers to the real interests of the work in Russia, which demands that all Party elements should rally together; 2) this line, and it alone, will expedite the process of emancipation of the legal organizations from the yoke of the Liquidators, by digging a gulf between the Mek (an abbreviation for Menshevik—ED.[66]) workers and the Liquidators, and dispersing and disposing of the latter." (LENIN AND STALIN, Russ. ed., Vol. I, pp. 529–30.)

Thanks to ~~the defence and completion of Lenin's party line~~ *a skilful combination of illegal and legal work*, the Bolsheviks were able to ~~take part~~ *become a serious force* in the *legal* workers' ~~groups~~ *organizations. This was revealed, incidentally, in the great influence which the Bolsheviks exercised on the workers' groups* at four legally held congresses that took place *at that period*—a congress of people's universities, a women's congress, a congress of factory physicians, and a temperance congress. The speeches of the Bolsheviks at these congresses were of great political ~~and agitational~~ value and awakened a response all over the country. For example, at the congress of people's universities, the Bolshevik workers' delegation exposed the policy of tsardom which stifled all cultural activity, and contended that no real cultural progress in the country was conceivable unless tsardom were abolished. The workers' delegation at the congress of factory physicians told of the frightfully unsanitary conditions in which the workers had to live and work, and drew the conclusion that factory hygiene could not be properly ensured until tsardom was overthrown.

The Bolsheviks gradually squeezed the Liquidators out of the various legal organizations that still survived. The peculiar tactics of a united front *with the Plekhanov pro-Party group* ~~likewise~~ enabled the Bolshevik*s*~~-Leninists~~ to win over a number of Menshevik worker organizations (in the Vyborg district, Ekaterinoslav, *etc.*).

In this difficult period the Bolsheviks set an example of how legal work should be combined with illegal work.

~~5. Stalin's Struggle for the Preservation and Strengthening of the Illegal Bolshevik Organizations in Transcaucasia~~

~~Comrade Stalin's activity in Transcaucasia during this period serves as an example of the struggle for party-mindedness and the preservation and strengthening of the proletarian party in the most grim circumstances of the reaction.~~

~~The Transcaucasian Bolsheviks under the leadership of Comrade Stalin built and strengthened their organizations in the deep underground, successfully implementing the Leninist tactic of using every kind of legal organization and opportunity for revolutionary propaganda and agitation.~~

~~Stalin and the Transcaucasian Bolsheviks under his command defended Leninist views on the inevitability of a new revolution, defended the inevitability of a new revolution,[67] mercilessly exposed the Constitutional-Democrats, Mensheviks, Socialist-Revolutionaries and bourgeois nationalists and prepared the proletariat for new revolutionary struggles.~~

~~In the 1907–12 period, under the leadership of Comrade Stalin, the Baku Bolshevik party organization matured and became stronger and more~~

~~tempered in the struggle with the Mensheviks, winning the overwhelming majority of all Social-Democratic workers over to their side. All the workers' regions in Baku were in Bolshevik hands. Baku turned into a base of the Transcaucasian Bolshevik organizations, an indestructible fortress of the Leninist party. The Baku Party Committee created around itself a firm group of activists taken from the most advanced workers. During the years of reaction, the Transcaucasian Bolsheviks under Comrade Stalin staged an organized retreat in the best of order, with the least damage to the revolutionary movement.~~

~~The Bolsheviks' Baku organization staged several major strikes in January and February 1908, which had an organized, militant character. During these strikes, the workers advanced political demands. Lenin pointed out that these mass political strikes had a very important meaning, in that they had held off to a certain extent the attack of the counter-revolution.~~

~~Arrested in March 1908, Comrade Stalin secretly maintained contact from prison with the comrades who remained at large, assisting them with advice and instructions. There was even a time when the prison inmates under Comrade Stalin prepared the entire editorial content for one issue of the illegal newspaper BAKINSKY RABOCHY (BAKU WORKER).~~

~~Stalin was banished from Baku in the fall of 1908 to the Vologda region, to Solvychegodsk, from where he escaped during the summer of 1909 to return to Baku, where he once again energetically took charge of further strengthening the Transcaucasian Bolshevik organization.~~

~~Comrade Stalin systematically spoke at district and interdistrict party meetings and led the preparation and direction of strikes. He further developed the merciless struggle to expose and destroy the Menshevik, Socialist-Revolutionary, Dashnak and other petty-bourgeois parties.~~

~~It was no coincidence that Baku was a Bolshevik fortress at a time when there were strong Mensheviks in Tiflis. In Tiflis, there were few workers in large-scale industry; most common was light and artisanal industry, as well as many trade establishments and the "trade proletariat" associated with them (salesmen, etc.). Class contradictions were not as clearly visible here as they were, for instance, in Baku and other centres of heavy industry.~~

~~By nature a petty property owner, the handicraftsman was not suited to a collective, organized struggle against the big bourgeoisie. The petty property owner was isolated and it was difficult for him to join an organization. Private property restrained him, as did the hope of somehow "becoming someone" and adapting to the status quo. The existence of a large number of petty bourgeoisie and workers from petty industry, where the class contradictions between workers and owners were not as sharp—all this turned out to be rich soil for the conciliator Mensheviks.~~

~~In Baku, the presence of heavy industry, a large number of workers, and the sharply defined class contradictions between the bourgeoisie and the proletariat formed a rich soil for Bolshevism's growth. The Bolsheviks' sharp class position found an active response among the Baku workers.~~

~~Led by Comrade Stalin, the Baku Party organization operated without interruption throughout the years of reaction. Despite its repressive policies, the tsarist government was unable to deal it a crushing blow. The Baku organization took the most active of roles in all forms of the labour movement, becoming a mass party organization in the fullest sense of the word.~~

~~Comrade Stalin's struggle for the Leninist line in Transcaucasia had a major all-Party significance. The Transcaucasian party organizations and the Baku committee, first and foremost, provided Lenin with support in his struggle with the Menshevik Liquidators (and Trotskyites, among others), Otzovists and conciliators.~~

~~In his historic articles—the "Letters from the Caucasus" and an array of addresses—Comrade Stalin revealed the treachery of the Georgian Mensheviks and exposed through their example the content of all-Russian liquidationism.~~

~~5.6.~~ Prague Party Conference, 1912. Bolsheviks Constitute Themselves an Independent ~~Social-Democratic Labour~~ *Marxist* Party

~~The proletarian party had to purge itself of OPPORTUNISTS and Menshevik-Liquidators in order to successfully gather the forces of the working class for a new revolutionary rising in the most difficult conditions of the Stolypin reaction.~~

~~We have already seen how the Mensheviks equipped themselves during the 1905 revolution and how they broke up the forces of the working class with their opportunistic, conciliatory policy. In the period of reaction, the Mensheviks' attraction to the Constitutional-Democrats and their determination to break away from the Party program became more visible. The Mensheviks renounced all revolutionary tasks and slogans. They wanted to reconcile the working class to the temporary victory of the counter-revolution. The Mensheviks proposed destroying and eliminating the illegal revolutionary proletarian party. In its place, they wanted to create a legal "Stolypin Labour Party," which would not have threatened the tsarist government and the bourgeoisie, who were not even thinking about revolution.~~

The fight against the Liquidators and Otzovists, as well as[68] *against the Trotskyites, confronted the Bolsheviks with the urgent necessity of uniting all the Bolsheviks and forming them into an independent Bolshevik Party. This was absolutely essential not only in order to put an end to the opportunist trends within the Party which were splitting the working class, but also in order to complete the work of mustering the forces of the working class and preparing it for a new upward swing of the revolution.*

But before this task could be accomplished the Party had to be rid of opportunists, of Mensheviks.

~~It was becoming clear that~~ *No Bolshevik now doubted that it was unthinkable* for the Bolsheviks to ~~formally~~ remain in one ~~Social-Democratic~~ party with the Mensheviks ~~would only harm the cause of the revolution. Further formal membership in the same party with the Mensheviks no longer made sense, as the Menshevik-Liquidators among the party workers were already largely unmasked. The Liquidators had almost no supporters in the illegal Social-Democratic party organizations in Russia.~~

~~In order to defeat the Menshevik-Liquidators in the non-party organizations—the surviving trade unions, co-operatives and hospital and labour insurance offices, etc.—it was necessary to complete the rupture and cast them out of the proletarian party.~~

~~The split with the Mensheviks also had to be resolved because the existence of the formally united organization (and the single Party Central Committee) gave the Mensheviks (and the Trotskyites, among others) the opportunity along with the conciliators to create a lot of red tape and sabotage the proceedings of any Party meeting or revolutionary affair.~~ *The treacherous conduct of the Mensheviks in the period of the Stolypin reaction, their attempts to liquidate the proletarian party and to organize a new, reformist*[69] *party, made a rupture with them inevitable. By remaining in one party with the Mensheviks, the Bolsheviks in one way or another accepted moral responsibility for the behaviour of the Mensheviks. But for the Bolsheviks to accept moral responsibility for the open treachery of the Mensheviks was unthinkable, unless they themselves wanted to become traitors to the Party and the working class. Unity with the Mensheviks within a single party was thus assuming the character of a betrayal of the working class and its party. Consequently, the actual rupture with the Mensheviks had to be carried to its conclusion: a formal organizational rupture and the expulsion of the Mensheviks from the Party.*

Only in this way was it possible to restore the revolutionary party of the proletariat with a single program, single tactics, and a single class organization.

Only in this way was it possible to restore the real (not just formal) unity of the Party, which the Mensheviks had destroyed.

This task was to be performed by the Sixth General Party Conference, for which the Bolsheviks were making preparations.

But this was only one aspect of the matter. A formal rupture with the Mensheviks and the formation by the Bolsheviks of a separate party was, of course, a very important political task. But the Bolsheviks were confronted with another and even more important task. The task of the Bolsheviks was not merely to break with the Mensheviks and formally constitute themselves a[70] *separate party, but above all, having broken with the Mensheviks, to create a new party, to create a party of a new type, different from the usual Social-Democratic parties of the West, one that was free of opportunist elements and capable of leading the proletariat in a struggle for power.*

In fighting the Bolsheviks, the Mensheviks of all shades, from Axelrod and Martynov to Martov and Trotsky, invariably used weapons borrowed from the arsenal of the West-European Social-Democrats. They wanted in Russia a party similar, let us say, to the German or French Social-Democratic Party. They fought the Bolsheviks just because they sensed something new in them, something unusual and different from the Social-Democrats of the West. And what did the Social-Democratic parties of the West represent at that time? A mixture, a hodgepodge of Marxist and opportunist elements, of friends and foes of the revolution, of supporters and opponents of the Party principle, the former gradually becoming ideologically reconciled to the latter, and virtually subordinated to them. Conciliation with the opportunists, with the traitors to the revolution, for the sake of what?—the Bolsheviks asked the West-European Social-Democrats. For the sake of "peace within the Party," for the sake of "unity"—the latter replied. Unity with whom, with the opportunists? Yes, they replied, with the opportunists. It was clear that such parties could not be revolutionary parties.

The Bolsheviks could not help seeing that after Engels' death the West-European Social-Democratic parties had begun to degenerate from parties of social revolution into parties of "social reforms," and that each of these parties, as an organization, had already been converted from a leading force into an appendage of its own parliamentary group.

The Bolsheviks could not help knowing that such a party boded no good to the proletariat, that such a party was not capable of leading the working class to revolution.

The Bolsheviks could not help knowing that the proletariat needed, not such a party, but a different kind of party, a new and genuinely Marxist party, which would be irreconcilable towards the opportunists and revolutionary towards the bourgeoisie, which would be firmly knit and monolithic, which would be a party of social revolution, a party of the dictatorship of the proletariat.

It was this new kind of party that the Bolsheviks wanted. And the Bolsheviks worked to build up such a party. The whole history of the struggle against the "Economists," Mensheviks, Trotskyites, Otzovists and idealists of all shades, down to the empirio-criticists, was a history of the building up of just such a party. The Bolsheviks wanted to create a new party, a Bolshevist party, which would serve as a model for all who wanted to have a real revolutionary Marxist party. The Bolsheviks had been working to build up such a party ever since the time of the old ISKRA. *They worked for it stubbornly, persistently, in spite of everything. A fundamental and* *decisive part was played in this work by the writings of Lenin—*WHAT IS TO BE DONE?, TWO TACTICS, *etc. Lenin's* WHAT IS TO BE DONE? *was the ideological preparation for such a party. Lenin's* ONE STEP FORWARD, TWO STEPS BACK *was the organizational preparation for such a party. Lenin's* TWO TACTICS OF SOCIAL-DEMOCRACY IN THE DEMOCRATIC REVOLUTION *was the political preparation for such a party. And, lastly, Lenin's* MATERIALISM AND EMPIRIO-CRITICISM *was the theoretical preparation for such a party.*

It may be safely said that never in history has any political group been so thoroughly prepared to constitute itself a party as the Bolshevik group was.

The conditions were therefore fully ripe and ready for the Bolsheviks to constitute themselves a party.

It was the task of the Sixth Party Conference to crown the completed work by expelling the Mensheviks and formally constituting the new party, the Bolshevik Party.

~~In the exhausting struggle with the Menshevik-Liquidators, the Bolsheviks prepared to convene the Sixth All-Russian Party Conference, which was held in Prague in January 1912. Major work on the preparations for the Prague Conference was done by Sergo Ordjonikidze, who traveled to an array of Party organizations and gave a report at the conference on the activity of the organizing commissions that convened it.~~

~~Comrade Stalin completely supported Lenin's line on the rupture with the Liquidators. On Lenin's orders, Comrade Stalin did an enormous amount of work to convene the all-party Prague Conference. At the beginning of July 1911, Comrade Stalin made his third escape from exile and returned to St. Petersburg. In St. Petersburg, Comrade Stalin organized and directed the struggle against the Liquidators—the Mensheviks and Trotskyites—and drew together and strengthened the Bolshevik organizations in St. Petersburg. In the summer of 1911, Comrade Stalin traveled to Baku and Tiflis in order to organize the convening of the all-Russian all-party conference. But in September 1911, Comrade Stalin was arrested in St. Petersburg and banished to Vologda region (for the fourth time) and was therefore unable to attend the Prague Conference.~~

~~The Prague Conference was fated to play an exceptionally important role in the history of our Party. It was to revive the proletarian party under the leadership of the Bolsheviks on the basis of a complete organizational rupture with the Mensheviks and the complete expulsion of opportunists from the party.~~ *The Sixth All-Russian Party Conference was held in Prague in January 1912.* Over twenty ~~Bolshevik~~ *Party* organizations were represented ~~at the conference, which~~. *The conference, therefore,* had the significance of a regular *Party* congress.

In the statement of the conference which announced that the shattered central apparatus of the Party had been restored and a Central Committee set up, it was declared that the period of reaction ~~was~~ *had been* the most difficult the Russian Social-Democratic Party had experienced since it had taken shape as a definite organization. In spite of all persecution, in spite of the severe blows dealt it from without and the treachery and vacillation of the opportunists ~~from~~ within, the party of the proletariat had preserved intact its banner and its organization.

"Not only have the banner of the Russian Social-Democratic Party, its program and its revolutionary traditions survived, but so has its organization, which persecution may have undermined and weakened, but could never utterly destroy. ~~The proletariat is critical to capitalist society, since it will not be able to hang on without expanding the number of proletarians and without increasing their unity and ability to strike back~~"—the statement of the conference declared ~~in an atmosphere of indestructible faith in the masses~~.

The conference recorded the first symptoms of a new rise of the working-class movement *in Russia* and a revival in Party work.

In its resolution on the reports presented by the local organizations, the conference noted that "energetic work is being conducted everywhere among the Social-Democratic workers with the object of strengthening the local illegal Social-Democratic organizations and groups."

The conference noted that the most important rule of Bolshevik tactics in periods of retreat, namely, to combine illegal work with legal work within the various legally existing workers' societies and unions, was being observed in all the localities.

~~At the Sixth (Prague) Party Conference, the most important organizational questions were resolved.~~

The Prague Conference elected a Bolshevik Central Committee of the Party, consisting of Lenin, Stalin, Ordjonikidze, Sverdlov, Spandaryan, *Goloshchekin*[71] and others. Comrades Stalin and Sverdlov were elected to the Central Committee in their absence, as they were in exile at the time. Among the elected alternate members of the Central Committee was Comrade Kalinin.

For the direction of ~~ALL~~ revolutionary work in Russia a practical centre (the Russian Bureau of the C.C.) was set up with Comrade Stalin at its head and including Comrades Y. Sverdlov, S. Spandaryan, S. Ordjonikidze, M. Kalinin *and Goloshchekin.*[72]

~~As the leader of the Russian Bureau of the Central Committee, Comrade Stalin escaped from exile shortly after the conference and traveled to all the important regions of Russia, built the Party, organized PRAVDA and led the Duma faction. Comrade Stalin personally steered the work of the Bolshevik Party during the period of the new wave of the labour movement according to Lenin's directions.~~

The Prague Conference reviewed the whole preceding struggle of the Bolsheviks *against opportunism* ~~for the purge and strengthening of the proletarian party~~ *and decided to expel the Mensheviks from the Party.*

~~The Bolsheviks had separated themselves out as a separate political trend—a faction or group—already in 1903 at the Second Party Congress of the R.S.D.L.P., and supported a line toward a rupture with the opportunists. During the Revolution of 1905–07, the Bolsheviks acted according to their own special revolutionary tactics, which differed sharply from the conciliatory tactics of the Mensheviks, who did not want to take the revolution to its conclusion. But before the Prague Conference, the Bolsheviks had kept their own party organization in the form of a faction and had waged their struggle against Menshevism within the context of a party which still formally united them with the Mensheviks.~~

~~The Bolsheviks used this formal unity in order to expose the Mensheviks, to tear the workers that the Mensheviks had deceived away from them and to bring about the defeat of Menshevism. At the Fifth London Congress of the R.S.D.L.P. (1907), which was convened as a conference of the entire party, it was the Bolshevik line that was victorious.~~

~~In the years of reaction following the Fifth Party Congress, the Mensheviks slid further and further down the path toward betrayal of the revolution. It became necessary to deal with all the survivals of the formal alliance with the Mensheviks—all the more because the overwhelming majority of the workers in the illegal party organizations was firmly on the Bolsheviks' side.~~

~~Therefore,~~ *B*y expelling the Menshevik*s*~~-Liquidators~~ from the Party, the Prague Conference formally inaugurated the independent existence of the Bolshevik Party ~~under a Bolshevik Central Committee, which united Bolshevik party organizations all across the country into a single Bolshevik Party~~.[73]

~~In this is found the basic, historical significance of the Prague Conference, which played the role of a Party Congress. Henceforth, the struggle with all non-Bolshevik tendencies was also simplified in an organizational sense to a significant extent.~~

Having routed the Menshevik*s*~~-Liquidators~~ ideologically and organizationally and expelled them from the Party, the Bolsheviks preserved the *old* banner of the ~~proletarian~~ Party—of the R.S.D.L.P. That is why the Bolshevik Party continued until 1918 to call itself the Russian Social-Democratic Labour Party, ~~but with~~ *adding* the word "Bolsheviks" ~~being added~~ in brackets.

Writing to Gorky at the beginning of 1912, on the results of the Prague Conference, Lenin said:

> "At last we have succeeded, in spite of the Liquidator scum, in restoring the Party and its Central Committee. I hope you will rejoice with us over the fact." (Lenin, COLLECTED WORKS, Russ. ed., Vol. XXIX, p. 19.)

~~"It is well known," said Comrade Stalin,~~ Speaking of the significance of the Prague Conference, ~~that~~ *Comrade Stalin said:*

> "This conference was of the utmost importance in the history of our Party, for it drew a boundary line between the Bolsheviks and the Mensheviks and amalgamated the Bolshevik organizations all over the country into a united Bolshevik Party." (Verbatim Report of the Fifteenth Congress of the C.P.S.U.[B.], Russ. ed., pp. 361–362.)

After the expulsion of the ~~Liquidator-~~Mensheviks ~~from the proletarian party~~ and ~~after~~ the constitution by the Bolsheviks of an independent party, the Bolshevik Party became ~~still~~ *firmer and* stronger. THE PARTY STRENGTHENS ITSELF BY PURGING ITS RANKS OF OPPORTUNIST ELEMENTS—that is one of the ~~qualities~~ *maxims* of the Bolshevik Party, which is a party of a new type fundamentally different from the ~~reformist~~ *Social-Democratic* parties of the Second International. Although the parties of the Second International called themselves Marxist parties, in reality they tolerated foes of Marxism, avowed opportunists, in their ranks *and allowed them to corrupt and to ruin the Second International*. The Bolsheviks, *on the contrary*, waged a ~~principled~~ *relentless* struggle against the opportunists, ~~and~~ purged the proletarian party of the filth of opportunism *and succeeded in creating a party of a new type, a Leninist Party, the Party which later achieved the dictatorship of the proletariat.*

If the ~~open~~ opportunists ~~of the Menshevik-Liquidator kind~~ had remained within the ranks of the proletarian party, the Bolshevik Party could not have come out on the broad highway and led the proletariat, it could not have taken power and set up the dictatorship of the proletariat, it could not have emerged victorious from the Civil War *and built Socialism*.

~~The fact that the Bolsheviks were able to cast the Menshevik-Liquidators out of the proletarian party at the Prague Conference had an important meaning for the subsequent fate of the revolution.~~

~~If it is taken into account that a whole decade lay between the Fifth Party Congress (London, 1907) and the Sixth Party Congress (Petrograd, 1917), then it becomes clear what kind of enormous significance the decisions of the Prague Conference had in the middle of that ten-year period. These decisions gave rise to the Bolshevik Central Committee under Lenin and Stalin and united the Bolshevik Party organizations into an independent Party.~~

The Prague Conference decided to ~~advance~~ *put forward* as the chief *immediate* political slogans of the Party *the demands contained in the minimum program*: a democratic republic, an 8-hour day, and the confiscation of the landed estates.

It was under these revolutionary slogans that the Bolsheviks conducted their campaign in connection with the elections to the Fourth State Duma.

It was these slogans that guided the new rise of the revolutionary movement of the working-class masses in the years 1912–*14*.

~~7. Struggle of the Bolsheviks against Opportunism and for a Rupture in the Second International~~

~~The struggle of the Bolshevik Party during the time of the Stolypin reaction, in the period of the defeat of the revolution, had an enormous international significance. The Bolsheviks showed how a militant party of the proletariat ought to struggle in the most difficult conditions of police persecution and reaction and how necessary it was to combine the most varied forms of legal activity—in the parliament, trade unions, enlightenment societies, labour insurance offices, clubs and so on—with illegal activity. The Party showed how necessary it was to use even such an anti-popular parliament as the State Duma for the organization of the revolutionary struggle of the worker and peasant masses. But the Bolsheviks did not carry out their main work in the Duma during this period. They built an illegal party organization, without the existence of which it would have been impossible to convey to the masses a consistent proletarian line.~~

~~Along with this, the Bolsheviks demonstrated the forms in which to struggle with all the opportunistic tendencies on the Right and "Left" and with Centrism, and did not hesitate to expel the opportunistic elements from their ranks. At this time, the Bolshevik Party was the only party of a new type (that is, a party that was utterly hostile to opportunism and able to lead the proletariat to seize power) within the ranks of the Second International. At the Second International's congresses and in the International Socialist Bureau, where Lenin was a member, the Bolsheviks defended their own special line. This was a line that unified Leftist Marxist elements within the International, separated these elements from the opportunists and split with opportunism. At the Stuttgart Congress in 1907, Lenin and Rosa Luxemburg made changes to a resolution about war: they demanded recognition of the imperative of revolutionary struggle against war and raised the concrete question about the means of struggling against war. Lenin struggled against the Centrist elements in the Second International including, among others, those within German Social-Democracy. Lenin welcomed Klara Zetkin, who struggled against the opportunism of German Social-Democracy and all of the Second International.~~

~~Lenin did everything that was in his power for the formation of a consistent Left Wing within the Second International. He warmly supported the line on the rupture with the opportunists among the revolutionary elements of the Dutch, Italian and other Socialist parties. Lenin supported the struggle of the~~

~~Left German Social-Democrats for the transition from purely legal parliamentary methods of struggle to "mass actions"—general strikes, demonstrations—for the development of anti-war work and so on.~~

~~At the Stuttgart and Copenhagen conferences of the Second International, Lenin made efforts to combine the Left elements of the various parties of the Second International on an international scale. And if these efforts were not successful, then that was because the Leftist elements in the Second International were not yet ready for the rupture and didn't understand its imperative. This Leninist critique had an enormous significance for the cause of the Left's political training within the Second International, and the overcoming of their quasi-Menshevik mistakes. In the international labour movement, the Bolsheviks were the only party that pursued the revolutionary struggle with consistency.~~

~~The Prague Conference signified a breakup and rupture not only with the opportunists in Russia. The Prague Conference at the same time was an extension of the Bolshevik line on splitting and breaking with the opportunists and Centrists in the Second International.~~

Brief Summary

The years 1908–12 were a most difficult period ~~of the Bolshevik Party's struggle~~ *for revolutionary work*. After the defeat of the ~~1905–07~~ revolution, when the revolutionary movement was on the decline and the masses were fatigued, the Bolsheviks ~~were forced to temporarily retreat~~ *changed their tactics and passed* from the *direct* struggle against tsardom to a roundabout struggle. In the ~~unprecedentedly~~ difficult conditions that prevailed during the Stolypin reaction, the Bolsheviks made use of the slightest legal opportunity to maintain their connections with the masses (from sick benefit societies and trade unions to the Duma platform). The Bolsheviks indefatigably worked to muster forces for a new rise of the revolutionary movement.

~~The Bolsheviks preserved their faith in the masses and their connection to the masses. The Bolsheviks acted on the premise that the basic tasks of the bourgeois-democratic revolution in Russia had not been resolved (the peasants had not received the landed estates, the popularly hated tsarist government remained in place). As a result, a new revolutionary rising was imperative and inevitable.~~

In the difficult conditions brought about by the defeat of the revolution, the disintegration of the oppositional trends, the disappointment with the revolution, and the increasing endeavours of intellectuals who had deserted the Party (Bogdanov, Bazarov and others) to revise its theoretical foundations, the Bolsheviks were the only force in the Party who did not furl the Party banner, who remained faithful to the Party program, and who beat off the attacks of the "critics" of Marxist theory (Lenin's MATERIALISM AND EMPIRIO-CRITICISM*).* What ~~was helping~~ *helped* the leading core of the Bolsheviks, centred around Lenin, to ~~not lose hope during the period of revolutionary defeat and Stolypin reaction~~ *safeguard the Party and its revolutionary principles* was that this core had been tempered by Marxist-Leninist ideology and had grasped the perspectives of the revolution. "Not for nothing do they say that we are as firm as a rock," Lenin stated in referring to the Bolsheviks.

The Mensheviks at that period were drawing farther and farther away from the revolution. They became Liquidators, demanding the liquidation, abolition, of the illegal revolutionary ~~organization of the proletarian~~ party *of the proletariat;*~~. The Mensheviks~~ *they* more and more openly renounced the Party program and ~~ALL~~ the revolutionary aims and slogans *of the Party,*[74] and ~~proposed organizing a "Stolypin Labour Party" of the Zubatov type~~ *endeavoured to organize their own, reformist party, which the workers christened a "Stolypin Labour Party."*[75] ~~The Trotskyites also occupied a Liquidationist position.~~ *Trotsky supported the Liquidators, pharisaically using the slogan "unity of the Party" as a screen, but actually meaning unity with the Liquidators.*

On the other hand, some of the Bolsheviks, who did not understand the necessity for the adoption of new and roundabout ways of combating tsardom, demanded that legal opportunities should not be utilized and that the workers' deputies in the State Duma be recalled. These Otzovists were driving the Party towards a rupture with the masses and were hampering the mustering of forces for a new rise of the revolution. Using "Left" phraseology as a screen, the Otzovists, like the Liquidators, in essence renounced the revolutionary struggle. *The Liquidators and Otzovists united against Lenin in a common bloc, known as the August Bloc, organized by Trotsky.*

In the struggle ~~on two fronts~~ against the Liquidators and Otzovists ~~and against the conductors of bourgeois influence over the proletariat~~, *in the struggle against the August Bloc,* the Bolsheviks ~~defended and preserved~~ *gained the upper hand and succeeded in safeguarding* the illegal ~~revolutionary organization of the~~ *proletarian* party ~~and preserved their contact with the masses~~.

The outstanding event of this period was the Prague Conference of the R.S.D.L.P. (January 1912). At this conference the Mensheviks~~-Liquidators~~ were expelled from the Party, and the formal unity of the Bolsheviks with the Mensheviks within one party was ended forever. From a ~~faction or~~ *political* group, the Bolsheviks formally constituted themselves an independent party, the Russian Social-Democratic Labour Party (Bolsheviks). The Prague Conference inaugurated *a party of a new type, the party of Leninism,* the ~~independently existing~~ BOLSHEVIK Party.

~~The Prague Conference elected a Bolshevik Central Committee led by Lenin and Stalin. Stalin headed the Russian Bureau of the Central Committee, which personally led revolutionary work in Russia.~~

~~Under the revolutionary slogans of the Prague Conference, the Bolshevik Party came to stand at the head of the new wave of the labour movement in 1912–14.~~

~~Expulsion of the Menshevik-Liquidators from the proletarian party made it stronger and more battle-ready.~~

The purge of the ranks of the proletarian party of opportunists, Menshevik*s*~~-Liquidators~~, effected at the Prague Conference, had an important and decisive influence on the subsequent development of *the Party and* the revolution. ~~Having Mensheviks in their ranks~~ *If the Bolsheviks had not expelled the betrayers of the workers' cause, the Menshevik compromisers*, the proletarian party would have been unable *in 1917* to rouse the masses for the fight for the dictatorship of the proletariat.

CHAPTER FIVE

The Bolshevik Party during the New Rise of the Working-Class Movement before the First Imperialist War (1912–1914)

1. ~~Revolutionary~~ Rise *of the Revolutionary Movement*[1] in the Period 1912–14

~~The temporary victory of the counter-revolution was inseparably connected with the decline of the workers' mass struggle. Feelings of fatigue and depression gripped a large part of the working class during the years of reaction. Gradually,[2] the working class again gathered its forces and began to take to the offensive.~~ *The triumph of the Stolypin reaction was shortlived. A government which would offer the people nothing but the knout and the gallows could not endure. Repressive measures became so habitual that they ceased to inspire fear in the people. The fatigue felt by the workers in the years immediately following the defeat of the revolution began to wear off. The workers resumed the struggle. The Bolsheviks' forecast that a new rise in the tide of revolution was inevitable proved correct.* In 1911 the number of strikers already exceeded 100,000, whereas in each of the previous years it had been no more than 50,000 or 60,000. The Prague *Party* Conference, *held in January 1912, could already* register~~ed~~ the beginnings of a revival of the working-class movement. But the real rise in the revolutionary movement began in *April and May*[3] 1912, when mass political strikes broke out in connection with the shooting down of workers in the Lena goldfields.

~~Lenin wrote in an article entitled "The Revolutionary Upsurge":~~

> ~~"The huge May Day strike of the proletariat of all Russia and the accompanying street demonstrations, revolutionary proclamations and revolutionary speeches to gatherings of workers have clearly shown that Russia has entered the phase of an upsurge in the revolution." (Lenin, Collected Works, Russ. ed., Vol. XV, p. 533.)~~

On April 4, 1912, *during a strike* in the Lena goldfields in Siberia, over 500 workers were killed or wounded upon the orders of a tsarist officer of the

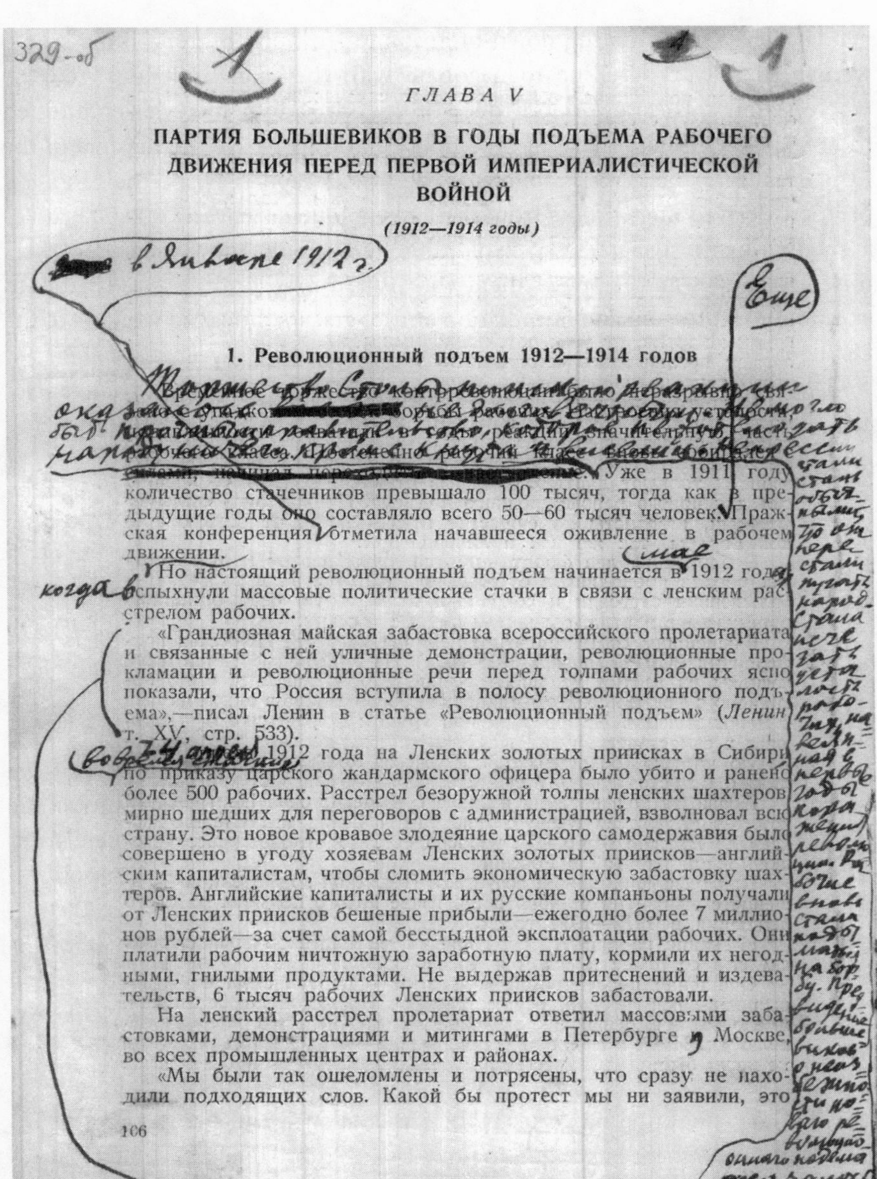

ГЛАВА V

ПАРТИЯ БОЛЬШЕВИКОВ В ГОДЫ ПОДЪЕМА РАБОЧЕГО ДВИЖЕНИЯ ПЕРЕД ПЕРВОЙ ИМПЕРИАЛИСТИЧЕСКОЙ ВОЙНОЙ

(1912—1914 годы)

1. Революционный подъем 1912—1914 годов

[illegible] Уже в 1911 году количество стачечников превышало 100 тысяч, тогда как в предыдущие годы оно составляло всего 50—60 тысяч человек. Пражская конференция отметила начавшееся оживление в рабочем движении.

Но настоящий революционный подъем начинается в 1912 году вспыхнули массовые политические стачки в связи с ленским расстрелом рабочих.

«Грандиозная майская забастовка всероссийского пролетариата и связанные с ней уличные демонстрации, революционные прокламации и революционные речи перед толпами рабочих ясно показали, что Россия вступила в полосу революционного подъема»,—писал Ленин в статье «Революционный подъем» (Ленин, т. XV, стр. 533).

[illegible] 1912 года на Ленских золотых приисках в Сибири по приказу царского жандармского офицера было убито и ранено более 500 рабочих. Расстрел безоружной толпы ленских шахтеров, мирно шедших для переговоров с администрацией, взволновал всю страну. Это новое кровавое злодеяние царского самодержавия было совершено в угоду хозяевам Ленских золотых приисков—английским капиталистам, чтобы сломить экономическую забастовку шахтеров. Английские капиталисты и их русские компаньоны получали от Ленских приисков бешеные прибыли—ежегодно более 7 миллионов рублей—за счет самой бесстыдной эксплоатации рабочих. Они платили рабочим ничтожную заработную плату, кормили их негодными, гнилыми продуктами. Не выдержав притеснений и издевательств, 6 тысяч рабочих Ленских приисков забастовали.

На ленский расстрел пролетариат ответил массовыми забастовками, демонстрациями и митингами в Петербурге и Москве, во всех промышленных центрах и районах.

«Мы были так ошеломлены и потрясены, что сразу не находили подходящих слов. Какой бы протест мы ни заявили, это

106

First page of Chapter Five with Stalin's editing from the summer of 1938. RGASPI, f. 558, op. 11, d. 1211, l. 329.

gendarmerie. The shooting down of an unarmed body of Lena miners who were peacefully proceeding to negotiate with the management stirred the whole country. This new bloody deed of the tsarist autocracy was committed to break an economic strike of the miners and thus please the masters of the Lena goldfields, the British capitalists. The British capitalists and their Russian partners derived huge profits from the Lena goldfields—over 7,000,000 rubles annually—by most shamelessly exploiting the workers. They paid the workers miserable wages and supplied them with rotten food unfit to eat. Unable to endure the oppression and humiliation any longer, six thousand workers of the Lena goldfields went on strike.

The proletariat of St. Petersburg, Moscow and all other industrial centres and regions replied to the Lena shooting by mass strikes, demonstrations and meetings.

> "We were so dazed and shocked that we could not at once find words to express our feelings. Whatever protest we made would be but a pale reflection of the anger that seethed in the hearts of all of us~~," wrote the workers in their resolutions~~. ~~"~~Nothing can help us, neither tears nor protests, but an organized mass struggle"*—the workers of one group of factories declared in their resolution.*

The furious indignation of the workers was further aggravated when the tsarist Minister Makarov, who was interpellated by the Social-Democratic group in the State Duma on the subject of the Lena massacre, insolently declared: "So it was, so it will be!" The number of participants in the political protest strikes against the bloody massacre of the Lena workers rose to 300,000.

The Lena events were like a hurricane which rent the atmosphere of ~~imaginary~~ "peace" created by the Stolypin regime.

This is what Comrade Stalin wrote in this connection in 1912 in the St. Petersburg Bolshevik newspaper, ZVEZDA (STAR):

> "The Lena shooting has broken the ice of silence and the river of the people's movement has begun to flow. The ice is broken! . . . All that was evil and pernicious in the present regime, all the ills of much-suffering Russia were focussed in the one fact, the Lena events. That is why it was the Lena shooting that served as a signal for the strikes and demonstrations."~~—Comrade Stalin wrote in the St. Petersburg Bolshevik newspaper, ZVEZDA (THE "1912 PRAGUE CONFERENCE" COLLECTION, p. 160.)~~

The efforts of the Liquidators and Trotskyites to bury the revolution had been in vain. The Lena events showed that the forces of revolution were alive, that a tremendous store of revolutionary energy had accumulated in the working class. The May Day strikes of 1912 involved about 400,000 workers. These strikes bore a marked political character and were held under the Bolshevik revolutionary slogans of a democratic republic, an 8-hour day, and the confiscation of the landed estates. These main slogans were designed to unite not only the broad masses of the workers, but also the peasants and soldiers for a revolutionary onslaught on the autocracy.

> *"The huge May Day strike of the proletariat of all Russia and the accompanying street demonstrations, revolutionary proclamations, and revolutionary speeches to gatherings of workers have clearly shown that Russia has entered the phase of a rise in the revolution"—wrote Lenin in an article entitled "The Revolutionary Rise." (Lenin, COLLECTED WORKS, Russ. ed., Vol. XV, p. 533.)*

~~Frightened~~ *Alarmed* by the revolutionary spirit of the workers, the Liquidators came out against the strike movement; they called it a "strike fever." The Liquidators and their ally, Trotsky, wanted to substitute for the revolutionary struggle of the proletariat a "petition campaign." They invited the workers to sign a petition, a scrap of paper, requesting the granting of "rights" (abolition of the restrictions on the right of association, the right to strike, etc.), which was then to be sent to the *State* Duma. The Liquidators managed to collect only 1,300 signatures at a time when ~~millions~~ *hundreds of thousands*[4] of workers backed the revolutionary slogans of the Bolsheviks.

The working class followed the path indicated by the Bolsheviks.

~~What was~~ The economic situation in the country at that period *was as follows*:

In 1910 industrial stagnation had already been succeeded by a revival, an ~~expansion~~ *extension* of production in the main branches of industry. ~~So, for instance,~~ Whereas the output of pig iron had amounted to 186,000,000 poods in 1910, and to 256,000,000 poods in 1912, in 1913 it ~~was~~ *amounted to* 283,000,000 poods. The output of coal rose from 1,522,000,000 poods in 1910 to 2,214,000,000 poods in 1913. ~~The amount of refined cotton grew from 2,214,000 in 1909 to almost 26 million poods in 1913.~~

The expansion of capitalist industry was accompanied by a rapid growth of the proletariat. A distinguishing feature of the development of industry was the *further* concentration of production in large plants. Whereas in 1901 the number of workers engaged in large plants employing 500 workers and over amounted to 46.7 per cent of the total number of workers, the corresponding figure in 1910 was already about 54 per cent, *or* over half the total number of workers. Such a degree of concentration of industry was unprecedented. Even in a country so industrially developed as the United States only about one-third the total number of workers were employed in ~~the~~ larg~~est~~[5] plants at that period.

The growth of the proletariat and its concentration in large enterprises, combined with the existence of such a revolutionary party as the Bolshevik Party, were converting the working class of Russia into the greatest force in the political life of the country. The barbarous methods of exploitation of the workers practised in the factories, combined with the intolerable police regime of the tsarist underlings ~~(so numerous were the instances of workers being subjected to torturous beatings!)~~ lent every big strike a political character. ~~Every serious strike left the Russian proletariat more battle hardened and revolutionary to the end. The struggle with capitalists over the spoils seized by the counter-revolution in 1905 and the increasing cost of living rallied newer and newer strata of workers, confronting them with political questions in the sharpest of ways.~~ *Furthermore, t*he intertwining of the economic[6] and political[7] struggles imparted exceptional revolutionary force to the mass strikes.

~~The death sentences for mutinous sailors, the persecution of worker newspapers, the trials of strikers, the reduction and limitation of workers' rights during the elections to the Fourth Duma and in labour insurance claims, the closure of trade unions, administrative harassment of workers, the ugly exploitation that precipitated massive accidents in the enterprises, and so on—all of this generated a powerful response from the working class in the form of mass strikes.~~

In the van of the revolutionary working-class movement ~~was~~ *marched* the heroic proletariat of St. Petersburg; St. Petersburg was followed by the Baltic Provinces, Moscow and the Moscow Province, the Volga region and the south of Russia. In 1913 the movement spread to the Western Territory, Poland and the Caucasus. In all, 725,000 workers, according to official figures, and over one million workers according to fuller statistics, took part in strikes in 1912, and 861,000 according to official figures, and 1,272,000 according to fuller statistics, took part in strikes in 1913. In the first half of 1914 the number of strikers already amounted to about one and a half million.

Thus ~~the conditions of~~ the revolutionary rise of 1912–14, the sweep of the strike movement, created a situation *in the country* similar to that which had existed at the beginning of the Revolution of 1905.

The revolutionary mass strikes of the proletariat were of moment to the WHOLE PEOPLE. They were directed against the autocracy, and they met with the sympathy of the vast majority of the labouring population. The manufacturers retaliated by locking out the workers ~~(the mass firing of workers)~~. In 1913, in the Moscow Province, the capitalists threw 50,000 textile workers on the streets. In March 1914, 70,000 workers were discharged in St. Petersburg in a single day. The workers of other factories and branches of industry assisted the strikers and their locked-out comrades by mass collections and sometimes by sympathy strikes.

The rising working-class movement and the mass strikes ~~stirred up newer and newer strata of workers and~~ *also stirred up the* peasants and drew them into the struggle. The peasants again began to rise against the landlords; they destroyed manors and kulak farmholds. In the years 1910–14 there were over 13,000 outbreaks of ~~revolutionary~~ peasant disaffection.

Revolutionary outbreaks also took place among the armed forces. In 1912 there was an armed revolt of troops in Turkestan. Revolt was brewing in the Baltic Fleet and in Sevastopol. ~~The revolutionary soldiers and sailors were harshly suppressed by the autocracy.~~

The revolutionary strike movement *and demonstrations*, led by the Bolshevik Party, ~~and the political demonstrations~~ showed that the working class was fighting not for partial demands, not for "reforms," but ~~for what WAS THE MASS PREPARATION FOR THE DECISIVE BATTLE~~ *for the liberation of the people from tsardom*. The country was heading for a new revolution.

In the summer of 1912, Lenin removed from *Paris to* Galicia (*formerly* Austria) in order to be nearer to Russia. Here he presided over two conferences of members of the Central Committee and leading Party workers, one of which took place in Cracow at the end of 1912, and the other in Poronino, a small town near Cracow, in the autumn of 1913. These conferences adopted decisions on important questions of the working-class movement: the rise in the revolutionary movement, the tasks of the Party in connection with the strikes, the ~~construction~~ *strengthening* of the illegal organizations, the Social-Democratic group in the Duma, the Party press, the labour insurance campaign~~, the national question and others~~.[8]

2. The Bolshevik Newspaper PRAVDA. *The Bolshevik Group in the Fourth State Duma*

A powerful instrument used by the Bolshevik Party to strengthen its organizations and to spread its influence among the masses was ~~the founding of~~ the Bolshevik daily newspaper PRAVDA (TRUTH), ~~which was organized by Comrade Stalin by a decision of the party~~ *published in St. Petersburg. It was founded, according to Lenin's instructions, on the initiative of Stalin, Olminsky and Poletayev.* PRAVDA was a mass working-class paper founded simultaneously with the new rise of the revolutionary movement. Its first issue appeared on April 22 (May 5, New Style), 1912. This was a day of real celebration for the workers. In honour of PRAVDA's appearance it was decided henceforward to celebrate May 5 as workers' press day.

Previous to the appearance of Pravda, the Bolsheviks already had a weekly newspaper called Zvezda, intended for advanced workers. Zvezda played an important part at the time of the Lena events. It printed a number of trenchant political articles by Lenin and Stalin which mobilized the working class for the struggle ~~against the tsarist government and capitalism~~. But in view of the rising revolutionary tide, a weekly newspaper no longer met the requirements of the Bolshevik Party. A daily mass political newspaper designed for the broadest sections of the workers was needed. Pravda *was such a newspaper.*

~~The stormy revolutionary protest of the working class against the brutal shooting of the Lena goldfield workers demonstrated that the period of the proletariat's fatigue and retreat after the defeat of the 1905 Revolution had come to an end. The workers were now powerfully awakened for a second revolution to follow the one in 1905. The Bolsheviks' line was proven correct, whereby they retained their faith in the power of the working class throughout the most grim years of the Stolypin reaction, predicting the inevitability of a new revolutionary rising.~~

~~The daily Bolshevik newspaper~~[9] Pravda played an exceptionally important part at this period. It gained support for Bolshevism among ~~the~~ broad~~est~~ masses of the working class. Because of incessant police persecution, fines, and confiscations of issues due to the publication of ~~revolutionary~~ articles and letters *not to the liking of the censor*, Pravda could exist only with the active support of tens of thousands of advanced workers. Pravda was able to pay the huge fines only thanks to large collections made among the workers. Not infrequently, considerable portions of confiscated issues of Pravda nevertheless found their way into the hands of readers, because the more active workers would come to the printing shop at night and carry away bundles of the newspaper.

The tsarist government suppressed Pravda eight times in the space of two and a half years; but each time, with the support of the workers, it reappeared under a new but similar name, e.g., Za Pravdu (For Truth), Put Pravdy (Path of Truth), Trudovaya Pravda (Labour Truth).

While the average circulation of Pravda was 40,000 copies per day, the circulation of Luch (Ray), the Menshevik ~~Liquidator~~ daily, did not exceed 15,000 or 16,000.

The workers regarded Pravda as their own newspaper; they had great confidence in it and were very responsive to its calls. ~~The revolutionary worker considered it his obligation to read the Bolshevik newspaper every day, obtaining it at all costs.~~ Every copy was read by scores of readers, passing from hand to hand; it moulded their class consciousness, educated them, organized them, and summoned them to the struggle.

What did Pravda write about?

Every issue contained dozens of letters from workers ~~themselves~~ describing their life, the ~~ugly forms of~~ *savage* exploitation and the various forms of oppression and humiliation they suffered at the hands of the capitalists, their managers and foremen. These were trenchant and telling indictments of capitalist conditions. Pravda often reported cases of suicide of unemployed and starving workers who had lost hope of ever finding jobs again.

Pravda wrote of the needs and demands of the workers of various factories and branches of industry, and told how the workers were fighting for their demands. Almost every issue contained reports of strikes at various factories. In big and protracted strikes, the newspaper helped to organize collections among the workers of other factories and branches of industry for the support of the strikers. Sometimes tens of thousands of rubles were collected for the strike funds, huge sums for those days when the majority of the workers received not more than 70 or 80 kopeks per day. This fostered a spirit of proletarian solidarity among the workers and a consciousness of the unity of interests of all workers.

The workers reacted to every political event, to every victory or ~~limited~~ defeat ~~of the proletariat~~, by sending to Pravda letters, greetings, ~~resolutions,~~ *protests,* etc. In its articles Pravda dealt with the tasks of the working-class movement ~~and all political events~~ from a consistent Bolshevik standpoint. A legally published newspaper could not call openly for the overthrow of tsardom. It had to resort to hints, which, however, the class-conscious workers understood very well, and which they explained to the masses. When, for example, Pravda wrote of the "full and uncurtailed demands of the Year Five," the workers understood that this meant the revolutionary slogans of the Bolsheviks, namely, the overthrow of tsardom, a democratic republic, the confiscation of the landed estates, and an 8-hour day.

Pravda organized the ~~proletariat~~ *advanced workers* on the eve of the elections to the Fourth Duma. ~~Pravda~~ *It* exposed the treacherous position of those who advocated an agreement with the liberal bourgeoisie, the advocates of the "Stolypin Labour Party"—the Menshevik*s*~~-Liquidators~~. Pravda called upon the workers to vote for those who advocated the "full and uncurtailed demands of the Year Five," that is, the Bolsheviks. The elections were indirect, held in a series of stages: first, meetings of workers elected delegates; then these delegates chose electors; and it was these electors who participated in the elections of the workers' deputy to the Duma. On the day of the elections of the electors Pravda published a list of Bolshevik candidates and recommended the workers to vote for this list. The list could not be published earlier without exposing those on the list to the danger of arrest. ~~The speeches of the workers' deputies in the Duma were published in full in Pravda (the bourgeois press refused to print them and remained silent on the issue).~~

Pravda helped to organize the ~~revolutionary~~ mass actions of the proletariat. At the time of a big lockout ~~(the mass firing of workers)~~ in St. Petersburg in the spring of 1914, when it was inexpedient to ~~resort to~~ *declare* a mass strike, Pravda called upon the workers to resort to other forms of ~~revolutionary~~ struggle, such as mass meetings in the factories and ~~revolutionary~~ demonstrations in the streets ~~on the anniversary of the Lena goldfield shootings~~. This could not be stated openly in the newspaper. But the call was understood by class-conscious workers when they read an article by Lenin bearing the modest title "Forms of the Working-Class Movement" and stating that at the given moment strikes should yield place to a higher form of the working-class movement—which meant a call to organize meetings and demonstrations.

In this way the illegal ~~(underground)~~ revolutionary activities of the Bolsheviks were combined with legal forms of agitation and organization of the masses of the workers through Pravda.

Pravda not only wrote of the life of the workers, their strikes and demonstrations, but also regularly described the life of the peasants, the famines from which they suffered, their exploitation by the feudal landlords. It described how as a result of the Stolypin "reform" the kulak farmers robbed the peasants of the best parts of their land. Pravda drew the attention of the class-conscious workers to the widespread and burning discontent in the countryside. It taught the proletariat that the objectives of the Revolution of 1905 had not been attained, and that a ~~second~~ *new* revolution was impending. It taught that in this second revolution the proletariat must act as the real leader and guide ~~(a hegemon)~~ *of the people*, and that in this revolution it would have so powerful an ally as the revolutionary peasantry.

The Mensheviks~~, by contrast,~~ worked to get the proletariat to drop the idea of revolution, to "stop thinking of the people, of the starvation of the peasants, of the domination of the Black-Hundred feudal landlords, and to fight only for "freedom of association" ~~(that is, the right to form trade unions)~~, to present "petitions" to this effect to the tsarist government." The Bolsheviks explained to the workers that this Menshevik gospel of renunciation of revolution, renunciation of an alliance with the peasantry, was being preached in the interests of the bourgeoisie, *that the workers would most certainly defeat tsardom if they won over the peasantry as their ally, and that bad shepherds like the Mensheviks should be driven out as enemies of the revolution.* ~~This is why the Bolshevik Pravda tirelessly directed the workers' attention to the condition of their ally—the peasantry.~~

What did Pravda write about in its "Peasant Life" section?

Let us take, as an example, several letters relating to the year 1913.

One letter from Samara, headed "An Agrarian Case," reports that of 45 peasants of the village of Novokhasbulat, Bugulma uyezd, accused of interfering with a surveyor who was marking out communal land to be allotted to peasants withdrawing from the commune, the majority were condemned to long terms of imprisonment.

A brief letter from the Pskov Province states that the "peasants of the village of Psitsa (near Zavalye Station) offered armed resistance to the rural police. Several persons were wounded. The clash was due to an agrarian dispute. Rural police have been dispatched to Psitsa, and the vice-governor and the procurator are on the way to the village."

A letter from the Ufa Province reported that peasant's allotments were being sold off in great numbers, and that "famine and the law permitting withdrawal from the *village* communes ~~opened the door for~~ *were causing increasing numbers of* peasants to lose their land. Take the hamlet of Borisovka. Here there are 27 peasant households owning 543 dessiatins of arable land between them. During the famine five peasants sold 31 dessiatins outright at prices varying from 25 to 33 rubles per dessiatin, though land is worth three or four times as much. In this village, too, seven peasants have mortgaged between them 177 dessiatins of arable land, receiving 18 to 20 rubles *per dessiatin* for a term of six years at a rate of 12 per cent per annum. When the poverty of the population and the usurious rate of interest are borne in mind, it may be ~~more than~~ safely said that half of the 177 dessiatins is bound to pass into the possession of the usurer, for it is not likely that even half the debtors can repay so large a sum in six years."

In an article printed in Pravda and entitled "Big Landlord and Small Peasant Land Ownership in Russia," Lenin strikingly demonstrated to the workers and peasants what tremendous landed property was in the hands of the parasite landlords. Thirty thousand big landlords alone owned about 70,000,000 dessiatins of land between them. An equal area fell to the share of 10,000,000 peasant households. On an average, the big landlords owned 2,300 dessiatins each, while peasant households, including the kulaks, owned 7 dessiatins each; *moreover, five million households of small peasants, that is, half the peasantry, owned no more than one or two dessiatins each.* These figures clearly showed that the root of the poverty of the peasants and the recurrent famines lay in the large landed estates, in the survivals of serfdom, of which the peasants could rid themselves only by a revolution led by the working class.

Through workers connected with the countryside, Pravda found its way into the villages and roused the politically advanced peasants to a revolutionary struggle.

~~Lenin and Stalin inspired Pravda and its leaders on an ideological level. Having escaped from the Narymsk territory at the end of the summer, Comrade Stalin personally directed Pravda from the second half of 1912 to the beginning of 1913. Lenin frequently sent articles on leadership to Pravda from~~

~~abroad. Pravda was genuinely the child of Lenin and Stalin. At Pravda, Comrade Molotov took the most active of roles.~~

At the time Pravda was founded the illegal Social-Democratic organizations were entirely under the direction of the Bolsheviks. On the other hand, the legal forms of organization, such as the Duma group, the press, the sick benefit societies, the trade unions, had not yet been fully wrested from the Mensheviks. The Bolsheviks had to wage a determined struggle to drive the Liquidators ~~(Mensheviks)~~ out of the legally existing organizations of the working class. Thanks to Pravda, this fight ended in victory.

Pravda stood in the centre of the struggle for the Party principle, for the building up of a MASS working-class *revolutionary* party. Pravda rallied the legally existing organizations around the illegal centres of the Bolshevik Party and directed the working-class movement towards one definite aim—preparation for revolution.

Pravda had a vast number of *worker* correspondents. In one year alone it printed over eleven thousand letters from workers. But it was not only by letters that Pravda ~~was connected~~ *maintained contact* with the working-class masses. Numbers of ~~visitors~~ *workers* from the factories visited the editorial office every day. In the Pravda editorial office was concentrated a large share of the organizational work of the Party. Here meetings were arranged with representatives from Party nuclei; here reports were received of Party work in the mills and factories; and from here were transmitted the instructions of the St. Petersburg Committee and the Central Committee of the Party.

As a result of two and a half years of persistent struggle against the Liquidators for the building up of a mass *revolutionary* working-class party, by the summer of 1914 *the Bolsheviks had succeeded in winning the support of* FOUR-FIFTHS of the politically ~~conscious~~ *active* workers of Russia ~~were~~ for the Bolshevik Party and for the Pravda tactics. This was borne out, for instance, by the fact that out of a total number of 7,000 workers' groups which collected money for the labour press in 1914, 5,600 groups collected for the Bolshevik press, and only 1,400 groups for the Menshevik press. But, on the other hand, the Mensheviks had a large number of "rich friends" among the liberal bourgeoisie and the bourgeois intelligentsia who advanced over half the funds required for the maintenance of the Menshevik newspaper. ~~The Liquidator-Mensheviks were likewise supported by the most elite among the best-paid workers, the so-called worker aristocracy—particularly several categories of printers. The main mass of the conscious workers supported the Bolsheviks. This was evident not only from the collections for Pravda, but in the trade union leadership elections and the elections for the leadership of the labour insurance councils (the organizations which dealt with issues connected to workers' labour insurance). The Bolsheviks won these elections.~~

~~Even the existence of Pravda itself, under the fire of police persecution, served as outstanding evidence of the consciousness, energy and solidarity of the Russian workers.~~

The Bolsheviks at that time were called "Pravdists." A whole generation of the revolutionary proletariat was reared by Pravda, the generation which ~~realized~~ *subsequently made* the October Socialist Revolution. Pravda was backed by tens and hundreds of thousands of workers. During the rise of the revolutionary movement (1912–14) the solid foundation was laid of a mass Bolshevik Party, a foundation which no persecution by tsardom could destroy during the imperialist war.

> "The Pravda of 1912 was the laying of the corner-stone of the victory of Bolshevism in 1917." (Stalin.)

Another legally functioning central organ of the Party was the Bolshevik group in the Fourth State Duma.

~~3. The Bolshevik Faction in the Fourth State Duma~~

In 1912 the government decreed elections to the Fourth Duma. Our Party attributed great importance to participation in the elections. The Duma Social-Democratic group and Pravda were the chief ~~legal~~ bases of the revolutionary work of the Bolshevik Party among the masses, *functioning legally on a countrywide scale.*

The Bolshevik Party acted independently, under its own slogans, in the Duma elections, simultaneously attacking both the government parties and the liberal bourgeoisie (Constitutional-Democrats). The slogans of the Bolsheviks in the election campaign were a democratic republic, an 8-hour day and the confiscation of the landed estates.

The elections to the Fourth Duma were held in the autumn of 1912. At the beginning of October, the government, dissatisfied with the course of the elections in St. Petersburg, tried to encroach on the electoral rights of the workers in a number of the large factories. In reply, the St. Petersburg Committee of our Party, on Comrade Stalin's proposal, called upon the workers of the large factories to declare a one-day strike. ~~Frightened~~ *Placed in a difficult*[10] *position*, the government was forced to yield, and the workers ~~elected~~ *were able* at their meetings *to elect* whom they wanted. The vast majority of the workers voted for the Mandate (Nakaz) *to their delegates and the deputy*, which had been drawn up by Comrade Stalin. The "Mandate of the Workingmen of St. Petersburg to Their Labour Deputy" called attention to the unaccomplished tasks of 1905.

> "We think," *the Mandate stated,* "that Russia is on the eve of the onset of mass movements, which will perhaps be more profound than in 1905. . . . As in 1905, in the van of these movements will be the most advanced class in Russian society, the Russian proletariat. Its only ally can be the much-suffering peasantry, which is vitally interested in the emancipation of Russia." ~~the Mandate stated.~~

The Mandate declared that the future actions of the people should take the form of a struggle on two fronts—against the tsarist government and against the liberal bourgeoisie, which was seeking to come to terms with tsardom.

Lenin attached ~~exceptionally~~ great importance to ~~this~~ *the* Mandate, which called the workers to a revolutionary struggle ~~and the overthrow of tsardom~~. And in their resolutions the workers responded to this call.

> ~~"Only the overthrow of tsardom and seizure of the democratic republic can furnish the workers with the right and genuine freedom of elections,"—the workers announced in their resolutions.~~

~~Comrade Stalin spoke at brief meetings in an array of factories. He was living in St. Petersburg illegally. His speeches at the assemblies entailed an enormous risk. The workers' organizations and the workers themselves took all means possible to shield Comrade Stalin from the police persecution that was always at his heels.~~

The Bolsheviks scored a victory *in the elections*, and Comrade Badayev was elected to the Duma by the workers of St. Petersburg.

The workers voted in the elections to the Duma separately from other sections of the population (this was known as the worker curia). Of the nine deputies elected from the worker curia, six were members of the Bolshevik Party: *Badayev,*[11] Petrovsky, ~~presently the chairman of the All-Ukrainian Central Executive Committee, Badayev,~~ Muranov, Samoilov, Shagov and Malinovsky (the latter subsequently turned out to be an agent provocateur). The Bolshevik deputies were elected from the big industrial centres, in which not less than four-fifths of the working class were concentrated. On the other hand, several of the elected Liquidators did not get their mandates from the worker curia, *that is, were not elected by the workers*. The result was that there were seven Liquidators in the Duma as against six Bolsheviks. At first the Bolsheviks and Liquidators formed a joint Social-Democratic group in the Duma. In October 1913, after a stubborn struggle against the Liquidators, who hampered the revolutionary work of the Bolsheviks, the Bolshevik deputies, on the instructions of the Central Committee of the Party, withdrew from the joint Social-Democratic group and formed an independent Bolshevik group.

The Bolshevik~~s~~ *deputies* made revolutionary speeches in the Duma in which they exposed the autocratic system and ~~gave speeches in which they~~ interpellated the government on cases of ~~the brutal~~ repression of the workers and on the inhuman exploitation of the workers by the capitalists.

~~During the period of all four Dumas, the Bolsheviks~~ *They also* spoke in the Duma ~~in speeches~~ on the agrarian question, ~~in which they called~~ *calling* upon the peasants to fight the feudal landlords, and ~~exposed~~ *exposing* the ~~liberal-bourgeoisie (the Cadets), pulling the peasantry out from under their influence~~ *Constitutional-Democratic Party, which was opposed to the confiscation and handing over of the landed estates to the peasants.*

~~Some of the Bolshevik deputies' speeches were written in advance by Lenin. These speeches by the Bolsheviks in the Duma had enormous agitational significance and the workers supported their deputies with sympathetic strikes.~~ The Bolsheviks introduced a bill *in the State Duma* providing for an 8-hour working day; of course it was not adopted by this Black-Hundred Duma, but it had great agitational value.

The Bolshevik group *in the Duma* maintained close connections with the Central Committee *of the Party* and with Lenin, from whom they received instructions. They were directly guided by Comrade Stalin while he was living in St. Petersburg. ~~In March 1913, Comrade Stalin was again arrested and banished to Siberia, from where he was freed only by the February Revolution.~~

The Bolshevik deputies did not confine themselves to work within the Duma, but were very active outside the Duma as well. They visited mills and factories and toured the working-class centres of the country where they made speeches, arranged secret meetings at which they explained the decisions of the Party, and formed new Party organizations. The deputies skilfully combined legal activities with illegal, underground work.

~~3.4. Bolshevik Leadership of All Forms of the Workers' Movement.~~ *Victory of the Bolsheviks in the Legally Existing Organizations. Continued Rise of the Revolutionary Movement. Eve of the Imperialist War*

The Bolshevik Party during this period set an example of leadership in all forms and manifestations of the class struggle of the proletariat. It built up illegal organizations. It issued illegal leaflets. It carried on secret revolutionary work among the masses. At the same time it steadily gained the leadership of the various legally existing organizations of the working class. The Party strove to win over the trade unions and gain influence in People's Houses, evening universities, clubs and sick benefit societies. These legally existing organizations had long served as the refuge of the Liquidators. The Bolsheviks started an energetic struggle to convert the legally existing societies into strongholds of ~~the illegal, revolu-~~

~~tionary~~ *our* Party. By skilfully combining ~~secret~~ *illegal* work with legal work, the Bolsheviks won over the ~~vast~~ majority of the trade union organizations in the two capital cities, St. Petersburg and Moscow. Particularly brilliant was the victory gained in the election of the Executive Committee of the Metal Workers' Union in St. Petersburg in 1913; of the 3,000 metal workers attending the meeting, barely 150 voted for the Liquidators. ~~Something similar took place in other cities.~~

The same may be said of so important a legal organization as the Social-Democratic group in the Fourth State Duma. Although the Mensheviks had seven deputies in the Duma and the Bolsheviks six, the Menshevik deputies, chiefly elected from non-working-class districts, represented barely one-fifth of the working class, whereas the Bolshevik deputies, who were elected from the principal industrial centres of the country (St. Petersburg,[12] *Moscow, Ivanovo-Voznesensk, Kostroma,*[13] *Ekaterinoslav and Kharkov), represented over four-fifths of the working class of the country. The workers regarded the six Bolsheviks (Badayev,*[14] *Petrovsky and the others) and not the seven Mensheviks as their deputies.*

~~The Bolsheviks paid particular attention to the organization of working women and played an active role in the women workers' movement. For the direction of work among women, the Bolsheviks published the journal RABOTNITSA (WORKING WOMAN) (publishing seven issues).~~

~~The Bolsheviks' LABOUR INSURANCE CAMPAIGN was a model of such participation in the economic struggle of the working class. The Black-Hundred State Duma developed a dock-tailed law on labour insurance for the workers. The Bolsheviks succeeded in making major improvements to this law and in taking over the leadership of the hospital labour insurance offices and the labour insurance institutions of St. Petersburg, Warsaw and an array of other cities. The Bolsheviks also published a journal entitled VOPROSY STRAKHOVANIYA (LABOUR INSURANCE QUESTIONS).~~ The Bolsheviks succeeded in winning over the legally existing organizations because, in spite of savage persecution by the tsarist government and vilification by the Liquidators and the Trotskyites, they were able to preserve the illegal Party and maintain firm discipline in their ranks, they staunchly defended the interests of the working class, had close connections with the masses, and waged an uncompromising struggle against ~~all~~ the enemies of the working-class movement.

Thus the victory of the Bolsheviks and the defeat of the Mensheviks in the legally existing organizations developed all along the line. Both in respect to agitational work from the platform of the Duma and in respect to the labour press and other legally existing organizations, the Mensheviks were forced into the background. The revolutionary movement took strong hold of the working class, which definitely rallied around the Bolsheviks and swept the Mensheviks aside.

To culminate all, the Mensheviks also proved bankrupt as far as the national question was concerned. The revolutionary movement in the border regions of

Russia demanded a clear program on the national question. But the Mensheviks had no program, except the "cultural autonomy" of the Bund, which could satisfy nobody. Only the Bolsheviks had a Marxist program on the national question, as set forth in Comrade Stalin's article, "Marxism and the National Question," and in Lenin's articles, "The Right of Nations to Self-Determination" and "Critical Notes on the National Question."

It is not surprising that after the Mensheviks had suffered such defeats, the August Bloc should begin to break up. Composed as it was of heterogeneous elements, it could not withstand the onslaught of the Bolsheviks and began to fall apart.

~~5. Struggle of the Bolsheviks against the Socialist-Revolutionaries, Liquidators and Otzovists~~

~~In the struggle for the masses, the Bolsheviks waged a stubborn fight with the Liquidators, Trotskyites, Socialist-Revolutionaries and Otzovists for the celebration of revolutionary slogans. Already then, the Populists (the Socialist-Revolutionaries) had aligned with the Liquidators against the Bolsheviks. Such was the case, for instance, during the struggle for the leadership of the trade unions. The Bolsheviks waged a struggle against the Populists' obfuscation of the opposition between labour and capital, against the Socialist-Revolutionaries' attempt to place an equals sign between the proletariat and petty landlords and against the preaching of individual terror by the Socialist-Revolutionaries. Thanks to the energetic Bolshevik struggle, the Socialist-Revolutionaries were not able to find a firm foothold within the working class and they continued to remain a rather small little group, just like the Otzovists.~~

~~But the main enemy of the working class was the Liquidators and their ally Trotsky. After the Prague Conference Trotsky mustered all his strength in order to rally together the Liquidators, the Vperyod-ites, the conciliators and others against the Bolshevik Party. He organized the August Bloc from the various anti-Leninist trends for the struggle with the Bolsheviks at a special conference in August 1912. The bloc had a Liquidator program. Demands were made for a "fully authoritative State Duma" instead of for a republic. Trotsky was the soul of the bloc, and he hypocritically concealed the Liquidator essence of the bloc underneath revolutionary phraseology. Lenin referred to Trotsky as Judas. All the participants in the bloc—the Liquidators, Trotskyites, Bundists, and others—were united by a mad hatred for Lenin, for Leninism and for Bolshevism. There were several provocateurs among the participants of the August conference.~~

Formed for the purpose of combating Bolshevism, the August Bloc soon went to pieces under the blows of the Bolsheviks. The first to quit the ~~August conference~~ *bloc* were the Vperyod-ites *(Bogdanov, Lunacharsky and others)*; next ~~to quit the bloc~~ went the Letts, *and the rest followed suit.*

~~Suffering continuous defeats~~ *Having suffered defeat in their struggle* against the Bolsheviks, the Liquidators appealed for help to the Second International. *The Second International came to their aid.* Under the pretence of acting as a "conciliator" between the Bolsheviks and the Liquidators, *and establishing "peace in the Party,"* the Second International ~~in fact wanted to subordinate the Bolsheviks to the Liquidators~~ *demanded that the Bolsheviks should desist from criticizing the compromising policy of the Liquidators.*[15] But the Bolsheviks were irreconcilable: they refused to abide by the decisions of the *opportunist* Second International and would agree to make no concessions.

~~6. Lenin's and Stalin's Struggle for the Bolshevik Program on the National Question~~

~~In 1912–14, the national question took on a particularly large significance. The autocracy was strangling the national movement. The persecution of national culture and the native languages of the Ukrainians and other peoples was bolstered; the harassment of Jews was strengthened. The liberal bourgeoisie also assumed a position that was hostile to the oppressed nationalities.~~

~~On the other side, among the oppressed nationalities, bourgeois nationalism was on the rise. Bourgeois nationalists preached the "harmony" (commonality) of interests between the bourgeoisie and working people of each nationality, denying that there was class struggle between the capitalists and workers of each nationality. Aside from that, the nationalists introduced feelings of mutual distrust and isolation into workers of each nationality, undermining their class unity. It was frequently the case, for instance, that when Polish workers would stage a strike, Jewish workers would not support them, and vice versa.~~

~~The Bundists and Liquidators shared this bourgeois nationalist point of view. They defended demands for so-called national-cultural autonomy. In other words, their only solution to the national question amounted to the organization of special cultural institutions (schools, hospitals and so on) for each nationality and to the right to use one's own native language.~~

~~The Bundists, for instance, demanded the organization of special Jewish hospitals. The Bundists announced at their conference that "the Jewish worker will feel bad among Polish workers and he will feel better among Jewish shopkeepers."~~

~~The Bolsheviks allocated a lot of attention to the correct solution to the national question. The Central Committee meeting that took place with party workers abroad in Poronin in the fall of 1913 cast a lot of attention to the national question.~~

~~Lenin and Stalin waged a struggle against the smallest compromise with nationalism and against the "national-cultural autonomy" slogan. They de-~~

~~fended the Marxist demand for the "right of self-determination for all nations within the state." They demanded full equality for all nations, even including the right of oppressed nations to secede from the Russian empire and form their own independent states. They demanded the elimination of any and all privileges (special rights) for Great Power nations and demanded recognition of the rights of every national minority. Criticizing the Bundists, Lenin also sharply criticized the views of Rosa Luxemburg, who had spoken out in the name of Polish Social-Democracy against the nations' right of secession and denied the significance of the national movements in the proletariat's struggle with tsardom and imperialism, in this way tearing the proletariat away from its allies in the revolution.~~

~~Lenin and Stalin aimed their main fire against Great Power nationalism as the main danger for the working class. The Bolsheviks contrasted the sowing of national antagonism and the artificial separation of one nation from another to PROLETARIAN INTERNATIONALISM and the merging of workers of all nationalities into single proletarian organizations and to the total emancipation and equality of all the oppressed peoples.~~

~~On the eve of the imperialist war, Lenin and Stalin, seeing its approach, sharpened their work on the national question. Lenin and Stalin foresaw the enormous significance that the national question would have during the period of the proletarian revolution and worked on it as a part of the general question of the proletarian dictatorship. The working masses among the oppressed and enslaved nationalities were the proletarian revolution's reserve and allies. Lenin and Stalin trained the working class in the spirit of internationalism, in the spirit of the brotherhood and equality of all peoples. To explain the party's policy on the national question, Lenin wrote two large works: "On the Right of Nations to Self-Determination," and "Critical Notes on the Nationality Question." During this time, in 1913, the major work "Marxism and the National Question" was written and published by Comrade Stalin in the Bolshevik journal PROSVESHCHENIE (ENLIGHTENMENT)—a work that Lenin regarded highly.~~

~~Lenin wrote about Stalin's work:~~

> ~~"In the theoretical Marxist literature . . . the basis of the S.-D. national program has recently been illuminated (the article by Stalin being the first to come to mind)." (Lenin, COLLECTED WORKS, Russ. ed., vol. XVII, p. 116.)~~

~~7. Eve of the Imperialist War~~

~~In the years that came before the imperialist war, the class contradictions between the bourgeoisie and the proletariat sharpened throughout the whole~~

~~world. There were mass strikes in an array of countries (Britain, France). A militant mood was palpable among the working masses in Germany. All of this together with the enormous revolutionary upsurge in Russia pointed to the nearing of the revolutionary storm. And together with this rose competition between the imperialist Great Powers, their struggle for markets and for a new division of the world. The imperialist Great Powers armed themselves to colossal proportions and feverishly prepared for war.~~

~~Already in 1912, war broke out in the Balkans—the forerunner of the coming imperialist war. In November 1912, the International Socialist Conference met in Basel (Switzerland), and there the question of the war was discussed. The Bolsheviks, among others, took part in this conference. The congress recognized the imperative of struggling with all available means against the approaching world war.~~

~~In 1914, the revolutionary upsurge in Russia continued to grow.~~

The victory of the Bolsheviks in the legally existing organizations was not, and could not have been, accidental. It was not accidental, not only because the Bolsheviks alone had a correct Marxist theory, a clear program, and a revolutionary proletarian party which had been steeled and tempered in battle, but also because the victory of the Bolsheviks reflected the rising tide of revolution.

The revolutionary movement of the workers steadily developed, spreading to town after town and region after region. In the beginning of 1914, the workers' strikes, far from subsiding, acquired a new momentum. They became more ~~frequent~~ and more stubborn~~, embracing~~ *and embraced* ever larger numbers of workers. On January 9, 250,000 workers were on strike, St. Petersburg accounting for 140,000. On May 1, over half a million workers were on strike, St. Petersburg accounting for more than 250,000. The workers displayed unusual steadfastness in the strikes. A strike at the Obukhov Works in St. Petersburg~~, for example,~~ lasted for over two months, and another at the Lessner Works for about three months. Wholesale poisoning of workers at a number of St. Petersburg factories was the cause of a strike of 115,000 workers ~~and~~ *which was accompanied by* demonstrations. The movement continued to spread. In the first half of 1914 (including the early part of July) a total of 1,425,000 workers took part in strikes.

In May a general strike of oil workers, which broke out in Baku, focussed the attention of the whole proletariat of Russia. The strike was conducted in a*n* ~~very~~ organized ~~and at the same time very stormy~~ way. On June 20 a demonstration of 20,000 workers was held in ~~the~~ Baku ~~region~~. The police adopted ferocious measures against the Baku workers. A strike broke out in Moscow as a mark of protest and solidarity with the Baku workers and spread to other districts.

~~The strike movement developed in a wide wave across all of Poland, especially in Warsaw and Lodz.~~ On July 3 a meeting was held at the Putilov Works in St. Petersburg in connection with the Baku strike. The police fired on the ~~meeting~~ workers. A wave of indignation swept over the St. Petersburg proletariat. On July 4, at the call of the St. Petersburg Party Committee, 90,000 St. Petersburg workers stopped work *in protest*; the number rose to 130,000 on July 7, 150,000 on July 8 and 200,000 on July 11.

Unrest spread to all the factories, and meetings and demonstrations were held everywhere. The workers even started to throw up barricades. Barricades were erected also in Baku and Lodz. In a number of places the police fired on the workers. The government adopted "emergency" measures to suppress the movement; the capital was turned into an armed camp; Pravda was suppressed.

But at that moment a new factor, one of international import, appeared on the arena. This was the imperialist war, which was to change the whole course of events. It was during the revolutionary developments of July that Poincare, the French President, arrived in St. Petersburg to ~~negotiate~~ *discuss* ~~on July 19~~ with the tsar *the war that was about to begin.*[16] A few days later, ~~on August 1, 1914,~~[17] Germany declared war on Russia. The tsarist government took advantage of the ~~long-organized~~ war to smash the Bolshevik organizations and to crush the working-class movement. The advance of the revolution was ~~delayed~~ *interrupted* by the World War, in which the tsarist government sought salvation from revolution.

Brief Summary

During the period of the new rise of the revolution *(1912–14)*, the Bolshevik Party headed the working-class movement and led it forward to a new revolution under Bolshevik slogans. The Party ~~brilliantly and~~ ably combined ~~secret~~ *illegal* work with legal work. *Smashing the resistance of the Liquidators and their friends—the Trotskyites and Otzovists—t*he Party gained the leadership of all forms of the legal movement and turned the legally existing organizations into bases of its revolutionary work.

In the fight against *the enemies of the working class and* their*r* agents ~~of the bourgeoisie~~ within the working-class movement, ~~the Liquidators, Trotskyites, Otzovists and the Socialist-Revolutionaries,~~ the Party ~~tempered~~ *consolidated* its ranks ~~for further struggle~~ *and extended its connections with the working class.* Making wide use of the Duma as a platform for revolutionary agitation, and having founded a splendid mass workers' newspaper, Pravda, the Party trained a new generation of revolutionary workers—the Pravdists. During the imperialist war this section of the workers remained faithful to the banner of internationalism and proletarian revolution. *It subsequently formed the core of the Bolshevik Party during the revolution of October 1917.*

On the eve of the imperialist war the Party led the working class in its revolutionary ~~fight~~[18] *actions*. These were vanguard engagements which were *interrupted by the imperialist war only* to be resumed ~~in 1917~~ *three years later* to *end in the* overthrow *of* tsardom. The Bolshevik Party~~—Lenin's and Stalin's Party—~~ entered the difficult period of the imperialist war with the banners of *proletarian* internationalism unfurled.

CHAPTER SIX

The Bolshevik Party in the Period of the Imperialist War. ~~And~~ The Second ~~Russian~~ Revolution *in Russia* (1914–~~February~~–March 1917)

1. Outbreak~~,~~ *and* Causes ~~and Character~~ of the *Imperialist* War

On July 14 (27, New Style), 1914, ~~as the workers began to build barricades in St. Petersburg, universal mobilization was announced, indicating that war had been declared~~ *the tsarist government proclaimed a general mobilization*. On July 19 (August 1, New Style) Germany declared war on Russia ~~and the First Imperialist War began like a thunder clap~~.

Russia entered the war.

Long before the actual outbreak of the war the Bolsheviks, headed by Lenin, had foreseen that it was inevitable. At international Socialist congresses Lenin had put forward proposals the purpose of which was to determine a revolutionary line of conduct for the Socialists in the event of war.

Lenin had pointed out that war is an inevitable concomitant of capitalism. Plunder of foreign territory, seizure and spoliation of colonies and the capture of new~~er and newer~~ markets had many times already served as causes of wars of conquest waged by capitalist states. For capitalist countries war is just as natural and legitimate a condition of things as ~~peace~~ *the exploitation of the working class.*

Wars became inevitable particularly when, at the end of the nineteenth century and the beginning of the twentieth century, capitalism definitely entered the highest and last stage of its development—imperialism. Under imperialism the powerful capitalist associations (monopolies) and the banks acquired a dominant position in the life of the capitalist states. Finance capital became master in the capitalist states. Finance capital demanded new markets, the seizure of new colonies, new fields for the export of capital, new sources of raw material.

But by the end of the nineteenth century the whole territory of the globe had already been divided up among the capitalist states. Yet in the era of imperialism the development of capitalism proceeds extremely unevenly *and by*

339

- ~~257~~ -

ГЛАВА У1

ПАРТИЯ БОЛЬШЕВИКОВ В ПЕРИОД ИМПЕРИАЛИСТИЧЕСКОЙ ВОЙНЫ. ВТОРАЯ РЕВОЛЮЦИЯ В РОССИИ.

(1914 г. - март 1917 г.).

1. Возникновение и причины империалистической войны.

14 (27) июля 1914 года царское правительство об"явило всеобщую мобилизацию. 19 июля (1 августа) Германия об"явила войну России.

Россия вступила в войну.

Еще задолго до начала войны Ленин, большевики предвидели ее неизбежность. На международных с"ездах социалистов Ленин выступал со своими предложениями, направленными к тому, чтобы определить революционную линию поведения социалистов в случае возникновения войны.

Ленин указывал, что войны - неизбежный спутник капитализма. Грабеж чужих земель, завоевание и ограбление колоний, захват новых рынков не раз служили причиной завоевательных войн капиталистических государств. Война для капиталистических стран является таким же естественным и законным состоянием, как эксплуатация рабочего класса.

В особенности войны стали неизбежны, когда капитализм в конце Х1Х и в начале ХХ века окончательно перерос в высшую и последнюю ступень своего развития - империализм. При империализме приобрели решающую роль в жизни капиталистических государств мощные об"единения (монополии) капиталистов и банки. Финансовый капитал стал хозя-

First page of Chapter Six from the summer of 1938. RGASPI, f. 558, op. 11, d. 1214, l. 339.

leaps: some countries, which previously held a foremost position, now develop their industry at a relatively slow rate, while others, which were formerly backward, overtake *and outstrip* them *by rapid leaps*. The relative economic and military strength of the imperialist states was undergoing a change. There arose a striving for a redivision of the world, and the struggle for this redivision made imperialist war inevitable. The war of 1914 was a war *for the redivision of the world and of spheres of influence. All* the imperialist states had long been preparing for *it*. The imperialists of all countries were responsible for the war.

But in particular, preparations for this war were made by Germany and Austria, on the one hand, and by France and Great Britain, as well as by Russia, which was dependent on the latter two, on the other. The Triple Entente, an alliance of Great Britain, France and Russia, was formed in 1907. Germany, Austria-Hungary and Italy formed another imperialist alliance. But on the outbreak of the war of 1914 Italy left this alliance and later joined the Entente. Germany and Austria-Hungary were supported by Bulgaria and Turkey.

Germany prepared for the imperialist war with the design of taking away colonies from Great Britain and France, and the Ukraine, Poland and the Baltic Provinces from Russia. By building the Baghdad railway, Germany created a menace to Britain's domination in the Near East. Great Britain feared the growth of Germany's naval armaments.

Tsarist Russia strove for the partition of Turkey and dreamed of seizing Constantinople and the straits leading from the Black Sea to the Mediterranean (the Dardanelles). The plans of the tsarist government also included the seizure of Galicia, a part of Austria-Hungary.

Great Britain strove by means of war to smash its dangerous competitor—Germany—~~German~~ *whose* goods before the war were steadily driving British goods out of the world markets. In addition, Great Britain intended to seize Mesopotamia and Palestine from Turkey *and to secure a firm foothold in Egypt*.

The French capitalists strove to take away from Germany the Saar Basin and Alsace-Lorraine, two rich coal and iron regions, *the latter of* which Germany had seized from France in the war of 1870–71.

Thus the imperialist war was brought about by profound antagonisms between two groups of capitalist states.

This rapacious war for the redivision of the world affected the interests of all the imperialist countries, with the result that Japan, the United States and a number of other countries were subsequently drawn into it.

The war became a world war.

The bourgeoisie kept the preparations for imperialist~~, predatory~~ war a profound secret from their people. When the war broke out each imperialist government endeavoured to prove that it *had not attacked its neighbours, but* had been attacked *by them*. The bourgeoisie deceived the people, concealing the true aims of the war and its imperialist, annexationist character. Each imperialist government declared that it was waging war in defence of its country.

The opportunists of the Second International helped the bourgeoisie to deceive the people. The Social-Democrats of the Second International vilely betrayed the cause of Socialism, the cause of the international solidarity of the proletariat. Far from opposing the war, they assisted the bourgeoisie in inciting the workers and peasants of the belligerent countries against each other on the plea of defending the fatherland.

That Russia entered the imperialist war on the side of the Entente, on the side of France and Great Britain, was not accidental. It should be borne in mind that before 1914 the most important branches of Russian industry were in the hands of foreign capitalists, chiefly those of France, Great Britain and Belgium, that is, the Entente countries.[1] ~~For instance,~~ *T*he most important of Russia's metal works were in the hands of French capitalists. In all, about three-quarters (72 per cent) of the metal industry depended on foreign capital. The same was true of the coal industry of the Donetz Basin. ~~Almost 20 percent of all oil was in British hands;~~[2] *O*ilfields owned by British and French capital accounted for about half the *oil* output of the country. A considerable part of the profits of Russian industry flowed into foreign banks, *chiefly British and French*. ~~In this way, Russian industry and Russian industrial and finance capital became interwoven chiefly with French as well as with British capital.~~ *All these circumstances, in addition to the t*housands of millions borrowed by the tsar from France and Britain in loans, chained tsardom to British and French imperialism and ~~made~~ *converted* Russia into a tributary,[3] a semi-colony[4] of these countries.

The Russian bourgeoisie went to war with the purpose of improving its position: to seize new markets, to make huge profits on war contracts, and at the same time to crush the revolutionary movement by taking advantage of the war situation.

Tsarist Russia was not ready for ~~this~~ war ~~in any way~~. Russian industry lagged far behind that of other capitalist countries. It consisted predominantly of out-of-date mills and factories with worn-out machinery. Owing to the existence of land ownership based on semi-serfdom, and the vast numbers of impoverished and ruined peasants, her agriculture could not provide a solid economic base for a prolonged war.

The chief mainstay of the tsar was the feudal landlords. The Black-Hundred big landlords, in alliance ~~(a union)~~ with the big capitalists, domineered the country and the ~~Fourth~~ State Duma. ~~Their base of support was the Black-Hundred "League of the Russian People," which was a fascist organization of sorts. The landlords~~ *They* wholly supported the home and foreign policy of ~~tsar Nicholas the Bloody~~ *the tsarist government*. The Russian imperialist bourgeoisie placed its hopes in the tsarist autocracy as a mailed fist that could ensure the seizure of new markets and new territories, on the one hand, and crush the revolutionary movement of the workers and peasants, on the other.

The party of the liberal bourgeoisie—the Constitutional-Democratic Party—*made a show of opposition, but* ~~fully~~ supported *the foreign policy of* the tsarist government *unreservedly* ~~at the start of the war~~.

From the very outbreak of the war, the petty-bourgeois parties, the Socialist-Revolutionaries and the Mensheviks, *using the flag of Socialism as a screen,* helped the bourgeoisie to deceive the people by concealing the imperialist, predatory character of the war. They~~, like the majority of the parties in the Second International,~~[5] preached *the necessity of* defending, *of* protecting the bourgeois "fatherland" *from the "Prussian barbarians"*; they supported ~~the tsarist government~~ *a policy of "civil peace,"* ~~and said that it was necessary to renounce any sort of revolutionary struggle~~ *and thus helped the government of the Russian tsar*[6] *to wage war, just as the German Social-Democrats helped the government of the German kaiser to wage war on the "Russian barbarians."*[7]

*Only the Bolshevik Party remained faithful to the great cause of revolutionary internationalism and firmly adhered to the Marxist position of a resolute struggle a*gainst the tsarist autocracy, against the landlords and capitalists, against the imperialist war ~~rose up the revolutionary working class, tempered in the revolutionary struggles of 1905. This most revolutionary of the world proletariats, with such a serious ally as the revolutionary Russian peasantry, fought under the leadership of the Bolshevik Party, the Lenin-Stalin Party. Both before and during~~ *From the very outbreak of* the war the Bolshevik~~s~~ *Party* ~~led the revolutionary struggle of the workers, peasants and working people from among the many nationalities oppressed by tsardom, as it had before the war~~ *maintained that it had been started, not for the defence of the country, but for the seizure of foreign territory, for the spoliation of foreign nations in the interests of the landlords and capitalists, and that the workers must wage a determined war on this war.*

~~We know that on the eve of the declaration of war, the Russian revolutionary movement had grown to such an extent that barricades were being built in the workers' regions of St. Petersburg and armed clashes were occurring.~~

~~But at the start of the war, the least conscious part of the workers, especially the semi-artisanal proletariat, just like a significant part of the peasantry, gave in to the bourgeois sentiment to defend the country and embrace chauvinism (hatred and contempt toward other peoples)—a sentiment foreign to the proletariat. These elements took part along with the bourgeoisie in patriotic parades, put on by the tsarist government, landlords, capitalists and clergy.~~

~~The world imperialist war lasted four years and claimed about 30,000,000 human lives—those killed, gravely wounded, or infected as the result of unheard-of epidemics that were fostered by the war. Heavy casualties were~~

~~borne by the army of tsarist Russia, which was led by untalented and traitorous generals and which was poorly armed and equipped.~~

~~The tsarist army suffered one defeat after another. The German artillery rained a hail of shells down upon the Russian soldiers. Every day, thousands of Russian soldiers perished—even hundreds of thousands in the major battles. The Russian army had too few cannons and almost no shells; there were not even enough rifles. Sometimes, there was only one rifle for every three soldiers. During the war, the tsarist Minister of War Sukhomlinov was revealed to be a traitor—he was connected to German spies. Tsarist ministers and generals aided in the Russian army's defeats. Together with the tsarina, a German by birth (Alix of Hesse), they passed military secrets to the Germans.~~

~~The tsarist army was forced to retreat. By 1916, the Germans had captured Poland, Lithuania and parts of Latvia. The war with all its weight fell upon the workers and peasants. During the war, the bourgeoisie and landlords profited from the suffering of the people and the deaths of millions. With every day, the workers and peasants endured more and more deprivation and want. The war ruined more and more of the Russian economy. 19 million of the most healthy and strong workers were taken into the army and ripped from the economy. The mills and factories came to a halt. The sowing of grain was curtailed—there were not enough labourers in the countryside. The population and the soldiers at the front began to starve; they were barefoot and clad in rags. Everything was being consumed by the war.~~

~~With every day of war, the working people's discontent mounted from the torment of the drawn-out, imperialistic, predatory war.~~

The working class supported the Bolshevik Party.

True, the bourgeois jingoism displayed in the early days of the war by the intelligentsia and the kulak sections of the peasantry also infected a certain section of the workers. But these were chiefly members of the ruffian "League of the Russian People" and some workers who were under the influence of the Socialist-Revolutionaries and Mensheviks. They naturally did not, and could not, reflect the sentiments of the working class. It was these elements who took part in the jingo demonstrations of the bourgeoisie engineered by the tsarist government in the early days of the war.

2. ~~Crash~~ *Parties* of the Second International *Side with Their Imperialist Governments. Disintegration of the Second International into Separate Social-Chauvinist Parties* ~~Lenin's Struggle for the Creation of a Third International~~

~~How were Socialists supposed to relate to this world war? The question of how to relate to war had been discussed before many times at international So-~~

~~cialist conferences. In 1907, Lenin and Rosa Luxemburg proposed that Socialists take advantage of the economic and political crisis triggered by war to accelerate the collapse of capital at the Stuttgart International Socialist Conference.~~

Lenin had time and again warned against the opportunism of the Second International and the wavering attitude of its leaders. He had always insisted that the leaders of the Second International only talked of being opposed to war, and that if war were to break out they would change their attitude, desert to the side of the imperialist bourgeoisie and become supporters of the war. What Lenin had foretold was borne out in the very first days of the war.

In 1910, at the Copenhagen Congress *of the Second International*, it was decided that Socialists in parliament should vote against war credits. At the time of the Balkan War of 1912, the Basel World Congress *of the Second International* declared that the ~~proletariat~~ *workers of all countries* considered it a crime to shoot one another[8] for the sake of increasing the profits of the capitalists. *That is what they said, that is what they proclaimed in their resolutions.*

But when the storm burst, when the imperialist war broke out ~~in 1914~~, and the time had come to ~~actually implement~~ *put* these decisions *into effect*, the leaders of the Second International proved to be traitors, betrayers of ~~internationalism~~ *the proletariat* and servitors of the bourgeoisie. *They became supporters of the war.*

On August 4, 1914, the German Social-Democrats in parliament voted for the war credits; they voted to support the imperialist war. So did the overwhelming majority of the Socialists in *France, Great Britain, Belgium and* other countries.

The Second International ceased to exist. Actually it broke up into separate social-chauvinist parties which warred against each other.

~~"After August 4, the Second International was a stinking corpse," Rosa Luxemburg remarked. The overwhelming majority of~~ The leaders of the Socialist parties betrayed the proletariat and adopted the position of ~~defencist~~ social-chauvinism and defence of the imperialist bourgeoisie. They helped the imperialist governments to hoodwink the working class and to ~~extinguish class struggle~~ *poison it with the venom of nationalism*. Using the defence of the fatherland as a plea, these social-traitors began to incite the German workers against the French workers, and the British and French workers against the German workers. ~~And just~~ Only an insignificant minority of the Second International kept to the internationalist position and went against the current; *true, they did not do so confidently and definitely enough, but go against the current they did.* ~~Amid the chaos of the worldwide imperialist war, this insignificant minority recreated an international association of the proletariat for the continuation of revolutionary class struggle~~.

Only the Bolshevik Party~~, the Lenin-Stalin Party,~~ immediately *and unhesitatingly* raised the banner of *determined* struggle against the imperialist war.

In the theses on the war that Lenin wrote in the autumn of 1914, he pointed out that the fall of the Second International was not accidental. The Second International had been ruined by the opportunists, against whom the foremost representatives of the revolutionary proletariat had long been warning.

The parties of the Second International had already been infected by opportunism before the war. The opportunists had openly preached renunciation of the revolutionary struggle; they had preached the theory of the "peaceful growing of capitalism into Socialism" ~~without revolution or the dictatorship of the proletariat~~. The Second International did not want to combat opportunism; it *wanted to live in peace with opportunism, and* allowed it to gain a firm hold. *Pursuing a conciliatory policy towards opportunism, the Second International itself became opportunist.*

The imperialist bourgeoisie systematically bribed the upper stratum of skilled workers, the so-called labour aristocracy, ~~(~~by means of higher wages and other sops~~)~~, using for this purpose part of the profits it derived from the colonies, from the exploitation of backward countries. This section of workers had produced quite a number of ~~leaders of~~ trade union~~s~~ and *co-operative leaders, members of municipal and parliamentary bodies, journalists and functionaries of* Social-Democratic organizations. When the war broke out, these people, ~~afraid~~ *fearing to lose their positions, became foes* of revolution~~, became~~ *and* [the] most zealous defenders of their own bourgeoisies, of their own imperialist governments.

The opportunists became social-chauvinists.

The social-chauvinists, the Russian Mensheviks ~~(Plekhanov and others)~~ and Socialist-Revolutionaries among their number, preached CLASS PEACE between the workers and the bourgeoisie ~~during the war~~ *at home and war on other nations abroad.* They deceived the masses by concealing from them who was really responsible for the war and declaring that the bourgeoisie of their particular country was not to blame. Many social-chauvinists ~~were even bribed by the bourgeoisie and~~ became ministers *of the imperialist governments of their countries* ~~(Vandervelde, Thomas, Sembat and others)~~.

No less dangerous to the cause of the proletariat were the covert social-chauvinists, the so-called Centrists.[9] The Centrists—Kautsky, Trotsky, Martov and others—justified and ~~covered for~~ *defended* the avowed social-chauvinists, *thus joining the social-chauvinists in betraying the proletariat; they masked their treachery by "Leftist" talk about combating the war, talk designed to deceive the working class.* ~~The Centrists preached only RESTRAINT~~ *As a matter of fact, the Centrists supported the war, for their proposal not to vote against war credits, but merely to abstain* when a vote on the credits was being taken~~, and not a struggle against war~~, *meant supporting the war.* Like the social-chauvinists, they demanded the renunciation of the class struggle during the war[10] *so as not to hamper their particular imperialist government in waging the war*. The Centrist Trotsky ~~was an enemy of Bolshevism~~ *opposed Lenin and the Bolshevik Party* on all the important questions of *the war and* Socialism.

~~The Centrist Kautsky announced that an international association of workers was necessary only in peacetime and during the war the International must not unite the workers or wage a struggle against war. Through such speeches the Centrists disarmed and disunited the working class. The Centrists—Kautsky, Martov and Trotsky—served the bourgeoisie more meanly and conspiratorially than the open defencists and social-chauvinists. Lenin therefore supported a total break with not only the open social-chauvinists, but with the Centrists.~~

~~"Kautsky is the most hypocritical of all, the most disgusting, the most harmful! . . . I hate and despise Kautsky now most of all. . . .," wrote Lenin in October 1914 in regard to Kautsky's betrayal of the cause of Socialism.~~

From the *very*[11] outbreak of the war Lenin began to muster forces for the creation of a new ~~Communist~~ International, the Third International. In the manifesto against the war it issued in November 1914, the Central Committee of the Bolshevik Party already called for the formation of the Third International in place of the Second International which had suffered disgraceful bankruptcy.

In February 1915, a conference of Socialists of the ~~allied~~ *Entente* countries was held in London. Comrade Litvinov ~~(Maximovich)~~, on Lenin's instructions, spoke at this conference demanding that the "Socialists" (Vandervelde, Sembat and Guesde) should resign from the bourgeois government of Belgium and France, completely break with the imperialists and refuse to collaborate with them. He demanded that all Socialists should wage a determined struggle against their imperialist governments and condemn the voting of war credits. But no voice in support of Litvinov was ~~yet~~ raised at this conference.

At the beginning of September 1915 the first conference of internationalists was held in Zimmerwald. Lenin called this conference the "first step" in the development of an international movement against the war. At this conference Lenin formed the Zimmerwald Left group. *But*[12] *w*ithin the Zimmerwald Left group *only*[13] the Bolshevik Party, headed by Lenin, took a correct and thoroughly consistent stand *against the war*. The Zimmerwald Left group published a magazine in German called the VORBOTE (HERALD), to which Lenin contributed articles.

In 1916 the internationalists succeeded in convening a second conference in the Swiss village of Kienthal. It is known as the Second Zimmerwald Conference. By this time groups of internationalists had been formed in nearly every country and the cleavage between the ~~correct~~ internationalist elements and the ~~defencists and~~ social-chauvinists had become more sharply defined. But the most important thing was that by this time the masses themselves had shifted to the Left under the influence of the war and its attendant distress. The manifesto drawn up by the Kienthal Conference was the result of an agreement between various conflicting groups; it ~~represented~~ *was* an advance[14] on the Zimmerwald Manifesto.

But like the Zimmerwald Conference, the Kienthal Conference did not accept the basic ~~slogans~~ *principles* of the Bolshevik~~s~~ *policy*, namely, the conversion of the imperialist war into a civil war, the defeat of one's own *imperialist* government in the war, and the formation of the Third International. Nevertheless, the Kienthal Conference helped to crystallize the internationalist elements of whom the *Communist* Third International was subsequently formed.

Lenin criticized the mistakes of the inconsistent internationalists *among the Left Social-Democrats,*[15] such as Rosa Luxemburg and Karl Liebknecht, but at the same time he helped them to take the correct position.

~~The Bolsheviks were the only party in the Second International which was consistently Marxist and loyal to the end to the ideas of revolutionary Marxism. The Bolshevik Party was the leader in the cause of forming a new Third Communist International, and it completed an enormous amount of work on the creation of this fighting international association of the working class.~~

3. *Theory and* Tactics of the Bolshevik~~s~~ *Party* ~~during the Years of the Imperialist War~~ *on the Question of War, Peace and Revolution*

The Bolsheviks were not mere pacifists who sighed for peace and confined themselves to the propaganda of peace, as the majority of[16] *the Left Social-Democrats did. The Bolsheviks advocated an active revolutionary struggle for peace, to the point of overthrowing the rule of the bellicose imperialist bourgeoisie. The Bolsheviks linked up the cause of peace with the cause of the victory of the proletarian revolution, holding that the surest way of ending the war and securing a just peace, a peace without annexations and indemnities, was to overthrow the rule of the imperialist bourgeoisie.*

~~From the start of the imperialist war, the Bolsheviks exposed its predatory character to the masses. They struggled with the lie that in the war, the workers were supposedly defending their "national interests," or that the war had for them some kind of national emancipatory significance.~~ In opposition to the Menshevik ~~slogan "Defence of the Fatherland!"~~ *and Socialist-Revolutionary renunciation of revolution and their treacherous slogan of preserving "civil peace" in time of war,* the Bolsheviks advanced the slogan of "CONVERTING THE IMPERIALIST WAR INTO A CIVIL WAR." This slogan meant that the *labouring people, including the* armed workers and peasants ~~masses~~ *clad in soldiers' uniform,* were to turn their ~~bayonets~~ *weapons* against their own bourgeoisie ~~for the overthrow of the capitalist system~~ *and overthrow its rule if they wanted to put an end to the war and achieve a just peace.*

~~In order to take advantage of the imperialist war underway in the interests of the revolution, it was necessary to advance another slogan as well.~~ *In opposition to the Menshevik and Socialist-Revolutionary policy of defending the bourgeois fatherland, the Bolsheviks advanced the policy of* "THE DEFEAT OF ONE'S OWN GOVERNMENT IN THE IMPERIALIST WAR." This ~~second slogan~~ meant voting against war credits, forming illegal revolutionary organizations in the armed forces, supporting fraternization among the soldiers at the front, ~~and~~ organizing revolutionary actions of the workers and peasants against the war, *and turning these actions into an uprising* against one's own *imperialist* government ~~of the bourgeoisie and landlords~~.

~~With this slogan, the Bolsheviks inculcated into the worker and soldier (peasant) masses an awareness of the diametrical opposition of the interests of the imperialistic fatherland and those of the labouring people and the imperative of converting the imperialist war into a civil war.~~ *The Bolsheviks maintained that t*he lesser evil for the people would be the *military* defeat of the ~~army of the~~ tsarist government in the imperialist war, ~~which~~ *for this* would facilitate the victory of the ~~revolution~~ *people* over tsardom *and the success of the struggle of the working class for emancipation from capitalist slavery and imperialist wars.* Lenin ~~and the Bolsheviks said~~ *held* that the ~~slogan~~ *policy* of working for the defeat of one's own imperialist government must be ~~advanced~~ *pursued* not only by the Russian revolutionaries, but by the revolutionary parties of the working class in ALL the belligerent countries.

It was not to EVERY KIND *of war that the Bolsheviks were opposed. They were only opposed to wars of conquest, imperialist wars. The Bolsheviks held that there are two kinds of war:*

a) JUST wars, wars that are not wars of conquest but wars of liberation, waged to defend the people from foreign attack and from attempt to enslave them, or to liberate the people from capitalist slavery, or, lastly, to liberate colonies and dependent countries from the yoke of imperialism; and

b) UNJUST wars, wars of conquest, waged to conquer and enslave foreign countries and foreign nations.

Wars of the first kind the Bolsheviks supported. As to wars of the second kind, the Bolsheviks maintained that a resolute struggle must be waged against them to the point of revolution and the overthrow of one's own imperialist government.

~~On this basis the Bolshevik Party developed its revolutionary work in the rear and at the front. The Bolsheviks' greatest dedication to the cause of the proletariat enabled them to succeed at this task, despite the persecution of the tsarist government and the destruction of Party and worker organizations. The Party fulfilled its proletarian duty bravely and resiliently, inspired by the great goal of preparing the people for revolution.~~

Of great importance to the working class *of the world* ~~and for the Bolshevik Party~~ was Lenin's theoretical work during the war. In the spring of 1916

Lenin wrote a ~~very important~~ book entitled IMPERIALISM, THE HIGHEST STAGE OF CAPITALISM. In this book he showed that imperialism is ~~a special step~~ *the highest stage* of capitalism, a stage at which it has *already become* transformed *from "progressive" capitalism* to parasitic capitalism, decaying capitalism, *and that imperialism is moribund capitalism*. Imperialism is the highest step of developed capitalism, after which it begins to die. ~~But this does not completely~~ *This, of course, did not* mean that capitalism would die away of itself[17] ~~without a fight~~, *without a revolution of the proletariat*, that it would just rot on the stalk. Lenin *always* taught that without a~~n armed uprising~~ *revolution* of the working class ~~it would be impossible for imperialism~~ *capitalism* ~~to~~ *cannot* be overthrown. *Therefore, while defining imperialism as moribund capitalism, Lenin at the same time showed that "imperialism is the eve of the social revolution of the proletariat."*

Lenin showed that in the era of imperialism the capitalist yoke becomes more and more oppressive, that under imperialism the revolt of the proletariat against the foundations of capitalism grows, and that the elements of a revolutionary outbreak accumulate in capitalist countries.

Lenin showed that in the era of imperialism the revolutionary crisis in the colonial and dependent countries becomes more acute, that the elements of revolt against imperialism, *the elements of a war of liberation from imperialism* accumulate ~~on the external, colonial front~~.

Lenin ~~demonstrated~~ *showed* that under imperialism the unevenness of development and the contradictions of capitalism have grown particularly acute, that the struggle for markets and fields for the export of capital, the struggle for colonies, for sources of raw material, makes periodical imperialist wars for the redivision of the world inevitable.

Lenin ~~demonstrated~~ *showed* that it is just ~~as a result of~~ this ~~particular~~ unevenness of development of capitalism ~~in its last, imperialistic step~~ that *gives rise to* imperialist wars ~~become inevitable. But wars between the imperialist Great Powers~~, *which* undermine the ~~general imperialist front~~ *strength of imperialism and make it possible to break the front of imperialism at its weakest point.*

~~Therefore,~~ *From all this Lenin drew the conclusion that* it was *quite* POSSIBLE for the *proletariat to* break ~~in~~ the imperialist front ~~to occur where it turned out to be the weakest~~ *in one place or in several places*, that the victory of Socialism was POSSIBLE first in several ~~countries~~ or even in one country, *taken singly, that the simultaneous victory of Socialism in all countries was impossible owing to the unevenness of development of capitalism, and that Socialism would be victorious first in one country or in several countries, while the others would remain bourgeois countries for some time longer.*

Here is the formulation of this brilliant deduction as given by Lenin in two articles written during the imperialist war:

1) "Uneven economic and political development is an absolute law of capitalism. Hence, the victory of Socialism is possible first in several or even in one capitalist country, taken singly. The victorious proletariat of that country, having expropriated the capitalists and organized its own Socialist production, would stand up AGAINST the rest of the world, the capitalist world, attracting to its cause the oppressed classes of other countries~~, raising them in a revolt against the capitalists, even using military power against the exploitative classes and their states in cases where it is necessary~~. . . ." (From the article, "The United States of Europe Slogan," written in August, 1915.—Lenin, SELECTED WORKS, Eng. ed., Vol. V, p. 141.)

2) "The development of capitalism proceeds extremely unevenly in the various countries. It cannot be otherwise under the commodity production system. From this it follows irrefutably that Socialism cannot achieve victory simultaneously IN ALL *countries. It will achieve victory first in one or several countries, while the others will remain bourgeois or pre-bourgeois for some time. This must not only create friction, but a direct striving on the part of the bourgeoisie of other countries to crush the victorious proletariat of the Socialist country. In such cases a war on our part would be a legitimate and just war. It would be a war for Socialism, for the liberation of other nations from the bourgeoisie." (From the article, "War Program of the Proletarian Revolution," written in the autumn of 1916.—Lenin,* COLLECTED WORKS, *Russ. ed., Vol. XIX, p. 325.)*

This was a NEW *and complete theory of the Socialist revolution, a theory affirming the possibility of the victory of Socialism in separate countries, and indicating the conditions of this victory and its prospects, a theory whose fundamentals were outlined by Lenin as far back as 1905 in his pamphlet,* TWO TACTICS OF SOCIAL-DEMOCRACY IN THE DEMOCRATIC REVOLUTION.

This theory fundamentally differed from the view current among the Marxists in the period of PRE-IMPERIALIST *capitalism, when they held that the victory of Socialism in one separate country was impossible, and that it would take place simultaneously in all the civilized countries. On the basis of the facts concerning imperialist capitalism set forth in his remarkable book,* IMPERIALISM, THE HIGHEST STAGE OF CAPITALISM, *Lenin displaced this view as obsolete and set forth a new theory, from which it follows that the simultaneous victory of Socialism in all countries is* IMPOSSIBLE, *while the victory of Socialism in one capitalist country, taken singly, is* POSSIBLE.

The inestimable importance of Lenin's theory of Socialist revolution lies not only in the fact that it has enriched Marxism with a new theory and has advanced Marxism, but also in the fact that it opens up a revolutionary perspective for the proletarians of separate countries, that it unfetters their initiative in the onslaught on their own, national bourgeoisie, that it teaches them to take advantage of a war situation to organize this onslaught, and that it strengthens their faith in the victory of the proletarian revolution.

Such was the theoretical and tactical stand of the Bolsheviks on the questions of war, peace and revolution.

It was on the basis of this stand that the Bolsheviks carried on their practical work in Russia.

~~This conclusion of Lenin's had the GREATEST SIGNIFICANCE for all subsequent struggles for Socialism. It taught the working class to be confident that it was possible to overthrow imperialism and organize Socialist production even in only one country, taken singly.~~

~~Taking its guidance from this PROGRAMMATIC Leninist principle, the Party organized the Great October Socialist Revolution.~~

~~Already during the war years, all the oppositionists—all the Mensheviks, Trotskyites and Bukharinites—aligned together against Lenin's conclusion about the possibility of the victory of Socialism in one country. Trotsky spoke against Lenin in particularly insolent terms.~~

~~After the victory of the Socialist Proletarian Revolution in 1917, all the opportunists and the enemies of Leninism again began to struggle against our Party under the command of Trotsky precisely in regard to this question, demonstrating the impossibility of the victory of Socialism in a single country, that is, the U.S.S.R.~~

~~Lenin defended the revolutionary Bolshevik tactics, struggling against the opportunists within the Bolshevik Party—Bukharin, Pyatakov, Kamenev, Zinoviev and others. During the war years, Bukharin slipped toward denying the need for a state during the transition period between capitalism and Socialism, that is, DENYING THE DICTATORSHIP OF THE PROLETARIAT. Lenin sternly criticized Bukharin's semi-Anarchistic errors.~~

~~Bukharin spoke against the Party's important tactical slogan "the defeat of one's own government in the imperialist war." Bukharin had already then allied together with Trotsky, Pyatakov, Radek and Sokolnikov on the most important questions.~~

~~Bukharin and Pyatakov shared all the vulgar errors of R. Luxemburg and Radek on the national question, further aggravating their mistakes.~~

~~Lenin and Stalin and the Bolshevik Party said that the national-emancipatory revolutionary movement of the oppressed peoples served as support and reserves for the proletarian revolution. The Party laid out a clear, Marxist program on the national question, which drew the oppressed peoples over to the side of the proletariat and the proletarian revolution. The Bolshevik Party~~

~~advanced the slogan on the right of nations to self-determination, all the way to their secession and formation of independent states.~~

~~Bukharin and Pyatakov denied the whole significance of the national question in the epoch of imperialism and spoke out against the Bolshevik program. In this way, they essentially aimed to weaken the revolution and aid imperialism.~~

~~Lenin warned Bukharin and Pyatakov that they had "STEPPED INTO A SWAMP AND THAT THEIR 'IDEAS' HAD NOTHING IN COMMON WITH MARXISM, NOR WITH REVOLUTIONARY SOCIAL-DEMOCRACY." (Lenin, COLLECTED WORKS, Russ. ed. Vol. XXX, p. 251)~~

~~Kamenev and Zinoviev frequently showed a willingness to compromise with the opportunists and betrayed Lenin. During the war, Zinoviev double-dealingly conspired with Shlyapnikov and other opportunists against Lenin.~~

~~Lenin's merciless struggle with opportunism within the Bolshevik Party was a key part of his struggle for the creation of the new Third Communist International.~~

~~4. Bolshevik Work in Russia during the War Years~~

~~The Bolshevik Party turned out to be the sole party in the Second International which in the most difficult of circumstances was able to remain true to the banner of Socialism, the banner of proletarian internationalism.~~

At the beginning of the war, in spite of severe persecution by the police, the Bolshevik members of the Duma—*Badayev,*[18] Petrovsky, ~~Badayev,~~ Muranov, Samoilov and Shagov—visited a number of organizations and addressed them on the policy of the Bolsheviks towards the war *and revolution*. ~~The Party expressed its point of view about the war in clear and thorough terms in a Central Committee manifesto. This manifesto was the most revolutionary document at the beginning of the imperialist war and the sole document which clearly said how the proletarian revolution was to be conducted during the war.~~ In November 1914 a conference of the ~~Social-Democratic~~ *Bolshevik* group in the State Duma was convened to discuss policy towards the war. On the third day of the conference all present were arrested. The court sentenced the Bolshevik members of the State Duma to forfeiture of civil rights and banishment *to Eastern Siberia* ~~(the deputies were deported to Yenisei Province, and Petrovsky was sent even further, to Yakutsk Province)~~. The *tsarist* government charged them with ~~"betraying the fatherland"~~ *"high treason."*

The picture of the activities of the Duma ~~worker-~~members unfolded in court did credit to our Party. The Bolshevik deputies conducted themselves manfully, transforming the tsarist court into a platform from which they exposed the ~~predatory~~ *annexationist* policy of tsardom.

Quite different was the conduct of Kamenev, who was also tried in this case. ~~Like a petty coward,~~ *Owing to his cowardice,* he abjured the policy ~~and decisions~~ of the Bolshevik Party ~~and betrayed Lenin's Party~~ at the first contact with danger. Kamenev declared in court that he did not agree with the Bolsheviks on the question of the war, and to prove this he requested that the Menshevik-Defencist Jordansky be summoned as witness. ~~Kamenev thus conducted himself in such a shameful, cowardly and mean manner at this most important of historical moments.~~

~~Lenin condemned Kamenev's shameful, treacherous conduct in the tsarist court and at the same time pointed to the enormous political significance of the whole trial.~~

~~Comrade Stalin spent the war in internal exile in Turukhansk. Comrade Stalin carried out a lot of work among the exiles, unmasking social-chauvinists, Mensheviks, Anarchists and Trotskyites. In his correspondence with Lenin, he ridiculed the Menshevik Plekhanov, the Anarchist Kropotkin and other social-chauvinists. In internal exile, Comrade Stalin hosted a meeting of exiled Bolsheviks to which Sverdlov, Spandaryan and others came. In this way, it served as a meeting of the Russian Bureau of the Central Committee. At this meeting, they demanded a report from Kamenev, who meanly squirmed about, justifying his actions. The Bolsheviks condemned his conduct as the behavior of a pathetic liberal. Their resolution on their relationship to the war, which Comrade Stalin worked out himself in the depths of exile, correctly pointed to the path for the Bolsheviks' struggle against the war.~~

~~Despite the harsh persecution of the Bolsheviks, Party work never broke down completely anywhere. Secret Bolshevik printing presses were at work virtually all the time. The St. Petersburg Party Committee released four issues of the Proletarsky golos (Proletarian's Voice) in 1915–16. From the start of the war, the hectographic journal Rabochy golos (Worker's Voice) was also published in St. Petersburg. The Bureau of the Central Committee released several issues of Osvedomitelny List (Information Bulletin). In 1916, a hectographic issue of the newspaper Golos Sotsial-demokrata (Voice of the Social-Democrat) was printed in Kharkov. In Irkutsk, an issue of the newspaper Tovarishch proletariya (Comrade Proletarian)—the organ of the "Union of Siberian Workers"—appeared in April 1915. In the Donetz Basin in 1915, the newspaper Yuzhnaya Pravda (Southern Pravda) was published as the organ of the regional organization of the Mountain Industrial district; Zvezda (Star) appeared in Yekaterinoslav and other cities. Throughout this time, leaflets were published against the war and on other issues, especially connected with the high cost of living, chauvinistic pogroms, and the bourgeoisie's attempt to draw the workers into co-operative activities through the War Industry Committees organized by the bourgeoisie.~~

~~In 1915, the publication of the Bolshevik journal Voprosy strakhovaniya (Labour Insurance Questions) was revived. Comrade Stalin hailed its appearance and collected money from among the exiles for this journal.~~

~~Despite the strictness of the censor, the Bolsheviks were able to take advantage of the legal press as well. Thus in Saratov, several issues of Nasha gazaeta (Our Newspaper) were published, while Zarya Povolzhya (Volga Dawn) appeared in Samara.~~

~~In 1915, the Bureau of the Central Committee was reestablished in Russia. Headed by Comrade Molotov, the Bureau led Bolshevik work in Russia at this time.~~

~~In May 1916, the Regional Bureau of the Central Committee was organized in Moscow under P. Smidovich, M. Savelyev and V. M. Molotov.~~

~~The Party's central organ Sotsial-Demokrat (Social-Democrat) was published abroad and distributed in Russia during the war, despite major difficulties. All in all, 25 issues of Sotsial-Demokrat were printed during the war.~~

~~Sotsial-Demokrat and other foreign publications informed the comrades working in Russia of the Central Committee's views on the war and on the struggle that was going on in regard to the question of the war within the international workers' movement.~~

~~The Bolsheviks were able to maintain their presence in a variety of educational societies, clubs and people's universities. There, they waged a harsh struggle with the Mensheviks and Socialist-Revolutionaries for influence over the working class. The Bolshevik Party struggled decisively against the bourgeois-Menshevik undertaking to involve the workers in the War Industry Committees.~~

The Bolsheviks worked very effectively against the War Industry Committees set up to serve the needs of war, and against the attempts of the Mensheviks to bring the workers under the influence of the imperialist bourgeoisie. It was of vital interest to the ~~industrial~~ bourgeoisie ~~and landlords~~ to make everybody believe that ~~this~~ *the imperialist* war was a people's war. During the war the ~~industrial~~ bourgeoisie managed to attain considerable influence in affairs of state and set up a~~n~~ *countrywide* organization of its own known as the Unions of Zemstvos and Towns. It was necessary for the bourgeoisie to bring the workers, *too,* under its leadership and influence. It conceived a way to *do* this ~~end~~, namely, by forming "Workers' Groups" of the War Industry Committees. The Mensheviks jumped at this idea. It was to the advantage of the bourgeoisie to have on these War Industry Committees representatives of the workers who would urge the working-class masses to increase productivity of labour in the factories producing shells, guns, rifles, cartridges~~, ammunition, chemicals~~ and other war material. "Everything for the war, all for the war"—was the slogan of the bourgeoisie. Actually, this slogan meant ~~everything for the bourgeoisie's~~

~~ENRICHMENT~~ *"get as rich as you can on war contracts and seizures of foreign territory."*[19] The Mensheviks took an active part in this pseudo-patriotic scheme of the bourgeoisie. They helped the capitalists by conducting an intense campaign among the workers to get them to take part in the elections of the "Workers' Groups" of the War Industry Committees. The Bolsheviks ~~rose up decisively~~ *were* against this scheme. They advocated ~~an active~~ boycott of the War Industry Committees and were successful in securing this boycott. But some of the workers, headed by a prominent Menshevik, Gvozdev, and an agent-provocateur, Abrosimov, did take part in the activities of the War Industry Committees. When, however, the workers' delegates met, in September 1915, for the final elections of the *"Workers' Groups" of the* War Industry Committees, it turned out that the majority *of the delegates* were opposed to participation in them.[20] A majority of the workers' delegates adopted a trenchant resolution opposing participation in the War Industry Committees and declared that the workers had made it their aim to fight ~~with the tsarist monarchy~~ *for peace and for the overthrow of tsardom.* ~~Attempts at this new Zubatov-like activity resulted in a shameful failure.~~

The Bolsheviks *also* developed *extensive* ~~revolutionary~~ activities in the army and navy. They explained to the soldiers and sailors who was to blame for the unparalleled horrors of the war and the sufferings of the people; they explained that there was only one way out for the people from the imperialist shambles, and that was revolution.

~~For only the first 30 months of the imperialist war, 14,500,000 soldiers were mobilized, among whom 6,226,000 soldiers and 60,000 officers were killed, poisoned by gas, wounded, shell-shocked or missing in action by May 1, 1917, according to information from the All-Russian Headquarters. More than 200,000 people were missing in action. Under the influence of the defeats, the Russian army began to decompose, while the number of those surrendering to the enemy or deserting rose.~~

~~During the war, the tsarist government was forced to replenish its command staff with more or less democratic elements, especially from the lower command staff, and this had an effect on the morale of the army. The fact that the government mobilized about 40 per cent of all workers also had an effect on the morale of the army. Among them were a good number from among the readership of the Bolshevik newspaper PRAVDA, which had been closed by the tsarist government on the eve of the war.~~

The Bolsheviks formed nuclei in the army and navy, at the front and in the rear, and distributed leaflets ~~and led conversations~~ *calling for struggle against the war.*

In Kronstadt, the Bolsheviks formed a "Central Collective of the Kronstadt Military Organization" which had close connections with the Petrograd Committee of the Party. A military organization of the Petrograd *Party* Committee ~~of the R.S.D.L.P.~~ was set up *for work among the garrison*. In August 1916, the chief of the Petrograd OKHRANA reported that "in the Kronstadt Collective, things are very well organized, conspiratorially, and its members are all taciturn and cautious people. This Collective also has representatives on shore."

~~This military organization released several leaflets—"When Will the War end?" and others that were printed in an underground printing plant.~~

~~Bolshevik work was more weakly developed within the Black Sea Fleet, where the influence of the Socialist-Revolutionaries and Mensheviks was still strong and where this would be reflected in the political morale of the Black Sea sailors in 1917.~~

At the front, the Party agitated for fraternization between the soldiers of the warring armies, emphasizing the fact that the world bourgeoisie was the enemy, and that the war could be ended only by converting the imperialist war into a civil war and turning one's weapons against one's *own* bourgeoisie *and its government*. Cases of refusal of army units to take the offensive became more and more frequent. There were already such instances in 1915, and even more in 1916.

Particularly extensive were the activities of the Bolsheviks in the armies on the Northern Front, *in the Baltic provinces.*[21] ~~Here, Latvian Bolsheviks conducted work together with Russian Bolsheviks, who had been drafted into the army (Myasnikov, Pozern and others).~~ At the beginning of 1917 General Ruzsky, Commander of the Army on the Northern Front, informed Headquarters that the Bolsheviks had developed intense revolutionary activities on that front.[22]

The war wrought a profound change in the life of the peoples, in the life of the working class of the world. The fate of states, the fate of nations, the fate of the Socialist movement was at stake. The war was therefore a touchstone, a test for all parties and trends calling themselves Socialist. Would these parties and trends remain true to the cause of Socialism, to the cause of internationalism, or would they choose to betray the working class, to furl their banners and lay them at the feet of their national bourgeoisie?—that is how the question stood at the time.

The war showed that the parties of the Second International had not stood the test, that they had betrayed the working class and had surrendered their banners to the imperialist bourgeoisie of their own countries.

And these parties, which had cultivated opportunism in their midst, and which had been brought up to make concessions to the opportunists, to the nationalists, could not have acted differently.

The war showed that the Bolshevik Party was the only party which had passed the test with flying colours and had remained consistently faithful to the cause of Socialism, the cause of proletarian internationalism.

And that was to be expected: only a party of a new type, only a party fostered in the spirit of uncompromising struggle against opportunism, only a party that was free from opportunism and nationalism, only such a party could stand the great test and remain faithful to the cause of the working class, to the cause of Socialism and internationalism.

And the Bolshevik Party was such a party.

~~4.5. Growth of the Revolutionary Movement and Crisis in the Country on the Eve of the February Revolution.~~ *Defeat of the Tsarist Army. Economic Disruption. Crisis of Tsardom*

~~When the tsarist government attacked the workers with harsh, repressive measures at the beginning of the war, the tide of the workers' movement noticeably subsided. But the strikes did not cease, even in 1914. In August 1914, the number of strikers numbered about 25,000. On May 1, 1915, 35,000 workers struck in Petrograd alone, with 400 being arrested and 100 dispatched to the front to fight. In all, there were 928 strikes in 1915, within which about 540,000 people took part; in 1916, there were already 1,600 strikes within which over 950,000 participants took part. There were also political strikes.~~

~~The strikes were frequently accompanied by shootings, inasmuch as martial law had been declared everywhere. Thus in Moscow in June 1915, 20 workers were killed or wounded, while 45 were killed in Kostroma. On August 10, 100 were killed and 40 wounded in Ivanovo-Voznesensk.~~

~~By the end of 1915, the lack of foodstuffs became painfully evident—there were no sugar, fats, meat or bread. The great majority of city dwellers were starving.~~

~~The war stimulated revolutionary sentiments among the peasantry as well. Under the influence of news from the front of the tsarist army's defeats, rising taxes, requisitioning, the drafting of all age categories and the mobilization of 2 million horses, hatred for those responsible for the war rose within the peasantry. The maimed returned home from the front to the countryside; they brought with them hatred for the tsarist regime and bitterness toward those responsible for their misfortunes—against the landlords and capitalists. The war was accompanied by ever newer mobilizations of men and horses and the requisitioning of livestock. The reports of the police and other forces spoke more frequently of a revolutionary mood among the peasantry.~~

~~At the same time, enormous discontent grew among the nationalities in the periphery who were oppressed by tsardom. The mass of oppressed nationalities sensed all the more sharply that tsarist Russia was a prison of peoples. This discontent overflowed into an uprising in 1916 in Central Asia involving almost all the peoples who populated the steppe territory (Kazakhstan) and Turkestan. The uprising was suppressed with extraordinary brutality.~~

~~This national liberation movement strengthened among the Poles, Finns, Ukrainians, Lithuanians and among the Transcaucasian nationalities.~~

The war had already been in progress for three years. Millions of people had been killed in the war, or had died of wounds or from epidemics caused by war conditions. The bourgeoisie and landlords were making fortunes out of the war. But the workers and peasants were suffering increasing hardship and privation. The war was undermining the economic life of Russia. Some fourteen million able-bodied men had been torn from economic pursuits and drafted into the army. Mills and factories were coming to a standstill. The crop area had diminished owing to a shortage of labour. The population and the soldiers at the front went hungry, barefoot and naked. The war was eating up the resources of the country.

The tsarist army suffered defeat after defeat. The German artillery deluged the tsarist troops with shells, while the tsarist army lacked guns, shells and even rifles. Sometimes three soldiers had to share one rifle. While the war was in progress it was discovered that Sukhomlinov, the tsar's Minister of War, was a traitor, who was connected with German spies, and was carrying out the instructions of the German espionage service to disorganize the supply of munitions and to leave the front without guns and rifles. Some of the tsarist ministers and generals surreptitiously assisted the success of the German army: together with the tsarina, who had German ties, they betrayed military secrets to the Germans. It is not surprising that the tsarist army suffered reverses and was forced to retreat. By 1916 the Germans had already seized Poland and part of the Baltic provinces.[23]

All this aroused hatred and anger against the tsarist government among the workers, peasants, soldiers and intellectuals, fostered and intensified the revolutionary movement of the masses against the war and against tsardom, both in the rear and at the front, in the central and in the border regions.

~~The tsarist government turned out to be unable to successfully wage the imperialist war and defend the interests of the Russian and allied bourgeoisie. Therefore, the bourgeoisie of Russia, France and Britain became more and more convinced of the imperative of changing the way Russia was ruled. The Russian bourgeoisie organized during the war under the auspices of the "All-Russian Zemstvo Union" and the "All-Russian Union of Towns." Both of these bourgeois organizations were created to aid in the war effort, but they were also used by the bourgeoisie for their own political organization. It was the Black-Hundred landlords, after all, who were in power at the tsarist court at this time. The industrial and financial bourgeoisie, whose economic power was increasing during the war, began to aspire toward political power.~~

~~Newer and newer defeats at the front in the imperialist war, the collapse of the economy, the fall in the productivity of the mills and factories and the upsurge in dissatisfaction among the soldiers—all of this forced a part of the bourgeoisie to search for a way to escape the terrible threat of total destruction~~

~~in this war. Among the bourgeoisie, conspiratorial groups began to form that set their goals on removing the most hated followers of the tsarist monarchy from power.~~

~~At the court, the tsar was in the grasp of the shadowy rogue Grigory Rasputin, the tsarina's lover who styled himself as a holy fool and a "man of God." Rasputin interfered in state affairs, influenced the hiring and firing of ministers and took bribes. But Rasputin was not the only one—in the tsarist court, a veritable "Rasputin-syndrome" weakened the system of tsarist state rule.~~

~~With the acknowledgment and encouragement of representatives of the foreign governments—Britain and France—a part of the bourgeoisie organized the murder of Rasputin, relying on several members of the tsar's family as well. This murder disgraced the tsarist regime even in the eyes of the most backward parts of the society.~~

~~The war continued. Every day, it was costing 40–50,000,000 gold rubles. A significant portion of this money went into the pockets of the Russian and foreign capitalists, who advocated war "to its victorious finish." But they saw the complete inability of the tsarist government to bring the war to such a conclusion.~~

Dissatisfaction also began to spread to the Russian imperialist bourgeoisie. It was incensed by the fact that rascals like Rasputin, who were obviously working for a separate peace with Germany, lorded it at the tsar's court. The bourgeoisie grew more and more convinced that the tsarist government was incapable of waging war successfully. ~~The bourgeoisie~~ *It* feared that the tsar might, in order to save his position, ~~secure~~ *conclude* a separate peace with ~~Germany~~ *the Germans. The Russian bourgeoisie therefore decided to engineer a palace coup with the object of deposing Tsar Nicholas II and replacing him by his brother, Michael Romanov, who was connected with the bourgeoisie. In this way it wanted to kill two birds with one stone: first, to get into power itself and ensure the further prosecution of the imperialist war, and, secondly, to prevent by a small palace coup the outbreak of a big popular revolution, the tide of which was swelling.*

~~Revolution was on the rise in the country. Therefore, the tsarist gang needed to secure a separate peace independent of the "Allies" in order to deal with the revolutionary movement within the country. But the bourgeoisie was against a separate peace, as ending the war would mean giving up the millions in profits that they were piling up during the war and the conquest of new markets.~~

~~The policy of the tsarist regime during the war also aroused dissatisfaction among the "ALLIES"—the governments of the Entente (Britain and France). The West-European capitalists looked "upon Russia like an auxiliary enterprise for their imperial ambitions" (STALIN).~~

In this the Russian bourgeoisie had the full support of the British and French governments who saw that the tsar was incapable of carrying on the war. They feared that he might end it by concluding a separate peace with the Germans. If the tsarist government were to sign a separate peace, the ~~imperialist~~ British and French governments would lose a war ally which not only diverted enemy forces to its own fronts, but also supplied France with ~~hundreds~~ *tens* of thousands of picked Russian soldiers. ~~This is why West-European capital~~ *The British and French governments therefore* supported the attempts of the ~~liberal~~ Russian bourgeoisie to bring about a palace coup.

~~The liberal bourgeoisie feared the revolutionary actions of the proletariat and attempted to head off the revolution, to prevent it.~~

~~The bourgeoisie fantasized about a palace coup, which would result in the installation of Michael Romanov in power in the place of Nicholas Romanov.~~

The tsar was thus isolated.

~~Unbelievable embezzlement, high-ranking bureaucratic corruption and treachery at the front led to newer and newer defeats for the army. The war caused a frightening disintegration and collapse throughout the economy and the ruin of transportation.~~

~~The discontent of the starving masses continued to rise. Disgust rose among the soldiers at the front, tormented by the war. Soldiers were dying in entire corps and armies in the swamps, the barbed wire and the poison gas. Within the soldier masses, the voice of the Bolsheviks—the opponents of the war who were pointing out to the soldiers who was truly responsible for the people's tragedy and how to end the war—was met with an ever more fiery response.~~

While defeat followed defeat at the front, economic disruption grew more and more acute. In January and February 1917 the extent and acuteness of the ~~crisis~~ *disorganization* of the food, raw material and fuel supply ~~rose to~~ *reached* a climax. The supply of foodstuffs to Petrograd and Moscow had almost ceased~~;~~. One factory after another closed down and this aggravated unemployment.[24] Particularly intolerable was the condition of the workers. Increasing numbers of *the* people were arriving at the conviction that the only way out *of the intolerable situation* was to overthrow the tsarist autocracy.

Tsardom was clearly in the throes of a mortal crisis.

The bourgeoisie thought of solving the crisis by a palace coup.

But the people solved it in their own way.

5.~~6.~~ The February ~~Bourgeois-Democratic~~ Revolution ~~of 1917~~. *Fall of Tsardom. Formation of Soviets of Workers' and Soldiers' Deputies. Formation of the Provisional Government. Dual Power*

The year 1917 was inaugurated by the strike of January 9. In the course of this strike demonstrations were held in Petrograd, Moscow, Baku and Nizhni-Novgorod. In Moscow about one-third of the workers took part in the strike of January 9. A demonstration of two thousand persons on Tverskoi Boulevard was dispersed by mounted police. A demonstration on the Vyborg Chaussée in Petrograd was joined by soldiers.

"The idea of a general strike," the *Petrograd* police reported, "is daily gaining new followers and is becoming as popular as it was in 1905."

The Mensheviks and Socialist-Revolutionaries tried to direct this incipient revolutionary movement into the channels the liberal bourgeoisie needed. The Mensheviks proposed that a procession of workers to the State Duma be organized on February 14, the day of its opening. But the working-class masses followed the Bolsheviks, and went, not to the Duma, but to a demonstration ~~against tsardom and for the struggle with the tsarist autocracy~~.

On February 18, 1917, a strike broke out at the Putilov Works in Petrograd. On February 22 the workers of ~~all~~ *most of* the big factories were on strike. On International Women's Day, February 23 (March 8), ~~1917,~~ at the call of the Petrograd Bolshevik Committee, working women came out in the streets to ~~protest~~ *demonstrate* against starvation, war and tsardom. ~~This demonstration was supported~~ *The Petrograd workers supported the demonstration of the working women* by a city-wide *strike* ~~movement of the proletariat~~. The political strike ~~grew~~ *began to grow* into a general political demonstration against the tsarist system.

On ~~the next day,~~ February 24 (March 9)~~;~~ the demonstration was resumed with even greater vigour. About 200,000 workers were already on strike.

On February 25 (March 10) the whole of working-class Petrograd had joined the revolutionary movement. The ~~various~~ *political* strikes *in the districts* merged into a general *political* strike *of the whole city*. Demonstrations and clashes with the police took place everywhere. Over the masses of workers floated red banners bearing the slogans: "Down with the tsar!" "Down with the war!" "We want bread!"

*On the morning of February 26 (March 11) t*he political strike and demonstration ~~assumed~~ *began to assume* the character of an ~~armed~~ uprising. The workers disarmed police and gendarmes and armed themselves. *Nevertheless* ~~On February 26 (March 11)~~, the clashes ~~took place~~ with the police ~~which~~ ended with the shooting down of a demonstration on Znamenskaya Square.

~~During the workers' clash with the police the workers not only defended themselves, but advanced forward, killing the commander of the police force.~~

General Khabalov, Commander of the Petrograd Military Area, announced that the workers must return to work by February 28 (March 13), otherwise they would be sent to the front. On February 25 (March 10) the tsar gave orders to General Khabalov: "I command you to put a stop to the disorders in the capital not later than tomorrow."

But "to put a stop" to the revolution was no longer possible.

On February 26 (March 11) the 4th Company of the Reserve Battalion of the Pavlovsky Regiment opened fire, not on the workers, *however,* but on squads of mounted police *who were engaged in a skirmish with the workers.* A most energetic and persistent drive was made ~~this time~~ to win over the troops, especially by the working women, who addressed themselves directly to the soldiers, fraternized with them and called upon them to help the people to overthrow the hated tsarist autocracy.

The *practical*[25] work of the *Bolshevik* Party at that time was directed by the Bureau of the Central Committee *of our Party* which had its quarters in Petrograd and was headed by Comrade Molotov. On February 26 (March 11) the Bureau of the Central Committee issued a manifesto calling for ~~the formation of a Provisional Revolutionary Government and~~ the continuation of the armed struggle against tsardom *and the formation of a Provisional Revolutionary Government.*

~~The workers obtained weapons where they could and entered into negotiations with the soldiers and sailors. More and more, the workers' strike began to transform into an armed uprising. Inspired by the Bolshevik Party, the workers rose for an assault on the tsarist autocracy.~~

On February 27 (March 12)~~, 1917,~~ the troops in Petrograd refused to fire on the workers and began to line up with the people in revolt. The number of soldiers who had joined the revolt by the morning of February 27 was still no more than ~~10,200~~ *10,000,* but by the evening it already exceeded ~~66,700~~ *60,000.* ~~THE REVOLUTION HAD WON. Tsardom had fallen.~~

The workers and soldiers who had risen in revolt began to arrest tsarist ministers and generals and to free revolutionaries from jail. The released political prisoners ~~eagerly took part in~~ *joined* the revolutionary struggle.

In the streets, shots were still being exchanged with police and gendarmes posted with machine guns in the attics of houses. But the troops rapidly went over to the side of the workers, and ~~the union of the struggle of the peasants (the soldiers) with the revolutionary struggle of the workers~~ *this* decided the fate of the tsarist autocracy.

When the news of the victory of the revolution in Petrograd spread to other towns and to the front, the workers and soldiers everywhere ~~deposed~~ *began to depose* the tsarist officials.

The *February* bourgeois-democratic revolution had won ~~and served as the prologue for the October Socialist Revolution that developed 8 months later~~.

*The revolution was victorious because its vanguard was t*he working class *which* headed the movement of millions *of peasants clad in soldiers' uniform* demanding "peace, bread and liberty." It was ~~precisely~~ the hegemony ~~(leadership)~~ of the proletariat that determined the success of the revolution.[26]

> "The revolution was made by the proletariat. The proletariat displayed heroism; it shed its blood; it swept along with it the broadest masses of the toiling and poor population," wrote Lenin ~~at the very beginning~~ *in the early days* of the revolution. (Lenin, Collected Works, Russ. ed., Vol. XX, pp. 23–4.)

The *First* Revolution, that of 1905, had ~~shaken tsardom and~~ prepared the way for the swift success of the Second ~~Russian February~~ Revolution, *that of 1917.*

> "Without the tremendous class battles," Lenin wrote, "and the revolutionary energy displayed by the Russian proletariat during the three years, 1905–07, the second revolution could not possibly have been so rapid in the sense that its initial stage was completed in a few days." (Lenin, Selected Works, Eng. ed., Vol. VI, pp. 3–4.)

~~The worldwide imperialist war created an unheard-of economic and political crisis which accelerated the pace of world history by an enormous amount. The Russian February bourgeois-democratic revolution was the first revolution born of the worldwide imperialist war.~~

~~In the Second Russian February Revolution, the Bolsheviks stood at the head of the masses and the revolutionary actions of the workers took place under the slogans of the Bolshevik Party.~~

~~7. Creation of the Soviets of Workers' and Soldiers' Deputies~~

Soviets arose in the very first days of the revolution. The victorious revolution rested on the support of the Soviets of Workers' and Soldiers' Deputies. The ~~proletariat~~ *workers and soldiers* who rose in revolt created Soviets of Workers' and Soldiers' Deputies. The Revolution of 1905 had shown that the Soviets were organs of armed uprising and at the same time the ~~rudiments~~ *embryo* of a new, revolutionary power. The idea of Soviets lived in the minds of the working-class masses, and they put it into effect as soon as tsardom was overthrown, *with this difference, however, that in 1905 it was Soviets only*[27] *of Workers' Deputies that were formed, whereas in February 1917, on the initiative of the Bolsheviks,*[28] *there arose Soviets of Workers' and Soldiers' Deputies.*

~~But~~ *While* the Bolsheviks were directly leading the struggle of the masses in the streets, *the compromising parties,* the Mensheviks and Socialist-Revolutionaries, ~~seized the majority of~~ *were seizing the* seats in the Soviets, *and building up a majority there. This was partly facilitated by the fact that the majority of the leaders of the Bolshevik Party were in prison or exile (Lenin was in exile abroad and Stalin and Sverdlov in banishment in Siberia) while the Mensheviks and Socialist-Revolutionaries were freely promenading the streets of Petrograd. The result was that* the Petrograd Soviet and its Executive Committee were headed~~, with the exception of a few Bolsheviks,~~ by representatives of the ~~petty-bourgeois~~ *compromising* parties: Mensheviks and Socialist-Revolutionaries. This was also the case in Moscow and a number of other cities. Only in Ivanovo-Voznesensk, Krasnoyarsk and a few other places did the Bolsheviks have a majority in the Soviets from the very outset.

~~At the time, the Bolshevik Party was organizationally weak. Many of the energetic activists of the Bolshevik Party were in internal exile. The chief of the Bolshevik Party, V. I. Lenin, was in emigration in Switzerland during the days of the February coup d'état. The most prominent leaders of the Bolshevik Party—Stalin and Sverdlov—were in internal exile in Siberia. Extant Bolshevik forces were occupied with the personal direction of the mass movement.~~

The armed people—the workers and soldiers—sent their representatives to the Soviet as to an organ of power of the people. They thought *and believed* that the Soviet of Workers' and Soldiers' Deputies would carry out all the demands of the revolutionary people, and that, in the first place, peace would be concluded.

But *the unwarranted trustfulness of the workers and soldiers served them in evil stead. The Socialist-Revolutionaries and Mensheviks had not the slightest intention of terminating the war, of securing peace. They planned to take advantage of the revolution to continue the war. As to the revolution and the revolutionary demands of the people, the Socialist-Revolutionaries and the Mensheviks considered that the revolution was already over, and that the task now was to seal it and to pass to a "normal" constitutional existence side by side with the bourgeoisie.* The *Socialist-Revolutionary and* Menshevik leaders of the Petrograd Soviet *therefore* did their utmost *to shelve the question of terminating the war, to shelve the question of peace, and* to hand over the power to the bourgeoisie.

~~At that time, the liberal bourgeoisie, which was aiming to halt the further development of the revolution, formed~~ On February 27 (March 12), 1917, *the liberal members of the Fourth State Duma, as the result of a backstairs*[29] *agreement with the Socialist-Revolutionary and Menshevik leaders, set up* a Provisional Committee of the State Duma, headed by Rodzyanko, the President of the Duma, a ~~very wealthy~~ landlord and a monarchist. ~~The Provisional Committee of the State Duma outlined the composition of the Provisional Government. The conciliatory leadership of the Petrograd Soviet came to the aid of the liberal bourgeoisie and at a joint session of the Provisional Committee of the State Duma and the Executive Committee of the Soviet of Workers' and Soldiers' Deputies on March 2, 1917, they formed~~ *And a few days later, the Provisional Committee of the State Duma and the Socialist-Revolutionary and Menshevik leaders of the Executive Committee of the Soviet of Workers' and Soldiers' Deputies, acting secretly from the Bolsheviks, came to an agreement to form a new government of Russia*—a bourgeois Provisional Government, headed by Prince Lvov, the man whom, prior to the February Revolution, even *Tsar* Nicholas II was about to make the Prime Minister of ~~the tsarist~~ *his* government.[30] The Provisional Government included Milyukov, the head of the Constitutional-Democrats, *Guchkov, the head of the Octobrists,*[31] and ~~7~~ *other* prominent *representatives of the* capitalist~~s~~ *class,* and, as the representative of the "democracy," ~~(with the permission of the Executive Committee of the Soviet)~~ the Socialist-Revolutionary Kerensky. ~~The Mensheviks and Socialist-Revolutionaries did everything that they could to strengthen the power of the bourgeoisie—the Provisional Government.~~

~~What made up this Provisional Government which replaced the tsarist government? Lenin pointed out that it was made up of representatives of the new class, specifically "the bourgeoisie and the landlords who had become bourgeois." The bourgeoisie had long ruled the country in economic terms, but during the war, when the autocracy couldn't handle the war and was forced to make concessions to the bourgeoisie, it solidified its political power as well.~~

And so it was that the Socialist-Revolutionary and Menshevik leaders of the Executive Committee of the Soviet surrendered the power to the bourgeoisie. Yet when the Soviet of Workers' and Soldiers' Deputies learned of this, its majority formally approved of the action of the Socialist-Revolutionary and Menshevik leaders, despite the protest of the Bolsheviks.[32]

Thus a new state power arose in Russia, consisting, as Lenin said, of representatives of the "bourgeoisie and landlords who had become bourgeois."

~~This was the Provisional Government which had come to power.~~

But alongside of the bourgeois government there existed another power—the Soviet of Workers' and Soldiers' Deputies. ~~The Soviet of Workers' and Soldiers' Deputies was the organ of the revolutionary-democratic dictatorship of the proletariat and the peasantry.~~ The soldier deputies on the Soviet were mostly peasants who had been mobilized for the war. The Soviet~~s~~ of Workers' and Soldiers' Deputies ~~were~~ *was* an organ of the alliance of workers and peasants against the tsarist regime, *and at the same time it was an organ of their power, an organ of the dictatorship of the working class and the peasantry.* ~~Without such an alliance, it would not have been possible to overthrow tsardom.~~

~~After the victory of the February bourgeois-democratic revolution,~~ *The* result was a~~n exceptionally~~ peculiar interlocking *of two powers,* of two dictatorships~~—a DUAL POWER~~: the dictatorship of the bourgeoisie ~~(the Provisional Government)~~, *represented by the Provisional Government,* and the dictatorship of the proletariat and peasantry ~~(the Soviet of Workers' and Soldiers' Deputies)~~, *represented by the Soviet of Workers' and Soldiers' Deputies.*

The result was a dual power.

How is it to be explained that the majority in the Soviets at first consisted of Mensheviks and Socialist-Revolutionaries?

How ~~then~~ is it to be explained that the victorious workers and peasants VOLUNTARILY surrendered the power to *the representatives of* the bourgeoisie? ~~How is it to be explained that the majority in the Soviets at first consisted of Mensheviks and Socialist-Revolutionaries?~~

Lenin explained it by pointing out that ~~tens of~~ millions of people, inexperienced in politics, had awakened and pressed forward to political activity. These were for the most part small owners, ~~petty bourgeoisie,~~ *peasants, workers who had recently been peasants,* people who stood midway between the ~~capitalists and hired labour~~ *bourgeoisie and the proletariat.* ~~Lenin explained it in terms that~~ Russia was *at that time* the most petty bourgeois of all the *big* European countries. And in this country, "a gigantic petty-bourgeois wave has swept over everything and overwhelmed the class-conscious proletariat, not only by force of numbers but also ideologically; that is, it has infected and imbued very wide circles of workers with the petty-bourgeois political outlook." (Lenin, SELECTED WORKS, Vol. VI, p. 49.)

It was this elemental petty-bourgeois wave that swept the petty-bourgeois Menshevik and Socialist-Revolutionary parties to the fore.

Lenin pointed out that another reason was the ~~insufficient numbers~~ *change in the composition* of the proletariat ~~in Russia~~ *that had taken place during the war* and the inadequate class-consciousness and organization of the proletariat at the beginning of the revolution. During the war big changes had taken place in the proletariat itself. About 40 per cent of the ~~old~~ *regular* workers had been drafted into the army. Many small owners, artisans, *and* shop-keepers ~~and other such people~~, to whom the proletarian psychology was alien, had gone to the factories in order to evade mobilization.

It was these petty-bourgeois sections of the workers that formed the soil which nourished *the petty-bourgeois politicians*—the Mensheviks and Socialist-Revolutionaries.

~~The petty-bourgeois masses turned out to be "well-meaning" (well-meaningly mistaken) defencists. The broad masses saw that the revolution had been victorious and that Russia had become a more free country in comparison with other bourgeois countries. And here the Provisional Government was calling for the defence of this free Russia against the German monarchy. The Mensheviks and Socialist-Revolutionaries supported these calls of the imperialistic bourgeoisie. The petty-bourgeois masses, trusting the bourgeoisie and their agents, became "well-meaning" defencists.~~

That is why large numbers of the people, inexperienced in politics, swept into the elemental petty-bourgeois vortex, and intoxicated with the first successes of the revolution, found themselves in its early months under the sway of the compromising parties and consented to surrender the state power to the bourgeoisie in the naive belief that a bourgeois power would not hinder the Soviets in their work.

The task that confronted the Bolshevik Party was, by patient work of explanation, to ~~win over the masses and the majority of the Soviets, isolate (separate) the conciliatory parties from the masses and~~ open the eyes *of the masses* to the ~~counter-revolutionary essence~~ *imperialist character* of the Provisional Government~~, which was supported by the petty-bourgeois leadership of the Soviet~~ *to expose the treachery of the Socialist-Revolutionaries and Mensheviks and to show that peace could not be secured unless the Provisional Government were replaced by a government of Soviets.*

~~From the first days of the February-March Revolution,~~ *And to this work* the Bolshevik Party addressed *itself* ~~the organization of the working masses~~ with the utmost energy. ~~The Bolshevik Party, while still in the minority in the Soviets and while being hounded by the Mensheviks, Socialist-Revolutionaries and all the bourgeois parties, conducted an enormous amount of work.~~

It resumed the publication of its legal periodicals. The newspaper PRAVDA appeared in Petrograd ~~5~~ *five* days after the February~~-March~~ Revolution, and the SOTSIAL-DEMOKRAT in Moscow a few days later. The Party ~~assumed~~ *was assuming* leadership of the masses, who were losing their confidence in the liberal bourgeoisie and in the Mensheviks and Socialist-Revolutionaries. ~~The Party led the economic and political struggle of the masses. It created military organizations everywhere. It assumed control of the revolutionary movement of the female masses and created Socialist youth groups that later would form the basis for the founding of the Young Communist League.~~ It patiently explained to the *soldiers and* peasants the necessity of acting jointly with the working class ~~for the completion and full realization of the bourgeois-democratic revolution. It strengthened the alliance of the workers and poor peasants for the Socialist Proletarian Revolution~~. *It explained to them that the peasants would secure neither peace nor land unless the revolution were further developed and the bourgeois Provisional Government replaced by a government of Soviets.*

Brief Summary

~~The period of the world imperialist war was the period of the fall of the Second International. The only workers' party in the Second International that preserved its loyalty to the proletarian banner of internationalism was the Bolshevik Party. It gave a correct evaluation of the war as a predatory, imperialist war. Alone, it united the working masses in uncompromising class struggle and rallied the masses to Socialist revolution as the only way out of the imperialist war and it tirelessly exposed the treachery of the Socialist-Revolutionaries,~~

~~Mensheviks and Anarchists, who supported the imperialist war, the bourgeoisie and capitalism. The Bolshevik Party used the sharpening of social contradictions during the war in order to prepare the masses for armed revolt. It led the February-March Revolution that overthrew tsardom.~~

~~The Bolshevik Party delivered a crushing blow to international social-chauvinism.~~

~~The struggle of Lenin and the whole Bolshevik Party against the Mensheviks, Socialist-Revolutionaries and Anarchists and against the Centrists and opportunists within the party had enormous significance for the rallying of genuinely internationalist elements of the workers' movement.~~

~~Lenin rallied the internationalist elements in the international movement at the Zimmerwald and Kienthal Conferences and made the first steps toward the formation of the Third International.~~

~~Victorious in February 1917, the Second Russian February Bourgeois-Democratic Revolution destroyed the tsarist autocracy. As a result of the treachery of the Socialist-Revolutionaries and the Mensheviks, who aimed at all cost to preserve the power of the bourgeoisie, a DUAL POWER was created which served as the source of a multitude of political crises. There was only one way out of the conditions thus created: to cross over into the second stage of the revolution—the overthrow of the power of the capitalists and capitalist landlords. The February revolution was the beginning of the conversion of the imperialist war into a civil war. This civil war now had to take the next step to accomplish the Socialist revolution.~~

~~The working class began to cross into the Socialist revolution immediately after the February revolution under the leadership of the Bolshevik Party.~~

The imperialist war arose owing to the uneven development of the capitalist countries, to the upsetting of equilibrium between the principal powers, to the imperialists'[33] *need for a redivision of the world by means of war and for the creation of a new equilibrium.*

The war would not have been so destructive, and perhaps would not even have assumed such dimensions, if the parties of the Second International had not betrayed the cause of the working class, if they had not violated the anti-war decisions of the congresses of the Second International, if they had dared to act and to rouse the working class against their imperialist governments, against the warmongers.

The Bolshevik Party was the only proletarian party which remained faithful to the cause of Socialism and internationalism and which organized civil war against its own imperialist government. All the other parties of the Second International, being tied to the bourgeoisie through their leaders, found themselves under the sway of imperialism and deserted to the side of the imperialists.

The war, while it was a reflection of the general crisis of capitalism, at the same time aggravated this crisis and weakened world capitalism. The workers of Russia and the Bolshevik Party were the first in the world successfully to take advantage of the weakness of capitalism. They forced a breach in the imperialist front, overthrew the tsar and set up Soviets of Workers' and Soldiers' Deputies.

Intoxicated by the first successes of the revolution, and lulled by the assurances of the Mensheviks and Socialist-Revolutionaries that from now on everything would go well, the bulk of the petty-bourgeoisie, the soldiers, as well as the workers, placed their confidence in the Provisional Government and supported it.

The Bolshevik Party was confronted with the task of explaining to the masses of workers and soldiers, who had been intoxicated by the first successes, that the complete victory of the revolution was still a long way off, that as long as the power was in the hands of the bourgeois Provisional Government, and as long as the Soviets were dominated by the compromisers—the Mensheviks and Socialist-Revolutionaries—the people would secure neither peace, nor land, nor bread, and that in order to achieve complete victory, one more step had to be taken and the power transferred to the Soviets.

CHAPTER SEVEN

The Bolshevik Party in the Period of Preparation and Realization of the October Socialist Revolution (April 1917–1918)

1. Situation in the Country after the ~~Victory of the Second Russian~~ February Revolution. *Party Emerges from Underground and Passes to Open Political Work. Lenin Arrives in Petrograd. Lenin's April Theses. Party's Policy of Transition to Socialist Revolution*

The course of events and the conduct of the Provisional Government daily furnished new proofs of the correctness of the Bolshevik line. It became increasingly evident that the Provisional Government stood not for the people but against the people, not for peace but for war, and that it was unwilling and unable to give the people peace, land or bread. The explanatory work of the Bolsheviks found a fruitful soil.

While the ~~working class in alliance with the soldiers and sailors and with weapons in hand~~ *workers and soldiers* were overthrowing the tsarist government and destroying ~~the old regime~~ *the monarchy root and branch*, the ~~bourgeois~~ Provisional Government ~~first and foremost tried~~ *definitely wanted* to preserve the monarchy. On March 2, 1917, it secretly commissioned Guchkov and Shulgin to go and see the tsar. The bourgeoisie wanted to transfer the power to Nicholas Romanov's brother, Michael. But when, at a meeting of railwaymen, Guchkov ended his speech with the words, "Long live Emperor Michael," the workers demanded that Guchkov be immediately arrested and searched. "Horse-radish is no sweeter than radish," they exclaimed indignantly.

It was clear that the workers would not permit the restoration of the monarchy.

~~Michael understood that the most dangerous thing he could do would be to don the crown that had been blown off Nicholas Romanov, so he also "abdicated." The traitor Kamenev set a congratulatory telegram to this "Citizen Romanov" during the first days of the revolution along with the merchants and officials of the city of Achinsk.~~

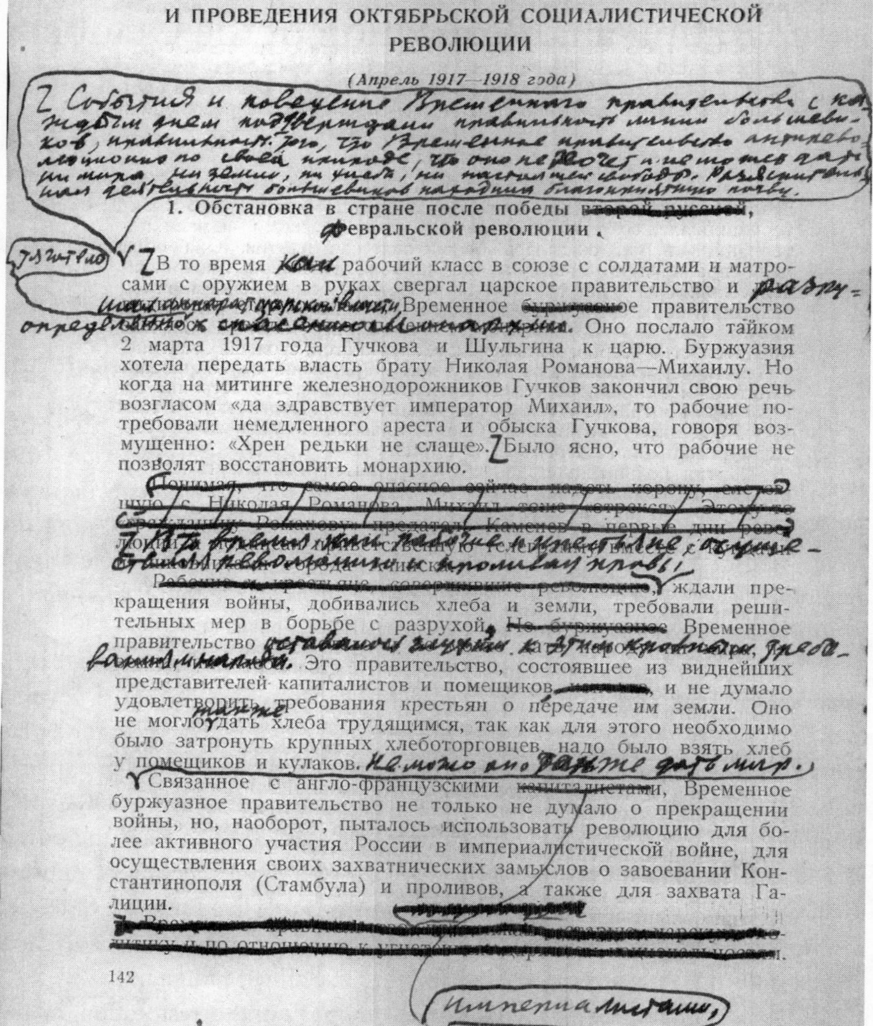

337

ГЛАВА VII

ПАРТИЯ БОЛЬШЕВИКОВ В ПЕРИОД ПОДГОТОВКИ И ПРОВЕДЕНИЯ ОКТЯБРЬСКОЙ СОЦИАЛИСТИЧЕСКОЙ РЕВОЛЮЦИИ

(Апрель 1917—1918 года)

1. Обстановка в стране после победы второй русской, февральской революции.

В то время как рабочий класс в союзе с солдатами и матросами с оружием в руках свергал царское правительство и [illegible] Временное буржуазное правительство [illegible]. Оно послало тайком 2 марта 1917 года Гучкова и Шульгина к царю. Буржуазия хотела передать власть брату Николая Романова—Михаилу. Но когда на митинге железнодорожников Гучков закончил свою речь возгласом «да здравствует император Михаил», то рабочие потребовали немедленного ареста и обыска Гучкова, говоря возмущенно: «Хрен редьки не слаще». Было ясно, что рабочие не позволят восстановить монархию.

Рабочие и крестьяне, совершившие революцию, ждали прекращения войны, добивались хлеба и земли, требовали решительных мер в борьбе с разрухой. Но буржуазное Временное правительство [illegible]. Это правительство, состоявшее из виднейших представителей капиталистов и помещиков, [illegible], и не думало удовлетворить требования крестьян о передаче им земли. Оно не могло дать хлеба трудящимся, так как для этого необходимо было затронуть крупных хлеботорговцев, надо было взять хлеб у помещиков и кулаков.

Связанное с англо-французскими капиталистами, Временное буржуазное правительство не только не думало о прекращении войны, но, наоборот, пыталось использовать революцию для более активного участия России в империалистической войне, для осуществления своих захватнических замыслов о завоевании Константинополя (Стамбула) и проливов, а также для захвата Галиции.

142

First page of Chapter Seven with Stalin's editing from the summer of 1938. RGASPI, f. 558, op. 11, d. 1211, l. 337.

~~The~~ *While the* workers and peasants who ~~had made~~ *were shedding their blood making* the revolution expected that the war would be terminated, [*and*] while they were fighting for bread and land and demanding vigorous measures to end the economic chaos~~. But~~, the ~~bourgeois~~ Provisional Government ~~was not willing or able to give the people either peace, land or bread~~ *remained deaf to these vital demands of the people.* Consisting as it did of prominent representatives of the capitalists and landlords, this government ~~of course~~ had no intention of satisfying the demand of the peasants that the land be turned over to them. Nor could they provide bread for the working people, because to do so they would have to ~~hurt~~ *encroach on the interests of* the big grain dealers and to take grain from the landlords and the kulaks *by every available means; and this the government did not dare to do, for it was itself tied up with the interests of these classes. Nor could it give the people peace.* Bound as it was to the British and French ~~capitalists~~ *imperialists*, the ~~bourgeois~~ Provisional Government had no intention of terminating the war; on the contrary, it endeavoured to take advantage of the revolution to make Russia's participation in the imperialist war even more active, and to realize its ~~predatory~~ *imperialist* designs of ~~conquering~~ *seizing* Constantinople ~~(Istanbul)~~, the Straits and Galicia.

It was clear that the people's confidence in the policy of the Provisional Government must soon come to an end.

~~The Provisional Government also maintained the old tsarist policy toward the nationalities which had been oppressed by tsardom. It looked upon the national movements in the periphery in Transcaucasia, the Ukraine and Finland with hostility. Having overthrown the tsar, the workers and peasants had effectively realized all their democratic freedoms: freedom of speech, freedom of association, freedom of assembly, freedom of the press, and so on. And despite the bourgeoisie's best efforts to impose order and limit these rights, it failed in its designs until the July days of 1917. The popular masses were aroused by this new political life and passionately attempted to make use of their newly won democratic rights in order to take an active role in politics and to understand and think through what they should do next.~~

~~Meetings and assemblies were held throughout the country and especially in the cities and the workers, soldiers and peasants formed organizations. The working people hungrily read newspapers, leaflets and brochures. But the broad worker and peasant masses did not have any political experience. They therefore believed the Mensheviks and Socialist-Revolutionaries, who deceived the people by saying that after the overthrow of the tsardom, all would be fine and the struggle would no longer be necessary.~~

~~The bourgeois lackeys—the Socialist-Revolutionaries and the Mensheviks—called upon the people to trust and support the Provisional Government~~

~~and convinced them to wait for the Constituent Assembly. The Constituent Assembly will be convened, they said, and it will provide peace, land and bread.~~

It was becoming clear that the dual power which had arisen after the February Revolution could not last long, for the course of events demanded the concentration of power in the hands of one authority: either the Provisional Government or the Soviets.

~~Part of the workers, solders and especially the peasantry at the start of the 1917 revolution believed the Provisional Government's promises to end the war with a just peace; they believed the promises of the Mensheviks and Socialist-Revolutionaries that the peasants would soon receive the land.~~

~~The petty-bourgeois masses, as Lenin put it, were "honestly mistaken" supporters of the war. This meant that they agreed to continue the war not for any of the spoils that the bourgeoisie was fighting for, but because they believed that what was at stake was the defence of Russia from German imperialism and not a redivision of the world.~~

It was true that the compromising policy of the Mensheviks and the Socialist-Revolutionaries still met with support among the masses. There were quite a number of workers, and an even larger number of soldiers and peasants, who still believed that "the Constituent Assembly will soon come and arrange everything in a peaceful way," and who thought that the war was not waged for purposes of conquest, but from necessity—to defend the state. Lenin called such people honestly mistaken supporters of the war. These people still considered the Socialist-Revolutionary and Menshevik policy, which was one of promises and coaxing, the correct policy. But it was clear that promises and coaxing could not suffice for long, as the course of events and the conduct of the Provisional Government were daily revealing and proving that the compromising policy of the Socialist-Revolutionaries and the Mensheviks was a policy of procrastination and of hoodwinking the credulous.

~~The Cadet-Octobrist Provisional Government attempted to "establish order," that is, to direct the revolution into channels that suited the needs of the bourgeoisie in order to later suppress it. But no matter how hard the Mensheviks and Socialist-Revolutionaries tried to eliminate every hint of revolution from the activities of the Soviet of Workers' and Solders' Deputies, the Soviet was forced BY THE DEMANDS OF THE SOLDIERS to pass the revolutionary "Order Number One" during the first days after the revolution.~~

~~This order granted the soldiers and sailors the same rights that all citizens had. The order eliminated the requirement to address officers as "Your Highness," "Your Excellency," and so on, and eliminated the need to salute officers when off duty. On the basis of this order, solders' and sailors' committees were elected in all units of the army and navy, which were themselves subordinated by this order to the Soviet and its solders' committees in all their political activities.~~

The Provisional Government did not always confine itself to a covert struggle against the revolutionary movement of the masses, to backstairs scheming against the revolution. It sometimes attempted to make an open assault on the democratic liberties, to "restore discipline," especially among the soldiers, to "establish order," that is, to direct the revolution into channels that suited the bourgeoisie. But all its efforts in this direction failed, and the people eagerly exercised their democratic liberties, namely, freedom of speech, press, association, assembly and demonstration. The workers and soldiers endeavoured to make full use of their newly won democratic rights in order to take an active part in the political life of the country, to get an intelligent understanding of the situation and to decide what was to be done next.

~~2. The Bolshevik Party after the Bourgeois-Democratic February Revolution~~

After the ~~overthrow of tsardom~~ *February Revolution*, the organizations of the Bolshevik Party, which had worked ~~secretly~~ *illegally* under the extremely difficult conditions of tsardom, emerged from underground and ~~were able~~ *began* to *develop political and organizational* work openly. The membership of the Bolshevik organizations at that time did not exceed 40,000 or 45,000. But these were all staunch revolutionaries, steeled in the struggle ~~with tsardom and trained by Lenin and Stalin. A considerable portion of the Bolsheviks were still in prison or far away in internal exile. Lenin was in Switzerland and Stalin, Sverdlov, Ordjonikidze and Kuibyshev had not yet managed to return from internal exile. Dzerzhinsky hadn't returned from his labour camp.~~

The Party Committees ~~were organized right after the February revolution first of all in the major industrial centres of Petrograd, Moscow, Ivanovo, Ekaterinoslav, and so on~~ *were reorganized on the principle of democratic centralism. All Party bodies, from top to bottom, were made elective.* ~~From the first day, the Party organizations began to conduct an enormous amount of agitational-propaganda work, form their nuclei in the enterprises, organize the workers, soldiers and peasants around the Soviets, and wage a struggle against the Mensheviks and Socialist-Revolutionaries. The first issue of PRAVDA was published on March 5 (18).~~

~~But Party members did not always assume the right line. Some Party committees in the provinces attempted to combine forces with the Mensheviks. Kamenev returned from exile in order to advance the Menshevik line of supporting the Provisional Government and called upon workers and peasants to continue the imperialist war.~~

~~Stalin returned from exile to Petrograd on March 12 (25). In his articles in PRAVDA, Stalin called for the creation of a firm alliance of workers and peasants~~

~~and explained that the organs of this alliance ought to be the workers' and soldiers' Soviets (the latter of which consisted chiefly of peasants in soldiers' uniforms on account of the war). He called for the Soviets to be strengthened and developed as the people's organs of revolutionary power.~~

~~On March 14, Stalin wrote in PRAVDA:~~

> ~~"We must strengthen . . . the Soviets, make them ubiquitous and link them together under the leadership of the Central Soviet of the Workers' and Soldiers' Deputies as the people's organ of revolutionary power. This is the direction in which revolutionary Social-Democracy must go."~~

~~Comrade Stalin delivered a rebuff to Kamenev and called upon the Party to expose the true origins of the imperialist war to the people, which meant "declaring war on war, making war impossible."~~

~~Comrade Stalin defended the arming of the workers and the imperative of creating detachments of the workers' (Red) guard. He called upon the peasants to not wait for the Constituent Assembly and to take over the landed estates and cultivate the land themselves.~~

When the Party began its legal existence, differences within its ranks became apparent. Kamenev and several workers of the Moscow organization, for example, Rykov, Bubnov and Nogin,[1] *held a semi-Menshevik position of conditionally supporting the Provisional Government and the policy of the partisans of the war. Stalin, who had just returned from exile, Molotov and others, together with the majority of the Party, upheld a policy of no-confidence in the Provisional Government, opposed the partisans of the war, and called for an active struggle for peace, a struggle against the imperialist war. Some of the Party workers vacillated, which was a manifestation of their political backwardness, a consequence of long years*[2] *of imprisonment or exile.*

The absence of the leader of the Party, Lenin, was felt.

On April 3 (16), 1917, after a long period of exile, Lenin returned to Russia.

Lenin's arrival was of tremendous importance to *the Party and* the revolution.

While still in Switzerland, Lenin, upon receiving the first news of the revolution, had written his "Letters From Afar" to the Party and to the working class of Russia, in which he said:

> "Workers, you have displayed marvels of proletarian heroism, the heroism of the people, in the civil war against tsardom. You must now display marvels of organization, organization of the proletariat and of the whole people, in order to prepare the way for your victory in the second stage of the revolution~~, that is, the Socialist stage of the revolution~~."[3] *(Lenin, SELECTED WORKS, Vol. VI, p. 11.)*

~~Lenin met Stalin at Byeloostrov Station in Finland. In the train car on the way to Petrograd, Lenin talked with solders and became acquainted with their sentiments.~~

Lenin arrived in Petrograd on the night of April 3. Thousands of workers, soldiers and sailors assembled at the Finland Railway Station and in the station square to welcome him. Their enthusiasm as Lenin alighted from the train was indescribable. They lifted their leader shoulder high and carried him to the ~~former tsar's~~ *main* waiting room of the station. There the Mensheviks Chkheidze and Skobelev launched into speeches of "welcome" on behalf of the Petrograd Soviet, in which they "expressed the hope" that they and Lenin would find a "common ~~path~~ *language*." But Lenin did not stop to listen; sweeping past them, he went out to the masses of workers and soldiers. Mounting an armoured car, he delivered ~~a brilliant~~ *his famous* speech in which he called upon the masses to ~~continue the~~ fight for the victory of the Socialist revolution. "Long live the Socialist revolution!" were the words with which Lenin concluded this first speech after long years of exile. ~~This brilliant chief of the revolution took his place at the head of the masses.~~

Back in Russia, Lenin flung himself vigorously into revolutionary work. On the morrow of his arrival ~~in Petrograd~~ he delivered a report on the subject of *the war and* the revolution at a meeting of Bolsheviks, and then repeated the theses of this report at a meeting attended by Mensheviks *as well as Bolsheviks.*

These were Lenin's famous April Theses, which provided the Party and the proletariat with a clear revolutionary line for the transition from the bourgeois to the Socialist revolution.

~~These~~ *Lenin's* theses were of immense significance *to the revolution and* to the subsequent work of the Party. The revolution was a momentous turn *in the life of the country*. In the new conditions of the struggle *that followed the overthrow of tsardom*, the Party needed a new orientation ~~after the overthrow of tsardom in order~~ to ~~go~~ *advance* boldly *and confidently* along the new road. *Lenin's theses gave the Party this orientation.*

Lenin's April Theses laid down for the Party a brilliant plan of struggle for the transition[4] from the bourgeois-democratic to the Socialist revolution, from the first stage *of the revolution*~~, when the tsar was overthrown,~~ to the second stage—the stage of the Socialist revolution~~, where it was necessary to overthrow the bourgeoisie and the landlords~~. The whole history of the Party had prepared it for this great task. As far back as 1905, Lenin had said *in his pamphlet, Two Tactics of Social-Democracy in the Democratic Revolution,* that after the overthrow of tsardom the ~~Party~~ *proletariat* would *immediately* proceed ~~by merit of the consciousness and organization of the proletariat~~ to bring about the Socialist revolution. *The new thing in the theses was that they gave a concrete, theoretically grounded plan for the initial stage of the transition to the Socialist revolution.*

~~Lenin's theses instructed that there was now a new task in front of the Party—the preparation for the Socialist revolution.~~

~~The theses provided answers to all the basic questions of the revolution.~~

The transitional steps in the economic field were: nationalization of all the land and confiscation of the landed estates, amalgamation of all the banks into one national bank to be under the control of the Soviet of Workers' Deputies, and establishment of control over the social production and distribution of products.

In the political field, Lenin proposed the transition from a parliamentary republic to a republic of Soviets. This was an important step forward in the theory and practice of Marxism. Hitherto, Marxist theoreticians had regarded the parliamentary republic as the best political form of transition to Socialism. Now Lenin proposed to replace the parliamentary republic by a Soviet republic as the most suitable form of political organization of society in the period of transition from capitalism to Socialism.

> *"The specific feature of the present situation in Russia," the theses stated, "is that it represents a* TRANSITION *from the first stage of the revolution—which, owing to the insufficient class-consciousness and organization of the proletariat, placed the power in the hands of the bourgeoisie—*TO THE SECOND STAGE*, which must place the power in the hands of the proletariat and the poorest strata of the peasantry." (Ibid., p. 22.)*
>
> *"Not a parliamentary republic—to return to a parliamentary republic from the Soviets of Workers' Deputies would be a retrograde step—but a republic of Soviets of Workers', Agricultural Labourers' and Peasants' Deputies throughout the country, from top to bottom." (Ibid., p. 23.)*

Under the new government, the ~~bourgeois~~ *Provisional* Government, ~~Lenin said,~~ the war continued to be a predatory imperialist war, *Lenin said*. It was the task of the Party to explain this to the masses and to show them that unless ~~capital was~~ *the bourgeoisie were* overthrown, it would be impossible to end the war by a truly democratic peace and not a rapacious peace.

As regards the ~~bourgeois~~ Provisional Government, the slogan Lenin put forward was: "No support for the Provisional Government!" ~~and explained to the masses the truth about all of its promises. Our task is not the establishment of an ordinary parliamentary republic, Lenin said, but the conquest of a Republic of Soviets of the Workers, Agricultural Labourers and Peasants from all across the country, from the bottom up.~~

~~In Lenin's theses there were also demands for the uncompensated seizure (confiscation) of all landed estates and their transfer to the jurisdiction of the Soviets of Agricultural Labourers' and Peasants' Deputies. The theses said that the goal of the Party was not to immediately realize Socialism, but instead to~~

~~take an array of transitional measures toward Socialism. The only immediate measure was a transfer of public production and foodstuffs distribution to the control of the Soviets of Workers' Deputies.~~

Lenin *further* pointed out *in the theses* that our Party was *still* in the minority in the Soviets, that the Soviets were dominated by a bloc of Mensheviks and Socialist-Revolutionaries, which was an instrument of bourgeois influence on the proletariat. Hence, the Party's task consisted in the following:

> "It must be explained to the masses that the Soviets of Workers' Deputies are the ONLY POSSIBLE form of revolutionary government, and that therefore our task is, as long as THIS government yields to the influence of the bourgeoisie, to present a patient, systematic, and persistent EXPLANATION of the errors of their tactics, an explanation especially adapted to the practical needs of the masses. As long as we are in the minority we carry on the work of criticizing and exposing errors and at the same time we preach the necessity of transferring the entire power of state to the Soviets of Workers' Deputies. . . ." (~~Lenin,~~ *I*bid., ~~Vol. XX,~~ p. 23.)

This meant that Lenin was not calling for a revolt against the Provisional Government, which at that moment enjoyed the confidence of the Soviets, that he was not demanding its overthrow, but that he wanted, by means of explanatory and recruiting work, to win a majority in the Soviets, to change the policy of the Soviets, and through the Soviets to alter the composition and policy of the government.

This was a line envisaging a peaceful development of the revolution.

Lenin further demanded that the "soiled shirt" be discarded, that is, that the Party no longer call itself a Social-Democratic Party. The parties of the Second International and the Russian Mensheviks called themselves Social-Democrats. This name had been tarnished and disgraced by the opportunists, the betrayers of Socialism. Lenin proposed that the Party of the Bolsheviks should be called the COMMUNIST PARTY, which was the name given by Marx and Engels to their party. This name was scientifically correct, for it was the ultimate aim of the Bolshevik Party to achieve Communism. Mankind can pass directly from capitalism only to Socialism, that is, to the common ownership of the means of production and the distribution of products according to the work performed by each. Lenin said that our Party looked farther ahead. Socialism was inevitably bound to pass gradually into Communism, on the banner of which is inscribed the maxim: "*From e*ach according to his abilities, to each according to his needs."

Lastly, Lenin ~~also posed the question of renewing the~~ *in his theses demanded the creation of a new* International, ~~that is,~~ the Third, Communist International, *which would be free of opportunism and social-chauvinism.*

Lenin's theses~~, which specifically defined the tasks of the revolution,~~ called forth a frenzied outcry from the bourgeoisie, the Mensheviks and the Socialist-Revolutionaries. ~~The entire Menshevik and bourgeois press fell upon Lenin and the Bolsheviks with the harshest of attacks, slander and accusations.~~

The Mensheviks issued a proclamation to the workers which began with the warning: "the revolution is in danger." The danger, in the opinion of the Mensheviks, lay in the fact that the Bolsheviks had advanced the ~~slogan "~~ALL POWER TO THE SOVIETS~~."~~ *demand for the transfer of power to the Soviets of Workers' and Soldiers' Deputies.*

Plekhanov in his newspaper, YEDINSTVO (UNITY), wrote an article in which he termed Lenin's speech a "RAVING SPEECH." He quoted the words of the Menshevik Chkheidze, who said: "Lenin alone will remain outside the revolution, and we shall go our own way." ~~What transpired, of course, was just the opposite. The revolution passed Plekhanov and Chkheidze by and followed Lenin and Stalin and the Bolshevik Party!~~

On April 14 a Petrograd City Conference[5] *of Bolsheviks* was held ~~which passed Lenin's theses; in its wake, other organizations also passed the theses~~. *The conference approved Lenin's theses and made them the basis of its work.*

Within a short while the local organizations of the Party approved Lenin's theses.

THE WHOLE PARTY, with the exception of a few ~~opportunists~~ *individuals of the type of Kamenev, Rykov and Pyatakov,*[6] received Lenin's theses with profound satisfaction ~~because they provided a brilliant plan for the struggle for victory in the Socialist revolution~~.

~~2.3. First Crisis of Power.~~ *Beginning of the Crisis of the Provisional Government.* April Conference *of the Bolshevik Party*

*While the Bolsheviks were preparing for the further development of the revolution, t*he ~~bourgeois~~ *Provisional* Government continued ~~in the meantime~~ to work *against the people*. On April 18, Milyukov, Minister of Foreign Affairs *in the Provisional Government*, informed the Allies that "the whole people desire to continue the World War until a decisive victory is achieved and that the Provisional Government intends fully to observe the obligations undertaken towards our allies."

Thus the ~~Russian capitalists and landlords~~ *Provisional Government* pledged ~~their~~ *its* loyalty to the tsarist treaties and promised to go on shedding as much of the people's blood as the imperialists might require for a "victorious finish."

On April 19 this statement ("Milyukov's note") became known to the workers and soldiers. On April 20 the Central Committee of the Bolshevik Party called upon the masses to protest against the imperialist policy of the ~~bourgeois~~ *Provisional* Government. On April 20–21 (May 3–4), 1917, not less than 100,000 workers and soldiers, *stirred to indignation by "Milyukov's note,"* took ~~to the street with slogans~~ *part in a demonstration. Their banners bore the demands*: "Publish the secret treaties!" "Down with the war!" "All power to the Soviets!" The workers and soldiers marched from the outskirts of the city to the centre, *where the Provisional Government was sitting*. On the Nevsky Prospect and other places clashes *with groups of bourgeois* took place.

The more outspoken counter-revolutionaries, like General Kornilov, demanded that fire be opened on the demonstrators, and even gave orders to that effect. But the troops refused to carry out the orders.

~~Demonstrations took place in Moscow and other cities.~~ During the demonstration, a *small* group of members of the Petrograd *Party* Committee (Bagdatyev and others) ~~released~~ *issued* a slogan demanding the immediate overthrow of the Provisional Government. The Central Committee of the Bolshevik Party sharply condemned the conduct of these "Left" ~~opportunists~~ *adventurers*, considering this slogan ~~premature~~ *untimely and incorrect*, a slogan that hampered the Party in its efforts to win over a majority in the Soviets ~~and the army~~ *and ran counter to the Party line of a peaceful development of the revolution.*

The events of April 20–21 signified the ~~FIRST CRISIS OF DUAL POWER~~ *beginning of the crisis of the Provisional Government.*

This was the first serious rift in the compromising policy of the Mensheviks and Socialist-Revolutionaries.

On May 2, 1917, under the pressure of the masses, Milyukov and Guchkov ~~left~~ *were dropped from* the Provisional Government.

The first COALITION ~~Ministry~~ *Provisional Government* was formed. It included, in addition to representatives of the bourgeoisie ~~and landlords~~, Mensheviks (Skobelev and Tsereteli) and Socialist-Revolutionaries (Chernov, Kerensky and others).

Thus the Mensheviks, who in 1905 had declared it impermissible for representatives of the Social-Democratic Party to take part in a REVOLUTIONARY *Provisional Government, now found it permissible for their representatives to take part in a* COUNTER-REVOLUTIONARY *Provisional Government.*

The Mensheviks and Socialist-Revolutionaries had thus deserted to the camp of the counter-revolutionary bourgeoisie.

On April 24, 1917, the Seventh (April) Conference of the Bolshevik Party assembled. For the first time ~~since the revolution~~ *in the existence of the Party* a Bolshevik Conference met openly. In the history of the Party this conference holds a place of importance equal to that of a Party Congress.

The All-Russian April Conference showed that the Party was growing by leaps and bounds. The conference was attended by 133 delegates with vote and by 18 with voice but no vote. They represented 80,000 organized members of the Party.

~~The number of Party members per organization varied thusly: Petrograd—16,000; Moscow—7,000; the Urals—16,000; Lugansk—1,500; Saratov—1,500; and Samara—2,700.~~

~~But there were also major workers' centres where Bolshevik organizations had not yet formed by that time, for instance in Sormovo and Tula.~~

> ~~"To the Russian proletariat," said Lenin, opening the conference, "has befallen the great honor of beginning this. But it must not forget that its movement and revolution comprise just one part of the worldwide proletarian revolutionary movement." (Lenin, Works, Russ. ed., Vol. XX, p. 239.)~~

The conference discussed and laid down the Party line on all basic questions of the *war and* revolution*:* ~~(~~*the current situation,* the war, the Provisional Government, the Soviets, the agrarian question, the national question, ~~and so on~~ *etc*~~)~~.

In his report, Lenin elaborated the principles he had already set forth in the April Theses. The task of the Party was to effect the transition from the first stage of the revolution, "which placed the power in the hands of the bourgeoisie . . . TO THE SECOND STAGE, which must place the power in the hands of the proletariat and the poorest strata of the peasantry" (LENIN). The course the Party should take was to prepare for the Socialist revolution. The ~~basic slogan~~ *immediate task of the Party* was set forth by Lenin in the slogan: "All power to the Soviets!"

The slogan, "All power to the Soviets!" meant that it was necessary to put an end to the dual power, that is, the division of power between the Provisional Government and the Soviets, to transfer the WHOLE POWER *to the Soviets, and to drive the representatives of the landlords and capitalists out of the organs of government.*

The conference resolved that one of the most important tasks of the Party was untiringly *to explain to the masses the truth that "the Provisional Government is by its nature an organ of the rule of the landlords and the bourgeoisie," as well as* to show ~~the masses the trickery and treachery of the Mensheviks and Socialist-Revolutionaries and to liberate the masses from the influence of these parties, which were aiding the bourgeoisie~~ *how fatal was the compromising policy of the Socialist-Revolutionaries and Mensheviks who were deceiving the people with false promises and subjecting them to the blows of the imperialist war and counter-revolution.*

Kamenev and Rykov opposed Lenin at the Conference. Echoing the Mensheviks, ~~these opportunists~~ *they* asserted that Russia was not ripe for a Socialist revolution, and that only a bourgeois republic was possible in Russia. They recommended the Party and the working class to confine themselves to "controlling" the Provisional Government. In reality, they, like the Mensheviks, stood ~~in this way~~ for the preservation of capitalism and of the power of the bourgeoisie.

Zinoviev, too, opposed Lenin at the conference; it was on the question whether the Bolshevik Party should remain within the Zimmerwald alliance, or ~~better,~~ break with it *and form a new International.* As the years of war had shown, *while* this alliance *carried on propaganda for peace, it did not* actually ~~was one~~ *break* with the *bourgeois* partisans of the war. Lenin therefore insisted on immediate withdrawal from this alliance and on the formation of a new, Communist International. Zinoviev ~~of course~~ proposed that the Party should remain within the Zimmerwald alliance. Lenin vigorously condemned[7] Zinoviev's proposal and called his tactics "arch-opportunist and pernicious."

The ~~Seventh All-Russian~~ April Conference also discussed the agrarian and national questions.

In connection with Lenin's report on the agrarian question, the conference ~~called upon the peasants to implement the seizure and immediate~~ *adopted a resolution calling for the* confiscation of the landed estates, which were to be placed at the disposal of the peasant ~~Soviets~~ *committees, and for the nationalization of all the land.* The Bolsheviks called upon the ~~revolutionary~~ peasants to fight for the land, showing them that the Bolshevik Party was the only revolutionary party, the only party that was really helping the peasants to ~~wage the fight with~~ *overthrow* the landlords. ~~The conference considered it imperative to create an organization of agricultural labourers and partial-proletarians in the countryside that would make the confiscated landed estates into model Soviet farms.~~

Of great importance was Comrade Stalin's report on the national question. Even before the revolution, *on the eve of the imperialist*[8] *war, Lenin and* Stalin ~~along with Lenin~~ had elaborated the fundamental principles of the ~~nationality~~ policy of the Bolshevik Party *on the national question*. Lenin and Stalin declared that the proletarian party~~, inasmuch as it is plotting the course toward the Socialist revolution,~~ must support the ~~revolutionary~~ national liberation movement of the *oppressed* peoples against imperialism. ~~Therefore~~ *Consequently*, the Bolshevik Party advocated the right of nations to self-determination even to the point of ~~complete~~ secession[9]~~, that is,~~ *and* formation of independent states. This was the view defended by Comrade Stalin, in his report delivered at the conference on behalf of the Central Committee.

Lenin and Stalin were opposed by Pyatakov, who, together with Bukharin, had already during the war taken up a ~~bourgeois~~ *national-chauvinist* stand on the national question. Pyatakov and Bukharin were opposed to the ~~Socialist revolution and against supporting revolutionary movements among the~~

~~oppressed nationalities. Therefore, they spoke out against the~~ right of nations to self-determination. ~~The Bukharin and Pyatakov line denied the proletariat its followers in the revolution and condemned the proletarian revolution to defeat.~~

The resolute and consistent position of the Party on the national question, its struggle for the complete equality of nations and for the abolition of all forms of national oppression and national ~~imparity~~ *inequality*, secured for the Party the sympathy and support of the oppressed nationalities~~, both in the period of struggle for the Socialist revolution and after the seizure of power in October 1917~~.

The text of the resolution on the national question adopted by the April Conference is as follows:

> *"The policy of national oppression, inherited from the autocracy and monarchy, is supported by the landlords, capitalists and petty bourgeoisie in order to protect their class privileges and to cause disunity among the workers of the various nationalities. Modern imperialism, which increases the striving to subjugate weak nations, is a new factor intensifying national oppression.*
>
> *"To the extent that the elimination of national oppression is achievable at all in capitalist society, it is possible only under a consistently democratic republican system and state administration that guarantee complete equality for all nations and languages.*
>
> *"The right of all the nations forming part of Russia freely to secede and form independent states must be recognized. To deny them this right, or to fail to take measures guaranteeing its practical realization, is equivalent to supporting a policy of seizure and annexation. It is only the recognition by the proletariat of the right of nations to secede that can ensure complete solidarity among the workers of the various nations and help to bring the nations closer together on truly democratic lines. . . .*
>
> *"The right of nations freely to secede must not be confused with the expediency of secession of a given nation at a given moment. The party of the proletariat must decide the latter question quite independently in each particular case from the standpoint of the interests of the social development as a whole and of the interests of the class struggle of the proletariat for Socialism.*
>
> *"The Party demands broad regional autonomy, the abolition of supervision from above, the abolition of a compulsory state language and the determination of the boundaries of the self-governing and autonomous regions by the local population itself in accordance with the economic and social conditions, the national composition of the population, and so forth.*

"The party of the proletariat resolutely rejects what is known as 'national cultural autonomy,' under which education, etc., is removed from the competence of the state and placed within the competence of some kind of national Diets. National cultural autonomy artificially divides the workers living in one locality, and even working in the same industrial enterprise, according to their various 'national cultures'; in other words it strengthens the ties between the workers and the bourgeois culture of individual nations, whereas the aim of the Social-Democrats is to develop the international culture of the world proletariat.

"The Party demands that a fundamental law shall be embodied in the constitution annulling all privileges enjoyed by any nation whatever and all infringements of the rights of national minorities.

"The interests of the working class demand that the workers of all the nationalities of Russia should have common proletarian organizations: political, trade union, educational institutions of the co-operatives and so forth. Only such common organizations of the workers of the various nationalities will make it possible for the proletariat to wage a successful struggle against international capital and bourgeois nationalism." (Lenin and Stalin, 1917, Eng. ed., pp. 118–19.)

Thus the ~~Seventh (~~April~~)~~ Conference exposed the opportunist, anti-Leninist stand of Kamenev, Zinoviev, Pyatakov, Bukharin, Rykov and their *small* following.

The ~~Party~~ *conference* unanimously supported Lenin ~~and Stalin~~ by taking up a precise stand on all important questions and adopting a course leading to the victory of the Socialist revolution.

3.~~4. Struggle of the Bolsheviks for the Masses~~ *Successes of the Bolshevik Party in the Capital. Abortive Offensive of the Armies of the Provisional Government. Suppression of the July Demonstration of Workers and Soldiers*

On the basis of the decisions of the April Conference, the Party developed extensive activities in order to win over the masses, and to train and organize them for battle. The Party line in that period was, by patiently explaining the Bolshevik policy and exposing the compromising policy of the Mensheviks and Socialist-Revolutionaries ~~with the bourgeoisie~~, to ~~separate them~~ *isolate these parties* from the masses and to win a majority in the Soviets.

~~In this period, the Party developed mass propaganda and agitation among the workers, soldiers, sailors and peasants.~~

In addition to the work in the Soviets, the Bolsheviks ~~worked~~ *carried on extensive activities* in the trade unions and in the factory committees.

Particularly extensive was the work of the Bolsheviks in the army. Military organizations began to arise everywhere. The Bolsheviks worked indefatigably at the front and in the rear to organize the soldiers and sailors. ~~The Bolsheviks did a lot to organize the Red Guard, especially in Petrograd and Moscow; they likewise organized work among female workers, playing an enormous role in the overthrow of tsardom and the victory of the revolution. It was at this time that the journal Rabotnitsa (Female Worker) began to be published.~~ *A particularly important part in making the soldiers active revolutionaries was played at the front by the Bolshevik newspaper, Okopnaya Pravda (Trench Truth).*

Thanks to Bolshevik propaganda and agitation, already in the early months of the revolution the workers in many cities held new elections to the Soviets, especially to the district Soviets, *drove out the Mensheviks and Socialist-Revolutionaries and elected followers of the Bolshevik Party in their stead.* ~~In this way, the Bolsheviks seized the Vyborg district Soviet and others in Petrograd. From below, the masses saw these new organizers, propagandists and agitators. Never had there ever been such a large number of popular mass assemblies and meetings at the factories and mills, the barracks and the ships, and in the streets and squares of the towns and villages.~~

~~The Bolsheviks, who actively took part in all the assemblies and meetings of the working people, tirelessly struggled with the compromisers—the Mensheviks and Socialist-Revolutionaries—unmasking their treachery and winning over the masses to their own side.~~

~~The bourgeois Provisional Government continued to conduct its old policies. And the popular masses felt the burden of war all the more sharply with each day, hated those responsible for the war all the more and all the more sought a way out of it. The continuing war and economic crisis hit the working class hardest of all. The capitalists led the attack on the workers. They answered the workers' strikes with lock-outs (mass firings of workers).~~

~~In May 1917, 108 enterprises were closed in Petrograd and 8,700 workers were fired. In June, 125 enterprises were closed and about 40,000 workers were fired. The Bolshevik slogan "Struggle for the Workers' Control of Production" caught up ever larger numbers of the working masses. Along with this grew the peasants' revolutionary movement. In June 1917, peasants in 43 provinces rose up against the landlords and the Provisional Government.~~

The work of the Bolsheviks yielded splendid results, especially in Petrograd.

A Petrograd Conference of Factory Committees was held from May 30 to June 3, 1917~~, at which~~. *At this conference* three-quarters of the delegates already supported the Bolsheviks. Almost the entire Petrograd proletariat supported the Bolshevik slogan—"All power to the Soviets!"

On June 3 (16), 1917, the First All-Russian Congress of Soviets met. The Bolsheviks were still in the minority *in the Soviets*; they had a little over 100 delegates *at this congress*, compared with 700 or 800 Mensheviks, ~~and~~ Socialist-Revolutionaries ~~of various stripes~~ *and others.*[10] ~~The Mensheviks and Socialist-Revolutionaries at this congress defended their alliance with the bourgeoisie and advanced their line supporting the Provisional Government; the speaker Tsereteli claimed that there was no party in the country that would say on behalf of a single class: "Give us power!" In Russia, there was no such party, declared Tsereteli. In the hush of the hall, Lenin's words were heard in answer to Tsereteli: "There is such a Party!" Lenin approached the tribune and said in response to Tsereteli that the party that "was ready to take power at any minute" was the Bolshevik Party.~~

At the First Congress of Soviets, the Bolsheviks insistently stressed the fatal consequences of compromise with the bourgeoisie and exposed the imperialist character of the war. Lenin made a speech at the congress in which he ~~strongly and persuasively indicated~~ *showed* the correctness of the Bolshevik line and declared that only a government of Soviets could give bread to the working people, land to the peasants, secure peace and lead the country out of chaos.

~~Under the pressure of the masses, who wanted to address their demands to the congress of Soviets,~~ *A mass campaign was being conducted at that time in the working-class districts of Petrograd for the organization of a demonstration and for the presentation of demands to the Congress of Soviets. In its anxiety to prevent the workers from demonstrating without its authorization, and in the hope of utilizing the revolutionary sentiments of the masses for its own ends, the Executive Committee of* the Petrograd Soviet ~~was forced~~ *decided* to call a demonstration for June 18 (July 1). *The Mensheviks and Socialist-Revolutionaries expected that it would take place under anti-Bolshevik slogans.* The Bolshevik Party began energetic preparations for this demonstration. Comrade Stalin wrote in PRAVDA that ". . . it is our task to make sure that the demonstration in Petrograd on June 18 takes place under our revolutionary slogans." ~~(STALIN).~~

The demonstration of June 18, 1917, was held at the graves of the martyrs of the revolution. It ~~was~~ *proved to be* a veritable review of the forces of the Bolshevik Party. It revealed the growing revolutionary spirit of the masses and their growing confidence in the Bolshevik Party. The slogans displayed by the Mensheviks and Socialist-Revolutionaries calling for confidence in the Provisional Government and urging the continuation of the war were lost in a sea of Bolshevik slogans. Four hundred thousand demonstrators ~~marched by~~ *carried banners* bearing the slogans: "Down with the war!" "Down with the ten capitalist Ministers!" "All power to the Soviets!"

It was a complete fiasco for the Mensheviks and Socialist-Revolutionaries, a fiasco for the Provisional Government in the capital of the country.

Nevertheless, the Provisional Government received the support of the First Congress of the Soviets and ~~with new energy~~ decided to continue the imperialist policy ~~and~~. On that very day, June 18, *the Provisional Government, in obedience to the wishes of*[11] *the British and French imperialists,* drove the soldiers at the front to take the offensive. The bourgeoisie regarded this as the only means of putting an end to the revolution. In the event of the success of the offensive, the bourgeoisie hoped to take the whole power into its own hands, *to push the Soviets out of the arena,* and to crush the Bolsheviks. Again, in the event of its failure, the entire blame could be thrown upon the Bolsheviks by accusing them of disintegrating the army. ~~The offensive was being demanded by the Allies, who threatened to stop supplying Russia with money.~~

~~The Russian army suffered a defeat at the front.~~

~~The defeat at the front, caused by the collapse of the economic and supply apparatus and by criminal carelessness and instances of treachery in the command staff, led to the weakening of the army and revolutionized the worker and peasant masses even more.~~ *There could be no doubt that the offensive would fail. And fail it did. The soldiers were worn out, they did not understand the purpose of the offensive, they had no confidence in their officers who were alien to them, there was a shortage of artillery and shells. All this made the failure of the offensive a foregone conclusion.*

The news of the offensive at the front, and then of its collapse, roused the capital. The indignation of the workers and soldiers knew no bounds. It became apparent that when the Provisional Government proclaimed a policy of peace it was hoodwinking the people, and that it wanted to continue the imperialist war. It became apparent that the All-Russian Central Executive Committee of the Soviets and the Petrograd Soviet were unwilling or unable to check the criminal deeds of the Provisional Government and themselves trailed in its wake. ~~In answer to this, the Cadets, Mensheviks and Socialist-Revolutionaries strengthened their persecution of Bolsheviks at the front and in the rear.~~

~~5. The Demonstration of July 3–5 and Its Suppression by the Provisional Government~~

~~The bourgeoisie's calculation was extremely simple: Summon the revolutionary masses onto the street, crush their uprising, defeat the Bolshevik Party and restore the monarchy to Russia. This was how the Parisian bourgeoisie proceeded in 1848.~~

~~But the Bolshevik Party guessed that this was their manoeuver. The Bolsheviks tried everything they could to restrain the masses from rising up, in order to wait until the tide of revolution rose not only in Petrograd, but also at the front and in the provinces. A premature uprising of only the Petrograd workers without the support of the front or the provinces would bring only harm to the revolution.~~

The revolutionary ~~impatience~~ *indignation* of the Petrograd workers and soldiers~~, however,~~ boiled over. On July 3 (16) spontaneous demonstrations started in the Vyborg District of Petrograd. They continued all day. The separate demonstrations grew into a huge general armed demonstration demanding the transfer of ~~all~~ power to the Soviets.[12] The Bolshevik Party was opposed to armed ~~revolt~~ *action* at that time ~~and was against the organization of an uprising~~, *for it considered that the revolutionary crisis had not yet matured, that the army and the provinces were not yet prepared to support an uprising in the capital, and that an isolated and premature rising might only make it easier for the counter-revolutionaries to crush the vanguard of the revolution*. But when it became obviously impossible to keep the masses from ~~revolting~~ *demonstrating*, the Party resolved to participate in ~~this~~ *the* demonstration in order to lend it a peaceful and organized character. This the Bolshevik Party succeeded in doing. Hundreds of thousands of men and women marched to the headquarters of the Petrograd Soviet and the All-Russian Central Executive Committee of Soviets, where they demanded ~~the rejection of the politics of compromise and an end to the war~~ *that the Soviets take the power into their own hands, break with the imperialist bourgeoisie, and pursue an active peace policy.*

Notwithstanding the pacific character of the demonstration, ~~troops loyal to the government~~ *reactionary units*—detachments of officers and cadets—were brought out against it. The streets of Petrograd ran with the blood of workers and soldiers. The most ~~backward~~ *ignorant and counter-revolutionary* units of the army ~~that were loyal to the government~~ were summoned from the front to suppress the workers.

After ~~dispersing~~ *suppressing* the demonstration of workers and soldiers, the Mensheviks and Socialist-Revolutionaries, in alliance with the bourgeoisie and Whiteguard *generals*, fell upon the Bolshevik Party. The Pravda premises were wrecked. Pravda, Soldatskaya Pravda (Soldiers' Truth) and a number of other Bolshevik newspapers were suppressed. A worker named Voinov was killed by cadets in the street *merely* for selling Listok Pravdy (Pravda Bulletin). Disarming of the Red Guards began. Revolutionary units of ~~troops~~ *the Petrograd garrison* were *withdrawn from the capital and* dispatched to the trenches. Arrests were carried out in the rear and at the front. On July 7 a ~~resolution~~ *warrant* was issued for Lenin's arrest. A number of prominent members of the Bolshevik Party were arrested. The Trud printing plant, *where the Bolshevik publications were printed*, was wrecked. The Procurator of the Petrograd Court of Sessions announced ~~about how~~ *that* Lenin and a number of other Bolsheviks were being charged with "*high* treason" and the organization of an armed uprising. The charge against Lenin was fabricated at the headquarters of General Denikin, and was based on the testimony of spies and agents-provocateurs.

Thus the coalition Provisional Government—which included such leading representatives of the Mensheviks and Socialist-Revolutionaries as Tsereteli, Skobelev, Kerensky and Chernov—sank to the depths of downright imperialism and counter-revolution. Instead of a policy of peace, it had adopted the policy of continuing war. Instead of protecting the democratic rights of the people, it had adopted the policy of nullifying these rights and suppressing the workers and soldiers by force of arms.

What Guchkov and Milyukov, the representatives of the bourgeoisie, had hesitated to do, was done by the "socialists" Kerensky and Tsereteli, Chernov and Skobelev.

The dual power had come to an end.

It ended in favour of the bourgeoisie, for the whole power had passed into the hands of the Provisional Government, while the Soviets, with their Socialist-Revolutionary and Menshevik leaders, had become an appendage of the Provisional Government.

The peaceful period of the revolution had ended, for now the bayonet had been placed on the agenda.

In view of the changed situation, the Bolshevik Party decided to change its tactics. It went underground, arranged for a safe hiding place for its leader, Lenin, and began to prepare for an uprising with the object of overthrowing the power of the bourgeoisie by force of arms and setting up the power of the Soviets.

~~With the aid of the Petrograd workers, Lenin hid in the outlying regions of Petrograd, near Razliv Station, before moving to Finland. Lenin communicated with the Party's Central Committee and Comrade Stalin through trusted intermediaries. Sergo Ordjonikidze came to visit Lenin. Lenin continued to lead the Party, passing his instructions through trusted people.~~

~~If Lenin had not gone into hiding, he would have been murdered just as the German Whiteguards and Mensheviks murdered Rosa Luxemburg and Karl Liebknecht in 1919.~~

~~The dual power of the Soviets and bourgeoisie was transformed after the July days into the singular power of the counter-revolutionary Provisional Government. Until July 4, a peaceful transfer of power to the Soviets had still been possible. Now, after all power had been seized by the Cadet-Black-Hundredist Gang, it would be possible to take power only by means of an armed uprising and civil war.~~

4.~~6.~~ The Bolshevik Party Adopts the Course of Preparing for Armed Uprising. Sixth Party Congress

The Sixth Congress of the Bolshevik Party met in Petrograd in the midst of a frenzied campaign of Bolshevik-baiting in the ~~entire~~ bourgeois and petty-bourgeois press. It assembled ten years after the Fifth (London) Congress and five years after the Prague Conference of the Bolsheviks. The congress, which was held ~~secretly~~ *illegally*, sat from July 26 to August 3, 1917. All that appeared in the ~~newspaper~~ *press* was an announcement of its convocation, the place of meeting was not divulged. ~~At first,~~ *The first* sittings were held in the Vyborg District, the later ones in a school near the Narva Gate, where a House of Culture now stands. The bourgeois press demanded the arrest of the delegates ~~and~~. *D*etectives frantically scoured the city trying to discover the meeting place of the congress, *but in vain*.

And so, five months after the overthrow of tsardom, the Bolsheviks were compelled to meet in secret, while Lenin, the leader of the proletarian party, was forced to go into hiding and took refuge in a shanty near Razliv Station. ~~Such was the "freedom" that reigned in the country after the July days.~~

He was being hunted high and low by the sleuths of the *Provisional* Government ~~of Kerensky~~ and was therefore unable to attend the congress; but he guided its labours from his place of concealment *through his close colleagues and disciples in Petrograd: Stalin, Sverdlov, Molotov, Ordjonikidze.* ~~Direct political leadership of the congress and the defence of the most important decisions of the Party fell to Comrade Stalin.~~

The congress was attended by 157 delegates with vote and 128 with voice but no vote. At that time the Party had a membership of about 240,000. On July 3, *i.e., before the workers' demonstration was broken up, when the Bolsheviks were still functioning legally,* the Party had 41 publications, of which 29 were in Russian and 12 in other languages.

The persecution to which the Bolsheviks and the working class were subjected during the July days, far from diminishing the influence of our Party, only enhanced it. The ~~speeches of~~ delegates from the provinces *cited numerous facts to* show~~ed~~ that the workers and soldiers had ~~ceased to believe~~ *begun to desert* the Mensheviks and Socialist-Revolutionaries *en masse*, ~~that the masses' revolutionary mood had grown and that the masses were increasingly united around the Bolshevik Party~~ *contemptuously styling them "social-jailers." Workers and soldiers belonging to the Menshevik and Socialist-Revolutionary parties were tearing up their membership cards in anger and disgust and applying for admission to the Bolshevik Party.*

The chief items discussed at the congress were ~~Comrade Stalin's reports:~~ the political report of the Central Committee and ~~the report on~~ the political situation. Comrade Stalin *made the reports on both these questions. He* showed with the utmost clarity how the revolution was growing and developing despite all the efforts of the bourgeoisie to suppress it. He pointed out that the revolution had placed on the order of the day the task of establishing workers' control over the production *and distribution of products*, of turning over the land to the peasants, and of transferring the power from the bourgeoisie to the ~~Soviets of workers' and soldiers' deputies~~ *working class and poor peasantry*~~, and~~. *He said* that the revolution was ~~taking on~~ *assuming* the character of a Socialist revolution.

The political situation in the country had changed radically after the July days. ~~Power had shifted dramatically to the right from the condition of an unstable equilibrium where it had been since the February Revolution: THE DUAL POWER OF THE PROVISIONAL GOVERNMENT AND SOVIETS SHIFTED TO THE SINGULAR POWER OF THE BOURGEOISIE. The government tried in every way to disarm the revolution and defeat the Bolsheviks.~~ *The dual power had come to an end. The Soviets, led by Socialist-Revolutionaries and Mensheviks, had refused to take over full power and had therefore lost all power. The power was now concentrated in the hands of the bourgeois Provisional Government, and the latter was continuing to disarm the revolution, to smash its organizations and to destroy the Bolshevik Party.* All possibility of a peaceful development of the revolution had vanished. ~~Leading the revolution forward became possible only through WRESTING POWER FROM THE BOURGEOISIE'S HANDS.~~ *Only one thing remained, Comrade Stalin said, namely, to take power by force, by overthrowing the Provisional Government.* And only ~~one class—~~the proletariat, ~~together~~ *in alliance* with the poor peasants, could take power by force.

The Soviets, still controlled by the Mensheviks and Socialist-Revolutionaries, had landed in the camp of the bourgeoisie, and ~~at that stage of the revolution~~ *under existing conditions* could be expected to act only as subsidiaries of the ~~counter-revolution~~ *Provisional Government*. Now, after the July days, *Comrade Stalin said,* the slogan "All power to the Soviets!" had to be ~~temporarily~~ withdrawn. However, the temporary withdrawal of this slogan did not in any way imply a renunciation of the struggle for the power of the Soviets. It was not the Soviets in general, as organs of revolutionary struggle, that were in question, but only the existing Soviets, the Soviets ~~which were in the grip of~~ *controlled by* the Mensheviks and Socialist-Revolutionaries. ~~And at that moment these Soviets did not want to take power and were unable to bring this revolutionary power into being.~~

> "The peaceful period of the revolution has ended," said Comrade Stalin, "a non-peaceful period has begun, a period of clashes and explosions." (Lenin and Stalin, 1917, Eng. ed., p. 302.)

The Party was headed ~~for Socialist revolution,~~ for armed uprising ~~against the bourgeoisie~~.

~~And at that decisive moment within the Party~~ There were some *at the congress* who, reflecting the bourgeois ~~and Menshevik~~ influence, opposed the adoption of the course of Socialist revolution. ~~Comrade Stalin rebuffed all the opponents of the proletarian Socialist revolution.~~

The Trotskyite Preobrazhensky~~, for instance,~~ proposed that the resolution on the ~~seizure~~ *conquest* of power should state that the country could be directed towards Socialism only in the event of a proletarian revolution in the West.

This Trotskyite motion was ~~sharply~~ opposed by Comrade Stalin. He ~~protested~~ *said*:

> "The possibility is not excluded that Russia will be the country that will lay the road to Socialism. . . . We must discard the antiquated idea that only Europe can show us the way. There is dogmatic Marxism and creative Marxism. I stand by the latter." (Ibid., p. 309.)

~~Comrade Stalin led the struggle at the congress on two fronts: on one side against the Trotskyites, who were working in league with Bukharin, and on the other, against the then Right Opportunists Rykov, Kamenev and others.~~ Bukharin, who held a Trotskyite position, asserted that the peasants supported the war, ~~and therefore~~ that they were in a bloc with the ~~imperialists~~ *bourgeoisie* and would not follow the ~~proletariat~~ *working class*.

> ~~"There are different kinds of peasants," Stalin replied to Bukharin. "There may be a bloc with the Rights, but there are also the lower peasants, who represent the poorest strata of the peasants. A bloc with them is impossible. They have not entered into a bloc with the major bourgeoisie, but follow them due to a lack of consciousness—they are being deceived and misled." (Verbatim Report of the Sixth Party Congress, Russ. ed., p. 138.)~~

Retorting to Bukharin, Comrade Stalin showed that there were different kinds of peasants: there were the rich peasants who supported the imperialist bourgeoisie, and there were the poor peasants who sought an alliance with the working class and would support it in a struggle for the victory of the revolution.

The congress rejected Preobrazhensky's and Bukharin's amendments and approved the resolution submitted by Comrade Stalin.

The congress discussed the economic platform of the Bolsheviks~~, every point of which was understood by the masses,~~ *and approved it. Its main points were t*he confiscation of the landed estates and the nationalization of all the land, the nationalization of the banks, ~~and~~ *the nationalization of* large-scale industry, and ~~establishment of genuine~~ workers' control *over production and distribution*~~—these were its main points. For their realization, the proletariat would have to seize power.~~

The congress stressed the importance of the fight for workers' control over production, which was later to play a significant part during the nationalization of the large industrial enterprises.[13]

In all its decisions, the Sixth Congress particularly stressed Lenin's ~~slogan~~ *principle* of an alliance between the proletariat and the poor peasantry ~~in the upcoming~~ *as a condition for the victory of the* Socialist revolution.

The ~~Sixth~~ *c*ongress ~~decisively spoke out against~~ *condemned* the Menshevik theory that the trade unions should be neutral.[14] It pointed out that the momentous tasks confronting the working class of Russia could be accomplished only if the trade unions remained militant class organizations ~~and waged their own struggle in tight cooperation with~~ *recognizing the political leadership of* the Bolshevik Party.

The congress adopted a resolution on the Youth Leagues, which at that time ~~(often on their own)~~ *frequently* sprang up ~~everywhere~~ *spontaneously*. As a result of the Party's subsequent efforts it succeeded in definitely securing the adherence of the*se* young organization*s* which became a reserve of the Party. ~~Everyone knows what an enormous role the Youth Leagues played in the revolution and in Socialist construction in the U.S.S.R.~~

The congress discussed whether Lenin should appear for trial. Kamenev, Rykov, Trotsky and others had held *even before the congress* that Lenin ought to appear before the counter-revolutionary court. ~~Even before the congress,~~ Comrade Stalin *was* vigorously opposed *to* Lenin's appearing for trial. ~~After Comrade Ordjonikidze's report,~~ *T*his was also the stand of the Sixth Congress, *for it considered that it would be a lynching, not a trial.* The congress ~~was decisively against taking a risk with this court, as~~ *had no doubt that* the bourgeoisie ~~doubtlessly~~ wanted only one thing—the physical destruction of Lenin as the most dangerous enemy of the bourgeoisie. The congress protested against the police persecution of the leaders of the revolutionary proletariat by the bourgeoisie, and sent a message of greeting to Lenin.

The Sixth Congress adopted new Party Rules. These rules provided that all Party organizations *shall* be built on the principle of DEMOCRATIC CENTRALISM.

This ~~means~~ *meant*:

1) That all directing bodies of the Party, from top to bottom, shall be elected;

2) That Party bodies shall give periodical accounts of their activities to their respective Party organizations;

3) That there shall be strict Party discipline and the subordination of the minority to the majority;

4) That all decisions of higher bodies shall be absolutely binding on lower bodies and on all Party members.

~~The principle of Democratic Centralism was already provided for by the decisions of the First Bolshevik Conference of the R.S.D.L.P. (December 1905).~~

~~But in the conditions of the Party's illegal existence, it had not been able to fully implement the principle.~~

The Party Rules provided that admission of new members to the Party shall be through local Party organizations on the recommendation of two Party members and on the sanction of a general membership meeting of the local organization.

The Sixth Congress admitted the MEZHRAYONTSI and *their leader,* Trotsky, into the Party. They were a *small* group that had existed in Petrograd since 1913 and consisted of *Trotskyite*-Mensheviks and a number of former Bolsheviks who had split away from the Party. During the war, the MEZHRAYONSTI were a Centrist organization. They fought the Bolsheviks ~~slogans about the transformation of the world war into a civil war, against the slogan calling for the defeat of the tsarist government in the war, and they denied the possibility of the victory of Socialism in Russia,~~ *but in many respects disagreed with the Mensheviks, thus occupying an intermediate, centrist, vacillating position*. During the *Sixth* Party *C*ongress the MEZHRAYONSTI ~~organization~~ declared that they were in agreement with the Bolsheviks on all points and requested admission to the Party. *The request was granted by the congress in the expectation that they would in time become real Bolsheviks. Some of the MEZHRAYONSTI, Volodarsky and Uritsky, for example, actually did become Bolsheviks. As to Trotsky and some of his close friends, they, as it later became apparent, had joined not to work in the interests of the Party, but to disrupt and destroy it from within.* ~~But, as it transpired, Trotsky deceived the Party and joined in order to drag in with him his Menshevik baggage. He "hid" his Menshevik weapon "out of sight," saving it for a rainy day, and later would frequently wield it against the Bolshevik Party until he was expelled from the Party (at the end of 1927) and exiled from the Land of Soviets (1929) as an enemy of the revolution and a counter-revolutionary.~~

The decisions of the Sixth Congress were all intended to prepare the proletariat and the poorest peasantry for an armed uprising. The Sixth Congress headed the Party for armed uprising, for the Socialist revolution.

The congress issued a Party manifesto calling upon the workers, soldiers and peasants to muster their forces for decisive battles with the bourgeoisie. It ended with the words:

> "Prepare, then, for new battles, comrades-in-arms! Staunchly, manfully and calmly, without yielding to provocation, muster your forces and form your fighting columns! Rally under the banner of the Party, proletarians and soldiers! Rally under our banner, down-trodden of the villages!"~~—called out the congress manifesto. The congress delegates left for home in order to prepare the workers and peasants for the completion of the Socialist Revolution.~~

5.~~7.~~ *General* Kornilov's Plot ~~and Its~~ *against the Revolution.* Suppression *of the Plot. Petrograd and Moscow Soviets Go Over to the Bolsheviks*

Having ~~come to power~~ *seized all power*[15] ~~with the aid of the Mensheviks and Socialist-Revolutionaries~~, the bourgeoisie ~~prepared~~ *began preparations*[16] to destroy ~~and disperse~~ the *now weakened* Soviets and to set up an open counter-revolutionary dictatorship. The millionaire Ryabushinsky insolently declared that the way out of the situation was "for the gaunt hand of famine, of destitution of the people, to seize the false friends of the people—the democratic Soviets and Committees—by the throat." At the front, courts-martial wreaked savage vengeance on the soldiers, and meted out death sentences wholesale. On August 3, 1917, General Kornilov, the Commander-in-Chief, demanded the introduction of the death penalty behind the lines as well.

On August 12, a Council of State, convened by the Provisional Government to mobilize the forces of the bourgeoisie and the landlords, opened in the Grand Theatre in Moscow~~, which~~. *The Council* was attended chiefly by representatives of the landlords, the bourgeoisie, *the generals,* ~~and~~ the officers *and Cossacks.* The Soviets were represented ~~at the Council of State~~ by Mensheviks and Socialist-Revolutionaries.

In protest against the convocation of the Council of State ~~in Moscow on August 12 (25)~~, the Bolsheviks on the day of its opening called a general strike *in Moscow* in which the majority of the workers ~~participated~~ *took part*. Simultaneously, strikes took place in a number of other cities.

~~In his speech at the meeting,~~ *T*he Socialist-Revolutionary Kerensky threatened *in a fit of boasting at the Council* to suppress "by iron and blood" *every attempt at a revolutionary movement, including* unauthorized attempts of the peasants to seize the lands of the landlords ~~before the decision of the Constituent Assembly~~.

The counter-revolutionary General Kornilov bluntly ~~proposed~~ *demanded* that "the Committees and Soviets be abolished."

Bankers, merchants and manufacturers flocked to Kornilov at General Headquarters, promising him money and support.

Representatives of the "Allies," *Britain and France,* also came to General Kornilov, demanding ~~quick~~ *that* action against the revolution *be not delayed.*

General Kornilov's plot against the revolution was coming to a head.

Kornilov ~~conspired and~~ made his preparations openly. In order to distract attention, the conspirators started a rumour that the Bolsheviks ~~would revolt~~ *were preparing an uprising* in Petrograd *to take place* on August 27—the end of the first six months of the revolution. The Provisional Government, headed by Kerensky, furiously attacked the Bolsheviks, and intensified the terror against the proletarian party. At the same time, General Kornilov massed troops in order to move them against Petrograd, ~~defeat the workers,~~ abolish the Soviets ~~and all worker organizations (first of all the Bolshevik ones)~~ and set up a ~~counter-revolutionary government~~ *military dictatorship*.

Kornilov had come to a preliminary agreement with Kerensky regarding his counter-revolutionary action. But no sooner had Kornilov's action begun than Kerensky made an abrupt right-about-face and dissociated himself from his ally. Kerensky ~~was frightened~~ *feared* that the masses who would rise against the Kornilovites and crush them would at the same time sweep away Kerensky's bourgeois government as well, unless it *at once* dissociated itself from the Kornilov affair. ~~Aside from that, Kerensky feared that Kornilov would appoint himself dictator.~~

On August 25 Kornilov moved the Third Mounted Corps under the command of General Krymov against Petrograd, declaring that he ~~wanted~~ *intended* to "save the fatherland." In face of the Kornilov ~~advance~~ *revolt*, the Central Committee of the Bolshevik Party called upon the workers and soldiers ~~not only in Petrograd, but in other cities~~ to put up active armed resistance to the counter-revolution. The workers hurriedly began to arm and prepared to resist. The Red Guard detachments grew enormously during these days. The trade unions mobilized their members. The revolutionary military units in Petrograd were also held in readiness for battle. Trenches were dug around Petrograd, barbed wire entanglements erected, and the railway tracks leading to the city were torn up. Several thousand armed sailors arrived from Kronstadt to defend the city. Delegates were sent to the "Savage Division" which was advancing on Petrograd ~~at the suggestion of S. M. Kirov~~; when these delegates explained the purpose of ~~this counter-revolutionary~~ *Kornilov's* action to the Caucasian mountaineers of whom the "Savage Division" was made up, they refused to advance. Agitators were also dispatched to other Kornilov units. Wherever there was danger, Revolutionary Committees and headquarters were set up to fight Kornilov.

In those days the mortally terrified Socialist-Revolutionary and Menshevik leaders, Kerensky among them, turned for protection to the Bolsheviks, for they were convinced that the Bolsheviks were the only effective force in the capital that was capable of routing Kornilov.

But while mobilizing the masses to crush the Kornilov revolt, the Bolsheviks did not ~~weaken~~ *discontinue* their struggle against the Kerensky government. They exposed the government of Kerensky, the Mensheviks and the Socialist-Revolutionaries, to the masses, pointing out that their whole policy was *in effect* assisting Kornilov's counter-revolutionary plot.

*The result of these measures was that t*he Kornilov revolt was crushed. General Krymov committed suicide. Kornilov and his fellow-conspirators, Denikin and Lukomsky, were arrested. (Very soon, however, Kerensky ~~let them go~~ *had them released*.)

~~The struggle with the Kornilov revolt elevated the authority and influence of the Bolshevik Party among the masses. The masses recognized their power. They saw clearly what sort of terrible danger was bearing down on the revolution from the direction of the landlords, bourgeoisie and generals, who supported the compromiser-Mensheviks and Socialist-Revolutionaries. After the Kornilov mutiny, the masses quickly slipped out from under the influence of the Mensheviks and Socialist-Revolutionaries.~~

The rout of the Kornilov revolt revealed in a flash the relative strength of the revolution and the counter-revolution. It showed that the whole counter-revolutionary camp was doomed, from the generals and the Constitutional-Democratic Party to the Mensheviks and Socialist-Revolutionaries who had become entangled in the meshes of the bourgeoisie. It became obvious that the influence of the Mensheviks and Socialist-Revolutionaries among the masses had been completely undermined by the policy of prolonging the unbearable strain of the war, and by the economic chaos caused by the protracted war.

The defeat of the Kornilov revolt further showed that the Bolshevik Party had grown to be the decisive force of the revolution and was capable of foiling any attempt at counter-revolution. Our Party was not yet the ruling party, but during the Kornilov days it acted as the real ruling power, for its instructions were unhesitatingly carried out by the workers and soldiers.

Lastly, the rout of the Kornilov revolt showed that the seemingly dead Soviets actually possessed tremendous latent power of revolutionary resistance. There could be no doubt that it was the Soviets and their Revolutionary Committees that barred the way of the Kornilov troops and broke their strength.

~~8. Organization of the Storm (September–October 1917)~~

~~THE REVOLUTIONARY CRISIS IN THE COUNTRY WAS INCREASING. By the fall, the economic collapse sharpened. Petrograd and Moscow received 30 per cent of the necessary amount of coal. For August and September, another 231 enterprises were closed and 61,000 workers were fired. The workers were starving. Not only did the strikes not cease, but they took on an even greater, more militant character. In the article "The Threatening Catastrophe and How to Struggle with It," Lenin wrote that the drawn-out war, and the hunger, ruin and poverty of the masses were the result of the policies of the Provisional Government.~~

~~The influence of the Bolshevik Party quickly grew and strengthened within the working class, peasantry and army. At the end of July, at the All-Russian Conference of Trade Unions, the Bolsheviks made up about a third of the delegates—36.6 per cent—and in September at the Democratic Assembly, there were 69 Bolsheviks out of 120 delegates (57.5 per cent).~~

The struggle against Kornilov put new vitality into the languishing Soviets of Workers' and Soldiers' Deputies. It freed them from the sway of the policy of compromise. It led them into the open road of revolutionary struggle, and turned them towards the Bolshevik Party.

The influence of the Bolsheviks in the Soviets grew stronger than ever.

Their influence spread rapidly in the rural districts as well.

The Kornilov revolt made it clear to the broad masses of the peasantry that if the ~~landlord-generals~~ *landlords and generals* succeeded in smashing *the Bolsheviks and* the Soviets, they would *next* attack the peasantry. ~~This is why the poor and middle strata of the peasantry began to come over to the side of the Bolsheviks. They understood that only the proletarian party could follow through with the revolution, crush the landlords and turn over the land to the peasants.~~ *The mass of the poor peasants therefore began to rally closer to the Bolsheviks. As to the middle peasants, whose vacillations had retarded the development of the revolution in the period from April to August 1917, after the rout of Kornilov they definitely began to swing towards the Bolshevik Party, joining forces with the poor peasants. The broad masses of the peasantry were coming to realize that only the Bolshevik Party could deliver them from the war, and that only this Party was capable of crushing the landlords and was prepared to turn over the land to the peasants.* The months of September and October 1917 witnessed a tremendous increase in the number of seizures of landed estates by the peasants. ~~The DESTRUCTION of the landed estates was under way.~~ *Unauthorized ploughing of the fields of landlords became widespread.* The peasants had taken the road of revolution and neither coaxing nor ~~the~~ punitive expeditions ~~that the Socialist-Revolutionary Kerensky and his bourgeois government was sending~~ could any longer halt them.

The tide of revolution was rising.[17]

~~The struggle with the Kornilov revolt gave the Bolsheviks the possibility of strengthening not only the military organizations and the Red Guard, but their influence in the Soviets. The Soviets in Petrograd, Moscow and an array of other cities became Bolshevik. The Party began to win over the regional Soviets.~~ *There ensued a period of revival of the Soviets, of a change in their composition, their BOLSHEVIZATION.* Factories, mills and military units held new elections and sent to the Soviets representatives of the Bolshevik Party in place of Mensheviks and Socialist-Revolutionaries. On August 31, the day following the victory over Kornilov, the Petrograd Soviet ~~passed a Bolshevik resolution~~ *endorsed the Bolshevik policy*. The old Menshevik and Socialist-Revolutionary Presidium of the *Petrograd* Soviet, *headed by Chkheidze*, resigned, *thus clearing the way for the Bolsheviks*. On September 5, the Moscow Soviet *of Workers' Deputies* ~~passed Bolshevik decisions~~ *went over to the Bolsheviks*. The Socialist-Revolutionary and Menshevik Presidium of the Moscow Soviet also resigned and left the way clear for the Bolsheviks. ~~An array of provincial Soviets (Ivanovo-Voznesensk, Lugansk) had already been won over by the Bolsheviks. The major cities' Soviets had become Bolshevik.~~

This meant that the chief conditions for a successful uprising were now ripe.

The slogan "All power to the Soviets!" was again on the order of the day.

But~~, as we already know,~~ it was no longer the old slogan, the slogan of transferring the power to Menshevik and Socialist-Revolutionary[18] Soviets. This time it was a slogan calling for an uprising[19] *of the Soviets against the Provisional Government*, the object being to transfer the *whole* power in the country to the BOLSHEVIK Soviets~~, which were in the hands of the proletariat and the poor peasantry~~ *now led by the Bolsheviks*.

Disintegration set in among the compromising parties.

Under the pressure of the revolutionary peasants, a Left wing formed within the Socialist-Revolutionary Party, known as the "Left" Socialist Revolutionaries, who expressed their disapproval of the policy of compromise with the bourgeoisie.

Among the Mensheviks, too, there appeared a group of "Lefts," the so-called "Internationalists," who gravitated towards the Bolsheviks.

~~The Mensheviks and the Socialist-Revolutionaries as a whole transformed from compromising petty-bourgeois parties into counter-revolutionary BOURGEOIS parties even before the October Revolution. Evaluating the counter-revolutionary policies of the Mensheviks after the July days, the Sixth Bolshevik Party Congress held that the Mensheviks "had crossed over to the camp of the enemies of the proletariat once and for all." (RESOLUTIONS OF THE C.P.S.U.[B], Russ. ed., Vol. 1, p. 269.) The Socialist-Revolutionary Party also crossed over to the bourgeois camp, once and for all.~~

~~The Bolsheviks waged a merciless struggle not only against the Socialist-Revolutionaries and Mensheviks, but against the Anarchists as well. What position did the Anarchists and the largest of their organizations, the Anarcho-Syndicalists, occupy during the imperialist war? Lenin called the Anarchists' leader, Prince Kropotkin and others, "social trench-diggers," because they helped the bourgeois drive the workers into the trenches and were defenders of the war.~~

~~During the period of the October Revolution, individual anarchists and their groups took part in the overthrow of the bourgeoisie and landlords. But the "Federation of Anarchists" contacted the Whiteguard general staff at this time and conducted negotiations concerning a joint struggle against the Bolsheviks and the Soviet Power, as they had in Moscow. The Anarchists interfered with the fighters' ranks, directing their attention chiefly to theft. The Anarchists freed criminals from prison, and these elements flowed into the Anarchist organizations.~~

~~Although opponents of any sort of state power, the Anarchists also struggled against the proletarian dictatorship. Seizing rich palaces, the Anarchists led raids on government institutions, seizing arms, which they passed on to enemies of the Soviet power. During the Civil War years, the Anarchists assisted the Whiteguards.~~

As to the Anarchists, a group whose influence was insignificant to start with, they now definitely disintegrated into minute groups, some of which merged with criminal elements, thieves and provocateurs, the dregs of society; others became expropriators "by conviction," robbing the peasants and small townfolk, and appropriating the premises and funds of workers' clubs; while others still openly went over to the camp of the counter-revolutionaries, and devoted themselves to feathering their own nests as menials of the bourgeoisie. They were all opposed to authority of any kind, particularly and especially to the revolutionary authority of the workers and peasants, for they knew that a revolutionary government would not allow them to rob the people and steal public property.

~~This is why it was imperative for the proletarian revolution to struggle against the Anarchists, as they took the side of the enemies of the Soviet power during the period of the proletarian dictatorship.~~

~~On the eve of the October Revolution,~~ *After the rout of Kornilov,* the Mensheviks and Socialist-Revolutionaries made one more attempt to stem the rising ~~movement~~ *tide* of revolution. With this purpose in view, on September 12, 1917, they convened an All-Russian Democratic Conference, consisting of representatives of *the Socialist parties,* the compromising Soviets, trade unions, Zemstvos, commercial and industrial circles and military ~~organizations~~ *units.* The conference set up a Provisional Council of the Republic, known as the Pre-parliament. *The compromisers hoped with the help of the Pre-parliament to halt the revolution and to divert the country from the path of a Soviet revolution to the path of bourgeois constitutional development, the path of bourgeois parliamentarism. But this was a hopeless attempt on the part of political bankrupts to turn back the wheel of revolution. It was bound to end in a fiasco, and end in a fiasco it did.* As a joke, the workers *jeered at the parliamentary efforts of the compromisers and* called ~~it~~ *the* PREDPARLAMENT *(Pre-parliament)* a "PREDBANNIK" ("pre-bath-house").

The ~~Bolsheviks~~ *Central Committee of the Bolshevik Party* decided to boycott the Pre-parliament. True, ~~they did not do this immediately, but after some wavering the Bolshevik faction did walk out of the Pre-parliament~~ *the Bolshevik group in the Pre-parliament, consisting of people like Kamenev and Teodorovich, were loath to leave it, but the Central Committee of the Party compelled them to do so.*

Kamenev *and Zinoviev* stubbornly insisted on participation in the Pre-parliament, striving thereby to divert the Party from its preparations for the uprising. Comrade Stalin, speaking at a meeting of the Bolshevik group *of the All-Russian Democratic Conference*, vigorously opposed participation in the Pre-parliament. He called the Pre-parliament a "Kornilov abortion."

Lenin and Stalin considered that it would be a grave mistake to participate in the Pre-parliament even for a short time, for it might encourage in the masses the false ~~understanding~~ *hope* that the Pre-parliament could really do something for the working people.

At the same time, the Bolsheviks made intensive preparations for the convocation of the Second Congress of Soviets, *in which they expected to have a majority*. Under the pressure of the Bolshevik Soviets, and notwithstanding the subterfuges of the Mensheviks and Socialist-Revolutionaries *on the All-Russian Central Executive Committee,* the Second All-Russian Congress of Soviets was called for the second half of October 1917.

6.9. ~~Preparation and Carrying-Out of the Armed Uprising.~~ *October Uprising in Petrograd and Arrest of the Provisional Government. Second Congress of Soviets and Formation of the Soviet Government. Decrees of the Second Congress of Soviets on Peace and Land.* Victory of the ~~October~~ Socialist Revolution. *Reasons for the Victory of the Socialist Revolution*[20]

~~After the Sixth Party Congress the Bolsheviks more energetically prepared for the armed uprising. At the end of September, Lenin wrote that the crisis had matured and that it was imperative to carefully prepare for the armed uprising.~~ *The Bolsheviks began intensive preparations for the uprising.* Lenin declared that, having secured a majority in the Soviets of Workers' and Soldiers' Deputies in both the capitals—Moscow and Petrograd—the Bolsheviks could and should take the state power into their own hands. Reviewing the path that had been traversed, Lenin stressed the fact that "the majority of the people are FOR us." In his articles and letters to the Central Committee and the Bolshevik organizations, Lenin ~~spoke in detail about~~ *outlined a detailed plan for* the uprising showing how the army units, the navy and the Red Guards should be used, ~~and~~ what key positions in Petrograd should be seized in order to ensure the success of the uprising, *and so forth*. ~~At this time, Stalin persistently explained to the workers and peasants through PRAVDA that there was no other way out aside from carrying out a Socialist revolution and transferring power into the hands of the Soviets.~~

On October 7, Lenin secretly[21] arrived in Petrograd from Finland ~~in order to personally lead the uprising~~. On October 10, 1917, the historic meeting of the Central Committee *of the Party* took place at which it was decided to launch the ~~revolutionary~~ *armed* uprising within the next few days. The historic resolution *of the Central Committee of the Party*, drawn up by Lenin, stated:

"The Central Committee recognizes that the international position of the Russian revolution (the revolt in the German navy which is an extreme manifestation of the growth throughout Europe of the world Socialist revolution; the threat of conclusion of peace by the imperialists with the object of strangling the revolution in Russia) as well as its military position (the indubitable decision of the Russian bourgeoisie and Kerensky and Co. to surrender Petrograd to the Germans), and the fact that the proletarian party has gained a majority in the Soviets—all this, taken in conjunction with the peasant revolt and the swing of popular confidence towards our Party (the elections in Moscow), and, finally, the obvious preparations being made for a second Kornilov affair (the withdrawal of troops from Petrograd, the dispatch of Cossacks to Petrograd, the surrounding of Minsk by Cossacks, etc.)—all this places the armed uprising on the order of the day.

"Considering therefore that an armed uprising is inevitable, and that the time for it is fully ripe, the Central Committee instructs all Party organizations to be guided accordingly, and to discuss and decide all practical questions (the Congress of Soviets of the Northern Region, the withdrawal of troops from Petrograd, the action of our people in Moscow and Minsk, etc.) from this point of view." (Lenin, SELECTED WORKS, Vol. VI, p. 303.)

Two ~~traitors~~ *members of the Central Committee*, Kamenev and Zinoviev, spoke and voted against this historic decision. Like the Mensheviks, they dreamed of a bourgeois parliamentary republic, and slandered the working class *by asserting* that it was not strong enough to carry out a Socialist revolution ~~and~~, *that* it was not mature enough to take power.

Although at this meeting Trotsky did not vote against the resolution directly, he ~~was actually against the armed uprising~~ *moved an amendment which would have reduced the chances of the uprising to nought and rendered it abortive.* He proposed that the uprising should not be started before the Second Congress of Soviets met, ~~which gave the Provisional Government the chance to get organized and destroy the revolutionary proletariat and its party~~ *a proposal which meant delaying the uprising, divulging its date, and forewarning the Provisional Government.*

The Central Committee of the Bolshevik Party sent its representatives to the Donetz Basin, the Urals, Helsingfors, Kronstadt, the South-Western Front and other places *to organize the uprising*. Comrades Voroshilov, *Molotov, Dzerzhinsky,*[22] Ordjonikidze, Kirov, Kaganovich, Kuibyshev, Frunze, *Yaroslavsky* and others were specially assigned by the Party to direct the uprising in the provinces. Comrade Zhdanov carried on the work among the armed forces in

Shadrinsk, in the Urals. Comrade Yezhov made preparations for an uprising of the soldiers on the Western Front, in Byelorussia.[23] The representatives of the Central Committee acquainted the leading members of the Bolshevik organizations in the provinces with the plan of the uprising and mobilized ~~the organizations~~ *them* in readiness to support the *uprising in* Petrograd ~~proletariat. The Party Central Committee distributed the responsibilities for the regions and provinces in the preparation for the uprising.~~

On the instructions of the Central Committee *of the Party*, a REVOLUTIONARY MILITARY COMMITTEE of the Petrograd Soviet was set up. This body became the legally functioning headquarters of the uprising.

Meanwhile the counter-revolutionaries, too, were hastily ~~mobilizing~~ *mustering* their forces. The officers of the army ~~mobilized into a counter-revolutionary officers' league~~ *formed a counter-revolutionary organization known as the Officers' League*. Everywhere the counter-revolutionaries set up headquarters for the formation of shock-battalions. By the end of October the counter-revolutionaries had 43 shock battalions ~~and one division~~ at their command. Special battalions of Cavaliers of the Cross of St. George were formed.

Kerensky's government *considered the question of transferring the seat of government from Petrograd to Moscow. This made it clear that it* was preparing to surrender Petrograd to the Germans in order to forestall the ~~Socialist Revolution~~ *uprising in the city. The protest of the Petrograd workers and soldiers compelled the Provisional Government to remain in Petrograd.*

On October 16 an enlarged meeting of the Central Committee of the ~~Bolshevik~~ Party was held. This meeting elected a ~~Revolutionary-Military-Fighting~~ *PARTY* CENTRE, headed by Comrade Stalin, to direct the uprising. This *Party* ~~Fighting~~ Centre was the leading core of the Revolutionary Military Committee of the Petrograd Soviet and had practical direction of the whole uprising.

At the meeting of the Central Committee the capitulators Zinoviev and Kamenev again opposed the uprising. Meeting with a rebuff, they came out openly in the ~~gravest treason~~ *press against the uprising,* against the Party. On October 18 the Menshevik newspaper, NOVAYA ZHIZN, printed a ~~treacherous notice~~ *statement* by Kamenev and Zinoviev declaring that the Bolsheviks were making preparations for an uprising, and that they (Kamenev and Zinoviev) considered it an adventurous gamble. ~~Both traitors~~ *Kamenev and Zinoviev thus* disclosed to the enemy the ~~Bolsheviks' plan~~ *decision of the Central Committee regarding the uprising, they revealed that an uprising had been planned to take place within a few days*. This was ~~explicit~~ treachery. Lenin wrote ~~about it~~ *in this connection*: "Kamenev and Zinoviev have BETRAYED the decision of the Central Committee *of their Party on the armed uprising*[24] to Rodzyanko and Kerensky." Lenin ~~proposed expelling the strikebreakers~~ *put before the Central Committee the question of Zinoviev's and Kamenev's expulsion* from the Party.

~~Informed by the strikebreakers, the traitors Kamenev and Zinoviev~~ *Forewarned by the traitors*, the ~~class enemy~~ *enemies of the revolution* at once began to take measures to *prevent the uprising and to* ~~quickly~~ destroy the *directing* staff of the revolution—the Bolshevik Party. The Provisional Government called a secret meeting which decided upon measures for combating the Bolsheviks. On October 19 the Provisional Government hastily summoned troops from the front to Petrograd. The streets were *heavily* patrolled. The counter-revolutionaries succeeded in massing especially large forces in Moscow. The Provisional Government drew up a plan: on the eve of the *Second* Congress of Soviets the Smolny—*the headquarters of the Bolshevik Central Committee*—was to be attacked and occupied and the Bolshevik ~~organization~~ *directing centre* destroyed. For this purpose the government summoned to Petrograd troops in whose loyalty it believed.

But the days and even the hours of the Provisional Government were already numbered. Nothing could now halt the victorious march of the ~~October~~ Socialist ~~proletarian~~ revolution.

On October 21 *the Bolsheviks sent* commissars of the Revolutionary Military Committee ~~were sent~~ to all revolutionary army units. Throughout the remaining days before the uprising energetic preparations for action were made in the army units and in the mills and factories. Precise instructions were also issued to the warships AURORA and ZARYA SVOBODY.

At a meeting of the Petrograd Soviet, Trotsky ~~followed Kamenev and Zinoviev~~ *in a fit of boasting* ~~and~~ blabbed to the enemy the date ~~of the~~ *on which the Bolsheviks had planned to begin the armed* uprising. In order not to allow Kerensky's government to ~~organize his forces and launch an offensive, on the night of October 24–25 the armed uprising was carried out according to Lenin's and Stalin's plans~~ *frustrate the uprising, the Central Committee of the Party decided to start and carry it through before the appointed time, and set its date for the day before the opening of the Second Congress of Soviets.*

Kerensky began his attack on the early morning of October 24 (November 6) ~~with the closure~~ *by ordering the suppression* of the central organ of the Bolshevik Party, RABOCHY PUT (WORKERS' PATH), ~~(PRAVDA)~~, *and the dispatch of armoured cars to its editorial premises and to the printing plant of the Bolsheviks.* By ~~11~~ *10* a.m., however, on the instructions of Comrade Stalin, Red Guards and revolutionary soldiers *pressed back the armoured cars and* placed a ~~patrol at~~ *reinforced guard over* the printing plant *and the* RABOCHY PUT *editorial offices. Towards 11 a.m.* RABOCHY PUT came out with a call[25] for the OVERTHROW of the Provisional Government. Simultaneously, on the instructions of the Party ~~Revolutionary-Military Fighting~~ Centre *of the uprising*, ~~specially prepared~~ detachments *of revolutionary soldiers and Red Guards* were rushed to the Smolny.

The uprising had begun.

On the night of October 24 Lenin arrived at the Smolny and assumed personal direction of the uprising. All that night *revolutionary* units *of the army* and detachments of the Red Guard kept arriving at the Smolny. The Bolsheviks directed them to the centre *of the capital*, to surround the Winter Palace, where the Provisional Government ~~had locked itself away~~ *had entrenched itself.*

On October 25 (November 7), Red Guards and revolutionary troops occupied the ~~main government institutions in Petrograd:~~ railway stations, post office, telegraph office, ~~the telegraph agency,~~ *the Ministries* and the State Bank.

The Pre-parliament was dissolved.

The Smolny, the headquarters of the Petrograd Soviet *and of the Bolshevik Central Committee*, became the headquarters of the revolution, from which all fighting orders emanated.

The Petrograd workers in those days showed what a splendid schooling they had received under the guidance of the Bolshevik Party. The revolutionary units of the army, prepared for the uprising by the work of the Bolshevik*s* ~~Fighting Organization~~, carried out fighting orders with precision and fought side by side with the Red Guard. ~~From the very start, the navy was on the side of the revolution~~ *The navy did not lag behind the army.* Kronstadt was a stronghold of the Bolshevik Party, and had *long since* refused to recognize the authority of the Provisional Government. The cruiser AURORA trained its guns *on the Winter Palace*, and on October 25 their thunder ushered in a new era, the era of the Great ~~Proletarian~~ Socialist Revolution.

On October 25 (November 7) *the Bolsheviks issued* a manifesto ~~was issued over Lenin's signature~~ "To the Citizens of Russia" announcing that the bourgeois Provisional Government had been deposed and that state power had passed into the hands of the Soviets.

The Provisional Government had taken refuge in the Winter Palace under the protection of cadets *and shock battalions*. On the night of October 25 the revolutionary workers, soldiers and sailors took the Winter Palace by storm and arrested the Provisional Government.

The *armed* uprising ~~of revolutionary workers, soldiers and sailors in the capital of the land~~ *in Petrograd* had won.

~~10. Second All-Russian Congress of Soviets (November 7–8, 1917). Formation of the Council of People's Commissars under Lenin's Command~~

The Second All-Russian Congress of Soviets opened in the Smolny at 10:45 p.m. on October 25 (November 7), 1917, when the uprising in Petrograd ~~had already begun~~ *was already in the full flush of victory and the power in the capital had actually passed into the hands of the Petrograd Soviet.*

The Bolsheviks secured an overwhelming majority at the congress~~, along with their followers among the non-Party delegates and the "Left" Socialist-Revolutionaries~~. The Mensheviks, Bundists and Right Socialist-Revolutionaries, seeing that their day was done, left the congress, announcing that they refused to take any part in its labours. In a statement which was read at the Congress of Soviets they referred to the October Revolution as a "military plot." The congress condemned the Mensheviks and Socialist-Revolutionaries and, far from regretting their departure, welcomed it, for, it declared, thanks to the withdrawal of the traitors the congress had become a real revolutionary congress of workers' and soldiers' deputies.

The congress proclaimed that all power had passed to the Soviets:

> "Backed by the will of the vast majority of the workers, soldiers and peasants, backed by the victorious uprising of the workers and the garrison which had taken place in Petrograd, the Congress takes the power into its own hands"—the proclamation of the Second Congress of Soviets~~, written in Lenin's hand,~~ read.

On *the night of* October 26 (November 8), 1917, the *Second* Congress of Soviets ~~with unheard-of enthusiasm~~ adopted ~~at Lenin's suggestion~~ the Decree on Peace. The ~~Soviet Government~~ *congress* called ~~for~~ *upon the belligerent countries to conclude* an immediate armistice for a period of not less than three months to permit negotiations for peace. While addressing itself to the governments and peoples of all the belligerent countries, the ~~Workers' and Peasants' Government of Russia~~ *congress* at the same time appealed to "the class-conscious workers of the three most advanced nations of mankind and the largest states participating in the present war, namely, Great Britain, France and Germany." It ~~was calling~~ *called* upon these workers to help "to bring to a successful "conclusion[26] the cause of peace, and at the same time the cause of the emancipation of the toiling and exploited masses of the population from all forms of slavery and all forms of exploitation."

~~At that time, on November 8, at 2 o'clock in the morning, on the basis of Lenin's report was~~ *That same night the Second Congress of Soviets* adopted the Decree on Land, which proclaimed that "landlord ownership of land is abolished forthwith without compensation."[27] The basis adopted for ~~the first~~ *this* agrarian law was a Mandate (Nakaz) of the peasantry, compiled from 242 mandates of peasants of various localities. In accordance with this Mandate private ownership of land was to be abolished forever *and replaced by public, or state ownership of the land*. The lands of the landlords, of the tsar's family and of the monasteries were to be turned over to all the toilers for their free use.

*By this decree t*he peasantry received from the ~~Great~~ October Socialist Revolution over 150,000,000 dessiatins (over 400,000,000 acres) of land that had formerly belonged to the landlords, the bourgeoisie, the tsar's family, the monasteries~~;~~ *and* the churches ~~and the kulaks~~.

Moreover, the peasants were released from paying rent to the landlords, which had amounted to ~~400–500,000,000~~ *about 500,000,000 gold* rubles annually.

All mineral resources (oil, coal, ores, etc.), forests and waters ~~were transferred to the jurisdiction of the workers' and peasants' state~~ *became the property of the people.*

*Lastly, t*he Second All-Russian Congress of Soviets ~~organized~~ *formed* the first Soviet Government—*the Council of People's Commissars*—~~the first of~~ which consisted entirely of Bolsheviks. Lenin was elected Chairman of the first Council of People's Commissars.

This ended the labours of the historic Second Congress of Soviets.

~~The workers, soldiers and peasants who took part in the work of the congress experienced enormous enthusiasm. They realized that a new path for world history was opening up, that they had contributed to the beginning of a new society—a society of working people, where power for the first time would belong not to the oppressors, but the oppressed. After the formation of the Soviet Government, the congress closed. Delegates from the congress hurriedly dispersed in order to assist in the victory of the revolution all over and organize the new power, the power of the workers and the peasants.~~

The congress delegates dispersed to spread the news of the victory of the Soviets in Petrograd and to ensure the extension of the power of the Soviets to the whole country.

Not ~~in every city~~ *everywhere* did power pass to the Soviets at once. While in Petrograd the Soviet Government was already in existence, in Moscow fierce and stubborn fighting continued in the streets several days longer. *In order to prevent the power from passing into the hands of the Moscow Soviet, the* counter-revolutionary Menshevik and Socialist-Revolutionary parties, together with Whiteguards and cadets, ~~waged~~ *started* an armed fight against the ~~revolutionary~~ workers and soldiers. *It took several days to rout the rebels and to establish the power of the Soviets in Moscow.*

~~Even~~ In Petrograd itself, *and in several of its districts,* counter-revolutionary attempts to overthrow the Soviet power were made *in the very first days of the victory of the revolution*. On November 10, 1917, Kerensky, *who during the uprising had fled from Petrograd to the Northern Front,* ~~and General Krasnov~~ mustered several Cossack units and dispatched them against Petrograd *under the command of General Krasnov*. On November 11, 1917, a counter-revolutionary organization calling itself the "Committee for the Salvation of the Fatherland

and the Revolution," headed by Socialist-Revolutionaries, raised ~~an uprising~~ *a mutiny* of cadets in Petrograd. But the ~~cadet uprising~~ *mutiny* was suppressed *by sailors and Red Guards without much difficulty* by the evening of the same day, and on November 13 General Krasnov was routed near the Pulkovo Hills. Lenin *personally* directed the suppression of the anti-Soviet mutiny, just as he had personally directed the October ~~coup d'état~~ *uprising.* His inflexible firmness and calm confidence of victory inspired and ~~organized~~ *welded* the masses. The enemy was smashed. Krasnov was taken prisoner and pledged his "word of honour" to terminate the struggle against the Soviet power. And on his "word of honour" he was released. But ~~he quickly organized another uprising against the Soviet power~~, *as it later transpired, the general violated his word of honour. As to Kerensky, d*isguised as a woman, ~~Kerensky ran away~~ *he managed to "disappear in an unknown direction."*[28]

~~At this time,~~ *I*n Moghilev, ~~from his~~ *at the* General Headquarters of the Army, General Dukhonin, the Commander-in-Chief, ~~began to organize counter-revolutionary forces~~ *also attempted a mutiny*. When the Soviet Government instructed him to start immediate negotiations for an armistice with the German Command, he refused *to obey*. Thereupon Dukhonin was dismissed by order of the Soviet Government. The counter-revolutionary General Headquarters was broken up and Dukhonin himself was killed by the ~~sailors and~~ soldiers, who had risen against him.

~~All the forces of the counter-revolution joined together against the victorious revolution. The turn-coats and traitors Kamenev and Zinoviev ACTED AS ONE WITH THE COUNTER-REVOLUTION, demanding the creation of a government including the Mensheviks and Socialist-Revolutionaries.~~ *Certain notorious opportunists within the Party—Kamenev, Zinoviev, Rykov, Shlyapnikov and others—also made a sally against the Soviet power. They demanded the formation of an "all-Socialist government" to include Mensheviks and Socialist-Revolutionaries, who had just been overthrown by the October Revolution.* On November 15, 1917, the Central Committee of the Bolshevik Party adopted a resolution rejecting agreement with these ~~petty-bourgeois~~ *counter-revolutionary* parties~~; these enemies of the Soviet power~~, *and proclaiming Kamenev and Zinoviev strikebreakers of the revolution*. On November 17, ~~the traitors~~ Kamenev, Zinoviev, Rykov and Milyutin, disagreeing with the ~~tactics~~ *policy* of the Party, announced their resignation from the Central Committee. That same day, November 17, Nogin, in his own name and in the names of Rykov, V. Milyutin, Teodorovich, A. Shlyapnikov, D. Ryazanov, Yurenev and Larin, members of the Council of People's Commissars, announced ~~that they also upheld "the position that it was necessary to form a Socialist government including all the Socialist parties"~~ *their disagreement with the policy of the Central Committee of the Party and their resignation from the Council of People's Commissars*. The desertion of this handful of cowards caused ~~immense~~ jubilation among the enemies of the October Revolution. The bourgeoisie and its henchmen proclaimed with malicious glee the collapse of Bolshevism and presaged the early end of the Bolshevik ~~Government~~ *Party*. But not for a moment ~~were the masses~~ *was the Party* shaken by this handful of deserters. The ~~entire Party~~ *Central Committee of the Party* contemptuously ~~brushed aside these pathetic bourgeois lackeys~~ *branded them as deserters from the revolution* and accomplices ~~of the counter-revolution~~ *of the bourgeoisie, and proceeded with its work.*

As to the "Left" Socialist-Revolutionaries, they, desirous of retaining their influence over the peasant~~-soldier~~ masses, ~~supported the Bolsheviks AGAINST THEIR WILL and FOR ONLY A SHORT TIME~~ *who definitely sympathized with the Bolsheviks, decided not to quarrel with the latter and for the time being to maintain a united front with them*. The Congress of Peasant Soviets which took place in November 1917 recognized all the gains of the October Socialist Revolution and endorsed the decrees of the Soviet Government. *An agreement was concluded with the "Left" Socialist-Revolutionaries and s*everal of their number were given posts on the Council of People's Commissars (Kolegayev, Spiridonova, Proshyan and Steinberg). ~~This coalition~~ *However, this agreement* lasted *only* until the signing of the Peace of Brest-Litovsk and the formation of the Committees of the Poor Peasants, when a deep cleavage took place among the peasantry and when the "Left" Socialist-Revolutionaries, coming more and more to reflect the interests of the kulaks, started a~~n uprising~~ *revolt* against the ~~Soviet power~~ *Bolsheviks* and ~~slid into the camp of counter-revolution~~ *were routed by the Soviet Government.*

In the interval from October 1917 to February 1918 the ~~proletarian~~ *Soviet* revolution spread throughout the *vast* territory of the country ~~in a "TRIUMPHAL MARCH."~~ *at such a rapid rate that Lenin referred to it as a "triumphal march" of Soviet power.* ~~Soviet power was established in the Ukraine. On the Don, 46 Cossack regiments joined the Soviet power and in the Cossack village of Kamensk, a military-revolutionary committee was organized for the struggle with counter-revolution on the Don. Soviet power was established in the Urals and Siberia. The workers' revolution was likewise victorious in Finland and Latvia. The Soviet power grew in strength during these first weeks and months almost throughout the large territory of formerly tsarist Russia.~~

The Great October Socialist Revolution had won.

~~The victory of the Soviet Socialist Revolution can be explained by the following reasons:~~

~~1. The bourgeois government of the Socialist-Revolutionary Kerensky had become utterly discredited in the eyes of the workers and peasants. Kerensky wanted to continue the war until victory was achieved, but the workers, peasants and soldiers demanded that the war be stopped and peace concluded. Ke-~~

~~rensky wanted to keep the land for the landlords, but the workers and peasants demanded the immediate seizure of the landlords' land for the benefit of the peasants. Kerensky wanted to curb the workers, but the workers and peasants demanded that the factory owners be curbed and placed under the control of the workers' organizations.~~

~~2. The second reason was that these demands served as the basis for a strong alliance between the workers and peasants in the form of Soviets of Workers' and Soldiers' Deputies against the bourgeois Provisional Government and its henchmen, the Socialist-Revolutionaries and Mensheviks, and in support of the Bolshevik Party.~~

~~3. The third reason was that the vast masses of the workers and peasants abandoned the compromising Socialist-Revolutionaries and Mensheviks, rallied around the Bolshevik Party, and recognized it as their leader and guide.~~

~~It was for these reasons that the October revolution was victorious.~~[29]

There were several reasons for this comparatively easy victory of the Socialist revolution in Russia. The following chief reasons should be noted:

1) The October Revolution was confronted by an enemy so comparatively weak, so badly organized and so politically inexperienced as the Russian bourgeoisie. Economically still weak, and completely dependent on government contracts, the Russian bourgeoisie lacked sufficient political self-reliance and initiative to find a way out of the situation. It had neither the experience of the French bourgeoisie, for example, in political combination and political chicanery on a broad scale nor the schooling of the British bourgeoisie in broadly conceived crafty compromise. It had but recently sought to reach an understanding with the tsar; yet now that the tsar had been overthrown by the February Revolution, and the bourgeoisie itself had come to power, it was unable to think of anything better than to continue the policy of the detested tsar in all its essentials. Like the tsar, it stood for "war to a victorious finish," although the war was beyond the country's strength and had reduced the people and the army to a state of utter exhaustion. Like the tsar, it stood for the preservation in the main of big landed property, although the peasantry was perishing from lack of land and the weight of the landlord's yoke. As to its labour policy the Russian bourgeoisie outstripped even the tsar in its hatred of the working class, for it not only strove to preserve and strengthen the yoke of the factory owners, but to render it intolerable by wholesale lockouts.

It is not surprising that the people saw no essential difference between the policy of the tsar and the policy of the bourgeoisie, and that they transferred their hatred of the tsar to the Provisional Government of the bourgeoisie.

As long as the compromising Socialist-Revolutionary and Menshevik parties possessed a certain amount of influence among the people, the bourgeoisie could use them as a screen and preserve its power. But after the Mensheviks and Socialist-Revolutionaries had exposed themselves as agents of the imperialist bourgeoisie, thus forfeiting their influence among the people, the bourgeoisie and its Provisional Government were left without a support.

2) The October Revolution was headed by so revolutionary a class as the working class of Russia, a class which had been steeled in battle, which had in a short space passed through two revolutions, and which by the eve of the third revolution had won recognition as the leader of the people in the struggle for peace, land, liberty and Socialism. If the revolution had not had a leader like the working class of Russia, a leader that had earned the confidence of the people, there would have been no alliance between the workers and peasants, and without such an alliance the victory of the October Revolution would have been impossible.

3) The working class of Russia had so effective an ally in the revolution as the poor peasantry, which comprised the overwhelming majority of the peasant population. The experience of eight months of revolution—which may unhesitatingly be compared to the experience of several decades of "normal" development—had not been in vain as far as the mass of the labouring peasants were concerned. During this period they had had the opportunity to test all the parties of Russia in practice and convince themselves that neither the Constitutional-Democrats, nor the Socialist-Revolutionaries and Mensheviks would seriously quarrel with the landlords or sacrifice themselves for the interests of the peasants; that there was only one party in Russia—the Bolshevik Party—which was in no way connected with the landlords and which was prepared to crush them in order to satisfy the needs of the peasants. This served as a solid basis for the alliance of the proletariat and the poor peasantry. The existence of this alliance between the working class and the poor peasantry determined the conduct of the middle peasants, who had long been vacillating and only on the eve of the October uprising wholeheartedly swung over towards the revolution and joined forces with the poor peasants.

It goes without saying that without this alliance the October Revolution could not have been victorious.

4) The working class was headed by a party so tried and tested in political battles as the Bolshevik Party. Only a party like the Bolshevik Party, courageous enough to lead the people in decisive attack, and cautious enough to keep clear of all the submerged rocks in its path to the goal—only such a party could so skilfully merge into one common revolutionary torrent such diverse revolutionary movements as the general democratic movement for peace, the peasant democratic movement for the seizure of the landed estates, the movement of the oppressed nationalities for national liberation and national equality,[30] *and the Socialist movement of the proletariat for the overthrow of the bourgeoisie and the establishment of the dictatorship of the proletariat.*

Undoubtedly, the merging of these diverse revolutionary streams into one common powerful revolutionary torrent decided the fate of capitalism in Russia.

5) The October Revolution began at a time when the imperialist war was still at its height, when the principal bourgeois states were split into two hostile camps, and when, absorbed in mutual war and undermining each other's strength, they were unable to intervene effectively in "Russian affairs" and actively to oppose the October Revolution.

This undoubtedly did much to facilitate the victory of the October Socialist Revolution.

~~The Great October Socialist Revolution was the start of the world proletarian revolution.~~

~~Under its direct influence, a workers' revolution took place in Finland in January 1918, while in November 1918, there were revolutions in Germany and Austro-Hungary which overthrew the monarchies of these countries. In March 1919, Soviet power was established in Hungary, and in April 1919 Soviet power emerged in Bavaria.~~

~~However, due to the treachery of the Social-Democratic chiefs and the weakness of the communist parties, the working class in these countries was unable to achieve the victory of Socialist Revolution.~~

7.~~11.~~ **Struggle of the Bolshevik Party to Consolidate the Soviet Power.** ***Peace of Brest-Litovsk. Seventh Party Congress***

~~The victorious proletarian dictatorship had to destroy and break down~~ *In order to consolidate the Soviet power,* the old, bourgeois state machine *had to be shattered and destroyed* and ~~set up~~ a new, Soviet state machine *set up* in its place. ~~In November 1917, all the pre-revolutionary legal institutions were abolished and all laws that had been promulgated by the tsarist and Provisional Government were rescinded. The Soviet power created its own class justice, based on the defence of the people's interests. In the place of the old state institutions and their bureaucratic apparatus, which arbitrarily decided the people's fate, the Soviet power created a new administrative apparatus—People's Commissariats in the centre and departments within the Soviets in the localities.~~ *Further, it was necessary to destroy the survivals of the division of society into estates and the regime of national oppression, to abolish the privileges of the church, to suppress the counter-revolutionary press and counter-revolutionary organizations of all kinds, legal and illegal, and to dissolve the bourgeois Constituent Assembly. Following on the nationalization of the land, all large-scale industry had also to be nationalized. And, lastly, the state of war had to be ended, for the war was hampering the consolidation of the Soviet power more than anything else.*

All these measures were carried out in the course of a few months, from the end of 1917 to the middle of 1918.

~~The Mensheviks and Socialist-Revolutionaries organized strikes of teachers, doctors, engineers and other groups from the bourgeois intelligentsia in Moscow and an array of other cities during the first days of Soviet power. This bourgeois intelligentsia had served the tsar. It had served the landlords and the capitalists. And when the working class and poor peasants took power into their own hands for the first time in history, this bourgeois intelligentsia refused to serve the people.~~

~~For a while, the Cadet and Menshevik-Socialist-Revolutionary press continued to function, pouring out a steady stream of lies and slander against the Bolshevik Party. In those first days, even the radio remained in the enemy's hands, and radio broadcasts beamed false updates around the world about the defeat of the Bolsheviks. On a daily basis, the bourgeois Menshevik-Socialist-Revolutionary newspapers predicted the imminent demise of the Soviet power, considering its days numbered.~~

~~The Soviet power arrested members of counter-revolutionary organizations, closed the main bourgeois newspapers and created the All-Russian Extraordinary Commission under a man with iron will and burning spirit—Feliks Edmundovich Dzerzhinsky—to struggle with the counter-revolution. The Workers' and Peasants' Red Army was created in the place of the old army, the origins of which date back to Lenin's January 15, 1918, decree.~~

The sabotage of the officials of the old Ministries, engineered by the Socialist-Revolutionaries and Mensheviks, was smashed and overcome. The Ministries were abolished and replaced by Soviet administrative machinery and appropriate People's Commissariats. The Supreme Council of National Economy was set up to administer the industry of the country. The All-Russian Extraordinary Commission (Vecheka) was created to combat counter-revolution and sabotage, and F. Dzerzhinsky was placed at its head.[31] *The formation of a Red Army and Navy was decreed. The Constituent Assembly, the elections to which had largely been held prior to the October Revolution, and which refused to recognize the decrees of the Second Congress of Soviets on peace, land and the transfer of power to the Soviets,*[32] *was dissolved.*

In order to put an end to the survivals of feudalism, the estates system, and inequality in all spheres of social life, decrees were issued abolishing the estates, removing restrictions based on nationality or religion, separating the church from the state and the schools from the church, establishing equality for women and the equality of all the nationalities of Russia.

A special edict of the Soviet Government known as "The Declaration of Rights of the Peoples of Russia" laid down as a law the right of the peoples of Russia to unhampered development and complete equality.

~~The Socialist measures of the Soviet power were of decisive significance for the cause of strengthening the victorious October Revolution. Legislation~~

~~on WORKERS' CONTROL over capitalist enterprises was published on November 27, 1917. On December 18, 1917, a decree was published on the creation of the Supreme Council of the National Economy—the organ through which the proletarian dictatorship would exercise leadership over the economic life of the country. The largest of these measures was the NATIONALIZATION OF THE BANKS.~~ *In order to undermine the economic power of the bourgeoisie and to create a new, Soviet national economy, and, in the first place, to create*[33] *a new, Soviet industry, the banks, railways, foreign trade, the mercantile fleet and all large enterprises in all branches of industry—coal, metal, oil, chemicals, machine-building, textiles, sugar, etc.—were nationalized.*

~~The Soviet Government annulled (renounced)~~ *To render our country financially independent of the foreign capitalists and free from exploitation by them,* the foreign loans contracted by the Russian tsar and the Provisional Government *were annulled*~~, inasmuch as the workers and peasants of the Soviet land did not want to pay for those loans that were made to the tsarist government and bourgeois provisional government for the realization of imperialist policies and the waging of imperialist war~~. *The people of our country refused to pay debts which had been incurred for the continuation of the war of conquest and which had placed our country in bondage to foreign capital.* ~~In December 1917, an array of joint-stock companies was nationalized, as were all railroads, foreign trade and the mercantile fleet.~~

These *and similar* measures ~~during the first period of the proletarian dictatorship~~ undermined the very root of the ~~economic strength~~ *power* of the ~~Russian~~ bourgeoisie, *the landlords, the reactionary officials and the counter-revolutionary parties,* and ~~dealt a blow to the international bourgeoisie and the capital that had been invested in Russian industrial and banking enterprises. At the time, these decrees and the Socialist measures of the Soviet power were well regarded by the working class and the working masses not only in our country, but abroad as well~~ *considerably strengthened the position of the Soviet Government within the country.*

~~Of absolutely critical significance was the LENIN-STALIN NATIONALITY POLICY. The October revolution destroyed national oppression and united together the working masses of all nationalities that had been oppressed by tsardom and the Kerensky government. Now, after the October coup d'état, the "Declaration of Rights of the Peoples of Russia" was published over Lenin's and Stalin's signatures. Recognition of the independence of Finland and the Ukraine followed thereafter. Sovnarkom ratified the Soviet power address "To All Working Muslims of Russia and the East," prepared by Comrade Stalin. In this address it was said that the Soviet power had decisively broken with the previous nationality policy of tsardom and the Provisional Government. A People's Commissariat of Nationality Affairs was formed under Comrade Stalin. The most important~~

steps in the Bolshevik Party's position on the national question BEFORE October were associated with Comrade Stalin's name, as are all issues associated with the Party's nationality policy AFTER October 1917.

The first decrees of the Soviet power that announced the new Socialist measures were also designed to completely uproot the remains of feudalism, serfdom and the societal estates system. The decrees separating the church from the state and school from the church, as well as the decrees on the court, the schools, on the elimination of estates and national and religious limitations and on the realization of women's equality put an end to barbaric survivals from the tsarist system.

The Soviet power had accomplished in a few weeks a thousand times more in this area than the Cadets, Mensheviks and Socialist-Revolutionaries had in 8 months in power.

The Bolshevik Party's tactics in regard to the question of the Constituent Assembly had great significance in the struggle for the strengthening of the Soviet power. The elections to the Constituent Assembly began in September 1917. They gave the Bolsheviks about 25 per cent of the votes, although in Petrograd the Bolsheviks received 45 per cent and in Moscow 50 per cent. In this way, the Bolsheviks in both capitals received about half of the vote. The majority of the proletariat was for the Bolsheviks. Half the army turned out to be on the Bolsheviks' side, and in the capitals and the units at the front and close to the capitals, the vast majority of the soldiers voted for the Bolsheviks. In this way, the Bolsheviks had the preponderance of all forces at the decisive moment and in the decisive place. Nevertheless, the enemies of the proletarian revolution—the bourgeois and petty-bourgeois parties—received about 62 per cent of the vote. This can be explained first and foremost by the fact that the voting lists were published well before the October Revolution, when the Socialist-Revolutionaries possessed significant influence and before the "Left" Socialist-Revolutionaries had split off from them (the voting lists remained unified). The voting did not represent the true alignment of forces in the country.

Why did the Bolsheviks participate in these elections? The Bolshevik Party believed that it was necessary to give the masses another chance to experience what the Socialist-Revolutionary and Menshevik majority at the Constituent Assembly had to offer. This would eliminate their faith in the all-powerful Constituent Assembly.

On January 5 (18), 1918, the first meeting of the Constituent Assembly was opened by Y. M. Sverdlov in the name of the All-Russian Central Executive Committee. The Socialist-Revolutionary and Menshevik majority at the Constituent Assembly refused to ratify the Soviet power's decrees and recognize the victories of the working class and working strata of the peasantry. The Constituent Assembly was therefore disbanded by a resolution of the All-Russian

~~Central Executive Committee on January 19, 1918. Members of the Constituent Assembly—Bolsheviks—quit the meeting of the Constituent Assembly after the declaration put together by Lenin was read. The "Left" Socialist-Revolutionaries left after the Bolsheviks did.~~

~~The disbanding of the Constituent Assembly, which was hostile to the Soviet power and the victories of the working people, was greeted with approval by the popular masses.~~

But the position of the Soviet Government could not be deemed fully secure as long as Russia was in a state of war with Germany and Austria. In order finally to consolidate the Soviet power, the war had to be ended. The Party therefore launched the fight for peace from the moment of the victory of the October Revolution.

~~12. Struggle of the Bolshevik Party for an End to the Imperialist War~~

The Soviet Government called upon "all the belligerent peoples and their governments to start immediate negotiations for a just, democratic peace." But the "allies"—Great Britain and France—~~had no intention of beginning negotiations without having realized their chief goal: the destruction of German imperialism~~ *refused to accept the proposal of the Soviet Government.* ~~Therefore, without waiting for the states to agree to negotiations~~ *In view of this refusal,* the Soviet Government, *in compliance with the will of the Soviets,* ~~started~~ *decided to start* negotiations with Germany and Austria.

The negotiations began on December 3 in Brest-Litovsk. On December 5 an armistice was signed.

The ~~peace~~ negotiations took place *at a time when the country was in a state of economic disruption*, when ~~the popular masses'~~ war-weariness ~~with the imperialist war~~ was ~~strong~~ *universal*, when our troops were ~~deserting~~ *abandoning* the trenches ~~en masse~~ and the front was collapsing. It became clear in the course of the negotiations that the German imperialists were out to seize huge portions of the territory of the former tsarist empire~~.~~, *and to turn* Poland, the Ukraine and the Baltic countries ~~were to be turned~~ into dependencies of Germany.

To continue the war under such conditions would have meant staking the very existence of the new-born Soviet Republic. The working class and the peasantry were confronted with the necessity of accepting onerous terms of peace, of retreating before the most dangerous marauder of the time—German imperialism—in order to secure a respite in which to strengthen the Soviet power and to create ~~from scratch~~ a new army, *the Red Army, which would be able to defend the country from enemy attack.*

All the counter-revolutionaries, from the Mensheviks and Socialist-Revolutionaries to the most arrant Whiteguards, conducted a frenzied campaign against the conclusion of peace. Their policy was clear: they wanted to wreck the peace negotiations, provoke a German offensive, ~~so that they could destroy the Soviet power with the assistance of the German imperialists~~ *and thus imperil the still weak Soviet power and endanger the gains of the workers and peasants.*

Their allies in this sinister scheme were ~~the traitor~~ Trotsky and his accomplice Bukharin, the latter, together with Radek and Pyatakov, heading a group which was hostile to the Party but camouflaged itself under the name of "Left Communists." ~~This~~ *Trotsky and the* group of "Left Communists" began a fierce struggle within the Party ~~Central Committee~~ against Lenin, demanding the continuation of the war. ~~This group was~~ *These people were* clearly playing into the hands of the German imperialists and the counter-revolutionaries within the country, for they ~~wanted~~ *were working* to expose the young~~, vulnerable~~ Soviet Republic, which had not yet any army, to the blows of German imperialism.

This was really a policy of provocateurs, skilfully masked by Left phraseology.

On February 10, 1918, the peace negotiations in Brest-Litovsk were broken off. Although Lenin and Stalin, *in the name of the Central Committee of the Party,* had insisted that peace be signed, Trotsky, who was chairman of the Soviet delegation *at Brest-Litovsk,* treacherously violated the direct instructions of the Bolshevik Party. He announced that the Soviet Republic refused to conclude peace on the terms proposed by Germany. ~~But~~ *A*t the same time ~~Trotsky announced~~ *he informed the Germans* that the Soviet Republic would not fight and would continue to demobilize the army. ~~The traitor Trotsky said to representatives of the German General Staff in a secret conversation that the Soviet power was powerless, a "corpse without anyone to bury it."~~

This was monstrous. The German imperialists could have desired nothing more from this traitor to the interests of the Soviet country.

The German government broke the armistice and assumed the offensive. The remnants of ~~the Russian~~ *our old* army *crumbled and* scattered *before the onslaught of the German troops*. The Germans advanced swiftly, seizing enormous territory and threatening Petrograd. ~~Predatory~~ German imperialism invaded the Soviet land with the object of overthrowing the ~~proletarian dictatorship~~ *Soviet power* and converting our country into its colony. The ruins of the old tsarist army could not withstand the armed hosts of German imperialism, and steadily retreated under their blows.

But the armed intervention of the German imperialists was the signal for a mighty revolutionary upsurge in the country. The Party and the Soviet Government issued the call—"The Socialist fatherland is in danger!" And in response the working class energetically began to form regiments of the Red Army. The young detachments of the new army—the army of the revolutionary people—heroically resisted the German marauders who were armed to the teeth. At Narva and Pskov the German invaders met with a resolute repulse. Their advance on ~~revolutionary~~ Petrograd was checked. February 23—the day the forces of German imperialism were repulsed—is regarded as the ~~founding day~~ *birthday* of the Red Army.

On February 18, 1918, the Central Committee of the Party had approved Lenin's proposal to send a telegram to the German government offering to conclude an immediate peace. But in order to secure more advantageous terms, the Germans continued to advance, and only on February 22 did the German government express its willingness to sign peace. The terms were now far more onerous than those originally proposed.

Lenin ~~and~~, Stalin *and Sverdlov* had to wage a stubborn fight on the Central Committee against *Trotsky,* Bukharin and the *other* Trotskyites before they secured a decision in favour of the conclusion of peace. Bukharin and Trotsky, Lenin declared, "actually HELPED the German imperialists and HINDERED the growth and development of the revolution in Germany." (Lenin, COLLECTED WORKS, Russ. ed., Vol. XXII, p. 307.)

On February 23, the Central Committee decided to accept the terms of the German Command and to sign the peace treaty. The treachery of Trotsky *and Bukharin* cost the Soviet Republic dearly. Latvia, Esthonia, not to mention Poland, passed into German hands; the Ukraine was severed from the Soviet Republic and converted into a vassal of the German state~~, as was Finland~~. The Soviet Republic undertook to pay an indemnity to the Germans.

Meanwhile, the "Left Communists" continued their struggle against Lenin, sinking ~~onto the path of counter-revolution and~~ *deeper and deeper into the slough of* treachery.

~~They published their own newspaper, in which they slandered the Party Central Committee and Lenin in every way.~~

The Moscow Regional Bureau *of the Party*, of which the "Left Communists" (Bukharin, Ossinsky, Yakovleva, Stukov and Mantsev) had temporarily seized control, passed a resolution of no-confidence in the Central Committee, a ~~provocative~~ resolution *designed to split the Party*. The Bureau declared that it considered "a split in the Party in the very near future scarcely avoidable." The "Left Communists" even went so far in their resolution as to adopt ~~a counter-revolutionary~~ *an anti-Soviet* stand. "In the interests of the international revolution," they declared, "we consider it expedient to consent to the possible loss of the Soviet power, which has now become purely formal."

Lenin branded this decision as "strange and monstrous."

At that time the real cause of this anti-Party behaviour of Trotsky and the "Left Communists" was not yet clear to the Party. ~~As~~ *But* the *recent* trial of the Anti-Soviet "Bloc of Rights and Trotskyites" (~~March~~ *beginning of* 1938) has now revealed~~;~~ *that* Bukharin and the group of "Left Communists" headed by him, together with Trotsky and the "Left" Socialist-Revolutionaries, ~~organized a conspiracy~~ *were at that time secretly conspiring* against the Soviet Government. *Now it is known that* Bukharin, *Trotsky* and ~~his~~ *their* fellow-conspirators ~~aspired~~ *had determined* to wreck the Peace of Brest-Litovsk, arrest ~~and assassinate~~ V. I. Lenin, J. V. Stalin and Y. M. Sverdlov, *assassinate them,* and form a new government consisting of Bukharinites, Trotskyites and "Left" Socialist-Revolutionaries. ~~One of the head "Left Communists," Unshlikht, led treacherous, counter-revolutionary negotiations with the Polish nationalists and their chief Pilsudsky.~~

While hatching this clandestine counter-revolutionary plot, the group of "Left Communists," *with the support of Trotsky,* ~~madly~~ *openly* attacked the Bolshevik Party, trying to split it and to disintegrate its ranks ~~by means of their treacherous speeches and resolutions~~. But at this grave juncture the Party rallied around Lenin, ~~and~~ Stalin *and Sverdlov* and ~~firmly~~ supported the Central Committee on the question of peace as on all other questions.

The "Left Communist" group was isolated and defeated ~~in the Party~~.

~~The Trial of the "Right-Trotskyite Bloc" in the spring of 1938 showed the "Left Communist" group in a new light. It turned out to be an espionage ring of forces hostile to Socialism within the ranks of the Bolshevik Party and the workers' movement, just like the Trotskyite movement. This was clear even then, in 1918. But the "Left Communists"—Bukharin and other supporters of Trotsky and the "Left" Socialist-Revolutionaries—during this period were the direct organizers of a counter-revolutionary coup d'état, which aimed to eliminate the Communist Party and the Soviet power.~~

*In order that the Party might pronounce its final decision on the question of peace t*he Seventh Party Congress was summoned ~~on March 6, 1918, chiefly in order that the Party might decide the question about the conclusion of a peace treaty~~.

The congress opened on March 6, 1918. This was the first congress held after our Party had taken power. It was attended by 46 delegates with vote and 58 delegates with voice but no vote, representing 145,000 Party members. Actually, the membership of the Party at that time was not less than 270,000. The discrepancy was due to the fact that, owing to the urgency with which the congress met, a large number of the organizations were unable to send delegates in time; and the organizations in the territories then occupied by the Germans were unable to send delegates at all.

Reporting *at this congress* ~~about war and peace~~ *on the Brest-Litovsk Peace,* Lenin said ~~at the Seventh Party Congress~~ that ". . . the severe crisis which our Party is now experiencing, owing to the formation of a Left opposition within it, is one of the gravest crises the Russian revolution has experienced." (Lenin, Selected Works, Vol. VII, pp. 293–94.)

The resolution submitted by Lenin on the subject of the Brest-Litovsk Peace was adopted ~~at the Seventh Party Congress~~ by ~~28~~ *30* votes against ~~9~~ *12*, with ~~1~~ *4* abstentions.[34]

On the day following the adoption of this resolution, Lenin wrote an article entitled "A Distressful Peace," in which he said:

> "Intolerably severe are the terms of peace. Nevertheless, history will claim its own. . . . Let us set to work to organize, organize and organize. Despite all trials, the future is ours." (Lenin, COLLECTED WORKS, Russ. ed., Vol. XXII, p. 288.)

In its resolution, the congress declared that further military attacks by imperialist states on the Soviet Republic were inevitable~~.~~*, and that t*herefore the congress ~~set its first and most~~ *considered it the* fundamental task *of the Party* to adopt the most energetic and resolute measures to strengthen the self-discipline and discipline of the workers and peasants ~~of Russia~~, to prepare the masses for self-sacrificing defence of the Socialist country ~~from the imperialists~~, to organize the Red Army, and to introduce universal military training ~~for adults~~.

Endorsing Lenin's policy with regard to the Peace of Brest-Litovsk, the congress condemned the position of Trotsky and Bukharin and stigmatized the attempt of the defeated "Left Communists" to continue their splitting activities at the congress itself.

The Peace of Brest-Litovsk gave the Party a respite in which to ~~organize the Red Army and strengthen the country's economy~~ *consolidate the Soviet power and to organize the economic life of the country.*

The peace made it possible to take advantage of the conflicts within the imperialist camp (the war of *Austria and* Germany with the Entente, which was still in progress) to disintegrate the forces of the enemy, *to organize a Soviet economic system and to create a Red Army.*

The peace~~, the "respite,"~~ made it possible for the proletariat to retain the support of the peasantry and to accumulate strength for the defeat of the Whiteguard generals in the Civil War.

In the period of the October ~~coup d'état~~ *Revolution* Lenin taught the Bolshevik Party how to advance fearlessly and resolutely when conditions ~~had been prepared for~~ *favoured* an advance. In the period of the Brest-Litovsk Peace Lenin taught the Party how to ~~temporarily~~ retreat *in good order* when the forces of the enemy are obviously superior to our own, in order to prepare with the utmost energy for a new offensive ~~against capitalism~~.[35]

History has fully proved the correctness of Lenin's line.

It was decided at the Seventh Congress to change the name of the Party and to alter the Party Program. The name of the Party was changed to the Russian

Communist Party (Bolsheviks)—R.C.P.(B.). Lenin proposed to call our Party a Communist Party because this name precisely corresponded to the aim of the Party, namely, the achievement of Communism.

A special commission, which included Lenin and Stalin, was elected ~~for the final work on the~~ *to draw up a new Party* program, Lenin's ~~rough~~ draft program having been accepted as a basis.

Thus the Seventh Congress accomplished a task of profound historical importance: it ~~destroyed~~ *defeated* the enemy *hidden within the Party's ranks*—the "Left Communists" and Trotskyites; it succeeded in withdrawing the country from the imperialist war; it ~~succeeded in obtaining at least a brief respite.~~ *secured peace and a respite;* ~~The congress gave firm directives on the creation~~ *it enabled the Party to gain time for the organization* of the Red Army; and it ~~gave~~ *set*[36] *the Party* the ~~firm directive~~ *task*[37] concerning the introduction of Socialist order in the national economy.

8.~~13.~~ Lenin's Plan for *the Initial Steps in* Socialist Construction ~~(Spring of 1918)~~*. Committees of the Poor Peasants and the Curbing of the Kulaks. Revolt of the "Left" Socialist-Revolutionaries and Its Suppression. Fifth Congress of Soviets and Adoption of the Constitution of the R.S.F.S.R.*

~~At the end of March, the Peace of Brest-Litovsk was ratified by the Fourth Extraordinary Congress of Soviets, despite the mad opposition of "Left" Socialist-Revolutionaries, supported by the "Left Communists."~~

Having concluded peace and thus gained a ~~"~~respite,~~"~~ the Soviet Government set about *the work of* Socialist construction. Lenin called the period from ~~October~~ *November* 1917 to February 1918 the stage of "the Red Guard attack on capital." During the first half of 1918 the Soviet Government succeeded in breaking the ~~resistance~~ *economic might* of the bourgeoisie, in concentrating in its own hands the key positions of the national economy (mills, factories, banks, railways, foreign trade, mercantile fleet, etc.), smashing the bourgeois machinery of state power, and victoriously crushing the first attempts of the counter-revolution to overthrow the Soviet power.

*But this was by no means enough. If there was to be progress, the destruction of the old order had to be followed by the building of a new. Accordingly, i*n the spring of 1918, ~~on the basis of these accomplishments,~~ a transition was begun "from the expropriation of the expropriators" to a new stage of Socialist construction—the organizational consolidation of the victories gained, *the building of the Soviet national economy*. Lenin held that the utmost advantage should be taken of the ~~"~~respite~~"~~ in order to begin to lay the foundation of the Socialist economic system. ~~It was time to raise the struggle with capitalism to the fore;~~ The Bolsheviks had to learn to organize and manage production *in a new way.*

The Bolshevik Party had convinced Russia, Lenin wrote ~~in that period~~; the Bolshevik Party had wrested Russia for the ~~poor~~ *people* from the hands of the rich, and now the Bolsheviks must learn to govern Russia.

Lenin held that the chief task at the given stage was to keep account of everything~~, that is, in the economy, that was~~ *the country* produced and to exercise control over the distribution of all products. Petty-bourgeois elements predominated in the economic system of the country~~; the many millions of handicraft enterprises and petty peasant farms were a breeding ground for capitalism~~. *The millions of small owners in town and country were a breeding ground for capitalism.* ~~These millions of petty producers~~ *These small owners recognized neither labour discipline nor civil discipline; they* would not submit to ~~any kind of~~ a system of state accounting ~~or~~ *and* control. What was particularly dangerous at this ~~grim~~ *difficult* juncture was the petty-bourgeois welter of speculation and profiteering, the attempts of the small owners and traders to profit by the people's ~~hunger~~ *want*~~; the workers suffered most of all from this speculation~~.

The Party started a vigorous war on slovenliness in work, ~~and in the area of labour organization~~ *on the absence of labour discipline in industry*. The masses were slow in acquiring new habits of labour. The struggle for labour discipline *consequently* became the major task of the period.

Lenin pointed to the necessity of developing Socialist emulation *in industry*; of introducing the piece rate system; of combating wage equalization; of resorting—in addition to methods of education and persuasion—to methods of compulsion with regard to those who wanted to grab as much as possible ~~for themselves~~ *from the state*, with regard to idlers and ~~those who profiteered and did not work~~ *profiteers*. He maintained that the new discipline—the discipline of labour, the discipline of comradely relations, Soviet discipline—was something that would be evolved by the labouring millions in the course of their daily, practical work, and that "this task will take up a whole historical epoch." (Lenin, SELECTED WORKS, Vol. VII, p. 393.)

All these problems of Socialist construction, of the new, Socialist relations of production, were dealt with ~~in a profound way~~ by Lenin in his celebrated work, THE IMMEDIATE TASKS OF THE SOVIET GOVERNMENT.

The "Left Communists," acting in conjunction with the Socialist-Revolutionaries and Mensheviks, fought ~~desperately against~~ Lenin over these questions too. Bukharin, Ossinsky and others were opposed to the introduction of discipline, one-man management *in the enterprises, the employment of bourgeois experts in industry,* and the ~~assertion~~ *introduction* of efficient business methods. They slandered Lenin by claiming that this ~~was~~ *policy would mean* a return to bourgeois conditions. At the same time, the "Left Communists" preached the Trotskyite view that Socialist construction and the victory of socialism in ~~one country~~ *Russia* were impossible.

The "Left" phraseology of the "Left Communists" served to camouflage their defence of the kulaks, idlers and profiteers who were opposed to discipline and hostile to *the* state regulation *of economic life*, to accounting and control. ~~The "Left Communists" regarded the Party line on the use of bourgeois specialists as a retreat from a proletarian policy. The Party led a decisive struggle against the "Left Communists" and against their defence of "petty-bourgeois disorderliness" (LENIN). The Party struggled for the strengthening of the Soviet power and Socialist discipline.~~

~~The Bolshevik Party completely destroyed the "Left Communists" in the summer of 1918, having unmasked once and for all the harm caused by their faux-revolutionary phrases in front of the masses and having shown the counter-revolutionary essence of "Left Communism."~~

~~14. Creation of Committees of the Poor, Struggle with the Kulaks and Development of the Socialist Revolution in the Countryside~~

~~After the elimination of the landlords, the Party set as its main task the destruction of the counter-revolutionary kulaks.~~ *Having settled on the principles of organization of the new, Soviet industry, the Party proceeded to tackle the problems of the countryside, which at this period was in the throes of a struggle between the poor peasants and the kulaks. The kulaks were gaining strength and seizing the lands confiscated from the landlords. The poor peasants needed assistance.* The kulaks fought the proletarian government and refused to ~~provide~~ *sell* grain to it at ~~a~~ fixed prices. They wanted to starve the Soviet state into renouncing Socialist measures. *The Party set the task of smashing the counter-revolutionary kulaks.* Detachments of industrial workers were sent into the countryside with the object of ~~struggling with counter-revolution, starvation and uniting the poor peasants in the struggle~~ *organizing the poor peasants and ensuring the success of the struggle* against the kulaks, who were holding back their grain surpluses.

> "Comrades, workers, remember that the revolution is in a critical situation," Lenin wrote. "Remember that YOU ALONE can save the revolution, nobody else. What we need is tens of thousands of picked, politically advanced workers, loyal to the cause of Socialism, incapable of succumbing to bribery and the temptations of pilfering, and capable of creating an iron force against the kulaks, profiteers, marauders, bribers and disorganizers." (Lenin, COLLECTED WORKS, Russ. ed., Vol. XXIII, p. 25.)

"The struggle for bread is a struggle for Socialism," Lenin said. And it was under this slogan that the sending of workers' detachments to the rural districts was organized. A number of decrees were issued establishing a food dictatorship and conferring emergency powers on the organs of the People's Commissariat of Food for the ~~struggle with the kulaks~~ *purchase of grain at fixed prices.*

A decree was issued on June 11, 1918, providing for the creation of Committees of the Poor Peasants. These committees played an important part in the struggle against the kulaks, in the redistribution of the confiscated land and the distribution of agricultural implements ~~and livestock~~, in the ~~requisitioning~~ *collection* of food surpluses from the kulaks, and in the supply of foodstuffs to the working-class centres and the Red Army. Fifty million hectares of kulak land passed into the hands of the poor and middle peasants. A large portion of the kulaks' ~~tools and~~ means of production was confiscated *and turned over to the poor peasants.*

The formation of the Committees of the Poor Peasants was a further stage in the development of the Socialist revolution in the countryside. The committees were strongholds of the dictatorship of the proletariat in the villages. It was largely through them that enlistment for the Red Army was carried out among the peasants.

The proletarian campaign in the rural districts and the organization of the Committees of the Poor Peasants consolidated the Soviet power in the countryside and were of tremendous political importance in winning over the middle peasants to the side of the Soviet Government.

At the end of 1918, when their task had been completed, *the Committees of the Poor Peasants were merged with the rural Soviets and* their existence was *thus* terminated.

At the Fifth Congress of Soviets which opened on July 4, 1918, ~~and where the overwhelming majority of all delegates were Bolsheviks,~~ the "Left" Socialist-Revolutionaries launched a fierce attack on Lenin in defence of the kulaks. They demanded the discontinuation of the fight against the kulaks~~. They spoke against~~ *and of* the dispatch of *workers'* food detachments *into the countryside.* ~~The speeches of the "Left" Socialist-Revolutionary Spiridonova and Karelin were especially hysterical. The "Left" Socialist-Revolutionary Kamkov proposed to send greetings to the army units, breaking revolutionary discipline.~~ When the "Left" Socialist-Revolutionaries saw that the majority of the congress was firmly ~~against~~ *opposed to* their policy, they started a~~n uprising~~ *revolt* in Moscow and seized Tryokhsvyatitelsky Alley, from which they began to shell the Kremlin. This foolhardy outbreak was put down *by the Bolsheviks* within a few hours ~~and the "Left" Socialist-Revolutionaries fled from Moscow~~. Attempts at revolt were made by "Left" Socialist-Revolutionaries in other parts of the country, but everywhere these outbreaks were speedily suppressed.

As the trial of the Anti-Soviet "Bloc of Rights and Trotskyites" has *now* established, the revolt of the "Left" Socialist-Revolutionaries was started with the knowledge and consent of Bukharin *and Trotsky* and was part of a general counter-revolutionary conspiracy of the Bukharinites, Trotskyites and "Left" Socialist-Revolutionaries *against the Soviet power*.

At this juncture, too, a "Left" Socialist-Revolutionary by the name of Blumkin, afterwards a*n* ~~mean~~ agent of Trotsky, made his way into the German Embassy and ~~provocatively~~ assassinated ~~Baron~~ Mirbach, the German Ambassador *in Moscow*, with the object of ~~starting a new~~ *provoking a* war with Germany. But the Soviet Government managed to avert war and to frustrate the provocateur designs of the counter-revolutionaries.

The Fifth Congress of Soviets adopted the First Soviet Constitution~~, which Comrade Stalin took an active part in developing~~—the Constitution of the Russian Soviet Federative Socialist Republic.

Brief Summary

During the eight months, February to October 1917, the Bolshevik Party accomplished the very difficult task of winning over the majority of the working class~~, the army, the fleet~~ and the majority in the Soviets, and enlisting the support of millions of peasants for the Socialist revolution. It wrested these masses from the influence of the petty-bourgeois parties (Socialist Revolutionaries, Mensheviks and ~~Anarcho-Syndicalists~~ *Anarchists*), by exposing the policy of these parties step by step and showing that it ran counter to the *interests of the* working people. The Bolshevik Party carried on extensive political work at the front and in the rear, preparing the masses for the ~~Great~~ October Socialist Revolution.

The events of decisive importance in the history of the Party at this period were Lenin's arrival from exile abroad ~~and Stalin's return from exile~~, his April Theses, the April *Party* Conference and the Sixth Party Congress. ~~Lenin's and Stalin's speeches and their leadership of the Party~~ *The Party decisions* were a source of strength to the working class and inspired it with confidence in victory; in them the workers found solutions to the important problems of the ~~struggle~~ *revolution*. The April Conference directed the efforts of the Party to the struggle for the transition from the bourgeois-democratic revolution to the Socialist revolution. The Sixth Congress headed the Party for an armed uprising against the bourgeoisie and ~~the~~ *its* Provisional Government.

The ~~petty-bourgeois~~ compromising Socialist-Revolutionary and Menshevik parties, the ~~Anarcho-Syndicalists~~ *Anarchists*, and the other non-Communist parties ~~within the working class~~ completed the cycle of their development: they all became ~~counter-revolutionary~~ bourgeois[38] parties even before the October

Revolution and ~~in its wake became agents of foreign espionage services~~ *fought for the preservation and integrity of the capitalist system*. The Bolshevik Party was the only party which led the struggle of the masses for the ~~proletarian dictatorship and the Socialist revolution~~ *overthrow of the bourgeoisie and the establishment of the power of the Soviets.*

At the same time, the ~~Party~~ *Bolsheviks* defeated the attempts of the capitulators ~~and strikebreakers~~ *within the Party*—Zinoviev, Kamenev, ~~and~~ Rykov, ~~and the traitors~~ Bukharin, Trotsky and Pyatakov ~~and others—who were spreading petty-bourgeois Menshevik influence within the Party,~~ to deflect ~~it~~ *the Party* from the path of Socialist revolution ~~or to forestall the revolutionary moment. Already in this period, disbelief in the victory of the Socialist, proletarian revolution brought together these enemies of Bolshevism, no matter the "shading" of their points of view~~.

~~Under the leadership of Lenin and Stalin, the Party successfully organized the workers and labouring peasantry for the overthrow of the power of the bourgeoisie and landlords. Headed by the Bolshevik Party, the workers, supported by the labouring peasantry, completed the Great October Socialist Revolution, which opened a new epoch in world history.~~ *Headed by the Bolshevik Party, the working class, in alliance with the poor peasants, and with the support of the soldiers and sailors, overthrew the power of the bourgeoisie, established the power of the Soviets, set up a new type of state—a Socialist Soviet state—abolished the landlords' ownership of land, turned over the land to the peasants for their use, nationalized all the land in the country, expropriated the capitalists, achieved the withdrawal of Russia from the war and obtained peace, that is, obtained a much-needed respite, and thus created the conditions for the development of Socialist construction.*

The ~~victorious~~ *October* Socialist Revolution ~~in the U.S.S.R.~~ *smashed capitalism,* deprived the bourgeoisie ~~and landowners~~ of the means of production~~, having~~ *and* converted the mills, factories, land, railways and banks into the ~~people's domain~~ *property of the whole people,* into public property.

~~The Socialist revolution liberated our country from its dependent, semicolonial existence by breaking the secret agreements with the imperialists, pulling the country out of the imperial war, abrogating the onerous foreign loans and carrying out the nationalization of enterprises which belonged to foreign capitalists.~~

~~The Socialist revolution created and strengthened the power of the working people and the proletarian dictatorship in an enormous country for the first time in human history. It brought to life a new type of state—a state of Soviets of Workers' and Peasants' Deputies, Soviets of the Deputies of the Working People.~~

It established the dictatorship of the proletariat and turned over the government of the vast country to the working class, thus making it the ruling class.

~~The October Socialist Revolution created the beginning of the international Socialist revolution of the proletariat.~~

The October Socialist Revolution thereby ushered in a new era in the history of mankind—the era of proletarian revolutions.

CHAPTER EIGHT

The Bolshevik Party in the Period of *Foreign Military Intervention and* Civil War (1918–1920)

1. ~~International Imperialism and the Soviet Republic. The Year 1918.~~ *Beginning of Foreign Military Intervention. First Period of the Civil War*

~~Completion of the Leninist economic plan during the summer of 1918 was disrupted by the Civil War. The war was started by the international bourgeoisie, in alliance with the Russian landlords and bourgeoisie and with the active support of the counter-revolutionary bourgeois Socialist-Revolutionaries, Mensheviks, Anarchists, Bundists, Petlyurites, Georgian Mensheviks, Mussavatists, Dashnaks and other bourgeois nationalist parties. The brief respite was over.~~

The conclusion of the Peace of Brest-Litovsk and the consolidation of the Soviet power, as a result of a series of revolutionary economic measures adopted by it, at a time when the war in the West was still in full swing, created profound alarm among the Western imperialists, especially those of the Entente countries.

The Entente imperialists feared that the conclusion of peace between Germany and Russia might improve Germany's position in the war and correspondingly worsen the position of their own armies. They feared, moreover, that peace between Russia and Germany might stimulate the craving for peace in all countries and on all fronts, and thus interfere with the prosecution of the war and damage the cause of the imperialists. Lastly, they feared that the existence of a Soviet government on the territory of a vast country, and the success it had achieved at home after the overthrow of the power of the bourgeoisie, might serve as an infectious example for the workers and soldiers of the West. Profoundly discontented with the protracted war, the workers and soldiers might follow in the footsteps of the Russians and turn their bayonets against their masters and oppressors. Consequently, the Entente governments decided to intervene in Russia by armed force with the object of overthrowing the Soviet Government and establishing a bourgeois government, which would restore the bourgeois system in the country, annul the peace treaty with the Germans and re-establish the military front against Germany and Austria.

ГЛАВА VIII

ПАРТИЯ БОЛЬШЕВИКОВ В ПЕРИОД ГРАЖДАНСКОЙ ВОЙНЫ

(1918—1920 годы)

1. Международный империализм и Советская республика. 1918 год

Выполнение ленинского хозяйственного плана летом 1918 года было сорвано гражданской войной. Войну начали международные империалисты в союзе с русскими помещиками и буржуазией, при активной поддержке со стороны контрреволюционных буржуазных партий эсеров, меньшевиков, анархистов, бундовцев, петлюровцев, грузинских меньшевиков, муссаватистов, дашнаков и прочих буржуазных националистических партий. Передышка кончилась.

Еще весной 1918 года германские войска заняли Украину, куда их призвали украинские буржуазные националисты (Украинская рада, петлюровцы). Советская власть на Украине была свергнута. Вместо Рады немцы вскоре поставили у власти гетмана Скоропадского—крупного помещика, бывшего царского генерала. Украина была превращена в немецкую колонию, откуда немцы спешно вывозили скот, хлеб и другие продукты. Украинские рабочие и крестьяне подвергались тяжелому гнету со стороны иноземных завоевателей и на зверства германских империалистов отвечали массовыми восстаниями. В то же время германский империализм задушил пролетарскую революцию в Финляндии. Немецкие войска стояли недалеко от Петрограда.

Наряду с германскими капиталистами на Советскую Россию набросились империалисты Англии, Франции и других стран Антанты. Они помогали белогвардейцам деньгами, снаряжением, оружием. Империалисты посылали в нашу страну войска, чтобы свергнуть советскую власть, превратить Россию в колонию, разделить ее на части. Гражданская война была войной против иноземного нашествия, против порабощения нашей родины империалистическими государствами, войной за свободу и независимость нашей родины. Большевистская партия подняла народные массы на *отечественную* войну против иностранных захватчиков и угнетателей.

Международный империализм был руководителем российской контрреволюции, вдохновителем ее планов борьбы с советской властью, организатором ее войны против пролетарской диктатуры. Гражданская война представляла собой, таким образом, не только борьбу пролетарской диктатуры против внутренней контрреволюции, против помещиков и буржуазии, —она являлась в то же время

178

Crossed-out first page of Chapter Eight, from the summer of 1938. RGASPI, f. 558, op. 11, d. 1211, l. 355.

The Entente imperialists launched upon this sinister enterprise all the more readily because they were convinced that the Soviet Government was unstable; they had no doubt that with some effort on the part of its enemies its early fall would be inevitable.

The achievements of the Soviet Government and its consolidation created even greater alarm among the deposed classes—the landlords and capitalists; in the ranks of the vanquished parties—the Constitutional-Democrats, Mensheviks, Socialist-Revolutionaries, Anarchists and the bourgeois nationalists of all hues; and among the Whiteguard generals, Cossack officers, etc.

From the very first days of the victorious October Revolution, all these hostile elements began to shout from the housetops that there was no ground in Russia for a Soviet power, that it was doomed, that it was bound to fall within a week or two, or a month, or two or three months at most. But as the Soviet Government, despite the imprecations of its enemies, continued to exist and gain strength, its foes within Russia were forced to admit that it was much stronger than they had imagined, and that its overthrow would require great efforts and a fierce struggle on the part of all the forces of counter-revolution. They therefore decided to embark upon counter-revolutionary insurrectionary activities on a broad scale: to mobilize the forces of counter-revolution, to assemble military cadres and to organize revolts, especially in the Cossack and kulak districts.

~~Already in the spring of 1918, German troops had occupied the Ukraine after they were summoned by the Ukrainian bourgeois nationalists (the Ukrainian Rada and the Petlyurites). The Soviet power in the Ukraine was overthrown. In the place of the Rada, the Germans quickly brought to power the Hetman Skoropadsky—a major landlord and former tsarist general. The Ukraine was transformed into a German colony, from which the Germans quickly began to extract livestock, grain and other foodstuffs. The Ukrainian workers and peasants endured heavy exploitation from the foreign conquerors and responded to the German atrocities with mass uprisings. At the same time, German imperialism stifled the proletarian revolution in Finland. German forces were then stationed close to Petrograd.~~

~~Along with the German capitalists, the imperialists of England, France and the other countries of the Entente attacked Soviet Russia. They assisted the Whiteguards with money, arms and weaponry. The imperialists sent troops to our country in order to overthrow the Soviet power and convert Russia into a colony and divide her into separate parts. The Civil War was a war against foreign intervention, a war against the imperialist governments' enslavement of our motherland, a war for the freedom and independence of our motherland. The Bolshevik Party mobilized the popular masses for a war for the FATHERLAND against the foreign invaders and oppressors.~~

~~International imperialism led the Russian counter-revolution and served as the inspiration for its plans for struggle with the Soviet power and the organizer for its war against the proletarian dictatorship. The Civil War was, in this way, not just a struggle of the proletarian dictatorship against the internal counter-revolution and the landlords and bourgeoisie, but it was at the same time a struggle of the proletarian revolution against worldwide imperialism, the goal of which was to stifle Soviet Russia at all costs. The imperialists were scared to death that the flame of proletarian revolution in Russia might spread to their countries.~~

Thus, already in the first half of 1918, two definite forces took shape that were prepared to embark upon the overthrow of the Soviet power, namely, the foreign imperialists of the Entente and the counter-revolutionaries at home.

~~It was only as a result of the imperialists' support of the Whiteguards that the Civil War dragged on for five years. Had there not been this support, and had there not been the intervention of the imperialist governments, Soviet Russia would have defeated the Whiteguards and changed over to peaceful construction in short order.~~

Neither of these forces possessed all the requisites needed to undertake the overthrow of the Soviet Government singly. The counter-revolutionaries in Russia had certain military cadres and man-power, drawn principally from the upper classes of the Cossacks and from the kulaks, enough to start a rebellion against the Soviet Government. But they possessed neither money nor arms. The foreign imperialists, on the other hand, had the money and the arms, but could not "release" a sufficient number of troops for purposes of intervention; they could not do so, not only because these troops were required for the war with Germany and Austria, but because they might not prove altogether reliable in a war against the Soviet power.

The conditions of the struggle against the Soviet power dictated a union of the two anti-Soviet forces, foreign and domestic. And this union was effected in the first half of 1918.

This was how the foreign military intervention against the Soviet power supported by counter-revolutionary revolts of its foes at home originated.

This was the end of the respite in Russia and the beginning of the Civil War, which was a war of the workers and peasants of the nations of Russia against the foreign and domestic enemies of the Soviet power.

~~On the periphery of the Soviet Republic, far from the industrial centres, the Whiteguards organized their forces, which were to return the landlords and capitalists to power. With German assistance, the Cossack General Krasnov formed an army on the Don which advanced on Tsaritsyn and Voronezh during the summer of 1918. In the South-East, the Cossack Dutov's forces made war on the Soviet power near Orenburg and Uralsk. In the Spring of 1918, the Japanese landed troops in Vladivostok. Gradually, they occupied almost~~

~~all of the far eastern Maritime Province. The "Allies," that is, the Anglo-French capitalists, organized an uprising of the Czechoslovak Corps against the Soviet power. The corps had been assembled already before the October revolution from Czech and Slovak prisoners-of-war for the fight against the Germans. The "Allies" requested that these corps be sent from the Ukraine to Vladivostok along the Trans-Siberian Railway, supposedly so that they could be transported to France by sea in order to continue the war against the Germans. In actuality, the idea of moving the corps was devised by the imperialists in order to stage an intervention and overthrow the Soviet power. Just as soon as the main force of the Czechoslovak corps reached the Volga at the end of May 1918, the corps on the order of the Anglo-French capitalists rose up in revolt against the Soviet power. The Czechoslovaks seized the whole railroad from Samara through Chelyabinsk to Irkutsk and even further. In this way, the middle stretches of the Volga, the Urals and Siberia to the Far East were occupied by the Czechoslovaks with the support of the Socialist-Revolutionaries and Mensheviks. A Whiteguard-Socialist-Revolutionary government was set up in Samara. A Whiteguard government of Siberia took shape in Omsk.~~

The imperialists of Great Britain, France, Japan and America started their military intervention without any declaration of war, although the intervention was a war, a war against Russia, and the worst kind of war at that. These "civilized" marauders secretly and stealthily made their way to Russian shores and landed their troops on Russia's territory.

The British and French landed troops in the North, occupied Archangel and Murmansk, supported a local Whiteguard revolt, overthrew the Soviets and set up a White "Government of North Russia."

The Japanese landed troops in Vladivostok, seized the Maritime Province, dispersed the Soviets and supported the Whiteguard rebels, who subsequently restored the bourgeois system.

In the North Caucasus, Generals Kornilov, Alexeyev and Denikin, with the support of the British and French, formed a Whiteguard "Volunteer Army," raised a revolt of the upper classes of the Cossacks and started hostilities against the Soviets.

On the Don, Generals Krasnov and Mamontov, with the secret support of the German imperialists (the Germans hesitated to support them openly owing to the peace treaty between Germany and Russia), raised a revolt of Don Cossacks, occupied the Don region and started hostilities against the Soviets.

In the Middle Volga region and in Siberia, the British and French instigated a revolt of the Czechoslovak Corps. This corps, which consisted of prisoners of war, had received permission from the Soviet Government to return home through Siberia and the Far East. But on the way it was used by the Socialist-Revolutionaries and by the British and French for a revolt against the Soviet Government.

The revolt of the corps served as a signal for a revolt of the kulaks in the Volga region and in Siberia, and of the workers of the Votkinsk and Izhevsk Works, who were under the influence of the Socialist-Revolutionaries. A Whiteguard-Socialist-Revolutionary government was set up in the Volga region, in Samara, and a Whiteguard government of Siberia, in Omsk, took shape.

~~With the assistance of Anglo-French forces, which landed in the North, the Whiteguards seized the Murmansk region and Archangel during the summer of 1918. In July, the Whiteguards rose in revolt in Yaroslavl, Rybinsk and Murom with the goal of clearing a path to Moscow for the counter-revolution. In Moscow itself at this time, there was an uprising of the "Left" Socialist-Revolutionaries. They were swiftly suppressed. The commander of the Red forces against the Czechoslovaks, the traitor Muravyev, a "Left" Socialist-Revolutionary, opened his lines to the enemy. Muravyev's uprising was quickly suppressed. The counter-revolutionary mutinies in Murom and Rybinsk were quickly eliminated as well. Only in Yaroslavl were the Whiteguards able to hold out for around two weeks. In an array of places, kulak uprisings were also sparked. Everywhere, the Socialist-Revolutionaries and Mensheviks supported the counter-revolutionary uprisings against the Soviets.~~

~~In the North Caucasus, General Denikin put together the Volunteer Army with the assistance and leadership of the Anglo-French capitalists. The Caucasus were seized by Turkish and German troops. Under their protection, and later under the protection of the British, the Georgian Mensheviks and Azerbaidjan Mussavatists (a bourgeois nationalist party) seized Georgia and Azerbaidjan. On the night of September 20, 1918, the British interventionists and Socialist Revolutionaries treacherously executed 26 Bolshevik commissars captured in Baku under the command of the Central Committee member Stepan Shaumyan.~~

~~Under the cover of the bourgeois flag of "democracy," the Mensheviks, Socialist-Revolutionaries, Anarchists and Bundists played a rotten and traitorous role in the Civil War while calling themselves Socialists. They took an active part in the Civil War on the side of the capitalists, landlords and Whiteguard generals. On the orders of the imperialists, they organized counter-revolutionary kulak uprisings during the summer of 1918. They assisted the counter-revolutionary generals in overthrowing Soviet power in an array of regions. In the Ukraine, they supported the German imperialists and on the Volga—the Czechoslovaks, in the North—the British, and in the Far East—the Japanese. The Socialist-Revolutionaries organized an array of terrorist attacks against leading Bolsheviks in order to sow confusion within the ranks of the Bolshevik Party. Their bullets gravely wounded Lenin (August 30, 1918) and killed Volodarsky and Uritsky. The Socialist-Revolutionaries and Anarchists threw a bomb into the Moscow Bolshevik Party Committee building. The working class responded to the White terror of the Socialist-Revolutionaries and~~

~~bourgeoisie with a mass Red terror against the bourgeoisie and its lackeys and agents.~~

~~During the Civil War, the landlords and capitalists, the kulaks, the well-off peasantry and Cossacks, a portion of the bourgeois specialists, the old bureaucrats and the whole petty-bourgeois intelligentsia took the side of the counter-revolution. On the side of the revolution were the proletariat and the poor peasantry. Between these two forces was the main part of the peasantry, the middle peasants, who tended toward the proletariat but whose temporary wavering in certain regions allowed the enemies of the proletarian revolution the chance to win temporary victories.~~

Germany took no part in the intervention of this British-French-Japanese-American bloc; nor could she do so, since she was at war with this bloc if for no other reason. But in spite of this, and notwithstanding the existence of a peace treaty between Russia and Germany, no Bolshevik doubted that Kaiser Wilhelm's government was just as rabid an enemy of Soviet Russia as the British-French-Japanese-American invaders. And, indeed, the German imperialists did their utmost to isolate, weaken and destroy Soviet Russia. They snatched from it the Ukraine—true, it was in accordance with a "treaty" with the Whiteguard Ukrainian Rada (Council)—brought in their troops at the request of the Rada and began mercilessly to rob and oppress the Ukrainian people, forbidding them to maintain any connections whatever with Soviet Russia. They severed Transcaucasia from Soviet Russia, sent German and Turkish troops there at the request of the Georgian and Azerbaidjan nationalists and began to play the masters in Tiflis and in Baku. They supplied, not openly, it is true, abundant arms and provisions to General Krasnov, who had raised a revolt against the Soviet Government on the Don.

Soviet Russia was thus cut off from her principal sources of food, raw material and fuel.

~~Toward the end of the summer of 1918, the Soviet Republic found itself in an extremely difficult position—a ring of fire. It was encircled on all sides by enemies. On September 2, the Soviet Republic was declared an armed camp. Military action at the front was met with temporary setbacks.~~ *Conditions were hard in Soviet Russia at that period. There was a shortage of bread and meat.* ~~At this time a frightful famine tormented~~ The workers ~~and the industrial centres~~ *were starving.* In ~~the capitals~~ *Moscow and Petrograd* a bread ration ~~made with linseed byproducts~~ of one-eighth of a pound was issued to them every other day, and there were times when no bread was issued at all. *The factories were at a standstill, or almost at a standstill, owing to a lack of raw materials and fuel. But the working class did not lose heart. Nor did the Bolshevik Party. The desperate struggle waged to overcome the incredible difficulties of that period showed how inexhaustible is the energy latent in the working class and how immense the prestige*[1] *of the Bolshevik Party.* ~~The industrial centres endured this difficult situation with foodstuffs for the duration of the Civil War.~~

~~During those terrible days, the Soviet Republic's workers and peasant masses heroically rose up to defend the Soviet power against the combined forces of the counter-revolution and the interventionists. Despite the hunger and deprivation, they rallied around Lenin, the Bolshevik Party and the Soviet power. The Bolsheviks issued the slogan, "All for victory, all for the defeat of the enemy!" For the defence of the country, THE BOLSHEVIK PARTY CREATED THE WORKERS' AND PEASANTS' RED ARMY. The Bolsheviks had begun to build the Red Army already at the start of 1918, during the German advance on Petrograd. The army was formed at first on a volunteer basis, and then, after the Czechoslovak mutiny was sparked, the Soviet power converted to compulsory military service for all working people. Those denied electoral rights and non-working elements were not accepted into the Red Army. They were used to form labour militias for work on the home front. Military specialists and former White officers were used with great care during the formation of the Red Army. The army placed them under strict proletarian control. While it was harnessing the military specialists, the Party punished them mercilessly for any instance of counter-revolutionary activity.~~

The Party proclaimed the country an armed camp and placed its economic, cultural and political life on a war footing. The Soviet Government announced that "the Socialist fatherland is in danger," and called upon the people to rise in its defence. Lenin issued the slogan, "All for the front!"—and hundreds of thousands of workers and peasants volunteered for service in the Red Army and left for the front. About half the membership of the Party and of the Young Communist League went to the front.[2] *The Party roused the people for a* WAR FOR THE FATHERLAND, *a war against the foreign invaders and against the revolts of the exploiting classes whom the revolution had overthrown. The Council of Workers' and Peasants' Defence, organized by Lenin, directed the work of supplying the front with reinforcements, food, clothing and arms. The substitution of compulsory military service for the volunteer system brought hundreds of thousands of new recruits into the Red Army and very shortly raised its strength to over a million men.*

~~The Czechoslovaks posed the greatest danger to the Soviet Republic during the summer of 1918. The Red Army found itself in a very difficult position: its provisions and armaments were very inferior to what the Whites had, as they had received everything they needed from the imperialists. Moreover, there no military knowledge, experience or discipline. But already toward the fall of 1918, there was a major breakthrough in military action and the Red Army began to defeat the Whiteguards. Kazan, Simbirsk (Ulyanovsk) and Samara (October 7) were liberated from the Czechoslovak troops. In October and November 1918, the Red forces on the Eastern Front went on the offensive almost~~

~~everywhere, clearing the Kama of the Whites and pushing the Czechoslovaks up against the Urals.~~

~~Military Communist commissars played a large role in the Red Army. They strengthened and rallied the units of the Red Army in an ideological and political sense and conducted major political work among the Red Army soldiers and the whole frontline population. This was very important, as it was necessary to expose the lies of the Whiteguard press and agitators, who sowed provocative rumors and panic.~~

~~At the end of 1918, the Council on the Workers and Peasants' Defence was formed under the leadership of Lenin, who was the inspiration for the defence of the republic. This council, which was later transformed into the Council for Labour and Defence (S.T.O.), held enormous significance for the organization of the defence at the front and in the rear, and for supplying the army with everything that it needed. In the struggle with the enemy, the front and rear were one and the same.~~

~~Along with Lenin, Comrade Stalin played an exceptional role in the defeat of the counter-revolution and intervention. He took the most active role in the formation of the Red Army and in devising strategic plans; he personally led the largest military operations. In the republic's most difficult moments, the Party sent Comrade Stalin to the most critical sections of the front. Everywhere, where conditions were tense, it was Comrade Stalin's iron will that inspired the troops and halted desertion, confidently rallying them to victory. Comrade Stalin's organizational talent assisted in the quick elimination of shortcomings and enemy breakthroughs.~~

~~In May 1918, Comrade Stalin was sent by Lenin to the Tsaritsyn Front to lead the fight against Krasnov and at the same time to take charge of all work concerning foodstuffs. All of Soviet Russia's starving urban centres depended on Comrade Stalin's success in this work. A brilliant, heroic defence of this city was waged in the summer and fall of 1918 under the leadership of Comrades Stalin and Voroshilov, the latter of whom had come to Tsarityn from the workers and peasants of the Donetz Basin region. Under the leadership of Comrade Stalin, the reorganized Red forces defended Tsaritysn and drove the Whites far away, preventing General Krasnov's troops from uniting with other Whiteguard troops on the Eastern Front. It was here, in Tsaritsyn, that at the initiative of Comrades Stalin and Voroshilov, major cavalry units started to form that would become the undefeatable First Mounted Army. Comrade Budyonny took on a major role in its organization from the start.~~

~~Having been dealt a setback at Tsaritysn, the Whites attempted to unite the Southern and Eastern Fronts where Comrade Kirov was located in Astrakhan at the end of 1918 and the start of 1919. A large mass of Whiteguards were gathering in Astrakhan. Kirov had to put down conspiracies several times.~~

~~Astrakhan had no grain or fuel. Trotsky issued a treacherous order to Comrade Kirov to abandon the city. But Kirov refused to obey this command and sent a report to Lenin in which he wrote that "as long as there is even a single Communist left in the Astrakhan region, the mouth of the Volga will remain Soviet." Lenin agreed with Kirov and gave the order not to surrender Astrakhan.~~

~~Organizing the defence of the republic at the front, it was necessary at the same time to struggle against counter-revolution in the rear. The All-Russian Extraordinary Commission for the Struggle with Counter-Revolution (V.Ch.K.) took on this tense work under the command of F. E. Dzerzhinsky. The Extraordinary Commission fought against the counter-revolution and uncovered Whiteguard and Socialist-Revolutionary-Menshevist-Anarchist conspiracies with the help of the working people that sometimes took on grandiose proportions. The Extraordinary Commission captured enemies in their secret organizations, hunted down Whiteguard headquarters and centres and waged a struggle with sabotage, diversionists and spies.~~

~~All the foreign espionage services were setting up networks for conspiracies, uprisings, spies and diversionists—the most important British agents and provocateurs; German spies; the leaders of the Polish espionage, diversionist and terroristic organization—the Polish Military Organization (P.O.V.); Araki, the organizer of all Japanese anti-Soviet adventurism and the head of the Japanese military mission in Vladivostok; and agents of French imperialism. They were preparing to stab Soviet Russia in the back at the decisive moment in the struggle on the fronts of the Civil War.~~

~~In 1918, the Extraordinary Commission under Comrade Dzerzhinsky uncovered and eliminated the largest conspiracy under the British agent Lockhart, which was in essence a conspiracy of all the espionage services of worldwide capitalism. This conspiracy's plans were discussed at foreign diplomatic meetings. The conspirators set their sights on contact with Trotsky and his Bukharinite followers in order to disrupt the peaceful respite and undermine the Brest Peace. They prepared the provocative rebellion of military units, the arrest of the entire All-Russian Central Executive Committee and the murder of Lenin.~~

~~Lockhart and his accomplices assembled a conspiracy consisting of many elements—the Czechoslovak mutiny; the military mutiny of "The Union for the Defence of the Motherland and Freedom," Savinkov's counter-revolutionary organization in Yaroslavl, Murom and Rybinsk; the counter-revolutionary mutiny of the "Left" Socialist-Revolutionaries; the murder of Uritsky and Volodarsky; and the attempted assassination of Lenin.~~

~~The Party sent the best Bolsheviks to work in the Extraordinary Commission. The honorable title "Chekist" became the term for a fearless fighter who was utterly committed to the cause of Communism.~~

Although the country was in a difficult position, and the young Red Army was not yet consolidated, the measures of defence adopted soon yielded their first fruits. General Krasnov was forced back from Tsaritsyn, whose capture he had regarded as certain, and driven beyond the River Don. General Denikin's operations were localized within a small area in the North Caucasus, while General Kornilov was killed in action against the Red Army. The Czechoslovaks and the Whiteguard-Socialist-Revolutionary bands were ousted from Kazan, Simbirsk[3] *and Samara and driven to the Urals. A revolt in Yaroslavl headed by the Whiteguard Savinkov and organized by Lockhart, chief of the British Mission in Moscow, was suppressed, and Lockhart himself arrested. The Socialist-Revolutionaries, who had assassinated Comrades Uritsky and Volodarsky and had made a villainous attempt on the life of*[4] *Lenin, were subjected to a Red terror in retaliation for their White terror against the Bolsheviks, and were completely routed in every important city in Central Russia.*

The young Red Army matured and hardened in battle.

The work of the Communist Commissars was of decisive importance in the consolidation and political education of the Red Army and in raising its discipline and fighting efficiency.

~~The Bolsheviks conducted an enormous amount of organizational and agitational work in the struggle with the Whiteguards and the interventionists. Toward the winter of 1918, the Red Army advanced to the East and South against the Czechoslovaks and Krasnov. The Soviet state apparatus had grown stronger. The tense situation with foodstuffs had eased somewhat, thanks to the tireless work of the food supply brigades. The leaders of these brigades, brave and energetic Bolsheviks, seized grain from the kulaks.~~

But the Bolshevik Party knew that these were only the first, not the decisive successes of the Red Army. It was aware that new and far more serious battles were still to come, and that the country could recover the lost food, raw material and fuel regions only by a prolonged and stubborn struggle with the enemy. The Bolsheviks therefore undertook intense preparations for a protracted war and decided to place the whole country at the service of the front. The Soviet Government[5] *introduced* WAR COMMUNISM. *It took under its control the middle-sized and small industries, in addition to large-scale industry, so as to accumulate goods for the supply of the army and the agricultural population. It introduced a state monopoly of the grain trade, prohibited private trading in grain and established the surplus-appropriation system, under which all surplus produce in the hands of the peasants was to be registered and acquired by the state at fixed prices, so as to accumulate stores of grain for the provisioning of the army and the workers. Lastly, it introduced universal labour service for all classes. By making physical labour compulsory for the bourgeoisie and thus releasing workers for other duties of greater importance to the front, the Party was giving practical effect to the principle: "He who does not work, neither shall he eat."*

All these measures, which were necessitated by the exceptionally difficult conditions of national defence, and bore a temporary character, were in their entirety known as War Communism.

The country prepared itself for a long and exacting Civil War, for a war against the foreign and internal enemies of the Soviet power. By the end of 1918 it had to increase the strength of the army threefold, and to accumulate supplies for this army.

Lenin said at that time:

> *"We had decided to have an army of one million men by the spring; now we need an army of three million. We can get it. And we will get it."*

2. *Defeat of Germany in the War.* Revolution in Germany ~~and Austro-Hungary. Establishment~~ *Founding* of the ~~Communist~~ *Third* International. Eighth Party Congress

While the Soviet country was preparing for new battles against the forces of foreign intervention, in the West decisive events were taking place in the belligerent countries, both on the war fronts and in their interior. Germany and Austria were suffocating in the grip of war and a food crisis. Whereas Great Britain, France and the United States were continually drawing upon new resources, Germany and Austria were consuming their last meagre stocks. The situation was such that Germany and Austria, having reached the stage of extreme exhaustion, were on the brink of defeat.

~~The October revolution stirred the working masses of every country. Hatred for those responsible for the war and the enormous suffering of the working masses in the capitalist countries spilled over into explicit uprisings against the imperialist governments. Revolution erupted in Germany and Austro-Hungary in November 1918. It was accelerated by the German military defeat. The revolting workers and soldiers overthrew the monarchy of Wilhelm II. The Austrian emperor was overthrown as well. Immediately after the revolution in Germany and Austro-Hungary, the Soviet Republic annulled the burdensome Brest Peace agreement, which had been forced upon our country by the German imperialists. It was the beginning of a time of a tremendous revolutionary upsurge of the masses. Lenin's prediction of the inevitability of revolution in the West-European countries was proven entirely correct. Units of the Red Army moved to the West and South on the heels of the retreating German troops. Soviet power proved victorious in an entire array of regions—in Esthonia, Latvia, Lithuania, Byelorussia—once they were liberated from their occupiers.~~

At the same time, the peoples of Germany and Austria were seething with indignation against the disastrous and interminable war, and against their imperi-

alist governments who had reduced them to a state of exhaustion and starvation. The revolutionary influence of the October Revolution also had a tremendous effect, as did the fraternization of the Soviet soldiers with the Austrian and German soldiers at the front even before the Peace of Brest-Litovsk, the actual termination of the war with Soviet Russia and the conclusion of peace with her. The people of Russia had brought about the end of the detested war by overthrowing their imperialist government, and this could not but serve as an object lesson to the Austrian and German workers. And the German soldiers who had been stationed on the Eastern front and who after the Peace of Brest-Litovsk were transferred to the Western front could not but undermine the morale of the German army on that front by their accounts of the fraternization with the Soviet[6] *soldiers and of the way the Soviet*[7] *soldiers had got rid of the war. The disintegration of the Austrian army from the same causes had begun even earlier.*

All this served to accentuate the craving for peace among the German soldiers; they lost their former fighting efficiency and began to retreat in face of the onslaught of the Entente armies. In November 1918 a revolution broke out in Germany, and Wilhelm and his government were overthrown.

Germany was obliged to acknowledge defeat and to sue for peace.

Thus at one stroke Germany was reduced from a first-rate power to a second-rate power.

~~In Germany, the proletarian revolution met with many more difficulties than in Russia. The Soviets that appeared in Germany were neither revolutionary organs, nor organs of state power. The tragedy of the working class of Germany and of the other European countries was that at the moment of the most bitter class struggle and revolutionary outrage among the masses, the workers lacked the sort of party to lead them that the Russian proletariat had had. Traitors of the working class—the German Mensheviks—stood at the head of the German revolution and the Soviets that were forming at this time. Carrying out the orders of their masters the bourgeoisie, they took control of the Soviets in order to strip them of their political power and influence, just as the Russian Mensheviks and Socialist-Revolutionaries had tried to do in Russia after the February 1917 revolution. The German Social-Democrats transformed the Soviets into an appendage of the bourgeois parliament. The German Mensheviks assisted the bourgeoisie in destroying the working class's revolutionary movement. The German Communists—that is, the "Spartacus" League under Karl Liebknecht and Rosa Luxemburg—had only begun to act. In January 1919, Luxemburg and Liebknecht were savagely murdered by German Whiteguardists, assisted by the Mensheviks. The proletariat paid homage to Rosa Luxemburg and Karl Liebknecht as heroes of the proletarian revolution.~~

As far as the position of the Soviet Government was concerned, this circumstance had certain disadvantages, inasmuch as it made the Entente countries, which had started armed intervention against the Soviet power, the dominant force in Europe and Asia, and enabled them to intervene more actively in the Soviet country and to blockade her, to draw the noose more tightly around the Soviet power. And this was what actually happened, as we shall see later. On the other hand, it had its advantages, which outweighed the disadvantages and fundamentally improved the position of Soviet Russia. In the first place, the Soviet Government was now able to annul the predatory Peace of Brest-Litovsk, to stop paying the indemnities, and to start an open struggle, military and political, for the liberation of Esthonia, Latvia, Byelorussia, Lithuania, the Ukraine and Transcaucasia from the yoke of German imperialism. Secondly, and chiefly, the existence in the centre of Europe, in Germany, of a republican regime and of Soviets of Workers' and Soldiers' Deputies was bound to revolutionize, and actually did revolutionize, the countries of Europe, and this could not but strengthen the position of the Soviet power in Russia. True, the revolution in Germany was not a Socialist but a bourgeois revolution, and the Soviets were an obedient tool of the bourgeois parliament, for they were dominated by the[8] *Social-Democrats, who were compromisers of the type of the Russian Mensheviks. This in fact explains the weakness of the German revolution. How weak it really was is shown, for example, by the fact that it allowed the German Whiteguards to assassinate such prominent revolutionaries as Rosa Luxemburg and Karl Liebknecht with impunity.*[9] *Nevertheless, it was a revolution: Wilhelm had been overthrown, and the workers had cast off their chains; and this in itself was bound to unloose the revolution in the West, was bound to call forth a rise in the revolution in the European countries.*

~~The revolutionary movement in Central Europe continued to develop. On March 21, 1919, a Soviet Republic was proclaimed in Hungary. It lasted more than four months. A Bavarian Soviet Republic also emerged. Both of these republics were stifled by the imperialists. Significant revolutionary movements at that time, in 1919, were also active in Switzerland, Poland, France and other countries. Communist parties formed in America and an array of other countries under the influence of the Russian revolution and the growing revolutionary movement in the West.~~

The tide of revolution in Europe began to mount. A revolutionary movement started in Austria, and a Soviet Republic arose in Hungary. With the rising tide of the revolution Communist parties came to the surface.

~~Lenin and the Bolsheviks had struggled to organize a Communist International for many years, to create an international association of the revolutionary workers of the world. Now that goal was realized.~~

A real basis now existed for a union of the Communist parties, for the formation of the Third, Communist International.

In March 1919, on the initiative of the Bolsheviks, headed by Lenin, *the First Congress of the Communist Parties of various countries, held in Moscow, founded* the Communist International ~~was founded by the First Congress of the Communist Parties of various countries, held in Moscow.~~[10] Although many of the delegates were prevented by the blockade and imperialist persecution from arriving in Moscow, the most important countries of Europe and America were represented at this First Congress. The work of the congress was guided by Lenin.

Lenin reported on the subject of bourgeois democracy and the dictatorship of the proletariat. He brought out the importance of the Soviet system, showing that it meant genuine democracy for the working people. The congress adopted a manifesto to the proletariat of all countries calling upon them to wage a determined struggle for the dictatorship of the proletariat and for the triumph of Soviets all over the world.

The congress set up an Executive Committee of the Third Communist International (E.C.C.I.)~~, which from that time has served as the military headquarters of the international revolutionary working-class movement~~.

Thus was founded an international revolutionary proletarian organization of a new type~~, based on the Bolshevik experience and on the basis of Lenin's teaching~~—*the Communist International—the Marxist-Leninist International.* ~~The foundation of the Communist International was an event of world-class historical significance.~~

~~3. Eighth Party Congress~~

~~The Civil War continued with varying success. Along with major victories were no fewer major defeats. At the start of 1919, the Germans left a significant portion of the Ukraine, but they were relieved by the "Allies" (England and France), who landed troops in Russia in the South. In the East at the end of 1918, the Red Army suffered a major defeat at Perm. Comrade Stalin, sent there by Lenin, was able to restore the situation and halt the Whites' advance. The danger from the East, however, from the Urals and Siberia, did not disappear. The Entente was preparing an even larger offensive against Soviet Russia.~~

~~In this unusually difficult and complex situation in the Civil War,~~ *T*he Eighth Congress of our Party met ~~in Moscow~~ in March 1919. *It assembled in the midst of a conflict of contradictory factors—on the one hand, the reactionary bloc of the Entente countries against the Soviet Government had grown stronger, and, on the other, the rising tide of revolution in Europe, especially in the defeated countries, had considerably improved the position of the Soviet country.*

The congress was attended by 301 delegates with vote, representing 313,766 members of the Party, and 102 delegates with voice but no vote.

In his inaugural speech, Lenin paid homage to the memory of *Y. M. Sverdlov,* one of the ~~most important~~ *finest* organizing talents in the Bolshevik Party, ~~Y. M. Sverdlov,~~ who had died on the eve of the congress.

The ~~Eighth Party~~ congress adopted a new *Party* Program[11]~~, which had been drafted by Lenin~~. This program gives a description of capitalism and of its highest phase—imperialism. ~~It pointed to the imperative of mercilessly struggling with open opportunists and chauvinists within the international workers' movement in order to advance the goal of victory of the world revolution.~~ It compares two systems of state—the bourgeois-democratic system and the Soviet ~~state~~ *system*. It details the specific tasks of the Party in the struggle for Socialism: completion of the expropriation of the bourgeoisie; administration of the economic life of the country in accordance with a single *Socialist* plan; participation of the trade unions in the organization of the *national* economy; Socialist labour discipline; utilization of bourgeois experts *in the economic field* under the control of Soviet bodies; gradual and systematic enlistment of the middle peasantry in the work of Socialist construction.

The congress adopted Lenin's proposal to include in the program in addition to a definition of imperialism as the highest ~~rung in the development~~ *stage* of capitalism, the description of industrial capitalism and simple commodity production contained in the old program adopted at the Second *Party* Congress. Lenin considered it essential that the program should take account of the complexity of our economic system and note the existence of diverse economic formations in the country, including small commodity production, as represented by the middle peasants. Therefore, during the debate on the program, Lenin vigorously condemned the anti-Bolshevik views of Bukharin, who proposed that ~~nothing should be said in the program about~~ *the clauses*[12] *dealing with* capitalism, small commodity production, the economy of the middle peasant, *be left out of the program*. Bukharin's views represented a Menshevik-Trotskyite denial of the role played by the middle peasant ~~as an ally of the working class~~ *in the development of the Soviet state.*[13] Furthermore, Bukharin glossed over the fact that the small *commodity* production of the peasants bred and nourished kulak elements.

Lenin further refuted the anti-Bolshevik views of Bukharin and Pyatakov on the national question. They spoke against the inclusion in the program of a clause on the right of nations to self-determination; they were against the ~~parity~~ *equality* of nations, claiming that it was a slogan that would hinder the victory of the proletarian revolution and the union of the proletarians of different nationalities. Lenin ~~defeated~~ *overthrew* these utterly pernicious, imperialist, chauvinist views *of Bukharin and Pyatakov*. ~~He pointed out as an example that we have recognized the right of nations to self-determination in those places where there is not already a proletarian dictatorship and where bourgeois power is still in place (in Finland). Were we to refuse to recognize this right, we would incite against ourselves a revolt within the PROLETARIAN part of those nationalities. The congress agreed wholeheartedly with Lenin on this issue. The~~

~~correct solution to the national question had enormous significance, strengthening the unity of the working class with the peasantry of those nationalities that had been oppressed under the tsar. The Leninist policy on the national question contributed to the successful conclusion of the Civil War. It furnished the Soviet power with the trust, sympathy and support of the periphery, which was populated by non-Russian peoples. Working people of these nationalities saw that the Soviet state embodied the fairest form of ethnic interrelations to be established by the proletariat and labouring peasant masses.~~

A ~~central~~ *serious* place in the deliberations of the Eighth Congress was devoted to policy towards the middle peasants. The ~~October revolution~~ *Decree on the Land* had resulted in a steady growth in the number of middle peasants, *who now comprised the majority of the peasant population*. The attitude and conduct of the middle peasantry, which vacillated between the bourgeoisie and the proletariat, was of momentous importance for the ~~victory in~~ *fate of* the Civil War and ~~for the cause of~~ Socialist construction. The outcome of the *Civil War largely* depended on *which way the middle peasant would swing,* which class would win his allegiance—the proletariat or the bourgeoisie. The Czechoslovaks, the Whiteguards, the kulaks, the Socialist-Revolutionaries and the Mensheviks ~~overthrew~~ *were able to overthrow* the Soviet power in the Volga region in the summer of 1918 because they were supported by a *large* section of the middle peasantry. The same was true during ~~a few~~ *the* revolts raised by the kulaks in Central Russia. But in the autumn of 1918 the mass of the middle peasants began to swing over to the Soviet power. The peasants saw that victories of the Whites were followed by the restoration of the power of the landlords, the seizure of *peasants'* land, and the robbery, flogging and torture of peasants. The activities of the Committees of the Poor Peasants, which crushed the kulaks, also contributed to the change in the attitude of the peasantry. ~~During the fall of 1918, the Poor Peasant Committees, which had fulfilled their task, were integrated into the peasant Soviets.~~ *Accordingly, i*n November 1918, Lenin issued the slogan:

> "Learn to come to an agreement with the middle peasant, while not for a moment renouncing the struggle against the kulak and at the same time firmly relying solely on the poor peasant." (Lenin, SELECTED WORKS, Vol. VIII, p. 150.)

Of course, the *middle* peasants did not cease to vacillate entirely, but they drew closer to the Soviet Government and began to support it more solidly. This *to a large extent* was facilitated by the policy towards the *middle* peasants laid down by the Eighth Party Congress.

The Eighth Congress marked a turning point in the policy of the Party towards the middle peasants.[14] Lenin's report and the decisions of the congress laid down a new line of the Party on this question. The congress demanded that the Party organizations and all Communists should draw a strict distinction and division between the middle peasant and the kulak, and should strive to win the former over to the side of the working class by paying close attention to his needs. The backwardness of the middle peasants had to be overcome by persuasion and not by compulsion and coercion. The congress therefore gave instructions that no compulsion be used in the carrying out of Socialist measures in the countryside (formation of communes and agricultural ~~collectives~~ *artels*). In all cases ~~where the~~ *affecting the* vital interests of the middle peasant ~~were affected~~, a practical agreement should be reached with him and concessions made with regard to the METHODS of realizing Socialist changes. The congress laid down the policy of a STABLE ALLIANCE with the middle peasant, the LEADING ROLE in this alliance to be maintained by the proletariat.

The new ~~slogan~~ *policy* towards the *middle* peasant ~~given~~ *proclaimed*[15] by Lenin at the Eighth Congress required that the proletariat should rely on the poor peasant, maintain a stable alliance with the middle peasant and fight the kulak. The policy of the Party before the Eighth Congress was *in general* one of NEUTRALIZING the middle peasant. This meant that the Party strove to prevent the middle peasant from siding with the kulak and with the bourgeoisie in general. But now this was not enough. The Eighth Congress passed from a policy of neutralization of the middle peasant to a policy of STABLE ALLIANCE with him for the *purpose of the struggle against the Whiteguards and foreign intervention and for the* successful building of Socialism.

The policy adopted by the congress towards *the middle peasants, who formed* the bulk of the peasantry, played a decisive part in ensuring success in the Civil War *against foreign intervention and its Whiteguard henchmen*. In the autumn of 1919, when the peasants had to choose between the Soviet power and Denikin, they supported the Soviets, and the proletarian dictatorship was able to vanquish its most dangerous enemy.

The problems connected with the building up of the Red Army[16] held a special place in the deliberations of the congress, where the so-called "Military Opposition" appeared in the field. This "Military Opposition" comprised quite a number of former members of the now shattered group of "Left Communists"; but it also included some Party workers who had never participated in any opposition, but were dissatisfied with the way Trotsky was conducting the affairs of the army. The majority of the delegates from the army were distinctly hostile to Trotsky; they resented his veneration for the military experts of the old tsarist army, some of whom were betraying us outright in the Civil War, and his arrogant and hostile attitude towards the old Bolshevik cadres in the army. *Instances of Trotsky's "practices" were cited at the congress.* ~~Things had gotten so~~

~~bad that~~ *For example,* he had ~~cruelly~~ attempted to shoot a number of prominent army Communists serving at the front, *just because they had incurred his displeasure.* This was directly playing into the hands of the enemy. It was only the intervention of the Central Committee and the protests of military men that saved the lives of these comrades. ~~By his treacherous actions, Trotsky consciously attempted to undermine the victory of the Red Army on the fronts of the Civil War.~~

But while fighting Trotsky's distortions of the military policy of the Party, the "Military Opposition" held incorrect views on a number of points concerning the building up of the army. Lenin and Stalin vigorously came out against the "Military Opposition," because the latter defended the survivals of the guerrilla spirit and resisted the creation of a regular Red Army, the utilization of the military experts of the old army and the establishment of that iron discipline, ~~which is imperative in an army~~ *without which no army can be a real army.* Comrade Stalin rebutted the "Military Opposition" and demanded the creation of a regular army inspired with the spirit of *strictest* discipline.

He said:

> "Either we create a real worker and peasant—primarily a peasant—army, strictly disciplined army, and defend the Republic, or we perish."

While ~~defeating~~ *rejecting a number of proposals made by* the "Military Opposition," the congress dealt a blow at Trotsky ~~as well~~ by demanding an improvement in the work of the central military institutions and the enhancement of the role of the Communists in the army.

A Military Commission was set up at the congress; thanks to its efforts the decision on the military question was adopted by the congress unanimously.

The effect of this decision was to strengthen the Red Army and to bring it still closer to the Party.

The congress further discussed Party and Soviet affairs and the guiding role of the Party in the Soviets. During the debate on the latter question the congress repudiated the view of the opportunist Sapronov-Ossinsky group which held that the Party should not guide the work of the Soviets.

Lastly, in view of the huge influx of new members into the Party, the congress outlined measures to improve the social composition of the Party and decided to conduct a re-registration of its members.

This initiated the first purge of the Party ranks.

~~The Eighth Party Congress had great significance for Party history. It worked out the Party's program, pointed out how the regular Red Army was to be formed, and determined the Party's policy in regard to the middle peasantry.~~

3.~~4.~~ Extension of Intervention. Blockade of the Soviet Country. ~~Defeat of the First and Second Kolchak Campaigns.~~ *Kolchak's Campaign and Defeat. Denikin's Campaign and Defeat. A Three-Months' Respite. Ninth Party Congress*

~~Having vanquished Germany, the Entente states decided to hurl large military forces against the Soviet Republic. Allied troops landed on the Black Sea coast. All of the forces of the counter-revolution on the Don and in the North Caucasus were placed under General Denikin, whom the imperialists actively supplied with weaponry and ammunition. Yudenich's Whiteguard corps formed in the North-West. The main blow was supposed to have been made from the East by Admiral Kolchak, who had formed a Whiteguard government in Siberia. Kolchak was aided by the Japanese, French and British. Therefore, the following song was sung about Kolchak:~~

> ~~"Uniform British,~~
> ~~Epaulettes from France,~~
> ~~Japanese tobacco,~~
> ~~Kolchak leads the dance."~~

Having vanquished Germany and Austria, the Entente states decided to hurl large military forces against the Soviet country. After Germany's defeat and the evacuation of her troops from the Ukraine and Transcaucasia, her place was taken by the British and French, who dispatched their fleets to the Black Sea and landed troops in Odessa and in Transcaucasia. Such was the brutality of the Entente forces of intervention that they did not hesitate to shoot whole batches of workers and peasants in the occupied regions. Their outrages reached such lengths in the end that after the occupation of Turkestan they carried off to the Transcaspian region twenty-six leading Baku Bolsheviks—including Comrades Shaumyan, Fioletov, Djaparidze, Malygin, Azizbekov, Korganov—and with the aid of the Socialist-Revolutionaries,[17] *had them brutally shot.*

The interventionists soon proclaimed a blockade of Russia. All sea routes and other lines of communication with the external world were cut.

The Soviet country was surrounded on nearly every side.

~~Kolchak was proclaimed "supreme ruler" of Russia—that is, essentially, the monarch or king. The whole Russian counter-revolution was placed under his command. The Eastern front again became the chief danger. During the spring of 1919, the Entente launched its FIRST campaign against the Soviet Republic. This was a joint campaign and presupposed a coordinated attack by Kolchak, Denikin, Poland, Yudenich and the integrated forces of the British interventionists and Russian Whiteguards in Turkestan and Archangel. The position of~~

~~the Soviet Republic at this time was very grim: she was forced to fight on six fronts while being cut off from her grain regions (Siberia, the Ukraine and the North Caucasus) and fuel (the Donetz Basin, Grozny and Baku). The centre of gravity for the first campaign of the Entente lay in Kolchak's region.~~

The Entente countries placed their chief hopes in Admiral Kolchak, their puppet in Omsk, Siberia. He was proclaimed "supreme ruler of Russia" and all the counter-revolutionary forces in the country placed themselves under his command.

The Eastern Front thus became the main front.

Kolchak assembled a huge army and in the spring of 1919 almost reached the Volga. The finest Bolshevik forces were hurled against him; Young Communist Leaguers and workers were mobilized. In April 1919, Kolchak's army met with severe defeat at the hands of the Red Army ~~under the command of M. V. Frunze~~ and very soon began to retreat along the whole front.

At the height of the advance of the Red Army on the Eastern Front, Trotsky put forward a ~~treacherous~~ *suspicious* plan: he proposed that the advance should be halted before it reached the Urals, ~~and~~ the pursuit of Kolchak's army discontinued, *and troops transferred from the Eastern Front to the Southern Front.* The Central Committee of the ~~Bolshevik~~ Party *fully realized that the Urals and Siberia could not be left in Kolchak's hands, for there, with the aid of the Japanese and British, he might recuperate and retrieve his former position. It therefore* rejected this plan and gave instructions to proceed with the advance. *Trotsky disagreed with these instructions and tendered his resignation, which the Central Committee declined, at the same time ordering him to refrain at once from all participation in the direction of the operations on the Eastern Front.* The Red Army *pursued its offensive against Kolchak with greater vigour than ever; it inflicted a number of new defeats on him and* freed of the Whites the Urals and Siberia, where the Red Army was supported by a powerful partisan movement in the Whites' rear.

In the summer of 1919, the imperialists assigned to General Yudenich, who headed the counter-revolutionaries in the north-west (in the Baltic countries, in the vicinity of Petrograd), the task of diverting the attention of the Red Army from the Eastern Front by an attack on Petrograd. Influenced by the counter-revolutionary agitation of former officers ~~who had served as military specialists~~, the garrisons of two forts in the vicinity of Petrograd mutinied against the Soviet Government. At the same time a counter-revolutionary plot was discovered at the Front Headquarters. The enemy threatened ~~the very city of~~ Petrograd. ~~The Central Committee sent Comrade Stalin in order to organize the struggle with Yudenich. Over the course of three weeks, Stalin made a breakthrough. Under his command, the mutinous forts were seized and the enemy was forced to retreat hurriedly.~~ *But thanks to the measures taken by the Soviet Government with the support of the workers and sailors, the mutinous forts were cleared of Whites, and Yudenich's troops were defeated and driven back into Esthonia.*

~~On November 27, 1919, the All-Russian Central Executive Committee awarded Comrade Stalin the Order of the Red Banner for his military service in the defence of Petrograd and his continuing selfless work on the Southern Front.~~

~~In the resolution about Comrade Stalin's award, it was written:~~

> ~~"At a time of mortal danger, when surrounded on all sides in a tight ring of enemies, the Soviet power deflected the enemy's blows; at a time in June 1919 when the enemies of the workers' and peasants' revolution were approaching Red Petrograd and had already taken Red Gorka—it was at this difficult hour for Soviet Russia that Joseph Vissarionovich Stalin, appointed to his post by the Presidium of the All-Russian Central Executive Committee, succeeded in rallying the trembling ranks of the Red Army through his energy and tireless work.~~
>
> ~~Being in the proximity of the front lines and falling under enemy fire, he inspired the ranks fighting for the Soviet Republic by personal example."~~

The defeat of Yudenich near Petrograd made it easier to cope with Kolchak, and by the end of 1919 his army was completely routed. Kolchak himself was taken prisoner and shot by sentence of the Revolutionary Committee in Irkutsk. ~~The Entente's FIRST campaign had ended with the defeat of the Whiteguards and imperialists.~~

That was the end of Kolchak.

The Siberians had a popular song about Kolchak at that time:

> *"Uniform British,*
> *Epaulettes from France,*
> *Japanese tobacco,*
> *Kolchak leads the dance.*
> *Uniform in tatters,*
> *Epaulettes all gone,*
> *So is the tobacco,*
> *Kolchak's day is done."*

Since Kolchak had not justified their hopes, the interventionists altered their plan of attack on the Soviet Republic. The troops landed in Odessa had to be withdrawn, for contact with the army of the Soviet Republic had infected them with the revolutionary ~~mood~~ *spirit* and they were beginning to rebel against their imperialist ~~governments~~ *masters*. For example, there was the revolt of French sailors in Odessa led by ~~the communist~~ André Marty.[18] ~~The main role in the struggle with the Soviets was now given to Denikin, who was supposed to be assisted by Yudenich and the White Poles. This was the Entente's SECOND campaign. The Entente launched its second campaign in the fall of 1919. This campaign entailed a joint attack by Denikin, Poland, and Yudenich (Kolchak had already been defeated). According to the Entente's plan, the main strike against the Soviet Republic was to come from Denikin on the Southern Front.~~ *Accordingly, now that Kolchak had been defeated, the Entente centred its attention on General Denikin, Kornilov's confederate and the organizer of the "Volunteer Army." Denikin at that time was operating against the Soviet Government in the south, in the Kuban region. The Entente supplied his army with large quantities of ammunition and equipment and sent it North against the Soviet Government.*

The Southern Front now became the chief front.

Denikin began his ~~offensive already in the spring of 1919~~ *main campaign against the Soviet Government in the summer of 1919*~~, during the first campaign~~. Trotsky had disrupted the Southern Front, and our troops suffered defeat after defeat. By the middle of October the Whites had seized the whole of the Ukraine, had captured Orel and were nearing Tula, which supplied our army with cartridges, rifles and machine-guns. The Whites were approaching Moscow. ~~Yudenich threatened Petrograd. By the fall of 1919, the Soviet Republic was in an extraordinarily dangerous position. Never before had it been so dangerous as it was now.~~ *The situation of the Soviet Republic became grave in the extreme. The Party sounded the alarm and called upon the people to resist.* Lenin issued the slogan, "All for the fight against Denikin!" Inspired by the Bolsheviks, the ~~proletariat~~ *workers and peasants* ~~gathered~~ *mustered* all their forces to ~~fight the mortal danger~~ *smash the enemy*.

The Central Committee sent Comrades Stalin, *Voroshilov, Ordjonikidze and Budyonny* to the Southern Front to *prepare the* rout *of* Denikin. Trotsky was removed from the direction of the operations of the Red Army in the south. Before Comrade Stalin's arrival, the Command *of the Southern Front, in conjunction with Trotsky,* had drawn up a plan to strike the main blow at Denikin~~'s rear~~ from Tsaritsyn in the direction of Novorossisk, through the Don Steppe, where there were no roads and where the Red Army would have to pass through regions inhabited by Cossacks, who were at that time largely under the influence of the Whiteguards. Comrade Stalin severely criticized this ~~wrecker's~~ plan and submitted to the Central Committee his own plan for the defeat of Denikin. According to this plan the main blow was to be delivered by way of Kharkov-Donetz Basin-Rostov. This plan would ensure *the rapid advance of our troops against Denikin, for they would be moving through working class and peasant regions where they would have* the open sympathy of the population ~~in the army's path through worker regions~~. *Furthermore,* the *dense network of* railway lines *in this region* would ~~make it easier to manoeuver, making it possible to quickly obtain the fuel that was so critical to the Soviet Republic—the coal of the Donetz Coal Basin~~ *ensure our armies the regular supply of all they required. Lastly, this plan would make it possible to release the Donetz Coal Basin and thus supply our country with fuel.*

The Central Committee of the Party accepted Comrade Stalin's plan. In the second half of October 1919, after fierce resistance, Denikin was defeated by the Red Army in the decisive battle*s* of Orel *and Voronezh*. ~~Near Voronezh, Budyonny's cavalry dealt him a defeat.~~ He began a rapid retreat, and, pursued by our forces, fled to the south. At the beginning of 1920 the whole of the Ukraine *and the North Caucasus* had been cleared of Whites.

During the decisive battles on the Southern Front, the imperialists again hurled Yudenich's corps against Petrograd in order to divert our forces from the south *and thus improve the position of Denikin's army*. The Whites approached the very ~~city~~ gates *of Petrograd*. The heroic proletariat of the premier city of the revolution rose in a solid wall for its defence. The Communists, as always, were in the vanguard. After fierce fighting, the Whites were defeated and *again* flung beyond our borders back into Esthonia.

~~Thus the Entente's second campaign ended in the total defeat of the imperialists.~~ *And that was the end of Denikin.*

~~5. War Communism~~[19]

~~The defence of the Soviet Republic from the Russian and international counter-revolution forced the Soviet power to change over to the policy of War Communism. What did this policy consist of? The Soviet power had inherited a ravaged country from the old regime. The Civil War destroyed the unified economic organism of the republic. The counter-revolution cut off the main grain-growing regions (the Ukraine, Siberia, the North Caucasus and others), as well as those regions that supplied industry with metal and fuel (the Urals, the Donetz Basin and Baku). The Soviet power was forced to subordinate all economic questions to the interests of defending the republic. It had to conduct an economic policy that would make it possible to realize the major military objective—the defeat of the enemy. It was to this end that not only the heavy and mid-scale industry was nationalized, but even a considerable portion of light industry and handicraft production by the end of the Civil War. Command of the whole economy was centralized and subordinated to special "heads" and "centres." This was necessary in order to correctly take into account and distribute the few supplies that the country still held in reserve. As a result of the~~

SIGNIFICANT REDUCTION IN SOWN ACREAGE, THE EXHAUSTION OF GRAIN RESERVES AND THE IMPOSSIBILITY OF ESTABLISHING ECONOMIC TRADE BETWEEN THE CITY AND COUNTRYSIDE, THE SOVIET POWER BANNED THE FREE SALE OF GRAIN AND SUSPENDED FREE TRADE.

The Soviet power firmly supported the GRAIN MONOPOLY and introduced the surplus-appropriation system, which entailed the seizure of all the peasantry's grain surpluses above the minimal norms necessary for satisfying subsistence needs, feeding livestock and sowing. At times, when there wasn't enough grain for the front, it became necessary to seize a portion of the grain allocated to the peasantry's subsistence minimums. By means of the surplus-appropriation system, the Soviet power obtained the bare minimum amount of foodstuffs for the defence of the country, the supply of the Red Army and the industrial centres. Grain that came into the state's possession went first to satisfy needs at the front, and then was distributed (by ration card) among workers at important enterprises, etc. In those years, there was no established distribution system. The transportation system had been destroyed. Everywhere, there were enormous shortages of industrial goods and essential items. This is why it was impossible to satisfy even the basic needs of the city or countryside. This is why the city was not in the condition to give the countryside a corresponding amount of goods in trade for its grain. A significant part of the foodstuffs that the city took from the countryside was taken as a loan, accruing debt. And the working class would pay back this debt to the peasantry in tractors and combines when the country was industrialized.[20]

The Soviet power introduced a UNIVERSAL LABOUR OBLIGATION for all classes. Forcing the bourgeoisie to engage in physical labour, to work for a living, the Soviet power realized the slogan: "HE WHO DOES NOT WORK, NEITHER SHALL HE EAT."

During the war years, a major role was played by the COMMUNIST SUBBOTNIKS, in which millions of people took part including Lenin, the chief of the Bolshevik Party, and all the Party workers. These subbotniks were a "great initiative" of Communist labour. They drew the Party even closer to the non-Party masses and helped complete an enormous amount of work associated with supporting the economy and straightening up and improving the condition of the cities, railway lines, Red Army barracks, hospitals, schools, etc.

This period of struggle was a period of military and political cooperation between the working class and the broad peasant masses. The working class, the hegemon of the revolution, which was directing the working people's struggle, endured enormous losses—more than any other class. The necessity of the alliance between the working class and the broad peasant masses coincided with the proletariat's task of defending the Soviet power and the gains of the October revolution. On this basis, the fire of the Civil War tempered the military

~~and political alliance of the proletariat and peasantry. BUT THIS MILITARY AND POLITICAL ALLIANCE WAS ONLY POSSIBLE BECAUSE IT HAD A CLEAR ECONOMIC BASE: the proletariat supplied our Red Army with weaponry and ammunition and directed the struggle against the internal and external counter-revolution and defended peasant land against the landlords. The proletariat made up the central backbone of the Workers and Peasants' Red Army, while the peasantry supplied the working class and Red Army with foodstuffs and swelled the ranks of the Red Army.~~

~~6. A Brief Respite toward the Beginning of the 1920s. The Party's Struggle with the "Democratic-Centralism" Anti-Party Group~~

The defeat of Kolchak~~, Yudenich~~ and Denikin ~~at the end of 1919~~ was followed by a brief respite[21]~~, which the Party used for the struggle with economic destruction~~.

When the imperialists saw that the Whiteguard armies had been smashed, that intervention had failed, and that the Soviet Government was consolidating its position all over the country, while in Western Europe the indignation of the workers ~~with the war~~ against *military intervention in* the Soviet Republic was rising, they began to change their attitude towards the Soviet state. In January 1920, Great Britain, France, and Italy decided to call off the blockade of ~~the R.S.F.S.R.~~ *Soviet Russia*~~, and on February 2, the Soviet state signed the first peace treaty with Esthonia~~.

This was an important breach in the wall of intervention.

It did not, of course, mean that the Soviet country was done with ~~counter-revolution~~ *intervention* and the Civil War. There was still the danger of attack by imperialist Poland. The forces of intervention had not *yet* been *finally*[22] driven out of the Far East, *Transcaucasia*[23] and the Crimea. But Soviet Russia had secured a temporary breathing space and was able to divert more forces ~~and attention to the struggle with economic destruction~~ *to economic development. The Party could now devote its attention to economic problems.*

During the Civil War many skilled workers had left industry owing to the closing down of mills and factories. The Party now took measures to return them to industry to work at their trades. The railways were in a ~~catastrophic~~ *grave* condition and several thousand Communists were assigned to the work of restoring them, for unless this was done the restoration of the major branches of industry could not be seriously undertaken. The organization of the food supply was extended *and improved*. The drafting of a plan for the electrification of Russia was begun. ~~Three~~ *Nearly five* million Red Army men were under arms and could not be demobilized owing to the danger of war. *A part of t*he Red Army was therefore ~~transformed~~ *converted* into LABOUR ARMIES and used in *the* economic ~~work~~ *field*. The Council of Workers' and Peasants' Defence was transformed into the Council of Labour and Defence, and a State Planning Commission (Gosplan) set up to assist it.

Such was the situation when the Ninth Party Congress opened.

The congress met at the end of March 1920. It was attended by 554 delegates with vote, representing 611,978 Party members, and 162 delegates with voice but no vote.

~~The Ninth Party Congress that took place from March 29 to April 5, 1920, mainly addressed economic questions. Opening the congress, Lenin warned that the imperialists might at any moment disrupt the brief respite and begin military action.~~

The congress defined the immediate tasks of the country ~~(~~in the sphere of transportation and industry~~)~~. It particularly stressed the necessity of the trade unions taking part in the building up of the economic life.

Special attention was devoted by the congress to[24] *a single economic plan for the restoration, in the first place, of the railways, the fuel industry and the iron and steel industry. The major item in this plan was a project for the electrification of the country, which Lenin advanced as "a great program for the next ten or twenty years." This formed the basis of the famous plan of the State Commission for the Electrification of Russia (GOELRO), the provisions of which have today been far exceeded.*

~~It was decided at the congress that the Communist Party should extend its influence through the Communist fraction of every trade union. This was resisted by Tomsky, the then-chairman of the All-Russian Central Council of Trade Unions, who proposed that the trade union fractions be subordinated not to the local Party committees, but directly to the fraction of the All-Russian Central Council of Trade Unions. This anti-Bolshevik proposal called attention to Tomsky's ambition to win the trade unions' "independence" from the Party. Thus this proposal was decisively rejected by the congress.~~

~~The Ninth Party Congress under Lenin's leadership defeated the advocates of "collegiality" who were speaking out against ONE-MAN MANAGEMENT in industry (Sapronov, Tomsky and Rykov). The opponents of one-man leadership used "collegiality" as a cover to conceal irresponsibility and petty-bourgeois disorder in industrial management. With this proposal, they played into the hands of the Mensheviks, who slanderously defined one-man management as denigrating working-class values and renouncing efforts to engage the broad working masses in the cause of management.~~

~~On the eve of the Ninth Party Congress, there were about 600,000 members in the Party. The core backbone of the Party consisted of workers. But during the Civil War years, no few "fellow travelers" had flooded into the Party. These "fellow travelers" entered the Party because it was in power. But in reality,~~

~~these elements were alien to Socialism and the Party's Socialist tasks and related to Party and state discipline with hostility. "Democratic-Centralism" (the Decists), a faction or group, took shape in 1919 from a number of these petty-bourgeois "fellow travelers" and waged a struggle against the Party. This group was fully formed by 1920.~~

~~Many former "Left Communists" joined the "Democratic-Centralism" group. This opposition group in the Party was also made up of new arrivals from the petty-bourgeois parties. In the first years after the October revolution, parts of the Socialist-Revolutionaries, Mensheviks, Anarchists, and the Social-Democratic Internationalists flooded into the Bolshevik Party. The Party of the "Revolutionary Communists," part of the former "Left" Socialist-Revolutionaries, the Ukrainian "Left" Socialist-Revolutionaries, the Borbists, the Ukrainian Communists, the Borotbists, the "Maximalists' Union" and the Communist part of the Bund, Poale Zion, etc., also flooded in. In the main, these new arrivals, who were far from ready to surrender their petty-bourgeois views, would eventually form the cadres of various factions and anti-party groups. The influence of petty-bourgeois elements was especially felt in an array of Party organizations in the Ukraine, which according to its social makeup was more petty bourgeois than central Russia. Thus the Democratic-Centralists were more powerful there than anywhere else.~~

~~The chieftain of the Democratic-Centralists was Sapronov; Maximovsky, Ossinsky, Kaminsky, Rafail, Drobnis and Boguslavsky also tended toward this group.~~[25] ~~Almost all of them~~[26] ~~would in the end become enemies of the people. Drobnis and Boguslavsky were shot in 1937 as active participants in a counter-revolutionary terroristic Trotskyite-espionage-fascist centre. The Democratic-Centralists obtained weapons for their struggle with the Party from the arsenal of the "Left Communists," Mensheviks and Socialist-Revolutionaries.~~[27] ~~They spoke out against the creation of a centralized Soviet apparatus, the proletarian dictatorship, the leading role of the Party in the Soviets, one-man management and labour discipline. The chieftains of this group were in most cases Soviet bureaucrats and officials.~~[28] ~~They struggled against Party discipline and the Central Committee's right to control the placement of Party workers. Under Lenin's leadership, the Ninth Party Congress delivered a decisive blow against this group of shouting demagogues, who under the cover of "Democratic-Centralism" were promoting the most dangerous petty-bourgeois rubbish and disorder.~~ *The congress rejected the views of an anti-Party group which called itself "The Group of Democratic-Centralism" and was opposed to one-man management and the undivided responsibility of industrial directors. It advocated unrestricted "group management" under which nobody would be personally responsible for the administration of industry. The chief figures in this anti-Party group were Sapronov, Ossinsky and V. Smirnov. They were supported at the congress by Rykov and Tomsky.*

~~The activity of this group was especially dangerous in the Ukraine. For the kulaks' benefit, they spoke out (together with the "Left" Socialist-Revolutionaries) against the organization of committees of poor peasants. They advanced the worst accusations of the "Left Communists" and "Left" Socialist-Revolutionaries in their struggle with the Party. Comrade Stalin was sent to the Ukraine by the decision of the Central Committee to struggle with the developing atamanism, batkovism, insubordination toward the centre ("all the power to the localities") and other forms of partisanism. Comrade Stalin exposed the anti-proletarian character of the opposition and rallied the best elements of the Party in the Ukraine around the Central Committee in order to struggle with the influence of the Democratic-Centralists and the Shlyapnikovite "Workers' Opposition" that was already lying in wait in the Ukraine at that time. The anti-party nature of the Democratic-Centralists was particularly exposed at the Fourth All-Ukrainian Party Conference in March 1920. There, the "Kharkov Opposition" under Sapronov supported enemies of the Soviet power, who contended that because of the Ukraine's "special circumstances," there was no need for the Ukraine to join the Soviet Union. The decision of this conference was not ratified by the Central Committee. The Central Committee of the Ukrainian Communist Party (Bolsheviks) that was elected at this conference was dismissed. To replace it, the Central Committee appointed a provisional Ukrainian Party Central Committee. The most malicious of the factional leaders were recalled from Ukraine.~~

~~In a special address to all the organizations of the Ukrainian Communist Party, the Central Committee explained the imperative of these actions in order to avoid a split in the Party. In the interests of purging the Ukrainian Party organizations of unprincipled adventurers and petty-bourgeois intellectual groups, a reregistration of all members of the Party was conducted in Ukraine in a month's time.~~

~~The Central Committee's letter pointed out that these elements inflicted the same damage that Whiteguard elements were capable of inflicting while serving in Soviet institutions.~~

~~Later, at the Ninth Party Conference in September 1920, a group of Democratic-Centralists spoke out yet again in order to make demagogical attacks on the Central Committee, criticizing shortcomings in the Party organizations' work from the perspective of an embittered petty bourgeoisie. Entering into a bloc with the Trotskyites in 1926–27, the Democratic-Centralists would once and for all pass into a counter-revolutionary group along with the Trotskyites, advancing a program for the violent overthrow of Soviet power. They thus~~

~~became, like the Trotskyites, spies of foreign espionage services. This group was eliminated by the organs of the proletarian dictatorship.~~

~~The brief respite at the beginning of 1920 did not last long. Quickly after the Ninth Congress, the Party again had to gather all of its strength in order to organize the defence of the republic from new enemies.~~

4.7. ~~Third Campaign of the Entente, the White Poles and Wrangel (1920)~~ *Polish Gentry Attack Soviet Russia. General Wrangel's Campaign. Failure of the Polish Plan. Rout of Wrangel. End of the Intervention*

~~After the defeat of Yudenich and the Kolchak and Denikin armies in the East and South, next followed the liberation of the Northern Territory and Turkestan from the Whites and interventionists. The imperialists, however, made one more desperate attempt to defeat Soviet Russia. This was the Entente's third campaign against the Soviet Republic. The main role in this campaign was given to Poland. In April 1920, they invaded the Ukraine and seized Kiev. In reply to the Polish advance, the Red Army staged a counter-offensive against Warsaw. In the South at this time, General Wrangel's new White army appeared. When Denikin was defeated, units of his broken army retreated from the North Caucasus to the Crimea, where General Wrangel took command. Having recovered in the Crimea, Wrangel during the summer of 1920 took the offensive and threatened the Donetz Basin.~~[29]

Notwithstanding the defeat of Kolchak and Denikin, notwithstanding the fact that the Soviet Republic was steadily regaining its territory by clearing the Whites and the forces of intervention out of the Northern Territory, Turkestan, Siberia, the Don region, the Ukraine, etc., notwithstanding the fact that the Entente states were obliged to call off the blockade of Russia, they still refused to reconcile themselves to the idea that the Soviet power had proved impregnable and had come out victorious. They therefore resolved to make one more attempt at intervention in Soviet Russia. This time they decided to utilize both Pilsudsky, a bourgeois counter-revolutionary nationalist, the virtual head of the Polish state, and General Wrangel, who had rallied the remnants of Denikin's army in the Crimea and from there was threatening the Donetz Basin and the Ukraine.

~~Poland~~ *The Polish gentry* and Wrangel, as Lenin put it, were the two hands with which international imperialism attempted to strangle Soviet Russia.

The plan of the Poles was to seize the Soviet Ukraine west of the Dnieper,[30] *to occupy Soviet Byelorussia, to restore the power of the Polish magnates in these regions, to extend the frontiers of the Polish state so that they stretched "from sea to sea," from Danzig to Odessa, and, in return for his aid, to help Wrangel smash the Red Army and restore the power of the landlords and capitalists in Soviet Russia.*

This plan was approved by the Entente states.

The Soviet Government made vain[31] *attempts to enter into negotiations with Poland with the object of preserving peace and averting war. Pilsudsky refused to discuss peace. He wanted war. He calculated that the Red Army, fatigued by its battles with Kolchak and Denikin, would not be able to withstand the attack of the Polish forces.*

The short breathing space had come to an end.

In April 1920, the Poles invaded the Soviet Ukraine and seized Kiev. At the same time, Wrangel took the offensive and threatened the Donetz Basin.

~~The Red Army seized Kiev back and defeated the Polish gentry's troops in Galicia, near the city of Lvov. Soviet troops also neared Warsaw. The victorious advance of the Red troops inspired an enormous revolutionary upsurge in the western countries. However, through the fault of the Revolutionary Military Council (Trotsky and his followers), the Red Army's advance took place without the corresponding consolidation of captured positions; the forward units of Red troops were sent far ahead, while the reserves and ammunition were left in the rear. Therefore, when the Polish forces broke through the front, the Red Army was obliged to retreat.~~[32]

In reply, the Red Army started a counter-offensive against the Poles along the whole front. Kiev was recaptured and the Polish war lords driven out of the Ukraine and Byelorussia. The impetuous advance of the Red troops on the Southern Front brought them to the very gates of Lvov in Galicia, while the troops on the Western Front were nearing Warsaw. The Polish armies were on the verge of utter defeat.

But success was frustrated by the suspicious actions of Trotsky and his followers at the General Headquarters of the Red Army. Through the fault of Trotsky and Tukhachevsky, the advance of the Red troops on the Western Front, towards Warsaw, proceeded in an absolutely unorganized manner: the troops were allowed no opportunity to consolidate the positions that they won, the advance detachments were led too far ahead, while reserves and ammunition were left too far in the rear. As a result, the advance detachments were left without ammunition and reserves and the front was stretched out endlessly. This made it easy to force a breach in the front. The result was that when a small force of Poles broke through our Western Front at one point, our troops, left without ammunition, were obliged to retreat. As regards the troops on the Southern Front, who had reached the gates of Lvov and were pressing the Poles hard, they were forbidden by Trotsky, that ill-famed "chairman of the Revolutionary Military Council," to capture Lvov. He ordered the transfer of the Mounted Army, the main force on the Southern Front, far to the North-East. This was done on the pretext of helping the Western Front, although it was not difficult to see that the best, and in fact only possible, way of helping the Western Front was to capture Lvov. But the withdrawal of the Mounted Army from the Southern Front, its departure from Lvov, virtually meant the retreat of our forces on the Southern Front as well. This wrecker's order issued by Trotsky thus forced upon our troops on the Southern Front an incomprehensible and absolutely unjustified retreat—to the joy of the Polish gentry.

This was giving direct assistance, indeed—not to our Western Front, however, but to the Polish gentry and the Entente.

Within a few days the advance of the Poles was checked and our troops began preparations for a new counter-offensive. But, unable to continue the war, and alarmed by the prospect of a Red counter-offensive, Poland was obliged to renounce her claims to the Ukrainian territory west of the Dnieper and to Byelorussia and preferred to conclude peace. In October 1920, ~~the Soviet power concluded~~ the Peace of Riga[33] *was signed* ~~with Poland. This peace treaty liberated the part of Byelorussian territory that before the start of the war had been held in Polish hands. Ukrainian Galicia and a portion of Byelorussia (Western Ukraine and Western Byelorussia) remained under the oppression of the Polish gentry.~~ *In accordance with this treaty Poland retained Galicia and part of Byelorussia.*[34]

Having concluded a~~n armistice~~ *peace* with Poland, the Soviet Republic decided to put an end to Wrangel. The British and French had supplied him with guns, rifles, armoured cars, tanks, aeroplanes and ammunition of the latest type. He had Whiteguard shock regiments, mainly consisting of officers. But Wrangel failed to rally any considerable number of peasants and Cossacks in support of the troops he had landed in the Kuban and the Don regions. Nevertheless, he advanced to the very gates of the Donetz Basin, creating a menace to ~~the~~ *our* coal region. The position of the Soviet Government at that time was further complicated by the fact that the Red Army was suffering greatly from fatigue. The troops were obliged to ~~manoeuver~~ *advance*[35] under extremely difficult conditions ~~for transport~~[36]*: while conducting an offensive against Wrangel, they had at the same time to smash Makhno's anarchist bands who were assisting Wrangel.*[37] But although Wrangel had the superiority in technical equipment, although the Red Army had no tanks, it drove Wrangel into the Crimean Peninsula and there bottled him up. In November 1920 the Red forces captured the ~~impregnable~~ *fortified* position of Perekop, ~~and~~ swept into the Crimea, *smashed Wrangel's forces and cleared the Peninsula of the Whiteguards and the forces of intervention.* ~~The capture of Perekop is associated with the name Frunze, one of the most talented organizers and commanders in the Red Army. In the history of the Civil War, the storming of Perekop shall remain in our memories forever. This was an example of the tremendous heroism of the Red Army, driven by hatred of the landlords and capitalists. Retreating, Wrangel evacuated 45,000 people from the Crimea by sea, a significant portion of whom were members of the bourgeoisie, who took with them their valuables.~~ The Crimea became Soviet territory.

The ~~Polish campaign~~ *failure of Poland's imperialist plans* and the defeat of Wrangel ~~basically~~ ended the period of ~~the Civil War~~ *intervention.*

~~Soon, the military struggle in Turkestan (against the Basmachi) ended.~~

At the end of 1920 there began the liberation of Transcaucasia ~~from the interventionists and Whiteguards~~: *Azerbaidjan was freed from the yoke of the bourgeois nationalist Mussavatists, Georgia from the Menshevik nationalists, and Armenia from the Dashnaks.* The Soviet power triumphed in Azerbaidjan, Armenia and Georgia.

This did not *yet* mean the end of all ~~armed struggle~~ *intervention.* That of the Japanese in the Far East lasted until 1922. *Moreover, n*ew attempts at intervention were made (Ataman Semyonov and Baron Ungern in the East, the Finnish Whites in Karelia in 1921~~, incursions by Polish units, etc.~~). ~~However,~~ *But* the principal enemies *of the Soviet country, the principal forces of intervention,* were shattered by the end of 1920.

The war of the foreign interventionists and the Russian Whiteguards against the Soviets ended in a victory for the Soviets.

The Soviet Republic preserved its independence *and freedom.*

~~The R.S.F.S.R. concluded its first peace treaties with Esthonia, Latvia, Poland and other countries, and it became possible to enter into direct diplomatic relations with Western Europe.~~

This was the end of foreign military intervention and Civil War.

This was a historic victory for the Soviet power.

~~The military and economic blockade and intervention were overturned by the combined efforts of the proletariat and peasant masses under the leadership of the Communist Party and with the support of the revolutionary proletariat of the western countries. From this moment, military objectives became a second priority. The tasks of economic construction and the construction of Socialism became the first priority. The war with Poland took place amid a growing revolutionary movement in the west. The example of the Soviet Republic inspired the multi-million man masses of working people to struggle in the capitalist countries. The size and influence of the West-European Communist parties quickly grew. The Comintern became a major force. An array of Social-Democratic parties and Anarcho-Syndicalist groups announced their desire to join the ranks of the Comintern. The swift rise of the Comintern and its organizations was a major event at that time. But at the same time, the growth of the Comintern presented a danger as well. The point is that the new arrivals from the Social-Democratic parties and Anarcho-Syndicalist groups brought into the Communist parties persistent Right-opportunist and "Leftist" views that they attempted to pass on to the Comintern. It became important to warn the Communist parties of the possibility that they might be diluted by opportunist elements, who had~~

~~not yet completely broken with the ideology of the Second International or Anarcho-Syndicalism.~~

~~The well-attended Second Comintern Congress took place under Lenin's leadership amid the heat of the war with Poland. The congress developed twenty-one conditions for admission to the Comintern that would block the way to opportunists and centralists. The Comintern would only admit those organizations that had broken with the opportunists and centralists and expelled them from their ranks. Along with this, the congress exposed the erroneous tactics of the "Lefts," who denied the necessity of working in the bourgeois parliaments and reactionary trade unions. The danger of the "Left" for the Communist parties was very big at that time. Groups appeared in an array of Communist parties that suffered from illness of "Leftism." They reflected views not of the proletariat, which was able to withstand systematic revolutionary class struggle, but of the petty bourgeoisie, which had been driven crazy by the horrors of capitalism.~~

~~Lenin's remarkable work from this period, "The Childhood Illness of 'Leftism' in Communism," generalized upon the experience of Bolshevik strategy and tactics and the experience of leading the proletariat's class struggle. It also revealed the total madness of opportunistic wavering. Lenin emphasized that one of the basic conditions for the Bolsheviks' success was the iron discipline within Party ranks that rested on the "granite theoretical base" of Marxism. He showed that the Bolshevik Party had grown, strengthened and become tempered in the struggle against opportunism from both the right and the "left."~~

~~The Second Comintern Congress passed important decisions on the role and construction of the Communist parties and on the national and colonial questions. The Second Comintern Congress played a major role in the Bolshevization of the western Communist parties.~~

8. Party Work during the Civil War Years

~~In the Civil War period, the Bolshevik Party worked under exceptionally difficult conditions. No fewer than 25 per cent of all Communists were mobilized for the front. In the frontline zones, all Communists were typically mobilized. In all sectors that were even slightly weak or dangerous, or where reinforcements were needed, the first to be sent in were Communists and Young Communist Leaguers. Several hundred thousand Communists and Young Communist Leaguers perished at the front. At the same time, Communists in the country's interior suppressed anti-Soviet mutinies and rebuffed the blows of the enemy, who was organizing terrorist attacks against Soviet officials. The counter-revolutionaries who captured Soviet officials, food supply officials and~~

Red Army soldiers subjected them to the harshest suffering and torture and sent them to a torturous death.

The Bolsheviks waged a large propaganda campaign in the city and countryside. Mass agitational efforts, which the Bolsheviks engaged in with exceptional energy, artfulness and resilience, were executed on an unusually large scale, as even the enemy himself was forced to admit. The Bolsheviks allocated enormous attention to work among the masses. Their agitation engaged with the widest breadth of the working people and was conducted in the most diverse ways. Despite the grim nature of the situation, the starvation and the poverty, the working class protected the republic with its life and selflessly supported the Bolsheviks. Massive rallies were continuously conducted in working-class regions and factories, where Party and Government leaders presented reports about the country's situation and the tasks of the revolution.

After the attempted assassination of Lenin in 1918, tens of thousands of workers flooded into the Party ranks. Moscow's "PARTY WEEK" in the fall of 1919 enrolled an additional 13,000 new members after 13 Bolsheviks were killed in a blast at the Leontyev Alley Moscow Party Committee building by a bomb thrown by the "Left" Socialist-Revolutionaries and Anarchists. This occurred just as Denikin was approaching Tula.

The major work accomplished at this time at the front was particularly noteworthy. Special agitational trains and frontline newspapers, as well as the activities of military political commissars, had an enormous significance in elevating the military readiness of the army and the resilience of the rear, as well as maintaining continuous communication and unity of purpose between front and rear.

The Bolshevik Party created underground organizations during the Civil War anywhere where the enemy captured even a small piece of the republic's territory. Neither persecution nor executions nor the most harsh and trying torture of arrested Bolsheviks was able to undermine the Party's work. The devotion of the Bolsheviks to the cause of Communism and the proletarian revolution was so great that they did not hesitate to make even the ultimate sacrifice in order to carry out the will and goals of the Party. The history of this underground work is replete with examples of Bolshevik heroism and self-sacrifice.

On the Southern Front, in Odessa, the members of the Bolshevik "foreign collegium," which had been created to disseminate propaganda among the soldiers and sailors of the interventionists, were executed after harsh torture by the imperialists' counterespionage agents. With the aid of foreign Communists such as André Marty,[38] this underground organization had succeeded in preparing revolutionary actions and staging an uprising within the French naval fleet in Odessa, forcing the Entente to withdraw troops who had been exposed to the Bolshevik propaganda.

On the Northern Front, General Miller and the former populist Chaikovsky took power in the name of the Constituent Assembly, allowing the Whiteguards and interventionists to stifle captured territories in the North and subject the population to inhuman suffering. On the "Islands of Death"—Mudyuga and Iokanga—the hangmen created a frightful prison camp, within which hundreds of Socialism's defenders were tortured to death.

The Bolsheviks conducted an enormous amount of Party work in the enemy's rear. Based on the workers' and partisans' movement, underground Siberian Communists upset the forces of the enemy and set the stage for the victory of the Red Army by organizing uprisings in Kolchak's rear.

On the Far Eastern front, the Bolshevik underground organized a partisan movement and prepared for the defeat of the Whiteguards and interventionists. The brutal enemy—the Japanese imperialists—burned to death Sergey Lazo, one of the partisan chiefs, in the boiler of a steam engine.

In this struggle, thousands of Communists died martyrs' deaths at the hands of the hangmen. During this period, tens of thousands of Communists went through this brutal school of struggle, becoming tempered, developing their powers and demonstrating their devotion to the Party and the Communist cause.

9. The Bolshevik Party—the Chief and Organizer of the Victory of the Proletarian Dictatorship during the Civil War

The Soviet state, led by the Bolsheviks, emerged victorious in the Civil War chiefly because of the firm military-political alliance that formed during the war years between the working class and the peasantry. It was only thanks to this alliance and the exceptional heroism of the worker and peasant masses that victory over the horde of our motherland's enemies became possible.

This greatest of all historical victories would have been unthinkable without the leadership of the Party under Lenin's command—its discipline, self-sacrifice and devotion to the proletarian cause, its theoretical rigor, its skilful tactics and strategy and its uncompromising struggle with any opposition that threatened to undermine the Party's military readiness.

Aided by all the exploitative elements in the country and the imperialists' powerful support, the whiteguard general attempted via blood, fire and iron to restore capitalism and overthrow the Soviet power. But all the imperialists' campaigns against Soviet Russia were defeated.

In the most difficult conditions of the Civil War, the Bolshevik Party continued to build its new Soviet state, laying the first bricks for the foundation of a Socialist economy and forging a new labour discipline. The Party strengthened the worker and peasant alliance; it lit the path of struggle with the torch

~~of the teachings of Marxism-Leninism; it unmasked, exposed and eliminated the intrigues of the enemies of the people; it organized merciless retribution against the counter-revolution; and it dedicated its best forces to organizing victory. During the Civil War years, the class of gentry landlords was defeated and eliminated,[39] as was the class of capitalists and the bourgeoisie. The kulaks were dealt a serious blow. All industry became the property of the proletarian state. All the land was[40] handed over for the peasants' use.~~

~~During the Civil War period, Lenin and Stalin mainly dedicated their attention to the military struggle at the front, the organization of the Red Army and the improvement of its armaments, provisions and political condition. Many times, when the Soviet power was threatened by great dangers, it was Lenin and Stalin who led her out of this danger. The Bolshevik Party correctly resolved the national question, dealing a firm blow to the international bourgeoisie. It assisted the working people of the oppressed nationalities in liberating themselves from the oppression of the landlords and capitalists.~~

~~The Bolshevik Party brought up within its ranks people who were able to overcome any obstacle that was demanded by the Party or the interests of the proletarian revolution. The Lugansk metal worker Klim Voroshilov became a military commander in the Red Army, one of the beloved leaders of the army during the Civil War period. The propagandist from Ivanovo-Voznesensk, Mikhail Vasilyevich Frunze, became one of the greatest military commanders of the Red Army and its leader. Sergey Mironovich Kirov preserved the front in the most difficult sector, in Astrakhan, in unbelievably difficult conditions; together with Sergo Ordjonikidze, they fulfilled Lenin's and Stalin's plans and demonstrated spectacular abilities in organizing the victory of the Red Army in the North Caucasus and Transcaucasia.~~

~~The Civil War advanced such popular heroes as Chapayev and Shchors, names which will be remembered for many generations.~~[41]

5. How and Why the Soviet Republic Defeated the Combined Forces of British-French-Japanese-Polish Intervention and of the Bourgeois-Landlord-Whiteguard Counter-Revolution in Russia

If we study the leading European and American newspapers and periodicals of the period of intervention, we shall easily find that there was not a single prominent writer, military or civilian, not a single military expert who believed that the Soviet Government could win. On the contrary, all prominent writers, military experts and historians of revolution of all countries and nations, all the so-called savants, were unanimous in declaring that the days of the Soviets were numbered, that their defeat was inevitable.

They based their certainty of the victory of the forces of intervention on the fact that whereas Soviet Russia had no organized army and had to create its Red Army under fire, so to speak, the interventionists and Whiteguards did have an army more or less ready to hand.

Further, they based their certainty on the fact that the Red Army had no experienced military men, the majority of them having gone over to the counter-revolution, whereas the interventionists and Whiteguards did have such men.

Furthermore, they based their certainty on the fact that, owing to the backwardness of Russia's war industry, the Red Army was suffering from a shortage of arms and ammunition; that what it did have was of poor quality, while it could not obtain supplies from abroad because Russia was hermetically sealed on all sides by the blockade. The army of the interventionists and Whiteguards, on the other hand, was abundantly supplied, and would continue to be supplied, with first-class arms, ammunition and equipment.

Lastly, they based their certainty on the fact that the army of the interventionists and Whiteguards occupied the richest food-producing regions of Russia, whereas the Red Army had no such regions and was suffering from a shortage of provisions.

And it was a fact that the Red Army did suffer from all these handicaps and deficiencies.

In this respect—but only in this respect—the gentlemen of the intervention were absolutely right.

How then is it to be explained that the Red Army, although suffering from such grave shortcomings, was able to defeat the army of the interventionists and Whiteguards which did not suffer from such shortcomings?

1. The Red Army was victorious because the Soviet Government's policy for which the Red Army was fighting was a right policy, one that corresponded to the interests of the people, and because the people understood and realized that it was the right policy, their own policy, and supported it unreservedly.

The Bolsheviks knew that an army that fights for a wrong policy, for a policy that is not supported by the people, cannot win. The army of the interventionists and Whiteguards was such an army. It had everything: experienced commanders and first-class arms, ammunition, equipment and provisions. It lacked only one thing—the support and sympathy of the peoples of Russia; for the peoples of Russia could not and would not support the policy of the interventionists and Whiteguard "rulers" because it was a policy hostile to the people.[42] *And so the interventionist and Whiteguard army was defeated.*

2. The Red Army was victorious because it was absolutely loyal and faithful to its people, for which reason the people loved and supported it and looked upon it as their own army. The Red Army is the offspring of the people, and if it is faithful to its people, as a true son is to his mother, it will have the support of the people and is bound to win. An army, however, that goes against its people must suffer defeat.

3. The Red Army was victorious because the Soviet Government was able to muster the whole rear, the whole country, to serve the needs of the front. An army without a strong rear to support the front in every way is doomed to defeat. The Bolsheviks knew this and that is why they converted the country into an armed camp to supply the front with arms, ammunition, equipment, food and reinforcements.

4. The Red Army was victorious because: a) the Red Army men understood the aims and purposes of the war and recognized their justice; b) the recognition of the justice of the aims and purposes of the war strengthened their discipline and fighting efficiency; and c) as a result, the Red Army throughout displayed unparalleled self-sacrifice and unexampled mass heroism in battle against the enemy.

5. The Red Army was victorious because its leading core, both at the front and in the rear, was the Bolshevik Party, united in its solidarity and discipline, strong in its revolutionary spirit and readiness for any sacrifice in the common cause, and unsurpassed in its ability to organize millions and to lead them properly in complex situations.

> *"It is only because of the Party's vigilance and its strict discipline," said Lenin, "because the authority of the Party united all government departments and institutions, because the slogans issued by the Central Committee were followed by tens, hundreds, thousands and finally millions of people as one man, because incredible sacrifices were made, that the miracle took place and we were able to win, in spite of repeated campaigns of the imperialists of the Entente and of the whole world." (Lenin, COLLECTED WORKS, Russ. ed., Vol. XXV, p. 96.)*

6. The Red Army was victorious because: a) it was able to produce from its own ranks military commanders of a new type, men like Frunze, Voroshilov, Budyonny[43] and others; b) in its ranks fought such talented heroes who came from the people as Kotovsky, Chapayev, Lazo, Shchors, Parkhomenko, and many others; c) the political education of the Red Army was in the hands of men like Lenin, Stalin, Molotov, Kalinin, Sverdlov, Kaganovich, Ordjonikidze, Kirov, Kuibyshev, Mikoyan, Zhdanov, Andreyev, Petrovsky, Yaroslavsky, Yezhov,[44] Dzerzhinsky, Shchadenko, Mekhlis, Khrushchev,[45] Shvernik, Shkryatov, and others; d) the Red Army possessed such outstanding organizers and agitators as the military commissars, who by their work cemented the ranks of the Red Army men, fostered in them the spirit of discipline and military daring, and energetically—swiftly and relentlessly—cut short the treacherous activities of certain of the commanders, while on the other hand, they boldly and resolutely supported the prestige and renown of commanders, Party and non-Party, who had proved their loyalty to the Soviet power and who were capable of leading the Red Army units with a firm hand.

> *"Without the military commissars we would not have had a Red Army," Lenin said.*

7. The Red Army was victorious because in the rear of the White armies, in the rear of Kolchak, Denikin, Krasnov and Wrangel, there secretly operated splendid Bolsheviks, Party and non-Party, who raised the workers and peasants in revolt against the invaders, against the Whiteguards, undermined the rear of the foes of the Soviet Government, and thereby facilitated the advance of the Red Army. Everybody knows that the partisans of the Ukraine, Siberia, the Far East, the Urals, Byelorussia and the Volga region, by undermining the rear of the Whiteguards and the invaders, rendered invaluable service to the Red Army.

8. The ~~Workers' and Peasants'~~ Red Army ~~and the workers' and peasants' Soviet state~~ was victorious because ~~they were~~ *the Soviet Republic was* not alone *in its struggle against Whiteguard counter-revolution and foreign intervention, because the struggle of the Soviet Government and its successes enlisted the sympathy and support of the proletarians of the whole world.* While the imperialists were trying to stifle the Soviet Republic by intervention and blockade, the workers of the imperialist ~~states~~ *countries* sided with the Soviets and helped them. Their struggle against the capitalists of the countries hostile to the Soviet Republic helped in the end to force the imperialists to call off the intervention ~~in order to free up their hands at home. More than once,~~ *T*he workers of Great Britain, France and the other intervening powers called strikes, ~~and~~ refused to load munitions consigned to the invaders and the Whiteguard generals,[46] *and set up Councils of Action whose work was guided by the slogan—"Hands off Russia!"*

> *"The international bourgeoisie has only to raise its hand against us to have it seized by its own workers," Lenin said. (Ibid., p. 405.)*

~~The world proletariat's international solidarity and aid for the Soviet Republic in her struggle with the international and Russian counter-revolution was the consequence and proof of the fact that the cause of the workers and peasants of the Soviet Union, struggling for the victory of Communism in the U.S.S.R., was also the cause of the workers and peasants of the entire world.~~

~~Tempered in the fire of the Civil War, and having defended its state's independence in her struggle with innumerable enemies, the country prepared to convert over to peaceful work. The Party had demonstrated its skill and abil-~~

~~ity to lead the people in an armed, military struggle for the existence of this independent country. Now, the Party had to lead the people to victory in the area of economic construction, win a better life for the working people on the peacetime front and build Socialism. The heroism that our people had shown during the Civil War years in the cause of defending the Republic of Soviets was an example for all the working people of the world in the struggle for liberation.~~

Brief Summary

~~In the Civil War period, the Bolshevik Party rallied the popular masses to the defence of the gains of the October Socialist Revolution against the Russian landlords and capitalists and international capitalism.~~

Vanquished by the October ~~Socialist~~ Revolution ~~already at the end of 1917~~, the ~~Russian~~ landlords and capitalists, *in conjunction* with the Whiteguard generals, ~~sold out their motherland, first to the German imperialists, and then to the imperialists of the Entente, becoming their lackeys and henchmen. In the wake of the German attack on the Soviet Republic (1918), three campaigns were organized against her (1919 and 1920)~~ *conspired with the governments of the Entente countries against the interests of their own country for a joint armed attack on the Soviet land and for the overthrow of the Soviet Government. This formed the basis of the military intervention of the Entente and of the Whiteguard revolts in the border regions of Russia, as a result of which Russia was cut off from her sources of food and raw material.*

The military defeat of Germany and the termination of the war between the two imperialist coalitions in Europe served to strengthen the Entente and to intensify the intervention, and created new difficulties for Soviet Russia.

On the other hand, the revolution in Germany and the incipient revolutionary movement in the European countries created favourable international conditions for the Soviet power and relieved the position of the Soviet Republic.

The Bolshevik Party roused the workers and peasants for a war FOR THE FATHERLAND, a war against the foreign invaders and ~~oppressors, which were aiming to enslave our motherland and convert her into a colony of foreign capital~~ *the bourgeois and landlord Whiteguards.* The Soviet Republic *and its Red Army* defeated ~~all the imperialists' campaigns~~ *one after another the puppets of the Entente—Kolchak, Yudenich, Denikin, Krasnov and Wrangel, drove out of the Ukraine and Byelorussia another puppet of the Entente, Pilsudsky, and thus beat off the forces of foreign intervention and drove them out of the Soviet country.*

Thus the first armed attack of international capital on the land of Socialism ended in a complete fiasco.

In the period of ~~Civil War~~ *intervention*, the ~~counter-revolutionary, bourgeois~~ parties which had been smashed by the ~~October Socialist~~ revolution, the

Socialist-Revolutionaries, Mensheviks, Anarchists *and nationalists* ~~and so on~~, supported the Whiteguard generals and the invaders, ~~and~~ hatched counter-revolutionary plots ~~within~~ *against* the Soviet Republic ~~on the imperialists' orders~~ *and resorted to terrorism against Soviet leaders.* ~~The Socialist-Revolutionaries, Mensheviks, Anarchists and other bourgeois~~ *These* parties, which had enjoyed ~~well-known~~ *a certain amount of* influence among the working class before the October Revolution, completely exposed themselves before the masses as counter-revolutionary parties during the Civil War.

The period of Civil War *and intervention* witnessed the ~~final~~ political collapse of these parties and the final triumph of the Communist Party *in Soviet Russia.*

CHAPTER NINE

The Bolshevik Party in the Period of Transition to the Peaceful Work of Economic Restoration (1921–1925)

1. Soviet Republic after the *Defeat of the Intervention and* End of the Civil War. *Difficulties of the Restoration Period*

~~Toward the end of 1920, the Soviet Republic emerged victorious from the bitter Civil War, having defeated the armed forces of the internal counter-revolution and intervention.~~

Having ended the war, the Soviet Republic turned to the work of peaceful economic development. The wounds of war had to be healed. The shattered economic life of the country had to be rebuilt, its industry, railways and agriculture restored.

~~The Bolshevik Party made the transition from armed struggle to~~ *But the work of* peaceful ~~economic~~ development *had to be undertaken* ~~amid~~ *in* extremely ~~tense, internal~~ *difficult* circumstances. The victory in the Civil War had not been an easy one. The country had been reduced to a state of ruin by four years of imperialist war and *three years of* war against the intervention.

The gross output of agriculture in 1920 was only about ONE-HALF of the pre-war output—that of the poverty-stricken Russian countryside of tsarist days. To make matters worse, in 1920 there was a harvest failure in many of the provinces. Agriculture was in ~~serious crisis~~ *sore straits*.

Even worse was the plight of industry, which was in a state of ~~the most profound,~~ complete dislocation. The output of large-scale industry in 1920 was a little over ONE-SEVENTH of pre-war. Most of the mills and factories were at a standstill; mines and collieries were wrecked and flooded. Gravest of all was the condition of the iron and steel industry. The total output of pig-iron in 1921 was only 116,300 tons, or about 3 per cent of the pre-war output. There was a shortage of fuel. Transport was disrupted. Stocks of metal and textiles in the country were nearly exhausted. There was an acute shortage of such prime necessities as bread, fats, meat, footwear, clothing, matches, salt, kerosene, and soap.

~~The political conditions within the country were extremely sharp. There were major class shifts within the country and the relationship between the~~

481

- 399 -

ГЛАВА IX

ПАРТИЯ БОЛЬШЕВИКОВ В ПЕРИОД ПЕРЕХОДА НА МИРНУЮ РАБОТУ ПО ВОССТАНОВЛЕНИЮ НАРОДНОГО ХОЗЯЙСТВА.

(1921-1925 годы)

1. Советская страна после ликвидации ~~иностранной~~ интервенции и гражданской войны. Трудности восстановительного периода.

Покончив с войной, Советская страна стала переходить на рельсы мирного хозяйственного строительства. Необходимо было залечить раны, нанесенные войной. Необходимо было восстановить разрушенное народное хозяйство, привести в порядок промышленность, транспорт, сельское хозяйство.

Но переход на мирное строительство пришлось проделать в чрезвычайно трудной обстановке. Победа в гражданской войне далась нелегко. Страна была разорена четырехлетней империалистической войной и трехлетней войной с интервенцией.

Общая продукция сельского хозяйства в 1920 году составляла лишь около половины довоенной. А ведь довоенный уровень - это был уровень нищенской царской российской деревни. Вдобавок в 1920 году многие губернии были охвачены неурожаем. Крестьянское хозяйство переживало тяжелое положение.

Еще хуже было положение промышленности, находившейся в состоянии разрухи. Продукция крупной промышленности в 1920 году была почти в семь раз меньше довоенной. Боль-

First page of Chapter Nine with Stalin's editing from the summer of 1938. RGASPI, f. 558, op. 11, d. 1215, l. 481.

~~classes had changed. Most transformed was the interrelationship between the working class and the peasantry. This was the result of enormous exhaustion from many years of war. "The people are worn out," said Lenin. Demand had expanded, production had not and all the reserves were depleted.~~

While the war was on, people put up with the shortage and scarcity, and were sometimes even oblivious to it. But now that the war was over, they suddenly felt that this shortage and scarcity were intolerable and began to demand that they be immediately remedied.

~~The middle peasants' wavering in the countryside increased sharply at the end of the Civil War.~~ *Discontent appeared among the peasants.* The fire of the Civil War had welded and steeled a military and political alliance of the working class and the peasantry. This alliance rested on a definite basis: the peasants received from the ~~proletarian dictatorship~~ *Soviet Government* land and protection against the landlords and kulaks; the workers received from the peasantry foodstuffs ~~as a loan~~ under the surplus-appropriation system.

Now this basis was no longer adequate.

The Soviet state had been compelled to appropriate all surplus produce from the peasants for the needs of national defence. Victory in the Civil War would have been impossible without the surplus-appropriation system, without the policy of War Communism. This policy was necessitated by the war and ~~ruin~~ *intervention.* As long as the war was on, the peasantry had acquiesced in the surplus-appropriation system *and had paid no heed to the shortage of commodities*; but when the ~~Civil~~ *w*ar ended and there was no longer any danger of the landlords returning, the ~~middle~~ peasants began to express dissatisfaction with having to surrender all their surpluses, with the surplus-appropriation system, *and to demand a sufficient supply of commodities.*

As Lenin pointed out, the whole system of War Communism had come into collision with the interests of the peasantry. ~~This posed a threat to the worker-peasant alliance. In this way, the transition from war to economic construction raised the question of lifting the worker-peasant alliance to new heights under the leadership of the proletarian dictatorship. With the transition to peacetime construction, a new economic base was needed for this alliance.~~

~~Petty-bourgeois~~ *The spirit of* discontent ~~weighed down upon~~ *affected* the working class as well. The proletariat had borne the brunt of the Civil War, had heroically and self-sacrificingly fought the Whiteguard and foreign hordes, and the ravages of economic disruption and famine. The best, the most class conscious, self-sacrificing and disciplined workers were inspired by Socialist enthusiasm. But the utter economic disruption had its influence on the working class, too. The few factories and plants still in operation were working spasmodically. The workers were reduced to doing odd jobs for a living, making cigarette lighters and engaging in petty bartering for food in the villages ("bag-trading"). The ~~economic~~ *class* basis of the dictatorship of the proletariat was being weakened;[1] the workers were scattering, decamping for the villages, ceasing to be workers and becoming declassed. Some of the workers were beginning to show signs of discontent owing to hunger and weariness. ~~It was from this that a serious danger for the proletarian dictatorship emerged.~~

~~In these sharp circumstances, the demobilization of the million-man army created enormous difficulties. Hundreds of thousands of demobilized peasants and workers were not able to immediately find employment or the means to support themselves.~~

The Party was confronted with the necessity of working out a new line of policy on all questions affecting the economic life of the country, a line that would meet the new situation.

And the Party proceeded to work out such a line of policy on questions of economic development.

But the class enemy was not dozing. He tried to exploit the distressing economic situation and the discontent of the peasants for his own purposes. Kulak ~~uprisings~~ *revolts*, engineered by Whiteguards and Socialist-Revolutionaries, broke out in Siberia, the Ukraine and the Tambov province (Antonov's rebellion). All kinds of counter-revolutionary elements—Mensheviks, Socialist-Revolutionaries, Anarchists, Whiteguards, bourgeois nationalists—became active again. The enemy adopted new tactics of struggle against the Soviet power. He ~~changed his colors and~~ began *to borrow a Soviet garb, and his slogan was no longer the old bankrupt "Down with the Soviets!" but* a *new* slogan: "For the Soviets, but without Communists!"

A glaring instance of the new tactics of the class enemy was the counter-revolutionary mutiny in Kronstadt. It began in March 1921, a week before the Tenth Party Congress. Whiteguards, in complicity with Socialist-Revolutionaries, Mensheviks and ~~the capitalist~~ *representatives of foreign* states, assumed the lead of the mutiny. The mutineers at first used a "Soviet" signboard to camouflage their purpose of restoring the power and property of the capitalists and landlords. They raised the cry: "Soviets without Communists!" ~~and "Free Trade!"~~ The counter-revolutionaries tried to exploit the discontent of the petty bourgeois masses in order to overthrow the power of the Soviets under a pseudo-Soviet slogan.

~~Why did the unit of the Kronstadt sailors go over to the mutineers?~~ *Two circumstances facilitated the outbreak of the Kronstadt mutiny: the deterioration in the composition of the ships' crews, and the weakness of the Bolshevik organization in Kronstadt.* Nearly all the old sailors who had taken part in the October Revolution were at the front, heroically fighting in the ranks of the Red Army. The naval replenishments consisted of new men, who had not been schooled in the revolution. These were a perfectly raw peasant mass who gave expression to the peasantry's discontent with the surplus-appropriation system. *As for t*he Bolshevik organization in Kronstadt, *it* had been *greatly* weakened ~~and corrupted~~ *by a series of mobilizations for the front.* ~~All of this explains how the Socialist-Revolutionaries, Mensheviks and Whiteguards were able to temporarily take control of Kronstadt.~~ *This enabled the Socialist-Revolutionaries, Mensheviks and Whiteguards to worm their way into Kronstadt and to seize control of it.*

The ~~Whiteguards~~ *mutineers* gained possession of a first-class fortress, the fleet, and a vast quantity of arms and ammunition. ~~All~~ *T*he international counter-revolutionaries were ~~reigning~~ triumphant. But their jubilation was premature. The mutiny was quickly put down by Soviet troops. Against the Kronstadt mutineers the Party sent its finest sons—delegates to the Tenth Congress, headed by Comrade Voroshilov. The Red Army men advanced on Kronstadt across a thin sheet of ice; it broke in places and many were drowned. The almost impregnable forts of Kronstadt had to be taken by storm; but loyalty to the revolution, bravery and readiness to die for the Soviets won the day. The fortress of Kronstadt fell before the onslaught of the Red troops. The Kronstadt mutiny was suppressed.

~~At the end of 1920 and the start of 1921, the Soviet Republic's condition was very serious. The revolution was in a critical stage.~~

2. *Party* Discussion on the Trade Unions ~~and the Party's Crisis~~. *Tenth Party Congress. Defeat of the Opposition. Adoption of the New Economic Policy (NEP)*

~~The Bolshevik Party's Central Committee and Lenin and Stalin saw what was happening in the country. They saw the difficulties that were connected with the transition from war to economic construction, but that is not all that they saw. They also saw the growing strength of the proletarian revolution which was capable of overcoming all difficulties and they recognized and pointed to the way out of these difficulties toward the victory of Socialism.~~

~~Lenin frequently said that the working class was to face a more difficult struggle on the economic front than on the fronts of the Civil War. This was a war against a capitalism that was born of small peasant farms. The roots of capitalism in our country had not yet been torn out: capitalism at that time had a more firm economic base in our country than Socialism. Only by creating large-scale industry and by introducing into the economy a new, technical base would it be possible to guarantee the victory of Socialism. The working class needed to create the advanced technique and give hundreds of thousands of tractors to the countryside in order to put the small peasant farms on the path to Socialism, on the path to large-scale, collectivized, mechanized farm-~~

~~ing. Only in this way was it possible to pull out the roots of capitalism in our country.~~

~~At Lenin's suggestion, the GOELRO Plan (the State Committee on the Electrification of Russia), approved by the Eighth Congress of Soviets at the end of 1920, served as the base for all economic construction. "Communism equals the Soviet power plus the Electrification of the entire country," Lenin said. Stalin defended Lenin's GOELRO plan with all his might against Trotsky, Rykov and other enemies of Socialism.~~

~~Lenin taught that in order to organize victory on the economic front, it was necessary to involve the million-man mass of workers and peasants in Socialist construction. It was both possible and necessary to include the peasants in the construction of Socialism. But for this, it was necessary to engage, persuade and convince them that there was no other way out of their servitude and need, or hunger and ruin, aside from the path of Socialism. It was necessary to find new ways to preserve and strengthen the alliance of the proletariat with the broad mass of the peasantry and at the same time to strengthen the proletarian dictatorship. The Trotskyites attempted to disrupt this approach, proposing instead to "tighten the screws" of War Communism.~~

The Central Committee of the Party, its Leninist majority, saw clearly that now that the war was over and the country had turned to peaceful economic development, there was no longer any reason for maintaining the rigid regime of War Communism—the product of war and blockade.

The Central Committee realized that the need for the surplus-appropriation system had passed, that it was time to supersede it by a tax in kind so as to enable the peasants to use the greater part of their surpluses at their own discretion. The Central Committee realized that this measure would make it possible to revive agriculture, to extend the cultivation of grain and industrial crops required for the development of industry, to revive the circulation of commodities, to improve supplies to the towns, and to create a new foundation, an economic foundation for the alliance of workers and peasants.

~~The political and economic situation in the country was sharp. In this difficult situation, an array of anti-Party groups acted against the Party. A bitter debate about the trade unions took shape within the Party.~~ *The Central Committee realized also that the prime task was to revive industry, but considered that this could not be done without enlisting the support of the working class and its trade unions; it considered that the workers could be enlisted in this work by showing them that the economic disruption was just as dangerous an enemy of the people as the intervention and the blockade had been, and that the Party and the trade unions could certainly succeed in this work if they exercised their influence on the working class not by military commands, as had been the case at the front, where commands were really essential, but by methods of persuasion, by convincing it.*

But not all members of the Party were of the same mind as the Central Committee. The[2] *small opposition groups—the Trotskyites, "Workers' Opposition," "Left Communists," "Democratic-Centralists," etc.—wavered and vacillated in face of the difficulties attending the transition to peaceful economic construction. There were in the Party quite a number of ex-members of the Menshevik, Socialist-Revolutionary, Bund and Borotbist parties, and all kinds of semi-nationalists from the border regions of Russia. Most of them allied themselves with one opposition group or another. These people were not real Marxists, they were ignorant of the laws of economic development, and had not had a Leninist-Party schooling,*[3] *and they only helped to aggravate the confusion and vacillations of the opposition groups. Some of them thought that it would be wrong to relax the rigid regime of War Communism, that, on the contrary, "the screws must be tightened." Others thought that the Party and the state should stand aside from the economic restoration, and that it should be left entirely in the hands of the trade unions.*

~~In order to understand why there were opportunistic groups within the Party and why the debate emerged, it is necessary to remember what sort of economic conditions and class forces prevailed in the country at that time. At present, the Socialist structure reigns supreme in the U.S.S.R. This was not the case, however, in 1921. We know that before the revolution, Russia was a petty-bourgeois country. The revolution had not yet managed to transform the economy. Socialism had made only its first steps. The Soviet Republic remained a small-peasant country. During the Civil War years, the middle peasant section of the peasantry had become stronger. The petty landholders expressed discontent with the surplus-appropriation system. The kulaks still enjoyed significant influence in the countryside. Private profiteering still played a significant role in trade. Petty-bourgeois unrest grew stronger and its influence penetrated into the working class and the Party.~~

~~The circumstances in the country and the condition of the working class were also reflected in the Communist Party. There were just 730,000 Party members in 1921. But among them, only 41–42 per cent were workers, with the remaining 58 per cent—peasants, employees, and members of the intelligentsia—lacking proletarian-class origins. The overwhelming majority of Party members had belonged to the Party for only one or two years and lacked political experience. There was quite a significant group in the Party at the time—several tens of thousands—who were new arrivals from other parties: Mensheviks, Bundists, Socialist-Revolutionaries, Ukrainian Borotbists and other nationalists. Many of them retained their old petty-bourgeois and bourgeois views, sowed doubt into the Party ranks, and actively took part in various oppositionist movements within the Party and a variety of double-dealing counter-revolutionary organizations.~~

It was clear that with such confusion reigning among certain groups in the Party, lovers of controversy, opposition "leaders" of one kind or another were bound to try to force a discussion upon the Party.

And that is just what happened.

The discussion started over the role of the trade unions, although the trade unions were not the chief problem of Party policy at the time.

~~The major turnabout from war to economic construction and the difficulties associated with this transition strengthened the doubts and wavering of opportunistic elements within the Russian Communist Party (Bolsheviks).~~

It was Trotsky who started *the discussion and* the fight against Lenin, *against the Leninist majority of the Central Committee. With the intention of aggravating the situation, h*e came out at a meeting of Communist delegates to the Fifth All-Russian Trade Union Conference, held at the beginning of November 1920, with the *dubious* slogans of "*tightening the screws*" *and* "shaking up the trade unions." Trotsky demanded that the trade unions be immediately "governmentalized." He was against the ~~trade unions' defence of the working class's material and cultural interests~~ *use of persuasion in relations with the working class, and was in favour of introducing military methods in the trade unions.* Trotsky was against any extension of democracy in the trade unions, against the principle of ~~elections~~ *electing trade union bodies* ~~and against Bolshevik methods of PERSUASION~~.

Instead of ~~Bolshevik~~ methods of persuasion, without which the activities of working-class organizations are inconceivable, the Trotskyites proposed methods of sheer COMPULSION, of ~~command~~ *dictation*~~, of bureaucratic decrees, etc~~. Applying this policy wherever they happened to occupy leading positions in the trade unions, the Trotskyites caused conflicts, disunity and demoralization in the unions. By their policy the Trotskyites were setting the mass of the non-Party workers against the Party, were splitting the ~~trade unions~~ *working class*~~, which threatened to disrupt the proletarian dictatorship~~.

As a matter of fact, the discussion on the trade unions was of much broader import than the trade union question. As was stated later in the resolution of the Plenum of the Central Committee of the Russian Communist Party (Bolsheviks) adopted on January 17, 1925, the actual point at issue[4] was "the policy to be adopted towards the peasantry, who were rising against War Communism, the policy to be adopted towards the mass of the non-Party workers, and, in general, what was to be the approach of the Party to the masses in the period when the Civil War was coming to an end." (RESOLUTIONS OF THE C.P.S.U.[B.], Russ. ed., Part I, p. 651.)

~~If the Party had not defeated the Trotskyites and other anti-Party oppositionist groups, and if the Party had not been able to turn from war commu-~~

~~nism to the New Economic Policy (as the Trotskyites hoped), the Soviet power would probably have met its fate.~~

Trotsky's lead was followed by other anti-Party groups: the "Workers' Opposition" (Shlyapnikov, Medvedyev, Kollontai and others), the "Democratic-Centralists" (Sapronov, Drobnis, Boguslavsky, Ossinsky, V. Smirnov and others), *the "Left Communists" (Bukharin, Preobrazhensky).*

The "Workers' Opposition" put forward a slogan demanding that the administration of the entire national economy be entrusted to an "All-Russian Producers' Congress." They wanted to reduce the ~~leadership~~ role of the Party to nought, and denied the ~~greatest~~ importance of the dictatorship of the proletariat to economic development. The "Workers' Opposition" contended that the interests of the trade unions were opposed to those of the Soviet state and the Communist Party. They held that the trade unions, and not the Party, were the ~~most important~~ *highest form* of working-class organization. ~~This is how the Anarchists and Syndicalists relate to the Party in Spain, France and other countries. This is why the Party termed the views of the "Workers' Opposition" to be an anarcho-syndicalist deviation.~~ *The "Workers' Opposition" was essentially an anarcho-syndicalist anti-Party group.*

The "Democratic-Centralists" (Decists) demanded complete freedom for factions and groupings. Like the Trotskyites, the "Democratic-Centralists" tried to undermine the leadership of the Party in the Soviets *and in the trade unions.* Lenin spoke of the "Democratic-Centralists" as a faction of "champion shouters," and of their platform as a Socialist Revolutionary-Menshevik platform.

Trotsky was assisted in his fight against Lenin and the Party by Bukharin. With Preobrazhensky, Serebryakov and Sokolnikov, Bukharin formed a "buffer" group. This group defended and shielded the Trotskyites, the most vicious of all factionalists. Lenin said that Bukharin's behaviour was the "acme of ideological depravity." Very soon, the Bukharinites openly joined forces with the Trotskyites against Lenin.

~~All of these enemies of Leninism, then, had already grouped together in order to struggle against the Party and its line.~~

Lenin and the Leninists concentrated their fire on the Trotskyites as the backbone of the anti-Party groupings. They condemned the Trotskyites for ignoring the difference between trade unions and military bodies and warned them that military methods could not be applied to the trade unions. ~~Lenin and Stalin spoke out against these groups. With eight other members of the Central Committee, they formed the "Platform of the Ten."~~ *Lenin and the Leninists drew up a platform of their own, entirely contrary in spirit to the platforms of the opposition groups.* In this platform, the trade unions were defined as a school of administration, a school of management, a school of Communism.[5] The trade unions should base all their activities on methods of persuasion. Only then would the trade unions rouse the workers as a whole to combat the economic disruption and be able to ~~draft~~ *enlist* them in the work of Socialist construction. ~~Strengthening working-class influence over the countryside also became the all-important task of the trade unions.~~

~~The basic questions in the discussion concerned the Party and its role, its relationship with the working class, and its methods of approaching the masses and leading them. Leninism teaches that the Communist Party is the leading power which directs all of the work of the Soviet state and the working-class organizations. The strength of the Soviet power is dependent on strengthening the Party's leadership throughout the system and the organizations of the proletarian dictatorship. The Party bases its work and influence on the masses' belief in the Party's correctitude. All the other anti-Party groups and their various platforms occupied a different position. They denied the role that the trade unions play as schools of Communism. The actions of all the anti-Party groups were designed to undermine the LEADING ROLE OF THE PARTY in the revolution and WEAKEN THE PROLETARIAN DICTATORSHIP. They were hostile to Marxism-Leninism.~~

~~The opposition's line expressed fear over the difficulties associated with the revolution. It promoted capitulation before the class enemy. The traitor Trotsky aimed to introduce disintegration and panic into the Party ranks. During the days of the Kronstadt mutiny, he announced that "the cock has already crowed" the last week of the Soviet power. All these groups—the Trotskyites, Bukharinites, Shlyapnikovites and Sapronovites—expressed dissatisfaction with the proletarian dictatorship and Lenin's leadership from the perspective of various strata of the petty bourgeoisie, the kulaks and the urban merchants, who dreamed of restoring capitalism. As it transpired, all of these groups later stooped so low as to betray their motherland by becoming agents (spies) of Japanese and German fascism and spies of other foreign espionage services. In terms of the Trotskyites, it was subsequently proven that at least by the fall of 1921, Trotsky was receiving money from German espionage services to conduct disruptive work against Lenin and our Party. And while he was at it, Trotsky agreed—one good turn deserves another!—to allow German espionage agents onto Soviet territory.~~

~~At the trial of the "Bloc of Rights and Trotskyites" in March 1938, it was established that on Trotsky's orders, the traitor Krestinsky conducted negotiations with the German generals Secht and Hasse. For 250,000 marks a year, the Trotskyites agreed to conduct counter-revolutionary Trotskyite work and aid the German bourgeoisie in creating espionage support facilities on Soviet territory to help agents cross the border without interference in order to supply German imperialists with secret information. This information was provided~~

~~to the enemy by Trotsky himself, as well as his fellow spies from the Trotskyite leadership: Krestinsky, Rosengoltz, Pyatakov and others. At that time, in 1920–21, the Party didn't know any of this, of course: it doesn't talk to traitors and spies, it destroys them.~~

~~Lenin understood the danger that the discussion presented on the eve of the difficult spring of 1921 and attempted to avoid it. But Trotsky and his follower Bukharin attempted to create a crisis within the Party, involving the Party in the discussion and distracting its attention and energy away from what was important: the task of building the economy. The opposition engaged in anti-Party, factional methods of struggle. It engaged in unprincipled demagogy against the Party and Lenin, treacherously hiding its factional, splitting ways. Setting down roots in the Ural Regional Party Committee, the Trotskyites Mrachkovsky, Sosnovsky and others who were subsequently exposed as dirty henchmen of German and Japanese fascism prevented the distribution of Party documents and articles written by Lenin. Lenin's platform on the tasks of the trade unions had to be distributed illegally there in secret.~~

~~The class enemy hurried to latch onto the opposition. Lenin warned the Party at that time that the Mensheviks and Socialist-Revolutionaries were taking cover among the opposition and that they were boiling with rabid hatred for the Bolsheviks and the Soviet power.~~

~~It subsequently transpired that more than a few provocateurs from the tsarist OKHRANA were exposed, who had long escaped unmasking and who had penetrated into the ranks of the Party, where they were actively taking part in various opposition movements with the goal of toppling the Soviet power. They did this because they sat quaking in their boots under the Soviet power, fearful of being unmasked.~~

~~It was a very critical and dangerous moment. Lenin published "The Crisis of the Party," an article which noted that a split in the Party was imminent if the Party was not healthy and strong enough to completely recover from this sickness in short order.~~

~~The Party understood the dangerous threat that lay before it and~~ *In this fight against the opposition groupings, the Party organizations* rallied around Lenin. The struggle took an *especially* acute form in Moscow. Here the opposition concentrated its main forces, with the object of capturing the Party organization of the capital. But these ~~enemies of Leninism~~ *factionalist intrigues* were frustrated by the spirited resistance of the Moscow Bolsheviks. An acute struggle broke out in the Ukrainian Party organizations as well. Led by Comrade Molotov, then the secretary of the Central Committee of the Communist Party of the Ukraine, ~~and Comrades Frunze, Chubar, Petrovsky and Manuilsky, who were also working in the Ukraine,~~ the Ukrainian Bolsheviks routed the Trotskyites and Shlyapnikovites. The Communist Party of the Ukraine remained a loyal support of Lenin's Party. In Baku, the routing of the opposition was led by ~~Sergo~~ *Comrade* Ordjonikidze. In Central Asia, the fight against the anti-Party groupings were headed by *Comrade* L. ~~M.~~ Kaganovich.

All the important *local* organizations of the Party ~~voted for~~ *endorsed* Lenin's platform. ~~Short messages about the results of the local discussions were published in PRAVDA by Comrade Stalin, who was leading the Party's struggle against the opposition along with Lenin, under the title "In the Name of Comrade Lenin's Platform." The attack against Leninism and the unity of our Party was defeated. The Leninist line was victorious. The Party emerged from the crisis stronger and more united.~~

~~3. Tenth Party Congress of the Bolsheviks~~

On March 8, 1921, the ~~Bolsheviks'~~ Tenth Party Congress opened. *The congress was attended by 694 delegates with vote, representing 732,521 Party members, and 296 delegates with voice but no vote.*

The congress summed up the discussion on the trade unions~~, having~~ *and* endorsed Lenin's platform by an overwhelming majority.

In opening the congress, Lenin said that the discussion had been an inexcusable luxury. He declared that the enemies had speculated on the inner Party strife and on a split in the ranks of the Communist Party.

Realizing how extremely dangerous the existence of factional groups was to the Bolshevik Party and the dictatorship of the proletariat, the Tenth Congress paid special attention to PARTY UNITY. The report on this question was made by Lenin. The congress passed condemnation on all the opposition groups and declared that they were "in fact helping the class enemies of the proletarian revolution."

The congress ordered the immediate dissolution of all factional groups and instructed all Party organizations to keep a strict watch to prevent any outbreaks of factionalism, non-observance of the congress decision to be followed by unconditional and immediate expulsion from the Party. The congress authorized the Central Committee, in the event of members of that body violating discipline, or reviving or tolerating factionalism, to apply to them all Party penalties, including expulsion from the Central Committee and from the Party.

These decisions were embodied in a special resolution on "Party Unity," moved by Lenin and adopted by the congress. ~~This became the iron law defending Party unity. Its significance in the subsequent struggle of the Party for Leninist unity was exceptionally great.~~

~~Let us summarize in detail the basic moments of the famous Tenth Party Congress's Leninist resolution.~~ *In this resolution, t*he congress reminded all Party members that unity and solidarity of the ranks of the Party, unanimity of will of the vanguard of the proletariat were particularly essential at that juncture, when a number of circumstances had, during the time of the Tenth Congress, increased the vacillation among the petty-bourgeois population of the country.

> "Notwithstanding this," read the ~~"Party Unity"~~ resolution, "even before the general Party discussion on the trade unions, certain signs of factionalism had been apparent in the Party, VIZ., the formation of groups with separate platforms, striving to a certain degree to segregate and create their own group discipline. All class-conscious workers must clearly realize the perniciousness and impermissibility of factionalism of any kind, for in practice factionalism inevitably results in weakening team work. At the same time it inevitably leads to intensified and repeated attempts by the enemies of the Party, who have fastened themselves onto it because it is the governing party, to widen the cleavage *(in the Party)* and to use it for counter-revolutionary purposes."

Further, in the same resolution, the congress said:

> "The way the enemies of the proletariat take advantage of every deviation from the thoroughly consistent Communist line was most strikingly shown in the case of the Kronstadt mutiny, when the bourgeois counter-revolutionaries and Whiteguards in all countries of the world immediately expressed their readiness to accept even the slogans of the Soviet system, if only they might thereby secure the overthrow of the dictatorship of the proletariat in Russia, and when the Socialist-Revolutionaries and the bourgeois counter-revolutionaries in general resorted in Kronstadt to slogans calling for an insurrection against the Soviet Government of Russia ostensibly in the interest of Soviet power. These facts fully prove that the Whiteguards strive, and are able to disguise themselves as Communists, and even as people "more Left" than the Communists, solely for the purpose of weakening and overthrowing the bulwark of the proletarian revolution in Russia. Menshevik[6] leaflets distributed in Petrograd on the eve of the Kronstadt mutiny likewise show how the Mensheviks took advantage of the disagreements in the R.C.P. actually in order to egg on and support the Kronstadt mutineers, the Socialist-Revolutionaries and Whiteguards, while claiming to be opponents of mutiny and supporters of the Soviet power, only with supposedly slight modifications." ~~(Resolutions of the C.P.S.U.(B.), Part I, Russ. ed. p. 373–74.)~~

The ~~Tenth Party Congress's~~ resolution declared that in its propaganda the Party must explain in detail the harm and danger of factionalism to Party unity and to the unity of purpose of the vanguard of the proletariat, which is a fundamental condition for the success of the dictatorship of the proletariat.

On the other hand, the congress resolution stated, the Party must explain in its propaganda the PECULIARITY of the latest tactical methods employed by the enemies of the Soviet power.

> "These enemies," ~~the congress stated~~ *read the resolution*, "having realized the hopelessness of counter-revolution under an openly Whiteguard flag, are now doing their utmost to utilize the disagreements within the R.C.P. and to further the counter-revolution in one way or another by transferring the power to the political groupings which outwardly are closest to the recognition of the Soviet power." *(RESOLUTIONS OF THE C.P.S.U.[B.], Russ. ed., Part I, pp. 373–74.)*

The ~~congress~~ *resolution further* stated that in its propaganda the Party "must also teach the lessons of preceding revolutions in which the counter-revolutionaries usually supported the petty-bourgeois groupings which stood closest to the extreme revolutionary Party, in order to undermine and overthrow the revolutionary dictatorship, and thus pave the way for the subsequent complete victory of the counter-revolution, of the capitalists and landlords. ~~(IBID.)~~

~~The Tenth Party Congress noted in its resolution:~~

> ~~"It is necessary that every Party organization strictly ensure that any unquestionably necessary criticism of the Party's shortcomings, any analysis of the general Party line or record of its practical experience and any investigation of its decision making and means of correcting its errors, etc., is turned over for discussion not to some group that has formed on the basis of any old "platform," etc., but to all members of the Party." (IBID.)~~

~~The Tenth Party Congress warned that "anyone speaking out critically must take into account the position of the Party, which is surrounded by its enemies." (RESOLUTIONS OF THE C.P.S.U.[B.], Russ. ed., Part I, p. 374.)~~

Closely allied to ~~Lenin's~~ *the* resolution on "Party Unity" was the ~~special~~ resolution on "The Syndicalist and Anarchist Deviation in our Party," also ~~written~~ *moved* by Lenin *and adopted by the congress*. In this resolution the Tenth Congress passed condemnation on the so-called "Workers' Opposition" ~~(Shlyapnikov, Medvedyev, etc.)~~. The congress declared that the propaganda of the ideas of the anarcho-syndicalist deviation was incompatible with membership in the Communist Party, and called upon the Party vigorously to combat this deviation.

~~At~~ *T*he Tenth Party Conference~~, Lenin's report was~~ passed ~~on~~ the *highly* important decision to replace the surplus-appropriation system by a tax in kind, to adopt the NEW ECONOMIC POLICY (NEP).

This turn from War Communism to NEP is a striking instance of the wisdom and farsightedness of ~~the Lenin-Stalin~~ *Lenin's* policy.

The resolution of the congress dealt with the substitution of a tax in kind for the surplus-appropriation system. The tax in kind was to be lighter than the assessments under the surplus-appropriation system. The total amount of the tax was to be announced each year before the spring sowing. The dates of delivery under the tax were to be strictly specified. All produce over and above the amount of the tax was to be entirely at the disposal of the peasant, who would be at liberty to sell these surpluses at will. *In his speech,* Lenin ~~was convinced~~ *said* that freedom of trade ~~at first~~ would *at first* lead to a certain revival of capitalism in the country. It would be necessary to permit private trade and to allow private manufacturers to open small businesses. But no fears need be entertained on this score. Lenin considered that ~~this well-known~~ *a certain* freedom of trade would give the peasant an economic incentive, induce him to produce more and would lead to a rapid improvement of agriculture; that, on this basis, the *state-owned* industries would be restored~~. We will get stronger~~ and private capital ~~will be~~ displaced~~.~~*; that s*trength and resources having been accumulated, a powerful industry could be created as the economic foundation of Socialism~~. Then we would embark on~~, *and that then* a determined offensive *could be undertaken* to destroy the remnants of ~~the capitalists and kulaks~~ *capitalism* in the country.

~~Such was Lenin's plan.~~ War Communism had been an attempt to take the fortress of ~~capitalism~~ *the capitalist elements in town and countryside* by assault, by a frontal attack. *In this offensive the Party had gone too far ahead, and ran the risk of being cut off from its base.* Now Lenin proposed *to retire a little, to retreat for a while nearer to the base,* to change from an assault of the fortress ~~of capitalism~~ to the slower method of siege, *so as to gather strength and resume the offensive.*

The Trotskyites~~, Zinovievites, Shlyapnikovites, Bukharinites and Rykovites~~ *and other oppositionists* held that NEP was NOTHING but a retreat. This interpretation suited their purpose, for their line was to restore capitalism. This was a most harmful, anti-Leninist interpretation of NEP. The fact is that only a year after NEP was introduced Lenin declared at the Eleventh Party Congress that THE RETREAT HAD COME TO AN END, and he put forward the slogan: "PREPARE FOR AN OFFENSIVE ON PRIVATE CAPITAL." (Lenin, COLLECTED WORKS, Russ. ed., Vol. XXVII, p. 213.) ~~Switching over to NEP, the Party solved the difficult~~

~~task of combining the interests of the peasant as a working man and a petty landlord with the interests of Socialist construction and the development of large-scale industry. In NEP the Party saw the only correct economic policy for the victorious proletariat; in NEP, the Party saw the path to the victory of Socialism.~~

> ~~"NEP," said Comrade Stalin, "is a special policy of the proletarian state that is designed to allow capitalism as long as the commanding heights are in the hands of the proletarian state, designed for the struggle of capitalist elements with Socialist ones, designed for the growing role of Socialist elements at the expense of the capitalist elements, designed for the victory of Socialist elements over the capitalist elements, and designed for the destruction of all classes and the construction of the foundation of a Socialist economy." (Stalin, On the Opposition, Russ. ed., p. 211.)~~

~~On the basis of NEP, the Bolshevik Party, the Lenin-Stalin Party, won world-historical victories, building the basis for a Socialist society.~~

The oppositionists, poor Marxists and crass ignoramuses in questions of Bolshevik policy as they were, understood neither the meaning of NEP nor the character of the retreat undertaken at the beginning of NEP. We have dealt with the meaning of NEP above. As for the character of the retreat, there are retreats and retreats. There are times when a party or an army has to retreat because it has suffered defeat. In such cases, the army or party retreats to preserve itself and its ranks for new battles. It was no such retreat that Lenin proposed when NEP was introduced, because, far from having suffered defeat or discomfiture, the Party had itself defeated the interventionists and Whiteguards in the Civil War. But there are other times, when in its advance a victorious party or army runs too far ahead, without providing itself with an adequate base in the rear. This creates a serious danger. So as not to lose connection with its base, an experienced party or army generally finds it necessary in such cases to fall back a little, to draw closer to and establish better contact with its base, in order to provide itself with all it needs, and then resume the offensive more confidently and with guarantee of success. It was this kind of temporary retreat that Lenin effected by the New Economic Policy. Reporting to the Fourth Congress of the Communist International on the reasons that prompted the introduction of NEP, Lenin plainly said, "in our economic offensive we ran too far ahead, we did not provide ourselves with an adequate base," and so it was necessary to make a temporary retreat to a secure rear.

The misfortune of the opposition was that, in their ignorance, they did not understand, and never understood to the end of their days, this feature of the retreat under NEP.

The decision of the Tenth Congress on the New Economic Policy ensured a durable economic alliance of the working class and the peasantry for the building of Socialism.

This prime object was served by yet another decision of the congress—the decision on the national ~~policy~~ *question*. The report on the national question[7] was made by Comrade Stalin. He said that we had abolished national oppression, but that this was not ~~all~~ *enough*. The task was to do away with the evil heritage of the past—the economic, political and cultural backwardness of the formerly oppressed peoples. They had to be helped to catch up with Central Russia.

~~In this sense, the Party took and implemented an array of measures. A federation (a union) of republics was put together and it was decided that in the national republics and regions, mills and factories would be built, the poor peasants would be organized, and decisive measures would be taken against the beys (kulaks).~~

~~Along with this,~~ Comrade Stalin further referred to two anti-Party deviations on the national question: dominant-nation~~,~~ *(*Great-Russian*)* chauvinism and local nationalism. The ~~Party~~ *congress* condemned both deviations as harmful and dangerous to Communism and proletarian internationalism. ~~The Party, however,~~ *At the same time, the congress* directed its main blow at the bigger danger, dominant-nation chauvinism, ~~at colonialism,~~ i.e., the survivals and hangovers of the attitude towards the nationalities ~~such as the bourgeois imperialists had displayed in regard to their colonial peoples,~~ such as the Great-Russian ~~nationalists~~ *chauvinists* had displayed towards ~~"aliens"~~[8] *the non-Russian peoples* under tsardom. ~~It would later transpire that the main danger in an array of the national republics and regions was local bourgeois nationalism, which would sell out to the imperialists and prepare for a foreign intervention with the goal of dividing the U.S.S.R. up among the bourgeois states.~~

~~It was in this way that the Bolshevik Party resolved the most important questions facing the people at the Tenth Party Congress in this difficult period during the shift from Civil War to peaceful construction and the restoration of the country's economy.~~

3.~~4. The Bolshevik Party during~~ The *First* ~~Years~~ *Results* of NEP. *Eleventh Party Congress. Formation of the Union of Soviet Socialist Republics. Lenin's Illness. Lenin's Co-operative Plan. Twelfth Party Congress*[9]

~~There was very little with which to begin to construct the foundation of the Socialist economy. It was necessary first of all to reach pre-war levels of production, that is, the level of what was a backward country for all intents and purposes. It was necessary to begin most of all with the restoration of~~

~~agriculture. And the economic troubles after the Tenth Party Congress only grew. The effects of the imperialist and civil war made themselves felt with all their strength, as did the effects of the blockade. During the summer of 1921, the Soviet Republic suffered a major harvest shortfall, accompanied by a famine. Up to 25 million people were starving. The situation on the Volga was particularly serious, where the population suffered frightfully from hunger despite the enormous aid that the Soviet power supplied.~~

~~The Soviet power mobilized all means within the country in order to aid the hungry and bought foodstuffs from abroad. Church valuables were seized (gold and silver) at the suggestion of the working people in order to help the starving. Campaigns continuously were conducted to collect donations for the hungry under the slogan "Every ten with enough to eat must feed one who is starving."~~

~~The capitalist world tried in every way to take advantage of this exceptionally difficult situation. In the fall of 1921, Petlyurite bandit units invaded the Ukraine and the White Finns launched a counter-revolutionary uprising in Karelia. In an array of regions, bandit gangs were still in operation, backed by the imperialists. The Mensheviks and Socialist-Revolutionaries remained very active. During the spring of 1921, they promoted their candidates for the Moscow and Petrograd Soviets under the guise of non-party candidates. Agricultural and handicraft co-operatives still remained in the hands of the Mensheviks, Socialist-Revolutionaries and Cadets. Diversionists and spies of the imperialist states organized an array of accidents, explosions and fires with the Mensheviks and Socialist-Revolutionaries.~~

~~During the transition to NEP, it was necessary to overcome the resistance of the anti-Leninist elements in the Party. Lenin said that we were introducing NEP "in all seriousness and for a long time." "But not forever," he added.~~ *The New Economic Policy was resisted by the unstable elements in the Party.* ~~The New Economic Policy could have been undermined~~ *The resistance came* from two quarters. First there were ~~those who shouted out~~ *the "Left" shouters, political freaks like Lominadze, Shatskin and others, who argued* that NEP was a renunciation of the gains of the October revolution, a return to capitalism, *the downfall of the Soviet power. Because of their political illiteracy and ignorance of the laws of economic development,* these people *did not understand the policy of the Party,* fell into a panic, and sowed dejection and discouragement ~~all around themselves.~~[10] ~~There were even a number of unstable Party members who left the Party ranks entirely as a result of their disagreement with NEP.~~ Then there were ~~those~~ *the downright capitulators, like Trotsky, Radek, Zinoviev, Sokolnikov, Kamenev, Shlyapnikov, Bukharin, Rykov and others,* who *did not believe that the Socialist development of our country was possible, bowed before the "omnipotence" of capitalism and, in their endeavour to strengthen the position of capitalism in the Soviet country,* ~~began to demand~~ *demanded* ~~greater~~ *far-reaching* concessions to private capital, both home and foreign, and ~~began to demand that the commanding heights be turned over to private capital~~ *the surrender of a number of key positions of the Soviet power in the economic field to private capitalists, the latter to act either as concessionaries or as partners of the state in mixed joint stock companies.*

Both groups were alien to ~~Bolshevism~~ *Marxism and Leninism.*

~~The enemies of the Bolshevik Party—Trotsky, Kamenev and Zinoviev—saw in NEP a retreat backward, to capitalism. Distorting the nature of NEP, they attempted to undermine the masses' belief in the new economic policy that was being implemented by the Communist Party.~~

~~The Party exposed the criminal-capitulatory character of all of these announcements. Lenin and Stalin tirelessly explained to the masses the true significance of the new economic policy. An enormous amount of explanatory work was done on an ideological level. Having heard Lenin's report on the tactics of the R.C.P.(B.), the Third Congress of the Comintern fully ratified the Bolshevik Party's new economic policy. The Bolsheviks had staged an orderly and temporary retreat in order to be able to soon return to the offensive against capitalism. The Party did not give the alarmists and capitulators an opportunity to do their dirty deeds.~~ *Both were exposed and isolated by the Party, which passed severe stricture on the alarmists and the capitulators.*

*This resistance to the Party policy was one more reminder that the Party needed to be purged of unstable elements. Accordingly, t*he Central Committee in 1921 organized ~~and carried out~~[11] a Party purge,[12] which helped to considerably strengthen the Party~~—an extremely important event~~. The purging was done at open meetings, in the presence and with the participation of non-Party people. Lenin advised that the Party be thoroughly cleansed "of rascals, bureaucrats, dishonest or wavering Communists, and of Mensheviks who have repainted their 'facade' but who have remained Mensheviks at heart." (Lenin, Collected Works, Russ. ed., Vol. XXVII, p. 13.)

Altogether, nearly 170,000 persons, or about 25 per cent of the total membership, were expelled *from the Party*[13] as a result of the purge.

The purge greatly strengthened the Party, improved its social composition, increased the confidence of the masses in it, and heightened its prestige. The Party became more closely welded and better disciplined.

The correctness of the New Economic Policy was proved in its very first year. Its adoption served greatly to ~~immediately~~ strengthen the alliance of workers and peasants *on a new basis*. The dictatorship of the proletariat gained in might and strength. Kulak banditry was almost completely liquidated. The middle peasants, now that the surplus-appropriation system had been abolished, helped the Soviet Government to fight the kulak bands. The Soviet Government retained all the key positions in the economic field: large-scale industry, the means of transport, the banks, the land, *and home* and foreign trade. The Party achieved a definite turn for the better on the economic front. Agriculture soon began to forge ahead. Industry and the railways could record their first successes. An economic revival began, still very slow but sure. The workers and the peasants felt and perceived that the Party was on the right track.

In March 1922, the Party held its Eleventh Congress. *It was attended by 522 voting delegates, representing 532,000 Party members, which was less than at the previous congress. There were 165 delegates with voice but no vote. The reduction in the membership was due to the Party purge which had already begun.*

At ~~it~~ *this congress* the Party reviewed the results of the first year of the New Economic Policy. These results entitled Lenin to declare at the congress:

> "For a year we have been retreating. In the name of the Party we must now call a halt. The purpose pursued by the retreat has been achieved. This period is drawing, or has drawn, to a close. Now our purpose is different—to regroup our forces." (Ibid., p. 238.)

Lenin said that NEP meant a ~~desperate,~~ life and death struggle between capitalism and Socialism. "Who will win?"—that was the question. In order that we might win, the bond between the working class and the peasantry, between Socialist industry and peasant agriculture, had to be made secure *by developing the exchange of goods between town and country to the utmost*. For this purpose the art of management and of *efficient* trading would ~~need~~ *have* to be learned.

At that period, trade was the main link[14] in the chain of problems that confronted the Party. Unless this problem were solved it would be impossible *to develop the exchange of goods between town and country,* to strengthen the *economic* alliance between the workers and peasants, impossible to advance agriculture, or to extricate industry from its state of disruption.

Soviet trade at that time was still very undeveloped. The machinery of trade was highly inadequate. Communists had not yet learned the art of trade; they had not studied the enemy, the Nepman, or learned how to combat him. The private traders, or Nepmen, had taken advantage of ~~our underdevelopment~~ *the undeveloped state of Soviet trade* to capture the trade in textiles and other goods in general demand. The organization of state and co-operative trade ~~was~~ *became* a matter of utmost importance. ~~The selection of people and the monitoring of implementation became the "key" to the whole affair, that is, the most important thing.~~

~~After the Eleventh Party Congress, the Central Committee elected Comrade Stalin to be General Secretary of the Central Committee. The Party viewed Comrade Stalin as the best and most devoted of Lenin's pupils and comrades-~~

~~in-arms and an experienced and firm chief who had built the Bolshevik Party with Lenin.~~

After the Eleventh Congress, work in the economic sphere was resumed ~~even more~~ *with redoubled vigour*. The effects of the recent ~~famine~~ *harvest failure* were successfully remedied. Peasant farming showed rapid recovery. The railways began to work better. Increasing numbers of factories and plants resumed operation.

In October 1922, the Soviet Republic celebrated a great victory: Vladivostok, *the last piece of Soviet territory to remain in the hands of the invaders,* was wrested by the ~~heroic~~ Red Army and the Far Eastern partisans from the hands of the Japanese.

The whole territory of the Soviet republic having been cleared of interventionists, and the needs of Socialist construction and national defence demanding a further consolidation of the union of the Soviet peoples, the necessity now arose of welding the Soviet republics closer together in a single federal state. All the forces of the people had to be combined for the work of building Socialism. The country had to be made impregnable. Conditions had to be created for the all-round development of every nationality in our country. This required that all the Soviet nations should be brought into still closer union.

In December 1922 the First All-Union Congress of Soviets was held, at which, on the proposal of Lenin and Stalin, a voluntary state union of the Soviet nations was formed—the Union of Soviet Socialist Republics (U.S.S.R.). Originally, the U.S.S.R. comprised the Russian Soviet Federative Socialist Republic (R.S.F.S.R.), the Trancaucasian Soviet Federative Socialist Republic (~~three republics entered into the~~ T.S.F.S.R.~~, Georgia, Azerbaidjan and Armenia~~), the Ukrainian Soviet Socialist Republic (Ukr. S.S.R.) and the Byelorussian Soviet Socialist Republic (B.S.S.R.). Somewhat later, three independent Union Soviet Republics—the Uzbek, Turkmen and Tadjik—were formed in Central Asia. *All t*hese republics have *now* united *in a single union of Soviet states—the U.S.S.R.*—on a voluntary and equal basis, each of them being reserved the right of freely seceding from the Soviet Union.

The formation of the Union of Soviet Socialist Republics meant the consolidation of the Soviet power and a great victory for the Leninist-Stalinist ~~nationality~~ policy of the Bolshevik Party *on the national question*.

In November 1922, Lenin made a speech at a plenary meeting of the Moscow Soviet in which he reviewed the ~~first~~ five years of Soviet rule and expressed the firm conviction that "NEP Russia will become Socialist Russia." This was his last speech to the country. That same autumn a great misfortune overtook the Party: Lenin fell seriously ill. His illness was a deep and personal affliction to the whole Party and to all the working people. All lived in trepidation for the life of their beloved Lenin. But even in illness Lenin did not discontinue his work ~~in the name of the revolution, to which he devoted all his energy and his entire life~~.[15] When already a very sick man, he wrote a number of highly important articles. In these last writings he reviewed the work already performed and outlined a plan for the building of Socialism in our country *by enlisting the peasantry in the cause of Socialist construction*. This contained ~~first of all the issue of the country's industrialization and its electrification~~ *his co-operative plan for securing the participation of the peasantry in the work of building Socialism.*

~~Lenin ascribed enormous significance to co-operatives.~~ Lenin regarded co-operative societies *in general, and agricultural co-operative societies in particular,* as a means of transition—a means within the reach and understanding of the peasant millions—from small, individual farming to large-scale producing associations, *or* ~~(~~collective farms~~)~~. Lenin pointed out that the line to be followed in the development of agriculture in our country was to draw the ~~majority of~~ peasants into the work of building Socialism through the co-operative societies, gradually to introduce the collective principle in agriculture, first in the selling,[16] and then in the growing of farm produce. With the dictatorship of the proletariat and the alliance of the working class and the peasantry, with the leadership of the peasantry by the proletariat made secure, and *with the existence of a Socialist industry,* Lenin ~~wrote~~ *said*, a properly organized *producing* co-operative system embracing ~~the whole population~~ *millions of peasants* ~~constituted everything necessary for the construction of a complete Socialist society~~ *was the means whereby a complete Socialist society could be built in our country.*

~~Lenin wrote about the imperative of improving the state apparatus and making it less costly, of observing a strict economy and thriftiness, in order to allocate all savings to the development of Socialist industry.~~

~~The industrialization of the country, its electrification and the transformation of peasant farms into co-operatives were things that Lenin tied into a single plan for Socialist construction in our country. Lenin considered the preservation of the worker-peasant alliance to have a decisive significance under the leadership of the proletariat. In the outline of his brochure "On the Foodstuffs Tax" (1921), Lenin wrote:~~

> ~~"10–20 years of correct relations with the peasantry and efforts to provide for victory on a world scale (even if it means the burden of supporting proletarian revolutions, wherever they may emerge), or else 20–40 years of Whiteguard terror." (Lenin, WORKS, Russ. Ed., vol. XXVI, p. 313.)~~

In April 1923, the Party held its Twelfth Congress. *Since the seizure of power by the Bolsheviks t*his was the first congress ~~(with the exception of the Fourth)~~ at which Lenin was unable to be present. *The congress was attended by 408* *voting delegates, representing 386,000 Party members. This was less than was represented at the previous congress, the reduction being due to the fact that in the interval the Party purge had continued and had resulted in the expulsion of a considerable percentage of the Party membership. There were 417 delegates with voice but no vote.*

The Twelfth Party Congress embodied in its decisions the recommendations made by Lenin *in his recent articles and letters.*

The congress sharply rebuked those who ~~did not believe in the possibility of building Socialism in our country with our own strength~~ *took NEP to mean a retreat from the Socialist position, a surrender to capitalism, and* who advocated a return to ~~imperialist~~ *capitalist* bondage. Proposals of this kind were made at the congress by Radek and Krassin, *followers of Trotsky*. They proposed that we should ~~make large concessions to the~~ *throw ourselves on the tender mercies of* foreign capitalists, surrender to them, in the form of concessions, branches of industry that were of vital necessity to the Soviet state. They proposed that we pay the tsarist government's debts annulled by the October Revolution~~, that is, transform into tributaries of the capitalist states. The Trotskyites kow-towed before the strength of the capitalist world~~. The Party ~~did not go for~~ *stigmatized* these capitulatory ~~Menshevik~~ proposals *as treachery*. It did not reject the policy of granting concessions, but favoured it only in such industries and in such dimensions as would ~~not threaten~~ *be of advantage to* the Soviet state.

Bukharin and Sokolnikov had even prior to the congress proposed the abolition of the state monopoly of foreign trade. ~~Accepting this traitorous proposal would have meant undermining our industry and becoming dependent on the imperialist predators.~~ *The proposal was also based on the conception that NEP was a surrender to capitalism.* Lenin had branded Bukharin as a champion of the profiteers, Nepmen and kulaks. The *Twelfth* Congress firmly repelled the attempts to undermine the monopoly of foreign trade.

The congress also repelled Trotsky's attempt to foist upon the Party a policy towards the peasantry that would have been fatal, and stated that the predominance of small peasant farming in the country was a fact not to be forgotten. It emphatically declared that the development of industry, including heavy industry ~~and especially metallurgy and machine-building~~, must ~~serve as the basis for the elevation of agriculture~~ *not run counter to the interests of the peasant masses, but must be based on a close bond with the peasants, in the interests of the whole working population*. These decisions were an answer to Trotsky, who had proposed that we should build up our industry by exploiting the peasants, ~~not worrying about the danger of rupturing the~~ *and who in fact did not accept the policy of an* alliance of the proletariat with the peasantry.

At the same time, Trotsky had proposed that big plants like the Putilov, Bryansk and others, which were of importance to the country's defence, should be closed down allegedly on the grounds that they were unprofitable. *The congress indignantly rejected Trotsky's proposals.* ~~Now, when Trotsky's spying and wrecking activities have become known, it is clear that he did all of this to disrupt the defencive capacity of the land of the Soviets.~~

On Lenin's proposal, *sent to the congress in written form,* the Twelfth Congress united the Central Control Commission of the Party and the Workers' and Peasants' Inspection into one body. To this united body were entrusted the important duties of safeguarding the unity of our Party, strengthening Party and civil discipline, and improving the Soviet state apparatus in every way.

~~A special~~ *An important* item on the agenda of the congress was the national question,[17] the report on which was made by Comrade Stalin. Comrade Stalin stressed the international significance of our ~~nationality~~ policy *on the national question.* To the oppressed peoples in the East and West, the Soviet Union was a model of the solution of the national question and the abolition of national oppression. He pointed out that energetic measures were needed to put an end to economic and cultural inequality among the peoples of the Soviet Union. He called upon the Party to put up a determined fight against deviations in the national question—Great Russian chauvinism and local bourgeois nationalism.

~~Great Russian chauvinists and bourgeois nationalists~~ *The nationalist deviators and their dominant-nation policy towards the national minorities* were ~~attacked~~ *exposed* at the congress. At that time the Georgian *nationalist* deviators, ~~Budu~~ Mdivani and others, were ~~bitterly~~ opposing the Party. They had been against the formation of the Transcaucasian Federation and were against the promotion of friendship between the peoples of Transcaucasia. The deviators were behaving like outright dominant-nation chauvinists towards the other nationalities of Georgia. They were expelling non-Georgians from Tiflis wholesale, especially Armenians; they had passed a law under which Georgian women who married non-Georgians lost their Georgian citizenship. The Georgian nationalist~~s~~ *deviators* were supported by Trotsky, Radek ~~and other Trotskyites.~~, *Bukharin*, ~~Even at that time, Trotskyism grouped together all anti-Party tendencies. The Georgian deviationists were supported in the Ukraine by the nationalist~~ Skrypnik and ~~the Trotskyite~~ Rakovsky.

Shortly after the congress, a special conference *of Party workers from the national republics* was called to discuss the national question. Here were exposed a group of Tatar bourgeois nationalists—Sultan-Galiev and others[18]*—and a group of Uzbek nationalist deviators—Faizulla Khodjayev and others.* ~~They were tied to enemies of the Soviet power and were aiming to create a bourgeois state at the behest of the imperialists. Sultan-Galievism served as an espionage network for the imperialists, penetrating into the Party ranks. The bourgeois nationalists, acting on the orders of the imperialist bourgeoisie, set their sights on dismembering the Soviet Union.~~

~~By~~ *T*he Twelfth Party Congress~~, the Party~~ reviewed the results of the New Economic Policy for the past two years. They were very heartening results and inspired confidence in ultimate victory.

> "Our Party has remained solid and united; it has stood the test of a momentous turn, and is marching on with flying colours," Comrade Stalin declared at the congress.

4.~~5.~~ Struggle ~~of the Party against the Trotskyite Opposition in 1923–24~~ *against the Difficulties of Economic Restoration. Trotskyites Take Advantage of Lenin's Illness to Increase Their Activity. New Party Discussion. Defeat of the Trotskyites. Death of Lenin. The Lenin Enrolment. Thirteenth Party Congress*

The struggle to restore the national economy yielded substantial results in its very first ~~few~~ years. By 1924 progress was to be observed in all fields. The crop area had increased considerably since 1921, and peasant farming was steadily improving. Socialist industry was growing and expanding. The working class had greatly increased in numbers. Wages had risen. Life had become easier and better for the workers and peasants as compared with 1920 and 1921. ~~Their political activity rose.~~

But the *effects of the* economic disruption still made ~~itself~~ *themselves* felt. Industry was still below the pre-war level, *and its development was still far behind the country's demand.* At the end of 1923 there were about a million unemployed; *the national economy was progressing too slowly to absorb unemployment.* ~~Eliminating unemployment was only possible through the further growth of the economy.~~ *The development of trade was being hindered by the excessive prices of manufactured goods, prices which the Nepmen, and the Nepman elements in our trading organizations, were imposing on the country.* ~~The Soviet currency (Sovznak) was unstable. Its value declined every day.~~ *Owing to this, the Soviet ruble began to fluctuate violently and to fall in value.* These factors ~~worsened~~ *impeded the improvement of* the condition of the workers and peasants.

In the autumn of 1923, the economic difficulties were ~~considerably~~ *somewhat* aggravated *owing to violations of the Soviet price policy by our industrial and commercial organizations.* There was a yawning gap between the prices of manufactures and the prices of farm produce. Grain prices were low, while prices of manufactures were *inordinately* high. Industry was burdened with excessive overhead costs which increased the price of goods. The money which the peasants received for their grain rapidly depreciated. To make matters worse, the Trotskyite Pyatakov, who was at that time on the Supreme Council of National Economy, gave managers and directors criminal instructions *to grind all the profit they could out of the sale of manufactured goods and* to force up prices to the maximum, *ostensibly for the purpose of developing industry. As a matter of fact, this Nepman policy could only narrow the base of industry and undermine it.* It became unprofitable for the peasantry to purchase manufactured goods, and they stopped buying them. The result was a sales crisis, from which industry suffered. Difficulties arose in the payment of wages. This provoked discontent among the workers. At some factories the more backward workers stopped work.

~~Class enemies hurried to take advantage of the Soviet power's economic difficulties. At first, the transition to NEP required a modest restoration of capitalism. This was, as Comrade Stalin pointed out, "the beginning of NEP, a period in which capitalism grew a bit more active." Socialist industry grew faster, but capitalist elements also rose up in the country as well. In the cities, a Nepman bourgeoisie appeared and began to grow, and in the countryside, the kulaks grew. In the area of industry, the Socialist position was very strong, but in the area of trade and credit, it was weak. In retail trade, private capitalists—or as they were called, Nepmen—still reigned. Three quarters of retail trade was in their hands. Credit in the countryside was almost entirely in the hands of the kulaks and usurers. The private dealer and usurer drove the peasant economy apart from Socialist industry like a wedge.~~

~~There were also weakness and shortcomings in the condition and work of the Communist Party. The social makeup of the Party in comparison to 1920–21 improved, but less than half of all Party members were workers. A significant number was composed of young Party members with little political experience. For instance, of 5,200 workers at the Putilov (now Kirov) factory in Leningrad, there were only 200 Party members. Internal Party democracy was not well developed.~~

The Central Committee of the Party~~, under the direction of Comrade Stalin,~~ adopted measures to remove these difficulties and anomalies. Steps were taken to overcome the sales crisis. Prices of consumers' goods were reduced. It was decided to reform the currency and to adopt a firm and stable currency unit, the chervonetz. The normal payment of wages was resumed. Measures were outlined for the development of ~~internal party democracy~~ *trade through state and co-operative channels and for the elimination of private traders and profiteers.*

What was now required was that everybody should join in the common effort, roll up his sleeves, and set to work with gusto. That is the way all who were loyal to the Party *thought and* acted. But not so the Trotskyites. ~~These traitors with Party cards in their pockets merely waited for a good opportunity to attack~~

~~the Party.~~ *They took advantage of the absence of Lenin, who was incapacitated by grave illness, to launch a new attack on the Party and its leadership. They decided that this was a favourable moment to smash the Party and overthrow its leadership.* They used everything they could as a weapon against the Party: the defeat of the revolution in Germany *and Bulgaria*[19] in the autumn of 1923, the economic difficulties *at home*, and Lenin's illness. ~~And~~ *I*t was at this moment of difficulty for the Soviet state, *when the Party's leader was stricken by sickness*, that Trotsky started ~~a new~~ *his* attack on the Bolshevik Party. ~~The new bourgeoisie, which was increasingly popular due to the NEP, increased its struggle against the Soviet power. The Trotskyites acted within the Party as the agents of the new Nepman bourgeoisie. In October 1923, Trotsky and forty-six of his oppositionist followers penned a declaration that was full of slander against the Party leadership.~~ *He mustered all the anti-Leninist elements in the Party and concocted an opposition platform against the Party, its leadership, and its policy. This platform was called the Declaration of the Forty-Six Oppositionists.* All the opposition groupings—the Trotskyites, Democratic-Centralists, and the remnants of the "Left Communist" and "Workers' Opposition" groups—united to fight the Leninist Party. ~~Among the forty-six signatories were all the future organizers of the counter-revolutionary Trotskyite Anti-Soviet Terrorist Centre—Pyatakov, Serebryakov, Radek, Smirnov, Muralov, Drobnis, Boguslavsky, Byeloborodov and others.~~ In their declaration, they prophesied a grave ~~mass,~~ economic crisis and the fall of the Soviet power*, and demanded freedom of factions and groups as the only way out of the situation.*

~~As Lenin had only just ended his activity in the Central Committee at the end of 1922 due to ill health, and as the Party continued to follow the path that Lenin had pointed out, this entire declaration was essentially directed against Lenin and the Leninist Central Committee.~~[20]

~~What was the way out that the opposition was proposing?~~[21] ~~The opposition demanded freedom for anti-Party factions and groups and proposed to create something like a permanent discussion club in the place of the Party which would give complete freedom of speech to those who did not share the Party line and did not obey its decisions. The Trotskyite opposition aimed to undermine Party discipline and unity.~~

This was a fight for the restoration of factionalism which the Tenth Party Congress, on Lenin's proposal, had prohibited.

The Trotskyites did not make a single definite proposal for the improvement of agriculture or industry, for the improvement of the circulation of commodities, or for the betterment of the condition of the working people. This did not even interest them. The only thing that interested them was to take advantage of Lenin's absence in order to restore factions within the Party, to undermine its foundations and its Central Committee.

~~On December 5, 1923, the Central Committee Politburo passed a resolution on internal Party democracy. The Central Committee made it completely possible to eliminate all the shortcomings of internal Party life on the basis of this decision. Being a double-dealer, Trotsky voted for this resolution, which was unanimously approved. But three days later, he issued a letter in which he advanced a whole array of new slanderous accusations against the Party.~~ *The platform of the forty-six was followed up by the publication of a letter by Trotsky in which he vilified the Party cadres and levelled new slanderous accusations against the Party.* In this letter Trotsky harped on the old Menshevik themes which the Party had heard from him ~~from the time of the Second Party Congress~~ *many times before.*

First of all the Trotskyites attacked the Party apparatus. They knew that without a strong apparatus the Party could not live and function. The opposition tried to undermine and destroy the Party apparatus, to set the Party members against it, and the young members against the old stalwarts of the Party. In this letter Trotsky played up to the students, the young Party members who were not acquainted with the history of the Party's fight against Trotskyism. To win the support of the students, ~~he~~ *Trotsky* flatteringly referred to them as the "Party's surest barometer," at the same time declaring that the *Leninist* old guard had degenerated. Alluding to the degeneration of the leaders of the Second International, he made the foul insinuation that ~~even~~ the old Bolshevik guard was going the same way. By this outcry about the degeneration of the Party, Trotsky tried to hide his own degeneration ~~into a counter-revolutionary~~ and his ~~counter-revolutionary~~ *anti-Party* scheming.

~~The Trotskyites set for themselves the task of destroying Bolshevik Party-mindedness and Party discipline and demanded tolerance for factions and groups within the Party. They wanted to change the Party's Leninist political line. The Trotskyites proposed raising the price of goods and establishing new, higher taxes for the peasants. They were against monetary reforms and the introduction of hard currency. The Trotskyites proposed going into servitude under the international bourgeoisie in exchange for loans and goods. Approving the Trotskyites' proposals would have meant undermining the industry that we had just set up on its own legs, as well as the worker-peasant alliance. Such policies would have led to the end of the proletarian dictatorship, the restoration of capitalism and the transformation of our motherland into a colony,[22] and this is what the Trotskyites intended to do.~~

The Trotskyites circulated both oppositionist documents, viz., the platform of the forty-six and Trotsky's letter, in the districts and among the Party nuclei and put them up for discussion by the Party membership.

They challenged the Party to a discussion.

Thus the Trotskyites forced a general discussion on the Party, just as they did at the time of the controversy over the trade union question before the Tenth Party Congress.

Although the Party was occupied with the far more important problems of the country's economic life, it accepted the challenge and opened the discussion.

The whole Party was involved in the discussion. The fight took ~~the very~~ *a* most bitter form. ~~Party meetings went on for days at a time, sometimes lasting all night without a break.~~ It was fiercest of all in Moscow, for the Trotskyites endeavoured above all to capture the Party organization in the capital. ~~For the Party, it was a matter of life and death. The Party rallied around Comrade Stalin and firmly defended the Party line. Only an insignificant minority within the Party supported Trotsky, mostly within Party organizations at the universities. In the course of these discussions, the Trotskyites were exposed and defeated.~~ *But the discussion was of no help to the Trotskyites. It only disgraced them. They were completely routed both in Moscow and all other parts of the Soviet Union. Only a small number of nuclei in universities and offices voted for the Trotskyites.*

In January 1924 the Party held its Thirteenth Conference. The conference heard a report by Comrade Stalin, summing up the results of the discussion. The conference condemned the Trotskyite opposition, declaring that it was a PETTY-BOURGEOIS DEVIATION *from Marxism*. The decisions of the conference were ~~then~~ *subsequently* endorsed by the Thirteenth Party Congress and the Fifth Congress of the Communist International. The international Communist proletariat supported the Bolshevik Party in its fight against Trotskyism.[23]

But the Trotskyites did not cease their subversive work. In the autumn of 1924, Trotsky ~~wrote~~ *published* an article entitled "The Lessons of October" in which he attempted to substitute Trotskyism for Leninism. It was a sheer slander on our Party and its leader, Lenin. This defamatory broadsheet was seized upon by all enemies of Communism and of the Soviet Government. The Party was outraged by this unscrupulous distortion of the heroic history of Bolshevism. Comrade Stalin denounced Trotsky's attempt to substitute Trotskyism for Leninism. He declared that "it is the duty of the Party to bury Trotskyism as an ideological trend."[24]

~~In the defeat of Trotskyism and the defence of Leninism's purity, Comrade Stalin's theoretical work had great significance. In 1924, Comrade Stalin gave a lecture at the Sverdlov Communist University on "The Foundations of Leninism," which later appeared in Stalin's book QUESTIONS OF LENINISM.~~ *An effective contribution to the ideological defeat of Trotskyism and to the defence of Leninism was Comrade Stalin's theoretical work,* FOUNDATIONS OF LENINISM *published in 1924.* This book is a~~n~~ ~~ingenious~~ *masterly* exposition and ~~further elaboration~~ *a weighty theoretical substantiation* of Leninism. It was, and is *today*, a trenchant weapon of Marxist-Leninist theory in the hands of Bolsheviks all over the world.[25]

In the battles against Trotskyism, Comrade Stalin rallied the ~~whole~~ Party *around its Central Committee* and mobilized it to carry on the fight for the victory of Socialism in our country. Comrade Stalin ~~made it clear to every Communist and worker that the defeat of Trotskyism would enable~~ *proved that Trotskyism had to be ideologically demolished if* the further victorious advance to Socialism *was to be ensured.*

Reviewing this period of the fight against Trotskyism, Comrade Stalin said:

> "Unless Trotskyism is defeated, it will be impossible to achieve victory under the conditions of NEP, it will be impossible to convert present-day Russia into a Socialist Russia."

But the successes attending the Party's Leninist policy[26] *were clouded by a most grievous calamity which now befell the Party and the working class.*

~~6. Lenin's Death. Stalin's Oath~~

On January 21, 1924, Lenin, our leader and teacher, the creator of the Bolshevik Party, passed away in the village of Gorki, near Moscow. Lenin's death was received by the ~~proletariat and~~ working ~~people~~ *class* of the whole world as a most cruel ~~toll~~ *loss.* ~~During~~ *On the day of* Lenin's funeral ~~workers all over the world~~ *the international proletariat* proclaimed a five-minute stoppage of work. Railways, mills and factories came to a standstill. As Lenin was borne to the grave, the working people of the whole world paid homage to him in overwhelming sorrow, as to a father and teacher, their best friend and defender.

The loss of Lenin caused the working class *of the Soviet Union* to rally even more solidly around the Leninist Party. In those days of mourning every *class-conscious* worker defined his attitude to the Communist Party, the executor of Lenin's behests. *The Central Committee of the Party received thousands upon thousands of applications from workers for admission to the Party. The Central Committee responded to this movement and proclaimed a mass admission of politically advanced workers into the Party ranks.* ~~Hundreds~~ *Tens* of thousands of workers flocked into the Party; they were people prepared to give their lives for the cause of the Party, the cause of Lenin. *In a brief space of time over t*wo hundred and forty thousand workers joined the ranks of the Bolshevik Party. They were the foremost section of the working class, the most class-conscious and revolutionary, the most intrepid and disciplined. This was the LENIN ENROLMENT~~, which improved the social makeup of the Party membership, strengthened the core of workers in the Party and strengthened the Party's connection to the broad non-Party masses~~.

The reaction to Lenin's death demonstrated how close are our Party's ties with the masses ~~and the millions of working people of the city and countryside~~, *and how high a place the Leninist Party holds in the hearts of the workers.*

~~Comrade Stalin—the loyal heir and great continuer of Lenin's cause—lifted Lenin's banner up high and then carried it forth.~~ In the days of mourning for Lenin, at the Second Congress of Soviets of the U.S.S.R., Comrade Stalin made a solemn vow ~~on January 26, 1924~~ *in the name of the Party*. ~~In the name of the entire Bolshevik Party, Comrade Stalin solemnly promised to fulfil Lenin's precepts and testaments.~~ He said:

> "We Communists are people of a special mould. We are made of a special stuff. We are those who form the army of the great proletarian strategist, the army of Comrade Lenin. There is nothing higher than the honour of belonging to this army. There is nothing higher than the title of member of the Party whose founder and leader is Comrade Lenin. . . .
>
> "Departing from us, Comrade Lenin adjured us to hold high and guard the purity of the great title of member of the Party. We vow to you, Comrade Lenin, that we will fulfil your behest with honour! . . .
>
> "Departing from us, Comrade Lenin adjured us to guard the unity of our Party as the apple of our eye. We vow to you, Comrade Lenin, that this behest, too, we will fulfil with honour! . . .
>
> "Departing from us, Comrade Lenin adjured us to guard and strengthen the dictatorship of the proletariat. We vow to you, Comrade Lenin, that we will spare no effort to fulfil this behest, too, with honour! . . .
>
> "Departing from us, Comrade Lenin adjured us to strengthen with all our might the alliance of the workers and the peasants. We vow to you, Comrade Lenin, that this behest, too, we will fulfil with honour! . . .
>
> "Comrade Lenin untiringly urged upon us the necessity of maintaining the voluntary union of the nations of our country, the necessity for fraternal co-operation between them within the framework of the Union of Republics. Departing from us, Comrade Lenin adjured us to consolidate and extend the Union of Republics. We vow to you, Comrade Lenin, that this behest, too, we will fulfil with honour! . . .
>
> "More than once did Lenin point out to us that the strengthening of the Red Army and the improvement of its condition is one of the most important tasks of our Party. . . . Let us vow then, comrades, that we will spare no effort to strengthen our Red Army and our Red Navy. . . .
>
> "Departing from us, Comrade Lenin adjured us to remain faithful to the principles of the Communist International. We vow to you, Comrade Lenin, that we will not spare our lives to strengthen and extend the union of the toilers of the whole world—the Communist International!" *(Joseph Stalin, THE LENIN HERITAGE.)*

~~The Bolshevik Party kept faithful to Comrade Stalin's great oath and fulfilled it with honor. Under the leadership of Comrade Stalin, the Bolsheviks succeeded in making the Socialist revolution in our country irreversible.~~ *This was the vow made by the Bolshevik Party to its leader, Lenin, whose memory will live throughout the ages.*

In May 1924 the Party held its Thirteenth Congress. It was attended by 748 voting delegates, representing a Party membership of 735,881. This marked increase in membership in comparison with the previous congress was due to the admission of some 250,000 new members under the Lenin Enrolment. There were 416 delegates with voice but no vote.

The congress unanimously condemned the platform of the Trotskyite opposition, defining it as a petty-bourgeois deviation from Marxism, as a revision of Leninism, and endorsed the resolutions of the Thirteenth Party Conference on "Party Affairs" and "The Results of the Discussion."

With the purpose of strengthening the bond between town and country, the congress gave instructions for a further expansion of industry, primarily of the light industries, while placing particular stress on the necessity for a rapid development of the iron and steel industry.

The congress endorsed the formation of the People's Commissariat of Internal Trade and set the trading bodies the task of gaining control of the market and ousting private capital from the sphere of trade.

The congress gave instructions for the increase of cheap state credit to the peasantry so as to oust the usurer from the countryside.

The congress called for the maximum development of the co-operative movement among the peasantry as the paramount task in the countryside.

Lastly, the congress stressed the profound importance of the Lenin Enrolment and drew the Party's attention to the necessity of devoting greater efforts to educating the young Party members—and above all the recruits of the Lenin Enrolment—in the principles of Leninism.

5.~~7.~~ The Soviet Union towards the End of the Restoration Period. *The Question of Socialist Construction and the Victory of Socialism in Our Country. Zinoviev-Kamenev "New Opposition." Fourteenth Party Congress. Policy of Socialist Industrialization of the Country*[27]

For ~~almost five~~ *over four* years the Bolshevik Party and the working class had been working strenuously ~~and selflessly~~ along the lines of the New Economic Policy. The heroic work of economic restoration was approaching completion. The economic and political might of the Soviet Union was steadily growing.

By this time the international situation had undergone a change. Capitalism had withstood the first revolutionary onslaught of the masses after the imperialist war. The revolutionary movement in Germany, Italy, Bulgaria, Poland and a number of other countries had been ~~temporarily~~ crushed. The bourgeoisie had been aided in this by the leaders of the compromising Social-Democratic parties. A temporary ebb in the tide of revolution set in~~, which slowed it down~~. There began a temporary, partial stabilization of capitalism~~—that is, a temporary strengthening of capitalism~~ *in Western Europe, a partial consolidation of the position of capitalism*. But ~~this~~ *the* stabilization of capitalism did not eliminate the basic contradictions rending capitalist society. On the contrary, the partial stabilization of capitalism aggravated the contradictions between the workers and the capitalists, between imperialism and the colonial nations, between the imperialist groups of the various countries. The stabilization of capitalism was preparing for a new explosion of contradictions, for ~~a new crisis of capitalism~~ *new crises in the capitalist countries.*

Parallel with the stabilization of capitalism, proceeded the stabilization of the Soviet Union. *But t*hese two processes of stabilization were fundamentally different in character. Capitalist stabilization presaged a new crisis of capitalism. The stabilization of the Soviet Union meant a further growth of the economic and political might of the Socialist country.

*Despite the defeat of the revolution in the West, t*he position of the Soviet Union in the international arena ~~was consolidated to a considerable degree~~ *continued to grow stronger, although, it is true, at a slower rate.*

In 1922, the Soviet Union had been invited to an international economic conference in Genoa, Italy. At the Genoa Conference the imperialist governments, *emboldened by the defeat of the revolution in the capitalist countries,* ~~brought~~ *tried to bring* new pressure to bear on the Soviet Republic, this time in diplomatic form. ~~Taking advantage of the difficult economic circumstances that our motherland was beset with as a result of the intervention,~~ *T*he imperialists presented brazen demands *to the Soviet Republic*. They demanded that ~~all~~ the factories and plants which had been nationalized by the ~~Great~~ October ~~Socialist~~ Revolution be returned ~~immediately~~ to the foreign capitalists; they demanded the payment of the debts of the tsarist government. In return, the imperialist states promised some trifling loans *to the Soviet Government*.

The Soviet Union rejected these demands~~, which amounted to the restoration of capitalism in our country, and refused to enter into the imperialists' servitude.~~ ~~Under the leadership of the Bolshevik Party, our motherland quickly restored the economy on its own, utilizing the advantages of the Socialist economic system.~~

The Genoa Conference was barren of result.

The threat of a new intervention contained in the ultimatum of Lord Curzon, the British Foreign Secretary, in 1923, also met with the rebuff it deserved.

Having tested the strength of the Soviet Government and convinced themselves of its stability, the capitalist states began one after another to ~~recognize~~ *resume diplomatic relations with* our country. In 1924 *diplomatic relations were restored with* Great Britain, France, Japan and Italy ~~recognized the Soviet state~~.

It was plain that the Soviet Union had ~~won~~ *been able to win* a prolonged breathing space, a period of peace.

The domestic situation had also changed. The self-sacrificing efforts of the workers and peasants, led by the Bolshevik Party, had borne fruit. The ~~furious~~ *rapid* development of the national economy was manifest. In the fiscal year 1924–25, agricultural output had already approached the pre-war level, amounting to 87 per cent of the pre-war output. In 1925 the large-scale industries of the U.S.S.R. were already producing about THREE-QUARTERS of the pre-war industrial output. In the fiscal year 1924–25, the Soviet Union was able to invest 385,000,000 rubles in capital construction work. The plan for the electrification of the country was proceeding successfully. Socialism was consolidating its key positions in the ~~whole~~ national economy. Important successes had been won in the struggle against private capital in industry and trade.

Economic progress was accompanied by a further improvement in the condition of the workers and peasants. The working class was growing rapidly. Wages had risen, and so had productivity of labour. The standard of living of the peasants had greatly improved. In 1924–25, the Workers' *and Peasants'* Government was able to assign nearly 290,000,000 rubles for the purpose of assisting the small peasants. The improvement in the condition of the workers and peasants led to greater political activity on the part of the masses. The dictatorship of the proletariat was now more firmly established. The prestige and influence of the Bolshevik Party had grown.

The restoration of the national economy was approaching completion. But mere economic restoration, the mere attainment of the pre-war level, was not enough for the Soviet Union, the land of Socialism in construction. The pre-war level was the level of a backward country. The advance had to be continued beyond that point. The prolonged breathing space gained by the Soviet state ensured the possibility of further development.

*But t*his raised the question in all its urgency: what were to be the perspectives, *the character* of our development, of our construction, what was to be the destiny of Socialism in the Soviet Union? *In what direction was economic development in the Soviet Union to be carried on, in the direction of Socialism, or in some other direction? Should we and could we build a Socialist economic system; or were we fated but to manure the soil for another economic system, the capitalist economic system?* Was it possible *at all* to build ~~Socialism~~ *a Socialist economic system in the U.S.S.R., and, if so, could it be built* in spite of the delay of the ~~world~~ revolution in the capitalist countries, in spite of the stabilization of capitalism? Was it at all possible to build ~~Socialism~~ *a Socialist economic system* by way of the New Economic Policy, which, *while it was strengthening and augmenting the forces of Socialism in the country in every way,* nevertheless still promoted *a certain growth of* capitalism?[28] *How was a Socialist economic system to be constructed, from which end should its construction begin?*

All these questions confronted the Party towards the end of the restoration period, and no longer as theoretical questions, but as practical questions, as questions of everyday economic policy.

All these questions needed straightforward and plain answers, so that[29] *our Party members engaged in the development of industry and agriculture, as well as the people generally,*[30] *might know in what direction to work, towards Socialism, or towards capitalism.*

Unless plain answers were given to these questions, all our practical work of construction would be without perspective, work in the dark, labour in vain.

The Party~~, armed with Leninist theory on the victory of Socialism in one country,~~ gave ~~affirmative~~ *plain and definite* answers to *all* these questions.

~~Yes, the construction of Socialism in one country was possible. Yes, WE ARE BUILDING A SOCIALIST SOCIETY, answered the Bolshevik Party at its Fourteenth Party Conference (April 1925).~~

~~Comrade Stalin frequently gave speeches with instructions on the necessity of demarcating and then separating the TWO SIDES to the issue regarding the victory of Socialism in one country. The first side of the issue concerned the relationship between the classes WITHIN THE COUNTRY. The working class could establish a solid alliance with the peasantry and overcome the bourgeoisie on its own; it could construct a fully Socialist society in the country. History proved the Leninist-Stalinist contention that "WE HAVE EVERYTHING NEEDED FOR THE CONSTRUCTION OF A FULLY SOCIALIST SOCIETY."~~

Yes, replied the Party, a Socialist economic system could be and should be built in our country, for we had everything needed for the building of a Socialist economic system, for the building of a complete Socialist society. In October 1917 the working class had vanquished capitalism POLITICALLY, *by establishing its own political dictatorship. Since then the Soviet Government had been taking every measure to shatter the economic power of capitalism and to create conditions for the building of a Socialist economic system. These measures were: the expropriation of the capitalists and landlords; the conversion of the land, factories, mills, railways and the banks into public property; the adoption of the New Economic Policy; the building up of a state-owned Socialist industry; and the application of Lenin's co-operative plan. Now the main task was to proceed to build a new, Socialist economic system all over the country and thus smash capitalism* ECONOMICALLY *as well. All our practical work, all our actions must be made to serve this main purpose. The working class could do it, and would do it. The realization of this colossal task must begin with the industrialization of the country. The Socialist industrialization of the country was the chief link in the chain; with it the construction of a Socialist economic system must begin. Neither the delay of the revolution in the West, nor the partial stabilization of capitalism in the non-Soviet countries could stop our advance—to Socialism. The New Economic Policy could only make this task easier, for it had been introduced by the Party with the specific purpose of facilitating the laying of a Socialist foundation for our economic system.*

~~In this way, the question from the perspective of the DOMESTIC OPPOSITION was resolved by history.~~

Such was the Party's answer to the question—was the victory of Socialist construction possible in our country?

~~But there was also the perspective of the AREA OF FOREIGN, INTERNATIONAL RELATIONS: the question about the interrelationship between our country and other countries, between our country and the capitalist countries, and about the interrelationship of the working class of our country with the bourgeoisie of other countries. The question was, could a victorious Socialist society in one country consider itself guaranteed against the threat of military invasion (intervention) if it were encircled by many strong capitalist countries? The question was, could a victorious Socialist society consider itself guaranteed against the danger of attempts to restore capitalism in our country? Could our working class and peasantry overcome the bourgeoisie of the other countries as they had overcome their own bourgeoisie, relying only on their own resources and making do without serious assistance from the working class of the capitalist countries?~~

~~To put it another way: could the victory of Socialism in our country be considered FINAL, that is, guaranteed against the threat of military attack and the attempt to restore capitalism, remembering here that Socialism had been victorious in only one country and that the capitalist encirclement continued to be felt?~~

~~To all of these questions connected with FOREIGN, INTERNATIONAL relations, Leninism's answer was negative.~~

~~Leninism teaches that "the FINAL victory of Socialism in the sense of a complete guarantee against a restoration of bourgeois relations is possible only on an international level." (RESOLUTION OF THE FOURTEENTH PARTY CONFERENCE.)~~

~~In 1938, Comrade Stalin explained the two sides to this issue once more in his answer to Comrade Ivanov, pointing out that "the second problem can be solved only by combining the serious efforts of the international proletariat with even the more serious efforts of the entire Soviet people."~~

But the Party knew that the problem of the victory of Socialism in one country did not end there. The construction of Socialism in the Soviet Union would be a momentous turning point in the history of mankind, a victory for the work-

ing class and peasantry of the U.S.S.R., marking a new epoch in the history of the world. Yet this was an internal affair of the U.S.S.R. and was only a part of the problem of the victory of Socialism. The other part of the problem was its international aspect. In substantiating the thesis that Socialism could be victorious in one country, Comrade Stalin had repeatedly pointed out that the question should be viewed from two aspects, the domestic and the international. As for the domestic aspect of the question, i.e., the class relations within the country, the working class and the peasantry of the U.S.S.R. were fully capable of vanquishing their own bourgeoisie ECONOMICALLY *and building a complete Socialist society. But there was also the international aspect of the question, namely, the sphere of foreign relations, the sphere of the relations between the Soviet Union and the capitalist countries, between the Soviet people and the international bourgeoisie, which hated the Soviet system and was seeking the chance to start again armed intervention in the Soviet Union, to make new attempts to restore capitalism in the U.S.S.R. And since the U.S.S.R. was as yet the only Socialist country, all the other countries remaining capitalist, the U.S.S.R. continued to be encircled by a capitalist world, which gave rise to the danger of capitalist intervention. Clearly, there would be a danger of capitalist intervention as long as this capitalist encirclement existed. Could the Soviet people by their own efforts destroy this external danger, the danger of capitalist intervention in the U.S.S.R.? No, they could not. They could not, because in order to destroy the danger of capitalist intervention the capitalist encirclement would have to be destroyed; and the capitalist encirclement could be destroyed only as a result of victorious proletarian revolutions in at least several countries. It followed from this that the victory of Socialism in the U.S.S.R., as expressed in the abolition of the capitalist economic system and the building of a Socialist economic system, could not be considered a* FINAL *victory, inasmuch as the danger of foreign armed intervention and of attempts to restore capitalism had not been eliminated, and inasmuch as the Socialist country had no guarantee against this danger. To destroy the danger of foreign capitalist intervention, the capitalist encirclement would have to be destroyed.*

Of course, as long as the Soviet Government pursued a correct policy, the Soviet people and their Red Army would be able to beat off a new foreign capitalist intervention just as they had beaten off the first capitalist intervention of 1918–20. But this would not mean that the danger of new capitalist intervention would be eliminated. The defeat of the first intervention did not destroy the danger of new intervention, inasmuch as the source of the danger of intervention—the capitalist encirclement—continued to exist. Neither would the danger of intervention be destroyed by the defeat of the new intervention if the capitalist encirclement continued to exist.

It followed from this that the victory of the proletarian revolution in the capitalist countries was a matter of vital concern to the working people of the U.S.S.R.

Such was the Party's line on the question of the victory of Socialism in our country.

The Central Committee demanded that this line be discussed at the forthcoming Fourteenth Party Conference, and that it be endorsed and accepted as the line of the Party, as a Party law, BINDING *upon all Party members.*

This line of the Party came as a thunderbolt to the oppositionists, above all, because the Party lent it a specific and practical character, linked it with a practical plan for the Socialist industrialization of the country, and demanded that it be formulated as a Party law, as a resolution of the Fourteenth Party Conference, binding upon all Party members.

~~The Fourteenth Party Conference condemned the Trotskyite theory of "permanent revolution," which claimed that the victory of Socialism in our country was impossible.~~[31] *The Trotskyites opposed this Party line and set up against it the Menshevik "theory of permanent revolution," which it would be an insult to Marxism to call a Marxist theory, and which denied the possibility of the victory of Socialist construction in the U.S.S.R.* ~~The Trotskyites denied the possibility of constructing Socialism in the U.S.S.R., consciously attempting to disrupt the construction of Socialism because Trotsky had by that time already conspired with the enemies of the Soviet power.~~[32] ~~Even then, Trotsky was acting in a way that was profitable for the imperialists. Already in 1925, he defended the development of kulak and capitalist agriculture in the countryside as imperative.~~

~~At that time the Rights (Bukharin, Rykov and Tomsky) were also trying to turn the Party away from the Leninist path. Bukharin advanced the slogan "Get Rich!" Bukharin's slogan "Get Rich!" was directed toward the kulaks and private dealers, the "Nepmen." This kulak slogan, advanced during the first stage of NEP as capitalism was being partially restored and when the kulaks were still powerful, was designed to enrich specific people or groups in order to help them subordinate and exploit the others. The slogan "Get Rich" was basically a rallying call for the RESTORATION of capitalism.~~

~~Bukharin also created the counter-revolutionary theory on the "peaceful passing of the kulak into Socialism." He created an anti-Leninist "school" of opportunists, future fascist agents, spies and wreckers from an array of kulak sons who had wormed their way into the Party. The Bukharinites claimed that there was actually no such thing as a kulak and that "the kulak is a boogeyman," an invention. Syrtsov appealed to the Siberian kulaks with the rallying call: "Save Up for a Better Day!" Krinitsky pursued this policy in Byelorussia as well.~~ *The Bukharinites did not venture to oppose the Party line outspokenly. But they furtively set up against it their own "theory" of the peaceful growing of the bourgeoisie into Socialism, amplifying it with a "new" slogan—"Get Rich!" According to the Bukharinites, the victory of Socialism meant fostering and encircling the bourgeoisie, not destroying it.*

~~The treacherous traitors and strikebreakers of October, Kamenev and Zinoviev, were united with the Trotskyites. Even before the Fourteenth Party Congress they spoke to one of the Central Committee meetings as genuine Trotskyites. They announced that the technical and economic backwardness of our country was an insurmountable obstacle on the path of Socialist construction. But Kamenev and Zinoviev hesitated to show the Party their true Trotskyite nature.~~ *Zinoviev and Kamenev ventured forth with the assertion that the victory of Socialism in the U.S.S.R. was impossible because of the country's technical and economic backwardness, but they soon found it prudent to hide under cover.*

The Fourteenth Party Conference (April, 1925) condemned all these capitulatory "theories" of the open and covert oppositionists and affirmed the Party line of working for the victory of Socialism in the U.S.S.R., adopting a resolution to this effect.

~~At the Fourteenth Party Conference these double-dealers voted for the Party line. And at the same time, these treacherous double-dealers began to secretly build their own anti-Party organization. They selected their people and hammered together the "New Opposition," Zinoviev in Leningrad and Kamenev in Moscow.~~ *Driven to the wall, Zinoviev and Kamenev preferred*[33] *to vote for this resolution. But the Party knew that they had only postponed their struggle and had decided to "give battle to the Party" at the Fourteenth Party Congress. They were mustering a following in Leningrad and forming the so-called "New Opposition."* ~~Together with Zalutsky (who was at that time a secretary of the Leningrad Party Committee), they circulated Menshevik, counter-revolutionary slander about the "growing over" of the Party. They created secret propagandistic circles, which were only open to "their own" people and where these propagandists pumped out anti-Party materials. They organized an anti-Party youth group under the leadership of the future terrorists Safarov and Naumov and attempted to transform the Leningrad Region Young Communist League into a second Y.C.L. centre. They spread the slander that the majority of the Central Committee, headed by Comrade Stalin, supported Trotsky. But in fact at this time it was actually Kamenev and Zinoviev who were putting together plans to form an alliance with Trotsky for a joint struggle against the Leninist Party. These despicable double-dealers wanted to represent Lenin's city at the congress by means of deception. Declaring their loyalty to the Party's Central Committee in front of the Party masses, the Zinovievites actually selected supporters for Leningrad's delegation to the Fourteenth Party Congress who were hostile to the Leninist Central Committee line.~~

~~In order to deceive the Party organization and place their supporters within the congress delegation, the head Zinovievites told their supporters to double-deal, to conceal their true goals and to speak out "at a quarter of their full voice" at the regional conferences, "at half voice" at the provincial Party conferences and "at full voice" at the Party congress.~~

~~The Zinovievites intended their activity at the congress to shake up the Party. They planned to frighten the Party and force it to make concessions to them. These traitors and double-dealers seriously miscalculated.~~

~~8. Fourteenth Party Congress—the Congress of Industrialization~~

The Fourteenth ~~Bolshevik~~ Party Congress opened in December 1925.

The situation within the Party was ~~unusually~~ tense and strained. Never in its history had there been a case when the whole delegation from an important Party centre like Leningrad had ~~presented its own special report~~ *prepared to come out in opposition to their Central Committee.* ~~This aroused the discontent of the entire congress.~~

The congress was attended by 665 delegates with vote and 641 with voice but no vote, representing 643,000 Party members and 445,000 candidate members, or a little less than at the previous congress. The reduction was due to a partial purge, a purge of the Party organizations in universities and offices to which anti-Party elements had gained entrance.

The political report of the Central Committee was made by Comrade Stalin. He drew a vivid picture of the growth of the political and economic might of the Soviet Union. Thanks to the advantages of the Soviet ~~structure~~ *economic system*, both industry and agriculture had been restored in ~~the shortest amount~~ *a comparatively short space* of time and were approaching the pre-war level. But ~~all the same,~~ *good as these results were, Comrade Stalin proposed that we should not rest there, for they could not nullify the fact that* our country still remained a backward, agrarian country. Two-thirds of the total production of the country was provided by agriculture and only one-third by industry. ~~The danger posed by the existence of the capitalist encirclement loomed over the Soviet state. It was necessary to tirelessly work for the full emancipation of our country from its dependency on trade with the capitalist countries.~~ *Comrade Stalin said that the Party was now squarely confronted with the problem of converting our country into an industrial country, economically independent of capitalist countries. This could be done, and must be done.* It was now the cardinal task of the Party to fight for the Socialist industrialization[34] of the country, *for the victory of Socialism.*

> "The conversion of our country from an agrarian into an industrial country able to produce the machinery it needs by its own efforts—that is the essence, the basis of our general line," said Comrade Stalin.

~~The Fourteenth Party Congress of the Bolshevik Party approved and passed this general line.~~ The industrialization of the country would ensure ~~the creation~~

~~of an economically independent, powerful state that was able to defend itself, as well as the victory of Socialism~~ *its economic independence, strengthen its power of defence and create the conditions for the victory of Socialism in the U.S.S.R.*

The Zinovievites ~~bitterly~~ opposed the *general* line of the Party. As against Stalin's plan of *Socialist* industrialization, the Zinovievite Sokolnikov put forward a ~~treacherous~~ *bourgeois* plan, ~~which consisted of renouncing industrialization and remaining an agricultural country~~ *one that was then in vogue among the imperialist sharks. According to this plan, the U.S.S.R. was to remain an agrarian country, chiefly producing raw materials and foodstuffs, exporting them, and importing machinery, which it did not and should not produce itself. As conditions were in 1925, this was tantamount to a plan for the economic enslavement of the U.S.S.R. by the industrially developed foreign countries, a plan for the perpetuation of the industrial backwardness of the U.S.S.R. for the benefit of the imperialist sharks of the capitalist countries.*

The adoption of this plan would have converted our country into an impotent agrarian, agricultural appendage of the capitalist world; it would have left it weak and defenceless against the ~~imperialist predators~~ *surrounding capitalist world, and in the end would have been fatal to the cause of Socialism in the U.S.S.R.* ~~The Zinovievites spoke out against the Leninist policy of an alliance with the middle peasants. They spread the slander that our state industry was supposedly not Socialist, but state capitalist. They denied the possibility of building Socialism in our country. They defended Trotsky and other enemies of Leninism. The Zinovievites aimed to disarm the working class and infect it with a lack of faith in the victory of Socialism. The Zinovievites attempted to force the Party to renounce the Leninist plan for the construction of Socialism through the workers' and peasants' efforts. They proposed renouncing the policy of industrialization and capitulating before the class enemy. Through their policy, the Zinovievites assisted the capitalist elements in our country and aided the capitalist encirclement.~~

The congress ~~dealt a devastating blow to the opposition~~ *condemned the economic "plan" of the Zinovievites as a plan for the enslavement of the U.S.S.R.*

Equally unsuccessful were the other sorties of the "New Opposition" as, for instance, when they asserted (in defiance of Lenin) that our state industries were not Socialist industries, or when they declared (again in defiance of Lenin) that the middle peasant could not be an ally of the working class in the work of Socialist construction.

The congress condemned these sorties of the "New Opposition" as anti-Leninist.

Comrade Stalin laid bare the Trotskyite-Menshevik essence of the "New Opposition." He showed that Zinoviev and Kamenev were only harping on the old tunes of the enemies of the Party with whom Lenin had waged so relentless a ~~war~~ *struggle.*

It was clear that the Zinovievites were nothing but ill-disguised Trotskyites.

Comrade Stalin stressed the point that the main task of our Party was to maintain a firm alliance between the working class and the middle peasant in *the work of* building Socialism. He pointed to two deviations on the peasant question existing in the Party at that time, *both of which constituted a menace to this alliance.* The first deviation was the one that underestimated and belittled the kulak danger, the second was the one that stood in panic fear of the kulak and underestimated the role of the middle peasant. To the question, which deviation was worse, Comrade Stalin replied: "One is as bad as the other. And if these deviations are allowed to develop they may disintegrate and destroy the Party. Fortunately there are forces in our Party capable of ridding it of both deviations."

And the Party did *indeed* rout both deviations, the "Left" and the Right, and rid itself of them.

~~It was necessary at that moment for the Party to concentrate its fire on the Trotskyites and Zinovievites, as they were aiming to break up the alliance of the working class and the main mass of the peasantry.~~

~~Waging a struggle against Leninism and the Leninist Party line, the Zinovievites attacked Comrade Stalin with particular spite.~~

~~All the enemies of the Party, all the agents of the bourgeoisie and kulaks—the Trotskyites, Zinovievites, Bukharinites and bourgeois nationalists—directed their main blows at Comrade Stalin as the most resolute defender of Leninism and Party unity. This was like when the opportunists and all the enemies of Bolshevism and agents of the bourgeoisie (the Economists, Mensheviks, Liquidators, Trotskyites, Socialist-Revolutionaries and others) had grouped together in mad hatred against Lenin. The enemies of Bolshevism hated Comrade Stalin for his faithfulness to Lenin's precepts, for his devotion to the cause of communism, for his principled, uncompromising attitude toward the opportunists, for his ability to detect and unmask the plans of the enemies of Leninism and the working class and because Comrade Stalin was more far-sighted than other political leaders.~~

~~The congress answered the slanderous attacks of the Zinovievite opposition against the Party leadership with a unanimous display of love and trust for Comrade Stalin. The congress, and with it the whole Party, rallied even more tightly around Comrade Stalin. The congress completely refuted and condemned the capitulatory proposals of the opposition.~~

~~In its decisions,~~ *Summing up the debate on the question of economic development,* the Fourteenth Party Congress *unanimously rejected the capitulatory plans of the oppositionists and* recorded *in its now famous resolution:*

"In the sphere of ECONOMIC DEVELOPMENT,[35] the congress holds that in our land, the land of the dictatorship of the proletariat, there is 'every requisite for the building of a complete Socialist society' (LENIN). The congress considers that the main task of our Party is to fight for the victory of Socialist construction in the U.S.S.R."

The Fourteenth Party Congress adopted new Party Rules.

Since the Fourteenth Congress our Party has been called the Communist Party of the Soviet Union (Bolsheviks)—the C.P.S.U.(B.). ~~Until then, it had been known as the Russian Communist Party (Bolsheviks)—the R.C.P.(B.).~~

Though defeated at the congress, the Zinovievites did not submit to the Party. They started a fight against the decisions of the Fourteenth Congress. Immediately following the congress, Zinoviev called a meeting of the Leningrad Provincial Committee of the Young Communist League, the leading group of which had been reared by Zinoviev, Zalutsky, Bakayev, Yevdokimov, Kuklin, Safarov and other double-dealers~~—counter-revolutionaries~~ in a spirit of hatred of the Leninist Central Committee of the Party. At this meeting, the Leningrad Provincial Committee passed a resolution unparalleled in the history of the Y.C.L.: it refused to ~~recognize as correct~~ *abide by* the decisions of the *Fourteenth* Party *C*ongress.

But the Zinovievite leaders of the Leningrad Y.C.L. did not in any way reflect the mind of the mass of Young Communist Leaguers of Leningrad. They were therefore easily defeated, and soon the Leningrad organization recovered the place in the Y.C.L. to which it was entitled.

~~During the period~~ *Towards the close* of the Fourteenth Congress a group of congress delegates—Comrades Molotov, Kirov, Voroshilov, Kalinin, Andreyev *and others*—were ~~dispatched~~ *sent* to Leningrad to explain to the members of the Leningrad *Party* organization the criminal, anti-Bolshevik nature of the stand taken up at the congress by the Leningrad delegation, who had secured their mandates under false pretences. ~~Stormy scenes marked the meetings at which the reports on the congress were made. Step by step, the members of the Central Committee won over one nuclei after another, one district after another. It was decided to call a new, extraordinary Party conference.~~ *An extraordinary conference of the Leningrad Party organization was called.* The overwhelming majority of the Party members of Leningrad (over 97 per cent) fully endorsed the decisions of the Fourteenth Party Congress and condemned the anti-Party Zinovievite *"New O*pposition." The latter already at that time were generals without an army.

The Leningrad Bolsheviks remained in the front ranks of the Party of Lenin-Stalin.

~~Sergey Mironovich Kirov played a major role in the defeat of the Leningrad opposition. A mighty Bolshevik, an outstanding organizer, a burning tribune (orator) who was always closely connected to the masses and an exacting~~

~~Bolshevik, he quickly won the affection and love of all the Leningrad workers. From that moment, Sergey Mironovich Kirov became the object of furious hatred on the part of the treacherous double-dealers from the Trotskyite-Zinovievite gang, who dreamed of killing him. This evil plan would be executed by the Trotskyite-Zinovievite Terroristic Centre on December 1, 1934, to the great sadness of the Party and working people.~~

~~The significance of the Fourteenth Party Congress in the history of the Party was enormous.~~ *Summing up the results of the Fourteenth Party Congress, Comrade Stalin wrote:*

> “The historical significance of the Fourteenth Congress of the C.P.S.U.,~~”—demonstrated Comrade Stalin, “~~lies in the fact that it was able to expose the very roots of the mistakes of the New Opposition, that it spurned their scepticism and sniveling, that it clearly and distinctly indicated the path of the further struggle for Socialism, opened before the Party the prospect of victory, and thus armed the proletariat with an invincible faith in the victory of Socialist construction.” (Stalin, LENINISM, Vol. I, p. 319.)

Brief Summary

The years ~~between 1921–25~~ *of* ~~(the~~ transition to the peaceful work of economic restoration~~)~~ constituted one of the most crucial periods in the history of the Bolshevik Party. In a tense situation, the Party was able to effect the ~~very~~ difficult turn from the policy of War Communism to the New Economic Policy ~~(NEP)~~. The Party reinforced the alliance of the workers and peasants on a new economic foundation. *The Union of Soviet Socialist Republics was formed.*

By means of the New Economic Policy, decisive results were obtained in the restoration of the economic life of the country. ~~The Union of Soviet Socialist Republics was created. The land of Soviets began to realize the grandiose plans for electrification~~ *The Soviet Union emerged from the period of economic restoration with success and entered a new period, the period of industrialization of the country.*

The transition from Civil War to peaceful Socialist construction was accompanied by great difficulties, especially in the early stages. The enemies of Bolshevism, the anti-Party elements in the ranks of the C.P.S.U.(B.), waged a ~~rabid~~ *desperate* struggle against the Leninist Party all through this period. These anti-Party elements were headed by ~~the accursed enemy of the Leninist Party,~~ Trotsky. His henchmen in this struggle were Kamenev, Zinoviev and Bukharin. *After the death of Lenin, the oppositionists calculated on demoralizing the ranks of the Bolshevik Party, on splitting the Party, and infecting it with disbelief in the possibility of the victory of Socialism in the U.S.S.R.* In point of fact, the Trotskyites were trying to form another party in the U.S.S.R., a political organization of the new bourgeoisie, a party of capitalist restoration. ~~The enemies counted on precipitating demoralization within the ranks of the Bolshevik Party after Lenin's death, dividing the Party. But they did not succeed in doing this.~~

The Party rallied under the banner of Lenin *around its Leninist Central Committee,* around ~~the great continuer of Lenin's cause,~~ Comrade Stalin, *and inflicted defeat both on the Trotskyites and on their new friends in Leningrad, the Zinoviev-Kamenev New Opposition.*

Having accumulated ~~enough~~ strength and resources, the Bolshevik Party brought the country to a new stage in its history—the stage of Socialist industrialization.

CHAPTER TEN

The Bolshevik Party in the Struggle for the Socialist Industrialization of the Country (1926–1929)

~~1. Which Difficulties and Enemies Did the Bolshevik Party Struggle with as It Pursued Its General Line for the Country's Socialist Industrialization~~ *Difficulties in the Period of Socialist Industrialization and the Fight to Overcome Them. Formation of the Anti-Party Bloc of Trotskyites and Zinovievites. Anti-Soviet Actions of the Bloc. Defeat of the Bloc*

After the Fourteenth Congress, the ~~Bolshevik~~ Party launched a vigorous struggle for the realization of the general line of the Soviet Government—the SOCIALIST INDUSTRIALIZATION of the country.

~~During the first period of the New Economic Policy, it had been necessary to begin with the restoration of agriculture and then on that basis, to build up industry. Now, further movement forward toward Socialism depended first of all on industry. Further economic development, including agriculture, depended on the production of machinery, the means of production—in other words, the development of LARGE-SCALE INDUSTRY. In pre-revolutionary Russia, machine building was very underdeveloped. Almost all machinery was imported from abroad. This was one of the signs of tsarist Russia's backwardness—her dependency on the more advanced, capitalistic countries.~~

In the restoration period the task had been to revive agriculture before all else, so as to obtain raw materials and foodstuffs, to restore and to set going the industries, the existing mills and factories.

The Soviet Government coped with this task with comparative ease.

But in the restoration period there were three major shortcomings:

First, the mills and factories were old, equipped with worn-out and antiquated machinery, and might soon go out of commission. The task now was to re-equip them on up-to-date lines.

Secondly, industry in the restoration period rested on too narrow a foundation: it lacked machine-building plants absolutely indispensable to the country.[1]

534

- 452 -

ГЛАВА X

ПАРТИЯ БОЛЬШЕВИКОВ В БОРЬБЕ ЗА СОЦИАЛИСТИЧЕСКУЮ ИНДУСТРИАЛИЗАЦИЮ СТРАНЫ.

(1926-1929 годы).

1. Трудности в период социалистической индустриализации и борьба с ними. Образование троцкистско-зиновьевского антипартийного блока. Антисоветские выступления блока. Поражение блока.

После XIV с'езда партия развернула борьбу за проведение в жизнь генеральной ~~линии~~ Советской власти на социалистическую индустриализацию страны.

В восстановительный период задача состояла в том, чтобы оживить, прежде всего, сельское хозяйство, получить от сельского хозяйства сырье, продовольствие и привести в движение, - восстановить промышленность, восстановить существующие заводы и фабрики.

Советская власть сравнительно легко справилась с этими задачами.

Но восстановительный период имел три больших недостатка.

Во-первых, он имел дело со старыми заводами и фабриками, с их старой, отсталой техникой, которые могли скоро выйти из строя. Задача/состояла в том,/ чтобы переоборудовать их на основе новой техники.

Во-вторых, восстановительный период имел дело с такой промышленностью, база которой была слишком узка, ибо в ~~списке~~ числе имевшихся заводов и фабрик ~~промышленности~~ отсутствовали десятки и сотни машиностроительных заводов, абсолютно необходимых для

First page of Chapter Ten with Stalin's editing from the summer of 1938. RGASPI, f. 558, op. 11, d. 1215, l. 534.

Hundreds of these plants had to be built, for without them no country can be considered as being really industrialized. The task now was to build these plants and to equip them on up-to-date lines.

Thirdly, the industries in this period were mostly light industries. These were developed and put on their feet. But, beyond a certain point, the further development even of the light industries met an obstacle in the weakness of heavy industry, not to mention the fact that the country had other requirements which could be satisfied only by a well-developed heavy industry. The task now was to tip the scales in favour of heavy industry.

All these new tasks were to be accomplished by the policy of Socialist industrialization.

It was necessary to build up a large number of NEW industries, industries which had not existed in tsarist Russia—new machinery, machine tool, automobile, ~~tractor,~~ chemical, and iron and steel plants—to organize the production of engines and power equipment, and to increase the mining of ore and coal. *This was essential for the victory of Socialism in the U.S.S.R.* ~~This was SOCIALIST INDUSTRIALIZATION, which was something that the Bolsheviks waged a particularly decisive struggle for after the Fourteenth Party Congress.~~

~~The international situation and the danger of a new intervention into the U.S.S.R. by the capitalist states demanded a FAST TEMPO of industrialization. Otherwise, our motherland would have been left unarmed and defenceless in the face of an enemy that possessed the latest military technique: aviation, tanks, chemical weapons, and so on. Technique in the capitalist states was advancing forward. Falling behind was impermissible.~~

~~"We are fifty to one hundred years behind the advanced countries. We must make good this distance in ten years. Either we manage it, or they will crush us," instructed Comrade Stalin in his speech "On the Tasks of the Business Managers." (Stalin, QUESTIONS OF LENINISM, Russ. ed., p. 445.) Only by breaking with the technical and economic backwardness that the Soviet Union inherited from the past would the U.S.S.R. be capable of defending its existence against the capitalist encirclement.~~

It was necessary to create a new munitions industry, to erect new works for the production of artillery, shells, aircraft, tanks and machine guns. This was essential for the defence of the U.S.S.R., surrounded as it was by a capitalist world.

~~Our country's home situation also demanded a fast tempo of industrialization. A hundred thousand tractors and agricultural machines were needed to ensure that Socialism was victorious in the countryside as well as in the city, so that millions of small peasant farms could be combined securely into collective farms. Without such Socialist amalgamation of small peasant farms, the restoration of capitalism remained a danger. Kulaks and capitalist elements rose up out of the small peasant farms. The bulk of the peasant masses~~

~~farming on individual plots were perpetually stuck in hardship due to kulak exploitation.~~

It was necessary to build tractor works and plants for the production of modern agricultural machinery, and to furnish agriculture with these machines, so as to enable millions of small individual peasant farms to pass to large-scale collective farming. This was essential for the victory of Socialism in the countryside.

All this was to be achieved by the policy of industrialization, for that is what the Socialist industrialization of the country meant.

~~These were the factors that demanded a fast tempo of Socialist industrialization in the U.S.S.R. Millions of rubles were necessary to build enormous mills, factories and electric stations in the shortest possible time.~~ *Clearly, construction work on so large a scale would necessitate the investment of thousands of millions of rubles. To count on foreign loans was out of the question, for the capitalist countries refused to grant loans. We had to build with our own resources, without foreign assistance.* ~~Accumulating this capital for the construction of large-scale industry was an extremely difficult task as~~ *But* our country was not rich at that point.

There lay one of the chief difficulties.

Capitalist countries as a rule built up their heavy industries with funds obtained from abroad, whether by colonial ~~robbery~~ *plunder*, or by exacting indemnities ~~(tribute)~~ from vanquished nations, or else by ~~oppressive~~ *foreign* loans ~~or concessions, for instance, as tsarist Russia had done~~. The Soviet Union could not *as a matter of principle* resort to ~~similar~~ *such infamous* means of obtaining funds *as the plunder of colonies or of vanquished nations. As for foreign loans, that avenue was closed to the U.S.S.R., as the capitalist countries refused to lend it anything.* The funds had to be found INSIDE the country.

And they were found. Financial sources were ~~available~~ *tapped* in the U.S.S.R. such as could not be tapped in any capitalist country. The Soviet state had taken over all the mills, factories, and lands which the ~~Great~~ October Socialist Revolution had wrested from the capitalists and landlords, *all the means of transportation, the banks, and home and foreign trade.* The profits from the state-owned mills and factories, *and from the means of transportation, trade and the banks* now went to further the expansion of industry, and not into the pockets of a parasitic capitalist class.

The Soviet Government had annulled the tsarist debts, on which the people had annually paid hundreds of millions of gold rubles in interest alone. By abolishing the right of the landlords to the land, the Soviet Government had freed the peasantry from the annual payment of about 500,000,000 *gold* rubles in rent. Released from this burden, the peasantry was in a position to help the state to build a new and powerful industry. The peasants had a vital interest in obtaining tractors and other agricultural machinery.

All these sources of revenue were in the hands of the Soviet state. They could yield hundreds and thousands of millions of rubles for the creation of a heavy industry. All that was needed was a business-like approach, the strictly economical expenditure of funds, rationalization of industry, reduction of costs of production, elimination of unproductive expenditure, etc.

And this was the course the Soviet Government adopted.

~~In 1925–26, the state budget grew to 4,000,000,000 rubles. The Party struggled for the strictest economy with state funds—it struggled to reduce the cost of the state apparatus, contract bloated institutional staffing and economize on all non-productive expenses. In this way, the Party proposed in 1926 to cut costs by about 300 million rubles, which could be devoted to the cause of industrialization. A lot of work was done in the mills and factories in order to rationalize production and reduce goods' production costs, which raised the enterprises' profitability and allowed the money saved to be invested in new industrial construction.~~

Thanks to a regime of strict economy ~~and rationalization~~, the funds available for capital development increased from year to year. ~~It was~~ *This made it* possible to start on gigantic construction ~~sites for large-scale industry~~ works like the Dnieper Hydro-Electric Power Station, the Turkestan-Siberian Railway, ~~and~~ the Stalingrad Tractor Works, *a number of machine-tool works, the AMO (ZIS)*[2] *Automobile Works,* ~~etc.~~ *and others.*

~~In 1928–29, the First Stalinist Five Year Plan for economic development was devised and ratified by the Sixteenth Party Conference (April 1929). This plan called for the construction of the foundation for a Socialist economy and called for major growth in large-scale industry and the formation of an array of new industrial branches of the economy.~~

~~1929, the first year of the Five Year Plan, was the year of the GREAT CHANGE. The plan for the first year of the Five Year Plan was overfulfilled, thanks to the labour heroism of the million-man working class and the development of Socialist emulation and shock work. In 1929, the most difficult problem for Socialist industry was solved—the problem of capital ACCUMULATION for the construction of large-scale industry.~~ Whereas in 1926–27 ~~1,065,000,000~~ *about 1,000,000,000* rubles were invested in industry, ~~in 1929–30~~ *three*[3] *years later* it was found possible to invest ~~4,775,000,000~~ *about 5,000,000,000* rubles ~~in state industry. It was surprising how much stronger all the branches of the economy had become, how much more secure the state budget had grown, and how much larger the sources of revenue were now!~~

Industrialization was making steady headway.

The capitalist countries looked upon the growing strength of the Socialist economic system in the U.S.S.R. as a threat to the existence of the capitalist system. Accordingly, the imperialist governments ~~sought an excuse for a new~~

~~intervention into the country of the Soviets and therefore hired wreckers to undermine Socialist construction. They dispatched and continue to dispatch spies, diversionists, wreckers and assassins to the Soviet Union~~ *did everything they could to bring new pressure to bear on the U.S.S.R., to create a feeling of uncertainty and uneasiness in the country, and to frustrate, or at least to impede, the industrialization of the U.S.S.R.*

In May 1927, the British Conservative Die-hards, then in office, organized a provocative raid on Arcos (the Soviet trading body in Great Britain). On May 26, 1927, the British Conservative Government broke off diplomatic and trade relations with the U.S.S.R.

On June 7, 1927, Comrade Voikov, the Soviet Ambassador in Warsaw, was assassinated by a Russian Whiteguard, a naturalized Polish subject.

About this time, too, in the U.S.S.R. itself, British spies and diversionists hurled bombs at a meeting in a Party club in Leningrad, wounding about 30 people, some of them severely~~; in an array of other places in the Soviet Union, diversionists set fire to mills, factories, military stores, etc~~.

In the summer of 1927, almost simultaneous raids were made on the Soviet Embassies and Trade Representations in Berlin, Peking, Shanghai and Tientsin~~; and diplomatic relations with France were upset. This was a broad, concerted plan of provocations on the part of the imperialists calculated to trigger a war against the U.S.S.R~~.

This created additional difficulties for the Soviet Government.

But the U.S.S.R. refused to be intimidated and easily repulsed the provocative attempts of the imperialists and their agents.

~~The enemies of the Party—the Trotskyites—were already helping the imperialist governments at this time. The Trotskyites increased their attacks on the Party and their efforts to cause a Party split at the very moment when the U.S.S.R.'s international position was most strained and when the British imperialists were threatening to declare war against the U.S.S.R.~~

No less were the difficulties caused to the Party and the Soviet state by the subversive activities of the Trotskyites and other oppositionists. Comrade Stalin had good reason to say that "something like a united front from Chamberlain to Trotsky is being formed" *against the Soviet Government*~~—said Comrade Stalin in his speech to a meeting of the Executive Committee of the Comintern at the end of May 1927 in regard to the hostile actions of the Trotskyites against the Party and the Soviet state~~. *In spite of the decisions of the Fourteenth Party Congress and the professions of loyalty of the oppositionists, the latter had not laid down their arms. On the contrary, they intensified their efforts to undermine and split the Party.*

~~It transpired later that this "united front" between Trotsky and the British imperialists was no coincidence: Trotsky had become an agent (a spy) of British espionage—the "Intelligence Service"—in 1926.~~

~~Strengthening its defensive capacity, the U.S.S.R. also advanced a firm diplomatic policy of peace, interfering with the plans of those who would begin a war. The Soviet Government expanded its trade relations with the capitalist countries, consistently strengthening its monopoly on foreign trade. The U.S.S.R. concluded an array of agreements at this time with capitalist countries: a non-aggression treaty with Turkey, a treaty and agreement with Germany about foreign credits, a treaty with Afghanistan, and a trade agreement with Turkey. Economic ties grew with countries like the United States and Italy.~~

~~In answer to the imperialists' plans for war, the Soviet Government proposed to all the capitalist countries that they immediately adopt a policy of total, worldwide disarmament.~~

~~The Bolshevik Party advanced its general line on the industrialization of the country amid sharpened class struggle with capitalist elements within the country. During the first years of NEP, private capital had seized for itself THREE QUARTERS of retail trade. The Party aimed for a decisive victory for the Socialist sector in the area of trade and continued with its line on further crowding private capital out of the market by developing co-operatives and state trade and intensifying the taxation of private dealers. In 1927–28, only A QUARTER of retail trade remained in the hands of private capital. Lenin's question "Who will win?" in the area of trade had been answered.~~

~~Of course, private capital desperately resisted this Socialist offensive. An army of profiteers attempted to corrupt the Soviet trade apparatus and co-operatives. This resistance of the Nepmen and new bourgeoisie against the Socialist offensive was REFLECTED in the Trotskyites, who during this period dramatically increased their struggle against the Bolshevik Party, the Party of Lenin and Stalin. The Trotskyites proposed to seize resources from the co-operatives and state trade in the interests of private capital. The Trotskyites aimed to break the alliance of the working class with the middle peasantry, aspiring to infect the working class with doubt over the possibility of building Socialism in one country.~~

~~During this period, the Socialist offensive against the kulaks developed under the leadership of the Bolshevik Party. The Party rigorously pursued a policy that limited the kulaks' exploitative tendencies (ambitions) and drove capitalist elements out of the countryside. The Fifteenth Party Congress, which took place in December 1927, called for the further development of the offensive against the kulaks and took an array of new measures that would limit the development of capitalism in the countryside and lead peasant agriculture to Socialism. The congress called for the development of collectivization. At the end of 1929, the Party passed from a policy of limiting the kulaks' exploitative tendencies to a policy of ELIMINATING THE KULAKS AS A CLASS on the basis of solid collectivization.~~

~~The kulaks, the most numerous of the exploitative classes, rabidly resisted the Socialist offensive. Class struggle in the countryside sharpened. Bourgeois specialist wrecking organizations were uncovered in industry which were connected to foreign espionage services and which were acting on the imperialists' orders.~~

~~The sharpening of class struggle and the rabid resistance of the kulaks against the Socialist offensive left its mark on the Party. During this period (1928), the Right deviation—the Bukharin-Rykov anti-Party faction and its kulak agents—formed within the Party. The Rightist Opportunists, who had formed their anti-Party faction even earlier, struggled openly against the general Party line, the country's industrialization, the Five-Year Plan, collectivization and the offensive against the kulaks.~~

~~The Trotskyites and Rights formed a united front with the foreign bourgeoisie, the urban Nepmen, the kulaks, the Shakhty wreckers and others. In their actions, all of them aimed for the revival (restoration) of capitalism in our country. This is why the Trotskyites and Rights were called capitalist restorationists.~~

~~It was impossible to even consider the successful construction of a Socialist foundation for the economy without the total defeat of the Trotskyites and Rights. This is why the struggle with the Trotskyites and Rights occupied such a large place in the life of our Party during this period.~~

~~2. Formation of the Trotskyite-Zinovievite Bloc with a Trotskyite Platform~~

~~The overwhelming majority of Party members realized what a huge task the Fourteenth Party Congress had placed before the country. The Party rallied around the Leninist-Stalinist Central Committee and around its chief, Comrade Stalin, in a stubborn struggle for the Socialist industrialization of the country.~~

~~The opponents of this general line, all the anti-Party elements, grouped together after the Fourteenth Party Congress under an anti-Party banner of Trotskyism, which quickly became an anti-Soviet, counter-revolutionary banner.~~

~~By April 1926, a bloc (union) of Trotskyites and Zinovievites was already plainly visible. By the July Central Committee Plenum, this bloc was completely formed. Kamenev and Zinoviev joined with Trotsky on a Trotskyite program and led a furious attack against Leninism and the Bolshevik Party and its Leninist-Stalinist Central Committee.~~

~~This new bloc was reminiscent of the August Bloc from the period of the Liquidators (1912). The situation was different, but the resemblance of these~~

~~bloces consisted in the fact that both were directed against the Leninist Party; both were stridently unprincipled combinations of the most diverse Rightist and "Leftist" groups; and the organizer of both blocs was precisely the same master of factionalism, the head traitor Judas Trotsky.~~

~~This Combined Opposition formed into a faction with its own program, its own centre and local groups and its own internal discipline. Its program was based on Trotsky's Menshevik views on the impossibility of the victory of Socialism in the U.S.S.R. and the Menshevik denial of the worker-peasant alliance. This Trotskyite bloc formed the rudiments, the embryo, of a new, anti-Bolshevik, fascist, counter-revolutionary Party. The Trotskyite bloc's method of struggle against the Party was double-dealing in relation to the Party and treacherous demagogy (deception) in relation to the masses.~~

~~The Trotskyites' program, however, did not fully express all of their actual goals.~~

~~The program served as camouflage. Its "Leftism" was designed to deceive its rank-and-file supporters and the masses: in fact, the leaders of this bloc were camouflaged fascists and already in this period had agreed to help the imperialists. But no matter how well the participants in this bloc camouflaged themselves, the counter-revolutionary essence of their program was visible in every one of their actions.~~

~~Already at the Fourteenth Party Congress the Zinovievite opposition (Sokolnikov) spoke against the slogan of Socialist industrialization, announcing that our country must remain an agrarian, agricultural country, and gave a sermon about his plan to transform the U.S.S.R. into an agrarian semi-colony for the capitalist industrial countries. Then the Zinovievites and Trotskyites instantly reorganized their front and raised false, hypocritical cries about how the Party supposedly did not care about industrialization.~~

~~Trotskyites (like Pyatakov) proposed in 1926 the so-called "subsiding curve" style of capitalist investment in industrial construction in a plan that was deliberately designed to wreck the economy. This "plan" proposed extraordinary, unbearably heavy capital expenditures in 1926–27 at the same time that the Trotskyites advanced the slogan of "super-industrialization." In subsequent years, however, when the state had more resources at its disposal, the Trotskyites proposed to reduce, to "subside" expenditures on industrialization. In this way, the Trotskyites aimed to "subside," to cripple the cause of Socialist industrialization. Other arch wreckers—the Mensheviks, who were finally fully unmasked in 1930–31—took part in the development of Pyatakov's "plan" alongside the Trotskyites. And the position on "subsiding" industrialization was supported by the Rights—Bukharin, Rykov, Tomsky, Uglanov and others. Pyatakov's plan to deliberately wreck the economy was exposed in time and rejected by the Party.~~

~~When capital resources were under discussion, the opposition demanded uncontrolled increases in prices on industrial goods and new taxes on the middle peasantry. The Trotskyites announced that the proletariat ought to think about the peasantry as a "colony." The Trotskyites—the enemies of the Party—wanted to destroy the essence of the proletarian dictatorship, which had been created by years of joint work by the worker-peasant alliance, and they wanted to pit the workers against the peasantry.~~

~~Under the cover of "Leftist" slogans, the Trotskyite-Zinovievite opposition even then aimed to do in the dictatorship of the proletariat and restore capitalism in our country.~~

~~Attempting to recruit the more backward part of the workers to their side, the Trotskyite opposition spoke out against the Party's programs to improve labour productivity and the rationalization of production. This was precisely what the self-seekers and loafers wanted. The Trotskyites wanted to use such promises to recruit part of the unemployed to their side as well. There was, after all, still unemployment in the U.S.S.R. at this time. Where did the unemployment come from? Industry had expanded rapidly, every year hiring many hundreds of thousands of new workers. But millions of poor and middle peasants, who worked on private peasant farms and who were unable to put their skills to good use in the countryside, were coming to the cities. A portion of those bureaucrats who had been let go during the contraction of swollen state bureaucracies also contributed to the number of unemployed.~~

~~The Party outlined a plan for the development of the Socialist economy that made it possible to eliminate this unemployment in the next 2–3 years, and this indeed eventually came to pass. But it cost the opposition nothing to promise that it would eliminate unemployment in the course of a single year. The opposition demanded that an additional 200 million poods of grain be seized from the peasantry. The Trotskyite I. Smirnov, who was later executed as the organizer of the Terroristic Counter-Revolutionary Trotskyite-Zinovievite Centre, declared plainly at that time that "nothing bad" would happen if the proletariat "temporarily" clashed with the middle peasantry. The Trotskyite Ossovsky presented the purely Menshevik demand that the formation of other parties in the U.S.S.R. be allowed in order to defend the interests of capitalist entrepreneurs. Kamenev and Trotsky spoke in support of the Menshevik Ossovsky and voted against expelling him from the Party.~~

~~Struggling against the Leninist theory on the possibility of the victory of Socialism in one country, the Trotskyites slanderously accused the Bolshevik Party of "national close-mindedness." It is well known that the Menshevik Trotsky made this stupid and treacherous accusation against Lenin already in 1915. But the Party in its actions demonstrated that it remained faithful to the cause of internationalism.~~

~~The Trotskyites spoke in defence of the most infamous document of the "Workers' Opposition," the so-called "Baku Letter," within which the counter-revolutionaries Shlyapnikov and Medvedyev proposed to eliminate the Comintern and other international revolutionary proletarian organizations. Shlyapnikov praised the Second International and demanded that the most important enterprises of Soviet industry in the U.S.S.R. be handed over to foreign capitalists in the form of concessions. They openly extended a hand to the proletariat's most evil enemy. The Trotskyite-Zinovievite bloc also defended those Mensheviks who were taking cover under the flag of Anarcho-Syndicalism.~~

~~At the same time, the Trotskyite-Zinovievite bloc was conducting destructive work within foreign communist parties abroad, supporting such spy-like splitter groups as the German ones under Korsch-Maslov, Ruth Fischer and Urbahns. The Trotskyites released articles hostile to the Party that were full of slander about the communist party.~~

~~Already in the summer of 1926, the Trotskyite-Zinovievite bloc conducted furious underground diversionary work against the Party, forming its own secret anti-Party groups in various cities and instructing its people to maintain contact through secret, coded correspondence. With the aid of these illegal factional groups, the Trotskyites prepared open protests hostile to the Party. In this, they gambled on the exacerbation of economic problems in 1926. In the summer of 1926, the Trotskyites and Zinovievites held a secret meeting with their supporters in the woods outside of Moscow. The July Central Committee Plenum ruled on the disruptive factional activity of the Trotskyite-Zinovievite opposition, deciding that the opposition had gone over to "the formation of an all-union illegal organization designed to resist the Party and trigger in this way a split in its ranks" (The C.P.S.U.(B.) in Its Decisions, Russ. ed., Part II, p. 115.)~~

In the summer of 1926 the Trotskyites and Zinovievites united to form an anti-Party bloc, made it a rallying point for the remnants of all the defeated opposition groups, and laid the foundation of their secret anti-Leninist party, thereby grossly violating the Party Rules and the decisions of Party congresses forbidding the formation of factions. The Central Committee of the Party gave warning that unless this anti Party bloc—which resembled the notorious Menshevik August Bloc—were dissolved, matters might end badly for its adherents. But the supporters of the bloc would not desist.

That autumn ~~of 1926~~, ~~before~~ *on the eve of* the Fifteenth Party Conference, ~~the Trotskyites and Zinovievites tried to make a series of sorties~~ *they made a sortie* at Party meetings in the factories of Moscow, ~~and~~ Leningrad *and other cities, attempting to force a new discussion on the Party. The platform they tried to get the Party members to discuss was a rehash of the usual Trotskyite-Menshevik anti-Leninist platform.* ~~At all of these meetings, the rank-and-file workers~~

~~delivered a rebuff to the opposition. The opposition was dealt a harsh defeat not just in Moscow, but across the whole Soviet Union.~~ *The Party members gave the oppositionists a severe rebuff, and in some places simply ejected them from the meetings. The Central Committee again warned the supporters of the bloc, stating that the Party could not tolerate their subversive activities any longer.*

~~Having received a devastating rebuff from the Party,~~ *T*he opposition then submitted to the Central Committee a ~~double-dealing, false~~ statement signed by Trotsky, Zinoviev, Kamenev and Sokolnikov ~~hypocritically~~ ~~"~~condemning~~"~~ their own factional work ~~in public~~ and promising ~~to refrain from illegal factional activity~~ *to be loyal* in the future. ~~In secret, however, the Trotskyites gave orders to their supporters in the anti-Party groups to continue—and not to curtail—their work to undermine the Bolshevik Party.~~ *Nevertheless, the bloc continued to exist and its adherents did not stop their underhand work against the Party. They went on banding together their anti-Leninist party, started an illegal printing press, collected membership dues from their supporters and circulated their platform.*

~~After their defeat in October 1926, the Trotskyites became convinced that they could no longer count on the working masses and began to even more intensely despise the working masses among whom they had just unsuccessfully attempted to find support. Among their own treacherous followers, the Trotskyites complained about the supposedly reactionary nature of the working class that hadn't supported them. The Trotskyites explained their defeat by saying that there "hadn't been enough difficulties" that they could take advantage of while making their case to the masses.~~

~~In order to increase the number of difficulties in the country, the Trotskyites—later to be exposed as enemies of the Party and the people—resorted to wrecking, espionage and preparing for foreign intervention and the defeat of the U.S.S.R. Fierce enemies of the working class, the Trotskyites resigned themselves to the brutal mass murder of workers, the destruction of mines and the organization of railroad crashes, etc.~~

~~The Fifteenth Party Conference in October–November 1926 and the Seventh Expanded Comintern Plenum that took place right afterward passed decisions condemning the Trotskyite-Zinovievite bloc as a Menshevik, Social-Democratic deviation.~~

~~In Comrade Stalin's report "On the Social-Democratic Deviation" and in the resolutions of the Fifteenth Party Conference and the Seventh Expanded Comintern Plenum, note was made of the Trotskyite-Zinovievites' defection to Menshevik-Social-Democratic positions.~~

~~In their decisions, the Fifteenth Party Conference and the Seventh Expanded Comintern Plenum pointed out that the Trotskyite opposition, under the cover of "Leftist" and pseudo-revolutionary phrases, was actually aiding the~~

~~enemies of the proletarian dictatorship and all the traitors to the communist cause.~~

~~The Trotskyites, just like the Mensheviks and Social-Democrats, had tried to sow doubt within the ranks of the proletariat both at home and abroad—doubt in its own strength, doubt in the proletarian revolution and doubt in the possibility of building Socialism in the U.S.S.R. In doing this, the Trotskyites aided capitalist agents within the U.S.S.R. and the international bourgeois.~~

~~The Fifteenth Party Conference noted that in terms of the most important tasks for the Party, it was necessary to "protect the unity of the Party by all available means, cutting off every and all attempts to revive factionalism and the breaking of Party discipline" (The C.P.S.U.[B.] in Resolutions, Russ. ed., Part II, p. 161.)~~

~~Trotskyism's identity as a Menshevik political trend within the working class stemmed most of all from its denial of the possibility that the working class and peasantry could build Socialism in the U.S.S.R. The Trotskyites tried to convince the workers of the U.S.S.R. that if world revolution did not help them soon, they would have to give up and surrender to the bourgeoisie. The dirty Trotskyites tried to convince the world proletariat that it wasn't worth it to defend the U.S.S.R., inasmuch as the victory of Socialism in the U.S.S.R. simply was not possible under any circumstances. The Trotskyite bourgeois counter-revolutionary theory on the impossibility of building Socialism in our country was masked with all sorts of false, pseudo-revolutionary phrases about the victory of world revolution, which the Trotskyites in reality aimed to disrupt and ruin.~~

~~Through their bourgeois theory, the Trotskyites aimed to corrupt the working class of the U.S.S.R., denying it any confidence in the possibility of building Socialism and eliminating capitalism. And who would be willing to build, to muster all their resources, if they thought they'd not be successful?~~

> ~~"Our working class," Comrade Stalin said at the Sixteenth Party Congress, "is expanding its commitment to labour not for the sake of capitalism, but for the sake of burying capitalism once and for all and building Socialism in the U.S.S.R. Deny the working class its confidence in the possibility of building Socialism and you eliminate the whole basis for Socialist emulation, the expansion of labour and shock work." (Stalin, Questions of Leninism, 10th Russ. ed., p. 418.)~~

~~In order to struggle successfully for the country's Socialist industrialization, it was therefore necessary most of all to defeat and bury the bourgeois Trotskyite theory on the impossibility of building Socialism in our country.~~

~~At the Fifteenth Party Conference and the Seventh Expanded Plenum of the Comintern, Comrade Stalin defended the struggle for Lenin's theory on the possibility of the victory of Socialism in one country against Trotskyism and elaborated upon this theory as only a genius could. And under this banner, the construction of Socialism in the U.S.S.R. was realized. Trotskyism as an ideology was utterly defeated.~~

~~At the Seventh Comintern Plenum, Comrade Stalin provided an exhaustive answer to the question about the causes of contradiction and disagreement in the proletarian Party and the causes of the recent opportunistic missteps. The source of disagreement was most of all a result of the pressure of the bourgeoisie and bourgeois ideology on the proletariat and its Party in the context of class struggle. In this struggle, the broad masses of the proletariat served, as always, as a reliable supporter of Marxism and Bolshevism. But there were some unreliable, chance, petty-bourgeois elements within the proletariat who were vulnerable to bourgeois influence.~~

~~The bourgeoisie was aided in its task by the heterogeneity of the working class. "Leftist" anarchist groups found support among recent arrivals from the non-proletarian classes—the peasantry, the petty bourgeoisie and the intelligentsia. Reformers, Mensheviks and open opportunists found a base of support chiefly among the working class "aristocracy," the small strata of workers who had been better paid under capitalism. At critical times in the developing class struggle and amid rising difficulties, these unreliable, petty-bourgeois elements were unable to keep up with the broad proletarian masses and fell under the influence of bourgeois ideology, which they in turn passed on to the Party rank-and-file. This fed internal party disagreements in the Party of the proletariat during the transitional period when capitalist elements were still present in society.~~

~~The party of the Second International dismissed these principal disagreements and did not want to struggle with opportunism within the workers' movement, allowing the opportunism to grow stronger. It thus fell under the influence of opportunism and itself passed over, betraying the cause of the proletarian revolution and Socialism. The Bolshevik Party, in contrast, from its very beginnings followed the precepts of Marx and Engels and waged an uncompromising, principled struggle with all the various forms of opportunism, growing and becoming tempered in this struggle.~~

> ~~"The entire history of our Party serves as confirmation of the principle that our Party's history is the history of overcoming internal party contradictions and on the basis of this principle, of unwaveringly strengthening our Party's ranks.~~

. . . Overcoming internal party disputes through struggle is one of the laws of our Party's development," Comrade Stalin said in his report to the Seventh Enlarged Comintern Plenum.[4]

At the Seventh Enlarged Comintern Plenum, Comrade Stalin exposed in front of the representatives of the international communist movement Trotsky's counter-revolutionary suppositions that the U.S.S.R. would apparently always be situated "UNDER THE CONTROL of the world economy." The Trotskyites aimed to SUBORDINATE the land of Soviets to the capitalist encirclement, making the U.S.S.R. an appendage of the world capitalist system. Comrade Stalin warned that with such views, the opposition was sliding toward capitulation and defeatism. And this is what transpired. Trotskyism slid completely over to capitulation and defeatism, treachery and a total betrayal of the Socialist motherland. It was already clear to the Comintern at this time and it was recorded in the resolutions on Stalin's report at the Seventh Comintern Plenum that "in ideological terms, the opposition within the C.P.S.U.(B.) poses a Rightist danger to the Party, occasionally masked by Leftist phraseology."

In December 1926 at the Seventh Expanded Plenum of the Comintern, the Trotskyites made a series of treacherous attacks against the Central Committee, advancing the claim that the proletarian dictatorship and the C.P.S.U.(B.) were supposedly "passing into" capitalist positions. The Seventh Comintern Plenum announced that such slanderous talk among the Trotskyites verged on counter-revolution.

The Seventh Comintern Plenum ratified the decision of the Fifteenth Party Conference on the Trotskyite opposition, demanding the elimination of this oppositionist bloc with the C.P.S.U.(B.).

Trotskyism quickly began transforming from a Social-Democratic, Menshevik deviation within the Party and from an anti-Leninist political trend within the working class into a specifically Menshevik party and an anti-Soviet group. Just as with the Mensheviks, the Trotskyites ended up on the wrong side of the barricades, having slid into the camp of counter-revolution and having become the most treacherous and rotten capitalist restorationists.

3. Transition of the Trotskyite Opposition to Anti-Soviet Activity

In view of the behaviour of the Trotskyites and Zinovievites, the Fifteenth Party Conference (November 1926) and the Enlarged Plenum of the Executive Committee of the Communist International (December 1926) discussed the question of the bloc of Trotskyites and Zinovievites and adopted resolutions stigmatizing the adherents of this bloc as splitters whose platform was downright Menshevism.

But even this failed to bring them to their senses. In 1927, ~~the Trotskyites' activity became more and more clearly anti-Soviet in character. The Trotskyites took advantage of the sharpening tension surrounding the U.S.S.R.'s international position in order to stage new attacks on the Party. The Trotskyites, in conjunction and in a "united front" with Chamberlain and the British imperialists,~~ *just when the British Conservatives broke off diplomatic and trade relations with the U.S.S.R., the bloc* attacked the Party *with renewed vigour.* ~~Just as trade relations with England were breaking down and the threat of war against the U.S.S.R. was on the rise, the Trotskyites released an anti-Party, Menshevik "Platform of the Eighty-Three" and began to secretly collect signatures of support for it among their supporters.~~ *It concocted a new anti-Leninist platform, the so-called "Platform of the Eighty-Three" and began to circulate it among Party members, at the same time demanding that the Central Committee open a new general Party discussion.*

This was perhaps the most mendacious and pharisaical of all opposition platforms.

In their platform, the Trotskyites and Zinovievites professed that they had no objection to observing Party decisions and that they were all in favour of loyalty, but in reality they grossly violated the Party decisions, and scoffed at the very idea of loyalty to the Party and to its Central Committee.

In their platform, they professed they had no objection to Party unity and were against splits, but in reality they grossly violated Party unity, worked for a split, and already had their own, illegal, anti-Leninist party which had all the makings of an anti-Soviet, counter-revolutionary party.

In their platform, they professed they were all in favour of the policy of industrialization, and even accused the Central Committee of not proceeding with industrialization fast enough, but in reality they did nothing but carp at the Party resolution on the victory of Socialism in the U.S.S.R., scoffed at the policy of Socialist industrialization, demanded the surrender of a number of mills and factories to foreigners in the form of concessions, and pinned their main hopes on foreign capitalist concessions in the U.S.S.R.

In their platform, they professed they were all in favour of the collective-farm movement, and even accused the Central Committee of not proceeding with collectivization fast enough, but in reality they scoffed at the policy of enlisting the peasants in the work of Socialist construction, preached the idea that "unresolvable conflicts" between the working class and the peasantry were inevitable, and pinned their hopes on the "cultured leaseholders" in the countryside, in other words, on the kulaks.

This was the most mendacious of all the platforms of the opposition.

It was meant to deceive the Party.

The Central Committee refused to open a general discussion immediately. It informed the opposition that a general discussion could be opened only in accordance with the Party Rules, namely, two months before a Party congress.

~~It was at that moment that the traitor Trotsky began to circulate his defeatist "Clemenceau Thesis." The point of this counter-revolutionary thesis was that the opposition not only would continue its struggle against the Party and Central Committee in the case of war, and not only that it would continue this struggle even if the enemy advanced to within a couple dozen kilometers of the capital, but that the opposition would aim to overthrow the Soviet Government. The leaders of this Trotskyite gang of traitors thus occupied a defeatist position in regard to the U.S.S.R. and were already aiding its enemies. Quickly, the Trotskyites made espionage, diversions, wrecking and terrorism their basic means of struggle against the Bolshevik Party and the proletarian dictatorship.~~

~~Many of the head Trotskyites (Trotsky himself, Rakovsky, Krestinsky, Rosengoltz and others) already at this time and even much earlier had become paid agents of foreign espionage services. Trotsky had become an agent of German espionage in 1921 and an agent of the British "Intelligence Service" in 1926, Krestinsky had become a German espionage agent in 1921, Rosengoltz had become a German agent in 1923 and a British agent, and Rakovsky had joined the "Intelligence Service" in 1924 and had become an agent of Japanese fascism in 1934.~~

~~The Trotskyites attempted to use the temporary defeat of the Chinese revolution in 1927 to attack the Comintern line. On the Chinese revolution, the Trotskyites adopted a Menshevik position, as they did on other issues. The denied the Chinese revolution's anti-imperialist, anti-feudal character. They denied that the Chinese peasantry could be a revolutionary force under the hegemony of the proletariat. The Chinese Trotskyites, led by Chen Duxiu, assisted the counter-revolutionary generals and imperialists when punitive battalions were sent after the Chinese communist party and Red Army. The Trotskyites worked hand-in-hand with the imperialists against the Chinese communist party.~~

~~Why did the Party not immediately expel the Trotskyites, these enemies of Leninism, from its ranks in 1927?~~

~~First, the Party did not yet know that Trotsky and an array of other Trotskyites were agents of foreign espionage services, nor did it know many other facts concerning their cleverly camouflaged counter-revolutionary activities.~~

~~Second, it was necessary to have the entire Party get involved in this conflict and convince the whole Party and the entire working class that we were dealing with enemies.~~

~~At the celebration dedicated to the 20th anniversary of the October revolution, Comrade Molotov explained that before expelling the enemies of Lenin-~~

ism and the Party from the Bolshevik ranks, we had to conduct a large investigation within the Party and the working class.

But the opposition understood the Party's patience in this matter in its own way. The opposition saw it as weakness on the part of the Party. Well before the Fifteenth Party Congress, the opposition even made the audacious demand to have a general party discussion and have its Menshevik platform printed and distributed. This was refused. In league with the Whiteguards at that time, the Trotskyites set up their own underground printing press. The Soviet Government arrested those complicit in this crime. After this, Trotsky, Zinoviev, Preobrazhensky, Serebryakov and others began to demand the immediate release of those under arrest. They secretly printed and distributed several thousand copies of their Menshevik platform well before the Fifteenth Party Congress.

Ordinary people possessing counter-revolutionary sentiments even took part in the Trotskyites' secret meetings. They rejoiced about finding a gang of criminals that would struggle against the C.P.S.U.(B.) and against the proletarian dictatorship. Things got so far out of control that the Trotskyites ended up seizing a lecture hall at the Moscow Higher Technical Institute by force. Even at that time, the leaders of the counter-revolutionary terrorist bloc encouraged terroristic methods in the struggle against the Party.

The entire Menshevik and Whiteguard press hailed the Trotskyite struggle against the Party, publicizing it and encouraging and supporting the Trotskyites as defenders of bourgeois "democracy" and opponents of the proletarian dictatorship. Trotsky's slogans were taken up by all of the proletarian dictatorship's enemies.

In the resolutions on party unity at the Tenth Party Congress, Lenin wrote that on the basis of the experience of all previous revolutions, the counter-revolution always would support petty-bourgeois groups close to the most revolutionary parties in order to shake up and overthrow the revolutionary dictatorship.

Lenin pointed out that in this revolution, the enemies of the Soviet power, convinced of the hopelessness of open counter-revolution under the Whiteguardist flag, aimed to advance the cause of counter-revolution by any means including the transfer of power to political groups THAT APPEARED very close to recognizing the Soviet power.

Lenin said that the Whiteguards and counter-revolutionaries were committed to this plan and would CHANGE THEIR STRIPES to become communists and even take up positions further to the "Left" if that would weaken and overturn the base for proletarian revolution in our country.

It was thus not accidental that the whole counter-revolution at home and the international bourgeoisie abroad actively supported the Trotskyites despite the fact that their stripes made them seem more "Leftist" than the communists.

~~The bourgeoisie at home and abroad gambled that they would be able to topple the Soviet power with the Trotskyites' assistance.~~

~~The Trotskyites, in turn, counted on the support of the bourgeoisie, especially from abroad. With their Party apparatus in ruins, the Trotskyites appealed openly to the imperialists for aid.~~

~~In this way, the experience with the Trotskyites confirmed Lenin's directions and warnings that the counter-revolution would stake a wager on political tendencies that were by all appearances close to recognizing the Soviet power, as well as on petty-bourgeois groups and "oppositions" that were struggling with the communist party.~~

~~If the Party had not defeated Trotskyism, it would have threatened the life of the proletarian dictatorship.~~

~~In 1927, the Party surveyed the results of the proletarian dictatorship's past decade and celebrated this activity with the proclamation of the seven-hour working day in mills and factories. 35 per cent of peasant farms were also freed from taxation, benefitting the poor peasantry. The opposition had fallen so low that it spoke out against the seven-hour working day.~~

In October 1927, that is, two months before the Fifteenth Congress, the Central Committee of the Party announced a general Party discussion, and the fight began. Its result was truly lamentable for the bloc of Trotskyites and Zinovievites: 724,000 Party members voted for the policy of the Central Committee; 4,000, or less than one per cent, for the bloc of Trotskyites and Zinovievites. The anti-Party bloc was completely routed. The overwhelming majority of the Party members were unanimous in rejecting the platform of the bloc.

Such was the clearly expressed will of the Party, for whose judgment the oppositionists themselves had appealed.

But even this lesson was lost on the supporters of the bloc. Instead of submitting to the will of the Party they decided to frustrate it. Even before the discussion had closed, perceiving that ignominious failure awaited them, they decided to resort to more acute forms of struggle against the Party and the Soviet Government. ~~On November 7, 1927, the Trotskyites tried to mount an anti-Soviet demonstration with counter-revolutionary slogans.~~ *They decided to stage an open demonstration of protest in Moscow and Leningrad. The day they chose for their demonstration was November 7, the anniversary of the October Revolution, the day on which the working people of the U.S.S.R. annually hold their countrywide revolutionary demonstration. Thus, the Trotskyites and Zinovievites planned to hold a parallel demonstration. As was to be expected, the supporters of the bloc managed to bring out into the streets only a miserable handful of their satellites.* ~~This pathetic group of Trotskyites was dispersed by the workers.~~ *These satellites and their patrons*[5] *were overwhelmed by the general demonstration and swept off the streets.*

~~This anti-Soviet demonstration showed that the Trotskyites were now prepared to go even further along the path of counter-revolution.~~ *Now there was no longer any doubt that the Trotskyites and Zinovievites had become definitely anti-Soviet. During the general Party discussion they had appealed to the Party against the Central Committee; now, during their puny demonstration, they had taken the course of appealing to the hostile classes against the Party and the Soviet state. Once they had made it their aim to undermine the Bolshevik Party, they were bound to go to the length of undermining the Soviet state, for in the Soviet Union the Bolshevik Party and the state are inseparable. That being the case, the ringleaders of the bloc of Trotskyites and Zinovievites had outlawed themselves from the Party, for men who had sunk to the depths of anti-Soviet action could no longer be tolerated in the ranks of the Bolshevik Party.*

~~Therefore, Trotsky and Zinoviev, the leading chieftains of the Trotskyite opposition, were expelled from the Party even before the Fifteenth Party Congress.~~ *On November 14, 1927, a joint meeting of the Central Committee and the Central Control Commission expelled Trotsky and Zinoviev from the Party.*

2. Progress of Socialist Industrialization. Agriculture Lags. Fifteenth Party Congress. Policy of Collectivization in Agriculture. Rout of the Bloc of Trotskyites and Zinovievites. Political Duplicity

By the end of 1927 the decisive success of the policy of Socialist industrialization was unmistakable. Under the New Economic Policy industrialization had made considerable progress in a short space of time. The gross output of industry and agriculture (including the timber industry and fisheries) had reached and even surpassed the pre-war level. Industrial output had risen to 42 per cent of the total output of the country, which was the pre-war ratio.[6]

The Socialist sector of industry was rapidly growing at the expense of the private sector, its output having risen from 81 per cent of the total output in 1924–25 to 86 per cent in 1926–27, the output of the private sector dropping from 19 per cent to 14 per cent in the same period.

This meant that industrialization in the U.S.S.R. was of a pronounced Socialist character, that industry was developing towards the victory of the Socialist system of production, and that as far as industry was concerned, the question—"Who will win?"—had already been decided in favour of Socialism.[7]

No less rapid was the displacement of the private dealer in the sphere of trade, his share in the retail market having fallen from 42 per cent in 1924–25 to 32 per cent in 1926–27, not to mention the wholesale market, where the share of the private dealer had fallen from 9 per cent to 5 per cent in the same period.

Even more rapid was the rate of growth of LARGE-SCALE *Socialist industry, which in 1927, the first year* AFTER *the restoration period, increased its output over the previous year by 18 per cent. This was a record increase, one beyond the reach of the large-scale industry of even the most advanced capitalist countries.*

But in agriculture, especially grain growing, the picture was different. Although agriculture as a whole had passed the pre-war level, the gross yield of its most important branch—grain growing—was only 91 per cent of pre-war, while the marketed share of the harvest, that is, the amount of grain sold[8] *for the supply of the towns, scarcely attained 37 per cent of the pre-war figure. Furthermore, all the signs pointed to the danger of a further decline in the amount of marketable grain.*

This meant that the process of the splitting up of the large farms that used to produce for the market, into small farms, and of the small farms into dwarf farms, a process which had begun in 1918, was still going on; that these small and dwarf peasant farms were reverting practically to a natural form of economy and were able to supply only a negligible quantity of grain for the market; that while in the 1927 period the grain crop was only slightly below that of the pre-war period, the marketable surplus for the supply of the towns was only a little more than one-third of the pre-war marketable surplus.

There could be no doubt that if such a state of affairs in grain farming were to continue, the army and the urban population would be faced with chronic famine.

This was a crisis in grain farming which was bound to be followed by a crisis in livestock farming.

The only escape from this predicament was a change to large-scale farming which would permit the use of tractors and agricultural machines and secure a several-fold increase of the marketable surplus of grain. The country had the alternative: either to adopt large-scale CAPITALIST *farming, which would have meant the ruin of the peasant masses, destroyed the alliance between the working class and the peasantry, increased the strength of the kulaks, and led to the downfall of* SOCIALISM *in the countryside; or to take the course of amalgamating the small peasant holdings into large Socialist farms, collective farms, which would be able to use tractors and other modern machines for a rapid advancement of grain farming and a rapid increase in the marketable surplus of gain.*

It is clear that the Bolshevik Party and the Soviet state could only take the second course, the collective farm way of developing agriculture.

In this, the Party was guided by the following precepts of Lenin regarding the necessity of passing from small peasant farming to large scale, co-operative, collective farming:

a) "There is no escape from poverty for the small farm." (Lenin, SELECTED WORKS*, Vol. VIII, p. 195.)*
b) "If we continue as of old on our small farms, even as free citizens on free land, we shall still be faced with inevitable ruin." (Lenin, SELECTED WORKS*, Vol. VI, p. 370.)*

c) *"If peasant farming is to develop further, we must firmly assure also its transition to the next stage, and this next stage must inevitably be one in which the small, isolated peasant farms, the least profitable and most backward, will by a process of gradual amalgamation form large-scale collective farms." (Lenin, SELECTED WORKS, Vol. IX, p. 151.)*
d) *"Only if we succeed in proving to the peasants in practice the advantages of common, collective, co-operative, artel cultivation of the soil, only if we succeed in helping the peasant by means of co-operative or artel farming, will the working class, which holds the state power, be really able to convince the peasant of the correctness of its policy and to secure the real and durable following of the millions of peasants." (Lenin, SELECTED WORKS, Vol. VIII, p. 198.)*

Such was the situation prior to the Fifteenth Party Congress.

~~4. Fifteenth Party Congress (December 2–19, 1927)—the Congress of Collectivization~~

~~The Bolshevik Party came to the Fifteenth Party Congress with an army of one and a quarter million members and candidate members, and with a strong and growing proletarian core.~~ *The Fifteenth Party Congress opened on December 2, 1927. It was attended by 898 delegates with vote and 771 delegates with voice but no vote, representing 887,233 Party members and 348,957 candidate members.*

~~By that time, on the basis of the Bolshevik Party line, the Soviet Union had realized new successes in the construction of a Socialist society.~~

~~The land of Soviets was confidently and quickly moving toward Socialism, every day excluding more and more capitalistic elements from the economy. The overall weight of Socialist industry in the economy had risen noticeably. The Fifteenth Party Congress instructed the Central Committee to continue without relenting in its implementation of the policies of Socialist industrialization.~~

~~At the same time, the Fifteenth Party Congress found that the agricultural economy was developing too slowly. This was due to the extraordinary backwardness of existing peasant agricultural technique and the low cultural level in the countryside. Most of all, the backwardness of the agricultural economy was due to the fact that the scattered small peasant holdings were not capable of developing as rapidly as large-scale Socialist industry was.~~

In his report on behalf of the Central Committee, Comrade Stalin referred to the good results of industrialization and the rapid expansion of Socialist industry, and set the Party the following task:

> *"To extend and consolidate our Socialist key position in all economic branches in town and country and to pursue a course of eliminating the capitalist elements from the national economy."*

Comparing agriculture with industry and noting the backwardness of the former, especially of grain growing, owing to the scattered state of agriculture, which precluded the use of modern machinery, Comrade Stalin emphasized that such an unenviable state of agriculture was endangering the entire national economy.

> "What is the way out?" Comrade Stalin ~~said~~ *asked* ~~in his political report to the Central Committee~~.
>
> "The way out," *he said,* "is to turn the small and scattered peasant holdings into large united farms based on the common cultivation of the soil, to introduce collective cultivation of the soil on the basis of a new and higher technique. *The way out is to unite the small and dwarf peasant farms gradually but surely, not by pressure, but by example and persuasion, into large farms based on common, co-operative, collective cultivation of the soil with the use of agricultural machines and tractors and scientific methods of intensive agriculture. There is no other way out.*"

The Fifteenth Congress passed a resolution calling for the fullest ~~support~~ *development* of COLLECTIVIZATION in agriculture. The congress adopted *a plan for* the extension and consolidation of the collective and state farms and formulated explicit instructions concerning the methods to be used in the struggle for collectivization in agriculture.

~~The successes of the Party's policy in the countryside and the strengthening of the alliance with the middle peasantry provided an opportunity to further develop the campaign against the kulaks. The Fifteenth Party Congress suggested:~~

At the same time, the congress gave directions:

> "To ~~conduct~~ *develop*[9] further the offensive against the kulaks and to adopt a number of new measures which would restrict the development of capitalism in the countryside and guide peasant farming towards Socialism." (RESOLUTIONS OF THE C.P.S.U.[B.], Russ. ed., Part II, p. 260.)

~~"THE FIFTEENTH PARTY CONGRESS WAS LARGELY A CONGRESS OF COLLECTIVIZATION" (STALIN). After the congress, the struggle for the collectivization of agriculture began to develop. The transition to collectivization was facilitated by policies supporting industrialization and the construction of tractor~~

factories.[10] ~~The solid collectivization of agriculture became possible due to the successes of industrialization in the U.S.S.R.~~

~~The congress gave instructions on how to put together the First Five-Year Plan of Socialist construction. This became possible because ten years of proletarian dictatorship had strengthened Socialist economic planning.~~

Finally, in view of the fact that economic planning had taken firm root, and with the object of organizing a systematic offensive of Socialism against the capitalist elements along the entire economic front, the congress gave instructions to the proper bodies for the drawing up of the First Five-Year Plan *for the development of the national economy.*

~~At the Fifteenth Party Congress, the leaders and participants in the Trotskyite-Zinovievite bloc were expelled from the Party.~~ *After passing decisions on the problems of Socialist construction, the congress proceeded to discuss the question of liquidating the bloc of Trotskyites and Zinovievites.*

~~During the discussion before the congress, oppositionists in the Party organizations found only about half a per cent of support for their anti-Party platform (725,000 Party members voted for the Central Committee and 4,000 against it).~~

~~The Trotskyite opposition never had roots within the main mass of the working class. Its foothold in society was based on those who had recently left the ranks of the bourgeoisie and petty bourgeoisie. In their struggle against the Party and their anti-Soviet speeches, the Trotskyites expressed the dissatisfaction of the urban bourgeoisie and petty bourgeoisie who were being excluded from the economy by the Socialist offensive.~~

> ~~". . . as a result of our movement forward, as a result of the growth of our industry and as a result of the growth of the specific scale of Socialist forms of economic management, one part of the petty bourgeoisie, especially the urban bourgeois, was ruined and sank out of sight. The opposition expressed these strata's grumbling and dissatisfaction with the proletarian revolution.~~
>
> ~~"This is where the social roots of the opposition are to be found," Stalin pointed out at the Fifteenth Party Congress. (Stenographic Report for the Fifteenth Party Congress, Russ. ed., p. 77.)~~

The congress recognized that "the opposition has ideologically broken with Leninism, has degenerated into a Menshevik group, has taken the course of capitulation to the forces of the international and home bourgeoisie, and has objectively become a tool of counter-revolution against the regime of the proletarian dictatorship." (~~Resolutions of the C.P.S.U.[B.], Russ. ed., Part II~~ *Ibid.*, p. 232.)

The congress found that the differences between the Party and the opposition had developed into differences of program, and *that* the Trotsky opposition had taken the course of struggle against the Soviet power. The congress therefore declared that adherence to the Trotsky opposition and the propagation of its views were incompatible with membership in the Bolshevik Party.

The congress approved the decision *of the joint meeting of the Central Committee and the Central Control Commission* to expel ~~the active members of the Trotskyite opposition, as well as the entire group of Democratic-Centralists (under Sapronov)~~ *Trotsky and Zinoviev from the Party and* resolved on the expulsion of ~~the~~ *all* active members of the ~~Trotskyite opposition~~ *bloc of Trotskyites and Zinovievites, such as Radek, Preobrazhensky, Rakovsky, Pyatakov, Serebryakov, I. Smirnov, Kamenev, Sarkis, Safarov, Lifshitz, Mdivani, Smilga*~~, as well as~~ *and* the whole "Democratic-Centralism" group (under Sapronov, *V. Smirnov, Boguslavsky, Drobnis and others).*

Defeated ideologically and routed organizationally, the adherents of the bloc of Trotskyites and Zinovievites lost the last vestiges of their influence among the people.

~~5. Transformation of Trotskyism from a Political Trend into a Gang of Brigands and Spies~~

~~Zinoviev, Kamenev, Yevdokimov and others, who had been expelled from the party for anti-Soviet activities, handed in double-dealing statements about their abandonment of Trotskyism. They recommended to their followers that they also hand in such double-dealing statements in order to at the very least "crawl on their bellies" back into the Party, as Zinoviev put it, so as to continue with their anti-Soviet activity under the cover of Party membership. Trotsky gave the same advice to his followers.~~[11]

~~Over the course of 1928, a considerable portion of the Trotskyites and Zinovievites handed in double-dealing statements at the request of their chieftains. But in actuality, the Trotskyites and Zinovievites did not cease their underground counter-revolutionary activity for a single moment. They gambled on the difficulties that were being experienced in the Soviet Union and recruited enemy elements of the Party in order to prepare new blows against the Bolshevik Party and the Soviet people. They instilled in their cadres a sense of rabid spite and hatred toward the Party and trained them to become spies, wreckers and assassins.~~

~~During this period, the Trotskyites and Zinovievites transformed once and for all from A POLITICAL TREND into a double-dealing, unprincipled GANG of brigands, spies, wreckers, diversionists and assassins.~~

The Trotskyites and Zinovievites had been utterly defeated by the Bolshevik Party in an ideological sense and to a great extent in an organizational sense, and had lost their entire base of support among the working class. They now decided TO SYSTEMATIZE THEIR RELATIONSHIP WITH THE PARTY AROUND THE IDEA OF DOUBLE-DEALING.[12]

Earlier, as a political trend, the Trotskyites had spoken out in defence of their anti-Leninist, Menshevik viewpoints and "platforms." Now, the Trotskyites and Zinovievites began TO CONCEAL their views; what's more, in their double-dealing statements the Trotskyites now denounced their own viewpoints and "platforms," while not really renouncing them.

The Trotskyites and Zinovievites began to praise the Party line to the skies, all the while remaining enemies.

The Trotskyites and Zinovievites ceased to be a political trend once and for all because groups cease to be political tendencies when their members conceal their views and do not struggle openly for them, instead praising their opponents' views.

Having ceased to be a political trend, the Trotskyites and Zinovievites turned into an unprincipled gang. In this way, they succeeded in preserving a considerable portion of their traitorous cadres. All of them, under the cover of agreement with the Party, nurtured a sense of rabid spite against the Communist Party, the Soviet people and the Soviet system.

It is not surprising that the Trotskyites and Zinovievites turned for assistance to the imperialists, who aimed to overthrow the Soviet power and restore capitalism in our country by means of a foreign intervention. This appeal for assistance from the imperialists was aided by the fact that there were already many agents of the foreign espionage services in the Trotskyite leadership, including Trotsky himself.

During this period, the Trotskyites completely switched all of their followers onto the path of espionage, wrecking and terror.

Expelled from the Party, Trotsky was exiled from the country in 1929 for anti-Soviet, counter-revolutionary activities. As soon as Trotsky settled abroad, he became a permanent correspondent for the foreign press and proffered all sorts of rotten rumors about the Party and the U.S.S.R. that were profitable for the imperialists. Having been tied to foreign espionage services for years, he now began to organize the "Fourth International." As was later revealed in the testimony of Pyatakov, Radek, Sokolnikov and other agents of his, and as was later demonstrated during the Trial of the Anti-Soviet "Bloc of Rights and Trotskyites," Trotsky agreed with the fascists about joint activities against the Soviet Union, about preparing the defeat of the Soviet Union in the event of war, and about the spy services' organization of terrorist, diversionary acts.[13]

~~Trotsky promised the imperialists that capitalism would be restored to the U.S.S.R. and that the Ukraine, the Far East and Byelorussia would be surrendered to the enemies.~~

~~In 1936–37, Trotsky was unmasked as the main organizer of the anti-Soviet Trotskyite-Zinovievite and the Trotskyite (Parallel) Centres, which committed the foul murder of S. M. Kirov along with the Rights. Having sold out to the imperialists and become bloody fascist mercenaries, the Trotskyite traitors conducted treacherous, fascist activities in order to assist in the restoration of capitalism in the U.S.S.R. Trotsky revealed himself as the most evil enemy of Socialism, the enemy of the Soviet people and all of the working people of mankind. The Trotskyite spies became the head detachment of international fascism.~~

Shortly after the Fifteenth Party Congress, the expelled anti-Leninists[14] *began to hand in statements, recanting Trotskyism and asking to be reinstated in the Party. Of course, at that time the Party could not yet know that Trotsky, Rakovsky, Radek, Krestinsky, Sokolnikov and others had long been enemies of the people, spies recruited by foreign espionage services, and that Kamenev, Zinoviev, Pyatakov and others were already forming connections with enemies of the U.S.S.R. in capitalist countries for the purpose of "collaboration" with them against the Soviet people. But experience had taught the Party that any knavery might be expected from these individuals, who had often attacked Lenin and the Leninist Party at the most crucial moments. It was therefore sceptical of the statements they had made in their applications for reinstatement. As a preliminary test of their sincerity, it made their reinstatement in the Party dependent on the following conditions:*

a) They must publicly denounce Trotskyism as an anti-Bolshevik and anti-Soviet ideology.

b) They must publicly acknowledge the Party policy as the only correct policy.

c) They must unconditionally abide by the decisions of the Party and its bodies.

d) They must undergo a term of probation, during which the Party would test them; on the expiration of this term, the Party would consider the reinstatement of each applicant separately, depending on the results of the test.

The Party considered that in any case the public acceptance of these points by the expelled would be all to the good of the Party, because it would break the unity of the Trotskyite-Zinovievite ranks, undermine their morale, demonstrate once more the right and the might of the Party, and enable the Party, if the applicants were sincere, to reinstate its former[15] *workers in its ranks, and if they were not sincere, to unmask them in the public eye, no longer as misguided individuals, but as unprincipled careerists, deceivers of the working class and incorrigible double-dealers.*

The majority of the expelled accepted the terms of reinstatement and made public statements in the press to this effect.

Desiring to be clement to them, and loath to deny them an opportunity of once again becoming men of the Party and of the working class, the Party reinstated them in its ranks.

However, time showed that, with few exceptions, the recantations of the "leading lights" of the bloc of Trotskyites and Zinovievites were false and hypocritical from beginning to end.

It turned out that even before they had handed in their applications, these gentry had ceased to represent a political trend ready to defend their views before the people, and had become an unprincipled gang of careerists who were prepared publicly to trample on the last remnants of their own views, publicly to praise the views of the Party, which were alien to them, and—like chameleons—to adopt any colouring, provided they could maintain themselves in the ranks of the Party and the working class and have the opportunity to do harm to the working class and to its Party.

The "leading lights" of the bloc of Trotskyites and Zinovievites proved to be political swindlers, political double-dealers.

Political double-dealers usually begin with deceit and prosecute their nefarious ends by deceiving the people, the working class, and the Party of the working class. But political double-dealers are not to be regarded as mere humbugs. Political double-dealers are an unprincipled gang of political careerists who, having long ago lost the confidence of the people, strive to insinuate themselves once more into their confidence by deception, by chameleon-like changes of colour, by fraud, by any means, only that they might retain the title of political figures. Political double-dealers are an unprincipled gang of political careerists who are ready to seek support anywhere, even among criminal elements, even among the scum of society, even among the mortal enemies of the people, only that they might be able, at a "propitious" moment, again to mount the political stage and to clamber on to the back of the people as their "rulers."

The "leading lights" of the bloc of Trotskyites and Zinovievites were political double-dealers of this very description.

~~3.6. Grain-Growing Difficulties in 1928 and the Sharpening of Class Struggle~~ ***Offensive against the Kulaks. The Bukharin-Rykov Anti-Party Group. Adoption of the First Five-Year Plan. Socialist Emulation. Beginning of the Mass Collective-Farm Movement***

~~Soon after the Fifteenth Party Congress, in February 1928, difficulties in grain growing were uncovered. There was a shortfall of 128 million poods in comparison with what was on hand at the beginning of 1927. The kulaks and profiteers drove up the price of grain and threatened the country with famine.~~

~~After several years of good harvests, the kulak farms had grown strong and built up major reserves, and now held onto their grain in order to drive up the~~

~~price. At this time, the kulaks still held in their hands about a fifth of the grain grown for the market and therefore had the ability to stage a "grain strike." More than anything else, it was necessary to break the kulaks' resistance in order to avoid an economic crisis.~~

~~The class struggle with the kulaks sharpened. The kulaks hid their grain and distilled it into alcohol, resorted to terrorism against Party and government officials, assassinated rural newspaper correspondents, and burned down collective farms and state granaries.~~

The agitation conducted by the bloc of Trotskyites and Zinovievites against the Party policy, against the building of Socialism, and against collectivization, as well as the agitation conducted by the Bukharinites, who said that nothing would come of the collective farms, that the kulaks should be let alone because they would "grow" into Socialism of themselves, and that the enrichment of the bourgeoisie represented no danger to Socialism—all found an eager response among the capitalist elements in the country, and above all among the kulaks. The kulaks now knew from comments in the press that they were not alone, that they had defenders and intercessors in the persons of Trotsky, Zinoviev, Kamenev, Bukharin, Rykov and others. Naturally, this could not but stiffen the kulaks' spirit of resistance against the policy of the Soviet Government. And, in fact, the resistance of the kulaks became increasingly stubborn. They refused en masse to sell to the Soviet state their grain surpluses, of which they had considerable hoards. They resorted to terrorism against the collective farmers and against Party workers and government officials in the countryside, and burned down collective farms and state granaries.

~~In this situation, the Party and Government had to resort to an array of extraordinary measures against the kulaks.~~ *The Party realized that until the resistance of the kulaks was broken, until they were defeated in open fight in full view of the peasantry, the working class and the Red Army would suffer from a food shortage, and the movement for collectivization among the peasants could not assume a mass character.*

In pursuance of the instructions of the Fifteenth Party Congress, the Party launched a determined offensive against the kulaks, putting into effect the slogan: rely firmly on the poor peasantry, strengthen the alliance with the middle peasantry, and wage a resolute struggle against the kulaks. ~~The Government increased the taxation of the well-off and rich strata of the countryside and introduced a law on self-taxation and a bond for the strengthening of the peasant economy.~~ *In answer to the kulaks' refusal to sell their grain surpluses to the state at the fixed prices,* the Party *and the Government* adopted a number of *emergency* measures~~, dealing a blow to the kulaks and profiteers who were driving up the price of grain (through the application of Article 107 of the Criminal Code on the court confiscation of surplus grain from kulaks and profiteers)~~

against the kulaks, applied Article 107 of the Criminal Code empowering the courts to confiscate grain surpluses from kulaks and profiteers in case they refused to sell them to the state at the fixed prices. ~~These extraordinary measures were conducted against the kulaks with the support of the poor peasantry~~, and granted the poor peasants a number of privileges, under which 25 per cent of the confiscated kulak grain was placed at ~~the~~ *their* disposal ~~of the village poor in the form of loans. The Party mobilized thousands of Party members for work in the countryside.~~ ~~Simultaneously, the production of industrial goods for the village market was expanded.~~

These emergency measures ~~eliminated the danger of a crisis that might have taken on larger proportions. At the same time, the Party corrected the excesses that had appeared in some places during the imposition of the extraordinary measures. The Party did not allow the extraordinary measures to affect the middle peasantry~~ *had their effect: the poor and middle peasants joined in the resolute fight against the kulaks; the kulaks were isolated, and the resistance of the kulaks and the profiteers was broken. By the end of 1928, the Soviet state already had sufficient stocks of grain at its disposal, and the collective-farm movement began to advance with surer strides.*

~~The Party announced the task of more quickly overcoming the BACKWARDNESS in agriculture, especially in the grain sector. Comrade Stalin pointed out that the fundamental solution to the difficulties with grain was to be found in the creation of collective and state farms that were furnished with equipment, armed with scientific information and capable of producing the most grain for market. This line on collectivization, which was approved by the Party at Comrade Stalin's suggestion, proved to be completely correct. Fulfilling this line, the Soviet country set out on the path to a prosperous life.~~

~~At the July 1928 Central Committee Plenum, the decision was made to organize new GRAIN-GROWING STATE FARMS. The grain-growing state farms were supposed to produce 100,000,000 poods of grain in the course of the next 4–5 years. The grain-growing state farms became genuine Socialist grain factories. In the future, M.T.S. (machine-tractor station) organizations would be formed on the basis of these grain-growing state farms—organizations that would play a decisive role in the conversion of millions of peasant holdings into Socialist farming.~~

~~The Party developed SELF-CRITICISM as one of the most important means for the improvement of work and correction of shortcomings. Self-criticism was to become the mightiest weapon of the Party, Young Communist League, trade unions and organs of the Soviet power in the struggle for the First Five-Year Plan and the Socialist offensive.~~

~~The Party concentrated all of its attention on the STRENGTHENING OF LABOUR AND PRODUCTION DISCIPLINE and the development of SOCIALIST EMULATION AND SHOCK WORK. On this basis, the productivity of labour also rose.~~

~~The Party mobilized the multi-million-man masses in the struggle for a fast tempo in Socialist industrialization and for the fulfilment of the First Stalinist Five-Year Plan.~~

~~But every step of the Socialist offensive was accompanied by the sharpening of class struggle. In 1928,~~ *That same year,* a large organization of wreckers, consisting of bourgeois experts, was discovered in the Shakhty district of the Donetz Coal Basin. The Shakhty wreckers were closely connected with the former mine owners—Russian ~~with~~ *and* foreign capitalists—and with a foreign military espionage service. Their aim was to ~~restore (reestablish) capitalism in the U.S.S.R., and they wanted~~ disrupt the development of Socialist industry *and to facilitate the restoration of capitalism in the U.S.S.R.* The wreckers had deliberately mismanaged the mines in order to reduce the output of coal, spoiled machinery and ventilation apparatus, caused roof-falls and explosions, and set fire to pits, plants and power stations. The wreckers had deliberately obstructed the improvement of the workers' conditions and had infringed the Soviet labour protection laws.

The wreckers were put on trial and met with their deserts.

~~After the trial of the Shakhty wreckers, an array of wrecking organizations were uncovered that conducted destructive activities in various branches of the economy.~~ The ~~C.P.S.U.(B.)~~ Central Committee *of the Party* directed all Party organizations to draw the necessary conclusions from the Shakhty case. Comrade Stalin declared that Bolshevik business executives must themselves ~~MASTER TECHNIQUE~~ *become experts in the technique of production,* so as no longer to be the dupes of the wreckers among the old bourgeois experts, and that the training of new~~, qualified~~ technical personnel from the ~~proletariat itself~~ *ranks of the working class* must be accelerated.

In accordance with a decision of the Central Committee, the ~~entire~~ training of young ~~proletarian~~ experts in the technical colleges was improved. Thousands of ~~the best~~ Party members, *members of the Young Communist League* and non-Party people *devoted to the cause of the working class* were mobilized for study~~, who in a few years became engineers and successfully struggled for the victory of the First and Second Five-Year Plans~~.

~~7. Formation of the Rightist Anti-Party Group and the Struggle with It~~[17]

~~It was precisely at this time of sharpened struggle with the kulaks and the switch to collectivization that the Rightist group took shape. The Party had always struggled against Rightist opportunists. But in the period before the Fifteenth Party Congress, it was the Trotskyites that posed the chief danger and the Rights pretended that they were struggling with them.~~

~~The Party had exposed Bukharin's Right-opportunist, kulak slogan "Get Rich," Syrtsov's slogan "Save Up for a Better Day,"[18] which also was directed at the kulak, Krinitsky's kulak-like statements, and so on. After the Trotskyites' defeat, the Right deviation became the chief danger.~~

~~The Rights began to actively speak out against the Party after the Fifteenth Party Congress and formed into an anti-Party faction. The factional struggle of the Right opportunists against the Party at this critical moment, when the broad restructuring of the country was getting underway, and when the resistance of the capitalist elements was sharpening, was not coincidental.[19]~~

~~The Rightist chieftains—Bukharin, Rykov and Tomsky—spoke out against Lenin and the Party repeatedly over the course of our Party's history and they were repeatedly beaten by Lenin for their opportunistic theories and deeds. Lenin warned that Bukharin was "devilishly unstable in politics." We know that not only during the war, but during 1917, the Brest period and the trade union debate, Bukharin acted as Trotsky's collaborator. Equally well known was Rykov's pseudo-Menshevik position over the course of his entire time in the Party, his strike-breaking activity during the October seizure of power and his desertion from the first Sovnarkom. It is well known that Tomsky also repeatedly betrayed the Party line in the past. The Rights' cadres started to line up even before their open assault on the Party. After Lenin's death, Bukharin organized his own anti-Leninist "school," which held that Bukharin had supposedly been right in his clashes with Lenin. Rykov likewise sought out counterrevolutionary cadres in the Soviet apparatus while Tomsky did the same in the trade unions.[20]~~

~~The Fifteenth Party Congress decided to further expand the offensive against the kulaks and took an array of new measures to limit the development of capitalism in the countryside and advance peasant agriculture onto the path to Socialism. The Rights resisted the Fifteenth Party Congress's decision about the decisive offensive against the kulaks and the private Nepman dealer. They were against industrialization and collectivization.~~

~~This is why the struggle against the Rights was especially necessary.~~

~~The Party anticipated that the growth of the Socialist economy would inevitably provoke A NEW SHARPENING OF CLASS STRUGGLE. The Rights preached a dangerous, malicious, opportunistic idea about the "subsiding" of class struggle that threatened to deaden Party vigilance. The Rights assured the country that with the passage of each day, and with each success of the Socialist offensive, class struggle would "soften" and "SUBSIDE." The Rights announced that the kulak would "pass over peacefully into Socialism." The Rights sedated the Party's revolutionary vigilance in order to more easily conduct their Right-opportunist actions.~~

Before the Party took the offensive against the kulaks, and while it was engaged in liquidating the bloc of Trotskyites and Zinovievites, the Bukharin-Rykov group had been more or less lying low, holding themselves as a reserve of the anti-Party forces, not venturing to support the Trotskyites openly, and sometimes even acting together with the Party against the Trotskyites. But when the Party assumed the offensive against the kulaks, and adopted emergency measures against them, the Bukharin-Rykov group threw off their mask and began to attack the Party policy openly. The kulak soul of the Bukharin-Rykov group got the better of them, and they began to come out openly in defence of the kulaks. They demanded the repeal of the emergency measures, frightening the simple-minded with the argument that otherwise agriculture would begin to "decay," and even affirming that this process had already begun. Blind to the growth of the collective farms and state farms, those superior forms of agricultural organization, and perceiving the decline of kulak farming, they represented the decay of the latter as the decay of agriculture. In order to provide a theoretical backing for their case, they concocted the absurd "theory of the subsidence of the class-struggle," maintaining, on the strength of this theory, that the class struggle would grow milder with every victory gained by Socialism against the capitalist elements, that the class struggle would soon subside altogether and the class enemy would surrender all his positions without a fight, and that, consequently, there was no need for an offensive against the kulaks. In this way they tried to furbish up their threadbare bourgeois theory that the kulaks would peaceably grow into Socialism, and rode roughshod over the well-known thesis of Leninism that the resistance of the class enemy would assume more acute forms as the progress of Socialism cut the ground from under his feet and that the class struggle could "subside"[21] *only after the class enemy was destroyed.*

~~The Rights were against the offensive against the kulaks and advanced the new slogan of one of their representatives, M. I. Frumkin, "From the Fifteenth Party Conference Back to the Fourteenth." But to turn back from the decisions of the Fifteenth Party Congress would have required the renunciation of the offensive against the kulaks. Two letters by Frumkin presented a summary of the Right-opportunist viewpoints and reflected the activities that the Rights were pursuing on the local level, disrupting Socialist construction. The Rights defended the prosperous kulak leadership in the countryside and the private dealer in the cities.~~[22]

It was easy to see that in the Bukharin-Rykov group the Party was faced with a group of Right opportunists who differed from the bloc of Trotskyites and Zinovievites only in form, only in the fact that the Trotskyite and Zinovievite capitulators had had some opportunity of masking their true nature with Left, revolutionary vociferations about "permanent revolution," whereas the Bukharin-Rykov group, attacking the Party as they did for taking the offensive against the kulaks, could not possibly mask their capitulatory character and had to defend the reac-

tionary forces in our country, the kulaks in particular, openly, without mask or disguise.

~~The Rights wanted to frighten the Party with slanderous rumors of the "degradation" (that is, the collapse) of agriculture and of the breakdown of the alliance between the working class and the peasantry that supposedly had taken place.~~

~~In September 1928, Bukharin published an opportunistic article in PRAVDA under the title "Observations of an Economist." He proposed to pursue industrialization less intensively and ease the "bottlenecks." Bukharin announced, for instance, that there were not enough bricks in the country for construction of new enterprises, although the production of bricks could have easily been expanded. He contended that there was an "overextension of capitalist expenditures" in the country and that it was necessary to reduce the tempo of industrialization.~~

The Party understood that sooner or later the Bukharin-Rykov group was bound to join hands with the remnants of the bloc of Trotskyites and Zinovievites for common action against the Party.

Parallel with their political pronouncements, the Bukharin-Rykov group "worked" to muster and organize their following. Through Bukharin, they banded together young bourgeois elements like Slepkov, Maretsky, Eichenwald, Goldenberg; through Tomsky—high bureaucrats in the trade unions (Melnichansky, Dogadov and others); through Rykov—demoralized high Soviet officials (A. Smirnov, Eismont, V. Schmidt, and others). The group readily attracted people who had degenerated politically, and who made no secret of their capitulatory sentiments.

~~About that time, the Rights~~ *About this time the Bukharin-Rykov group* gained the support of high functionaries in the Moscow Party organization (Uglanov, ~~Kotov, Penkov, Ukhanov, Ryutin, Giber, Yagoda, Kulikov, Mikhailov, Matveyev,~~ *Kotov, Ukhanov, Ryutin, Yagoda, Polonsky,* and others).[23] A section of the Rights kept under cover, abstaining from open attacks on the Party line. In the Moscow Party press and at Party meetings, it was advocated that ~~"ongoing~~ concessions ~~to the kulak"~~ must be made *to the kulaks* ~~(in fact, the Rights wanted concessions for the kulaks), complaints were aired about the apparently extraordinary~~, *that heavy* taxation of the kulaks *was inadvisable, that industrialization was burdensome to the people, and that the development of heavy industry was premature*. Uglanov opposed the Dnieper hydro-electric scheme and demanded that funds be diverted from heavy industry to the light industries. Uglanov and the other Right ~~opportunists~~ *capitulators* maintained that Moscow was and would remain a gingham city,[24] and that there was no need to build engineering works in Moscow. ~~The Right opportunists conducted secret, underground factional work within the Moscow Party organization against the Party and its Central Committee.~~

The Moscow Party organization unmasked Uglanov *and his followers* ~~and remained~~, *gave them a final warning and rallied* closer than ever around the ~~Lenin-Stalin~~ Central Committee *of the Party*. At a plenary meeting of the Moscow Committee *of the C.P.S.U.(B.)*, held in 1928, Comrade Stalin said that a fight must be waged on two fronts, with ~~special attention given to~~ *the fire concentrated on* the Right deviation. The Rights, *Comrade Stalin said,* were kulak agents inside the Party. ~~Insofar as the roots of capitalism in the country had not yet been torn up,~~

> "The triumph of the Right deviation in our Party would unleash the forces of capitalism, undermine the revolutionary position of the proletariat and increase the chances of restoring capitalism in our country," said Comrade Stalin. (Stalin, LENINISM, Vol. II.)[25]

~~During the summer of 1928, Bukharin made a criminal, treacherous attempt to ally with the Trotskyites and conducted secret negotiations with Kamenev for a joint struggle against the Party. A record of these hostile negotiations that was made by Kamenev was published in a counter-revolutionary leaflet by the Trotskyites in early 1929 and showed that the Rights had joined the path of double-dealing, deceit and underground struggle. And the Trotskyites and Rights eventually agreed to a program on restoring capitalism. It is not surprising that they subsequently conspired to conduct rotten, destructive work together against the Party.~~

~~Caught in their criminal negotiations with the Trotskyites, the leaders of the Right deviation—Bukharin, Rykov and Tomsky—launched harsh attacks on the Party. In February 1929, they spoke out to announce their own anti-Party, factional, Right-opportunist platform.~~

~~The April 1929 Central Committee Plenum condemned Bukharin, Rykov and Tomsky's Right-opportunistic activity. In Comrade Stalin's speech to the plenum "On the Right Deviation in the C.P.S.U.(B.)," he completely unmasked the anti-Leninist views of Bukharin and the others. The Party did everything in its power to return the Rights to the path of Party-mindedness and Leninism before drawing organizational conclusions about the Rights in the same way as it had about the Trotskyites, Zinovievites, Democratic-Centralists and Anarcho-Syndicalists. But the Rights continued with their anti-Party activity.~~

At the beginning of 1929 it was discovered that Bukharin, authorized by the group of Right capitulators, had formed connections with the Trotskyites, through Kamenev, and was negotiating an agreement with them for a joint struggle against the Party. The Central Committee exposed these criminal activities of the Right capitulators and warned them that this affair might end lamentably for Bukharin, Rykov, Tomsky and the rest. But the Right capitulators would not heed the warning. At a meeting of the Central Committee they advanced a new anti-Party platform, in the form of a declaration, which the Central Committee condemned. ~~The plenum warned the Rights where their factional activity was headed, that they were slipping toward Menshevism and counter-revolution.~~ *It warned them again, reminding them of what had happened to the bloc of Trotskyites and Zinovievites. In spite of this, the Bukharin-Rykov group persisted in their anti-Party activities.* Rykov, Tomsky and Bukharin ~~began to demand that they be allowed to resign~~ *tendered to the Central Committee their resignations*, believing that they would intimidate the Party thereby. ~~The plenum~~ *The Central Committee* passed condemnation on this saboteur policy of resignations. *Finally, a* plenum of the Central Committee, held in November 1929, declared that the propaganda of the views of the Right opportunists ~~and reconciliation with them~~ was incompatible with membership of the Party; it resolved that Bukharin, ~~(~~as the instigator and leader of the Right ~~opportunists~~ *capitulators*~~)~~, be removed from the Political Bureau of the Central Committee, and issued a grave warning to Rykov, Tomsky and other members of the Right opposition.

~~After that, the chieftains of the Right opposition "confessed" to their errors and the correctness of the Party's political line.~~[26] *Perceiving that matters had taken a lamentable turn, the chieftains of the Right capitulators submitted a statement acknowledging their errors and the correctness of the political line of the Party.*

~~But this was no more than a double-dealing manoeuver that the Trotskyites had tried before the Rights.~~ *The Right capitulators decided to effect a temporary retreat so as to preserve their ranks from debacle.*

This ended the first stage of the Party's fight against the Right capitulators.

~~About this time the Rights set up an underground organization against the Party and the Soviet power, creating groups and nests in various cities. The Bukharin "School"—Ryutin, Slepkov, Maretsky and others, under the leadership of Bukharin, Rykov, Tomsky and Uglanov—started down the path of counter-revolution, planning terrorist acts and a counter-revolutionary coup d'état, and entering into negotiations with the Trotskyites and Zinovievites about joint actions. The Rights worked out a line that defended the kulaks and antagonized the middle peasantry against collectivization; they implemented this policy along with Central Asian, Ukrainian and Byelorussian bourgeois nationalists. A. Smirnov, working in the People's Commissariat of Agriculture, supported this policy. The Rights planted wrecking elements in state agricultural agencies. Already at this time, the Rights had come to an agreement with the Socialist Revolutionaries and Mensheviks about a collective struggle against the communist party and the Soviet power.~~

~~The Rights became tied to fascist espionage services.~~[27]

~~In the trade union movement, the Right opportunists attempted to implement a Menshevik shop policy. The Rights spoke out against Socialist emulation and shock work. At the Ninth Trade Union Conference (December 1928), the Rights made a factional attack against the Party. In order to correct the anti-Bolshevik line advanced by Tomsky, Dogadov, Melnichansky and other Rights in the trade unions, the Party sent a group of comrades under L. M. Kaganovich to the congress. The Rights vigorously resisted the Central Committee's decision. In particular, they objected to Comrade Kaganovich's joining the All-Union Central Council of Trade Unions, knowing of his uncompromising stance in the struggle with opportunism and his principled consistency and straightforwardness. Under Tomsky, 93 delegates to the Ninth Congress of Trade Unions voted against the Central Committee's proposal after conspiring to do so beforehand. The Central Committee removed Tomsky from the trade union movement leadership, inasmuch as he was implementing an anti-Party line. The trade union bureaucrats among the Rights (the "Group of 93") became the "cadres" of an underground counter-revolutionary Rightist group.~~

~~Insofar as Trotskyism was defeated during this period, the centre of gravity for anti-Party elements shifted to the Rights. The Rights, after all, stood for the restoration of capitalism as had the Trotskyites, and the different "shading" of their views did not prevent them from acting as one against the Bolshevik Party. The Rights' struggle against the Party revived the imperialists' ideas of organizing an anti-Soviet bloc and then invading the U.S.S.R.~~

The new differences within the Party did not escape the attention of the external enemies of the Soviet Union. Believing that the "new dissensions" in the Party were a sign of its weakness, they made a new attempt to involve the U.S.S.R. in war and to thwart the work of industrialization before it had got properly under way. In the summer of 1929, ~~the imperialist governments attempted to test the defencive capacity of the Soviet Union.~~ *t*he imperialists provoked a conflict between China and the Soviet Union, and instigated the seizure of the Chinese Eastern Railway (which belonged to the U.S.S.R.) by the Chinese militarists, and an attack on our Far-Eastern frontier by troops of the Chinese Whites. ~~But the Special Red Banner Far East Red Army under the command of Comrade Blyukher not only wiped out the Chinese militarists' raid, but taught them a serious lesson by defeating the militarists' troops on Manchurian territory before returning across the border.~~ *But this raid of the Chinese militarists was promptly liquidated; the militarists, routed by the Red Army, retreated and the conflict ended in the signing of a peace agreement with the Manchurian authorities.*

The peace policy of the U.S.S.R. ~~was greeted with sympathy and support by the workers of all capitalist countries~~ *once more triumphed in the face of all obstacles, notwithstanding the intrigues of external enemies and the "dissensions" within the Party.*

~~Thanks to the growth of the U.S.S.R.'s economic and political might, its defensive capacity and its peace policy, it was able to quickly and successfully eliminate the conflict on the Chinese Eastern Railroad and reestablish diplomatic and trade relations with Great Britain.~~ *Soon after this diplomatic and trade relations between the U.S.S.R. and Great Britain, which had been severed by the British*[28] *Conservatives, were resumed.* ~~Trade relations with the capitalist states grew stronger.~~

While successfully repulsing the attacks of the external and internal enemies, the Party was busily engaged in developing heavy industry, organizing Socialist emulation, building up state farms and collective farms, and, lastly, preparing the ground for the adoption and execution of the First Five-Year Plan for the development of the national economy.

~~8. Sixth Comintern Congress (July 1928)~~[29]

~~The Sixth Comintern Congress gathered in Moscow in June 1928. In the capitalist countries at that time, the proletariat had already recovered from the defeats of the previous five years and had again resumed the struggle against the capitalists.~~

~~The Sixth Comintern Congress evaluated the successes of Socialism in the U.S.S.R. The congress ratified a program which had been worked out by Comrade Stalin. Entire sections of this program such as, for instance, the section on the dictatorship of the proletariat, were based on the results of the experience of building the first Socialist state in the world.~~

~~Bukharin denied the rotten and contradictory nature of the capitalist world's stabilization. He announced that postwar capitalism had become "organized capitalism" and would now supposedly have the power to deal with the anarchy of capitalist production and crises.~~

~~Bukharin made this rotten, counter-revolutionary theory one of the cornerstones of his counter-revolutionary work to transform his Rights into fascist cadres.~~

~~Comrade Stalin vigorously struggled with the Right-opportunist, Menshevist positions represented by Bukharin and others at the congress.~~

~~Only a year later, the harsh world economic crisis that began in 1929 reduced Bukharin's already-defeated Right-opportunist theory of "organized capitalism" to ashes.~~

~~The most important questions that were discussed at the Sixth Comintern Congress—concerning the danger of war, colonial policy and the Comintern program—were resolved with reference to the international significance of the C.P.S.U.(B.)'s revolutionary experience and the experience of building the Soviet state.~~

~~The Sixth Comintern Congress pointed all communist parties to the imperative of renewed struggle with the Right deviation and a refusal to reconcile with it. The Rightist deviation at this time was the chief danger in the Comintern as well. Bukharin and his group headed the struggle of anti-Bolshevik elements within the fraternal parties of the Comintern—in Germany, where the Rights (Brandler, etc.) waged a struggle against the leader of the German communist party, Comrade Telman, in Czechoslovakia and in America. Bukharin's speeches, like his article "On Organized Capitalism," showed that the Rights were kow-towing before imperialism and acting like defenders of the imperialist bourgeoisie. The Tenth Plenum of the Comintern's Executive Committee (1929) thus expelled Bukharin from the Comintern Presidium and declared the defence of Rightist deviationist views to be incompatible with membership in the communist party. The Communist Party was to purge its ranks of Rightist opportunists on the basis of this decision.~~

~~9. Sixteenth Party Conference (April 1929) and the First Five-Year Plan for the Economy~~

~~The Sixteenth All-Union Party Conference mobilized the Party for the Socialist offensive, for the Socialist reconstruction of the entire economy. Before the conference, the Rights (Rykov, Bukharin and Tomsky) had unveiled their own opportunistic program for a TWO-YEAR PLAN that was to displace the Five-Year Plan and disrupt the policies of the Socialist industrialization of the country. The conference rejected the proposal and ratified the so-called "OPTIMAL VARIANT OF THE FIVE-YEAR PLAN"—that is, a variant of the Five-Year Plan in which the tasks for the Socialist restructuring of the U.S.S.R. were maximally developed.~~ *In April 1929, the Party held its Sixteenth Conference, with the First Five-Year Plan as the main item on the agenda. The conference rejected the "minimal" variant of the Five-Year Plan advocated by the Right capitulators and adopted the "optimal" variant as binding under all circumstances.*

Thus, the Party adopted the celebrated First Five-Year Plan for the construction of Socialism.

The *Five-Year-P*lan fixed the volume of capital investments in the national economy in the period 1928–33 at 64,600,000,000 rubles. Of this sum, ~~16,400,000,000~~ *19,500,000,000* rubles were to be invested in industrial and electric-power development ~~(only 4,400,000,000 had been spent on the re-equipping of industry in the preceding four years). Of this sum, 3,100,000,000 rubles were to be spent on electrification. 10,000,000,000 rubles were to be spent on transport; 23,200,000,000 on agriculture,~~ *10,000,000,000 rubles in transport development and 23,200,000,000 rubles in agriculture.* ~~Such big expenditures on the development of large-scale industry, on electrification, transport and~~

~~agriculture, meant that the entire face of the country would change and that the foundation of a Socialist economy would be laid.~~

This was a colossal plan for the equipment of industry and agriculture of the U.S.S.R. with modern technique.

> "The fundamental task of the Five-Year Plan," said Comrade Stalin, "was to create such an industry in our country as would be able to re-equip and reorganize, not only the whole of industry, but also transport and agriculture—on the basis of Socialism." (Stalin, PROBLEMS OF LENINISM, Russ. ed., p. 485.)

~~As approved, the Five-Year Plan demanded that the enemies of the Five-Year Plan—the Rights and Trotskyites—be mercilessly rebuffed, along with anyone wavering from the Party line. The conference warned that the Rightist deviation represented an open rejection of Leninist Party policy, an "OPEN SHIFT OVER TO THE KULAKS' POSITION." The conference pointed out that the greatest danger within the Party was the Rightist deviation as a representation of the openly opportunistic surrender of Leninist positions in the face of pressure from the class enemy.~~

~~In regard to agriculture, the Party made collectivization and the construction of state farms the chief task of the Five-Year Plan. A network of machine and tractor stations was created, which played an enormous role in the development of Socialist agriculture.~~[30]

For all the immensity of this plan, it did not nonplus or surprise the Bolsheviks. The way for it had been prepared by the whole course of development of industrialization and collectivization and it had been preceded by a wave of labour enthusiasm which caught up the workers and peasants and which found expression in SOCIALIST EMULATION.

The Sixteenth Party Conference adopted an appeal *to all working people,* calling for the further development of Socialist emulation ~~in the city and country~~.

~~Socemulation~~ *Socialist emulation*[31] had produced many an instance of exemplary ~~new-style~~ labour *and of a new attitude to labour.* In many factories, collective farms and state farms, the workers and collective farmers drew up COUNTER-PRODUCTION PLANS for an output exceeding that provided for in the state plans. They displayed heroism in labour. They not only fulfilled, but exceeded the plans of Socialist development laid down by the Party and the Government. *The attitude to labour had changed. From the involuntary and penal servitude it had been under capitalism, it was becoming "a matter of honour, a matter of glory, a matter of valour and heroism." (Stalin.)*

New industrial construction on a gigantic scale ~~developed~~ *was in progress* all over the country;. The Dnieper hydro-electric scheme was in full swing;.

Construction work on the Kramatorsk and Gorlovka Iron and Steel Works and the reconstruction of the Lugansk Locomotive Works had begun in the Donetz Basin~~;~~. *N*ew collieries and blast furnaces came into being. The Urals Machine-Building Works and the Berezniki and Solikamsk Chemical Works were under construction in the Urals. Work was begun on the construction of the iron and steel mills of Magnitogorsk. The erection of ~~the first~~ *big* automobile plants in Moscow~~;~~ *and* Gorky ~~and Yaroslavl~~ was well under way, as was the construction of giant tractor plants, harvester combine plants, *and a mammoth agricultural machinery plant in Rostov-on-Don*. The Kuznetsk collieries, the Soviet Union's second coal base, were being extended. ~~The exploitation of natural mineral resources beyond the Arctic circle, in Khibingorsk (Kirovsk), began under the energetic participation of S. M. Kirov. Factories were also built in Siberia and Central Asia.~~ *An immense tractor works sprang up in the steppe near Stalingrad in the space of eleven months. In the erection of the Dnieper Hydro-Electric Station and the Stalingrad Tractor Works, the workers beat world records in productivity of labour.*

History had never known industrial construction on such a gigantic scale, such enthusiasm for new development, such labour heroism on the part of the working-class millions.

It was a veritable upsurge of labour enthusiasm, produced and stimulated by Socialist emulation.

~~An immense tractor works sprang up in the space of eleven months in the steppe near Stalingrad (the former Tsaritsyn), there where in 1918 Comrade Stalin and Voroshilov defeated the Whiteguards. In the erection of the Dnieper Hydro-Electric Station and the Stalingrad Tractor Works, the workers beat world records in productivity of labour.~~

~~All of this was realized only because the working class and peasantry unreservedly trusted the Bolshevik Party, which was leading our country to Socialism under the leadership of Comrade Stalin.~~

~~The development of self-criticism, the improvement of production meetings and the struggle for economy and Socialist rationalization helped to mobilize the masses for the fulfilment of the tasks of the First Five-Year Plan.~~

~~The Bolshevik Party summoned hundreds of thousands of workers and employees to ensure mass control over the economy and to verify the precise implementation of the decisions of the Party and Government. The Party called upon the workers and employees to struggle with bureaucratic distortions in the state apparatus and to purge it of class-alien, wrecking elements. The Party promoted workers and peasants into the Soviet apparatus on a massive scale to replace the alien elements that had been purged. The Party purge (1929) strengthened Party ranks, expelling from them all alien, unfit elements.~~

All of these measures were branches of the broader Socialist offensive, which was being conducted under the leadership of the Bolshevik Party, the Party of Lenin and Stalin.

10. A Year of Great Change (1929)

On the twelfth anniversary of the Great October Socialist Revolution, Comrade Stalin drew noteworthy conclusions in regard to the struggle for the construction of a Socialist society in our country in his article "A Year of Great Change," which was printed in PRAVDA.

> "The past year," wrote Comrade Stalin, "was a year of great change on all the fronts of Socialist construction. This breakthrough occurred in connection with the decisive Socialist OFFENSIVE against capitalist elements in the city and countryside. The unique characteristic of this offensive was that it has already given us an array of SUCCESSES in the most fundamental areas of Socialist economic restructuring (reconstruction)." (Stalin, PROBLEMS OF LENINISM, Russ. ed., p. 288.)

The main task of the Party was to bring the First Five-Year Plan to fruition, including the development of fast tempos in the industrialization of the country and the Socialist reconstruction of the countryside. The plan for industry was already overfulfilled during the first year of the Five-Year Plan, and the state budget was sound.

1929's results showed that one of the most difficult tasks of Socialist industrialization—that of ACCUMULATING the resources for building large-scale industry—had been solved in basic terms.

> "The past year has shown," wrote Comrade Stalin in his article, "that despite the visible and invisible financial blockade of the U.S.S.R., we were not forced into servitude under the capitalists and successfully solved the problem of accumulation with our own resources, laying down the foundations for large-scale industry." (Stalin, PROBLEMS OF LENINISM, Russ. Ed., p. 290.)

The November 1929 Central Committee Plenum approved the final figures for the 1929–30 year which far surpassed the dimensions of the Five-Year Plan. By November 15, 92 per cent of the grain-growing plan was complete—something that had never been accomplished before. This provided the proletarian state with basic foodstuffs. The Rightist doubters' "prophecy" about the inevitable slowdown of industrialization tempos utterly collapsed, as did talk

~~of the "degradation" of agriculture. The correctness of the Party's general line was brilliantly confirmed in all areas of economic activity.~~

~~The years of the great change provided no few examples of an upsurge of heroic labour and overfulfilling the norm.~~

~~This was a great transformation of people, a development of truly Socialist labour discipline, and a new Communist relationship to labour. All of the Party's work was restructured. The Party organizations turned their faces to the question of production and organized and led Socialist emulation, which quickly became the method of work not only in the city, but in the countryside. People's views about work changed. Labour changed from involuntary, hard prison labour, as it had been under capitalism, to "a matter of HONOR, a matter of GLORY, a matter of VALOR and HEROISM" (STALIN). The PRODUCTIVITY OF LABOUR rose in the Socialist enterprises and construction sites. Already during the first half of 1930, Socialist emulation embraced no less than two million workers.~~

~~Not just in the city, but in agriculture the year of the great change was a year of great victories for Socialism. In agriculture, this breakthrough was expressed in the turnabout of the main body of the peasant masses from the path of petty private farming onto the path of collective, Socialist economy.~~

This time the peasants did not lag behind the workers. In the countryside, too, this labour enthusiasm began to spread among the peasant masses who were organizing their collective farms. The peasants definitely began to turn to collective farming. In this a great part was played by the state farms and the machine and tractor stations. The peasants would come in crowds to the state farms and machine and tractor stations to watch the operation of the tractors and other agricultural machines, admire their performance and there and then resolve: "Let's join the collective farm." Divided and disunited, each on his tiny, dwarf individually-run farm, destitute of anything like serviceable implements or traction, having no way of breaking up large tracts of virgin soil, without prospect of any improvement on their farms, crushed by poverty, isolated and left to their own devices, the peasants had at last found a way out, an avenue to a better life, in the amalgamation of their small farms into co-operative undertakings, collective farms; in tractors, which are able to break up any "hard ground," any virgin soil; in the assistance rendered by the state in the form of machines, money, men, and counsel; in the opportunity to free themselves from bondage to the kulaks, who had been quite recently defeated by the Soviet Government and forced to the ground, to the joy of the millions of peasants.

On this basis began the mass collective-farm movement, which later developed rapidly, especially towards the end of 1929, progressing at an unprecedented rate, a rate unknown even to our Socialist industry.

In 1928 ~~collective farms sowed~~ *total crop area of the collective farms was* 1,390,000 hectares, ~~while~~ in 1929 it was 4,262,000 hectares~~; the middle peas-~~

~~ant joined the collective farm~~, *while in 1930 the ploughing plan of the collective farms was already 15,000,000 hectares.*

~~The swift rise in the collectivization of agriculture led to desperate resistance on the part of the kulaks, who mobilized all their power against the collective farm movement. Class struggle in the countryside related to the collectivization of agriculture heated up with enormous force: the kulaks' actions against the organization of the collective farms, their setting of fires, killing of cattle, spoilage of stored grain and murder of rural newspaper correspondents and active Young Communist League leaders, etc. It thus transpired that the warnings of Lenin and Stalin were justified and that the successes of Socialism would be accompanied by the most desperate, savage resistance on the part of the perishing parasites from within the exploitative elements.~~

> *"It must be admitted," said Comrade Stalin in his article, "A Year of Great Change" (1929), in reference to the collective farms, "that such an impetuous speed of development is unequalled even in our socialized large-scale*[32] *industry, which in general is noted for its outstanding speed of development."*

This was a turning point in the development of the collective-farm movement. This was the beginning of a mass collective-farm movement.

> *"What is the NEW feature of the present collective-farm movement?" asked Comrade Stalin in his article, "A Year of Great Change." And he answered:*
>
> *"The new and decisive feature of the present collective-farm movement is that the peasants are joining the collective farms not in separate groups, as was formerly the case, but in whole villages, whole VOLOSTS (rural districts), whole districts and even whole areas. And what does that mean? It means that THE MIDDLE PEASANT HAS JOINED THE COLLECTIVE-FARM MOVEMENT. And that is the basis of that radical change in the development of agriculture which represents the most important achievement of the Soviet Government. . . ."*

~~During this time, the Party advanced the slogan calling for~~ *This meant that the time was becoming ripe, or had already become ripe, for* the elimination of the kulaks as a class, on the basis of solid collectivization ~~of agriculture~~.

Brief Summary

During the period 1926–29, the Party grappled with and overcame immense difficulties on the home and foreign fronts in the fight for the Socialist industrialization[33] of the country. ~~During this period, the policy of the Socialist industrialization of the country and fast tempos for industrialization emerged fully victorious under the leadership of Comrade Stalin.~~ *The efforts of the Party and the working class ended in the victory of the policy of Socialist industrialization.*

In the main, one of the most difficult problems of industrialization had been solved, namely, the problem of accumulating[34] funds for the building of *a heavy* industry. The foundations were laid of a heavy industry capable of ~~redoing~~ *re-equipping* the entire national economy.

The First Five-Year Plan of Socialist construction was adopted. The building of new factories, state farms and collective farms was developed on a vast scale.

~~The First Five-Year Plan began to be successfully fulfilled. The Five-Year Plan's fulfilment established the technical and economic independence of the U.S.S.R. from the capitalist encirclement, strengthening the international position of the land of the Soviets.~~

This advance towards Socialism was attended by a sharpening of the class struggle in the country and a sharpening of the struggle within the Party. The chief results of this struggle were that *the resistance of the kulaks was crushed*, the bloc of Trotskyite~~s~~ and Zinovievite~~s~~ *capitulators* was ~~completely~~ exposed as ~~a counter-revolutionary~~ *an anti-Soviet* bloc, the Right~~s~~ *capitulators* were exposed as agents of the kulaks, the Trotskyites were expelled from the Party, and the views of the Trotskyites and the Right opportunists were declared incompatible with membership of the C.P.S.U.(B.).

Defeated *ideologically* by the Bolshevik Party ~~in ideological terms~~, and having lost all support among the working class, the Trotskyites ceased to be a political trend and became *an unprincipled, careerist clique of political swindlers,* a ~~double-dealing, predatory~~ gang of ~~spies~~ *political double-dealers.* ~~The Trotskyites turned for assistance to the imperialists, aiming to overthrow the Soviet power and restore capitalism through foreign intervention.~~

~~The Party persuaded the working class of the imperative of fast tempos for industrialization and rallied the working people, mobilizing them.~~ *Having laid the foundations of a heavy industry, the Party mustered the working class and the peasantry* for the fulfilment of the First Five-Year Plan for the Socialist reconstruction of the U.S.S.R. Socialist emulation developed all over the country among ~~the~~ millions *of working people*, giving rise to a mighty wave of labour enthusiasm and originating a new labour discipline.

This period ended with a year of great change, signalized by sweeping ~~victories~~ *gains* of Socialism *in industry*, ~~the victory of the general Party line in the city and the countryside, the strengthening of its influence over the masses,~~ *the first important successes in agriculture, the swing of the middle peasant towards the collective farms, and the beginning of a mass collective-farm movement.*

~~On the basis of the successes of Socialist industrialization, the Bolshevik Party launched the struggle for the solution to the next major task in the construction of a Socialist society—the task of the COLLECTIVIZATION of agriculture.~~

CHAPTER ELEVEN

The Bolshevik Party in the Struggle for the Collectivization of Agriculture (1930–1934)

1. International ~~Position of the U.S.S.R.~~ *Situation* in 1930–34. *Economic Crisis in the Capitalist Countries. Japanese Annexation of Manchuria. Fascists' Advent to Power in Germany. Two Seats of War*

While in the U.S.S.R. important progress had been made in the Socialist industrialization of the country and industry was rapidly developing, in the capitalist countries a devastating world economic crisis of unprecedented dimensions had broken out *at the end of 1929 and grew steadily more acute in the three following years.* ~~The partial stabilization of capitalism had come to an end.~~ The industrial crisis was interwoven ~~in the capitalist countries~~ with an agrarian crisis, *which made matters still worse for the capitalist countries.* ~~In order to maintain high prices and high profits, the capitalists destroyed a colossal amount of produce. Hundreds of millions of poods of grain were burned in ships' boilers or dumped into the sea. Grain and cotton harvests were destroyed, as were millions of head of cattle.~~

In the three years of economic crisis (1930–33), industrial output in the U.S.A. had sunk to 65[1] *per cent, in Great Britain to 86 per cent, in Germany to 66 per cent and in France to 77 per cent of the 1929 output. Yet in this same period industrial output in the U.S.S.R. more than doubled, amounting in 1933 to 201 per cent of the 1929 output.*[2]

This was but an additional proof of the superiority of the Socialist economic system over the capitalist economic system. It showed that the country of Socialism is the only country in the world which is exempt from economic crises.

The world economic crisis condemned 24,000,000 unemployed ~~(60,000,000 if their families are taken into account)~~ to starvation, poverty and ~~extinction~~ *misery*. The agrarian crisis brought suffering to tens of millions of peasants.

The world economic crisis further aggravated the contradictions between the ~~most important~~ imperialist states, between the victor countries and the vanquished countries, between the imperialist states and the colonial and

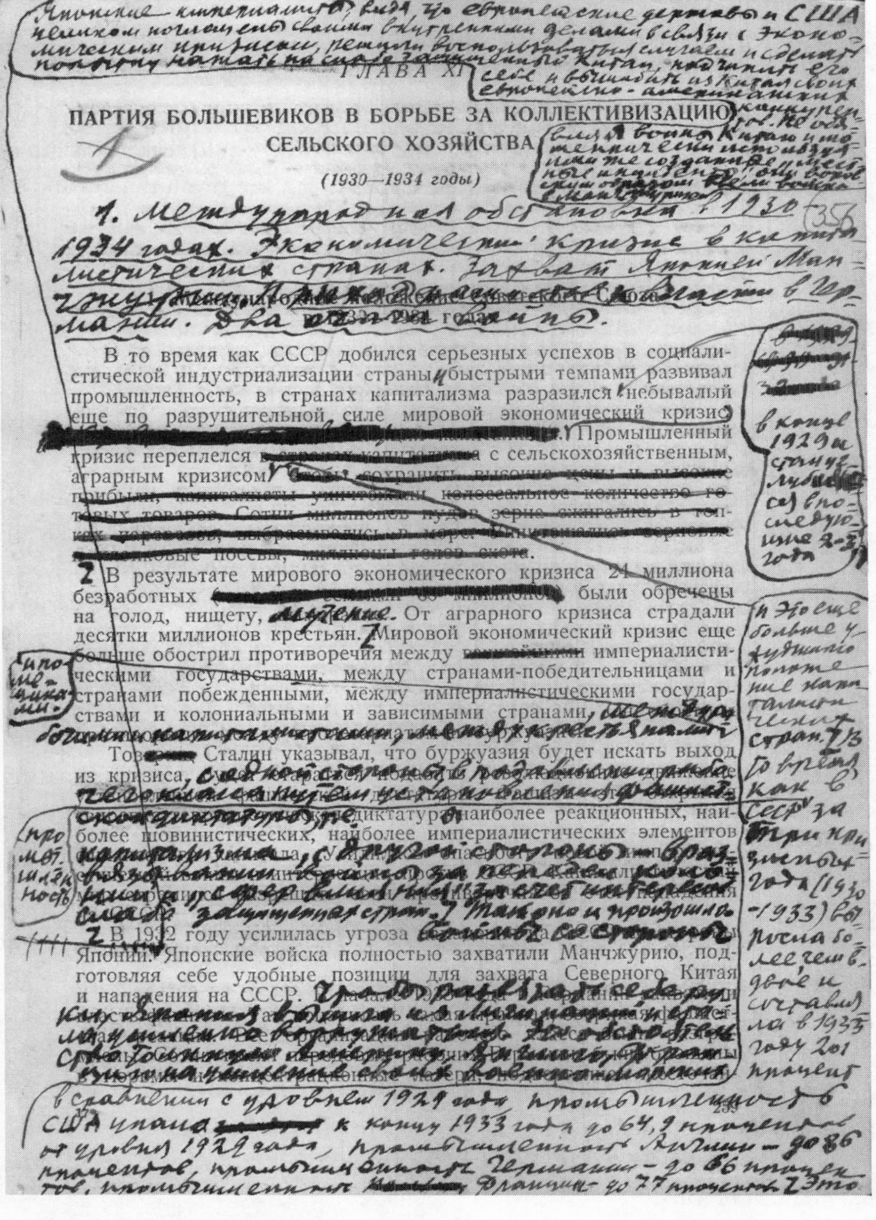

ГЛАВА XI

ПАРТИЯ БОЛЬШЕВИКОВ В БОРЬБЕ ЗА КОЛЛЕКТИВИЗАЦИЮ СЕЛЬСКОГО ХОЗЯЙСТВА

(1930—1934 годы)

В то время как СССР добился серьезных успехов в социалистической индустриализации страны и быстрыми темпами развивал промышленность, в странах капитализма разразился небывалый еще по разрушительной силе мировой экономический кризис. Промышленный кризис переплелся с сельскохозяйственным, аграрным кризисом.

В результате мирового экономического кризиса 24 миллиона безработных были обречены на голод, нищету, мучения. От аграрного кризиса страдали десятки миллионов крестьян. Мировой экономический кризис еще больше обострил противоречия между империалистическими государствами, между странами-победительницами и странами побежденными, между империалистическими государствами и колониальными и зависимыми странами,

Товарищ Сталин указывал, что буржуазия будет искать выход из кризиса,

диктатуры наиболее реакционных, наиболее шовинистических, наиболее империалистических элементов

В 1932 году усилилась угроза

Японии. Японские войска полностью захватили Манчжурию, подготовляя себе удобные позиции для захвата Северного Китая и нападения на СССР.

First page of Chapter Eleven with Stalin's editing from the summer of 1938. RGASPI, f. 558, op. 11, d. 1211, l. 356.

dependent countries, *between the workers and the capitalists, between the peasants and the landlords.* ~~It aggravated the contradictions between the proletariat and the bourgeoisie.~~

In his report on behalf of the Central Committee to the Sixteenth Party Congress, Comrade Stalin pointed out that the bourgeoisie would seek a way out of the *economic* crisis, ~~and would attempt to put down the revolutionary movement~~ *on the one hand, by crushing the working class* through the establishment of fascist dictatorship~~. Fascism is an openly savage, terroristic dictatorship~~, *i.e., the dictatorship* of the most reactionary, most chauvinistic, most imperialistic *capitalist* elements ~~of finance capital~~, *and, on the other hand, by fomenting war for the redivision of colonies and spheres of influence at the expense of the poorly defended countries.* ~~The danger of a new imperialist war and an invasion of the U.S.S.R. mounted. The capitalist world aimed to resolve its contradictions by attacking the U.S.S.R.~~

That is just what happened.

In 1932 the *war* danger ~~of an attack on the U.S.S.R.~~ was aggravated by Japan. *Perceiving that, owing to the economic crisis, the European powers and the U.S.A. were wholly engrossed in their domestic affairs, the Japanese imperialists decided to seize the opportunity and bring pressure to bear on poorly defended China, in an attempt to subjugate her and to lord it over the country.*[3] *Unscrupulously exploiting "local incidents" they themselves had provoked, the Japanese imperialists, like robbers, without declaring war on China, marched their troops into Manchuria.* The Japanese soldiery seized the whole of Manchuria, thereby preparing a convenient place d'armes for the conquest of North China and for an attack on the U.S.S.R. *Japan withdrew from the League of Nations in order to leave her hands free, and began to arm at a feverish pace.*

This impelled the U.S.A., Britain and France to strengthen their naval armaments in the Far East. It was obvious that Japan was out to subjugate China and to eject the European and American imperialist powers from that country. They replied by increasing their armaments.

But Japan was pursuing another purpose, too, namely, to seize the Soviet Far East. Naturally, the U.S.S.R. could not shut its eyes to this danger, and began intensively to strengthen the defences of its Far Eastern territory.

Thus, in the Far East, thanks to the Japanese fascist imperialists, there arose the first seat of war.

But it was not only in the Far East that the economic crisis aggravated the contradictions of capitalism. It aggravated them in Europe too. The prolonged crisis in industry and agriculture, the huge volume of unemployment, and the growing[4] *insecurity of the poorer classes fanned the discontent of the workers and peasants. The discontent of the working class grew into revolutionary disaffection. This was particularly the case in Germany, which was economically exhausted by the war, by the payment of reparations to the Anglo-French victors, and by the economic crisis, and the working class of which languished under a double yoke, that of the home and the foreign, the British and French, bourgeoisie. The extent of this discontent was clearly indicated by the six million votes cast for the German Communist Party at the last Reichstag elections, before the fascists came to power.*[5] ~~At the beginning of 1933, the fascists seized power in Germany. The darkest, most savage reaction reigned there. Hundreds of thousands of the most progressive workers were thrown into prison and concentration camps and subjected to the harshest forms of torture. Thousands of communists were executed. The chief of the German proletariat, Comrade Telman, was locked in a fortress.~~ *The German bourgeoisie perceived that the bourgeois-democratic liberties preserved in Germany might play them an evil trick, that the working class might use these liberties to extend the revolutionary movement. They therefore decided that there was only one way of maintaining the power of the bourgeoisie in Germany, and that was to abolish the bourgeois liberties, to reduce the Reichstag to a cipher, and to establish a terrorist bourgeois-nationalist dictatorship, which would be able to suppress the working class and base itself on the petty-bourgeois masses who wanted to revenge Germany's defeat in the war. And so they called to power the fascist party—which in order to hoodwink the people calls itself the National-Socialist Party—well knowing that the fascist party, first, represents that section of the imperialist bourgeoisie which is the most reactionary and most hostile to the working class, and, secondly, that it is the most pronounced party of revenge, one capable of beguiling the millions of the nationalistically minded petty bourgeoisie. In this they were assisted by the traitors to the working class, the leaders of the German Social-Democratic Party, who paved the way for fascism by their policy of compromise.*

These were the conditions which brought about the accession to power of the German fascists in 1933.

Analysing the events in Germany in his report to the Seventeenth Party Congress, Comrade Stalin said:

> *"The victory of fascism in Germany must be regarded not only as a symptom of the weakness of the working class and a result of the betrayals of the working class by the Social-Democratic Party, which paved the way for fascism; it must also be regarded as a symptom of the weakness of the bourgeoisie, of the fact that the bourgeoisie is already unable to rule by the old methods of parliamentarism and bourgeois democracy, and, as a consequence, is compelled in its home policy to resort to terroristic methods of rule. . . ." (J. Stalin, Seventeenth Congress of the C.P.S.U., "Report on the Work of the Central Committee of the C.P.S.U.[B.]," p. 17.)*

~~Comrade Georgy Dimitrov was thrown into prison on the rotten charge of setting fire to the Reichstag. Later it was established that it was the fascists themselves who had set the Reichstag fire. The heroic conduct of Comrade Dimitrov on the stand moved the whole world, dealt fascism a major blow and inspired all those struggling against fascism.~~ *The German fascists inaugurated their home policy by setting fire to the Reichstag, brutally suppressing the working class, destroying its organizations, and abolishing the bourgeois-democratic liberties. They inaugurated their foreign policy by withdrawing from the League of Nations and openly preparing for a war for the* FORCIBLE *revision of the frontiers of the European states to the advantage of Germany.*

~~Having seized power in Germany, fascism began frenzied preparations for war.~~ *Thus, i*n the centre of Europe, *thanks to the German fascists, there arose* a *second* seat of war ~~was created.~~ ~~The threat of an attack on the U.S.S.R. grew even further.~~

Naturally, the U.S.S.R. could not shut its eyes to so serious a fact, and began to keep a sharp watch on the course of events in the West and to strengthen its defences on the Western frontiers.

~~During this period, the traitors to our motherland—the Trotskyites, Zinovievites and Bukharinites—grew even closer to the fascists, negotiated with them about the form and scale of their assistance to one-another and created in the U.S.S.R. an array of organizations devoted to espionage, terrorism and diversion. At the moment that the struggle between the capitalist world and the country of Socialism became most intense, the Trotskyites, Zinovievites and Bukharinites went over to the fascists' camp, becoming its bloody servants.~~

~~The greater the success of Socialist construction, the more stubbornly the imperialists sowed wrecking and espionage organizations into the U.S.S.R. In 1930–31, several such counter-revolutionary, wrecking organizations were exposed. Shortly after the Shakhty affair, a counter-revolutionary organization comprised of bourgeois specialists—the "Promparty"—was uncovered. The trial of the "Promparty" participants demonstrated the close connection between the wreckers and foreign espionage agencies and general staffs. On their orders, the wreckers were preparing to inflict a major blow in the event of war.~~

~~Similarly exposed was the Kondratev-Chayanov kulak party, which was engaged in wrecking in agriculture and fomenting kulak uprisings that fought against the collective and state farms. In the Ukraine, an organization of this type was uncovered which was comprised of bourgeois nationalists—the "Union for the Liberation of the Ukraine"—and which acted on the orders of Polish and German espionage.~~

~~"The Union Bureau of Mensheviks," a Menshevik counter-revolutionary spying and wrecking organization, was also uncovered. The trial of the members of this organization demonstrated that the Mensheviks had completed~~

~~a round of the blackest treacheries, betrayals and crimes against the working class of the U.S.S.R. This trial occurred at the same time as the trial of the Second International, to which other Russian Mensheviks belonged.~~

~~1930 through 1934 were years of stubborn struggle for the Socialist redivision of the peasant economy, for the collectivization of agriculture and simultaneously for the elimination of the most numerous of the exploitative classes—the kulaks. During these years efforts were made to tear up the deepest roots of capitalism.~~

~~The elimination of the kulaks as a class meant the elimination of the kulak servitude in the village, the elimination of the most brutal, most vulgar, most savage class of exploiters, the mad enemies of the Soviet power. Lenin said that the kulak could easily make peace with the landlords, the tsar and the priest, even if they were at odds, but NEVER with the working class. In the history of foreign lands, kulaks had frequently restored the landlords, kings, priests and capitalists to power during earlier revolutions.~~

~~The elimination of the kulaks as a class meant the strengthening of the position of the workers and peasants' government amid the rising threat of military intervention from the capitalist encirclement. It is well known that during the Civil War period, the kulaks did not provide grain for the cities or the Red Army and aided the Whiteguards and interventionists by rebelling against the Soviet power and organizing bandit gangs. If the kulaks had been left in possession of the means of production and grain reserves, they certainly would have used all their class power not only to repeat these "grain strikes," but to commit other counter-revolutionary acts against the Soviet power in the case of a new intervention.~~

2. ~~Transition~~ *From the Policy of Restricting the Kulak Elements* to *the Policy of* Eliminating the Kulaks as a Class ~~on the Basis of Solid Collectivization~~. *Struggle against Distortions of the Party Policy in the Collective-Farm Movement. Offensive against the Capitalist Elements along the Whole Line. Sixteenth Party Congress*

The mass influx of ~~millions of poor and middle~~ *the* peasants into the collective farms in 1929 *and 1930* was a result of the whole preceding work of the Party and the ~~Soviet state~~ *Government*. The growth of Socialist industry, which had begun the mass production of tractors and machines for agriculture; the vigorous measures taken against the kulaks during the grain-purchasing campaigns of 1928 and 1929; the spread of agricultural co-operative societies, which gradually accustomed the peasants to collective farming; the good results obtained by the first collective farms *and state farms*—all this prepared the way for solid collectivization, *when the peasants of entire villages, districts and regions joined*[6] *the collective farms.*

Solid collectivization was not just a peaceful process—the overwhelming bulk of the peasantry simply joining the collective farms—but was a struggle of the peasant masses against the kulaks. Solid collectivization meant that all the land in a village area in which a collective farm was formed passed into the hands of the collective farm; but a considerable portion of this land was held by the kulaks, and therefore the peasants would expropriate them, driving them from the land, dispossessing them of their cattle and machinery and demanding their arrest and eviction from the district by the Soviet authorities.

Solid collectivization therefore meant the elimination of the kulaks.

This was a policy of eliminating the kulaks as a class, on the basis of solid collectivization.

~~A large role in turning the peasantry onto the collective farm path was also played by the STATE FARMS. Thousands of peasants went to see how tractors work and how grain was harvested by machine in the major state farms. Here they saw with their own eyes the advantages of large-scale mechanized agriculture, for which it was necessary to combine together into collective farms.~~[7]

~~After the Fifteenth Congress (1927) the Bolshevik Party did a lot of work to develop the collective farm movement. The collective farms were given enormous aid in the form of credits and machinery. Machine and tractor stations (M.T.S.) were organized that began to work the collective farm fields with tractors, demonstrating to the peasants in the most visible of terms the advantages of collective farming. Already in the middle of 1929, collectivization began to take over entire districts, especially in the grain-growing regions and territories. At the end of 1929, the mighty collective farm movement included a million peasant plots and gave rise to a new confluence of class power in the country.~~

~~The middle peasant had joined the collective farm.~~

~~On the basis of this GREAT CHANGE, which was expressed in the decisive turnabout of the middle peasant masses onto the collective farm path, Comrade Stalin announced the slogan calling for ELIMINATION OF THE KULAKS AS A CLASS on the basis of solid collectivization in his historic speech at the Conference of Marxist Agriculturalists (December 27, 1929).~~

> ~~". . . The collective farm movement," announced Comrade Stalin, "has taken on the character of a mighty, growing, ANTI-KULAK avalanche, sweeping kulak resistance from its path and breaking the kulaks as it lays a path for broad Socialist construction in the countryside." (Stalin, QUESTIONS OF LENINISM, p. 299.)~~[8]

By this time, the U.S.S.R. had a strong enough material base to allow it to ~~strike a blow at~~ *put an end to* the kulaks, break their resistance, eliminate them as a class and replace kulak farming by collective and state farming.

In 1927 the kulaks still produced over 600,000,000 poods of grain ~~and took to market outside the village~~, *of which* about 130,000,000 poods *were available for sale*. In that year the collective and state farms had only 35,000,000 poods of grain available for sale. In 1929, thanks to the Bolshevik Party's firm policy of developing state farms and collective farms, and likewise to the progress made by Socialist ~~industrialization~~ *industry in supplying the countryside with tractors and agricultural machinery*, the collective farms and state farms had become an important factor. In that year the collective farms and state farms already produced no less than 400,000,000 poods of grain, of which over 130,000,000 poods were marketed. This was more than the kulaks had marketed in 1927. And in 1930 the collective farms and state farms were ~~supposed~~[9] to produce ~~according to the plan~~, *and actually did produce*,[10] ~~about~~ *over*[11] 400,000,000 poods of grain for the market, which was incomparably more than had been marketed by the kulaks in 1927.

*Thus, t*hanks to the changed alignment *of class forces* in the economic life of the country, and the existence of the *necessary* material base for the replacement of the kulak grain output by that of the collective and state farms, the Bolshevik Party was able to proceed from the policy of RESTRICTING ~~the exploitative tendencies of~~ the kulaks to a new policy~~, the policy~~ of ELIMINATING THEM AS A CLASS, *on the basis of solid collectivization*.

~~The slogan calling for the elimination of the kulaks as a class, announced by Comrade Stalin on the basis of the Leninist teaching on class struggle in the transition period, entailed a new iteration in the development of that theory. The slogan calling for the elimination of the kulaks as a class on the basis of solid collectivization identified the way to destroy the last base of capitalist exploitation in our country. The slogan played a decisive role in the victory of the collective farms.~~

~~In his speech "On the Questions of Agrarian Policy in the U.S.S.R.," Comrade Stalin subjected an array of anti-Marxist, bourgeois and Right-opportunistic theories that were attempting to halt the Socialist reconstruction of the countryside to a devastating critique. Among the various anti-Marxist theories, Comrade Stalin exposed the Right-opportunistic theory of "spontaneity" in Socialist construction, pointing out that "the Socialist city must bring along with it the petty peasant village, SOWING the countryside with collective farms and state farms and converting the village onto a new Socialist footing." (Stalin, QUESTIONS OF LENINISM, Russ. ed., p. 304.)~~

~~Comrade Stalin underscored that the U.S.S.R. possessed all the most important preconditions for the rapid growth of the collective farm movement, such as the NATIONALIZATION OF THE LAND and the absence of private property, which might otherwise root the peasant to his individual land holding.~~

Prior to 1929, the Soviet Government had pursued a policy of restricting the kulaks. It had imposed higher taxes on the kulak, and had required him to sell grain to the state at fixed prices; by the law on the renting of land it had to a certain extent restricted the amount of land he could use; by the law on the employment of hired labour on private farms it had limited the scope of his farm. But it had not yet pursued a policy of eliminating the kulaks, since the laws on the renting of land and the hiring of labour allowed them to carry on, while the prohibition of their expropriation gave them a certain guarantee in this respect. The effect of this policy was to arrest the growth of the kulak class, some sections of which, unable to withstand the pressure of these restrictions, were forced out of business and ruined. But this policy did not destroy the economic foundations of the kulaks as a class, nor did it tend to eliminate them. It was a policy of restricting the kulaks, not of eliminating them. This policy was essential up to a certain time, that is, as long as the collective farms and state farms were still weak and unable to replace the kulaks in the production of grain.

At the end of 1929, with the growth of the collective farms and state farms, the Soviet Government turned sharply from this policy to the policy of eliminating the kulaks, of destroying them as a class. It repealed the laws on the renting of land and the hiring of labour, thus depriving the kulaks both of land and of hired labourers. It lifted the ban on the expropriation of the kulaks. It permitted the peasants to confiscate cattle, machines and other farm property from the kulaks for the benefit of the collective farms. The kulaks were expropriated. They were expropriated just as the capitalists had been expropriated in the sphere of industry in 1918, with this difference, however, that the kulaks' means of production did not pass into the hands of the state, but into the hands of the peasants united in the collective farms.

This was a profound revolution, a leap from an old qualitative state of society to a new qualitative state, equivalent in its consequences to the revolution of October 1917.

The distinguishing feature of this revolution is that it was accomplished FROM ABOVE, *on the initiative of the state, and directly supported* FROM BELOW *by the millions of peasants, who were fighting to throw off kulak bondage and to live in freedom on the collective farms.*

This revolution, at one blow, solved three fundamental problems of Socialist construction:

a) It eliminated the most numerous class of exploiters in our country, the kulak class, the mainstay of capitalist restoration;

b) It transferred the most numerous labouring class in our country, the peasant class, from the path of individual farming, which breeds capitalism, to the path of co-operative, collective, Socialist farming;

c) It furnished the Soviet regime with a Socialist base in agriculture—the most extensive and vitally[12] necessary, yet least developed, branch of national economy.

This destroyed the last mainsprings of the restoration of capitalism within the country and at the same time created new and decisive conditions for the building up of a Socialist economic system.

Explaining the reasons for the policy of eliminating the kulaks as a class, and summing up the results of the mass movement of the peasants for solid collectivization, Comrade Stalin wrote in 1929:

> *"The last hope of the capitalists of all countries, who are dreaming of restoring capitalism in the U.S.S.R.—'the sacred principle of private property'—is collapsing and vanishing. The peasants, whom they regarded as material manuring the soil for capitalism, are abandoning en masse the lauded banner of 'private property' and are taking to the path of collectivism, the path of Socialism. The last hope for the restoration of capitalism is crumbling." (Stalin,* LENINISM*, "A Year of Great Change," Eng. ed.)*

The ~~slogan~~ *policy* of eliminating the kulaks as a class was embodied in the historic resolution on "The Rate of Collectivization and State Measures to Assist the Development of Collective Farms" adopted by the Central Committee of the C.P.S.U.(B.) on January 5, 1930. ~~On the basis of this decision, the Central Committee, the Central Executive Committee and the U.S.S.R. Council of People's Commissars approved a resolution on February 1, 1930, that forbade the rental of land and the use of hired labour in peasant holdings in districts where there was solid collectivization. Regional executive committees were given the right in districts of solid collectivization to take all necessary measures in the struggle with the kulaks, including even the total confiscation of kulak property and the deportation of the kulaks themselves beyond the district borders. These measures were necessary to break the kulaks' resistance and relied on the support of the poor peasant masses, who were demanding the exile of the kulaks.~~ In this decision ~~from January 5, 1930,~~ full account was taken of the diversity of conditions in the various districts of the U.S.S.R. and the varying degrees ~~of their preparation~~ *to which the regions were ripe*[13] for collectivization.

Different[14] rates of collectivization were established, for which purpose the Central Committee of the C.P.S.U.(B.) divided the regions of the U.S.S.R. into three groups.

The first group included the principal grain-growing areas: viz., the North Caucasus *(the Kuban, Don and Terek)*, the Middle Volga and the Lower Volga, which were ripest for collectivization since they had the most tractors, the most state farms, and the most experience in fighting the kulaks, gained in past grain-purchasing campaigns. The Central Committee proposed that in this group of grain-growing areas collectivization should in the main be completed in the spring of 1931.

The second group *of grain-growing areas*, the Ukraine, the Central Black-Earth Region, Siberia, the Urals, Kazakhstan and others could complete collectivization in the main in the spring of 1932.

The other regions, territories and republics (Moscow Region, Transcaucasia, the republics of Central Asia, *etc.*) could extend the process of collectivization to the end of the Five-Year Plan, that is, to 1933.

In view of the growing speed of collectivization, the Central Committee of the Party considered it necessary to accelerate the construction[15] of plants for the production of tractors, harvester combines, tractor-drawn machinery, etc. Simultaneously, the Central Committee demanded that "the tendency to underestimate the importance of horse traction at the present stage of the collective-farm movement, a tendency which was leading to the reckless disposal and sale of horses, be resolutely checked."

State loans[16] to collective farms for the year 1929–30 were doubled (500,000,000 rubles) ~~and help was to be supplied with land surveying~~ *as compared with the original plan.*

The expense of the surveying and demarcation of the lands of the collective farms was to be borne by the state.

The ~~Central Committee~~ resolution ~~of January 5, 1930,~~ contained the highly important direction that the CHIEF FORM of the collective-farm movement at the given stage must be the agricultural artel, in which only the PRINCIPAL means of production are collectivized.

The Central Committee most seriously warned[17] Party organizations "against any attempts whatsoever to force the collective-farm movement by 'decrees' from above, which might involve the danger of the substitution of mock-collectivization for real Socialist emulation in the organization of collective farms." (RESOLUTIONS OF THE C.P.S.U.[B.], Russ. ed., Part II, p. 662.)

In this resolution the Central Committee made it clear how the Party's new policy in the countryside should be applied.

The policy of eliminating the kulaks as a class and of solid collectivization stimulated a powerful collective-farm movement. The peasants of whole villages and districts joined the collective farms, sweeping the kulaks from their path and freeing themselves from kulak bondage.

~~Such were the Central Committee's exhaustive directives on the tempo of collectivization and the elimination of the kulaks as a class, on the basis of which the Party organizations developed the struggle for a new level in the collective farm movement. But in the course of this struggle, some became "dizzy with success." Many Party organizations and Party workers made crude mistakes as a result of the DIRECT VIOLATION of the Central Committee's directives.~~

~~These errors could have led to extremely dangerous consequences if the Central Committee had not corrected these distortions of the Party line in a firm and decisive manner.~~

~~3. Struggle with Distortions of the Party Line in the Collective Farm Movement~~

~~Already during the second half of February 1930 it was becoming evident that along with collectivization's genuine, serious successes, there were also DISTORTIONS OF THE PARTY LINE in various districts in the U.S.S.R.~~

But with all the phenomenal progress of collectivization, certain faults on the part of Party workers, distortions of the Party policy in collective farm development, soon revealed themselves. Although the Central Committee[18] *had warned Party workers not to be carried away by*[19] *the success of collectivization, many of them began to force the pace of collectivization artificially, without regard to the conditions of time and place, and heedless of the degree of readiness of the peasants to join the collective farms.*

*It was found that t*he ~~Lenin-Stalin~~ VOLUNTARY principle of forming collective farms was being violated, and that in a number of districts the peasants were being FORCED into the collective farms under threat of being dispossessed, disfranchised, and so on. ~~Some of the middle peasants and even poor peasants had been "dekulakized." In some districts, the number of the "dekulakized" reached 15 per cent, and the disfranchised—15–20 per cent.~~

~~As it later transpired, hidden Rightists and Trotskyites had intentionally implemented a policy of "excesses" in many districts: Kabakov and Zubaryev in the Urals, Sheboldayev, Larin and Pivovarov in the North Caucasus, and Goloded and Chervyakov in Byelorussia.~~[20] ~~In an array of districts, hidden enemies of the people intentionally introduced measures that antagonized the peasants and Cossacks. They did this in order to wreck collectivization.~~

In a number of districts, preparatory work and patient explanation of the underlying principles of the Party's policy with regard to collectivization were being replaced[21] by bureaucratic decreeing from above, by exaggerated, fictitious figures regarding the formation of collective farms, by an artificial inflation of the percentage of collectivization. ~~For instance, in a few regions, collectivization levels "grew" from 10 to 90 per cent. Of course, these collective farms existed only on paper.~~

Although the Central Committee had specified that the chief form of the collective-farm movement must be the agricultural artel, in which only the PRINCIPAL means of production are collectivized, in a number of places pigheaded attempts were made to skip the artel form and pass straight to the commune; dwellings, milch-cows, small livestock, *poultry,* etc., not exploited for the market, were ~~allowed to be~~ collectivized ~~by FORCE~~.

Carried away by the initial success of collectivization, *persons in authority in*[22] certain regions violated the Central Committee's explicit instructions regarding the pace and time limits of collectivization. ~~For instance,~~ *I*n their zeal for inflated figures, the leadership of the Moscow Region gave the cue to their subordinates to complete collectivization by the spring of 1930, although they had no less than three years (till the end of 1932) for this purpose. Even grosser were the violations ~~of the Central Committee's directives on the pace of collectivization~~ in Transcaucasia and Central Asia. ~~During the Trial of the Anti-Soviet "Bloc of Rights and Trotskyites," Zelensky, an active participant and an old provocateur of the tsarist OKHRANA, confessed that while holding a leadership position in Central Asia in 1930, he had pursued wrecking goals when he announced the provocative slogan "Catch Up and Surpass the Most Collectivized Districts."~~

~~Crude distortions in the Party line on the collective farm movement also occurred on the basis of direct violations of the Central Committee directives issued in the resolution of January 5, "On the Tempo of Collectivization." Heavy-handed administration and excesses aroused serious dissatisfaction among the middle peasantry. The local Party and Soviet organizations' errors were widely exploited by the CLASS ENEMY.~~

*Taking advantage of these distortions of policy f*or their own provocative ends, the kulaks and their toadies would themselves propose that communes be formed instead of agricultural artels, and that dwellings, small livestock and poultry be collectivized forthwith. Furthermore, the kulaks ~~began to madly~~ instigate*d* the ~~middle~~ peasants to slaughter their animals before entering the collective farms, arguing that "they will be taken away anyhow." The class enemy calculated that the distortions and mistakes committed by the local organizations in the process of collectivization would incense the peasantry and provoke ~~mutinies~~ *revolts*[23] against the Soviet Government. ~~Captured wreckers from the Kondratev-Chayanov kulak gang talked about this in their later testimony.~~

As a result of the mistakes of Party organizations and the downright provocateur actions of the class enemy, in the latter half of February 1930, against the general background of the unquestionable success of collectivization, there were dangerous signs of serious discontent among the peasantry in a number of districts. Here and there, the kulaks and their agents even succeeded in inciting the peasants to outright anti-Soviet actions.

Having received a number of alarming signals of distortions of the Party line that might jeopardize collectivization, the ~~Bolshevik~~ Central Committee of the Party immediately proceeded to remedy the situation, to set the Party workers the task of rectifying the mistakes as quickly as possible. On March 2, 1930, by decision of the Central Committee, Comrade Stalin's ~~historic~~ article, "Dizzy with Success," was published. This article was a warning to all who had been so carried away by the success of collectivization as to commit gross mistakes and depart from the Party line, to all who were trying to coerce the peasants to join the collective farms. The article ~~again~~ laid the utmost emphasis on the principle that the formation of collective farms must be voluntary,[24] and on the necessity of making allowances for the diversity of conditions in the various districts of the U.S.S.R. when determining the pace and methods of collectivization. Comrade Stalin ~~again~~ reiterated that the chief form of the collective-farm movement was the agricultural artel,[25] in which only the principal means of production, chiefly those used in grain growing, are collectivized, while household land, dwellings, ~~a major~~ part of the dairy cattle, small livestock, poultry, etc., are not collectivized.

~~Comrade Stalin demonstrated the scale of the harm and danger of the pigheaded attempts to jump directly from the agricultural artel straight to the commune.~~

> ~~"Angering the peasant-collective farmer with the 'communalization' of dwellings and all of the dairy cows, small livestock and poultry, when the grain problem has still NOT BEEN RESOLVED, and when the artel structure of the collective farms HAS NOT YET BEEN SOLIDIFIED? IS IT NOT CLEAR that this sort of 'policy' could only be convenient and profitable for our accursed enemies?" wrote Comrade Stalin.~~

Comrade Stalin's ~~"Dizzy with Success"~~ article was of the utmost political moment. It helped the Party organizations to rectify their mistakes and dealt a severe blow to the ~~plans of the~~[26] enemies of the Soviet Government who had been hoping to take advantage of the distortions of policy to set the peasants ~~against the Bolshevik Party,~~ against the Soviet Government. The broad mass of the peasants now saw that the line of the Bolshevik Party had nothing in common with the pigheaded "Left" distortions of local authorities. ~~Each copy of the paper in which Comrade Stalin's article appeared was circulated among tens, and even hundreds, of peasant households. In a political sense,~~ The article set the minds of the peasants.

~~Far from all Party workers on the local level immediately grasped the imperative of quickly correcting the mistakes committed during collectivization. The Central Committee's instructions, presented in Comrade Stalin's "Dizzy with Success" article, were met with resistance by a portion of the Party workers who didn't understand the imperative of renouncing all methods of administrative pressure and who didn't want to admit to the mistakes that had been made that required correction. Those collective farms that had been organized~~

~~by heavy-handed administrative pressure began to collapse. The number of collective farms that existed only on paper plummeted in an array of districts.~~

~~In order to strengthen the collective farms and put the collective farm movement on the right path, it was necessary most of all to correct the mistakes and GIVE THE BOLSHEVIK COLLECTIVE FARM CADRES A LESSON ON THE BASIS OF THESE MISTAKES.~~

~~Therefore,~~ *I*n order to complete the work begun by Comrade Stalin's article in rectifying distortions and mistakes, the Central Committee of the C.P.S.U. (B.) ~~again struck~~ *decided to strike* another blow at them ~~with all its might~~, and on March 15, 1930, published its resolution on "Measures to Combat the Distortions of the Party Line in the Collective-Farm Movement."

This resolution made a detailed analysis of the mistakes committed, showing that they were the result of a departure from the Leninist-Stalinist line of the Party, the result of a flagrant breach of Party instructions.

The Central Committee ~~demonstrated~~ *pointed out* that these "Left" distortions were of direct service to the class enemy~~, and that the future growth of the collective farm movement and the elimination of the kulaks as a class would be impossible without the elimination of the distortions in the Party line~~.

~~The Central Committee required the Party organizations to halt the practice of using force in collectivization while at the same time supporting further efforts TO INCORPORATE the peasantry into the collective farms on a voluntary basis and STRENGTHEN already-existing collective farms. Proposals focused most of this attention on the economic improvement of the collective farms and on securing the successes already realized during collectivization. Proposals also called for the immediate correction of mistakes and excesses.~~ The Central Committee gave directions that "persons who are unable or unwilling earnestly to combat distortions of the Party line must be REMOVED from their posts and REPLACED." (RESOLUTIONS OF THE C.P.S.U.[B.], Part II, p. 663.)

The Central Committee changed the leadership of certain regional and territorial Party organizations (Moscow Region, Transcaucasia) which had committed political mistakes and ~~had not rectified~~ *proved incapable of rectifying* them.

On April 3, 1930, Comrade Stalin's "Reply to Collective Farm Comrades" was published, in which he indicated the ROOT CAUSE of the mistakes in the peasant question and the major mistakes committed in the collective-farm movement, VIZ., an incorrect approach to the middle peasant, violation of the Leninist principle that the formation of collective farms must be voluntary, violation of the Leninist principle that allowance must be made for the diversity of conditions in the various districts of the U.S.S.R. ~~in regard to collective farm construction~~, and the attempts to skip the artel form and to pass straight to the commune.

~~Comrade Stalin pointed out in his political report to the Sixteenth Party Congress that attempts to pressure the middle peasantry and the "Leftist" excesses represented "a certain attempt, albeit unintended, to revive Trotskyite traditions in our everyday practices and the Trotskyite relationship to the middle peasantry." The Party decisively rebuffed these attempts to revive the Trotskyite relationship to the middle peasantry.~~

~~The greatest danger for the Party remained the RIGHT DEVIATION. But the "Leftist" excesses in the collective farm movement created a fertile climate for the STRENGTHENING of the Right deviation.~~

~~Pointing to the connection between "Leftist" opportunism and the Right deviation, Comrade Stalin said:~~

> ~~"The uniqueness of the present moment stems from the fact that the struggle with 'Leftist' excesses offers a way and means for successful struggling with Right opportunism." (Stalin, QUESTIONS OF LENINISM, Russ. ed., p. 338.)~~

~~The Party corrected the mistakes and excesses of the collective farm movement. If the Party had not been able to correct the errors in the shortest possible time, the entire business of collectivization would have faced the threat of collapse. As a result of the anti-middle peasant mistakes, the alliance of the workers with the toiling peasantry had threatened to break down, which would have undermined the very foundation of the Soviet state. Anti-collective farm actions in an array of districts that grew over into isolated incidents of anti-Soviet action under the influence of the kulaks testified to the seriousness of the situation. Most alarming in all of this was the fact that there were "frequent attempts on the part of Party organizations to cover up the situation and blame everything on the hesitating middle peasants instead of admitting to and correcting the mistakes on their own." (CENTRAL COMMITTEE APPEAL, Russ. ed., April 2, 1930.)~~

~~"THIS WAS ONE OF THE MOST DANGEROUS PERIODS IN THE LIFE OF OUR PARTY," said Comrade Stalin at the February–March 1937 Central Committee Plenum as he recalled the spring of 1930.~~

The result of all these measures was that the Party secured the correction of the distortions of policy committed by local Party workers in a number of districts.

It required the utmost ~~Leninist-Stalinist~~ firmness on the part of the Central Committee and its ability to go "AGAINST THE CURRENT" in order to promptly correct that *considerable* body of Party workers who, carried away by success, had been rapidly straying from the Party line ~~on the question of the peasantry and collective farm construction~~.

The Party succeeded in correcting the distortions of the Party line in the collective-farm movement.

This made it possible to consolidate the success of the collective farm movement ~~and the securing of a decisive victory for the collective farm system~~.

It also made possible a new and powerful advance of the collective farm movement.

Prior to the Party's adoption of the policy of eliminating the kulaks as a class, an energetic offensive against the capitalist elements with the object of eliminating them had been waged chiefly in the towns, on the industrial front. So far, the countryside, agriculture, had been lagging behind the towns, behind industry. Consequently, the offensive had not borne an all-round, complete and general character. But now that the backwardness of the countryside was becoming a thing of the past, now that the peasants' fight for the elimination of the kulak class had taken clear shape, and the Party had adopted the policy of eliminating the kulak class, the offensive against the capitalist elements assumed a general character, the partial offensive developed into an offensive along the whole front. By the time the Sixteenth Party Congress was convened, the general offensive against the capitalist elements[27] *was proceeding all along the line.*

~~4. Sixteenth Congress of the C.P.S.U.(B.)~~

The Sixteenth Party Congress met on June 26, 1930. It was attended by 1,268 delegates with vote and 891 delegates with voice but no vote, representing 1,260,874 Party members and 711,609 candidate members.

The Sixteenth ~~C.P.S.U.(B.)~~ Party Congress~~, which took place from June 26 to July 13, 1930,~~ is known in the annals of the Party as "the congress of the sweeping offensive[28] of Socialism ALONG THE WHOLE FRONT, of the elimination of the kulaks as a class, and of the realization of solid collectivization." (STALIN.)

~~During previous stages of the struggle for Socialism, the Party had successfully developed the Socialist offensive on certain parts of the economic front (in the area of trade, industrialization and the construction of collective and state farms). This was an attempt at a GENERAL Socialist offensive and at extracting the deepest roots of capitalism. The period of the Sixteenth Party Congress was a period of a general Socialist offensive ALONG THE ENTIRE FRONT, a period of strengthened construction work both in the area of industry and agriculture.~~[29]

Presenting the political report *of the Central Committee* ~~at the Sixteenth Party Congress~~, Comrade Stalin showed what ~~massive~~ *big* victories had been won by the Bolshevik Party in developing the Socialist offensive.

SOCIALIST INDUSTRIALIZATION[30] had progressed so far that the share of industry in the total production of the country now predominated over that of agriculture. In the fiscal year 1929~~/30~~*–30*, the share of industry already comprised no less than 53 per cent of the total production of the country, while the share of agriculture was about 47 per cent.

In the fiscal year 1926–27, at the time of the Fifteenth Party Congress, the TOTAL output of industry ~~(both major and minor)~~ had been *only* 102.5 per cent[31] of the pre-war output; in the year 1929–30, *at the time of the Sixteenth Congress*, it was already about 180 per cent.

Heavy industry—the production of means of production, *machine-building*—was steadily growing in power.

> ". . . We are on the eve of the transformation of our country from an AGRARIAN to an INDUSTRIAL country," declared Comrade Stalin at the congress, amidst hearty acclamation.

*Still, t*he high RATE of industrial development, Comrade Stalin explained, was not to be confused with the LEVEL of industrial development. Despite the unprecedented rate of development of Socialist industry, we were still FAR BEHIND the advanced capitalist countries as regards the LEVEL of industrial development. This was so in the case of electric power,[32] in spite of the phenomenal progress of electrification in the U.S.S.R. This was the case with metal.[33] According to the plan, the output of pig-iron in the U.S.S.R. was to be 5,500,000 tons in the year 1929–30, when the output of pig-iron in Germany in 1929 was 13,400,000 tons, and in France 10,450,000 tons. In order to make good our technical and economic backwardness in the minimum of time, our rate of industrial development had to be further accelerated,[34] and a most resolute fight waged against the opportunists who were striving to reduce the rate of development of Socialist industry.

> ". . . People who talk about the necessity of REDUCING the rate of development of our industry are enemies of Socialism, agents of our class enemies," said Comrade Stalin." (Stalin, LENINISM, "Political Report of the Central Committee to the Sixteenth Congress of the C.P.S.U.," Eng. ed.)

After the program of the first year of the First Five-Year Plan had been successfully fulfilled and surpassed, a slogan originated among the masses—"FULFIL THE FIVE-YEAR PLAN IN FOUR YEARS." A number of branches of industry (oil, peat, general machine-building, agricultural machinery, electrical equipment) were carrying out their plans so successfully that their five-year-plans could be fulfilled in two and a half or three years. This proved that the slogan "The Five-Year Plan in Four Years" was quite feasible, and thus exposed the opportunism of the ~~unfaithful~~ *sceptics*[35] who doubted it.[36]

The Sixteenth Congress instructed the Central Committee of the Party to "ensure that the SPIRITED BOLSHEVIK TEMPO of Socialist construction be maintained, and that the FIVE-YEAR PLAN BE ACTUALLY FULFILLED IN FOUR YEARS."

By the time of the Sixteenth Party Congress, a momentous change had taken place in the development of agriculture in the U.S.S.R.[37] The *broad masses of the* peasantry had turned towards Socialism. On May 1, 1930, collectivization in the principal grain-growing regions embraced 40–50 per cent of the peasant households (as against 2–3 per cent in the spring of 1928). The crop area of the collective farms reached 36,000 hectares.

Thus the *increased* program (30,000,000 hectares), laid down in the resolution of the Central Committee of January 5, 1930, was more than fulfilled. The five-year program of collective farm development had been fulfilled more than one and a half times in the space of two years.

~~In 1930, by Central Committee decision, financing for the collective farms was bolstered and major BENEFITS were established for them. Collective farmers also were given farming equipment taken from those who had been dekulakized that was worth more than 400 million rubles.~~

In three years the amount of produce marketed by the collective farms had increased more than forty-fold. Already in 1930 more than half the marketed grain in the country came from the collective farms, *quite apart from the grain produced by the state farms*.

*This meant that from now on t*he fortunes of agriculture ~~and its fundamental problems now~~ would ~~begin to~~ be decided not by the individual peasant farms, but by the collective and state farms.

While, before the mass influx of the ~~middle~~ peasantry into the collective farms, ~~Socialist relations in the U.S.S.R.~~ *the Soviet power* had leaned ~~almost exclusively~~ *mainly* on Socialist industry, now it began to lean also on the rapidly expanding Socialist sector of agriculture, ~~(~~the collective and state farms~~)~~.

The collective farm peasantry, as the Sixteenth Party Congress stated in *one of* its resolutions, had become "a real and firm mainstay of the Soviet power."

~~5. Underground Struggle of the Bukharinites and Trotskyites against the Party and Soviet State~~[38]

~~In the fall of 1930, the double-dealing, anti-Party group of Syrtsov, Lominadze and Shatskin, known as the Rightist-"Leftist" Bloc, was uncovered. This group, consisting of Trotskyite elements—the "Lefts" (Lominadze, Shatskin)—and Rightist elements, came together on the basis of the views of the Bukharinite-kulak Right deviation.~~

~~The "Leftist" group (Lominadze, Shatskin, etc.) formed from petty-bourgeois, careerist elements with Trotskyite views and sensibilities in roughly 1928.~~

The "Lefts," like other anti-Party groups, gathered together into a faction and recruited supporters chiefly among university students and the highest levels of the Young Communist League. During 1928, the "Lefts" defamed the Central Committee, alleging that the Central Committee was not struggling enough with the Right deviation. But this was just an act: in fact the "Lefts" themselves soon drew close to the Rightist elements and formed a formal bloc with them for a joint, double-dealing struggle against the Party.[39]

The Rightist-"Leftist" Bloc aimed to reduce the Bolshevik tempo of industrialization and supported the "contraction of the capital construction front." Hostile to the Party, these people availed themselves of the most revolting forms of double-dealing to mask themselves while working in executive posts.

Eventually, the participants of this bloc were identified along with other Trotskyites and Bukharinites as enemies of the people, as treacherous slaves and spies of German and Japanese fascism.

The December 1930 Central Committee and the Central Control Commission Plenum removed Rykov, the Chairman of the U.S.S.R. Council of People's Commissars, from his post. In spite of formally admitting to his mistakes, Rykov had tried in every way to brake the Soviet administration. Comrade Stalin's closest ally and a steadfast fighter for communism, Comrade Molotov, was elected as the Chair of the U.S.S.R.'s Council of People's Commissars.

After the exposure of the Rightist-"Leftist" Bloc, two more counter-revolutionary groups were uncovered in 1932 and 1933 within which Bukharinites and Trotskyites were working together: the Ryutin-Galkin-Slepkov group and the Eismont-Tolmachyev-A. Smirnov group.

When these groups were caught red-handed, they attempted to cover their tracks and conceal their connection to the leaders of the Right deviation—Bukharin, Rykov, Tomsky and Uglanov—who in reality led all of these organizations. They likewise hid their connection to the Trotskyite centres. It is for this reason that only part of these groups' revolutionary activity was uncovered before 1936–37.

It turns out that these separate Trotskyite and Bukharinite groups (Syrtsov-Lominadze, Ryutin-Slepkov, Eismont-Smirnov, etc.), as well as the other Trotskyite groups and "centres" that were exposed at various times, were actually all connected to one-another. These groups had an authentic program supporting the restoration of capitalism—the rebirth of the kulaks and the destruction of the collective farms, the ceding of Socialist enterprises created by the heroic labour of the working class to foreign capital. At the same time, they prepared an uprising against the Party and Soviet Government, engaged in wrecking in all sectors of the economy and prepared for the defeat of the U.S.S.R. in the event of war, in order to restore capitalism with the aid of an imperialist military intervention.

~~It stands to reason that with such a program, the enemies of the people did not dare to reveal themselves to the workers and the peasantry. The Trotskyite-Bukharinite villains despaired over their inability to attract masses of any kind to their cause and were driven as mad as the devil by their hatred for the Party and the people, leading them to go over to terroristic, wrecking and espionage activities against the Party and Soviet Government. With the aid of the fascists, they prepared to drown our country in the blood of the working people and take away from them all the victories of Socialism.~~

~~The counter-revolutionary Ryutin group had a platform calling for the restoration of capitalism in our country. This group prepared a villainous, terroristic assassination attempt against the C.P.S.U.(B.) leadership. As was established later, this so-called "Ryutin" platform was put together by the leaders of the Right deviation (Bukharin, Rykov, Tomsky, Uglanov, A. Smirnov and others). These traitors conducted concealed diversionary work over the course of a number of years even as they remained within the Party ranks and as a few of them even remained within the Central Committee.~~

~~The treacherous Eismont-Smirnov group recruited supporters from among corrupt elements who had passed into the bourgeoisie; it also prepared a villainous, terroristic attempt on the lives of the Party and Government leaders. A. Smirnov conducted negotiations with the Socialist-Revolutionaries about a joint struggle against the C.P.S.U.(B.) and the Soviet power.~~

~~As it later transpired, all these groups were just offshoots of a combined Trotskyite-Bukharinite organization devoted to espionage, wrecking and terrorism, which was carefully hidden and which possessed an array of many-tentacled groups: the "Bloc of Rights and Trotskyites." The Party was unable to reach the genuine roots of these groups, the treacherous joint Trotskyite-Bukharinite organization, in 1932–33. This was accomplished only in 1936–37.~~

~~The Party marched forward towards new Socialist victories, waging a merciless war against all counter-revolutionary groups that were striving to restore capitalism in our country, throwing them from the path and exposing their counter-revolutionary essence.~~

3. Policy of Reconstructing All Branches of the National Economy. Importance of Technique. Further Spread of the Collective-Farm Movement. Political Departments of the Machine and Tractor Stations. Results of the Fulfilment[40] of the Five-Year Plan in Four Years. Victory of Socialism along the Whole Front. Seventeenth Party Congress

When heavy industry and especially the machine-building industry had been built up and placed securely on their feet, and it was moreover clear that they were developing at a fairly rapid pace, the next task that faced the Party was to reconstruct all branches of the national economy on modern, up-to-date lines. Modern technique, modern machinery had to be supplied to the fuel industry, the metallurgical industry, the light industries, the food industry, the timber industry, the armament industry, the transport system, and to agriculture. In view of the colossal increase in the demand for farm produce and manufactured goods, it was necessary to double and treble output in all branches of production. But this could not be done unless the factories and mills, the state farms and collective farms were adequately supplied with up-to-date equipment, since the requisite increase of output could not be secured with the old equipment.

Unless the major branches of the national economy were reconstructed, it would be impossible to satisfy the new and ever growing demands of the country and its economic system.

Without reconstruction, it would be impossible to complete the offensive of Socialism along the whole front, for the capitalist elements in town and country had to be fought and vanquished not only by a new organization of labour and property, but also by a new technique, by technical superiority.

Without reconstruction, it would be impossible to overtake and outstrip the technically and economically advanced capitalist countries, for although the U.S.S.R. had surpassed the capitalist countries in rate of industrial development, it still lagged a long way behind them in level of industrial development, in quantity of industrial output.

In order that we might catch up with them, every branch of production had to be equipped with new technique and reconstructed on the most up-to-date technical lines.

The question of technique had thus become of decisive importance.

The main impediment was not so much an insufficiency of modern machinery and machine-tools—for our machine-building industry was in a position to produce modern equipment—as the wrong attitude of our business executives to technique, their tendency to underrate the importance of technique in the period of reconstruction and to disdain it. In their opinion, technical matters were the affair of the "experts," something of second-rate importance, to be left in charge of the "bourgeois experts"; they considered that Communist business executives need not interfere in the technical side of production and should attend to something more important, namely, the "general" management of industry.

The bourgeois "experts" were therefore given a free hand in matters of production, while the Communist business executives reserved to themselves the function of "general" direction, the signing of papers.

It need scarcely be said that with such an attitude, "general" direction was bound to degenerate into a mere parody of direction, a sterile signing of papers, a futile fussing with papers.

It is clear that if Communist business executives had persisted in this disdainful attitude of technical matters, we would never have been able to overtake the advanced capitalist countries, let alone outstrip them. This attitude, especially in the reconstruction period, would have doomed our country to backwardness, and would have lowered our rates of development. As a matter of fact, this attitude to technical matters was a screen, a mask for the secret wish of a certain section of the Communist business executives to retard, to reduce the rate of industrial development, so as to be able to "take it easy" by shunting the responsibility for production on to the "experts."

It was necessary to get Communist business executives to turn their attention to technical matters, to acquire a taste for technique; they needed to be shown that it was vital for Bolshevik business executives to master modern technique, otherwise we would run the risk of condemning our country to backwardness and stagnation.

Unless this problem were solved further progress would be impossible.

Of utmost importance in this connection was the speech Comrade Stalin made at the First Conference of Industrial Managers in February 1931.

> *"It is sometimes asked," said Comrade Stalin, "whether it is not possible to slow down the tempo a bit, to put a check on the movement. No, comrades, it is not possible! The tempo must not be reduced! . . . To slacken the tempo would mean falling behind. And those who fall behind get beaten. But we do not want to be beaten. No, we refuse to be beaten!*
>
> *"Incidentally, the history of old Russia is one unbroken record of the beatings she suffered for falling behind, for her backwardness. She was beaten by the Mongol khans. She was beaten by the Turkish beys. She was beaten by the Swedish feudal lords. She was beaten by the Polish and Lithuanian gentry. She was beaten by the British and French capitalists. She was beaten by the Japanese barons. All beat her—for her backwardness. . . .*
>
> *"We are fifty or a hundred years behind the advanced countries. We must make good this distance in ten years. Either we do it, or they crush us. . . .*
>
> *"In ten years at most we must make good the distance we are lagging behind the advanced capitalist countries. We have all the 'objective' opportunities for this. The only thing lacking is the ability to make proper use of these opportunities. And that depends on us. ONLY on us! It is time we learned to use these opportunities. It is time to put an end to the rotten policy of non-interference in production. It is time to adopt a new policy, a policy adapted to the times—the policy of interfering in everything. If you are a factory manager, then interfere in all the affairs of the factory, look into everything, let nothing escape you, learn and learn again. Bolsheviks*

must master technique. It is time Bolsheviks themselves became experts. IN THE PERIOD OF RECONSTRUCTION TECHNIQUE DECIDES EVERYTHING.” (Stalin, LENINISM, “The Tasks of Business Managers,” Eng. ed.)

The historic importance of Comrade Stalin’s speech lay in the fact that it put an end to the disdainful attitude of Communist business executives to technique, made them face the question of technique, opened a new phase in the struggle for the mastery of technique by the Bolsheviks themselves, and thereby helped to promote the work of economic reconstruction.

From then on technical knowledge ceased to be a monopoly of the bourgeois “experts,” and became a matter of vital concern to the Bolshevik business executives themselves, while the word “expert” ceased to be a term of disparagement and became the honourable title of Bolsheviks who had mastered technique.

From then on there were bound to appear—and there actually did appear—thousands upon thousands, whole battalions of Red experts, who had mastered technique and were able to direct industries.

This was a new, Soviet technical intelligentsia, an intelligentsia of the working class and the peasantry, and they now constitute the main force in the management of our industries.

All this was bound to promote, and actually did promote, the work of economic reconstruction.

Reconstruction was not confined to industry and transport. It developed even more rapidly in agriculture. The reason is not far to seek: agriculture was less mechanized than other branches, and here the need for modern machinery was felt more acutely than elsewhere. And it was urgently essential to increase the supply of modern agricultural machines now that the number of collective farms was growing from month to month and week to week, and with it the demand for thousands upon thousands of tractors and other agricultural machines.

~~6. The Party’s Struggle to Strengthen the Collective Farms and against Kulak Diversion and Wrecking. Organization of the M.T.S. Political Departments~~

The year 1931 witnessed a further advance in the collective farms *movement*. In the principal grain-growing districts over 80 per cent of the peasant farms had already amalgamated to form collective farms. Here, solid collectivization had in the main already been achieved.[41] In the less important grain-growing districts and in the districts growing industrial crops about 50 per cent of the peasant farms had joined the collective farms. By now there were 500,000 collective farms and 4,000 state farms, which together cultivated two-thirds[42] of the total crop area of the country, the individual peasants cultivating only one-third.[43]

This was a tremendous victory for Socialism in the countryside.

But the progress of the collective-farm movement was so far to be measured in breadth rather than in depth: the collective farms were increasing in number and were spreading to district after district, but there was no commensurate improvement in the work of the collective farms or in the skill of their personnel. This was due to the fact that the growth of the leading cadres and trained personnel of the collective farms was not keeping pace with the numerical growth of the collective farms themselves. The consequence was that the work of the new collective farms was not always satisfactory, and the collective farms themselves were still weak. They were also held back by the shortage in the countryside of literate people indispensable to the collective farms (book-keepers, stores managers, secretaries, etc.), and by the inexperience of the peasants in the management of large-scale collective enterprises. The collective farmers were the individual peasants of yesterday; they had experience in farming small plots of land, but none in managing big, collective farms. This experience could not be acquired in a day.

~~However, the collectives farms were far from secure. Their work demonstrated an array of serious shortcomings which the kulak used to collapse or undermine many collective farms.~~[44] *The first stages of collective farm work were consequently marred by serious defects. It was found that* work was still badly organized *in the collective farms*; labour discipline was slack. In many collective farms the income was distributed ~~at first~~ not by the ~~amount of labor~~ *number of work-day-units*, but by the number of mouths to feed in the family. It often happened that slackers got a bigger return than conscientious hard-working collective farmers. ~~This, in turn,~~ *These defects in the management of collective farms* lowered the incentive *of their members*. There were many cases of members absenting themselves from work even at the height of the season, leaving part of the crops unharvested ~~in places~~ until the winter snows, *while the reaping was done so carelessly that large quantities of grain were lost.* ~~There were enormous losses of grain at harvest time and~~ The absence of individual responsibility for machines and horses~~; no one would take responsibility for anything.~~ *and for work generally, weakened the collective farms and reduced their revenues.* ~~The collective farm economy itself also suffered from this during the first few years.~~

The situation was particularly bad wherever *former* kulaks *and their toadies* had managed to worm their way into ~~the leadership of~~ collective farms and ~~other~~ *to secure* positions *of trust in them*. Not infrequently former kulaks would betake themselves to districts where they were unknown, and there make their way into the collective farms with the deliberate intention of sabotaging and doing mischief. ~~Frequently~~ *Sometimes,*[45] owing to lack of ~~revolutionary~~ vigilance ~~and class blindness~~ on the part of ~~some~~ Party workers and Soviet officials, kulaks managed to get into collective farms even in their own districts

~~in order to wreck there~~. *What made it easier for former kulaks to penetrate into the collective farms was that* ~~The kulaks~~ *they* had radically changed *their* tactics. ~~In 1929–30,~~ *Formerly*[46] the kulaks had fought the collective farms openly~~; spreading foolish, wild stories about how all collective famers and their wives were going to sleep together, "under a hundred-meter blanket." The priests and kulaks distributed all sorts of "documents," which had apparently fallen from the skies, in which God forbade them to join the collective farms. The kulaks~~ *and* had savagely persecuted collective farm leading cadres and ~~first~~ *foremost* collective farmers, nefariously murdering them ~~with sawn-off shotguns~~, burning down their houses and ~~sheds~~ *barns*. By these methods they had thought to intimidate the peasantry and to deter them from joining the collective farms. ~~This~~ *Now that their*[47] open struggle ~~of the kulaks~~ against the collective farms had failed~~. The middle peasant had joined the collective farm. The kulak had lost his wager. It was then that the kulaks began everywhere to change over to a new tactic—the tactic of wrecking, of corrupting the collective farms FROM THE INSIDE. For this, the kulaks snuck into the collective farms, becoming members of the leadership, brigadiers, bookkeepers, managers, grooms and so on. Now that the kulaks were able to conceal themselves~~, *they changed their tactics. T*hey laid aside their sawn-off shotguns and posed as innocent, unoffending folk who would not hurt a fly. *They pretended to be loyal Soviet supporters.* ~~Frequently,~~ Once inside the collective farms ~~the kulaks~~ *they stealthily* carried on their ~~frightful~~ sabotage ~~"on the sly."~~ They strove *to disorganize the collective farms from within,* to undermine labour discipline and to muddle the *harvest* accounts and the records *of work performed*. It was part of their sinister scheme to destroy the ~~horse herds~~ *horses of the collective farms*[48] by deliberately infecting them with glanders, mange and other diseases, or disabling them by neglect or other methods, in which they were often successful. They did damage to tractors and farm machinery.

~~In a word, the kulaks who snuck into the collective farms resorted to the most varied forms of WRECKING in order to collapse and destroy the collective farms. The kulaks and their agents committed acts of diversion, delayed the spring sowing, tilled the fields shallowly so that the fields would fill full of weeds, and stole seed from the seeders so that the fields were left essentially unsown. The kulaks wrecked the harvest and grain threshing, allowing it to rot in the fields or burning the fields to the roots. The kulaks and do-nothings stole the collective farms' harvest, robbing the honest collective farmers.~~

~~The kulaks were assisted by wreckers in the People's Commissariat of Agriculture and in the various institutes devoted to agriculture and animal husbandry: they confused the collective farms' crop rotations, delayed the seeding process and virtually destroyed the best sorts of seed, especially on the local level. It even transpired that the wreckers (among whom were found even a few~~

~~"professors") inoculated livestock in the collective and state farms with rinderpest, Siberian anthrax and meningitis.~~

~~The wreckers' work was facilitated by the fact that there were Rights working in the People's Commissariat of Agriculture—Chernov, Yakovlev, Lisitsyn and Muralov—who issued wreckers' orders and infected livestock with infectious diseases—Siberian anthrax, rinderpest and meningitis; who confused the crop rotations, spoiled various sorts of seed, contaminated seed with mites and so on.~~

~~Kulaks and opportunists, as well as concealed, masked enemies of the Party, organized the diversion of grain storage in an array of districts in 1932, especially in the Kuban. In several regions and territories (Kuban, the North Caucasus, the Lower Volga and part of the Ukraine) there were instances of clear counter-revolutionary wrecking in agriculture that were simultaneously committed by concealed Trotskyites, Bukharinites, Socialist-Revolutionaries and Whiteguards, so as to undermine the collective farms and restore capitalism and the kulaks.~~

~~The Soviet power took decisive measures against this kulak diversion: deportation from the district for wrecking in the collective farms and diversion of grain stores, the purge of kulaks from the collective farms and the passage of the law of August 7, 1932, on the protection of Socialist property.~~

~~In order to successfully fight kulak wrecking and diversion, it was necessary to mobilize the Party organizations in the countryside and raise their level of vigilance.~~

~~Comrade Stalin did this in his speech "On Work in the Countryside" at the 1933 Central Committee and Central Control Commission Plenum.~~

~~He noted that the majority of rural communists did not understand the new situation in the countryside that was created by the opening of trade in collective farm grain. In this new context, it was necessary to emphasize grain collection from the very beginning, instilling in collective farmers an awareness of the imperative of honoring their commitments to the Government as a matter of first priority. This was not done, despite the fact that the collective farm system had increased rather than decreased the amount of care and responsibility that it required from the Party and Government in regard to agricultural development. It therefore became necessary to strengthen the communist leadership of the collective farms. Former Whiteguard officers, Petlyurites and other such enemies of the workers and the peasants grouped together in the collective farms where there was no such leadership.~~

~~Comrade Stalin warned that the class enemy might sneak its way into the collective farm leadership and use the farms in order to wreck and ruin things.~~

~~The communists in the countryside had not yet succeeded in transforming the front in the struggle with the kulak and did not understand the changes in~~

~~the class enemy's tactics, their shift from a direct attack on the collective farms to stealthy diversion. They did not understand all of their responsibilities in the business of collective farm construction. This was one of the reasons for the shortcomings in their work in the countryside.~~

The kulaks were often[49] *able to deceive the collective farmers and commit sabotage with impunity because the collective farms were still weak and their personnel still inexperienced.*

To put an end to the sabotage of the kulaks and to expedite the work of strengthening the collective farms, the latter had to be given urgent and effective assistance in men, advice and leadership.

This assistance was forthcoming from the Bolshevik Party. ~~In the places where communists genuinely took charge and where they took interest first of all in WHO stood at the helm of the collective farms and WHO was leading them—those collective farms were able to correctly fulfil their obligations before the Soviet state and steadily grew stronger in an economic sense from one day to the next.~~

> ~~". . . WE have the power, WE possess the means of governance, WE are called to run the collective farms and WE must bear the entire responsibility for the work in the countryside," declared Comrade Stalin (Stalin, PROBLEMS IN LENINISM, p. 523).~~

~~The January 1933 Central Committee Plenum issued~~ *In January 1933, the Central Committee of the Party adopted* a decision to organize POLITICAL DEPARTMENTS in the machine and tractor stations ~~and state farms~~ *serving the collective farms.* Some 17,000 Party members were sent *into the countryside* to work in these ~~M.T.S.~~ political departments and ~~8,000 to work in state farm political departments~~ *to aid the collective farms.* ~~All of these Party workers were individually chosen by the Central Committee.~~

This assistance was highly effective.

In two years (1933 and 1934) the political departments of the machine and tractor stations did a great deal *to build up an active body of collective farmers,* to eliminate the defects in the work ~~in the countryside that had been pointed out in Comrade Stalin's speech "On Work in the Countryside" and the decisions of the January 1933 Central Committee Plenum~~ *of the collective farms, to consolidate them, and to rid them of kulak enemies and wreckers.* ~~The political departments of the machine and tractor stations did great work in the cultivation of COLLECTIVE FARM ACTIVISTS from among the collective farmers who were devoted to the party. With the help of these activists and the collective farm masses, the political departments purged the collective farms of hostile, wrecking and kulak elements. Labor discipline on the collective farms rose.~~

~~The collective farms grew strong in an organizational, managerial and political sense and became Bolshevik.~~

The political departments performed their task with credit: they strengthened the collective farms both in regard to organization and efficiency, trained skilled personnel for them, improved their management and raised the political level of the collective farm members.

Of ~~the~~ great~~est~~ importance in stimulating the collective farmers to strive for the strengthening of the collective farms was the First *All-Union* Congress of Collective Farm Shock Workers (February 1933) and the speech made by Comrade Stalin at this congress.

Contrasting the old, pre-collective farm system in the countryside with the new, collective farm system, Comrade Stalin said:

> *"Under the old system the peasants each worked in isolation, following the ancient methods of their forefathers and using antiquated implements of labour; they worked for the landlords and capitalists, the kulaks and profiteers; they lived in penury while they enriched others. Under the new, collective farm system, the peasants work in common, co-operatively, with the help of modern implements—tractors and agricultural machinery; they work for themselves and their collective farms; they live without capitalists and landlords, without kulaks and profiteers; they work with the object of raising their standard of welfare and culture from day to day." (Stalin, Problems of Leninism, Russ. ed., p. 528.)*

Comrade Stalin showed in this speech what the peasants had ~~already~~ achieved by adopting the collective farm way. The Bolshevik Party had helped millions of poor peasants to join the collective farms and to escape from servitude to the kulaks. By joining the collective farms, and having the best lands and the finest instruments of production at their disposal, millions of poor peasants who had formerly lived in penury had now as collective farmers risen to the level of middle peasants, and had attained material security.

This was the first step in the development of collective farms, the first achievement.

The next step, *Comrade Stalin said,* was to raise the collective farmers—both former poor peasants and former middle peasants—to an even higher level, *to make all the collective farmers prosperous and all the collective farms Bolshevik.* ~~"Make All Collective Farmers Prosperous"—this was the slogan that Comrade Stalin announced at the First Congress of Collective Farm Shock Workers. This slogan was inextricably tied to another slogan that was simultaneously announced by Comrade Stalin: "Make the Collective Farms Bolshevik."~~

~~Comrade Stalin showed the collective farm peasantry the path to prosperity in his speech.~~

> ~~"Only one thing is required of you—to work honestly, to divide the collective farm's income according to labour performed, to protect the collective farm's assets, to maintain the tractors and machines, to provide for the horses, to fulfil the tasks of your worker-peasant state, and to strengthen the collective farms and kick out all the kulaks and petty kulaks who have worked their way in. . . ."~~
>
> "Only one thing is now needed for the collective farmers to become prosperous," Comrade Stalin said, "and that is for them to work in the collective farms conscientiously, to make efficient use of the tractors and machines, to make efficient use of the draught cattle, to cultivate the land efficiently, and to cherish collective farm property~~," said Comrade Stalin to the collective farmers~~. (Ibid., pp. 532–3.)

~~His words~~ *Comrade Stalin's speech* made a profound impression on the millions of collective farmers and became a practical program of action for the ~~strengthening of the~~ collective farms ~~and the growth of agriculture~~.

By the end of 1934 the collective farms had become a strong and invincible force.[50] They already embraced *about* three-quarters[51] of all the peasant households *in the Soviet Union* and *about* 90 per cent of the *total* crop area.

In 1934, ~~all the work for converting 55 million hectares for tillage was done solely by the M.T.S. tractors.~~ *t*here were already 281,000 tractors and 32,000 harvester combines at work in the Soviet countryside. The spring sowing in that year was completed fifteen to twenty days earlier than in 1933, and thirty to forty days earlier than in 1932, *while the plan of grain deliveries to the state was fulfilled three months earlier than in 1932.*

This showed how firmly established the collective farms had become in two years, thanks to the tremendous assistance given them by the *Party and the* workers' and peasants' state~~, which had armed the collective farms with mechanized technique. The Bolshevik Party's dispatch of thousands of tough Bolshevik organizers also played a large role~~.

~~On the basis of the upsurge of agriculture in 1934, the plan of grain deliveries to the state was fulfilled three months earlier than in 1932.~~

This solid victory of the collective farm system and the *attendant* improvement of agriculture enabled the ~~abolition of~~ *Soviet Government to abolish the* rationing of bread and ~~some~~ *all* other products *and to introduce the unrestricted sale of foodstuffs*. ~~A decision to this effect was passed by the November 1934 Central Committee Plenum.~~

Since the political departments of the machine and tractor stations had served the purpose for which they had been temporarily created, the ~~November 1934~~ Central Committee ~~Plenum~~ decided to convert them into ordinary Party bodies by merging them with the district Party Committees in their localities.

~~7. January 1933 Central Committee and Central Control Commission Plenum. Results of the First Five-Year Plan~~

~~Already by the time of the Twelfth Party Conference (January 30–February 4, 1932), it was clear that the First Stalinist Five-Year Plan would be fulfilled in four years. Therefore, the conference issued directives to prepare a SECOND Five-Year Plan for the economy of the U.S.S.R. (1933–37).~~

~~The results of the First Five-Year Plan were summarized in Comrade Stalin's historic report to the January 1933 Central Committee and Central Control Commission Plenum.~~

~~This plenum served as a major event in the life of the Party. Due to the importance of some of its issues, it was no less important than some of the Party congresses.~~

~~The results of the First Five-Year Plan, which were completed not in five years, but in four, drew the attention of the whole world. The entire world—both our friends and our enemies—studied Comrade Stalin's report.~~[52]

~~The capitalist countries' economies were collapsing as a result of the world economic crisis. The level of industrial production in an array of capitalist countries in 1932 declined to half of the level of industrial production in 1928 (in the U.S.A.—to 56 per cent, in Germany—to 55 per cent, in Poland—to 54 per cent). At the same time, the economy of the U.S.S.R. grew at a furious pace. By the end of 1932, the level of industrial production in the U.S.S.R. grew by more than two times to 219 per cent of 1928 levels, and by more than THREE TIMES in comparison to pre-war levels.~~

~~Therefore, the Central Committee Plenum pointed out in its decisions that the completion of the Five-Year Plan in four years was "a fact—one of the most superlative facts in modern history."~~

~~Seeing the successes of the Five-Year Plan, the working class all around the world became all the more convinced of the superiority of the Soviet system over the capitalist one. In the capitalist countries, unemployment, poverty and hunger grew to unheard-of levels. In the U.S.S.R., unemployment was completely eliminated and the workers' and peasants' material well-being was growing already at the beginning of 1931.~~

~~In the struggle for the Five-Year Plan, the U.S.S.R. was forced to overcome enormous difficulties both externally and internally. The Soviet Union did not received any loans from the capitalist countries. It was able to build its Socialist~~

~~large-scale industry only through the use of internal resources, only through the greatest amount of economizing on everything.~~

~~The Soviet Union existed under the continuous threat of a new, armed intervention from the imperialists. It built its industry in the conditions of a financial and economic blockade. The working class of the U.S.S.R. overcame all of these difficulties under the leadership of the Bolshevik Party and made use of the advantages of the Socialist economic system, creating its own advanced technical base for the Socialist reconstruction of the entire economy.~~

~~From the backward, petty peasant-dominated country that was Old Russia, the U.S.S.R. stepped forward into the first ranks of the most technically and economically advanced countries.~~

~~Giant examples of the ferrous and nonferrous metallurgical, chemical and energy producing industry rose up during this period: the Magnitogorsk and Kuznetsk ferrous metallurgy works, the Urals copper works, the Ridderovsk polymetal works, the Volkhovsk aluminum works, the Chernorechensk and Berezinovsk nitric factories, the Dnieper hydroelectric station and the Zuevsk, Chelyabinsk and Shterovsk electric stations. New, mighty mines appeared in the Donetz Basin, Kuznetsk Basin and other districts. A new coal-and-metallurgy base was created in an unheard-of short time in the East—the Ural-Kuznetz Basin, the pride of our country.~~

~~MACHINE-BUILDING giants rose up. Machine building was one of the core areas of large-scale industry. It was necessary to completely rebuild this sector in the Soviet Union. Enormous TRACTOR factories were built and put into production in order to furnish agriculture with millions of mechanical horsepower per year—the Stalingrad and Kharkov tractor factories. Construction of the Chelyabinsk tractor factory was also completed.~~

~~The production of combines and other complex agricultural equipment was established.~~

~~The production of mighty railroad engines and rolling stock grew, as did the production of heavy turbines and generators for electric stations, the production of equipment for ferrous metallurgy and the production of equipment for the fuel industry (powerful digging machinery, drilling equipment for oil extraction, cracking, etc.).~~

~~New branches of the machine-building industry were also created, such as the automobile and aviation industry. The Moscow Stalin Plant and the Gorky Molotov Plant, equipped with the latest word in technique, began to produce hundreds of thousands of automobiles. Powerful, first-class aviation plants rose up in our country. The machine tools industry was reestablished, as was the production of tools and equipment. The result was that in aggregate, Soviet machine-building grew by TEN times in comparison to the prewar period.~~[53]

~~The specific output of all industrial production within the overall economy of the U.S.S.R. grew from 48 per cent at the beginning of the Five-Year Plan (1928) to 70 per cent by the end of the fourth year of the Five-Year Plan (1932). In this way, the U.S.S.R. was transformed from a backward, agrarian country into an advanced, INDUSTRIAL superpower. Our Union was transformed into a mighty country prepared for all eventualities and capable of creating on a massive scale all modern means of defence.~~[54]

~~In agriculture, more than 200,000 collective farms, armed with tractors and combines, along with about 5,000 state farms devoted to grain and animal husbandry, rose up over the course of the First Five-Year Plan in the place of a sea of petty peasant holdings. The kulaks were defeated, but not completely eliminated. The toiling peasantry was freed of kulak subjugation and exploitation. A firm economic base in the countryside, a base for a collective economy, was laid under the Soviet power.~~[55]

~~In Comrade Stalin's report on the results of the First Five-Year Plan, he said:~~

> ~~"The collective farms have taken root and the path back to individual agricultural operations has been closed off for good. Now, the task consists of strengthening the collective farms in AN ORGANIZATIONAL WAY, kicking out all the wrecking elements and selecting genuine and tested Bolshevik cadres for the collective farms and making the collective farms genuinely BOLSHEVIK."~~

~~Comrade Stalin's speeches in which he announced his slogans on the construction of Socialist industry and Socialist agriculture had great meaning for the mobilization of the Party and the masses in the struggle for the victory of the First Five-Year Plan.~~

~~Comrade Stalin announced the slogan of eliminating the kulaks as a class on the basis of solid collectivization, the slogan "Make All Collective Farmers Prosperous," and "Make the Collective Farms Bolshevik." During the years of the Bolshevik Party's intense struggle for the collectivization of agriculture, Comrade Stalin's articles, speeches and slogans mobilized the masses in the struggle for the collective farms like a projector illuminating the path to the collective farms' construction. They captured the minds of tens of millions of people because they were understandable to them.~~

~~Comrade Stalin's speech "On the Tasks of the Industrial Managers" (February 1931), which advanced the slogans "The Bolsheviks Must Master Technique" and "In the Reconstruction Period, Technique Decides Everything,"~~[56] ~~had enormous significance for the successful struggle for Socialist industry.~~

~~On June 23, 1931, Comrade Stalin presented the speech "New Circumstances—New Tasks in the Building of the Economy" at a meeting of industrial~~

managers. He laid out in front of the industrial managers SIX CONDITIONS that had to be met in order to successfully develop our industry and the entire Socialist economy.

These six conditions were as follows: 1) it is necessary to put together a work force through agreements with the collective farms and the mechanization of labour; 2) it is necessary to eliminate the fluidity of the work force, eliminate wage leveling and correctly set wages and improve workers' living conditions; 3) it is necessary to put an end to the absence of individual responsibility and improve the organization and positioning of labour in enterprises; 4) it is necessary to make it so that the working class of the U.S.S.R. has its own technical intelligentsia; 5) it is necessary to correct the relationship with the engineers and technical specialists of the old school, paying more attention to them and involving them in work more energetically; 6) it is necessary to establish and strengthen the practice of balancing profits and losses and promoting industry-wide capital accumulation.

The appearance of these six conditions demanded the restructuring of all ongoing work: "One must work in a new way and lead in a new way." The restructuring of industrial work on the basis of Comrade Stalin's directives formed one of the conditions for the victory of the First Five-Year Plan.

The successes of Socialist industry and Socialist agriculture were also accompanied by the development of state, co-operative and collective farm trade. Private dealers, merchants and profiteers were finally excluded from the trade system during the years of the First Five-Year Plan. During the first stage of NEP, trade had developed which had been regulated by the state but which had allowed for the participation of private dealers and capitalist elements. Now, SOVIET trade had grown up and taken root—trade without capitalists, whether petty or large-scale, and trade without profiteers. This sort of trade had never been heard of before in human history.

As a result of the rise of industry and agriculture during the years of the First Five-Year Plan, the workers' and peasants' material conditions improved in a fundamental way.

UNEMPLOYMENT was eliminated for good, as were feelings of uncertainty over what tomorrow might bring the workers.[57] This was one of the most basic victories of the First Five-Year Plan. In the vast majority of enterprises in the U.S.S.R., people enjoyed a 7-hour working day—the shortest in the world—and only 6 hours a day in dangerous types of production.

Already as a result of the First Five-Year Plan, almost all of the poor peasantry was included in collective farm construction. On this basis, the stratification of the peasantry into kulaks and poor peasants was eliminated, as was the kulak subjugation and impoverishment in the countryside. No fewer than 20 million poor peasants were saved from a life of poverty and ruin by the

~~collective farms and were now well taken care of. Even before the collective farms, the Soviet power had taken care of poor peasants in every possible way, but only by means of the collective farms did it become possible to direct the whole of the poor peasantry onto the path to a prosperous life. This was also one of the most basic victories of the First Five-Year Plan.~~[58]

~~The results of the First Five-Year Plan had an enormous INTERNATIONAL impact. Bourgeois and Social-Democratic leaders announced that the Five-Year Plan was a Bolshevik fantasy, madness and an unrealizable dream, and that the Five-Year Plan would be fulfilled no earlier than in half a century. The Mensheviks, Trotskyites and all the enemies of Leninism declared that it was impossible to build Socialism in one country. The results of the Five-Year Plan, Stalin said in his report, "have shown that it is completely possible to build a Socialist society in one country, inasmuch as the economic foundation of such a society has already been built in the U.S.S.R."~~

~~Summarizing its international significance, Comrade Stalin pointed out that "the Five-Year Plan as not the private affair of the U.S.S.R., but the business of the entire world proletariat, and the Five-Year plan's successes are mobilizing the revolutionary forces of the working class in all countries against capitalism."~~

All these achievements, both in agriculture and in industry, were made possible by the successful fulfilment of the Five-Year Plan.

By the beginning of 1933 it was evident[59] *that the First Five-Year Plan had already been fulfilled ahead of time, fulfilled in four years and three months.*

This was a tremendous, epoch-making victory of the working class and peasantry of the U.S.S.R.[60]

Reporting to a plenary meeting of the Central Committee and the Central Control Commission of the Party, held in January 1933, Comrade Stalin reviewed the results of the First Five-Year Plan. The report made it clear that in the period which it took to fulfil the First Five-Year Plan, the Party and the Soviet Government had achieved the following major results.

a) The U.S.S.R. had been converted from an agrarian country into an industrial country, for the proportion of industrial output to the total production of the country had risen to 70 per cent.[61]

b) The Socialist economic system had eliminated the capitalist elements in the sphere of industry and had become the sole economic system in industry.

c) The Socialist economic system had eliminated the kulaks as a class in the sphere of agriculture, and had become the predominant force in agriculture.

d) The collective farm system had put an end to poverty and want in the countryside, and tens of millions of poor peasants had risen to a level of material security.

e) The Socialist system in industry had abolished unemployment, and while retaining the 8-hour day in a[62] *number of branches, had introduced the 7-hour day in the vast majority of enterprises and the 6-hour day in unhealthy occupations.*

f) The victory of Socialism in all branches of the national economy had abolished the exploitation of man by man.

The sum and substance of the achievements of the First Five-Year Plan was that they had completely emancipated the workers and peasants from exploitation and had opened the way to a prosperous and cultured life for all working people in the U.S.S.R.

~~The Second Five-Year Plan was supposed to build on this new industrial construction by directing special attention to the MASTERY of established enterprises. Comrade Stalin pointed out that it was important to combine the enormous pathos (emotional uplift) of the new construction, which we enjoy as a result of the First Five-Year Plan, with the pathos, the enthusiasm, for mastering the new enterprises and technique. If during the First Five-Year Plan, the unshakeable foundation of the Socialist economy had been created, then the task of the Second Five-Year Plan was to build the edifice of Socialism, the complete technical reconstruction of the whole economy, the development and strengthening of Socialist productive relations and the final elimination of the capitalist elements within the U.S.S.R.~~

~~In sum, the realization of the First Five-Year Plan in the area of industry, agriculture and trade throughout all the sectors of the economy was a victory for Socialism. Capitalist elements were cast out of all areas of the economy.~~

~~The survivals of the dying capitalist classes—the industrialists, the dealers, the kulaks, the last of the noble landowning classes, former Whiteguard officers and all such "declassé" elements—snuck around throughout our factories and plants, our institutions and trade organizations, and our railroad and maritime transport enterprises. These "former people" especially aimed to sneak into the collective and state farms.~~

~~This sort of people nurtured a hatred of the Soviet power and the working people and a rabid hostility toward the new forms of economic activity, everyday practices and culture. Powerless to attack the Soviet power head-on, the survivals of those classes hostile to Socialism began to harm the workers, collective farmers, the Soviet power and the Party; they began to organize the theft and embezzlement of the society's Socialist property.~~

~~More than a few of these "former people" even stole their way into the Party in order to conduct wrecking activities.~~

~~Foreign espionage agencies, especially the fascist ones, recruited spies, wreckers, saboteurs and killers from among the survivals of the capitalist classes and their agents.~~

~~In his report on the results of the First Five-Year Plan, Comrade Stalin warned the Party that "the growth of the power of the Soviet state is destined to strengthen the resistance of the last remains of the dying classes." Comrade Stalin pointed out that it was precisely because they are dying that they will adopt the sharpest, most desperate forms of struggle."~~

> ~~"A strong and powerful dictatorship of the proletariat—that is precisely what we need now in order to scatter the survivals of the dying classes to the wind and defeat their thieving machinations," said Comrade Stalin.~~

~~Comrade Stalin warned the Party that due to the new intensity of the struggle with the last survivals of the capitalist classes in our country,~~

> ~~"defeated groups may come back to life and start to stir, drawing from old counter-revolutionary parties such as the Socialist-Revolutionaries, Mensheviks and bourgeois nationalists from the centre and the periphery, as well as fragments of old counter-revolutionary oppositional elements composed of Trotskyites and Right deviationists.~~
>
> ~~This is why revolutionary vigilance is a quality which is especially necessary for Bolsheviks to possess at the present time," said Comrade Stalin (Questions of Leninism, Russ. ed., p. 510).~~

~~The January Plenum of the Central Committee and Central Control Committee ratified the economic plan for the first year of the Second Five-Year Plan (1933). According to this plan, the general growth of industrial production in 1933 was to be 16.5 per cent more than 1932, while large-scale industry was to grow by 21.1 per cent. This plan represented the next stage in the business of building a Socialist society in the U.S.S.R.~~

~~Comrade Stalin's speech at the January Central Committee Plenum on work in the countryside had an exceptionally important meaning for ongoing efforts to strengthen the collective farm system.~~

~~Comrade Stalin's directives and the decisions of the January Central Committee Plenum mobilized the entire Party to correct the shortcomings of its work in the countryside and to defeat once and for all the kulaks and other enemies of the people, who were trying to corrupt the collective and state farms from the inside. The entire Party mobilized to reinforce the collective farms in both political and organizational ways.~~

~~The January Central Committee Plenum also passed a decision creating political departments in the M.T.S.s and the state farms.~~

~~The question of the anti-Party Bukharin-Rykovite group of Eismont, Tolmachyev, A. Smirnov and others was discussed at the January Plenum of the~~

~~Central Committee and Central Control Commission. At the moment when the Party was taking accounts of the great victories of the First Five-Year Plan, this treacherous, double-dealing group set its sights on undermining the policies of Socialist industrialization and restoring capitalism, particularly the kulaks.~~

~~The Bukharinites, like the Trotskyites, expressed the intense resistance of the survivals of the dying capitalist classes, who had resorted to ever more desperate, mad forms of struggle against the Party and Soviet power. The Rights (Bukharin, Rykov and others), like the Trotskyites, completely ceased to be a political trend (roughly between 1929–30) and transformed into a highway robber-like gang of spies, wreckers and killers.~~

~~Only part of the counter-revolutionary activities of the double-dealing Eismont-Tolmachyev group were exposed in 1933. Only later, in 1936, 1937 and 1938 were all of the monstrous, counter-revolutionary crimes and plans of these Trotskyite-Bukharinite enemies of the people uncovered.~~

~~The January Central Committee and Central Control Commission Plenum made the decision to conduct a Party purge over the course of 1933 and to halt Party admissions. The purge had the task of ensuring the Party's iron proletarian discipline and cleansing its ranks of all unreliable, unsteadfast and corrupt elements, as well as of all double-dealers.~~

~~8. The Seventeenth Party Congress—the Congress of Victors (January 26–February 10, 1934)~~

In January 1934 the *Party held its* Seventeenth ~~Party~~ Congress ~~took place, which summed up a decade of work without Lenin but under the banner of Lenin and the leadership of Stalin. The Party arrived at the Seventeenth Party Congress united as one and monolithic.~~ *It was attended by 1,225 delegates with vote and 736 delegates with voice but no vote, representing 1,874,488 Party members and 935,298 candidate members.*

The congress reviewed the work of the Party since the last congress. It noted the decisive results achieved by Socialism in all branches of economic and cultural life and placed on record that the general line of the Party had triumphed along the whole front.

The Seventeenth Party Congress is known in history as the "Congress of Victors."

~~The Seventeenth Party Congress had a major international significance. It summed up the great victories of Socialism in the context of the most severe economic crisis. The congress demonstrated to the working people of the capitalist world that the way out of capitalist slavery, unemployment, poverty and hunger was in the struggle for the dictatorship of the proletariat and the creation of a Socialist society.~~

Reporting on the work of the Central Committee, Comrade Stalin ~~showed~~ *pointed to* the ~~enormous~~ *fundamental* changes that had taken place in the U.S.S.R. during the period *under review*.

> "During this period, the U.S.S.R. has become radically transformed and has cast off the integument of backwardness and mediaevalism. From an agrarian country it has become an industrial country. From a country of small individual agriculture it has become a country of collective, large-scale mechanized agriculture. From an ignorant, illiterate and uncultured country it has become—or rather it is becoming—a literate and cultured country covered by a vast network of higher, intermediate and elementary schools teaching in the languages of the nationalities of the U.S.S.R. (Stalin, Seventeenth Congress of the C.P.S.U., "Report on the Work of the Central Committee of the C.P.S.U.[B.]," p. 30.)

By this time 99 per cent of the industry of the country was Socialist industry. Socialist agriculture—the collective farms and state farms—embraced ~~already 84.5~~ *about 90* per cent[63] of the *total* crop area *of the country* ~~for grain, whereas the share of individual plots amounted to only 15.5 per cent~~. *As to trade, t*he capitalist elements had been completely ousted from this domain.

When the New Economic Policy was being introduced, Lenin said that there were the elements of five social-economic formations in our country. The first was patriarchal economy, which was largely a natural form of economy, i.e., which practically carried on no trade. The second formation was small commodity production, as represented by the majority ~~of peasants who sell grain~~ *of the peasant farms, those which sold agricultural produce, and by the artisans*. In the first years of NEP this economic formation ~~was the dominant force~~ *embraced the majority of the population*. The third formation was private capitalism, which had begun to revive in the early period of NEP. The fourth formation was state capitalism, chiefly in the form of concessions, which had not developed to any considerable extent. The fifth formation was Socialism: Socialist industry, which was still weak, state farms and collective farms, which were ~~completely~~ economically insignificant at the beginning of NEP, state trade and co-operative societies, which were also weak at that time.

Of all these formations, Lenin said, the Socialist formation must gain the upper hand.

The New Economic Policy was designed to bring about the complete victory of Socialist ~~elements~~ *forms* of economy.

And by the time of the Seventeenth Party Congress this aim had *already* been ~~reached~~ *achieved*.

> *"We can now say," said Comrade Stalin, "that the first, the third and the fourth social-economic formations no longer exist; the second social-economic formation has been forced into a secondary position, while the fifth social-economic formation—the Socialist formation—now holds unchallenged sway and is the sole commanding force in the whole national economy." (Ibid., p. 33.)*

~~The Socialist formation had become the unchallenged, sole commanding force in the whole national economy.~~

~~Accompanied by the thunder of applause from the participants in the Seventeenth Party Congress, Stalin announced: "Everyone sees that the Party line has been victorious," that is, the path that was chosen to move forward toward the victory of Socialism has turned out to be the right one. The policy of Socialist industrialization of the country has won out. The policy of eliminating the kulaks as a class on the basis of solid collectivization has won out. It has been proven on the example of our country that the victory of Socialism in a single country is completely possible.~~

~~Comrade Stalin's report to the Seventeenth Party Congress was, as S. M. Kirov aptly put it, the most brilliant document of the epoch. This report depicted the great Socialist construction site and its successes and at the same time laid out the gigantic prospects for work in the coming years. Comrade Stalin's report presented the plan for COMPLETING THE CONSTRUCTION of a Socialist society during the Second Five-Year Plan, as well as how this plan was to be fulfilled. This is why Comrade Kirov made a proposal that was unanimously supported by the congress to treat all the conditions and conclusions of Stalin's report as Party law.~~

~~In his report, Comrade Stalin focused Party and non-Party workers' attention on the next tasks in the area of industry and agriculture, transportation and Soviet trade. He pointed to those areas of the economy that were falling behind, like ferrous and non-ferrous metallurgy and animal husbandry. It was imperative to develop trade and decisively improve the work of transportation, without which the Socialist economy would not be able to move forward.~~

An important place in Comrade Stalin's report was given to the question of ideological-political leadership. He warned the Party that although its enemies, the opportunists and nationalist deviators of all shades and complexions, had been defeated, remnants of their ideology still lingered in the minds of some Party members and often asserted themselves. The survivals of capitalism in economic life and particularly in the minds of men provided a favourable soil for the revival of the ideology of the defeated anti-Leninist groups. The development of people's mentality does not keep pace with their economic position.

As a consequence, ~~people with bourgeois views and tendencies~~ *survivals of bourgeois ideas still* remained ~~in the U.S.S.R.~~ *in men's minds and would continue to do so* even though capitalism had been abolished in economic life. ~~From another point of view, Comrade Stalin pointed out~~ *It should also be borne in mind* that the surrounding capitalist world, against which we had to keep our powder dry, was working to revive and foster the*se* survivals ~~in the U.S.S.R.'s economy, as well as men's minds~~.

~~The presence of capitalist survivals in the economy and especially in men's minds (bourgeois views and tendencies) facilitated the emergence of a variety of anti-Party and opposition groups and their transformation into agents of imperialism and spies of foreign espionage agencies.~~

~~All these enemies of the people turned out to be people who were rotten and corrupt to the core with an ideology that is alien to the proletariat, and who were infected with bourgeois views and tendencies (careerism, covetousness, etc.). Among the Rightist-Trotskyite spies and killers were also people who carried religious prayers about in their pockets (Rosengoltz).~~

~~Comrade Stalin brought up several serious questions about ideological-political work, which pointed out that there was a lack of clarity and confusion and even direct deviations from Leninism within several strata of the Party ranks. For instance, some understood the slogan of the Seventeenth Party Congress on the movement toward a classless society to mean that it was possible to relax in regard to class struggle, relax in regard to the dictatorship of the proletariat and in general to do away with the state. This confusion resembled the well-known origins of the ideas of the Bukharin Right deviation on the peaceful "convergence" of capitalist elements under Socialism.~~

~~There was also confusion on the issue of agricultural artels and communes and the slogan "Make All Collective Farmers Prosperous."~~

Comrade Stalin *also* dwelt on the survivals of capitalism in men's minds on the national question, where ~~these survivals~~ *they* were particularly tenacious. The Bolshevik Party was fighting on two fronts, both against the deviation to Great-Russian chauvinism and against the deviation to local nationalism. In a number of republics (the Ukraine, Byelorussia, and others) the Party organizations had relaxed the struggle against local ~~bourgeois~~ nationalism, and had allowed it to grow to such an extent that it had allied *itself* with *hostile forces,* the forces of intervention, and had become a danger to the state. In reply to the question, which deviation in the national question was the major danger, Comrade Stalin said:

> "The major danger is the deviation against which we have ceased to fight, thereby allowing it to grow into a danger to the state." (~~Stalin, QUESTIONS OF LENINISM, Russ. ed., p. 587.~~ *Ibid., p. 81.*)

Comrade Stalin called upon the Party to be more active in ideological-political work, systematically to expose the ideology and the remnants of the ideology *of the hostile classes and* of the trends hostile to Leninism.

He ~~showed~~ *further pointed out* in his report ~~how the Central Committee had ORGANIZED the struggle for a way to bring to life the slogans and decisions of the Party. The Central Committee recruited masses of workers and peasants for this struggle (which involved development, self-criticism, competition and shock work among labourers, and the purge of state and economic organizations)~~ *that the adoption of correct decisions does not in itself guarantee the success of a measure. In order to guarantee success, it was necessary to* PUT THE RIGHT PEOPLE IN THE RIGHT PLACE, *people able to give effect to the decisions of the leading organs and to* KEEP A CHECK ON THE FULFILMENT OF DECISIONS. *Without these organizational measures there was a risk of decisions remaining scraps of paper, divorced from practical life.* ~~Organizing this practical work for the victory of Socialism, the Central Committee was guided by~~ *Comrade Stalin referred in support of this to* Lenin's famous maxim that the chief thing in organizational work was THE CHOICE OF PERSONNEL AND THE KEEPING OF A CHECK ON THE FULFILMENT OF DECISIONS. *Comrade Stalin said that the disparity between adopted decisions and the organizational work of putting these decisions into effect and of keeping a check on their fulfilment was the chief evil in our practical work.*

~~In Comrade Stalin's report, two types of Party workers who put a brake on work and slowed the movement forward were subjected to harsh criticism.~~

~~One such type of Party worker were those who were known for their service in the past, but who now, as "celebrities," did not believe that Party and Soviet laws applied to them. Such arrogant "celebrities" did not consider it their responsibility to implement the Party's and Government's decisions and destroyed the basis for Party and state discipline. The second type, the so-called "honest babblers," were not capable of leading and could not organize a single thing.~~

In order to keep a better check on the fulfilment of Party and Government decisions, the Seventeenth Party Congress set up a Party Control Commission under the Central Committee of the C.P.S.U.(B.) and a Soviet Control Commission under the Council of People's Commissars of the U.S.S.R. in place of the combined Central Control Commission and Workers' and Peasants' Inspection, this body ~~fulfilling~~ *having completed* the tasks ~~of Party and Soviet control~~ for which it had been set up by the Twelfth Party Congress.

Comrade Stalin formulated the organizational tasks of the Party in the new stage as follows:

"1) Our organizational work ~~from now on~~ must be adapted to the requirements of the political line of the Party;

2) Organizational leadership must be raised to the level of political leadership;

3) Organizational leadership must be made fully equal to the task of ensuring the realization of the political slogans and decisions of the Party." ~~(Stalin, Questions of Leninism, Russ. ed., pp. 595-6.)~~

In conclusion, Comrade Stalin warned the Party that although Socialism had achieved great ~~and unusual~~ successes, *successes* of which we could be justly proud, we must not allow ourselves to be carried away, to get "a swelled head," to be lulled by success.

> ". . . We must not lull the Party, but sharpen its vigilance; we must not lull it to sleep, but keep it ready for action; not disarm it, but arm it; not demobilize it, but hold it in a state of mobilization for the fulfilment of the Second Five-Year Plan," said Comrade Stalin. (~~Questions of Leninism.~~ p. 596. *Ibid., p. 96.*)

The Seventeenth Congress heard reports from Comrades Molotov and Kuibyshev on the Second Five-Year Plan for the development of the national economy. ~~Its~~ *The* program *of the Second Five-Year Plan* was even vaster than that of the First Five-Year Plan.[64] By the end of the Second Five-Year Plan period, in 1937, industrial output was to ~~grow~~ *be increased* approximately eightfold in comparison with pre-war. Capital development investments in all branches in the period of the Second Five-Year Plan were to amount to ~~133.4 trillion~~ *133,000,000,000* rubles, as against a little over ~~50.5 trillion~~ *64,000,000,000*[65] rubles in the period of the First Five-Year Plan.

This immense scope of new capital construction work would ensure the complete technical RE-EQUIPMENT of all branches of the national economy. ~~The U.S.S.R. had to transform and did transform during the Second Five-Year Plan into the most technically advanced country in Europe.~~

The Second Five-Year Plan was to complete in the main the mechanization of agriculture. Aggregate tractor power was to increase from 2,250,000 hp. in 1932 to over 8,000,000 hp. in 1937. The plan provided for the extensive employment of scientific agricultural methods (correct crop rotation, use of selected seed, autumn ploughing, *etc.*).

A tremendous plan for the technical reconstruction of the means of transport and communication was outlined.

The Second Five-Year Plan contained an extensive program for the further improvement of the material and cultural standards of the workers and peasants.

The Seventeenth Congress paid great attention to matters of organization and adopted decisions on the work of the Party and the Soviets in connection with a report made by Comrade Kaganovich. The question of organization had acquired even greater importance now that the general line of the Party had won and the Party policy had been tried and tested by the experience of millions of workers and peasants. The new and complex tasks of the Second Five-Year Plan called for a higher standard of work in all spheres.

> "The major tasks of the Second Five-Year Plan, VIZ., to completely eliminate the capitalist elements, to overcome the survivals of capitalism in economic life and in the minds of men, to complete the reconstruction of the whole national economy on modern technical lines, to learn to use the new technical equipment and the new enterprises, to mechanize agriculture and increase its productivity—insistently and urgently confront us with the problem of IMPROVING WORK IN ALL SPHERES, FIRST AND FOREMOST IN PRACTICAL ORGANIZATIONAL LEADERSHIP," it was stated in the decisions of the congress on organizational questions. (RESOLUTIONS OF THE C.P.S.U.[B.], Russ. ed., Part II, p. 591.)

The Seventeenth Congress adopted new Party Rules, which differ from the old ones firstly by the addition of a preamble. This preamble gives a *brief* definition of the Communist Party, and *a definition of* its role in the struggle of the proletariat and its place in the organism of the dictatorship of the proletariat. The new rules enumerate in ~~greater~~ detail the duties of Party members. Stricter regulations governing the admission of new members and a clause concerning sympathizers' groups were introduced. The ~~entirely~~ new rules give a more detailed exposition of the organizational structure of the Party, and formulate anew the clauses dealing with the Party nuclei, or primary organizations, as they have been called since the Seventeenth Party Congress. The clauses dealing with inner Party democracy and Party discipline were *also* formulated anew.

~~The Seventeenth Party Congress went down in history as the CONGRESS OF VICTORS. The victory of Socialism was clear and obvious. The entire Party and all the working people repeated with great joy the words of Comrade Stalin, "The Party line has been victorious."~~

~~But the enemies of Socialism, the enemies of the people who were harboring spite, prepared counter-revolutionary conspiracies with foreign espionage agencies, wanting to take away the victories of Socialism from the working people.~~

~~At the Seventeenth Party Congress, Bukharin, Rykov, Tomsky, Kamenev and Zinoviev made repentant speeches in which they admitted that the Party line had been victorious. But the speeches were nothing more than conscious double-dealing to mask these enemies of the people. Presenting artificially sweet speeches at the congress, these wretched mercenaries of fascism~~

~~simultaneously prepared the villainous murder of Comrade Kirov and other leaders of the Party and Government, sold out our motherland to the imperialists and planned to arrest the entire Seventeenth Party Congress and stage an anti-Soviet coup d'état. On trial in March 1938, Rykov confessed that they were dismayed by the unity of the Party around Comrade Stalin: they saw the total hopelessness of their plans to seize power from the inside and from that moment these conspirators became even more active in their conversion over to terroristic means of struggle and direct ties with the fascists.~~

4.9. Degeneration of the Bukharinites into Political Double-Dealers. Degeneration of the Trotskyite Double-Dealers into a Whiteguard Gang of Assassins and Spies. **Foul Murder of S. M. Kirov ~~by a Trotskyite-Bukharinite Band of Fascist Mercenaries~~. Measures of the Party to Heighten Bolshevik Vigilance**

The achievements of Socialism in our country were a cause of rejoicing not only to the Party, and not only to the workers and collective farmers, but also to our Soviet intelligentsia, and to all honest citizens of the Soviet Union.

But they were no cause of rejoicing to the remnants of the defeated exploiting classes; on the contrary, they only enraged them the more as time went on.

They infuriated the lickspittles of the defeated classes—the puny remnants of the following of Bukharin and Trotsky.

These gentry were guided in their evaluation of the achievements of the workers and collective farmers not by the interests of the people, who applauded every such achievement, but by the interests of their own wretched and putrid faction, which had lost all contact with the realities of life. Since the achievements of Socialism in our country meant the victory of the policy of the Party and the utter bankruptcy of their own policy, these gentry, instead of admitting the obvious facts and joining the common cause, began to revenge themselves on the Party and[66] *the people for their own failure, for their own bankruptcy; they began to resort to foul play and sabotage against the cause of the workers and collective farmers, to blow up pits, set fire to factories, and commit acts of wrecking in collective and state farms, with the object of undoing the achievements of the workers and collective farmers and evoking popular discontent against the Soviet Government. And in order, while doing so, to shield their puny group from exposure and destruction, they simulated loyalty to the Party, fawned upon it, eulogized it, cringed before it more and more, while in reality continuing their underhand, subversive activities against the workers and peasants.*

At the Seventeenth Party Congress, Bukharin, Rykov and Tomsky made repentant speeches, praising the Party and extolling its achievements to the skies. But the congress detected a ring of insincerity and duplicity in their speeches; for what the

Party expects from its members is not eulogies and rhapsodies over its achievements, but conscientious work on the Socialist front. And this was what the Bukharinites had showed no signs of for a long time. The Party saw that the hollow speeches of these gentry were in reality meant for their supporters outside the congress, to serve as a lesson to them in duplicity, and a call to them not to lay down their arms.

Speeches were also made at the Seventeenth Congress by the Trotskyites Zinoviev and Kamenev, who lashed themselves extravagantly for their mistakes, and eulogized the Party no less extravagantly for its achievements. But the congress could not help seeing that both their nauseating self-castigation and their fulsome praise of the Party were only meant to hide an uneasy and unclean conscience. However,[67] *the Party did not yet know or suspect that while these gentry were making their cloying speeches at the congress they were hatching a villainous plot against the life of S. M. Kirov.*

On December 1, 1934, ~~at 4:30 in the afternoon,~~ S. M. Kirov~~, a member of the Presidium of the U.S.S.R. Central Executive Committee, a member of the Politburo, and secretary of the Central Committee and the Leningrad Party Committee,~~ was *foully* murdered in the Smolny, in Leningrad, by a shot from a revolver.

The assassin was caught red-handed and turned out to be a member of a secret counter-revolutionary group made up of members of an anti-Soviet group of Zinovievites in Leningrad.

S. M. Kirov was loved by the Party and the ~~masses~~ *working class*, and his murder stirred the people profoundly, sending a wave of wrath and ~~the greatest~~ *deep* sorrow through the country.

The investigation established that in 1933 and 1934 an underground counter-revolutionary terrorist group had been formed in Leningrad consisting of former members of the Zinoviev opposition and headed by a so-called "Leningrad Centre." The purpose of this group was to murder leaders of the Communist Party. S. M. Kirov was chosen as the first victim. The testimony of the members of this counter-revolutionary group showed that they were connected with representatives of foreign capitalist states and were receiving funds from them.

The exposed members of this organization were sentenced by the Military Collegium of the Supreme Court of the U.S.S.R. to the supreme penalty—to be shot.

Soon afterwards the existence of an underground counter-revolutionary organization called the "Moscow Centre" was discovered. The preliminary investigation and the trial revealed the villainous part played by Zinoviev, Kamenev, Yevdokimov and other leaders of this organization in cultivating the terrorist mentality ~~in~~ *among* their followers, and in *plotting* the murder of members of the Party Central Committee and of the Soviet Government.

To such depths of duplicity and villainy had these people sunk that Zinoviev, who was one of the organizers and instigators of the assassination of S. M. Kirov, and who had urged the murderer to hasten the crime, wrote an obituary of Kirov *speaking of him in terms of eulogy, and demanded that it be published.*

The Zinovievites simulated remorse in court; but they persisted in their duplicity even in the dock. They concealed their connection with Trotsky. They concealed the fact that together with the Trotskyites they had sold themselves to fascist espionage services. They concealed their spying and wrecking activities ~~in preparation for an intervention~~. They concealed *from the court* their connections with the ~~Rights~~ *Bukharinites*, and the existence of a united Trotsky-Bukharin gang of fascist hirelings.

As it later transpired, the murder of Comrade Kirov was the work of this united Trotsky-Bukharin gang.

Even then, in 1935, it had become ~~completely~~ clear that the Zinoviev group was a camouflaged Whiteguard organization whose members fully deserved to be treated as Whiteguards. ~~The Central Committee demanded an end to the complacency and weakening of Party vigilance that had helped Comrade Kirov's mean murderers in their bloody villainy. At the same time, the Central Committee demanded that major corrections be made to the study of Party history and the study of every sort of anti-Party group in our Party's history. Party members were required to know the enemy's methods. They were required to study the tactics and methods that had been used to overcome and defeat these wretched groups in the past.~~

~~During the summer of 1936,~~ *A year later* it became known that the actual, real and direct organizers of the murder of Kirov were Trotsky, Zinoviev, Kamenev and their accomplices, and that they had also made preparations for the assassination of other members of the ~~Politburo~~ Central Committee. Zinoviev, Kamenev, Bakayev, Yevdokimov, Pikel, I. N. Smirnov, Mrachkovsky, Ter-Vaganyan, Reingold and others were committed for trial. Confronted by direct evidence, they had to *admit* publicly, in open court, ~~admit~~ that they had ~~continued to deceive the party and government and that they had~~ *not only* organized the assassination of Kirov, but had ~~gone so far as to utilize the assistance of the German fascist secret police—the Gestapo—becoming Gestapo agents in the process~~ *been planning to murder all the other leaders of the Party and the Government.* Later investigation established the fact that these villains ~~and traitors~~ had been engaged in espionage and in organizing acts of diversion~~, and that they had committed to aiding the fascists to prepare for an armed intervention into the U.S.S.R~~. The full extent of the monstrous moral and political depravity of these men, their despicable villainy and treachery, concealed by hypocritical professions of loyalty to the Party, were revealed at a trial in Moscow ~~from August 19–24,~~ *in* 1936. ~~The open court proceedings and the publication of the~~

~~confessions of the accused and the investigative materials made an enormous impression, not only on the working people in the U.S.S.R., but on the whole world.~~

~~In the history of the political struggle with tsardom, the names of the greatest traitors, the agents of the tsarist government, are well-known: Azef, Malinovsky, Serebryakov, etc. But the treachery of these foul snakes paled in comparison to the infamy of the Trotskyite-Zinovievite terroristic centre that was uncovered during the August trial.~~

The chief instigator and ringleader of this gang of assassins and ~~mean capitalist restorationists~~ *spies* was *Judas* Trotsky. Trotsky's assistants and agents in carrying out ~~Trotsky's directives~~ *his counter-revolutionary instructions* were Zinoviev, Kamenev and ~~other Trotskyites, Zinovievites, Bukharinites and Rykovites~~ *their Trotskyite underlings*. They were preparing to bring about the defeat of the U.S.S.R. in ~~a war against imperialism~~ *the event of attack by imperialist countries*; they had become defeatists with regard to the ~~proletarian~~ *workers' and peasants'* state; they had become *despicable* tools~~, accomplices~~ and agents of ~~fascism~~ *the German and Japanese fascists*.

The main lesson which the Party organizations had to draw from the trials ~~was the increase of Bolshevik vigilance~~ *of the persons implicated in the foul murder of S. M. Kirov* was *that they must put an end to their own political blindness and political heedlessness, and must increase their vigilance and the vigilance of all Party members.* ~~Communists must not for a single minute forget the words of Comrade Stalin: "It is necessary to keep in mind that the growth of the power of the Soviet state will strengthen the resistance of the last hold-overs of the dying classes."~~

~~This is why revolutionary vigilance was a quality that was now especially necessary for all Bolsheviks.~~

~~It was necessary to learn to recognize the enemy, who, having camouflaged himself, had penetrated into the core of our organizations and positioned his people to soil and wreck the Party.~~

~~The Trotskyite bandits took advantage of their connections in order to penetrate into the apparatus of the Presidium of the U.S.S.R. Central Executive Committee and the territory of the Kremlin in order to commit terrorist acts. In June 1935, the Central Committee Plenum issued a decision concerning A. Yenukidze, expelling him from the Central Committee and the Party. It later transpired that A. Yenukidze had been one of the most active members of the counter-revolutionary Trotskyite-Bukharinite espionage and terroristic organization. Over the course of many years, the wretched traitor of our motherland A. Yenukidze had deceived the Party and the Soviet people and carried out the biddings of the fascists and prepared terrorist acts while being closely tied to one of the fascist states' general staff.~~

In a circular letter to Party organizations on the subject of the foul murder of S. M. Kirov, the Central Committee of the Party stated:

> *"a) We must put an end to the opportunist complacency engendered by the enormous assumption that as we grow stronger the enemy will become tamer and more inoffensive. This assumption is an utter fallacy. It is a recrudescence of the Right deviation, which assured all and sundry that our enemies would little by little creep into Socialism and in the end become real Socialists. The Bolsheviks have no business to rest on their laurels; they have no business to sleep at their posts. What we need is not complacency, but vigilance, real Bolshevik revolutionary vigilance. It should be remembered that the more hopeless the position of the enemies, the more eagerly will they clutch at 'extreme measures' as the only recourse of the doomed in their struggle against the Soviet power. We must remember this, and be vigilant.*
>
> *"b) We must properly organize the teaching of the history of the Party to Party members, the study of all and sundry anti-Party groups in the history of our Party, their methods of combating the Party line, their tactics and—still more the tactics and methods of our Party in combating anti-Party groups, the tactics and methods which have enabled our Party to vanquish and demolish these groups. Party members should not only know how the Party combated and vanquished the Constitutional-Democrats, Socialist-Revolutionaries, Mensheviks and Anarchists, but also how it combated and vanquished the Trotskyites, the 'Democratic-Centralists,' the 'Workers' Opposition,' the Zinovievites, the Right deviators, the Right-Leftist freaks and the like. It should never be forgotten that a knowledge and understanding of the history of our Party is a most important and essential means of fully ensuring the revolutionary vigilance of the Party members."*

~~10. Struggle of the Party to Put Its Affairs in Order~~

Of enormous importance in this period was the purge of the Party ranks *from adventitious and alien elements*, begun in 1933, and especially the careful verification of the records of Party members~~, undertaken at Comrade Stalin's initiative,~~ and the exchange of old Party cards for new ones *undertaken after the foul murder of S. M. Kirov*.

Prior to the verification *of the records of Party members*, ~~the worst~~ irresponsibility and negligence in the handling of Party cards had prevailed in many Party organizations. In a number of ~~places~~ *the organizations* ~~there was~~ utterly ~~unbearable~~ *intolerable* CHAOS IN THE REGISTRATION OF COMMUNISTS *was revealed*, a state of affairs which enemies had been turning to their nefarious ends, using the possession of a Party card as a screen for espionage, wrecking, etc. Many leaders of Party organizations had entrusted the enrolment of new members and the issuance of Party cards to persons in minor positions, and often even to Party members of untested reliability.

In a circular letter to all organizations dated May 13, 1935, on the subject of the registration, safekeeping and issuance of Party cards, the Central Committee instructed all organizations to make ~~the most~~ *a* careful verification of the records of Party members and "to establish Bolshevik order in our own Party home."

~~This~~ *The* verification of the records of Party members was of great political value. In connection with the report of Comrade Yezhov, Secretary of the Central Committee,[68] on the results of the verification of the records of Party members, a plenary meeting of the Central Committee *of the Party* adopted a resolution on December 25, 1935, declaring that this verification was an organizational and political measure of enormous importance in strengthening the ranks of the C.P.S.U.(B.).

After the verification of the records of Party members and the exchange of Party cards, the admission of new members into the Party was resumed. In this connection the Central Committee of the C.P.S.U.(B.) demanded that new members should not be ~~brought~~ *admitted* into the Party wholesale, but on the basis of a strictly individual enrolment of "people really advanced and really devoted to the cause of the working class, the finest people of our country, drawn above all from among the workers, and also from among peasants and active intelligentsia, who had been tried and tested in various sectors of the struggle for Socialism."

In resuming the admission of new members to the Party, the Central Committee instructed Party organizations to bear in mind that hostile elements would persist in their attempts to worm their way into the ranks of the C.P.S.U.(B.). Consequently:

> "It is the task of every Party organization to increase Bolshevik vigilance to the utmost, to hold aloft the banner of the Leninist Party, and to safeguard the ranks of the Party from the penetration of alien, hostile and adventitious elements." (Resolution of the Central Committee of the C.P.S.U.[B.], September 29, 1936, published in PRAVDA No. 270, 1936.)

Purging and consolidating its ranks, destroying the enemies of the Party and relentlessly combating distortions of the Party line, the Bolshevik Party rallied closer than ever around ~~Comrade Stalin~~ *its Central Committee* under whose leadership the Party and the Soviet land now passed to *a new stage*—the completion of the construction of a *classless*, Socialist society.

Brief Summary

In the period 1930–34 the Bolshevik Party solved what was, after the winning of power, the most difficult historical problem of the proletarian revolution, namely, to get the millions of small peasant owners to adopt the path of collective farming, the path of Socialism. ~~The most numerous of the exploiting classes, the kulaks, were eliminated. The kulaks' desperate resistance was broken, and they switched over from an open attack against the collective farms to diversion and wrecking within the collective farms.~~

The elimination of the kulaks, the most numerous of the exploiting classes, and the adoption of collective farming by the bulk of the peasants led to the destruction of the last roots of capitalism in the country, to the final victory of Socialism in agriculture, and to the complete consolidation of the Soviet power in the countryside.

After overcoming a number of difficulties ~~and trials, the collective farms under Bolshevik leadership at the end of 1934~~ *of an organizational character, the collective farms* became firmly established and entered upon the path of prosperity. ~~The roots of capitalism in our country were torn out for good.~~

The effect of the First ~~Stalinist~~ Five-Year Plan was to lay an unshakable foundation of a Socialist economic system in our country in the shape of a first-class *Socialist* heavy industry and collective ~~mechanical~~ *mechanized* agriculture~~. It~~, *to* put an end to unemployment ~~forever~~, *to abolish the exploitation of man by man, and to create the conditions for the steady improvement of the material and cultural standards of our working people.* ~~The material well-being of the working people of our motherland grew, as did their cultural level.~~

~~The Second Five-Year Plan of Socialist construction provided for the total elimination of the capitalist elements, the construction of a Socialist society and the further improvement of the working people' material and cultural conditions, as well as a flourishing of their culture.~~

These colossal achievements were attained by the working class, the ~~peasants~~ *collective farmers*, and the working people of our country generally, thanks to the *bold, revolutionary and* wise policy of the ~~C.P.S.U.(B.) and its chief, Comrade Stalin~~ *Party and the Government*.

The surrounding capitalist world, ~~which was planning to attack the U.S.S.R. throughout this period and still plans to do so~~ *striving to undermine and disrupt the might of the U.S.S.R.*, ~~organized groups of wreckers and spies~~ *worked with redoubled energy to organize gangs of assassins, wreckers and spies* within the U.S.S.R. This hostile activity of the capitalist encirclement became particularly marked with the advent of fascism to power in Germany *and Japan*. In the Trotskyites~~;~~ *and* Zinovievites ~~and Bukharinites~~, fascism found faithful servants who were ready to spy, sabotage, commit acts of terrorism and diversion, and to work for the defeat of the U.S.S.R. in order to restore capitalism. ~~The Trotskyite-Bukharinite gang of mercenaries would be exposed and destroyed during the next period, between 1935 and 1937.~~

The Soviet Government punished these degenerates with an iron hand, dealing ruthlessly with these enemies of the people and traitors to the country.

CHAPTER TWELVE

The Bolshevik Party in the Struggle to Complete the Building of the Socialist Society. Introduction of the New Constitution[1] (1935–1937)

1. International ~~and Home~~ Situation in 1935–37. *Temporary Mitigation of the Economic Crisis. Beginning of a New Economic Crisis. Seizure of Ethiopia by Italy. German and Italian Intervention in Spain. Japanese Invasion of Central China. Beginning of Second Imperialist War*

~~The 1935–37 period was distinguished by a very complex international situation. All the contradictions of the capitalist system became especially aggravated during this period. Preparations for war and a new division of the world increased among the imperialist states, as did their hostility to the U.S.S.R.~~

~~The fascist states and warmongers had already dragged about a quarter of humanity into war by 1937. The fascist robbers first attacked the weak states, taking advantage of the conniving and cowardly nature of the bourgeois-capitalist states' foreign policy.~~

~~In 1935, fascist Italy attacked Ethiopia and subjugated her. In 1936, Germany and Italy organized a fascist mutiny of Spanish generals and led a war against the revolutionary Spanish people. At the beginning of 1938, Germany forced Austria to change the makeup of her government through the threat of intervention and then seized Austria. The Japanese fascist military clique, which had been involved for a long time in what amounted to a war against China, moved in 1937 to take over all of China. But the Chinese people united together in a united national front against the Japanese invaders and oppressors and resisted them heroically.~~[2]

~~Between 1935–37, a number of changes took place in the capitalist world economy. The world economic crisis already in 1933–34 began to transform into a special type of depression.~~ *The economic crisis that had broken out in the capitalist countries in the latter half of 1929 lasted until the end of 1933. After that industry ceased to decline, the crisis was succeeded by a period of stagnation, and was then followed by a certain revival, a certain upward trend.* ~~During previous industrial economic crises, depressions (stagnation) gradually gave way~~

ГЛАВА XII

ПАРТИЯ БОЛЬШЕВИКОВ В БОРЬБЕ ЗА ЗАВЕРШЕНИЕ СТРОИТЕЛЬСТВА СОЦИАЛИСТИЧЕСКОГО ОБЩЕСТВА И ПРОВЕДЕНИЕ НОВОЙ КОНСТИТУЦИИ

(1935—1937 гг.)

1. Международная и внутренняя обстановка 1935—1937 годов

Период 1935—1937 годов отличался крайне сложной международной обстановкой. В этот период особо обострились все противоречия капиталистической системы. Усилилась подготовка империалистических государств к войне за новый передел мира и враждебность их к СССР.

Фашистские государства, поджигатели войны, втянули уже в 1937 году, примерно, четвертую часть человечества в войну. Фашистские разбойники нападают в первую очередь на слабые государства, пользуясь при этом попустительством и трусливой политикой буржуазно-демократических государств.

В 1935 году фашистская Италия напала на Абиссинию и поработила ее. Германия и Италия организовали в июле 1936 года фашистский мятеж испанских генералов и повели войну против революционного испанского народа. В начале 1938 года Германия угрозой интервенции заставила изменить состав правительства в Австрии, усилив в нем фашистские элементы, а затем захватила Австрию. Японская фашистская военщина, давно уже ведущая фактическую войну против Китая, в 1937 году приступила к захвату всего Китая. Но китайский народ объединился в единый национальный фронт против японских захватчиков и угнетателей и оказал им героическое сопротивление.

За 1935—1937 годы произошли некоторые изменения в экономике мирового капитализма. Мировой экономический кризис уже в 1933—1934 годах стал переходить в депрессию особого рода. Во время прошлых экономических промышленных кризисов депрессия (застой) постепенно сменялась промышленным оживлением, затем бурным подъемом промышленности, далеко превосходящим докризисный уровень. Та депрессия особого рода, а затем некоторое оживление промышленности, которыми сменился мировой экономический кризис, начавшийся в 1929 году, не привели к новому подъему и расцвету капиталистической промышленности. Мировое капиталистическое промышленное производство в 1936 году в целом еще не вернулось к докризисному периоду, составляя 95—96% промышленной продукции 1929 года. А в 1937 году в странах капитализма (в первую очередь в Соединенных штатах Америки) начался уже новый экономический кри-

19* 291

First page of Chapter Twelve with Stalin's editing from the summer of 1938. RGASPI, f. 558, op. 3, d. 77, l. 291.

~~to an industrial revival, and then a strong expansion of industry, far surpassing pre-crisis levels. This special type of depression, and then the marginal revival of industry that followed the world economic crisis that began in 1929, did not lead to a new expansion and blossoming of capitalist industry.~~ *But this upward trend was not of the kind that ushers in an industrial boom on a new and higher basis.* World capitalist industry ~~in 1936 as a whole~~ was unable to reach the level of ~~the pre-crisis period~~ *1929*, attaining *by the middle of 1937 only* 95–96 per cent of ~~1929's~~ *that* level. And *already* in *the second half of* 1937, a new economic crisis began ~~in the capitalist countries~~, ~~(~~affecting first of all the United States of America~~)~~. By the end of 1937, the number of unemployed in ~~America~~ *the U.S.A.* had *again* risen to ten million. In Great Britain, *too,* unemployment was rapidly increasing.[3]

The capitalist countries thus found themselves faced with a new economic crisis before they had even recovered from the ravages of the preceding one.

~~The conditions for the working class and all the labourers were especially hard in the countries with fascist dictatorships. In these countries, workers' blood flowed like rivers and the ferocious fascist gangs mistreated the popular masses. Fascism enslaved the workers, reducing their pay to the poverty level, extending their working day, establishing prison-like conditions in the workplace and bringing to ruin the peasant masses.~~

~~The fascists kept the workers and peasants on starvation rations as they prepared for war and a redivision of the world with the capitalist states and as they prepared to attack our motherland. The official slogan of fascist Germany became "guns before butter," which in reality meant "guns instead of bread." Fascism drove many millions of labourers to complete impoverishment. Over the course of the 1936–37 winter, about 11 million people in Germany were officially considered poor. The fascist governments of Germany, Poland, and Italy eliminated workers' unemployment insurance, even though the cities were burgeoning with millions of unemployed. Instead of providing the unemployed with assistance, the fascist governments organized forced labour camps for them.~~

The result was that the contradictions between the imperialist countries, as likewise between the bourgeoisie and the proletariat, grew still more acute. As a consequence, the aggressor states redoubled their efforts to recoup themselves for the losses caused by the economic crisis at home at the expense of other, poorly defended, countries. The two notorious aggressor states, Germany and Japan, were this time joined by a third—Italy.

In 1935, fascist Italy attacked Ethiopia and subjugated her. She did so without any reason or justification in "international law"; she attacked her like a robber, without declaring war, as is now the vogue with the fascists. This was a blow not only at Ethiopia, but also at Great Britain, at her sea routes from Europe to India and to Asia generally. Great Britain vainly attempted to prevent Italy from establishing herself in Ethiopia. Italy later withdrew from the League of Nations so as to leave her hands free, and began to arm on an intensive scale.

Thus, on the shortest sea routes between Europe and Asia, a new war knot was tied.

Fascist Germany tore up the Versailles Peace Treaty by a unilateral act, and adopted a scheme for the FORCIBLE *revision of the map of Europe. The German fascists made no secret of the fact that they were seeking to subjugate the neighbouring states, or, at least, to seize such of their territories as were peopled by Germans. Accordingly, they planned first to seize Austria, then to strike at Czechoslovakia, then, maybe, at Poland—which also has a compact territory peopled by Germans and bordering on Germany—and then . . . well, then "we shall see."*

In the summer of 1936, Germany and Italy started military intervention against the Spanish Republic. Under the guise of supporting the Spanish fascists, they secured the opportunity of surreptitiously landing troops on Spanish territory, in the rear of France, and stationing their fleets in Spanish waters—in the zones of the Balearic Islands and Gibraltar in the south, the Atlantic Ocean in the west, and the Bay of Biscay in the north. At the beginning of 1938 the German fascists seized Austria, thus establishing themselves in the middle reaches of the Danube and expanding in the south of Europe, towards the Adriatic Sea.

The German and Italian fascists extended their intervention in Spain, at the same time assuring the world that they were fighting the Spanish "Reds" and harboured no other designs. But this was a crude and shallow camouflage designed to deceive simpletons. As a matter of fact, they were striking at Great Britain and France, by bestriding the sea communications of these countries with their vast African and Asiatic colonial possessions.

As to the seizure of Austria, this at any rate could not be passed off as a struggle against the Versailles Treaty, as part of Germany's effort to protect her "national" interests by recovering territory lost in the first Imperialist War. Austria had not formed part of Germany, either before or after the war. The FORCIBLE *annexation of Austria was a glaring imperialist seizure of foreign territory. It left no doubt as to fascist Germany's designs to gain a dominant position on the West European continent.*

This was above all a blow at the interests of France and Great Britain.

Thus, in the south of Europe, in the zone of Austria and the Adriatic, and in the extreme west of Europe, in the zone of Spain and the waters washing her shores, new war knots were tied.

In 1937, the Japanese fascist militarists seized Peiping, invaded Central China and occupied Shanghai. Like the Japanese invasion of Manchuria several years earlier, the invasion of Central China was effected by the customary Japanese method, in robber fashion, by the dishonest exploitation of various "local incidents" engineered by the Japanese themselves, and in violation of all "international standards," treaties, agreements, etc. The seizure of Tientsin and Shanghai placed the keys of the immense China market in the hands of Japan. As long as Japan holds Shanghai and Tientsin, she can at any moment oust Great Britain and the U.S.A. from Central China, where they have huge investments.

Of course, the heroic struggle of the Chinese people and their army against the Japanese invaders, the tremendous national revival in China, her huge resources of man-power and territory, and, lastly, the determination of the Chinese National Government to fight the struggle for emancipation to a finish, until the invaders are completely driven out from Chinese territory, all go to show beyond a doubt that there is no future for the Japanese imperialists in China, and never will be.

But it is nevertheless true that for the time being Japan holds the keys of China's trade, and that her war on China is in effect a most serious blow at the interests of Great Britain and the U.S.A.

Thus, in the Pacific, in the zone of China, one more war knot was tied.

All these facts show that a second imperialist war has actually begun. It began stealthily, without any declaration of war. States and nations have, almost imperceptibly, slipped into the orbit of a second imperialist war. It was the three aggressor states, the fascist ruling circles of Germany, Italy and Japan, that began the war in various parts of the world. It is being waged over a huge expanse of territory, stretching from Gibraltar to Shanghai. It has already drawn over five hundred million people into its orbit. In the final analysis, it is being waged against the capitalist interests of Great Britain, France and the U.S.A., since its object is a redivision of the world and of the spheres of influence in favour of the aggressor countries and at the expense of the so-called democratic states.

A distinguishing feature of the second imperialist war is that so far it is being waged and extended by the aggressor powers, while the other powers, the "democratic" powers, against whom in fact the war is directed, pretend that it does not concern them, wash their hands of it, draw back, boast of their love of peace, scold the fascist aggressors, and . . . surrender their positions to the aggressors bit by bit, at the same time asserting that they are preparing to resist.

This war, it will be seen, is of a rather strange and one-sided character. But that does not prevent it from being a brutal war of unmitigated conquest waged at the expense of the poorly defended peoples of Ethiopia, Spain and China.

It would be wrong to attribute this one-sided character of the war to the military or economic weakness of the "democratic" states. The "democratic" states are, of course, stronger than the fascist states. The one-sided character of the developing world war is due to the absence of a united front of the "democratic" states against the fascist powers. The so-called democratic states, of course, do not approve of the "excesses" of the fascist states and fear any accession of strength to the latter. But they fear even more the working-class movement in Europe and the movement of national emancipation in Asia, and regard fascism as an "excellent antidote" to these "dangerous" movements. For this reason the ruling circles of the "democratic" states, especially the ruling Conservative circles of Great Britain, confine themselves to a policy of pleading with the overweening fascist rulers "not to go to extremes," at the same time giving them to understand that they "fully comprehend" and on the whole sympathize with their reactionary police policy towards the working-class movement and the national emancipation movement. In this respect, the ruling circles of Britain are roughly pursuing the same policy as was pursued under tsardom by the Russian liberal-monarchist bourgeois, who, while fearing the "excesses" of tsarist policy, feared the people even more, and therefore resorted to a policy of pleading with the tsar and, consequently, of CONSPIRING *with the tsar against the people. As we know, the liberal-monarchist bourgeoisie of Russia paid dearly for this dual policy. It may be presumed that history will exact retribution also from the ruling circles of Britain, and of their friends in France and the U.S.A.*

~~The foreign policy of the U.S.S.R. during this period was, as before, directed to support the struggle for peace and against war.~~ *Clearly, the U.S.S.R. could not shut its eyes to such a turn in the international situation and ignore the ominous events. Any war, however small, started by the aggressors, constitutes a menace to the peaceable countries. The second imperialist war, which has so "imperceptibly" stolen upon the nations and has involved over five hundred million people, is bound all the more to represent a most serious danger to all nations, and to the U.S.S.R. in the first place. This is eloquently borne out by the formation of the "Anti-Communist Bloc" by Germany, Italy and Japan. Therefore, our country, while pursuing its policy of peace, set to work to further strengthen its frontier defences and the fighting efficiency of its Red Army and Navy.* ~~With these goals in mind, in September~~ *Towards the end of* 1934 the U.S.S.R. joined the League of Nations~~, looking at it as a sort of "bump," in Stalin's words, on the road to war~~. *It did so in the knowledge that the League, in spite of its weakness, might nevertheless serve as a place where aggressors can be exposed, and as a certain instrument of peace, however feeble, that might hinder the outbreak of war. The Soviet Union considered that in times like these even so weak an international organization as the League of Nations should not be ignored.* In May 1935 a treaty of mutual assistance against possible attack by ~~enemies and~~ aggressors was signed between France and the U.S.S.R. A similar treaty was *simultaneously* concluded between the Soviet Union and Czechoslovakia.[4] *In March 1936 the U.S.S.R. signed a treaty of mutual assistance with the Mongolian People's Republic, and in August 1937 a pact of non-aggression with the Republic of China.*

~~In the name of the Soviet Government, Comrade Litvinov stubbornly defended the peaceful foreign policy of the U.S.S.R. in front of the whole world~~

~~at the League of Nations and other international conferences. In front of the whole world, Soviet diplomacy exposed and will continue to expose in the future the policies and plans of the fascist states and warmongers (aggressors). Soviet diplomacy likewise exposed in front of the working people of the world the foreign policy of the bourgeois-democratic states, which encouraged the aggressors and the bloody intervention of German, Italian, and Portuguese fascism in Spain.~~

~~Our entire country and all the people of the U.S.S.R. raised their voice in the defence of the Spanish people and the Spanish revolution. Tens of millions of rubles were raised in the shortest possible time to aid the Spanish people and Spanish women and children. Several ships, laden with food, clothing, and shoes, were sent to Spain. Soviet aid gave encouragement and strength to the ranks of the Spanish working people, who were bravely fighting against the interventionists and Spanish mutineers.~~

~~From besieged Madrid, the Central Committee of the heroic Spanish communist party sent greetings to Comrade Stalin in the name of the Spanish people, writing that the brotherly aid of the working people of the U.S.S.R. had strengthened the Spanish people's faith in victory.~~

~~Comrade Stalin replied to Jose Dias, the general secretary of the Central Committee of the Spanish Communist Party, in a telegram which will go down in the history of the international proletariat's struggle as one of the most glorious documents of our era.~~

> ~~"The working people of the Soviet Union," wrote Comrade Stalin, "are only fulfilling their duty in providing all the aid that they can to the revolutionary Spanish masses. They have decided for themselves that the liberation of Spain from the fascist, reactionary yoke is not a private Spanish affair, but the general business of all advanced and progressive mankind."~~[25]

~~The U.S.S.R. looked with great sympathy upon the brave struggle of the Chinese people against the Japanese invaders and a non-aggression pact was signed with republican China at precisely the moment that Japanese imperialism fell upon the Chinese people.~~

~~Under the leadership of its chief and teacher Comrade Stalin, the C.P.S.U.(B.) has represented the interests of not only the working people of the U.S.S.R., but of all advanced and progressive mankind.~~

~~The hostility of the capitalist encirclement towards the U.S.S.R.—the country of victorious Socialism—then further increased, first of all among the fascist states. Preparing for war with the U.S.S.R., the reactionary-fascist forces of~~

~~the capitalist countries took advantage of the Trotskyite-Bukharinite gang of traitors, bourgeois nationalists and other enemies of the Soviet people.~~

~~In 1937, the Bolshevik Party and Soviet people uprooted many hidden nests of Trotskyite-Bukharinites and other double-dealers, spies, wreckers, and saboteurs. The glorious Soviet counterintelligence, directed by Stalin's loyal student N. I. Yezhov, dealt a devastating blow to the plans of the fascist general staffs. The Trotskyite-Bukharinite gang of fascist henchmen, bourgeois nationalists and other enemies of the Soviet people wanted to restore power to the capitalists and landlords and drown the victories of the Socialist revolution in oceans of blood.~~

~~According to the confessions of fascist henchmen who were caught in the act, 1937 was the appointed date for the fascist states' attack on our motherland. The Soviet punitive organs' destruction of the spy nests and wreckers interfered with these plans' realization.~~

~~The growing strength of the well-equipped Red Army was a stern warning to all those who want to attack the U.S.S.R. The well thought-out, consistent policy of peace that the Soviet Union pursued and will continue to pursue in the future increased the support that it enjoyed from all those in favour of peace and from all of mankind's working people. The Stalinist policy of peace exposed the aggressive policies of the militant circles of the capitalist countries and complicated their attack against the U.S.S.R.~~

~~1935–37 was to be the period for the struggle to complete the construction of the Socialist society. During the previous periods, a powerful, first-class industry had been created, as had a powerful and mechanized agriculture, under the leadership of the Bolshevik Party, the Lenin-Stalin Party. In order to harness the new technique of our first-class factories and mills, and of our state farms and collective farms, people were needed who had mastered technique. This was the most important condition for the successful completion of the construction of the Socialist society.~~

~~In May 1935, Comrade Stalin advanced a new slogan in his speech to the graduates of the Red Army Academies: "Cadres decide everything." Comrade Stalin underscored with all his strength the task of taking care of people and~~ paying attention to the cadres.[6]

> ~~"It is time to realize that OF ALL THE VALUABLE CAPITAL THAT THE WORLD POSSESSES, THE MOST VALUABLE AND MOST DECISIVE IS PEOPLE, CADRES. IT MUST BE REALIZED THAT IN THE PRESENT CONDITIONS 'CADRES DECIDE EVERYTHING.' If we have good and numerous cadres in industry, agriculture, transport and the army—our country will be invincible," pointed out Comrade Stalin.~~[7]

~~The slogan advanced by Comrade Stalin and the growth of the toiling masses' welfare gave life to the powerful Stakhanovite movement, which in 1935 was already well developed. During these years, the Bolshevik Party conducted a gigantic mobilization of the masses in the struggle for the mastery of technique and the Socialist productivity of labour.~~

~~Dozens of meetings of the progressive workers of Socialist industry, agriculture and transport with Party and state leaders shared the pioneers' experience with the entire country.~~

~~This Stalinist concern for people moved and will continue to move the Soviet people to accomplish heroic feats. The fairy tale-like rescue of the crew of the icebreaker Chelyuskin, which sank far away in the Arctic Sea, attracted the attention of the entire world. The brave flyers—Molokov, Vodopyanov, Levanevsky, Lyapidevsky, Kamanin, and Slepnev—saved the entire expedition. These heroic flyers were dubbed Heroes of the Soviet Union. The crew of the Chelyuskin knew that the Central Committee Politburo, headed by Comrade Stalin, was supervising the rescue effort's progress and that the entire country was thinking of them and providing help. This contributed to the Chelyuskinites' bravery.~~

~~In 1937, Soviet patriots showed the entire world new, wonderful examples of heroism and self-sacrifice. An expedition of Soviet aeroplanes raised the red flag at the North Pole. Four fearless researchers conducted unprecedented scientific work on a drifting sheet of ice in order to uncover the secrets of the Arctic.~~

~~These four Soviet heroes—Papanin, Shirshov, Krenkel and Fyodorov—spent more than 8 months on the ice floe, enduring enormous danger and showing exceptional courage. When storms threatened their fracturing ice sheet, and when their lives were in danger, the Soviet Government and Party set up a rescue team and on February 19, 1938, the icebreakers Murman and Taimyr broke through the ice into the Greenland Sea and rescued the four heroes and their legendary station "North Pole."~~

~~Soviet flyers' non-stop flights to America across the Arctic stunned the whole world. Yet again, the power of Soviet technique and the spirit, bravery and skill of Soviet flyers was shown to the entire world.~~

~~The Heroes of the Soviet Union who made these flights—Chkalov, Baidukov and Belyakov, and then Gromov, Yumashev and Danilin, who simultaneously set a world distance record—did so as conquerors of nature and the bearers of world progress and civilization. But along with this, their flights also served as a stern warning to the enemies of the Soviet Union. It's not for nothing that the world press emphasized over and over that the Soviet flyers could reach several countries that are particularly hostile to the Soviet Union much easier than America.~~

~~In February 1935, the Seventh Congress of Soviets of the Union of Soviet Socialist Republics reached the decision to alter the Constitution of the U.S.S.R. (the Fundamental Law). The change of the Constitution was necessitated by the vast changes that had taken place in the U.S.S.R. since 1924, since the ratification of the Soviet Union's first Constitution. During this period the relationship of class forces within the country had completely changed: a new Socialist industry had been created, the kulaks had been smashed, the collective farm system had triumphed, and Socialist ownership had been established in the city and countryside as the basis of Soviet society. This made it possible to move toward further democratization of the electoral system and the introduction of universal, equal and direct suffrage with a secret ballot.~~[8]

~~The new Constitution of the U.S.S.R., the Constitution of Victorious Socialism, was drafted by a special Constitution Commission under the chairmanship of Comrade Stalin. After a nationwide discussion, the draft was unanimously ratified by the Extraordinary Eighth All-Union Congress of Soviets on December 5, 1936, following a report by Comrade Stalin.~~

~~1937 went down in the history of Socialism as the first year of the implementation of the U.S.S.R.'s Stalin constitution. After its implementation, Socialist democracy became fully developed and the unbreakable connection between the Bolshevik Party and Soviet people became even more strong and manifold.~~

~~During the elections to the U.S.S.R. Supreme Soviet on December 12, 1937, about 90 million of 91.1 million votes, or 98.6 per cent, voted for candidates from the communist and non-Party bloc. No other party or government in the world has ever had such a brilliant electoral victory.~~

~~The elections to the U.S.S.R. Supreme Soviet show the great moral and political unity of the Soviet people. All the Soviet people have rallied tightly around the communist Party and Comrade Stalin, whose name acts as the symbol and standard of the Soviet people's moral and political unity.~~

2. Further Progress of Industry and Agriculture in the U.S.S.R. Second Five-Year Plan Fulfilled Ahead of Time. Reconstruction of Agriculture and Completion of Collectivization. Importance of Cadres. Stakhanov Movement. Rising Standard of Welfare. Rising Cultural Standard. Strength of the Soviet Revolution

Whereas, three years after the economic crisis of 1930–33, a new economic crisis began in the capitalist countries, in the U.S.S.R. industry continued to make steady progress DURING THE WHOLE OF THIS PERIOD. *Whereas by the middle of 1937 world capitalist industry, as a whole, had barely attained 95–96 per cent of the level of production of 1929, only to be caught in the throes of a new crisis in the second half of 1937, the industry of the U.S.S.R. in its steady cumulative progress had by the end of 1937 attained 428 per cent of the output of 1929, or over 700 per cent of the pre-war output.*[9]

These achievements were a direct result of the policy of reconstruction so persistently pursued by the Party and the Government.

The result of these achievements was that the Second Five-Year Plan of industry was fulfilled ahead of time. It was completed by April 1, 1937, that is, in four years and three months.

This was a most important victory for Socialism.

Progress in agriculture presented very much the same picture. The total area under all crops increased from 105,000,000 hectares in 1913 (pre-war) to 135,000,000 hectares in 1937. The grain harvest increased from 4,800,000,000 poods in 1913, to 6,800,000,000 poods in 1937, the raw cotton crop from 44,000,000 poods to 154,000,000 poods, the flax crop (fibre) from 19,000,000 poods to 31,000,000 poods, the sugar-beet crop from 654,000,000 poods to 1,311,000,000 poods, and the oil-seed crop from 129,000,000 poods to 306,000,000 poods.[10]

It should be mentioned that in 1937 the collective farms alone (without the state farms) produced a marketable surplus of over 1,700,000,000 poods of grain, which was at least 400,000,000 poods more than the landlords, kulaks and peasants together marketed in 1913.[11]

Only one branch of agriculture—livestock farming—still lagged behind the pre-war level and continued to progress at a slower rate.

As to collectivization in agriculture, it might be considered completed. The number of peasant households that had joined the collective farms by 1937 was 18,500,000 or 93 per cent of the total number of peasant households, while the grain crop area of the collective farms amounted to 99 per cent of the total grain crop area of the peasants.[12]

The fruits of the reconstruction of agriculture and of the extensive supply of tractors and machinery for agricultural purposes were now manifest.

As a result of the completion of the reconstruction of industry and agriculture the national economy was now abundantly supplied with first-class technique. Industry, agriculture, the transport system and the army had received huge quantities of modern technique—machinery and machine tools, tractors and agricultural machines, locomotives and steamships, artillery and tanks, aeroplanes and warships. Tens and hundreds[13] *of thousands of trained people were required, people capable of harnessing all this technique and getting the most out of it. Without this, without a sufficient number of people who had mastered technique, there was a risk of technique becoming so much dead and unused metal. This was a serious danger, a result of the fact that the growth in the number of trained people, cadres, capable of harnessing, making full use of technique* WAS NOT KEEPING PACE WITH, *and even* LAGGING FAR BEHIND, *the spread of technique. Matters were further complicated by the fact that a considerable number of our industrial executives did not realize this danger and believed that technique would just "do the job by itself." Whereas, formerly, they had underrated the importance of technique and treated it with disdain, now they began to overrate it and turn it into a fetish. They did not realize that without people who had mastered technique, technique was a dead thing. They did not realize that to make technique highly productive, people who had mastered technique were required.*

Thus the problem of cadres who had mastered technique became one of prime importance.

The executives who displayed an excessive zeal for technique and a consequent underestimation of the importance of trained people, cadres, had to have their attention turned to the study and mastery of technique, and to the necessity of doing everything to train numerous cadres capable of harnessing technique and getting the most out of it.

Whereas formerly, at the beginning of the reconstruction period, when the country suffered from a dearth of technique, the Party had issued the slogan, "technique in the period of reconstruction decides everything," now, when there was an abundance of technique, when the reconstruction had in the main been completed, and when the country was experiencing an acute dearth of cadres, it became incumbent on the Party to issue a new slogan, one that would focus attention, not so much on technique, as on people, on cadres capable of utilizing technique to the full.

Of great importance in this respect was the speech made by Comrade Stalin to the graduates from the Red Army Academies in May 1935.

> *"Formerly," said Comrade Stalin, "we used to say that 'technique decides everything.' This slogan helped us to put an end to the dearth in technique and to create a vast technical base in every branch of activity for the equipment of our people with first-class technique. That is very good. But it is not enough, it is not enough by far. In order to set technique going and to utilize it to the full, we need people who have mastered technique, we need cadres capable of mastering and utilizing this technique according to all the rules of the art. Without people who have mastered technique, technique is dead. In the charge of people who have mastered technique, technique can and should perform miracles. If in our first-class mills and factories, in our state farms and collective farms and in our Red Army we had sufficient cadres capable of harnessing this technique, our country would secure results three times and four times as great as at present. That is why emphasis must now[14] be laid on people, on cadres, on workers who have mastered technique. That is why the old slogan, 'technique decides everything,' which is a reflection of a period already passed, a period in which we suffered from a dearth of technique, must now be replaced by*

> *a new slogan, the slogan 'cadres DECIDE EVERYTHING.' That is the main thing now. . . .*
>
> *"It is time to realize that of all the valuable capital the world possesses, the most valuable and most decisive is people, cadres. It must be realized that under our present conditions 'cadres DECIDE EVERYTHING.' If we have good and numerous cadres in industry, agriculture, transport and the army—our country will be invincible. If we do not have such cadres—we shall be lame on both legs."*

Thus the prime task now was to accelerate the training of technical cadres and rapidly to master the new technique with the object of securing a continued rise in productivity of labour.

The most striking example of the growth of such cadres, of the mastering of the new technique by our people, and of the continued rise in productivity of labour was the Stakhanov movement. It originated and developed in the Donetz Basin, in the coal industry, and spread to other branches of industry, to the railways, and then to agriculture. It was called the Stakhanov movement after its originator, Alexei Stakhanov, a coal-hewer in the Central Irmino Colliery (Donetz Basin). Stakhanov had been preceded by Nikita Izotov, who had broken all previous records in coal hewing. On August 31, 1935, Stakhanov hewed 102 tons of coal in one shift and thus fulfilled the standard output fourteen times over. This inaugurated a mass movement of workers and collective farmers for raising the standards of output, for a new advance in productivity of labour. Busygin in the automobile industry, Smetanin in the shoe industry, Krivonoss on the railways, Musinsky in the timber industry, Yevdokia Vinogradova and Maria Vinogradova in the textile industry, Maria Demchenko, Maria Gnatenko, P. Angelina, Polagutin, Kolesov, Borin and Kovardak in agriculture—these were the first pioneers of the Stakhanov movement.

They were followed by other pioneers, whole battalions of them, who surpassed the productivity of labour of the earlier pioneers.

Tremendous stimulus was given to the Stakhanov movement by the First All-Union Conference of Stakhanovites held in the Kremlin in November 1935, and by the speech Comrade Stalin made there.

> *"The Stakhanov movement," Comrade Stalin said in this speech, "is the expression of a new wave of Socialist emulation, a new and higher stage of Socialist emulation. . . . In the past, some three years ago, in the period of the first stage of Socialist emulation, Socialist emulation was not necessarily associated with modern technique. At that time, in fact, we had hardly any modern technique. The present stage of Socialist emulation, the Stakhanov movement, on the other hand, is necessarily associated*

> *with modern technique. The Stakhanov movement would be inconceivable without a new and higher technique. We have before us people like Comrade Stakhanov, Busygin, Smetanin, Krivonoss,*[15] *the Vinogradovas and many others, new people, working men and women, who have completely mastered the technique of their jobs, have harnessed it and driven ahead. We had no such people, or hardly any such people, some three years ago. . . . The significance of the Stakhanov movement lies in the fact that it is a movement which is smashing the old technical standards, because they are inadequate, which in a number of cases is surpassing the productivity of labour of the foremost capitalist countries, and is thus creating the practical possibility of further consolidating Socialism in our country, of converting our country into the most prosperous of all countries."*

Describing the methods of work of the Stakhanovites, and bringing out the tremendous significance of the Stakhanov movement for the future of our country, Comrade Stalin went on to say:

> *"Look at our comrades, the Stakhanovites, more closely. What type of people are they? They are mostly young or middle-aged working men and women, people with culture and technical knowledge, who show examples of precision and accuracy in work, who are able to appreciate the time factor in work and who have learned to count not only the minutes, but also the seconds. The majority of them have taken the technical minimum courses and are continuing their technical education. They are free of the conservatism and stagnation of certain engineers, technicians and business executives; they are marching boldly forward, smashing the antiquated technical standards and creating new and higher standards; they are introducing amendments into the designed capacities and economic plans drawn up by the leaders of our industry; they often supplement and correct what the engineers and technicians have to say, they often teach them and impel them forward, for they are people who have completely mastered the technique of their job and who are able to squeeze out of technique the maximum that can be squeezed out of it. Today the Stakhanovites are still few in number, but who can doubt that tomorrow there will be ten times more of them? Is it not clear that the Stakhanovites are innovators in our industry, that the Stakhanov movement represents the future of our industry, that it contains the seed of the future rise in the cultural and technical level of the working class, that it opens to us the path by which alone can be achieved those high indices of productivity of labour which are essential for the transition from Socialism to Communism and for the elimination of the distinction between mental labour and manual labour."*

The spread of the Stakhanov movement and the fulfilment of the Second Five-Year Plan ahead of time created the conditions for a new rise in the standard of welfare and culture of the working people.

~~2. Strengthening Socialist Productive Relations~~

~~The Second Five-Year Plan was pursued under the slogan of strengthening and developing the Socialist economy in the city and countryside. With each year, the new Socialist productive relations in the countryside were strengthened. The old habits of yesterday's petty landholders were transformed and a new habit of co-operative collective labour was devised.~~

~~The collective farms moved far ahead, armed by Soviet power with the newest agricultural techniques, tractors and combines. Labour organization in the collective farms was improved. The distribution of income according to labour through the work-day-unit struck a blow against slackers and provided support to committed collective farmers. Improvements were made to the use of tractors and vehicles and their productivity rose. Harvest-time work in the collective farm fields was improved. Rich livestock farms emerged among the collective farms and collective farmers acquired cows, pigs and other auxiliary forms of production.[16]~~

~~In February 1935, right after the Seventh All-Union Congress of Soviets, the Second Congress of Collective Farm Shock Workers assembled in the Kremlin.[17] In the two years since the First Congress of Collective Farm Shock Workers (February 1933), collective farm construction had developed in many ways. Kulak wrecking in the majority of collective farms had been exposed and defeated. A strong group of collective farm activists had taken shape. The collective farm peasantry had confidently set out on the path to Socialism, to the creation of a prosperous collective farm life, under the leadership of the Bolshevik Party and with the help of its non-Party activists. It was the great Stalin who pointed to this path in his historic address at the First Congress of Collective Farm Shock Workers. Comrade Stalin's statement "WORK HONESTLY AND PRESERVE THE COLLECTIVE FARM'S BOUNTY" became the collective farmers' maxim and part of the collective farms' everyday life.~~

~~There was still a lot of various sorts of disorganization, dislocation and difficulties at the time of the First Congress of Collective Farm Shock Workers. It was not possible to entirely resolve such an enormous affair for peasants who were entirely unaccustomed to it. What's more, kulak survivals on the collective farms were engaged in a lot of wrecking and dissembling at that time.~~

~~In 1932, even the strong, leading collective farms were still distributing three to four kilograms of grain per day-work-unit. But in 1934, the leading~~

collective farms began to give sometimes seven and sometimes twelve or more kilograms of grain per day-work-unit.

The successes of the collective farms and the wonderful, cultured collective farm life were clearly reflected in the delegates' addresses at the Second All-Union Congress of Collective Farm Shock Workers.

A new set of rules for the agricultural artel was ratified at the Second All-Union Congress of Collective Farmer Shock Workers. This set of rules stated that collective farm and artel members were obligated to strengthen their collective farms, work honestly, distribute collective farm income according to labour, protect public property, preserve the collective farm's assets, protect tractors and vehicles, ensure proper care for work horses and fulfil the assignments of the worker-peasant state. In doing this, they would make their collective farms operate in a Bolshevik way and make all of the collective farmers prosperous.

In this way, all the fundamental slogans advanced by Comrade Stalin at the First Congress of Collective Farm Shock Workers that had subsequently entered into everyday collective farm life were written into the collective farms' set of rules. Comrade Stalin took part in the development of the congress rules commission with other leading collective farmers.

"Reconciling the collective farmers' personal interests with the public interests of the collective farms—this is where the key to strengthening the collective farm is located," said Comrade Stalin. And this was how the new set of rules for agricultural artels was constructed, earning it the moniker of a Stalinist set of collective farm rules. Under the new set of collective farm rules, the collective farmers' personal interests were deftly reconciled with the public interests of the collective farm. The fundamental, critical means of production on collective farms were socialized (draft animals, agricultural implements, reserve seed, feed for the socialized cattle, work buildings, etc.). But along with this, every collective farm household was allowed to have its own small private holdings: it received land for a garden (from a quarter to half a hectare, and in outlying areas, up to 1 hectare). Depending on the region, every peasant household was allowed to have for its own use between 1–3 cows, 1–3 sows and their offspring, 10 to 25 sheep, an unlimited number of poultry, etc. These private holdings were to be held by the collective farmer as an auxiliary form of production. Through these holdings, the collective farmer's private everyday needs, his family's needs and his personal tastes could be satisfied without negatively affecting the public interests of the collective farm.

The new set of Stalinist rules for collective farm life, worked out through the experience of millions, crowned and solidified the victory of the collective farm system.

~~The new set of rules stated that land used by the collective farm that is the people's public property is signed over to the collective farm for its permanent use, that is, in perpetuity. Land is assigned to the collective farm by Government act, a copy of which is given to the collective farm leadership.~~

~~In November 1935, collective farm shock workers of the beet sector attended a reception with Party and Governmental leaders.~~[18] ~~These were genuine heroes of Socialist labour who brought in unheard-of harvests by their stubborn labour—500 and more centners of beets per hectare. This led to a whole movement of "Five Hundreders." The initiator and virtuoso of this whole affair was Maria Demchenko, who promised Comrade Stalin that she would harvest 500 centners a hectare at the Second Congress of Collective Farm Shock Workers. She kept her word and inspired others by her example.~~

~~Only the collective farm movement, which emancipated women and gave them their independence, could give rise to such labour heroines in the countryside.~~

~~At the beginning of December 1935, a meeting of combine operators with the Party and state leaders took place.~~[19] ~~In the course of just that year, combine productivity had on average doubled. Peasant sons and daughters who had never even seen machinery before and didn't know anything about it had been transformed in the shortest time into excellent combine operators. They began to surpass the norms of the capitalist countries. This meeting was evidence that new cadres had begun to appear in the collective farms who had mastered technique.~~

~~In connection with the steady rise in the working people's material well-being, the consumption of grain in our country grew as well. At the meeting with the combine drivers Comrade Stalin assigned a new task for those tilling the land in a Socialist way—achieve an annual production of 7–8 billion poods of grain in the nearest future (in 1935, about five and a half billion poods were brought in).~~

~~In the wake of the combine operators' meeting, the leaders in the grain harvest, the tractor drivers and threshing machine drivers, had an all-union meeting.~~[20] ~~More than 1,200 delegates attended this meeting. The masters of grain harvests and the skilful drivers who are advancing the Socialist tilling of the land talked of their successes and how they had achieved them. Their glorious work served as an example for others and their experience was passed on to tens and hundreds of thousands of leading collective farmers.~~

~~In February 1936, a meeting of stockbreeders took place at which 1,400 delegates were present; in October 1936, there was a meeting of leading workers in industrial crops—the cotton and linen growers.~~[21]

~~These meetings of collective farm shock workers from various agricultural sectors with Party and Governmental leaders had enormous meaning for the~~

strengthening and development of the Socialist economy in the countryside. The meetings of shock workers in industry and agriculture acted as a powerful way of mobilizing the masses for further improvements in all areas in the Socialist economy and the total mastery of techniques that now arm both industry and agriculture.

These meetings clearly demonstrated that labour in the U.S.S.R. was not just a top priority of its citizens, but a matter of honor, glory, valour and heroism. Along with Comrade Stalin and the Party and Governmental leaders, the entire country saluted the heroes and heroines of Socialist labour in industry and agriculture. The Government decorated them with awards. Surrounded by this attention and care, they promised the teacher and father of all the working people, Comrade Stalin, that they would achieve new, even more outstanding results.

Between 1935–37, the powerful development of Socialist industry continued and a decisive breakthrough was reached in the transport sector. In order to improve this work, a meeting was convened of workers in metallurgy and light industry. In April 1936, a meeting of railroad transport workers took place under the leadership of L. M. Kaganovich. Here, the Party's attention toward a full-blooded, properly working transport sector gave big results. The transport workers completed their first task—loading no less than eighty thousand freight cars a day—and promised to expand to a hundred thousand freight cars a day. This was a major accomplishment. Before Comrade Kaganovich took charge of transport, the old bourgeois specialists among the railroad executives contended that the sector's maximum loading capacity was no more than fifty-four thousand freight cars a day. But in 1937, the daily loading rate surpassed this old maximum norm by almost half.

It is in this way that the struggle for the completion of the construction of Socialist society in our country proceeded.

3. Rise of the Working People's Well-Being

1937 demonstrated that thanks to the Bolshevik Party's efforts, the entire collective farm peasantry had been set on the path to prosperity by the Stalinist collective farm rules. More than a few collective farms distributed to their members 20–25 kilograms of grain per labour-day-unit, not including other sorts of produce. For the first time in our country's history, the harvest reached 6.8 billion poods of grain, while in tsarist Old Russia, only 4–5 billion poods were brought in.

In 1937, our countrymen focused on fulfilling the task that Stalin had assigned them: 7–8 billion poods of grain.

The fast rise in well-being in the countryside in a place that had fallen into poverty under the tsar aroused feelings of profound Soviet patriotism among

~~the broadest masses and strengthened feelings of gratitude and love for the Bolshevik Party and for the chief of the Party and people, Comrade Stalin.~~

~~On the basis of this powerful development of Socialist industry and agriculture, the urban population's well-being increased dramatically and both the size and overall well-being of the working class grew as well. In 1936, the number of workers and executives reached 25,800,000. Actual salaries more than doubled during the Second Five-Year Plan.~~

During the period of the Second Five-Year Plan real wages of workers and office employees had more than doubled. The total payroll increased from 34,000,000,000 rubles in 1933 to 81,000,000,000 rubles in 1937. The state social insurance fund increased from 4,600,000,000 rubles to 5,600,000,000 rubles in the same period. ~~In the wake of the elimination of the rationing system, prices for bread and other produce in the collective farm markets fell significantly. Government decrees repeatedly lowered prices on many goods. 32,000,000,000 rubles were spent on housing construction during the Second Five-Year Plan.~~ In 1937 alone, about 10,000,000,000 rubles were expended on the state insurance of workers and employees, on improving living conditions and on meeting cultural requirements, on sanatoria, health resorts, rest homes and on medical service.

In the countryside, the collective farm system had been definitely consolidated. This was greatly assisted by the RULES OF THE AGRICULTURAL ARTEL, *adopted by the Second Congress of Collective Farm Shock Workers in February 1935, and the assignment to the collective farms of the land cultivated by them* IN PERPETUAL TENURE. *The consolidation of the collective farm system put an end to poverty and insecurity among the rural population. Whereas formerly, some three years earlier, the collective farmers had received one or two kilograms of grain per work-day-unit, now the majority of the collective farmers in the grain-growing regions*[22] *were receiving from five to twelve kilograms, and many as much as twenty kilograms per work-day-unit, besides other kinds of produce and money income. There were millions of collective farm households in the grain-growing regions who now received as their yearly returns from 500 to 1,500 poods of grain, and in the cotton, sugar beet, flax, livestock, grape growing, citrus fruit growing and fruit and vegetable growing regions, tens of thousands of rubles in annual income. The collective farms had become prosperous. It was now the chief concern of the household of a collective farmer to build new granaries and storehouses, inasmuch as the old storage places, which were designed for a meagre annual supply, no longer met even one-tenth of the household's requirements.*

In 1936, in view of the rising ~~material~~ *standard of* welfare of the people, the ~~Soviet~~ Government passed a law prohibiting abortion, at the same time adopting an extensive program for the building of maternity homes, nurseries, milk centres and kindergartens. In 1936, 2,174,000,000 rubles were assigned for these measures, as compared with 875,000,000 rubles in 1935. A law was passed providing for considerable ~~monetary~~ grants to large families. *Grants to a total of over 1,000,000,000 rubles were made in 1937 under this law.* ~~This law was one of the indicators of the rise in the masses' well-being.~~

~~The Party succeeded in conducting Socialist construction on a colossal scale. It is thanks to this that we see the growth in the masses' cultural consumption. And nowhere in the world is there such an unheard-of thirst for genuine, profound knowledge.~~

~~The reconstruction of the cities received powerful development. The Moscow Metro—the best in the world—and the Moscow-Volga Canal serve as brilliant examples of this growth. Everyday social institutions likewise have grown to unprecedented levels.~~

~~A large number of theaters, stadiums, parks and pioneer palaces have appeared. The popular arts in the U.S.S.R. have developed to unprecedented levels. Ten-day festivals have taken place in Moscow devoted to Ukrainian, Georgian, Uzbek and Azeri national art, showcasing the cultural growth among the peoples of the U.S.S.R. under the slogan national in form, Socialist in content.~~

~~A new Socialist intelligentsia was established and nurtured from among the working people. Before the revolution, only the children of the bourgeoisie, kulaks and landlords completed school and higher education. Thanks to the October revolution, the working people's children and the working people themselves have begun to receive state-funded higher education. Thanks to Soviet power, many hundreds of thousands of working-class and peasant children have become highly qualified specialists and well-educated and cultured people. This new intelligentsia enjoys the broadest opportunities to take advantage of its knowledge. It plays a respected role among the working people because of its active participation in Socialist construction.~~

~~The Party and Government improved the material conditions of those engaged in intellectual rather than physical labour—doctors, teachers and other school executives.~~ *The introduction of universal compulsory education and the building of new schools led to the rapid cultural progress of the people.* Schools were being built in large numbers all over the country. ~~In the country of the Soviets, universal compulsory education was introduced.~~[23] ~~The number of school children has increased almost five times in the twenty years since the revolution, reaching more than 38 million (including adults) in 1937. The number of higher educational institutions has increased by 7.7 times.~~ *The number of pupils in elementary and intermediate schools increased from 8,000,000 in 1914 to 28,000,000 in the school year 1936–37. The number of university students increased from 112,000 to 542,000 in the same period.*[24]

~~The U.S.S.R. become a country where science and the arts flourished at the same time science and art were in decline in an array of capitalist countries.~~ *This was a veritable cultural revolution.*

~~The Academy of Sciences and the U.S.S.R.'s scientific institutions were given the task of resolving questions connected with the Socialist reconstruction of society. Science became one of communism's firm supporters. The most famous scholars and academicians took an honored place among the ranks of the builders of Socialism. Nowhere else in the world did science enjoy as much support from the Government as in the U.S.S.R.~~

The rise in the standard of welfare and culture of the masses was a reflection of the strength, might and invincibility of our Soviet revolution. Revolutions in the past perished because, while giving the people freedom, they were unable to bring about any serious improvement in their material and cultural conditions. Therein lay their chief weakness. Our revolution differs from all other revolutions in that it not only freed the people from tsardom and capitalism, but also brought about a radical improvement in the welfare and cultural condition of the people. Therein lies its strength and invincibility.

> *"Our proletarian revolution," said Comrade Stalin at the First All-Union Conference of Stakhanovites, "is the only revolution in the world which had the opportunity of showing the people not only political results but also material results. Of all workers' revolutions we know only one which managed to achieve power. That was the Paris Commune. But it did not last long. True, it endeavoured to smash the fetters of capitalism, but it did not have time enough to smash them, and still less to show the people the beneficial material results of revolution. Our revolution is the only one which not only smashed the fetters of capitalism and brought the people freedom, but also succeeded in creating the material conditions of a prosperous life for the people. Therein lies the strength and invincibility of our revolution."*

~~4. The Stakhanovite Movement and the Struggle for Socialist Labour Productivity~~

~~Lenin pointed out more than once that capitalism would be utterly defeated when Socialism gave rise to a new, much higher labour productivity.~~

~~A new labour discipline took shape during the years of the first and second Five-Year Plans. It dated back to the "great departure"—1919's Communist volunteer SUBBOTNIK labour days. One of the reasons for the victory of the First Five-Year Plan and Socialist industrialization's fast tempos was the powerful movement surrounding Socialist emulation and shock work. On the basis of this movement, the Bolshevik Party defeated the opportunists who attempted to show that the production plans were "unrealistic," and successfully struggled against saboteurs, wreckers, self-promoters and slackers.~~

~~During the Second Five-Year Plan, the working class of the U.S.S.R. moved from its great spirit of enthusiasm for new building to an enthusiasm for the mastery of new factories and new technologies. The acquisition of basic technical knowledge took on particular importance. Technical education at the workplace became widely developed. Socialist emulation in 1935 rose to the highest of heights.~~

~~Amid the steady growth in the working people's welfare and Stalin's concern for the people, attention to the Soviet Union's cadres—a special, new group of people—also increased. A movement to raise Socialist labour productivity emerged and grew rapidly, bravely adopting new innovations in the field of technique and breaking old norms. It was called the Stakhanov movement after its originator, Alexei Stakhanov, a coal-hewer in the Central Irmino Colliery (Donetz Basin).~~

~~This shock worker of the mines had been preceded by Nikita Izotov, who had broken all previous records in coal hewing. On August 31, 1935, Stakhanov hewed 102 tons of coal in one shift and thus fulfilled the standard output fourteen and a half times over. This inaugurated a mass movement of workers and collective farmers for raising labour productivity through the mastery of new techniques. The remarkable work of Busygin in the automobile industry, Smetanin in the shoe industry, Krivonoss on the railways, Yevdokia and Maria Vinogradova in the textile industry, Maria Demchenko, Maria Gnatenko, and Pasha Angelina in agriculture served as examples for the leading workers and collective farmers—these were the first pioneers of the Stakhanov movement. A mighty Stakhanov movement developed.~~

~~Tens and hundreds of thousands of Stakhanovites grew out of this—leading workers and collective farmers. A huge strata of people took shape, entirely devoted to the Lenin-Stalin Party, despite the fact that non-Party Bolsheviks were not formally included within the organization.~~

~~Tremendous stimulus was given to the Stakhanov movement by the First All-Union Conference of Stakhanovites held in the Kremlin in November 1935.~~

> ~~"The basis of the Stakhanovite movement," said Comrade Stalin, "came most of all from our fundamental improvement in the workers' material conditions. Life has become better, comrades. Life has become more joyful. And when life is joyous, work is successful. It is thanks to this that we have high rates of productivity. It is thanks to this that we have labour heroes and heroines." The second source of the Stakhanov movement was the absence of exploitation in the U.S.S.R.: everyone works for themselves, for their class, and for their society. Everyone who works well enjoys the glory of being a labour hero. The third source of the Stakhanov movement was the existence of new techniques that were~~

> organically tied to the Stakhanov movement. The Stakhanov movement would have been inconceivable without the country's industrialization. But in order for the new techniques to deliver results, a fourth condition was necessary: "it is necessary to possess people, cadres drawn from the workers, who are capable of mastering the techniques and moving them forward."

The Stakhanov movement "will go down in the history of our Socialist construction as one of its most glorious pages" (Stalin). It surpassed the norms of labour productivity that existed until then in the U.S.S.R. and in the capitalist countries. The Stakhanov movement facilitated the further strengthening of Socialism in our country, as well as the U.S.S.R.'s transformation into one of the richest and most opulent countries in the world.

Leading workers and collective farmers, working according to their strength and ability, made the most of their benches, tractors and combines. They were motivated by a high sense of Socialist consciousness. Moreover, the higher the level of labour productivity among workers and collective farmers, the more produce they receive. This is the law of Socialism and the first step towards communism: "From each according to his ability; to each according to his work."

The Stakhanov movement prepared conditions to support still higher levels of labour productivity and the abundance of consumer goods necessary for the transition from Socialism to communism, whereupon the law of society will become "From each according to his ability; to each according to his needs."

The Stakhanov movement contained within it the beginnings of the elimination of the division between mental and physical labour. The movement for the elevation of the worker's cultural and technical level to that of an engineer or technician has attracted millions of workers. By the end of 1936, two thirds of all workers in large-scale industry had either enrolled or completed courses on technique. During the Stalinist Five-Year Plans, about 9 million people completed public school and 393,000 enrolled in higher education.

It was in this way that solutions were devised and continue to be devised for the historic task of creating a Socialist form of organized labour, a new sense of Socialist discipline, and a new form of labour productivity higher than that under capitalism.

5. The U.S.S.R.'s Great Friendship of the Peoples[25]

The 1935–37 period coincided with the fifteenth anniversary of the organization of an array of national republics (Georgia, Armenia, Azerbaidjan, the Byelorussian S.S.R., and others) and their liberation from the rule of the Whiteguards, Mensheviks and interventionists. Numerous delegations of working

~~people and notables from these republics were hailed at receptions by Party and Governmental leaders. These delegations further solidified the U.S.S.R.'s great Friendship of the Peoples. At the meeting of leading collective farmers from Tadjikistan and Turkmenia with the Party and Governmental leaders, Comrade Stalin said:~~

> ~~". . . the Friendship of the Peoples of the U.S.S.R. is a major and serious victory. This is because as long as this friendship lasts, our country's peoples will be free and invincible. No one can frighten us, whether internal or external enemies, while this friendship remains alive and well."~~

~~As a result of the implementation of the Lenin-Stalin nationality policy, the peoples of the U.S.S.R. have ceased to be backward, their economy has improved, their culture has developed and their national cadres have grown.~~

~~In 1936, the formation of the Kazakh, Kirgiz, Georgian, Azeri and Armenian union republics were proclaimed. The autonomous regions of Kabardino-Balkaria, Komi, Marii, North Osetia and Chechen-Ingushetia were converted to the category of autonomous republics. The Lenin-Stalin nationality policy rallied all of the U.S.S.R.'s peoples around the Party's banner and showed the working people of the world a model way in which to correctly resolve the national question.~~

~~Lenin and Stalin have frequently pointed out that private property and capital inevitably DIVIDE people and enflame national discord. Conversely, collective ownership and labour just as inevitably UNITE people, undermine national discord and eliminate national oppression. The Soviet victory in October 1917 and the establishment of the proletarian dictatorship supplied a key condition for the elimination of national oppression in the U.S.S.R. and the creation of a friendship of equal and free peoples.~~

~~The more that the Socialist system is strengthened and the more that collective Socialist ownership in the national republics is strengthened, the more that the U.S.S.R.'s Friendship of the Peoples will grow. This is one of the foundations of the Soviet people's indestructible moral and political unity, which was displayed so forcefully in the elections to the U.S.S.R.'s Supreme Soviet.~~

~~6. Seventh Comintern Congress (June–August 1935)~~[26]

~~Amid an extraordinarily complex international situation in August 1935, the Seventh Congress of the Communist International assembled. The congress was held under the slogan of unifying all anti-fascist forces.~~

~~In a notable speech, Comrade Dimitrov identified the factors that enabled the establishment of a fascist dictatorship in Germany. The main factor was the~~

~~traitorous policies of the reactionary Social-Democratic leaders. The Social-Democratic chiefs followed a coalition-oriented policy and entered into an understanding with the bourgeoisie. They created a split in the workers' movement and weakened the proletariat and its power to influence the peasantry and petty working people in the countryside. They allowed the fascists to organize their forces unopposed and called upon the masses to retreat while they themselves surrendered to the fascists.~~

~~The Communist Parties were not strong enough to rebuff the Social-Democrats and rally the masses into decisive battle against fascism. At times, the Communist Parties failed to approach the masses correctly and promoted agitation that was insufficiently concrete and failed to take into account the workers' everyday concerns.~~

~~Fascism demonstrated itself to be the worst enemy of the working people and humanity. It aroused the burning hatred of the working people and all honorable people with its savage policies. Deceived by their party chiefs, hundreds of thousands of Social-Democratic workers failed to resist the fascists' seizure of power and now endure harsh persecution previously used only against the Communists. They now are beginning to sober up to their mistakes and are ready to join the Communists in the struggle against fascism.~~

~~The Seventh Comintern Congress, therefore, advanced the task of creating a united front for the struggle against fascism. As a resolution of the Seventh Comintern Congress said on the basis of Comrade Dimitrov's report, "The establishment of a united front for the working class' struggle is the main task of the international workers' movement in the present historical stage."~~

~~The congress noted that Communist Parties should advance the sort of slogans and forms of struggle that coincide with the everyday interests of the masses and correspond to their ability to fight at this stage. Thus the congress suggested that the Communists stage anti-fascist and anti-war rallies and events with the Social-Democratic parties, reformers, trade unions, and other working people's organizations.~~

~~The Seventh Congress pointed out that a united proletarian front would require the uniting of the labouring masses in the struggle with fascism under the proletariat's leadership. Communists were to seek out the creation of a broad ANTIFASCIST POPULAR FRONT that would unite the toiling peasantry, urban petty bourgeoisie and the toiling masses among the oppressed peoples within a struggle against fascism and war. In its decisions, the Seventh Congress provided a detailed plan for the establishment of a united anti-fascist popular front and for the struggle against fascism and the warmongers.~~

~~The Seventh Comintern Congress' line on the unification of all anti-fascist forces completely justified itself. This is visible in the success of the popular front in France. It is visible in the heroic struggle of the Spanish popular front~~

~~against fascism. A united front is also being created in China in the form of a national bloc against the Japanese invaders.~~

~~The congress heard a report by Comrade Manuilsky on the results of Socialist construction in the U.S.S.R. In its resolution on this report, the congress pointed out that the victory of Socialism in the U.S.S.R. was a victory of WORLDWIDE SIGNIFICANCE and that it would bring about a profound shift in the consciousness of working people in every country. The victory of Socialism in the U.S.S.R. gave the toiling masses of the capitalist countries, colonies and semi-colonies confidence in their strength and belief in the imperative and reality of overthrowing capital and building Socialism.~~

~~The Seventh Congress determined that the first duty of the working class and the working people of the entire world and all sections of the Comintern was "TO AID IN THE STRENGTHENING OF THE U.S.S.R. AND STRUGGLE AGAINST HER ENEMIES IN EVERY WAY POSSIBLE."~~

~~Today, the working people of the entire world are rallying ever more tightly around the U.S.S.R. Inspired by Socialism's world-class historical victory across one-sixth of the world, the toiling masses of the capitalist countries are increasingly disgusted by the power of capital and increasingly determined to put an end to the loathsome fascism.~~

3.7. *Eighth Congress of Soviets. Adoption of the* New ~~Stalinist~~ Constitution *of the U.S.S.R.*

In February 1935, the Seventh Congress of Soviets of the Union of Soviet Socialist Republics passed a decision to change the Constitution of the U.S.S.R., which had been adopted in 1924. The change of the Constitution was necessitated by the vast changes that had taken place in the life of the U.S.S.R. since the first Constitution of the Soviet Union had been adopted in 1924. During this period the relation of class forces within the country had completely changed; a new Socialist industry had been created, the kulaks had been smashed, the collective farm system had triumphed, and the Socialist ownership of the means of production had been established in every branch of national economy as the basis of Soviet society. The victory of Socialism made possible the further democratization of the electoral system and the introduction of universal, equal and direct suffrage with secret ballot.

The new Constitution of the U.S.S.R. was drafted by a Constitution Commission set up for the purpose, under the chairmanship of Comrade Stalin. The draft was thrown open to nationwide discussion, which lasted five and a half months. It was then submitted to the Extraordinary Eighth Congress of Soviets.

The Eighth Congress of Soviets, specially convened to approve or reject the draft of the new Constitution of the U.S.S.R., met in November 1936.

~~Profound changes throughout the whole economy and in the class composition of the Soviet state placed before the Party and Government the issue of developing a new constitution. The new Constitution, created by Comrade Stalin, recorded all the great conquests of the first two decades of the proletarian dictatorship.~~[27]

Reporting to ~~the Central Committee Plenum on 1 June 1936 and to~~ the congress ~~in November 1936~~ *on the draft of the new Constitution*, Comrade Stalin enumerated the principal changes that had taken place in the Soviet Union since the adoption of the 1924 Constitution.

The 1924 Constitution had been drawn up in the early period of NEP. At that time the Soviet Government still permitted the development of capitalism alongside of the development of Socialism. The Soviet Government planned in the course of competition between the two systems—the capitalist system and the Socialist system—to organize and ensure the victory of Socialism over capitalism in the economic field. The question, "Who will win?" had not yet been settled. Industry, with its old and inadequate technical equipment, had not attained even the pre-war level. Even less enviable was the picture presented by agriculture. The state farms and collective farms were mere ~~points~~ *islands*[28] in a boundless ocean of individual peasant farms. The question then was not of eliminating the kulaks, but merely of restricting them. The Socialist sector accounted for only about 50 per cent of the country's trade.

Entirely different was the picture presented by the U.S.S.R. in 1936. *By that time* the economic life of the country had undergone a complete change. The capitalist elements had been entirely eliminated ~~everywhere~~ and the Socialist system had triumphed in all spheres of economic life. There was now a powerful Socialist industry which had increased output seven times compared with the pre-war output and had completely ousted private industry. Mechanized Socialist ~~agricultural~~ farming in the form of collective farms and state farms, equipped with up-to-date machinery and run on the largest scale in the world, had triumphed in agriculture. By 1936, the kulaks had been completely eliminated as a class, and the individual peasants no longer played any important role in the economic life of the country. Trade was entirely concentrated in the hands of the state and the co-operatives. The exploitation of man by man had been abolished forever. Public, Socialist ownership of the ~~tools and~~ means of production had been firmly established as the unshakable foundation of the new, Socialist system in all ~~spheres~~ *branches* of economic life. In the new, Socialist society, crises, poverty, unemployment and destitution had disappeared forever ~~and~~. *T*he conditions had been created for a prosperous and cultured life for all members of Soviet society.

The class composition of the population of the Soviet Union, *said Comrade Stalin in his report,* had changed correspondingly ~~in accord with these changes~~.

The landlord ~~and old bourgeoisie~~ class and the *old big imperialist bourgeoisie* had already been eliminated in the period of the Civil War. During the years of Socialist construction all the exploiting elements—capitalists, merchants, kulaks and profiteers—had been eliminated. Only insignificant remnants of the eliminated exploiting classes persisted, *and their complete elimination was a matter of the very near future.* ~~But these survivals of the hostile classes were supported by the capitalist encirclement.~~

The working people of the U.S.S.R.—workers, peasants and intellectuals—had undergone profound change in the period of ~~Soviet power~~ *Socialist construction.*

The working class had ceased to be an exploited class bereft of means ~~and tools~~ of production, as it is under capitalism. It had abolished capitalism, taken away the means ~~and tools~~ of production from the capitalists *and turned them into public property.* It had ceased to be a proletariat in the proper, the old meaning of the term. The proletariat of the U.S.S.R., possessing the state power, had been transformed into an entirely new class. It had become a working class ~~of the U.S.S.R.~~ *emancipated from exploitation*, a working class which had abolished the capitalist economic system and had established Socialist ownership of the means ~~and tools~~ of production. *Hence, i*t was a working class *the like of* which *the* history *of mankind* had never known before.[29]

No less profound were the changes that had taken place in the ~~nature~~ *condition* of the peasantry of the U.S.S.R. *In the old days, o*ver twenty million scattered individual peasant households, small and middle, had delved away in isolation on their small plots, using backward technical equipment. They were exploited by landlords, kulaks, merchants, profiteers, usurers, etc. *Now a*n entirely new peasantry had grown up in the U.S.S.R. There were no longer any landlords, kulaks, merchants and usurers ~~exploiting~~ *to exploit* the peasants. The overwhelming majority of the peasant households had joined the collective farms, which were based not on private ownership, but on collective ownership *of the means of production, collective ownership* which had grown from collective labour. *This was a new type of peasantry, a peasantry emancipated from all exploitation.* It was a peasantry the like of which the history of mankind had never known before.

The intelligentsia in the U.S.S.R. had also undergone a change ~~in fundamental terms~~. It had for the most part become an entirely new intelligentsia. The majority of its members came from the ranks of the workers and peasants. *It no longer served capitalism, as the old intelligentsia did; it served Socialism.* It had become an equal member of the Socialist society. Together with the workers and peasants, it was building a new Socialist society. *This was a new type of intelligentsia, which served the people and was emancipated from all exploitation.* ~~There had never been such a labouring intelligentsia anywhere.~~ *It was an intelligentsia the like of which the history of mankind had never known before.*[30]

Thus the old class dividing lines between the working people of the U.S.S.R. were being obliterated, the old class exclusiveness ~~of separate socialist toilers in the city and country~~ was disappearing. The economic and political contradictions between the workers, the peasants and the ~~socialist intelligentsia~~ *intellectuals* were declining and becoming obliterated.[31] *The foundation for the moral and political unity of society had been created.*

These profound changes in the life of the U.S.S.R., these decisive achievements of Socialism in the U.S.S.R., were reflected in the new Constitution.

According to the new Constitution, Soviet society consists of two friendly classes—the workers and peasants—class distinctions between the two still remaining. ~~Therefore,~~ *T*he Union of Soviet Socialist Republics~~, as it is written in the U.S.S.R.'s Constitution,~~ is a Socialist state of workers and peasants.

The political foundation of the U.S.S.R. is formed by the Soviets of Deputies of the Working People, which developed and grew strong as a result of the overthrow of the power of the landlords and capitalists and the achievement of the dictatorship of the proletariat.

All power in the U.S.S.R. belongs to the working people of town and country as represented by the Soviets of Deputies of the Working People.

~~The working class, as the most revolutionary, conscious and organized, and as the most progressive class of the U.S.S.R., leads~~[32] ~~and will lead Soviet society in the future. The construction of Socialism and the introduction of the new Constitution has expanded and strengthened the base of the working-class dictatorship in the U.S.S.R., transforming it into a more flexible, more powerful system of state control over society.~~

The highest organ of state power in the U.S.S.R. ~~according to the new Constitution~~ is the Supreme Soviet of the U.S.S.R.[33]

The Supreme Soviet of the U.S.S.R., consisting of two Chambers with equal rights, the Soviet of the Union and the Soviet of Nationalities, is elected by the citizens of the U.S.S.R. for a term of four years on the basis of universal, equal and direct suffrage by secret ballot.

Elections to the Supreme Soviet of the U.S.S.R., as to all Soviets of Deputies of the Working People, are UNIVERSAL. This means that all citizens of the U.S.S.R. who have reached the age of eighteen, irrespective of race or nationality, religion, standard of education, domicile, social origin, property status or past activities, have the right to vote in the election of deputies and to be elected, with the exception of the insane and persons convicted by court of law to sentences including deprivation of electoral rights. ~~All restrictions on electoral rights that were previously in effect have now been eliminated.~~

Elections of deputies are EQUAL. This means that each citizen is entitled to one vote and that all citizens participate in the elections on an equal footing.

Elections of deputies are DIRECT. This means that all Soviets of Deputies of the Working People, from rural and city Soviets of Deputies of the Working People up to and including the Supreme Soviet of the U.S.S.R., are elected by the citizens by direct vote.

The Supreme Soviet of the U.S.S.R. at a joint sitting of both Chambers elects the Presidium of the Supreme Soviet and the Council of People's Commissars of the U.S.S.R.

The economic foundation of the U.S.S.R. is the Socialist system of economy and the Socialist ownership of the ~~tools and~~ means of production. ~~It is written in the new Constitution that~~ *In the U.S.S.R. is realized the Socialist principle:* "From each according to his ability, to each according to his work." ~~and "He who does not work, does not eat."~~

All citizens of the U.S.S.R. are guaranteed the right to work, the right to rest and leisure, the right to education, the right to maintenance in old age and in case of sickness or disability.

~~In this vein,~~ *W*omen are accorded equal rights with men in all spheres of life.[34]

The equality of the citizens of the U.S.S.R., irrespective of their nationality or race, is an indefeasible law.

Freedom of conscience and freedom of anti-religious propaganda is recognized for all citizens.

In order to strengthen Socialist society, the ~~Stalin~~ Constitution guarantees freedom of speech, press, assembly and meeting, the right to unite in public organizations, inviolability of person, inviolability of domicile and privacy of correspondence, the right of asylum for foreign citizens persecuted for defending the interests of the working people or for their scientific activities, or for their struggle for national liberation.

The new Constitution also imposes serious duties on all citizens of the U.S.S.R.: the duty of observing the laws, maintaining labour discipline, honestly performing public duties, respecting the rules of the Socialist community, safeguarding and strengthening public, Socialist property, and defending the Socialist fatherland.

> "To defend the fatherland is the sacred duty of every citizen of the U.S.S.R." ~~Universal military service is established by law.~~

~~The Soviet country received the most democratic constitution in the world. The new Stalin Constitution secured the great victories of the toiling peoples of the U.S.S.R. The public discussion of the Constitution lasted six and a half months until the Constitution was ratified by the Extraordinary Eighth~~

~~Congress of the Soviets in December 1936. This discussion provided the masses with a major experience in political schooling. They recognized even more profoundly what an enormous meaning the C.P.S.U.(B.) had and continues to have in their struggle.~~[35]

~~The Constitution identified a LEADERSHIP role for the Communist Party of the Soviet Union (Bolsheviks) in the dictatorship of the working class and noted that the Party serves as THE ADVANCE GUARD OF THE WORKING PEOPLE in their struggle for the strengthening and development of the Socialist system.~~

Dealing with the right of citizens to unite in various societies, *one of the articles*[36] *of* the Constitution states ~~that~~:

> "The most active and politically conscious citizens in the ranks of the working class and other strata of the working people unite in the Communist Party of the Soviet Union (Bolsheviks), which is the vanguard of the working people in their struggle to strengthen and develop the Socialist system and which represents the leading core of all organizations of the working people, both public and state." ~~(From Article 126 of the U.S.S.R. Constitution.)~~

~~The Constitution should not be confused with the Party program. The Constitution, in contrast to the Party program, details not what is to be achieved, but what already exists, what has already been accomplished and won. This is a collection of fundamental victories of the workers and the peasants of our country in the form of an immutable law. The Constitution arms the working people of the U.S.S.R. in spirit, rallies them forward and endows them with a sense of pride in their Socialist motherland, their power and their Party.~~

~~For the workers of the capitalist countries, however, our Constitution does serve as a plan of struggle. It shows what is possible for the workers and working people to accomplish if they overthrow the capitalist system. It was greeted with sympathy by working people all over the world. The new Constitution's mention of the working people's already completed victories is a wonderful form of Communist propaganda for the fraternal communist parties. These victories supply proof of the correctitude of the Marx-Engels-Lenin-Stalin teachings. The Stalin Constitution demonstrates that only internationalism and the brotherhood of the peoples can lead the people to peace. The Stalin Constitution provides proof of the superiority of Soviet democracy over the democracy of the bourgeois states, refuting all the fascists' fabrications and lies and their racist, nationalistic theories, and indicting their struggle against the vestiges of democracy in the capitalist countries.~~

~~On the eve of the twentieth anniversary of the proletarian dictatorship, the Extraordinary Eighth Congress of Soviets summarized the results of the great~~

~~victories won by the Bolshevik Party and the Soviet power. It demonstrated to the working people of the whole world the trustworthy, tried-and-true path laid by the Bolshevik Party, the Lenin-Stalin Party—the path to emancipation from class oppression, inequality, exploitation, racial and national hatred, cultural decline and distortion, poverty, unemployment and war.~~

The Eighth Congress of Soviets unanimously approved and adopted the draft of the new Constitution of the U.S.S.R.

The Soviet country thus acquired a new Constitution, a Constitution embodying the victory of Socialism and workers' and peasants' democracy.

In this way[37] *the Constitution gave legislative embodiment to the epoch-making fact that the U.S.S.R. had entered a new stage of development, the stage of the completion of the building of a Socialist society and the gradual transition to Communist society, where the guiding principle of social life will be the Communist principle: "From each according to his abilities, to each according to his needs."*

4.~~8.~~ ~~Defeat~~ *Liquidation* of the ~~Counter-Revolutionary~~ *Remnants of the* Bukharin-Trotsky ~~Germano-Japanese~~ Gang of Spies, ~~Saboteurs,~~ Wreckers and ~~Terrorists~~ *Traitors to the Country. Preparations for the Election of the Supreme Soviet of the U.S.S.R. Broad Inner-Party Democracy as the Party's Course. Election of the Supreme Soviet of the U.S.S.R.*

~~Soviet power has been victorious in one sixth of the world. Five sixths of the world still remains in the hands of the capitalist states. The U.S.S.R. remains located within a capitalist encirclement. The bourgeois states are doing everything they can in order to weaken the U.S.S.R.'s economic and military strength and attack her at a convenient time. In order to undermine the U.S.S.R.'s strength and restore capitalism to the U.S.S.R., the international bourgeoisie are taking advantage of the remnants of the defeated exploitative classes who remain in the country and the remnants of the anti-Soviet, counter-revolutionary parties—the Socialist-Revolutionaries, Mensheviks, Anarcho-Syndicalists, and so on.~~

~~The capitalist encirclement has used and will continue to use all the former oppositionist currents in the country—Trotskyites, Rights (the Bukharinite-Rykovites), "Lefts," nationalists of every stripe and republic of the U.S.S.R.—as their agents and henchmen. In the course of their struggle against the Party, all of these former oppositionist currents became ENEMIES OF THE PEOPLE, agents (spies) of foreign espionage services, murderers and wreckers.~~[38]

~~As long as the capitalist encirclement exists, foreign espionage services—most of all the fascist ones—will continue to send wreckers, spies, murderers and saboteurs to the U.S.S.R. whom they have recruited from people and groups hostile to the Soviet system and Bolshevik Party.~~

~~In January 1937,[39] the trial of the anti-Soviet Trotskyite centre took place, a group which had been uncovered in 1936 after the exposure of the Trotskyite-Zinovievite centre and its members Zinoviev, Kamenev, Mrachkovsky, Smirnov and others. It had already been clear at that time that there was another parallel Trotskyite centre. This centre transpired to consist of Pyatakov, Radek, Sokolnikov and Serebryakov. These mutineers and traitors to the Socialist motherland took advantage of the positions and trust granted to them by the Party and Government. They surrounded themselves with the remnants of the Trotskyites and other counter-revolutionary elements; maintaining a connection to the bloody Judas Trotsky, they entered into direct contact with representatives of foreign espionage services, especially those of German and Japanese fascism. They organized and carried out terrorist attacks on the fascists' orders; they sabotaged railroads; they caused train accidents claiming many lives, mine explosions and factory and mill accidents; they wrecked in industry, transportation and other sectors of the economy.~~

~~The Trotskyites' goal was the overthrow of the Soviet power[40] and the restoration of capitalism, the return of the landlords and capitalists to power and the partitioning of the U.S.S.R. Lacking roots and necessary forces within the country, they relied on the aid and cooperation of German, Japanese and Polish fascism and served as agents in the espionage services of these and other imperialist states. In return for this aid, they promised to cede the Ukraine to the Germans, Byelorussia to the Poles and the Far East to the Japanese. The traitor Trotsky concluded a treaty with Hitler's deputy Hess according to which Trotsky promised that in the event of the fall of Soviet power he would cede the Ukraine to Hitler, support fascist Germany's foreign policy and hand over to German entrepreneurs for their exploitation the most important enterprises in the U.S.S.R. for the production of iron ore, manganese, oil, gold, timber and so on. Counter-revolutionary Trotskyism was a real "find" for the fascist espionage services. Trotskyism long ago had ceased to be a political current within the working class and became a gang of wreckers, spies and saboteurs and the advance guard of Germano-Japanese fascism in the U.S.S.R. and the most counter-revolutionary capitalist elements in other countries.~~

~~These scoundrels, the worst enemies of the people, obtained for German, Japanese and Polish headquarters secret information on the U.S.S.R.'s defences. The biggest German firms were also included in this espionage and diversionary work and sent agents to the U.S.S.R. under the guise of "specialists." The Trotskyites received payment for their services from Japanese and German espionage services and directly from German industrialists as early as 1921–22. All the main participants in this affair were shot, and Sokolnikov and Radek were sentenced by the court to a ten-year prison term. This trial exposed before the entire world the Trotskyites' nightmarish crimes. As a result, they were~~

~~expelled from an array of working-class organizations abroad within which the Trotskyites had still enjoyed some trust before the trials. Their treacherous role in Spain, France, China, the U.S.A. and other countries[41] had become completely obvious. Everywhere, the Trotskyites served as fascist collaborators, followers and agents.~~

~~At the same time that it was dealing with the Trotskyites, the Party also defeated the Bukharin-Rykovite counter-revolutionary gang[42] and the bourgeois nationalists who worked in league with the Trotskyites and Bukharinites.~~

~~After the start of the exposure of the Trotskyite anti-Soviet centre's terrorist activity, information came to light about the direct connection of the Trotskyite terrorists with the right leaders Bukharin, Tomsky, Rykov, Uglanov and Kotov. During the court's investigation, Sokolnikov and Radek testified about their counter-revolutionary discussions with Bukharin and Tomsky. After the February–March Central Committee Plenum established Bukharin's and Rykov's guilt as mutineers and traitors, it expelled them from the Party and turned them over to the N.K.V.D. for investigation.~~

~~At the time of the February–March Central Committee Plenum (1937), it was established that the Rights (Bukharin, Rykov and others) had long since ceased—like the Trotskyites—to be a political trend and had turned long ago into a robber-like gang of spies, terrorists and wreckers.~~

~~The Trotskyites and Bukharinites had combined together into one Trotskyite-Bukharinite gang of fascist henchmen. This gang had an array of branches, an array of secret, double-dealing nests of spies and wreckers. The villainous murder of S. M. Kirov, the Party's favourite, was planned by the Trotskyite-Bukharinite fascist henchmen.[43]~~

~~Tomsky, who was a candidate member of the Central Committee and who occupied an executive position as head of the Government publishing house O.G.I.Z. turned out to be one of the worst enemies of the Party. Over the course of many years, he trained counter-revolutionary cadres for a fascist coup. When the Party and N.K.V.D. found the opportunity to expose the criminal activity of the Rights once and for all, Tomsky shot himself in order to hide the evidence of his crimes. Exactly the same thing happened with the other double-dealers and traitors Gamarnik and Lyubchenko.[44] Rudzutak, Antipov, Yakovlev, Yagoda, Yenukidze, Karakhan,[45] Sheboldayev, Kabakov, Razumov and others all turned out to be involved in a counter-revolutionary conspiracy with the Bukharinites and Trotskyites. Over the course of many years these accursed enemies of the people did the fascists' bidding and prepared a counter-revolutionary coup.~~

~~In March 1938, the trial of the anti-Soviet "Bloc of Rights and Trotskyites" took place.[46]~~

~~This trial demonstrated that the Rights and Trotskyites had been connected with the Menshevik and Socialist-Revolutionary parties for a long time. The~~

~~court again showed that the Party of the Second International—the Mensheviks under Dan[47] and others—was little more than a foreign fascist espionage service franchise, both within the U.S.S.R. and abroad, and that the Mensheviks, just like the Trotskyites, were also an international espionage organization. The court showed that the Socialist-Revolutionaries also had served as despicable henchmen for the imperialists, as spies for fascist espionage services and as hired assassins.~~

~~The destruction of the "Bloc of Rights and Trotskyites" and other counterrevolutionary organizations during this period by Comrade Yezhov's N.K.V.D. organs and the trial dealt a blow against international fascism and exposed a particularly heinous and threatening conspiracy against the C.P.S.U.(B.), against the lives of the Party and Government leaders, against the Soviet state and against the Soviet people.~~

~~In March 1938, the loathsome criminal gang of the "Bloc of Rights and Trotskyites" was brought before the Military Collegium of the U.S.S.R. Supreme Court. This conspiratorial group had taken shape in 1932–33 and acted on the orders of the espionage services of foreign states hostile to the U.S.S.R., most significantly Germany, Japan, England and Poland. Its goals were to spy for foreign states, wreck, sabotage, commit acts of terror, to undermine the defensive power of the U.S.S.R., to assist foreign military intervention against the U.S.S.R, to prepare the way for the U.S.S.R.'s defeat, to bring about the dismemberment of the U.S.S.R. and to hand over the Ukraine, Byelorussia, the Central Asian republics, Georgia, Armenia, Azerbaidjan, the Maritime Region and the Far East for the benefit of the imperialistic fascist states.~~[48]

~~The anti-Soviet "Bloc of Rights and Trotskyites" set as its objective the overthrow of the U.S.S.R.'s Socialist system and the restoration of the capitalist system and bourgeois rule in the U.S.S.R.~~

~~The trial established that Bukharin, Rykov, Yagoda, Rakovsky, Krestinsky, Grinko, Sharangovich, Chernov, Faizulla Khodjayev, Ikramov, Zelensky, Ivanov, Zubaryev and other participants in this heinous gang of traitors joined up with fascists and imperialists in order to obtain from them armed assistance against the Communist Party and Soviet power. They spied for foreign states and handed over to them top secret material of state significance. They systematically committed diversionary acts in industry, transportation and agriculture; they poisoned people and livestock and infected them with contagious diseases; they wrecked the sowing; they consciously soured the peasants on collectivization; they carried out wrecking in finance and trade; and they took advantage of all means possible to undermine the country's defensive power. The "Bloc of Rights and Trotskyites" organized an array of terrorist attacks against the leaders of the C.P.S.U.(B.) and the Soviet Government.~~

~~This bloc, acting in concert with the leaders of the previously exposed counter-revolutionary groups, staged terrorist attacks against S. M. Kirov, V. R. Menzhinsky, V. V. Kuibyshev and A. M. Gorky.~~[49] ~~The last three were poisoned by these heinous conspirators with the aid of Pletnev, Levin and Kazakov,~~[50] ~~several doctors and professors who had been drawn into the affair. Several of the leaders of this group—Krestinsky, Rakovsky, Chernov, Grinko, Rosengoltz, Sharangovich and others—had been paid agents of international espionage like Trotsky for a number of years. Zelensky, Ivanov and Zubaryev,~~[51] ~~other participants of this bloc, had been paid agents of the tsarist secret police back during the Party's underground period and had turned over dozens of revolutionaries to the tsarist butchers.~~

~~The entire right-Trotskyite gang sold out the Socialist motherland both wholesale and retail, wrecking, spying and organizing acts of diversion and terror.~~

In 1937, new facts came to light regarding the fiendish crimes of the Bukharin-Trotsky gang. The trial of Pyatakov, Radek and others, the trial of Tukhachevsky, Yakir and others, and, lastly, the trial of Bukharin, Rykov, Krestinsky, Rosengoltz and others, all showed that the Bukharinites and Trotskyites had long ago joined to form a common band of enemies of the people, operating as the "Bloc of Rights and Trotskyites."

The trials showed that these dregs of humanity, in conjunction with the enemies of the people, Trotsky, Zinoviev and Kamenev, had been in conspiracy against Lenin, the Party and the Soviet state ever since the early days of the October Socialist Revolution. The insidious attempts to thwart the Peace of Brest-Litovsk at the beginning of 1918, the plot against Lenin and the conspiracy with the "Left" Socialist-Revolutionaries for the arrest and murder of Lenin, Stalin and Sverdlov in the spring of 1918, the villainous shot that wounded Lenin in the summer of 1918, the revolt of the "Left" Socialist-Revolutionaries in the summer of 1918, the deliberate aggravation of differences in the Party in 1921 with the object of undermining and overthrowing Lenin's leadership from within, the attempts to overthrow the Party leadership during Lenin's illness and after his death, the betrayal of state secrets and the supply of information of an espionage character to foreign espionage services, the vile assassination of Kirov, the acts of wrecking, diversion and explosions, the dastardly murder of Menzhinsky, Kuibyshev and Gorky—all these and similar villainies over a period of twenty years were committed, it transpired, with the participation or under the direction of Trotsky, Zinoviev, Kamenev, Bukharin, Rykov and their henchmen, at the behest of espionage services of bourgeois states.

The trials brought to light the fact that the Trotsky-Bukharin fiends, in obedience to the wishes of their masters—the espionage services of foreign states—had set out to destroy the Party and the Soviet state, to undermine the defensive power of the country, to assist foreign military intervention, to prepare the way for the defeat of the Red Army, to bring about the dismemberment of the U.S.S.R., to hand over the Soviet Maritime Region to the Japanese, Soviet Byelorussia to the Poles, and the Soviet Ukraine to the Germans, to destroy the gains[52] *of the workers and collective farmers, and to restore capitalist slavery in the U.S.S.R.*

These Whiteguard pigmies, whose strength was no more than that of a gnat, apparently flattered themselves that they were the masters of the country, and imagined that it was really in their power to sell or give away the Ukraine, Byelorussia and the Maritime Region.

These Whiteguard insects forgot that the real masters of the Soviet country were the Soviet people, and that the Rykovs, Bukharins, Zinovievs and Kamenevs were only temporary employees of the state, which could at any moment sweep them out from its offices as so much useless rubbish.

These contemptible lackeys of the fascists forgot that the Soviet people had only to move a finger, and not a trace of them would be left.

The Soviet court sentenced the ~~"Bloc of Rights and Trotskyites"~~ *Bukharin-Trotsky fiends* to be shot.

The People's Commissariat of Internal Affairs carried out the sentence.

The Soviet people ~~unanimously~~ approved the ~~court's verdict—the verdict of the people~~ *annihilation of the Bukharin-Trotsky gang and passed on to next business.* ~~The Soviet land was thus purged of a dangerous gang of heinous and insidious enemies of the people, whose monstrous villainies surpassed all of the darkest crimes and most vile treason of all times and all peoples.~~

~~Before that happened, a counter-revolutionary organization was uncovered in the Workers' and Peasants' Red Army high command consisting of Tukhachevsky, Yakir, Uborevich, Kork, Eideman, Feldman, Primakov and Putna. They were unmasked while violating their military duty (their oath) and betraying the motherland. They had prepared fascist military cadres in Red Army units, planned a coup d'état on behalf of the fascists and prepared for the defeat of the Red Army in the case of war with the fascists. All of them spied for the U.S.S.R.'s enemies. All of them were sentenced to be shot in a verdict handed down by the Military Collegium of the Supreme Court.~~

~~The Party likewise eliminated bourgeois nationalist espionage groups in Byelorussia, the Ukraine, Karelia, the republics of Central Asia, Tataria and Transcaucasia. These groups carried out the imperialists' orders and planned to restore the landlords, capitalists, beys and khans to power.~~

~~The exposure of these groups and their elimination demonstrated how correct Comrade Stalin had been to warn the Party of the increasing inevitability of conflict during the period of Socialism's greatest success in the U.S.S.R. It demonstrated how correct he was to continuously demand the strengthening of~~

~~Party vigilance in regard to the enemies of the people. Over the course of 1937, the Party accomplished a lot of work devoted to rooting out the spies and wreckers who had snuck into the Party organization and defeating and eliminating the nests of Trotskyite spies. It transpired that among the enemies of the people were an array of old, unexposed provocateurs who had been infiltrated into the Party years earlier by the tsarist secret police. The N.K.V.D. under Comrade Yezhov, beat the enemy with swift and precise blows. This struggle with hidden, masked enemies and double-dealers also increased Party members' vigilance. The February–March 1937 Central Committee Plenum played an exceptional role in the mobilization of the Party in the struggle with the enemies of the people.~~

~~The elimination of these groups of spies and saboteurs dealt a major blow to the foreign capitalist states' espionage services that have been sending spies and saboteurs into the U.S.S.R. through the Trotskyites, Bukharinites, bourgeois nationalists and their own secret agent networks. The German, Polish and Japanese headquarters' hope that they would be able to depend on the Trotskyite-Bukharinite counter-revolutionary organization within the country during wartime were dashed.~~

And the next business was to prepare for the election of the Supreme Soviet of the U.S.S.R. and to carry it out in an organized way.

~~9. The Bolshevik Party's Further Struggle for the Strengthening of Its Ranks. C.P.S.U.(B.) Central Committee Plenum (February–March 1937)~~

~~The Central Committee Plenum that took place in February–March 1937 passed important decisions on the restructuring of the Party organizations' work.~~

~~On the eve of the plenum, on February 18, 1937, Sergo Ordjonikidze, one of the leaders of the Party, died. Sergo Ordjonikidze was a Central Committee Politburo member, the People's Commissar of Large-Scale Industry and an outstanding figure in our Party who had devoted his glorious, heroic life to the cause of the working class and communism. Sergo Ordjonikidze was dearly beloved by the popular masses.~~

The Party threw all its strength into the preparations for the elections. It held that the putting into effect of the new Constitution of the U.S.S.R. signified a turn in the political life of the country. This turn meant the complete democratization of the electoral system, the substitution of universal suffrage for restricted suffrage, equal suffrage for not entirely equal suffrage, direct elections for indirect elections, and secret ballot for open ballot.

Before the introduction of the new Constitution there were restrictions of the franchise in the case of priests, former White Guards, former kulaks, and persons not engaged in useful labour. The new Constitution abolished all franchise restrictions for these categories of citizens by making the election of deputies universal.

Formerly, the election of deputies had been unequal, inasmuch as the bases of representation for the urban and rural populations differed. Now, however, all necessity for restrictions of equality of the suffrage had disappeared and all citizens were given the right to take part in the elections on an equal footing.

Formerly, the elections of the intermediate and higher organs of Soviet power were indirect. Now, however, under the new Constitution, all Soviets, from rural and urban up to and including the Supreme Soviet, were to be elected by the citizens directly.

Formerly, deputies to the Soviets were elected by open ballot and the voting was for lists of candidates. Now, however, the voting for deputies was to be by secret ballot, and not by lists, but for individual candidates nominated in each electoral area.

This was a definite turning point in the political life of the country.

The new electoral system was bound to result, and actually did result, in an enhancement of the political activity of the people, in greater control by the masses over the organs of Soviet power, and in the increased responsibility of the organs of Soviet power to the people.

In order to be fully prepared for this turn, the Party had to be its moving spirit, and the leading role of the Party in the forthcoming elections had to be fully ensured. But this could be done only if the Party organizations themselves became thoroughly democratic in their everyday work, only if they fully observed the principles of democratic centralism in their inner-Party life, as the Party Rules demanded, only if all organs of the Party were elected, only if criticism and self-criticism in the Party were developed to the full, only if the responsibility of the Party bodies to the members of the Party were complete, and if the members of the Party themselves became thoroughly active.

~~In a report to the Central Committee Plenum on the preparation for the working people's Soviet elections, Comrade Zhdanov pointed to the need for Party organizations to be restructured on a democratic footing in order to take charge of the major turnabout in the country's political life that had been brought about by the introduction of the new U.S.S.R. constitution.~~

> ~~"What is demanded of the Party, and what do the Central Committee Plenum resolutions say is required for the Party to take charge of this turnabout and these new, fully democratic elections?~~
>
> ~~For this, the Party itself must institute consistent, democratic practices and fully implement the basics of democratic centralism within the Party, as demanded by the Party rules. This would give the Party all the conditions necessary for the election of all Party organs; it would allow~~

~~for the full development of criticism and self-criticism; it would make the Party organs fully answerable to the Party masses; and it would allow the Party masses to become fully mobilized."~~

A report made by Comrade Zhdanov at the plenum of the Central Committee at the end of February 1937 on the subject of preparing the Party organizations for the elections to the Supreme Soviet of the U.S.S.R. revealed the fact that a number of Party organizations were systematically violating the Party Rules and the principles of democratic centralism in their everyday work, substituting co-option for election, voting by lists for the voting for individual candidates, open ballot for secret ballot, etc. It was obvious that organizations in which such practices prevailed could not properly fulfil their tasks in the elections to the Supreme Soviet. It was therefore first of all necessary to put a stop to such anti-democratic practices in the Party organizations and to reorganize Party work on broad democratic lines.

~~The Central Committee Plenum pointed out that the Party was being harmed by the violation of the principle of democratic centralism and inter-party democracy. Facts uncovered in the Azov-Black Sea Basin regional Party committee, the Kiev regional Party committee, the Central Committee of the Ukrainian Communist Party (Bolsheviks), in the Urals and in an array of other organizations showed how dangerous this sort of violation of the Party rules was in terms of allowing enemies to slip into the organizations. Therefore, the Central Committee Plenum required all Party organizations to return to electing the leading organs of their Party organizations as required by the Party statute and the principles of democratic centralism. They were to hold elections for all Party organs on the basis of a secret ballot, to end the practice of co-opting members of the Party Committees, to forbid voting by list in the election of Party organs, and to guarantee all Party members the unlimited right to challenge the candidates and criticize them.~~ *Accordingly, after hearing the report of Comrade Zhdanov, the Plenum of the Central Committee resolved:*

"a) To reorganize Party work on the basis of complete and unqualified observance of the principles of inner-Party democracy as prescribed by the Party Rules.

"b) To put an end to the practice of co-opting members of Party Committees and to restore the principle of election of directing bodies of Party organizations as prescribed by the Party Rules.

"c) To forbid voting by lists in the election of Party bodies; voting should be for individual candidates, all members of the Party being guaranteed the unlimited right to challenge candidates and to criticize them.

"d) To introduce the secret ballot in the election of Party bodies.

"e) To hold elections of Party bodies in all Party organizations, from the Party Committees of primary Party organizations to the territorial and regional committees and the Central Committees of the national Communist Parties, the elections to be completed not later than May 20.

"f) To charge all Party organizations strictly to observe the provisions of the Party Rules with respect to the terms of office of Party bodies, namely: to hold elections in primary Party organizations once a year; in district and city organizations—once a year; in regional, territorial and republican organizations—every eighteen months.

"g) To ensure that Party organizations strictly adhere to the system of electing Party Committees at general factory meetings, and not to allow the latter to be replaced by delegate conferences.

"h) To put a stop to the practice prevalent in a number of primary Party organizations whereby general meetings are virtually abolished and replaced by shop meetings and delegate conferences."

In this way the Party began its preparations for the forthcoming elections.

This decision of the Central Committee was of tremendous political importance. Its significance lay not only in the fact that it inaugurated the Party's campaign in the election of the Supreme Soviet of the U.S.S.R., but also, and primarily, in the fact that it helped the Party organizations to reorganize their work, to apply the principles of inner-Party democracy, and to meet the elections to the Supreme Soviet fully prepared.

~~Comrade Stalin's report to the Central Committee Plenum "On the Shortcomings of Party Work and the Measures to Eliminate Trotskyite Double-Dealers and Others" had enormous meaning for the strengthening of the Party organizations and the elevation of revolutionary Bolshevik vigilance. Comrade Stalin subjected the mistakes and shortcomings of an entire array of Party organizations to harsh criticism. Many organizations and their leading organs turned out to be rife with double-dealers, Trotskyites, Bukharinites and bourgeois nationalists. And there had been, as it transpired, no lack of warnings and signals. The first serious warning was the murder of S. M. Kirov, which showed that the enemies of the people were double-dealing and would continue to double-deal, disguising themselves as Bolsheviks in order to ingratiate themselves into favour and slip into the Party organizations. In January 1935 and July 1936, the Party Central Committee warned the Party organizations about opportunistic complacency and everyday gullibility and reminded them about the imperative of Party vigilance and the exposure of skilfully hidden enemies.~~

~~In spite of these warnings, many Party leaders were captivated by Trotskyite, Bukharinite and bourgeois nationalist wreckers who were thus able to continue~~

their counter-revolutionary work. This happened for the most part because many Party workers, distracted by economic construction, gradually stepped back from Party political work and ceased to lead in a political sense. Political nonchalance, self-deception and everyday complacency appeared as a result of a fixation on our enormous economic successes.

Comrade Stalin uncovered the roots of this political nonchalance and called for lessons to be learned from the exposure of the Trotskyite and other double-dealers, pointing to the Party comrades' two fundamental mistakes.

First, they forgot that the Soviet Union was located within the context of a capitalist encirclement, which was sending and would continue to send wreckers, spies, saboteurs and murderers into our country.

The second mistake consisted in the fact that, as Comrade Stalin said, "our Party comrades have failed to notice and let slip by the fact that Trotskyism today is no longer what it was, let's say, about 7–8 years ago, and that since that time Trotskyism and the Trotskyites have undergone a serious evolution, changing the face of Trotskyism on a fundamental level, and that in light of this, the struggle with Trotskyism and the methods of this struggle must also change. Our Party comrades have not noticed that Trotskyism has ceased to be a political trend within the working class and that Trotskyism has transformed from a political current within the working class that it was 7–8 years ago into a rabid, unprincipled gang of wreckers, saboteurs, spies and murderers, acting on the order of foreign states' espionage services."

Many Party leaders had lost their taste for ideological work and the political training of Party members and non-Party members among the masses. As a result, very important sections of political training work were entrusted to weak, untrained executives and this led them to become rotten or even to play into the enemy's hands in places.

The major weakening of criticism and self-criticism during this time turned out to be particularly dangerous. The most important ruling organs of the Party, such as the regional and city committee plenums, and the city activist groups and Party conferences, turned from a means of mass Party control over the Party organs into empty parades and boastful rallies about our successes. All of this led to an atmosphere of complacency, mutual appreciation and "bovine ecstasy." The Central Committee Plenum mercilessly condemned this as a deviation from the Party line.

The Central Committee Plenum decisively spoke out against the unprofessional selection of Party workers, patron-client networks and the practice in some places in which "families" had been created of "one's own" people who defended each other from criticism instead of creating ruling groups of responsible Party workers. The Trotskyites, Bukharinites and bourgeois nationalists took advantage of all of these shortcomings and distortions. They exploited the

~~"yes-man" situation that took shape in an array of locations, as it allowed them to sneak into the Party organizations' good graces and engage in wrecking.~~

~~The Central Committee Plenum condemned this spiritless, inattentive relationship toward Party members and the lack of an individualistic approach; it condemned the incorrect, indiscriminate expulsion of people from the Party (for instance, under the premise of "passivity"), as it artificially sowed discontent within the Party ranks which could be utilized by the enemy. The Central Committee Plenum underscored with all of its might how important it was for Party organizations to master Bolshevism, how imperative Marxist-Leninist study and training was for the cadres, and how necessary their political enlightenment and retraining was. To this end, an entire educational system of courses was created for various groups of Party workers.~~

~~Despite this decision of the C.P.S.U.(B.) Central Committee, however, a year later, in January 1938, the Central Committee Plenum was forced to return to the issue of shortcomings in the work of Party organizations. The January Central Committee Plenum (1938) discussed a report presented by Comrade Malenkov and issued a decision "On the Mistakes of Party Organizations during the Expulsion of Communists from the Party and On the Formalistic and Bureaucratic Relationship to the Appeals of those Excluded from the Ranks of the C.P.S.U.(B.) and On Measures for Eliminating these Shortcomings." On the basis of this decision, the Party called for struggle against the mass, indiscriminate expulsion of Party members from the Party ranks; against the spiritless, formalistic and bureaucratic relationship to the fate of Party members accused of unfounded slander; and against careerists who have built careers on vigilance-for-show.~~

~~The Central Committee Plenum demanded the exposure of cleverly hidden enemies who were trying to conceal their hostility to the U.S.S.R. and preserve their place in the Party ranks by shrill calls for vigilance. It also demanded the exposure of those trying to defeat our Bolshevik cadres and sow doubt and excessive suspicion within our ranks through the mechanism of Party repression.~~

~~The Central Committee Plenum vowed to put an end to this spiritless, formalistic and bureaucratic relationship to the fate of Party members; to bring to justice those leaders who tolerated the existence of such a relationship; to complete the processing of appeals within a three-month period of time; to publish expulsion decrees in the press and to rehabilitate people in the press if their reputations turned out to have been compromised without cause; to bring slanderers to justice; and to curtail the practice of firing those excluded from the Party without transferring them to a different job.~~

~~It was in this way, in this new period at the end of the Second Five-Year Plan, that the Party elevated the life of the Party organization to a major priority; corrected the errors and distortions in the Party line that had been allowed by an array of Party organizations; and raised Bolsheviks' revolutionary vigilance.~~

~~10. Elections to the Supreme Soviet (December 12, 1937)~~

The Party decided to make the idea of an election bloc of Communists and the non-Party masses the keynote of its policy in developing the election campaign. The Party entered the elections in a bloc, an alliance with the non-Party masses, by deciding to put up in the electoral areas joint candidates with the non-Party masses. This was something unprecedented and absolutely impossible in elections in bourgeois countries. But a bloc of Communists and the non-Party masses was something quite natural in our country, where hostile classes no longer exist and where the moral and political unity of all sections of the population is an incontestable fact.

On December 7, 1937, the Central Committee of the Party issued an Address to the electors, which stated:

> *"On December 12, 1937, the working people of the Soviet Union will, on the basis of our Socialist Constitution, elect their deputies to the Supreme Soviet of the U.S.S.R. The Bolshevik Party enters the elections in a bloc, an alliance with the non-Party workers, peasants, office employees and intellectuals. . . . The Bolshevik Party does not fence itself off from non-Party people, but, on the contrary, enters the elections in a* BLOC, *an* ALLIANCE, *with the non-Party masses, in a bloc with the trade unions of the workers and office employees, with the Young Communist League and other non-Party organizations and societies. Consequently, the candidates will be the joint candidates of the Communists and the non-Party masses, every non-Party deputy will also be the deputy of the Communists, just as every Communist deputy will be the deputy of the non-Party masses."*

The Address of the Central Committee concluded with the following appeal to the electors:

> *"The Central Committee of the Communist Party of the Soviet Union (Bolsheviks) calls upon all Communists and sympathizers to vote for the non-Party candidates with the same unanimity as they should vote for the Communist candidates.*
>
> *"The Central Committee of the Communist Party of the Soviet Union (Bolsheviks) calls upon all non-Party electors to vote for the Communist candidates with the same unanimity as they will vote for the non-Party candidates.*
>
> *"The Central Committee of the Communist Party of the Soviet Union (Bolsheviks) calls upon all electors to appear at the polling stations on December 12, 1937, as one man, to elect the deputies to the Soviet of the Union and the Soviet of Nationalities.*

"There must not be a single elector who does not exercise his honourable right of electing deputies to the Supreme organ of the Soviet state.

"There must not be a single active citizen who does not consider it his civic duty to assist in ensuring that all electors without exception take part in the elections of the Supreme Soviet.

"December 12, 1937, should be a great holiday celebrating the union of the working people of all the nations of the U.S.S.R. around the victorious banner of Lenin and Stalin."

On December 11, 1937, the eve of the elections, Comrade Stalin addressed the voters of the area in which he was nominated and described what type of public figures those whom the people choose, the deputies to the Supreme Soviet of the U.S.S.R., should be. Comrade Stalin said:

"The electors, the people, must demand that their deputies should remain equal to their tasks; that in their work they should not sink to the level of political philistines; that in their posts they should remain political figures of the Lenin type; that as public figures they should be as clear and definite as Lenin was; that they should be as fearless in battle and as merciless towards the enemies of the people as Lenin was; that they should be free from all panic, from any semblance of panic, when things begin to get complicated and some danger or other looms on the horizon, that they should be as free from all semblance of panic as Lenin was; that they should be as wise and deliberate in deciding complex problems requiring a comprehensive orientation and a comprehensive weighing of all pros and cons as Lenin was; that they should be as upright and honest as Lenin was; that they should love their people as Lenin did."

The elections to the Supreme Soviet of the U.S.S.R. took place on December 12 amidst great enthusiasm. ~~The elections to the U.S.S.R. Supreme Soviet were a celebration of the great Stalin Constitution.~~ *They were something more than elections; they were a great holiday celebrating the triumph of the Soviet people, a demonstration of the great friendship of the peoples of the U.S.S.R.*

~~About 90 million Soviet voters voted for candidates from the bloc of the Communists and the non-Party masses, for the Soviet Government.~~ *Of a total of 94,000,000 electors, over 91,000,000, or 96.8 per cent, voted. Of this number 89,844,000, or 98.6 per cent, voted for the candidates of the bloc of the Communists and the non-Party masses. Only 632,000 persons, or less than one per cent, voted against the candidates of the bloc of the Communists and the non-Party masses. All the candidates of the bloc were elected without exception.*

~~The whole Soviet people voted for the new Socialist system with unheard-of unanimity. This system had already graphically shown its superiority to the broadest popular masses.~~ *Thus, 90,000,000 persons, by their unanimous vote, confirmed the victory of Socialism in the U.S.S.R.*

This was a remarkable victory for the bloc of the Communists and the non-Party masses.

~~The entire Soviet people, standing together and united as never before, voted for the policies of the Bolshevik Party, the Lenin-Stalin Party, and showed the Party great trust. By their vote, the Soviet people demonstrated that they were prepared to defend with their lives the Socialist system and their motherland's Soviet soil from the imperialist predators and fascist warmongers. The Soviet people showed with their vote their readiness to utterly destroy the despicable traitors and Trotskyite-Bukharinite henchmen.~~ *It was a triumph for the Bolshevik Party.*

~~The Bolshevik Party completely deserved the great trust offered to it by the entire Soviet people by merit of its heroic work.~~ *It was a brilliant confirmation of the moral and political unity of the Soviet people, to which Comrade Molotov had referred in a historic speech he delivered on the occasion of the Twentieth Anniversary of the October Revolution.*

~~At the start of this book, we described what a backward, poor, dark and uncultured country Old Russia was, and how unbearably difficult it was for the workers and peasants living there.~~

~~Under the rule of the workers and the peasants, and through the leadership of the Bolshevik Party, our country was transformed into a leading, cultured, powerful Socialist Great Power.~~

~~These successes have been accomplished by our people under the leadership of the Bolshevik Party.~~

~~In our country, the capitalist system of economics and the exploitative classes have been eliminated forever, as have the private ownership of the tools and means of production and the exploitation of one man by another. Socialist ownership of the means of production made up 98.7 per cent of the productive forces of the national economy in 1936. Socialist ownership of the tools and means of production has been confirmed as the inalienable foundation of Soviet society.~~

> ~~"This world-historical victory was won by our people under the Bolshevik Party," it was said in an appeal to voters by the Central Committee of the Communist Party of the Soviet Union (Bolsheviks).~~
>
> ~~"Anyone who wishes the working people of the Soviet Union to be forever free of the yoke of exploitation will vote for the Bolshevik~~

~~Party and the candidates of the bloc of the Communists and non-Party masses."~~

~~Over the course of two Stalinist Five-Year-Plans, the U.S.S.R. has been transformed into a powerful industrial Great Power. About four fifths (77.4 per cent) of all economic production now consists of industrial production. A first-class industry has been created, equipped with modern techniques. The volume of our Socialist factory and mill production in 1937 surpassed the volume of pre-war industrial production by more than eight times. Industry in the U.S.S.R. has climbed to first place in Europe and second place in the entire world.~~

~~Such are the results of the Bolshevik Party's struggle for the country's Socialist industrialization.~~

~~In the pre-revolutionary countryside, there were about 30–40 million poor peasants doomed to hunger and poverty. The Soviet system, under the leadership of the Bolshevik Party, has eliminated the landlords, destroyed kulak servitude and handed over to the peasantry over 150 million hectares of the landlords' and kulaks' land.~~

~~Under the leadership of the Bolshevik Party, the collective farm system won out, freeing the peasants from poverty forever and providing them with the opportunity for a prosperous and cultured life in the U.S.S.R. In our motherland's agricultural economy, more than 243,000 collective farms have taken life and matured, furnished with more than enough tractors, combines and other agricultural machinery. 18.5 million peasants have united within the collective farms, as well as 99.1 per cent of the arable land.~~

~~If combined with that of the state farms, collective farm agriculture in 1937 produced two times more as an economic sector than agriculture did in the pre-war period. Socialist agriculture provides for a fast, uninterrupted rate of growth that creates an abundance of goods.~~

~~Such are the results of the Bolshevik Party's struggle for the collectivization of agriculture.~~

~~In pre-revolutionary Russia, as in any capitalist country, there was always a great deal of unemployment. In Soviet society, unemployment has been destroyed for all time and the Soviet economy remains unacquainted with the crises that are characteristic of capitalism. All citizens of our country are guaranteed by law and by the great Stalin Constitution the right to work, the right to rest, and the right to material support in old age. Material well-being is increasing steadily, as is the cultural life of the working people of the U.S.S.R.~~

~~The transition from capitalism to Socialism is largely complete in our country, which in October 1917 first broke through the imperialist front, overthrew the power of the bourgeoisie and established a proletarian dictatorship. The workers and peasants of the U.S.S.R., along with the Soviet intelligentsia,~~

~~form the labouring people of a Socialist society that is already built in general terms.~~

~~In this way, Lenin's theory on the possibility of building a Socialist society in our country has been realized. The working class of the U.S.S.R., led by the Lenin-Stalin Party, has demonstrated that Socialism is neither a utopia nor a daydream. Under the leadership of the working class, the working people of our country have realized a system of free labouring peoples in the city and countryside; a system that excludes every sort of oppression and exploitation.~~

~~A moral and political unity that until now has been unheard-of has been created in our country as a result of the victory of Socialism in our society.~~

~~The Soviet people have rallied tightly around the Bolshevik Party, around the great continuer of Lenin's deeds, Comrade Stalin.~~

~~The elections to the U.S.S.R. Supreme Soviet were a demonstration of the limitless love and devotion of the popular masses to the Bolshevik Party, to its Stalinist Central Committee, and to Comrade Stalin.~~

~~Comrade Molotov, in his report on the twentieth anniversary of the October revolution, said:~~

> ~~"The moral and political unity of the people in our country has its own embodiment. We have a name that has become the symbol of the victory of Socialism. This name is also the symbol of the moral and political unity of the Soviet people. You know what that name is: Stalin!"~~

~~Comrade Stalin is the inspiration and organizer of the victories of the First and Second Five-Year-Plans and the world-class historical victory of Socialism in the U.S.S.R. He armed the Party and the working class with Lenin's theory on the possibility of building a Socialist society in one country, without which it would have been impossible to imagine mobilizing the Party and masses for the completion of this great plan. Comrade Stalin defended Lenin's teachings on the possibility of the victory of Socialism in one country in an ideological struggle with opportunists and developed it further as only a genius could.~~

~~In practice, the U.S.S.R. has fully justified the great words of Marx about how a theory takes on material power when it is mastered by the masses. Inspired by the great Lenin-Stalin ideas of building a Socialist society in our country, the labouring masses have built and brought this society to completion through heroic and stubborn labour under the leadership of the Bolshevik Party. Without this revolutionary theory, the working class and its Party would not have been able to move forward. Continuing Lenin's cause, Comrade Stalin added concrete definition to Marxist-Leninist theory and furthered its development.~~

~~Stalin developed the Marxist-Leninist teachings on THE DICTATORSHIP OF THE PROLETARIAT, working out the forms that the working class' class conflict takes at the various stages of Socialist construction, as well as the ways in which to eliminate the capitalist elements and classes in general.~~

~~Stalin developed the Marxist-Leninist teachings on THE NATIONAL-COLONIAL question as a part of the general question concerning the dictatorship of the proletariat and the international revolution. Along with Lenin, Comrade Stalin was the creator of the Lenin-Stalin nationality policy of the Bolshevik Party and the creator of the Friendship of the Peoples of the Soviet Union.~~

~~Developing Lenin's teachings about the possibility of building Socialism in our country, Comrade Stalin developed a general plan on this basis for a Socialist offensive on all fronts and worked out the methods, forms and paths for the construction of Socialist society.~~

~~Stalin developed and enriched Lenin's teachings on SOCIALIST INDUSTRIALIZATION, as the most important condition for the victory of Socialism in our country. Stalin made an invaluable contribution to Marxist-Leninist theory by working out how to reorganize the peasantry in a Socialist way under the leadership of the working class; and by working out how THE COLLECTIVIZATION OF AGRICULTURE was to proceed—under what conditions and according to what method. Comrade Stalin invented the slogan calling for the elimination of the kulak as a class on the basis of solid collectivization.~~

~~Comrade Stalin is the creator of the new U.S.S.R. Constitution—the Stalinist Constitution of victorious Socialism and developed Socialist democracy.~~

~~Comrade Stalin developed and enriched Lenin's teachings on the Party and its role in the dictatorship of the proletariat, brilliantly working out the strategy and tactics of the working-class Party. Stalin developed and continued Lenin's analysis of the social origins of opportunist currents within the working class and the Party, demonstrating the special characteristics of opportunism in the various stages of class struggle.~~

~~Generalizing about the entire experience of the world proletarian revolution and the experience of Socialist construction in the U.S.S.R., Comrade Stalin advanced and continues to advance practical slogans for the leadership of the struggle at all major stages and then demands that they be fulfilled. At every new stage, Comrade Stalin identified without error precisely which forms of struggle and organization would best facilitate the mobilization of the multimillion strong masses.~~

~~Comrade Stalin, the continuer of Lenin's cause, has tirelessly armed and united the Bolshevik Party in an ideological sense, leading it though all its difficulties toward the victory of Socialism. His book QUESTIONS OF LENINISM, and all his articles and speeches, have been and continue to be the most important leadership for every Bolshevik—whether Party member or non-Party mem-~~

~~ber—in the struggle for the construction of Socialist society and the victory of Communism.~~

~~Comrade Stalin's speeches and directives have been and continue to be the most important leadership for work on the ideological front and for the exposure of every sort of bourgeois theory and theoretical survival that is hostile to Marxism-Leninism. An exceptional role in this connection was played by Comrade Stalin's speech "On the Questions of Agrarian Policies in the U.S.S.R." and his letter "On Several Questions Concerning the History of Bolshevism," which raised the Party's vigilance in regard to counter-revolutionary Trotskyism and Trotskyite contraband on the ideological front, and also Stalin's report to the Seventeenth Party Congress. In his report to the February–March Central Committee Plenum (1937), Comrade Stalin pointed to the continuing evolution of counter-revolutionary Trotskyism and the Bukharinite Rightist deviation, mobilizing the Party to uproot the Trotskyite-Bukharinite double-dealers, spies, wreckers, murders and saboteurs.~~

~~The slogan calling for the MASTERY OF BOLSHEVISM and the elimination of political nonchalance advanced by Comrade Stalin raised the Party's vigilance even more and heightened its fighting ability in the struggle against the remains of the hostile capitalist classes and the agents of the capitalist encirclement.~~

~~On the basis of Lenin's teachings on imperialism, Comrade Stalin gave a profound analysis of the STRUGGLE OF TWO SYSTEMS—capitalist and Socialist—in the context of the worldwide capitalist crisis and the growing international proletarian revolution. In his reports and speeches, Comrade Stalin laid out an array of fundamental questions regarding the international revolutionary movement.~~

~~STALIN'S NAME STANDS IN A LINE WITH THE GREAT NAMES OF THE WORLD PROLETARIAT'S THEORISTS AND CHIEFS: MARX, ENGELS AND LENIN.~~

~~Comrade Stalin has taught the Bolsheviks—Party members and non-Party members—THE LENINIST STYLE OF WORK, combining the Russian revolutionary sweep-of-the-hand with an American sense of professionalism.~~

~~Comrade Stalin has brilliantly demonstrated who a political figure of the Leninist type ought to be.~~

~~Comrade Stalin said the following in his speech at an election campaign meeting of voters in the Stalin voting district in Moscow on December 11, 1937:~~

> ~~"The electors, the people, must demand that their deputies should remain equal to their tasks; that in their work they should not sink to the level of political philistines; that in their posts they should remain political figures of the Lenin type; that as public figures they should be as clear and definite as Lenin was; that they should be as fearless in battle and as merciless towards the enemies of the people as Lenin was; that they~~

should be free from all panic, from any semblance of panic, when things begin to get complicated and some danger or other looms on the horizon, that they should be as free from all semblance of panic as Lenin was; that they should be as wise and deliberate in deciding complex problems requiring a comprehensive orientation and a comprehensive weighing of all pros and cons as Lenin was; that they should be as upright and honest as Lenin was; that they should love their people as Lenin did."[53]

All Comrade Stalin's activities serve as the most clear, lofty example of a political figure of the Leninist type: his entire struggle for the interests of the Party and the people against all the enemies of Marxism-Leninism, the enemies of Socialism and the enemies of the people; and his service to the cause of the working class and the cause of the proletarian revolution and world Communism.

Conclusion[1]

What are the chief conclusions to be drawn from the historical path traversed by the ~~C.P.S.U.(B.)~~ *Bolshevik Party*?

What does the history of the ~~C.P.S.U.(B.)~~ *Party* teach us?[2]

1) The history of the Party teaches us, *first of all*, that *the victory of the proletarian revolution*, the ~~conquest~~ *victory* of the dictatorship of the proletariat, ~~as well as its preservation, strengthening and expansion in the interests of the total victory of Socialism and the construction of a Socialist society in the U.S.S.R., would have been~~ *is* impossible without a *revolutionary* ~~communist~~ party *of the proletariat*, ~~which is strong by merit of its unity and rigid discipline, formed on the basis of its Party members' consciousness and their devotion to the proletarian revolution, and by merit of its inseparable connection to the masses and their support~~ *a party free from opportunism, irreconcilable towards compromisers and capitulators, and revolutionary in its attitude towards the bourgeoisie and its state power.*

~~Leninism teaches us that the dictatorship of the proletariat is a STUBBORN STRUGGLE, both bloody and bloodless, violent and peaceful, militant and civil and institutional and administrative, against THE FORCES AND TRADITIONS OF THE ANCIEN RÉGIME, and that without a party, which is rigid and battle-hardened, without a Party, which enjoys the trust of all that is honest within the working class, and without a Party, which is able to follow the mood of the masses and influence them, it is impossible to wage such a struggle.~~ *The history of the Party teaches us that to leave the proletariat without such a party means to leave it without revolutionary leadership; and to leave it without revolutionary leadership means to ruin the cause of the proletarian revolution.*

The history of the Party teaches us that the ordinary Social-Democratic Party of the West-European type, brought up under conditions of civil peace, trailing in the wake of the opportunists, dreaming of "social reforms," and dreading social revolution, cannot be such a party.

The history of the Party teaches us that only a party of the new type, a Marxist-Leninist party, a party of social revolution, a party capable of preparing the

ЗАКЛЮЧЕНИЕ

Каков же основной итог исторического пути, пройденного ВКП(б)? Чему учит нас история партии?

История партии учит нас тому, что завоевание диктатуры пролетариата, удержание ее, закрепление и расширение в интересах полной победы социализма и построения социалистического общества в СССР невозможно было бы без коммунистической партии, сильной своей сплоченностью и железной дисциплиной, которая основана на сознательности членов партии и их преданности пролетарской революции, сильной своими неразрывными связями с массами и поддержкой масс.

Ленинизм учит, что диктатура пролетариата есть *упорная борьба*, кровавая и бескровная, насильственная и мирная, военная и хозяйственная, педагогическая и администраторская, против *сил и традиций старого общества*, и что без партии, железной и закаленной в борьбе, без партии, пользующейся доверием всего честного в рабочем классе, без партии, умеющей следить за настроением масс и влиять на него, вести такую борьбу невозможно.

Такой именно партией и является Всесоюзная коммунистическая партия (большевиков).

История нашей партии является историей борьбы против других, враждебных большевизму, партий и уничтожения их, является историей завоевания нашей партией такого положения, при котором она стала единственной легальной партией в стране, не делящей своего руководства ни с какой другой партией.

Положение нашей партии в стране как единственно легальной партии (монополия компартии) не есть нечто искусственное и надуманное.

Товарищ Сталин в своей беседе с первой американской рабочей делегацией показал, что монополия нашей партии выросла из жизни как результат того, что партии эсеров и меньшевиков (и другие некоммунистические партии в рабочем классе) окончательно обанкротились и сошли со сцены в условиях нашей действительности.

Чем были партии эсеров и меньшевиков в прошлом?—ставил вопрос товарищ Сталин. Они были проводниками буржуазного влияния на пролетариат.

322

First page of Conclusion with Stalin's editing from the early summer of 1938. RGASPI, f. 558, op. 3, d. 77, l. 322.

proletariat for decisive battles against the bourgeoisie and of organizing the victory of the proletarian revolution, can be such a party.

The ~~Communist~~ *Bolshevik* Party ~~of the Soviet Union (Bolsheviks)~~ *in the U.S.S.R.* is such a party.

> *"In the pre-revolutionary period," Comrade Stalin says, "in the period of more or less peaceful development, when the parties of the Second International were the predominant force in the working-class movement and parliamentary forms of struggle were regarded as the principal forms, the Party neither had nor could have had that great and decisive importance which it acquired afterwards, under conditions of open revolutionary battle. Defending the Second International against attacks made upon it, Kautsky says that the parties of the Second International are instruments of peace and not of war, and that for this very reason they were powerless to take any important steps during the war, during the period of revolutionary action by the proletariat. That is quite true. But what does it mean? It means that the parties of the Second International are unfit for the revolutionary struggle of the proletariat, that they are not militant parties of the proletariat, leading the workers to power, but election machines adapted for parliamentary elections and parliamentary struggle. This, in fact, explains why, in the days when the opportunists of the Second International were in the ascendancy, it was not the party but its parliamentary group that was the chief political organization of the proletariat. It is well known that the party at that time was really an appendage and subsidiary of the parliamentary group. It goes without saying that under such circumstances and with such a party at the helm there could be no question of preparing the proletariat for revolution.*
>
> *"But matters have changed radically with the dawn of the new period. The new period is one of open class collisions, of revolutionary action by the proletariat, of proletarian revolution, a period when forces are being directly mustered for the overthrow of imperialism and the seizure of power by the proletariat. In this period the proletariat is confronted with new tasks, the tasks of reorganizing all party work on new, revolutionary lines; of educating the workers in the spirit of revolutionary struggle for power; of preparing and moving up reserves; of establishing an alliance with the proletarians of neighbouring countries; of establishing firm ties with the liberation movement in the colonies and dependent countries, etc., etc. To think that these new tasks can be performed by the old Social-Democratic parties, brought up as they were in the peaceful conditions of parliamentarism, is to doom oneself to hopeless despair and inevitable defeat. If, with such tasks to shoulder, the proletariat remained under the leadership of the*

old parties it would be completely unarmed and defenceless. It goes without saying that the proletariat could not consent to such a state of affairs.

"Hence the necessity for a new party, a militant party, a revolutionary party, one bold enough to lead the proletarians in the struggle for power, sufficiently experienced to find its bearings amidst the complex conditions of a revolutionary situation, and sufficiently flexible to steer clear of all submerged rocks in the path to its goal.

"Without such a party it is useless even to think of overthrowing imperialism and achieving the dictatorship of the proletariat.

"This new party is the party of Leninism." (J. Stalin, LENINISM, *Eng. ed.)*

2) The history of the Party further teaches us that a party of the working class cannot perform the role of leader of its class, cannot perform the role of organizer and leader of the proletarian revolution, unless it has mastered the advanced theory of the working-class movement, the Marxist-Leninist theory.

The power of the Marxist-Leninist theory lies in the fact that it enables the Party to find the right orientation in any situation, to understand the inner connection of current events, to foresee their course and to perceive not only how and in what direction they are developing in the present, but how and in what direction they are bound to develop in the future.

Only a party which has mastered the Marxist-Leninist theory can confidently advance and lead the working class forward.

On the other hand, a party which has not mastered the Marxist-Leninist theory is compelled to grope its way, loses confidence in its actions and is unable to lead the working class forward.

It may seem that all that is required for mastering the Marxist-Leninist theory is diligently to learn by heart isolated conclusions and propositions from the works of Marx, Engels and Lenin, learn to quote them at opportune times and rest at that, in the hope that the conclusions and propositions thus memorized will suit each and every situation and occasion. But such an approach to the Marxist-Leninist theory is altogether wrong. The Marxist-Leninist theory must not be regarded as a collection of dogmas, as a catechism, as a symbol of faith, and the Marxists themselves as pedants and dogmatists. The Marxist-Leninist theory is the science of the development of society, the science of the working-class movement, the science of the proletarian revolution, the science of the building of the Communist society. And as a science it does not and cannot stand still, but develops and perfects itself. Clearly, in its development it is bound to become enriched by new experience and new knowledge, and some of its propositions and conclusions are bound to change in the course of time, are bound to be replaced by new conclusions and propositions corresponding to the new historical conditions.

Mastering the Marxist-Leninist theory does not at all mean learning all its formulas and conclusions by heart and clinging to their every letter. To master the Marxist-Leninist theory we must first of all learn to distinguish between its letter and substance.

Mastering the Marxist-Leninist theory means assimilating THE SUBSTANCE *of this theory and learning to use it in the solution of the practical problems of the revolutionary movement under the varying conditions of the class struggle of the proletariat.*

Mastering the Marxist-Leninist theory means being able to enrich this theory with the new experience of the revolutionary movement, with new propositions and conclusions, it means being able to DEVELOP IT AND ADVANCE IT *without hesitating to replace—in accordance with the substance of the theory—such of its propositions and conclusions as have become antiquated by new ones corresponding to the new historical situation.*

The Marxist-Leninist theory is not a dogma but a guide to action.

Before the Second Russian Revolution (February 1917), the Marxists of all countries assumed that the parliamentary democratic republic was the most suitable form of political organization of society in the period of transition from capitalism to Socialism. It is true that in the seventies Marx stated that the most suitable form for the dictatorship of the proletariat was a political organization of the type of the Paris Commune, and not the parliamentary republic. But, unfortunately, Marx did not develop this proposition any further in his writings and it was committed to oblivion. Moreover, Engels' authoritative statement in his criticism of the draft of the Erfurt Program in 1891, namely, that "the democratic republic . . . is . . . the specific form for the dictatorship of the proletariat" left no doubt that the Marxists continued to regard the democratic republic as the political form for the dictatorship of the proletariat. Engels' proposition later became a guiding principle for all Marxists, including Lenin. However, the Russian Revolution of 1905, and especially the Revolution of February 1917, advanced a new form of political organization of society—the Soviets of Workers' and Peasants' Deputies. As a result of a study of the experience of the two Russian revolutions, Lenin, on the basis of the theory of Marxism, arrived at the conclusion that the best political form for the dictatorship of the proletariat was not a parliamentary democratic republic, but a republic of Soviets. Proceeding from this, Lenin, in April 1917, during the period of transition from the bourgeois to the Socialist revolution, issued the slogan of a republic of Soviets as the best political form for the dictatorship of the proletariat. The opportunists of all countries clung to the parliamentary republic and accused Lenin of departing from Marxism and destroying democracy. But it was Lenin, of course, who was the real Marxist who had mastered the theory of

Marxism, and not the opportunists, for Lenin was advancing the Marxist theory by enriching it with new experience, whereas the opportunists were dragging it back and transforming one of its propositions into a dogma.

What would have happened to the Party, to our revolution, to Marxism, if Lenin had been overawed by the letter of Marxism and had not had the courage to replace one of the old propositions of Marxism, formulated by Engels, by the new proposition regarding the republic of Soviets, a proposition that corresponded to the new historical conditions? The Party would have groped in the dark, the Soviets would have been disorganized, we should not have had a Soviet power, and the Marxist theory would have suffered a severe setback. The proletariat would have lost, and the enemies of the proletariat would have won.

As a result of a study of pre-imperialist capitalism Engels and Marx arrived at the conclusion that the Socialist revolution could not be victorious in one country, taken singly, that it could be victorious only by a simultaneous stroke in all, or the majority of the civilized countries. That was in the middle of the nineteenth century. This conclusion later became a guiding principle for all Marxists. However, by the beginning of the twentieth century, pre-imperialist capitalism had grown into imperialist capitalism, ascendant capitalism had turned into moribund capitalism. As a result of a study of imperialist capitalism, Lenin, on the basis of the Marxist theory, arrived at the conclusion that the old formula of Engels and Marx no longer corresponded to the new historical conditions, and that the victory of the Socialist revolution was quite possible in one country, taken singly. The opportunists of all countries clung to the old formula of Engels and Marx and accused Lenin of departing from Marxism. But it was Lenin, of course, who was the real Marxist who had mastered the theory of Marxism, and not the opportunists, for Lenin was advancing the Marxist theory by enriching it with new experience, whereas the opportunists were dragging it back, mummifying it.

What would have happened to the Party, to our revolution, to Marxism, if Lenin had been overawed by the letter of Marxism and had not had the courage of theoretical conviction to discard one of the old conclusions of Marxism and to replace it by a new conclusion affirming that the victory of Socialism in one country, taken singly, was possible, a conclusion which corresponded to the new historical conditions? The Party would have groped in the dark, the proletarian revolution would have been deprived of leadership, and the Marxist theory would have begun to decay. The proletariat would have lost, and the enemies of the proletariat would have won.

Opportunism does not always mean a direct denial of the Marxist theory or of any of its propositions and conclusions. Opportunism is sometimes expressed in the attempt to cling to certain of the propositions of Marxism that have already become antiquated and to convert them into a dogma, so as to retard the further development of Marxism, and, consequently, to retard the development of the revolutionary movement of the proletariat.

It may be said without fear of exaggeration that since the death of Engels the master theoretician Lenin, and after Lenin, Stalin and the other disciples of Lenin, have been the only Marxists who have advanced the Marxist theory and who have enriched it with new experience in the new conditions of the class struggle of the proletariat.[3]

And just because Lenin and the Leninists have[4] *advanced the Marxist theory, Leninism is a further development of Marxism; it is Marxism in the new conditions of the class struggle of the proletariat, Marxism of the epoch of imperialism and proletarian revolutions,*[5] *Marxism of the epoch of the victory of Socialism on one-sixth*[6] *of the earth's surface.*

The Bolshevik Party could not have won in October 1917 if its foremost men had not mastered the theory of Marxism, if they had not learned to regard this theory as a guide to action, if they had not learned to advance the Marxist theory by enriching it with the new experience of the class struggle of the proletariat.

Criticizing the German Marxists in America who had undertaken to lead the American working-class movement, Engels wrote:

> *"The Germans have not understood how to use their theory as a lever which could set the American masses in motion; they do not understand the theory themselves for the most part and treat it in a doctrinaire and dogmatic way, as something which has got to be learned off by heart and which will then supply all needs without more ado. To them it is a dogma and not a guide to action." (Letter to Sorge, November 29, 1886.)*

Criticizing Kamenev and some of the old Bolsheviks who in April 1917 clung to the old formula of a revolutionary democratic dictatorship of the proletariat and the peasantry at a time when the revolutionary movement had gone on ahead and was demanding a transition to the Socialist revolution, Lenin wrote:

> *"Our teaching is not a dogma, but a guide to action, Marx and Engels always used to say, rightly ridiculing the learning and repetition by rote of 'formulas' which at best are only capable of outlining* GENERAL *tasks that are necessarily liable to be modified by the* CONCRETE *economic and political conditions of each separate* PHASE *of the historical process. . . . It is essential to realize the incontestable truth that a Marxist must take cognizance of real life, of the* CONCRETE REALITIES, *and must not continue to cling to a theory of yesterday. . . ." (Lenin,* COLLECTED WORKS, *Russ. ed., Vol. XX, pp. 100–101.)*

3)[7] ~~THE HISTORY OF OUR PARTY IS THE HISTORY OF THE STRUGGLE AGAINST OTHER PARTIES HOSTILE TO BOLSHEVISM AND THE PARTY AND THE HISTORY OF THEIR DESTRUCTION. The history of our Party is the history of our Party's victory in conditions within which it was the sole legal party that did not share leaders with any other party in the country.~~

~~The conditions within which our Party presently stands as the sole legal party (i.e., the Communist Party's monopoly) are neither artificial nor contrived.~~

~~Comrade Stalin, in his conversation with the American worker delegation, pointed out that the Socialist-Revolutionaries and Mensheviks (as well as other non-communist parties within the working class) had completely bankrupted themselves and vanished from sight in the conditions of our everyday reality.~~

~~Comrade Stalin then asked: so what were the Socialist-Revolutionaries and the Mensheviks in the past? They were the agents of the bourgeoisie's influence over the proletariat.~~

~~What was it that cultivated and then nurtured the existence of these parties before October 1917? It was the presence of the bourgeoisie and, in the last instance, the presence of the bourgeois power, which supported these parties. The basis for the existence of these parties, therefore, vanished with the overthrow of the bourgeoisie.~~

~~It is clear why these parties lost all their support and all their influence among the workers and labouring strata of the peasantry.~~

~~The struggle between the Communist Party and the Socialist-Revolutionaries and Mensheviks for influence within the working class began long ago. Its origins date to the first hints of a mass revolutionary movement in Russia, in the years before 1905. The period between 1903 and October 1917 was a period of intense struggle for the support of the working class in our country, a period of struggle between the Bolsheviks, the Mensheviks and the Socialist-Revolutionaries for influence within the working class. During this time, the working class experienced three revolutions. In the fires of these revolutions, it tested and verified these parties—their suitability for the cause of proletarian revolution and their proletarian revolutionary spirit.~~

~~And so it transpired that on the eve of October 1917, when history took account of all past revolutionary struggles and when history measured the weight of the various working class parties struggling with one another on her scales, the working class at long last finally settled on the Communist Party as the sole proletarian party.~~

~~What can explain the fact that the working class chose the Communist Party? Is it not a fact that the Bolsheviks were an insignificant minority within the Petrograd Soviet in April 1917, for instance? Is it not a fact that the Socialist-Revolutionaries and Mensheviks enjoyed a huge majority in the soviets at that time? Is it not a fact that by October the entire government and its coercive~~

~~apparatus lay in the hands of the Mensheviks and Socialist-Revolutionaries, who had formed a bloc with the bourgeoisie?~~

~~The answer is that the Communist Party stood for ending the war and an immediate democratic peace while the Socialist-Revolutionaries and Mensheviks supported "the war to its victorious conclusion"—the continuation of the imperialist war. The answer is that the Communist Party stood for the overthrow of the Kerensky government, for the overthrow of the bourgeois power, for the nationalization of the mills and factories and the banks and the railroads, while the Mensheviks and Socialist-Revolutionaries fought for the Kerensky government and defended the bourgeoisie's rights to the mills and factories and the banks and railroads. The answer is that the Communist Party stood for the immediate confiscation of the landlords' land for the peasantry, while the Socialist-Revolutionaries and Mensheviks set the question aside until the Constituent Assembly, the convening of which they had postponed for an indefinite period of time.~~

~~Why should it be surprising that the workers and poor peasants decided at long last in favour of the Bolsheviks? Why should it be surprising that the Socialist-Revolutionaries and Mensheviks quickly vanished from sight? This is why the Communist Party came to power.~~

~~The subsequent period, the period after October 1917, the period of the Civil War, was the period in which the Mensheviks and Socialist-Revolutionaries finally met their fate and the Bolsheviks realized their ultimate triumph. The Mensheviks and the Socialist-Revolutionaries simplified this triumph for the Communist Party.~~

~~Having been defeated and having vanished from sight during the October coup d'état, the remains of the Menshevik and Socialist-Revolutionary parties began to link up with the counter-revolutionary kulak uprisings, form alliances with Kolchak and Denikin, and join the service of the Entente, sealing their fate in the eyes of the workers and peasants, once and for all.~~

~~Turning from bourgeois revolutionaries to bourgeois counter-revolutionaries, the Socialist-Revolutionaries and Mensheviks helped the Entente try to strangle the new Soviet Russia as the Bolshevik Party surrounded itself with everything that was alive and revolutionary and raised ever more new detachments of workers and peasants in the struggle for a Socialist fatherland and against the Entente. It is completely natural that the Communists' victory during this period should have brought about the complete defeat of the Socialist-Revolutionaries and the Mensheviks. Why should it be surprising that after all of this, the Communist Party would become the sole party of the working class and poor peasantry?~~

~~As Comrade Stalin explained, it thus transpired that the Communist Party came to have a monopoly as the only legal party in the country.~~

~~There is no basis in the U.S.S.R. for the existence of multiple parties, nor for the right to form different parties. A party is a part of a larger class—it represents the most advanced part of that class. Multiple parties, and the right to form parties, may only exist in societies where there are antagonistic classes with interests that are hostile and irreconcilable in regard to one another—where there are capitalists and workers, landlords and peasants, kulaks and poor peasants, and so on. But in the U.S.S.R., there are no longer any classes such as the capitalists, the landlords, the kulaks, etc. There are just two classes in the U.S.S.R., the workers and peasants, the interests of which are not only not conflictual, but just the opposite—harmonious.~~

> ~~"It thus has transpired," observed Comrade Stalin in his report on the draft U.S.S.R. Constitution, "that in the U.S.S.R. there is no basis for the existence of multiple parties, nor for the right to form parties. In the U.S.S.R., there is the basis for just one party, the Communist Party. Only one party may exist in the U.S.S.R.—the Communist Party, which boldly defends the workers' and peasants' interests to the utmost. And there can hardly be any doubt about the job that the Party has done in defending the interests of these classes thus far."~~

~~The entire course of the proletarian revolution has confirmed Lenin's well-known postulate that~~

> ~~"the unity of the proletariat in the epoch of social revolution may be realized only by a radically revolutionary Marxist party, and only by a merciless struggle against all other parties." (Lenin, COLLECTED WORKS, Russ. ed., Vol. XXVI, p. 50.)~~

~~Aside from the Socialist-Revolutionaries and the Mensheviks, there was one more petty-bourgeois political trend within the working class—Anarcho-Syndicalism—with which the Bolshevik Party waged an ongoing, uncompromising struggle. It was defeated by the Bolshevik Party precisely in the way that the Socialist-Revolutionaries and Mensheviks were defeated.~~

~~The Anarchists were opposed to the working class's political struggle and this tactic of opposing political struggle divided the workers and aided only the bourgeoisie. The Anarchists were against any form of government and opposed to the dictatorship of the proletariat.~~

~~What form did the Anarcho-Syndicalists take during the October Socialist Revolution and Civil War? The Anarcho-Syndicalists turned into a counter-revolutionary, BOURGEOIS party. During the Civil War, they—along with the Socialist-Revolutionaries—entered into conspiracies at the behest of inter-~~

~~national espionage services (the explosion in the Moscow Party Committee's headquarters in 1919 and other counter-revolutionary actions). The Anarchists waged an armed struggle against the Soviet power (Makhno's gang, the Kronstadt mutiny). Pretending to be "on the Left," as the anarchist's phrase goes, they became enemies of the Soviet power just as any Whiteguards.~~

~~All non-communist, petty-bourgeois parties within the working class—the Socialist-Revolutionaries, Mensheviks, Anarcho-Syndicalists[8] and so on—became counter-revolutionaries and BOURGEOIS parties even before the October revolution and in its wake transformed into agents of foreign espionage services, into a gang of spies, wreckers, assassins and diversionists. The Socialist-Revolutionaries and the Mensheviks set out on this path already during the Civil War, when they took part in a variety of counter-revolutionary conspiracies organized by imperialist espionage services (the Lockhart plot and others).~~

~~Without the defeat of the bourgeois Socialist-Revolutionaries, Menshevik and Anarcho-Syndicalist parties, which had supported the preservation of capitalism and then its restoration, it would have been impossible to overthrow capitalism, establish and then strengthen the dictatorship of the proletariat, win in the Civil War and build Socialism.~~

~~Without the defeat and destruction of these enemies of the people, who had become spies of foreign espionage services, the Soviet people would not be able to enjoy the benefits of a free, joyous, prosperous and cultured life, and would instead now be groaning under the yoke of the capitalists and landlords, under the yoke of fascism.~~[9]

The history of the Party further teaches us that unless the petty-bourgeois parties which are active within the ranks of the working class and which push the backward sections of the working class into the arms of the bourgeoisie, thus splitting the unity of the working class, are smashed, the victory of the proletarian revolution is impossible.

The history of our Party is the history of the struggle against the petty-bourgeois parties—the Socialist-Revolutionaries, Mensheviks, Anarchists and nationalists—and of the utter defeat of these parties. If these parties had not been vanquished and driven out of the ranks of the working class, the unity of the working class could not have been achieved; and if the working class had not been united, it would have been impossible to achieve the victory of the proletarian revolution.

If these parties, which at first stood for the preservation of capitalism, and later, after the October Revolution, for the restoration of capitalism, had not been utterly defeated, it would have been impossible to preserve the dictatorship of the proletariat, to defeat the foreign armed intervention, and to build up Socialism.

It cannot be regarded as an accident that all the petty-bourgeois parties, which styled themselves "revolutionary" and "socialist" parties in order to deceive the people—the Socialist-Revolutionaries, Mensheviks, Anarchists and nationalists—became counter-revolutionary parties even before the October Socialist Revolution, and later turned into agents of foreign bourgeois espionage services, into a gang of spies, wreckers, diversionists, assassins and traitors to the country.

> *"The unity of the proletariat in the epoch of social revolution may be realized only by a radically revolutionary Marxist party, and only by a merciless struggle against all other parties. (Lenin,* Collected Works, *Russ. ed., Vol. XXVI, p. 50.)*

4)[10] ~~The history of the Party is the history of the Party's struggle against anti-Leninist oppositionist tendencies, groups and factions within the Bolshevik Party, and the history of their destruction.~~

~~The source of contradictions and disagreements within the proletarian Party stems from two sets of conditions. First is the pressure that the bourgeoisie and bourgeois ideology bring to bear on the proletariat and its Party in the context of class struggle, where these antagonistic classes exist alongside one another. This pressure, which frequently bears down on the least resilient strata of the proletariat, also affects the least resilient strata of the proletarian Party. Second is the heterogeneity of the working class and the presence of petty-bourgeois elements within its ranks.~~

~~Leninism teaches that the Party is the unity of will, which is incompatible with the existence of factions.~~

~~What are factions? They are groups with their own particular platforms and anti-Leninist views that emerge within the Party. They aim to close themselves off and foster their own group discipline, which is at odds with Party discipline. The existence of factions effectively aids the bourgeoisie by undermining Party unity and rigid Party discipline, without which the dictatorship of the proletariat becomes impossible to realize. The foundation of factions within the Bolshevik Party represents a step toward the founding of a different, anti-Bolshevik party, which is necessarily hostile to the cause of Socialism.~~

> ~~Lenin said: "He who weakens even by just a little bit the rigid Party discipline of the proletarian Party (especially during its dictatorship period) is someone who effectively aids the bourgeois against the proletariat." (Lenin, Collected Works, Russ. ed., Vol. XXV, p. 190.)~~

~~At Lenin's suggestion, the Tenth Party Congress passed a special resolution "On Party Unity," which called for the "total elimination of all factions" and called for Party members "to immediately dissolve, without exception, all groups that have formed on the basis of this or that program" under the threat~~

~~of "unconditional, immediate expulsion from the Party." The Tenth Party Congress resolution pointed out that any revival or tolerance of factions in the future would result in expulsion from the Party.~~

~~The congress warned that any sort of factional activity was dangerous for the revolution, since it "strengthens the repeated attempts of corrupt enemies close to the leading Party to deepen and exploit divisions in the interests of the counter-revolution."~~

~~In this decision, the Tenth Party Congress pointed to the experience of ALL PREVIOUS REVOLUTIONS, where counter-revolutionary forces had supported petty-bourgeois groups close to the most revolutionary parties in order to shake up and overthrow the revolutionary dictatorships. This cleared the way for the eventual victory of the counter-revolution and the capitalists and landlords.~~

~~The experience of our revolution confirms the correctness of Lenin's evaluation of the harm and danger of factionalism within the proletarian Party.~~

~~History has shown that the capitalist encirclement took advantage of all of the oppositionist groups and tendencies within the Bolshevik Party that appeared after the October revolution.~~

~~All the opposition trends within our Party—the Trotskyites, Rights (Bukharin, Rykov), "Lefts" (Lominadze, Shatskin), the "Workers' Opposition" (Shlyapnikov, Medvedyev, etc.), the "Democratic-Centralists" (Sapronov), and nationalists of every stripe and republic—became enemies of the people and agents (spies) of foreign espionage services in the course of the struggle.~~[11]

~~In this way, all of the oppositionist tendencies struggling against the Party ended up like the Socialist-Revolutionaries, Mensheviks and other parties hostile to Bolshevism.~~

~~How did this transpire?~~

~~Most importantly, these trends closed themselves off into factions. The existence of closed factions with anti-Leninist views and with their own factional discipline led to attempts to deceive and double-deal, and then to conditions in which the various opposition tendencies became more and more hostile to our Party.~~

~~The Bolshevik Party exposed all these anti-Leninist trends in ideological terms before the working class.~~

~~The Bolshevik Party utterly defeated and buried Trotskyism in ideological terms. The Party showed that the Trotskyite prophecy denying the possibility that the working class and peasantry of our country could build Socialism in the U.S.S.R. was a Menshevik, bourgeois prophecy. The Party showed that the Trotskyite denial of the possibility that much of the peasantry could be drawn over to the cause of Socialist construction of the countryside revealed the Menshevik, bourgeois essence of Trotskyism. The Party showed that by denying the imperative of rigid discipline within the Party, and by demanding the right~~

to form factions and groups, the Trotskyites were provoking a split within the Party and the formation of a second party hostile to Bolshevism.

The Party defeated Trotskyism. In the discussion on the eve of the Fifteenth Party Congress, the Trotskyites won only about half a per cent of the Party's vote.

The Party defeated the kulak Right deviation, which was furiously struggling against the Socialist industrialization of the country, against collectivization and against the elimination of the kulaks as a class. The Party defeated the Right deviation in ideological terms, demonstrating that the Rights (Bukharin, Rykov and others) effectively sided with the view denying the possibility of Socialism being victorious in our country. The Party showed that the Rights' line was a line that would disarm the working class and arm the kulaks, and that the Rights' line was directed toward the preparation of conditions for the reestablishment (restoration) of capitalism.

The Party defeated the so-called "Workers' Opposition" (Shlyapnikov, Medvedyev and others), which ended up demanding freedom of the press for all counter-revolutionary parties and groups, "from the monarchists to the anarchists and all in between." The platforms of these parties and groups vomited counter-revolutionary Menshevik bile at the Party, demanding that our major industries be handed over to the imperialists as concessions, that the Comintern be eliminated, etc.

The Party defeated the "Democratic-Centrists" (Sapronov's people), who were related to the Trotskyites and whom Lenin had characterized as a Socialist-Revolutionary-Menshevist group. The Party also defeated the "Lefts" (the Lominadze-Shatskin group).

The Party defeated all of the bourgeois nationalists[12] of every stripe and republic of the U.S.S.R. who snuck their way into our ranks. All these bourgeois-nationalist groups[13] aimed to destroy the great Friendship of the Peoples of the U.S.S.R. and sell all the peoples of the Soviet Union who had been emancipated from national oppression by the Great October Revolution back into the slavery of the imperialist states.

Like the Trotskyites and Rights, the nationalists aimed for the restoration of capitalism. All of them followed the same treacherous path as the Trotskyites and Rights—from closed factions and groups that were hostile to the Party to their transformation into spies of foreign espionage services and serfs of the imperialist states.

The Party defeated and exposed all of the enemies of Bolshevism and Leninism who tried to corrupt and undermine the Party from the inside.

Had our Party not defeated all of these anti-Party oppositionist trends and groups, it would not have been able to lead the Soviet people to the victory of Socialism.

~~What was it that united all of these political tendencies and parties that were so hostile to Leninism? What moved them to organize every sort of unprincipled, anti-Party bloc?~~

~~They were drawn together and united by their lack of faith in the power of the people and the construction of Socialism in our country and by their belief in almighty, all-powerful capitalism. They were united by their rabid hatred of the Party. Disguised and undisguised capitulation—this was the essence of all the opposition to the Party.~~

~~From capitulation, the former oppositionist trends went on to sell themselves as spies, wreckers, assassins and diversionists to the imperialists. It was not accidental that in 1927–28, just as the Bolshevik Party was beginning to realize its great program of Socialist industrialization, and just as the Party switched over to the collectivization of agriculture and began to tear out the deepest roots of capitalism in our country, and just as class struggle inside the country sharpened beyond the hostility of the capitalist encirclement toward the U.S.S.R.—it was not accidental that it was during these years that the Trotskyites and then the Rights launched rabid, frenzied attacks against the Party. It was in precisely this period of Socialist advance that the capitulatory, treacherous essence of all these tendencies and groups revealed itself with particular clarity.~~

~~Thanks to the support of the masses, the Bolshevik Party was able to boldly and decisively cast the capitulators off its historical path, like a mighty railway engine casts off sparks.~~

~~Defeated in ideological terms and having lost their basis within the working class, all the oppositionist groups and trends formed a gang of accursed enemies of the people, concealing their true face under the mask of double-dealing and the most rotten hypocrisy and trickery. They appealed for aid from the imperialists and became spies-for-hire for foreign espionage services, selling out their motherland.~~

~~This transformation was aided by the fact that the most evil enemies of the people, Trotsky and Bukharin, had led a struggle against Lenin and the Bolshevik Party over the course of many decades. As is well known, as early as 1903–04, Trotsky acted as Bolshevism's most evil enemy. Already in 1918, Trotsky and Bukharin had forged a counter-revolutionary conspiracy and had plotted to overthrow the Soviet Government, arrest and kill Lenin, Stalin and Sverdlov, and form their own counter-revolutionary Trotskyite-Bukharinite-Socialist-Revolutionary government.~~

~~This transformation over to espionage, treachery, wrecking, terror and diversion was aided by the fact that among the former anti-Party oppositionists were more than a few spies of foreign espionage services, old provocateurs from the tsarist OKHRANA and other similarly savage enemies of the Soviet power.~~

~~The Trial of the Anti-Soviet "Bloc of Rights and Trotskyites" in March 1938 demonstrated with unusual power and strength that as long as the capitalist encirclement exists, it will sow spies, wreckers and assassins into our country.~~

~~This is not surprising: if the imperialist states systematically dispatch masses of spies against one another, then they must dispatch many more of their spies against the country of victorious Socialism in order to prepare for an attack.~~[14]

~~But why did the Bolshevik Party emerge victorious from this struggle with so many enemies? Why was it able to lead the working class and all the working people of the U.S.S.R. to the victory of Socialism? Is it possible to view this as some sort of historical accident?~~

~~No, the victory of the Bolshevik Party was not an accident. Two basic conditions explain the reasons for the Bolshevik Party's victory in the struggle with its enemies.~~

~~First, the Bolshevik Party was and still is the only Marxist, tempered party that is armed with such an advanced theory as the teachings of Marxism-Leninism.~~

~~"Only a party armed with advanced theory can perform the role of the vanguard," observed Lenin. The teachings of Marxism-Leninism demonstrate the developmental laws of human society and scientifically express the fundamental interests of the advanced class, the class of the proletariat. The revolutionary theory of Marxism-Leninism teaches the proletariat to understand its great historical mission and teaches that the proletariat has been summoned by the very march of history to overthrow the slavery of capitalism, establish the dictatorship of the proletariat and build a classless Socialist society.~~

~~This revolutionary theory gives the revolutionary movement confidence, the power to properly orient itself, and an understanding of the internal connectedness of external events. It also helps its practitioners understand not only how and in what direction various classes are developing in the present, but how and in what direction they are bound to develop in the future.~~

~~Leninism teaches that "revolutionary theory is not dogma" and that "it comes together only in tight connection with practice in a genuinely mass movement that is genuinely revolutionary" (Lenin, "The Childhood Disease of 'Leftism' in Communism"), since theory must contribute to practice, since "theory must provide answers to questions raised by practice" (Lenin) and since theory must be verified in practice.~~

~~The Bolshevik Party is the only Marxist Party where revolutionary theory is inseparably connected to revolutionary practice. The Bolshevik letter never differs from its substance.~~

~~The Bolshevik Party is the only Marxist Party that has been able to demonstrate in everyday life the unbreakable union of theory and practice, where theory and practice are found in complete organic unity.~~

~~"There are two types of Marxists," Comrade Stalin wrote on Lenin's fiftieth jubilee. "Both of them work under the banner of Marxism and consider themselves to be 'genuine' Marxists. And yet they are far from identical. More than that: between them is a vast gap, since the methods of their work are diametrically opposed to one-another.~~

~~"The first group usually limits itself to the external appearance of Marxism and its triumphant statements. Unable or unwilling to actually probe deeply into the essence of Marxism and unable or unwilling to bring it to life, this group transforms Marxism's living, revolutionary postulates into lifeless formulas that don't say anything. This group bases its actions not on experience and not on an accounting of its practical work, but on quotations taken from Marx. It doesn't draw its instructions and directives from the analysis of living reality, nor from analogous situations or historical parallels. The fundamental malady of this group is the difference between its letter and substance. It is from this malady that come the demoralization and permanent dissatisfaction with fate that always betrays this group. The name for this group is Menshevism (in Russia) and opportunism (in Europe). At the London Party Conference, Comrade Tyshko (Jogiches) accurately characterized this group when he said that it doesn't so much stand for the Marxist point of view as it LIES DOWN for it.~~

~~"The second group, by contrast, shifts the emphasis from the external appearance of Marxism to its execution, its realization in everyday life. This group pays attention most of all to the ways and means for realizing Marxism, the corresponding conditions, and any changes in these ways and means. It draws its instructions and directives not from historical analogies and parallels, but from the study of surrounding conditions. It bases its actions not on quotations and sayings, but on practical experience, verifying each one of its steps, learning from its mistakes and teaching others about how to build a new life. This explains why this group's letter never differs from its substance and why the teachings of Marx retain their full, living, revolutionary power. Marx's well-known dictum applies well to this group, whereby it is not enough for Marxists to merely explain the world. They must go further in order to change it. The name for this group is Bolshevism and Communism."~~

~~The party of the Second International, the Russian Mensheviks, the Trotskyites and the Bukharinites, all of whom were by the letter "Marxists" and "Bolsheviks," long ago became agents of the bourgeoisie and traitors to Marxism-Leninism in substance. Marxism-Leninism long ago became for them a means~~

~~of camouflage and trickery. It is precisely for this reason that they met their fate in the stinking swamp of counter-revolution.~~

~~Only our Bolshevik Party has been faithful to the end to the great, triumphant banner of Marx, Engels, Lenin and Stalin. This is why Marxism has been victorious over one-sixth of the world's surface. The world bourgeoisie, which rabidly hates Marxism, has claimed to have destroyed Marxism many times. But in order to destroy Marxism, it is necessary to destroy the working class, whose fundamental interests it expresses. And the working class is impossible to destroy.~~

The history of the Party further teaches us that unless the Party of the working class wages an uncompromising struggle against the opportunists within its own ranks, unless it smashes the capitulators in its own midst, it cannot preserve unity and discipline within its ranks, it cannot perform its role of organizer and leader of the proletarian revolution, nor its role as the builder of the new, Socialist society.

The history of the development of the internal life of our Party is the history of the struggle against the opportunist groups within the Party—the "Economists," Mensheviks, Trotskyites, Bukharinites and nationalist deviators—and of the utter defeat of these groups.

The history of our Party teaches us that all these groups of capitulators were in point of fact agents of Menshevism within our Party, the lees and dregs of Menshevism, the continuers of Menshevism. Like the Mensheviks, they acted as vehicles of bourgeois influence among the working class and in the Party. The struggle for the liquidation of these groups within the Party was therefore a continuation of the struggle for the liquidation of Menshevism.

If we had not defeated the "Economists" and the Mensheviks, we could not have built the Party and led the working class to the proletarian revolution.

If we had not defeated the Trotskyites and Bukharinites, we could not have brought about the conditions that are essential for the building of Socialism.

If we had not defeated the nationalist deviators of all shades and colours, we could not have educated the people in the spirit of internationalism, we could not have safeguarded the banner of the great amity of the nations of the U.S.S.R., and we could not have built up the Union of Soviet Socialist Republics.

It may seem to some that the Bolsheviks devoted far too much time to this struggle against the opportunist elements within the Party, that they overrated their importance. But that is altogether wrong. Opportunism in our midst is like an ulcer in a healthy organism, and must not be tolerated. The Party is the leading detachment of the working class, its advanced fortress, its general staff. Sceptics, opportunists, capitulators and traitors cannot be tolerated on the directing staff of the working class. If, while it is carrying on a life and death fight against the bourgeoisie, there are capitulators and traitors on its own staff, within its own fortress, the working class will be caught between two fires, from the front and the rear. Clearly, such a struggle can only end in defeat. The easiest way to capture a fortress is from within. To attain victory, the Party of the working class, its directing staff, its advanced fortress, must first be purged of capitulators, deserters, scabs and traitors.

It cannot be regarded as an accident that the Trotskyites, Bukharinites and nationalist deviators who fought Lenin and the Party ended just as the Menshevik and Socialist-Revolutionary parties did, namely, by becoming agents of fascist espionage services, by turning spies, wreckers, assassins, diversionists and traitors to the country.

> *"With reformists, Mensheviks, in our ranks," Lenin said, "it is* IMPOSSIBLE *to achieve victory in the proletarian revolution, it is* IMPOSSIBLE *to retain it. That is obvious in principle, and it has been strikingly confirmed by the experience both of Russia and Hungary. . . . In Russia, difficult situations have arisen* MANY TIMES, *when the Soviet regime would* MOST CERTAINLY *have been overthrown had Mensheviks, reformists and petty-bourgeois democrats remained in our Party. . . ." (Lenin,* COLLECTED WORKS, *Russ. ed., Vol. XXV, pp. 462–63.)*
>
> *"Our Party," Comrade Stalin says, "succeeded in creating internal unity and unexampled cohesion of its ranks primarily because it was able in good time to purge itself of the opportunist pollution, because it was able to rid its ranks of the Liquidators, the Mensheviks. Proletarian parties develop and become strong by purging themselves of opportunists and reformists, social-imperialists and social-chauvinists, social-patriots and social-pacifists. The Party becomes strong by purging itself of opportunist elements." (Stalin,* LENINISM, *Eng. ed.)*

5) ~~Precisely because our Party is armed with the advanced, revolutionary theory of Marxism-Leninism and has been able to connect theory and practice, it has never been afraid of criticism. Indeed, it considers self-criticism to be the basic method of training cadres to the present day. Leninism teaches that the relationship of a political party to its errors is one of the best and most reliable indicators of that Party's seriousness and its commitment to its class responsibilities and the toiling masses. All of the parties and groups that were hostile to Bolshevism feared self-criticism and attempted to hide their mistakes, trying to "whitewash over troubling questions and conceal their shortcomings with a façade of prosperity, which dulled critical thought and put a brake on the Party's revolutionary training on the basis of its own mistakes." (Stalin, "On the Foundations of Leninism," QUESTIONS IN LENINISM, Russ. ed., pp. 11–12.)~~

~~The strength of the Bolshevik Party consists in the fact that it has never covered up its mistakes; on the contrary, it has openly discussed them and used~~

~~them to teach its cadres. It also has turned self-criticism into a fundamental method for training Bolshevik cadres.~~

~~This is the first, fundamental condition and key to the invincibility of the Bolshevik leadership.~~

The history of the Party further teaches us that a party cannot perform its role as leader of the working class if, carried away by success, it begins to grow conceited, ceases to observe the defects in its work, and fears to acknowledge its mistakes and frankly and honestly to correct them in good time.

A party is invincible if it does not fear criticism and self-criticism, if it does not gloss over the mistakes and defects in its work, if it teaches and educates its cadres by drawing the lessons from the mistakes in Party work, and if it knows how to correct its mistakes in time.

A party perishes if it conceals its mistakes, if it glosses over sore problems, if it covers up its shortcomings by pretending that all is well, if it is intolerant of criticism and self-criticism, if it gives way to self-complacency and vainglory and if it rests on its laurels.

> *"The attitude of a political party towards its own mistakes," Lenin says, "is one of the most important and surest ways of judging how earnest the party is and how it* IN PRACTICE *fulfils its obligations towards its class and the toiling* MASSES. *Frankly admitting a mistake, ascertaining the reasons for it, analysing the conditions which led to it, and thoroughly discussing the means of correcting it—that is the earmark of a serious party; that is the way it should perform its duties, that is the way it should educate and train the* CLASS, *and then the* MASSES." *(Lenin,* COLLECTED WORKS, *Russ. ed., Vol. XXV, p. 200.)*

And further:

> *"All revolutionary parties, which have hitherto perished, did so because they* GREW CONCEITED, *failed to see where their strength lay,* AND FEARED TO SPEAK OF THEIR WEAKNESSES. *But we shall not perish, for we do not fear to speak of our weaknesses and will learn to overcome them." (Lenin,* COLLECTED WORKS, *Russ. ed., Vol. XXVII, pp. 260–61.)*

6) ~~The key to the Bolshevik leadership's invincibility is found in its inseparable connection with the masses.~~

~~Leninism teaches that the Party must not only teach the masses, but learn from them as well.~~

~~Leninism teaches that the experience of the leadership in isolation is insufficient for correct leadership, and that it is imperative to complement leader-~~

~~ship experience with the experience of the masses, the experience of the Party masses, the experience of the working class and the experience of the people.~~

~~Leninism teaches that the Party must carefully hearken to the voice of the masses, to the voice of rank-and-file Party members, to the voice of the so-called "little people," and to the voice of the people.~~

~~Leninism teaches that to lead correctly, a leader must:~~

~~First, identify the correct solution to a question, which is impossible to do without taking into account the experience of the masses;~~

~~Second, implement the correct solution, which is impossible to do without the direct help of the masses;~~

~~Third, verify the solution's implementation, which again is impossible to do without the direct help of the masses.~~

~~Leninism teaches that to lead and to complement one's leadership experience with the experience of the Party masses, the working class, the working people and the so-called "little people" is possible only if leaders are tightly connected to the people—only if they are connected to the Party masses, the working class, the peasantry and the labouring intelligentsia.~~

~~The connection with the masses, the strengthening of these connections, and the readiness to hearken to the voice of the masses—this is where the power and invincibility of the Bolshevik leadership can be found.~~

~~In his report to the February–March Central Committee Plenum (1937), Comrade Stalin invoked the brilliant artistic imagery of Antaeus, the invincible hero of ancient Greek mythology.~~

~~When Antaeus was hard pressed in the struggle with an enemy, he would touch the earth—his mother, who gave birth to him and nurtured him—and that would give him new strength that would make him impossible to vanquish. There was only one way to defeat Antaeus—to separate him from the earth.~~

~~The Bolshevik Party is reminiscent of Antaeus, the hero of ancient Greek mythology. The Bolsheviks have the same powerful and invincible connection to their mother, the popular masses, who gave birth to the Bolsheviks and nurtured them.~~

~~Leninism teaches that as long as the Bolsheviks preserve their connection with the broad popular masses, they will be invincible. This is the key to the invincibility of the Bolshevik leadership.~~

Lastly, the history of the Party teaches us that unless it has wide connections with the masses, unless it constantly strengthens these connections, unless it knows how to hearken to the voice of the masses and understand their urgent needs, unless it is prepared not only to teach the masses, but to learn from the masses, a party of the working class cannot be a real mass party capable of leading the working class millions and all the labouring people.

A party is invincible if it is able, as Lenin says, "to link itself with, to keep in close touch with, and, to a certain extent if you like, to merge with the broadest masses of the toilers—primarily with the proletariat, but also with the non-proletarian toiling masses." (Lenin, COLLECTED WORKS, Russ. ed., Vol. XXV, p. 174.)

A party perishes if it shuts itself up in its narrow party shell, if it severs itself from the masses, if it allows itself to be covered with bureaucratic rust.

> *"We may take it as the rule," Comrade Stalin says, "that as long as the Bolsheviks maintain connection with the broad masses of the people they will be invincible. And, on the contrary, as soon as the Bolsheviks sever themselves from the masses and lose their connection with them, as soon as they become covered with bureaucratic rust, they will lose all their strength and become a mere cipher.*
>
> *"In the mythology of the ancient Greeks there was a celebrated hero, Antaeus, who, so the legend goes, was the son of Poseidon, god of the seas, and Gaea, goddess of the earth. Antaeus was very much attached to the mother who had given birth to him, suckled him and reared him. There was not a hero whom this Antaeus did not vanquish. He was regarded as an invincible hero. Wherein lay his strength? It lay in the fact that every time he was hard pressed in a fight with an adversary he would touch the earth, the mother who had given birth to him and suckled him, and that gave him new strength. Yet he had a vulnerable spot—the danger of being detached from the earth in some way or other. His enemies were aware of this weakness and watched for him. One day an enemy appeared who took advantage of this vulnerable spot and vanquished Antaeus. This was Hercules. How did Hercules vanquish Antaeus? He lifted him from the earth, kept him suspended in the air, prevented him from touching the earth, and throttled him.*
>
> *"I think that the Bolsheviks remind us of the hero of Greek mythology, Antaeus. They, like Antaeus, are strong because they maintain connection with their mother, the masses, who gave birth to them, suckled them and reared them. And as long as they maintain connection with their mother, with the people, they have every chance of remaining invincible.*
>
> *"That is the clue to the invincibility of Bolshevik leadership." (J. Stalin, DEFECTS OF PARTY WORK.)*

~~* * *~~

~~What are the conclusions that every Bolshevik must draw for himself from the historical experience of our Party?~~

~~Every Bolshevik must be faithful to the great banner of Marx, Engels, Lenin and Stalin, MASTER BOLSHEVISM, arm himself with the revolutionary theory that illuminates the path for people engaged in practical work and learn to combine the mastery of revolutionary theory with practical work.~~

~~Every Bolshevik must preserve his connection to the masses, every day and in every way, remembering that this is the key to the invincibility of the Bolshevik leadership. Every Bolshevik must also be able to both teach the masses and learn from them.~~

~~Every Bolshevik must learn all the lessons of our Party's past experience with the parties, groups and trends that were hostile to Bolshevism, especially from the last trials of the anti-Soviet Trotskyite centres and the anti-Soviet "Bloc of Rights and Trotskyites."~~

~~Remembering the Party's entire historical experience, every Bolshevik must defend and protect Party UNITY and not permit the formation of any sort of faction or group, which inevitably end up on the counter-revolutionary path.~~

~~Every Bolshevik must struggle to develop Bolshevik self-criticism, the sort of self-criticism that will strengthen the Party and the proletarian dictatorship. Every Bolshevik must remember Lenin's instructions that important criticism of short-comings and errors in our Party's work must be brought up for discussion not just in any old Party group meeting, but within the Party membership as a whole.~~

~~Every Bolshevik must DEFEND the Party from the penetration of spies and double-dealers and must study the insidious methods of the enemy and the methods of foreign espionage services and their agents, the exposed double-dealers.~~

~~We must not for a single minute forget that we live within the capitalist encirclement, surrounded by the wolves of capitalism and why we must know about their "wolfish ways." Bolsheviks must master all the means of exposing and destroying double-dealers, enemies of the people and spies of foreign espionage services.~~

~~This is what the last period of struggle with the enemies of the people teaches us.~~

~~In the cause of defeating and uprooting the enemies of the people,~~[15] ~~the Bolshevik Party relies on the limitless support of the popular masses. This is already clear to one and all. The Party's cause has become a personal issue for the entire Soviet people. The entire Soviet people is tightly united around the Bolshevik Party and considers it their recognized chief, organizer and inspirer. The Bolshevik Party is the vanguard of the working people of the U.S.S.R. in the struggle to strengthen and develop the Socialist system.~~

~~The Bolshevik Party is continuing its world historical struggle for the final victory of Socialism and Communism in our country and throughout the world.~~

~~In the name of these high goals, the Bolshevik Party will defeat and destroy all the enemies of Socialism and the enemies of the people in the future just as boldly and decisively as it has defeated and destroyed them in the past.~~

~~Aid in all of this is supplied by the entire glorious historical path of the Bolshevik Party, the Lenin-Stalin Party.~~[16]

Such are the chief lessons to be drawn from the historical path traversed by the Bolshevik Party.

THE END[17]

Notes

Editors' Introduction

1. "Izdanie proizvedenii I. V. Stalina v Sovetskom Soiuze s 7 noiabria 1917 goda po 5 marta 1953 goda: Statisticheskie tablitsy," in Sovetskaia bibliografiia: Sbornik statei i materialov, issue 1 (34) (Moscow: Izd-vo Vsesoiuznoi knizhnoi palaty, 1953), 224.

2. See Robert C. Tucker, Stalin in Power: The Revolution from Above (New York: W. W. Norton, 1990), 532–536; Jochen Hellbeck, "Introduction," in Autobiographical Practices in Russia / Autobiographische Praktiken in Russland, ed. Jochen Hellbeck and Klaus Heller (Gottingen: G&R Unipress, 2004), 23.

3. Most of the extant literature dates to the glasnost' era: I. L. Man'kovskaia, "Kommunisticheskaia partiia Sovetskogo Soiuza: Istoriografiia," in Sovetskaia istoricheskaia entsiklopediia, 14 vols. (Moscow: Sov. entsiklopediia, 1965), 7:717–718; George Enteen, "The Writing of Party History in the USSR: The Case of Em. Iaroslavskii," Journal of Contemporary History 21:2 (1986): 327; I. Man'kovskaia and Iu. Sharapov, "Kul't lichnosti i istoriko-partiinaia nauka," Voprosy istorii KPSS 5 (1988): 63–64; N. N. Maslov, "'Kratkii kurs istorii VKP(b)'—entsiklopediia kul'ta lichnosti Stalina," Voprosy istorii KPSS 11 (1988): 51–67; Maslov, "Iz istorii rasprostraneniia Stalinizma (Kak gotovilos' postanovlenie TsK 'O postanovke partiinoi propagandy v sviazi s vypuskom 'Kratkogo kursa istorii VKP(b)")," Voprosy istorii KPSS 7 (1990): 94–108; Maslov, "I. V. Stalin o 'Kratkom kurse istorii VKP(b),'" Istoricheskii arkhiv 5 (1994): 4–33.

More recently, see Michal Głowiński, "'Nie puszczać przeszłości na żywioł': 'Krótki kurs WKP(b)' jako opowiadanie mityczne," in Rytuał i demogogia: Trzynaście szkiców o sztuce zdegradowanej (Warsaw: Open, 1992), 24–45 (published in Russian as M. Glovinskii, "'Ne puskat' na samotek': 'Kratkii kurs VKP(b) kak mificheskoe skazanie," Novoe literturnoe obozrenie 22 [1996]: 142–160); Fabio Bettanin, La Fabrica del Mito: Storia e politica nell'Urss staliniana (Naples: Edizioni Scientifiche Italiani, 1998); P. B. Grechukhin, V. N. Danilov, "Vykhod 'Kratkogo kursa istorii VKP(b)' i predvoennoe sovetskoe obshchestvo," in Istoriograficheskii sbornik: Mezhvuzovskii sbornik nauchnykh trudov (Saratov: Izd-vo Saratovskogo un-ta, 2001), 53–64; V. Bukharev, "Ideal'nyi uchebnik Bol'shevizma: Traditsiia i lingvokul'tura 'Kratkogo kursa istorii VKP(b),'" in Novyi mir istorii Rossii, ed. G. Bordiugov et al. (Moscow: AIRO XX, 2001), 316–333; I. V. Stalin, Istoricheskaia ideologiia v SSSR v 1920–1950-e gody: Perepiska s istorikami, stat'i i

ZAMETKI PO ISTORII, STENOGRAMMY VYSTUPLENII—SBORNIK DOKUMENTOV I MATERIALOV, vol. 1, 1920–1930-E GODY, ed. M. V. Zelenov (St. Petersburg: Nauka-Piter, 2006); N. B. Arnautov, "Rol' 'Kratkogo kursa istorii VKP(b)' 1938 g. v agitatsionno-propagandisticheskoi politike partii," in ISTORICHESKIE ISSEDOVANIIA V SIBIRI: PROBLEMY I PERSPEKTIVY—SBORNIK MATERIALOV II REGIONAL'NOI MOLODEZHNOI NAUCHNOI KONFERENTSII, ed. A. K. Kirillov (Novosibirsk: Institut istorii SO RAN, 2008), 213–220; Arnautov, "Mifologiia 'Kratkogo kursa istorii VKP(b)': Istoriograficheskii aspect," VESTNIK NGU: SERIIA ISTORIIA, FILOLOGIIA 8:1 (2009): 165–168; Rustem Nureev, "The Short Course of the History of the All-Union Communist Party: The Distorted Mirror of Party Propaganda," in THE LOST POLITBURO TRANSCRIPTS: FROM COLLECTIVE RULE TO STALIN'S DICTATORSHIP, ed. Paul R. Gregory et al. (New Haven: Yale University Press, 2008), 165–178; Evgenii Dobrenko. "Stalinskii stil'," in Diktatory pishut: Literaturnoe tvorchestvo avtoritarnykh pravitelei XX veka, eds. A. Koschorke, K. Kaminskii (Moscow: Kul'turnaia revoliutsiia, 2014): 104–191; Sandra Dahlke, INDIVIDUUM UND HERRSCHAFT IM STALINISMUS: EMEL'JAN JAROSLAVSKIJ (1878–1943) (Munich: Oldenbourg, 2010), 318–339; David Brandenberger, PROPAGANDA STATE IN CRISIS: SOVIET IDEOLOGY, INDOCTRINATION AND TERROR UNDER STALIN, 1927–1941 (New Haven: Yale University Press, 2011), esp. chaps. 2, 7, 10, 11; O. V. Grushaev, "Istoriia izucheniia partiino-pravitel'stvennoi politiki 1930-kh gg. v oblasti istoricheskogo obrazovaniia," VESTNIK TGU 3 (107) (2012): 288–292; E. A. Minaev, "Reformirovanie sistemy prepodavaniia sotsial'no-ekonomicheskikh distsiplin kak instrumenta ideino-politicheskogo vospitaniia sovetskogo studentchestva vo vtoroi polovine 1930-kh godov," GOSUDARSTVENNOE UPRAVLENIE—ELEKTRONNYI VESTNIK 39 (2013): 180–194; KRATKII KURS ISTORII VKP(B): TEKST I EGO ISTORIIA, ed. M. V. Zelenov and D. Brandenberger, 2 vols. (Moscow: ROSSPEN, 2014–).

Other publications are derivative and full of errors, e.g., ISTORIIA VKP(B): REPRINTNOE IZDANIE, ed. R. A. Medvedev (Moscow: Logos, 2004), iii–xliv; Medvedev, "Kak sdelan 'Kratkii kurs,'" SVOBODNAIA MYSL' 21:3 (2004): 130–146; Medvedev, CHTO CHITAL STALIN (Moscow: Prava cheloveka, 2005), 196–248.

4. I. V. Stalin, "O nekotorykh voprosakh istorii bol'shevizma," PROLETARSKAIA REVOLIUTSIIA 6 (1931): 3–12.

5. Brandenberger, PROPAGANDA STATE IN CRISIS, chaps. 2, 4–5; Henry Steele Commager, THE SEARCH FOR A USABLE PAST AND OTHER ESSAYS IN HISTORIOGRAPHY (New York: Knopf, 1967), 3–27. The term "usable past" dates to Van Wyck Brooks, "On Creating a Usable Past," DIAL 64 (1918): 337–341.

6. "Zakrytoe pis'mo TsK VKP(b): Uroki sobytii, sviazannykh s zlodeiskim ubiistvom tov. Kirova," IZVESTIIA TsK KPSS 8 (1989): 96, 100.

7. "Glubzhe izuchat' istoriiu partii," PRAVDA, March 7, 1935, 1; "'O nekotorykh zadachakh Marksistsko-Leninskogo obrazovaniia:' iz rechi tov. P. Postysheva na plenume Kievskogo gorodskogo partiinogo komiteta 22 fevralia 1935 goda," PRAVDA, March 5, 1935, 2.

8. So many records from Kul'tprop have been lost that the only evidence of this meeting is found in Ye. M. Yaroslavsky's diary entry from March 10, 1935. This diary, which remains to the present day in private hands, is cited in Dahlke, INDIVIDUUM UND HERRSCHAFT, 332–333.

9. Yaroslavsky to Stalin (March 11, 1935), RGASPI, f. 89, op. 1, d. 84, ll. 9–10. P. N. Pospelov confirmed the seriousness of this proposal in 1972—see D. Rudnev, "Kto pisal 'Kratkii kurs,'" *Politika* 9 (1991): 63. See *Kratkaia istoriia VKP(b)*, ed. V. G. Knorin et al. (Moscow: Partizdat, 1934); E. M. Iaroslavskii, *Istoriia VKP(b)*, 2 vols. (Moscow: Partizdat, 1933, 1934).

10. RGASPI, f. 558, op. 11, d. 1118, l. 99; "Zabotlivo vyrashchivat' partiinye kadry," *Pravda*, March 26, 1935, 1; Central Committee resolution of March 27, 1935, "O sozdanii v gorkomakh VKP(b) otdelov partkadrov," *Pravda*, March 28, 1935, 2; "Reshitel'no uluchshit' partiinuiu rabotu," *Pravda*, March 29, 1935, 1; "O zadachakh partiino-organizatsionnoi i politichesko-vospitatel'noi raboty: Postanovlenie plenuma Leningradskogo gorodskogo komiteta VKP(b) ot 29 marta 1935 goda," *Pravda*, March 30, 1935, 2–3.

11. The connection between the Kirov murder and the verification campaign is questioned in J. Arch Getty, *Origins of the Great Purges: The Soviet Communist Party Reconsidered, 1933–1938* (New York: Cambridge University Press, 1991), 58; *The Road to Terror: Stalin and the Self-Destruction of the Bolsheviks, 1932–1939*, ed. J. Arch Getty and Oleg Naumov (New Haven: Yale University Press, 1999), 150. A direct connection is posited in O. V. Khlevniuk, *Politbiuro: mekhanizmy politicheskoi vlasti v 1930-e gody* (Moscow: Rosspen, 1996), 146–147; Bettanin, *La fabrica del mito*, 133–134. Although Getty is right that the verification campaign was announced before Kirov's murder, it was clearly shaped by the December crisis—see, for instance, RGASPI, d. 558, op. 11, d. 1118, ll. 101–102.

12. See undated Central Committee resolution "O reorganizatsii Kul'tpropa TsK VKP(b)," *Pravda*, May 14, 1935, 1. A. I. Stetsky retained control of the new Agitprop department.

13. Central Committee resolution of June 14, 1935 "O propagandistskoi rabote v blizhaishee vremia," *Pravda*, June 15, 1935, 1. This resolution is discussed in N. Rubinshtein, "Nedostatki v prepodavanii istorii VKP(b)," *Bol'shevik* 8 (1936): 32–42.

14. See Stetsky to Stalin (June 8, 1935), RGASPI, f. 17, op. 163, d. 1066, ll. 118–119; Stetsky to Stalin (June 15, 1935), f. 71, op. 3, d. 62, ll. 287–285; Yaroslavsky to Stalin (June 2, 1935), f. 558, op. 11, d. 842, ll. 7–8. Stesky's first letter, which Stalin transformed into a Politburo resolution entitled "O populiarnom uchebnike," indicated that the collectively written, popular textbook was to be written by a prominent brigade of authors (Knorin, Yaroslavsky, Pospelov, M. A. Moskalyev, L. M. Gulyaev, N. M. Voitinsky, A. P. Kuchkin, F. A. Anderson, S. E. Rabinovich, and B. N. Ponomaryev) and was due in early August. Yaroslavsky mentioned these developments in correspondence that summer and fall—see f. 71, op. 3, d. 57, ll. 41–42ob; op. 1, d. 9, ll. 10–14, 18; d. 28, ll. 157–158, 178–193.

15. *Soveshchanie po voprosam partiinoi propagandy i agitatsii pri TsK VKP(b), 4–7 dekabria 1935 g.* (Moscow: Partizdat, 1936), 10, 29, 135; RGASPI, f. 558, op. 3, d. 74.

16. Hints about the volume's shortcomings are visible in "O partiinoi propagande: rech' sekretaria TsK VKP(b) tov. A. Andreeva na otkrytii Vysshei shkoly propagandistov im. Ia. M. Sverdlova pri TsK VKP(b), 7 fevralia 1936 g," *Pravda*, February 26, 1936, 2; A. I. Stetskii, "Ob institutakh Krasnoi professury," *Bol'shevik* 23–24 (1935): 54–55.

17. Compare, for instance, the membership of the Bolshevik military organization in early 1917 as listed in the September 1936 and August 1937 printings of E. M. Iaroslavskii, Ocherki po istorii VKP(b), 2 vols. (Moscow: Partizdat, 1936, 1937), 1:376 versus 1:306.

18. Compare, for instance, the list of party members assisting Stalin during the 1917 revolution as listed in August 1937 and January 1938 printings of Iaroslavskii, Ocherki po istorii VKP(b), 1:335 versus 1:323.

19. Yaroslavsky reported being repeatedly asked about new textbooks whenever he gave public talks—see RGASPI, f. 89, op. 8, d. 807, l. 4.

20. "'O nedostatkakh partiinoi raboty i merakh likvidatsii trotskistskikh i inykh dvurushnikov'—Doklad t. Stalina na plenume TsK VKP(b)," Pravda, March 29, 1937, 2–4; "Materialy fevral'sko-martovskogo plenuma TsK VKP(b) 1937 g.," Voprosy istorii 10 (1994): 13; Voprosy istorii 3 (1995): 11, 14–15; Orgburo resolution of March 25, 1937, "O vypolnenii resheniia Plenuma TsK ob organizatsii partiinykh kursov, leninskikh kursov i kursov po istorii i politike partii," RGASPI, f. 17, op. 114, d. 623, l. 1. According to Stalin's proposal, the commission charged with overseeing the organization of these courses was to be chaired by Andreev and include Stetsky, A. A. Zhdanov, N. I. Yezhov, Ya. B. Gamarnik, N. S. Khrushchev, G. M. Malenkov, and Ya. A. Yakovlev.

21. RGASPI, f. 558, op. 11, d. 1219, ll. 1–6. The manuscript, entitled Kratkaia istoriia VKP(b), does not appear to have survived; it was probably related to his two-volume Ocherki po istorii VKP(b).

22. Draft Politburo resolution "Ob uchebnike istorii VKP(b)," RGASPI, f. 17, op. 163, d. 1144, ll. 1–5ob. Stalin edited this text at least once between April 6 and 14.

23. At the Politburo meeting, the commission in charge of organizing the new party courses was reassigned to Zhdanov and expanded to include Stetsky, Yezhov, Gamarnik, Khrushchev, Malenkov, Yakovlev, I. A. Akulov, B. M. Tal, N. N. Popov, Yaroslavsky, Knorin, Pospelov, N. L. Rubinshtein, L. Z. Mekhlis, and A. I. Ugarov. See Politburo resolution of April 16, 1937, "Ob organizatsii kursov usovershenstvovaniia dlia partkadrov, soglasno rezoliutsii poslednego plenuma TsK(b) po punktu 4 poriadka dnia plenuma," RGASPI, f. 17, op. 114, d. 800, l. 2. The only detailed material on these courses is stored at RGVA, thanks to the major role Gamarnik played in their development on the eve of his suicide in May 1937. Duplicates at the former central party archive are missing along with dozens of other Agitprop files from this period. See RGVA, f. 9, op. 29, d. 323, ll. 82, 100–119; RGASPI, f. 17, op. 3, d. 989, l. 16. An outline of the lower-tier curriculum was published as "Programma po istorii VKP(b) dlia partiinykh kruzhkov (proekt)," Bol'shevik 11 (1937): 68–90.

24. Politburo resolution of April 16, 1937, "Ob uchebnike po istorii VKP(b)," RGASPI, f. 17, op. 163, d. 1144, ll. 5–5ob; f. 558, op. 1, d. 3212, l. 27. It was published as "K izucheniiu istorii VKP(b)," Pravda, May 6, 1937, 4. Many of the provisions of this resolution were developed further in the Politburo resolution of May 11, 1937, "Ob organizatsii partiinykh kursov," RGASPI, f. 17, op. 114, d. 840, ll. 46–48.

25. Hints of this collaborative work appear in "'Zavtra menia uzhe ne budet.' Iz vospominanii ostavlennykh Mil'doi Iur'evnoi Knorinoi (1907–1977)," Gorizont 8 (1990): 25–26.

26. Yaroslavsky signaled his frustration with Stetsky's critique of his Kratkaia istoriia VKP(b) in marginalia written on the typescript—see RGASPI, f. 558, op. 11, d. 1219, ll.

1–6. *Ocherki po istorii VKP(b)* was an updated edition of Yaroslavsky's famous *Istoriia VKP(b)* (1933–1935), which he had struggled to keep in print in 1936. See Central Committee resolution of May 28, 1936, "Ob izdanii knigi t. Iaroslavskogo 'Istoriia VKP(b),'" RGASPI, f. 17, op. 163, d. 1109, ll. 85–86; E. Iaroslavskii, *Ocherki istorii VKP(b)*, 2 vols. (Moscow: Partizdat, 1936).

27. V. Knorin, "K voprosu ob izuchenii istorii VKP(b)," *Bol'shevik* 9 (1937): 1–6. Both Yaroslavsky and Knorin were to complete revisions to their older texts by July 1, 1937. See Politburo resolution of May 11, 1937, "Ob organizatsii partiinykh kursov," RGASPI, f. 17, op. 3, d. 987, ll. 51–54.

28. RGASPI, f. 629, op. 1, d. 10, ll. 21–97.

29. A. Litvin, *Bez prava na mysl': Istoriki v epokhu Bol'shogo Terrora—ocherki sudeb* (Kazan': Tatarskoe knizhnoe izd-vo, 1994), 20–21; A. N. Artizov, "Sud'by istorikov shkoly M. N. Pokrovskogo (seredina 1930-kh godov)," *Voprosy istorii* 7 (1994): 34–48; "1937 god: Institut Krasnoi professury (Stenograficheskii otchet 5–6 maia, 1937)," *Otechestvennaia istoriia* 2 (1992): 119–146.

30. RGASPI, f. 71, op. 1, d. 10, ll. 22–26. I. D. Orakhelashvili, another major party historian, was banished to Astrakhan that spring and arrested in July.

31. Knorin was arrested on June 22; his deputies, Anderson and P. Ia. Viskne, were arrested at about the same time. Stalin claimed to G. M. Dimitrov that Knorin had been exposed as "a Polish and German spy"; he was also apparently accused of wrecking on the ideological front along with Ya. A. Yakovlev, Stetsky, and Tal. See Georgi Dimitrov, *Dnevnik (9 Mart 1933–6 Fevuari 1949)* (Sofia: Universitetsko izdatelstvo "Sv. Kliment Okhridski," 1997), 128; RGANI, f. 3, op. 8, d. 335, ll. 97–100, published in *Reabilitatsiia: Kak eto bylo—Dokumenty Prezidiuma TsK KPSS i drugie materialy. Mart 1953–fevral' 1956*, ed. A. Artizov et al., 3 vols. (Moscow: Mezhdunarodnyi fond "Demokratiia," 2000), 1:273.

32. Adoratsky to Andreev (November 28, 1937), RGASPI, f. 71, op. 3, d. 98, l. 232.

33. RGASPI, f. 558, op. 11, dd. 1203–1207; Yaroslavsky to Stalin (July 1, 1937), d. 1203, l. 1. Days after Knorin's arrest, responsibility for the flagship textbook was reassigned to Yaroslavsky and Pospelov—see Politburo resolution of June 28, 1937, "O leninskikh kursakh," RGASPI, f. 17, op. 3, d. 989, ll. 14–15.

34. The galleys with Stalin's marginalia are at RGASPI, f. 558, op. 3, d. 381. Stetsky probably met with Stalin on July 31—see *Na prieme u Stalina: Tetradi (zhurnaly) zapisei lits, priniatykh I. V. Stalinym (1924–1953 gg.)* (Moscow: Novyi khronograf, 2008), 217.

35. RGASPI, f. 558, op. 11, d. 1219, ll. 21–35.

36. Pospelov mentions this recommendation in an undated letter to Yaroslavsky and Stetsky written during late 1937—see RGASPI, f. 629, op. 1, d. 64, l. 73. The new chapter titles, authors, and projected lengths are at l. 78; new outlines to the introduction and several chapters are at ll. 74–77, 79–84.

37. Yaroslavsky attempted to supply this more advanced reader in early 1938 by expanding his 1936 *Sketches on the History of the CPSU(B)*. These efforts were abandoned after it became clear that Stalin intended to profoundly redesign the *Short Course*. See RGASPI f. 89, op. 8, dd. 832–833.

38. RGASPI, f. 89, op. 8, d. 807, l. 3.

39. Yaroslavsky to Pospelov (August 29, September 13, 19, 1937), RGASPI, f. 89, op. 12, d. 2, ll. 234–238; f. 629, op. 1, d. 101, ll. 5–6; also d. 64, l. 78; for Yaroslavsky's later reminiscences, see f. 89, op. 8, d. 807, ll. 1–2.

40. On the completion of the manuscript, see Pospelov to Stalin (November 5, 1937), RGANI, f. 3, op. 22, d. 175, l. 123. The galleys of ISTORIIA VKP(B): KRATKII UCHEBNIK are at RGASPI, f. 558, op. 11, d. 1208, ll. 2–295.

41. See David Brandenberger, "Stalin as Symbol: A Case Study of the Cult of Personality and Its Construction," in STALIN: A NEW HISTORY, ed. Sarah Davies and James Harris (Cambridge: Cambridge University Press, 2005), 249–270.

42. Pospelov's revisions were delivered to Stalin shortly after a firm deadline was set by the Orgburo resolution of February 16, 1938, "Voprosy 'Partiinykh kursov,'" RGASPI, f. 17, op. 114, d. 840, l. 32. For Pospelov's draft introduction, part of which is dated February 26, see f. 558, op. 11, d. 1217, ll. 2–24.

43. For the March 4 and 5 meetings, 1938, see NA PRIEME U STALINA, 232.

44. RGASPI, f. 558, op. 11, d. 1208, l. 1; f. 89, op. 8, d. 831, l. 3. After this meeting, Pospelov transformed the text's eleventh chapter into an article for immediate publication. See P. N. Pospelov, "Partiia Bol'shevikov v bor'be za kollektivizatsiiu sel'skogo khoziaistva," PROLETARSKAIA REVOLIUTSIIA 9 (1938): 91–133.

45. Stalin's editing of his own notes is rendered in struck-through text; his insertions appear in italics; his emphases in small capital letters. RGASPI, f. 558, op. 11, d. 1217, ll. 26–28.

46. Three copies of the third version's galleys are at RGASPI, f. 558, op. 3, dd. 75–77.

47. NA PRIEME U STALINA, 234.

48. Zhdanov's emphases are rendered in small capital letters. RGASPI, f. 77, op. 3, d. 157, ll. 2ob–3ob.

49. For Zhdanov's April 3 meeting with Pospelov, see RGASPI, f. 77, op. 4, d. 45, l. 21ob. For the drafts, one of which is dated April 8, see d. 24, ll. 151–161, 135–150.

50. For Zhdanov's April 15 meeting with Pospelov, see RGASPI, f. 77, op. 4, d. 45, l. 21ob; for his notes from the meeting, see op. 3, d. 157, l. 133.

51. Four copies of the fourth version's galleys dating to April 24, 1938, are stored at RGASPI, f. 17, op. 120, d. 383; over a hundred pages of another copy (pp. 51–120, 141–177, 259–290) covered with Stalin's corrections are at f. 558, op. 11, dd. 1209–1211. Pospelov's additions to the fourth version are described in a letter to Zhdanov—see Pospelov to Zhdanov (April 24, 1938), f. 17, op. 120, d. 383, ll. 1–2.

52. Stalin looked over the text on April 24 or 25 and identified about a dozen objections that Pospelov acknowledged on April 26—see RGASPI, f. 17, op. 120, d. 383, l. 539ob.

53. On Yaroslavsky's May 1938 speech, see RGASPI, f. 89, op. 8, d. 831, l. 1; on Zhdanov's June 9 speech, see f. 77, op. 1, d. 692, l. 175.

54. The commission formally consisted of Stalin, Molotov, and Zhdanov. See Politburo resolution of April 25, 1938, "Ob izdaniiakh 'Kratkikh kursov' i 'uchebnikov' dlia prepodavaniia v partiinykh i komsomol'skikh shkolakh, kursakh i kruzhkakh," RGASPI, f. 17, op. 3, d. 998, l. 1.

55. Stalin's early editing is reflected in the margins of a copy of the third version of the galleys; he abandoned this work later that summer. See RGASPI, f. 558, op. 3, d. 77.

56. RGASPI, f. 89, op. 8, d. 807, l. 3. Stetsky's arrest on April 26 may have contributed to Stalin's loss of confidence in the "collective farm." The dating of Stalin's editing is based on periods during which he did not regularly receive visitors in his Kremlin office—see *Na prieme u Stalina*, 236–238.

57. Stalin to the Politburo and authors of the *Short Course* (August 16, 1938), RGASPI, f. 558, op. 11, d. 1219, ll. 36–37.

58. Although Stalin's initial editing retitled the book the *Short Popular Course*, he cut this emphasis during the last stages of his editing. See RGASPI, f. 558, op. 11, d. 1217, l. 1.

59. RGASPI, f. 17, op. 120, d. 383.

60. Instead, Stalin stressed the growing internecine strife *between* capitalist countries—tensions he viewed as evidence of the start of "a second imperialist war."

61. "'O nedostatkakh partiinoi raboty i merakh likvidatsii trotskistskikh i inykh dvurushnikov'—Doklad t. Stalina na plenume TsK VKP(b)," 2–4. On theory and practice, see David Priestland, *Stalinism and the Politics of Mobilization: Ideas, Power and Terror in Inter-war Russia* (Oxford: Oxford University Press, 2007).

62. Brandenberger, *Propaganda State in Crisis*, chaps. 4–5.

63. Brandenberger, "Stalin as Symbol"; Sarah Davies, "Stalin and the Making of the Leader Cult in the 1930s," in *The Leader Cult in Communist Dictatorship: Stalin and the Eastern Bloc*, ed. Balázs Apor, Jan Behrends, Polly Jones, and E. A. Rees (Basingstoke: Palgrave, 2005), 36–37.

64. Brandenberger, *Propaganda State in Crisis*, chap. 5.

65. The recipients were Andreev, Yezhov, Kaganovich, Kalinin, Molotov, Petrovsky, Voroshilov, Zhdanov, Khrushchev, and Mikoian.

66. See RGASPI, f. 558, op. 11, d. 1219, ll. 54, 74, 79–80; 44, 83, 93; 50, 75; 45–48.

67. RGASPI, f. 558, op. 11, d. 1217, l. 1. Years later, Pospelov paraphrased Stalin's explanation for the change to the book's title page: "if the book comes out under the editorship of the Central Committee commission, this will give it a lot of weight and ensure it the trust of the mass reader. We need to indicate that the *Short Course* has the approval of the Central Committee. This will put an end to the differences in the evaluation of events that were found in the old party history texts." Rudnev, "Kto pisal 'Kratkii kurs,'" 64. Pospelov may have been referring to Stalin's address to the September 1938 propagandists' conference—see RGASPI, f. 558, op. 11, d. 1122, ll. 35–36.

68. Yaroslavsky to Stalin (August 17, 1938), RGASPI, f. 558, op. 11, d. 1219, l. 38.

69. Pospelov to Stalin (August 17, 1938), RGAPSI, f. 558, op. 11, d. 1219, ll. 39–40.

70. Most of the substantial comments were offered by Pospelov and Yaroslavsky. See RGASPI, f. 558, op. 11, d. 1219.

71. *Na prieme u Stalina*, 239–240. A. N. Poskrebyshev is not listed in Stalin's office logbook for these sessions, but Yaroslavsky remembered him as being involved. RGASPI, f. 89, op. 8, d. 807, l. 5.

72. RGASPI, f. 89, op. 8, d. 807, ll. 4–5. Pospelov's account of the sessions echoes Yaroslavsky's—see Rudnev, "Kto pisal 'Kratkii kurs,'" 64. For the minor, aesthetic changes resulting from this editing, compare RGASPI, f. 558, op. 11, dd. 1212–1216, to the text published in *Pravda*, September 9–19.

73. Pospelov recounted a story of Stalin's to an audience at the Higher Party School in December 1938 about how A. E. Badayev had asked him in 1912 what the best book was for someone just beginning to study Marxism. This request, according to Stalin, was satisfied only with the advent of the SHORT COURSE 26 years later. See RGASPI, f. 629, op. 1, d. 13, ll. 100–101. PROLETARSKAYA REVOLYUTSIYA hoped to publish this speech in its Stalin jubilee issue in December 1939; the fact that it failed to appear indicates that the party hierarchy wished to limit public speculation about Stalin's contributions to the text.

74. Just before the text's appearance, rumors swept through Moscow about the imminent release of a new history edited by Stalin. Pospelov appears to have been responsible for the gossip—see August 14, 1938, entry in "Diary of Vladimir Petrovich Stavskii," in INTIMACY AND TERROR: SOVIET DIARIES OF THE 1930s, ed. Veronique Garros, Natalia Korenevskaya, and Thomas Lahusen (New York: New Press, 1995), 225–226.

75. "Gluboko izuchat' istoriiu partii Lenina-Stalina," PRAVDA, September 9, 1938, 1; see also "Vospityvat' molodezh' v dukhe bol'shevistskikh traditsii," PRAVDA, September 11, 1938, 1; "Obespechit' glubokoe izuchenie istorii VKP(b)," PRAVDA, September 17, 1938, 1.

76. Quickly, the initial print run was increased to eight million—see Politburo resolution of November 2, 1938, "'O dopolnitel'nom izdanii knigi 'Kratkii kurs istorii VKP(b),'" RGASPI, f. 17, op. 3, d. 1003, l. 7.

77. Central Committee resolution of November 14, 1938, "O postanovke partiinoi propagandy v sviazi s vypuskom 'Kratkogo kursa istorii VKP(b),'" PRAVDA, November 15, 1938, 1–2.

78. SOVKINOZHURNAL 47, dir. N. Karmazinskii and I. Setkina (Soiuzkinokhronika, 1938); SOVKINOZHURNAL 55, dir. N. Karmazinskii et al. (Soiuzkinokhronika, 1938); SOVKINOZHURNAL 7, dir. N. Karmazinskii et al. (Soiuzkinokhronika, 1938); SSSR NA EKRANE 5 (Soiuzkinokhronika, 1939); etc.

79. A. M. Pankratova suggested that the appearance of the text provided scholars with a template that allowed them to return to research and publishing without fear of denunciation. See Arkhiv RAN, f. 1577, op. 2, d. 30, ll. 45–53, published in ISTORIK I VREMIA: 20–50-E GODY XX VEKA—A. M. PANKRATOVA, ed. Iu. S. Kukushkin (Moscow: Mosgorarkhiv, 2000), 217–220. For an example of the way that the SHORT COURSE shaped historical research, see the discussion of M. V. Nechkina's work on Russian underdevelopment in A. M. Dubrovskii, ISTORIK I VLAST': ISTORICHESKAIA NAUKA V SSSR I KONTSEPTSII ISTORII FEODAL'NOI ROSSII V KONTEKSTE POLITIKI I IDEOLOGII (1930–1950 GG.) (Briansk: BGU, 2005), 361–407.

80. P. Iudin, "Istoriia partii i literatura," LITERATURNAIA GAZETA, November 7, 1938, 3; "Vooruzhit' bol'shevizmom khudozhestvennuiu intelligentsiiu," TEATR 12 (1938): 5–9; Central Committee resolution of August 7, 1939, "O Muzee V. I. Lenina," RGASPI, f. 17, op. 116, d. 12, l. 44; f. 71, op. 10, d. 374, ll. 20–23. This reorganization was originally proposed in September 1938—see f. 17, op. 120, d. 307, ll. 53, 150.

81. RGASPI, f. 17, op. 120, d. 307, l. 3.

82. RGASPI, f. 558, op. 11, d. 1122, l. 10.

83. RGASPI, f. 17, op. 163, d. 1218, ll. 44–45. Barely literate, Khrushchev dictated everything he "wrote." Personal communication with William Taubman, April 13, 2003.

84. RGASPI, f. 17, op. 2, d. 773, l. 127, cited in O. V. Khlevniuk, 1937-I: STALIN, NKVD I SOVETSKOE OBSHCHESTVO (Moscow: Respublika, 1992), 78.

85. At least some of those best suited to work with the SHORT COURSE reacted negatively to the book's tendentiousness. Party executive A. G. Solovyov reported right after the textbook's publication that his colleague, S. Zhbankov, was very dissatisfied with how it turned out. Quoting Zhbankov, Solovyov wrote: "Com[rade] Stalin gives himself too much credit. He doesn't deny that he wrote it and yet at the same time the textbook contains no less than a hundred mentions of himself and quotations [from his speeches and writing]. What's the point in this? It's not serious at all. Moreover, he credits himself with things that never happened. For instance, the leadership of the Bolshevik faction in the Fourth Duma. And there's a huge amount of attention cast on the recent show trials of the enemies of the people, as if he is trying to justify himself. No, there's no way you can say the textbook is high quality." Solovyov concluded later: "there is some truth to what Zhbankov is saying." See diary entry from October 13, 1938, in A. G. Solov'ev, "Tetradi krasnogo professora (1912–1941 gg.)," in NEIZVESTNAIA ROSSIIA: XX VEK, 4 vols. (Moscow: Istoricheskoe nasledie, 1993), 4:199.

86. RGASPI, f. 17, op. 120, d. 307, ll. 7–11. Others agreed—see ll. 68–72, 80–85, 113–114.

87. RGASPI, f. 558, op. 11, d. 1122, ll. 3–4. For Stalin's notes on the speech, see ll. 112–115, 116–123.

88. RGASPI, f. 17, op. 163, d. 1218, ll. 42–44.

89. For evidence that Stalin arrived at this determination during the conference, compare his opening remarks (RGASPI, f. 558, op. 11, d. 1122, ll. 1–18) with his closing speech where the proposal is first made (ll. 112–115, 19–27).

90. See RGASPI, f. 17, op. 163, d. 1218, ll. 33–56; Central Committee resolution of November 14, 1938, "O postanovke partiinoi propagandy v sviazi s vypuskom 'Kratkogo kursa istorii VKP(b).'"

91. Brandenberger, PROPAGANDA STATE IN CRISIS, 220–221; MATERIAL K VII GLAVE "KRATKOGO KURSA ISTORII VKP(B)" (V POMOSHCH' IZUHAIUSHCHIM ISTORIIU VKP(B)) (Voronezh: Voronezhskoe obl. kn. izd-vo, 1939); V POMOSHCH' IZUCHAIUSHCHIM ISTORII VKP(B): K IV GLAVE KRATKOGO KURSA ISTORII VKP(B)" (Stalingrad: Oblastnoe knigoizdatel'stvo, 1941); etc. Use of the provincial texts was discouraged due to problems in quality control. See also centrally printed supplements, e.g., V POMOSHCH' IZUCHAIUSHCHIM ISTORIIU VKP(B): KONSUL'TATSII K I GLAVE "KRATKOGO KURSA ISTORII VKP(B)" (Moscow: Moskovskii rabochii, 1939); etc.

92. Brandenberger, PROPAGANDA STATE IN CRISIS, chap. 11.

93. E. M. Iaroslavskii, O TOVARISHCHE STALINE (Moscow: Gos. izd-vo polit. lit-ry, 1939); "Iosif Vissarionovich Stalin (Kratkaia biografiia)," PRAVDA, December 20, 1939, 2–6; reprinted in BOL'SHEVIK 23–24 (1939): 12–56; PROLETARSKAIA REVOLIUTSIIA 4 (1939): 9–64; PARTIINOE STROITEL'STVO 23–24 (1939): 7–41; IOSIF VISSARIONOVICH STALIN (KRATKAIA BIOGRAFIIA) (Moscow: Gos. izd-vo polit. lit-ry, 1939). The text was written by Volin, M. S. Pozner, P. S. Cheremnykh, and V. D. Mochalov and edited by M. B. Mitin, G. F. Aleksandrov, Pospelov, and I. I. Mints. See RGASPI, f. 629, op. 1, d. 55, l. 52; R. Koniushaia, "Iz

vospominanii ob izdanii sochinenii I. V. Stalina i ego kratkoi biografii," Edinstvo, January 19, 1995, 3.

94. See David Brandenberger, National Bolshevism: Stalinist Mass Culture and the Formation of Modern Russian National Identity, 1931–1956 (Cambridge: Harvard University Press, 2002), chaps. 3–6.

95. RGASPI, f. 89, op. 9, d. 169, ll. 4–5.

96. RGASPI, f. 89, op. 8, d. 813, l. 3.

97. Layout reformatted. G. V. Shumeiko, Iz letopisi Staroi ploshchadi: istoricheskii ocherk (Moscow: n.p. 1996), 97–98.

98. RGASPI, f. 17, op. 125, d. 1, ll. 5, 94, 47–47ob, 17, 92–93, 103–104.

99. Moguchee oruzhie bol'shevizma, dir. S. Gurov, I. Kravchunovskii, and M. Fideleva (Moscow: TsSKKh, 1940).

100. G. D. Komkov, "Ideino-politicheskaia rabota partii v massakh v pervyi period Velikoi Otechestvennoi voiny," Voprosy istorii KPSS 6 (1960): 44–58; Brandenberger, National Bolshevism, chaps. 7–9.

101. See Aleksandrov to A. S. Shcherbakov (March 31, 1944), RGASPI, f. 17, op. 125, d. 221, ll. 28–90; Volin to Malenkov (December 5, 1944), RGASPI, f. 17, op. 125, d. 254, ll. 220–221.

102. John Curtiss and Alex Inkeles, "Marxism in the USSR—The Recent Revival," Political Science Quarterly 61:3 (1946): 349–364.

103. RGASPI, f. 17, op. 3, d. 1054, ll. 8–10; I. V. Stalin, O Velikoi Otechestvennoi voine Sovetskogo soiuza (Moscow: OGIZ, 1946).

104. Malenkov to the Politburo (January 17, 1946), RGASPI, f. 17, op. 163, d. 1477, l. 94; op. 3, d. 1055, ll. 65–70. On the history of Stalin's Works, see V. G. Mosolov, IMEL—tsitadel' partiinoi ortodoksii: iz istorii Instituta marksizma-leninizma pri TsK KPSS, 1921–1956 (Moscow: Novyi khronograf, 2010), 436–452.

105. Politburo resolution of January 19, 1946, "Ob izdanii sochinenii I. V. Stalina," RGASPI, f. 17, op. 3, d. 1055, ll. 4, 63–70; see also op. 163, d. 1477, l. 86; "Ob izdanii Sochinenii I. V. Stalina," Pravda, January 20, 1946, 2.

106. V. S. Kruzhkov to Stalin (October 23, 1946), RGASPI, f. 558, op. 11, d. 1222, ll. 1–2, 3–23, 24–205.

107. Aleksandrov and P. Fedoseyev to Stalin (January 7, 1947), RGASPI, f. 558, op. 11, d. 1223, ll. 1, 2–140.

108. Aleksandrov and Fedoseyev were replaced at the helm of Agitprop by M. A. Suslov and D. T. Shepilov in August 1947. Shepilov's August 1948 version of their material dropped its discussion of Munich, collective security, and Japanese aggression. See Shepilov to Poskrebyshev (August 12, 1948), RGASPI, f. 558, op. 11, d. 1224, ll. 1, 2–138.

109. Stalin explained to Pospelov during a December 1946 editorial meeting that his biography was to be used as an introduction to party ideology and history. See Brandenberger, "Stalin as Symbol: A Case Study of the Cult of Personality and Its Construction," 265.

110. Work on the political economy textbook had begun in the late 1930s; it was published only in 1954—see Politicheskaia ekonomiia: uchebnik (Moscow: Gos. izd-vo

politicheskoi literatury, 1954); Ethan Pollock, Stalin and the Soviet Science Wars (Princeton: Princeton University Press, 2006), 168–211.

111. Although Stalin left no marginalia on the documents, he retained Shepilov's draft until February 1953; Aleksandrov and Fedoseyev's manuscript was discovered at his dacha after his death. See RGASPI, f. 558, op. 11, d. 1223, l. lob; d. 1224, l. 1ob.

112. For Stalin's postwar editing of the Short Course, see RGASPI, f. 558, op. 11, d. 1218, ll. 1–3, 145–146, 154, 159ob–162; d. 1221, ll. 99, 101, 104, 106, 115, 123, 126, 339–342.

113. Vavilov's August 19, 1949, notes on his meeting with Stalin are at RGASPI, f. 558, op. 11, d. 717, l. 110. The authors are grateful to O. L. Leibovich for this citation.

114. The layout of the 1951 galleys differed from the 1946 galleys, but neither reflected anything but the most routine printers' changes to the 1938 original. See RGASPI, f. 558, op. 11, d. 1225, ll. 1–569.

115. Note the reversals experienced by other prominent books of the period including G. F. Aleksandrov, Istoriia zapadnoevropeiskoi filosofii (Moscow: Izd-vo Akademii nauk SSSR, 1946); E. S. Varga, Izmeneniia v ekonomike kapitalizma v itoge vtoroi mirovoi voiny (Moscow: Gos. izd-vo polit. lit-ry, 1946).

116. RGASPI, f. 17, op. 3, d. 1079, l. 53; d. 1083, l. 36; d. 1086, l. 99; d. 1092, l. 27; etc.

117. On the promotion of the Short Course abroad, see A Szovjetuni'o Kommunista (Bolsevik) P'artj'anak Tört'enete: rövid tanfolyam (Budapest: Szikra Kiadas, 1948); Istoria partidului Comunist (bolsevic): curs scurt (Bucharest: Editura Partidului Municitoresc Romän, 1948); Historia Wszechzwiazkowej Komunistycznej Partii (bolszewików): krótki kurs (Warszawa: Ksiazka i Wiedza, 1949); Dejiny Vsesvazové komunistické strany (bolseviku): strucný výklad (Prague: Svoboda, 1949); Sulian gong chan dang (bu) li shi jian yao du ben (Beijing: Jie fang she, 1949); Istoriia na vsesuiuznata kommunisticheska partiia (bolsheviki): kratuk kurs (Sofia: Izd-vo na Bulgarskata komunisticheska partiia, 1949); Geschichte der Kommunistischen Partei der Sowjetunion (Bolschewiki) Kurzer Lehrgang (Berlin: Dietz Verlag, 1952). See also John Reshetar, "The Educational Weapon," Annals of the American Academy of Political and Social Science 271 (1950): 135–144; Hua-Yu Li, Mao and the Economic Stalinization of China, 1948–1953 (Lanham: Rowman and Littlefield, 2006), 61–120; Hua-Yu Li, "Instilling Stalinism in Chinese Party Members: Absorbing Stalin's Short Course in the 1950s," in China Learns from the Soviet Union, 1949–Present, ed. Thomas Bernstein and Hua-Yu Li (Plymouth: Lexington Books, 2010), 107–130.

118. See the postwar V pomoshch' izuchaiushchim istoriiu VKP(b) series; A. M. Pankratova, "Kratkii kurs istorii VKP(b)" i sovetskaia istoricheskaia nauka: stenogramma publichnoi lektsii, prochitannoi 24 sent. 1948 g. v Moskve (Moscow: Vsesoiuznoe obshchestvo po rasprostraneniiu politicheskikh i nauchnykh znanii, 1948); "Moguchee oruzhie ideinogo vospitaniia kadrov," Pravda, September 30, 1946, 1; etc.

119. See, for instance, Leningradskii kinozhurnal 28, dir. M. Levkov (Leningradskaia st. kinokhroniki, 1946); Novosti dnia 49 (TsSDF, 1948); Leningradskii kinozhurnal 28, dir. L. Kikaz (Leningradskoe st. kinokhroniki, 1948); V. Il'enkov, Bol'shaia doroga (Moscow: Sovetskii pisatel', 1949), 117.

120. Brandenberger, National Bolshevism, chaps. 11–13.

121. See, for example, F. Golovenchenko, "Znachenie 'Kratkogo kursa istorii VKP(b)' dlia ideologicheskoi raboty," Bol'shevik 18 (1948): 6–16.

122. IMEL discussions about a new, multivolume academic history of the party in 1954 revealed staffers to have been completely dependent on the Short Course. See RGASPI, f. 71, op. 4, d. 179, ll. 92, 94–97.

123. For the final working version of the galleys, see RGASPI, f. 71, op. 10, d. 142. Critical feedback about the Short Course is at dd. 13, 146; a catalog of disputed translations and citations is at d. 145.

124. For a retrospective description of this process, see TsAOPIM, f. 212, op. 3, d. 50, l. 75, 77, 86.

125. TsAOPIM, f. 212, op. 3, d. 50, l. 66.

126. Compare the galleys of vol. 15 (1951) and vol. 16 (1952) to vol. 15 (1954) (RGASPI, f. 558, op. 11, d. 1225 and d. 1092 versus d. 1091); compare vol. 14 (1946) to vol. 14 (1954) (f. 558, op. 11, d. 1073 versus d. 1072).

127. Authorship was also reassigned between 1953 and 1954 in new drafts of Stalin's Short Biography and the Great Soviet Encyclopedia—see RGASPI, f. 71, op. 10, d. 264, l. 63; d. 257, ll. 162–167ob.

128. Presidium resolution of March 3, 1955, "O sozdanii truda po istorii Velikoi Otechestvennoi voiny i vtoroi mirovoi voiny v tselom," RGANI, f. 3, op. 22, d. 176, l. 4.

129. RGASPI, f. 71, op. 4, d. 183, l. 8, 71; d. 151, l. 245.

130. The editorial brigade was headed by M. D. Stuchebnikova; it was staffed by N. I. Shatagin, A. V. Lukashev, V. S. Kirillov, Yu. N. Petrov, R. I. Markova, T. F. Grabar', I. V. Zagloskina, I. M. Mishakova, I. I. Krasyukova, V. A. Astapenkova, and several other specialists on loan from Agitprop. See RGASPI, f. 71, op. 4, d. 151, l. 245.

131. TsAOPIM, f. 212, op. 3, d. 37, ll. 4–5.

132. For the draft text of the February 9 Pospelov commission report to the Presidium, see APRF, f. 3, op. 24, d. 489, ll. 23–91, published in Reabilitatsiia: kak eto bylo, 1:317–348. Generally, see V. P. Naumov, "K istorii sekretnogo doklada N.S. Khrushcheva na XX s"ezda KPSS," Novaia i noveishaia istoriia 4 (1996): 156–165; R. G. Pikhoia, Sovetskii Soiuz: istoriia vlasti, 1945–1991 (Moscow: Izd-vo RAGS, 1998), 136–143.

133. For the February 9 Presidium protocols, see RGANI, f. 3, op. 8, d. 389, ll. 58–62, published in Reabilitatsiia: kak eto bylo, 1:349–351; also Iu. V. Aksiutin, "Novoe o XX s"ezde KPSS," Otechestvennaia istoriia 2 (1998): 108–123.

134. N. S. Khrushchev, "Otchetnyi doklad Tsentral'nogo komiteta Kommunisticheskoi partii Sovetskogo soiuza XX s"ezdu partii 14 fevralia 1956 g.," in XX s"ezd Kommunisticheskoi partii Sovetskogo soiuza: stenograficheskii otchet, 2 vols. (Moscow: Izd-vo polit. lit-ry, 1956), 1:101–102, 114.

135. See "Rech' A. I. Mikoiana," in ibid., 1:325–326. Pankratova presented a more modest report at the congress that echoed Mikoian's findings—see "Rech' A. M. Pankratovoi," in ibid., 1:619–623. Mikoian's calls for a new, accessible history textbook based on original

research drew upon several oblique passages in Khrushchev's opening address and similar calls in the party press in 1955. See ibid., 1:114; N. Eroshkin and A. Nelidov, "Arkhivnye fondy—na sluzhbu istoricheskoi nauki," Izvestiia, April 15, 1955, 3; etc.

136. Anastas Mikoian, Tak bylo: Razmyshleniia o minuvshem (Moscow: Vagrius, 1999), 595.

137. For the Pospelov commission's February 18 report for the congress, see APRF, f. 52, op. 1, d. 169, ll. 1–29ob, published in Reabilitatsiia: kak eto bylo, 1:353–364. Pospelov's draft is at RGASPI, f. 629, op. 1, d. 54, ll. 73–112.

138. "'O kul'te lichnosti i ego posledstviiakh:' Doklad Pervogo sekretaria TsK KPSS tov. Khrushcheva N. S. XX s"ezdu Kommunisticheskoi partii Sovetskogo Soiuza 25 fevralia 1956 goda," in Doklad N. S. Khrushcheva o kul'te lichnosti Stalina na XX s"ezde KPSS—dokumenty, ed. K. Aimermakher (Moscow: Rosspen, 2002), 51–119, here 106. Although Khrushchev worked on his draft of the speech with Shepilov, the latter claimed that his contributions to the speech were restricted to international affairs and the war. See D. T. Shepilov, "Vospominaniia," Voprosy istorii 11–12 (1998): 4–5.

139. "O kul'te lichnosti i ego posledstviiakh," 117. Although Khrushchev read an early typescript copy of Stalin's version of the Short Course in August 1938 (RGASPI, f. 558, op. 11, d. 1219, ll. 43, 55), it is unlikely that he was aware of the editorial process that the text had undergone that summer. Pospelov did remember these changes, but was not a member of Khrushchev's inner circle and did not contribute to the last stages of the Secret Speech when commentary on the Short Course was added. Nor did Pospelov ever publicly object to Khrushchev's characterization of Stalin's editing in subsequent years, perhaps because he and Yaroslavsky were the ones responsible for the hagiography that Khrushchev attributed to Stalin.

140. "O kul'te lichnosti i ego posledstviiakh," 117–118.

141. The Central Committee resolution inspired by the Secret Speech did little to clarify the contours of the new official line. See Central Committee resolution of June 30, 1956, "O preodolenii kul'ta lichnosti," Pravda, July 2, 1956, 1–2; M. Chulanov, "Postanovlenie TsK KPSS ot 30 iunia 1956 g. 'O preodolenii kul'ta lichnosti i ego posledstvii' v kontekste svoego vremeni," in Avtoritarnye rezhimy v tsentral'noi i vostochnoi Evrope (1917–1990-e gody), ed. A. S. Sytalkin and T. Islamov (Moscow: Institut slavianovedeniia RAN, 1999), 140–195. Another unpublished resolution was somewhat more detailed, but did not resolve the confusion—see Presidium Resolution of April 26, 1956, "O podgotovke populiarnogo marksistskogo uchebnika po istorii Kommuniticheskoi partii Sovetskogo soiuza," RGANI, f. 3, op. 14, d. 18, l. 1; op. 12, d. 35, ll. 37–42, published in Doklad N. S. Khrushcheva o kul'te lichnosti na XX s"ezde KPSS, 297–304.

142. Generally, see Polly Jones, Myth, Memory, Trauma: Rethinking the Stalinist Past in the Soviet Union, 1953–1970 (New Haven: Yale University Press, 2013), 18, 66–68, 75, etc.; L. A. Sidorova, Ottepel' v istoricheskoi nauke: sovetskaia istoriografiia pervogo poslestalinskogo desiatiletiia (Moscow: Pamiatniki istoricheskoi mysli, 1997); A. V. Pyzhikov, Politicheskie preobrazovaniia v SSSR, 50–60-e gody (Moscow: Kvadrat S-Fantera, 1999), 70–90.

143. See Istoriia Kommunisticheskoi partii Sovetskogo Soiuza, ed. B. M. Ponomarev et al. (Moscow: Gospolitizdat, 1959); Istoriia KPSS, ed. A. V. Fedorov (Leningrad: Izd-vo Leningradskogo universiteta, 1960); Istoriia Kommunisticheskoi partii Sovetskogo Soiuza v 6-ti t-kh, ed. P. N. Pospelov (Moscow: Izd-vo polit. lit-ry, 1964). Generally, see V. V. Bulanov, "Vliianie kritiki kul'ta lichnosti na izmenenie kursov gumanitarnykh predmetov obshcheobrazovatel'noi shkoly (1956–63)," in Gumanisticheskie idei, sotsial'no-pedagogicheskie eksperimenty, biurokraticheskie izvrashcheniia v razvitii otechestvennoi shkoly: mezhvuzovskii sbornik nauchnykh trudov, ed. V. Volkov (St. Petersburg: Obrazovanie, 1993), 104–123.

144. See, for instance, Ronald Meek, "The Teaching of Economics in the USSR and Poland," Soviet Studies 10:4 (1959): 346–348. The Short Course remained a part of the Maoist canon after 1956 and was published in Chinese until the mid-1970s. See Li, "Instilling Stalinism in Chinese Party Members," 107–130.

145. Roger Markwick, Rewriting History in Soviet Russia (Houndmills: Palgrave, 2000). The official was S. P. Trapeznikov, head of the Central Committee Department of Science and Education; he made the comment at a 1965 forum on social studies pedagogy. See P. V. Volobuev, "Takie liudy byli vsegda," Sovetskaia kul'tura, May 6, 1989, 4.

146. D. A. Volkogonov, Triumf i tragediia—politicheskii portret I. V. Stalina v dvukh knigakh, 2 vols., 2 pts. (Moscow: Izd-vo APN, 1989), 2/2:144.

147. Collapsing all the sins of Soviet historiography since 1917 into his indictment of the Short Course, Maslov declared that it was this sort of thinking that Gorbachev's opponents now clung to in their struggle "against perestroika in ideology, against the liberation of free thought, and against glasnost' and democracy." See Maslov, "'Kratkii kurs istorii VKP(b)'—entsiklopediia kul'ta lichnosti Stalina," 66–67. This essay was reprinted multiple times during the period, including Maslov, "'Kratkii kurs istorii VKP(b)'—entsiklopediia kul'ta lichnosti Stalina," in Surovaia drama naroda: Uchenye i publitsisty o prirode stalinizma, ed. Iu. N. Senokosov (Moscow: Izd-vo polit. Litry, 1989), 334–352; Maslov, "Ideologiia Stalinizma: Istoriia utverzhdeniia i sushchnost' (1929–1956)," no. 3, Novoe v zhizni, nauke, tekhnike—Seriia "Istoriia i politika KPSS" (Moscow: Znanie, 1990); Maslov, "Ob utverzhdenii ideologii stalinizma," in Istoriia i stalinism, ed. A. N. Mertsalov (Moscow: Izd-vo polit. lit-ry, 1991), 37–86.

148. Volkogonov, Triumf i tragediia, 2/2:144–148.

149. For Stalin's first, abortive round of editing, see the marginalia in Stalin's copies of Yaroslavsky and Pospelov's third and fourth versions—RGASPI, f. 558, op. 3, d. 77; f. 120, op. 120, d. 383. For Stalin's incomplete second round of editing, consisting of unbound pages from another set of the fourth version's galleys and Stalin's own typescript and handwritten interpolations, see f. 558, op. 11, dd. 1209–1211. Five drafts of chapter 4, including typescript with handwritten editing and interpolations, are at d. 1210, ll. 297–328 (Stalin's subsection); ll. 237–296; ll. 149–236; d. 213, ll. 238–314; ll. 161–237. A complete copy of Stalin's last round of revisions—a typescript with marginalia from between August 16 and September 9—is at d. 1212, ll. 1–157; d. 1213, ll. 238–314; d. 1214, ll. 315–444; d. 1215, ll. 445–576; d. 1216, ll. 568–670.

150. See, for example, Zhdanov's and Pospelov's marginalia on manuscripts from August 1938: RGASPI, f. 77, op. 4, d. 22; RGANI, f. 3, op. 22, dd. 174a–174g.

151. Many archival documents associated with the history of the SHORT COURSE are reproduced in KRATKII KURS ISTORII VKP(B): TEKST I EGO ISTORIIA, ed. M. V. Zelenov and D. Brandenberger, 2 vols. (Moscow: ROSSPEN, 2014), vol. 1. The second volume of this set, which supplies a critical edition of the original text in Russian, is in preparation.

152. Archival materials associated with Stalin's revisions of the SHORT COURSE are edited almost exclusively in the general secretary's distinctive handwriting. Exceptions to this rule are identified by footnotes throughout the present critical edition.

153. NA PRIEME U STALINA: TETRADI (ZHURNALY) ZAPISEI LITS, PRINIATYKH I. V. STALINYM (1924–1953 GG.) (Moscow: Novyi khronograf, 2008), 236–238.

154. June 1977 interview with I. I. Mints, summarized in Robert Tucker, STALIN IN POWER: THE REVOLUTION FROM ABOVE, 1929–1941 (New York: Norton, 1990), 531–532. More generally, see I. I. Mints, "Podgotovka Velikoi proletarskoi revoliutsii: k vykhodu pervogo toma 'Istorii grazhdanskoi voiny v SSSR,'" BOL'SHEVIK 21 (1935): 15–30; Mints, "Stalin v grazhdanskoi voine: mify i fakty," VOPROSY ISTORII 11 (1989): 48.

155. RGASPI, f. 558, op. 11, d. 1217, ll. 2–24.

156. Stalin objected to such exceptionalism in regard to the empire first in 1934—see I. Stalin, "O stat'e Engel'sa 'Vneshniaia politika russkogo tsarizma,'" BOL'SHEVIK 9 (1941): 3–4.

157. This commentary coincided with Stalin's views on heroes during the 1930s. See "Beseda s nemetskim pisatelem Emilem Liudvigom," BOL'SHEVIK 8 (1932): 33.

158. Yaroslavsky had developed this rather forced interpretation of the Prague Conference during the early 1930s. See E. M. Iaroslavskii, KRATKAIA ISTORIIA VKP(B) (Moscow: Gosizdat, 1930), 195–199; Iaroslavskii, ISTORIIA VKP(B), 2 vols. (Moscow: Partizdat, 1933), 1:224–227.

159. Intended as a synthesis of Marxist thought for mass consumption, Stalin's treatise on dialectical and historical materialism has been assailed for its schematicism. See, for instance, Leszek Kołakowski, MAIN CURRENTS OF MARXISM: THE FOUNDERS, THE GOLDEN AGE, THE BREAKDOWN (New York: W. W. Norton & Co., 2005), 865–868, 908–910; Andrzej Walicki, MARXISM AND THE LEAP TO THE KINGDOM OF FREEDOM: THE RISE AND FALL OF THE COMMUNIST UTOPIA (Stanford: Stanford University Press, 1997), 431–440. For a more balanced evaluation, see Erik van Ree, "Stalin as Marxist Philosopher," STUDIES IN EASTERN EUROPEAN THOUGHT 52:4 (2000): 259–308; van Ree, THE POLITICAL THOUGHT OF JOSEPH STALIN: A STUDY IN TWENTIETH CENTURY REVOLUTIONARY PATRIOTISM (London: RoutledgeCurzon, 2002), esp. chap. 17.

160. Stalin's draft manuscripts of the section suggest that he worked on it alone and that much of his editing focused on maximizing its accessibility and clarity. See RGASPI, f. 558, op. 11, d. 1210, ll. 297–338; ll. 249–286; ll. 164–210; d. 1213, ll. 251–292; ll. 174–215. As he was writing this section, Stalin may have read and underlined sections of DIALEKTICHESKII I ISTORICHESKII MATERIALIZM V 2 CHASTIAKH: UCHEBNIK DLIA KOMVUZOV I VTUZOV, ed. M. V. Mitin (Moscow: OGIZ, 1934)—see RGASPI, f. 558, op. 3, d. 55, ll. 105–109, 140, 269, 281–290.

161. Retaining this detail, Stalin stripped some of the agitators of their Latvian ethnicity.

162. The relationship between the Bolsheviks' Revolutionary Military Center and the Petrograd Soviet's Revolutionary Military Committee is often considered one of Stalin's most significant revisions of party history. In a polemic with Trotsky in 1924, Stalin contended that while Trotsky had contributed to the October revolution as chair of the Revolutionary Military Committee, this body had been subordinate to the Revolutionary Military Center, which Stalin himself had chaired. After Yaroslavsky elaborated upon this distinction in 1927, it became a standard part of both Stalin's master narrative and Trotsky's allegations of historical fraud. See I. Stalin, "Trotskizm ili Leninizm," PRAVDA, November 24, 1924, 6; E. Iaroslavskii, PARTIIA BOL'SHEVIKOV V 1917 GODU (Moscow: Gos. izd-vo, 1927), 85–86, 90; L. D. Trotskii, "Pis'mo v Istpart TsK VKP(b) 'O poddelke istorii Oktiabr'skogo perevorota, istorii revoliutsii i istorii partii,'" in STALINSKAIA SHKOLA FAL'SIFIKATSII: POPRAVKI I DOPOLNENIIA K LITERATURE EPIGONOV (Berlin: Granit, 1932), 13–100, 9–10.

163. Stalin preserved mention of his report on the national question to the Seventh Party Conference but cut most of Pyatakov's and Bukharin's objections, rendering his opponents inarticulate and downgrading the overall importance of the debate.

164. Perhaps because the party was still growing in strength during the summer of 1917, Stalin deleted mention of Lenin's famous repartee at the First Congress of Soviets that the Bolsheviks were ready to take power.

165. On the general secretary's changing views on this revolutionary year, see David Brandenberger, "Stalin's Rewriting of 1917," THE RUSSIAN REVIEW 76:4 (2017): 667–689.

166. On the changing contours of nationality and internationalism in the text, see David Brandenberger and Mikhail Zelenov, "Stalin's Answer to the National Question: A Case Study in the Editing of the 1938 SHORT COURSE," SLAVIC REVIEW 73:4 (2014): 859–880; Brandenberger, "The Fate of Interwar Soviet Internationalism: A Case Study of the Editing of Stalin's 1938 SHORT COURSE ON THE HISTORY OF THE ACP(B)," REVOLUTIONARY RUSSIA 29:1 (2016): 1–27.

167. On the SHORT COURSE's about-face regarding the purges, see David Brandenberger, "Ideological Zig Zag: Official Explanations for the Great Terror, 1936–1938," in THE ANATOMY OF TERROR: POLITICAL VIOLENCE UNDER STALIN, ed. James Harris (Oxford: Oxford University Press, 2013), 143–160.

168. Stalin's new narrative finessed the attainment of unity about a year before the actual end of the Terror.

169. This translation was quickly republished abroad by left-leaning and communist-aligned houses in London, New York, San Francisco, and elsewhere—see "V Soedinennykh Shtatakh gotoviatsia k massovomu rasprostraneniiu istorii VKP(b)," ISTORICHESKII ARKHIV 5 (2013): 137–146. Further English-language printings in the USSR appeared both during and after the war through 1953; abroad, the book appeared in substantial runs into the mid-1970s, usually in connection with Maoist movements that did not abandon the text after 1956. See HISTORY OF THE COMMUNIST PARTY OF THE SOVIET UNION (BOLSHEVIKS) (Moscow: State Foreign Languages Publishing House, 1939, 1945; London: Red Star, 1939, 1943, 1976; New York: International, 1939, 1975; San Francisco: Proletarian, 1939, 1972, 1976; etc.).

170. See Politburo resolution of September 27, 1938, "O perevode knigi 'Istoriia VKP(b)' na inostrannye iazyki," RGASPI, f. 17, op. 3, d. 1002, l. 28. See also Politburo resolution of September 23, 1938, "Ob izdanii 'Istorii VKP(b)' na iazykakh soiuznykh i avtonomnykh respublik," l. 25.

171. RGASPI, f. 17, op. 120, d. 258, ll. 102–113.

172. Mary M. Leder, My Life in Stalinist Russia: An American Woman Looks Back, ed. Francis Bernstein (Bloomington: Indiana University Press, 2001), 75, 86–87, 90, 118, 139–141, 144, 154–155. Curiously, none of the foreign communists involved in the project ever disclosed their work on the Short Course. See About Turn: The British Communist Party and the Second World War—The Verbatim Record of the Central Committee meetings of 25 September and 2–3 October 1939 (London: Lawrence and Wishart, 1990), 103; J. R. Campbell, Soviet Policy and Its Critics (London: Victor Gollancz, 1939).

173. The use of "technique" instead of "technology" to represent the Russian term tekhnika was apparently dictated by the leading Russian-English dictionary of the time, Anglo-Russkii slovar', ed. V. K. Muller and S. K. Boianus (Moscow: Sovetskaia entsikopediia, 1935), 1395–1396. The authors are grateful to Brian Kassof for his explanation of this idiosyncracy.

174. Although the party was known in Russian between 1935 and 1952 as the All-Union Communist Party (Bolsheviks), it was referred to in official English-language propaganda as CPSU(B) after the mid-1920s.

Title Page and Table of Contents

1. Late in his revisions, Stalin added Zhdanov to the book's editorial board, first at the head of the list and then at the end. Somewhat later, he crossed out the entire board and wrote in its place "*A COMMISSION OF THE C.C. OF THE C.P.S.U.(B.).*" See RGASPI, f. 558, op. 11, d. 1217, l. 1.

2. The explanation of terms is not reproduced in this critical edition.

3. The recommended reading list is not reproduced in this critical edition.

Chapter 1. The Struggle for the Creation of a Social-Democratic Labour Party in Russia (1883–1901)

1. Early in Stalin's editing, Zhdanov wrote in the margins beside this paragraph "*or from their share of the harvest*"—see RGASPI, f. 17, op. 120, d. 383, l. 542ob. Stalin later incorporated this theme into his revisions.

2. Stalin eliminated the emphasis initially placed on the phrase "a prison of nations" midway through his editing. See RGASPI, f. 558, op. 11, d. 1209, l. 5.

3. Early in Stalin's editing, Zhdanov recommended the correction "~~was still~~ *remained*"—see RGASPI, f. 17, op. 120, d. 383, l. 543ob. Although Stalin did not accept the suggestion, he did reframe the paragraph to underscore the persistence of Russian underdevelopment.

4. "Owner" was rendered incorrectly as "worker" in the official 1939 English translation.

5. Stalin's late cut "~~not return before the owner had satisfied their demands, that is~~" may have been recommended by Zhdanov. See RGASPI, f. 558, op. 11, d. 1219, l. 46.

6. Stalin's late interpolation "*Russian*" may have been recommended by Pospelov. See RGANI, f. 3, op. 22, d. 174a, l. 14. See note 7 below.

7. Stalin's late cut "~~in Russia~~" may have been recommended by Pospelov. See RGANI, f. 3, op. 22, d. 174a, l. 14. See note 6 above.

8. Early in Stalin's editing, Zhdanov wrote in the margins beside this paragraph "*three sources*"—apparently a reference to Lenin's 1913 article "The Three Sources and Three Constituent Parts of Marxism." See RGASPI, f. 17, op. 120, d. 383, l. 545. Stalin ignored the reference and later cut the entire paragraph.

9. Stalin eliminated the emphasis initially placed on the word "First" midway through his editing. See RGASPI, f. 558, op. 11, d. 1209, l. 21.

10. Stalin eliminated the emphasis initially placed on the word "Secondly" midway through his editing. See RGASPI, f. 558, op. 11, d. 1209, l. 21.

11. Stalin eliminated the emphasis initially placed on the word "Thirdly" midway through his editing. See RGASPI, f. 558, op. 11, d. 1209, l. 22.

12. Stalin's late correction to his interpolation "*~~was easily organizable~~ easily lent itself to organization*" may have been recommended by Pospelov. See RGANI, f. 3, op. 22, d. 174a, l. 21.

13. Stalin's late correction to his interpolation "*revolution~~ary movement~~*" may have been recommended by Pospelov. See RGANI, f. 3, op. 22, d. 174a, l. 21.

14. Stalin sometimes signed his parenthetic explanations as "—*Ed.*"

15. Stalin's late cut to his interpolation after the word "*its*"—"*~~present~~*"—may have been recommended by Zhdanov or Pospelov. See RGASPI, f. 77, op. 4, d. 22, l. 28; RGANI, f. 3, op. 22, d. 174a, l. 21.

16. Stalin's late revision of his own sentence—the interpolation "*Moreover,*" the correction "*~~was less easily organizable~~ lent itself less easily,*" and the interpolation "*to organization*"—may have been recommended by Pospelov. See RGANI, f. 3, op. 22, d. 174a, l. 22.

17. Stalin's late correction to his interpolation—"*~~announced~~ maintained*"—may have been recommended by Pospelov. See RGASPI, f. 89, op. 16, d. 8, l. 19; RGANI, f. 3, op. 22, d. 174a, l. 22.

18. Stalin's late cut to his interpolation after the word "*individuals*"—"*~~, heroes,~~*"—may have been recommended by Yaroslavsky. See RGASPI, f. 89, op. 16, d. 8, l. 21.

19. Stalin's late interpolation "*Heroes,*" may have been recommended by Zhdanov, Yaroslavsky, or Pospelov. See RGASPI, f. 77, op. 4, d. 22, l. 31; f. 89, op. 16, d. 8, l. 21; RGANI, f. 3, op. 22, d. 174a, l. 24.

20. Stalin's late addition to his interpolation—"*, outstanding individuals,*"—may have been recommended by Pospelov. See RGANI, f. 3, op. 22, d. 174a, l. 24.

21. Stalin eliminated the emphasis initially placed on the phrase "openly voice the interests of the kulaks" midway through his editing. See RGASPI, f. 558, op. 11, d. 1209, l. 28.

22. Stalin eliminated the emphasis initially placed on the phrase "any practical connections with the working class movement" midway through his editing. See RGASPI, f. 558, op. 11, d. 1209, l. 29.

23. Stalin eliminated the emphasis initially placed on the phrase "the victorious Communist revolution" midway through his editing.

24. Stalin initially rewrote this sentence to read "It is this *formal act,* that ~~constitutes~~ *constituted* the *unquestionably great revolutionary propagandist* significance of the First Congress of the R.S.D.L.P." He then revised the sentence to read "It is this *formal act, which played a great revolutionary propagandist role,* that ~~constitutes~~ *constituted* the ~~*unquestionably great revolutionary propagandist*~~ significance of the First Congress of the R.S.D.L.P." Pospelov may have recommended these revisions. See RGANI, f. 3, op. 22, d. 174a, l. 35.

Chapter 2. Formation of the Russian Social-Democratic Labour Party. Appearance of the Bolshevik and the Menshevik Groups within the Party (1901–1904)

1. Stalin's late addition to his interpolated Lenin quotation—*"Lenin wrote,"*—may have been recommended by Pospelov. See RGANI, f. 3, op. 22, d. 174a, l. 53.

2. Stalin's late correction to his interpolated Lenin quotation—"~~*such an*~~ *this*"—may have been recommended by Pospelov. See RGANI, f. 3, op. 22, d. 174a, l. 53.

3. Stalin's late cut of this Lenin quotation may have been recommended by Zhdanov. See RGASPI, f. 77, op. 4, d. 22, l. 60.

4. Stalin's late cut to his interpolation after the word "the"—"~~*conscious, organized*~~"—may have been recommended by Zhdanov or Pospelov. See RGASPI, f. 77, op. 4, d. 22, ll. 61–62; RGANI, f. 3, op. 22, d. 174a, l. 54.

5. Stalin's late correction to his interpolation—"~~*revolutionary movement of the workers and exploited masses*~~ *class struggle of the proletariat*"—may have been recommended by Pospelov. See RGANI, f. 3, op. 22, d. 174a, l. 54.

6. Stalin's late correction to his interpolation—"~~*toward the liberation of the working-class from capitalism*~~ *of Socialism*"—may have been recommended by Pospelov. See RGANI, f. 3, op. 22, d. 174a, l. 54.

7. Stalin's late cut to his interpolated Lenin quotation after the word "*wrote*"—"~~*in his book* WHAT IS TO BE DONE?~~"—may have been recommended by Pospelov. See RGANI, f. 3, op. 22, d. 174a, l. 54.

8. Stalin's late addition to his interpolation—"*was a matter for all classes, but primarily for the bourgeoisie, and that therefore it*"—may have been recommended by Pospelov. See RGANI, f. 3, op. 22, d. 174a, l. 55.

9. Stalin's late addition to his interpolation—"*better working conditions,*"—may have been recommended by Pospelov. See RGANI, f. 3, op. 22, d. 174a, l. 56.

10. Stalin's late correction to his interpolation—"~~*party*~~ *Social-Democrats*"—may have been recommended by Zhdanov or Pospelov. See RGASPI, f. 77, op. 4, d. 22, l. 63; RGANI, f. 3, op. 22, d. 174a, l. 56.

11. Early in Stalin's editing, Zhdanov wrote in the margins beside this paragraph "*A second time about the Economists.*" See RGASPI, f. 17, op. 120, d. 383, l. 556ob. Stalin later rewrote the section.

12. Stalin's late cut to his interpolation after the word "*theory*"—"~~*and Social-Democracy, as the cradle of socialist consciousness,*~~"—may have been recommended by Zhdanov. See RGASPI, f. 77, op. 4, d. 22, l. 63.

13. Stalin's late correction to his interpolation—"~~*said*~~ *showed*"—may have been recommended by Pospelov. See RGANI, f. 3, op. 22, d. 174a, l. 57.

14. Stalin's late correction to his interpolation—"~~*After all,*~~ *The*"—may have been recommended by Pospelov. See RGANI, f. 3, op. 22, d. 174a, l. 57.

15. Stalin's late division of his sentence into two may reflect Pospelov's recommendation. It initially read: "*The economic struggle of the workers against the employers and the government was a trade union struggle for better terms in the sale of their labour power to the capitalists, while the workers wanted to fight not only for better terms in the sale of their labour power to the capitalists, but also for the abolition of the capitalist system itself which condemned them to sell their labour power to the capitalists and to suffer exploitation.*" See RGANI, f. 3, op. 22, d. 174a, l. 57.

16. Stalin's late addition to his interpolation—"*and thus clear the way to Socialism*"—may have been recommended by Pospelov. See RGANI, f. 3, op. 22, d. 174a, l. 57.

17. Stalin's late cut to his interpolation after the word "*was*"—"~~*famously*~~"—may have been recommended by Pospelov. See RGANI, f. 3, op. 22, d. 174a, l. 58.

18. Stalin's late cut to his interpolation after the word "*of*"—"~~*even*~~"—may have been recommended by Pospelov. See RGANI, f. 3, op. 22, d. 174a, l. 59.

19. Stalin's late cut to his interpolation after the word "*the*"—"~~*spontaneous*~~"—may have been recommended by Pospelov. See RGANI, f. 3, op. 22, d. 174a, l. 59.

20. Stalin's late addition to his interpolation—"*, thus helping the bourgeoisie*"—may reflect an interpolation suggested by Pospelov. See RGANI, f. 3, op. 22, d. 174a, l. 59.

21. Stalin's late cut to his interpolation after the word "*a*"—"~~*proletarian*~~"—may have been recommended by Pospelov. See RGANI, f. 3, op. 22, d. 174a, l. 59.

22. Stalin's late cut to his interpolation after the word "*a*"—"~~*petty-bourgeois*~~"—may have been recommended by Pospelov. See RGANI, f. 3, op. 22, d. 174a, l. 59.

23. Stalin's late correction to his interpolation—"~~*typical opportunists*~~ *reformists*"—may have been recommended by Pospelov. See RGANI, f. 3, op. 22, d. 174a, l. 60.

24. Stalin's late correction to his interpolation—"~~*which led to*~~ *showing that they principally consisted in*"—may have been recommended by Pospelov. See RGASPI, f. 558, op. 11, d. 1219, l. 47.

25. Stalin's late cut to his interpolation after the word "*spontaneous*"—"~~*, free-flowing*~~"—may have been recommended by Pospelov. See RGANI, f. 3, op. 22, d. 174a, l. 61.

26. Stalin's late correction to his interpolation—"~~*explanation*~~ *exposition*"—may have been recommended by Pospelov. See RGANI, f. 3, op. 22, d. 174a, l. 61.

27. Stalin's late correction to his interpolation—"~~*allow*~~ *grant*"—may have been recommended by Zhdanov or Pospelov. See RGASPI, f. 77, op. 4, d. 22, l. 47; RGANI, f. 3, op. 22, d. 174a, l. 68.

28. The sentence is stronger in the original Russian (lit., "The congress rejected the Bund's *organizational* nationalism").

29. Late in Stalin's editing, he cut a Lenin quotation that he had earlier interpolated into the text after this paragraph:

> *"From the point of view of Martov," wrote Lenin, "the border line of the Party remains quite indefinite, for 'every striker' may 'proclaim himself a Party member.' What is the use of this*

vagueness? A wide extension of the 'title.' Its harm is that it introduces a DISORGANIZING *idea, the confusing of class and Party.' (Lenin,* COLLECTED WORKS, *Russ. ed., Vol. VI, p. 211.)*

This cut may have been recommended by either Yaroslavsky or Pospelov. See RGASPI, f. 89, op. 8, d. 16, l. 73; RGANI, f. 3, op. 22, d. 174a, l. 76.

30. Stalin's late addition *"Lenin wrote,"* may have been recommended by Pospelov. See RGANI, f. 3, op. 22, d. 174a, l. 76. This correction is connected to the deletion of a Lenin quotation above—see note 29.

31. Stalin's late decision to deemphasize the phrase *"a mere agglomeration of persons"* within his interpolation may reflect a recommendation by Pospelov. See RGANI, f. 3, op. 22, d. 174a, l. 77.

32. Stalin's late cut to his interpolation after the word *"can"*—*"~~have the chance to~~"*—may have been recommended by Pospelov. See RGANI, f. 3, op. 22, d. 174a, l. 77.

33. Stalin's late cut to his interpolation after the word *"opportunity"*—*"~~and obligation~~"*—may have been recommended by Pospelov. See RGANI, f. 3, op. 22, d. 174a, l. 79.

34. Stalin's late addition to his interpolation—*"—and is obliged to guide—"*—may have been recommended by Pospelov. See RGANI, f. 3, op. 22, d. 174a, l. 79.

35. Stalin's late decision to deemphasize the phrase *"without connections with the non-Party masses, and without multiplying and strengthening these connections"* within his interpolation may reflect a recommendation by Pospelov. See RGANI, f. 3, op. 22, d. 174a, l. 79.

36. Stalin's late correction to his interpolation—*"~~working-class~~ masses"*—may have been recommended by Pospelov. See RGANI, f. 3, op. 22, d. 174a, l. 79.

37. Stalin's late cut to his interpolation after the word *"confidence"*—*"~~and support~~"*—may have been recommended by Pospelov. See RGANI, f. 3, op. 22, d. 174a, l. 79.

38. Stalin's late addition to his interpolation—*"of its class"*—may have been recommended by Pospelov. See RGANI, f. 3, op. 22, d. 174a, l. 79.

39. Stalin's late correction to his Lenin quotation—*"~~have dispensed~~ dispense"*—may have been recommended by Pospelov. See RGANI, f. 3, op. 22, d. 174a, l. 81.

40. Stalin's late interpolation to his Lenin quotation—*"complete"*—may have been recommended by Pospelov. See RGANI, f. 3, op. 22, d. 174a, l. 81.

41. Stalin's late interpolation *"Thus,"* may have been recommended by Pospelov. See RGANI, f. 3, op. 22, d. 174a, l. 84.

42. Stalin's late interpolation *"when the Russo-Japanese war had already begun,"* may have been recommended by Pospelov. See RGANI, f. 3, op. 22, d. 174a, l. 84.

43. Stalin's late correction to his interpolation—*"~~organizations~~ groups"*—may have been recommended by Pospelov. See RGANI, f. 3, op. 22, d. 174a, l. 84.

Chapter 3. The Mensheviks and the Bolsheviks in the Period of the Russo-Japanese War and the First Russian Revolution (1904–1907)

1. Evidently, Pospelov's editing of Stalin's revisions to this chapter has not been preserved. See RGANI, f. 3, op. 22, d. 174a.

2. Stalin's late correction to his interpolation—*"~~a popular institution~~ popular representation"*—may have been recommended by Zhdanov. See RGASPI, f. 77, op. 4, d. 22, l. 107.

3. Stalin's early cut of this paragraph may have been recommended by Zhdanov. See RGASPI, f. 17, op. 120, d. 383, l. 571ob.

4. Stalin removed the emphasis placed on the first two sentences of this quotation midway through his editing.

5. Stalin's late cut to his interpolation after the word “*these*”—“‘~~*God-forsaken*~~’”—may have been recommended by Yaroslavsky. See RGASPI, f. 558, op. 11, d. 1219, ll. 51–52.

6. Stalin's late cut “~~A. M. Gorky helped the Bolsheviks in this affair.~~” may have been recommended by Zhdanov. See RGASPI, f. 77, op. 4, d. 22, l. 140.

7. Stalin's late correction to his interpolation—“~~*forty*~~ *thirty*”—may have been recommended by Zhdanov. See RGASPI, f. 77, op. 4, d. 22, l. 161.

Chapter 4. The Mensheviks and the Bolsheviks in the Period of the Stolypin Reaction. The Bolsheviks Constitute Themselves as an Independent Marxist Party (1908–1912)

1. Stalin's late correction “~~all~~ *both*” may have been recommended by Pospelov. See RGANI, f. 3, op. 22, d. 174b, l. 182.

2. Stalin's late decision to deemphasize the word “manoeuvre” may have been recommended by Pospelov. See RGANI, f. 3, op. 22, d. 174b, l. 184.

3. Stalin's late correction “~~destroyed~~ *broke down*” may have been recommended by Pospelov. See RGANI, f. 3, op. 22, d. 174b, l. 184.

4. Stalin's late cut “~~or~~” may have been recommended by Pospelov. See RGANI, f. 3, op. 22, d. 174b, l. 184.

5. Stalin's late decision to deemphasize the word “landlords” may have been recommended by Pospelov. See RGANI, f. 3, op. 22, d. 174b, l. 185.

6. Stalin's late decision to deemphasize the word “kulaks” may have been recommended by Pospelov. See RGANI, f. 3, op. 22, d. 174b, l. 185.

7. Stalin's late decision to deemphasize the word “trusts” may have been recommended by Pospelov. See RGANI, f. 3, op. 22, d. 174b, l. 185.

8. Stalin's late decision to deemphasize the word “syndicates” may have been recommended by Pospelov. See RGANI, f. 3, op. 22, d. 174b, l. 185.

9. Stalin's late decision to deemphasize the word “imperialist” may have been recommended by Pospelov. See RGANI, f. 3, op. 22, d. 174b, l. 186.

10. Stalin's late correction to his interpolation—“~~*obsolete*~~ *fundamental*”—may have been recommended by Pospelov. See RGANI, f. 3, op. 22, d. 174b, l. 190.

11. Stalin's late addition of this sentence to his interpolation may have stemmed from Yaroslavsky's protest that “*in this chapter, there is nothing about god-builders or god-seekers. In my mind, these reflections of the reactionary thought of the 1908–1912 period should be mentioned, if only in passing, as they captured the minds of a portion of the Bolsheviks.*” See RGASPI, f. 558, op. 11, d. 1219, l. 68. Pospelov recommended a slightly different wording: “*Some of the intellectuals went so far as to advocate the founding of a new religion (the so-called ‘god-seekers’ and ‘god-builders’).*” See RGANI, f. 3, op. 22, d. 174b, l. 189ob.

12. Stalin's late interpolation “*—Ed.*” may have been recommended by Pospelov. See RGANI, f. 3, op. 22, d. 174b, l. 193.

13. Stalin's late correction to his interpolation—"~~*Marxism-Leninism*~~ *the Marxist-Leninist party*"—may have been recommended by Pospelov. See RGANI, f. 3, op. 22, d. 174b, l. 194.

14. Stalin's late revisions to his interpolation may reflect a correction suggested by Pospelov: "~~*These dialectics, which were dialectics of thought, were later transformed into dialectics of nature, which regard*~~ *This dialectical method of thought, later extended to the phenomena of nature, developed into the dialectical method of apprehending nature, which regards*"—see RGANI, f. 3, op. 22, d. 174b, l. 196.

15. Stalin's late correction to his interpolation—"~~*clash*~~ *interaction*"—may have been recommended by Pospelov. See RGANI, f. 3, op. 22, d. 174b, l. 196.

16. On the reverse side of the page, Pospelov wrote "*dialectics against metaphysics.*" See RGANI, f. 3, op. 22, d. 174b, l. 195ob.

17. Stalin's late correction to his interpolation—"~~*unbeatable*~~ *invincible*"—may have been recommended by Pospelov. See RGANI, f. 3, op. 22, d. 174b, l. 197.

18. Stalin's late addition to this Lenin quotation—"*in general*"—may have been recommended by Pospelov. See RGANI, f. 3, op. 22, d. 174b, l. 207.

19. Stalin's late decision to emphasize "*MATTER THINKS*" within this Lenin quotation may reflect a recommendation by Pospelov. See RGANI, f. 3, op. 22, d. 174b, l. 208.

20. Stalin's late correction to his interpolation—"~~*this*~~ *Marx's words*"—may have been recommended by Pospelov. See RGANI, f. 3, op. 22, d. 174b, l. 213.

21. Stalin's late cut to his interpolation after the word "*society*"—"~~*, the more fully they express the interests of the leading forces of society*~~"—may have been recommended by Pospelov. See RGANI, f. 3, op. 22, d. 174b, l. 213.

22. Stalin's late correction to his interpolation—"~~*grips*~~ *has gripped*"—may have been recommended by Pospelov. See RGANI, f. 3, op. 22, d. 174b, l. 214.

23. A new subheading—"*3) Historical Materialism.*"—was added after this paragraph in 1945.

24. This line was changed to "*a) What, then,*" in 1945.

25. Stalin's late addition to his interpolation—"*fuel, instruments of production,*"—may have been recommended by Zhdanov or Pospelov. See RGASPI, f. 77, op. 4, d. 22, l. 201; RGANI, f. 3, op. 22, d. 174b, l. 218.

26. Stalin's late addition to his interpolation—"*fuel,*"—may have been recommended by Zhdanov or Pospelov. See RGASPI, f. 77, op. 4, d. 22, l. 201; RGANI, f. 3, op. 22, d. 174b, l. 218.

27. Stalin's late decision to emphasize the phrase "*INSTRUMENTS OF PRODUCTION*" within his interpolation may reflect a recommendation by Pospelov. See RGANI, f. 3, op. 22, d. 174b, l. 218.

28. Stalin's late decision to emphasize the word "*PEOPLE*" within his interpolation may reflect a recommendation by Pospelov. See RGANI, f. 3, op. 22, d. 174b, l. 218.

29. Stalin's late cut to his interpolation after the word "*utilize*"—"~~*her*~~"—may have been recommended by Zhdanov or Pospelov. See RGASPI, f. 77, op. 4, d. 22, l. 202; RGANI, f. 3, op. 22, d. 174b, l. 219.

30. Stalin's late correction to his interpolation—"~~*exploitation*~~ *subordination*"—may have been recommended by Zhdanov or Pospelov. See RGASPI, f. 77, op. 4, d. 22, l. 202; RGANI, f. 3, op. 22, d. 174b, l. 219.

31. This line was changed to "*b) THE FIRST FEATURE*" in 1945.

32. This line stems from Stalin's marginalia on the cover sheet of an earlier draft of this chapter: "*Thus productive relations, economic relations and man's manner of life take shape in connection with the condition of productive forces and the means of production; man's manner of thought takes shape in connection with his MANNER OF LIFE. Whatever is the MANNER OF LIFE, such is the MANNER OF THOUGHT.*" See RGASPI, f. 558, op. 11, d. 1210, l. 148.

33. This line was changed to "*c) THE SECOND FEATURE*" in 1945.

34. Stalin's late correction to his interpolation—"~~*and then a*~~ *with a corresponding*"—may have been recommended by Pospelov. See RGANI, f. 3, op. 22, d. 174b, l. 221.

35. Stalin's late cut to his interpolation after the word "*slave*"—"~~*which is equated to an implement of labor,*~~"—may have been recommended by Pospelov. See RGANI, f. 3, op. 22, d. 174b, l. 223.

36. Stalin's late correction to his interpolation—"~~*hunter's means of production*~~ *husbandry of the hunter*"—may have been suggested by Zhdanov or Pospelov. See RGASPI, f. 77, op. 4, d. 22, l. 206; RGANI, f. 3, op. 22, d. 174b, l. 223.

37. Stalin's late correction to his interpolation—"~~*subjugation*~~ *possibility of subjugation,*"—may have been recommended by Zhdanov or Pospelov. See RGASPI, f. 77, op. 4, d. 22, l. 206; RGANI, f. 3, op. 22, d. 174b, l. 223.

38. Stalin's late cut to his interpolation after the word "*majority*"—"~~*of the people*~~"—may have been recommended by Zhdanov or Pospelov. See RGASPI, f. 77, op. 4, d. 22, l. 206; RGANI, f. 3, op. 22, d. 174b, l. 223.

39. Stalin's late addition to his interpolation—"*and free*"—may have been recommended by Pospelov. See RGANI, f. 3, op. 22, d. 174b, l. 223.

40. Stalin's late correction to his interpolation—"~~*represents*~~ *is*"—may have been recommended by Pospelov. See RGANI, f. 3, op. 22, d. 174b, l. 223.

41. Stalin's late cut to his interpolation after the word "*handicraftsmen*"—"~~*(their land, implements of production and the fruits of their labor)*~~"—may have been recommended by Zhdanov or Pospelov. See RGASPI, f. 77, op. 4, d. 22, l. 208; RGANI, f. 3, op. 22, d. 174b, l. 225.

42. Stalin's late correction to his interpolation—"~~*obsolete*~~ *primitive*"—may have been recommended by Zhdanov or Pospelov. See RGASPI, f. 77, op. 4, d. 22, l. 208; RGANI, f. 3, op. 22, d. 174b, l. 225.

43. Stalin's late correction to his interpolation—"~~*labor*~~ *production*"—may have been recommended by Zhdanov or Pospelov. See RGASPI, f. 77, op. 4, d. 22, l. 208; RGANI, f. 3, op. 22, d. 174b, l. 225.

44. Stalin's late correction to his interpolation—"~~*armed with scientific knowledge*~~ *run on scientific lines*"—may have been recommended by Zhdanov. See RGASPI, f. 77, op. 4, d. 22, l. 208.

45. Stalin's late revision to his interpolation—"~~*which produce material goods through social labor, capitalism undermines its own foundation*~~ *capitalism lends the process of production a social character and thus undermines its own foundation*"—may have been recommended by Pospelov. See RGANI, f. 3, op. 22, d. 174b, ll. 225–225ob.

46. Stalin's late correction to his interpolation—"~~*halt*~~ *suspend*"—may have been recommended by Pospelov. See RGANI, f. 3, op. 22, d. 174b, l. 226.

47. Stalin's late decision to deemphasize the word "*capitalist*" within his interpolation may have been recommended by Pospelov. See RGANI, f. 3, op. 22, d. 174b, l. 227.

48. Stalin's late correction to his interpolation—"~~*a Socialist form of ownership*~~ *Socialist ownership*"—may have been recommended by Pospelov. See RGANI, f. 3, op. 22, d. 174b, l. 227.

49. Stalin's late decision to deemphasize the word "*social*" within his interpolation may have been recommended by Pospelov. See RGANI, f. 3, op. 22, d. 174b, l. 227.

50. Stalin's late decision to deemphasize the word "*social*" within his interpolation may have been recommended by Pospelov. See RGANI, f. 3, op. 22, d. 174b, l. 227.

51. Stalin's late interpolation to his Marx quotation—"*primarily*"—may have been recommended by Pospelov. See RGANI, f. 3, op. 22, d. 174b, l. 228.

52. This line was changed to "*d) THE THIRD FEATURE*" in 1945.

53. Stalin's late correction to his interpolation—"~~*more than once*~~ *not infrequently*"—may have been recommended by Pospelov. See RGANI, f. 3, op. 22, d. 174b, l. 231.

54. Stalin's late addition to his interpolation—"*(emphasis added—ED.)*"—may have been recommended by Pospelov. See RGANI, f. 3, op. 22, d. 174b, l. 232.

55. Stalin's late cut to his interpolation after the word "*contrary,*"—"~~*in classist society,*~~"—may have been recommended by Pospelov. See RGANI, f. 3, op. 22, d. 174b, l. 232.

56. Stalin's late correction to his interpolation—"~~*most often*~~ *usually*"—may have been recommended by Pospelov. See RGANI, f. 3, op. 22, d. 174b, l. 232.

57. Stalin's late addition to his interpolation—"*by the conscious action of the new classes,*"—may have been recommended by Pospelov. See RGANI, f. 3, op. 22, d. 174b, l. 232.

58. Stalin eliminated the emphasis initially placed on the word "liquidate" during his editing. See RGASPI, f. 558, op. 11, d. 1213, l. 216.

59. Stalin's late correction "~~in~~ *that*" may have been recommended by Pospelov. See RGANI, f. 3, op. 22, d. 174b, l. 237.

60. Stalin's late interpolation "*was inevitable also*" may have been recommended by Pospelov. See RGANI, f. 3, op. 22, d. 174b, l. 237.

61. Stalin eliminated the emphasis initially placed on the phrase "had taught the working class to fight for its rights in mass revolutionary struggle" during his editing. See RGASPI, f. 558, op. 11, d. 1213, l. 217.

62. Stalin's late interpolation "*within the Party*" may have been recommended by Pospelov. See RGANI, f. 3, op. 22, d. 174b, l. 237.

63. Stalin eliminated the emphasis initially placed on the word "fellow-travelers" during his editing. See RGASPI, f. 558, op. 11, d. 1213, l. 222.

64. Stalin eliminated the emphasis initially placed on the two words "August Bloc" midway through his editing.

65. Stalin's late cut "~~And~~" may have been recommended by Yaroslavsky or Pospelov. See RGASPI, f. 558, op. 11, d. 1219, l. 68; RGANI, f. 3, op. 22, d. 174b, l. 244.

66. Stalin's late interpolation "*—ED.*" may have been recommended by Pospelov. See RGANI, f. 3, op. 22, d. 174b, l. 246.

67. Typesetter's error in Yaroslavsky and Pospelov's last version of the SHORT COURSE.

68. Stalin's late correction to his interpolation—"~~*and*~~ *as well as*"—may have been recommended by Pospelov. See RGANI, f. 3, op. 22, d. 174b, l. 248.

69. Stalin's late correction to his interpolation—"~~*petty-bourgeois Stolypin Labour*~~ *reformist*"—may have been recommended by Pospelov. See RGANI, f. 3, op. 22, d. 174b, l. 248.

70. Stalin's late cut to his interpolation after the word "*a*"—"~~*new*~~"—may have been recommended by Pospelov. See RGANI, f. 3, op. 22, d. 174b, l. 251.

71. Stalin's late interpolation of F. I. Goloshchekin's last name may have been recommended by Pospelov. See RGANI, f. 3, op. 22, d. 174b, l. 253. Goloshchekin was subsequently removed from all successive printings of the SHORT COURSE after his arrest on October 15, 1939.

72. See note 71.

73. Stalin eliminated the emphasis initially placed on this entire paragraph midway through his editing.

74. Stalin's late interpolation "*of the Party*" may have been recommended by Pospelov. See RGANI, f. 3, op. 22, d. 174b, l. 256.

75. Stalin's late correction "~~proposed organizing a 'Stolypin Labour Party' of the Zubatov type~~ *endeavoured to organize their own, reformist party, which the workers christened a 'Stolypin Labour Party'*" may have been recommended by Pospelov. See RGANI, f. 3, op. 22, d. 174b, ll. 255ob–256.

Chapter 5. The Bolshevik Party during the New Rise of the Working-Class Movement before the First Imperialist War (1912–1914)

1. Stalin's late correction "~~REVOLUTIONARY~~ RISE *OF THE REVOLUTIONARY MOVEMENT*" may have been recommended by Pospelov. See RGANI, f. 3, op. 22, d. 174b, l. 281.

2. Early in Stalin's editing, Zhdanov proposed the interpolation "*But*"—see RGASPI, f. 17, op. 120, d. 383, l. 592ob. Stalin later interpolated his own text, preserving the sense of the correction.

3. Early in Stalin's editing, Zhdanov wrote "*When*" in the margins near this sentence. Stalin's later interpolation "*April and May*" may have been prompted by this note or similar concerns expressed by Pospelov. See RGASPI, f. 17, op. 120, d. 383, l. 592ob; RGANI, f. 3, op. 22, d. 174b, l. 281.

4. Stalin's late correction "~~millions~~ *hundreds of thousands*" may have been recommended by Zhdanov. See RGASPI, f. 77, op. 4, d. 23, l. 4.

5. Stalin's late correction "~~the~~ larg~~est~~" may have been recommended by Pospelov. See RGANI, f. 3, op. 22, d. 174b, l. 285.

6. Stalin eliminated the emphasis initially placed on the word "economic" midway through his editing.

7. Stalin eliminated the emphasis initially placed on the word "political" midway through his editing.

8. Stalin's late cut "~~, the national question and others~~" may have been recommended by Pospelov. See RGANI, f. 3, op. 22, d. 174b, l. 286.

9. Stalin's late cut "~~The daily Bolshevik newspaper~~" may have been recommended by Pospelov. See RGANI, f. 3, op. 22, d. 174b, l. 287.

10. Stalin's late correction to his interpolation—"*~~an awkward difficult~~*"—may have been recommended by Pospelov. See RGANI, f. 3, op. 22, d. 174b, l. 296.

11. Stalin's late decision to list A. E. Badayev first instead of second may have been prompted by Pospelov. See RGANI, f. 3, op. 22, d. 174b, l. 297.

12. Stalin's late correction to his interpolation—"*~~Leningrad~~ St. Petersburg*"—may have been recommended by Zhdanov or Pospelov. See RGASPI, f. 77, op. 4, d. 23, l. 20; RGANI, f. 3, op. 22, d. 174b, l. 300.

13. Stalin's late addition to his interpolation— "*Ivanovo-Voznesensk, Kostroma,*"—may have been recommended by Pospelov. See RGANI, f. 3, op. 22, d. 174b, l. 300.

14. Stalin's late decision to list Badayev first instead of second may have been recommended by Pospelov. See RGANI, f. 3, op. 22, d. 174b, l. 300.

15. Stalin's late correction "~~in fact wanted to subordinate the Bolsheviks to the Liquidators~~ *demanded that the Bolsheviks should desist from criticizing the compromising policy of the Liquidators*" may have been recommended by Pospelov. See RGANI, f. 3, op. 22, d. 174b, l. 301.

16. Stalin's late revisions to this sentence—the correction "~~negotiate~~ *discuss* ~~on July 19~~" and the interpolation "*the war that was about to begin*"—may have been recommended by Pospelov. See RGANI, f. 3, op. 22, d. 174b, l. 303.

17. Stalin's late cut "~~August 1, 1914,~~" may have been recommended by Pospelov. See RGANI, f. 3, op. 22, d. 174b, l. 303.

18. Early in Stalin's editing, Zhdanov wrote in the margins beside this paragraph "*Interrupted by the beginning of the war*"—see RGASPI, f. 17, op. 120, d. 383, l. 599ob. Stalin incorporated this point into his revisions.

Chapter 6. The Bolshevik Party in the Period of the Imperialist War. The Second Revolution in Russia (1914–March 1917)

1. Stalin eliminated the emphasis initially placed on the passage "the most important branches of Russian industry were in the hands of foreign capitalists, chiefly those of France, Great Britain and Belgium, that is, the Entente countries" midway through his editing.

2. Stalin's late cut "~~Almost 20 percent of all oil was in British hands;~~" may have been recommended by Pospelov. See RGANI, f. 3, op. 22, d. 174b, l. 307.

3. Stalin eliminated the emphasis initially placed on the word "tributary" midway through his editing.

4. Stalin eliminated the emphasis initially placed on the word "semi-colony" midway through his editing.

5. Stalin's late cut "~~, like the majority of the parties in the Second International,~~" may have been recommended by Zhdanov or Pospelov. See RGASPI, f. 77, op. 4, d. 23, l. 29; RGANI, f. 3, op. 22, d. 174b, l. 308.

6. Stalin's late revision to his interpolation—the correction "*~~tsarist government~~ Russian government*" and the interpolation "*of the tsar*"—may have been recommended by Pospelov.

See RGANI, f. 3, op. 22, d. 174b, l. 310. Stalin's revision was subsequently transformed into "*the government of the Russian tsar*" with his permission.

7. Stalin's late interpolation "*, just as the German Social-Democrats helped the government of the German kaiser to wage war on the 'Russian barbarians'*" may have been recommended by Zhdanov. See RGASPI, f. 77, op. 4, d. 23, l. 29. Pospelov agreed, although he recommended "*kaiser Wilhelm*" instead of "*the government of the German kaiser*"—see RGANI, f. 3, op. 22, d. 174b, l. 310.

8. Stalin eliminated the emphasis initially placed on the phrase "a crime to shoot one another" midway through his editing.

9. Stalin eliminated the emphasis initially placed on the word "Centrist" midway through his editing.

10. Stalin eliminated the emphasis initially placed on the phrase "the renunciation of the class struggle during the war" midway through his editing.

11. Stalin's late interpolation "*very*" may have been recommended by Pospelov. See RGANI, f. 3, op. 22, d. 174b, l. 314.

12. Stalin's late interpolation to this sentence—"*But*"—may have been recommended by Pospelov. See RGANI, f. 3, op. 22, d. 174b, l. 314.

13. Stalin's late interpolation to this sentence—"*only*"—may have been recommended by Pospelov. See RGANI, f. 3, op. 22, d. 174b, l. 314.

14. Stalin eliminated the emphasis initially placed on the words "an advance" midway through his editing.

15. Stalin's late interpolation "*among the Left Social-Democrats*" may have been recommended by Pospelov. See RGANI, f. 3, op. 22, d. 174b, l. 315.

16. Stalin's late interpolation "*the majority of*" may have been recommended by Pospelov. See RGANI, f. 3, op. 22, d. 174b, l. 315.

17. Stalin eliminated the emphasis initially placed on the expression "die away of itself" midway through his editing.

18. Stalin's decision to list Badayev first instead of second may have been prompted by Pospelov. See RGANI, f. 3, op. 22, d. 174b, l. 321.

19. Stalin's late interpolation "*and seizures of foreign territory*" may have been recommended by Zhdanov or Pospelov. See RGASPI, f. 77, op. 4, d. 23, l. 43; RGANI, f. 3, op. 22, d. 174b, l. 323.

20. Stalin eliminated the emphasis initially placed on the phrase "the majority were opposed to participation in them" midway through his editing.

21. Stalin's late interpolation "*, in the Baltic provinces*" may have been recommended by Pospelov. See RGANI, f. 3, op. 22, d. 174b, l. 323.

22. Early in his editing, Stalin cut this paragraph—see RGASPI, f. 17, op 120, d. 383, l. 431. Later, he partially restored it, although without mention of the Latvian Bolsheviks.

23. Stalin's late correction to his interpolation—"*, ~~Lithuania, a part of Latvia~~ and part of the Baltic provinces*"—may have been recommended by Pospelov. See RGANI, f. 3, op. 22, d. 174b, l. 327.

24. Stalin's late division of this sentence into two may have been prompted by Zhdanov or Pospelov. It originally read "The supply of foodstuffs to Petrograd and Moscow had al-

most ceased; one factory after another closed down and this aggravated unemployment." See RGASPI, f. 77, op. 4, d. 23, l. 48; RGANI, f. 3, op. 22, d. 174b, l. 328.

25. Stalin's late interpolation "*practical*" may have been recommended by Pospelov. See RGANI, f. 3, op. 22, d. 174b, l. 331.

26. Stalin eliminated the emphasis initially placed on this sentence midway through his editing.

27. Stalin's late addition of "*only*" to his interpolation may have been recommended by Pospelov. See RGANI, f. 3, op. 22, d. 174b, l. 332.

28. Stalin's late addition of "*on the initiative of the Bolsheviks*" to his interpolation may have been recommended by Pospelov. See RGANI, f. 3, op. 22, d. 174b, l. 332.

29. Stalin's late interpolation "*backstairs*" may have been recommended by Pospelov. See RGANI, f. 3, op. 22, d. 174b, l. 334.

30. Stalin's late revisions to this sentence may have reflected changes recommended by Pospelov. Stalin's previous draft was closer to that found in Yaroslavsky and Pospelov's last version of the SHORT COURSE: "~~The conciliatory leadership of the Petrograd Soviet came to the aid of the liberal bourgeoisie~~ And *a few days later*, at a joint session of the Provisional Committee of the State Duma and the Executive Committee of the Soviet of Workers' and Soldiers' Deputies ~~on March 2, 1917~~, they formed *a new government of Russia*—a bourgeois Provisional Government, headed by Prince Lvov, the man whom, prior to the February Revolution, even Nicholas II was about to make the Prime Minister of the tsarist government." See RGANI, f. 3, op. 22, d. 174b, l. 334.

31. Stalin's late interpolation "*Guchkov, the head of the Octobrists,*" may have been recommended by Pospelov. See RGANI, f. 3, op. 22, d. 174b, l. 334.

32. Stalin's late revisions of this sentence may have reflected suggestions made by Pospelov. In Stalin's previous draft, his version was considerable shorter: "*And so it was that the Soviet of Workers' and Soldiers' Deputies voluntarily handed over state power in the country to the bourgeoisie.*" See RGANI, f. 3, op. 22, d. 174b, l. 334.

33. Stalin's late correction to his interpolation—"~~*capitalists'*~~ *imperialists'*"—may have been recommended by Pospelov. See RGANI, f. 3, op. 22, d. 174b, l. 337.

Chapter 7. The Bolshevik Party in the Period of Preparation and Realization of the October Socialist Revolution (April 1917–1918)

1. Stalin's late addition of V. P. Nogin's last name to this list may have been prompted by Pospelov. See RGANI, f. 3, op. 22, d. 174v, l. 351.

2. Stalin's late correction to his interpolation—"~~*sentences*~~ *years*"—may have been recommended by Zhdanov or Pospelov. See RGASPI, f. 77, op. 4, d. 23, l. 63; RGANI, f. 3, op. 22, d. 174v, l. 352.

3. Stalin eliminated the emphasis initially placed on this Lenin quotation midway through his editing.

4. Stalin eliminated the emphasis initially placed on the word "transition" midway through his editing.

5. Stalin eliminated the emphasis initially placed on the words "Petrograd City Conference" midway through his editing.

6. Stalin's late addition of Yu. L. Pyatakov's last name to this list may have been prompted by Pospelov. See RGASPI, f. 558, op. 11, d. 1219, ll. 77–78; RGANI, f. 3, op. 22, d. 174v, l. 357.

7. Stalin eliminated the emphasis initially placed on the phrase "Lenin vigorously condemned" midway through his editing.

8. Stalin's late correction to his interpolation—"*~~first world~~ imperialist*"—may have been recommended by Pospelov. See RGANI, f. 3, op. 22, d. 174v, l. 362.

9. Stalin eliminated the emphasis initially placed on the phrase "the right of nations to self-determination even to the point of ~~complete~~ secession" midway through his editing.

10. Stalin's late interpolation "*and others*" may have been recommended by Zhdanov. See RGASPI, f. 77, op. 4, d. 23, l. 77.

11. Stalin's late cut to his interpolation after the word "*of*"—"*~~'our allies'~~*"—may have been recommended by Pospelov. See RGASPI, f. 558, op. 11, d. 1219, l. 78.

12. Stalin eliminated the emphasis initially placed on the phrase "general armed demonstration demanding the transfer of power to the Soviets" midway through his editing.

13. Stalin may have interpolated this paragraph at Molotov's recommendation. See RGASPI, f. 558, op. 11, d. 1219, l. 79.

14. Stalin eliminated the emphasis initially placed on the word "neutral" midway through his editing.

15. Stalin's late correction "~~come to power~~ *seized all power*" may have been recommended by Pospelov. See RGANI, f. 3, op. 22, d. 174v, l. 374ob.

16. Stalin's late correction "~~prepared~~ *began preparations*" may have been recommended by Pospelov. See RGANI, f. 3, op. 22, d. 174v, l. 374ob.

17. Stalin's late cut to his interpolation after the word "*rising*"—"*~~even more~~*"—may have been recommended by Pospelov. See RGANI, f. 3, op. 22, d. 174v, l. 382.

18. Stalin eliminated the emphasis initially placed on the adjectives "Menshevik and Socialist-Revolutionary" midway through his editing.

19. Stalin eliminated the emphasis initially placed on the phrase "a slogan calling for an uprising" midway through his editing.

20. Stalin's late interpolation "*REASONS FOR THE VICTORY OF THE SOCIALIST REVOLUTION*" may have been recommended by Pospelov. See RGANI, f. 3, op. 22, d. 174v, l. 386.

21. Stalin replaced the word "secretly" with "*illegally*" during his editing. When the SHORT COURSE was officially published in English in 1939, "illegally" was incorrectly rendered as "secretly."

22. Stalin's late addition of F. E. Dzerzhinsky's last name to the list may have been recommended by Molotov or Pospelov. See RGASPI, f. 558, op. 11, d. 1219, l. 80; RGANI, f. 3, op. 22, d. 174v, l. 388.

23. This sentence mentioning N. I. Yezhov was removed from all successive editions of the Short Course after his arrest on April 10, 1939.

24. Stalin's interpolation "*of their Party on the armed uprising*" may have been recommended by Pospelov. See RGANI, f. 3, op. 22, d. 174v, l. 389.

25. Late in Stalin's editing, Pospelov recommended the interpolation "*in an article by Comrade Stalin*"—see RGANI, f. 3, op. 22, d. 174v, l. 391. The general secretary rejected this suggestion.

26. Stalin's late change to the quotation marks may have been recommended by Pospelov. See RGANI, f. 3, op. 22, d. 174v, l. 393.

27. Stalin eliminated the emphasis initially placed on the quotation "landlord ownership of land is abolished forthwith without compensation" midway through his editing.

28. Stalin's late revisions to this sentence may have been suggested by Zhdanov. See RGASPI, f. 77, op. 4, d. 23, l. 107.

29. Yaroslavsky and Pospelov borrowed these three points word-for-word from A. V. Shestakov's 1937 textbook on Soviet history. In doing so, they unknowingly plagiarized an interpolation that Stalin had made in that manuscript during its editing—see KRATKII KURS ISTORII SSSR, ed. A. V. Shestakov (Moscow: Gos. uchebno-pedagog. izd-vo, 1937), 198–199; RGASPI, f. 558, op. 11, d. 1584, l. 94. Stalin apparently spotted this upon receiving Yaroslavsky and Pospelov's final version on April 24 and wrote in the margins: "*From the October Revolution and tactics of the Russian communists*"—a request that the historians replace the three points with a direct quotation from his introduction to the book NA PUTIAKH K OKTIABRIU (Moscow: GIZ, 1925), vii–lvi—see RGASPI, f. 17, op. 120, d. 383, l. 447ob. Pospelov promptly wrote into the margins of a second copy of the galleys: "*what Comrade Stalin addressed in his work 'The October Revolution and the Tactics of the Russian Communists.'*" He then added "*Replace with the following interpolation: 'Three circumstances of an external nature . . .' to the words '. . . the October Revolution won its victory.'*" On April 26, he returned to Stalin this copy of the galleys, accompanied by a typescript addendum:

> The victory of the Soviet Socialist Revolution can be explained by the following reasons *which Comrade Stalin pointed to in his work* THE OCTOBER REVOLUTION AND THE TACTICS OF THE RUSSIAN COMMUNISTS:
>
> *"Three circumstances of an external nature determined the comparative ease with which the proletarian revolution in Russia succeeded in breaking the chains of imperialism and thus overthrowing the rule of the bourgeoisie.*
>
> *"Firstly, the circumstance that the October Revolution began in a period of desperate struggle between the two principal imperialist groups, the Anglo-French and the Austro-German; at a time when, engaged in mortal struggle between themselves, these two groups had neither the time nor the means to devote serious attention to the struggle against the October Revolution. This circumstance was of tremendous importance for the October Revolution; for it enabled it to take advantage of the fierce conflicts within the imperialist world to strengthen and organize its own forces.*
>
> *"Secondly, the circumstance that the October Revolution began during the imperialist war, at a time when the labouring masses, exhausted by the war and thirsting for peace, had come to believe that the only logical way out was through proletarian revolution. This circumstance was of extreme importance for the October Revolution, for it put the mighty weapon of peace at its disposal, made it easier for it to link the Soviet revolution with the ending of the hated war, and thus created mass sympathy for it both in the West, among the workers, and in the East, among the oppressed peoples.*
>
> *"Thirdly, the existence of a powerful working-class movement in Europe and the fact that a revolutionary crisis was maturing in the West and in the East, brought on by the*

protracted imperialist war. This circumstance was of inestimable importance for the revolution in Russia, for it ensured the revolution faithful allies outside Russia in its struggle against world imperialism.

"But in addition to circumstances of an external nature, there were also a number of favourable internal conditions which facilitated the victory of the October Revolution.

"Of these conditions, the following must be regarded as the chief ones:

"Firstly, the October Revolution enjoyed the most active support of the overwhelming majority of the working class in Russia.

"Secondly, it enjoyed the undoubted support of the poor peasants and of the majority of the soldiers, who were thirsting for peace and land.

"Thirdly, it had at its head, as its guiding force, such a tried and tested party as the Bolshevik Party, strong not only by reason of its experience and discipline acquired through the years, but also by reason of its vast connections with the labouring masses.

"Fourthly, the October Revolution was confronted by enemies who were comparatively easy to overcome, such as the rather weak Russian bourgeoisie, a landlord class which was utterly demoralized by peasant "revolts," and the compromising parties (the Mensheviks and Socialist-Revolutionaries), which had become completely bankrupt during the war.

"Fifthly, it had at its disposal the vast expanses of the young state, in which it was able to manoeuver freely, retreat when circumstances so required, enjoy a respite, gather strength, etc.

"Sixthly, in its struggle against counter-revolution the October Revolution could count upon sufficient resources of food, fuel and raw materials within the country.

"The combination of these external and internal circumstances created that peculiar situation which determined the comparative ease with which the October Revolution won its victory." (Stalin, THE OCTOBER REVOLUTION AND THE TACTICS OF THE RUSSIAN COMMUNISTS, IN PROBLEMS IN LENINISM, Russ. ed., p. 75–76.)

Stalin ignored this proposal and rewrote the section to express different priorities. See RGASPI, f. 17, op. 120, d. 383, ll. 623ob, 539ob, 266–268.

30. Stalin's late addition to his interpolation—"*the movement of the oppressed nationalities for national liberation and national equality*"—may have been recommended by Molotov. See RGASPI, f. 558, op. 11, d. 1219, l. 80.

31. Stalin's late addition to his interpolation—"*, and F. Dzerzhinsky was placed at its head*"—may have been recommended by Zhdanov or Pospelov. See RGASPI, f. 77, op. 4, d. 23, l. 113; RGANI, f. 3, op. 22, d. 174v, l. 402.

32. Stalin's late corrections to his interpolation—the addition of the phrase "*the transfer of power to the Soviets*" and the repositioning of the word "*and*"—may have been recommended by Pospelov. See RGASPI, f. 77, op. 4, d. 23, l. 113; RGANI, f. 3, op. 22, d. 174v, l. 403.

33. Stalin's late addition to his interpolation—"*to create*"—may have been recommended by Zhdanov or Pospelov. See RGASPI, f. 77, op. 4, d. 23, l. 114; RGANI, f. 3, op. 22, d. 174v, l. 403.

34. Stalin's late corrections "~~28~~ *30* votes against ~~9~~ *12*, with ~~1~~ *4* abstentions" may have been recommended by Zhdanov or Pospelov. See RGASPI, f. 77, op. 4, d. 23, l. 121; f. 558, op. 11, d. 1219, l. 78.

35. Stalin replaced "against capitalism" with "*against the enemy*" during his editing. The latter phrase was erroneously excluded from the official 1939 English translation.

36. Stalin's late correction "~~gave~~ *set*" may have been recommended by Pospelov. See RGANI, f. 3, op. 22, d. 174v, l. 411.

37. Stalin's late correction "~~firm directive~~ *task*" may have been recommended by Pospelov. See RGANI, f. 3, op. 22, d. 174v, l. 411.

38. Stalin eliminated the emphasis initially placed on the word "bourgeois" midway through his editing.

Chapter 8. The Bolshevik Party in the Period of Foreign Military Intervention and Civil War (1918–1920)

1. Stalin's late correction to his interpolation—"~~*pressure*~~ *prestige*"—may have been recommended by Zhdanov or Pospelov. See RGASPI, f. 77, op. 4, d. 23, l. 136; RGASPI, f. 3, op. 22, d. 174v, l. 436.

2. Stalin's late addition to his interpolation—"*About half the membership of the Party and of the Young Communist League went to the front.*"—may have been recommended by Zhdanov or Pospelov. See RGASPI, f. 77, op. 4, d. 23, l. 136; RGANI, f. 3, op. 22, d. 174v, l. 436.

3. Stalin's late cut to his interpolation after the word "*Simbirsk*"—"~~*(Ulyanovsk)*~~"—may have been recommended by Zhdanov or Pospelov. See RGASPI, f. 77, op. 4, d. 23, l. 137; RGASPI, f. 3, op. 22, d. 174v, l. 437.

4. Stalin's late correction to his interpolation—"~~*wounded*~~ *had made a villainous attempt on the life of*"—may have been recommended by Pospelov. See RGASPI, f. 3, op. 22, d. 174v, l. 437.

5. Stalin's late correction to his interpolation—"~~*Party*~~ *Soviet Government*"—may have been recommended by Pospelov. See RGASPI, f. 3, op. 22, d. 174v, l. 438.

6. Late in Stalin's editing, he corrected his interpolation—"~~*Russian*~~ *Soviet*"—see RGASPI, f. 558, op. 11, d. 1215, l. 454.

7. See note 6.

8. Stalin's late cut to his interpolation after the word "*the*"—"~~*Menshevik-*~~"—may have been recommended by Zhdanov. See RGASPI, f. 77, op. 4, d. 23, l. 141.

9. Stalin's late revision of one of his interpolated sentences may have been at Pospelov's recommendation: "~~*The full extent of the weakness of this revolution was visible not least in the fact that it allowed the German Whiteguard assassination of such prominent revolutionaries as Karl Liebknecht and Rosa Luxemburg to go unpunished*~~ *This in fact explains the weakness of the German revolution. How weak it really was is shown, for example, by the fact that it allowed the German Whiteguards to assassinate such prominent revolutionaries as Rosa Luxemburg and Karl Liebknecht with impunity.*" See RGASPI, f. 77, op. 4, d. 23, l. 141; RGANI, f. 3, op. 22, d. 174v, ll. 440ob–441.

10. Stalin may have rewritten this sentence at Zhdanov's recommendation—see RGASPI, f. 77, op. 4, d. 23, l. 141.

11. Stalin eliminated the emphasis initially placed on the word "*Program*" midway through his editing.

12. Stalin's late correction to his interpolation—"~~*places*~~ *clauses*"—may have been recommended by Zhdanov or Pospelov. See RGASPI, f. 77, op. 4, d. 23, l. 144; RGANI, f. 3, op. 22, d. 174v, l. 443.

13. Initially, Stalin corrected the end of this sentence to read "~~as an ally of the working class~~ *in Soviet development*." Later, Pospelov offered a correction to Stalin's interpolation: "~~*Soviet development*~~ *socialist construction*"—see RGANI, f. 3, op. 22, d. 174v, l. 443. Stalin eventually settled on "~~*Soviet development*~~ *the development of the Soviet state.*"

14. Stalin eliminated the emphasis initially placed on this sentence midway through his editing.

15. Stalin's late correction "~~given~~ *proclaimed*" may have been recommended by Zhdanov or Pospelov. See RGASPI, f. 77, op. 4, d. 23, l. 146; RGANI, f. 3, op. 22, d. 174v, l. 446.

16. Stalin eliminated the emphasis initially placed on the phrase "the building up of the Red Army" midway through his editing.

17. Stalin's late addition to his interpolation—"*with the aid of the Socialist-Revolutionaries,*"—may have been recommended by Yaroslavsky or Pospelov. See RGASPI, f. 558, op. 11, d. 1219, l. 87; RGANI, f. 3, op. 22, d. 174v, l. 449.

18. Mention of André Marty's name was cut from all successive printings of the SHORT COURSE after he was expelled from the French Communist Party in December 1952. See RGASPI, f. 71, op. 3, d. 215, l. 108.

19. Early in his editing, Stalin cut this entire section on war communism. See RGASPI, f. 558, op. 3, d. 77, ll. 190–192.

20. Early in his editing, Stalin cut the last two sentences of this paragraph. See RGASPI, f. 17, op. 120, d. 383, l. 460. Later, he deleted much of the rest of this section.

21. Stalin eliminated the emphasis initially placed on the expression "a brief respite" midway through his editing.

22. Stalin's late interpolation "*finally*" may have been recommended by Pospelov. See RGANI, f. 3, op. 22, d. 174v, l. 454.

23. Stalin's late interpolation "*Transcaucasia*" may have been recommended by Yaroslavsky. See RGASPI, f. 558, op. 11, d. 1219, l. 87.

24. Stalin's late correction "~~*to*~~*ward*" may have been recommended by Zhdanov. See RGASPI, f. 77, op. 4, d. 23, l. 156.

25. Early in his editing, Stalin made the cut "~~; Maximovsky, Ossinsky, Kaminsky, Rafail, Drobnis and Boguslavsky also tended toward this group~~"—see RGASPI, f. 17, op. 120, d. 383, l. 461ob. Later, Stalin reframed this discussion and deleted much of the remaining detail.

26. Early in his editing, Stalin made the correction "~~them~~ *the Democratic-Centralists*"—see RGASPI, f. 17, op. 120, d. 383, l. 461ob. Later, Stalin reframed this discussion and deleted much of this detail.

27. Early in his editing, Stalin made the cut "~~Drobnis and Boguslavsky were shot in 1937 as active participants in a counter-revolutionary terroristic Trotskyite-espionage-fascist cen-~~

~~tre. The Democratic-Centralists obtained weapons for their struggle with the Party from the arsenal of the “Left Communists,” Mensheviks and Socialist-Revolutionaries.~~” See RGASPI, f. 17, op. 120, d. 383, l. 461ob. Later, Stalin reframed this discussion and deleted much of the remaining detail.

28. Early in his editing, Stalin made the cut “~~The chieftains of this group were in most cases Soviet bureaucrats and officials.~~” On April 26, Pospelov recommended the interpolation “*The members of this group were recruited from bureaucratic elements within the Soviet administration and from among self-important officials.*” See RGASPI, f. 17, op. 120, d. 383, ll. 461ob, 539ob, 639ob. Later, Stalin reframed this discussion retaining elements of Pospelov’s suggestion.

29. Early in his editing, Stalin wrote into the margins next to this paragraph “*The Poles’ plan (1772).*” See RGASPI, f. 558, op. 3, d. 77, l. 195. Later, he cut the paragraph and rewrote the section’s introduction.

30. Stalin’s late correction “~~*’s east bank*~~ *west of the Dnieper*” may have been recommended by Zhdanov. See RGASPI, f. 77, op. 4, d. 23, l. 157.

31. Stalin’s late correction to his interpolation—“~~*unsuccessful*~~ *vain*”—may have been recommended by Zhdanov. See RGASPI, f. 77, op. 4, d. 23, l. 157.

32. Early in his editing, Stalin wrote in the margins next to this paragraph “*This isn’t what’s needed. Needs to be developed.*” See RGASPI, f. 558, op. 3, d. 77, l. 195. Later, he cut the paragraph and reframed the discussion.

33. Stalin eliminated the emphasis initially placed on the phrase “Peace of Riga” midway through his editing.

34. Stalin’s late corrections to this interpolated sentence—the addition of “*Poland retained*” after the word “*treaty*” and the cut “~~*remained Polish*~~” after the word “*Byelorussia*”—may have been recommended by Pospelov. See RGANI, f. 3, op. 22, d. 174v, l. 459.

35. Stalin’s late correction “~~manoeuver~~ *advance*” may have been recommended by Pospelov. See RGANI, f. 3, op. 22, d. 174v, l. 459ob.

36. Stalin’s late cut “~~for transport~~” may have been recommended by Pospelov. See RGANI, f. 3, op. 22, d. 174v, l. 459ob.

37. Stalin’s late interpolation “*while conducting an offensive against Wrangel, they had at the same time to smash Makhno’s anarchist bands who were assisting Wrangel*” may have been recommended by Pospelov. See RGANI, f. 3, op. 22, d. 174v, l. 460.

38. Mention of André Marty’s name was cut from all successive printings of the Short Course after he was expelled from the French Communist Party in December 1952. See RGASPI, f. 71, op. 3, d. 215, l. 108.

39. Early in his editing, Stalin made the cut “~~and eliminated~~”—see RGASPI, f. 17, op. 120, d. 383, l. 464ob. He later deleted the entire section.

40. Early in Stalin’s editing, Pospelov recommended the interpolation “*nationalized and*”—see RGASPI, f. 17, op. 120, d. 383, l. 642ob. Stalin ignored the suggestion and later deleted the entire section.

41. Early in his editing, Stalin wrote in the margins next to this paragraph “*Lazo, Parkhomenko.*” See RGASPI, f. 558, op. 3, d. 77, l. 200. Later, he deleted the entire section.

42. Earlier drafts of this sentence did not include specific mention of Russia. See RGASPI, f. 558, op. 11, d. 1215, l. 476.

43. During his editing, Stalin cut M. I. Tukhachevsky's last name from this list. Later, he cut S. K. Timoshenko's and G. I. Kulik's last names, perhaps at Pospelov's recommendation. See RGASPI, f. 558, op. 11, d. 1215, l. 478; RGANI, f. 3, op. 22, d. 174v, l. 464.

44. Mention of Yezhov's last name was removed from all successive printings of the SHORT COURSE after his arrest on April 10, 1939.

45. Stalin's late addition of N. S. Khrushchev's last name to this list may have been at Pospelov's recommendation. See RGANI, f. 3, op. 22, d. 174v, l. 464.

46. Early in his editing, Stalin wrote in the margins next to this paragraph "'*Hands off Sov. Russia.*'" See RGASPI, f. 558, op. 3, d. 77, l. 200. Later, he interpolated the slogan into its concluding sentence.

Chapter 9. The Bolshevik Party in the Period of Transition to the Peaceful Work of Economic Restoration (1921–1925)

1. Stalin eliminated the emphasis initially placed on the expression "being weakened" midway through his editing.

2. Stalin's late cut to his interpolation after the word "*The*"—"~~*remains of the*~~"—may have been recommended by Zhdanov or Pospelov. See RGASPI, f. 77, op. 4, d. 23, l. 173; RGANI, f. 3, op. 22, d. 174v, l. 485.

3. Stalin's late correction to his interpolation—"~~*training*~~ *schooling*"—may have been recommended by Zhdanov, Yaroslavsky, or Pospelov. See RGASPI, f. 77, op. 4, d. 23, l. 173; f. 558, op. 11, d. 1219, l. 98; RGANI, f. 3, op. 22, d. 174v, l. 485.

4. Stalin eliminated the emphasis initially placed on the phrase "the actual point at issue" midway through his editing.

5. Stalin eliminated the emphasis initially placed on the phrase "school of Communism" midway through his editing.

6. Stalin eliminated the emphasis initially placed on the word "Menshevik" midway through his editing.

7. Stalin eliminated the emphasis initially placed on the term "the national question" midway through his editing.

8. Stalin replaced the archaic, chauvinistic term "alien" [inorodets] with the more modern usage "*the non-Russian peoples*" [nerusskie] midway through his editing.

9. Early in his editing, Stalin wrote in the margins alongside this subheading "*The XI Party Congress established the Union of Sov*[*iet*] *Soc*[*ialist*] *Repub*[*lics*]." See RGASPI, f. 558, op. 3, d. 77, l. 213. Ultimately, he credited the founding of the USSR to the 1922 First All-Union Congress of Soviets later in the section.

10. Early in his editing, Stalin wrote in the margins next to this line "*The Leftists were freaks such as Lominadze, Shatskin, etc.*" See RGASPI, f. 558, op. 3, d. 77, l. 213. Later, he incorporated this language into his revisions.

11. Stalin's late cut "~~and carried out~~" may have been recommended by Zhdanov. See RGASPI, f. 77, op. 4, d. 23, l. 185.

12. Stalin eliminated the emphasis initially placed on the expression "a Party purge" midway through his editing.

13. Stalin's late interpolation "*from the Party*" may have been recommended by Zhdanov or Pospelov. See RGASPI, f. 77, op. 4, d. 23, l. 185; RGANI, f. 3, op. 22, d. 174v, l. 497.

14. Stalin eliminated the emphasis initially placed on the expression "the main link" midway through his editing.

15. Stalin's late cut "~~in the name of the revolution, to which he devoted all his energy and his entire life~~" may have been recommended by Zhdanov or Pospelov. See RGASPI, f. 77, op. 4, d. 23, l. 189; RGANI, f. 3, op. 22, d. 174v, l. 501.

16. Early in his editing, Stalin left a question mark in the margins and cut the phrase "~~first in the selling~~." Pospelov then recommended the interpolation "*Lenin's co-operative plan included all forms of agricultural economic cooperation, from the lowest (supply and sales) to the highest (collective farm production).*" See RGASPI, f. 17, op. 120, d. 383, ll. 472ob, 539ob, 650ob. Stalin later ignored these concerns.

17. Stalin eliminated the emphasis initially placed on the phrase "the national question" midway through his editing.

18. Stalin made a different set of interpolations early in his editing: "a group of Tatar *and Uzbek* bourgeois nationalists—Sultan-Galiev, *F. Khodzhaev* and others" See RGASPI, f. 558, op. 3, d. 77, l. 218.

19. Stalin's late interpolation "*and Bulgaria*" may have been recommended by Zhdanov, Yaroslavsky, or Pospelov. See RGASPI, f. 77, op. 4, d. 23, l. 196; f. 558, op. 11, d. 1219, l. 98; RGANI, f. 3, op. 22, d. 174v, l. 508.

20. Stalin cut this paragraph early in his editing—see RGASPI, f. 17, op. 120, d. 383, l. 474ob.

21. Stalin cut this sentence early in his editing—see RGASPI, f. 17, op. 120, d. 383, l. 474ob.

22. Stalin underscored the term "colony" early in his editing. Days later, Pospelov recommended the interpolation "*for the imperialist countries*"—see RGASPI, f. 17, op. 120, d. 383, ll. 475, 539ob, 653. Later, Stalin cut the entire paragraph.

23. When Pospelov submitted to Stalin the final version of his and Yaroslavsky's SHORT COURSE prototype, he appended a typescript that was to be interpolated after this paragraph. It read:

> *The Central Committee Plenum which took place in January 1925 pointed out during its summary of the struggle of the Party with Trotskyism in the 1918–24 period that in the 1923 discussion, the issue concerned an economic and political alliance with the peasantry, the policy on pricing, currency reform, the imperative of orienting Party policy around the core workers, the preservation of the Party's leading role in the economy and state organs, the struggle with "free" factions and groupings, and the preservation of the Bolshevik cadres' leading role—in other words,* THE PRESERVATION OF THE LENINIST PARTY LINE DURING THE NEP PERIOD.
>
> *Trotskyism during this period once again (as in 1918 and 1921) pushed the Party toward policies that could prove fatal for the revolution, insofar as Trotskyite policy undercut the Party's economic successes at their very origins. The Trotskyite opposition already in this period had begun to reason according to the formula "the worse the better" and had begun* TO GAMBLE ON THE SETBACKS EXPERIENCED BY THE PARTY AND SOVIET POWER.

In the 1923 discussion, the Party exposed Trotskyism as an expression of petty-bourgeois capitulationism, fright and disbelief in the strength of our revolution. The Party demonstrated that Trotskyism represented a Menshevik misunderstanding of the role of the proletariat in relation to the non-proletarian and pseudo proletarian strata of the working people. The Party demonstrated that Trotskyism was aiming in a Menshevik way to reduce the role of the Party in the revolution and Socialist construction, undermine the ideological unity of the Party, and spread doubt within the Party about the possibility of successful Socialist construction.

Pospelov also proposed to Stalin that the following paragraph open somewhat differently: "*After the 1923 discussion,* ~~But~~ the Trotskyites did not cease their subversive work." See RGASPI, f. 17, op. 120, d. 383, ll. 539ob, 653, 296. Stalin ignored these suggestions.

24. Late in his editing, Stalin eliminated the emphasis initially placed on the phrase "to bury Trotskyism as an ideological trend"—perhaps at Pospelov's suggestion. See RGANI, f. 3, op. 22, d. 174v, l. 511.

25. When Pospelov submitted to Stalin the final version of his and Yaroslavsky's SHORT COURSE prototype, he appended a typescript that was to be interpolated after this paragraph. It read:

Comrade Stalin, in his speech "Trotskyism or Leninism" (November 1924) and his article THE OCTOBER REVOLUTION AND THE TACTICS OF THE RUSSIAN COMMUNISTS *(December 1924) exposed the Menshevik, bourgeois essence of Trotskyism as a political trend that was hostile to Leninism.*

Comrade Stalin exposed Trotsky's attempts to replace Leninism with the Trotskyite-Menshevik theory of "permanent revolution" and rebuffed Trotsky's insolent slander that Bolshevism had somehow "rearmed" itself in 1917.

Comrade Stalin demonstrated that Leninism was an integral theory which had emerged in 1903 and passed through the trials of three revolutions and was now marching forward as the militant banner of the world proletariat.

Comrade Stalin defeated the Trotskyite theory of "permanent revolution" and showed that this false theory was a variety of Menshevism and entailed THE REPUDIATION OF THE DICTATORSHIP OF THE PROLETARIAT.

"What is the dictatorship of the proletariat according to Lenin?

"The dictatorship of the proletariat is a power which rests on an alliance between the proletariat and the labouring masses of the peasantry for 'the complete overthrow of capital' and for 'the final establishment and consolidation of socialism.'

"What is the dictatorship of the proletariat according to Trotsky?

"The dictatorship of the proletariat is a power which comes 'into hostile collision' with 'the broad masses of the peasantry' and seeks the solution of its 'contradictions' only 'in the arena of the world proletarian revolution.'

"What difference is there between this 'theory of permanent revolution' and the well-known theory of Menshevism which repudiates the concept of dictatorship of the proletariat?

"Essentially, there is no difference.

"There can be no doubt at all. 'Permanent revolution' is not a mere underestimation of the revolutionary potentialities of the peasant movement. 'Permanent revolution' is an underestimation of the peasant movement which leads to the repudiation of Lenin's theory of the dictatorship of the proletariat.

"Trotsky's 'permanent revolution' is a variety of Menshevism'"—wrote Comrade Stalin in his article The October Revolution and the Tactics of the Russian Communists.

The Trotskyite theory of "permanent revolution" denied the Leninist theory of the proletarian revolution, denied the possibility of the victory of Socialism in one country. Trotskyism preached doubt in the strength and abilities of our revolution and doubt in the strength and abilities of the Russian proletariat.

"Hitherto," Comrade Stalin pointed out in his article The October Revolution and the Tactics of the Russian Communists, *"only one aspect of the theory of 'permanent revolution' has usually been noted—lack of faith in the revolutionary potentialities of the peasant movement. Now, in fairness, this must be supplemented by another aspect—lack of faith in the strength and capacity of the proletariat in Russia.*

"What difference is there between Trotsky's theory and the ordinary Menshevik theory that the victory of socialism in one country, and in a backward country at that, is impossible without the preliminary victory of the proletarian revolution 'in the principal countries of Western Europe?'

"Essentially, there is no difference.

"There can be no doubt at all. Trotsky's theory of 'permanent revolution'is a variety of Menshevism," wrote Comrade Stalin.

See RGASPI, f. 17, op. 120, d. 383, ll. 539ob, 653, 297–298. Stalin ignored the suggested interpolation.

26. Stalin's late cuts to his interpolation—"*But the successes attending ~~Leninism in its struggle with Trotskyism~~ the Party ~~Central Committee~~'s Leninist policy*"—may have been recommended by Zhdanov or Pospelov. See RGASPI, f. 77, op. 4, d. 23, l. 200; RGANI, f. 3, op. 22, d. 174v, l. 512.

27. Early in his editing, Stalin wrote in the margins alongside this heading "*The question of the build[ing] of soc[ial]ism.*" See RGASPI, f. 558, op. 3, d. 77, l. 223. He later underscored this theme in his revisions to the section.

28. Early in his editing, Stalin wrote in the margins next to this paragraph "*The question about what we were building became practical—was it socialism or a bourgeois state.*" See RGASPI, f. 558, op. 3, d. 77, l. 225. He later underscored this theme in his revisions to the section.

29. Stalin's late addition to his interpolation—"*that*"—may have been recommended by Pospelov. See RGANI, f. 3, op. 22, d. 174v, l. 520.

30. Stalin's late addition to his interpolation—"*as well as the people generally,*"—may have been recommended by Pospelov. See RGANI, f. 3, op. 22, d. 174v, l. 520.

31. Early in his editing, Stalin drew two heavy, parallel lines in the margins next to this paragraph. Days later, Pospelov recommended the interpolation "*The Party completely*

exposed the Menshevik, capitulatory nature of Trotskyism"—see RGASPI, f. 17, op. 120, d. 383, ll. 477ob, 539ob, 655ob. Stalin ignored the suggestion and later reworked much of the section.

32. Early in Stalin's editing, Pospelov proposed the cut "~~because Trotsky had by that time already conspired with the enemies of the Soviet power~~"—see RGASPI, f. 17, op. 120, d. 383, ll. 477ob, 539ob, 655ob. Stalin ignored the suggestion and later reworked much of the section.

33. Stalin's late corrections to his interpolation—"~~*were forced*~~ *preferred*"—may have been recommended by Zhdanov or Pospelov. See RGASPI, f. 77, op. 4, d. 23, l. 213; RGANI, f. 3, op. 22, d. 174v, l. 525.

34. Stalin eliminated the emphasis initially placed on the term "industrialization" midway through his editing.

35. Stalin eliminated the emphasis initially placed on the term "economic development" midway through his editing. The term was inexplicably reemphasized in the official 1939 English translation.

Chapter 10. The Bolshevik Party in the Struggle for the Socialist Industrialization of the Country (1926–1929)

1. Stalin's late cuts to his interpolation—"*it lacked* ~~*a whole list of*~~ *machine-building plants* ~~*in industry*~~ *absolutely indispensable to the country*"—may have been recommended by Zhdanov or Pospelov. See RGASPI, f. 77, op. 4, d. 24, l. 1; RGANI, f. 3, op. 22, d. 174g, l. 541.

2. Stalin's late interpolation "*(ZIS)*" may have been recommended by Yaroslavsky or Pospelov. See RGASPI, f. 558, op. 11, d. 1219, l. 99; RGANI, f. 3, op. 22, d. 174g, l. 545.

3. Stalin's late correction to his interpolation—"~~*two*~~ *three*"—may have been recommended by Zhdanov. See RGASPI, f. 558, op. 11, d. 1219, l. 91.

4. Early in his editing, Stalin wrote in the margins beside this quotation "*AT THE END OF THE BOOK.*" See RGASPI, f. 558, op. 3, d. 77, l. 240.

5. Stalin's late addition to his interpolation—"*and their patrons*"—may have been recommended by Zhdanov. See RGASPI, f. 77, op. 4, d. 24, l. 10.

6. Stalin's late cut to his interpolation after the word "*ratio*"—"~~*, while consumer manufacturing in industry rose to 68 per cent*~~"—may reflect a cut suggested by Mikoian. See RGASPI, f. 558, op. 11, d. 1219, l. 93.

7. Stalin's corrections to his interpolation—the addition "*and that as far as industry was concerned,*" and the cut after the word "*win?*"—"~~*as far as industry was concerned,*~~"—may have been recommended by Zhdanov. See RGASPI, f. 77, op. 4, d. 24, l. 11.

8. Stalin's late correction to his interpolation—"~~*released*~~ *sold*"—may have been recommended by Zhdanov. See RGASPI, f. 77, op. 4, d. 24, l. 12.

9. Stalin's late correction "~~conduct~~ *develop*" may have been recommended by Pospelov. See RGANI, f. 3, op. 22, d. 174g, l. 555.

10. Early in his editing, Stalin drew a question mark in the margins near this sentence and made the cut "~~and the construction of tractor factories.~~" RGASPI, f. 17, op. 120, d. 383, l. 486ob. He later cut the paragraph and reworked the section.

11. Early in his editing, Stalin revised this paragraph: "~~Zinoviev, Kamenev, Yevdokimov and others~~ *The supporters of Trotsky and Zinoviev*, who had been expelled from the party ~~for anti-Soviet activities~~, handed in ~~double-dealing~~ statements about their abandonment of Trotskyism. They recommended to their followers that they also hand in such ~~double-dealing~~ statements in order to ~~at the very least "crawl on their bellies"~~ *get* back into the Party, ~~as Zinoviev put it, so as to continue with their anti-Soviet activity under the cover of Party membership. Trotsky gave the same advice to his followers~~." Stalin then wrote in the margins next to this paragraph "*They were admitted back into the* PARTY." See RGASPI, f. 558, op. 3, d. 77, l. 245. Stalin later cut the entire section.

12. Early in his editing, Stalin wrote in the margins beside this paragraph "*Begin with this*." See RGASPI, f. 558, op. 3, d. 77, l. 246. He later cut the entire section.

13. Early in his editing, Stalin wrote in the margins beside this paragraph "*There weren't yet any fascists in power*." See RGASPI, f. 558, op. 3, d. 77, l. 246. He later cut the paragraph and reworked the section.

14. Stalin's late addition to his interpolation—"*anti-Leninists*"—may have been recommended by Zhdanov or Pospelov. See RGASPI, f. 77, op. 4, d. 24, l. 16; RGANI, f. 3, op. 22, d. 174g, l. 556.

15. Stalin's late correction to his interpolation—"~~*needed*~~ *its former*"—may have been recommended by Pospelov. See RGANI, f. 3, op. 22, d. 174g, l. 558.

16. Early in his editing, Stalin underscored the phrase "MASTER TECHNIQUE" and wrote "*TEACHER*" in the margins beside this paragraph. See RGASPI, f. 558, op. 3, d. 77, l. 249. He later reworked the sentence.

17. Early in his editing, Stalin wrote in the margins beside this heading "*Until this time,* BUKHARIN *and Co. were held* IN RESERVE *against the party*." See RGASPI, f. 558, op. 3, d. 77, l. 249. He later reworked much of this part of the chapter.

18. Early in his editing, Stalin made the cut "~~Syrtsov's slogan 'Save Up for a Better Day,'~~" and wrote in the margins beside this paragraph "*The theory of* PASSING INTO." See RGASPI, f. 558, op. 3, d. 77, l. 249. He later cut the paragraph and reworked this part of the chapter.

19. Early in his editing, Stalin wrote in the margins beside this paragraph "*The 'Rights' and 'Lefts' in the end were of the same essence*." See RGASPI, f. 558, op. 3, d. 77, l. 249. He later cut the paragraph and reworked this part of the chapter.

20. Early in his editing, Stalin wrote in the margins beside this paragraph "*Needed*" and then added "*The Trotskyists' agitation against collectivization and the victory of socialism in the U.S.S.R. was met with support within the bourg*[eois] *elements in the country, most of all among the kulaks. The Kulaks knew from many comments in the press that not all were in agreement with the policies of Soviet power and that there were such people as Trotsky, Zinoviev and Kamenev, as well as Bukharin, Rykov and others, who were waiting for the right conditions.*" Stalin then crossed this out and wrote "*While there was no dec*[isive] *support for an offensive against the kulaks, right opportunists like Bukh*[arin] *and Rykov bided their time and remained in reserve. They didn't directly help the Trots*[kyite]–*Zin*[ovievite] *bloc and even spoke out against it when the Central Committee's dec*[isive] *off*[ensive] *against the kul*[aks]

began [and their] *half-Men*[shevik] *heart couldn't take it any longer.*" See RGASPI, f. 558, op. 3, d. 77, l. 249. He later cut the paragraph and reworked this part of the chapter.

21. Stalin's addition of quotation marks may have been at Pospelov's recommendation. See RGANI, f. 3, op. 22, d. 174g, l. 564.

22. Early in his editing, Stalin wrote into the margins beside this paragraph "*I.e., don't attack, but allow for its development.*" See RGASPI, f. 558, op. 3, d. 77, l. 250. He later cut the paragraph and reworked it.

23. Early in his editing, Stalin left a question mark in the margins and cut all of the last names in this sentence—Kotov, Penkov, Ukhanov, Ryutin, Giber, Yagoda, Kulikov, Mikhailov, and Matveyev—except for Uglanov. Pospelov revised the sentence days later, leaving only Uglanov and Yagoda in place. See RGASPI, f. 17, op. 120, d. 383, ll. 489ob, 539ob, 667ob. Stalin subsequently underlined the names and wrote "*Needed*" in the margins—see RGASPI, f. 558, op. 3, d. 77, l. 250. In the end, he restored Kotov, Ukhanov, Ryutin, Yagoda, and Polonsky to the text, the last one perhaps at Pospelov's suggestion. See RGANI, f. 2, op. 22, d. 174g, l. 565.

24. Stalin eliminated the emphasis initially placed on the expression "gingham city" midway through his editing.

25. Early in his editing, Stalin wrote in the margins beside this paragraph "*The Right and the Left opportunists had a similar essence.*" See RGASPI, f. 558, op. 3, d. 77, l. 251.

26. Early in his editing, Stalin wrote in the margins beside this paragraph "*The end of 1929.*" See RGASPI, f. 558, op. 3, d. 77, l. 251.

27. Early in his editing, Stalin wrote in the margins beside this line "*There weren't any fascist* ESPIONAGE SERVICES *yet (in 1929).*" See RGASPI, f. 558, op. 3, d. 77, l. 252. He later cut this line and much of the rest of the section.

28. Stalin's late addition to his interpolation—"*British*"—may have been recommended by Pospelov. See RGANI, f. 3, op. 22, d. 174g, l. 568.

29. Early in his editing, Stalin crossed out the whole section on the Comintern. See RGASPI, f. 558, op. 3, d. 77, ll. 253–254.

30. Early in his editing, Stalin wrote in the margins near this paragraph "*Title: technique decides everything during the period of reconstruction*"—see RGASPI, f. 558, op. 3, d. 77, l. 254. He later crossed out the marginalia and then the paragraph.

31. Stalin's late correction "~~Socemulation~~ *Socialist emulation*" may have been recommended by Zhdanov or Pospelov. See RGASPI, f. 77, op. 4, d. 24, l. 29; RGANI, f. 3, op. 2, d. 174g, l. 569.

32. Stalin's late correction to a quotation from an article—the interpolation "*large-scale*"—may have been recommended by Pospelov. See RGANI, f. 3, op. 22, d. 174g, l. 571.

33. Stalin eliminated the emphasis initially placed on the phrase "Socialist industrialization" midway through his editing.

34. Stalin eliminated the emphasis initially placed on the term "accumulating" midway through his editing.

Chapter 11. The Bolshevik Party in the Struggle for the Collectivization of Agriculture (1930–1934)

1. Stalin's late correction "~~*64.9*~~ *65*" may have been recommended by Zhdanov. See RGASPI, f. 77, op. 4, d. 24, l. 34.

2. Stalin derived aspects of his statistical data from 20 let Sovetskoi vlasti. Statisticheskii sbornik. Tsifrovoj material dlia propagandistov (Moscow: Partizdat, 1937), 17—see RGASPI, f. 558, op. 3, d. 57, l. 17.

3. Stalin's late correction to his interpolation—"~~*kick their European and American rivals out of China*~~ *lord it over the country*"—may have been recommended by Zhdanov or Pospelov. See RGASPI, f. 77, op. 4, d. 24, l. 36.

4. Stalin's late correction to his interpolation—"~~*strengthening*~~ *growing*"—may have been recommended by Zhdanov. See RGASPI, f. 77, op. 4, d. 24, l. 36.

5. Stalin's late addition to his interpolation—"*before the fascists came to power*"—may have been recommended by Zhdanov. See RGASPI, f. 77, op. 4, d. 24, l. 37.

6. Stalin's late correction to his interpolation—"~~*began to join*~~ *joined*"—may have been recommended by Zhdanov. See RGASPI, f. 77, op. 4, d. 24, l. 39.

7. Early in his editing, Stalin wrote in the margins next to this paragraph "*Move to the previous* [sub]*chapter*." See RGASPI, f. 558, op. 3, d. 77, l. 261. He later cut the paragraph.

8. Early in his editing, Stalin wrote in the margins next to this paragraph "*This to the prev*[ious] [SUB]*CHAPTER*." See RGASPI, f. 558, op. 3, d. 77, l. 262. He later cut the paragraph.

9. Stalin's late cut "~~supposed~~" may have been recommended by Zhdanov or Pospelov. See RGASPI, f. 77, op. 4, d. 24, l. 40; RGANI, f. 3, op. 22, d. 174g, l. 585.

10. Stalin's late interpolation "*, and actually did produce,*" may have been recommended by Pospelov. See RGANI, f. 3, op. 22, d. 174g, l. 585.

11. Stalin's late correction "~~about~~ *over*" may have been recommended by Zhdanov or Pospelov. See RGASPI, f. 77, op. 4, d. 24, l. 40; RGANI, f. 3, op. 22, d. 174g, l. 585.

12. Stalin's late revisions to his interpolation may have been recommended by Pospelov: "~~*most*~~ *vitally*"—see RGANI, f. 3, op. 22, d. 174g, l. 588.

13. Stalin's late correction "~~of their preparation~~ *to which the regions were ripe*" may have been recommended by Pospelov. See RGANI, f. 3, op. 22, d. 174g, l. 589.

14. Stalin eliminated the emphasis initially placed on the word "Different" midway through his editing.

15. Stalin eliminated the emphasis initially placed on the words "to accelerate the construction" midway through his editing.

16. Stalin eliminated the emphasis initially placed on the word "loans" midway through his editing.

17. Stalin eliminated the emphasis initially placed on the word "warned" late in his editing. See RGASPI, f. 558, op. 11, d. 1216, l. 579.

18. Stalin's late cut to his interpolation after the word "*Committee*"—"~~*resolution of January 5, 1930,*~~"—may have been recommended by Zhdanov. See RGASPI, f. 77, op. 4, d. 24, l. 46.

19. Stalin's late correction to his interpolation—"~~caught up in~~ *carried away by*"—may have been recommended by Zhdanov. See RGASPI, f. 77, op. 4, d. 24, l. 46.

20. Early in his editing, Stalin added in the margins the interpolation "*Vareikis in the C*[entral] *B*[lackearth] *R*[egion]." See RGASPI, f. 558, op. 3, d. 77, l. 264. Later, he cut the entire paragraph along with others in this section.

21. Stalin eliminated the emphasis initially placed on the expression "were being replaced" midway through his editing.

22. Stalin's late interpolation "*persons in authority in*" may have been recommended by Zhdanov or Pospelov. See RGASPI, f. 77, op. 4, d. 24, l. 47; RGANI, f. 3, op. 22, d. 174g, l. 592.

23. Stalin's late correction "~~mutinies~~ *revolts*" may have been recommended by Zhdanov or Pospelov. See RGASPI, f. 77, op. 4, d. 24, l. 47; RGANI, f. 3, op. 22, d. 174g, l. 592.

24. Stalin eliminated the emphasis initially placed on the word "voluntary" midway through his editing.

25. Stalin eliminated the emphasis initially placed on the phrase "the chief form of the collective-farm movement was the agricultural artel" midway through his editing.

26. Stalin's late cut "~~plans of the~~" may have been recommended by Pospelov. See RGANI, f. 3, op. 22, d. 174g, l. 594.

27. Stalin's late addition to his interpolation—"*against the capitalist elements*"—may have been recommended by Zhdanov. See RGASPI, f. 77, op. 4, d. 24, l. 51.

28. Stalin eliminated the emphasis initially placed on the expression "the sweeping offensive" midway through his editing.

29. Early in his editing, Stalin wrote in the margins next to the paragraph "*It was a period of RECONSTRUCTION.*" See RGASPI, f. 558, op. 3, d. 77, l. 268. He later cut the paragraph.

30. Stalin eliminated the emphasis initially placed on the term "Socialist industrialization" midway through his editing. This emphasis was inexplicably restored in the official 1939 English translation.

31. Early in his editing, Stalin left a question mark in the margins next to this line. See RGASPI, f. 558, op. 3, d. 77, l. 269.

32. Stalin eliminated the emphasis initially placed on the term "electrical power" midway through his editing.

33. Stalin eliminated the emphasis initially placed on the word "metal" midway through his editing.

34. Stalin eliminated the emphasis initially placed on the term "further accelerated" midway through his editing.

35. Stalin's late correction "~~unfaithful~~ *sceptics*" may have been recommended by Zhdanov and Pospelov. See RGASPI, f. 77, op. 4, d. 24, l. 53; RGANI, f. 3, op. 22, d. 174g, l. 598.

36. Early in his editing, Stalin wrote in the margins next to this paragraph "*The Slogan 'The Five-Year Plan in 4 years.'*" See RGASPI, f. 558, op. 3, d. 77, l. 269.

37. Stalin eliminated the emphasis initially placed on the phrase "a momentous change had taken place in the development of agriculture in the U.S.S.R." midway through his editing.

38. Early in his editing, Stalin cut the entire section on the Bukharinites and Trotskyites' struggle. See RGASPI, f. 558, op. 3, d. 77, ll. 270–272.

39. Early in his editing, Stalin wrote into the margin next to this paragraph *"This should be moved to the* [sub]*chapter on the Kirov murder."* See RGASPI, f. 558, op. 3, d. 77, ll. 270–272. He later cut the paragraph.

40. Stalin's late correction to his interpolation—*"~~PERFORMANCE~~ FULFILMENT"*—may have been recommended by Pospelov. See RGANI, f. 3, op. 22, d. 174g, l. 600.

41. Early in his editing, Stalin wrote in the margins beside this paragraph *"All of this represented an enormous victory for socialism in the countryside. But the construction of collective farms took place in breadth rather than in depth as it encompassed more and more regions. This created a situation in which the growth of leading cadres did not follow the growth in work* [. . .]." Stalin then crossed out this interpolation. See RGASPI, f. 558, op. 3, d. 77, l. 272.

42. Stalin eliminated the emphasis initially placed on the term "two-thirds" midway through his editing.

43. Stalin eliminated the emphasis initially placed on the term "one-third" midway through his editing.

44. Early in his editing, Stalin wrote in the margins next to this sentence a semi-legible note about the "leadership's weakness and inexperience" in these areas. See RGASPI, f. 558, op. 3, d. 77, l. 272. Later, he cut the sentence and rewrote it.

45. Stalin's late correction "~~Frequently~~ *Sometimes*" may have been recommended by Pospelov. See RGANI, f. 3, op. 22, d. 174g, l. 607.

46. Stalin's late interpolation *"Formerly"* may have been recommended by Zhdanov. See RGASPI, f. 77, op. 3, d. 159, l. 366.

47. Stalin's late correction "~~This~~ *Now that their*" may have been recommended by Zhdanov. See RGASPI, f. 77, op. 3, d. 159, l. 366.

48. Stalin's late correction "~~horse herds~~ *horses of the collective farms*" may have been recommended by Zhdanov or Pospelov. See RGASPI, f. 77, op. 4, d. 24, l. 60; RGANI, f. 3, op. 22, d. 174g, l. 607.

49. Stalin's late revisions to his interpolation—the addition "*often*" and the corrections "*deceive~~d~~*" and "*commit~~ted~~*"—may reflect editing suggested by Pospelov. See RGANI, f. 3, op. 22, d. 174g, l. 608.

50. Stalin eliminated the emphasis initially placed on the term "invincible force" midway through his editing.

51. Stalin eliminated the emphasis initially placed on the measurement "three-quarters" midway through his editing.

52. Early in his editing, Stalin wrote in the margins next to the paragraph *"Technique decides everything."* He then added *"The report made it clear that in past period, in the period which it took to fulfil the five-year plan in the U.S.S.R., the following major results were realized."* See RGASPI, f. 558, op. 3, d. 77, l. 276. Later, he cut the paragraph along with others in this section.

53. Early in his editing, Stalin underscored the phrase "Soviet machine-building" and wrote into the margin *"2)"*—see RGASPI, f. 558, op. 3, d. 77, l. 277. Later, he cut the paragraph along with others in this section.

54. Early in his editing, Stalin wrote into the margin *"2)"*—see RGASPI, f. 558, op. 3, d. 77, l. 278. Later, he cut the paragraph along with others in this section.

55. Early in his editing, Stalin wrote into the margin *"3)"*—see RGASPI, f. 558, op. 3, d. 77, l. 277. Later, he cut the paragraph along with others in this section.

56. Early in his editing, Stalin underscored the phrase "'The Bolsheviks Must Master Technique' and 'In the Reconstruction Period, Technique Decides Everything'"—see RGASPI, f. 558, op. 3, d. 77, l. 278. Later, he cut the paragraph along with others in this section.

57. Early in his editing, Stalin wrote in the margins next to the paragraph *"5) Unemployment in the city was eliminated."* See RGASPI, f. 558, op. 3, d. 77, l. 279. Later, he cut the paragraph along with others in this section.

58. Early in his editing, Stalin underscored the phrase "UNEMPLOYMENT was eliminated for good" and wrote in the margins next to the paragraph *"5) misery and poverty in the countryside were eliminated."* See RGASPI, f. 558, op. 3, d. 77, l. 279. Later, he cut the paragraph along with others in this section.

59. Stalin's late correction to his interpolation—"*~~discovered~~ evident*"—may have been recommended by Pospelov. See RGANI, f. 3, op. 22, d. 174g, l. 611.

60. Stalin's formulation of this sentence stems from marginalia in his early editing. See note 41.

61. The formulation of this statement can be traced back to Stalin's marginalia in his copy of 20 LET SOVETSKOI VLASTI—see RGASPI, f. 558, op. 3, d. 57, l. 12.

62. Stalin's late cut to his interpolation after the word *"a"*—"*~~small~~*"—may have been recommended by Pospelov. See RGANI, f. 3, op. 22, d. 174g, l. 611.

63. Stalin's correction is derived from data in 20 LET SOVETSKOI VLASTI, 45—see RGASPI, f. 558, op. 3, d. 57, l. 45

64. Stalin's late corrections to this sentence may have been recommended by Zhdanov. See RGASPI, f. 77, op. 4, d. 24, l. 73.

65. Stalin's correction "~~50.5 trillion~~ *64,000,000,000*" may have been recommended by Zhdanov. See RGASPI, f. 77, op. 4, d. 24, l. 73.

66. Stalin's late addition to his interpolation—"*the Party and*"—may have been recommended by Zhdanov. See RGASPI, f. 77, op. 4, d. 24, l. 75.

67. Stalin's late revisions to his interpolation—"*However,*"—may have been recommended by Zhdanov or Pospelov. See RGASPI, f. 77, op. 4, d. 24, l. 76; RGANI, f. 3, op. 22, d. 174g, l. 621.

68. The phrase "the report of Comrade Yezhov, Secretary of the Central Committee," was removed from all subsequent printings of the SHORT COURSE after Yezhov's arrest on April 10, 1939.

Chapter 12. The Bolshevik Party in the Struggle to Complete the Building of the Socialist Society. Introduction of the New Constitution (1935–1937)

1. Early in his editing, Stalin wrote in the margins beside the chapter title:

> *1. the two centers of war that emerged during the previous period now matured and developed in activity*
> *2. Characteristically, a division of spheres of influence now took place without the declaration of war*
> *3. Domestically, class differences narrowed*

See RGASPI, f. 558, op. 3, d. 77, l. 291. He later revised the beginning of the chapter along these lines.

2. Early in his editing, Stalin wrote in the margins beside this paragraph "*more or less democr*[atic] *st*[ates] *and the fascist state*[s] = *the dispute between them*." See RGASPI, f. 558, op. 3, d. 77, l. 291. He later cut the paragraph and revised this section of the chapter.

3. Early in his editing, Stalin wrote in the margins underneath this paragraph "*The League of Nations*." See RGASPI, f. 558, op. 3, d. 77, l. 291. He later incorporated this organization into his revisions below.

4. Early in his editing, Stalin wrote in the margins beside this paragraph "*for the first* [sub] *chapter*." See RGASPI, f. 558, op. 3, d. 77, l. 292. He later reframed this paragraph instead.

5. Early in his editing, Stalin wrote in the margins beside this paragraph "*for* [sub]*chapter I*." See RGASPI, f. 558, op. 3, d. 77, l. 293. He later cut the quotation and almost all discussion of the Spanish civil war.

6. Early in his editing, Stalin wrote in the margins beside this paragraph "= FOR [sub] *chapter 2*." He then wrote "*With the disappearance of exploitation, the hostile classes also disappeared. Two classes and the intelligentsia were left and the border between them was being erased. This symbolized the solidarity of the Soviet people and the stability of the home front in the case of war*." See RGASPI, f. 558, op. 3, d. 77, l. 293. He later cut the paragraph and revised the section; elements of his marginalia are reflected in the chapter's third section below.

7. Early in his editing, Stalin wrote in the margins beside this quotation "*After technique was supplied = cadres* DECIDE EVERYTHING. *For [*SUB*]*CHAPTER *2*." See RGASPI, f. 558, op. 3, d. 77, l. 294. This quotation was incorporated into a revised discussion of cadres in the chapter's second section below.

8. Early in his editing, Stalin added the interpolation "*All of these successes of socialism had to be built into the new constitution*." He then crossed out the paragraph, circled it and wrote in the margins "*Const.*"—apparently a reference to the chapter's third section on the 1936 Stalin Constitution. See RGASPI, f. 558, op. 3, d. 77, l. 294. Stalin later shifted this paragraph and the one following it to the head of the third section.

9. Stalin based some of this statistical data on 20 LET SOVETSKOI VLASTI. STATISTICHESKII SBORNIK. TSIFROVOI MATERIAL DLIA PROPAGANDISTOV (Moscow: Partizdat, 1937), 17—see RGASPI, f. 558, op. 3, d. 57, l. 17.

10. Stalin based some of this statistical data on 20 LET SOVETSKOI VLASTI, 50—see RGASPI, f. 558, op. 3, d. 57, l. 50.

11. Stalin based some of this statistical data on 20 LET SOVETSKOI VLASTI, 45—see RGASPI, f. 558, op. 3, d. 57, l. 45.

12. Stalin based some of this statistical data on 20 LET SOVETSKOI VLASTI, 43—see RGASPI, f. 558, op. 3, d. 57, l. 43.

13. Stalin's late addition to his interpolation—"*and hundreds*"—may have been recommended by Zhdanov. See RGASPI, f. 77, op. 4, d. 24, l. 93.

14. Stalin's late addition to his interpolation—"*now*"—may have been recommended by Pospelov. See RGANI, f. 3, op. 22, d. 174g, l. 645.

15. A typesetter's error cut I. K. Pronin's last name from this quotation in 1938; it was restored in 1945.

16. Early in his editing, Stalin wrote in the margins beside this paragraph "*for* [sub] *ch*[apter] *2*." See RGASPI, f. 558, op. 3, d. 77, l. 296. Stalin later cut the paragraph but incorporated the theme into the chapter's second section below.

17. Early in his editing, Stalin wrote in the margins beside this sentence "*1)*"—apparently a reference to part of section two below. See RGASPI, f. 558, op. 3, d. 77, l. 296. Stalin then cut the paragraph.

18. Early in his editing, Stalin wrote in the margins beside this sentence "*2)*"—apparently a reference to part of section two below. See RGASPI, f. 558, op. 3, d. 77, l. 297. Stalin then cut the paragraph.

19. Early in his editing, Stalin wrote in the margins beside this sentence "*3)*"—perhaps a reference to section three below. See RGASPI, f. 558, op. 3, d. 77, l. 297. Stalin then cut the paragraph.

20. Early in his editing, Stalin wrote in the margins beside this sentence "*4)*"—see RGASPI, f. 558, op. 3, d. 77, l. 298.

21. Early in his editing, Stalin wrote in the margins beside this sentence "*5)*" and followed it up with "etc."—see RGASPI, f. 558, op. 3, d. 77, l. 297.

22. Stalin's late addition to his interpolation—"*in the grain-growing regions*"—may have been recommended by Zhdanov or Pospelov. See RGASPI, f. 77, op. 4, d. 24, l. 99; RGANI, f. 3, op. 22, d. 174g, l. 649.

23. Early in his editing, Stalin wrote in the margins beside this sentence "*Schools*"—see RGASPI, f. 558, op. 3, d. 77, l. 300. He later revised the paragraph.

24. Stalin based some of this statistical data on 20 LET SOVETSKOI VLASTI, 81—see RGASPI, f. 558, op. 3, d. 57, 81.

25. Early in his editing, Stalin wrote in the margins beside this heading "*for the* [sub] *chapter on the* CONS[TITUTION]"—see RGASPI, f. 558, op. 3, d. 77, l. 300. Stalin did not incorporate this theme into his revisions of the chapter's third section.

26. Early in his editing, Stalin cut the whole section on the Comintern—see RGASPI, f. 558, op. 3, d. 77, ll. 303–305.

27. Early in his editing, Stalin wrote in the margins beside this paragraph "*In November 1936, the Extraord*[inary] *VIII Congress of Soviets assembled to ratify the new const*[itution]"—see RGASPI, f. 558, op. 3, d. 77, l. 305. He later cut this paragraph but added information on the congress below.

28. Stalin's late correction "~~points~~ *islands*" may have been recommended by Zhdanov. See RGASPI, f. 77, op. 4, d. 24, l. 103.

29. Early in his editing, Stalin wrote in the margins at the head of this paragraph "*Free from exploitation*"—see RGASPI, f. 558, op. 3, d. 77, l. 306. He later incorporated the theme into his revisions below.

30. Late in his editing, Stalin may have revised this paragraph at Pospelov's suggestion. See RGANI, f. 3, op. 22, d. 174g, l. 656.

31. Early in his editing, Stalin wrote in the margins beside this paragraph "*These profound ch*[anges] *were reflected in the new constitution*"—see RGASPI, f. 558, op. 3, d. 77, l. 307. He added a similar line to the text below.

32. Early in his editing, Stalin underscored the word "leads" and wrote in the margins "*st*[ate] *leadership*"—see RGASPI, f. 558, op. 3, d. 77, l. 307. He later cut this paragraph and its discussion of working-class sovereignty.

33. Early in his editing, Stalin drew a line in the margins along this paragraph and the four that follow it and then wrote "*more briefly*"—see RGASPI, f. 558, op. 3, d. 77, l. 307.

34. Stalin made the correction "~~life~~ *activity*" during his editing. This expression was accidentally returned to its original form in the official 1939 English translation.

35. Early in his editing, Stalin wrote in the margins beside this paragraph "*This is for the beginning of the* [sub]*chapter*"—see RGASPI, f. 558, op. 3, d. 77, l. 308. He later cut the paragraph; its theme was reflected in his revisions to the head of the section.

36. Stalin's late correction "~~*paragraphs*~~ *articles*" may have been recommended by Zhdanov or Pospelev. See RGASPI, f. 77, op. 4, d. 24, l. 109; RGANI, f. 3, op. 22, d. 174g, l. 649.

37. Stalin's late revisions to his interpolation may reflect a correction suggested by Pospelov: "~~*Henceforth*~~ *In this way*"—see RGANI, f. 3, op. 22, d. 174g, l. 659.

38. This is almost a direct quotation of Stalin's March 3, 1938, advice to Yaroslavsky and Pospelov. See RGASPI, f. 558, op. 11, d. 1217, ll. 26–28; f. 77, op. 3, d. 157, ll. 2ob–3ob; and page 9 of the Introduction. Early in his editing, Stalin wrote in the margins beside this paragraph "*Say here that the trial summed up the activity of these* GENTLEMEN"—see RGASPI, f. 558, op. 3, d. 77, l. 309. He later revised the entire section, using different epithets.

39. Early in his editing, Stalin drew a circle around the phrase "In January 1937," underscored it and then wrote in the margins "*1) one trial*"—see RGASPI, f. 558, op. 3, d. 77, l. 310. He later cut the paragraph and revised the entire section.

40. Early in his editing, Stalin underscored the expression "overthrow of the Soviet power" and wrote in the margins "*ABOUT YENUKIDZE*"—see RGASPI, f. 558, op. 3, d. 77, l. 310. He later cut the paragraph and revised the entire section.

41. Early in his editing, Stalin wrote in the margins beside this paragraph "*an international gang of* SPIES"—see RGASPI, f. 558, op. 3, d. 77, l. 311. He later cut the paragraph and revised the entire section.

42. Early in his editing, Stalin underscored the phrase "Bukharin-Rykovite counter-revolutionary gang" and wrote in the margins "*2) the other trial*"—see RGASPI, f. 558, op. 3, d. 77, l. 311. He later cut the paragraph and revised the entire section.

43. Early in his editing, Stalin wrote in the margins beside this paragraph "*Begin with this*"—see RGASPI, f. 558, op. 3, d. 77, l. 311. He later revised the entire section.

44. Early in his editing, Stalin circled the last names Gamarnik and Lyubchenko and wrote in the margins "*Lominadze*"—see RGASPI, f. 558, op. 3, d. 77, l. 311. He later cut the paragraph and revised the entire section.

45. Early in his editing, Stalin underscored the last names Yakovlev, Yagoda, Yenukidze and Karakhan and then circled Yagoda, Yenukidze and Karakhan. See RGASPI, f. 558, op. 3, d. 77, l. 311. He later cut the paragraph and revised the entire section.

46. Early in his editing, Stalin circled the phrase "In March 1938," underscored the words "trial of the anti-Soviet" and wrote in the margins "*trial II*"—see RGASPI, f. 558, op. 3, d. 77, l. 311. He later cut the paragraph and revised the entire section.

47. Early in his editing, Stalin wrote "*Spy*" in the margins beside Dan's name. See RGASPI, f. 558, op. 3, d. 77, l. 311. He later cut the paragraph and revised the entire section.

48. Early in his editing, Stalin wrote in the margins beside this paragraph "*Some of them = former members of the tsarist secret police*"—see RGASPI, f. 558, op. 3, d. 77, l. 312. He later cut the paragraph and revised the entire section.

49. Early in his editing, Stalin underscored the last names Kirov, Menzhinsky, Kuibyshev and Gorky. See RGASPI, f. 558, op. 3, d. 77, l. 312. He later cut the paragraph and revised the entire section.

50. Early in his editing, Stalin circled the last names Pletnev, Levin and Kazakov. See RGASPI, f. 558, op. 3, d. 77, l. 312. He later cut the paragraph and revised the entire section.

51. Early in his editing, Stalin circled the last names Zelensky, Ivanov and Zubaryev. See RGASPI, f. 558, op. 3, d. 77, l. 312. He later cut the paragraph and revised the entire section.

52. Stalin's late correction to his interpolation—"~~*accomplishments*~~ *gains*"—may have been recommended by Zhdanov. See RGASPI, f. 77, op. 4, d. 24, l. 111.

53. Early in his editing, Stalin wrote in the margins beside this paragraph "*Need this*" and then "*End with this and a small concluding bit*"—see RGASPI, f. 558, op. 3, d. 77, l. 321. He later cut the paragraph and revised the entire section around the theme of representative democracy and constitutional governance.

Conclusion

1. Early in his editing, Stalin wrote across the title to the conclusion:

Four basic conclusions from the history of the CPSU.

As is visible from history, the party defeated its enemies and was victorious.

Why it was victorious:

First conclusion: It liberated itself from every type of opportunism. The party is the headquarters of the working class, its front[*line*] *fortress.*

Second conclusion: it was theoretically equipped . . .

Third conclusion: it was unafraid of criticism and self-criticism, thanks to which it liberated itself from mistakes.

Fourth conclusion: it never broke its ties with its mother—with the popular masses, with the workers and peasants and all the toilers.

See RGASPI, f. 558, op. 3, d. 77, l. 322.

2. Early in his editing, Stalin wrote diagonally across the first page of the conclusion:

Two conclusions on the history of the CPSU

1) It cannot be done without the party

2) The struggle with the tendencies [three illegible words]

= *Not right*

He then rewrote these theses in red pencil:

1. Without the party, there would be no leadership of the proletarian struggle or revolution of the proletariat. To leave the proletariat without the party would be to leave it without leadership in the U.S.S.R.
2. The party must be "monolithic"

See RGASPI, f. 558, op. 3, d. 77, l. 322.

3. Late in his editing, Stalin may have revised this paragraph at Pospelov's recommendation. Originally, it read *"It may be said without fear of exaggeration that since the death of Engels, Lenin has been the only theoretician who has advanced the Marxist theory and enriched it with new experience within the conditions of imperialism and Soviet power in the U.S.S.R."* Stalin rejected an additional interpolation recommended by Pospelov: *"After Lenin, it was Comrade Stalin who developed the creative theory of Marxism-Leninism and who continues to develop it to the present day, arming the Bolshevik party, Soviet people and world proletariat with revolutionary theory."* See RGANI, f. 3, op. 22, d. 174g, ll. 677–678.

4. Stalin's late correction to his interpolation—"~~*has*~~ *and the Leninists have*"—may have been recommended by Zhdanov or Pospelov. See RGASPI, f. 77, op. 4, d. 24, l. 127; RGANI, f. 3, op. 22, d. 174g, l. 677.

5. Stalin may have based this statement on his marginalia from the coversheet of an earlier version of the conclusion: "'*Leninism is a further development of Marxism in the* ~~*new conditions of social development of society, in the conditions of imperialism and*~~ *new context, in the context of imperialism and prolet*[arian] *revolutions' (or something like that).*" See RGASPI, f. 558, op. 11, d. 1211, l. 392.

6. Stalin's late correction to his interpolation—"~~*1/6*~~ *one-sixth*"—may have been recommended by Zhdanov or Pospelov. See RGASPI, f. 77, op. 4, d. 24, l. 127; RGANI, f. 3, op. 22, d. 174g, l. 677.

7. Early in his editing, Stalin numbered this section "*2)*"—see RGASPI, f. 558, op. 3, d. 77, l. 322. He later cut the paragraph and revised much of the section.

8. Early in his editing, Stalin added the interpolation "*nationalists in the republics of the U.S.S.R.*"—see RGASPI, f. 558, op. 3, d. 77, l. 325.

9. Early in his editing, Stalin wrote in the margins beside this paragraph "*This is the first conclusion of the history of the C.P.S.U.'s development*"—see RGASPI, f. 558, op. 3, d. 77, l. 325. He later cut the paragraph and revised the entire section.

10. Early in his editing, Stalin numbered this section "*3)*"; he then added the interpolation "*Furthermore, the history of the C.P.S.U. teaches that*"—see RGASPI, f. 558, op. 3, d. 77, l. 325. On the coversheet of a later draft of the conclusion, he wrote "*on the conciliators in point 3—divide them.*" See RGASPI, f. 558, op. 11, d. 1211, l. 392. He later completely rewrote the section, significantly reducing the overall proportion of the conclusion devoted to the struggle with the opposition.

11. This is almost a direct quotation of Stalin's March 3, 1938, advice to Yaroslavsky and Pospelov. See RGASPI, f. 558, op. 11, d. 1217, ll. 25–46, here 26–28; f. 77, op. 3, d. 157, ll. 2ob–3ob; and page 9 of the Introduction. Early in his editing, Stalin made the correction

"nationalist~~s~~ *deviators*"—see RGASPI, f. 558, op. 3, d. 77, l. 326. He later cut the paragraph and revised the entire section.

12. Early in his editing, Stalin made the correction "~~bourgeois~~ nationalist~~s~~ *deviators*"—see RGASPI, f. 558, op. 3, d. 77, l. 326. He later cut much of this section.

13. Early in his editing, Stalin made the correction "~~bourgeois~~ nationalist ~~groups~~ *deviators*"—see RGASPI, f. 558, op. 3, d. 77, l. 326. He later cut much of this section.

14. Early in his editing, Stalin wrote the following into the margins beside this paragraph:

4) Theory
5) Connection with the masses
And internationalists against Great Russian chauvinism, against nation[al] *chauvinism*
Include in this point the uncompromising struggle with opportunism

See RGASPI, f. 558, op. 3, d. 77, l. 328. This recommendation was partially reflected in the following thirty-three paragraphs (pp. 658–663), which Pospelov and Yaroslavsky interpolated into the fourth version of the Short Course galleys on April 26, 1938. See RGASPI, f. 17, op. 120, d. 383, ll. 529–530ob. Stalin later cut these additions and rewrote their discussions of theory and the party's connection with the masses.

15. Early in his editing, Stalin interpolated the phrase "*and during its activism.*" See RGASPI, f. 17, op. 120, d. 383, l. 531. He later cut the entire section.

16. Early in his editing, Stalin wrote in the margins beside this paragraph "*And the connection with the masses and the masses' trust of the* PARTY*?*" See RGASPI, f. 558, op. 3, d. 77, l. 328. He later incorporated this theme into his revisions to the final section of the conclusion above.

17. Stalin's late interpolation "*The End*" may have been recommended by Pospelov. See RGANI, f. 3, op. 22, d. 174g, l. 685.

Index

Names, events, and locations are arranged alphabetically and spelled according to their usage in the text. Modern orthographic renderings follow in parentheses when needed, as do the given names of those known by their *nom de guerre*.